GRANDPA'S SCRAPBOOK

BY
LEONARD BOND CHAPMAN
(1834–1915)

HIS GENEALOGICAL COLUMNS
AS PUBLISHED IN
THE DEERING [MAINE] NEWS
FROM 1894–1904

REFORMATTED AND INDEXED BY
THOMAS SHAW HENLEY

HERITAGE BOOKS
2012

HERITAGE BOOKS
AN IMPRINT OF HERITAGE BOOKS, INC.

Books, CDs, and more—Worldwide

For our listing of thousands of titles see our website
at
www.HeritageBooks.com

Published 2012 by
HERITAGE BOOKS, INC.
Publishing Division
100 Railroad Ave. #104
Westminster, Maryland 21157

Copyright © 2001 Thomas Shaw Henley

All rights reserved. No part of this book may be reproduced or transmitted in any form or by any means, electronic or mechanical, including photocopying, recording or by any information storage and retrieval system without written permission from the author, except for the inclusion of brief quotations in a review.

International Standard Book Numbers
Paperbound: 978-0-7884-1881-5
Clothbound: 978-0-7884-9121-4

TABLE OF CONTENTS.

	PAGE.
COMPILER'S NOTES	VII.
DESCENDANTS OF EDWARD CHAPMAN OF IPSWICH, MA	IX.
PHOTOGRAPHS OF LEONARD BOND CHAPMAN'S HOME	XXIX.
PHOTOGRAPHS OF CHAPMAN GRAVESTONES	XXXI.
"GRANDPA'S SCRAPBOOK," BY LEONARD BOND CHAPMAN	1.
INDEX	343.

COMPILER'S NOTES

Leonard Bond Chapman, born Stroudwater Village, Deering, Maine (now Portland) was the publisher of the newspaper, "The Deering News." This newspaper was published during the late 1800s to the early 1900s with offices at 98 Exchange Street, Portland, Maine. Leonard's most enduring legacy, "Grandpa's Scrapbook" was published in this newspaper, along with specific articles about area notables and places.

Leonard Bond Chapman, son of Henry and Hannah (Bond) Chapman, was born on his father's farm located on Congress Street where it passes through Stroudwater. Here he listened to the stories about ancestors and other early settlers of the area. From these stories he developed a life long interest of local history and genealogy that culminated in the Scrapbook.

In my research for the book, "Descendants of Thomas Skillin of Falmouth (now Portland), Maine,"
I referenced the Scrapbook, but found that without an index, it was difficult to use. This project is meant to correct this oversite. Leonard Bond Chapman produced many other individual printings, but none as extensive as this Scrapbook.

This project includes a large percentage of the available published Scrapbook articles; the missing ones are due to mechanical printing problems with the original newspaper leaving them unreadable. The surviving articles, Chapman genealogical data, and the index, should provide todays researchers with a refreshing look into the local history and genealogy of Portland, Westbrook, and Scarborough, Maine.

Thomas Shaw Henley, Compiler
Portland, Maine

EDWARD CHAPMAN,

OF

IPSWICH, MASS., IN 1644,

AND SOME OF HIS DESCENDANTS.

COMPILED BY

REV. JACOB CHAPMAN AND DR. W. B. LAPHAM.

PORTLAND:
PRINTED BY B. THURSTON & CO.
1878.

DESCENDANTS OF

EDWARD CHAPMAN, OF IPSWICH.

CHAPMAN.

Several persons bearing the name of Chapman came early to New England, and we are not aware that any two of them were related. The name is quite common in England, and also in the United States. Edward was at Windsor, Conn., in 1662; John at Boston in 1634, and at New Haven in 1639; Robert was at Saybrook, Conn., in 1640; and William at New London in 1669. The genealogies of the Connecticut families of this name have been carefully compiled by Rev. F. W. Chapman, late of that State, now deceased, and published in a substantial volume. Jacob Chapman was at Boston in 1642, and Richard and wife Mary were at the same place in 1652, and previously of Braintree.

Ralph Chapman, from Southworth, England, came to New England in the ship "Elizabeth", in 1635, aged 20. He was at Duxbury, Mass., in 1640, and his marriage with Lydia Wills is the first recorded in that ancient town. He subsequently moved to Marshfield where he worked at his trade, that of ship carpenter. In Marshfield he left three sons and two daughters. His grandson John, son of Ralph, jr., moved to Newport, R. I., but returned to Pembroke, Mass., and died there in 1811, aged 104 years, 2 months, and several days. When 102 years of age, he rode nine miles on horseback to visit a granddaughter, and returned the same day. The descendants of Ralph Chapman of Duxbury and Marshfield have been quite numerous in Nobleborough, and in other parts of Maine.

Edward Chapman, of Ipswich, Mass., some of whose descendants are recorded in the following pages, appears to have been of a family distinct from any other New England family of Chapmans, though an examination of English family records would probably show that most, if not all, of these several New England families descended from the same common ancestor.

Our thanks are especially due to Dea. Joseph Dow, of Hampton, N. H., to David Murray and Comfort York, of Newmarket, N. H., and L. B. Chapman, of Deering, Me., for valuable aid rendered in the compilation of these records.

THE FAMILY OF EDWARD CHAPMAN.

A Grantee of Ipswich, Ms., in 1644.

FIRST GENERATION.

The word *Chapman* is Anglo-Saxon, "*Ceapman*." It is spelled "*Kaufman*" in German. It means, in old English, a cheapener, a market man, a merchant.

Edward Chapman, miller, of Ipswich, is said to have come from the northeast of England, not far from Hull, in Yorkshire. The probability of this tradition is supported by the facts that others from the same vicinity of the name, Chapman, are recorded, as recommended by their parish priests to be members of the Episcopal Church, and so were permitted by the authorities to leave

DESCENDANTS OF EDWARD CHAPMAN.

the country. Edward Chapman and the Puritans of that period could not expect such permission.

He is said to have landed in Boston. In 1642 he married first, Mary, daughter of Mark Symonds, the mother of his five children. She died June 10, 1658, and he married second, Dorothy, daughter of Richard Swain, and widow of Thomas Abbott of Rowley, who survived him. He died April 18, 1678. He seems to have been an industrious, energetic, christian man, who accumulated some property, and preferred to keep it in his own hands till he saw how his children would take care of their own earnings. He was cautious, firm and decided in his opinions.

WILL OF EDWARD CHAPMAN, SEN.

Fr. Records of Deeds, &c., Essex Co., Mass., Ipswich Series, v. 4, p. 169.

In the name of God, Amen, I, Edward Chapman of Ipswich, in the county of Essex, being weake of Body, but through the mercy of God, Injoying my understanding and Memory, do make and ordain this my last will and testament.

Imprimis. I committ my soule into the hands of Jesus Christ, my blessed Savjour and Redeemer, in hope of a joyful resurrection unto life, at the last day, my body to decent buriall. And for my outward estate, God hath graciously lent unto me, I dispose as followeth; viz. My beloved wife, there being a covenant and contract between us, upon marriage, my will is that it be faithfully fullfilled, twenty pounds of that contained in the covenant, to be in such household goods as she shall desire. Also my will is that my beloved wife Dorothy Chapman shall have the use of the parlour end of the house, both upper and lower roomes, with the little cellar that hath lock and key to it, with free liberty of the oven, and well of water, with ten good bearing fruit trees near that end of the house wch. she is to make use of, to have the fruit off them, also the garden plot fenct in below the orchard, and one quarter of the barne, at the farther end from the house, also to have the goeing of one cow in the pasture, and all during the time she doth remaine my widdow.*

---
* Dorothy Chapman m., 13 Nov., 1678, Archelaus Woodman, of Newbury

DESCENDANTS OF EDWARD CHAPMAN.

Item. My son Symon, haveing alreadye done for him beyond my other children, my will is that he shall have thirty pounds payed him, by my executor, as followeth, viz., to be paid five pound a year, to begin the first five pounds three years after my decease, and five every yeare, next after, and this, to be his full portion. And for four *pounds* that is comeing to him of his Grandfather Symonds' gift, which is yet behynd, my will is that it shall be payed unto him, out of that six acre lott lyeing at Wattells neck, wch. was his grandfather's, as it shall be prized by indifferent men.

Item. I give and bequeath unto my son Nathaniel Chapman, thirty pounds, to be payed unto him by my executor, by five pound a year, the first five pounds to be payed three years after my decease, and the rest by five pound a year, the next following years; and that to be his full portion.

Item. I give and bequeath to my daughter, Mary, the wife of John Barry, the sum of thirty pounds, to be payed unto her, by five pounds a year, the first five pounds to be payed three years after my decease, and so every year after, five pounds a year, untill it be all payed. All the aforesayd Legacies to be payed in current country pay, unto sd. children. Also I give unto my sayd daughter Mary, one coverlett that is black and yellow.

Item. I appoynt my son, Samuel, to be my sole executor, of this my last will and testament, and do give unto him all my house and lands and chattels, he paying and performing all my will, unto my wife, and brothers and sister as above exprest, and also all my debts and funeral charges. I say I give unto him, my son Samuel Chapman, all the rest of my estate, both reall and personall. My will further is that all my children shall rest satisfied with what I have done for them, and if any of them shall through discontent, make trouble about this my will, that then they shall forfeitt and loose what I have herein bequeathed unto them or him, unto them that shall be so molested by them. In witness that this is my last will and testament, I have heare unto put my hand and seale, this 9th of April, 1678.

EDWARD CHAPMAN, ⌐ mark and seale.

Syned and sealed and published by Edward Chapman, to be his last will, in presence of us, MOSES PINGRY, Sen'r,
Proved April 30, 1678. ROBERT LORD, Sen'r.

DESCENDANTS OF EDWARD CHAPMAN.

I. EDWARD[1] and Mary (Symonds) Chapman, of Ipswich, Ms. In his last days, Edward Chapman had some trouble with his son, Nathaniel. Mark Symonds, his father-in-law, had left with him, in trust, certain lands, which were to be given to his children when they became of age. In Sept., 1677, after he had given John some real estate, Nathaniel sued his father for his share of the legacy left by his grandfather Symonds. By mutual consent, "Dea. Moses Pingry and Symon Stacy of Ipswich, and Ezekiell Northend, of Rowley," were chosen to divide that land into five equal parts, and Nathaniel was to choose "his share, according to his birth." Some of the other children left their shares in possession of their father till his death. When he made his will, April 9, 1678, he gave Nathaniel another equal share, and added, "My will is that all my children be satisfied with that I have done for them. And if any of them shall, through discontent, make trouble about this, my will is that they shall forfeit and lose what I have herein bequeathed to him or them." They had:

2. I. SIMON[2] (or Symonds), born 1643, a carpenter, who married Mary, daughter of John Bruer, Sen., of Ipswich, and had two children named when her father made his will in 1684. She died Feb. 23, 1724; he died Aug. 25, 1735, aged over 93; the oldest "town-born child when he died." Their children:

† 3 i Edward[3], b. in Rowley, 11 May, 1669; m. Mary ———.
  4 ii Simon, b. and died 2 July, 1674.
    iii John[3].
  5 iv Mary[3], b. 12 March, 1677.
             Born in Ipswich:
  6 v Samuel[3], b. 28 Oct., 1680; m. 2. Feb., 1703-4, Ester Harris, and had:
      i Ester[4], b. 29 Nov., 1704.
      ii Abigail[4], b. 20 Dec., 1706.
      iii Sarah[4], b. 20 April, 1708.
      iv Samuel[4], b. 10 Feb., 1712.
      v Dorothy[4], b. 28 April, 1716.
      vi Margaret[4], b. 23 Nov., 1718.
      vii Mary[4], bapt. 22 April, 1722.
  7 vi Joseph[3], b. March, 1682; m., 5 Feb., 1707, ——— Winworth, of Rowley.
  8 vii Stephen[3], b. 30 Oct., 1685.

DESCENDANTS OF EDWARD CHAPMAN.

9. II. NATHANIEL², married 30 December, 1674, Mary Wilborn, called the daughter of Andrew Peters. Nathaniel was a carpenter, and is said to have died July 2, 1691.

10. III. MARY², born   , married 24 Jan., 1676, John Barry.

† 11. IV. SAMUEL CHAPMAN², born 1654, was a wheelwright and farmer. He married 20 May, 1678, Ruth, daughter of Samuel Ingals. On the death of his father, April 18, 1678, he was appointed, by the will, "sole executor of the will." He took the homestead, and was allowed three years to settle the estate, and then six years to pay the other heirs, in six annual installments. He then became residuary legatee.

12. V. JOHN², born   , married 30 Sept., 1675, Rebecca Smith, and died 1677. Sept. 1, 1677, his father gave him a house and lands, as he said, "in consideration of his dutifulness to me and living with me to the day of date," &c., "dureing the terme of his naturall life, and to his son John Chapman, after him, if he liveth to the age of 21 years." Two months after this his son John died, and the property fell, by the deed, into the hands of the widow, Rebecca, till the child became of age. Her son:

13. JOHN CHAPMAN³, born July 7, 1676, married 28 Oct., 1702, Elizabeth Davis, and had:

14 i   Martha⁴, b. 10 Feb., 1703.
15 ii Elizabeth⁴, b. 19 Oct., 1704.
16 iii Rebecca⁴, b. 10 May, 1713.
† 17 iv John⁴, b. 2 Jan., 1715.
18 v   Davis⁴, b. 26 Jan., 1717.

3. EDWARD CHAPMAN³ (Simon², Edward¹), and Mary his wife, had:

19 i John⁴.
20 ii Edward⁴,* m. 1st, 1727, Oct. 29, Ruth Jewett; 2d, 1731, Dec. 9, Sarah Kilbourn, of Rowley.

---

* This man was born about 1700, was a farmer, and lived to be over a hundred years of age. He married 1st Oct. 29, 1727, Ruth Jewett, 2d Dec. 9, 1731, Sarah Kilbourn, both of Rowley, and had:
  i Amos⁵, b. about 1745, m. 1st a Warner of Ipswich, and had Amos⁶, Edward⁶, and Simon⁶; m. 2d Olive Foster, of Ipswich, and had Moses⁶, who died young; Joseph⁶, b. Dec. 24, 1778, m. 1801, Mary Summers, of Ipswich, and had 1 son and 8 daughters. He d. 4 April, 1846, aged 67.
  ii Joseph W.,⁵ a farmer, who lives in Ipswich on land 150 years in the family. He was born Dec. 8, 1814, m. Nov. 18. 1845, Eliza B. Moulton, and had Elizabeth Ann⁶ and Edward Irving⁶.

DESCENDANTS OF EDWARD CHAPMAN.

21 iii   Jonathan.[4]
22 iv   Daniel[4], b.   ; m. 1733, Mary Jewell.
23 v   Susanna[4], b.   ; m. 1731, March 22, John Nealand.
24 vi   Frances, b. 1697; d. 24 Aug., 1730.
25 vii   Mary ———; d. 27 Oct., 1731, unm.

11. SAMUEL CHAPMAN[2] (Edward[1]) was a man of piety and influence in the community. His wife, Ruth, died in Ipswich, June 22, 1700, and he soon removed with his children to North Hill in Hampton, and settled on a place called Brumble Hill, on the north side of the road to Stratham, where he died Jan. 26, 1722.

In May, 1719, he presented to the council of New Hampshire, a petition from the North Hill people for a meeting-house, etc., in their part of the town. The selectmen of Hampton were present to oppose him; but the petition was granted. Owing, however, to some difficulties, the separate organization was not completed till their meeting-house was built, and a church formed, on the 17th of November, 1738. So he did not live to see his hopes accomplished. The stone over his grave says, "Samuel Chapman, died Jan. 26, 1722, in ye 68th year of his age."

The town of North Hampton was incorporated Nov. 26, 1742. The pastor settled over this colony was Rev. Nathaniel Gookin, son of the former pastor of the old church in Hampton.

They had, born in Ipswich:

† 26 i   Samuel[3], b. 12 Feb., 1679; m. 11 March 1702, Phebe Balch of Manchester, and removed to Hampton, N. H., and about twelve years later to Greenland, where he died April 21, 1742. He was, in Hampton, a cordwainer, afterward a farmer. His wife Phebe died April 11, 1738.
27 ii   John[3], b.   ; m. 16 March, 1705, Dorothy, dau. of James and Elisabeth Chase, and died Oct. 17, 1705.
† 28   John[4] his posthumous son, was b. in Hampton, Nov. 20, 1705.
29 iii   Joseph[3], b. 6 April, 1685, and died unm. in Hampton, March, 1750. He left lands, etc., and his brother Job administered on the estate.
30 iv   Ruth[3], b. 10 Jan., 1687; she m. ——— Eaton, and in 1750, received her share of her brother Joseph's estate.
31 v   Edward[3], b.   ; d. in Ipswich, 17 Oct., 1688.
32 vi   Mary[3], b. 2 Jan., 1691; d. unm. in Hampton, 13 March, 1740, aged 49.

DESCENDANTS OF EDWARD CHAPMAN.

† 33 vii Job³, b. about 1693; m. 1st Mary Chase, who d. 5 April, 1736, aged 43. He m. 2d Rachel Goss, of Rye, Jan., 1737. He inherited the homestead, where he died in 1765, aged over 70.

84 viii Edmund,³ b. about 1697. A farmer, in company with his brother Joseph. [I have a deed of marsh land sold them in 1725, by Christopher Page. It was inherited by Job⁵, their nephew — J. C.] He died unmarried in Hampton, Feb. 20, 1739, aged 42.

17. JOHN CHAPMAN⁴ [supposed] (John³, John², Edward¹), of Ipswich, born 1715, married Joanna Perkins, of Ipswich. In 1779, a John Chapman, of Ipswich, Mass., whose wife was (I think) Joanna, bought land in Londonderry, N. H., where his son Joseph had settled some years before. He was a maker of leather breeches. Children:

† 35 i John⁵, b. 17 April, 1777, in Ipswich; d. in Tewkesbury, Mass., Oct., 1847.
86 ii Jeremiah⁵.
87 iii Daniel⁵.
88 iv Joseph⁵, supposed to have settled in Londonderry, N. H.
89 v Elizabeth⁵.

33. JOB³ and MARY (CHASE) CHAPMAN of North Hampton,* had:

40 i James⁴, b.   , bapt. 1719.
41 ii Mary⁴, bapt. 1719.
42 iii Elisabeth⁴, bapt. 1722.
43 iv Samuel⁴, b. 2 July, 1726; m. ———; lived on the homestead, and had a son, Samuel⁵, b.   , 1756.

By 2d wife, Rachel:

44 v Ruth⁴, bapt. Jan. 15, 1738, and three other daughters.

35. JOHN⁵, born 1777, blacksmith, married in Tewkesbury, Mass., 1803, Clarissa, daughter of J. Jaques, of Wilmington, Mass., and had children:

† 45 i John Brown⁶, b. in Tewkesbury, 23 Sept., 1805, and died 1867, June 29th, at Nashua, N. H.
46 ii Clarissa Jaques⁶, b. 31 July, 1810.
47 iii Henry Jaques⁶, b. Nov., 1812.
48 iv Mary Parker⁶, b. 10 March, 1820, and died 22 Feb., 1846.

---

* The descendants of Job are to appear in the History of Hampton, by Dea. Joseph Dow.

DESCENDANTS OF EDWARD CHAPMAN.

45. JOHN BROWN CHAPMAN[6], merchant, married in Pembroke, N. H., 27 Feb., 1832, Mehitable Wiggin (daughter of Nehemiah) Cochrane, of Pembroke, N. H., and had children:

- 49 i   Mary Elizabeth[7], b. 4 May, 1836.
- 50 ii   John Wesley[7], b. 2 Dec., 1838, and died Sept. 30, 1840.
- 51 iii   Clara Ann[7], b. 7 Aug., 1840.
- 52 iv   John Henry[7], b. 14 Sept., 1844.
- 53 v   George Barrows[7], b. 1 June, 1846.

26. SAMUEL CHAPMAN[3] (called Samuel Chapman, jr.), (Samuel[2], Edward[1]), and his wife Phebe, had seven children born in Hampton and three in Greenland:

- 54 i   Phebe[4], b. 29 Dec., 1702; m. Robert Hinkson, and lived in Epping, where she was a widow in 1756, with five small children. Her father administered on the estate.
  - i   Samuel (Hinkson) became a joiner in Concord.
  - ii   John (Hinkson) of Concord.
  - iii   Ruth (Hinkson) of Epping.
  - iv   Abigail (Hinkson) of Epping.
- † 55 ii   Paul[4], b. 4 Nov., 1704; baptized in Greenland in 1717. He spent some years with his uncle Joseph in Hampton. He m. Mary, dau. of Capt. Samuel and Elinor (Haines) Weeks, and settled on the homestead with his sisters, where he d. Oct. 18, 1754. His widow died about 1762. He was a cooper and farmer in Epsom where he owned lands, and for a time was town clerk.
- † 56 iii   Samuel[4], b. 7. Dec., 1706; m. 1st ——— York; was taxed in Newmarket 1732 or earlier. He is supposed to have lived in Stratham, and had seven sons and five daughters.
- 57 iv   Martha[4], b. 9 Sept., 1708; d. in Greenland, unm., 1767.
- 58 v   Penuel[4], b. 28 May, 1711; m. ———, 1743, Sarah Lebbee of Rye, and lived some years in North Hampton, then in Exeter, excepting a few years of absence, twenty years. He owned land in Epsom, and for a time was town clerk.
- 59 vi   Joseph[4], b. 10 June, 1713; was taxed in Exeter (N. Market section) in 1732, with Samuel[4], and is supposed to have spent his life in Newmarket. He was living there in 1776. He m. ———, and had:
  - i   Smith[5], m. ———, and had:
    - Levi.
    - Smith.
    - Kate.
    - Nancy.
    - Mary, m. Thomas York.

DESCENDANTS OF EDWARD CHAPMAN.

  ii Levi⁵, m. and had:
    Levi.
    Eben, killed in Newmarket, 1845.
    Irene, d. unm.
    Mary, m. G. Batchelder.
60 vii Benjamin⁴, bapt. in Greenland, 1717.
61 viii Jonathan⁴, bapt. in Greenland, 1719; m. Mary ———, who, with her daughter Salina, was bapt. in Rye, 1751, and daughter Phebe bapt. 1752. In 1751 he bought land in Barrington, N. H., where he lived in 1761, with a son Anthony
62 ix Ruth⁴, bapt. in Greenland, 1719.
63 x Abigail⁴, b. , 1721; d. unm. 13 Oct., 1754, aged 33.

28. JOHN CHAPMAN⁴ (John³, Samuel², Edward¹), born in Hampton, Nov. 20, 1705; married Huldah Hoyt. In March, 1736, he sold his lands in Hampton to Wm. Russell, and lived some years in Kensington, whence he went to Epping, where his wife joined the church in 1755. He and his sons were there in 1776.

      Children:

64 i Mary⁵, b. in Hampton, , 1730.
65 ii John⁵, b. Jan. , 1734.
66 iii Edmund⁵, b. in Kensington, Oct. 20, 1736; bapt. 1738. In 1775 he took a letter from Epping to the Baptist church in Lower Gilmanton.
67 iv Hannah⁵, b. Feb. 1739.

56. SAMUEL CHAPMAN⁴ (Samuel³, Samuel², Edward¹), born in Hampton, Dec. 7, 1706; baptized in Greenland, 1717. He married first ——— York.

      Children:

68 i John⁵, b. in Newmarket, 5 July, 1730.
69 ii Mary⁵, b. 8 March, 1732.
† 70 iii Samuel⁵, b. 9 March, 1734; m. Mary Barber, who was b. Feb. 4, 1729, and d. 30 Dec., 1816. Samuel died 9 April, 1809, aged 75 years and 1 month.
71 iv Benjamin⁵, b. 4 Jan., 1737; m. ——— Bracket, and had:
   i Paul⁶, b. Nov. 9, 1761; m. 1st ———; 2d Nancy, dau. of Smith Chapman. He had by 1st wife:
    i Nancy⁷, wife of Elder Wm. Demeritt, of Durham.
    ii Mary⁷, m. Benjamin Brackett.
    iii Sally⁷, m. Arthur Branscomb.
    iv Lydia⁷, m. John Shackford.
    v Paul, jr.⁷, m. 1829, Mary French, of Deerfield.

DESCENDANTS OF EDWARD CHAPMAN.

   ii Lydia⁵.
   iii Noah⁵, d.
   iv John⁵.
   v Joseph⁵, who lived in Meredith, N. H.
72 v Phebe⁵, b. 10 June, 1739; d. 14 May, 1750.
73 vi Edmund⁵, b. 18 Feb. 1741.
74 vii Noah⁵, b. 24 March, 1743, and d. 8 Aug. 1759, killed by lightning in the house.
75 viii Elisabeth⁵, b. 14 Jan., 1745, and d. 30 May, 1760.
† 76 ix Eliphaz⁵, b. 7 March, 1750; m. Aug. 12, 1772, Hannah Jackman, b. July 24, 1758, of Newburyport.
77 x Martha⁵, b. 11 Aug., 1749.
78 xi David⁵, b. 7 Dec., 1752; m. Elis. Clark of Stratham.
   By second wife:
79 xii Hannah⁵, b. ——, m. —— Daniels, who went to Danville, Vt., where her father spent his last days, living to be near 90 years of age.

55. PAUL CHAPMAN⁴ (Samuel³, Samuel², Edward¹), and his wife Mary, had:

80 i Samuel⁵, b. Jan. 6, 1745; m. ——. He lived, most of his days in Wakefield and vicinity, but with his wife, found a home, about 1828, with their widowed dau. Betsey, in Tamworth, where his wife d. Aug. 12, 1831, and he, June 24, 1833. They had:
   i Betsey⁶, b. in Greenland, 25 April, 1772. She d. in Tamworth, 18 Sep., 1850. She m. 25 Feb., 1798, Wm. Goodwin, who d. Sep. 17, 1817, leaving eight children:
    i Jeremiah (Goodwin), b. 1800.
    ii Betsey (Goodwin), b. 2 Oct., 1801, and d. 1840, June 10. She m. Matthew Gannet, of Tamworth.
    iii Nathan (Goodwin), b. 1803; d.
    iv William (Goodwin), b. 1804; m. Mary Folsom.
    v Mary (Goodwin), b. 1807, Nov. 2; m. M. Gannet, and d.
    vi Samuel (Goodwin), b. 1808, Dec. 26.
    vii Lydia (Goodwin), b. 1811, d. 11 June, 1851.
    viii George W. (Goodwin), b. 4 July, 1813; m. Julia Moulton, and lived, in 1878, in Tamworth.
   ii Lydia⁶, b. in Wakefield; m. 27 May, 1799, Samuel Goodwin of Rochester, a brother of her sister's husband. They had eight children:
    i Chapman (Goodwin).
    ii Betsey (Goodwin).

DESCENDANTS OF EDWARD CHAPMAN.

  iii Samuel (Goodwin).
  iv Lydia (Goodwin).
  v Woodbury (Goodwin).
  vi Olive (Goodwin).
  vii Daniel (Goodwin).
  viii William (Goodwin).

† 81 ii Job^5, b. in Greenland, Nov. 1, 1747; bapt. Nov. 8, 1747. He m. 8 Jan., 1771, in Kensington, Penelope Philbrook of Hampton, (supposed) dau. of Benjamin^5 Elias^4, John^3, John^2, Thomas^1. Her brother Eliphalet, and sister Mary, wife of Col. John Wingate, lived in Wakefield, N. H.

 Paul^5, b. 25 May, 1749, and died 17 Sep., 1753.

 John^5, b. 28 July, 1751, and died 22 Sep., 1753. They died, it is said, of that fatal epidemic, putrid sore throat.

81. JOB CHAPMAN^5 bought his brother Samuel's share of the estate, and lived on the homestead about twenty years. In 1793 he went to Deerfield, and in 1802 he settled, with all his seven children, in Tamworth, where he died March 26, 1837, aged 89 years and 5 months. His wife Penelope died there May 10, 1838, aged 87. He was a very quiet and peaceable citizen, fond of reading, interested in politics, but not ambitious for office, nor eager for wealth. Their children, born in Greenland:

82 i Benjamin^6, b. 1773; m. Sept., 1795, Sarah Wedgwood of Deerfield Was a farmer in Tamworth, and d. June 16, 1826. No child.

83 ii Job^6, b. 1776; d. unm., June 9, 1822.

† 84 iii Eliphalet^6, b. 1778; a farmer in Tamworth; m. 1803, Peggy Kennison of Deerfield, who d. Aug. 10, 1826, of a fever. She left 9 children. In June, 1863, Eliphalet d. in Newton, Mass., aged 85.

† 85 iv Samuel^6, b. 11 May, 1781; a cooper and then a farmer. He m. in Tamworth, Feb. 10, 1808, Elisabeth (or Betsey) Smith, dau. of Levi and Joanna (Weeks) Folsom. Mrs. Folsom was a dau. of Dr. John Weeks, an eminent physician of Hampton, who died when she was a child. She was a woman of remarkable intelligence and piety. She was b. Dec. 31, 1755; m. in Newmarket, Dec. 4, 1777, and soon removed into the wilderness of Tamworth, where she patiently endured the trials of frontier life, and trained up a large family of children.

86 v Mary^6, b. 1784; m. 1st in 1806, Bradbury Jewell, of Tamworth, and had:
  i Bradbury (Jewell), b. 1807, and d. 1843.
  ii David (Jewell), b. , who died unmarried.

DESCENDANTS OF EDWARD CHAPMAN.

   Her husband d. , and she m. 2d, 1844, Phinehas Wentworth, of Barrington, and d. 1864.

87 vi John⁶, b. 1788, and m. 22 Oct. 1800, Mercy Ballard. He d. 21 June, 1812, and his widow m. 17 Feb., 1819, David Luce of Industry, Me. They had:

   Lucy Chapman,⁷ b. 1811, who m. Henry Luce of Industry, Me.

88 vii Joseph⁶, b. in Greenland, 1791; m. 1st 1813, Huldah Howard, who d. May 7, 1826, leaving two children; m. 2d in 1827, Julia Atkinson of Hollis, Me., who lives with the son, Simeon. He was a lumberman, a cooper, and a farmer, and died in Tamworth, Sept. 15, 1869.

  i Rebecca⁷, b. 12 April, 1817, who m. April 30, 1840, Enoch Perkins of Great Falls, where she died April 20, 1859. She had two daughters:
   i Clara A. (Perkins), b. 16 Dec., 1850.
   ii Frances J. (Perkins), b. 17 Dec., 1852.
  ii Simeon⁷, b. 1824, who, in 1878, lives unmarried on the homestead.

70. SAMUEL CHAPMAN⁵ (Samuel⁴, Samuel³, Samuel², Edward¹), born March 9, 1734; married Aug. 4, 1754, Mary Barber, who was born Feb. 4, 1729; lived in Newmarket, N. H., and had the following children:

  i Jenny⁶, b. June 4, 1755; d. 10 Nov., 1814, unm.
  ii Mary⁶, b. Aug. 29, 1757; d. 7 March, 1815, unm.
  iii Elizabeth⁶, b. Dec. 18, 1759; d. 6 March, 1852.
† 89 iv Samuel⁶, b. in Newmarket, N. H., Jan. 13, 1762; d. in Parsonsfield, Me., April 23, 1851. Hannah Quinby, his first wife, died Sept. 27, 1801, and he m. 2d Olive Deshon, of Saco, b. Nov. 21, 1771; d. April 22, 1860.
† 90 v Shadrach, b. in Newmarket, N. H., March 6, 1764; d. at Westbrook, Me., in 1812. He was married to Lydia Starbird, who was born at Westbrook, Me., Nov. 20, 1768, and died Feb. 18, 1851.
91 vi Comfort⁶, b. Feb. 23, 1766; d. May 12, 1783.
† 92 vii John⁶, b. July 20, 1768; m. 1st Hannah Davis, b. in Lee, Mass., 1770; 2d, Betsey Odlin, of Exeter.
  viii Rhoda⁶, b. Oct. 30, 1770; m. Davis, of Lee; no children.
† 93 ix Andrew McLary⁶, born in Newmarket, Aug. 22, 1773; m. Eleanor Jones, of Epping, N. H.; d. at Parsonsfield, Me., April 14, 1850. She d. May 24, 1868, aged 91 years 4 months 15 days.

89. SAMUEL CHAPMAN⁶ (Samuel⁵, Samuel⁴, Samuel³, Samuel², Edward¹).

Previous to the settlement of Rev. Eliphaz Chapman at

DESCENDANTS OF EDWARD CHAPMAN.

Bethel, three of his nephews came from Newmarket, N. H., to this State,—Samuel, Shadrach, and Andrew McLary Chapman.

Samuel purchased a tract of land situated on what was then and still is known as the "North road," Parsonsfield, in York county, most of which, if not all, was in a wild state. He cleared a portion of it, planted an orchard, and erected a comfortable dwelling. Through the back portion of the tract ran a small stream of water, and being possessed of considerable mechanical ability, he built a saw and grist mill, with dwelling-house for mill men. His efforts both as a farmer and miller were quite successful. The mill gradually went to decay, likewise the first farmhouse, and nothing now remains as a mark of the mill spot for the visiting eye but the old mill-stones resting upon the bank of the sluggish little stream. He thought for himself; was stern and decided in his convictions. In his religious opinions he was independent, believing firmly in common honesty—that man should deal fairly with his brother man. His children by the first marriage were:

 i Betsey[7], b. in Parsonsfield, Jan. 9, 1790; m. Samuel Clafford, of Corinth, Vt., and had 6 children:
   Caroline.
   Mary.
   George.
   Robert, b. at Parsonsfield, Me.
   William.
   Betsey, b. at Plainfield, Vt., at which place both Samuel and Betsey died.
 ii Hale[7], b. in Parsonsfield, June 9, 1792; d. May 31, 1800.
† 94 iii Henry[7], b. in Parsonsfield, Nov. 9, 1794.
 iv Mary[7], b. in Parsonsfield, July 30, 1796.
 v Hannah[7], b. in Parsonsfield, March 24, 1799; m. Richard Campernell, of Newfield, and had:
   Fannie[8], b. April 6, 1838; m. Henry Long, and d. 1872.

By 2d wife, Olive Deshon:

† 95 vi Mark[7], b. July 17, 1804; m. Ruth M. Wedgewood.
 vii Pamelia[7], b. Dec. 6, 1805; m. John Gammon, jr., and had:
   Mary O. (Gammon), b. Feb. 17, 1827; m. George Warren.
   John G. (Gammon), b. Nov. 30, 1832; d. May 16, 1844.
 viii Caroline[7], b. Nov. 16, 1807; d. April 16, 1812.
† 96 ix Hale[7], b. March 29, 1810.
† 97 x Andrew McLary[7], b. Feb. 19, 1812.

DESCENDANTS OF EDWARD CHAPMAN.

90. SHADRACH CHAPMAN⁶ (Samuel⁵, Samuel⁴, Samuel³, Samuel², Edward¹), being by trade a blacksmith, settled and married his wife at Stroudwater Village, Westbrook, where much ship-building was done at that time. He was industrious in business, and a zealous advocate of the Methodist form of religious worship, and kept an open house for the believers in the Methodist doctrine. His wife, who long survived him, was possessed of large conversational power, and for many years after the death of her husband was a school-teacher in her native town. She embraced the Swedenborgian doctrine, and died firm and outspoken in the belief that her soul would remain with her friends on earth after the death of the body. Children:

   i   Mary⁷, b.   ; d. in 1838, unmarried.
   ii Nancy C.⁷, b. Nov. 18, 1791; m. at Westbrook, Oct. 25, 1810, Tristram C. Stevens, who was born Nov. 6, 1799, and d. Sept. 3, 1870. He was a ship-joiner. She died at Deering, Sept. 24, 1874. Deering was a part of Westbrook till 1871, at which time the town was divided. Their children were:
        Tristram (Stevens).
        Henry (Stevens).
        David (Stevens).
        Ann M. (Stevens).
        Henry (Stevens).
        Lydia M. (Stevens).
        Charles B. (Stevens).
        Olive J. (Stevens).
        Michael (Stevens).
   iii Samuel⁷, b.   ; d. in Westbrook, unmarried.

92. JOHN CHAPMAN⁶, of Newmarket (Samuel⁵, Samuel⁴, Samuel³, Samuel², Edward¹), b. 20 July, 1768, had:

   i   Comfort⁷, b. in Lee, 1 March, 1791, who m. in 1812, Elijah York, of Lee. Mrs. York is living in Lee, N. H., and has aided in this work. They had:
        i David D. (York), b. 11 Oct., 1813.
        ii Mary J. (York), b. 14 July, 1816.
   ii Rebecca⁷, b.   ; m. Benj. D. Watson: no children.
   iii Woodbridge⁷, d. in infancy.
        By 2d wife, Betsey Odlin:
† 98 iv Geo. W.⁷, b. 26 Sept., 1804; m. Sally Burnham, b. 14 March, 1802, and d. April   , 1878.
   v   Hannah⁷.
   vi Hale.⁷

DESCENDANTS OF EDWARD CHAPMAN.

vii Noah[7].
viii Wm. O.[7], b.   ; m. Caroline Adams, and lives in Kittery, Me. Their children are:
  i Wesley[8].
  ii George[8].
  iii Olivia[8].
  iv Ednah[8].

93. ANDREW McLARY CHAPMAN[6] (Samuel[5], Samuel[4], Samuel[3], Samuel[2], Edward[1]), not being robust in health, his parents looked more particularly after his education than that of the other members of the family. His early manhood was spent at school-teaching, but he finally purchased a tract of land in Parsonsfield, where he erected buildings in keeping with the times, tilled the soil, and performed the duties of Justice of the Peace. Though physically somewhat weak, yet he managed to keep his farm in good condition, and buildings in excellent repair till the time of his death, all of which he left to his son Andrew McLary. In stature he was slim; in demeanor, circumspect and grave. In religious matters he was somewhat interested, being a member of the church. His wife was a help-mate in every particular. Industrious, ingenious, and frugal in every respect. Children:

  i Judith G.[7], b. Nov. 11, 1801; m. 1st, Dr. David Howard, of Bridgewater, Mass. He d. at Madison, aged 34; m. 2d, Dr. Daniel S. Hobbs, b. in Effingham, Nov. 10, 1800. She had, all born in Madison:
    i Eleanor C. (Howard), b. May 9. 1825; m. Wm. Gile, of Kent, O.
    ii Huldah C. (Howard), b. April 19, 1827; m. John N. Lord, b. in Freedom, N. H., Dec., 1817.
  By second husband, Dr. Daniel S. Hobbs:
    iii Josiah H. (Hobbs), b. Dec. 22, 1835.
    iv Almira H. (Hobbs), b. May 28, 1837.
  ii Rhoda D.[7], b. July 10, 1802; m. July, 1825, Josiah H. Hobbs, b. at Effingham, N. H., Nov. 2, 1796, who d. June 18, 1854, and had, all born in Wakefield, N. H.:
    i Sarah H. (Hobbs), b. Feb. 7, 1828; m. Cyrus K. Sanborn, Jan. 14, 1851.
    ii Benjamin (Hobbs), b. Sept. 10, 1829; d. July 19, 1839.
    iii Ellen C. (Hobbs), b. April 30, 1831; m. Hon. Edward A. Rollins, of Philadelphia, Oct. 5, 1855.
    iv Josiah O. (Hobbs), b. Feb. 1, 1833; d. May 9, 1834.

DESCENDANTS OF EDWARD CHAPMAN.

  vi Harriet N. (Hobbs), b. June 11, 1838.
  vii Benjamin (Hobbs), b. Feb. 1, 1840; m. Hattie M. Chase, and d. Aug. 22, 1866.
  viii Laura B. (Hobbs), b. June 22, 1865.
  ix George Frank (Hobbs), b. May 6, 1841; m. Emma J. Christie, Nov. 19, 1874.
  x Mary A. (Hobbs), b. Dec. 22, 1842; m. Henry N. Clapp, July 26, 1870.
 iii Zebulon D.⁷, b. Oct., 1804; d. unmarried, Sept. 12, 1837.
 iv Almira⁷, b. Oct. 30, 1806; m. Sept. 11, 1825, Algernon S. Howard, b. in Bridgewater, Mass., Oct. 17, 1796. He lived first in Tamworth, N. H., and died at Sangerville, Me., Aug. 5, 1859. They had, b. in Tamworth, N. H.:
  i Andrew McChapman (Howard), b. Sept., 1826; m. Susan Rollins.
  ii Adonis (Howard), b. July 11, 1828; d. Aug. 12, 1828.
  iii Henry C. (Howard), b. July 28, 1829; m. Flora Harriman.
  v Mary A. C. (Howard), b. July 22, 1831; m. John D. Coy.
  v Octava W. (Howard), b. Aug. 28, 1833; m. Wm. H. Hyde.
  vi Algernon S. (Howard), b. in Bangor, Me., Sept. 26, 1835; m. Annie E. Bearse.

  Born in Sangerville, Me.:
  vii Grace S. (Howard), b. Nov. 2, 1837; m. Charles H. Knowlton.
  viii Charles A. (Howard), b. Aug. 10, 1839; m. Hattie E. Johnson.
  ix Adonis D. (Howard), b. Sept. 28, 1841.
  x Lorenzo D. (Howard), b. July 3, 1843; d. May 4, 1864.
  xi Nelson (Howard), b. April 18, 1845; m. Mary Clark.
  xii Almira (Howard), b. April 13, 1847; d. Aug. 9, 1864.
  xiii Annette (Howard), b. Sept. 9, 1851; m. Frank A. Lewis.
 v Mary Ann⁷, b. Feb. 16, 1810; m. Sept. 13, 1831, True Perkins, b. in Tamworth, N. H., May 17, 1806. They lived in Tamworth. She d. Oct. 22, 1867; he d. July 3, 1878. They had, all born in Tamworth:
  i Edwin R. (Perkins), b. Feb. 20, 1833; m. Aug. 24 1858, Hattie Pelton, b. in La Grange, N. Y., May 31 1837. They settled in Cleveland, O.
  ii Mary Ann (Perkins), b. Dec. 30, 1834; m. March 10, 1857, Henry B. Nealley, b. in Northwood, N. H., May 16, 1820. They settled at Manhattan, Kansas. He d. in the army, Jan., 1862.
  iii Winslow T. (Perkins), b. Jan. 4, 1837.

DESCENDANTS OF EDWARD CHAPMAN.

    iv George W. (Perkins), b. July 1, 1842; m. in Boston, Mass., March 31, 1862, Minerva R. Berry, b. in West Westminster, Vt., Nov. 8, 1842, and settled in Boston.

    v Andrew McChapman (Perkins), b. Aug. 22, 1850; d. Jan. 16, 1863.

vi Andrew McLary[7], born in Parsonsfield, May 8, 1821; m. Mary A. Bickford, b. in Parsonsfield, Aug. 22, 1820, resides on the homestead, and had:

    i George Francis[8], b. July 5, 1842; m. Nov. 29, 1863, Mary E. Hussie, of Limerick, b. June 11, 1842, and had:

        Ida Belle, d. Aug. 9, 1869, aged 6.
        Minnie May, b. Dec. 31, 1865.
        Ida Belle, b. July 5, 1868.
        George F., b. March 30, 1870.

    ii Almira H.[8], b. Aug. 2, 1844; d. Jan. 4, 1859, aged 14 years 6 mos. 2 days.

    iii Malvina[8]; b. Nov. 10, 1846, m. June 7, 1869, James E. Kezar, of Parsonsfield, and have:

        Adda M. (Kezar).
        Abner (Kezar).
        Mary (Kezar).

    iv Altae E.[8], b. Feb. 22, 1851.

    v Carrie E.[8], b. Sept. 11, 1855; m. Aug. 11, 1875, Silas V. Kilborn, of Bridgton, b. Feb. 14, 1855.

94. HENRY CHAPMAN[7], the third child of Samuel of Parsonsfield and of Hannah Quinby his wife, born Nov. 9, 1794, died March 31, 1873; married Hannah Bond, of Westbrook, who was a grand-daughter of Abraham and Sarah (Swan) Russell, of Bethel and Fryeburg. He was a ship-carpenter and farmer, in Westbrook, Me., where he lived and died. They had:

    i Lorenzo Mark[8], b. in Westbrook, Sept. 5, 1824.

    ii Albion Parris[8], b. July 7, 1826; m. March 28, 1864, Lizzie M. Foss, of Portland, b. July 7, 1826, and have:

        George Albion, b. March 20, 1869.
        Arthur, b. August 10, 1873.

    iii George Henry[8], b. June 20, 1829.

    iv Leonard Bond[8], b. Feb. 3, 1834; m. Aug. 7, 1859, Ruby F. Merrill, b. July 4, 1837, dau. of Edmond Merrill, of Bethel; resides in Deering, Me., and have:

        Albion Leonard, b. in Deering, Aug. 20, 1863.

    v Sarah Bond, b. Oct. 13, 1836; m. in Portland, Oct. 1862, Abraham Hill of Cambridge, Mass., b. July 28, 1832; went to Algona Iowa, where he died Feb. 3, 1870.

Leonard Bond Chapman Home
44 Capisic St., Portland, ME
January 2001

xxxi

Evergreen Cemetery, Stevens Ave.
Portland, ME, Lot 266, Section Q
Magnolia Ave

GRANDPA'S SCRAPBOOK

BY

LEONARD BOND CHAPMAN
(1834-1915)

Aug 1894

GRANDPA'S SCRAP BOOK

The Hamlet of Woodfords.

[In the matter under this head last week there appeared two errors that I noticed. The name Josiah should have been Isaiah Woodford, and then Rev. Mr. Jordan is not pastor of All Souls' church, for that is a Universalist denomination, as its name indicates, but the Free church at Morrill's located on the same avenue.]

In 1804 Isaac Adams conveyed to Cornelius Adams for $200, a house lot where the blacksmith shop of F. S. Ayer stands. Of the relation of these two I know nothing, and but little of the Adams name.

June 17, 1804, Cornelius Adams and Rebecca Davis were married.

October 16, 1806, Harriet Briggs Adams was born.

April 3, 1809, William Davis Adams was born.

In 1814 a Margaret Adams was taxed for 6 acres of land at $25 per acre, and 3 acres of pasturing at $9 per acre. An Adams lived on what is now Ocean St., in the small house near that of Mr. F. E. C. Robbins, and a Margaret Adams died Dec. 6, 1824. I presume this record refers to her.

In 1814 there was a Rebecca Adams widow, residing at Woodfords, and for $40 Isaac Knight deeded her a privilege as long as she lived to occupy a "certain building formerly used as a shoemaker's shop, now standing on my premises and on the easterly side my present house, with privilege to pass over the land to the street."

In 1820 an Isaac Adams resided in Paris, this state, who, for $400 sold to Joshua Young Atkins of Portland, the house which was subsequently occupied by Dea. Addison P. Woodford.

As a Mary Adams signed with Isaac it is presumed by me that this Isaac Adams of Paris, in 1820, was the person who built both of the Woodford houses now standing.

In 1806 this Knight sold to the Woodford Brothers the house where Josiah Woodford lived, now the residence of Mrs. John J. Chenery, for $1,300, which has since been added to in size very much.

In 1800 they bought of him the now so called Mosier house, paying $2,500 for the same, selling at the same time the one story house for $1,200, now used by Ayer for his blacksmith work, thus showing it was built by the Woodfords a little prior to 1800, or they obtained it in some mysterious way.

When Knight built the Mosier house although he had a two-acre lot he failed to set the house on it, hence the crook in Woodford street. From the adjacent lot owner a jib shaped piece was purchased, as the angle in the street plainly shows.

The year the town of Westbrook was incorporated, Isaac Knight was taxed for a house and lot $270; shop 25—the present shop of F. S. Ayer.

Chauncey Woodford was taxed at that time for one house, $70; shop, $25; four acres mowing land at $18; 25 pasturing, $7.

Ebenezer D. Woodford, house, $700; barn, $50; shop, $80; 2 1-2 acres mowing, $30; cow, $14; stock in trade, $200; "1 horse added, $40."

Isaiah Woodford, house, $400; barn, $25; shop, $60; 2 acres land, $30; cow, $14; house, $40; stock, $100, "deduct stock in trade."

Concerning the road between Woodfords and Morrills, every one who has endeavored to find a record of it has failed, so far as my observation goes, but I am more fortunate. This road is a town road only, and was laid out Mar. 20, 1811, by the selectmen of Falmouth, and accepted May 6 of that year. The record reads:

"Begin near Widow Bishop's house in middle of road, 12d. 20mo. east 405 rods to a small bridge between Morse and Woodford in the old road."

To this Capt. Isaac S. Stevens and Zachariah B. Stevens, his son, who later the fine old house next southerly Universalist meeting house now ng on Stevens Plains, objected, ie matter was given a sheriff's ho met at the shop of Bela Shaw, st, 1813, and reported: "Road inexpedient and ought to be discontinued."

Soon after the town re-located it in the same place. It was the small land damage awarded to which the Messrs. Stevens objected, they owning much through which the proposed way was to pass.

It does not now appear as there ever was a bridge between Saunders street, where the Morse house stood, and the Woodford house now standing.

This record "breaks the thread" of brother Elder's argument before the Supreme court when he stated in reference to the widening of Forest avenue that the old way connected with another county road, and so was continued as a county road on—on—on—to Bridgton.

Forest avenue was laid in April, 1824, and commenced in the "mouth of the Bishop road," a town way only, as before stated.

As the question of widening of this avenue is still before the public I will here give the first part of the record:

"Begining at a point three rods on a course north 78 degrees east from the northerly corner of the tavern house of Mr. Smith, (father to F. O. J. Smith) and in the mouth of the Bishop road—

Sept. 1894

GRANDPA'S SCRAP BOOK

Benjamin Stevens.—The Progenitor of the Stevens Race of Woodfords and Stevens Plains.

This name was put on record in 1738 when Isaac Sawyer and wife Martha sold Benjamin Stevens of Falmouth, blacksmith, five acres of land at a place called Back Cove, for a consideration of £150, adjoining Sawyer's land and two and one-half acres of marsh and flats previously laid out to him by the town of Falmouth. Whence he came I have no knowledge. The name appears in Falmouth records before his time, also in Gorham, this state, where it increased in numbers.

In a law suit of 1756 a John Stevens o Gorham testified: "Am 46 years of age About 1740 moved with my family from a place called Back Cove in Falmouth to Saccarappa; lived in the end of a house with one Conant; news of an Indian raid at Gorham reached us, and while absent up there, the wife of Thomas Haskell moved into the Conant part of the house. On my return moved into a smaller house built by one Isaac Winter, a logger; and remained by permission of Waldo and Westbrook. In 1744 when news came that there was to be a French war we all removed to Stroudwater."

The cellar hole of Haskell's house that stood on the bank of what is now Geo. Libby's field, not far from Frost street, and back of the dwelling of John Neilson, may now be plainly seen. Chas. Frost got the house from him somehow, and Parson Smith alludes to the matter in his journal. (p. 92 printed edition of 1849.

In 1762 Isaac Sawyer of Back Cove alludes to his heirs as Thomas Sawyer, (to whom he gives at that time his farm of 119 acres) Edward Sawyer, Abraham Sawyer, daughters, Elizabeth Jenks, Judith Brackett, and son-in-law, Benjamin Stevens. (Cumberland Co. Reg. of Deeds, vol. 2, p. 64.)

These records furnish conclusive proof of the relationship between the Back Cove Sawyers and Stevens (or the Sawyers of the hamlet of Woodfords for there was another set near Lunt's Corner, also called Back Cove at that time.

Here is a copy of the will of Benjamin Stevens:

In the name of God Amen. The Nineteenth Day of April Anno Domini one Thousand Seven hundred and fifty-eight, I, Benjamin Stevens of Falmouth in the County of York and Province of Massachusetts Bay in New England, Blacksmith being in good bodily Health and of a sound & disposing Mind & Memory Thanks be given to God, But calling unto Mind ye Mortality of my Body, and knowing that it is appointed for all Men once to die make & ordain this my last Will and Testament, That is to Say, principally & first of all I give & recommend my Soul into the hands of God that gave it, and my Body I recommend to the Earth to be buried in a decent Christian Burial at ye Discretion of my Executrix, nothing daunting but at the General Resurrection I shall receive the Same again by the Mighty Power of God, and as touching Such worldly Estate, wherewith it hath pleased God to bless me in this Life, I give demise and dispose of the Same in ye following Manner & Form. Imprimis, It is my Will that all my just Debts & funeral Charges be first paid out of my Estate.

Item. I give & bequeath unto my Son Benjamin one-half my Smith's Tools he to have His Choice of ye Bellows & Anvil.

Item. I give & bequeath unto my well beloved Son Joshua the other half of my Smith's Tools in Case he inclines to learn the Smith's Trade, otherwise to be left to my well beloved Wife Martha, to be by her disposed of for ye Use of ye Family.

Item. I give & bequeath unto my well beloved Wife, Martha Stevens, the Use & Improvement of all the remaining part of my Estate during the time of her continuing my Widow, but in case of a second marriage, but one third from time to time.

Item. I give & bequeath unto my several Children, vizt: Benjamin, Martha, Joshua, Isaac Sawyer & Sarah two-thirds of my Estate real & personal, (Smith's Tools excepted) to be divided equally between them, at the time my Wife should Marry (in case that should be) and the remainder thereof at the time of her Decease to be divided among them in the Same Manner to them their Heirs & Assigns forever.

And I do constitute, make & ordain my beloved wife Martha Sole Executrix of this my last Will & Testament. In Witness whereof I have here unto Set my Hand & Seal ye Day and year before written.

BENJ. STEVENS (Seal.)

Signed, Sealed, published pronounced & declared by ye said Benj. Stevens as his last Will & Testament in the presence of us the Subscribers.

EUNICE PEARSON.
LUCIA CUSHING.
MOSES PEARSON.

It was probated October 1, 1759, at which time a letter of administration was granted the widow; then in 1760 the county was divided and the probate court business transferred to Portland, and as all the records of the court were destroyed in 1866 by fire nothing more can be learned in this direction. His last earthly abode was in the house now owned and occupied by Geo. W. Codman, Esq.

CHILDREN OF BEN. AND MARTHA STEVENS.

1—Benjamin. His intention of marriage with Elizabeth Bailey, supposed daughter of Dea. John Bailey, was published Aug. 2, 1755. She was born Nov. 6, 1733. In 1806 a son William was living, and this is all I can learn of this branch.

2—Martha married Lemuel Cox April 24, 1755. He was not a real estate owner in the county, at least he has no record after 1760, and this is all I know of this pair.

3—Joshua, who retained the homestead, born 1742, married Susannah Sawyer Feb. 5, 1763. This opens up too large a field of observation for further consideration at this time, so defer the matter till next week.

Sept 1894

GRANDPA'S SCRAP BOOK

[Under this head historical and genealogical memoranda will be furnished the readers of the News that appears worthy of preservation, particularly of remote periods in our history within the city limits and immediate vicinity.]

I dropped the record of the Back Cove Stevens family in last week's News with the name of Joshua, third son of Benjamin Stevens. He was born in 1742 as then stated, married Susannah Sawyer, Feb. 5, 1763. Who she was I have no knowledge.

In the Portland Gazette of May 12, 1800, I find the following obituary notice:

Died at Back Cove, on Wednesday evening last after a short illness, Capt. Joshua Stevens. He was an upright, honest man. He lived beloved and died lamented. He has left a widow and twelve affectionate children to mourn his loss. The religion he possessed inspired him with a belief of a reserection to eternal life by Lord Jesus Christ, enabling him with fortitude to meet the King of Terrors, and submit to the fate of man. "Mark the perfect man, and behold the righteous, for the end of that man is peace."

This Benjamin Stevens was a Revolutionary soldier. I first meet the name on old muster rolls as a sergeant in Capt. John Brackett's company. He built the venerable appearing dwelling now occupied by the venerable William Woodford, standing opposite the parental home, now occupied by George B. Cordman, Esq. At one time it was used as an inn by Benjamin Stevens, son of Joshua. Joshua was a blacksmith as well as a "gentleman."

In 1890 I fortunately met a Joshua Stevens, grandson of the Revolutioner. He was then in the eighty sixth year of his age with a mind unimpaired—a visitor then in Portland. He rendered me valuable aid "from his memory." On the 23rd of July, 1891, I published in the Eastern Argus quite a lengthy article entitled "Stevens." The facts therein contained may help someone in genealogical research, hence the notice here of the article.

I cannot place correctly as to time of birth the twelve children of Joshua. There were five sons and seven daughters as follows:

1st, Nobby, married Samuel Ray, Jan. 26, 1792, had a son Jonathan and a daughter, who was a mute. They lived northerly of Lunt's Corner on the Shattuck road in the ancient house now standing.

2—Martha, married Josiah Harbour. He lived easterly of Lunt's Corner and had three children: Alexander, James, Edward and Mary.

3—— —— married —— Greenleaf. He was a shoe maker and had children; Joseph, Amos, Henry and Jane.

4—Dolla, married Samuel Clary Apr. 2 1802. He was a tinman, resided in Portland and had children: Samuel, Clara who married a Winship, whose son was connected with a Portland bank several years, now deceased; Sally, married Marshal; Caroline, married Williams, second Williams, and Eleanor, married —— Garland.

5—Susannah, died unmarried.

6—Nancy, born Feb. 14, 1788, married George Bishop of Morrill's Corner, Feb. 14, 1806; he was born in Falmouth, Jan. 24, 1787. Children: Adeline, born in Falmouth, Oct. 21, 1806. Catherine, Oct. 17, 1808. Mary, Oct. 7, 1812. Wm. Oct. 19, 1814. Mollie, born in Westbrook. Julia Ann, March 11, 1821. Geo. and Edward (twins) May, 2 1825, died Apr. 20, 1827. Edwin, born Dec. 10, 1828. Adeline, born Dec. 1, 1830, died young. Julie Ann, born Sep. 12, 1842. Catharine McDonald died, Oct. 15, 1842. Mr. Bishop was first a house carpenter, then trader. He was many years town clerk, treasurer and justice of the peace. His residence still stands at Morrill's, and occupied by his son George who is unmarried. His shop stood between his dwelling and the steam railroad track. His grave may be seen in the so called Allen's Corner graveyard. He last acted as town clerk in 1854, and died in 1861 aged 82 years. A Mrs. Mary Bishop died Apr. 20, 1820 aged 75 years, probably his mother.

7—Miriam, married Jonathan Sawyer Jr., Feb. 6, 1794. Children: Lewis, born Sept. 18, 1801, died Jan. 23, 1847. Frederick, born Apr. 24, 1809, married, and died Dec. 21, 1858. Succeeded his father on Spring street. Was a trombone player in the old Bradley church. Lucy Ann C., born Oct. 4, 1811, died unmarried Feb. 6, 1849. Samuel Cox, born March 6, 1814.

Jonathan Sawyer was a shoemaker, and in 1793, for £85, he bought of Josiah Bailey eight acres of land on Spring street "including buildings," where Capt. Benj. H. Lewis now resides. It was the country home place prior to 1775 of Joseph Bailey who lived in Portland on Middle, opposite foot of Free street. Jonathan Sawyer died June 11, 1838, aged 75, thus showing he was born in 1763.

All these have gravestones in Pine Grove cemetery.

A Jonathan Sawyer Jr., married Sally Sawyer, Jan. 20, 1806.

A Jonathan Sawyer married Elizabeth Noyes, March 1, 1823.

There died a "wife of Jonathan Sawyer, April 2, 1807;" and Jan. 27, 1821 a wife of Jonathan Sawyer also died; still another died also named, according to gravestone, Elizabeth N. (oyes) Sawyer, March 17, 1855, aged 86 years. As she is buried by the side of Jonathan she must have been a wife.

Jonathan Sawyer Jr., was taxed in 1814, house $250, barn $30, seven acres of land at $16 per acre, two oxen $40, two cows $28, horse $40, swine $5.

Another Jonathan Sawyer was taxed same time, house $300, barn $35, shop $25, eleven acres of land, cow $14 and chaise $35. I don't know where this last one was located.

Sept 15, 1894

GRANDPA'S SCRAP BOOK

[Under this head historical and genealogical memoranda will be furnished the readers of the News that appears worthy of preservation, particularly of remote periods in our history within the city limits and immediate vicinity.]

Where the name "Benjamin Stevens" occurs, immediately under the copy of the obituary notice, in the last article under this head, "Benjamin" should be Joshua.

I have alluded to the seven daughters of Capt. Joshua Stevens, but there may be omissions made in the immediate offspring; now comes notices of the five sons—twelve children in all.

8—Joshua, of whom I can learn nothing, so can say nothing.

9—Jonathan, married February 1, 1797, Tabitha Toby. He was a blacksmith, built the dwelling that now stands easterly of the old house occupied by Wm. Woodford. The Jonathan Stevens house is now owned by the Saunders' heirs; and the shop set in front of it. Jonathan and his brothers, Joseph and Benjamin, constituted a sort of family, close corporation society, Jonathan occupying the house as above stated, Benjamin the parental homestead of their father, Capt. Joshua Stevens, while Joseph lived next westerly; the other brother, named Lemuel, occupying the homestead of the grandfather Benjamin, now the home of Geo. C. Codman, Esq.,—and strange as it may seem all four of the houses stand today, and Mr. Wm. Woodford remembers the Lemuel Stevens house as a very shabby affair outside in his early boyhood, and Mr. Codman is of the opinion from the fact that not a door or window casing stands plumb throughout the entire structure the crew must have been drunk all the time during its construction. These four brothers were blacksmiths, the money earned falling into a common till, then there was not much of this in ye olden times. Joshua, son of Jonathan, with whom I met in 1894, informed me that much of the work of the shop consisted of spike-making, and it was no uncommon thing to take a back load in a bag and carry them to Portland, even to Presumpscot Falls, where vessels were built.

In town meeting at Portland May 6, 1805: Voted, to raise one thousand dollars to build a bridge from high water mark, in Green street, to the line that separates this town from Falmouth towards Reed's point.

Isaac Sawyer came to Back Cove (now Woodfords) in 1720, but there was no land communication with Portland Neck till the building of Green street bridge, only via what is now Deering street up Haggett's hill to Congress street, and then the road to the bridge at Green street was not opened from Woodfords till twenty years after the building of the bridge. It is readily seen that everything then was slow, particularly so to go to market with a back load of iron spikes.

In 1814 Lemuel Stevens was taxed for a house $400; barn $15; cow $15; horse $40.

His three brothers were taxed in common: Three houses $2000; three barns $150; chaise house $15; shop $20; 21 acres tillage and mowing at $25; 15 acres of pasturing at $10; 22 acres of unimproved land $8; 2 oxen $40; 6 cows $84; horse $40; and one swine $5.

In 1806 the old Benjamin Stevens homestead was conveyed to the above named Jonathan, Joseph and Benjamin for a consideration of $150, as follows, but the deed was not recorded till twenty years later. The record shows the relationship at that time and is here given in brief:

We, Elizabeth (Bailey) Stevens, relict of Benjamin Stevens, late of Falmouth, deceased, in her right, William Stevens, son of said Benjamin in his right; Isaac Sawyer Stevens (progenitor of the Stevens Plains branch) in his right; William Toby and Submit, his wife, in her right; Sally Cox in her right; Hezekiah Hall and Betsey, his wife, in her right; Moses Cox in his right; Submit York, single woman, in her right; Job Haskell and Polley, his wife, in her right; and Daniel Bailey and Sarah, his wife, in her right. (married May 27, 1802, Daniel Bailey and Sarah Stevens) all our rights etc., in a certain tract of land in Falmouth, containing seven acres, bounded * * * being the homestead whereof Joshua Stevens, late of Falmouth, died seized.

The three brothers conveyed the buildings and 80 square rods of land to Lemuel Stevens, who let it go to Oliver Everett, who transferred to James W. and Lydia P. Sterns of Salem, Mass., in 1823, who in turn sold to Ebeneza D. Woodford in 1829 and then Ebeneza D., for $600 paid in 1846, sold the premises to Stephen Felton, who let it go to John Russell, a book peddler, now deceased.

Susannah (Sawyer) Stevens, widow of Joshua Stevens, died Aug. 1, 1830, aged 87 years—gravestone in George street burying ground.

SEPTEMBER 1894

GRANDPA'S SCRAP BOOK

[Under this head historical and genealogical memoranda will be furnished the readers of the News that appears worthy of preservation, particularly of remote periods in our history within the city limits and immediate vicinity.]

Jonathan Stevens, whose name appeared in my last chapter under this heading as 9th on the list of twelve children of Capt. Joshua Stevens removed to Portland about the year 1825, where he had a blacksmith's shop at the head of Central wharf. His remains were deposited in a tomb he built in the Eastern cemetery of Portland. He was the father of ten children all born at Woodfords: 1 Eunice; 2, Eliza, 3 Mary; 4, Joshua; 5, Martha; 6, Marion; 7, Frances; 8, Daniel; 9, Caroline; 10, Cornelia.

1—Eunice, born Oct. 30, 1798, married Oct. 9, 1823, Ebenezer Collins Stevens, a tailor of Portland, born in New Gloucester.

A son of this union named Eben Stanwood Stevens, married, first, Angelina A. Patterson, Apr. 30, 1846, who died May 20, 1850, aged 24 years. He married, second, Clara Davis, widow, whose maiden name was Clara Chapman, born at Damariscotta April 25, 1819. He was a merchant tailor. Children: 1, Nellie C. Stevens, born Aug. 25, 1855, died June 1875; 2, Edward Wilford Stevens, born July 27, 1858; and George Mellen Stevens, born Sept. 4, 1860.

Another daughter of Ebenezer C., named Julia Ann Stevens, born in Portland, Nov. 15, 1833, married June 9, 1859, Gore B. Chapman, born in Damariscotta, March 15, 1830, carriage maker foot Preble street, deceased, had Wilford G. Chapman, Esq., present city solicitor of Portland, married daughter of Hon. Josiah Drummond, and a daughter unmarried.

Martha C. (Stevens) Robinson, daughter of Ebenezer C. Stevens, is mother of ex-County Attorney Robinson and Geo. S. Robinson, clerk to Conant and Patrick, Portland; and Eben S. Robinson who died last winter at Providence, R. I. A son of Ebenezer C. is named George.

Gore Bugbee Chapman and Clara (Chapman Davis) Stevens, children of John Chapman of Nobleboro and Mary Bugbee, his wife, of Bristol. Gore and Clara, brother and sister to the veteran dentist, Rufus C. Chapman of Damariscotta, and John E. Chapman, clothing dealer, Bangor.

Of the New Gloucester Stevens I know but little. Isaac, son of Capt. Isaac S. Stevens of Stevens Plains moved there with his second wife whose name was Hannah Wier, widow, where they had as many as six children, Sarah becoming the wife of Mr. Africa P. Cotton of this city.

MISS SALLY STEVENS.

Miss Sally Stevens, who died on the 8th inst. at her home in New Gloucester, was born in that town Nov. 21, 1807. Ebenezer C. Stevens, late of this city, and Dr. John P. Stevens, late of New Gloucester, were her brothers. Her grandfather, William Stevens, was one of the first settlers of New Gloucester, and one of eight who formed the first church in that town. She was one of the earliest members of the old Third Parish of this city, having united with it during the pastorate of Rev. Charles Jenkins, father of the present pastor of the State Street church.

For nineteen years the sole survivor of nine brothers and sisters, it was inevitable that her life's late afternoon should be filled with the lengthening shadows of the distant past, but with mind undimmed and trust implicit she hopefully awaited her call to rest. Her long life was well spent; its duties were well performed.

"And Love will dream, and Faith will trust,
(Since He who knows our need is just,)
That somehow, somewhere, meet we must."

R.

The foregoing quotation is from the Portland Argus, March 12, 1894.

Rev. S. Foxcroft was settled there in 1754, and the town was incorporated 1774; so the Woodford Stevens name could not have been transported to New Gloucester.

2—Eliza, born June 15, 1800; married —— Jordan, ship carpenter, one child, all of whom are dead.

3—Mary, born Aug. 15, 1802; married Simon T. Rice, a joiner, resided in Portland, had two daughters, one of whom married Peter Frost, a tailor, the other Chas. Fernald.

4—Joshua, born Sept. 20, 1840.

And here I will put in the closing part of the article that appeared in the Portland Argus of July 23, 1891, to which allusion has been made in a former chapter under this heading. Albert A. Stevens, a son of this Joshua, resides at 345 Main street, Charlestown, Mass.

It was on the 20th day of last September that we called on Joshua Stevens, then sojourning in Portland. He was born at Woodfords in 1804 in the Saunder's house, hence just 86 years of age at that time, and son of Jonathan before mentioned, and Tabethy Toby, his wife. He was recovering then from illness caused by a continuous journey of fifteen hundred miles. For several years, in fact since the great fire of 1866 when he was a resident here, he has led a kind of cosmopolitan life, stopping but a few months in a place.

It was not a difficult task to interest him in a retrospective view of events of long ago. At times he indulged in a little revery, braiding his long white beard upon a couple of his fingers as a maiden does her front hair on a hair pin, then describe in an entertaining manner not only events of boyhood but manhood as well.

At the age of twenty-one Mr. Stevens told his father that in his judgment it would be an evidence of progress to move to Portland and thereby put a stop to carrying spikes—products of the hammer and anvil—to market in a bag on one's back as was the custom of the Stevens Back Cove community, and the father readily agreed with the son. At the head of Central wharf they established their new place of business. At that time, he said, there was but little money circulating—it was barter, barter. Children were poorly clad—a pair of pants made of blue drilling, a cheap straw hat, and a coarse pair of shoes was the every day attire of most of the young men. It was seldom one arrived to a go-to-meeting suit, and then only in the summer months. He told of his going over to the Bradley meeting house in the winter time with shoes and the snow a foot deep, running his finger between stocking and shoe to clean out the snow, then sitting two hours in the great meeting house, now gone, without a fire.

In 1827 he was married to Lucy A. Claridge of Blackstrap, Falmouth, and soon thereafter his father built him a good brick house. The same year Neal Dow built his—the only two brick houses built that year in Portland. And Gen. Dow says his was built in 1829.

It stood at the corner of Franklin and Cumberland streets and was destroyed in the great fire of 1866, after which Rev. Dr. Carruthers lived on the same spot in a house built on the same foundation, Mr. Stevens concluding to quit Portland as a place of perpetual residence.

At about the age of forty (1845) Mr. Stevens engaged in the sale of "Blacksmiths' coal," no other being used in this region for fuel, then "trucking," followed by "street sprinkling," taking Elisha Hinds as a business partner. So Mr. Joshua Stevens can be set down as the pioneer street sprinkler of Portland as a business enterprise. Then about every one residing on Free street was considered wealthy, and at the end of the season each occupant of a dwelling paid $5 for sprinkling. It was the best paying street of any in the city.

"Well do I recollect," said Mr. Stevens, when Chas. E. Jose, then engaged in dry goods traffic, came and said, "If you do not sprinkle Middle street we shall all be compelled to quit it," and the contracts I made with him for the whole business part of the street.

"Sure," said he, "Capt. Joshua Stevens was my paternal grandfather, and I had twelve aunts and uncles," all of whom he accounted, and placed very readily, one being the wife of George Bishop who was a trader at Morrill's Corner and served the town of Westbrook long and faithfully as town clerk.

We called his attention to the hostlery of Brewer and Broad at Stroudwater. "Ah," said he, "the people then entered into a good time more spiritedly than now. Broad's was my favorite resort, and a little incident that took place in connection with one of my visits I want to relate." And, laughingly, he said: "In playing a social game of cards the vanquished side would put a dime into a bowl on the table to pay the expense of the entertainment. It was Saturday night, and before we were aware we were trespassers upon the Sabbath on the occasion to which I allude; so one of our party suggested that the $3 remaining in the bowl after paying all expenses of the house be left at the residence of a certain parson on the way to town. The old gentleman was accordingly aroused

CONTINUED:

from his Sunday morning slumbers and the case stated; he received the donation in his extended hand, remarking at the same time gruffly, "Why didn't you play longer?"

The builders have been removed from earth, and we seek almost in vain for recorded events of the period in which they participated; but ten monumental residences of the long departed representatives of the Steven's name still stand in the town of Deering, some past, and the rest near a full round century in age, each possessing unwritten history—history that can never be correctly told.

L. B. C.

5—Martha, born Aug. 4, 1806, married Ebenezer True, who had a blacksmith's shop on Portland street, and now resides 113 Oak street.

6—Marion, born April 28, 1808, married Albert J. Merrill, a house joiner, born in the present town of Falmouth, but last lived at 74 Lincoln street, Portland, with a young wife from whom he departed, and this world as well, a short time since, leaving a young child.

7—Frances, born Oct. 3, 1810, married William Duran, a junk dealer in Portland, who had four children, all dead but one who keeps a clothing store in Boston, Mass.

8—Daniel, born Aug. 12, 1813, married Sarah Kimball. He was a blacksmith, had a shop at head of railway wharf, had seven daughters and two sons.

9—Caroline, born Nov. 9, 1816, died young, or at age of 16 years.

10—Cornelia——

Sept 1894

GRANDPA'S SCRAP BOOK

[Under this head historical and genealogical memoranda will be furnished the readers of the News that appears worthy of preservation, particularly of remote periods in our history within the city limits and immediate vicinity.]

In the printed list of the names of the members of the First Congregationalist church of Westbrook, now Deering (Church street) made in 1833, the only list in existence, (the manuscript record was burned at the time of the destruction of the store of Dea. Hiram H. Dow at Brighton Corner, who was church clerk at the time) I find the names of Capt. Joshua Stevens and wife Susannah Stevens; Jonathan Stevens whose family record I presented in my last chapter, "Mrs. Stevens," who I take to be the wife of Jonathan; Capt. Isaac S. Stevens and wife Sarah (Brackett) Stevens of Stevens' Plains; Nathaniel Stevens son of Capt. Isaac S., and wife Abigail (Bailey) Stevens, alias "Uncle Nat" who died at Stroudwater, June 1, 1853. These are the only Stevens names appearing, excepting Jane L. Stevens. This last I have not located, she was a member in 1833.

Joseph Stevens, one of the twelve children of Capt. Joshua Stevens, lived in the house on northerly side of Ocean street, nearest what is now Forest avenue and the railroad. His first wife was Mary Toby, married Jan. 28, 1802.

I have the names of four children that were recorded and two that are not.

1—Harriet, born Oct. 10, 1803, married —— Downes, firm of Downes & Stevens of Portland, tailors.

2—Louisa, born July 30, 1805, married Isaac Bailey Nov. 8, 1827. Mr. Bailey was born near Saccarappa and his father died when Isaac was about a year of age. He was Orthodox in his belief in eternal punishment for sinners, and his name appears on the church list before alluded to; and he lived on Ocean street where (Collector) Isaac Sawyer's house stood. (Further notice of him under the head of Bailey family.)

3—Lucy, born May 11, 1808, married John Crockett Sept. 30, 1834. Mr. Crockett came from Shapleigh, N. H. I find his name on the church list of 1833, and very frequently on the journal as opening the Sabbath school with prayer. He was at that time an inmate of the family of Dea. E. D. Woodford, and worked at comb making, and when the business collapsed he engaged with Messrs Corey & Co., furniture manufacturers, but his last days were spent on Market near Federal street, Portland, where he ran a second hand furniture emporium. He was an outspoken disbeliever in shams and pretences, and his voice was frequently heard in temperance meetings. He died three or four years ago. He married a second time but had no children by first wife.

After the death of Joseph Stevens' first wife he married Jane Sawyer, daughter of (Collector) Isaac Sawyer. This Mr. Sawyer was called Collector Sawyer because he was many years town and parish collector.

4—Joseph, born Oct. 30, 1813, of whom I know nothing.

5—Charles, a mute who died recently.

6—Henry Jewett, who lives somewhere "up country."

NOTE.—I find recorded under date of June 11, 1812, a marriage between Joseph Stevens and Jane Jones. Jane Sawyer may have been Jane Jones, a widow, who knows?

DEERING NEWS.

Saturday, October, 6, 1894.

GRANDPA'S SCRAP BOOK

[Under this head historical and genealogical memoranda will be furnished the readers of the News that appears worthy of preservation, particularly of remote periods in our history within the city limits and immediate vicinity.]

That I may arrange more chronologically for the printer my notes of the Woodfords Corner Stevens family, and supply some omissions not at hand I defer till next week further consideration of this name, and present some extracts from

SKILLIN'S JOURNAL.

Silas Skillin, who lived and died a few years since at Long Creek, Cape Elizabeth, had a brother at North Yarmouth, now deceased, who was interested in the family history, and kept something of a journal. He was father to Silas Skillin, Esq., residing at Falmouth Foreside, who was the Democratic nominee for senator of the last campaign, and who, a few years ago, allowed me to make extracts from the journal, some of which, to supply a special request, I now present to the public as copied then.

DEATHS.

Aug. 3, 1824, Lydia Wescott, aged 37
Feb. 1, 1825, William Wescott, (Post) 97
Jan. 11, 1827, Mrs. Post Wescott, 94
Apr. 19, 1822, Josiah Wescott, 88
Jan. 1, 1826, Mary Wescott, 86
Feb. 10, 1852, Joseph ——— 79
Aug. 31, 1853, Betsey Wescott, 68
Apr. 27, 1850, Mary Ann Wescott, 35

Before the establishment of a mail system there were men who were called post riders. They carried letters and small packages and travelled horseback. They were not government but private officials. "Post" Wescott lived in the extreme northwesterly end of Cape Elizabeth, or his home may have been over the town line in Scarboro. The part of Cape Elizabeth in which he lived is very pleasantly situated and may have received the name of Running Hill from the occupation of Mr. Wescott for ought I know.

Nov. 14, 1796, Elizabeth Skillin, 29
Apr. 10, 1830, Samuel York, 82
Oct. 30, 1830, Nathan Johnson, 85
Oct. 31, 1830, Mrs. Robert Johnson, 40
    1830, Rufus Skillin, C. E., 42
Feb. 21, 1832, Maj. Samuel Skillin, 57
May 28, 1833, John Johnson, 90
May 11, 1833, Reuben Skillin, 73
June 27, 1838, Widow Samuel York, 75
Aug. 20, 1838, John Skillin, 82
May 13, 1840, Alexander Johnson, 63
Aug. 13, 1840, Hezekiah Skillin, C. E., 36
Dec. 31, 1841, Lydia, wife of Isaac
    Skillin, 75
May 4, 1843, Isaac Skillin, 81-1 26
Sept. 2, 1844, Eunice, wife of Thomas
    Johnson, 76
Dec.— 1844, Joseph Skillin, C. E., 89-9
May 20, 1844, John L. Johnson, 60
May 20, 1845, Thomas Johnson, 76
May 27, 1845, May Johnson, 45
Apr. 25, 1846, Richard Johnson, 80-6
Dec. 31-18, 1848, Rebecca, wife of
    John Babb, 80
May 26, 1848, Randall Johnson, 81
May 16, 1857, Jane Skillin, C. E., 84-5-19
Nov. 8, 1857, Sally Trickey, 82
Jan. 27, 1859, George Johnson, 70
June 5, 1859, Andrew Skillin, 40
Aug. 29, 1859, Fannie Johnson, 79
May 12, 1859, James Johnson, 69
July 2, 1859, Andrew R. Johnson, 24
Oct. 31, 1860, Mrs. Polly Skillin, 71
Feb. 16, 1861, Capt. John Skillin, 83-6
Feb. 29, 1861, David Trickey, 85-0-15
Apr. 7, 1861, Tiza Skillin, 61-6
May 1, 1861, David Pratt, 83
Oct. 5, 1861, Capt. Robert Johnson, 71
May 10, 1862, Capt. John Babb, 80
July 10, 1862, Jason Skillin, C. E., 73
Jan. 3, 1862, Wm. H. Skillin, C. E., 30
Mar. 28, 1863, Lucy S., wife of
    Zebulon Trickey, 82-2
Feb. 13, 1849, John Skillin, Portland, 66-5
May 8, 1849, Zebulon Skillin, 63
Aug. 12, 1849, Mary Skillin, 57
Nov. 16, 1849, Lydia, wife of John
    Skillin, 53
Jan. 22, 1851, Daniel Skillin, C. E.,
    86-7-23
    1851, Ann, widow of Nehemiah, 89
Apr. 7, 1853, Marion, wife of Randall
    Johnson, 86
Aug. 18, 1855, Harriet Johnson, 52
Nov. 1, 1855, David York, 62
Oct. 17, 1855, Lucy Ward, 92
May 6, 1856, David Johnson, 87
Aug. 25, 1856, Frances E. Skillin, 23
Sept. 1, 1856, Ephraim Broad C. E., 82-8
Sept. 17, 1856, James Skillin, 69
Feb. 10, 1857, Joseph(?) Johnson, 59
Apr. 26, 1863, Daniel Trickey, 92

Oct. 7, 1863, Jane, wife of Benjamin
    Skillin, Portland, 76-7
March 15, 1864, Catherine Skillin,
    C. E., 81-7
    1864, Amos Broad, N. H., 80
May 16, 1864, Mary Skillin, 31
Apr. 20, 1865, Betsey Broad, 78
Jan. 25, 1865, Thomas Johnson,
    Jr., 64-2 19
Sept. 17, 1865, Simeon Skillin,
    Portland, 78-4
Oct. 13, 1865, Thomas Broad, 72-2
Dec. 16, 1865, Hannah Skillin, C. E., 50
Mar. 12, 1866, Robert Johnson, 84
Apr. 25, 1866, Betsey Skillin,
    C. E., 81-3-20
Feb. 28, 1867, Mary Slemmons Lunt, 77-4
July 27, 1867, Hannah M. Skillin, 74-4-27
Sept. 16, 1867, Almira Broad, 70
Oct. 29, 1867, Thaddeus Skillin,
    C. E., 85-7-14

THE DEERING NEWS.

Saturday, October 13, 1894.

GRANDPA'S SCRAP BOOK

[Under this head historical and genealogical memoranda will be furnished the readers of the News that appears worthy of preservation, particularly of remote periods in our history within the city limits and immediate vicinity.]

No. 203 Cumberland St.
Portland, Me., Oct. 4, 1894.
Mr. L. B. Chapman, Editor of the Deering News.

My Dear Sir;—I am very much interested in the "Scrap Book" column of your paper, being a real double Stevens as my father and mother were both possessed of the name, and I remember to have heard them say many times, one was a third cousin, while the other was fourth in the line of Stevens relationship, and this is all I know of early family ties. But I am pleased to learn from your Scrap Book articles of my mother's great grandfather, Benjamin Stevens, and children of which we have no record, also that my Christian name is the same as my mother's great grandmother.

In my father's family we have items of family history dating back to 1632. You mention Capt. Isaac S. Stevens and son Isaac. My father had a brother Isaac and there are many names alike in both families.

In the News on the 22d of last month, there are a few mistakes though, they do not trouble me, but as the papers will probably be kept, if you think favorable you may print all I communicate, in way of corrections and additions.

My grandmother's name was Tabither not Tabitha. She was the mother of nine children, not ten;—seven daughters and two sons as follows, and this I copy from the Bible record; and each of the sons had nine children, seven daughters and two sons.

Jonathan Stevens, born in Westbrook (now Deering,) Aug. 20, 1774.
Tabither Toby, born April 14, 1776, married Feb. 1, 1797.

Children.

1. Eunice, born Oct. 30, 1798. (Mrs. E. C. Stevens.)
2. Eliza, born June 13, 1800, (Mrs. Jordan.)
3. Mary, born Aug. 13, 1802, (Mrs. Rice.)
4. Joshua, born Sept. 20, 1804.
5. Martha, born Aug. 4, 1806, (Mrs. True.)
6. Mariam, born April 28, 1808, (Mrs. Merrill.)
7. Frances, born Oct. 3, 1810, (Mrs. Duron.)
8. Daniel, born Aug. 12, 1813.
9. Cornelia B., born Nov. 6, 1816, died April 18, 1834, unmarried.

The parents of the above named Jonathan Stevens were Capt. Joshua Stevens, born in Falmouth, (now Deering, Woodfords district,) died there May 7, 1800, Susanna Sawyer, his wife, born April 3, 1743, died Aug. 1, 1830.
Married (according to Deering News) Feb. 5, 1763.

Children.

1. Nabby, born in Falmouth, Nov. 9, 1768, (Mrs. Ray).
2. Miriam, born in Falmouth, June 10, 1770, (Mrs. Sawyer).
3. Martha, born in Falmouth, June 11, 1772, (Mrs. Barbour).
4. Jonathan, born in Falmouth, Aug. 20, 1775, who married Tabither Toby, Feb. 1, 1779).
5. Joshua, born in Falmouth, Apr. 3, 1777.
6. Benjamin, born in Falmouth, March 9, 1779.
7. Joseph, born in Falmouth, March 9, 1779, (twins).
8. Susannah, born in Falmouth, June 9, 1781, (unmarried).
9. Dolly, born in Falmouth, May 14, 1783, (Mrs. Clary).
10. Lemuel, born in Falmouth, March 1, 1784.
11. Sally, born in Falmouth, Feb. 16, 1786, (Mrs. Greenleaf).
12. Nancy, born in Falmouth, Feb. 18, 1788, (Mrs. Bishop).

In the foregoing list the offspring are arranged according to time of birth, and will aid in the endeavor to arrange records correctly, as you say you are unable to place the names according to time of birth.

I will now present a few facts on my father's side of the Stevens' relationship.

Deacon William Stevens, who settled in New Gloucester, was born in the town of Stratham, N. H. Paul Stevens, his son, of New Gloucester was born there Jan. 31, 1762, died June, 1818. Lydia Collins, his wife, was born Apr. 12, 1767.

Children.

1. William, born May 12, 1792.
2. Ebenezer Collins, born Jan. 21, 1794.
3. Abigail, born Apr. 10, 1796.
4. Joel, born Apr. 13, 1798.
5. Isaac, born July 1, 1800.
6. Dr. John P., May 21, 1803.
7. David, born May 12, 1805.
8. Sally, born Nov. 20, 1807.
9. Lydia, born July 4, 1811.

Ebeneza Collins Stevens, son of Paul Stevens, married Eunice, the eldest child of Jonathan Stevens of Westbrook, as before stated.

Children.

1. Eunice Maria.
2. Eben Stanwood.
3. George Washington.
4. Eunice Caroline.
5. Julia Ann, (Mrs. Chapman).
6. Martha Amelia, (Mrs. Robinson).
7. Edward Payson.

Sometime I hope to put my memoranda in shape and so establish the relationship of the two families.

Very Respectfully,
MARTHA A. ROBINSON.

Mrs. Gore B. Chapman and our correspondent are the only members of this family that survive. In the News referring to the family of Jonathan Stevens and decendants of Sept. 22nd, the name of Martha A. Robinson appears as Martha C. which is an error; and the correct name of her son is George R. not George C.; and her son Eben S. lived in Sharon, Mass., and died there, not in Providence, R. I. as stated in the News.

Mrs. Martha A. (Stevens) Robinson married Franklin Robinson. He is the son of Woodbury Robinson, a sea captain, whose two brothers, Samuel and Eben were also mariners. Captain Robinson had a brother John and brother William, also two sisters. Franklin in company with his two brothers, he being youngest of the three, opened a dry goods store under the Preble House at the time the old mansion house was converted to an inn. He is now with Eastman Bros. & Bancroft, the dry goods firm of Portland.

George W. Stevens, brother to Mrs. Robinson died at New Gloucester May 6, 1891 but was buried from his residence No. 203 Cumberland street, Portland.

OBITUARY.

George W. Stevens of this city died on the 6th inst., at New Gloucester, aged 62 years. He was the second son of the late Eben Collins Stevens, who, prior to 1865, for many years carried on the tailoring business on Middle street (near the head of Plum street) in this city. The deceased was a man of kindly, unassuming nature, who quietly lived and died. His sunny disposition made him many loving friends, while his strict honesty and upright ness gained for him the respect of his acquaintances. He was a most devoted son to his mother, who in her ninety-third year survives him at his home in this city. He leaves two sisters by whom he was dearly loved. He was never married.—*Portland Argus.*

Daniel Stevens, born Aug. 12, 1813, at Woodfords, son of Jonathan and Tabither (Toby) Stevens, married Oct. 22, 1835, Sarah Saunders Kimball, who was born January 22, 1813.

Children.

Sarah K., married James M. Allen.
Daniel H., married May A. Allison.
Mary E., married Samuel D. Latham. He died, she married second Geo. W. Lord.
Harriet A., married Willard C. G. Carney.
Lucy M., married Curtis H. Parsons.
Elizabeth A., married Emerson W. Hovey.
William K., married Maud P. Libby, 2d, Susan Harris.
Lillie B. Stevens—unmarried.
Ida G., married Clarence O. Buck. All born and married in Portland, Maine.

Daniel Stevens was by occupation a blacksmith, a member of the order of Masons, and a true and worthy type of the Stevens name. Of the eighteen

CONTINUED:

grandchildren, twelve still survive. Walter Chenery Parsons evinces a wonderful capacity for designing for one so young, who was awarded a medal at the Columbian Centennial. Daniel Stevens Latham is a physician practicing at Auburn, R. I.

A memorandum, or papers relating to the Stevens name, left by Dr. John Stevens, states that the father of Deacon William Stevens of New Gloucester, died in Westbrook, and his name was William.

THE DEERING NEWS.

Saturday, October 20, 1894.

GRANDPA'S SCRAP BOOK

[Under this head historical and genealogical memoranda will be furnished the readers of the News that appears worthy of preservation, particularly of remote periods in our history within the city limits and immediate vicinity.]

Benjamin Stevens, sixth son of Jonathan and Tabither (Toby) Stevens, and twin brother to Joseph, was born, as has been stated, at Falmouth, March 9, 1779, and married Jan. 9, 1801 Charlotte Webb of Stroudwater village.

A Henry Webb married Ann Riggs March 20, 1789, and a Henry Webb purchased a lot and built a house which was afterward purchased by Benjamin Burnham. I think Charlotte Webb was his daughter. Another daughter named Lucy married, first—Cobb, second, Michael Stevens of Stroudwater who last lived on Oak street, Portland, southerly of Free street, where Lucy died about eight years ago.

There was a son who was remembered by one now departed as coming home the last time when a young man dressed in blue with gold colored bands on collar of jacket and around his sleeves.

CHILDREN.

Henry Webb, William, Nancy W., Edward P. and Harriet Rebecca.

1. Henry Webb born at Falmouth July 12, 1802, married Jane L. Noyes Feb. 9, 1825.

2. William born at Falmouth Aug. 9, 1805.

From the Eastern Argus: "Sept. 9, 1823, Died on way from Africa, William Stevens, aged 19."

3. Nancy W. born at Falmouth Jan. 9, 1807, married Apr. 26, 1827 William Woodford. (For family connections of William see back numbers of the News.)

CHILDREN.

1. William, resides in Chicago, Ill.
2. Albert H., resides at Woodfords.
3. Harriett Rebecca, married Fred O. Bailey, and resides on Oak street, Deering.

4. Edward P. born at Falmouth, Feb. 21, 1810, married Dorcas C. Knight born Sept. 21, 1800, married Jan. 17, 1830. He died June 20, 1871. She died Dec. 24, 1883.

CHILDREN.

1. Esther Ann Bean Stevens, born Aug. 15, 1833, married Enoch B. Bennett.
2. Benjamin F. Stevens, born Oct. 28, 1836, died Oct. 21, 1844.
3. Charles L. Stevens, born July 28, 1839, married Edmond P. Merrill.
4. Franzella K. Stevens, born Dec. 12, 1841, married Alexander Hannah.
5. Benjamin F. Stevens, born July 18, 1847, married Annetta Jane Merrill of Cumberland, resides at Woodfords.

Edward P. Stevens was a blacksmith, and lived on Ocean street, Woodfords, in the long one story house, now owned by Thomas M. Johnston.

5. Harriet Rebecca married Oct. 3, 1844 James N. Reed, who resides now near foot of Pleasant street, Woodfords. She is deceased.

Lemuel Stevens, tenth son of Jonathan and wife Tabatha (Toby) Stevens, born in Falmouth March 1, 1784, married Sally Peaks April 1806. He was a blacksmith as before stated, and removed from the old parental homestead at Woodfords to Portland where he died July 13, 1839. Sally, his wife, died Jan. 14, 1850, aged 65 years. Graves at Pine Grove Cemetery.

Sally Peaks and Sopha Peaks, the last one of the two becoming the wife of David Stevens of Stroudwater who was a brother to the aforementioned Michael Stevens, were children of Widow Peaks and she was a Tombs.

Col. James Webb who lived next southerly to Henry Webb is supposed to have been a brother to Col. James.

The following extract is from the Portland Advertiser of Sept. 6, 1825:

DIED.

Col. James Webb, aged 72 years. "He served through the whole of the Revolutionary war and as an ensign bore the standard at Monmouth, N. J., in one of the most severe battles in the war of the Revolution."

On page 25 of pension record book presented to the Maine Historical Society by Z. K. Harmon appears the following:

"Col. James Webb had two daughters, one was Mrs. Albert Winslow, the other was Mrs. Johnson of Portland."

I learn there was a son by the name of Thomas.

Col. James Webb married second Widow Peaks. He and his wives fill nameless graves in the old Stroudwater cemetery. This may meet the eye of some one who can make valuable additions.

2. Elizabeth Ann, born in Falmouth Oct. 11, died Jan. 29, 1828.

3. James Webb Stevens resides at No. 13 Hill street, Portland.

THE DEERING NEWS.

Saturday, October 27, 1894.

GRANDPA'S SCRAP BOOK

[Under this head historical and genealogical memoranda will be furnished the readers of the News that appears worthy of preservation, particularly of remote periods in our history within the city limits and immediate vicinity.]

Benjamin Stevens was sixth *child* of Jonathan Stevens and not sixth *son*, and Lemuel was tenth *child* and not tenth son of the same parents as stated in the last issue of the News.

The name of the eldest child of Lemuel Stevens was accidentally omitted in my last chapter under this head which made the record somewhat difficult to understand. He had three children:—Sophia, Elizabeth Ann, and James W.

Sophia Ann, born in Falmouth Feb. 6, 1807, married Elbridge Tobie, a tanner by occupation, who lived on Green street, Portland. He was born Dec. 6, 1800, died Feb. 14, 1884. She died Apr. 22, 1881. Graves in Pine Grove cemetery. The other two children, Elizabeth Ann and James W. Stevens were alluded to in my last chapter.

The wife of Jonathan Stevens and the first wife of Joseph Stevens were sisters, born on Hampshire street, Portland.

Elbridge Robie it is said came from New Gloucester. All do not spell the name the same way.

Mrs. Martha A. Robinson, whose name has appeared in these records, possesses a large daguerreotype of Jonathan Stevens and James F. Stevens of Woodfords has a family record of Capt. Joshua Stevens, supposed to have been made by George Bishop, Esq.

AN EXTRACT FROM JOURNAL OF REV. CALEB BRADLEY.

"March 27, 1848, I married at my house in Westbrook, (now Deering) Ferdenaud Burnell and Marcena G. Stevens.—Feb. 28, 1825, I married the father and mother of the bride; and Jan. 9, 1802, I married the grandmother and grandfather of the said bride."

Mr. Burnell was a shoemaker at Woodfords, his shop occupying the site of the old Westbrook bank, was town clerk several years, and died suddenly while holding the office, spring of 1891.

The dates in Parson Bradley's journal differ somewhat from those I have used, found in other places.

I have often heard it said Deacon Ebenezer D. Woodford gave a lot of land for meeting house purposes. Here is an abstract from the record dated 1828.

Ebenezer D. Woodford, Gentleman, of Westbrook, To the Inhabitants of school district No. 3, for $1 and other valuable considerations, a certain lot of land, etc. Beginning bounds 13 rods and 21 links from the northerly corner of the Hilton house.

"On condition that the school house erected thereon shall always be open at all times when instruction is not carried on in said house, is the use there as a school house for all persons of the various religious denominations to meet therein for the purpose of public and social and private worship of God meaning hereby to confine it to the various denominations of Christians at all reasonable hours of the day, and evening, and if the said inhabitants shall ever shut said house and preclude such religious meeting, then said land to revert to said Woodford and his heirs.

EBENEZER D. WOODFORD.
MARY WOODFORD."

THE DEERING NEWS.

Saturday, November 3, 1894.

GRANDPA'S SCRAP BOOK

[Under this head historical and genealogical memoranda will be furnished the readers of the News that appears worthy of preservation, particularly of remote periods in our history within the city limits and immediate vicinity.]

Rev. Thomas Smith is reported in the printed copy of his journal on page 55 of 1849 as stating that in 1715 Messrs. Skillin and Brackett settle on their father's old farms at Back Cove.

In a foot note the compiler says: "The Brackett was Zachariah, son of Anthony by his second marriage, he returned from Hampton where his mother, Susannah, daughter of Abraham Drake, originated."

This farm is now the one occupied by Henry Deering, to whose grandfather, James Deering, it was sold by Joseph Noyes who purchased it of Zachariah Brackett in 1740, after which Brackett removed to Ipswich, Mass., where he died in 1751. He was a brother to Joshua Brackett who lived on Congress street, Portland, opposite the head of High and Anthony where Brackett street joins Danforth.

Three sons of this Zachariah settled in the part of Falmouth now the city of Deering.

Opposite the head of Church street stands a one and a half story dwelling house with ell and stable, all painted white and in good state of repair. The house was built about forty-five years ago by Alexander Barker whose wife was a sister to Hannah and Jane Walker now residing at Stroudwater where they were born. Today the premises are owned and occupied by Mr. William E. Watson and Hannah Frances (Brackett) Watson, his wife, without children, who is a representative of the fifth generation of Bracketts, calling Zachariah and family the first. In this house after a long search for information relative to Zachariah and family, I am fortunate in finding a well worn Bible without date of publication in consequence of much use of the book. With the aid of the records the old Bible contains, all of which are here presented, a very large number of the inhabitants of Deering and other places can now trace their origin back through Zachariah and descendants to Anthony Brackett, the father of Zachariah, killed by the Indians in Falmouth in 1689.

The record commences with the name of "Zachariah Brackett and wife Hannah." All else of the first record of this Zachariah is added by myself, the rest is as appears in the old Bible.

CHILDREN OF ZACHARIAH BRACKETT AND WIFE HANNAH.

1 Sarah, born March 1, 1709; married 1st Isaac Sawyer, Jr., of Back Cove, settled easterly of Lunt's Corner, where he left an estate, and several minor children. The widow married 1754 Jonathan Morse. The Sawyers then are descendants.
2 Jane, b. Jan. 13, 1710, Daniel Mosier of Gorham.
3 Anthony, Jr, b. Aug. 25, 1712, m. Abigail Chapman, whose parents lived on a farm located near adjacent to the Union Station, Portland, if the station is not upon it, and whose residence stood about where that of the late Fred Clark stands. They had three sons when she died: Jeremiah, David and John. A grandson of John, who lived in the town of Harrison is Rev. S. B. Brackett, No. 2409 Wabash avenue, Chicago, Ill. Capt. John Brackett was born April 11, 1761, went into the Revolutionary army at the age of 17 years and served three years. The wife of Capt. Brackett was Molly Walker of Westbrook, a sister to Deacon Walker. Capt. John died Feb. 22, 1844; she died Sept. 18, 1843.
Anthony, Jr., married second 1764 a daughter of Joshua Brackett, his cousin, and widow of Job Lane of Woodfords by whom he had Abigail, born Feb. 1766, married Daniel Green, of Portland. He lived on the Nathan Tibbetts place a few steps southeasterly of the residence of William E. Watson, on the site of the residence of Mrs. Abbie Tibbets.
4 Abraham, b. July 3, 1714.
5 Zachariah, b. Nov. 30, 1716, married Judith Sawyer 1742, daughter of Isaac Sawyer of Back Cove, and settled on Stevens Plains, the maternal ancestor of the Stevens of that region.
6 Thomas, b. 1718, married March 11, 1744 Mary Snow, daughter of John Snow, a ship carpenter, who came from Kittery and lived foot of George street. He settled at Morrill's Corner, back of the "Morrill House."

CONTINUED:

7 Susannah, born Feb. 13, 1720, married John Baker of Back Cove 1740.
8 Joshua, born Jan. 7, 1723, married Esther, daughter of John Cox of Portland and died in Westbrook 1816.
9 Abigail, born Aug. 21, 1727, married James Merrill.

I now present the record as found without additions, though rearranged so as to present it in order. The numbers are placed to the left that reference may be easy.

10 ABRAHAM Brackett and wife Joanna married Dec. 13, 1743. Children;
11 1 Hannah b. Sept. 4, 1744.
12 2 Abigail b. Feb. 7, 1747.
13 3 Susannah b. Oct. 7, 1748.
14 4 Eunice b. Dec. 20, 1750.
15 5 Elizabeth b. Mar. 4, 1752.
16 6 Abraham b. Aug. 8, 1753.
17 7 Joanna b. Mar. 19, 1755.
18 8 Nathaniel b. Sept. 4, 1756.
19 9 Joanna b. Sept. 4, 1760.
20 10 Abigail b. Apr. 2, 1762.
21 11 James b. Mar. 5, 1764.
22 12 ABRAM b. Aug. 20, 1765.
23 13 Sarah b. Mar. 7, 1767.
24 14 Anthony b. Mar. 30, 1769.
25 15 Samuel b. Nov. 5, 1770.
26 ABRAM and wife Hannah (Lunt) Brackett married Oct. 10, 1787. He died Nov. 19, 1838; she died Apr. 19, 1845.
27 1 Polly b. Feb. 14, 1788, married Oliver Sprague Feb. 25, 1806. She died Dec. 27, 1829. They lived in Sidney. Paul Stevens lives on the homestead.
28 2 Marcy b. May 1, 1789, died Dec. 13, 1851.
29 3 Joan b. Dec. 2, 1790, married Robert Packard Sept. 3, 1809. She died Dec. 1, 1857.
30 4 Esther b. Oct. 13, 1792, married Levi Moore Dec. 1811. She died July 29, 1862. They resided in Sidney.
31 5 Abigail b. Aug. 20, 1794, married Collins Moore Nov. 1812.
32 6 Sarah F. b. July 30, 1796, married Daniel Jacobs Nov. 12, 1822. Resided in Sidney.
33 7 Benjamin b. June 20, 1798, died Feb. 11, 1799.
34 8 Betsey A. b. June 5, 1800, died March 18, 1822.
35 9 Mariah H. b. June 17, 1802, married Paul T. Stevens Sept. 3, 1829. She died Oct. 14, 1843.
36 10 Abraham D. B. July 11, 1803 married Eliza Longley July 8, 1830. He died Apr. 9, 1850. Resided in Sidney.
37 11 Ruth S. b. Nov. 3, 1805 married Thomas Avery Dec. 23, 1828. She died July 12, 1882. Resided in Sidney.
38 12 Amos L. b. Jan. 22, 1808, married Eliza M. Hodgkins Nov. 1838. He died May 29, 1857.
39 13 Enos L. b. Aug. 20, 1809, married Miranda C. Brackett 2nd Nancy Robinson Dec. 1830. Died May 21, 1853.
40 14 STEPHEN B. b. Nov. 29, 1811, married Luisa M. Lunt Dec. 31, 1840. She born in Brunswick. He made the record here presented.
41 15 Benjamin F. Feb. 19 1814. Mary Shaw Feb. 9, 1837. He died Jan 11, 1852.
42 STEPHEN B. Brackett born Nov. 29, 1811, Louisa M. his wife born Feb. 14, 1818. Married Dec. 31, 1840. He died Aug. 17, 1864. Children. She died March 19, 1894, at Deering.
43 Joseph Henry Brackett born Nov. 23, 1841, died Aug. 29 1889.
44 1 Elora Brackett born June 3, 1843, died May 19, 1870
45 2 Mary Addia born Sept. 25, 1846.
46 3 Chas. E. born Dec. 18, 1848, died Apr. 25 1865.
47 4 Louisa Ellen born Dec. 29, 1851, died Apr. 15, 1874.
48 5 Hannah Frances b. May 10, 1853 (Mrs. William E. Watson of Stevens Plains or Deering)
49 6 Lizzie b. Sept. 23, 1856, Lizzie B. Emerson died May 24, 1889. (Abraham Drake Brackett died July 1896 aged 92 years.)
50

THE DEERING NEWS.

Saturday, November 10, 1894.

GRANDPA'S SCRAP BOOK

[Under this head historical and genealogical memoranda will be furnished the readers of the News that appears worthy of preservation, particularly of remote periods in our history within the city limits and immediate vicinity.]

Anthony Brackett Jr. (No. 3) did not marry for a second wife the widow of Job Lane as stated in my last chapter but Job Lunt, and where Job Lunt lived I cannot now say but *not* at Woodfords. Then the name of Abbie Tibbetts should appear as Miss not as Mrs.

The land upon which the hamlet of Stevens Plains is situated was granted to Phineas Jones by the town of Falmouth in 1737, and the record shows that James Douty had a residence at that time at what is now known as Abbott's, and sometimes as Allen's Corner.

The locality was given the name in 1744 of Pitch Pine Plains when Phineas Jones made a conveyance of the premises to Zachariah Brackett. After the occupancy by Capt. Isaac Sawyer Stevens "Pitch Pine" was dropped, and Stevens substituted therefor, which, as a local territorial distinguisher, has been in use ever since. A more appropriate topographical name could not have been applied, and outside the location of the few residents of this part of Old Falmouth and relationship of same, it is unnecessary for me to speak, the name itself covering the situation in every respect, only to say that a highway had been located through the forest, over the Plains, to connect the mills at Stroudwater with those of Presumpscot Falls, North Yarmouth, and other places in an easterly direction when Zachariah Brackett took up his abode there. By a plan made in 1811 it seemed that this road ran from what is now the head of Pleasant street to a point some few rods southeasterly of what is Morrill's Corner, thence to the track now in use in the direction of Presumpscot Falls.

Upon the westerly side of this forest track over this forest clad region, opposite a point a short distance southerly of the Universalist church edifice, say, at the foot of the present house lots located on the easterly side of the present way Zachariah Brackett reared his humble abode. Allusion has been made to the spot and its first occupants in an article before this. Zachariah and his bride Judith Sawyer, daughter of Isaac Sawyer of Ocean street, Back Cove, and is now noticed that the place may be known in connection with the Brackett name in the hereafter.

Zachariah's abode was a sort of "half way" place between the then stirring places of Stroudwater and Presumpscot Falls, and in after years there can be no doubt but was possessed of a "retailer's license" and soon after the occupancy of the spot by Zachariah a sign board must have read, "Friendly Inn," Z. Brackett, Proprietor. The size of the dwelling for a hotel at that time was not a consideration to be taken into account, but what transpired on the spot where the cellar indentation may still be seen by those who desire to behold the place cannot be known, not even the time of births of children, or time of deaths of first occupants till record facts are found and publicly used.

Neighbors to Zachariah who were not related were scarce, in fact there were none. His brother Thomas lived in back of the "Morrill House" at what is now known as Morrill's Corner, his wife's parents down where the late Isaac Bailey lived a half century, or they may have lived at first nearer the shore, and Benjamin Stevens, whose wife was a sister to his own, lived where Geo. C. Codman, Esq., does at this time, in the very house, I believe, Benjamin Stevens built; and to establish the relationship beyond doubt I will allude to a copy of an abstract of a record, in fact, here insert it:

Isaac Sawyer of Back Cove, heirs: Thomas Sawyer, Edward Sawyer, Abram Sawyer, daughters Elizabeth Jenks, Judith Brackett, son-in-law, Benjamin Stevens." (Cumb. Co. Reg. of Deeds, vol. 2, p. 64, Date, 762.)

If this is not sufficient here is another evidence:

Isaac Sawyer to my son Thomas Sawyer, "being the land whereon I now dwell containing 119 acres, exclusive of 7 1-2 acres included in the bounds aforesaid which I have heretofore sold my son-in-law, Benjamin Stevens, which land I purchased in 1726 and 1741."

In my last chapter I showed the fact that Zachariah Brackett was the fifth child of Zachariah Brackett, Sen., born Nov. 30, 1716. His wife was Judith Sawyer, as appeared by the foregoing, and the publication of marriage was made Nov. 7, 1742.

CHILDREN.

1 Sarah, born Oct. 18, 1740, m. Capt. Isaac G. Stevens.
2 Josiah.
3 Joseph.
4 Abigail.
5 Susannah, married Merrill Sawyer.
6 Judith, married Nathaniel Merrill of North Yarmouth.
7 Rebecca, married Joseph Wire of Livermore.

In some cases records of families are very meagre, this is one. I give here all I know of it, but more research will probably reveal more.

I have in a former chapter stated that Capt. Isaac S. Stevens was a son of Benjamin Stevens, born Sept. 1, 1748. Sarah Brackett, daughter of Zachariah Brackett, was born Oct. 17, 1748, as before stated, and the nuptial ceremony was performed Nov. 24 1769.

Of all his relation his name is the most prominent on the record pages of the past. In 1775 I first meet it emblazoned as a defender of his country on a "muster roll of Capt. Samuel Knight's company stationed upon the coast of Falmouth from July 10, 1775 to Jan. 1776," where he served as a sergeant.

Upon another record, (Mass. Archives vol. 24, p. 126,) the fact appears he was discharged from Fort Edwards, being a distance of 424 miles from Falmouth. Joseph Brackett was one of his companions from his native town.

Aug. 20, 1776, he appears on record as ensign under Capt. John Wentworth of Cape Elizabeth; Second Lieut. Joshua Brackett of Falmouth; and Josiah Brackett as private, but his achievements as a soldier of the Revolutionary army can never be known. His commission is in the possession of his descendants residing on the Plains.

In 1787 for a consideration of £60 the Zachariah Brackett homestead was sold to Enoch Ilsley who for the small sum of $212 sold it to "Isaac Stevens" in 1789, as follows:

All right in our father's farm, Zachariah Brackett, he possessed and owned at time of his death in Falmouth, bounded by land belonging to heirs of John Snow on southeast, land belonging to Nelson Rackliff on northwest, by land in possession of heirs of John Snow and George Berry and by county road on the northeast, and by land in possession of Isaac Stevens and John Blake on the southwest, with all the fences and house standing on said land, whereon our said father formerly lived.

With the war of the Revolution over, himself, the proprietor of a "hotel," with a growing family. I here leave the name of Captain Isaac Sawyer Stevens till next week.

THE DEERING NEWS.

Saturday, November 17, 1894.

GRANDPA'S SCRAP BOOK

[Under this head historical and genealogical memoranda will be furnished the readers of the News that appears worthy of preservation, particularly of remote periods in our history within the city limits and immediate vicinity.]

I left in the last issue of the News the name of Captain Isaac Sawyer Stevens as the proprietor of an inn and farm valued at two hundred and twelve dollars, and answering to the name of plain "Isaac Stevens."

To the careful observer considerable of an historical order is summoned up in the above that does not appear on the surface at first glance, particularly the name itself, to the genealogical student.

Of all characters that I have tracked upon the "sands of time" this hero of the days of the American Revolution has been the worst to follow.

He was christened Isaac Sawyer Stevens, in perpetuation of the name of his maternal grandfather, Isaac Sawyer, but when he arrived at legal maturity, or the time he could "handle a musket and smoke a pipe," he appears as Isaac Stevens, plain and simple. Later he appears, or I should say there appears on manuscript record pages the names of Isaac Stevens, wife Sarah; Isaac Stevens, wife Mahitable; Isaac Stevens, wife Hannah; Isaac Stevens; Capt. Isaac S. Stevens; Isaac Stevens Sen., Isaac Stevens Jr., Falmouth; Isaac Stevens, Jr., New Gloucester. And in the grave yard enclosure, westerly side of Windham road, about a mile from Morrill's Corner, located on a sunny slope, one of the best within the city, stands an unpretending white slab inscribed as follows:

ISAAC S. STEVENS
DIED
OCTOBER 23, 1820,
AGED 72 YEARS.

In reference to his death I find in the Eastern Argus of October 31, 1820, this only:

"DIED, Captain Isaac S. Stevens, aged 72 years. Capt. S. leaves a widow, seven children and fifty grand children to lament his loss."

His family record runs as follows: Capt. Isaac Sawyer Stevens, born at Falmouth. Sept. 17, 1748. Sarah Brackett, his wife, born at Falmouth October 18, 1749, married Nov. 24, 1769. He died October 23, 1820; she died February 23, 1830. Children, all born on Stevens Plains:

1 Sarah, born Aug. 17, 1771.
2 Isaac Jr., born March 20, 1773.
3 Molly, born June 24, 1776.
4 Zachariah B., born March 20, 1778.
5 Nathaniel, born March 21, 1780.
6 Lucy, born March 3, 1782.
7 Josiah, born March 3, 1784.
8 William, born December 11, 1785.
9 Nabby born April 17, 1791.

I have shown that there are upon manuscript records a small multiplicity of Isaacs as a prefix to the name of Stevens which are very perplexing, or were to me at one time, but after much study I found that the eight Isaacs represented just two persons—sire and son—no more, and after Isaac Jr. became of age, who had two wives and died at New Gloucester, he went by the name of Isaac Stevens Jr., while his father was known as Isaac S. Stevens.

I have also shown that Capt. Stevens was an inn keeper after the close of the war of the Revolution, his inn must have been more productive of dimes and dollars than his farm. But withall he was a blacksmith and lived in the days of good cheer when the recitals of scenes of the Revolution to bar room denizens were all absorbing themes accompanied by songs of revelry and flip drinking. His abode soon became the suburban resort of Portland and vicinity military, and May training and military muster days, more than a half score of companies, thirteen at one time of which I find record, congregated there. In course of time came a new dwelling house, addition, dance hall attached, bowling alleys and places for amusements peculiar to the time and occasion. The dwelling thus built stands to-day on the westerly side of Stevens Plains avenue, a little obliquely with the line of the street, a reminder of old fashioned architecture—houses without pediment ends but overhanging cornices, gable peaked front door finish and heavy window caps and sills.

THE DEERING NEWS.

Saturday, December 1, 1894.

GRANDPA'S SCRAP BOOK

[Under this head historical and genealogical memoranda will be furnished the readers of the News that appears worthy of preservation, particularly of remote periods in our history within the city limits and immediate vicinity.]

The first recorded land title on what is now known as Stevens' Plains reads in brief as follows: "Laid out to Phineas Jones fifty acres of land in Falmouth adjoining on both sides the road that leads from Stroudwater to Presumpscot Great Dam, beginning bounds at a birch tree which is in the westerly corner of one hundred acres of land on which John Snow now lives, etc., etc., which fifty acres of land is to satisfy the one half of one hundred acres lot sold by Henry Wheeling Jr. etc." This was in 1738. In 1741 Stephen Jones sold for 150£ to Abraham and Zachariah Brackett the 50 acres laid out Phineas Jones which he says he purchased March 28 1741, but I find nothing to show that Abraham ever disposed of his interest in the purchase.

Capt. Isaac S. Stevens purchased the title to a twenty acre lot not located at time of purchase, but allowing it was located on the westerly side of Stevens' Plains avenue he then had title to seventy acres only, fifty of which he purchased of the heirs of his father-in-law, Zachariah Brackett, and twenty as above indicated.

In some mysterious way Captain Isaac's land possession grew so as to make him trouble as I will soon show.

In a former chapter under this head, or an article entitled Stevens' Plains which appeared as a News editorial, it was stated that all the houses on the Plains in the year 1811 were occupied by persons of the name of Stevens. An old plan made at that date lead me into an error.

In 1803 for a consideration of $75 "Isaac Stevens" sold Thomas Brisco a one and one-half acre lot commencing bounds at "a stake standing south 40 degrees east 4 rods distant from the south east corner of said Thomas Brisco's house."

The next year Captain Isaac sold Samuel Clary (before noticed) for $50 a house lot on westerly side of the highway adjoining Thomas Brisco's lot. In 1806 for $300 Clary, "tinman of Portland," sold the lot "with house thereon" to Elizah North. In 1807 Elizah sold half of the house and lot for $150 to Elisha North, then Elisha sold to Thomas Brisco. Brisco, his wife and five adopted daughters, four of whom married and reared families, were "characters" who will be noticed hereafter. They all sleep the sleep that knows no awaking in adjoining lots in Pine Grove cemetery. The house lot was located in the south westerly angle made by Stevens' Plains avenue and the entrance to Evergreen cemetery.

In 1809 for a consideration of $105 Captain Isaac conveyed to Zachariah Brackett a one acre lot located on the westerly side of the highway "40 rods from the front door of my dwelling house." This I believe to have been the lot where the brick house stood that was burned a few years ago, now owned by Mr. Best, and this record establishes the fact that the Capt. Isaac S. Stevens house, now known as the old William Stevens house, was standing in 1809.

THE DEERING NEWS.

Saturday, December 8, 1894.

GRANDPA'S SCRAP BOOK

[Under this head historical and genealogical memoranda will be furnished the readers of the News that appears worthy of preservation, particularly of remote periods in our history within the city limits and immediate vicinity.]

Of Cæsar Thomes I know but little to record here. At the adoption of the charter by the Commonwealth of Massachusetts all slaves were made free and he among the rest.

Upon the Superior Court records of 1805 I find the case of Isaac S. Stevens vs. Cæsar Thomes which was an appeal from the court of common pleas in an action to recover possession of three acres and forty-one rods of land, the bounds of which commenced 49 rods southerly of Stevens' front door in his residence on the westerly side of the road leading over Stevens' Plains, the lot being 34 rods long and 8 rods deep, in which case Stevens recovered the costs amounting to $53.

In 1811 I find a record of much larger dimensions,—an action of ejectment brought by the town of Falmouth against Captain Stevens to recover 370 acres of land valued at $500, the recorded bounds of which read as follows:

Located on westerly side of the highway, easterly side line being the county road, northwesterly by land laid out to Paines Jones, southwesterly on land laid out to John Blake and on the Mile Square Lot. Stevens claimed to "hold by possession of more than six years since action was commenced," and he recovered $47.53 costs of court and held the land against the claim of the town.

The lot was located on the westerly side of the road upon which is located a large part of Evergreen cemetery. The trial lasted four days. Wm. Brackett was a witness who received pay for 7 miles travel; Joseph Brackett 20 miles travel; Joshua Brackett 20 miles travel; and Peter Brackett, 12 miles travel.

The papers in the case are meager, but a plan of considerable historical value is found, which locates the site of the residence of Zachariah Brackett, the first occupant of the soil, as I have before intimated; the dwelling of Isaac Stevens, Jr., Zachariah B. Stevens, Joseph Stevens and Capt. Isaac S. Stevens. The paper upon which the plan is drawn is inscribed as follows:

"Plan of land including

The plains whereon the Stevens dwell adjoining The Mile Square (so called) by a scale of 40 rods to an inch.

pr. JAMES TORREY, Survr.

Falmouth, 11th m 1811.

N. B. The pricked lines by desire of I. S. Stevens."

What is now known as Central avenue forms the northeasterly side line of the "Mile Square Grant" of land to Sylvanus Davis in 1680 by Governor Danforth, within which grant Capis' mill privilege is located and to which all the land titles of the mile square region are traceable.

The disputed title as it appears on the on the plan extended on what is now Stevens' Plains avenue from Central avenue to the railroad track at Morrill's Corner and contained, as indicated by the figures, 146 acres.

In 1813 Capt. Stevens made a mortgage deed to Cumberland Bank, for a consideration of $200, of his landed possessions on the easterly side and as the document presents a mirror of the situation on the easterly side of the avenue at that date, I here present an abstract:

"About 35 acres of land, 5 acres of which is tillage and 30 acres of pasturage. Commence bounds at southerly line of a lot Zachariah B. Stevens purchased of Ebenezer H. Sawyer, on easterly side of county road, southerly by county road leading to Portland till it comes to land owned by Isaac Sawyer (with the exception of half an acre sold to Oliver Buckley) thence by said Sawyer's land and Henry Knight's land and Samuel Sawyer's land, then by Zach. B. Stevens' land to first bounds, together with four barns, two sheds, two shops and one slaughter house thereon."

The copies of original documents and references thereto, present an outline view of Stevens' Plains in 1811-13. Captain Stevens was really a sort of land king and must have been pretty nearly a monarch of all his eyes surveyed, in which position I will leave him till next week.

THE DEERING NEWS.

Saturday, December 15, 1894.

GRANDPA'S SCRAP BOOK

[Under this head historical and genealogical memoranda will be furnished the readers of the News that appears worthy of preservation, particularly of remote periods in our history within the city limits and immediate vicinity.]

But few children will leave the parental roof, or the immediate surroundings of "home" if there is sufficient subsistance for all. Proof of this assertion is found in the fact that in the case of Captain Isaac S. Stevens his children did not wander off—did not go to far countries for husbands and wives, but obtained them near at hand and settled near at home. I think all the sons by "profession" were "knights of the anvil." From what is now Presumpscot trotting park on Stevens Plains avenue to near the burying place on the Windham road they were strung out. It was a wonderful long string of relations. A string nearly two miles in length, comprizing the homestead of Captain Isaac, and the families of nine children, William, the eight child retaining the homestead. And why should they not have remained near the parental abode? The sire evidently was possessed of magnetic attraction for his children, as well as the public generally. The story of adventure while a soldier, had a charm for all, then he had an abundance of land as I have shown. It did not require so much then as now to start one fairly well in the world. Then there was pleasure and gaity at home at stated times for Captain Isaac's broad fields was a place of rendezvous for regimental gatherings, real military gala days. In a copy of the Argus of Oct. 15, 1800, I find a record that shows that on that day there were assembled on the Plains a "troop of Cavalry;" a company of artillery; three companies of light infantry; and thirteen companies of heavy infantry.

Of Capt. Isaac's family I have already shown that Sarah was the eldest, born August 17, 1771 and married Nathaniel Haskell, who was a blacksmith and who lived on the Windham road not far south easterly of the old cemetery, but on the opposite side of the road from the cemetery—in fact on the place now owned by the heirs of H. H. Harris deceased.

In 1812 for a consideration of $2,500 Peter Brackett of Falmouth sold to Nathaniel Haskell of New Gloucester "all my homestead farm in Falmouth, with all the buildings."

The farm was subsequently sold by Nathaniel Haskell Jr. to I. P. Woodbury, who sold it to L. B. Dennett Esq., lawyer of Portland, who in turn sold it to H. H. Harris. And this is all I know of the Haskell branch of the Stevens family.

Isaac Stevens Jr., born March 20, 1773, was the second child of Captain Isaac. He married Dec. 15, 1795, Mehitable Knight, who was born Aug. 20, 1774. She died, he married second, Hannah Wier a widow.

Children by first wife:

1 Harriet, born March 31, 1798.
2 Augusta, born April 20, 1800.
She married Hiram Sawyer May 15, 1828, and resided on Windham road.
3 Lewis, born Jan. 28, 1802. He went to sea and never returned.

Children by second wife:

4 Cloracy
5 Abbie
6 Mary
7 Lorene
8 Hudson
9 Sarah married Africa Cotton, and resides in Deering. I do not put this last part of the list down as correct.

The quaint appearing old long one story dwelling house, one half constructed of wood, the other of brick, standing on westerly side of Forest avenue just southerly of the electric car house was his place of abode prior to his removal to New Gloucester, and in this building I am told he kept "a hotel." The building is represented on the plan to which allusion has been made.

In 1813, or thereabouts, Captain Isaac conveyed to his son Isaac, for a consideration of $500, a tract of land located where the house to which allusion has just been made stands; it contained forty-two acres, and the record says, "being the same land whereon said Stevens' dwelling house stands on."

In 1813 Isaac Jr. "blacksmith" conveyed an acre of this lot to Henry Blake for $100, adjoining George Bishop's land.

Concerning the Blakes my notes need classification. Jasper Blake came early after the last settlement of Falmouth and bought land easterly of Lunt's Corner upon which John H. Blake resides. John bought into the northeasterly corner of the mile square tract. He decended from Jasper—son I think.

"James Blake had children as follows:
1 Henry, born April 21, 1789. This is he who purchased the acre lot I think of Isaac Stevens Jr., and built the house now standing. He had a daughter Almira born Jan. 26, 1817.
2 Mary, born July 21, 1791 died Nov. 17, 1816.
3 Almira, born Dec. 19, died Nov. 17, 1816.
4 James, born Dec. 12, 1794.
5 Frank, born Sept. 30, 1799.
6 John, born Aug. 28, 1803.

This is all I know of Isaac Stevens Jr. and the Blakes of Morrill's Corner except Henry Blake was a house carpenter and at one time he and George Bishop were in company.

THE DEERING NEWS.

Saturday, December 22, 1894.

GRANDPA'S SCRAP BOOK

[Under this head historical and genealogical memoranda will be furnished the readers of the News that appears worthy of preservation, particularly of remote periods in our history within the city limits and immediate vicinity.]

In 1798 for a consideration of $1200 Joshua Racklyft, shipwright, and Benjamin Racklyft, rigger, both of Newburyport, conveyed to William Kenney and Zachariah Sawyer of Falmouth 105 acres of land, "being all the land our honored father purchased of Phineas Jones by deed dated May 15, 1738."

William Kenney was an uncle to Zachariah Sawyer by marriage, as I will presently show—Kenney's wife being a daughter of Captain Isaac S. Stevens, while the wife of Sawyer was a daughter of Isaac Stevens, Jr.

This lot was located next northwesterly of the lot conveyed by Captain Stevens to his son Isaac, and the dwelling of George Bishop was located in the southeasterly corner of it, or very close to it.

Whether the Bracklyfts (spelled several ways) ever occupied the lot I cannot state positively, but I think they did.

There was in "ye olden times" a dwelling standing somewhere near where the Bishop house of today stands, and it is traditional that when Portland was burned in 1775, the mother of Geo. Bishop wheeled away all the household goods saved and took up her abode in the house to which allusion is made.

In the year 1798 Kenney for $500 conveyed his interests in one half of the lot being 52½ acres, "commencing bounds at the most northerly corner of the lot, thence running by the road southeasterly 58 rods.

Then for a consideration of $500, in 1799, "Zachariah Sawyer, mariner, conveyed to Kinney his interest in the other half of the 105 acre lot, and then in 1800 for a consideration of $800, Kinney conveyed the lot to Chauncy Woodford, whose wife was a daughter to Capt. Stevens. Woodford lived in what is now called the Purington house, and I presume he built it.

Upon further examination of my notes I find that the Widow Bishop lived in an "old house" that stood just northerly of the Portland & Rochester railroad track, and in it the widow taught private schools.

Zachariah Sawyer belonged to the family of Sawyers who lived easterly of Lunt's Corner where descendants still reside. He was not only a mariner but he was a brick mason also. He married Sarah Thompson, Jan. 17, 1797 and the record says "both of Portland," but it is traditional that she was a Buxton woman.

CHILDREN.

1 Nathaniel, born Sept. 25, 1797.
2 Amos, born Oct. 18, 1798.
3 William, born Aug. 1, 1800.

These three all died young and within thirteen days of each other.

4 Hiram, born Feb. 10, 1802, married May 15, 1828 Augusta Stevens, daughter of Isaac Stevens, Jr., born April 20, 1800. He retained the homestead of his father, both living to see "ripe old age," and both died within three or four years.
5 Joanna, born Jan. 8, 1804, and died unmarried.
6 Sarah, born July 15, 1806, married Jeremiah Jackson, son of Henry Jackson, of Jackson's Hotel that stood where the Morrill's house stands at Morrill's Corner.
7 Zachariah, born March 15, 1808.
8 Hannah, born April 16, 1810 and died unmarried.
9 Jane, born Jan. 17, 1812, married Moses Chase.
10 Dorcas, born July 2, 1814, and died unmarried.
11 William, born July 29, 1816, died young.
12 Harriet, born Feb. 23, 1818, married Levi Bradish Stevens, son of Nathaniel Stevens, born Dec. 22, 1811, and was a brother to Maria (Stevens) Maxfield whose obituary appeared in the News two weeks since. Levi lived at Morrill's Corner where children survive him.

THE DEERING NEWS.

Saturday, December 29, 1894.

GRANDPA'S SCRAP BOOK

[Under this head historical and genealogical memoranda will be furnished the readers of the News that appears worthy of preservation, particularly of remote periods in our history within the city limits and immediate vicinity.]

In my last article I committed an error in saying that William Kenney was an uncle to Zachariah Sawyer; there was no relationship, but William Kenney was an uncle to Hiram Sawyer by marriage, Kenney's wife being a sister to Isaac Stevens, Jr., who was a brother to Kenney's wife.

I stated with reference to the three eldest children of Zachariah Sawyer that they all died within thirteen days of each other.

In the very imperfect record of the funerals attended by the Rev. Caleb Bradley I find the following:

March 3, 1802, a child of Zach. Sawyer, 1 year, 7 months.
March 7, 1802, a child of Zach. Sawyer, 4 years, 7 months.
March 19, 1802, a child of Zach. Sawyer, 3 years, 6 months.

In a former article I alluded to Cæsar Thomas with whom Capt. Isaac S. Stevens had a law suit. In the record from which the foregoing was obtained I select the following:

February 15, 1801, the wife of Cæsar Thomas, (colored) aged 50 years.
February 19, 1819, Cæsar Thomas, (colored) aged 80 years.

This gentleman of color owned land, and had a habitation at one time where Belknap's tripe factory stood near Brighton Corner.

The third child of Capt. Isaac S. Stevens, named Molly, born on Stevens Plains, Jan. 24, 1776, married Nov. 5, 1795, a William Kenney of Portland, born there Oct. 31, 1774. She died August 29, 1840; he died Nov. 7, 1844.

He purchased his first land in 1798 located on the westerly side of Windham road between Morrill's Corner and the old cemetery, where he lived, a few rods northerly of the brook that crossed the highway. About thirty-two years ago the house was burned. It was then used by his descendants as an inn.

The first house, a one-story dwelling now standing, which is the first after passing the brook, was the homestead of Stetson Kenney. The William Kenney homestead stood a few rods northerly of the residence of Stetson, upon the site of which Freeman Kenney now resides, who is a son of Stetson. William's wife was the mother of ten children:

1. Samuel, born Feb. 29, 1796. Died of consumption, unmarried, and was buried from the homestead.
2. William Jr., (sometimes called William Henry) born June 17, 1798; married Louisa Hancock, lived at Morrill's Corner, has three children, at least alive, one of whom resides in this city.
3. Clarisa, born August 1, 1802, married James Webb (I think) of Gorham and resided in Bridgton, where they had born to them two girls and ten boys.
4. Isaac Stevens, born July 1, 1804; died, unmarried, on the homestead.
5. Stetson, born Oct. 17, 1806, married Susan Brackett of Gray. He lives as above indicated.
6. Nabby P., born Nov. 17, 1808, married William Baldwin, removed to Laurenceville, Ill., where both died.
7. Sarah, born Nov. 13, 1810, married James Irish of Gorham, and removed to the same place as that of her sister, Nabby P.
8. Louisa, born May 28, 1813, married first —— Nason of Gorham, by whom she had Mary S., and Louisa, second, Samuel H. Lunt, and had Augusta S. and Hattie E. Both husbands have passed beyond the veil, but Mrs. Nason-Lunt, the only surviving child of William Kenney, resides with two of her daughters on the westerly side of the Windham road a little southerly of the brook, the second house I think. I allude to the brook because it is a landmark and will in consequence aid "generations unborn", when the record of the Kenney family is finally made.
9. Sophia W., born Dec. 6, 1815, married Frederick Pride, who lived on the homestead when the house was burned.
10. Frances A., born Oct. 27, 1819, married Thomas Nason, who also lived on the homestead at time of destruction of dwelling house.

This is all I know of the Kenney family.

Mrs. Lunt possesses a record made by a young lady of Gorham in 1836 of the Kenney children which is unusually elaborate as to size and particularly in workmanship, but dates differ somewhat from those here presented. The list from which I have copied was made prior to the birth of the last child, so I am inclined to the opinion that it is nearer correct than that of Mrs. Lunt's.

A6 1894

GRANDPA'S SCRAP BOOK

The Hamlet of Woodfords.

I closed my chapter under this head last week, with Jacob Adams and Thomas Morse residing together as innkeepers in the dwelling known later as the Saunders house, but the printer made me say, or he called the word street in the manuscript shop, and then where he says Adams sold the farm to Morse for £2000, it should read $2000.

In 1804 they sold to Joseph Stevens, blacksmith, a half acre of land for $100, where the brick house stands, a few rods southerly of the foot of Pleasant street. John Dole at that time was his guardian, and Adam's wife was named Peggy.

July 20, 1805, Jacob Adams died. Where he was buried or what became of his wife, I have no knowledge. After this, or in the year 1807, Isaac Knight and Polly, his wife, and daughter of Jacob Adams, relinquished all claim to the estate of her father.

April 9, 1800, Rev. Caleb Bradley records in his journal the deaths of Peggy Adams, aged 19; Aug. 8, 1800, Joseph Adams, age not given; Sept. 19, 1802, Thankful Adams, aged 17 years; but I have no means of knowing whose children they were.

In 1809 there was a land boom. Morse sold a lot between the corner and the Asa Taylor house to Artemas Prentiss, for $230; another to Jonathan Haskell at same place for $250, and to Elijah North thirteen acres where the Presumpscot Trotting Park is located, who built the great house there which was burned a few years since. At about this time Elisha Higgins, Jr., built the house now seen at Higgins' Corner, and the house of the late Edward Newman was commenced, all of which will be noticed hereafter.

April 12, 1807, died—wife of Thomas Morse, aged 33 years. (Journal Rev. Caleb Bradley.

Eastern Argus, May 14, 1809, advertisement of Thomas Morse:

A fine stand for a Tavern, good buildings, well watered, and sixty acres of land."

In 1810 Thomas Morse sold to Christopher S. Kimball, tanner, for $200, "the homestead farm where I now dwell." The transfer notices the lots sold by Morse as follows:

Woodfords—Wm. Lunt, Cornelius Adams, Artemias Prentiss, John Tucker and Joseph Stevens.

In 1813, and later, Christopher Sargent Kimball was mixed up with Cotton Kimball, in ownership, and John Jones, Esq., as adm. on the estate of Morse, in 1814, held an execution for $2,500 against the place.

In 1817, Cotton Kimball of Haverhill, for a consideration of $30, sold to Joseph Stevens, blacksmith, a little lot "cut off and laying on the northeasterly side of the road recently opened from Shaw's Corner (now Morrill's) to the county road." This piece must have been where the railroad crosses Ocean street.

In 1823, for $1,700, Cotton Kimball, through his attorney Wm. Kimball, sold the place to Jonathan Smith of Portsmouth, N. H., father to Hon. F. O. J. Smith, deceased, and the next year Smith conveyed it to Samuel Saunders, Smith keeping a public house while residing there.

HIGHWAYS.

York Deeds, vol. 27, p. 36, time, 1750, abstract of depositions of Isaac and Abram Sawyer, (father and son), Isaac being 67 and Abraham 34 years of age, testify and say that, "in the year 1732, witnessed the running of a line between the farms now owned by Pote and Skillings at Back Cove, beginning at a stake in the middle of the gully (Coyle's gully) at about highwater mark in the footpath where people used to pass, about three rods southward of an old back of a chimney, from which stake down into Back Cove, and from said stake into the woods as the fence now stands."

This record has attached to it much historical value, for it gives the time of birth of the first permanent dwellers upon the soil of Back Cove, after its last settlement (near Woodfords) the fact that the first ways of travel by land were by paths, and fixes the site of one of the dwellings near Woodfords prior to the destruction of Falmouth by the Indians.

In 1735 a highway three rods wide was laid out from Moses Pearson's wharf, a point where the Rochester railroad extension crosses Grove street towards Woodfords, thence along where Deering street is located through the "corner", and along Ocean Street. As then located it is now in use. In now viewing the situation, where the Rochester road crosses the highway, it seems incredible that once there was water and a wharf there, but such are the written facts.

In 1749 there was a survey made and a public way two and a half rods wide laid out between the farms of Samuel Lunt and William Pote (Spring street). Daniel Godfrey of Saccarappa was the surveyor and the return was made Mar. 17 of that year. The course was same as now to the Congregational meeting house, thence southerly, intersecting the county road about where the town house stands, but the way was never accepted by the town.

In 1752 the present course of Spring street was adopted, at which time Pote was dead and Sawyer died the same year, being three rods wide. This change and other records all tend to show that the old house on Spring St., nearly opposite foot of High, in which John Newman, deceased, lived so many years, was built just prior to 1750, and one cause of the change of location was to accommodate it, which was built by one John Bailey, Jr., aided by his father, Deacon John Bailey, a prominent character about Falmouth in ye olden times, and here I must lay aside the consideration of highway records till next week, at which time I hope for space to allude to the first Woodfords and others of the hamlet of Back Cove.

GRANDPA'S SCRAP BOOK

Woodfords.
PART SECOND—CONTINUED.

March 23, 1889, I obtained from Mrs. Matilda M. Packard, daughter of John Dain, who resided in the queer shaped old brick Dain house, No. 16 Portland st., who has since died, the following Mr. Dain was a Revolutionary soldier, and shortly after obtaining the facts, I published an account of him in the Portland Argus.

John Proctor, born May 28, 1747; Esther Proctor, born Jan. 15, 1759.

Children—Hannah, born Dec. 31, 1790, married, Jan. 11, 1818 to John Dain; Esther, born Dec. 31, 1792; Frederick, born Dec. 11, 1849; James, born Jan. 22, 1797.

Died—John Proctor, Oct. 14, 1820; Edward Mountford, father to said Esther Proctor, born Feb. 27, 1732; Hannah, wife of Edmund Mountford, born 1730; Elizabeth Mountford, born Dec. 27, 1729, being the sister of the said Edmund Mountford; Samuel Mountford, born June 19, 1737.

Died—Edmund Mountford April 30, 1806; Hannah, his wife, Dec. 1, 1813; Elizabeth Mountford Dec. 28, 1818; Samuel Mountford Oct. 29, 1819.

Nathaniel Proctor, brother of John, born Oct. 27, 1753; Sarah, wife of Nathaniel Proctor, born on Long Island 1765; Captain Nathaniel Proctor died Dec. 29, 1825; Mary Mountford, born June 1754. She died March 1, 1825.

A foot note on page 87 of Pason Smith's journal relating to this name is interesting from which it appears with other facts that Samuel Mountford remained single till he was 70 years of age after which he married twice.

I have here presented the record obtained of Mrs. Packard just as found, but none of the names here presented are names of descendents of Charity Lunt for her husband was William Proctor. The record is here presented as a record of relatives by marriage, and that it may be preserved.

March 6, 1756, intention of marriage was made public between Mary Lunt and John Goodwin, but whether or not Jane married I have not learned. And this is all I know relative to the descendants of Samuel Lunt, of Woodfords.

In 1773 Charity Lunt conveyed to Daniel Lunt, blacksmith, for a consideration of £98: 13s., the farm, and at this point in time her name disappeared from records. Who Daniel Lunt was I am unable to learn, but he held the place till Feb. 14, 1778, when he conveyed it to one Jacob Adams, a cordwainer, of the part of Falmouth now known as Portland. As the price was £420, Lunt must have built the "Saunders house" that sat where Saunders store is located and was burned a few years ago, or money had greatly depreciated between the dates of 1773 when the widow Lunt sold it, and 1778 when purchased by Adams.

JACOB ADAMS.

This man was the son of Jacob Adams of Portland, a sailor, and had a sister who married a man by the name of Woodman and another who married a Knight. A court record shows he had trouble with Peter Noyes about the first of his residing here but as there are no "papers of the case on file" nothing more can be learned from court records till 1793 when he received an innholders license.

Adams was a "cordwainer," a cordwainer in ye olden time being a person who understood the art of making leather as well as shoes.

Of the personality of this man, of his offspring, or career I can learn but little though records indicate that he was a stirring person. He added to his original purchas land at Higgins Corner, and on the "corner" where now resides Mrs. John J. Chenery he built a brick shoe maker's shop, and with all he was an inn keeper.

In 1796 the first innovation upon the homestead lot was made when 131¾ square rods of land was sold from the south westerly corner of the farm to Thomas Knight, housewright, for a consideration of £16, upon which Knights had built a house, which, twenty years later, was posessed by Asa Taylor whose wife was a daughter of the first Higgins, who lived and died in the old John Newman house, built prior to 1750, and now standing on Spring, opposite the foot of High street.

Asa Taylor was born in Sandburton, N. H., Dec. 28, 1778, married Tamzia Higgins March 17, 1811. She was born in Falmouth, March 19, 1785. Children: Freeman Todd Taylor, born April 28, 1813; Emily Ann Taylor, born Jan. 1, 1817.

Thomas Knight's lot consisted of three purchases, the first of Adams in 1796 as noted in the foregoing, the second, of Jonathan Sawyer., Jr., in 1804, and the third, of Thomas Morse, in 1806. In 1813, for a consideration of $1,200, Knight and wife Joanna, convey the lot to Henry Knight, who in 1815 conveys a half acre to Joseph Cox, comb maker, and in 1816 the two acres remaining to Asa Taylor for $885. Cox built the house now known as the Thomas J. Riggs place, and between the Cox house on the east now standing and on the Cox lot and the original site of the Knight's house on the west, the Woodford's Congregational meeting house stands.

Joseph Cox married Charlotte, daughter of Isaac Sawyer then known as Collector Sawyer, who resided on Ocean street, where the late Isaac Bailey, deceased, lived many years.

Their children were:

Enoch, born Aug 5, 1816; Susanna Sawyer, June 5, 1818; Lemuel, Sep. 17, 1820; Sarah, Sep. 22. 1822; Charles Edward, June 25, 1825; Jane Stevens, Dec. 31, 1827.

In 1797 further innovations were made by Jacob Adams upon the homestead farm of himself and Samuel Lunt, by the sale of two acres of land where the so-called Mosier house now stands, occupied many years by Deacon Ebenezer D. Woodford, whose daughter married Mosier, hence the present name, to one Isaac Knight, "also the brick shoe maker's shop standing on the westerly side of the road, with the land it stands on and the land lying between said shop and the two roads running by the same."

In 1799, two years later than the record of the last sale, Adams conveys to this same Knights sixty square rods of land where the brick shop stood with a frontage of five rods, extending back on Spring street, or "lane" as it was then called, twelve rods, "excepting what I heretofore sold him," meaning the brick shoe maker's shop and land upon which it sat.

This Knight's wife was Polly or Mary daughter of Jacob Adams, to whom he was married in 1799, and this Knight built the so-called Mosier house as now seen and the original part of the John J. Chenery house on the opposite corner.

Anthony Morse lived near Presumscott falls and in 1794 sold his farm to "my two sons," Ephraim and Thomas Morse. In 1799 Jacob Adams for a consideration of £2,000 conveys to Thomas Morse and wife Jane (Bailey) "my homestead farm at Back Cove (lots sold to Thomas Knights and Isaac Knights excepted) and Thomas Morse, with Adams residing with him, continued the business of an innholder, where I leave them till next week.

Aug 1894

GRANDPA'S SCRAP BOOK

Woodfords.

The first European permanent occupants of Ancient Falmouth of whom there are manuscript records were Geo. Cleeve and Richard Tucker. By Ancient Falmouth, is meant the present town of Falmouth, Cape Elizabeth, Portland, Westbrook and Deering, here arranged in order as to time of incorporation. Cleeve and Tucker were adventurers and landed at a point a few rods north easterly of India street, Portland, but the story of the landing and incidents connected therewith is too well known to receive notice here.

At that time the northerly shore of Back Cove was more attractive on account of its well watered and productive soil than any other of the region hereabouts, and its close connection with deep water communication. To those two first occupants are traceble, with one exception, all the present land titles from Deering point along the shore of the Cove to the Falmouth and Deering territorial dividing line, but I will not say at this time at what point a settlement was first made; this I will do later on.

In the year 1658 there was a "land boom" at a point on the Cove line now known as Woodfords and several lots were taken up. March 25th of that year Phineas Rider received a deed of fifty-five acres at "Back Cove and at the water side," between the lots of Wmphrey Durram and Geo Ingarsoll, five and forty poles by the water side, and soe on yt breadth north westerly into the woods eight scoore poole untill the 55 acres bee ended." The consideration was five shillings before the delivery, "also yearly rent of twelve pence and one days work for one man every year forever, the days work to be paid at any time in the year after six days warning."

This tract was what is now embraced with the bounds of Spring and Woodfords streets on the south, the waters of Back Cove on the east, a line between the Saunder heirs, and Geo. C. Codman, Esq., on the north, extending back westerly to the westerly side of the First Congregational meeting house, the back end being a few rods wider than the front or water end.

Somewhere on this lot it appears Phineas Rider lived, but his personality can be described only through the aid of conjecture, so it is better not to attempt it. In the Massachusetts achives his name is found among others in papers of 1660. In 1666 he was a juror, and 1670 a member of "Falmouth and Scarborugh commission court."

In 1675 came the untamed savage in warlike attire, destroying life and property with lighted torch and sharpened tomahawk, the entire population fleeing for safety.

On the 12th of April 1678 articles of peace were signed, captives released, refugees allowed to occupy their former homes then desolate.

With the fall of Fort Loyall in May of 1690, located at the foot of India street, Portland, not only the prosperity of the settlement around Back Cove was overthrown again but hope was eclipsed, and not only was there desolation at Back Cove but throughout all Falmouth. The Indian and the wild beast were the supreme rulers, and this state of affairs continued many years or till 1726 at Black Cove, when Isaac Sawyer came who will be noticed in a chapter by itself in the hereafter.

In 1738 Thomas Flint, a millright sold to Jonathan Flint, who was a sailor, a half of the lot before described for a reasonable compensation and the other half for a few shillings, thus showing there was doubt as to ownership of the entire lot. These brothers were residents of Salem. In the conveyance the names of adjoining lot owners are given thus locating before the Indian War, the original occupants or neighbors of Phineas Rider.

In 1743 for £97 Jonathan Flint and wife Mary joining, convey the lot "with dwelling house" to Samuel Lunt of Kittery who was a cordwainer, and this man took up his abode on the now so-called Saunders farm.

On the 17th day of June, 1752, "being in God's righteous Providence upon a Bed of Sickness and pain, and not knowing how soon He may take me out of the World, by Death," made his will as follows:

First—I give to my dear children, Samuel Lunt, Job Lunt, Charity Proctor, Mary Lunt and Jane Lunt each of them the sum of twenty shillings lawful money to be paid them by my wife out of my estate.

Second—I give to my dear wife Charity Lunt the whole and every part of my Estate real and personal, after my debts are paid and the forementioned Legacies to my Children, to be to her use, profit and disposal entirely forever.

The will was signed in the presence of Isaac Ilsley who lived where Hawkin's shoe factory stands, John Snow who lived at foot of George street, close to the water of the Cove, and Dorothy Pote who lived near the present residence of George Rackleff, and as the will was probated in 1752 he must have died that year.

This chapter will be continued in the next number of the News.

THE WEIGHT OF AUTHORITY

A draft of a letter written by Charles Thorton Libby to Leonard Bond Chapman about 1914 or 1915 to correct some egregious errors in published Portland history

My dear Mr. Chapman:

In looking into the question of the 200th anniversary of the founding of Portland, whether it should commemorate the year 1715, about which year Parson Smith's narrative says that ZACHARIAH BRACKETT and BENJAMIN SKILLIN came back to their father's lands, or 1716, when the officers and garrison who had been mustered out at Falmouth Foreside fort came across and really founded our city, or 1718 when they were permitted to hold a town meeting, I have run into the predicament of questioning the accuracy of no lesser authorities on our city's history that Hon. William Willis and William M. Sargent. As the mistakes concern Benjamin Skillin and the Skillin lands on the Deering side of Back Cove, I feel like putting the matter up to you, rather than combat the weight of authority myself.

Mr. Sargent undertook to correct the History of Portland by making two Benjamins[!] Skillin out of Willis's one. Mr. Willis said that the BENJAMIN SKILLIN who came here early, and who lived at Back Cove until nearly one-hundred years old, was living at Marblehead in 1719. Mr. Sargent said that this Marblehead man was a nephew of the Back Cove man. I find that Mr. Sargent was right in there being two BENJAMINS SKILLIN, but reversed their identity, and fell into several other errors, urging that the Marblehead BENJAMIN SKILLIN was an only child (of THOMAS SKILLIN, Jr.), probably posthumous, etc., and the deed which he executed (to MR. JOHN WASS) conveyed nothing because he owned nothing. As against this it may be seen that this BENJAMIN SKILLIN himself mentioned his brother Joseph, and also a disposition is found on record by the widow of THOMAS SKILLIN, JR. in which she testifies that she was a married woman with three children at the time the inhabitants in 1676 fled to the garrison on Cushing's Island to escape the Indians.

So many of the old records have now been printed and indexed that it has been comparatively easy to straighten out these two BENJAMINS SKILLIN. BENJAMIN SKILLIN, the uncle, son of THOMAS SKILLIN, SR., after arriving in Salem among the penniless Maine refugees in 1676, must have found an opening at Rowley, where he was taxed in 1677 or soon after, and where he married his second wife, a daughter of ELDER NEHEMIAH JEWETT. Children by her and by his first wife, Susannah _____, are recorded at Ipswich, and his son NEHEMIAH SKILLIN was remembered in his grandfather Jewett's will, 1719. The following is an incomplete and perhaps not entirely correct family record of this Benjamin who at Marblehead, in 1719, with wife Mary, deeded one-half of the Back Cove farm of his father THOMAS SKILLIN, SR. to JOHN WASS.

BENJAMIN SKILLIN married 1st., Susannah _____; 2nd, intentions published April 24, 1708, to Mary Jewett.

Children:

    Elizabeth, daughter of Benjamin and Susannah, birth recorded at Ipswich December 25, 1693; marriage recorded at Marblehead December 21, 1714, to Edmund Clark.

    John, son of Benjamin and Susannah, birth recorded at Ipswich March 29, 1704; intentions of marriage recorded at Ipswich, he then of Marblehead, November 11, 1727, to Eunice Kimball.

    Nehemiah, intentions of marriage recorded at Ipswich, he then of Marblehead, October 3, 1730, to Mercy Kimball.

    Mary, daughter of John [i.e., Benjamin?] and Mary, birth recorded at Ipswich 13: 3 mo.:1711.

Mr. Sargent said that EDMUND CLARK'S wife was a daughter of THOMAS SKILLIN, Sr., because he deeded the other half of the farm to JOHN WASS, but Mr. Sargent overlooked the deed by which Clark bought this half-interest FROM JOSEPH SKILLIN, also of Marblehead, 1719. In a hearing by the committee on Eastern Claims, about 1715, JOSEPH SKILLIN of Marblehead and BENJAMIN SKILLIN claimed their father THOMAS SKILLIN'S homestead, on the ground that the widow and son John were only to have use of it during the minority of the two youngest sons. Contrary to Mr. Sargent's statement, JOHN WASS, who bought their two half-interests, deeded the original Skillin farm to ISAAC SAWYER, 1726, who lived on it all his life, and titles come down through them to the present day. Col. Westbrook did indeed pay something to JOHN SKILLIN of Boston, nephew of Joseph and Benjamin, for his interest, but the enterprising colonel only got 4 pounds out OF ISAAC SAWYER and JOSEPH PRIDE for a quit claim. Mr. Sargent was misled by Mr. Willis' mistake in thinking there was but one Skillin farm on Back Cove, and by his own mistake in thinking that our BENJAMIN SKILLIN was the son, instead of the grandson, of the first Skillin.

Coming now to our Benjamin, the nephew of the other, who as PARSON SMITH said came back to his father's farm, where he and his son Isaac after him lived nearly 70 years, the earlier records of this man are found at Greenland, N.H. His mother, whose first husband was Thomas Skillin, Jr. was the daughter of GEORGE LEWIS of "Lewis his Neck," East Deering, and after the first flight to Salem, in 1676, and her husband's death, she seems to have come to Greenland, N.H., where Philip Lewis was a prominent citizen, very likely her uncle, as she had a brother of the same name. At any rate she married for her second husband Philip Lewis' son JOTHAM LEWIS, whose four children were remembered in their grandfather's will, 1700. Her son BENJAMIN SKILLIN served in the Greenland company of scouts, 1712, signed the Greenland petition, 1714, described himself as of Portsmouth, (Greenland was then the north parish of Portsmouth), with wife Deliverance, in a deed dated September 17, 1717, conveying 23 ¾ acres of land adjoining land of his mother, widow MARY LEWIS, (this deed assented to by her), and at the end of that year, 1717, had five children baptized in the Greenland church: ISAAC, BENJAMIN, LYDIA, MARY, and JANE.

Both the uncle and the nephew BENJAMIN SKILLIN were illiterate, like most of those who escaped with their lives from the useless and disastrous early attempts to wrest Maine from the Indians. The uncle made his mark with three perpendicular strokes, and the nephew with a rude production of the antique B, for BENJAMIN, shaped more like a modern C. The younger BENJAMIN made this mark when he sold one of his town grants here, the latter original deed being preserved with the Willis Papers.

Mr. Willis' mistake in assuming that the farm on which BENJAMIN SKILLIN and his son lived was the original Skillin grant led him into the greater error of saying in his history that the six southerly grants by GEORGE CLEEVE on Back Bay, to MICHAEL MITTON, NATHANIEL MITTON, HUMPHREY DURHAM, PHINEAS RIDER, GEORGE INGERSOLL and THOMAS SKILLIN, were all of them bought into the Deering farm. This would have taken almost to George Street. On the contrary it was the third grant, to HUMPHREY DURHAM, (but not that part of it between Forest Avenue and Back Cove), that made the northermost[!] portion of the Deering farm. This HUMPHREY DURHAM disposed of his grant and removed to the east side of the Presumpscot [river] before 1675, where he was killed by the Indians, and THOMAS SKILLIN, JR. acquired it.

Of the two farms between the two Skillin farms, the Rider farm was sold by JAMES KNAPP in 1730 to WILLIAM POTE, (who in 1739 bought up other Rider heir's interest from PHINEAS JONES), and later came down to Rev. THOMAS BROWN. This farm, as you have pointed out, includes the greater part of Woodfords. Its southern bounds at Back Cove was the creek into which Coyle's gully leads down, but on Forest Avenue it fell considerably south of the gully. ALFORD DYER'S land, which he afterwards sold to Mr. Ricker, was Durham-Skillin land, but the Tolford lot was Rider land.

GEORGE INGERSOLL, the Cleeve grantee of the next lot north, also removed from the Back Cove settlement, and MR. RICHARD PATTISHALL, a Boston merchant, became the owner. He sold it to JOHN WHITEFOOT, 1674, who sold the southerly half of it to ZACHARIAH WHITE, 1684. PHILIP WHITE, nephew of Zachariah, sold to THOMAS FLINT of Salem, who removed first to Portland and then to Harpswell. His son JONATHAN FLINT sold to SAMUEL LUNT of Kittery, 1743, who removed here and lived on it. Lunt's widow, Charity, gave it to DANIEL LUNT in 1773, who soon sold it to JACOB ADAMS, innkeeper. Adams deeded it to Thomas and Jane Morse, (his daughter?), and it became known as the Morse farm. COTTON KIMBALL of Haverhill acquired it in some way and sold to EBEN WOODFORDS a strip 8 rods in width along the Rider line until it reached the center of the creek which Clifton Street leads down into, then by the creek to Back Cove. This small lot, partly a part[!] of the original Ingersoll grant and partly a gore between the Rider and Ingersoll grants, now holds many thousand dollars' worth of handsome residences. Mr. Kimball sold the remainder of the Lunt farm to JONATHAN SMITH, who sold to SAMUEL SAUNDERS.

This gore came about in this way. The same ZACHARIAH WHITE in 1687 bought from HENRY BAILEY and his wife Mary 20 acres off the north side of the Rider grant which he claimed to have bought from JOHN RIDER. Very likely the wife was John Rider's daughter, granddaughter of PHINEAS RIDER. This lot was deeded to the Flints and to Lunt along with the other. How much value was set by this title may be seen from the fact that SAMUEL LUNT only allowed five shillings for it in a separate deed. Nevertheless he and WILLIAM POTE, in 1749, fixed up their bounds in a way that gave Lunt a gore 21 rods across the head a half-mile inland and tapering down to nothing on Back Cove.

The northern half of the Ingersoll grant was still the property of JOHN WHITEFOOT when the English were driven into the sea. Over forty years later his heirs sold to the new settlers and after passing through several hands JOHN WAITE sold to ISAAC SAWYER in 1741. This purchase added to the Skillin grant would have given Sawyer a frontage of over a quarter of a mile on Back Cove, but he had already sold to JOSEPH PRIDE (in 1738, and in 1762 Pride sod to MARK KNIGHT) the northerly half of the Skillin grant, thus leaving him with the equivalent of one Cleeve grant, half Ingersoll and half Skillin. Before long, however, he gave 7 ½ acres off the southern side to his son-in-law, BENJAMIN STEVENS, blacksmith, which came down through JOSHUA STEVENS to JOSEPH STEVENS as the Stevens homestead. The Steven's later bought still more of the Sawyer lands.

ISAAC SAWYER sold to his son Thomas in 1762 and after THOMAS SAWYER'S death, in 1779, his son Jonathan seems to have had what lay between Ocean Street and Back Cove. He sold to JOSHUA STEVENS three acres next to his own, then 13 acres to SIMON GOOKIN, and the balance as far as the Knight line to his brother, ISAAC SAWYER. The Gookin lot was willed to DOROTHY GOOKIN, who sold it in 1800 to SIMEON HILTON. MARY HILTON sold 8 rods by the Cove to JOSHUA STEVEN"S heirs, 9 rods by the Cove to ISAAC SAWYER, and 5 ¾ acres next to Ocean Street to EBENEZER D. WOODFORDS. ISAAC SAWYER'S widow, Susannah, about 1820 sold 7 acres to JOSEPH STEVENS, adjoining Woodford's land and his own, and 9 ½ acres to OLIVER BUCKLEY who sold to the Allens, adjoining THOMAS KNIGHT.

The original Skillin grant was owned by MR. JOHN WASS from 1719 to 1726, and then by ISAAC SAWYER, or Sawyer and Pride, until 1762. In that year ISAAC SAWYER gave the southerly half to his son and JOSEPH PRIDE sold the northerly half to MARK KNIGHT. The Knight half, about 29 rods on the Cove, has come down in that family to the present day.

Of the three rows of elm trees coming down across the country to the Cove, the northerly one marks the northerly Knight line, about a hundred feet south of George Street, which is the northernmost[!] line of Cleeve's 50 and 55 acre grants. The plainest line of trees and bushes, marks the southerly Knight line, next to the Allen lot. The third line, reaching the bank just south of Chenery Street, looks to me like the original southern Sawyer line, half way of the Ingersoll grant, but you will know best.

As I have not spent the necessary time on this to be thorough, you will no doubt find errors to correct, but you may feel absolutely sure regarding the two Benjamins Skillin and the two Skillin farms. Beyond any doubt there were two Thomases Skillin, father and son, who both had farms on Back Cove, (two other farms between them), and both had sons Benjamin.

As regards the Durham-Skillin farm, the deed to THOMAS SKILLIN, JR. was presumably destroyed with the other Casco records by the Indians, but the Bracketts, who inherited the two Mitton grants, repeatedly gave THOMAS SKILLIN and BENJAMIN SKILLIN as their northern abutters, and ISAAC LARRABY[!], who only knew this region before the first Indian war, made oath in a disposition that the land north of CAPT. ANTHONY BRACKETT was Skillin's. Sixty years later Col. Waldo and PHINEAS JONES competed in buying up the Durham heir's rights to his farm east of the Presumpscot River, but made no claim at Back Cove. From BENJAMIN SKILLIN down, a very few deeds tell the story:

    BENJAMIN SKILLIN to ISAAC SKILLIN, 1742, vol. 9, page 116
    ISAAC SKILLIN to DR. N. COFFIN, 1787, vol. 14, page 238
    Dr. Coffin to BENJAMIN LARRABEE, 1799, vol. 30. Page 9
    Larrabee to Green and Ford, 1811, vol. 16, page 353

Mrs. Green and Mrs. Ford, who were Larrabee's daughters, divided it into checkers, and all west of Forest Avenue came into the hands of CAPT. JAMES DEERING. East of Forest Avenue, the southern checker was bought from Mrs. Ford by WILLIAM FREEMAN, ESQ., who built "Freeman's Cottage" on it. Both this checker and the Green checker were purchased by Moses Hall, who lived there till his death.

A disposition of ISAAC SAWYER and ABRAHAM SAWYER taken in 1750, to perpetuate the bounds between Durham and Rider grants is suggestive of conditions in the previous century.

"In 1732 MR. STEPHEN JONES, surveyor, run the line between the land in the possession of MR. BENJAMIN SKILLIN and MR. WILLIAM POTE'S farm lying at Back Cove** beginning at a stake in the middle of a gully at about high water mark in the foot path where people used to pass, about three rods south of an old back of a chimney** etc."

I am sending all this to you in the hope that by correcting and bringing down to date you will be able to make it good material for the Argus [newspaper] historical page.

Very truly yours,

    C.T. Libby [Charles Thornton Libby, compiler of the "Libby Genealogy"]

Handwritten draft original: Charles Thornton Libby papers, Maine Historical Society
Copied and made available by: GLENN B. SKILLIN

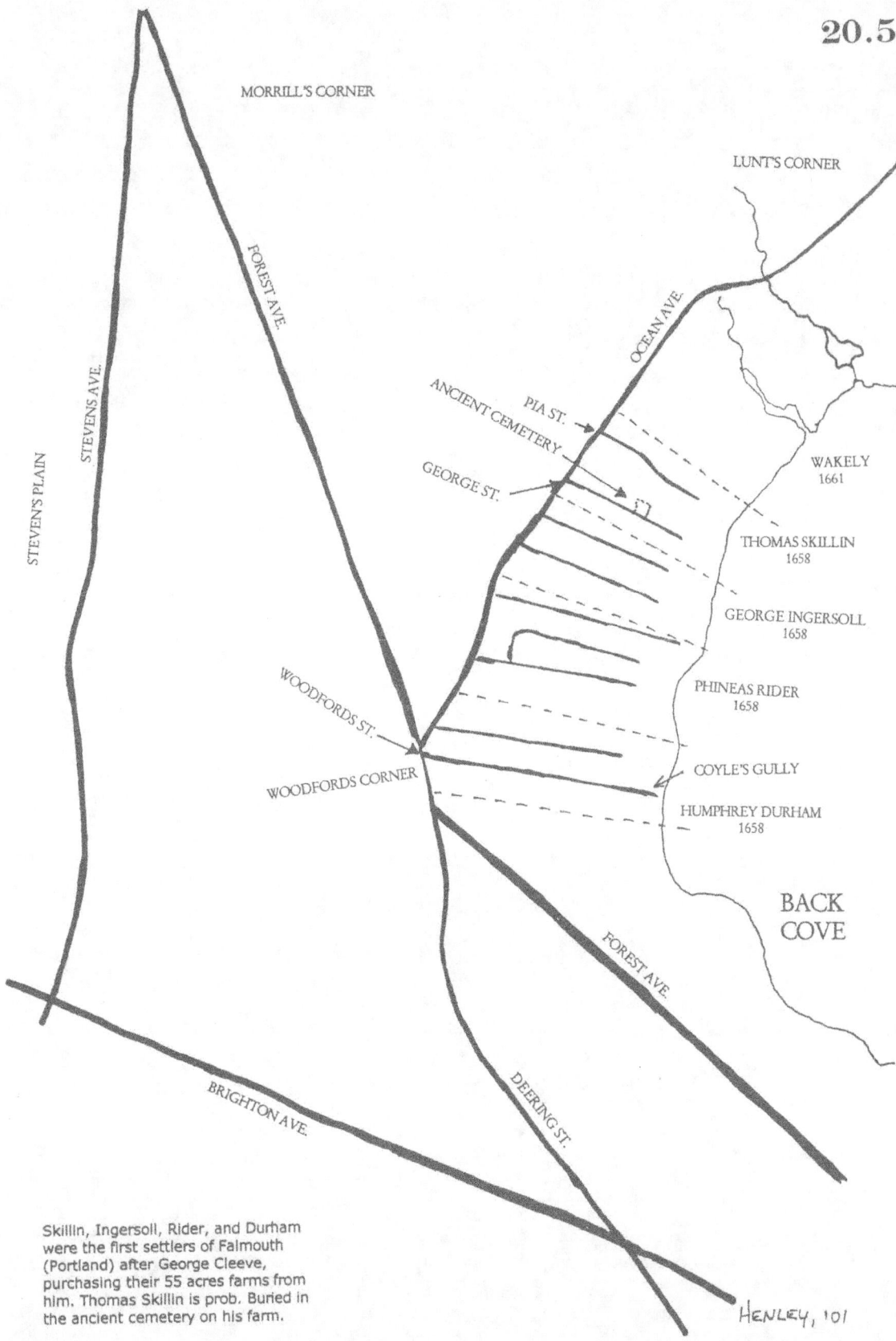

GRANDPA'S SCRAP BOOK

Timothy Galvin.

Ninety years ago and later the name of Timothy Galvin was a household word hereabouts. He was an Irishman, born in Ireland, February 2, 1766, married March 12, 1793, Joanna Ilsley. The Ilsleys lived where Hawkins' Shoe Factory is located on Ocean street.

In 1799 he purchased the quarter of an acre of land to which allusion was made in the last issue of the News, and erected the house now standing on the southwesterly corner of Veranda and Main streets, East Deering, then known as Secomb's Point.

The name by which he was more commonly known was Master Galvin. He was short in stature, quick in motion, an excitable temper, full of wit, slight brogue, stood high as a mathematician, a surveyor of land, shopkeeper and schoolmaster. His name however is seldom found in historical research. Mr. Chas. A. Bradley has a fine plan made by him, which is the only piece of work of his I have discovered.

In 1810 the two story school house was commenced that was located on the site of the present one at Stroudwater, and Master Galvin was notified that when finished another teacher would be employed as he did not understand grammar sufficiently well to teach it, whereupon he obtained a grammar and went to work on it. When the school house was ready he was also ready to teach grammar as well as other branches of study.

Here is a copy of an original receipt for money paid for teaching there:

Rec'd of Charles Pierce as school committee $115.37 for keeping winter school (Stroudwater) 1815.
TIMOTHY GALVIN.
March 16, 1816.

Other memoranda where the above was obtained throws further light on matters of schools at Stroudwater at that time and expense thereof:

Rec'd of Charles Pierce in his capacity as school committee, $36.63, in full for my services in keeping his district school in summer of 1815.
LYDIA CHAPMAN.

1815 Amount of money raised and belonging to School District No. 3 in Westbrook—148 scholars C 99 per head, $146.52.

Agreeable to a vote of the district the above to be schooled out in the following manner, viz:

For man's school, $109.88
For woman's school, $36.63
 CAPT. ENOCH PREBLE,
 CHARLES PIERCE,   } School Committee.
 STETSON LOBDELL,

1815 3d District paid George Warren, Jr., for eleven weeks keeping school, 16 per month, $44.
James Means 11 weeks, board $3 per week, $33.
1816 1st District paid Timothy Galvin per month, $33.

Where the third district was located at that time I cannot say, but Messrs. Pierce and Means lived at Stroudwater and were traders; so did Lobdell. Capt. Preble owned the land and barn where Albert A. Chesley lives just out of Stroudwater, and a house lot at Back Cove.

When the first valuation of Westbrook was made in 1815, Master Galvin was taxed for a house, $350, barn $30, ¼ a lot of land $20, lot of Hussey $40.

April 6, 1821, he sent a communication that read as follows:

Mr. Randall Johnson, clerk of the First Congregational Parish of Westbrook: Let me not be considered a member of this parish. I am in belief a Universalist.
Sir Yours,
TIMOTHY GALVIN.

By thus doing he prevented being taxed to support Congregational preaching in the town.

In 1822 for $2,200 he sold his home and shop standing on land of Jane and Peter Lunt to his son, George Ilsley Galvin of Boston, Mass., and in 1837, Galvin, then of Calais, Me., sold the same to Thomas P. Galvin, and Thomas P., in 1841, sold to Abraham W. Whitman and William Adil of Portland.

Master Galvin died in 1836 and a small white stone marks his grave, and thus states the time, in the old East Deering cemetery.

Of his offspring I know but little. Harriet died Sept. 21, 1805, aged 5 years, 2 months; grave stone at East Deering. Others were named George Ilsley, Eliza, Edward and Thomas. They were all small in stature. Eliza was rather above the average of the "outside world" in personal charms, and is said to have married a Unitarian minister. Thomas engaged in mercantile pursuits in Philadelphia, and is said to have obtained wealth.

If the boys were in swimming or sliding, or engaged in any other amusement and discovered by Master Galvin he joined them, and fifty years ago his little speeches were repeated and acts described, but now allusion to him is seldom heard. The hand of time has nearly effaced all recollection of his name, and I seek in vain for a written notice of his achievements.

A few years since I had the pleasure of meeting with Mrs. Eleanor (Tate) Jordan of Gorham, this state, since deceased. She was born in Stroudwater village, had a distinct recollection of Master Galvin, and a vivid way of describing what she called his pranks.

She said that she was at times his pet and on the occasion of a spelling match before the exercise commenced he told her of the manner in which he wanted her to spell the word grape. So when the time came he requested the class to spell the word grape in Irish. After all had failed he requested her to spell it,' and she said, "po-ta-to—potato.' "That's right," said he "take the head of the class."

From another source I learn that he once informed his scholars that when a person stands back to a stove, with hands back of himself, palms out, with fingers turned up like fish hooks, it is no harm to place a coal of fire in them, so he was observed in the position and one of the large boys crept up behind him stealthily, dropped a live coal in one of his hands and returned to his seat. He said, "The teaching justifies the example."

The next chapter under this head will relate to some of the first settlers at Woodfords.

June 1894
GRANDPA'S SCRAP BOOK

Two hundred and fifty years have elapsed since the land upon which our city is located was first settled by white men, and one hundred and seventy-four years since the first land grant was made near the time of the last occupancy, and under the above named head we shall commence next week the publication of records of births, marriages and deaths; notices of persons, families and events connected therewith worthy of preservation, and continue the practice from week to week, at such length as circumstances will allow, of those who lived in the distant past, and in some cases of recent date. There are but few people who do not leave a record of some sort that can be found in some place in part or in whole. Many such are in grandpa's scrap book, printed and in manuscript, a result of years of careful research and preservation.

Morrill's Corner.

Merrill & Buxton have opened the Geo. Wilson store where they have a fine line of groceries, meats, vegetables, fruit, confectionery, etc. See ad.

Democratic County Convention.

The Democratic county convention was held Thursday forenoon in City Hall, Portland. There was a large number of delegates present and spectators. The organization was as follows:

Chairman—Joseph A. McGowen.
Secretaries—C. F. Plummer, E. S. Osgood, John A. McGowan and F. R. Fay.

Then the following nominations for senators were made:

Eastern District—Silas Skillings of Falmouth.
Northern District—Edward S. Alien of Bridgton.
Western District—Leroy B. Mason of Windham.
Southern District—William H. Stevens.

The ballot for sheriff was as follows:

Whole number of votes   138
Necessary for a choice   70
George A. Morrill   89
Warren B. Chute   36
William M. Pennell   13

The other nominations were as follows.
Treasurer—Thomas B. Haskell of Cape Elizabeth.
Clerk of Courts—Virgil C. Wilson of Portland.
Register of Deeds—William M. Pennell of Brunswick.
County Commissioner—L. W. Dyer of Deering.

Mr. Farnsworth moved that the resolutions passed by the state convention be adopted by this convention as their resolutions and platform. This motion was carried. The convention then adjourned.

THE DEERING NEWS.

Saturday, January 5, 1895.

GRANDPA'S SCRAP BOOK

[Under this head historical and genealogical memoranda will be furnished the readers of the News that appears worthy of preservation, particularly of remote periods in our history within the city limits and immediate vicinity.]

Where the name Cæsar Thomas appears in my last it should be Cæsar Thomes.

In 1814 William Kenney was taxed as follows: "House $250; two barns $50; also house on Plains $200; slaughter house $20; fifteen acres mowing and tillage at $16; thirty-seven pasturage at $7. 'Deduct house on Plains and charge to John Coulbourn.' Two oxen, $40; three cows $42; two swine $10; and one horse $40."

The name of Samuel Kenney appears as owner of ½ a shop, value not named, and Samuel Kenney, Jr., as a poll tax payer. And this is all the reference there is to the name of Kenney on the list at that time.

I have alluded very briefly in a former chapter under this head to the fact that Thomas Brackett, brother to Zachariah, who lived on Stevens' Plains, lived in back of the Morrill house. Quite a long story is connected with the fact, but I allude now to the name only to explain some other facts. In a future issue of the News I will bring the matter out clearly.

In the News of Dec. 15, I allude to Nathaniel Haskell who married Sarah, the eldest daughter of Capt. Isaac S. Stevens, and in 1812 purchased of Peter Brackett, his wife signing with him, the L. B. Dennett, now the H. H. Harriss farm, located on the Windham road, not far from Morrill's Corner.

In 1814 there was a Nathaniel Haskell, farmer, millman, etc., residing at Saccarappa, and a Nathaniel Haskell and Nathaniel Haskell, Jr., residing on the Peter Brackett place, the last two being taxed as follows:

"One house $40; one barn $30; outhouse; $42; one shop $30; fifteen acres mowing and tillage $17; seventy acres unimproved $6; two oxen $40; four cows $56; one 2-year-old $7; three yearlings $15; one horse $40; a 2-year-old colt $15; and four swine $20."

Hiram Sawyer told me a year or so before he died that he remembered the Peter Brackett house as "a small, poor thing," as shown by the valuation record, and that the so-called William Snell house, next adjoining the junction of the new road from Cumberland Mills with the Windham road, was built by Zachariah Brackett, son of Peter Brackett.

Those interested in the early history of the residents of this part of Deering now under observation by the writer will read the two following letters with interest. Considering the age of the writer she makes an excellent exhibit. I here present the letters as written.

West Auburn, Me., Dec. 29, 1890.

Dear Sir:—I received your letter last night and will answer to the best of my ability, and will say first, that I shall be very much pleased if I can aid you.

The Brackett you write about, who married a woman by the name of Snow, was my great-grandfather, and my father, Nathaniel Brackett, told me her name was Nancy Snow and all she cared to do was to read and scold.

Brackett lived where Benjamin Bailey lived near Morrill's Corner, where his daughter Octavia (Libby) lives now. I have forgotten her last name but you can readily find the place.

My grandfather, Peter Brackett, married Sally Sawyer of Back Cove. He moved to West Gloucester, this state, before I was born and I am seventy-six years of age. They both died there. He was a soldier of the war of the Revolution. I used to hear him say he was one of the number who guarded Major Andre's place of execution.

My grandfather had one brother who settled in Peru, this state. William Brackett lived to be nearly ninety years of age. I saw him when he was ninety.

There were eleven children in my grandfather's family—all dead. My father died in 1879, aged 82 years; my mother died in 1873.

My grandfather had one sister who married Benjamin Bailey; her name was Polly; she died and he married Content Elliot, whose daughter Octavia lives where my great-grandfather lived near Morrill's Corner.

And there were other sisters; one married a Merrill of Windham, Me., and I think one married a man by the name of Pride.

There are, or were, two maiden women by the name of Wilson who live about two miles from Morrill's Corner that have, so Mr. S. P. Mayberry told me, a Brackett genealogy. Their mother was a daughter of Polly and Benjamin Bailey.

My grandmother Brackett had six brothers, all but one followed the sea. Four were sea captains. Their names were: Thomas, Robert, William, Ephraim and Asa. A sister of these married Amos Knight who settled and died in the town of Wayne, Me.

There is Smith and Dean's journal I saw the last time I was in Portland to stop. That will tell you of the Bracketts. Thomas B. Reed has Brackett blood in him, I presume, as he is interested in the Brackett genealogy.

I saw, when at Peaks Island a few years ago, a man who told me he was a Brackett and descended from Anthony Brackett who was killed by the Indians in 1690 in a battle between the French and English.

CONTINUED:

Will you please tell me if there is any of the old town of Westbrook still a town or is it all cut up into cities?

I will not write you any more tonight, but if at any time I can aid you I will. You are not the only one who has written me. I just got a letter from a William Sawyer of Wilmot street, Portland and one from a man in Boston I never saw.

Respectfully Yours,
SARAH A. BRACKETT.

WEST AUBURN, Jan. 18, 1892.

DEAR SIR:—I think I wrote you all I know about my great-grandfather, Thos. Brackett, who lived and died near Morrill's Corner.

His son William lived to be a very old man. He had by his first wife three sons, Seth, Simon, Thomas, and a daughter Betsey—all dead. In his old age he married Belsa (?) Smith, and this is all I know of him.

My grandfather, Peter Brackett, had as many as three sisters, Mrs. Bailey Mrs. Pride and Mrs. Merrill of Windham. I never saw any of them, save Mrs. Bailey. I think by inquiring of Mr. Isaiah Daniels of Portland you can find out all about the Merrills as he married a Miss Merrill for his first wife, and her father was a cousin to my father.

Of my grandfather, Peter Brackett, I will now tell you what I know of his family.

Peter Brackett, born at Falmouth, Nov. 1, 1755; died Oct. 27, 1832. Sarah Sawyer, his wife, born at Falmouth, June 1, 1765; died Feb. 12, 1839. I don't know when they were married. They had twelve children. Peter lived and died in West Gloucester. He married Polly Haskell. They had nine children. Zachariah married Mary Cleaves. He died in Waterville. They had seven children—about all dead. Daniel died before I can remember, and Susan, too. Hannah married Merrill Berry of Gray, and they had four children—all dead. Olive married John Bailey, who lived near Morrill's Corner, and they had six children, one a Mrs. Burnham who lives near the Corner, and a Mrs. Roberts who lived over the Presumpscot river.

My father, Nathaniel Brackett, was born in Falmouth, March 16, 1791. My mother was Eunice Humphrey of Gray. He died June 29, 1879, aged 82 years and about three months. She died Jan. 8, 1873, aged 71 years. They had eight children and I am the oldest. Two are dead. Susan married Stetson Kenney of Morrill's Corner where his daughter, Mrs. Theodore Buck, now resides, and near her brother, Freeman Kenney, had seven children. I think Harriet married William Thomas of Oxford. They had five or six children. Mary married Wm. Crockett. I think he was a New Gloucester man. He died in Gorham, Me., had seven sons and all living but two. Lois married Nathan Doughty of Gray—both dead. They had three children. And this is all I can remember of my grandfather's family.

I forgot my aunt Sophia Brackett. She married James Thompson and they had six children—all dead.

I think I wrote you in my other letter about the Sawyers.

My grandmother Sally (Sawyer) Brackett had six brothers and one sister, Mrs. Jennie Knight who died in Wayne. They had seven children I think: William, Daniel, Amos and four daughters. I think one married a Joel Sawyer of Portland, and the most of them I think are dead.

My grandmother's family are all dead. Her brothers were: Ephraim, Thomas, Robert, Daniel and Asa Sawyer, and all were masters of vessels. Daniel was shipwrecked and all hands on board lost the first night he sailed as master. * * * (?) Had a son who lived in Portland by the name of John, on Munjoy Hill, my father said, and two daughters, one of whom married John Emery of Portland, son of the late Judge Emery, and one a man by the name of Knight. I never saw them.

I live in the house used by Mrs. Jane Prince (?) She is one year older than I am. I was born Sept. 21, 1815. The place is five miles from the depot. The stage to North Auburn, Brettness' Mills and West Auburn, goes past my door twice every day.

Yours Respectfully,
SARAH A. BRACKETT.

THE DEERING NEWS.

Saturday, January 12, 1895.

GRANDPA'S SCRAP BOOK

[Under this head historical and genealogical memoranda will be furnished the readers of the News that appears worthy of preservation, particularly of remote periods in our history within the city limits and immediate vicinity.]

What appears in to-days News under this head was prepared for last week but the article was found to be longer than space allowed for it would admit.

Where it is stated in Miss Sarah A. Brackett's second letter that her mother Eunice (Humphrey) Brackett, died Jan. 8, 1873, aged 71 years, an error was committed in consequence of the aged hand made a figure seven that resembled in appearance the figure four, etc. The following extract from the Portland Argus of Jan. 1843 will set the matter right:

"Died in New Gloucester, Jan. 8, 1843. Mrs. Eunice, wife of Capt. Nathaniel Brackett, aged 49 years and 9 months. She has left a husband, eight children, and an aged father and mother and a large concourse of relatives and acquaintances to mourn the loss of one who was beloved by all who knew her. She was in full hope of immortality."

CUMBERLAND CO. REG. OF DEEDS
Vol. 68, p. 388.

1813—William Brackett Esq. and William Brackett Jr., and Betty his wife, to Zachariah Brackett, thirteen acres and twenty rods of land—"reserving ¼ acre for the burying ground and privelege of passage."

This lot was located in Westbrook near Pride's bridge or Pride's corner.

Benjamin Bailey Jr., (Son of John Jr. and grandson of Deacon John Bailey born 1764, on Spring Street Deering) in the old John Newman house, married Mary Brackett, Apr. 22, 1788. She was a daughter of Thomas Brackett, and born Sept. 14 1760. Thomas died May 23, 1803 aged 85 years. Benjamin's wife died Oct. 16 1823; he married second Content Elliot of Presumpscott Falls, march 27, 1825. She died Jan. 6, 1866 he, Aug. 16, 1844.

One child by first wife named Mary, born Apr. 4, 1789, married "on Sunday evening," Nov. 26, 1809 Henry Wilson, born Feb. 14 1782 a descendant of Major Wilson, of Falmouth a soldier of the Revolution.

CHILDREN.
1 Mary, born and died Jan. 27 1811.
2 Angeline, born Oct. 1, 1812.
3 Mary Ann born Dec. 20, 1816, in the house that stood near the Benjamin Bailey house—then after it was moved to its present location on the Shattuck road there were born
4 Benjamin.
5 Henry, died at home unmarried.
6 Albert M., who resides at No. 123 Cumberland street, Portland retired from active business.

For a period of some forty years he was a member of the firm of Littlefield & Wilson, stair builders and machine wood workers. His son, Virgil C. Wilson, unmarried, who graduated at Bowdoin College in 1880, is a lawyer in Portland
7 Almira

Mary Ann who taught school many years, with her sisters Angeline and Almira reside in the old homestead house on the Shattuck road.

Benjamin Bailey had children by his second wife:
2 Benjamin F. Bailey, born Aug. 13 1826.
3 Octavia, born May 24, 1829, who retains the homestead and is known as Mrs. Samuel F. Libby.

Benjamin Bailey was an uncle by marriage to the venerable Charles Maxfield of Stroudwater, Charles mother being a sister to Benjamin. This Bailey family was large—containing twelve or thirteen members. More relating to it hereafter.

John Bailey Jr. was a son of Joseph Bailey Jr., and grandson of Deacon John Bailey. His father Joseph W. was a brother to Benjamin Bailey, the before named, and married December 7, 1783, Sally Waterhouse of Stroudwater, a daughter of William Waterhouse the first person by the name in that village. He Joseph W. was a blacksmith and was drowned at Lisbon while crossing a river. The widow married Nov. 29 1804 Isaac Fly of Standish, or thereabouts. He was a ship carpenter and they resided in a one story house, now the lower story of the dwelling of the late George W. Morton, that stands where it always has, next northeastly of the Stroudwater river mill, supposed to have been built in the time of Col. Thos. Westbrook. It originally sat end to road. Mrs. Fly was known in her last days as "Aunt Fly" and was a superior woman.

CHILDREN:
1 Sally, married a man by the name of Riley and removed to the State of Ohio.
2 Jane, married May 26, 1808, Daniel Webb of Saccarappa.
3 Rebecca, married March 6, 1806 John Brown, who was lost at sea. At one time she taught a private school at Stroudwater where Charles Fickett resides, in which house William Waterhouse died, March 5, 1805. His obituary consists of three words: "An honest man." Mrs. Brown has three daughters and one son; she died in Woburn, Mass. at which some of her family lived.
4 Joseph, a hatter, by trade, went to Portsmouth, N. H., and it is said he soon became mayor of that city.
5 Elizabeth married Feb. 11, 1813 Joseph Quinby, son of Joseph Quinby of Saccarappa, whose wife was a sister to Captain Jesse Partridge, a Revolutionary soldier who built the house at Stroudwater where Andrew Hawes, Esq., resides. The second Joseph Quinby who married Elizabeth Bailey had six children: 1—Joseph; 2—Nathaniel; 3—Captain Isaac F. Quinby; 4—Elizabeth Ann; 5—Charlotte; 6—Joseph B.
Captain Isaac F. Quinby went through the war of the Rebellion, is a wide-awake and one of the richest and most active business men of Saccarappa. He was the first county treasurer under the Republican party.
6 William died unmarried.
7 John born 1796, married Olive Brackett, noticed by Miss Sarah A. Brackett. He lived when young with his uncle Benjamin Bailey. His dwelling that stood southeasterly of the brook that crossed the Windham road, where the cellar rocks now may be seen, was burned a few years ago. He died Aug. 4, 1870, aged 74 years; she died July 22, 1872 aged 78 years. A son Charles resides at Cumberland Mills.

Saturday, January 19, 1895.

GRANDPA'S SCRAP BOOK

[Under this head historical and genealogical memoranda will be furnished the readers of the News that appears worthy of preservation, particularly of remote periods in our history within the city limits and immediate vicinity.]

When it reads Joseph W. Bailey in connection with the name of John Bailey Jr., in my article of last week under this head the "W" should be left out and "Jr" added to make the record correct. Then the name "Brown" should appear as Brawn, where it reads "3 Rebecca, married March 6, 1800," etc. And where it says at the close of the article, John Bailey's house was "burned a few years ago" there is an error. His house stands today, next southerly of the site of the one burned, a small sized one and half story house and is occupied by a son of the John who married Olive Brackett.

As two of the sons of Capt. Isaac S. Stevens married two of the daughters of Deacon James Bailey I propose to put in here some records connected with the name of Deacon James Bailey before proceeding further with the Stevens family. The names of the Stevenses who married into the Bailey family were Nathaniel who married Abigail Bailey and William who married Sally, sister to Abigail, upon all of which light will be let on when the right time comes.

And here I desire to allude to the fact that while most people are well informed on general matters, few have any knowledge of their own parentage beyond their grandparents, and dates are absolete.

Most people hereabouts have heard of the "Skillings claim" "to Monument Square" located in Portland till recently known as Market Square. Those who have not, can do so by referring to vol. 3, second series of Maine Historical Society publications, page 281—91, inclusive; and to vol. 2, page 105 of Maine His. and Gen. Recorder.

Daniel Bailey married into the family of Samuel Skillings and wife Rhoda (Bailey) Skillings. The time of birth of Deborah and time of marriage I have not obtained. She was the widow Dunn when Bailey married her. Her next eldest sister, named Elizabeth, was born April 25, 1713. They lived about a fourth of a mile in a westerly direction from the Reform school buildings on the westerly side of the road passing through a place called Long Creek, in the town of Cape Elizabeth and on the northerly side of the old mill pond. I think the house owned by D. W. Clark stands upon the site of the Daniel Bailey house.

In the pasture at the rear of the house may be seen the old Skillings burying place, unprotected and unreserved at time of sale of property. It contains a full hundred graves with a few lettered stones a copy of the inscriptions of which may be found in the Maine Gen. and His. Recorder, vol. 4, page 227, but no records of a single Bailey appear.

In Vol. 1, p. 69—1759, Cumberland Co. Rg. of Deeds the names of, the heirs of Samuel Skillings appear among which is the name of Deborah Bailey; and same volume, same year, p. 255, Deborah Bailey, administratrix on estate of her late husband, Daniel Bailey, may be seen, thus establishing the fact of the death of her husband.

April 25, 1757, a letter of administration was granted her, and inventory made May 16. The homestead, house, barn, twenty-five acres of land with thirty acres adjoining on the South side were appraised £116-13-4, upon which there was a mortgage of £50. They had two oxen, two steers, one cow, one horse. Deborah was appointed guardian of James and Deborah, while James Merrill was appointed for Abigail and Daniel.

Vol. 14, p. 149—1773, Cumberland Co. Reg. Deeds, James Bailey, of Falmouth, joiner, and George Smith of Cape Elizabeth, tailor, and Deborah his wife, for a con. of £22-8, to George Capson Roberts of Cape Elizabeth—land and buildings of Daniel Bailey, late of Falmouth.

Signed,
JAMES BAILEY.
SARAH BAILEY.
GEORGE SMITH.
DEBORAH SMITH.

Vol. 15, p. 100—1766 Con. £11-4 John Gideon Bailey of Newbury, Mass., cordwainer, to George Capson Roberts of Long Creek—one fifth part as heir to my father, Daniel Bailey, deceased, and brother, Daniel Bailey, deceased.

Signed,
JOHN G. BAILEY.

Vol. 15, p. 102—1792, Con. £7-6, We Smith Woodward Cobb of Falmouth, Lousewright, and Abigail, my wife, late Abigail Bailey, daughter of Daniel Bailey deceased, to George C. Roberts.

Signed,
SMITH W. COBB.
ABIGAIL COBB.

I find this Cobb was alive and living in Portland in 1794.

Now I will arrange the names of the heirs of Daniel Bailey:
1 James.
2 Deborah, married Sept. 3, 1772, Geo. Smith, a tailor.
3 John G., who went to Newbury.
4 Betty, alias Elizabeth, married Oct. 22, 1780, Richard Wescott of Scarboro.
5 Daniel who died according to deed referred to herein.

This is all I know of the foregoing named except

DEACON JAMES BAILEY.

This character was born Aug. 1st, 1749, Sarah Paine, his wife, was born May 23, 1753, and were married March 20, 1773. I have stated in a former chapter that he commenced married life on the wild land located on the Windham road where he died, but I find at this writing no foundation for the statement.

Aug 30, 1788 he purchased land there. His possessions were on both sides of the highway, and immediately northerly of the old burying ground, on the ridge on the westerly side of the road he reared his dwelling—a large two story house, and out houses—the cellar of which is still to be seen.

In 1814 he was taxed as follows: One house $450; one barn $65; one chaise house $20; shop $60; thirteen acres mowing and tillage at $13 per acre; twenty pasturing at $8; seventeen acres at $7; five acres at $5; four 3-year-old oxen $40; three cows $42; one 2-year-old $7; one 1-year-old $5.

Of his mechanical abilities I have no knowledge other than he built the Bradley barn at Bradley's Corner.

He was deacon of the old First Congregational church, the meeting house of which society stood where the so-called Bradley meeting house stands at this time, but as the records of the church are destroyed I cannot state the time. In a printed copy of membership made in 1833 his name is marked "deceased," but that of Sally Bailey appears immediately under his, who I presume represented his widow at that time.

He was the father of twelve children, the names of which with dates of births and other facts I will present in my next.

Saturday, January 26, 1895.

GRANDPA'S SCRAP BOOK

[Under this head historical and genealogical memoranda will be furnished the readers of the News that appears worthy of preservation, particularly of remote periods in our history within the city limits and immediate vicinity.]

I closed my last article under this head with the statement of the fact that Deacon James Bailey and wife, Sarah (Paine) Bailey were the parents of twelve children. Their names were respectively: Nabby, Elizabeth, George, Daniel, Nabby, Nathaniel, George, Sally, Alexander, Sophia, James Paine and Nancy Paine.

1. Nabby, born Dec. 17, 1773, died Nov. 24, 1780.
2. Elizabeth, born Dec. 19, 1775, married first, a man by name of Walker, second, Ebenezer Hilton Sawyer. Elizabeth had children by first husband.

Ebenezer Hilton Sawyer's first wife was Rebecca Berry, daughter of George Berry, Jr., whose house stood on the site of the house of the late David Torrey, southerly side of road from Morrill's Corner to Allen's Corner which was burned about the year 1835. George Berry, Jr., was son of Mayor George Berry who spent his last days on earth with his son Obediah in the house now owned and occupied by Mr. John J. Frye, Ocean street. Maj. George died Feb. 22, 1776; George, Jr., died Apr. 3, 1816 in Denmark, this state, to which place he removed in 1808, with a son. Rebecca was the tenth child in a family of eleven children. I don't know when she was born, but Eunice, the youngest child of the family, first saw the light of day Sept. 24, 1761.

Maj. George Berry's second child, brother to George, Jr., was named Josiah; and he married Thankful Butler. He died Feb. 12, 1815, aged 79; she died Nov. 28, 1821, aged 78. Into this family of Josiah Berry, Zachariah B. Stevens married, who was a son of Capt. Isaac B. Stevens. Ex-postmaster and ex-selectman Alfred R. Huston of Woodfords is also a descendant of Josiah Berry. He resided just westerly of Lorenzo P. Hawkins' shoe factory, Ocean street.

Ebenezer H. Sawyer was a cordwainer, an occupation now known as shoemaker. He built the one story house standing opposite the Morrill house, in a southeasterly direction, where, I think, Oliver B. Howard lives at this time.

Oliver B. is son of Abijah Howard. Abijah went from Randolph, Mass., to Buckfield, Me., from which place he came to what is now Deering. He died Feb. 20, 1834, aged 70 years. Sally, his wife, died Apr. 23, 1848, aged 82 years.

Vol. 30, p. 501, Cumb. Co. Reg. Deeds. Time 1799; consideration $180—George Berry conveyed to Ebenezer Hilton Sawyer 18¼ acres of land commencing bounds 3¼ rods from most northwesterly corner of said Sawyer's house. This established the fact in my mind that the house now standing was built prior to 1799.

In 1809 Sawyer sold the buildings to Zachariah B. Stevens with thirty acres of land for $1300, and next year Stevens sold the buildings and nineteen acres to Abijah Howard for $1200.

In 1814 Howard was taxed for one house $250; one barn $20; one shop $15; four acres mowing at $18 per acre; 13 acres of unimproved at $7 per acre; two cows $28; one horse $40; and two swine at $10. Abijah Howard, Jr., was taxed one-half shop $40; stock in trade $100.

In 1771 the location of the house of Geo. Berry, Jr., is given in the survey of a road, as I have located it, running easterly from Morrill's Corner.

Ebenezer Hilton Sawyer and Rebecca Berry, his first wife, had:

1. Jeremiah, the father of Nathaniel K. Sawyer, born in Otisfield, to which place Ebenezer removed and died. Nathaniel K. now resides here in Deering, opposite the Westbrook Seminary, in the Dr. Eben Stone house.
2. William B. died in Paris, France, to which place he went as a medical student in company with D. R. Wood of Portland.

Then Ebenezer had by his second wife who was Elizabeth (Bailey) Walker:

3. A daughter died young.
4. George, who went south.
5. Josiah, alive, and lives in the western country.
6. Rebecca, married Daniel Holden of Otisfield.
7. Charles, died at home unmarried.
8. Louis H., married —— Holden and went to the western country.

3. George, born April, 12, 1778; died Nov. 4, 1780.
4. Daniel, born July 23, 1780, married May 26, 1802, Ann Stevens, but I do not know of what family. He was a house carpenter and removed to Harrison, or somewhere thereabouts. They had ten children: George, Eliza, William, Martha, Ann Joel, who is supposed to be alive and resides in the town of Sweden. He married second, Rebecca Jumper of Harrison, and they had children: Abbie W., who married her cousin, Lafayette, son of Alexander Bailey noticed farther on in this chapter of records, and now resides with her son, Clarence W., in this city, Phebe Ann, Annie, who died young, and Mary M.
5. Abigail, born Aug. 20, 1782, married Nathaniel Stevens, who died at Stroudwater June 1, 1853, the father of nine children, whose record will appear in order as a child of Capt. Isaac S. Stevens.
6. Nathaniel, born Aug. 3, 1784, died May 9, 1786.
7. George, born June 26, 1786.
8. Sally, born July 8, 1778, m. Nov. 26, 1807, William Stevens, son of Capt. Isaac S. Stevens. This record will appear in order as a child of Capt. Isaac S. Stevens.
9. Alexander, b. Nov. 8, 1790, married Sept. 17, 1815, Sally Jackson of Baldwin, born June 9, 1796. He died June 3, 1882; she died Aug. 9, 1883.

In 1813 Deacon James Bailey conveyed to his son Alexander land on the opposite side of the highway where Alexander built a house and where he ever lived thereafter, and where his son Eldridge G. now resides. In 1822 the deacon conveyed his homestead to his two sons, Alexander and James P. Bailey. It can with truth be said that Alexander was a "knight of goad stick" for for many years he teamed between Duck Pond and Portland hauling curbstones.

CHILDREN:

1. Orren, died young.
2. Charles L. born Oct. 10, 1818.

He first worked with his father, who was a house carpenter; then he was a clerk in a dry goods store in Boston. His health becoming impaired he returned to his native place, started a "traveling emporium" of dry goods, taught school, (several terms at Morrill's Corner) served on the school committee, built the two-story building on Windham road now used for a schoolhouse, near which he resides. His children were Ferdinand E., a dealer in paints, etc., with whom his father is engaged, Orren M., Ida M. and Frank M.

3. Alexander, his wife, a sister to the wife of his brother George W. Bailey. Was a house carpenter, and killed by a railroad train at Morrill's corner. He lived first house, southwesterly of the Windham road where his widow now resides.
4. Lafayette, married Abigail W., daughter of his uncle Daniel Bailey, born Dec. 11, 1825. He lived opposite the old Alexander Bailey place. Has a son Clarence W., lives near Allen's Corner with whom the widow resides.
5. George W., born Jan. 2, 1827, married Apr. 28, 1850, Sarah A., daughter of Hezekiah Doughty of Gray, born there March 9, 1824. She died June 7, 1892. They lived on Windham-road, westerly side and northerly the residence of his father, where he was a farmer and house joiner. Children: 1, Leon M.; 2, Jeremiah P.; 3, Lena F.; 4, Cora A.; 5, Georgio E.; 6, Minnetta E., the wife of Geo. W. Ward who resides on Windham road, the second house southerly the old cemetery, same side of the highway, where his wife's father makes his home.
6. Monroe, died young.
7. Catherine F., resides with her brother Elbridge G., on the homestead.
8. Elbridge G., married Emma Hatford of Hiram.
10. Sophia, born Nov. 12, 1792, married Wm. Hicks May, 25, 1815. He was a calker. He married second, Widow Patterson.

CONTINUED:

11 James Paine' born July 26, 1795, married Oct. 20, 1818, Caroline Hilton. He purchased the property next southerly of the old cemetery, living in the house now owned and occupied by Thomas J. Ward father to George W. before mentioned, being the third from the cemetery on a southerly course. Down back of the house he made brick, but in 1841 he sold the place to Lydia, wife of Alfred Dyer, a tailor of Portland, and James P. removed to the town of Harrison, where he has decendants. It was he who made the last reservation to the old burying ground.

12 And last, Nancy Paine, born Sept. 24, 1797. Married Rufus Read May 25, 1815. He lived on Windham Road, and had a large family.

THE DEERING NEWS.

Saturday, February 2, 1895.

GRANDPA'S SCRAP BOOK

[Under this head historical and genealogical memoranda will be furnished the readers of the News that appears worthy of preservation, particularly of remote periods in our history within the city limits and immediate vicinity.]

In my last chapter under this head I stated that the fourth son of Dea. James Bailey, named Daniel, born July 23, 1780, married May 26, 1802, Ann Stevens, "but I do not know of what family." I now notice that according to our Cumberland County Registry of Deeds, Vol. 105, p. 30, in the year 1806, Daniel Bailey and "Sarah in her right" signed off all claim to the old Stevens house where Geo. C. Codman lives at Woodfords. I am not sure that Daniel married Ann. I only know that he married a woman by the name of Stevens.

Zachariah Brackett Stevens, the fourth child of Capt. Isaac Sawyer Stevens, and Sarah (Brackett) Stevens, was born on Stevens' Plains Mar. 21, 1778. Like all the rest of the family he was taught to perform manual labor, the first being at the bellows and anvil with his father.

In 1798, Nov. 8, he united in marriage with Miriam P. Berry, born June 1, 1778. She was a daughter of Josiah Berry and wife Thankful (Butler) Berry, and granddaughter of Major George Berry, the famous Indian hunter in his time, whose commission honors the hall of the Maine Historical society, Portland. This Berry name was noticed in my last chapter to which I now refer. The gravestones of Josiah and wife Thankful may be seen in the George street burying ground, a notice of which appeared in the Portland Argus, Sep. 29, 1888, followed by one of Dr. William B. Lapham of Augusta, deceased, a descendant of Major George, Oct. 17, '88, both articles of interest to those interested in these families. Josiah Berry died Feb. 12, 1815, aged 79 years; his wife Thankful Nov. 28, 1821, aged 78 years.

Nancy the wife of Josiah Beals, another daughter of Josiah Berry whose headstone is at the same place, died July 3, 1855, aged 85 years.

Major Berry had three sons, whose records in part can be found, and a daughter Elizabeth who married Jeremiah Pote, he born Jan. 18, 1724, whose father was Capt. Wm. Pote and lived at Woodfords with his family after 1733. This Jeremiah was a sea captain and merchant in Portland but was an avowed loyalist. On the breaking out of the war of the Revolution he removed to the Provinces and died at St. Andrews, 1796.

When Zachariah B. Stevens was first married he lived in the house of his father, now standing on the westerly side of the avenue, which has been noticed as the last abode of his father, Capt. Isaac.

Zachariah B. built soon after his marriage the fine old mansion house now standing next south westerly of the Universalist meeting house which occupies the south westerly corner of the Westbrook Seminary lot. In his new home he accommodated the traveling public, by furnishing coffee to teamsters and hay for oxen and horses. But I think the smallest part of the house now standing was built first as Zachariah, in describing some land, about the year 1830, alludes to "my new house," which is probably the part of the residence next the Universalist meeting house. Opposite, on the other side of the highway, stood his blacksmith shop. As early as 1814 he repudiated the Puritanical idea of future punishment. In 1821 Cordelia, his youngest daughter, first saw the light of day in the ell part of the ancestral home she now occupies. In 1823 he was coroner, and he filled the offices of selectman, deputy sheriff, postmaster, and what else I cannot say. In 1842 his shop was destroyed by fire, an in the Portland Argus of Apr. 11, of that year, I find as follows:

Fire broke out this morning about o'clock at Stevens' Plains, in the blacksmith shop of Z. B. Stevens, and soon communicated to the tin ware shop of his son Samuel B. Stevens. Both shops were consumed. Mr. S. B. Stevens lost his books, ware, tinplate, etc., amounting to $1500, insured $300. The fire extended to the shop of Rufus Dunham block tin manufacturer, which was also destroyed with the contents. Loss $100 to $1200. The citizens turned out with great spirit, and disputed the ground with the fire adversary so successfull that the buildings nearly contiguous to those destroyed were saved including large amount of property.

I give here only an outline of the career of Zachariah. He was positive in his convictions. He did not occupy middle ground on any question. With him it was a friend or an enemy, but he more friends than enemies.

The schedule of property upon which he paid a tax in 1814 is an interesting item in this brief notice as follows:

One house, $350; one barn, $65; one shop $40; one outhouse $20; ¼ house $100; 7 acres mowing at $18; 10 pasturing at $8; 40 acres unimproved at $ Add 16 mowing and tillage; cheever $400; also ¼ house, $100; barn, $60; deduct for house $100 and barn $60; two oxen, $40; two cows, $28; one horse, $40 one chaise, $50; one swine, $5. Add on cow, $14; one swine; $5.

As guardian to Caroline and Theophilus Hilton, money at interest $600.

The house of William Stevens, brother to Zachariah, who succeeded the father Capt. Isaac, and is now standing, was taxed on a valuation of $650; that of Josiah, another brother, $350, now standing; that of Isaac, Jr., another brother, $300, the one story, half brick, now standing, and that of Nathaniel, still another brother, $125, that stood where Samuel B. Stevens lived, his house now occupied by Granville M. Stevens.

These figures show the taxable values of the period noted, and the fact that four of the five houses that stood in 1814, all occupied by sons of Capt. Stevens, stand today, respected by a few for their dust of antiquity possessed and former occupants.

ZACHARIAH B. STEVENS,

Died May 17, 1856, aged 78 years, a much respected citizen; his wife Miriam (P. Berry) died Dec. 13, 1865 aged 87 years. They had four children: 1, Samuel Butler; 2, Alfred; 3, Emeline; 4, Cordelia.

THE DEERING NEWS.

Saturday, February 9, 1895.

GRANDPA'S SCRAP BOOK

[Under this head historical and genealogical memoranda will be furnished the readers of the News that appears worthy of preservation, particularly of remote periods in our history within the city limits and immediate vicinity.]

Samuel Butler Stevens, the eldest child of Zachariah B. and wife, Miriam P. Berry, was born on Stevens' Plains Sept. 23, 1799. His wife, Sarah B. Frances, daughter of Caleb Frances, was born at Sterling, Mass., Nov. 11, 1799, married October 17, 1821.

April 15, 1814, Capt. Isaac S. Stevens conveyed to his son, Nathaniel Stevens, a blacksmith, a lot of land commencing bounds thereof at the corner of Thomas Brisco's lot on westerly side of the highway, then running southerly by the road eight rods, etc., "containing one acre and being the same land whereon the dwelling house of said Nathaniel stands." The consideration was but $20. The next year for a consideration of $500 he conveyed to his son Nathaniel thirty-seven acres, adjoining.

In 1822, Oliver Buckley, for a consideration of $737.50 conveyed to Samuel B. Stevens the premises (or part thereof) "being the same I purchased of Nathaniel Stevens Nov. 26, 1818." And thus we have the origin of the fine old homestead of Samuel B. Stevens, standing opposite the head of Oak street on Plains avenue, but the house has been added to, and so transformed that if divested of its additions it would not know itself.

Of this character I can say but little—his children and grandchildren are with us.

He was a tin plate maker, and horn comb manufacturer. His place of business was destroyed as shown in my last article under this head.

His last years were spent as a civil engineer. He assisted in establishing the location of the old York & Cumberland railroad—now the Portland & Rochester road. His wife was a superior woman—a painter by nature of rare ability, as her work indicates.

He died July 24, 1848; she July 6, 1890. Children:

1. Almena Maria, born Apr. 20, 1823. Married Judge Charles R. Starr of Kankakie, Ill., and died there May 29, 1887.
2. Augustus E., born Sept. 20, 1825. An iron merchant of Portland, of which city he was mayor 1866-7.
3. Samuel H., born July 15, 1827; was mail agent between Portland and Boston ten years; conductor on Portland & Ogdensburg railroad; general agent Boston & Maine railroad; now engaged with music instruction. Resides in Portland.
4. Granville M., born Jan. 30, 1833. Was several years engaged in the iron business with his brother; collector of taxes town of Deering two years, where he now resides under the parental roof of his father.
5. Lilla Cathleen, born Dec. 4, 1838, died Dec. 19, '39.
6. Frank G., born Dec. 25, 1840. Was engaged some years with the firm of Augustus E. Stevens & Co. Was in the war of the rebellion; register of deeds Cumberland Co. two terms; now traveling agent with N. Y. & N. England railroad.

At the close of the war of the rebellion Granville M. and Frank B. Stevens built on the old Thomas Brisco lot two of the finest residences of the town. As they were exactly alike they were known as the "Twin houses," one of which, the one nearest the cemetery entrance, was consumed by fire fall of 1893.

For a period of some twenty-five years Granville M. was secretary of the Westbrook Seminary Association, and many years the secretary of the Universalist church society, and being a family of musicians, both vocal and instrumental, years agone, they often appeared before the public. Fifty years ago I attended a concert given by a quartette one of which was Samuel H., and there may have been more Stevens in it.

Alfred, the second child of Zachariah B. Stevens was born Sept. 3, 1803, married Oct. 17, 1826 Nancy Goodrich Buckley, born on Stevens' Plains, Feb. 22, 1806. He died there Sept. 9, 1884; she is still alive.

Emeline, the third child of Zachariah B., was born Nov. 13, 1811, married Rufus Dunham. She died, he married again.

Cordelia, the fourth and last child of Zachariah B., was born Dec. 28, 1821, married Sept. 10, 1844 Levi Q. Pierce, born at Stroudwater, Sept. 28, 1815, son of Charles Pierce and Peggy Porterfield, his wife.

Mr. Pierce was a merchant tailor at Saccarappa village, a man of commanding person, a ready debator and fine singer. He died Apr. 29, 1858, aged 42 years. After his death his widow returned to the home of her youth and now occupies the old ancestral home—the house in which she was born, and for several years taught the art of drawing and painting at Westbrook Seminary, and must in consequence, now be widely known. Two children:

Emeline I., born at Saccarappa Sept. 13, 1846, died June 27, 1884, at Stevens' Plains. She taught district school and music.

Florence, born Feb. 13, 1852, died Dec. 30, 1872—both unmarried.

Cordelia and Levi Q. were married by the Rev. Zenas Thompson who always made it a point on such occasions to give a word of advice to those embarking on the unknown ways of life.

At the time when an attack was expected on Portland during the war of 1812-15, and preparations were made for the same, a half dozen heavy frame chairs were brought from that city and stored in the attic of the house of Zachariah B. Stevens, where they remained till Miss Cordelia thought of, and commenced preparations for the marriage event, when two of them were pulled from the place of long seclusion, scraped, varnished, and bottoms worked and put on so the pair of chairs, like the pair that were to be united in wedlock, appeared "neat as a pin."

In front of these chairs the bride and groom were arranged, and at the close of the ceremony the reverend gentleman said in his pleasing way: "Now if ever matters do not go pleasant with you and the stream of married life becomes rough, just stand up before these chairs and reproduce in your minds the event of the present hour."

In the upstairs hall of the ancient abode may be seen the chairs that formed the background of the tableau of Sept. 10, 1844, the silvery drapery of the occasion continuing in retrospect of the remaining participant.

THE DEERING NEWS.

Saturday, February 16, 1895.

GRANDPA'S SCRAP BOOK

[Under this head historical and genealogical memoranda will be furnished the readers of the News that appears worthy of preservation, particularly of remote periods in our history within the city limits and immediate vicinity.]

In the news of March 17, 1894, I alluded to Charles Pierce and wife, Peggy Poterfield, and presented quite a lengthy account of the Poterfield family, and in the News of Jan. 12 of this year, in an article under the head of North Deering, again, in which two errors appear; one that he was a teacher when in fact he was a trader; the other that Polly Poterfield was a niece to Peggy Poterfield when in fact she was a sister. In my article under this head last week the name again appeared. I now have more data which I propose to preserve in this number of the News.

"FAMILY RECORD OF BENJ. PIERCE."

"Mr. Benjamin Pierce was married to Miss Lydia Frost of Kittery, daughter of Major Charles Frost, Nov. 8, 1692.

1. Daniel born Aug. 6, 1693.
2. Charles, born Feb. 3, 1695.
3. Elizabeth, born Nov. 14, 1697.
4. Daniel, born Oct. 11, 1698.
5. Benjamin, born June 13, 1700.
6. Abigail, born Jan. 26, 1702.
7. John, born Nov. 7, 1704.
8. Humphrey, born March 22, 1705.
9. Thomas, born Nov. 1, 1706.
10. Joseph, born May 18, 1708.
11. Samuel, born Sept. 21, 1709.
12. Eleazer, born May 19, 1711.

The above record is taken from his book of records for the town of Newbury and state of Massachusetts, drawn off from the book May 30, 1810.

There is a note on this old manuscript which reads, "he had 3 wives," but as the note is on the side of the record paper and at the end and between the names of Samuel and Eleazer it is not clear to whom the reference is made.

From which one of the foregoing persons Charles Pierce of Stroudwater descended I have not informed myself. His Bible is in possession of Mrs. Cordelia Pierce from which I am permitted to make the following copy:

Charles Pierce, born July 23, 1774; died Oct. 26, 1827.

Peggy Porterfield, born March 1, 1781; died Apr. 2, 1858.

They were married Oct. 11, 1807.

CHILDREN.

1. Edward, born Aug. 12, 1811. Married, 1838, Abigail Doughty Shaw, b n Jan. 6, 1814. He died Sept. 2, 1870.
2. Mary, born May 30, 1813, married 1855 Olof N. Thurnburg. Margaret Wilhelmena, their only child, died Apr. 7, 1858, aged 2 years, 2 months, 20 days.
3. Levi, born Sept. 28, 1815, married Sept. 10, 1844, Cordelia Stevens. The "Q." which stands for Quinby, used by him, does not appear in the Bible record. For the rest of the record of this Levi see my last chapter under this head, also the Poterfield article.

At the old Stroudwater cemetery may be seen a stone inscribed as follows:

This stone is erected
in the memory of
CHARLES PIERCE,
who was born in Haverhill, Mass., July 23, 1777,
and departed this life
Oct. 26, 1827, Æt. 50 years,
3 months, 3 days

As in Adam all die, even so in crist shall all be made alive; for this corruptible must put on incorruption, and this mortal must put on immortality.

The gravestone of his wife as well as daughter Mary (Pierc) Thurnburg, husband and daughter, may be seen at same place.

The dwelling Mr. Pierce built stood between the house now on the corner and river, which has been noticed in former articles, was one story, parlor in end, then living room, between which was the front door, and off the living room, in the other end were two bedrooms, with "cellar kitchen" under the half next the river. Between the house and river stood the barn. The distance between the street line and front of house was not more than three feet, in which space, stood several rose bushes, but all are now gone as well as every descendant.

The road in front of the residence was established about the time Mr. Pierce built his residence.

Portland Advertiser, Saturday, Feb. 14, 1824:

On Thursday morning last we were visited with the severest storm and gale of wind that has been felt since Sep., 1815. The violence of the gale was principally between 3 and 4 o'clock in the morning. In this town but little damage was done. The upper Presumpscot bridge was swept away, and the lower lost a pier. A bridge and grist mill on the new road to Scarborough, and a fulling mill on the road from Stroudwater bridge to Broad's tavern were also carried away.

The "fulling mill" stood near where Stevens' mill now stands. The Pierce barn, as well as the bridge that stood near it, was also carried away, and the Charles Chesley barn on the opposite side of the river. The story seems strange, but in addition to the record I have heard it many times. And what is more strange a rooster was carried along with the debris and secured next morning where he was perched on the ridge-pole of the roof of the Pierce barn, which was where the smelt houses are now seen on the ice of Fore river.

Here is what I have of the record of the family of

BELA SHAW:

Bela Shaw, born in Middleboro, Mass., Nov. 20, 1787.

Hannah Doughty, born in Falmouth (Allen's Corner) Dec. 6, 1792. Married June 30, 1811.

CHILDREN.

1. Martha Dunbar, born July 2, 1812.
2. Abigail Doughty, born June 6, 1814. Married Edward Pierce as before noticed.
3. Frances Ellen, born Nov. 23, 1820.
4. Sumner (I am told). This Shaw was a trader at Morrill's Corner, built the house Dr. Parker lives in, and Ferdinand E. Bailey occupies the old shop which stood in the fork of the roads where the drinking fountain stands. This is all I know of this family of Shaws.

THE DEERING NEWS.

Saturday, February 23, 1895.

GRANDPA'S SCRAP BOOK

[Under this head historical and genealogical memoranda will be furnished the readers of the News that appears worthy of preservation, particularly of remote periods in our history within the city limits and immediate vicinity.]

I did not intend to convey the idea that there are no descendants left of Charles Pierce, only none at Stroudwater. He has a grandson, at least, living in the state of Connecticut, whose father was Edward Pierce.

The mother of Charles Pierce was named Rebecca. March 12, 1802, she gave power of attorney for herself and heirs to sell a piece of land with half a house in Newburyport, estate of Joseph Pierce, deceased, late of Atkinson, N. H.

In 1801, he had a sister Mary living in Haverhill, and in a letter of that date "an old gentleman" is spoken of who, evidently, was the father to Charles and who died the next year.

Jan. 12, 1804, "Charter Party" papers were made out relative to the Brigantine "Maine," 127 tons, Samuel Freeman, master, between Pierce and Capt. John Quinby—the last was one-fourth owner. She was to sail to the West Indies and back to Portland, and Pierce was to pay Quinby at the rate of $1.84 per ton a month and he received $194.03.

In 1816 Charles Pierce had a brother Samuel who lived in Haverhill.

At this period rum was sold at three cents per glass; eggs 17 cents per dozen; corn $1.17 per bushel; flour, $14 per barrel; clear lumber $16 per 1,000 feet; "one pipe of wine, 122 gallons, $131.76;" cheese, 9 cents per pound; quart of rum, 26 cents; six pounds of sugar, 84 cents; molasses, 50 cents per gallon; one mast, $20; one-half pound of tea, 53 cents, and "Sept. 27, 1804, one-half pound bison tea, 75 cents." "One quarter of veal, 70 cents." "Wharfage on 35,492 feet of boards at 5 cents, $1.77."

"PORTLAND HAT COMPANY.
Daniel How—Treasurer."
"Share No. 69, $25.00
Charles Pierce, holder. Sept. 8, 1810."

July 3, 1807, Charles Pierce commissioned Ensign of Stroudwater Light Infantry Company "annexed to First Regiment, Second Brigade, Sixth Division, Military of Massachusetts."

In 1805 the ladies presented this company with a standard, and the record of presentation is in my possession, including speeches, with a counter demonstration at Broad's tavern, in the orchard, the oration on which occasion was printed and sold, but I am unable to find a copy. The standard was presented to the Maine Historical Society four or five years ago, or less, by Miss Ann Broad. The speeches, toasts and other facts will soon be reproduced in the News. Rev. Caleb Bradley delivered the oration on presentation of standard.

In 1811 Mr. Pierce leased for one year the two-story house that stood back of the house now on the corner, and towards the old burying ground, to Dr. Jacob Hunt for $45 the second physician of Stroudwater.

1815.

"Amount of money raised and belonging to school district No. 3 in Westbrook, 148 scholars at 99 per head, $146.52."

"Agreeable to a vote of the district the above to be schooled out in the following (vict) $109.88 for man's school; $36.63 for woman's school."

CAPT. ENOCH PREBLE, } School
CHARLES PIERCE, } Committee.
STETSON LOBDELL, }

"Received of Charles Pierce in his capacity of school committee $36.63 in full for my services in keeping his district school in the summer of 1815."

LYDIA CHAPMAN.

The next year she received $34.43. (The districts seem so be mixed in the records.)

Mrs. Chapman's maiden name was Lydia Starbird, born Nov. 20, 1768, in the Riggs house, alias Jones house, alias Daniel Fowler house, that stood near Bradley's Corner, which was torn down some three years ago, and three houses—one single, and double—built on the site. The year she was born the Starbird house, now standing between Stroudwater and Saccarappa, was built by her father. She married Shadrach Chapman of Newmarket, N. H., July 16, 1786. He a blacksmith, born March 6, 1764, at Newmarket, N. H., and died at Stroudwater Aug. 8, 1812; she died there Feb. 18, 1851.

CHILDREN.

1. Mary, died 1838, unmarried; buried in the Starbird burying ground, on the farm where there are some twenty graves, but not a lettered stone. The lot is reserved in deed of conveyance.
2. Nancy, born Nov. 18, 1791, married Oct. 25, 1810, Tristram C. Stevens, born at Stroudwater Nov. 6, 1789, died there Sept. 3, 1870. She died Sept. 24, 1874. They had 9 children.
3. Samuel, died unmarried Aug. 15, 1811.

The Widow Chapman was a teacher many years.

"Rec'd of Charles Pierce $115.37 for keeping winter school 1815.
March 16, 1816.
TIMOTHY GALVIN.

Galvin was noticed in the News July 14, '94.

"1815. Paid George Warren, Jr., for keeping school at $10 per month, $44."

"Paid Jones Means eleven weeks' board at $3 per week, $33."

"1816 Dr. 1st school district. Paid Timothy Galvin at $33 per month."

The schoolhouse at Stroudwater in which these teachers labored was a new one; was two stories high, and stood on the site of the present structure, in the southwesterly corner of the old Town Landing lot.

Dec. 10, 1810, the district voted $400 to build it.

May 17, 1811, voted $150 to finish schoolhouse.

May 11 voted $50 additional.

Sept. 9, accepted report of school committee, $693.20.

Oct. 11, accepted report committee, $724.21, and raised $200 additional.

The small stove would not heat the room, so May 28, 1815, it was voted to raise $100 to put in a brick box of a thing in the middle of the room, and bills were paid for the same as follows:

WESTBROOK, Oct. 10, 1815.
DATE   SCHOOL DISTRICT No 1.   AMT.
Oct. 10. To Chas. Pierce, Dr., two
        casks lime, $5.50
        Hauling lime,   .40
        Hauling bricks,   .25
        2½ pints of rum for
            workmen,   .32
        Paid S. Lobdell for
            2000 bricks at $4.00 $8.00
        Paid Zenas Pratt for
            hauling some, $2.00
        1-lb. nails 10c, 2½ pints
            1 glass rum,   .50
        Paid Thos. Pierce mason,
                                $12.00
        Paid Chas. Crispan   9.50
        Paid Benjamin Remick   1.75
        Paid for iron,   .50
        Paid for hinges, screws
            and latches,   .58
        Paid Joseph Quinby,
            joiner, $5.00
        2½ pints rum for workmen,
                                   .32
Nov. 6 To 1½ pint and 1 gil rum
            for men   .24
        Plank and boards   .75
        Shingles   .25
        Paid Thomas Pierce,   1.50
        Paid   "   "   3.00
        Paid Chas. Crispan   3.00
        Paid T. C. Steves,   .25
Dec. 28, To 25 feet clear Boards
            for spout   .50
1816, Jan. 23, Paid Benj. Remick for
            keys and iron,   1.42
        Paid Benj. Remick,   .08
        Moody & Swett,   2.00
        3 glasses rum   .12
        Cash for Sundries   1.00
                               ──────
                                $60.73
Cr. Amt. of Sale Small Stove.   14.50
                               ──────
Balance on the district, $40.23

The patent or brick box stove was a failure and was soon removed.

Continued:

In 1814 Charles Pierce was taxed as follows: One house, $250; one barn, $75; one store, $40; one house and lot, $150; one-half acre lot, $50 Deduct stock, $40. One-third Chesley's house and lot. Add 3 cows, $42; one horse, $40; one chaise, $35; one swine, $5; stock in trade, $200; vessel, $300. Deduct stock in trade, $200; deduct for real, $326; do. personal, $328.

July 11, 1815, articles of agreement were entered into, by Mr. Pierce and Jacob Quincy of Portland relative to the line of a schooner on stocks at Stroudwater, of 104 tons, "carpenters' admeasurement." Quincy agreed to pay Pierce at the rate of $20 per ton, "said hull to be butt bolted," one-half cash down and a three months' note.

It appears by the record that Solomon Morton, father of George W. Morton whose widow, Ann Maria (Stevens) Morton now occupies the homestead of Solomon, commenced the vessel and got the frame up which stood on "Shipyard Point," the point of land between the Morton house and Mill Creek, but on account of the "hard times" of that period Morton in common with many others failed.

THE DEERING NEWS.

Saturday, March 9, 1895.

GRANDPA'S SCRAP BOOK

[Under this head historical and genealogical memoranda will be furnished the readers of the News that appears worthy of preservation, particularly of remote periods in our history within the city limits and immediate vicinity.]

Mary Pierce, second child of Charles Pierce and wife Peggy (Porterfield) Pierce, noticed in my article in the News under this head Feb. 16, '95, was a character and deserves more than a one line notice in Grandpa's Scrap Book which she shall have. She was born at Stroudwater, as before stated, May 13, 1813, in the house now gone to which allusion has not only been made, but the house described.

Her father, whose shop stood —— received a paralytic shock which rendered one side of him useless. Her mother was a corpulent woman, weighing 204 pounds at the time of her death which was very sudden, she falling from her chair and taken up lifeless. She was a strong minded woman, and rather masculine in voice, and few were the boys of the village who did not have an occasional battle of words with her, yet she was full of compassion and rendered words of advice freely, even referring to the manner in which she trained her own children.

Mary, on arriving at womanhood, adopted the calling of a tailoress. At the time of my earliest recollection she was employed with her brother Edward who had established himself as a merchant tailor at Saccarappa.

After the disablement of her father a few things were kept in the dwelling for sale.

Polly Porterfield, sister to Peggy, hence aunt to Mary, fell in her young womanhood and fractured her thigh bone, and then she engaged in trade in the dwelling of her aunt Peggy, but the time I cannot state. Meeting with success she built the one story shop on the corner of the cross roads, a rod or so easterly of the residence of her aunt Peggy, to which the husband of Mary, in 1861 or 2, added a story, and is now the homestead of Mr. Thomas W. Jackson.

It was painted yellow, two rooms; the shop part being on the right as one entered the front door from the Buxton road side. In the Saccarappa end there was a door which was opened only in the summer. The shop had shutters made of matched boards painted green, with letters, W. I. GOODS, in black. On the back side was a shed-roof addition, very low, the top of which could be easily reached from the fence, and when smelting time came in the fall we boys could always find a little piece of lead for a sinker around the chimney of this flat roof, provided "Aunt Peggy" did not discover us before procurement.

When Aunt Polly felt her time on earth was drawing to a close she gave Mary the few, (say four) thousand dollars she had accumulated, and Mary took upon herself the management of the establishment.

Temporarily residing in the village was a young man by the name of Olof N. Thurnburg and a brother Charles, said to be natives of Sweden, who worked for Hon. Jonathan Smith in his tannery, who became enamored with Mary, or her home and fortune. Of course everybody was surprised when the fact was made public, and for a while the villagers had but little else to talk about.

The marriage day came in 1855, and Mary took home her "boy husband." He was compactly built, light complexion, gentlemanly deportment, round face, spoke broken English, and in personal appearance was rather above the average of mankind.

As a trader at Stroudwater he was a failure, so he opened a restaurant in Portland, between Preble and Elm on Congress street, of which place he was proprietor at the time of his death.

Then Mary re-stocked the shop at Stroudwater with goods, and the establishment became in the evening of the day the headquarters of the boys and young men of the neighborhood, Mary always joining in the conversation—in fact she rather enjoyed the company of the young folks—a characteristic of the old Porterfield race, a name now extinct hereabouts, though there are descendants still, bearing other names.

There were no greater events that I know of in the lives of these persons than what I have mentioned. Aunt Polly had a fine complexion, rather large nose, but not thick, and was far less demonstrative than her sister Peggy. She had a bright eye with a penetrating glance, as did Aunt Peggy and her daughter Mary. The chronography of Mary was good, and her memory of dates, particularly of births and marriages, was remarkable.

When I was just old enough to commence driving I took my father's horse and carried her over to the Shaw's who lived in what is now the Dr. Parker house at Morrill's Corner, and the younger of the two women present made some candy by dissolving brown sugar in certain parts of water and vinegar and treated us. I was taken into the kitchen and let into the secret of the manufacture, which was one of the great events of my young life, and served to furnish me with home amusement more than one stormy day.

Mary was dark complexioned, rather corpulent, appeared as well in one dress as another, liked to hear the village news but used much caution in repeating, a rolling walk, with a shrill voice when talking to countrymen in the distance, though near to was mellow and musical.

Poor Mary! The afternoon before her death I stepped into the shop to speak to her relative to matters pertaining to her parents, and she said: "I don't feel at all smart just now, but you come over Sunday and we will see what we can find of records up stairs." The next morning to my surprise I learned that she had departed this life, and I obtained nothing.

In the old cemetery, only a few rods distant, may be seen two modest appearing grave stones inscribed as follows:

OLOF THURNBURG,
Died
Sep. 24, 1867.
Aged 35 years.

MARY S. THURNBURG,
Wife of
Olof Thurnburg,
died
Sept. 12, 1887.
Aged 74 years.

He was a member of the order of Free Masons. In addition to the above named is a stone to the memory of their only child, as well of the parents of Mary.

THE DEERING NEWS.

Saturday, March 16, 1895.

GRANDPA'S SCRAP BOOK

[Under this head historical and genealogical memoranda will be furnished the readers of the News that appears worthy of preservation, particularly of remote periods in our history within the city limits and immediate vicinity.]

Nathaniel Stevens, the fifth son of Capt. Isaac S. Stevens, was born on Stevens' Plains, Nov. 22 1780, as stated in the News, Nov. 17, '94 which see for list of names, etc., of his sisters and brothers. He selected for a wife Abigail, daughter of Dea. James Bailey, born Aug. 20, 1782, a record of whose family connections appeared in the News under this head, Jan. 26, of this year. He was a blacksmith and commenced married life on the Plains.

In 1814 he was taxed as follows: One house, $125; one barn, $30; one shed, $20; 4 acres mowing and tillage at $20; forty-three acres pasturing and unimproved at $9; one cow, $14. Deduct thirty-six acres and change to Buckley. It was in 1814 that he purchased the last lot of his father for $500 and at about the same date he received a deed of his father of an acre of land, "being the same land whereon the said Nathaniel's dwelling house stands," the house being the "original" house of Samuel B. Stevens, before alluded to as the present abode of Granville M. Stevens, Esq., which is the second house southerly of the Universalist church building, Stevens' Plains avenue. I am particular in some of these matters in order to accommodate the fellow who hunts for landmarks a hundred years hence, for I often say it is a pity some people cannot come back to earth and put matters pertaining to themselves and families into better shape.

It was in the year 1818 that Nathaniel sold his house to Oliver Buckley for $400, who, in 1822, sold it to Samuel B. Stevens for $737.50.

From the Plains Nathaniel moved to where Mr. Geo. Woodbury Johnson now lives, on the Saco road about a mile southwesterly of Stroudwater.

The strange appearing part of Mr. Johnson's residence where he keeps his wood, etc., was then known as a Trickey house. It was a two-story building and stood end to the road. It was built probably by the sons of the Trickey who came to Stroudwater. James Johnson, Esq., father to George W., moved it to its present location and cut it down part of a story, and built the one his son now occupies. In the Trickey building Sophia, daughter of Nathaniel, taught a private school. On the opposite side of the road stood the blacksmith shop.

The Trickey name was David, who last occupied the building, and who married, Sept. 1, 1768 Mary Hobbs; she died Aug. 7, 1799, aged 54 years; he died Apr. 5, 1814, aged 73 years. It was in 1733 that the premises came into the possession of Zebulon Trickey, father to David. David's brother Zebulon settled about three-fourths of a mile westerly, where the Trickeys now reside. The lot had a house upon it when purchased by Trickey. In 1757 the premises figured in a big law suit; the papers "in the case" contain much history.

From this place Nathaniel moved to Bridgton Corner, to the Plains and then back into the large square house that stood next southeasterly of where the post office is located at Stroudwater. The house was burned about twenty years ago when owned by Thomas Jackson. The post office is located in the house on the westerly side of Westbrook street, opposite the head of Waldo street, where John Hobart lived fifty years ago. There Nathaniel kept a public house.

Mrs. Reynolds, his daughter, who now resides in Portland, remembers the time well—remembers seeing the venerable Lafayette when he was driven through the place in 1824, the carriage drawn by the fine pair of grays we have heard so much about, and she remembers attending the private school of Mrs. Shadrach Chapman, taught in the Stevens house opposite where the public schoolhouse now stands.

After this Nathanael moved from "pillow to post," his last place of abode being in a two story house, wood colored, that stood next southerly of the Dr. Jacob Hunt house, now owned by heirs of Mrs. McDonald, or Mrs. Susie (McDonald) Morton, which was built by Dr. Jeremiah Barker of Gorham in the year 1800. It was while he lived at this last place I knew him.

He worked with his son at the bellows and anvil. He was compactly built, somewhat corpulent, a nose rather larger than the average size, heavy eyebrows and answered to the name of "Uncle Nat." The contrast of the "spandy white" window shades and the black exterior of his place of abode I now see in imagination as though of yesterday. His belief in a universal salvation was unbounded. Originally both he and his wife were members of the old Congregational church. Before me as I write is the temperance pledge he signed in 1852 and his signature in the original. His wife died Dec. 4, 1849, at Stroudwater, aged 67 years; he died there June 1, 1853, aged 73.

On the record book of the temperance society I find this:

June 3

Voted to attend the funeral of Brother Nathaniel Stevens and that the burial service be performed at the grave.

Voted to purchase badges of mourning and that the expense be paid from the club treasury.

Alvan B. Rand, who lived some two or more miles from Stroudwater on the Saco road, was chaplain.

The first service, or that of the relatives of the deceased and friends, and there were many, was holden at Westbrook Seminary, from which place we all walked in order to the ancient burying place on the Windham road, where may be seen gravestones suitably inscribed that mark the place of deposit of their earthly remains.

Their children were as follows: 1, Sally; 2, Sophia; 3, Maria; 4, Leonard; 5, Levi B.; 6, Elizabeth B.; 7, Ellen N.; 8, Frances; 9, and last, Abigail.

THE DEERING NEWS.

Saturday, March 23, 1895.

GRANDPA'S SCRAP BOOK

[Under this head, historical and genealogical memoranda will be furnished the readers of the News that appears worthy of preservation, particularly of remote periods in our history within the city limits and immediate vicinity.]

I closed my article last week under this head with the statement that Nathaniel Stevens and wife, Abigail Bailey, had nine children and gave their names. I now consider the matter in detail.

1.

Sally, born Nov. 4, 1802, on Stevens Plains, married William Grant, born on the Windham road near the Quaker meetinghouse. He was by occupation a calker, and resided in the house that stands back from the street some four rods, a story and a half high, next house southerly from the corner of Oak street, on Forest avenue, westerly side thereof. He died May 22, 1871; she died April 1, 1891. No records obtainable other than what is here given. Children:
1. Albion K. P., married and died in Connecticut; no issue.
2. Henry, unmarried, went whale fishing and never returned.
3. Nathaniel Stevens, married, resides in Boston.
4. Maria Elizabeth Stevens, married Thomas Wright of Windham; he died; she retains the homestead of her father where she resides.
5. Frances died when about 16 years of age.
6. Corcelia Ellen died young.
7. Samuel, unmarried, went into the war of the late rebellion and died.
8. Orman Franklin, married, died in California, no issue.
9. Marsha Adelia, married David Richardson of Deering.
10. Edward Lyman, married, resides in Deering.

2.

Sophia, born March 9, 1804, married James Hicks of what is now Deering, April 10, 1825. He worked at brickmaking and wool-pulling; lived at various places; at one time on Forest avenue in what is known as the Ramsey house, attached to the green houses there, which was originally Deacon James Bailey's carpenter shop moved from the old homestead place on Windham road and converted into a dwelling by his brother, William Hicks, of whom he bought it, just prior to which date he lived in a house next southerly which he owned. After the death of his wife, Sophia Bailey, he married one Elizabeth White and resided in the town of Harrison, but returned to Portland where he died Jan. 30, 1860, aged 70 years, 4 months, and was buried in the Bailey burying ground, Windham road, where a family monument that contains but little information may be seen. Children:
1. Edwin, born Aug. 24, 1826, died when young at Stroudwater with his Grandfather Stevens while living in the house now occupied by Walter Fickett.
2. James Wallace, died young.
3. Frances Ellen born May 14, 1829, married Daniel F. Hussey. He is dead; the widow resides in Portland.
4. Julia, born July 12, 1833, married John Tate of Stroudwater, three children; then he died. He owned and they lived where Mr. Augustus Tate resides in the most ancient house in Deering or Portland. Of the three children Ada E. survived, married at Stroudwater, Samuel E. Dill, and they reside at Vassalboro. She married 2nd, Joseph C. Parker, of Stroudwater, where they reside. Seven children.
5. Watson, born Apr. 15, 1835 married in the State of Wisconsin and now resides in Syracuse, N. Y. Eight children.
By second wife James Hicks had Ann, born in Harrison, Jan. 19 1846; she married Austin D. Sulivan, firm of Sulivan & Osgood, grocers, corner of Portland & Green streets, he of Appleton. She died—he married second.

3.

Maria, born March 18, 1806, married March 20, 1828, Josiah Maxfield, born at Stroudwater March 20, 1799. The rest of this record will appear next week.

4.

Leonard, born Aug. 26, 1808, married 1831, Hannah Morton of Stroudwater Mar. 17, 1841 born Nov. 11, 1807. He died in Stroudwater, Aug. 10 1862 in the ancient dwelling standing on Bond street, next westerly of the present residence of Joseph C. Parker, which is on the corner of Westbrook and Bond streets. She died at Bar Harbor, Apr. 11, 1893. He was a blacksmith; thinish face, rather prominent nose, medium size and a powerful man at the anvil. His shop in his last days stood between the present shop of the same sort and the grocery shop of Andrew Hawes, Esq. his shop being the storehouse of Mr. Hawes' shop. His three sons went into the Union army, war of the rebellion. Their names were George Leonard, Franklin Whitman, and John Fairfield. The first two died in service; the other resides at Dorchester, Mass. Children:
1. Eliza A., born Apr. 11, 1832, married Andrew J., son of Isaac Johnson of Stroudwater; he now resides at Manchester, N. H.
2. George L., born Sep. 9. 1833, died at Baton Rouge, La., Sep. 25, 1867; married Caroline, daughter of Isaac Johnson, and sister to Andrew J., above noticed. She resides at Stroudwater.
3. Lucy Maria, born March 20, 1835, (No record of her death.)
4. Franklin W., born Dec. 19, 1837, died unmarried David's Island, N. Y. Harbor, Oct. 18, 1865. Remains brought home to Deering.
5. Abbie Elizabeth, born March 15, 1839, married Samuel Skillin; they reside in the northerly part of Cape Elizabeth.
6. Martha Ellen, born Feb. 20, 1842, now living at Dorchester, Mass., unmarried.
7. John Fairfield, born Oct. 1, 1844, married Ella A. Delano, Nov. 17, 1869, now residing at Dorchester Mass.
8. Lucy Anna, born, Jan. 16, 1846 married George E. Wescott, now residing at Bar Harbor.
9. Mary M., born Aug. 5, 1848, died Aug 5, 1850.

5.

Levi Bradish, born Dec. 22, 1811, married Harriet Sawyer, 12th and youngest daughter of Hiram Sawyer, whose record appeared in the News of Dec. 22, 1894, born Feb. 20, 1818. He was a block tin worker at Morrill's corner so long as the business lasted. He had not been married many years when his household goods were all consumed in a house that stood where the house now stands next northerly of the Free church, Stevens' Plains avenue. Tall, erect, white hair and beard of same color, his personal appearance was fine. She died Aug. 5, 1860; he died Feb. 25, 1889. They had Georgiana; Henry Hunt—named for Dr. Hunt of Stroudwater—Augusta. None ever married. The son died young, the daughter occupies the homestead of their father that stands nearly opposite the Free church building.

6

Elizabeth Brisco, born Apr. 8, 1813, married Alpheus Bailey, son of George Bailey, born March 31, 1783, married Betsey Webb, Jan. 21, 1808, daughter of Col. James Webb of Stroudwater, who was a Revolutionary soldier. George Bailey built the house where Charles E. Bailey, brother to Alpheus, now resides. George was the sixth child in a family of 14 children, and was a wheelwright, the shop standing near the house in which Alpheus died. His wife died while visiting her sister, Mrs. Jackson in Cape Elizabeth, Jan. 11, 1894. No issue.

7

Ellen North, born Aug. 7, 1816, married at Portland, where they resided, June 28, 1840, Leonard O. Reynolds, who was born Feb. 2, 1814, in the town of Minot, and was son of William Reynolds who came to Maine from Bridgewater, Mass. He was a dealer in choice brands of groceries in the shop next westerly of Union hall, Congress street, Portland. He died Apr. 24, 1882; resided 144 Brackett street. Children: Millie M., Edward Everett, Alice Alberta, Lena Eugene, (adopted) The widow resides in the homestead with the unmarried daughters.

8

Frances, born Jan. 10, 1820, married Miles Hobart, son of John, who resided in the present post office building at Stroudwater, Westbrook street, head of Waldo. They resided in Providence, R. I., where they have children and where the widow now resides. He was a sail maker.

CONTINUED:

9 AND YOUNGEST.

Abigail, born Apr. 25, 1824, married Henry Small Jackson, born Apr. 28, 1820, on the Saco road in Cape Elizabeth, just over the town line. He was a farmer and much respected citizen. Thomas Jackson, his father, was born there, March 14, 1784, died there Oct. 20, 1854. His wife, Mary McKenney, born Nov. 27, 1783, died there Oct. 6, 1842. Thomas Jackson, grandfather to Henry S., died there Sept. 15, 1819, aged 80 years. He was son of Francis Jackson, who settled there in 1736. This last Thomas married widow Abigail Damm, March 20, 1780. She died June 20, 1813, aged 73 years.

The Jackson homestead becoming out of repair Henry S., bought the Deacon Cummings farm a mile and a half westerly, and about 30 years ago had the old Jackson dwelling removed. The widow resides on the Cummings place. Children: Amanda S., Henry B., Lucy T., Ida Lizzie, Nellie G., George W., (twins) and Florence M.

NOTE.—I made an error last week in the location of the original house of Samuel B. Stevens, built by Nathaniel Stevens. I should have said, second house southerly of the main entrance to Evergreen cemetery, and not church, on Stevens Plains avenue, westerly side.

THE DEERING NEWS.

Saturday, March 30, 1895.

GRANDPA'S SCRAP BOOK

[Under this head historical and genealogical memoranda will be furnished the readers of the News that appears worthy of preservation, particularly of remote periods in our history|within the city limits and immediate vicinity.]

In my last article under this caption I stated that the record of Maria, the third child of Nathaniel Stevens and wife Abigail Bailey, who united in marriage with Josiah Maxfield, "will appear next week." Here is the commencement.

WILLIAM MAXFIELD AND SOME OF HIS DESCENDANTS.

His birthplace is a matter of conjecture among the descendants hereabouts, but there is a family tradition that his youth was spent with one Mayberry at Windham, which place was settled in 1737, by Thomas Chute and Wm. Mayberry, from Marblehead, Mass., and at one time was called New Marblehead.

Nov. 4, 1753, according to the records of Old Falmouth in manuscript, matrimonial "intentions" between this William and Susannah Webb were made public, she, according to another family tradition, being an aunt to Eli Webb, the father to Nathan Webb, the present judge of our U. S. District Court.

In 1756, I find he received a grant of land in Windham, the town in which he resided; what else he owned I cannot say.

By the marriage with Susannah Webb there was at least one child that was given the name of William. As he was not born till 1760 it is reasonable to suppose there were other children, though Mr. Charles Maxfield, his nephew, now in the 92nd year of life, residing at Stroudwater, never heard of any other children. This William, Jr., married with Isabella Webster of Cape Elizabeth and settled at Stroudwater. He never owned real estate of which there is record. He worked about the wharves, rafted lumber, piloted vessels up and down Fore River, and in the war of 1812-15 he played a part for which his widow received a pension.

Here is a copy of an extract from the day book of Jonathan Sparrow, dated at Stroudwater, May 14, 1804.

William Maxfield,   Cr.
By piloting schooner Harmeney
 up and down the river, $2 00
By ¼ day work on boom,   .50
By work 2 days farming,   2.00

The above shows the price of labor at that date. Here are a few items of charges of that year that show somewhat what it cost to live: Three yards of velvet, $5.25; one bushel corn, $1.00; one and a half gallons rum, $1.75; one barrel flour, $8.50; two pounds sugar, $.34; nineteen pounds of pork, $2.38; one pound of tea $1.50; one fur hat, $3.17; four and three-fourths yards calico, $2.95; one nineteen and one-half inch mast, $19.50, etc., etc.

On the fly-leaf of the old book are several records of agreements. One reads: "Rhoda Partridge Came to board with me July 13, 1804, at 9s. per week, ($1.50), also took one of my chambers at $15.00 per year. Left the chamber Oct. 8, 1805, which is 17 months and 5 days."

Sparrow lived where the cellar hole may now be seen, head of Waldo street. After this Rhoda built a house, westerly end of the Stroudwater iron bridge and southerly side of the highway, on leased ground, which is now the so-called Walker house, to which a half-story has been added. It was moved to its present location by David Stevens. It was in this house that William Maxfield lived several years. He died in the house now occupied by Mr. E. Milton Jacobs and family; his widow removed to Portland where she resided with her daughter, Mrs. Nathaniel Shaw, and where she died, No. 58 Brown street.

In the old cemetery at Stroudwater may be seen a pair of moss-covered gravestones inscribed thus:

WILLIAM MAXFIELD,
Died,
May 1, 1840,
Aged 80 years.

ISABELLA,
Widow of Daniel Maxfield,
Died Apr. 25, 1852,
Aged 93 years.

Their children were:
1 Susan, died young.
2 Eliza Haskell Shaw, married Nathaniel Shaw of Portland, published Nov. 5, 1831; one child, Daniel Winslow Shaw. Nathaniel died March 12, 1869, aged 82 years; Eliza H. died May 2, 1872, aged 75. She was his second wife. Mrs. Mary E. Ayers, a child by first marriage occupies the homestead. Daniel Winslow Shaw entered the Union army as a member 1st Maine cavalry and at last accounts resided in Chelsea, Mass.
3 Apphia, died unmarried.
4 Susan, died with Mrs. Shaw Dec. 2, 1841, aged 38 years.
5 Webster.
6 George. These two last left home when young men and became mariners.

William Maxfield, Sen., married second at Windham, July 21, 1763, Mary Wescott and had children: 1, Elizabeth; 2, Ann; 3, Daniel; 4, Josiah; 5, Mary; and 6, Eliakim.
1 Elizabeth, (alias Betsey), baptized May 12, 1765, married Sept. 17, 1795, Mark Haskell of Saccarappa village.

On page 91 of Smith & Dean's Journal edition of 1849, appears the following:

Apr. 30, 1740 I rode to Stroudwater to talk with Mr. Slemmons, who is offended with me. * * * Mr. Frost also made known that he is offended with me for some passages in a sermon which he thought reflected on his taking Haskell's house, etc.

The cellar hole of the house then referred to is now plainly shown on the easterly bank of the gully through which the Portland & Ogdensburg railroad passes, about half way from Congress to Frost street, its location established by records.

Deacon Solomon Haskell, son of Thomas Haskell, the first of the name hereabouts, and father to Mark, resided between Cumberland Mills and Saccarappa. His first wife, named Mary, died April 27, 1801, aged 77 years.

"Portland Argus, May 5, 1807. Married, Solomon Haskell and Mrs. Eleanor Quinby. He 84 years old; she 73."

Grave stone record: Solomon Haskell died May 22, 1816, aged 92 years.

Mary, wife of Solomon, died April 27, 1801, aged 77 years.

Journal record of Rev. Caleb Bradley: Died, August 1822, Deacon Haskell's widow, aged 90 years.

In the Saccarappa village cemetery, located a few rods from the public library, upon a high bank looking down upon the passing trains of cars over the Portland & Rochester railroad, is a row

CONTINUED:

of Haskell graves containing thirteen lettered stones, and others near by, and at the head of the long row stands that of Solomon, with a blank space where the stone of the second wife should appear.— This brief notice may tend to save her name as her headstone cannot.

In the village cemetery at Saccarappa are two stones inscribed as follows:

In Memory of
MARK HASKELL,
who died
Feb. 20, 1827, aged 65 years.

"Jesus I give my spirit up,
And trust it in thy hand,
My dying flesh shall rest in hope,
And rise at thy command."

ELIZABETH,
wife of Mark Haskell,
Died
Dec. 20, 1850, aged 85 years.

The last worldly home of this pair was the building now used as the stable to the residence of Jeremiah R. Andrews, located nearly in the centre of the village.

2 Ann, baptised Nov. 1, 1767, married —— Watson, and there is a family tradition that they lived at Bethel, whose daughter Martha married a man by the name of Clark. [Norman Clark, born Dec. 18, 1784, married Martha Watson of Norway. History of Bethel p. 512.]

3 Daniel, b ptized Dec. 24, 1769, and here I must pause till next week.

NOTE. In the record of the marriage of Leonard Stevens that appeared last week there was an error; it should have read—married, May 17, 1831.

THE DEERING NEWS.

Saturday, April 6, 1895.

GRANDPA'S SCRAP BOOK

[Under this head historical and genealogical memoranda will be furnished the readers of the News that appears worthy of preservation, particularly of remote periods in our history within the city limits and immediate vicinity.]

I closed my article last week under this head with the name of Daniel, third child of William Maxfield of Windham, baptized there Dec. 24, 1769. He married Dec. 25, 1796 at Falmouth, (the part that is now Deering) Lydia Bailey, daughter of John Bailey, Jr., who lived in the John Newcomb house on Spring, opposite foot of High street, which house is now standing. This John Bailey, Jr., was born in Newbury, Mass., Oct. 30, 1722, and married Jane Brady Jan. 3, 1749. He died in the month of March 1776, (p. 233 Rev. Thos. Smith's Journal, edition of 1849. He was son of Deacon John Bailey who died in the house now occupied by Miss Helen M. Bailey, Aug.

26, 1770. (Court Records at Portland) which was then one story and which was built about the year 1760.

Lydia Bailey, born Apr. 15, 1776, was the youngest child in a family of 12 or 13 children, and when she became the wife of Daniel Maxfield was making her home with her sister, the wife of Capt. Jesse Partridge, a Revolutionary soldier who came down from Saccarappa after the war was over and purchased of the Smalls what is now known as the Quinby farm, and built the house where Hon. Andrew Hawes now resides, on the Saccarappa road next northerly to the old Stroudwater cemetery.

Small located there just prior to 1744, but his deed is not a matter of record. In the year of 1744 I find in Nathaniel Knight's account book who lived at Stroudwater Falls, a mile southerly of Saccarappa, charges against Joseph Small, and in 1745 against Joseph Small, Jr., "To one gun, £9 10; To Pasturing ye Oxen & yr father's, £1 10."

The dwelling of Mrs. Caroline Stevens, (widow of George L. Stevens noticed two weeks ago) was built by the Smalls. It stood immediately opposite the driveway to the Quinby dwelling, a few feet northerly of it, and when Capt. Partridge built what is now called the Quinby house, the Small house was moved to the opposite side of the highway and became the residence of Daniel Maxfield when he was married.

Capt. Jesse Partridge died Dec. 21, 1795, aged 53 years without issue; his widow Rebecca Bailey, sister to the wife of Daniel Maxfield, married Andrew Titcomb, whose first wife was Mary Dole, daughter of Capt. Daniel Dole, who built the ancient mansion house standing opposite, in the year 1770. Rebecca (Bailey) (Partridge) Titcomb died May 5, 1808, aged 58 years.

A corner of the farm, comprising some six acres, was sold to the Doles by the Smalls, otherwise, strange to say, the bounds remain now as established when the Smalls made the purchase. The site of the dwelling has a commanding view and is one of the finest locations in Deering, the higher land back of the house being particularly pleasant.

Daniel Maxfield was a mariner, but being made a prisoner by an English cruiser, carried to a distant land, confined in an unhealthy place he returned to his home only to die, leaving six children, the widow residing in the Small house till the marriage of her daughter Mary Jane with whom she removed to Bangor where she died. In the Stroudwater cemetery stand two grave stones inscribed as follows:

In Memory of
DANIEL MAXFIELD,
who died
Feb. 27, 1812.
Æ - | - 42.

In Memory of
LYDIA,
widow of
Daniel Maxfield.
Died
Sept 24, 1861.
Aged 85 yrs., 5 mos.,
& 9 days.

Children: 1, Daniel was a farmer in the town of Bradford; 2, Josiah; 3, Andrew; 4, Charles; 5, Mary Jane, and 6, William.

2 Josiah, born at Stroudwater March 20, 1799. Of his boyish life I know but little. He was 45-8 years of age when I observed him first, and tended the tide mills now managed by Mr. Walter Fickett. The mills were only about a dozen years old at that time. Like his father he started out for a mariner and before me is a curious old paper of which I will here present a copy.

Isaac Ilsley, Collector of the District of Portland and Falmouth, hereby certify, that Josiah Maxfield is an American seaman, aged eleven years, or thereabouts, of the height of 4 feet 4¼ inches, light complexion, light brown hair, light eyes, was born in Falmouth, State of Massachusetts, has this day produced the proof, in the manner directed by the Act entitled, "An Act for the Relief and Protection of American Seamen," and pursuant to the said Act, I do hereby certify that the said Josiah Maxfield is a citizen of the United States of America In witness whereof, I have here unto set my hand and Seal of Office this thirtieth day of August 1810.

ISAAC ILSLEY,
Collector.

No. 225.

The seal consists of an impression representing two ships, light house and custom house.

A boy in these times would think it hard to go to sea at the age of eleven years.

Major and Hon. Archelaus Lewis built the house in which the post office room is located, on Westbrook, opposite the head of High street, which he sold in 1809 for $2500 and moved to Cumberland Mills.

Lewis owned a lot at Long Creek, or vicinity, which he used for a pasture. It is traditional that Josiah lived with Lewis and on one occasion when young Josiah went over with the cows an Indian camped there named Nicholas, somewhat under the influence of drink, caught the boy and threatened to kill him. Josiah thinking it no harm to punish an Indian, particularly one that had threatened to take the life of another, got a gun and using a spike for a bullet, secreted himself behind the fence and when the Indian made his appear-

CONTINUED:

ance be fired. The sequel was, young Josiah was arrested, carried before Justice Lewis, young Moses Quinby of the first graduating class of Bowdoin appearing for Josiah who was fined $1 and discharged. He finally learned the trade of a brick mason and became an expert. He built the Martin Hawes house, the only brick house in Stroudwater, and the brick house on Spring street where Capt. Eben T. Harmon now lives.

As I have said, when he came under my observation he was the miller at the tide mills, which not only ground corn but plaster, running three pairs of stones, two for plaster in the building now standing and one for corn in the building that is gone.

In this last was a work bench where Josiah often busied himself between tides in making goad sticks, etc. He liked to tell a good story and exhibit his work, and on one occasion he bent his stick so both ends touched and said to the countryman: "Do that." The countryman in turn, tied his in a knot, throwing it onto the floor said: "Do that with your darned varnished up things." At that point the exhibition closed.

The mills were quite a resort for the boys—always something to amuse them.

Mr. Maxfield was always pleasant—rather enjoyed the society of the boys—thinking always that his own were rather better than the rest of the world. He had a round red face, always clean shaved, medium height, and well proportioned in his physical make up.

The shot bag containing a hint of silver coins obtained from the sale of plaster which he carried in his trousers pocket I plainly see in my mind's eye at this time, and when he and Captain Dexter Brewer who kept the Brewer House, and Capt. Jonathan Smith, proprietor of the village tannery, with one or two others formed a group in front of the mill and Miss Josephine Brewer came along and asked her father for a cent and he told her he had none and asked Mr. Maxfield to give her one which he did, I thought him a most wonderful good man. And that bull's eye watch of his, thick as it was wide with the gold fob, oh, my!

And then when he was elected moderator of the school meeting and "swore" Martin Hawes in as clerk, I looked on with far more wonderment than now upon the doings of our Congress at Washington.

But my space for this week's news will be more than full if I do not stop here.

NOTE. The grave stone inscription should read Isabella, wife of William, and not Daniel Maxfield; Eliza Haskell Maxfield and not Shaw.

THE DEERING NEWS.

Saturday, April 13, 1895.

GRANDPA'S SCRAP BOOK

[Under this head historical and genealogical memoranda will be furnished the readers of the News that appears worthy of preservation, particularly of remote periods in our history within the city limits and immediate vicinity.]

The deed of the Smalls to Partridge is a short one and I will here give it a place:

Falmouth, Nov. 5, 1782, We, Joseph Small and James Small, of Falmouth, in consideration of £300 paid by Jesse Partridge of Saccarappa, convey a certain farm at Stroudwater whereon we now dwell, be the same more or less, beginning bounds upon the town road leading to Saccarappa at the line of the burying place, thence south 60 degrees west to Stroudwater river, thence by and up the said river to the line of Nathan Chick's land, thence by his land to the town road aforesaid, thence by the same to the bounds first mentioned, with the house and barn thereon, excepting out of the above described six acres sold to Daniel Dole, being the same farm we purchased from our father Joseph Small deceased.

It was February 25, 1772, that the six acres were sold to Capt. Daniel Dole, for £32, and strange as it may seem, as I said in my last article under this head, the bounds of this farm and six acre lot remain as originally established.

From Stroudwater the Smalls removed to the town of Gray.

One of the Chicks married into the Small family as did a man by the name of Samuel Starbird, a Revolutionary soldier, and Eleanor Small April 6, 1751 married Edward Chapman, the grandfather of the late Edward Chapman, the last being born Nov. 11, 1814, and died a couple of years ago at Stroudwater Falls. Eleanor, the widow, married second, Jan. 8, 1779 James Frost of the town of Gorham. The great grandfather of the late Edward owned a farm and his residence stood a little westerly of Union railroad depot, in Portland, who made his will Jan. 3, 1750. His son Edward, the grandfather of the late Edward, owned a farm and lived in from the Buxton road next beyond the James Babb farm, where the cellar, well and foundation of a barn may now be seen.

I stated in my last article that the Small dwelling house was moved to the opposite side of the highway to make room for the present so-called Quinby house, and became the residence of Daniel Maxfield and wife Lydia (Bailey) Maxfield. It was a well built house and in the year 1764 or 5, tradition says, it was constructed.

It had a room on the left hand on entering the front door, that served for a parlor; on the right, a room of equal size for a living room and then two bed rooms next—or in the end—and one story high, in other words—a parlor in one end, two bed rooms in the other end, chimney, entry and living room in the middle, and all in a row, the chimney and entry being between the parlor and living room, windows small and high up from the floor, two each side the front door, so the parlor contained two in front, the living room one, the corner bed room one. The ends contained two windows below and one in the gable, making three in each end.

I will now continue the record of Josiah Maxfield commenced in my last article, who was the second child of Daniel Maxfield and wife, Lydia (Bailey) Maxfield.

Josiah Maxfield was born at Stroudwater in the Small house Mar. 20, 1790, m. Mar. 20, 1828, Marcia Stevens, daughter of Nathaniel Stevens, born March 18, 1807, on Stevens' Plains. (See News of March 23.) He died at Lewiston, March 9, 1878, and was buried there, to which place he moved from Stroudwater after all his children had been born. His widow died at Lynn, Mass., Nov. 17, '94 where she resided with her daughter, Mrs. Randall Johnson. (See News Dec. 8, '94 for obituary.)

He commenced married life in the Small house, when it stood opposite the Quinby house, but removed it to its present site where it may now be seen, unchanged in outward appearances. Its present occupant has been noticed in a previous article.

CHILDREN OF JOSIAH MAXFIELD.

1 Daniel V., born Feb. 14, 1830, married Lizzie Gammon of Oxford, Sept. 4, 1854. He died at Lewiston Feb. 27, 1862. The widow resides in Massachusetts.
2 George Webster, born Dec. 23, 1831, married Rose E. Hearn, of Clinton, Jan. 1860. He resides in Canaan.
3 Caroline C., born Nov. 1, 1833, died Jan. 10, 1861, unm.
4 Mary Francis, born May 20, 1836, married June 7, 1858 Randall Johnson, son of Isaac Johnson, who resided about a mile westerly of Stroudwater on one of the finest farms in the town. Randall died at Lynn, Mass., Nov. 14, 1889. Isaac, father to Randall, died Jan. 13, 1875, aged 73 years 6 mo. Abigail, his wife died March 15, 1852, aged 42 years. She was Abigail Frost of Gorham. After her death Isaac married his wife's sister, the widow Leavitt of Saccarappa, who now resides there on Brown street. Isaac was the son of Randall Johnson who died May 26, 1848, aged 81 years. Miriam, his widow, died April 7, 1853, aged 80 years. This line of Johnsons are descended from John Johnson, who at the time of the purchase of the wild land where Randall and Isaac resided, which was Oct. 2, 1747, was a "farmer of Scarborough."
5 Ellen R., born May 13, 1838, died Oct. 21, 1861.
6 Andrew J., born Oct. 28, 1840, married June 8, 1864 Angie Poland of Lewiston, She died June 1865. He married 2nd, June 1870, Rose Burnham of Lewiston; she died Dec. 1886. He resides in Appleton, Wis.
7 Wallace, born May 4, 1843, married Frank J. Nay Feb. 2, 1864 of Skowhegan. She died June 1870; he married 2nd Nellie Judkins of Lewiston Sept. 20, 1871. He resides at Lewiston.
8 Elizabeth Stevens, born Jan. 17, 1847, married Frank Adams of Auburn, 1865; she died Dec. 30, 1868.
9 Henrietta M., born June 8, 1849, married Russell Taylor of Lewiston, Oct. 1869.
10 Josiah B., born March 2, 1855, died June 23, 1861.

NOTE. The name John *Newcome* where it appears in the first paragraph of my last article should read John *Newman*.

THE WEBB FAMILY.

I am in receipt of the following communication and lay it before the readers of the News in this connection with feelings of gratitude to the writer:

TO THE EDITOR OF THE NEWS:—In the "Scrap Book" article of your issue of March 30, allusion is made to Wm. Maxfield and his wives Susanna Webb and Mary Wescott.

It would seem from a passage in the centennial history of Windham by the late Thomas L. Smith, that Maxfield was among the early residents of that town, where on the 27th day of August, 1747, he barely escaped capture by the Indians. He was then a young man living with Wm. Mayberry, and with Wm. Bolton who was taken, was attacked in the road about twenty rods above the present dwelling house of Charles Hunnewell and a few rods below the blockhouse which stood on the present Anderson hill. Both men "were well armed with muskets. * * * Maxfield retreated, walking backward in the direction of the fort (blockhouse), keeping the Indians at a respectful distance by occasionally presenting his musket. * * * In this manner he made good his retreat till a body of armed men came from the fort to his relief."

According to data which I collected some years since, Maxfield married Susanna Webb in 1763. She was the daughter of Samuel and Bethiah (Farrar) Webb, and the sister of Eli Webb who once lived on the farm since known as the Rea farm near Mallison Falls in Windham. This Eli Webb was the grandfather of Eli of Portland, who was the father of Judge Nathan Webb. Hon. Edmund N. Morrill, the present governor of Kansas is of the same family, his mother being a sister of Eli Webb of Portland.

The old Patriarch Samuel Webb (who was born at a place called Redriff near London) accompanied, later in life, his son Seth to Deer Isle in this state where he died in 1785 in the 90th year of his age. Capt. Seth Webb of Deer Isle who recently represented his town in the state legislature is one of his descendants through his son Seth.

The Webb families of Windham, are I believe with one or two exceptions, descended from Samuel, the Englishman, who by the way, taught the first school in that town. Among the other families is that of ex-Mayor Mahlon H. Webb of Westbrook, whose great-grandfather John Webb (who married Susannah Swett) was a brother I am told of James Webb who lived near the beginning of the century at Stroudwater.

Susannah Webb, the first wife of Wm. Maxfield, according to my notes died some time before 1763 leaving a son and daughter.

His second wife, Mary Wescott, whom he married in March 1763, was a sister of the wife of James Babb, who was the grandmother of the present James Babb, Esq., of Westbrook. After Maxfield's death, his widow married a Mr. Cook of Otisfield or vicinity. Mrs. Mark Haskell was one of Maxfield's children. Your correspondent is in error in supposing that the original Haskells lived between Saccarappa and Cumberland Mills. The "Haskell place" so called, nearest the last named village was purchased by the late Nathaniel Haskell (a son of Solomon Haskell, Jr.) from Wm. Valentine, father of Hon. Leander Valentine some time in the first half of the present century. The first Haskells in what is now Westbrook lived on the north side of the river at Saccarappa. Later Solomon and Benjamin, sons of the first Thomas Haskell, purchased from the Waldo heirs the "Tyng hundred acres," beginning at or near the present Ridge at Saccarappa. Subsequently Benjamin conveyed his interest to his brother Solomon who left the tract to his sons Solomon, Jr., and Mark. Benjamin Haskell above mentioned, lies buried on Scotch hill with other members of his family on land now owned by the Westbrook Manufacturing company, while Solomon and his sons, Solomon, Jr., and Mark, and others of his descendants are buried in the so called Saccarappa cemetery on the "Tyng hundred acres."
R.

THE GRANT FAMILY.

WILLIAMSPORT, PA., Mar. 27, 1895.

EDITOR DEERING NEWS:—Being a member of the Stevens family, whose genealogy you have been publishing for a number of weeks, and in which said genealogy I am, of course, interested, and to the extent that it may be as nearly correct as practicable, I beg to inform you that in your issue of the 24th inst., which I have not had the pleasure of reading yet but which is on file for me at my home in Deering, I am advised that you are in error with reference to my immediate family, in this, that you say with reference to "Albion K. Grant" that "he married and lived and died in Connecticut" and "left no issue." Here are the facts: Albion K. P. Grant married Isabella W. Small, daughter of Col. Geo. and Dolly Small of the village of Saccarappa, went to Meriden, Conn., in 1871 and died there in 1883. His wife died in Meriden, July 5, 1894. Their children are Emma F., who died in Westbrook in 1864; Geo F., married Hattie F. Allen and resides in Deering; and Mabel C., married A. A. Twichell and resides in New Haven, Conn.

Yours, etc.,
GEO. F. GRANT.

NOTE. I obtained the information relative to the Grant family from a member thereof and supposed it to be correct. This statement applies also to what I said relative to the location of the residence of Solomon Haskell which statement "R." corrects as appears by his communication.

THE DEERING NEWS.

Saturday, April 20, 1895.

GRANDPA'S SCRAP BOOK

[Under this head historical and genealogical memoranda will be furnished the readers of the News that appears worthy of preservation, particularly of remote periods in our history within the city limits and immediate vicinity.]

[Easter Argus, Oct. 7, 1813.]
DESTRUCTIVE FIRE.

Wednesday, the 24th of September, at Saccarappa, were destroyed by fire, the paper mill, with its whole apparatus, about twenty tons of rags (excepting four or five tons partly consumed, preserved after the fire subsided) and about twenty reams of writing paper; three saw mills; the clothier's dye house; and a large building containing a grist mill, and fulling mill, and two machines for carding wool.

The cloth, most of the wool, and the carding machinery were fortunately saved.

The fire originated in the paper mill, and was first discovered between one and two o'clock in the afternoon. All persons had left it as early as nine or ten in the forenoon.

In 10 or 12 minutes after the fire was first discovered this group of buildings were all in flames. Many other buildings, sawmills, houses and barns, from four or five to fifteen or twenty rods distant, and in one or two instances at a much greater distance, took fire from the light coals carried by the wind, which by extraordinary exertion were extinguished.

Much praise is due to all present for their activity, and especially to the females who rendered very essential service, and without whose aid the fire would probably have spread much further as many men of the place and vicinity were absent at the muster at Gorham.

The paper mill belonged to Messrs. Partridge & Tower, one sawmill to Samuel A. Proctor, one to Joshua Webb, and one to Joseph Partridge, Nathan and Moses Quinby, and the heirs of G. W. Quinby; the gristmill to Nathan and Moses Quinby; the carding machine to Moses Longfellow, and the fulling mill and dye house to Benjamin B. Foster. The loss cannot be estimated at less than 10 to 20 thousand dollars.

THE DEERING NEWS.

Saturday, April 27, 1895.

GRANDPA'S SCRAP BOOK

[Under this head historical and genealogical memoranda will be furnished the readers of the News that appears worthy of preservation, particularly of remote periods in our history within the city limits and immediate vicinity.]

In the quotation from the Portland Argus of Oct. 7, 1813 that appeared under this head last week the name of Quinby occurs.

Benjamin Quinby, the first on record at Saccarappa, was there in 1770. He came from Somersworth, N. H. He married, May 6, 1779, Eleanor Starbird. It was his widow, Mrs. Eunice (Starbird) Haskell, who on the fifth day of Nov. 1807, at the age of 73 years united in marriage with Solomon Haskell, senior, who was 84 years old at that time, she being his second wife, to which allusion was made in the News of March 30 of this year. I allude to the matter here to show who Eleanor was before marriage.

It is difficult to find the children of Benjamin Quinby.

In the year 1775 he sold a share of his mill to Joseph Quinby of Portland—the relationship I have no means of knowing.

In 1798, Benjamin Quinby conveyed to his daughter-in-law Sally Quinby, "wife of my late son Simeon Quinby, de'd" and his children, Nancy, Charles and Charlotte, one-fourth part of mill called Quinby mill, consideration $30.

In 1799 Benjamin Quinby, Jr., of Somersworth, N. H., clothier, agreed to maintain "Benjamin Quinby and wife Eleanor."

In 1799 Sarah Quinby is alluded to as the widow of Simeon Quinby, and the daughter of Capt. John Brackett of Saccarappa who I wrote up in the Argus of Apr. 23, 1889, and the article was copied into the Westbrook Chronicle of that period. (Be careful for there were two Capt. John Bracketts; the second born where Nathan Tibbett's house stands at Bradley's Corner. He was a Revolutionary soldier but made captain after, while the first died in service.)

May 2, 1778 there was a Nathan Quinby of Falmouth who married Resinah Partridge. In 1791 he bought the Bailey farm on the northeasterly side of the Presumpscot opposite Saccarappa, which he sold to Timothy Pike. In 1805 he speaks of my son Abel Quinby, and in 1817 he sells to Hiram Quinby "my house and barn" which seems to have been located back of where the Universalist chapel stood on northerly side of Main street in the village.

In 1797, Joseph Quinby and Azabah Partridge, Nathan Quinby and Rosinah Partridge Benjamin Quinby and Eleanor Starbird, Benjamin Quinby, Jr., and Jacob Quinby, appear on record and this Joseph was, as I understand the matter, the grandfather of Capt. Isaac F. Quinby of Saccarappa.

Nathan and Joseph Quinby it seems married sisters, whose brother was Capt. Jesse Partridge and who died at Stroudwater.

A Jacob Quinby died here Nov. 27, 1805 aged 62 years which shows he was born in 1743. He probably was the ancestor of Joseph, Nathan and Benjamin as above.

In 1814 the assessor's books show as follows:

1—Benjamin Quinby, one house, $175; barn, $35; shop, $40; two acres mowing land; two acres pasturing; two cows; one horse; swine; stock in trade $100.
2—Charles Quinby, blacksmith shop, $100; and nine acres of land.
3—Simeon, part of a house, $95.
4—Nathan, house, $20; barn, $25.
5—Hiram, poll tax.
6—Franklin, two cows; swine; ¼ of Quinby sawmill.
7—Samuel, poll tax.
8—Moses, house, $250; barn, $35; 20 acres mowing land; 25 acres pasturing, 2 oxen; 3 cows; 1 horse; 2 swine.
9—Sally (widow), house and lot $250; barn $20; store $40; 7 acres land; 1 cow; 1 swine.
10—Jacob, Jr., poll tax.

MARRIAGES.

Nov. 17, 1799, Sally Quinby–Thomas Mayberry.
July 21, 1800, Eunice Quinby–Caleb Bartlett.
Oct. 13, 1808, Lydia Quinby–Joseph Partridge.

CHILDREN.

1 Nancy Partridge born at Saccarappa, June 3, 1809.
2 Joseph Partridge, Nov. 13, 1811.
3 Benjamin Q. Partridge, June 11, 1813.
4 Geo. W. Partridge, May 30, 1815.
George Washington Quinby, married ——.

In the old worse than neglected burying ground above Saccarappa is a stone that reads Geo. W. Quinby, died 1813, aged 32.
Their daughter Nancy born Oct. 25, 1807.
Benjamin Quinby married ——.

1 Mary Quinby born Oct. 11, 1808.
2 Geo. Quinby born Dec. 20, 1810.
3 Sophronia born Feb. 13, 1813.
4 Lucretia born Dec 10, 1814.

Dec. 1, 1808, Martha Quinby–Isaac Cox
Levi Quinby–Hannah ——.

1 Frederick Quinby born Feb. 25, 1810
2 Nathan Quinby born Nov. 26, 1812.

Feb. 17, 1811, Nancy Quinby–Charles Alden of Limerick.
Feb. 11, 1813, Joseph Quinby–Elizabeth Bailey. (For further particulars see News, Jan 12, '95.) Capt. Isaac Fly Quinby comes in here.

CONTINUED:

Abigail Quinby-Wm. Slemmons Jr., he of Buxton road a mile and a half westerly of Stroudwater, son of Robert Slemmons of Stroudwater, married Oct. 10, 1784, Sally Rounds. He died Apr. 1823 aged 76; she Jan. 15, 1845, aged 8 years. The grandfather of William lived on the farm now owned by Mr. F. A. Johnson on the westerly side of Stroudwater village, whose name was William.

CHILDREN OF WILLIAM AND ABIGAIL.
1 John, born Aug. 8, 1815; a doctor who died in the State of Indiana.
2 George, born Aug. 29, 1817, alive and well.
3 Harriet, born Dec. 29, 1819.
4 Catharine, born July 1, 1823.
5 Oliver, born Nov. 20, 1825, died Jan. 22, 1850. Grave at Stroudwater.
6 Sarah, born Apr. 1, 1828.
7 Abbie, born June 25, 1830. See "Poets of Maine," p. 435.

After all the children were born Col. Slemmons, the father, moved with his family to Corydon, Ind.

Apr. 4, 1814, Tamson Quinby-Peter Libby.
Jan. 6, 1817, Chas. Quinby-Mary Roberts.
Mar. 17, 1817, Mary Quinby-Levi Tole.
Mar. 6, 1821, Moses Quinby-Betsey Walker.
Dec. 27, 1821, Hiram Quinby-Sally Jameson.
Dec. 10, 1822, Elizabeth Quinby-James Proctor.
Nov. 30, 1823, Rhoda Quinby-John Babb, Jr.

In this list none of the descendants of Joseph Quinby of Portland appear.

THE DEERING NEWS.

Saturday, May 4, 1895.

GRANDPA'S SCRAP BOOK

[Under this head historical and genealogical memoranda will be furnished the readers of the News that appears worthy of preservation, particularly of remote periods in our history within the city limits and immediate vicinity.]

Note.—Where the name Mrs. Eunice (Starbird) Haskell appears in the second paragraph of my article last week, under this head, it should read, Mrs. Eleanor (Starbird) Quinby.

1806, Moses Quinby and Abigail his wife, at Saccarappa, conveyed for a consideration of $1100 to Benjamin B. Foster of Cambridge, Mass., the Quinby mill privilege and "old dwelling house adjoining."

1815 Foster was taxed as follows: House, $200; barn, $40; fulling mill, shop and dye house—;two acres mowing land at $21 per acre; four acres pasturing at $10; one cow, $14; one swine, $5; one horse, $40; one chaise $80; Benjamin B. Foster, two machines, $200.

From Benjamin B. are descended the Preble street, Portland, Dye house Fosters as well as the wife of Daniel Dole, Sen., of Stroudwater, who celebrated the 50th anniversary of their wedding a year or two since.

The following names are copied from the journal of Rev. Caleb Bradley.

DEATHS.

1805, Mrs Quinby.
Nov. 27, 1805, Jacob Quinby, aged 62 years. (This death was noticed in my last article.)
Feb. 26, 1807, Mrs. Quinby aged 92 years.
Aug. 14, 1813, Geo. W. Quinby aged 32. (Copied from gravestone by myself and noticed in my last article.)
Sept. 12, 1817, Thankful Quinby.
Apr. 1813, the wife of Moses Quinby.
Oct. 28, 1821, the widow of Benjamin Quinby, aged 34.
Aug, 1822, Mary Quinby, aged 15.
Aug 1822, Dea. Haskell's widow, aged 90. (Before noticed.)
May 13, 1825, wife of Abel Quinby.

I have here presented dates and names in full as they appear in the journal and all the journal contains relative to the name.

Henry C. Quinby, a student of Harvard College—11 Gray's Hill, Cambridge, Mass., a great-grandson of Moses Quinby, Esq., dec'd., of Stroudwater, is at work on a history of the Quinby name.

The First Congregational church record of 1833 contains the following four names:
1 Betsey Quinby, deceased.
2 Simeon Quinby.
3 Sarah Quinby.
4 Charlotte Quinby, dismissed to another church.

Apr. 3, 1827, ninety-six persons bought of Nathaniel and Sarah Haskell the lot where the village cemetery is located at Saccarappa, and on the list appear the names of
1 Simeon Quinby.
2 Moses Quinby.
3 Moses Quinby, 3d.
4 Charles Quinby.

The entire list will be given to the public very shortly.

On the original manuscript list of voters of Westbrook, dated Feb. 18, 1827, appear the names of
1 Benjamin Quinby.
2 Moses Quinby.
3 Hiram Quinby.
4 Charles Quinby.
5 Abel Quinby.
6 Abel Quinby, Jr.
7 Moses Quinby, Esq. (Stroudwater.)
8 Moses Quinby, 3d.
9 Simeon Quinby.
10 Joseph Quinby.

William Slemons, Jr.,) Selectmen
Zachariah B. Stevens, } of
Benjamin Quinby,) Westbrook.

It will be noticed that William S., Jr., spells his name with one m.

In 1735 Robert Slemons paid a tax on real estate of five shillings; on personal property, one shilling and six pence. His dwelling stood in from the present road to Buxton from Stroudwater, on the ridge where the elm tree stands, on the dividing line between the Dr. Hunt lot and the Henry Chapman "Goose Island" lot, between Stroudwater river and the Chapman residence,—then there was no Buxton road. His son William built the house now occupied by Mr. F. A. Johnson, about ¼ of a mile westerly of the original Slemmons house which was built by Gowen Wilson who sold to Josiah Plumer, who sold to Slemons in 1742. Robert's son William, a copy of whose will is now before me, made Dec. 13, 1784, married, Falmouth, Sept. 16, 1744, Catheren Poterfield; his son, William, Jr., and brother to Robert the grandfather of Geo. Slemmons, Esq., who lives on the Buxton road in Westbrook, noticed in my article of last week as son of Colonel William, married Jan. 15, 1781, Polly, daughter of Joseph Quinby, who lived in Portland till the bombardment of the neck in 1775, and built three or four years later the house now owned and occupied by Joseph C. Parker, opposite the Stevens mill.

When Hon Leander Valentine was a boy, (he is now living at Saccrappa) there was not a house from Bridge street westerly on the northerly side of Main street. On a lane running northerly, starting a little easterly of what is now Saco street he places four houses on the westerly side thereof.
1 Thomas Akers, nearest Main street.
2 Nathan Quinby.
3 Abel Quinby.
4 Geo. Babb.

He places Moses Quinby on the westerly side of the Saco road, some little distance from the village. On Bridge street, over the river, next beyond a three story brick house built by Joshua Webb, he places the residence of Simeon Quinby.

On the northerly side of Island he places the Quinby mill and it was on this Island the fire occurred in 1813, of which an account was re-produced by the News two weeks since.

Robert Slemmons, the grandfather of the present George, lived on the ridge southerly from the residence of George.

He took the land in its wild state and cleared the farm. The road passed that way then, which was changed some over fifty years ago to its present location. George occupies a part of the homestead.

This is all I have to say relative to the Saccarappa Quinby name.

THE DEERING NEWS.

Saturday, May 11, 1895.

GRANDPA'S SCRAP BOOK

[Under this head historical and genealogical memoranda will be furnished the readers of the News that appears worthy of preservation, particularly of remote periods in our history within the city limits and immediate vicinity.]

THE MAXFIELD FAMILY OF STROUDWATER, ETC.

[A continuation of the record that appeared in the News of April 13.]

Daniel Maxfield, third child of Daniel and Lydia (Bailey) Maxfield, born at Stroudwater, married, resided and died a successful contractor and builder at Bangor. A son of his, named Daniel W. Maxfield, a dentist of that city, is collecting material, I am told, for a family genealogy.

Charles, the fourth child, born Feb. 23, 1808 learned the trades of shoemaking and brick laying. He has always lived in Stroudwater on the southerly side of the Buxton and Saco road from the village, about ten rods westerly of the Chapman residence. His dwelling originally stood (that is before he purchased it) on the easterly side of Stevens Plains and shop on State street, Portland. He united in marriage May 27, 1827, with Julia Ann Mitchell, daughter of Peleg Mitchell. Mr. Mitchell came here from Massachusetts, and he with Jonas Hamilton, and Joseph Chenery of Watertown, Mass., June 6, 1798, purchased at what is now known as Bradley's, the northwesterly corner lot on which there was a tanyard and pottery. What is now known as the Bradley parsonage had just been built and dedicated as a public house. On the opposite side of what is now Congress street lived one Harry Miles a "gentleman of color." Mr. Mitchell purchased the lot on which Miles lived, in 1804, of the First Parish of Portland and the house was removed. Hamilton sold to Chenery and Mitchell. A man by the name of Silas Hamilton was a trader in a small building that stood northerly of the present residence of Mr. Augustus Tate at Stroudwater, where he died, June 2, 1821 aged 47 years, suddenly. He was taxed in 1815 as follows: ½ store, $80. Add part of the Chesley house, $130; (which had reference to the first house now standing after crossing the iron bridge at Stroudwater, upon which Hamilton held a mortgage;) stock in trade, $200.

In 1807 Mr. Mitchell purchased thirty acres of land back of the so called Bradley meeting house and extending by the highway nearly to Capisic pond, and built the dwelling house now standing next westerly of the meeting house, which is one story but large on the ground, and in good repair for a building of its age, and long occupied by the late Moses G. Dow, Esq., whose widow still retains the premises. Mr. Mitchell lived first on the corner in the house here Mrs. Knights resides, opposite the Bradley parsonage, though the house has been much changed since.

In 1812 Mitchell & Chenery divided their partnership interest in the tannery establishment. This Joseph Chenery was a grandfather to Daniel D. Chenery, the present county treasurer, and father to Edward Chenery who married for a second wife a daughter of Peleg Mitchell. The last two died in Portland quite recently.

Joseph Chenery was drowned at Stroudwater Dec. 4, 1817, walking off the wharf next easterly the tide mill when it was intensely dark.

In the year 1787 Joseph Riggs speaks of and gave up to Sarah Waldo on a foreclosed mortgage as follows:

My house, and other houses, shops, barn, and buildings, except a small new house on the corner, which my son Enoch has built, and he is to have liberty to move by or before the first of March, 1789.

It is a family tradition that Peleg Mitchell built the original house, now the Knights house, but it seems Enoch Riggs had one built there as above indicated, which I believe was never moved.

The history of this locality is interesting and entitled to an extended notice.

The inscriptions of two grave stones at Stroudwater read as follows:
Peleg Mitchell, died Apr. 2, 1859, aged 83 years.
Ann, wife of Peleg Mitchell, died Apr. 30, 1840, aged 65 years.
Other stones in the immediate vicinity are inscribed:
Julia Ann, wife of Charles Maxfield, born Aug. 13, 1808, died Oct. 12, 1874.
Charles Maxfield, died Sep. 7, 1857, aged 19 years 2 months.
Lansia (an infant).
Adelaide B. Maxfield, died Oct. 2, 1862, aged 18 years, 2 months.
Louisa S. Maxfield, born Sept. 19, 1848, died Jan. 16, 1892.

These were all children of our aged and respected citizen, Mr. Chas. Maxfield, and with the five children living comprises his family.

Mary Jane, the fifth child of Daniel and Lydia (Bailey) Maxfield, born Aug. 13, 1808, married, Feb. 28, 1828, Francis J. Cummings, son of 'Squire Cummings who resided in the northerly part of Cape Elizabeth where the widow of the late Henry S. Jackson now resides, whose husband purchased the Cummings farm of Francis J. Cummings.

Francis J. spent most of his married life in Bangor, returning and residing a few years on the homestead of his father and then removing to Bangor where he and his wife died.

A Cummings family monument at Stroudwater is inscribed as follows:
George Andrew, died May 14, 1830, aged 1 month, 14 days.
Frances Caroline, died June 19, 1833, aged 4 years, 6 months.
Andrew Jackson, died July 30, 1832, aged 2 years, 2 months.
Frances Caroline, died Jan. 2, 1836, aged 10 months.
Charles Maxfield, died Apr. 28, 1836, aged 2 years, 9 months.
Charles Winslow, died Apr. 25, 1841, aged 8 months.
Martha Ella, died July 6, 1846, aged 5 months.
Mary Eliza Shaw, died Jan. 5, 1848, aged 5 years, 3 months.
Malatta Frances, died Jan 25, 1854, aged 15 years, 4 months.
Children of Francis J. and Mary Jane Cummings.
"Sleep on, sweet babes, and take your rest, God called you home when He thought best."

The father and mother were interred on the same lot, but there is nothing visible to indicate the fact. In addition to the above named children there was one more, named Susan Maria, who married a man by the name of Skillings.

Of the number and time of births of the children of Peleg Mitchell other than here presented I have no reliable data.

In my article of March 30 I stated that William Maxfield of Windham had by his last wife six children; the fourth of whom was named

Josiah, married here, (then Falmouth) Feb. 21, 1802, Nancy Partridge of Saccarappa. In 1803 he was living here; in 1809 in Raymond. He left a large family and I am told that Mr. A. D. Maxfield, who resides near the corner of Spring and High streets is grandson.

August 12, 1804, Daniel Dole of Stroudwater and Catharine Partridge were united in marriage—she was a sister to the wife of Josiah Maxfield.

Dec. 26, 1816, Solomon Haskell, Jr., died aged 64 years.

May 17, 1804, Sarah, his wife, aged 40 years. (Gravestone record.)

Nov. 6, 1806, Solomon Haskell and Polly Partridge were married. She, I understand, was a widow whose maiden name was Bailey, sister to the wife of Capt. Jesse Partridge, and to the mother of Charles Maxfield, born in the old John Newman house on Spring street.

5 Mary Maxfield, married Aug. 19, 1790, Nathan Cook of Casco.

6 and last. Eliakim Maxfield, married July 23, 1797, Rebecca Mann of Falmouth. Their son William, who, I think, was the eldest child, married Jan. 6, 1828, Mary Waterhouse of Portland and in consideration of a gift of the homestead located in Casco or Raymond, or vicinity, he, on the 30th day of October, 1828, agreed to maintain his parents and minor children and send them to school. They were as follows: 1, George; 2, James; 3, Rebecca; 4, Eliza Ann; 5, Almira; to which list must be added, William, the eldest, Mary, Eliakim, and one died young

THE DEERING NEWS.

Saturday, May 18, 1895.

GRANDPA'S SCRAP BOOK

[Under this head historical and genealogical memoranda will be furnished the readers of the News that appears worthy of preservation, particularly of remote periods in our history within the city limits and immediate vicinity.]

August 18, of last year, under this heading, Chauncy Woodford's name was alluded to, which allusion closed with these words: Notice of him hereafter. His name appears here on record Nov. 23, 1799, when he married Lucy, 6th child of Capt. Isaac Sawyer Stevens, of Stevens' Plains. (For her family connections see News of Nov. 17.) He was a brother to Isaiah and Deacon Ebenezer D. Woodford, who lived at the hamlet of Woodfords, whose names appear in the same article to which reference is here made, though the name of Isaiah appears as Josiah which error was corrected in the next issue of the News. He was a brother to Martha Woodford also, born August 21, 1783, and married March 2, 1805, Elijah North. Chauncy was born March 1, 1774. For his place of birth and descendant of his two brothers who settled at Woodfords see back numbers of the News.

In the so-called Bailey cemetery located on the westerly side of the Windham road may be seen three Woodford grave stones—no more—and two are inscribed as follows:

CHAUNCY WOODFORD
died Apr. 24, 1841,
Æt. 68 years.

LUCY,
wife of
Chauncy Woodford,
died June 27, 1854,
aged 73 years.

"Rest weary Soul,
Thy good works follow thee."

In the year 1800 he purchased the lot upon which he settled; located on the westerly side of the very commencement of Windham road, at what is now called Morrill's Corner, and built as is supposed what is known at this time as the Purrington house, owned and occupied today by Adam W. Wilson and sister. In 1815 Chauncy was taxed as follows: One house $70; one shop $25; four acres mowing and tillage land at $18; twenty-eight pasturing at $7. From the fact that he was taxed only $70 for a house I think the present building must have been added to considerable since.

In the shop here noted and other small ones to which he added a building for horse power he manufactured large quantities of combs, and had peddle carts running in all directions, which brought back wool, yarn, dried apples, etc., as well as cash.

His name appears upon the old Congregational church record, but not that of his wife prior to 1833.

Perhaps I had better here give all the names of Woodford appearing at that date besides Chauncy: Margaret, Thomas Edward, Eben'r D. (the deacon); Mary, Margaret (again); Jane; Orin F.; Eliza; Addison (deacon), who was not I am told a descendant of either of the three brothers, but son of another brother who did not come here.

The children of Chauncy were named: 1, Hellena; 2, Joseph; 3, Isaac; 4, Infant, died Nov. 1814 aged 1 yr. 3 mo.; 5, Silas; and 6, Isaiah.

In the employ of Chauncy was one Philo Hall, born in the town of Willingford, Ct., May 13, 1799. He acted the part of a peddler along the coast of our state, using as a vehicle a boat or sloop.

June 16, 1801, Hellena, the eldest child of Chauncy was born, and July 3, 1828, she and Philo Hall were united in marriage.

In 1829 Mr. Hall, "manufacturer of brittania ware," for a consideration of $85, purchased of George Bishop, Esq., 19 square rods of land at Morrill's Corner * * * "the said Hall to build a brick house 39 x 36 upon the ground floor within three feet of the first side course of the bounds of the lot, on front on a line of the other buildings, namely, H. Blake and J. Alden."

The house he built stands today, three story high, with an addition in the rear, in the corner of which main house is a shop at this time and over the door of which is the sign of "LEVI CRAM." When first built it must have been quite imposing—even now it is attractive in its attire of light colored paint though built of brick.

Philo being possessed of musical talent which he indulged, being able to play several instruments, he had constructed in his house now noticed a hall where he kept dancing schools—in fact he was an inn keeper and his abode became one of gayety. And within a couple of hours I have heard that John T. Winslow, Esq., was a pupil of his, who I hope will tell the public something about the matter.

CHILDREN OF PHILO HALL.

1 Henry Clay Hall, born Dec. 17, 1828—died young.
2 George F., born July 21, 1830, married a daughter of Hiram Sawyer who was noticed in the News of Dec. 22 of last year under this heading. He has resided some twenty years where his father was born in Connecticut, in the state of Michigan, and now with his wife occupies the homestead of his wife's father on the Windham road.
3 Mary Jane, died in the state of Connecticut, at the age of 20 years, married.
4 Frances Ellen, married in Connecticut a man by the name of Rice of New York state in which state they resided.

Two other children of Mr. Hall died young.

In the old Windham road cemetery stands a lone stone inscribed as follows:

HELLENA,
wife of
Philo Hall,
died July 21, 1839,
aged 37 years.

Oct. 4, 1842 Philo Hall married, second, Mary Ann Field, the public record says, "of Boston," but she was of Yarmouth or Freeport, and one child was born to them who was named Silas L. Hall. He married and resided in Willingford, Ct., to which place his parents removed and died, the father in August of 1864.

2 Joseph Woodford, born May 14, 1804, married April 2, 1825, Eliza Knight, born April 9, 1804, daughter of Nathaniel, a ship carpenter and farmer, who married Betsey Thompson of Buxton. He resided on the road from Morrill's Corner to Presumpscot river, where Peter Gammon now resides. She died May 1, 1835, aged 63 years; he died Jan. 5, 1868, aged 95 yrs. 6 mo. 24 days. There were ten children in this Knight family as follows:
1, Fannie; 2, Theodore; 3, Lavina; 4, Isaac; 5, Eliza, (married Joseph Woodford); 6, Charles; 7, Mary; 8, Maria; 9, Sarah; 10, Nathaniel, a farmer, residing in Denmark, this state.

Joseph Woodford resided on the homestead at Morrill's Corner till the collapse of comb making when he removed to the town of Leeds and engaged in farming where he remained 14 years when he died, July 28, 1878. Interred in Pine Grove cemetery this city. His widow resides with her son Charles F., on the outskirt of Saccarappa village towards Stroudwater, who is engaged with the Portland & Rochester railroad company at Portland.

CHILDREN.

1 Adeline B. Woodford, born Aug. 29, 1826, married April 15, 1848, Edwin M. Buckley of Stevens' Plains. (The Buckley record to appear later.)
2 Helen F., born June 13, 1828, married Lucius Prince, 2nd Robert Hall. She died in Chicago June 19, 1890.
3 Charles F., born Feb. 28, 1832, married Oct. 21, 1880 Marshall Knight of Pleasant Hill, Falmouth, who resided in the family of Dr. Parker, Morrill's Corner, several years.
4 Lorenzo, born Nov. 30, 1832, died Feb. 10, 1830.
5 Ella E., born Feb. 1842, married Pitt Stevens, son of Alfred and grandson of Zachariah B. Stevens, all of Stevens' Plains.
6 and youngest, Clara, born March 4, 1848, married Loretto Hartland Foss, engineer, residing 41 Ellsworth street, Portland.

CONTINUED:

3 Isaac Woodford, born March 23, 1807, married Jane Hanson, and had one son who went to Aroostook county. Isaac resided after marriage as before under the parental roof. The third Woodford stone in the Bailey cemetery is inscribed as follows:

ISAAC WOODFORD
died March 22, 1837,
aged 30 years.

His gentle virtues blossomed like a rose,
Promised much benefit to man but soon,
Ah sudden gained a passport to the skies.

4 Infant, died young, (noticed before.)
5 Silas Woodford, born Jan. 14, 1814, died at home Dec. 13, 1839, unmarried.
6 and youngest, Josiah Woodford, born July 15, 1819, died unmarried on the home place March 11, 1858, but I do not find a grave stone.

He invented a folding pocket comb, made of horn, and in two parts, fine teeth on one side and coarse on the other which met with public favor.

The widow of Joseph Woodford as appears from the records here presented is 91 years of age, and remarkably smart for one of her years, whose personal appearance must in youth have been unusually prepossessing, and with the needle has ever been an expert, particularly in the winter of life, which has ever been full of sunshine. Three years ago she visited her daughter, Mrs. Buckley, and in the course of the six weeks she was with her, made a quilt complete, including quilting and binding the outside of which contains 2368 pieces.

THE DEERING NEWS.

Saturday, May 25, 1895.

GRANDPA'S SCRAP BOOK

[Under this head historical and genealogical memoranda will be furnished the readers of the News that appears worthy of preservation, particularly of remote periods in our history within the city limits and immediate vicinity.]

When the matter of annexation was before the public a few years since, one of the points of argument in favor of the project was that James Parker's shop at Woodfords had been broken into and annexation would stop such business, because Portland would station a policeman at that place.

Should the News present at this time a list of the thefts in Portland for a period of twelve months the people of Deering would be surprised.

In one day thirteen persons were detected and arrested in the act of stealing in one shop in New York city a short time since.

Annexation of Deering to Portland where the ratio of the crime is largely in favor of Portland would not make less the temptation to do evil in this city.

"The poor ye have always," so, too, we shall always have among us thieves whatever the government may be in style or name.

In the Portland Argus of August 4, 1847, we find the following:

We learn from the Advertiser that, last week the store of Martin Hawes at Stroudwater, was entered, his change and a piece of cotton drilling stolen. Last Wednesday night, the store of Dexter Brewer was broken open and quite a lot of merchandise taken, among which were one piece of satinett, one do. white drilling, pins, needles, inch augers, bundles of knives and forks, plated spoons, tea, raisins, medicine, and what little change there was in the till.

The next night the store of John Haskell was attempted to be opened, but the thief did not succeed.

A liberal reward will be paid for conviction of the thief or thieves."

An examination of the clerk's records of Westbrook of that period does not show that a town meeting was called to see if the inhabitants would vote to be annexed to some other town, or employ a police force. People of that time were philosophical in their acts and in most respects, considering their surroundings and opportunities, head and shoulders above the people of today.

In 1847 there were four shops at Stroudwater. Martin Hawes, a very estimable man of few words outside his immediate friends, occupied the easterly half of the building now owned and occupied by his son as a warehouse. It was built, tradition says, by Jonathan Sparrow, father to William, now of Pleasant street, this city, and Hon. Archelaus Lewis about the year of 1807, two very active men at that time, both of whose names demand a larger space in history than they fill, but justice shall be done both if the writer lives long enough.

Capt. Dexter Brewer was proprietor of the Brewer House burned a few years since, that occupied a commanding site on the bank of Fore river opposite the village of Stroudwater. His shop in which he did but little business, and which was occupied but a short time, stood where the guide-board may now be seen on the northerly side of Frost where it joins Congress street. The building was two story, and arranged for a dwelling in the second story. Originally it stood just southerly of the hydrant opposite the shop of Andrew Hawes, Esq., and was built by Hon Archelaus Lewis and Capt. John Quinby, about the year 1787, on the Town wharf, and by a vote of the town the privilege to occupy the premises was to cover a period of twenty years. When occupied by Dexter Brewer the building was painted white and had outside steps to the second story. It was, shortly after the breaking, sold to Tristram Stevens and moved to a site on Tate street, Portland, where it was converted into a dwelling house and where it now stands and owned by him.

Dexter Brewer and his brother David were in the crockery ware trade in Portland prior to Dexter's coming to Stroudwater and the sign read, "D. & D. Brewer." When Dexter opened the shop to which we now particularly allude he had the "D. & D." painted over and the name "Dexter" placed thereon, but after a little use the old letters were plainly visible and for a long time I supposed the painter had made a mistake which Dexter had corrected.

When the building stood at Stroudwater it had an entrance on the outside via a pair of stairs to the second story, but I do not know the exact use to which the upper part was put. I remember entering it just once. The walls were painted to represent landscapes and my youthful eyes rested upon the work with feelings of the keenest admiration. It was done by David Stevens, a shoemaker of Stroudwater, born there April 11, 1789, married Sophia Peaks. I think he occupied the room at the time I visited it. He was of medium height, corpulent, dark complexion, black hair, without whiskers, black, piercing eye, and fond of sport, particularly wild duck shooting. He was designed by nature for an artist and had he lived in these times would undoubtedly have been one of more than local fame. After this he occupied a small building that stood to the easterly end of the shop building now owned and occupied by Andrew Hawes, Esq.

The father of David Stevens was Tristram Stevens, born at Newburyport, Oct. 19, 1751. Margaret Patrick, his wife, was born at Stroudwater Aug. 17, 1754. She was a daughter of David Patrick, who was a mason and a maker of brick. At the time of her birth David was at work on the top of the chimney, now to be seen, a massive pile of brick protruding from the so-called Tate house, nearly opposite the schoolhouse on Westbrook street, Stroudwater. Tristram and Margaret were married Dec. 12, 1776. David Patrick's house now stands upon the southwesterly corner made by Westbrook street crossing Congress street at Stroudwater, and known as the Frazier house at this time. David Stevens was the sixth child of Tristram and wife, Margaret (Patrick) Stevens. Tristram Stevens, Jr., son of Tristram C. Stevens, and grandson of Tristram Stevens, senior, of Stroudwater, sold the Patrick house to Seth Frazier, hence its present name.

The shop of John Haskell stood two-thirds the distance between the present residence of Mr. Chas. E. Bailey, opposite the Libby Corner schoolhouse on Congress street and the old Bailey house, which is the next easterly of the Chas. E. Bailey place on the same side of Con-

CONTINUED:

gress street. It was one story and small on the ground, and was built by Jeremiah Bailey. It was consumed by fire in August of 1857. It stood front to the street, a window each side the door, without paint, and the ridgepole sagged in the middle. A notice of Mr. Haskell, the last occupant, will appear next under this head.

THE DEERING NEWS.

Saturday, June 1, 1895.

GRANDPA'S SCRAP BOOK

[Under this head historical and genealogical memoranda will be furnished the readers of the News that appears worthy of preservation, particularly of remote periods in our history within the city limits and immediate vicinity.]

Of the antecedents of Jonathan Haskell, I have but little or comparatively no knowledge. He was born at Harvard, Mass., I think, February 15, 1766, and was a cooper. Hannah Robins with whom he was united in marriage was born June 24, 1766, and to them were born six daughters and a son as follows:

1. Nancy, born Jan. 9, 1786, married John Butler and lived in Leminster, Mass.
2. Hannah, born Sep. 2, 1788, married Abel Whitney, and lived in Lowell, Mass. She was his second wife and died Aug. 2, 1868.
3. Susan, born April 4, 1791, married Ebenezer Willard, who died at Harvard, Mass., Jan. 4, 1878. She died Feb. 29, 1876.
4. Mary, born Apr. 3, 1795, married Eben Larkeman. She died Nov. 22, 1866.
5. Nabby, born March 12, 1801 married Elijah Wyer, resided at Potuckett, R. I., and died there.
6. Almirad, born Dec. 23, 1803, married Nathan Tibbetts of Waterboro, March 2, 1822. She died May 17, 1882; he May 4, 1883.
7. John, born Sep. 22, 1812, died Nov. 10, 1890.

I have said before in the News that in "ye olden time" there stood on the northerly side of the brook that crosses Stevens Plains avenue at Bradley's and westerly side of the way a kiln owned by the Riggs family who first resided where Mr. Daniel D. Chenery now resides, that was used for the purposes of burning brick and pottery. It was constructed of brick, banked with earth and in the three or four feet that appeared above the earth embankment were holes to let in the light of day. This was the impromptu home of Jonathan Haskell on coming to the District of Maine and the place where John Haskell was born.

As I have stated, Nathan Tibbetts was born in the town of Waterboro; his nephew, Mark Tibbetts occupies the site of the Tibbets parental abode, the old house building having been removed.

When a young man Nathan lived in the family of Captain Thomas Seal at Capisic on the easterly side of the highway —"Capisic" being the name of a hamlet that existed some less than a hundred years since, and "Captain" was affixed to the Seal name because he was a mariner and commanded vessels when a young man. Opposite the Seal house near the salt water Nathan Tibbetts made brick for a while where an old well and pieces of bricks may still be seen.

Associated with the triangular perhaps jib shaped is a more appropriate name— piece of land from Bradley's to the northerly line of the present home lot of Mr. John B. Curtis between the highway and the back line of the lots are many historical facts. In the year 1735 the place came into the possession of Anthony Brackett, Jr., whose name is noticed in the News of Nov. 3, of last year, under this head. Brackett's dwelling stood on the opposite of the highway passing the brick kiln and a little to the northerly thereof.

It was two story and stood end to the street. In the year 1823 the house came into the possession of Nathan Tibbetts. In 1809 one William Homes of Scarboro conveyed a half acre of land containing the house to Thomas Pierce for $150. Thomas mortgaged it to Charles Pierce of Stroudwater, who was some sort of a cousin, who conveyed it to Nathan Tibbetts for $100,—"being the same that William Homes and wife sold Thomas Pierce." The conveyance of 1809 stated that Pierce lived on the premises.

Mr. Tibbetts removed the old house and erected a neat one story dwelling. He was an axeman in the establishment of the northeastern boundary line, wrote a good hand and being an easy talker was entertaining in conversation. He was well built, rather a good face, and above the average size of mankind.

CHILDREN.

1. Frances, born March 3, 1823, died in Portland, west end of Congress street, March 29, 1892. He was a shop keeper, his shop standing over the city line in Deering.
2. Rufus, born Jan. 23, 1826, died in Portland, Oct. 20, 1889. By occupation he was first a brick mason, then was clerk for William Parker several years, then manufactured brick. Parker's shop stood corner of Congress and Grove streets, not far from which Rufus Tibbetts resided.
3. Hannah, born June 29, 1828, died Sept. 2, 1890. She was the wife of John H. Whitney of Sebago.
4. Abbie, born Aug. 10, 1832; unmarried and retains the Tibbetts homestead. The original house was raised two years ago and a story put under it.

Of the boyhood of John the seventh child and only son of Jonathan Haskell I know nothing. When the tide mills were built at Stroudwater he drove an ox team for Capt. Dexter Brewer and hauled stone for the foundation. In 1837, I think this was the year, he purchased a house lot of Daniel Mason, and the carpenter shop that stood on the easterly end of the Daniel Mason house, and constructed the dwelling now standing next easterly of the First Congregational meetinghouse, where the heirs of the late Arthur Milliken reside, who own the place.

In 1847 John Haskell engaged in trade as noticed in my article of last week, but his shop was burned a year later than then stated. The following is from the Portland Transcript of August 21, 1858:

A small store at Libby's corner, Westbrook (now Deering) was destroyed by fire on Friday morning of last week. It is supposed it was robbed, and then set on fire. As the fire progressed a quantity of powder exploded, scattering the fragments in all directions. The loss is estimated at $400 or $500. No insurance.

While he was in trade he served several terms as school district clerk and two years on the board of selectmen.

After the destruction of his shop he did not engage in active business, but in a very quiet way carried on a private banking business, ever residing in the original Tibbetts house. In figure he was short, a musical voice, clean shaved, plainly dressed and a very quiet citizen.

A few rods westerly of the soldiers' lot in Evergreen cemetery may be seen a fine pedestal monument of solid granite with an undressed base of some material upon which appears one in raised and the other in sunken letters, the names,

TIBBETTS,
HASKELL.

Two white marble slabs are inscribed as follows:

FATHER,
Nathan Tibbetts,
Died
May 4, 1843.
Æt. 87 yrs., 3 m.

MOTHER,
Almira Tibbetts,
Died
May 17, 1882,
Æt. 78 yrs., 4 m.

Then other stones on the lot are inscribed as follows:

Rufus Tibbetts, 1826–1889.
Rufus Tibbetts, 1852–1853.
Nathan W. Tibbetts, 1858–1859.
Jonathan Haskell, 1766–1823.
Hannah Haskell, 1766–1846.
John Haskell, 1812–1890.
Hannah W. Whitney, 1828–1890.

THE DEERING NEWS.

Saturday, June 8, 1895.

GRANDPA'S SCRAP BOOK

[Under this head historical and genealogical memoranda will be furnished the readers of the News that appears worthy of preservation, particularly of remote periods in our history within the city limits and immediate vicinity.]

Josiah Stevens like all the other male members of the Stevens family was a blacksmith, and was the seventh child of Capt. Isaac Sawyer Stevens and wife Sarah Brackett, (for whose record see News of Nov. 17, last year,) was born on Stevens Plains, March 3, 1784, married Sally, daughter of John Blake, Jan. 14, 1807, John being a descendant of Jasper Blake who lived a little easterly of Lunt's Corner. He came from Hampton, N. H., in 1736, and purchased of Cornelius Hall the land where John H. Blake, a descendant, now resides, upon which there was a house and garrison "thereon standing" at time of purchase. In 1738 there were 80 acres in the Jasper Blake lot and 54 square rods, Isaac Sawyer, Jr., and Thomas Sawyer owning land on the westerly side of Jasper, where Isaac Sawyer, Jr., resided and died in 1749, leaving several minor children, whose widow married second, Apr. 3, 1754, Jonathan Morse. (More of this later.)

In 1680 the Lieutenant Governor of Massachusetts granted Sylvanus Davis & Co., the Capisic mill privilege, and a mile square of land to go with it. As I write a copy of the original plan of which is before me. In the northwesterly corner of this mile square lot, (Central avenue, formerly called the Blake road, forming the northerly boundary line,) John Blake purchased 110 acres of land, in 1766 which is now owned by Portland and connected with Evergreen Cemetery. Southerly and adjoining at the same time Jeremiah Riggs, Jr., and brother Stephen purchased 59 acres of Isaac Winslow whose wife was a daughter of Brig. Gen. Samuel Waldo. On this last lot "Glenwood" is located, where the house lots are now being sold so rapidly.

Into this Blake family Josiah Stevens married at the time above shown.

In 1809 Capt. Isaac S. Stevens sold Zachariah Brackett an acre of land for $105, which was located on the westerly side of the road, south 14s, west 49 rods and 18 links distant "from the front door of my dwelling house."

In 1814 Capt. Isaac, for $500, conveyed his son, Josiah Stevens, 40 acres and 80 square rods of land commencing bounds on westerly side of road and southerly corner of land. "I conveyed to my son William," southerly by road 35 rods, 18 links to land sold Zachariah Brackett, this Brackett lot, now the lot of Martin W. Best, corner New street, where the brick house stood, built by Walter B. Goodrich and burned a few years since. "It is the same land whereon his (Josiah Stevens) dwelling house now stands." So it appears by this record, and the only one I find except a plan made three years earlier which carries the date back to 1811, the large two story house now recognized as the Alfred Stevens house was in existence at that date.

In 1815 Josiah Stevens was taxed as follows: One house, $350; barn, $30; shop and outhouse, $70; eight acres mowing, $20; per acre; twenty-nine pasturing at $7 per acre; 2 cows, $28; and one swine, $5.

Windham road gravestone record:

In Memory of
JOSIAH STEVENS,
Who Died
Dec. 24, 1818,
Æt. 34 years.

FOUR CHILDREN.

1 Mary, married Joel H. Murray, 1839, and died Apr. 28, 1849. He was born at Brunswick, Apr. 24, 1808, died Dec. 26, 1894. He worked at combmaking then in a tan yard, and lived on what is now called Forest avenue, not far from Morrill's Corner. Of his children all are dead except one, a daughter, married and resides in a neighboring town. A stone in Bailey burying ground is inscribed, Catherine S. Murray, died Aug. 29, 1846, aged 10 mos. 6 days.

2 Catharine, born 1812, married Samuel K. Bailey, who was a shoemaker, born 1812. Their remains are interred at the Bailey graveyard Windham road. Gravestone record.

SAMUEL K. BAILEY.
Died
Apr. 1, 1863,
Æt. 57 years.
CATHARINE,
wife of
SAMUEL K. BAILEY,
and
Dau. of Josiah & Sally Stevens,
Died May, 18, 1842,
Æt. 30 years.

CHILDREN OF SAMUEL K. BAILEY.

First—Josiah Stevens Bailey, born 1831, married Henrietta C. Knight, daughter of Thomas Knight, Jr., and wife Elizabeth Pierce whose father, Thos. Pierce, built the house standing on Stevens Plains avenue about half-way from Brighton road to Church street and occupied by Isaiah Ingalls. It originally stood close to the street, and end thereto, in the corner of the lot with several tall fir trees in front. It was moved to its present site on the side of the hill by the late Arthur Milliken. Thomas Knight built the house that originally stood where Nevens joins Spring street, then he removed to Ocean Street. The widow of Josiah S. Bailey resides on the homestead Forest avenue.

Second—Samuel Smith Bailey, married; resided and died in the town of Jay.

Third—"Stillman G. Bailey, died East New York, Nov. 24, 1862, aged 23 years. A Volunteer in Co. D, 21st Maine Regiment." Thus reads as above the inscription on a stone standing in the Windham road cemetery.

After the death of his wife Samuel K. Bailey went to the town of Vassalboro where he married a widow Rackleff with three daughters, and where he last resided and died.

3 A gravestone record in the Windham road graveyard reads, "John B., only son of Josiah and Sally Stevens died July 28, 1826, aged 12 years.

4 Nancy B. Stevens, born 1818, (the year her father died,) married Storer Libby. She died March 18, 1864 aged 36 years; he died Sep. 13 1887, aged 68 years, 9 months, 27 days. Remains of both buried in Pine Grove cemetery. He retained the John Blake farm, the house thereof standing being on the high ground, one story and weather wood color outside, while the other Blake house stood on the lower ground on a southwesterly course. The John Blake house was at what is now known as Central avenue, formerly called the "Blake road." Nov. 20, 1871, Libby sold the John Blake part of the Blake farm to the city of Portland for cemetery purposes, containing 51 acres for $13,925. Storer Libby and wife had children: 1—Franklin W., married, died Jan. 26, 1883, aged 34 years 9 months. (Gravestone record.) 2—Oscar S., died Aug. 10, 1867, aged 17 years, 6 months. (Gravestone record, Pine Grove cemetery.) 3—Mary. 4—Oscar, who was an adopted son.

THE DEERING NEWS.

Saturday, June 15, 1895.

GRANDPA'S SCRAP BOOK

[Under this head historical and genealogical memoranda will be furnished the readers of the News that appears worthy of preservation, particularly of remote periods in our history within the city limits and immediate vicinity.]

In the printed edition of Rev. Thomas Smith's journal, issued in 1849, notes by Willis, on page 165, may be seen as follows:

May 11, 1756. Capt. Milk with forty men, Capt. Haley with a company and Capt. Skillin with another, went out in pursuit of the Indians. * * * We hear Capt. Berry is also gone with a scout. [Berry lived where John J. Fray resides on Ocean street. Ed. News.]

14. This morning, one Brown was killed and Winship was wounded and scalped at Marblehead (Windham.) Manchester fired upon them, and we hope killed an Indian, as did Capt. Skillin another. The Indians fled affrighted and left five packs, a bow and a bunch of arrows, and several other things.

Then follows an account of the engagement.

The journal at this period is replete with entries relative to the war.

May 3, 1758, he says: "One Ingersoll and one Willard are come to town with recruiting orders for ninety more men out of this part of the country, which makes the people quite mad, that when we had cheerfully enlisted our quota (five hundred) they should now get a pressing.

21. Our soldiers sailed for Kittery in three transport sloops.

No connected story can be given of what transpired hereabouts at the time to which I now allude. A war between England and other powers was sure to make trouble here between the English and the Indians, and as there was no telling when the savages would appear guards were stationed in various places and persons designated by the government to give warning.

In vol. 95, p. 451, Massachusetts Archives is preserved an original paper, dated 1757. It is entitled

ALARM LIST.

Following is a copy:
1. Lieutenant Nathaniel Knight.

He resided near Stroudwater Falls, adjacent the residence of the late Edw. Chapman. His account book now before me as I write does not indicate trouble with the Indians. He was a nephew of Col. Thomas Westbrook. His dwelling was burned some seventy-five years ago.

2. Sergt. Robert Slemmons.

He resided in the so-called Phinney house, renovated and repaired last year by the Cummings Brothers, in Westbrook, on the Buxton road, a mile and a half westerly of Stroudwater.

3. Sergt. James Johnson.
4. Sergt. John Johnson.
5. Sergt. George Johnson.

A Johnson lived where our present George Johnson resides, on the Buxton road; John Johnson where Geo. B. Leavitt now resides a few rods easterly; and another Johnson built the Pratt house on the Stroudwater road, a mile easterly of Saccarappa.

6. Sergt. John Haskell.

He lived westerly of Saccarappa, on the road to Gorham. His place of abode is noticed in a survey of a highway filed in the office of our County Commissioners.

7. Sergt. Jeremiah Riggs.

He lived where Daniel D. Chenery now resides at Bradley's Corner,—came here to Bradley's in 1735.

8. Sergt. John Crockett.

He resided near Stroudwater Falls, and was a brother-in-law to Lieut. Nathaniel Knight. His house was on the easterly side of the road and opposite that of his brother-in-law.

9. Sergt. William Knight.

This one I cannot place.

10. Sergt. John Bailey.

Whether this means Dea. John or John, Jr., who built the house on Spring street, opposite High, now known as the John Newman house I cannot determine.

11. George Tate.

He was the King's mast agent, resided at Stroudwater. His house still standing. Was sent here by the English government.

12. Sergt. Thomas Thomes.

He resided at Libby's Corner, southerly of Douglass street, on the northerly side of Congress street.

13. Sergt. Edward Gilman.

Of this one, as well as William Knight, I have not placed.

14. David Patrick, clerk.

He resided in what is now called the Frazier house at Stroudwater, and wrote an excellent hand.

Strange as it may seem, seven at least of the houses then occupied I can now locate which are standing, if the Pratt house was then in existence, which was standing in 1773 as now seen, and six of them are located in Deering.

Capt. Samuel Skillings resided at Long Creek, Cape Elizabeth. For a sketch of him see vol. III, p. 281, Collection Maine Historical Society, 2d Series, and for a genealogy, Watson's Maine Historical and Genealogical Recorder, vol. II, p. 100; also Portland Argus, March 15, 1889, and Aug. 19, 1889.

The roll of his company is as follows, and is recorded in the Massachusetts archives;

1 Samuel Skillings, Captain, *Long Creek.
2 Joseph Small, Lieut., Stroudwater.
3 Chipman Cobb, Sgt., Capisic.
4 Solomon Haskell, Sgt., Saccarappa.
5 John Wilson, Corporal.
6 Anthony Brackett, Corporal, Bradley's Corner, where the late John Haskell resided.
7 William Slemmons, Stroudwater, where Fred A. Johnson resides.
8 James Thompson.
9 James Johnson, Jr.
10 John Johnson, Jr.
11 Robert Johnson.
12 William Porterfield, westerly of Stroudwater.
13 Thomas Jackson, westerly of Stroudwater.
14 Richard Nason, Jr., westerly of Stroudwater.
15 Isaac Nason.
16 Jonathan Nason.
17 Zebulon Trickey, westerly of Stroudwater.
18 William Lamb.
19 Joseph Small, Jr, Stroudwater.
20 David Small, Stroudwater.
21 Daniel Small, Stroudwater.
22 Nathan Chick, northwesterly of Stroudwater.
23 Abel Gold,
24 Samuel Conant, Saccarappa.
25 Bartholomew Thompson, Saccarappa.
26 Nicholas Thompson, Saccarappa.
27 Benjamin Haskell, Saccarappa.
28 John Haskell, Saccarappa.
29 Peter Babb,
30 Thomas Pennell, Capisic.
31 Clement Pennell, Capisic.
32 John Pennell, Jr.
33 Andrew Cobb.
34 Joseph Riggs, Bradley's Corner.
35 Jeremiah Riggs, Bradley's Corner.
36 Stephen Riggs, Bradley's Corner.
37 Jonah Blethen,
38 John Thombs, Jr. Libby's Corner.
39 Edward Chapman, Stroudwater Falls
40 Joseph Mussett, Stroudwater Falls, Mussett's wife was an aunt to this Edward Chapman.
41 William Bayley.
42 David Bayley.
43 William Wescott, Jr., Long Creek.
44 Ebenezer Done, Long Creek.
45 Richard Wescott, Long Creek.
46 Nathaniel Done, Long Creek.
47 Josiah Skillings, Long Creek.
48 Samuel Skillings, Jr., Long Creek.
49 John Warren.
50
51 Gilbert Warren.
52 David Patrick, Jr., Stroudwater.
53 William Webb.
54 Benjamin Godfrey, Saccarappa.
55 William Balden.
56 John Green.
57 Jacob Dalinge, Sr.
58 Jacob Dalinge, Jr.
59 Peter Lawrence.
60 Thomas Jones.
61 Nathaniel Knight, Jr.
62 George Knight.
63 William Knight, Jr.
64 Joseph Knight.
65 Samuel Knight.
66 Nathaniel Starbird.
67 John Starbird,
68 Nicholas Smith.
69 Abraham Crockett.
70 Stephen Sawyer.
71 James Frost. Later built a house at Capisic.
72 Joseph Frost.
73 Joshua Crockett.
74 Edward Done, Long Creek.
75 Edward Gilman, Jr.
76 Richard Crockett.
77 Nathan Starbird.
78 William Tate, Stroudwater.
79 Elias Hoffman.

CONTINUED:
80 Veluis Shier.
81 John Green.
82 John Gripes.
83 Robert Frances.
84 James Frances.
85 David McDonald, Stroudwater.
86 John McDonald, Stroudwater. The house stood southeasterly of the present post office.
87 Valentine Tilter.
88 Makel Grouse.
89 Nicholas Shoulders.
90 Peter Puff.
91 Edward Caskallon.
92 Valentine Skeminel.
93 Philip Cook.
94 John Cook.

*The names of the places of residence are placed by the writer of this article.

THE DEERING NEWS.

Saturday, June 29, 1895.

GRANDPA'S SCRAP BOOK

[Under this head historical and genealogical memoranda will be furnished the readers of the News that appears worthy of preservation, particularly of remote periods in our history within the city limits and immediate vicinity.]

Before the break of day, Apr. 21, 1775, the rider of a galloping steed shouted hereabouts—"To arms! to arms! The fight at Lexington has commenced." He was an "express from Boston." Then there was excitement in this section. The musket was taken from its accustomed resting place when not in use, a mother's benediction and lover's embrace followed in quick succession, and before the sun disappeared in the western horizon of that day, of that eventful period, Capt. John Brackett of Saccarappa, and his company of "Minute Men" were on the move for the place of encounter, but when the company reached the town of Wells it was ordered back.

In Vol. xi, p. 218, of Massachusetts Archives, at Boston statehouse, an original manuscript may be seen on file, of which the following is a copy:

A List of a party of Minute Men, under command of Capt. John Brackett, who were on their march to Head Quarters immediately after Lexington Battle, April 21, 1775.

1 John Brackett—Capt.
2 James Johnson—Lieut.
3 Jesse Partridge—2nd Lieut.
4 Morris Clark—Sergt.
5 Daniel Lunt, do
6 Amos Noyes—Corporal.
7 Edmund Merrill, do
8 Samuel Thoms.
9 Archelaus Lewis.
10 David Partridge.
11 Jotham Partridge.
12 Willm. Conant.
13 David Thompson.
14 Willm. Babb.
15 George Waterhouse.
16 Peter White.
17 Saml. Starbird.
18 Daniel Gold.
19 Adriel Warren.
20 John Starbird.
21 Pepperel Frost.
22 Benja. Bailey.
23 George Johnson.
24 Moses Gammon.
25 John Thoms.
26 Wm. Berry.
27 Ichabod Wilson.
28 James Doughty.
29 John Knight.
30 John Huston.
31 Peter Babb.
32 Nathl. Knight.
33 Nathl. Chapman.
34 Robert Tate.

The company was in service five days, marching from home 30 miles. Privates received, each, 7s. 1p. All received 22£ 11s. 2p.

Then Capt. Brackett commenced to recruit a company, and July 3 of that year, Parson Smith says: "Capt. Brackett and company marched to Cambridge," and in a foot note the reviser of the journal in the edition of 1849 says: "Capt. Brackett, I believe, was Joshua, son of Zachariah," when in fact he was the oldest child of Anthony Brackett who owned and lived on a tract of land comprising the southwesterly part of Portland. He married Sarah Knight.

In 1720 Nathan Knight came to Dunston and purchased a small lot there which became Nov. 15, 1748, the home place of Richard King of the family of Kings of Dunstan. Knight was a brother in-law of Col. Thomas Westbrook of Stroudwater marrying the Colonel's sister. Nathan was admitted to Scarboro church Sep. 12, 1731.

Sarah Knight was the third child in the family of Nathan Knight and was married to Brackett Feb. 14, 1733. She died and he married second, Widow Hicks whose maiden name was Proctor. The children were, Capt. John, Thomas, James, Mary, Joshua, Elizabeth, Keziah, Sarah, Nathaniel, and Sarah. Widow Hicks lived beyond Morrill's Corner on the Windham road.

Joshua Brackett who lived at the head of High street was a brother to Anthony and married, Dec. 9, 1744, Esther Cox. Another brother lived on the James Deering place, but left town in 1744. His name was Zachariah, and his family appeared in the News of Nov. 3, last year. I am explicit because Willis, compiler of the second edition of Parson Smith's Journal is in error as to the parents of Capt. John Brackett.

The residence of Nathaniel Knight, son of Nathan, that stood near Stroudwater Falls, alluded to in my last article, was destroyed by fire Sept. 4, 1829. An official copy of the will of Nathaniel, son of Nathaniel and grandson of Nathan, is before me while I now write.

On the back of the paper upon which the names of the "Minute Men" appear, is written as follows, the names of Johnson and Partridge because Capt. Brackett was dead.

CAMBRIDGE, Dec. 14, 1775.

These within is a true acct. of Capt. Brackett and his company's travel and expense till they rec'd counter orders to return home.

JAMES JOHNSON, Lieut.,
JESSE PARTRIDGE, 2nd Lieut.

Brackett sickened soon after reaching the seat of war and on his way home died at Ipswich, Mass., and in the month of September 1776, his widow, Mary, married Peltiah March, a tanner, of Saccarappa.

THE DEERING NEWS.

Saturday, July 6, 1895.

GRANDPA'S SCRAP BOOK

[Under this head historical and genealogical memoranda will be furnished the readers of the News that appears worthy of preservation, particularly of remote periods in our history within the city limits and immediate vicinity.]

The names of the Regimental staff officers and members of the company with which Capt. John Bracket was connected were as follows: (Vol. LVI, p. 215, Mass. archives, Sept. 29, 1775.)

Col., Edward Phinney, Gorham.
Lieut. Col., Samuel March, Scarboro.
Major, Jacob Brown, North Yarmouth.
Adj't, George Smith, North Yarmouth.
2d Major, Moses Banks, North Yarmouth.
Surgeon, Stephen Swett, Gorham.

The company started for Boston July 3, 1775.

1 John Brackett, Capt., died Sept. 24, 1775, at Ipswich, Mass.
2 James Johnson, 1st Lieut., died Sept. 24, 1775 at Ipswich, Mass.
3 Jesse Partridge, 2d Lieut., died Sept. 24, 1775, at Ipswich, Mass.
4 Daniel Lunt, Sergeant, died Sept. 24, 1775, at Ipswich, Mass.
5 Morris Clark, Sergeant, died Sept. 24, 1775, at Ipswich, Mass.
6 Joshua Stevens, Sergeant.
7 Archaleus Lewis, Sergeant.
8 Charles Frost, Corporal.
9 James Douty Corporal.
10 James Means, Corporal.
11 Enoch Knight, Corporal.
12 Zebulon Knight, Drummer.
13 Joseph Knight, Fifer.
14 John Blair.
15 James Brackett.
16 Jeremiah Brackett.
17 William Brackett.
18 George Crockett.
19 George Douty.
20 Moses Gammon.
21 Daniel Gold.
22 George Hammond.
23 Samuel Hicks.
24 Pearson Huntress.
25 John Hustone.
26 George Johnson, Jr.
27 Joseph Johnson.
28 John Knight.
29 John Lunt.
30 Stephen Marriner.
31 John McDonald.
32 Uriah Nason.
33 Amos Noyes.
34 David Partridge.
35 Nathan Partridge.
36 Jeremiah Pennel.
37 Joseph Pennel.
38 John Porterfield.
39 John Priest.
40 Joseph Quinby.
41 John Robinson.
42 Enoch Riggs.
43 John Sawyer.
44 Elias Starbird.
45 John Starbird.
46 Samuel Starbird.
47 John Thoms, Jr.
48 Elijah Ward.
49 Adriel Warren, Jr.
50 Henry Webb.
51 James Webb.
52 John Webb.
53 Joseph Wilson.
54 Mark Wilson.
55 Daniel Crockett, Windham.
56 Stephen Manchester, Windham.
57 John Young, Windham.
58 Josiah Peabody, Gorham.
59 James Westmore, Gorham.

For further particulars see "Vol. 46, T, Muster and Pay rolls, Bundle 25," Bound Book, Mass. archives.

I gave the parents' names of Capt. Brackett in my last. Anthony Brackett, his father, owned an interest in the Saccarappa mill privilege.

In 1753, Charles Gerrish, an edge tool maker, the grandfather of John J. Gerrish, Esq., residence 48, Eastern Promenade, Portland, sold to "George Tate (the King's mast agent) of Botherhith in the county of Surry in Great Britain, now resident of Falmouth, Merchant,— All that certain piece of land in Falmouth on the northerly side of Stroud Water river near the lower mill and fronting northerly on the Marst Yard, (where Frank Mason now resides), at the most easterly corner of a lot of land inclosed and improved by David Patrick (where Michael Stevens now lives), thence running about South East as the fence now stands by said mast yard seventy feet to a stake (the present brick house) and from said stake and the aforesaid corner running back seventy feet in width by said Patrick's improvements about two hundred feet towards the bank of the river aforesaid till it comes within ten feet of the flowing or usual running of a spring fresh et being the same lot of land I, the said Charles Gerrish, purchased of Samuel Waldo, Esq., July 17, 1749."

The deed of which the foregoing is an abstract contains much historical data. On the lot Tate built the house now to be seen, though the original house had a row of windows where it is now roof on front, thus making it three story, which was changed about the year 1800. Gerrish went to Saccarappa and in 1755 he sold a lot on the westerly side of Saccarappa to James Frost, "reserving one-fourth of an acre on the northerly side where some children are buried for a burying ground." This gives a clue to the delapidated burying ground which reflects anything but credit upon the people of Westbrook.

For a consideration of 120£ in 1762 Capt. John Brackett purchased the seven acre lot of Prof. Gerrish going up back in the country, Durham. I think, into the woods where he cleared a farm, and became a citizen of importance.

Who the wife of Capt. Brackett was I have never learned. He was a land surveyor, and to his original purchase of seven acres he added other lots in other places. In 1769 he surveyed the highway from Saccarappa to Gorham. Brackett's children were: 1—John; 2—Mary; 3—Lucy; 4—Sally.

In 1761, the George Tate above noticed sold to one John Warren a 62 acre lot of land about a mile easterly from Saccarappa and on the northerly side of the Stroudwater road, for the small consideration of 17£. On this lot John Warren lived, thrived and died. The one story house and large barn, now gone, are still well remembered by many. On the county atlas, made in 1871, the spot is marked "S. Conant."

JOHN WARREN'S FAMILY RECORD

John Warren born in Berwick March 5, 1731; married Dec. 25, 1755 Jane Johnson of Falmouth; and she was born June 15, 1740. He died Jan. 1, 1807; she, Nov. 18, 1809. They were interred at Stroudwater from which place they were removed to the Warren tomb at the Saccarappa village cemetery.

CHILDREN.

1 John Warren, Jr., born Nov. 9, 1756. He entered the army of the war of the Revolution and died unmarried, May 23, 1776.
2 Polly, March 7, 1758.
3 David, Nov. 17, 1760.
4 Elizabeth, June 28, 1763.
5 Sally, Jan. 9, 1776.
6 James, Jan. 25, 1769.
7 Jane, Sept. 24, 1771.
8 Margaret, Jan. 11, 1774.
9 John, Jr., May 23, 1776. It is a family tradition that the news of the death of the first John was received the day this John was born, hence the date of the death of the first was made to correspond with the birth of the last.
10 Robert, June 27, 1778.
11 Nathaniel, Feb. 25, 1781. died 1783.
12 Nancy, Oct. 24, 1782.

It is traditional that Jane Johnson, who became the wife of John Warren, Sen., was a daughter of James Johnson who in 1749, came from Scarboro and settled on the wild land a mile westerly of Stroudwater where his great-grandson George Johnson now resides, and Jane was a younger sister to John Johnson, the grandfather to the present George, John being born May 14, 1737, but in the list of names furnished the Portland Transcript of last week (June 26) of the names of James Johnson's children that of Jane does not appear. In the Cumberland County History, published in 1880 may be seen a likeness of George and some of the names of his relatives.

The Transcript list is as follows:

1 George, born 1728, died 1793, married a Miss Jackson. [This was Mary Jackson, daughter of Francis Jackson who lived on the Saco road about a half mile southerly of the James Johnson homestead. Jackson located there 1736. The dwelling was removed some 25 years ago. Francis' daughter Sarah became Sarah Brewer and built the one story house now standing on Bond street, Stroudwater, the 2nd house on the right from Westbrook.—ED. NEWS.]
2 Flora, married a Patten of Bath, Me.

CONTINUED:

3 Eleanor, married a Means of Stroudwater. [A Means lived a spell in a log house that stood on Stevens' Plains avenue, near Bradley's Corner. The fact will be shown later by manuscript records.—ED. NEWS.]
4 James, died 1831, married Elizabeth Porterfield [Apr. 12, 1759.—ED. NEWS.] who lived a half mile westerly of the Johnsons. They lived at Thompson's Pond Poland.
5 John, born May 14, 1737; married Eleanor Lamb. He died May 28, 1733.
6 Margaret, born 1739, married Oct. 21, 1765, Alexander McLellan of Gorham, Me. He died and she married John Miller of Gorham.

Thus the Portland Transcript contributor gives the names of the descendants of James Johnson.

Here is a list of the children of the above named John, obtained of Silas Skillin, Esq., of Cumberland Foreside, made by his father at North Yarmouth where he resided.

John Johnson born May 14, 1737, died at Westbrook May 28, 1833.

Eleanor Lamb, his wife, born at Falmouth, Nov. 15 1740, died May 20, 1820. [These two names appear on one stone at Stroudwater cemetery.—ED. NEWS.]

CHILDREN.

1 Richard Johnson, born 1764, died at Westbrook, Apr. 25, 1846.
2 Elizabeth, died at North Yarmouth, Nov. 14, 1796. She was Mrs. Isaac Skillin, married July 13, 1786.
3 Hannah, died at Gorham. (Mrs. Matthew Johnson.)
*4 William, born 1771, died while on a visit at Gorham, May, 18, 1796.
5 Jane, born Nov. 29, 1772, died at Cape Elizabeth, May 18, 1857. (Mrs. Daniel Skillin.)
6 Rebecca, born March 11, 1774, died Feb., 1863. (Mrs. Joseph Chenery who was grandmother to Daniel D. Chenery, the present county treasurer of this county.)
7 Sally died Nov. 8, 1857. (Mrs. Daniel Trickey.)
*8 Alexander, born Apr. 28, 1777, died May 13, 1840. [Sally (Johnson) Johnson, his wife, born in the next house easterly where George B. Leavitt lives, died June 3, 1876, aged 83 years.—ED. NEWS.]
9 Dorcas, born April 28, 1780, died Dec. 6, 1864. (Mrs. Wm. Roberts.)
*10 John Lamb Johnson, born May 1784, died May e5, 1844, not married.

*These are the only graveyard memorials, four in number, at Stroudwater, erected to the memory of the James Johnson branch of the Johnson name.

Next week the name of Capt. Brackett and recollections of persons and events connected therewith will be further considered.

THE DEERING NEWS.

Saturday, July 13, 1895.

GRANDPA'S SCRAP BOOK

[Under this head historical and genealogical memoranda will be furnished the readers of the News that appears worthy of preservation, particularly of remote periods in our history within the city limits and immediate vicinity.]

The statement in my last article that James Johnson, Jesse Partridge and Daniel Lunt died at Ipswich, Mass. Sept. 25, 1775, was an error I was very sorry to see. Capt. John Brackett only died at that time and place. And as I have been disappointed in not receiving certain copies by mail of records I expected to come to hand in season for use this week a further consideration of this Capt. Brackett matter must be suspended for the present.

Mr. Josiah S. North.

The friends and relatives of Mr. Josiah Stevens North, born Jan. 22, 1819, in the house built by his father, Elisha North, that stood within the enclosure of what was originally known as Presumpscot Trotting Park, but now Woodfords Park, which house was burned soon after the park was constructed, has recently submitted to amputation of a leg in consequence of a frost-bite of a toe that occurred five or six years ago, and is now at a hospital at Lewiston. This course was the only alternative to save his life, gangreen having made its appearance. His wife sends us the following which we cheerfully reprint. We think it was prepared for publication by the late William Jordan who resided on College street, Stevens Plains, father to Rev. William T. Jordan, recent pastor of the Free church of that locality.

OLD WESTBROOK WAS ALWAYS DEMOCRATIC—ITEMS OF EARLY HISTORY.

To the Editor of the Portland Argus:

Our Congress has expired to give place to a better one, we hope; the Legislature of Maine has adjourned; and now, who was the first tin-peddler, (in Maine) and where is the last? For we see none nowadays. The people in Deering, of the present generation, ought to be able to answer these questions—can they? A few now living can remember when nearly all the tin-ware and horn combs ("hair combs") used in Maine were manufactured in what is now Deering, between Morrill's Corner and Woodford's, on the road over "Stevens Plains," and when hundreds of active young men were employed in peddling these wares, all over the state. This one place was headquarters for all. There might have been three of four small "custom tinshops" between Kittery and Eastport. The tin-peddler was "a butt" for everybody, and they were men who could stand butting. But who was the first one? We think "Old Brisco" was that man. He had no children, but adopted daughters who married tinmen and have raised good families. We think Mr. Brisco might have been tinman, peddler, and tinker, but he left no mark on "The Plains" to show that he ever lived there. Then came from Connecticut the brothers Elisha and Elijah North and Oliver Buckley, who were tinmen, set up "tinshops," peddled some, took apprentices to learn the trade, but soon sold all their wares by others, whom they hired as peddlers. Then came, also from Connecticut, the brothers Isaiah, Chauncy and Ebenezer D. Woodford, combmakers, and went to work at their trade. Isaiah died young, leaving a young family, Chauncy lived and did business with ordinary success, at what is now Morrill's Corner. Eben D. lived and did business at what is now Woodford's. Later the business was carried on by Woodford & Jordan with large success, the firm manufacturing more combs than enough to supply Maine, selling largely in Boston, New York and Philadelphia. Then the Stevenses, whether they were natives or came from elsewhere, is not known to the writer, went into the tin and comb business more or less. It was all Westbrook then. About 1830 the "wave" began to be too close. Campbell and Mills, and apprentice and a peddler, swarmed out, went to Bangor and set up tin shops for custom work and peddling, soon occupying all that part of the state as their field. Soon others did the same more or less extensively, in towns along the coast and on the Kennebec and Penobscot rivers. Consequently, the business began to fall off at Westbrook. Cooking stoves and furnaces were not known in those days, but the Tin Kitchen was used for baking meats before the open fire, and later the "Tin Baker," for baking bread and meats had a short run preceding the introduction of stoves and furnaces; when they came the Tin Kitchens and Bakers went out of sight.

The call for stoves and furnaces increased so fast that custom stove and tinshops were soon opened in nearly every town in the state and the tin peddler's calling was gone, and the successors of the Norths, Stevenses, and Buckley had to abandon tinware. About the same time the fashions changed, the wearing of combs by the ladies fell off so much that the business of the Woodfords, Stevens, and Woodford & Jordan was worthless and they gave that up.

To-day, in April 1883, not a lady's horn comb is made in Maine, we believe no tin shop exists in Deering, (none to make peddlers' ware, if any) nor do we know of a single tin peddler in the state, but likely there may be a few. What a change; a complete turn over. Nobody suffered by it. The change occurred in the last days of the first comers and when their successors were about taking their places, they made no complaints, but turned their attention to other kinds of business or scattered to do better elsewhere. They had not then been trained to seek remedies for every unpleasant change, from Congressional legislation or a protective tariff as some of their descendents may now be doing simply because it is the fashion.

This is sent to the Argus to be printed to remind Deering people that their predecessors are not forgotten by one who scattered. And, Mr. Editor, if you print this we will give you another, telling how some of the peddlers have got through the world, for it will be interesting many readers to learn how they to

"Grandmarm Porterfield," the Mother Goose of Stroudwater a half Century ago, Descendants and Will.

EDITOR THE NEWS:—The names of William Porterfield and William Porterfield, jr., appear upon the original list of tax payers of the parish of Cape Elizabeth of 1735, the first paying a tax on real estate and personal property, while the latter paid only a poll tax. Hereabouts the name is now extinct. From whence came these persons is a mystery, but conjecture places them among the band of Scotch-Irish emigrants who landed here some fifteen years anterior to the date above given. Their first descendants were somewhat peculiar in their inclinations, abounding in sociability and mirthfulness.

In 1737, January 7, a William Porterfield married a Mary Jamerson, and 1747 a William Porterfield purchased a hundred acre lot about a mile and a half westerly of Stroudwater, the place now being known as the Boothby farm. April 12, 1759, James Johnson and Elizabeth Porterfield were married. May 15, 1774, Hannah Porterfield and John Lamb were united in marriage.

The relationship between these persons I do no know, but one Capt. John Porterfield succeeded his father William in the possession of the hundred acre homestead, receiving it by will, dated May 4, 1790. The wife of Capt. John was Catherine Slemmons to whom he was united in marriage April 25, 1788. She was born where Fred A. Johnson lives at Stroudwater, her father noticing her in his will dated Dec. 13, 1784, by a bequest of £53, 6s. lawful money. Capt. John's wife had children, Mary who died unmarried; Betsey married Dec. 25, 1819, James Rounds of Saco; 2nd—Dunn and died at Stroudwater a few years since; William, married Feb. 16, 1819, Dorothy Bailey, born near Libby's Corner, Jan. 5, 1791, had one child; died unmarried; he married 2nd Mary Ann Larrabee of Brunswick. In 1851 they sold the farm and went to Corridon, Ind., where both died childless. The dances and annual corn-huskings at his place of abode, his thin face, long neck, white horse, old chaise, and pretty faced second wife are still remembered. He was last of the name hereabouts.

In 1743 John's brother William was born, and at Brunswick in 1746, Elizabeth Wilson was born who became William's wife. In 1764 he made a purchase of real estate about two-thirds the way from Stroudwater to Saccarappa, where Mr. Edward Trickey now resides, and built the large low-posted one story dwelling, removed a few years since by Mr. Trickey to make room for the fine residence now observable. To them were born eight children as follows:

(1.) Eleanor born Nov. 17, 1773, married June 27, 1802, Jonathan Sparrow then of Stroudwater. (An extended notice of this couple I hope to give soon.)

(2.) Lettice born July 3, 1776, married Nov. 1, 1803, William Larrabee of Brunswick. He was son of Benjamin and Lydia (Bailey) Larrabee, she of this vicinity, married Oct. 12, 1762. Their children were: 1, David, 2, Margaret, 3, Elizabeth, born 1809, married Nathan Fickett of Stroudwater, mother of our street commissioner, and still living; 4, William, a farmer at Dover, this state; 5, Mary Ann, who married William Porterfield, to whom allusion has been made.

(3.) James born Apr. 27, 1778, married Mary Ann Motely who was reared by the side of the Presumpscot river between the site of the old townhouse and Pride's Corner. He "lived at home," engaged in lumber speculation, purchasing interests in mills at Saccarappa and Cougin. In 1815 he was taxed for a 300 dollar house; 120 dollar barn; 35 dollar shed; 105 acres of land; one-half of two sawmills; 6 oxen, 5 cows, horse, chaise and 3 swine, but adversity overtook him and he died childless, Sept. 9, 1826.

(4.) Mary born Jan. 18, 1779, whose hand and affections were sought by John Warren of Saccarappa, but she declined and engaged in trade at Stroudwater, continuing there till her death, Apr. 3, 1854, unmarried.

(5.) Peggy born March 1, 1782, married Oct. 11, 1807, Charles Pierce of Haverhill, Mass., born there July 23, 1777, a descendant of Lydia Frost, daughter of Maj. Charles Frost and Benjamin Pierce, who were married Nov. 8, 1692. Mr. Pierce was a stirring man. He kept shop. In 1804 he was one of the "charter party" of the brigantine "Maine," of 127 tons, at $1.85 per ton a month. In 1815-16, he was a member of the school committee. In 1815 I find an agreement by him signed to sell a schooner then on the stocks at Stroudwater of 104 tons at $20 per ton, "but bolted," "one-half cash down, and a three months' note." These memorandums show what it cost to build a vessel then and what they paid. He was stricken with paralysis but lived some time in a helpless state, and diedOct. 26, 1827. He weighed a few pounds over two hundred and fell dead from a chair Apr. 2, 1853. Their dwelling was a good, one-story building, with a "cellar kitchen which he built, and it stood between the shop of Polly Porterfield, as everyone called her, and the river, on the Buxton road, where the cellar may now be seen.

These things "Aunt Peggy" as she was called behind her back, disliked. First, to be called "Peggy:" second, to have snowballs or stones thrown at her martin-house, perched on a standard on the barn roof, and third, to have stones thrown into her very sour fruited apple-tree on a neighboring lot—three things we boys would sometimes do.

She was the mother of three children: (1.) Edward, born Aug. 12, 1811, married Abigail Doughty Shaw, born Jan. 6, 1814, daughter of Bela Shaw, born in Middleboro, Mass., Nov. 20, 1787, and wife Hannah Doughty of old Falmouth, born Dec. 6, 1792, married June 30, 1811. Mr. Shaw was a trader at Morrill's Corner, lived where Dr. Parker does; while Edward Pierce built the house on part of the homestead lot, occupied by the late Capt. Wm. Sinnett.

(2.) Mary born May 30, 1813. She succeeded her aunt Polly as shopkeeper, married Olof Thornbury, had one child, but all are dead.

(3.) Levi Quinby, born Sept. 28, 1815, was a successful merchant tailor, at Saccarappa, where he built a nice, comfortable dwelling on Main street, now removed. He was a man of commanding demeanor, fine conversationalist, as was his sister Mary and aunt Polly and mother, a ready debater and excellent singer. He was a local worker in the organization of the Republican party, and a member of the advance guard in temperance work. He married Cordelia Stevens of Stevens Plains who resides there a widow.

(6.) Ann, born Nov. 18, 1783, married Charles Pratt Dec. 13, 1814, and resided at Saccarappa. She died Jan. 1863.

(7.) Thomas, born Apr. 16, 1786, with Richard Palmer was burned to death in a logging camp at Waterford, March 23, 1813.

(8.) William, born Feb. 27, 1788, married Zenobia Collins, a Quakeress of Durham where he resided, leaving one child named Charles, who remains on the homestead unmarried.

In the old cemetery at Stroudwater one of the lettered stones reads as follows:

In Memory of
Mr. William Porterfield,
who died
Aug. 16, 1788,
Aged 45 years.

At the time of his demise it appears by the foregoing that the youngest of his eight children was only six months of age. To describe the ordeal of the widowed mother, one must draw largely upon imagination. The soil of the hundred acre farm was excellent; and it is more than probable, all been bereft of their natural growth of timber, thus affording a means of subsistence, by cultivation of the former and sales of the latter. Her early childhood was spent when the Indians were feared. She saw the smoke and flame of the burning of Portland in 1775, and listened to the

CONTINUED:

reports of success and failure of the army of the Revolution, so but few thus inclined were better qualified and equipped than she to entertain by recital of stories of adventure, escape and destruction, bereft of which privilege life to her in its decline would, undoubtedly, have been irksome. The exact time of her removal to Stroudwater I cannot here state. Her aged form, has nearly vanished from my memory, only a faint shadow remains. Her abode in the second story of an aged house that stood on the top of the hill, on the left, as one ascends towards the reform school, a spot that now at times commands a landscape view of more than ordinary beauty, wore a sombre appearance with its time-blackened walls, and darkened lower story windows by outside board shutters placed there during the expected Indian raid upon the hamlet in 1744. And though gloomy without, with its snow white floor within, with its boxes, baskets and bags, conveniently arranged with its bright minded occupant at home, it was a domicile the young of the village found delight in visiting, for she was a Mother Goose indeed, though her stories, sayings and riddles were of a higher order than the original.

Her will is a document containing the very essence of brevity, and the following is a copy from the original:

WESTBROOK, May 27, 1826.
This is my last will and testament that this book is to be Elizabeth Larrabee's, daughter of William Larrabee, of Brunswick.

ELIZABETH PORTERFIELD,
LYDIA CHAPMAN,
MARY PIERCE.

The "book" willed was a Bible which is now the companion of the legatee Mrs. Elizabeth (Larrabee) Fickett.

Mrs. Chapman, writer of the will and witness to the signature, was Lydia (Starbird) Chapman, many years a school teacher at Stroudwater, who was born Nov. 20, 1768, the year the Starbird House was built, now standing on a very pleasant location a short distance from the place where Mrs. Porterfield spent the early part of her married life.

By the side of the stone in the old Stroudwater cemetery reared to the memory of William Porterfield stands one inscribed as follows:

Elizabeth,
wife of William
Porterfield,
died Oct. 12, 1844,
Æ98.

L. B. C.

Aug 1894

GRANDPA'S SCRAP BOOK

The Hamlet of Woodfords.

In my last a cipher was left off the amount represented as paid by Christopher S. Kimball to Thomas Morse for the Jacob Adams farm in 1810. It should be $2000 instead of $200 as it appeared, and then Morse died March 30, 1811. (Rev. Caleb Bradley's journal.)

THE WOODFORD BROTHERS.

Chauncey Woodford appears on record in Falmouth, Nov. 23, 1799, at which time he married Lucy, daughter of Cop. Isaac Sawyer Stevens, the first Stevens who lived on Stevens' Plains, but not the first of the name in Falmouth. He settled at Morrill's Corner. Notice of him hereafter.

JOSIAH WOODFORD.

He was a younger brother, born Aug. 19, 1779, married Peggy Sawyer, Jan. 13, 1803, daughter of Isaac (collector) Sawyer; she was born August 25, 1783. He died July 12, 1819; she died Sept. 24, 1858.

CHILDREN.

1—William, born in Falmouth, July 21, 1805, married Nancy W., daughter of Benjamin and Charlotte (Webb) Stevens, April 26, 1827; she was born Jan. 7, 1807- He is still alive and occupies the ancient homestead of his wife's father at Woodfords.

2—Jane, born in Falmouth, May 14, 1807, married Nov. 17, 1844, John Read, who occupied and owned the old Samuel Sawyer house and farm many years, a prominent citizen, and died at Woodfords, Aug. 6, 1889.

Mr. Read was son of Noah Read, of Windham, where he was born a Quaker, Aug. 10, 1793, where he kept a public house many years. He married, Jan. 29, 1818, Nancy Horton, by whom he had four children; 2nd, Eunice Hodsdon, by whom he had two children. His last wife died without issue, Aug. 25, 1882. He has children residing at Woodfords.

3—Thomas D., born in Falmouth, July 15, 1809, married April 16, 1835, Frances W. Bradley of Saco, and died in Franklin, N. H., where they resided.

4—Margaret, born in Westbrook, May 27, 1811, married Edward Chenery, who was a wheelwright at that time, lived many years at Bradley's Corner, where she died, leaving two children, William, now the treasurer in the Portland P. O., where he has been many years. Mr. Chenery died in Portland where he last lived with a second wife.

5—Darius, born Sept. 18, 1813, died at the age of one year and three months.

6—Eliza, born Oct. 13, 1815, married Jan. 15, 1845, Dea. William Jordon, born in Casco. She died. Her monument in the Pine Grove cemetery says: Eliza W... wife of William Jordan, died March 26, 1851, aged 35 years. He died last winter, leaving a widow and a son, who is pastor of All Souls' Church, Morrill's Corner.

7—Darius, born Dec. 27, 1814, died young.

8—Harriet B., the last child, became the wife of John Read, son of John Read, who married Harriet's sister Jane.

DEA. EBENEZER D. WOODFORD.

He was the youngest of the three brothers, born at Farmington, Hartford Co., Ct., June 28, 1788. On his way here he met a young woman on the stage coach then but 15 years of age, named Mary Frances, born at Sterling, Worcester Co., Mass., June 28, 1788, one of five sisters, nieces of "Aunt Brisco" who resided on Stevens' Plains where the Goss house stood, recently burned, and she became his wife. They were married January 16, 1805. He died April 5, 1849; she died October 12, 1871. Her gravestone says she was born December 20, 1789, but an old record has it as I have recorded it above.

CHILDREN.

1—Philip Rose, born September 30, 1806, married and resided in Massachusetts.

2—Mary, born September 3, 1808, died the 8th day of same month.

3—Edward, born August 10, 1810. A college graduate, studied for the ministry but "never had charge of a society." He is alive.

4—Harriet Frances, born April 3, 1813, died July 28, 1813.

5—Oren, born August 8, 1814, married Mary Ann Merrill, resided in Chicago, Ill., where he died.

6—Mary Ann, born December 25, 1816, died February 26, 1817.

7—Charles D. born June 13, died September 13, 1818.

8—Mary E. born July 16, 1820, married John J. Chenery, brother to Edward Chenery who married a daughter of Isaiah Woodford. Their father was drowned at Stroudwater one very dark and stormy night. John J. was born September 16, 1816, at Bradley's Corner, where Daniel Chenery now resides. He left a widow still alive and several children.

9—Ebenezer D., born August 2, 1828, died young.

10—Julia Harris, born May 26, 1836, married A. J. Mosier and resides in Boston. She retains the homestead of her father while the widow of John Chenery retains the homestead of Isaiah Woodford.

THE DEERING NEWS

Saturday, July 20, 1895.

GRANDPA'S SCRAP BOOK

[Under this head historical and genealogical memoranda will be furnished the readers of the News that appears worthy of preservation, particularly of remote periods in our history within the city limits and immediate vicinity.]

PINE GROVE CEMETERY.

The records of the clerk of Pine Grove Cemetery Association are all contained in what was once a blank book, 7x8 inches square and ¾ inch thick. It was opened to the purpose for which it was used Oct. 12, 1841, closed Feb. 12, 1894, a period of over half a century.

Walter B. Goodrich filled the place till his death, a period of 27 years; then Frank G. Stevens held the position 16 years, who was followed by Walter F. Goodrich one year (1885); then came William Jordan who served till 1893, making in the meantime but five pages of records.

The commencement is as follows:

To George Bishop, Esquire, one of the Justices of the Peace, within and for the County of Cumberland:

We, the subscribers, inhabitants of the town of Westbrook, feeling desirous of incorporating ourselves as a body politic for the purpose of purchasing land and suitably preparing the same for a burying ground, do hereby request you to issue a warrant for the calling of a meeting of said subscribers to be holden at the Seminary in said Westbrook, on the eighteenth day of October next, at two o'clock in the afternoon, to act on the following articles, to wit:

1st. To choose a moderator.
2nd. To choose a clerk.
3rd. To choose a collector and treasurer.
4th. To raise money for the purpose of purchasing a lot of land, and suitably fencing the same and preparing it for a burying ground.
5th. To act on any other matter that may be deemed legal and proper relating to said burying ground.

Westbrook, Me. Sept. 27, 1841.

S. B. Stevens,   Levi Morrill,
Freeman Porter,   (Rev.) Zenas Thompson,
Oliver Buckley,   Gerry Cook,
Walter B. Goodrich, Samuel Jordan,
C. S. Buckley,   Simeon Hersey,
Elisha Higgins,   E. D. Woodford,
Alfred Stevens,   John Read,
Rufus Dunham,   A. G. Fobes,
Rufus Morrill,   Jeremiah Butler,
Nathan L. Woodbury. Joseph Cox,
             John R. True.

WESTBROOK SEMINARY, Oct. 18, 1841. Agreeable to above warrant and notification the proprietors met, when the meeting was called to order by S. B. Stevens, who, having read the warrant and notice, proceeded to ballot for and choose

S. B. Stevens—Moderator.
A. G. Fobes—Clerk.
Walter B. Goodrich—Collector and Treasurer.

The clerk was then sworn by the moderator.

VOTED—To adjourn to meet at this place at 4 o'clock this afternoon.

At the adjourned meeting it was voted to raise $250 and assess the amount upon the several members of the coporation in equal proportions to defray the expenses of purchasing land, building fences and other necessary attendant expenses.

VOTED—That this association assume the name of

PINE GROVE CEMETERY.

VOTED—That we empower W. B. Goodrich, the collector and treasurer, to confer with and purchase of Oliver Buckley a lot of land laying in the rear of and adjoining the westerly side of the land belonging to the Westbrook Seminary, and receive a deed thereof in behalf of the proprietors of the Pine Grove Cemetery.

VOTED:—That Oliver Buckley, Samuel Jordan, Levi Morrill, Alfred Stevens and Jeremiah Beale be a committee to contract for and cause to be constructed a suitable fence around the contemplated land now to be purchased.

VOTED—That S. B. Stevens, (Rev.) Zenas Thompson and Samuel Jordan be a committee to arrange, lay out and lot off the above named land when purchased,

Upon a fly leaf in the clerk's book is written as follows: "Deed of land purchased for cemetery recorded in Cumberland Registry, Book 177, page 134. Consideration $100." Then appears the following:

DESCRIPTION.

Beginning at a post in the northerly corner of the Seminary lot, thence north, 68 degrees west, 22 rods to a stake; thence south, 26 degrees 30 minutes west 21 rods to a stake; thence south, 63 degrees and 30 minutes east, 22 rods to a post; thence north 26 degrees 30 minutes east, 23 rods to first bounds mentioned, containing three acres and four square rods.

May 21, at 4 o'clock p. m., 1842, a meeting of the proprietors of the cemetery company was holden at the Seminary when it was

VOTED—That the plan reported by the committee chosen "to arrange, lay out and lot off" the Pine Grove Cemetery lot be accepted and the land layed out agreeable thereto.

VOTED—That each and every proprietor meet at the Pine Grove Cemetery on Saturday the 28th instant, (May 28, 1842) at 8 o'clock in the morning, and to labor all day, or be assessed the sum of $1 as an equivalent therefor, and that these meetings be continued each succeeding Saturday under the superintendance of one of the proprietors whose duty it shall be to be faithful in attendance, or to employ some other person, out of the proprietors, to take his place as the same, until a sum not exceeding $100 equally and severally assessed shall be expended.

May 28, 1842, 5 o'clock P. M.

VOTED—That we authorize W. B. Goodrich to contract for sixty-four granite posts 24 inches long, 6 inches square, the top flat and severally numbered on top with black paint.

WESTBROOK SEMINARY, June 12, 1842. 5 o'clock P. M.

VOTED—To raise a committee of three to draft a code of by-laws for the government and better regulation of this association to be presented for their consideration at the next meeting, and Nathan L. Woodbury, Walter B. Goodrich and John Read were chosen said committee.

VOTED—That the committee whose duty was to "arrange, layout and lot off the cemetery lot" be requested to number the several lots upon the plan.

VOTED—To make a disposition of the lots to the several proprietors at the next meeting of the same.

June 25, 1 o'clock P. M.

VOTED—To accept the report of the committee to whom was assigned the duty of numbering the plan, and that the plan as numbered by the committee be placed upon file and a draft of same be drawn on the clerk's book of records of the association.

VOTED—That the choice of one lot to each proprietor be sold forthwith to the highest bidder, and that the chairman, Mr. Gerry Cook, be the auctioneer.

Following is a transcript of the record:

First choice to N. L. Woodbury, $1.50 for No. 17; 2, Levi Morrell, $2.50, 16; 3d Jeremiah Beedle, $2.50, 49; 4, Gerry Cook, $2.00, 24; 5, Samuel Jordan, $1.50, 9; 6, Freeman Porter, $1.00, 10; 7, Chas. S. Buckley, $1.00, 7; 8, John Read, .75, 8; 9, W. B. Goodrich, .50, 47; 10, Rufus Morrill, .50, 23; 11, E. D. Woodford, .50, 62; 12, John K. True, .25, 31; 13, Simeon Hersey, .25, 22; 14, Elisha Higgins, .25, 57; 15, Rufus Durham, .25, 59; 16, (Rev.) Zenos Thompson, .25, 29; 17, Alfred Stevens, .13, 41; 18, Joseph Cox, .6, 2; 19, S. B. Stevens, .14, 50; 20, A. G. Fobes, .14, 48. Total, $15.97.

VOTED—That any one of the proprietors may exchange his for any one of the unsold lots within one week from this day, by giving notice thereof to the secretary of the number he may have selected.

VOTED—That Messrs. Levi Morrell, Dunham and True be a committee to nominate a president, vice-president and five others that shall constitue a board of directors and also a secretary.

The committee reported as follows:
President—Nathan S. Woodbury.
Vice President—John Read.
   Samuel B. Stevens,
   Samuel Jordan,
   Rufus Morrell,   } Directors.
   John K. True,
   Walter B. Goodrich,
A. G. Fobes, Secretary.

VOTED—To reconsider the vote whereby No. 13 was appropriated for a stranger's lot and substitute No. 30.

VOTED—To see the surplus wood cut from the cemetery lot, forthwith which was auctioned off to Chas. S. Buckley for $5.

VOTED—To adjourn.

Copy of Original Plan Numbered by Committee.

21 Rods.

22 Rods								Main Avenue—1 1-2 Rods Wide.							
61. Henry Stevens	60. John Dunham	59. George Libby	58. Rufus Dunham	57. T. J. Riggs	56. H. Francis	55. Jeremiah Bedell			45. Daniel Davis	44. Adams	43. Wm. Eldridge	38. Alfred Dyer	37. Wm. Jordan	34. Albion Libby	33. J. F. Moses
62. Daniel Choat				54.					52. David Thompson						
63. O. & E. Sawyer			53. E. D. Woodford			50. Saml. B. Stevens	47. Walter B. Goodrich		51. Chandler Rackliff	40. Wm. H. Hanson	42. B. Larrabee	39. Fred'k Sawyer			
64. Amos Greenleaf					Eliana Higgins	59. Jeremiah Bedell	48. A. G. Fobes			41. Alfred Stevens		40. John Newman			
	60. John Boyd	9. Saml. Jordan	8. C. S. Buckley	10. Freeman Porter	11. Jeremiah H. Kemp	15. Almon Leach	14. Edward Newman		16.	17. N. L. Woodbury	25. Wm. H. Small	26. Dr. Henry Hunt	27. Hiram Howard	28. Levi Q. Pierce	29. J. A. Thompson
Gate.									Levi Morrill						
	No. 1. Robert Allen				12. S. J. Jordan	13. George Wilson	18. Henney & Haffock				24. Gerry Cook	23. Rufus Morrill	22. Simeon Hersey	21. Jonathan Sargent & Hubbard	20. Jonathan Smith
	J. Cox 2.	3. Wm. Stevens	6. Albert Bennett	5.	H. H. Dow		19. F. Hall								
	Wm. S Cammon			W. J. Thorn											

65. John Larrabee	82. Mrs. Boody
66. Henry Blake	81. John R. True
67. Chase	80. A. P. Sweetair
68. Aaron Winslow	
69. John Swett	
70. S. Libby	
71. Jonas Dyer	
72. John Chase	
73. Joshua Lunt	
74. B. W. Ballard	
75. Daniel Anderson	
76. Johnson & Lobdell	
77. Jason Wilson	
78. Mrs. Gurney	
Tomb	
79. Strangers	

Seminary Grounds.

THE DEERING NEWS.

Saturday, July 27, 1895.

GRANDPA'S SCRAP BOOK

[Under this head historical and genealogical memoranda will be furnished the readers of the News that appears worthy of preservation, particularly of remote periods in our history within the city limits and immediate vicinity.]

BY-LWS OF THE PINE GROVE CEMETERY, ADAPTED 1842.

ARTICLE 1.—The annual meeting of the association shall be holden at the Seminary in Westbrook on the last Saturday in June annually.

ARTICLE 2.—The officers of the association shall consist of a president, vice-president, treasurer and secretary, who shall be chosen at the annual meeting and shall hold their offices for one year, or until others shall be chosen in their places, the chairman of the board of directors shall be the treasurer.

ARTICLE 3.—The president shall preside at all meetings of the association, and in his absence the vice president shall preside. The secretary shall call all meetings of the association by giving personal notice, or leaving written notice at their usual places of abode of each of the proprietors and shall keep a record of all doings of the association.

ARTICLE 4.—The directors shall have the general supervision and control of the affairs of the association.

ARTICLE 5.—In case of death or resignation of any of the officers the directors shall have a right to fill vacancies and the officer or officers elected by them shall hold their offices until the next annual meeting.

ARTICLE 6.—No person shall have a right to cut any tree or trees, standing upon his lot until he shall have obtained permission of the directors so to do.

ARTICLE 7—Any proprietor wishing to make improvements on his lot shall first obtain permission from the board of directors which shall be in writing stating what improvements are to be made, and said permit shall be signed by the president and secretary.

ARTICLE 8.—No proprietor shall be permitted to use his lot for any other purpose except to bury his deceased relatives or friends or to ornament and improve it as he may be permitted by the board of directors.

ARTICLE 9—The directors shall have full power and authority to sell and convey by deed in their own name, for and in behalf of the proprietors, any lot or lots, which may at any time remain unsold, in said Pine Grove Cemetery, to such persons as they may deem proper, but if said directors shall disagree as to the propriety of selling to any applicant, they shall lay the application of such person before the proprietors at their annual meeting next for action and then proceed as said proprietors shall direct.

ARTICLE 10.—No person shall be entitled to a deed or to occupy or improve any lot in said Pine Grove Cemetery until he shall have paid for the same.

ARTICLE 11.—The treasurer shall keep a full account of all monies received by him and the manner in which it shall have been expended, and at the annual meeting shall lay before the proprietors a true account of the same, and he shall be responsible to said proprietors for all monies received, and shall pay over to his successor in office all monies which shall remain in his hands.

ARTICLE 12.—It shall be the duty of the directors to commence and prosecute to a final decision in law every person who shall injure, destroy or disfigure any of the property of said Pine Grove Cemetery.

ARTICLE 13.—It shall be be the duty of the secretary to call a special meeting of the proprietors of said Pine Grove Cemetery at the written request of any five of said proprietors, setting forth the purpose of said meeting and the time of holding the same.

ARTICLE 14.—The foregoing articles may be altered or amended at any annual meeting of the proprietors by a majority of the original proprietors of said Pine Grove Cemetery or their heirs or assigns.

VOTED—To accept and adopt the foregoing as the standing by-laws of the Pine Grove Cemetery.

At the same meeting at which the by-laws were adopted it was

VOTED—That a committee of three be appointed to select one lot to be appropriated for the burial of strangers, also one lot for ministers of all denominations.

VOTED—That Samuel Jordan, S. B. Stevens and Rufus Morrill be a committee, who, having attended to their duty, reported that they had selected lot No. 21 for strangers and No. 28 for ministers.

VOTED—That the same committee select a lot to be appropriated to Westbrook Seminary and lot No. 13 was selected and dedicated.

VOTED—That the vote whereby lot No. 21 was appropriated for a strangers' lot be reconsidered and lot No. 30 be substituted.

VOTED—To sell the surplus wood cut on the cemetery lot be sold forthwith at auction, which was struck off to Charle. Buckley for $5.

Nothing appears on the record worthy of note till 1843 when it was

VOTED—That the original proprietors be severally a committee to dispose of one lot each for the sum of $12.

From 1843 till 1848 there are no entries in the secretary's book, when it was

VOTED—That Saml. B. Stevens, Freeman Porter and Rufus Dunham be authorized to spend $100 for painting fence, setting trees, etc.

In 1850 an attempt was made to change article 9 of the by-laws but the attempt failed. At that time there was $41.49 in the treasury.

In 1851 there was $55.49 in the treasury, and there was due the association $64.

VOTED—That lots No. 28 and 13 appropriated for the seminary and ministers be sold, they not having been occupied.

VOTED—That George Libby, Samuel Jordan and Benj. W. Ballard be a committee to build a receiving tomb.

VOTED—To spend $25 for the purpose of the tomb and procurement of a hearse house if necessary after the subscription is expended.

VOTED—That Oliver Buckley, the owner of land on the western side of the cemetery be permitted to bring into the cemetery as much land on that side of the cemetery as he pleases as the directors of the cemetery may agree to.

In 1851 officers were elected as follows:

Alfred Stevens—Pres.
Walter B. Goodrich—Sec.
William Eldridge—Vice Pres.
Alfred Stevens,
Samuel Jordan,
F. Porter, } Directors.
George Libby,
John Reed,

There was then in the treasury $106.68. Eight votes were passed that were recorded, some of which I here present.

That Geo. Libby be paid for building the tomb and hearse house.

That Messrs Reed and Libby be a committee to remove the fence and place it out on the line between the cemetery and William Kenney's and make what new fence is necessary.

That the request of the sewing circle in relation to furnishing dressing for setting trees and shrubs on the main avenue be referred to the directors.

That the directors be authorized to lay out the land which is to be enclosed by the removal of the fence to Kenney's line as they see fit, and affix such prices on the lots as they may think proper. (The small lots on the side of the plane here annexed show the comparative size of the addition.)

That the vote whereby lot No. 21 was appropriated for a stranger's lot be reconsidered and the same, offered for sale.

That the bodies deposited on lot No. 21 be removed to lot No. 70.

That Messrs. George Libby and Freeman Porter be a committee to procure a hearse.

That the owners of lots be allowed to place stones as they see fit.

In 1853, there was $76.96 in the treasury and there was $108 due for lots sold; and it was voted to loan what money was not in use.

In 1854, a hearse was purchased of Mr. John Sawyer and $150 paid for the same.

At this meeting a movement was made to procure the right of way through Evergreen Cemetery owned by Portland to Pine Grove Cemetery, "provided we take away our fence and give them privilege to draw water from our well."

In 1855, it was voted to purchase two shares in the Atlantic & St. Lawrence R. R. Co. at $80 each. The next year there was a balance of $129.81 in the treasury.

In 1857, permission was granted by a vote of the Portland city government to allow the Pine Grove Cemetery Association to pass through Evergreen Cemetery, and a unanimous vote was passed to remove the fence between the two lots.

The old fence was sold to the highest bidder who was E. H. Forbes at 25 cents per rod, "there being 43 rod." $155.03 in the treasury.

THE DEERING NEWS.

Saturday, Aug. 3, 1895.

GRANDPA'S SCRAP BOOK

[Under this head historical and genealogical memoranda will be furnished the readers of the News that appear worthy of preservation, particularly of remote periods in our history within the city limits and immediate vicinity.]

RECORDS OF PINE GROVE CEMETERY.

When and by whom the well was constructed the clerk's records do not show, but at the meeting of the association holden July 9, 1883, it was voted "to accept Mr. Geyer's offer of $200 for the 'Well lot,'"—the well, I presume, having been filled.

In 1858 Elisha Higgins was chosen president who held the place till 1865, when Freeman Porter was chosen his successor.

In 1859 there was $208.02 in the treasury, and in 1860 there was $215.68 when it was voted to collect the Town order, also the interest on all other demands and deposit the amount in the Portland Savings Bank.

VOTED—That any one who may be allowed to take the hearse, besides the sexton, shall return the same in as good condition as when taken.

VOTED—That E. B. Forbes be allowed the privilege to make a carriage gateway in the fence on the northerly side of the cemetery and against the second carriage avenue from the Seminary grounds.

In 1861 there was $211.05 in the hands of the treasurer, "not including all the back interest."

In 1862 there was $229.04 in the treasury, deposited in the Savings Bank.

VOTED—That the treasurer be authorized to pay to the Ladies' Sewing Circle the amount they paid to John R. Sawyer from their funds for hearse runners.

The amount paid for taking care of the grounds was $5 annually—this was for walks—not lots.

In 1863 cash in Savings bank $229.35; cash on hand $82; note $10.59.

The sexton reported he had received $2 for use of hearse, and E. B. Forbes was continued in the office on an annual salary of $5 which included care of the grounds.

In 1864 the question of taking into the enclosure a piece of Mr. Forbes' was brought up, and Walter B. Goodrich, Geo. Libby and Wm. Eldridge were appointed a committee to confer with him, and Aug. 13, 1864 the committee reported, which report was accompanied with a plan, and the motion of Mr. Geo. Libby to accept Mr. Forbes' proposition, on motion of Hon. Samuel Jordan, was laid on the table, and a committee was chosen to ascertain what Mr. Forbes would take for his land, "with right of way from Plains road to cemetery." The committee consisted of Sam'l Jordan, Chandler Rackleff and N. K. Sawyer. This committee reported that Mr. Forbes would sell the whole lot for $1100, or the 60 lots at $20 each, and wait for his pay till the lots were sold. The meeting thought the price too high.

Total amount of cash in treasury $270.05.

VOTED—That the gate opened to the cemetery by Mr. Forbes be permanently closed till otherwise ordered by the proprietors.

1866, Whole number of burials during the year, 4. Albert Jones was sexton.

IN 1867 VOTED—That an assessment of fifty cents be put upon each lot owner for the purpose of clearing up the grounds to be collected by Albert Jones. $318.28 in the treasury.

IN 1869, VOTED:—To inquire into the expediency of building a new receiving tomb, but when it was ascertained $1,500 would be required the matter was dropped.

IN 1872, VOTED.—That Samuel Jordan, N. K. Sawyer and Granville M. Stevens be a committee to confer with E. B. Forbes with the view of uniting the two yards and obtaining a permanent passageway through his property.

VOTED.—To close the Seminary entrance, and to sell the lot used for an entrance from the Seminary grounds.

VOTED.—That lot No. 55, now standing in the name of Miss Harriet R. Francis be changed to A. S. Alden at request of H. R. Francis.

In 1872, one Gavit made a plan for a receiving tomb to cost $1,500 and a committee was chosen to solicit subscriptions, but nothing came of the movement.

In 1874, a committee consisting of Francis Purrington, Alfred Stevens and E. B. Sawyer was chosen to confer with E. B. Forbes with regard to removing division fence between the two lots.

VOTED.—To close all gates and passageways in connection with the Seminary grounds.

From this time forward, a period of six years no officers were chosen, a quorum not being present at meetings, until July 17, 1880, the following named persons were chosen:

Pres.—E. B. Forbes.
Vice Pres.—George Mead Stevens.
Sec.—Frank G. Stevens.
Treas.—Alfred Stevens.
Directors.—Rufus Dunham, Rufus Morrill, Alfred Stevens, Walter F. Goodrich, Granville M. Stevens.

In 1883, there was $390 in the treasury, and in 1885 $432.67.

In 1886, the second article in the call for the annual meeting reads:

To hear the report of the secretary as to deeding the said cemetery to the city of Portland to become a part of Evergreen Cemetery, but no quorum was present. The treasurer reported $718.18 in the treasury

In 188 there was no attendance of members at the annual meeting.

In 1888, no attendance, $1,367.48 in treasury.

Deering, Me., Feb. 12, 1894.

At the meeting of the surviving officers of the Pine Grove Cemetery Association held this day at he residence of Granville M. Stevens for the purpose of filling vacancies in the Board of officers occasioned by death, there being present Messrs. Walter F. Goodrich, George Mead Stevens, and Rufus Morrill the following named persons were unanimously elected.

Pres.—James N. Read in place of Rufus Dunham, dec'd.

Sec.—Frederick Dunham in place of William Jordan, dec'd.

Director—Joseph S. Dunham in place of Rufus Dunham, dec'd.

Chairman—Walter F. Goodrich.

And here the old book of records was closed it being full.

On a fly leaf in the back of the book is a record which I here present in full.

"1861—List of names of proprietors in Pine Grove Cemetery."

No. of Lot.		No. of Lot.	
1	Robert Allen & Hunt	40	John Newman
2	E. Cox	41	Alfred Stevens
3	Wm. and Geo. M. Stevens	42	Oliver Buckley
		43	B. Larabee
4	Wm. Scammon	44	Adams
5	Wm. Thorn & James Johnson	45	D. Davis
		46	W. Hanson
6	Albert Bennett	47	Walter B. Goodrich
7	Charles Buckley	48	Albert Forbes
8	John Read	49	J. Bedell
9	Samuel Jordan	50	Sarah B. Stevens
10	Freeman Porter	51	Chandler Rackleff
11	J. Kemp & A. Jones	52	David Thompson
12	S. Jordan and Hiram Dow	53	Geo. Libby
		54	Thos. J. Riggs
13	Geo. Wilson and ——	55	Isabell Alden
14	Edward Newman	56	J. Bedell
15	Almon Leach	57	Elisha Higgins
16	Levi Morrill	58	Mrs. Woodford
17	N. L. Woodbury	59	Rufus Dunham
18	Hancock and Henry	60	John Dunham
19	E. B. Fobes	61	Hood and Stevens
20	Jonathan Smith	62	Daniel Choat
21	J. Sargent	63	Charles and Eben Sawyer
22	Hersey and Saunders		
23	Rufus Morrill	64	Amos Greenleaf and John Homes
24	Gerry Cook and W. Polleys		
		65	John Larabee
25	W. Small	66	Henry Blake
26	Dr. Henry Hunt	67	Capt. Chase & Mrs. Larabee
27	Hiram Howard		
28	Capt. T. Scal	68	Aaron Winslow
29	J. A. Thompson	69	J. Swett
30	A. Sweetser	70	Lothrop Libby
31	N. K. Sawyer	71	James Dyer
32	Mrs. Boody	72	John Chase
33	J. F. Moses	73	Joshua Lunt
34	Stevens and Pierce	74	B. W. Ballard
35	Wm. Jordan	75	Daniel Anderson
36	Leonard O. Raynolds	76	Johnson and Lobdell
37	Wm. Eldridge and Walker	77	Jason Wilson
		78	Mis. Gurney
38	A. Dyer and Kimball	79	Strangers
39	Frederick Sawyer		

This closes our notes on Pine Grove Cemetery.

THE DEERING NEWS

Saturday, Aug. 10, 1895.

GRANDPA'S SCRAP BOOK

[Under this head historical and genealogical memoranda will be furnished the readers of the News that appears worthy of preservation, particularly of remote periods in our history within the city limits and immediate vicinity.]

THE FIRST PARISH OF DEERING.

As it is known by those who have informed themselves, the present towns and cities, namely: Falmouth, Cape Elizabeth, South Portland, cities of Portland, Westbrook and Deering were at one time one parish with the meeting house in what is now Portland, with Rev. Thomas Smith as pastor, who lived on Congress, opposite India street. Cape Elizabeth was first made into a separate parish, then what is now Falmouth and called the third parish, then the fourth or Stroudwater parish was created and comprised territorially what is now known as Westbrook and Deering.

Some months ago a chest was discovered in an unused room of the First Parish stone church edifice containing valuable papers among which were several that let in light upon the Stroudwater, or fourth parish as it was called, which was incorporated, or the church connected therewith was organized, April 8, 1765.

July 1757
To the Inhabitants of the 1st Parish in Falmouth
The Petition of the Inhabitants of Stroudwater Capisick Sacarapy and Stroudwater falls in said Parish Humbly Sheweth

That haveing for many Years past laboured under great Difficultys in attending the publick Worship of God, and being willing and desirous of having a Gospell Minister Setled amongst our Selves, humbly pray we may be set off as a Seperate Parish and that the dividing Lines may be between the Parishes as follows viz: begining at the little Bridge at the Narrow of the Neck, (Union Station, Congress street. ED. NEWS) thence running North 26 degrees West to Presumpscut River, thence Northwest to the head line of Falmouth Courses to the Second Parish line in Said Town and to Joyn to the Sd Second Parish as the line is now Run and . . . .
Your Petitioners as in Duty bound Shall Ever Pray
Falmouth ye 16th of July 1757

Geo Tate	Sam Waldo junr
David Patrick	
his	
Richd Nason	
mark	Joanna Frost
Zebulun Trickey	John Johnson
Samuel Conant	James Johnson
James Frost	Robert Johnson
Charles Gerrish	Jeremiah Riggs
David Small	Joseph Riggs
Nathaiel Knight	Edwd Chapman
Solomon Haskell	Thomas Pennell
John Wilson	Chipman Cobb
Nichs Smith	Anthony Bracket jur
Edward Gilman	Thomas Haskell
Nathan Starbird	Benjamin Godfrey
Aaron Goole	Benjamin Haskell
James Johnson Jur	
John Johnson Jur	

March 1764
To the Freeholders and other Inhabitants of the first Parish in Falmouth assembled at their Annual Meeting in March 1764.
The petition of a number of the Freeholders and Others of the said Parish humbly sheweth

That they live at a great Distance from the place of publick Worship there, and have by means thereof with great Difficulty for many years past attended the same, and being as they imagine able to build a Meeting House & support a Minister among themselves; Humbly request said Parish to set them off by the Name of the fourth Parish in in Falmouth, and that the dividing Lines may be as follows, vizt to begin at Martins Point and thence to run Southerly adjoining Presumpscut River to back Cove, thence to continue round Back Cove to Land late belonging to William Pote* deceas'd, thence Northwesterly adjoining said Land to the Head thereof and thence Southerly on the Head of said Land & Isaac Skillin's and thence Southerly to the fore River so as to include John Thomas's Land, thence over said River to intersect the Line of the Second Parish in said Town, on the westerly Bank of said River thence Westerly adjoining the Line of said Second Parish to the Head thereof, and that all the Lands (and Inhabitants that are so inclined) between the Lines herein before mentioned, and the Line of the the third Parish in Falmouth & Head of the Township, be set off and remain for a fourth Parish in said Town, and your Petitioners as in Duty bound will ever pray.

Edward Gilman	James Babb
John wilson	John Starbird
Jeremiah Hobs	David Small
John Crockit	Geo Tate
Joseph Small	James Johnston
William Webb	John Johnson
Wm Lamb	Joseph Riggs
James Therell	John Warren
Daniel Small	Thomas Haskell
Nathaniel (?)	Solomon Haskell
Samuel Cole	Benja Haskell
Samuel Conant	John Haskell
Richard Nason	John Sanborn
Isaac Nason	Peter Babb

(This petition is in the handwriting of Geo. Tate.)

*(Woodford and Spring streets form the northerly boundary line of the Wm. Pote farm which extended westerly somewhat beyond Grant street and southerly to Coyle's gully, and southerly of this came the Skillings farm, the dwelling of which stood by the side of Deering street where the cellar hole and well may now be seen. John Thomes house stood immediately westerly of the George Libby brick residence at Libby's Corner.)

TO BE CONTINUED.

THE DEERING NEWS

Saturday, Aug. 17, 1895.

GRANDPA'S SCRAP BOOK

[Under this head historical and genealogical memoranda will be furnished the readers of the News that appears worthy of preservation, particularly of remote periods in our history within the city limits and immediate vicinity.]

CONTINUED FROM LAST WEEK.

(List of Names given in March 17th 1765, by Jos. Riggs vizt Henry Knight & others 43 in all to be of ye 4th Parish, Recordd in ye Parish Records Page 83 pr Stepn Longfellow Parh Clerk. Jos. Riggs gave them into the Clerke 27th March 1765. Just before ye opening the Parish Meeting.)

falmouth (August) ye 17: 1764 wee whose Names are under written (with our) Estates Living Eastward of the Line of (the) fourth parrish which was sett of as a (fourth) parrish by the first parrish Last march do Now (Return) our Names & Estates to Joyn to the fourth (parrish) in building a meeting house at ye north side of Sacarapey Road (Join) ye County Road* & Seetle a gospell (mi)nister with them Therefore desеir Mr Steven (Longfe)llor the first parrish Clark to Record the above Sd and Likewise our Names under written in the first parrish Book as it was Voted by the first parrish Last march

Henry Knight	Joseph Conant Jur
Hugh Barlow	John Webb
Andrew Gibbs	Joshua Brackett Juner
George Houstoun	Thos Brackett
James Bryant	Mark Knight
Moses Knight	Henery Knight Jun
Paul Huston	Nathan Merrill
Nathaniel Wilson	William Gibbs
James Merrill	William Procter
Joseph Conant	John Procter
John Barber Juner	
Richard Knight	
Joshua Knight	James Douty
Isaac Hardy	
Bartho Conant	
Nchles Tomson	Josiah Baker
Isaac Skilling	John Jenks
Lemuel Hicks	John Bayley Junr
Anthony Mors	John Barber
Zechariah Brackett	Samuel Knight
thomas Douty	Joseph Pride
Joseph Hall	William Pride
Joshua Swett	George Walker
Stephen Swett	

(The parts in parentheses above were torn from the original and supplied by the Parish Record Book. The text is in the handwriting of Henry Knight.)

*The site selected for the meeting house is the site of the present so-called Bradley meeting house located on Church street. After the fourth parish was set off the location of the dividing line with the first became a matter of dispute with the first which was settled by the general court of the commonwealth.

Long Island.

Sunday night's meeting was largely attended. Rev. William Knight McGowan of New York city gave a very fine address to the young pupils. The Christian Endeavor is progressing and the meeting Sunday night was led by Miss Philena Griffin.

Last Thursday the annual anniversary of the Ladies' Auxiliary was held at their new building near the 1st tenth and 20th. The dedication of the building took place at 10.30 in the morning, opened by prayer from Major Gould of Portland. Col. Shaw, who gave the land to the society for the building, gave a very fine address. Capt. Nye, Dr. Day, Mrs. Ingalls, Mrs. Frost and others also delivered some remarks suitable to the occasion and thoroughly enjoyed. There was also some very fine singing. Fruit punch and cake were served at the Auxiliary all day for the benefit of the Grand Army people and guests. A year ago at the last meeting, it was voted that each lady should earn one dollar, to be given this year with an account of their experiences in earning it. The meeting was a very interesting as well as a laughable one. The amount earned was $46, and was put in the treasury toward paying the debt for the new building. Even the weather put on its best appearance for the benefit of this society and the day will be long remembered by them. The party broke up about 5 o'clock, looking forward to the next reunion to be held next year.

Quite a number of Boston people have been visiting at the island for the past two weeks. Mrs. Mary Restall and baby Harry from Everett are boarding at Mrs. C. A. Clarke's. Miss Laura Restall, Miss Matilda Benson and Messrs. George and Charles Restall from Everett are boarding at Mrs. M. A. Johnson's. Mr. and Mrs. Littlefield and family are at their new cottage. Mr. and Mrs. Gowell of Lewiston are visiting their son, Rev. W. H. Gowell.

Mrs. Ira L. Hall has been visiting her sister, Mrs. Charles Barker, for the past week on House Island.

Mr. William Parker and family and Mr. E. Tobin and family from Malden are stopping at the Mirabile Visu Cottage.

Capt. Anice Wallace has returned from his sword-fishing trip after being gone eight weeks. He got a fair catch.

Capt. Warren B. Woodbury has returned after a trip of two weeks. Caught 22 fish.

THE DEERING NEWS.

Saturday, Aug. 31, 1895.

GRANDPA'S SCRAP BOOK

[Under this head historical and genealogical memoranda will be furnished the readers of the News that appears worthy of preservation, particularly of remote periods in our history within the city limits and immediate vicinity.]

REV. THOMAS BROWNE.

THE FIRST MINISTER OF THE FOURTH, OR STROUDWATER PARISH OF FALMOUTH.

NOTE.—The fourth parish of Falmouth prior to the incorporation of Falmouth Neck, which was set off from Falmouth in 1786 and named Portland, and the Stroudwater parish are synonymous terms. When the Neck was incorporated the fourth parish became the third parish of Falmouth. When Westbrook was set off from Falmouth in 1814 the third parish of Falmouth became the first parish of Westbrook. When Deering was set off from Westbrook in 1871, the first parish of that town became the first parish of Deering but the name of "First Parish of Westbrook" was not changed to that of Deering by an act of the state legislature till last winter. Stroudwater is the name of a village located first in Falmouth, second in Westbrook, now in Deering though its location is the same today as it ever has been since its record name commenced in 1728.

The state Reform school farm, located at a place called Long Creek within the town of Cape Elizabeth which town was included once within the limits of Falmouth, is some over a mile southerly from Stroudwater village, and originally comprised 400 acres, connected with which is much historical data of an interesting character to those sufficiently old to live in the past. The farm was once the property of Geo. Munjoy and was located almost wholly on the northerly side of the creek and below the falls where the mill stood. In the course of time it came into the possession of Gen. Samuel Waldo and when the General's son, Col. Samuel Waldo, became of age his father "In Consideration of the Natural Love good will and Parental affection which I hath and doth bear for and towards my beloved and dutiful son Samuel Waldo of Falmouth Gent. as also for divers other good causes and Considerations convey the 400 acre farm to him my said son," beginning bounds at the point of Long creek, thence running up Fore river, 200 rods,etc.,etc. The date of the transaction was May 11, 1744. Of the condition of the farm I have no knowledge other than that of conjecture which has been practiced too much already by those too indolent or lazy to hunt for historical truths.

On a tract of land joining Back Cove upon which is located the part of the city of Deering now known as "Woodfords," having for its northerly boundary line the streets called Woodford and Spring, extending westerly a little beyond Grant street and southerly as far as Coyl's gully estimated at 57¼ acres, located one William Pote who was admitted a citizen of Falmouth in 1728. He built his dwelling, a two story house that stood end to the road, barn on opposite side of the highway, where Dr. Albion Topleff's house now stands on Deering street. He and his wife had eight sons and one daughter, not seven as Willis claims; but more of this Pote family hereafter.

On the second day of Sept., 1765, Rev. Thomas Browne purchased this Pote farm paying "£400 lawful money," and the natural inference is that he occupied the premises, yet in 1771, I find him in Cape Elizabeth and occupying what is now the state Reform school farm, for a petition on file in the Massachusetts archives addressed to the General Court reads as follows.

We your petitioners, Assessors for the District of Cape Elizabeth, in behalf of said District, Hereby Show—That the Rev. Mr. Thomas Browne, who is minister of the third Parish in Falmouth, hath hired and does live on and improve the most Valuable Farm in said District which farm belonged to the late Col. Samuel Waldo, Esq., of Falmouth Deceased, which Farm Cattle & Co. we have just put down in the foregoing list in page 9. We think it a great damage to and infringement on our Rights A said district that a minister of another town should hire and live on so valuable a farm in this district and pay no taxes for the same, which said Mr. Browne utterly refuses to do, because he is a settled minister in Falmouth. We your Petitioners. Humbly pray your Excellency's and Honor's Directions whether sd. Mr. Browne shall be Taxed for said Farm or not. And Your Petitioners as in Duty Bound shall ever pray.

DAVID STROUT,
THOMAS SIMONTON,
BENJAMIN JORDAN.

Cape Elizabeth, Sep. 23, 1771.

The page referred to shows that he was taxed for two horses, four oxen, eighteen cows, seventy sheep and goats, two hundred acres of pasturage, four acres of tillage, one hundred acres of English and upland mowing, forty acres of fresh meadow, producing fifty-two tons of English and twenty-eight tons of meadow hay. "The annual worth of the farm after deducting necessary repairs is £85.62.

It is traditional that Col. Samuel Waldo used the Reform School farm as his country seat, the dwelling standing upon the site of the present residence of Mr. Charles P. Trickey, Col. Samuel's Portland Neck home being located on Middle street a little easterly of Exchange, who died March 16, 1770, and Parson Smith says in his journal "was buried with great parade under the church, with a sermon, and under arms," he being an active Episcopalian. His remains were afterwards removed to Boston. He was the chief promoter of disagreements in the parish and the promoter of the Stroudwater agitation that culminated in the organization of the Fourth Parish.

From the fact that Col. Samuel Waldo died in 1770, and being a man of wealth, it is natural to presume that Rev. Mr. Browne rented the farm or country seat of Waldo's widow, and purchased the stock of cattle, etc.

In 1802 for a consideration of $7,420 Sarah Tyng Waldo, widow, sold to Zenas Pratt 371 acres of this lot, ninety-eight acres being located on the westerly side of the road passing through it upon which, or part of which, Mr. Chas. P. Trickey now resides, to whom allusion has been made in this article. It is traditional that the Waldo house which tradition also says stood where Mr. Trickey's present dwelling stands was burned. Then the home place of Rev. Mr. Browne in 1771 was upon the site of the present place of abode of Mr. Chas. P. Trickey, opposite the entrance to the Reform School, and one if the finest of the whole region hereabouts; and Mr. Trickey informs me that about twenty rods northerly of his residence stood the house built for Waldo's farm hand's and a 100 feet barn, where he has dug up brick of very thin make, a silver knee buckle and a silver spoon on the premises.

In 1828 Enoch Trickey father to Charles purchased the place containing fifty acres of land "including buildings" for $1050.

Everything else relative to the sojourn of Rev. Mr. Brown on the State Reform school farm other than what is given here is to me shrouded in mystery.

A pen picture of the man found in "The Eastern Herald and Gazette of Maine," published at Falmouth, now Portland, "Saturday, Oct. 21st, 1709," is full of interest, and I here insert a complete transcript.

Died at Falmouth, on Wednesday last Rev. Thomas Brown, aged 63, his funeral will be held from his house this afternoon at three o'clock where his friends and acquaintances are requested to attend without further invitation.

From the same, Monday Oct. 30th, 1797.

On Wednesday the 18th inst. departed this life at Falmouth (now Deering) in the sixty-fourth year of his age, the Rev. Thomas Brown, minister of the Second Congregational church in that town.

He was a son of Harvard University graduated in the year 1752.

Saturday, Aug. 24, 1895.

GRANDPA'S SCRAP BOOK

[Under this head historical and genealogical memoranda will be furnished the readers of the News that appears worthy of preservation, particularly of remote periods in our history within the city l mits and i imediate vicinity.]

REV. THOMAS BROWNE.

THE FIRST MINISTER OF THE FOURTH, OR STROUDWATER PARISH OF FALMOUTH.

In the northeasterly corner of the old Stroudwater village cemetery the oldest stone of which bears the date of 1730, stands a memorial slab of slate stone inscribed as follows:

Here lies interred
the mortal part of
the Revd. THOMAS BROWNE,
who expired in hope of
a glorious immortality,
on the 18th day of October, 1797;
in the 64th Year of his Age.

And they that be wise shall shine
as the brightness of the firmament;
And they that turn many to
righteousness, as the stars forever and ever.

A step westerly is one that was erected to the name of his wife, but having fallen apart in consequence of a flaw in the stone in an attempt four or five years ago to place it in an upright position, the two pieces now lay upon the grave. The inscription is as follows:

SACRED
to the memory of
LYDIA
late wife of the Rev. T. Browne,
WHO
died at Falmo. Oct. 13, 1805:
AGED
LXIX.

"But wisdom is the gray hair to man, &
an unspoted life is old age."

The cemetery lot comprises about an acre of land, extending from the road connecting the village of Stroudwater with the village of Saccarappa, back westerly to the Stroudwater river. The earliest reference made to the place in manuscript records thus far found is in the year 1744, in a mortgage deed, made by the Smalls who occupied the farm next northerly, and now known by the name of Quinby farm, in favor of Gen. Samuel Waldo. A part of the lot is ill adapted to the use for which it was given to the parish in 1787 by one of the heirs of the Waldos, and like other places of its character, many interred there, particularly the early settlers of the place, have no distinguishing marks. The steeple of the old meeting house, a half mile or a little over distant and the third one that marks the site of the original building erected for church purposes where Rev. Thomas Browne expounded divine law is plainly to be seen in an easterly direction from the site of the Browne memorial stones, the point where they are located being some ten feet above the highway from which a charming view of the surrounding country may be seen. Only two names of Browne appear as above represented.

Connected with this name is a long story—a story that carries one back in time as well as forward, from the date when Parson Brown came here, who studies it, but I can only here present the skeleton, or threads of genealogical ramifications, for, to array the name in an historical-biographical manner in more than a plain attire would make a fair sized volume.

Whether or not the names of "Brown" and "Browne" grew out of each other I cannot say from data discovered, nor do I know any thing of the relationship, or whether there is any or not between the two. Everybody knows the commonness of the name "Brown" but the other is uncommon. Where the last originated, or time, I have no knowledge as I have not had an opportunity to search manuscript records at Haverhill.

Thomas Browne married Martha, widow of Richard Oldham, and lived in Cambridge, Mass. His son Ichabod, born Sept. 5, 1666, lived in Cambridge, Mass., also. His son John, born Nov. 1, 1696, at Little Cambridge (Brighton), Mass., graduated at Harvard, 1714. He married Joanna Cotton, daughter of Rev. Roland Cotton of Sandwich, "an eminently worthy and pious lady." She had four brothers who were clergymen.

Rev. John Browne succeeded Rev. Mr. Checkley of the first parish of Haverhill, Mass., and was installed at that place, May 13, 1719, and continued the pastor of the society till his death which occurred Dec. 2, 1742.

His children were:

1 Elizabeth, born Oct 25, 1721.
2 Martha, born ——— 6, 1723, died Oct. 5, 1736.
3 John, born March 9, 1724, graduated Harvard, 1741, preached at Cohasset, Mass.
4 Nathaniel, born Sept. 20, 1725, died Oct. 21, 1736.
5 Cotton, born Jan. 21, 1726, graduated at Harvard, preached at Brookline, died Apr. 13, 1751.
6 Ward, born July 19, 1728, graduated at Harvard 1748 and died same year.
7 Meriel, born July 5, 1730.
8 Abigail, ———, married Rev. Edward Brooks of Medford, Mass., who graduated at Harvard 1755, and was ordained, or installed, at North Yarmouth July 4, 1765, where he remained five years and was then dismissed because he was too liberal minded to suit a

MISSING DATA

turned [...] ansfield where he died March, 1781, aged 48 years. His widow died Nov. 1800, aged 69 years—"a woman of rare excellence." They had four children:

Peter C., born in North Yarmouth 1765, and became a capitalist in Boston, Mass.

Cotton B., born 1767, a merchant in Portland, where he made his first purchase of land in 1802. He resided at the time of his death in the large brick house, southeast corner of Oak and Free streets which his heirs sold to John Bradley in 1835. The late Bishop Brooks of Boston was a descendant but I have not time to place him now. Cotton B. owned the 17 acre field at Stroudwater, recently purchased by the Messrs. Cummings Bros., which bears his name.

One of the daughters married Samuel Gray of Medford; the other Nathaniel Hall of Boston.

9 Thomas, born May 17, 1734, the subject of this article.
10 Samuel, born Sept. 17, 1736; died Nov. 8, 1736.

The three children died with "putred sore throat," now called diphtheria, and Rev. John Browne published a book of considerable size upon the disease.

Within the Eastern cemetery inclosure, not far from the westerly end line, and two-thirds back from Congress street, may be seen a monument composed of two pieces of chiseled granite, six feet long, two feet wide and eighteen inches thick, or thereabouts, one placed upon the other, surmounted by a brown sand stone slab, with a moulded edge, one-half of which is inlaid with a piece of white marble, inscribed as follows:

JOHN CHIPMAN, ESQr
Barrister at Law
Was born October 23d A.D. 1722,
and died July 1 A.D. 1768
of an apoplexy
with which he was suddenly seized
in the Court House
in Falmouth
while he was arguing a cause
before the Superior Court of Judicature
&c
then sitting.
To the rememberance of his great learning
Uniform integrity
and singular humanity and benevolence
this monument is dedicated
by a number of his brethren
at
the Bar.

Saturday, Sept. 7, 1895.

GRANDPA'S SCRAP BOOK

[Under this head historical and genealogical memoranda will be furnished the readers of the News that appears worthy of preservation, particularly of remote periods in our history within the city limits and immediate vicinity.]

REV. THOMAS BROWNE,

THE FIRST MINISTER OF THE FOURTH, OR STROUDWATER PARISH OF FALMOUTH.

The First Parish of Falmouth did not look with favor upon so many divisions of its original territory. The situation may be gleaned from the journals of Rev. Mr. Smith and his assistant, Rev. Mr. Dean, as follows:

"March 28, 1764, Stroudwater again set off. A great struggle to get me, an assistant, and all the principal men for it; but———headed the young men and Stroudwaterer's in the opposition and prevented it."

"July 17. The new meeting house men with the Stroudwater men, made the utmost opposition to Mr. Dean's settlement, but in vain."

Oct. 4. Mr. Browne, late of Mansfield, came here in order to preach at Stroudwater."

"Nov. 25, Sunday. Our Sabbath frolicers now ride to hear Browne, as they used to do to hear Wiswell." This has reference to the New Casco minister (Now Falmouth:)

"March 12, 1765. Col. Waldo brings the news that Stroudwater is made a parish by the court."

"27th. Forty returned their names and were therefore set off to Stroudwater parish."

"The church acted in concert with the Parish and dismissed for the purpose of forming the Stroudwater church, Messrs. John Johnson; Nathaniel Knight; Joseph Riggs; John Bailey; Solomon Haskell; Clement Pennel; Benjamin Haskell; Jeremiah Riggs; Henry Knight; James Merrill; Anthony Morse; and such of their wives as are of our communion." This is the list furnished by Willis in a foot note to Smith's journal, but the church list printed in 1833 present three addition names, namely: James Johnson Joseph Riggs and Thomas Haskell. I will here present the 1833 list with locations and some other fact--ffourteen persons all told.

1.—DEA. JOHN BAILEY, and FIRST CLERK OF THE PARISH.

He had a family of nine children, eight by first wife and one by second, and was a tailor but did not work at the business. With others he received a grant in 1730 of Saccarappa Falls, an interest in which he held till his death which was Aug. 26, 1770. He was collector of taxes in 1735; in 1750 he was toll; collector of the Stroudwater bridge. His first dwelling house stood on the site of Michael Mitton near foot of High street, Portland. (Deposition of George Knight seventy-two years of age, Vol. 51 p. 297—time 1807, Cum. Co. Reg. Deeds.). His second dwelling was that of Spring street, opposite High street, this city, now standing in its original simplicity. His third and last earthly abiding place, the lower story of the dwelling house of the late Capt. Francis H. Baily, where his maiden sister Helen now resides near Libby's Corner, on Congress street, Deering. Since the death of Dea. John a story has been added,

2.— THOMAS HASKELL.

On page ninety-one, April 30, 1740, edition of 1849 of Parson Smith's printed journal appears the following:

"I rose to Stroudwater, * * Mr. Frost also made known that he is offended with me for some passages in a sermon which he thought reflected on his taking Haskell's house, etc."

The cellar hole of the house to which reference is made may now be seen at this late day on the easterly bank of the gully between Frost and Congress streets but manuscript records show that Frost purchased the lot and buildings. Frost resided on what is now known as the Brewer house lot, and died Jan. 4th 1756. Haskell removed to Saccarappa, then to Winahan, and from the church of that town was dismissed Aug. 14, 1765, to join the Stroudwater church. They had ten children. The site of his first dwelling is easily located by an old highway record.

3.— NATHANIEL KNIGHT.

Nathan Knight came to Dunston, in Scarboro, in 1720. As near as I can ascertain he had eight children. Nathaniel being the eldest. Nathan was admitted to the Scarboro church, Sep. 12 1731. Col. Thomas Westbrook was admitted to the same church in 1728. Nathan's wife was Mary Westbrook sister to Colonel Thomas W. Family tradition says Nathaniel married Pricilla Berry.

CHILDREN.

1 Mary born March 6, 1726.
2 Sarah, born March 17, 1728, baptized, Scarboro, Aug. 25, same year.
3 John, born June 10, 1730, died Aug. 3, 1744. Family tradition says he was carried off by Indians at that time. Baptized July 29, same year.
4 Hannah, born Aug. 20, 1732.
5 Elizabeth, born Sept. 16, 1734, died Jan. 22, 1736.
6 Nathaniel, born Aug. 1, 1737, married his cousin Ruth Elden of Buxton, Dec. 12, 1782, daughter of his aunt Martha (Knights) Elden of Biddeford. (For Eldens see history of Buxton.) He was well advanced in years when he married, but became the father of 5 children. A copy of the will of this Nathaniel is before me as well as the account book of his father Nathaniel, from which I will make one extract.

Feb. 9, 1728, to "Thos. Westbrook Dr. 1 Day carrying things to Stroudwater, £0.8.0."

The two Nathaniel Knights, father and son, lived at Stroudwater Falls, on the Edward Chapman farm where the cellar hole of the Knights mansion house may be still seen which house was destroyed by fire. They were farmers, traders and millers.

There is a family tradition that one of the above named daughters of Nathaniel Knights Senior married Solomon Haskell and one a Conant, and one a Joseph White. "R." in his history of Westbrook, June 29, says Solomon Haskell married Mary White who was a widow.

7 George, born Feb. 27, 1739, married Jan. 1, 1771, Elizabeth (or Betsey) Slemmons, he called George Knight 3d.) She was born in the house now occupied by Fred A. Johnson, at the westerly edge of Stroudwater village—one of the finest locations in the city. This George Knights lived on the Buxton road, southerly side, and westerly of the road, a half mile, that leads to Stroudwater Falls from the Buxton road. He is mentioned in Wm. Slemmons, will now before me. She was a sister to the wife of Andrew P. Frost, who succeeded Chas. Frost in the possession of the Brewer House farm—a very stirring man.

8 Priscilla and last, born May 29, 1742, died Sept. 24, 1743.

The descendants of this branch of the Knights name are quite numerous, comprising all by the name who settled in the neighborhood of George Knight 3rd.

4—HENRY KNIGHT.

I know nothing of the parents of the character. The name of his wife was Priscilla, same as the wife of Nathaniel before mentioned. He lived in 1761 on Congress street head of India, Portland, and was a neighbor to Parson Smith. He made a will Apr. 3, 1751, which was probated Apr. 20, 1773, but I am unable to find a copy. He was a house carpenter. His son Mark, in 1761, purchased of Joseph Pride 45 acres "with buildings," crossed by Ocean street, where the fill in the highway is now being made and where descendants still live. In 1775 this lot of 45 acres came into the possession of Henry Knight Jr., brother to Mark, where Henry Jr. lived and died Oct. 20, 1871, aged 84 years, as I understand and the situation, Henry, senior, lived, it appears, in the vicinity of Lunt's Corner, and Henry M. got the 45 acre lot in the settlement of the estate of Henry, senior, and exchanges with Mark, his brother. And this is all I have to say at this time relative to the Knight family.

TO BE CONTINUED.

THE DEERING NEWS.

Saturday, Sept. 14, 1895.

GRANDPA'S SCRAP BOOK

[Under this head historical and genealogical memoranda will be furnished the readers of the News that appears worthy of preservation, particularly of remote periods in our history within the city limits and immediate vicinity.]

REV. THOMAS BROWNE.

THE FIRST MINISTER OF THE FOURTH, OR STROUDWATER PARISH OF FALMOUTH.

Continued from last week.

5—JAMES JOHNSON.

In 1749 James Johnson came from the town of Scarboro and occupied the wild land where his great-grandson, George Johnson, resides a mile westerly of Stroudwater on the road to Buxton. (For his children see News of July 6, this year, also His. Cumberland Co., p. 393, pub. in 1880.) The original dwelling stood on the opposite side of the highway, a few rods westerly of the present Johnson home, and was constructed of logs. The next one was two story on front, one story on back side, but about the year 1848 the back side was raised a story, new roof added and left as now observed, occupying a commanding position. None of his male descendants prior to 1833 joined the Stroudwater church.

6—JOHN JOHNSON.

He was a brother to James noticed above and occupied the farm lot next easterly, extending to the fork of the roads and back to Stroudwater river. April 2, 1751, a plan of these lots was recorded at Alfred in York county. Mr. George B. Leavitt, whose mother became the second wife of Isaac Johnson, the last occupant of the premises by the name of Johnson, now owns the premises, the site of the old mansion house being one of the finest within the city. Like his brother, none of his male descendants joined the church, prior to 1833.

7—JEREMIAH RIGGS.

He came from Cape Ann, Mass., and received a town grant of a house lot in what is now Portland in the year 1726. His wife was Rachel Haskell and he had a family when he came. Parson Smith notes his advent. In 1734 he purchased of Rev. Thomas Smith and others the old John Ingalls farm, now known as the Fowler farm, situated on the southerly side of Congress street at Bradley's Corner, and five acres of Col. Thomas Westbrook on the opposite side of the highway, where the so-called Fowler house stood till recently, and where Mr. Daniel D. Chenery now resides in a house the bottom story of which is supposed to be the original house of Jeremiah Riggs. He had seven children as near as I can ascertain: 1—Joseph; 2—Wheeler; 3—Abigail; 4—Hannah; 5—Jeremiah, Jr.; 6—Mary; 7—Stephen.

Jeremiah, the patriarch, and particularly Joseph became pillars of the Stroudwater church. It was at the home of Joseph Riggs the meeting was holden Sept. 10, 1764, to "agree to settell the Gospell" among them, the original record of the parish being safe and in a good state of preservation, and in possession of Mr. Daniel D. Chenery.

Joseph, Jr., was a tanner, as well as his father, and made brick and pottery back of his residence. He was born in 1722 and married Ann Bagley. He was an inn keeper, and in the year 1774, purchased 310 acres of land in the "Mill square lot", which included Capisic mill privilege, agreeing to pay for same 641£. In 1777 he bonded his home to the Waldoes, and in 1787 he relinquished it to Sarah Waldo as follows:

Five acres of land with my house, all other houses, shops, barn and buildings, except a small new house on the corner, which my son Enoch has built, and he is to have liberty to move by or before the first of March, 1789.

"My late father," Jeremiah Riggs, is alluded to in the document.

The house exempted is supposed by me to be the original part of the house standing in the corner opposite the Parson Bradley homestead.

In the year 1801 he made a deposition as follows:

I, Joseph Riggs, 70 years of age, testify and say, that the gore of land between the five acres which was conveyed to me by my father, Jeremiah Riggs, in the year 1746, and the present road leading from Portland to Stroudwater, was formerly in the possession of my said father sixty-five years ago and until his death; after which it was possessed by my brother, Jeremiah Riggs.

In 1810 Ann Riggs of Windham, widow of James Riggs, "now upwards of 85 years," made a statement relative to certain facts of her girlhood in Portland which are interesting. (Vol. 20, p. 380, Cum. Co. Reg. of Deeds.) Two or three of her daughters resided in Windham.

Where the father to Joseph Riggs died I do not know, nor do I know where Joseph died or the time.

The following is from the Portland Argus of Jan. 19, 1821:

Died in Westbrook, Mrs. Ann Riggs, aged 89 years. Buried from house of John Jones, Esq.

Jeremiah Riggs, Jr., brother to Joseph, born July 17, 1731, married Ann Barbour, Sept. 22, 1752, daughter of James Barbour.

In the old cemetery at Stroudwater stand two monumental slabs inscribed as follows:

In
memory of
MR. JEREMIAH
RIGGS,
who died Dec.
1800
Æt. 70.
Tho' the body sinks, the spirit soars.

In memory of
ANNA,
wife of
Jeremiah Riggs,
who died
June 17, 1821
Æt. 87.

Jeremiah Riggs, Jr., lived in the so-called Fowler house, was a farmer and was engaged in navigation. The last place of his earthly abode, known in later years as the Fowler house, a fine two story, square building with a long ell, with oak posts and clear pine shaved laths, was taken down in June of 1802.

Capt. John Jones married two of his daughters, Lucy and Mary, one the widow of Capt. Stickney.

Capt. John Jones came into possession of the Jeremiah Riggs, Jr., homestead in 1800, for which he paid $5,000.

Daniel Fowler married a daughter of Capt. Jones, hence the name.

The above named two sons were brothers to Wheeler Riggs, who settled in Portland, and to Stephen, who lived near the city line westerly of Nason's Corner, on what is now the Anson C. Trask farm. Joseph and Stephen Riggs married sisters.

THE DEERING NEWS.

Saturday, Sept. 21, 1895.

GRANDPA'S SCRAP BOOK

[Under this head historical and genealogical memoranda will be furnished the readers of the News that appears worthy of preservation, particularly of remote periods in our history within the city limits and immediate vicinity.]

REV. THOMAS BROWNE.

THE FIRST MINISTER OF THE FOURTH, OR STROUDWATER PARISH OF FALMOUTH.

Continued from last week.

CORRECTION. In my article under this caption of Sept. 7, where it reads Henry Knight, Jr., brother to Mark Knight, "died Oct. 20, 1891, aged 84 years," it should be Oct. 20, 1817. Then where "Henry M." appears. near the close of the article, it should read Henry Knight, Jr.

Again. In my article of Sept. 14, where it reads: "In 1810 Ann Riggs of Windham, widow of James Riggs"— James should be Joseph Riggs.

The credit of children given Jeremiah Riggs, senior, was copied from a foot note of Willis' edition of Smith & Dean's journal, p. 50, but it seems there were two daughters, Ruth and Rachel not comprised in the list who married respectively Thomas and Clement Pennell, said to be brothers as I shall show.

8—JAMES MERRILL.

James Merrill, senior, lived in the part of Falmouth now known as Falmouth. His residence stood easterly of Presumpscot Falls, and southerly of the highway leading to North Yarmouth, in from the way a fourth of a mile. A large, nearly new house occupied by a descendant by the name occupies the spot. It is not far from the little burying ground by the main road side.

April 6, 1753, he made his will and mentioned as his seventh child James Merrill. And this is the person who constituted one of the Stroudwater parish and church. He built his abode on the northerly side of the highway that bounds the northerly side of the three cornered piece of land on the northerly side of Presumpscot Falls, between the westerly corner of the lot and the brick schoolhouse, standing still, westerly of the James Merrill house which is standing now—a square house recently renovated and changed somewhat internally, and occupied by a descendant.

9—CLEMENT PENNELL.

In the year 1735 Thomas Pennell was at Portland, and was by occupation a ship carpenter. His intention of marriage with Rachel Riggs was filed Jan. 10, 1735, and to them was born a son Feb. 21, 1738-9. (Old Falmouth Mss. records.)

In 1739 he purchased of Col. Thomas Westbrook 60 acres of land at Capisic which was under attachment in favor of Gen. Samuel Waldo. The lot commenced at the salt water of Rapick creek and extended towards what is now known as Brighton Corner. There was at that time at Capisic under attachment: "A sawmill, a gristmill, three dwelling houses and two barns." One of the mills used the water as it passed down from the other. To Samuel Cobb and his son Chipman Cobb, Westbrook, sold the mill and privilege as well as the lot to Pennell—the only real objectionable thing I have found Westbrook guilty of in his long public career.

In the copy of the Falmouth town clerk records (manuscript) appears the following:

Time—1742, 5th article in the warrant. "To hear the request of Thomas Pennell viz: to see whether the town will allow him to keep a gate by his house in the road that leads from Saccarappa to Kapissick." March 23, 1743, the request was granted.

In 1758, Waldo commenced an action of ejecture against both Cobb and Pennell. Papers and plans are filed at Alfred courthouse. John Thomes who resided at Libby's Corner and kept a public house made a deposition as follows:

I, John Thomes, aged about 50 years, testify and say, that in the year 1735, Samuel Cobb did live in the house Thomas Pennell now lives in—the house that Col. Westbrook purchased of John Perrey, (or Perney).

There are other papers of like character. Waldo recovered but the court brought in that Waldo should pay Cobb the sum of 1100£ and Pennell 1117£.

After this transaction Thomas Pennell purchased a farm and buildings in Windham from which place he removed with his family to Harpswell. Ex-County Treasurer Pennell is a descendant. (See history of that town)

In 1767, Samuel Waldo in making a land sale alludes to a house at Capisic as the house lately possessed by Thomas Pennell and where Mr. Partridge now resides.

In the year 1741, June 10, Clement Pennell and Ruth Riggs were, according to old Falmouth records, published. In 1750 his brother sold him an acre of land at Capisic. Both were ship carpenters.

May 2, 1766, he purchased a quarter of an acre of land of Waldo, and Nov. 10, 1769, a half quarter, the residence of Mr. Warren Harmon, built by Levi Russell Starbird now standing on the lot.

In 1766, this same Clement Pennell purchased ten acres of land next northwesterly of where Mr. Edward D. Starbird now resides between Capisic and Nason's Corner and later five acres more. On this lot in the corner next to the Starbird house, since built, Clement Pennell erected his last earthly abiding place a low posted, long building with two front doors, described to me this very day by Mr. Elbridge G. Riggs who was born in 1813, and possesses a wonderful memory, and has resided most of his long life near the spot.

August 8, 1781, Ruth Pennell was a widow, according to a record in our Cumberland County Registry of Deeds, vol. 12, p. 118, and the soul executor of the last will of Clement Pennell her late husband, and she and her children named respectively as follows: 1—Abigail Adams; 2—Molly Fickett; Clement Pennell Jr., married, Nov. 7, 1784, Esther Hinnigham; 4—Eunice Goold who conveyed the lot where the Warren Harmon house stands to-day to Joseph Pennell, and he in turn, alluding to the place as the property of my late father, Clement Pennell, sells the place to Andrew P. Frost, for £60 who resided where the old Brewer house cellar may be seen. And in the division of the estate of Andrew P. Frost, it went to Peter T. Clark's wife who was a daughter to Frost, and they sold it to Capt. Thomas Seal, in 1813, for $500, "being the same lot Joseph Pennell purchased of A. P. Frost in 1781."

After the death of Clement the widow Ruth kept an inn where the wayfarer obtained his flip as the records of the old Court of Sessions plainly show, she receiving a license in 1776 which was continued till her death.

In the year 1797, John Goold, yeoman; Clement Pennell, yeoman; Samuel Pennell, yeoman; Nabby Adams, widow; and Nabby Fickett, widow, for a consideration of $10, paid by Thomas Pennell conveyed the premises to the said Thomas.

This Thomas Pennell, son of Clement, occupied the premises and made bricks where the Brighton road is now located. He married first; Eunice Knight, March 5, 1789, and had: 1—Nancy, born Feb. 1, 1791, married Levi Starbird, March 18, 1810, who built the house now occupied by Mr. Edward D. Starbird. 2—Henry; 3—Almira. At this time his wife died and he married Apr. 28, 1809, Sally Jones of Standish. Under date of Nov. 15, 1808, Parson Bradley records the death of "Mrs. Pennell, aged 43 years." This was probably the first wife of Thomas Pennell. 4—Thomas; 5—Jones. who died in Portland recently; 6—Charles; 7—George; 8—Sopha; 9—John now residing at Saccarappa who has a daughter, a school teacher, a son, a lawyer in the West, and is the father of Mr.

CONTINUED:

Henry B. Pennell, member of the firm of Cook, Everett and Pennell, wholesale druggists, Portland. 10 and youngest—Ephraim who is alive and resides in Massachusetts.

His second wife was a Methodist, so the story runs, and not finding a meeting to meet her views of theology prevailed upon her husband to sell here and remove to Buxton and occupy a farm, but both died at Saccarappa.

Ruth Riggs was with her husband Clement a member of the Congregational church and for several years, according to the parish record, had the charge of the meeting house.

THE DEERING NEWS.

Saturday, Sept. 28, 1895.

GRANDPA'S SCRAP BOOK

[Under this head historical and genealogical memoranda will be furnished the readers of the News that appears worthy of preservation, particularly of remote periods in our history within the city limits and immediate vicinity.]

REV. THOMAS BROWNE.

THE FIRST MINISTER OF THE FOURTH, OR STROUDWATER PARISH OF FALMOUTH.

Continued from last week.

CORRECTION. Where the name of "Esther Hanningham" appears in my article of last week as the representative of the wife of Clement Pennel, Jr., it should be Esther Kunningham.

I stated last week as follows: In 1767, Samuel Waldo in making a land sale alludes to a house at Capisic as the house lately possessed by Thomas Pennell and where Mr. Partridge now resides.

Upon making a further examination of my scrap book material I find the record more explicit than I gave it, so I will here make an addition to what I related last week.

The Thomas Pennel house lot was 7¼ rods on front and when Waldo made the sale of the half acre to James Frost which was 8 rods in front and 10 rods deep, Waldo says the northeasterly corner of the lot sold to Frost is 14¼ rods southeasterly from the southerly corner of the house recently occupied by Thomas Pennell, etc. The two story house built by Frost stood just a little southerly of Mr. Warren Harmon's present cooper shop. In this Frost house Capt. Thomas Seal resided the first of his married life. Thus it is readily seen by those familiar with the locality that the Thomas Pennell house stood northeasterly of the present house which is the residence of Mr. Warren Harmon, and not exactly on the spot of the Harmon house as stated last week. This Frost lot formed the northerly side of the approach to the Town landing, and I am particular as to location because there is a good deal that is historical and genealogical connected with Capisic 200 years ago as well as of the period of which I now write, all of which I hope to bring to the light of day. Mr. Elbridge G. Riggs remembers the house well, says it was painted yellow, and another now gone, told me the same as to color, etc.

In my last I alluded to a Joseph Pennel as one of the children of Clement Pennel, who purchased the interest of several of the heirs of that part of his father's estate located where the Warren Harmon dwelling house now stands.

In the history of Cumberland county published in 1880 by Everts & Peck, on page 380, may be seen an engraving of William L. Pennell, deceased, and on page 392 that of his brother, James Pennell, who resides at Saccarappa village, Westbrook. This William L. and James are descended from Clement Pennel through Joseph above mentioned.

William L. Pennell says:

I was born in the town of Gray, Cumberland county, Me. The family was descended from Clement Pennell, one of three brothers, who emigrated from the Isle of Jersey and settled in Deering, then Falmouth. He married Ruth Riggs, (as I have stated from manuscript records). Their son Joseph, (above noticed) grandfather to Wm. L., married for his first wife Hannah Ward by whom he had eight children. His second wife was Charlotte Nash, by whom he also had eight children. Joseph Pennell, William L. Pennell's father, was the second child by the first wife. He was born in the town of Gray, Aug. 7, 1778, and married Elizabeth Stone of Kennebunk. Wm. L. Pennell was born April 15, 1821.

For the rest see the history from which I have copied the foregoing.

In 1872 William L. Pennell was high sheriff of this county, which position he held four years. In 1878 he purchased a home at Cumberland Mills, engaged in trade there, died in this city at Deering Center, where he resided with his daughter, Mrs. Boody.

Of the parents of John Goold who became the husband of Eunice Pennell daughter of Clement Pennell, senior, I have no knowledge. Mr. Elbridge G. Riggs, alluded to in my last article, thinks he came from New Market, N. H. His dwelling stood in front of where the dwelling of Orrin G. Chipman's stands on the southerly side of the highway, a third of a mile from Nasons Corner towards Westbrook, built by one Henry Coffin about 25 years ago. He purchased the two acre lot, which was twenty-five rods wide on the highway and on the northerly side of the "mile square" lot of Stephen Riggs March 15, 1775 for which he paid 5£ 6s. In 1801 he and wife Eunice sold their interest in the estate of Clement Pennell deceased, father to Eunice and purchased 7¼ acres of Sam'l. Harper, adjoining the two acres, and in 1824 he conveyed all his personal property and real estate to his son Samuel Goold. In Parsons Bradley's diary dated August 1826, appears the following: Died, Mr. Goold aged 80 years. This must have been the wife of John Goold.

Mr. Elbridge G. Riggs informs me that John Goold was 99 years, 9 months, and 9 days old when he died and furnished me with part of the following from his memory, excepting dates.

John Goolds wife had eight children as follows:

1 Clement, married Oct. 3, 1802, Polly Miles, and removed to Limington. Capt. William Miles who built the brick house at Capisi which was removed about 40 years ago, where the barn stands southerly of the residence of Mr. Warren Harmon married Nov. 25, 1802, Judith Knight. He died and the widow married Nov. 2 1809 John A. Kinson. The relationship between Capt. Wm. Miles and Polly Miles I do not know.
2 Eunice married Jan. 31, 1808 Isaac Winship of Portland; and resided on Congress street easterly of Union Station, in that city.
 Calvin Jordan's son Luther whose father lived at the corner of Portland and Forest St., Portland, married one of his daughters.
3 Betsey died unmarried on the Trask farm where she kept house for her brother Samuel.
4 Clarissa married Sept. 1 1811, Daniel Trask father to Mr. Ansel C. Trask who resides on the old Stephen Riggs farm, or I should say, a part of the farm. This Mr. Ansel C. Trask is now alive, though aged, born in 1812, says that his father was a hatter by trade in Portland, and that he went to live with his grandfather John Goold when he was one year old and remained with him till he was 24; that he was an only child; Rev. J. H. Trask, now of Conway is his son; and that whatever of papers and books there were belonging to the family were burned at the time of the destruction by fire of the old Stephen Riggs house in which he lived.
6 Nabby married Oct. 18, 1827 Joseph son of Samuel Copps who built the small house that stood in front of the site of the late abode of Clement Pennell, house removed a few years since by Mr. Albion P. Chapman who now owns the land. The house was good, a room each side the front door but very small. It was built by Samuel Harper who lived westerly of Nason's corner, and Mr. Riggs says Harper scolded a good deal about its size.
7 Samuel did not marry but bought the Stephen Riggs place where he and his sister Betsey resided.
8 William married Sept. 26 1824, Mary Copps daughter of Samuel Copps and lived where Mr. Elbridge G. Riggs

63

CONTINUED:

lives on part of the Stephen Riggs farm, in from the road a few rods on the northerly side thereof. He died in the house he built.

In the old Stroudwater cemetery where it is claimed the remains of the descendants of Clement Pennell are interred of those who departed this life at Capisic but one memorial stone stands; it is inscribed as follows:

Abigail,
wife of
JOSEPH COPPS
died
July 3, 1852.
Æt 60.

There may have been more children of John Goold, but this is the list as Mr. Riggs remembers it.

None by the name of Goold or Copps became members of the 1st Congregational church prior to 1833, and only Clement Pennell and wife by the name of Pennell.

THE DEERING NEWS.

Saturday, Oct. 5, 1895.

GRANDPA'S SCRAP BOOK

[Under this head historical and genealogical memoranda will be furnished the readers of the News that appears worthy of preservation, particularly of remote periods in our history within the city limits and immediate vicinity.]

REV. THOMAS BROWNE.

THE FIRST MINISTER OF THE FOURTH, OR STROUDWATER PARISH OF FALMOUTH.

Continued from last week.

AN OMISSION. From some unexplainable cause the notice of the fifth child of John Goold did not appear in my last article. She was the wife of Edmund Mann of Fort Hill, Gorham, Me., and the mother of Hon. James Mann, State senator, custom house official, politician, etc.

The name of Samuel Copps, Jr., and Peggy, his wife, appear incidentally upon public records in the year of 1814 for the first time. Strange as it may appear the name of Joseph, their son, is the only representative of the "Copps" name on the Cumberland Registry of Deeds. From whence came Samuel, Jr., to Capisic I have no knowledge. Mr. Elbridge G. Riggs thinks he came from Lebanon, N. H. He lived first in a house that stood where the house of Mr. Edward Goold now stands in the corner of the lot about four rods southerly of the residence of Mr. A. P. Chapman. This Edward Goold house was built by Edward Winslow, on the site of the Copps house, which was a small one-story building with very small glass, standing end to road and fronting southerly. Edward Goold resides now in Portland, and is not of the John Goold family. Nor are the Goolds westerly of Nason's Corner of the John Goold family.

The time and by whom the Copps house was built I cannot state. In the year 1797 a tract of land that extended from Capisic bridge along the road northwesterly to the A. P. Chapman lot and back westerly to the salt water was conveyed by Jacob Noyes to Samuel Butts who engaged in trade at Capisic; consideration, $2,900; quantity, fifty-five acres. This conveyance included the Copps lot but no buildings are mentioned. The "garden dyke" made by Gardner Goold, back of the residence of Warren Harmon, who was once in trade at Capisic, and then at Stroudwater, is alluded to, also the one made by Joseph Noyes, both of which are very plainly visible at this time though thrown up a hundred years ago, but the parents of this Gardner Goold I cannot locate, nor does the record refer to a dwelling on the premises conveyed, but exceptions are made of three or four small lots sold from the Butts lot prior to the date of 1797 when he made the purchase.

Last spring when I presented some memoranda in this column relative to the Pierces I said: "I cannot locate the shop of Charles Pierce at Stroudwater." I am now able to state that it stood near the present location of Quinby hall, and the original bill of sale is now before me which I here present in full:

Know all men That I Asa Knight of Fa'mouth in consideration of the sum of Eighty dollars to me paid by Charles Pierce of said Falmouth the receipt whereof I do hereby acknowledge, do hereby bargain & sell unto the said Charles Pierce a certain store standing at Capisic & standing on land owned by Messrs. Goodwin & Graffam being the same lately occupied by Mr. Samuel Butts. And I do covenant with the said Pierce that said store is free of incumbrances, & that I have good right to sell & convey the same.—

April the 24, 1810.
ASA KNIGHT.

In presence of
MOSES QUINBY.

There is no record of a land title in the name of Goodwin and Graffam that I can find.

The building was moved to Stroudwater, and after it passed from the possession of Pierce it was cut into halves, one piece becoming the shoemaker's shop of David Stevens, the other, after standing a while where the old Dr. Jacob Hunt hay scales stood, later owned by Andrew Hawes, Esq., in the back of the road, was removed to Capt. Jonathan Smith's tannery where the ruins of which tannery may now be seen though started by one Bryant of Watertown, Mass, just a hundred years ago. The building was small, low posted, with a two foot projecting cornice on front. The Stevens part stood easterly of Mr. Hawes' shop where he now trades.

In the year of 1803 for a consideration of $4,631 fifty acres of this lot was conveyed by Butts to one John Deering, the mill privilege being excluded which was included in the conveyance of 1797 "excepting a ¼ acre belonging to A. P. Frost.

In 1808 part of this lot, commencing at the corner of what is now the Chapman lot and extending southeasterly by the road thirty-two rods to the easterly corner of the schoolhouse, which was to a point near the present barn of Mr. Edward D. Starbird, was conveyed to John Quinby for a consideration of $900, but no buildings mentioned. In 1814 the mortgage of Samuel Copps is referred to, and in 1821 buildings are mentioned, and though the name of Samuel Copps does not appear on record as owner of the property it is more than probable he built the house with additional small [illegible] born 1811 now alive, and to whom allusion has been made as residing on the old Stephen Riggs place at the present time, informs me that his earliest recollection of going to school was in the Copps house when his daughter, who became the wife of Wm. Goold, was teacher.

Samuel Copps was deserving of the appellation of "knight of the goad stick." Many years he was on the highway with two pair of oxen. Capt. Thomas Seal and Col. Jeremiah Bailey were co partners in the lumber business. Capt. Seal lived at Capisic where the large cellar hole may be seen, where the dwelling was burned about 30 years ago, which was pleasantly situated, and for Capt. Seal Mr. Copps worked, spending his last days on the opposite side of the highway from the Capt. Seal house, but a few rods southerly of it, where he died, Capt. Seal owning the house, which was constructed from one of the porches of the old meeting house in which Rev. Thomas Browne preached when the meeting house was taken down. The Seal house in which Copps lived was destroyed by fire in the afternoon in the winter when occupied by John Seal, son of Capt. Thomas Seal, some thirty years ago.

Here is what Rev. Caleb Bradley says in his journal relative to the death of Samuel Copps:

March 13, 1838. It is said Mr. Copps is now dying—a man of 70 years old.

The above named Copps died this afternoon—thus in the midst of life we are with death. Man is but vanity and dust in all his flower and prime. Mr. Copps, the deceased, has travelled from Saccarappa to Portland and from Congin to Portland for more than 30 years—say 260 times a year which multiplied by 30 makes 7800 days, and this multiplied by 6 miles per day will make 46,800 miles going, then for coming, double this sum —93,600 miles travel in thirty years, (as driver of a four-ox team.) We shall see him pass no more. His days are gone,

CONTINUED:

and his purposes broken off.

March 15. It is three o'clock p. m. Just returned from the funeral of Samuel Copps, 68 years. (Rev.) Mr. Lane made the prayer. (Here follows five lines written in Latin. After this English which includes the meaning of the Latin, as follows). It is the consideration of another world, seeing through a glass darkly, which makes death so much to be dreaded. Sin is the sting of death and to obtain a victory over both of them, if a victory be obtained, is through our Lord Jesus Christ. There is no victory but through faith in the Saviour. All things can be accomplished through the strength of the Redeemer, and without Him nothing can be brought to pass, therefore Christians are exhorted by the Apostle to "be steadfast, unmoveable, abounding in the work of the Lord, always knowing that your labor is not in vain in the Lord."

THE DEERING NEWS.

Saturday, Oct. 12, 1895.

GRANDPA'S SCRAP BOOK

[Under this head historical and genealogical memoranda will be furnished the readers of the News that appears worthy of preservation, particularly of remote periods in our history within the city limits and immediate vicinity.]

JOHN FICKETT.

A FEW FACTS RELATIVE TO HIS DESCENDANTS HEREABOUTS.

I found I was getting far off in my presentation of memoranda relative to Parson Browne and original members of his so-called Stroudwater church society, so have dropped the heading for the present, but will return shortly to the consideration of the record of his descendants and unnoticed members of his church.

In my article of Sept. 21, I stated, from records, that in 1781, Polly (Pennell) Fickett, daughter of Clement Pennell was a widow.

March 24, 1776, Parson Smith records the fact among others that:

"The peri pneumonia disorder, is very mortal; that at Stroudwater, Mr. Wyer; Mrs. Riggs, Fickett and Trickey have died."

Taking the name of "Fickett" in the above to mean Benjamin Fickett, in an obituary I furnished the Portland Argus of Apr. 14, 1890, I stated that Benjamin Fickett of Stroudwater died in 1776, but I am satisfied from later discovered facts, which I will present, that I was in error in this statement, and believe the person by the name of Fickett to whom Parson Smith referred was Nathaniel Fickett, husband of Polly Pennell who were united in marriage Jan. 25, 1765, and resided between Stroudwater and Saccarappa.

In an article that appeared in the News of Sept. 14, I alluded briefly to the Ficketts of Stroudwater, and should have said that Samuel was an uncle to the other three named, to have the relationship plain.

Mr. Jerome B. Fickett, the successful dealer in paints and oil at No. 403 4 Fore street, Portland, was born Jan. 16, 1815, hence is 80 years old, and has taken some interest in the genealogy of the Fickett name. He is now in active business has, in his possession some memoranda of the descendants of Thomas Fickett which has materially assisted me in what I now present.

In a deposition by John Fickett in Scarboro in 1670 he stated that he was at that date twenty-five years of age Vol. 4 p. 141, Me. His. & Gen. Recorder. He owned a small lot of land at Black Point, but there is no record title obtainable that I can find. His life is veiled in mystery to me.

Thomas, grandson of John Fickett first appears on record in this State as follows:

Dec. 8, 1731, John Fickett of Portsmouth, N. H., tanner, for a consideration of "10£ paid by my brother Thomas Fickett of Kittery, shipwright, convey all claim to the estate of my grandfather and grandmother Fickett and of my father John Fickett dec'd, of land in Scarboro."

July 18, 1744, Rebeckah Gey of Marblehead, Mass., widow woman "for 5£ relinquished to Thomas Fickett of Falmouth, shipwright, all claim in the estate of my father and mother in Scarboro, John Fickett and Abigail Fickett." These records, are the only ones at Alfred, show conclusively the origin of the Fickett name hereabouts and connections.

May 11, 1737, for a consideration of 85£ Thomas Fickett of Scarboro, shipwright, conveyed his six acres of land at Black Point, Scarboro, "together with my house thereon standing," to Robert Bailey of Falmouth, bounds commencing at a pitch pine stump northern side of Jamacia Brook running over to the cove of Andrew Libby's lot, 20 rods. "Then Seth Fogg's lot is mentioned as a boundary on one side. And this joins Nonesuch river as another record shows. Those who desire to known where John Fickett lived in Scarboro 200 years ago, and his grandson Thomas, 50 years later, after reading this, can probably find the spot without much difficulty.

June 8, 1737, Robert Bailey of Falmouth conveyed to Thomas Fickett of Scarboro, shipwright, for a consideration of 150£, "104 acres of land in Falmouth, on Purpooduck side, or southerly side, of Fore river over to a place called Barren Hill." The title of this property, or a part of it, is still in the Fickett name.

Thomas Fickett married, tradition says, Mary Moulton of Scarboro, but did not move to Barren Hill in 1731 as tradition has it, but in 1737, as I have shown by the record. His wife had six sons and two daughters named as follows: 1, John; 2, Benjamin; 3, Jonathan; 4, Daniel; 5, Nathaniel; and 6, Abner. One daughter married Ichabod Libby of Scarboro; the other, Charles Patrick of Stroudwater.

The foregoing list of names was made by Ebeneza Fickett, dec'd, son of William and grandson of Thomas. Ebeneza I am informed, was grandfather to Mr. Jason T. Fickett now a wood and coal dealer, No. 59 Lincoln street, Portland, but I have rearranged his classification to make it correspond as well as I can with time of births.

But before proceeding further I will present some memoranda from Scarboro and Cape Elizabeth church records as follows:

July 18, 1736. Baptized Thomas and Mehitable, children of Thomas and Mary Fickett.

Aug. 1, 1736. John, Mary and Benjamin, children of Thomas and Mary Fickett.

Sept. 25, 1737, Benjamin, son of Thomas and Mary Fickett. (The other Benjamin must have died.)

Sept. 7, 1780. Joshua, son of Abner and Abigail Fickett, offered for baptism by his grandparents.

Sept. 2, 1781. Vincent Fickett and Hannah Fickett, his wife, owned the covenant.

Children of Vincent Fickett and Hannah his wife, baptized: Joseph, Sept. 2, 1781; Clarissa, daughter, Sept. 14, 1783; Joseph, Aug. 4, 1785; Hannah, Nov. 24, 1793.

MARRIAGES.

Oct. 27, 1764, Ichabod Libby and Mary Fickett.

June 25, 1765, Nathaniel Fickett and Molly Pennell.

June 6, 1768, Charles Patrick and Mehitable Fickett, he of Falmouth.

Apr. 10, 17—, Benjamin Fickett and Deborah Sawyer.

Aug. —, 1774, John Fickett, Jr., and Lucy Stanford. (Grandfather to Mr. J. B. Fickett of Portland, herein noticed.)

Oct. 17, 1775, Abner Fickett and Abigail Brown.

Aug. 6, 1780, Zebulon Fickett and Sarah Fickett.

Sept. 7, 1780, Vincent Fickett and Hannah Brown.

Oct. 19, 1780, Nathaniel Fickett and Susanna Brown.

Jan. 1, 1788, Jonathan Fickett, Jr., and Lydia Cox, he of Falmouth.

Oct. 21, 1790, Isaac Fickett and Mary Dyer.

Dec. 24, 1795, Benjamin Fickett and Sarah Stanford.

Mar. 8, 1798, Joshua Fickett and Mary Hunnewell.

TO BE CONTINUED.

THE DEERING NEWS.

Saturday, Oct. 19, 1895.

GRANDPA'S SCRAP BOOK

[Under this head historical and genealogical memoranda will be furnished the readers of the News that appears worthy of preservation, particularly of remote periods in our history within the city limits and immediate vicinity.]

JOHN FICKETT.

A RECORD OF SOME OF HIS DESCENDANTS AND FACTS CONNECTED THEREWITH.

Continued from last week.

John Fickett, the eldest son of his father Thomas, married, 1749, Isabella Roberts, and resided as I understand the situation, at Barren Hill, Cape Elizabeth. A record of his marriage appears on Old Falmouth records, p. 448. The same year Thomas, his father, was chosen surveyor of highways, the only office he held. He died Feb. 9, 1823 aged 96 years; his wife died Feb. 9, 1828 aged 96 years. They had nine children: 1, Benjamin; 2, Vincent, married according to record presented last week, Sept. 7, 1780, Hannah Brown; 3, Nathaniel; 4, John, Jr., married August, 18, 1774, Lucy Stauford, grandfather to Jerome B. Fickett of Portland, as stated last week; 5, William, the father to Ebeneza, noticed last week as furnishing certain memoranda to Jerome B. Fickett, married, Abigail Fickett April, 17, 1783, who was a daughter of Benjamin Fickett of Stroudwater, noticed further along in this article; 6, Isaac; 7, Hannah who married John Dinsmore; 8, Mary who married Richard Collins, and 9, Sally who married Aug. 6, 1780 Zebulan Fickett.

The last named moved to a place called at the time "Narraguagus." After considerable research I found a private letter which states that Narraguagus is, or was, the name of a postoffice situated in the part of Harrington now known as Milbridge, and 24 miles from Machias.

The second child of Thomas who was named Benjamin, married Feb. 2, 1760, Sarah Sawyer of Cape Elizabeth, and resided at Stroudwater where he was a shipwright.

In 1786 for a consideration of 7£ he purchased of Henry Webb, Mariner, of that place, who built the "uncle Ben Burnham" house, sixteen square rods of land and built a two story house close to where Mr. Cypress L. Dill now lives on the southerly side of Mill creek, or in other words, Mill Lane, or still more modern, Bond street.

In 1799, for $666 he sold the lot and house to Josiah Fickett of Portland, shipwright, his cousin, born at Stroudwater, and went to Gorham, Me. In 1802 Josiah sold to James and Chas. Ferguson for $700, and in 1823 Ferguson sold a half to Nathaniel Crockett for $233. In about the year of 1845 the house was hauled to Portland and located on Portland street opposite foot of New High where it was used as a tenement house quite a number of years ago. Children:

1 Jonathan, Jr., married Jan. 1, 1788 Lydia Cox.
2 Zebulon.
3 Moses, married Jan. 27, 1791, by the Rev. Thomas Browne, Sally Warren, fifth child of John Warren, born Jan. 9, 1766, which John Warren lived a mile southeasterly of Saccarappa on the Stroudwater road, northerly side.
4 Benjamin.
5 Ezra.
6 Nathaniel.
7 Abigail, married, as before stated, Apr. 17, 1783 William Fickett who, Ebeneza says, "was my father," and as I have shown, the fifth child of John the son of Thomas.
8 A daughter who married Chas. Smith, a blacksmith.

The third child of Thomas Fickett was Jonathan, a shipwright who first lived in the "Garrison House," the Stroudwater home place of Col. Thomas, Westbrook, that stood on the southwesterly corner of what is known as Westbrook and Bond streets, Stroudwater, where the large house now stands, occupied by Ficketts, and built by Samuel Fickett a 100 years since, who was the third child of Jonathan Fickett. And here let me state that I have recently found a plan made for court use in 1757 when a writ of ejectment was issued against the Zebulon Trickey heirs who lived where Mr. George Woodbury Johnson now resides on the Saco road, a mile southwesterly of Stroudwater, which plan was made from memoranda of 1737, and which shows the "Garrison house" stood where the Fickett house alluded to above now stands, and the milldam on the Stroudwater river was some 40 rods above the present dam and the mill contained a double and a single set of saws. Other papers, in manuscript, show that the paper mill, such as it was, stood about where the steam pleasure launch, the We Two, now lands.

Jonathan Fickett's wife was named Elizabeth, but further than this I know nothing of her, nor do I find a record of the marriage.

Jonathan Fickett leased of William Slemmons who owned the mill privilege, "ship yard point," as it was then called, where he built vessels, and where he built his dwelling, on leased ground and where the cellar hole of the house is still visible on the northerly side of the creek, some over half the way down to the point from the road, which house was one story and was moved to a point nearly opposite the village school, between what are known now and ever have been as the Stevens house, and Tate house, upon which a raid was made by "us boys" one winter night with snow balls and clubs, when it was unoccupied, leaving but little whole glass in the front windows, after which it was removed by one James Creddiford, a tin peddler, who bought old houses as well as rags. The house removed, renovated, and remodeled is now owned and occupied by Mr. Stewart Worster, Brighton corner.

In the year 1785, Dec. 24, he purchased a tract of land back of the Waterhouse lot, where Frederick Waterhouse, great grandson of William Waterhouse, the original of the name at Stroudwater now resides, back of the Benjamin Fickett lot, and back of the Henry Webb lot, all of which lots fronted on the "Town Landing" lot where great mast logs were landed in Col. Westbrook's day,—the Jonathan Fickett purchase commencing at Fore river, extending westerly to the highway and along by the highway to what is now known as the Brook's field.

Dec. 8, 1796, he purchased of Enoch Ilsley for a consideration of "453£ lawful money" land on the opposite side of the road, commencing bounds at the "corner where the road runs westerly from the Main Post road a little to the northeast of "Harrow House" so called, thence south etc., etc., "together with the buildings thereon"—Harrow house meaning the Garrison house.

The "buildings thereon" stood where the Dr. Jacob Hunt house stands now owned by Mrs. Susie (McDonald Morton) removed to make room for the Hunt house, built by Dr. Jeremiah Barker in 1800.

TO BE CONTINUED.

THE DEERING NEWS.

Saturday, Oct. 26, 1895.

GRANDPA'S SCRAP BOOK

[Under this head historical and genealogical memoranda will be furnished the readers of the News that appears worthy of preservation, particularly of remote periods in our history within the city limits and immediate vicinity.]

JOHN FICKETT.

A RECORD OF SOME OF HIS DESCENDANTS
AND FACTS CONNECTED THEREWITH.
Continued from last week.

The children of Jonathan Fickett of Stroudwater, who was alluded to in my article of last week as the third child of Thomas Fickett of Cape Elizabeth which Thomas was a grandson of John Fickett of Scarboro, were named respectively as follows: 1—Mary; 2—Asa; 3—Samuel; 4—Josiah; 5—Ephraim; 6—Enoch; 7—Elizabeth; 8—Phebe, and 9—Nancy.

1 Mary married Daniel Herrick, a saddler, and in 1794 Jonathan Fickett for a consideration of 10£ sold his son-in-law Herrick a house lot next southerly of the old Dr. Jeremiah Barker place at Stroudwater, alluded to in my last article as now owned by Mrs. Susie (McDonald) Morton and the Dr. Jacob Hunt house who succeeded Dr. Barker. Feb. 27, 1796, Herrick sold the lot and two story house "thereon standing" to Daniel Bryant for $600 who had started the tannery, yet to be noticed. Concerning Herrick I know but little. He lived in Stroudwater and died there in 1836, aged 78 years. Concerning his wife I know nothing. They had two children—Daniel who married Martha Small, and Polly who married Samuel Stevens. Daniel Herrick, Jr., was a ship carpenter and removed to New York city.

Samuel Stevens, eldest child of Tristram Stevens and wife Margaret Patrick, was born at Stroudwater Aug. 28, 1777. I have no record of the marriage or their deaths. In company with his brother Tristram he built the large square house now standing opposite the school house at Stroudwater same as it was built, with some slight change in the front door and stair case, which house is now occupied by Mr. Michael Stevens, youngest child of Tristram, and is one of the finest of the old style, and very pleasantly located. Samuel Stevens was a ship carpenter and occupied the northerly half of the house. I remember him as a small man, with a round, pleasant face, but very lame, and in his last days made shoe pegs. I remember six of his children: Samuel, Isaac, Frederick, Amanda, Elizabeth and Frances.

In making the pegs a slice was sawed from the end of a hard wood log, planed to an even thickness, then one side grooved so as to form points in the block, then the four sides were split off so as to form a square, the outside pieces being waste which the boys prized highly, and called them combs, it being a frequent occurrence for a boy to have a pocket full of the waste.

2 Asa, born Feb. 14, 1769, married Jan. 29, 1792, Dorcas Plummer of Portland, born there June 30, 1766, daughter of Moses Plummer.

July 1815, Parson Bradley makes an entry as follows: Died—Mrs. Plummer, wife of Moses.

When an invasion of Portland was expected during the war of 1812-15 Moses Plummer removed to the house now occupied by Mr. Walter Fickett and mother at Stroudwater and it is probable that Mrs. Plummer died while at Stroudwater.

Jane Thurston's mother—Jane of Portland who claims to own that city—was a sister to Dorcas (Plummer) Fickett. [See Thurston Gen. Vol. I, p. 194, & Vol. II, p. 206.]

Nov. 9, 1795, for a consideration of $300 Jonathan Fickett conveyed a house lot to his son Asa, located on the easterly side of what is now called Westbrook street, consisting of a fourth of an acre, and on the lot he built a medium sized one story house that stood some over fifty years on the site of the present dwelling of Mr. Geo. B. Jacobs which dwelling was erected by Elias Jacobs, whose wife was Asa Fickett's youngest child by a second wife. Asa was a ship joiner, but spent his last days at farming.

To give an idea of what it cost to get the joiner work of a vessel done I will here make a transcript from Jonathan Sparrow's account book now before me who carried on ship building at Stroudwater:

August 25, 1804. This day I have agreed with Asa Fickett to do or cause to be done the joiner work of the schooner Dave and find the stuff for one hundred and seventy dollars, to be paid for by him the said Fickett, (meaning, I presume, that Fickett was to pay for the lumber required.)

Here is another:

February 19, 1805. This day agreed with Samuel Stevens, to do the joiner work on the brig Samson both in board and out complete for one hundred and seventy dollars.

A few years later Asa Fickett built the house now occupied by Mr. Elias M. Jacobs, brother to George, located a few rods southerly, which house was many years the residence of Capt. Jonathan Smith and family, but Asa never occupied the last named premises.

In 1814 Asa was taxed as follows: Two houses $500; one barn $40; seven acres mowing & tillage at $22 per acre; two cows $28; one horse $40; and one swine $5.

This is quite conclusive that the two story house as now seen had been commenced in 1814, but it was never occupied by Asa and family.

The dates of Jonathan and wife, the parents of Asa, I am unable to obtain. In Parson Bradley's journal, however, is this statement which refers probably to Jonathan: Oct. — 1809, Died—Mr. Fickett.

The name of the second wife of Asa was Eliza Edwards of Bar Mills.

In the old Stroudwater cemetery stand three memorial slabs with inscriptions as follows:

In memory of
MRS. DORCAS,
wife of
Mr. Asa Fickett,
Died Dec. 11, 1819,
Æt. 53.

She stretched out her hand to the poor:
Yea, she reached forth her hands to the needy
A tender mother, and a virtuous wife
Through all the various scenes of life.

In memory of
ASA FICKETT,
who died
Sept. 6, 1835,
Æt. 66.

Blessed are the dead which die in the Lord, henceforth; yea, saith the Spirit, that they may rest from their labors and their works do follow them.

ELIZA,
Wife of
Asa Fickett,
Died
Feb. 22, 1866,
Aged 79 years, 3 mo.

It is traditional that the lines upon the memorial stone of Dorcas are not mere sentiment, but portray her real character which was exemplary in the fullest degree.

(TO BE CONTINUED.)

Saturday, Nov. 2, 1895.

GRANDPA'S SCRAP BOOK

[Under this head historical and genealogical memoranda will be furnished the readers of the News that appears worthy of preservation, particularly of remote periods in our history within the city limits and immediate vicinity.]

JOHN FICKETT.

A RECORD OF SOME OF HIS DESCENDANTS AND FACTS CONNECTED THEREWITH.

Continued from last week.

The notice in Parson Bradley's journal I referred to last week which reads: "Oct.—1809—Died Mr. Fickett," does not have reference to Jonathan Fickett as I then thought nor his wife Betsey, nor Elizabeth, as I find it recorded both ways, the very last time as Betsey, for further research reveals the fact that in 1803 he disposed of his last real estate in Stroudwater, consisting of 33 acres of land, to certain of his sons, reserving a life lease, and purchased land in the town of Poland to which place he and wife removed. It seems his wife had a life interest there, in certain real estate obtained by will of one Peter Brooks, physician, which on the third day of Dec. 1812, they sold to Seth Hillard "excepting about two square rods where Peter Brooks and others are buried." Three years after this transaction Jonathan again appears on record in the town of Poland for the last time at which place I leave his name where unquestionably his earthly remains as well as his wife are deposited.

Asa Fickett alluded to in my last article as the second child of Jonathan, above noticed, and wife Dorcas Plummer, had children as follows: 1, Susan; 2, Charles; 3, Theophilus; 4, George; 5, Frances; 6, Nelly; 7, George (the first George died;) 8, James; 9, Nahum; 10, Jennette. Then Asa had by his second wife, Eliza Edwards, one child named Ellen, making eleven in all.

1. Susan Fickett, born ———— married Aug. 6, 1813, John M. Milliken, Jr, born at Dunston Landing, Scarboro, but I know nothing of his parentage or early life. He was a shoemaker. In 1822 he was an inn keeper in Scarboro. He kept an inn also at Stroudwater, but I do not know the date. The house stood at the head of what is now Waldo street westerly side of Westbrook street, where the cellar hole and foundation stones are now observable, next to the Milliken house in which the postoffice is kept, and which was the last earthly abiding place of John M(ulbury) Milliken and wife Susan Fickett. The house was used as a public house many years both before and after he occupied it and was burned about twenty years ago.

From Stroudwater Mr. Milliken removed to New York city, where he first engaged in shoe making then in politics, acting as city assessor of the eleventh ward, day constable, dock master and collector of rents for his brother-in-law, Frank Fickett, returning to Stroudwater in 1849. Soon thereafter he purchased the property next northerly of the place where he was an inn holder which place I have located at Stroudwater, now occupied by his son Frances F. Milliken. His children were:

1 Frances, died young.
2 Elizabeth.
3 William, married and died in New York.
4 Charles, married and died in Australia.
5 George, born Feb. 18, 1822. He always lived in Stroudwater, and was lame from sickness when a child. He married Nov. 14, 1857 Amanda, daughters of Samuel Stevens, hence his second cousin, and both died a few years since in the house where his brother Francis, now resides. No children.
6 James, married, and is supposed to be alive in New York.
7 Nahum, died young.
8 Frances F., born in New York Sept. 19, 1833, married Martha Spaulding of Buxton, and with her and three daughter reside as above seated. She is postmaster, the office is in their dwelling house. He attends to the receiving and delivery of the mail at the railroad crossing on Congress street, at which place mail matter is received and delivered twice each day. The notice is for the future—not for this day.
9 Ascena, married John Maner of New York.

John M. Milliken was a ready conversationalist, a genial companion, and in his last years, with his long white hair, long white beard, and mustache appeared very patriarchal. So desirous was he that his grave should be marked that several years before his earthly departure he procured the stone now seen in the old Stroudwater grave yard and had it deposited under his bed. This being the case it is but a simple act of justice to here present the inscription as follows.

JOHN M. MILLIKEN,
Died
October 9, 1875,
Æt. 86.

Look aloft, the spirit's risen,
Death cannot the soul imprison,
'Tis in the heaven the spirits dwell
Glorious thought invisible.

SUSAN,
wife of
JOHN M. MILLIKEN,
Died
Nov. 14, 1858,
Aged 66.

"This word" she cried, "is not my place,
I seek a place in heaven,
A country far from mortal sighs,
Yet, O, by faith I see
The land of rest, the saints delight,
The heaven prepared for me."

2 The second child of Asa Fickett was born March 11——named Charles and drowned when three years of age.
3 Theophilus, born Nov. 17 1795. He died when 19 years of age. He was born an invalid, but was an excellent scholar and a marvel with a pen. I know of two pieces of his pen work—one at the residence of Mr. Walter Fickett, Stroudwater, the other at the residence of Mr. William Sparrow, Pleasant street, this city. A small wagon was built for him, as he could not walk, and other scholars would haul him to the school house and back home.
4 George, born July 31, 1797, and died when three months of age.
*5 Francis, born Oct. 8, 1798.
6 Nelly, born March 27, 1800, and died when four years of age.
*7 George, born March 16, 1802.
*8 James, born Nov. 18, 1803.

* These three went to New York; were mechanics and engaged in shipbuilding, but George returned to Portland and died there. (See News Sep. 14, this year, for notice of Fickett.)
9 Nahum, born June 17, 1809. Notice of him in my next article.
10 Jennette, born June 17, 1809, died at Stroudwater, Apr. 13, 1890, where she resided with her brother Nahum. Memorial stone in Stroudwater cemetery. For obituary notice see Portland Argus Apr. 14, of that year
11 Ellen, by second wife as noticed above, and youngest of the family. Her memorial in the Stroudwater cemetery and that of her husband are inscribed as follows.

FATHER.
Elias Jacobs.
DIED
June 18, 1858,
Aged 33 years.

MOTHER.
Ellen F.,
wife of
ELIAS JACOBS,
DIED
July 30, 1875,
Aged 52 years, 4 mos.

TO BE CONTINUED.

Saturday, Nov. 9, 1895.

GRANDPA'S SCRAP BOOK

[Under this head historical and genealogical memoranda will be furnished the readers of the News that appears worthy of preservation, particularly of remote periods in our history within the city limits and immediate vicinity.]

JOHN FICKETT.

A RECORD OF SOME OF HIS DESCENDANTS AND FACTS CONNECTED THEREWITH.

Continued from last week.

The two story dwelling house now owned and occupied by Mr. George B. Jacobs stands upon the site of the old Asa Fickett house and was built by the father of George B.

Nahum Fickett, 9th child of Asa, who I promised to notice this week, was born, as before stated, June 17, 1809. After spending some years in New York with his brothers where he worked both as a black smith and as a ship joiner he returned to Stroudwater and in company with James Parker who lived on Mill Land, now Bond street, engaged in ship joiner work as a contractor.

Benjamin Larraby married, Oct. 12 1762, Lydia Bailey, he of Brunswick, she of Falmouth, but her exact place in the large Bailey family I cannot now fix. His son William, who lived at a place called New Meadows in the town of Brunswick, married, Nov. 1, 1803, Lettice Poterfield, born July 3, 1776, a little over the city limits of Deering, in Westbrook, where Edward Trickey, Esq., resides, on the road from Stroudwater to Saccarappa village. She was sister to Mrs. Peggy (Poterfield) Pierce and Polly Poterfield which Polly kept a shop at Stroudwater where Mr. Thomas W. Jackson resides. (For further notice of the Poterfields, see News of March 17 last year.) The children of William Larraby were as follows:
1. Daniel.
2. Margaret.
3. Elizabeth, born June 25 1809, and when 19 years of age came to Stroudwater to assist her aunt Polly in her store.
4. William P., who was a farmer in the town of Dover, Me., and died there June 23, of this year. He left children: William; Charlotte;——; and Edmond
5. Mary Ann, who preceeded her as clerk for her aunt but married William Poterfield and went to live with him as his second wife on what is now known as the Boothby farm, a mile westerly of Stroudwater. This William Poterfield was the son of Capt. John Poterfield and wife Catherine Slemmons, married Apr. 25, 1788. William was the youngest of their children, and married first, Feb. 16, 1819, Doritha Bailey, who was born in the old Col. Jeremiah Bailey house at Libby's Corner, Jan. 5, 1791 by whom he had one child, that died when a young woman, unmarried.

It was in 1851 for a consideration of $2500 that William Poterfield sold to William Boothby his interest in the farm. The recorded deed contains this bit of history:

"My late father, John Poterfield dec'd rec'd from his father, Wm. Poterfield, by will May 4, 1790; my grandfather William rec'd from Samuel Waldo by Deed, Nov. 11, 1747."

From the farm William and wife Mary Ann moved to Carridan, Ind., where both died without issue. She was remarkably prepossessing and when I saw them seated in the "one horse chaise," or met them at the "village store," she so pretty, he so plain in his suit of black with high coat collar, neck stock, large nose and scant white hair, the difference in their appearance was remarkable to my youthful eyes, but in conversation he was a pleasing man.

Elizabeth Larraby, above noticed, became the wife of Nahum Fickett and they commenced married life in the dwelling built by his father now owned and occupied by Mr. Elias M. Jacobs, which he exchanged soon thereafter for the fine old specimen of the residences of ye olden time where his widow and son Walter with his family reside. A hundred years nearly have passed since the bounds of the acre lot upon which the house stands were established and house built, and nearly a hundred since the two southerly lots were located and not a foot has been added or taken from them. In establishing the bounds of one of these lots the "stump of a white oak tree" is alluded to as standing on the back end of the dividing line between the lots now owned by Mr. Chas. Fickett and Mrs. Susie (McDonald) Morton at rear end, the tree that stood upon the stump thus noticed being referred to at a prior date as standing back of the residence of Col. Thomas Westbrook.

The site of this centurial abode of the Ficketts is the most interesting study of all for the local historian. Much pertaining to it and the locality can never be known, but not unfrequently newly discovered recorded facts dispel the maze of conjecture and establish the truth of tradition. But recently in the Probate Court records at Boston, Mass., in the inventory of the personal estate of Gen. Samuel Waldo who owned the premises in 1759, I found the recorded fact there were four mounted small cannon on the spot at that time.

A few persons still remember the ancient, low posted barn that stood forty years ago adjacent the present Fickett lot on the westerly side which was taken down by Dr. Henry Hunt and the tradition that the planked floor of the corner was where cannon stood. The recent discovery of facts establishes the truthfulness of the tradition.

The children of Nahum Fickett were named as follows:

1. Frances Augustus, married Amos W. Waterhouse of Scarboro. She died Jan. 16, 1860, aged 24 years; he died in consequence of a fall from a building in Portland, Oct. 10, 1865, aged 37 years. They resided in Stroudwater. No children.
2. Edward, married, and resides, or his post office address is University, Cal.
3. Franklin, died Aug. 12, 1888 aged 41 years. He resided in Stroudwater where his widow and sons reside.
4. Charles, married, and resides in Stroudwater.
5. Walter, married, and resides in Stroudwater.

Nahum Fickett, was straight in figure, average in size, very dark or black hair, small side whiskers, and when young must have been above the average in personal appearance. He was industrious, frugal, honest, a ready conversationalist, and accommodating as a neighbor. Without visible profession, when the great summons came, he said; "I am prepared." In the old village cemetery may be seen this reminder of him.

NAHUM FICKETT,
Died
Nov. 25, 1866,
Aged 60 years.

TO BE CONTINUED.

Nov. 16, 1895.

'S SCRAP BOOK

[...and historical and genealogical
...ill be furnished the readers of the
...ppears worthy of preservation, par-
...ly of remote periods in our history within
...ity limits and immediate vicinity.]

JOHN FICKETT.

[RECORD OF SOME OF HIS DESCENDANTS
AND FACTS CONNECTED THEREWITH.

Continued from last week.

Referring to past articles and references relative to the matter under consideration and will here state that Samuel Fickett, the third child of Jonathan and wife Elizabeth alias Betsey—, continued, or assisted in continuing, the shipbuilding business at his father's old place of business on "shipyard point" where the cellar hole of Jonathan's family abode may still be seen to which reference has been made, till about the year of 1808-10, the non-intercourse policy of the general government and embargo act killing business at Stroudwater. But Samuel Fickett being a man of persistency started up a business in Portland where he built large ships and commenced the large house now standing at the foot of State street, and the westerly side thereof, but the depression in business during the war of 1812-15 was too much and like scores of others he went down financially, so that, in the year 1816, his Stroudwater house where Walter Fickett now resides was taken to satisfy an execution of $589.68 in favor of one John Hobert of Portland, and Samuel removed to New York. The record of this transaction refers to the lot as where the so-called "Garrison house formerly stood and where the roads intersect." Mr. Jerome B. Fickett, to whom reference has been in former articles, claims it was this Samuel who built the first steam ship that crossed the Atlantic and not his nephew Frank as has been stated. At New York he far more than regained the value of former losses.

He was born in the year 1771, married Elizabeth Dyer of Cape Elizabeth, and after her decease had two other wives. He became a member of the society of Friends and held offices of trust in New York city where he died. His children, as far as I can learn, were named; Gardner, Mary, Scott, Martha, Fannie, Elizabeth and Walter.

I will now continue the notice of the children of Jonathan Fickett in consecutive order.

Josiah Fickett married Mary Swett of Windham. They had children: ...oh, Jane, Harr. Adeline, Cyrus, ... and Harriet.

Josiah Fickett built the house
...erly side of the
...ocally known at

the "old road," now
...ich house was occupied
...ar by Capt. George Morton,—a
two story house, fronting easterly,
road, which was purchased about
by Nahum Fickett, Mr.——Pride
cupies the site. The house was
about twenty years ago when
by one Reed, Apr. 18, 1812 for a
ation of $670. George Morton,
iner, of Plymouth, purchased
e subject to a mortgage of $1,200
1808, probably the time the
was built. From Stroudwater
with his family removed to St.
n, down in the Provinces, and after
ort stay there went to New York
where he died.

Ephraim, who was a shipwright,
New York city where he died.

...e Ficketts had a shop at the
the yard and close to the mill
...ox oridge. Enoch was a clerk then
his brothers. He died August, 1820,
ed 42 years. (Parson Bradley's journal.)

7 Elizabeth, who married, 1792, Robert Waterhouse of Stroudwater, son of William. In 1795, William conveyed to his son Robert his homestead house and part of lot. He died Aug. 7, 1808 aged 38 years. She died in New York city Aug. 13, 1829, aged 56 years.

Following is the copy of an obituary that appeared in the Portland Argus Aug. 25, 1808.

Died in Falmouth Robert Waterhouse, shipwright, aged 39 years. An honest and influential citizen, who lived beloved, and died universally lamented. He has left a wife and seven children to lament the loss of an affectionate husband and kind father.

The children were named respectively follows:

Sopha, married Thomas Broad, who spent their last years near Stroudwater.

Betsey, married June 15, 1836, Moses Hanson. They resided at Stroudwater.

Almira, married Wm. Roberts of Saccarappa, and went to the town of Harrison.

Charlotte died unmarried.

Frederick, married Aug. 17, 1823 Sarah J. Mange of Libby's Corner. He was a shipwright.

Alpheus, married first, in New York, and had one child. His wife died, married, July 20, 1836, Celia Han- and occupied the homestead of father at Stroudwater, where his

...ottie. (This Waterhouse family will receive a more extended notice later.)

7 Robert.

8 Phebe Fickett married Capt. Samuel Thomes of Libby's Corner, Dec. 31, 1808, Samuel and Asa Fickett for a consideration of $400 conveyed to Phebe (Thomes) Fickett, the lot now owned by Frances F. Milliken, on Westbrook street, at the southerly edge of the village. The house of Samuel Thomes on the lot is alluded to in the conveyance. It was a small affair.

An abstract from the record of another conveyance, made in 1823, reads as follows:

James Brewester Rand of Lovell to Henry H. Roody of Portland, * * * stake standing easterly side of road 17 rods, 4 links from northerly corner of a small house belonging to Samuel Thomes, now occupied by Nathaniel Skillin, 40 square rods of land etc.

This has reference to a house that stood where Mrs. Caroline Stevens now resides, which lot Rand says: "I purchased of Asa Fickett, July, 1812."

The Thomes house was moved to the northerly side of the school house that stood where the present school house stands, and was occupied by the Walker family, two members of which, Hannah and Jane, far advanced in years, recently died.

In the Stroudwater cemetery stands a stone inscribed as follows:

In memory of

PHEBE,

the friend and companion

of

Samuel Thomes,

who died

Aug. 23, 1830,

Æt. 42.

She left eight children, who, with their father, all went to New York city.

9th and last. Nancy, married William Crockett of Gorham, a shipwright, and went to New York city. They had eight children.

TO BE CONTINUED.

THE DEERING NEWS.

Saturday, Nov. 23, 1895.

GRANDPA'S SCRAP BOOK

[Under this head historical and genealogical memoranda will be furnished the readers of the News that appears worthy of preservation, particularly of remote periods in our history within the city limits and immediate vicinity.]

JOHN FICKETT.

A RECORD OF SOME OF HIS DESCENDANTS AND FACTS CONNECTED THEREWITH.

Concluded.

I presented last week all I have to say at this time relative to the Stroudwater branch of the male portion of the Fickett family, and now return to the list of the children of Thomas Fickett of Barren Hill, Cape Elizabeth, as arranged in the News of Oct. 12, this year, and here present—

4th, Daniel Fickett. He went to Narragaugus in this state, as did his brother Zebulon, noticed in a previous article under this head, and this is all I know of him.

5th, Nathaniel. Of this son of Thomas Fickett, Ebenezer Fickett, grandson of Thomas, which Ebenezer I noticed in my article of Oct. 12, says:

He settled between Stroudwater and Saccarappa, and had one son named Clement whom I saw when a boy, also two daughters; one of whom married a Josiah Walker, the other Jonathan Newbegin.

To this I add: Nathaniel Fickett married, Jan. 25, 1765, Polly Pennell of Falmouth, now Deering, (Capisic district). This Pennell family of which Polly was a member has been noticed in previous numbers of the News of late dates to which I refer. In the year 1768, three years after the date of his marriage, he purchased of Francis Waldo a farm lot of land located on the easterly side of the road leading from Stroudwater to Saccarappa, on the northerly side of the Starbird's, and where the Westbrook cemetery is now located. On this lot he located and erected the shelter for himself and family. The cellar hole and old apple trees are well remembered by the writer hereof. Of his descendants I here present the following memoranda:

Sept. 27, 1791. Married—Betsey Fickett and Richard Tobie, he of New Gloucester.

Apr. 22, 1792. Polly Fickett and Jonathan Newbegin.

Nov. 11, 1800. Patience Fickett and Solomon Strout of Limington.

—— —— Ann Fickett and Josiah Walker.

In 1793, the heirs of Nathaniel Fickett were:

1 Joseph Walker of Freeport and Ann, his wife.
2 Richard Tobie of New Gloucester and Betsey, his wife.
3 Jonathan Newbegin of Falmouth and Polly, his wife.

In 1815 for a consideration of $665, Solomon Strout, adm., of Limington, sold rty-five acres of land and "small house .d barn" to George and Alexander Babb—"the estate of Clement Fickett," which covered the homestead of Nathaniel Fickett.

I presume that Moses Fickett noticed, in a previous article, in going over from Cape Elizabeth to see his relative Nathaniel, became acquainted with Sally Warren whose home he was obliged to pass on the way, and married her Jan. 27, 1791.

Clement Fickett, who, Ebenezer Fickett says he once saw, which I have noticed above, was son of Nathaniel, and succeeded him in the possession of the parental home.

Next southerly of Nathaniel Fickett lived the Starbirds—their land joined the Fickett's, and next to the highway here noticed, and in the southerly corner of the Westbrook cemetery, covering a portion of the Fickett farm, a burying place was commenced. The last time I visited it twenty grave mounds were visible, some marked by a rudely shaped ledge stone, but not one was lettered. When the property was disposed of the burial place was reserved, but the size or location of bounds are not stated.

Mr. G. S. Fickett, of North Sebago, is a great grandchild to Clement, and Clement Fickett of No. 63 Myrtle street, Portland, is a descendant of Clement, the original. And this is all I know of this branch.

6th, Abner, and last son, but Ebeneza only states the fact there was an Abner. Of him I have no knowledge.

Of the two daughters of Thomas Fickett, Ebeneza says: "One married Ichabod Libby of Scarboro; the other, Charles Patrick of Stroudwater.,'

This Chas. Patrick was the second child of David Patrick, which David appears as early as 1737 in court records, and on the town records of Falmouth in 1741. He and Mehitable Fickett were married June 2, 1767, and in the year 1781 purchased land in the town of Gorham, Me., where he thereafter resided and reared a family.

This closes my notice of the Ficketts; my next will relate to the Patrick family of Stroudwater.

Saturday, Nov. 30, 1895.

GRANDPA'S SCRAP BOOK

[Under this head historical and genealogical memoranda will be furnished the readers of the News that appears worthy of preservation, particularly of remote periods in our history within the city limits and immediate vicinity.]

DAVID PATRICK.

THE NAMES OF SOME OF HIS DESCENDANTS AND FACTS CONNECTED THEREWITH.

From whence came David Patrick, the exact time he arrived, and the site of his first landing place at the hamlet of Stroudwater, painstaking research does not disclose. The clang of the mile-saw by day and the bark of the wolf by night were familiar sounds to the few denizens of the locality at the time of his advent of which he became one. He was a mechanic—a brick-maker and brick mason. His chirography was of the best of the time. Opposite of the present school house, he moulded the vergin clay into brick shaped cubes; the clay, for the purpose being obtained evidently from the hole now to be seen northwesterly of the school house some twenty-five rods distant, on land then owned by him, and still is possession of a descendant. The first record notice of him I find on the books of the Inferior Court of Common Pleas, Boston, Mass., in the case of Richard Fry vs. David Patrick, of Falmouth an abstract of which is as follows:

A large brass kettle, two chairs, a brass skillet, a powdering tub and a half barrel of soap valued at £20. Non suit.''

This Richard Fry was a character, apparently a crazy character, who figured in the early history of Stroudwater and vicinity in various ways, several of his communications addressed to the Great and General Court of the Commonwealth being our file in the Massachusetts archives. some written in jail where he was confined. He was connected with the Stroudwater paper mill project and some of his statements are very misleading. The court record to which allusion is above made relates evidently in some way to the paper mill failure. He preferred charges he could not sustain, and the one against David Patrick may have been one of the sort. Patrick in some way was connected with the paper mill I find a record made in 1743 which shows Patrick lived at that period "in a house built with some conveniences for paper makers," the record giving the names of the several peices of furniture contained in the house. In the year 1741 he was elected surveyor of lumber in Falmouth. In 1743 he made a purchase of Gen. Saml. Waldo of two pieces of two pieces of land, one containing "three acres and twelve perches" one "lying on ye southerly side of Fore river nigh unto the Great Bridge built over the same.'' (York Co. Records, Vol. 26, p. 47. This is the piece upon which the ancient shops of Stroudwater are built, and comprises the entire lot extending from the highway in front of the shops northerly to Mr. Daniel Dole's fence, and westerly to the Saccarappa road. The other lot contained "one fourth of an acre of land lying at Stroudwater aforesaid and adjoining a cottage lately inhabited by our William Libby."

To fix by records the site exactly of the "cottage" of William Libby, is too much of a task for me; but I am of the opinion that if the one story house standing next northerly of the old Stevens mansion, and in the southwesterly angle made by Congress and Westbrook streets crossing each other, is not the repaired Libby "cottage" of 1743, then the present house occupies the site thereof.

It is more than probable that David Patrick, when he moved from the house with "some conveniences for paper makers." moved into the Libby cottage, for thirty years later I find his widow living there.

The river at this point must have been boomed,'' and the cottage was erected for the accommodation of laborers in the employ of Messrs. Westbrook & Waldo, the land kings of the region. Where the school house now stands was the "mast landing place" of that time, which, a few years later, was officially dedicated to public purposes, as manuscript records show, but later became a bone of contention, the dispute terminating in a law suit, settled by a rule of court.

It is apparent that the present Stevens lot comprises more than a fourth of an acre at this time. This fact, with the present position of the old Mary Patrick house. indicates to my mind that the highway as then used was located nearer the Stroudwater river than now.

To David's name there is no grave memorial, nor to any one by the name of Patrick in the region of Stroudwater, but the top of the great chimney in the ancient abode of the once "King's Mast Agent," George Tate, may be seen a piece of the work of "the hand that is laid away," performed at the time of the birth of Margaret Patrick, daughter of David, which was Aug. 17, 1754.

The time David Patrick departed this life records do not show, but Mary, his wife, according to the records of Parson Bradley, died August, 1806, aged 95, thus showing she was born in 1711. Allowing her husband to have been five years her senior he must have been born in 1706.

It is traditional that his wife's maiden name, was Mary Hawkins, and a record of which the following is an abstract shows there were seven children that reached years of maturity who were named respectively: 1—William; 2—Charles; 3—Eleanor; 4—Margaret; 5—Elizabeth; 6—Mary; and 7th Betsey.

William Tate of London, mariner, to Tristram Stevens, consideration $70, being all right and title in the estate of David Patrick, deceased, said right being the right of the said William's mother, Eleanor (Patrick) Tate of Falmouth, being the one-seventh part of the estate of Mary Patrick.

There is a tradition that the indentation which I attribute to the removal of clay for brick purposes was caused by an attempt to dig through from Fore to the Stroudwater river and so run lumber and logs through a sluice from the last to the first named rivers. Mine is conjecture, the other tradition—hence record truth is needed to establish the facts.

NOTE. The transposition of punctuation marks made one part of my article last week misleading. It should have read, in the notice of Josiah Fickett, as follows:

The house was burned about twenty years ago when occupied by one Reed. Apr. 18, 1812 for a consideration of $670 George Morton, Jr., mariner, of Plymouth, Mass., purchased the place subject to a mortgage, etc.

TO BE CONTINUED.

THE DEERING NEWS.

Saturday, Dec. 7, 1895.

GRANDPA'S SCRAP BOOK

[Under this head historical and genealogical memoranda will be furnished the readers of the News that appears worthy of preservation, particularly of remote periods in our history within the city limits and immediate vicinity.]

DAVID PATRICK.

THE NAMES OF SOME OF HIS DESCENDANTS AND FACTS CONNECTED THEREWITH.

On the first day of February, 1803, the highway from what now appears as the intersection of Bond and Congress streets, running easterly over Stroudwater river, crossing the Saccarrappa road, now known as Westbrook street, thence down the hill, passing the ancient shops, to the old bridge, locally known as the "long bridge," was established. Prior to that period all the travel was via of Bond street, from Portland westward to Buxton. The record of the event contains important historical facts in several respects and is as follows:

ROAD FROM BUXTON TO PORTLAND.—DAMAGES IN FALMOUTH.

Heirs of George Knight, dec'd.	$ 60
Richard Johnson	100
Adam Sloan	28
John Johnson	60
Wm. Slemmons	80
Joseph H. Ingraham and those who own the small lot between Stroudwater river and Saccarappa road.	220
Mary Patrick	20
Total,	$578

Wm. Slemmons lived where Mr. Joseph Parker now resides and owned the Hunt, Maxfield Chapman property, etc. The terminating courses of the highway were as follows: "North 55 d. E.—10 rods, crossing Stroudwater river to near an old road; thence N. 69d. E.—18 rods and 18 links; thence N. 48 1-2 d. E.—13 rods and 20 links to a stake in the county road, 14 rods and 11 links on a course N. 20 d. E. from the well near the northerly corner of Capt. James Means' dwelling house and two rods and 20 links from the southerly corner of the store of Archelaus Lewis, Esq., on a course of N. 30 d. West from whence the road into Portland was laid before."

The reference "to near an old road" means the way between the schoolhouse and Walker house, on Congress street, which was formally laid out in the month of Dec. 1770, and approved by the town April 1771. It was eight rods wide, and shows that Mrs. Mary Patrick's barn stood on the opposite side of the road from her house and about where the guide board now stands, which barn is still remembered by our aged citizen, Mr. Chas. Maxfield.

This record fixes the site, (for the well still remains,) of an ancient land mark, that was fully described in the News of May 25th, this year, to which I now refer.

David Patrick was slow in relinquishing his title to real estate by sale. He seems to have preferred the lease; he did however for a consideration of 6£. 13s. 4p. in the year 1757, March 26, sell to "George Tate of Surry county, Great Britain, now of Falmouth, a small lot located southerly side of Fore River nigh unto the Great Bridge, commencing bounds at David Patrick's first bounds" which lot was forty-five feet on front and extending back fifty feet, upon which Tate built a warehouse in connection with his mast business. The blacksmith shop of Mr. Walter Fickett is now located upon the lot, or a part of it.

In the year 1782 Patrick was dead and Tate sold the lot "with wharf, and store or warehouse, with all the orerafts in said store," to Jonathan Webb whose wife at that time was a daughter of Tate's second wife, Tate marrying Mary Coverly, Apr. 15, 1779, and Webb being united to her daughter Mary by marriage in March, of 1781.

In the year 1784, Charles Patrick came down from Gorham, and being reinforced by Wm. Patrick and Tristram Stevens, on the 4th day of May of that year, "with force and arms entered the close of Jonathan Webb and broke down five lengths of fence to the value of 40 shillings," a dispute having arose as to the bounds of the lot which were later established by a rule of the court.

TO BE CONTINUED.

THE DEERING NEWS.

Saturday, Dec. 14, 1895.

GRANDPA'S SCRAP BOOK

[Under this head historical and genealogical memoranda will be furnished the readers of the News that appears worthy of preservation, particularly of remote periods in our history within the city limits and immediate vicinity.]

DAVID PATRICK.

THE NAMES OF SOME OF HIS DESCENDANTS AND FACTS CONNECTED THEREWITH.

Continued from last week.

In my first article under this caption, two weeks ago, I gave the number of David Patrick's children as seven who reached years of maturity and their respective names, but I am not sure the classifiation is correct; in fact I am convinced it is not, but will not attempt a change here.

1 William, son of David, I do not know where he was born, who he married, the number of his children, or when he died. The site of his abode is the site of the so-called Walker house now standing on the northerly side of Congress street, opposite the school house, standing in the southeasterly angle where Westbrook street crosses Congress, at Stroudwater. It was a story and part of a story structure, the part being about three feet high under the eaves, with port-holes protected with shutters, supposed to have been arranged for protection in case of Indian invasion. Our venerable citizen, Mr. Chas. Maxfield, now more than 90 years of age, discribed it to me more than once, years ago when his mind was active and recollection good.

Parson Bradley states in his diary that the wife of William Patrick died Sept. 18, 1800, aged 56 years, thus showing she was born in the year 1744.

A daughter of this William, named Harlot, May 1, 1802, married Wm. Stoddard, and Sept. 3, 1803 there died, "a child of Wm. Stoddard."

August 24, 1775, a David Patrick and Elizabeth Potter were united in marriage, he evidently a son of William.

March 25, 1827, a William B. Peters and Elizabeth P. Patrick were united in marriage.

In the year 1839, the following named persons were heirs at law to Harlot P. Stoddard, at which time the homestead lot was conveyed to David Stevens, grandson of Tristram Stevens, whose wife was Margaret Patrick. And David Stevens moved the present house from a point on Congress street, next southwesterly of the iron bridge built over Stroudwater river, to which house Alexander Walker added a half story.

I think it was in the latter part of summer the building was moved to its present location, and small birch trees were used as skids under the shoes. Aunt Peggy Pierce, who has been noticed as living at the time at the other end of the present landing of the iron bridge, but on the northerly side of the highway, established in 1803, and noticed in my last article, said the bark removed from the skids was excellent stuff to start fires and if we boys would collect it she would pay us, and so we worked "with might and main." In course of time the house arrived at its place of destination, the bark was all gathered, and Aunt Peggy obtained two cents worth of peppermints and when divided we had two each. That was my first business adventure, or performance of manual labor for hire of which I have recollection, and was fifty-six years ago, if the house was moved the year the lot was purchased by David Stevens.

The heirs to the ownership of the lot when Stevens bought it were as follows: Harriet Stoddard and William Stoddard of Portland; Elizabeth P. Peters of Portland, widow; Benjamin Harmon, chaise maker, and Mary Elizabeth, his wife, in her right; Hariot Amelia Stoddard, singlewoman; William P. Stoddard, yeoman, of Portland and Charles S. Stoddard of Cambridge, Mass. The lot is nine rods wide on front.

2. Charles Patrick, married June 9, 1767, Mehitable Fickett of Cape Elizabeth, and in 1781 purchased land in Gorham, Me., where he resided. He has been noticed in the News in connection with the Fickett family, particularly Nov. 23.

3. Mary, married with William Tate, who succeeded his father, George Tate, "the King's mast agent," in possession of the Tate mansion, now standing, and built the shop in 1784, now occupied by Andrew Hawes, Esq. This Tate was a trader at Stroudwater and will be noticed later.

4. Margaret, born Aug. 17, 1754, and Dec 8, 1775, married Tristram Stevens, the first of the name at Stroudwater, who came from Newburyport.

TO BE CONTINUED.

Bailey's Island.

Mr. George Leeman has built him a new store on the island and fitted it up with groceries and intends to try his luck at storekeeping. Mr. Leeman is a very smart, enterprising young man and we wish him great success.

THE DEERING NEWS.

Saturday, Dec. 21, 1895.

GRANDPA'S SCRAP BOOK

[Under this head historical and genealogical memoranda will be furnished the readers of the News that appears worthy of preservation, particularly of remote periods in our history within the city limits and immediate vicinity.]

Extracts from Rev. Caleb Bradley's Journal.

Feb. 15, 1837, four persons presented themselves for examination for admittance to the church namely; Mrs North Charlotte Stevens, Ed. Newman and Josiah S. North.

March 16, 1837. Business dull, breadstuff high; yellow corn $1.33, white $1.20; flour $12.50; beef steak 11 cents; butter 16¼; potatoes 50 cents. Many are in a state of distress—almost starvation. One great reason why breadstuff is so high, there is so much grain used by distilleries 1,200,000 used in the state of N. Y., in a year.

Apr. 8, 1837, p. m. Stroudwater yarn company met at Thackers and found things favorable.

Apr. 7. Spent a long a. m. in the city on business. 4 bails of cotton by steamer Portland this morning. Helped load it, paid an Irishman three cents for his assistance.

Aug. 7. Albert Chesley and one of Mr. Wm. Graves children died this morning of fever. Rev. Mr. Lane attended the funeral of Mr. Grave's child and Rev. Mr. Whitman, Mr. Chesleys. Nearly twenty are sick with the typhus fever. Nothing but trouble all about.

Apr. 5th 1837. This day city officers elected (Portland) Levi Cutter, (whig) Mayor, had (a) struggle—rub and go.

6th. A caucus today at Mr. North's relating to town affairs etc.

11th. Town meeting today—great excitement. Temperance and antitemperance; the last carried their points. All the town antitemperance—disgraceful, abonable, unaccountable, too bad!

It seems as though the devil is suffered to reign and has come down in great wrath, thinking his time is short, and I pray it may be in this town, or we shall be ruined.

May 26, 1837. Went to Gorham. Centennial celebration in this place. Josiah Pierce made an address, rather an interesting day.

June 30, 1837. The mill (at Stroudwater) came nigh burning this day, but Providence ordered it otherwise. This took place at 9 a. m.

Oct. 1st. The Westbrook Stroudwater Thread company met and concluded to call a meeting and organize agreeable to an act of incorporation on the 18th of this month at the Cumberland house in Portland, at 7 o'clock p. m.

6th. The water runs over the dam at Stroudwater, business enough, water sufficient for factory and mill.

18th. Fair day, but rather cool. Cattle show today, a multitude of people and many cattle. General Appleton delivered an address before the society in our meeeting house, much order and decorum were observable. (Rev.) Mr. Jameson (of Scarboro) made a prayer. A premium of $10 was given for hay cut on my farm, seventeen tons 400ct and 67lbs on five acres and 29 rods of land.)

THE DEERING NEWS.

Saturday, Dec. 28, 1895.

GRANDPA'S SCRAP BOOK

[Under this head historical and genealogical memoranda will be furnished the readers of the News that appears worthy of preservation, particularly of remote periods in our history within the city limits and immediate vicinity.]

DAVID PATRICK.
THE NAMES OF SOME OF HIS DESCENDANTS

AND FACTS CONNECTED THEREWITH.

Continued from two weeks ago.

I stated at the close of my article two weeks ago that Margaret, daughter of David and Mary Patrick of Stroudwater was born Aug. 17 1754 and Dec. 8 1775, united in marriage with Tristram Stevens, a joiner, who came from Newburyport and succeeded his father-in-law in possession by purchase most of the homestead, Chas. Patrick disposing of his interest to Stevens in the year 1781; Richard Pain and wife Elizabeth who was David's daughter, Pain being at the time of the transaction, a blacksmith residing at Gorham, Me. The transfer of Tate has been alluded to in a former article. A claim was made by the Patrick heirs to the lot where Mr. Thomas W. Jackson now resides where Aunt Polly Porterfield traded so many years, and thence northerly, including part of the lot now used for burial purposes, where a house stood within the present grave yard enclosure, which will be noticed later, but upon what grounds the claim was founded I have never discovered.

Who built originally, whether Patrick or Stevens, or some one before their time, the ancient one story dwelling now standing next northerly of the large Tristram Stevens mansion, owned and occupied at the present time by his son Michael, I am unable to state. In ye olden time when less regard was paid to appearances than now, a long, lowposted building stood in front of the house, end to the highway, and on the southerly side of the front door, which building was used as a carpenter shop. The date of the disappearance, and by whom the building was removed I cannot at this time state.

Of the characteristics of Tristram Stevens I have no knowledge. He was born Oct. 19 1751 at Newburyport, Mass., and died Nov. 21 1803, thus showing him to be 52 years of age at the time of his demise. His wife Margaret Patrick, was born, as has been shown, Aug. 17 1754, and died——.

CHILDREN.

1. Samuel, born Aug. 28 1777, married Polly Herrick, and has been noticed in connection with the Fickett family, Polly's mother being a Fickett.
2. Tristram Coffin, born Nov. 6 1779. He was a joiner, and in connection with his brother Samuel built the mansion now standing which both occupied till death called them away. He is to be further noticed later.
3. Margaret born Jan. 28 1781, died Oct. 14 1785 from the effects of a kick of a horse.
4. Nancy born Nov. 30 1783, married with a man by the name of Leonard, a blacksmith, and resided at Windham, or vicinity, and has children named Margaret; Samuel; Nancy; Albert and perhaps more.
5. Eleanor, born Nov. 20 1785, married Paul Morrrill of Newburyport who was a tobacco merchant. After his death she returned to Stroudwater and lived in the Uncle Ben Burnham house that stood in the south easterly angle made by Westbrook and Bond streets at Stroudwater, which house was taken down about 25 years ago by Mr. Robert Waterhouse to make room for the house now occupied by Mr. Fred Libby. The children were name respectively—if I am correctly informed—1. Ellen, who married Geo. S. Barstow of Portland whose daughter married Rev. Mr. Boles, a Universalist preacher, and another Mr. Geo. S. Hunt of Portland; 3. Paul; 4. Elizabeth married Mr. Wm. E. Short, whose son resides in Portland, a member of the firm of Loring, Short and Harmon, book sellers; 4. Samuel; and 5, Margaret Ann.
6. Michael born Nov. 30 1787.

TO BE CONTINUED.

THE DEERING NEWS.

Saturday, January 4, 1896.

GRANDPA'S SCRAP BOOK

[Under this head historical and genealogical memoranda will be furnished the readers of the News that appears worthy of preservation, particularly of remote periods in our history within the city limits and immediate vicinity.]

DAVID PATRICK.

THE NAMES OF SOME OF HIS DESCENDANTS AND FACTS CONNECTED THEREWITH.

Continued from last week.

I stated at the close of my last article that Michael Stevens, sixth child of Tristram Stevens and wife Margaret Patrick, was born Nov. 30 1787. Michael united in marriage June, 11 1811, at Stroudwater, with Mrs. Lucy Cobb. She was the widow of one Daniel Cobb Jr., with whom she married March 9, 1809. Further than this I know nothing of Cobb. She was the daughter of Henry Webb, mariner, who was lost at sea. Henry married, March 20, 1780, with Ann Riggs of Bradley's Corner, and was a brother to Col. James Webb, a Revolutionary soldier, who settled in Stroudwater, also to Sally Webb who married Gen. John Kilby Smith, March 2, 1785, who, after the close of the war of the Revolution, was a trader at Stroudwater in a small building that stood on the easterly side of what is now known as Waldo street, about half way up the hill. Of these Webbs a more extended notice will be made shortly. Henry Webb resided in the Uncle Ben Burnham house, noticed last week as the residence at one time of Mrs. Eleanor (Patrick) Merrill, which was built by Henry Webb in 1786, or I should say, he purchased the lot that year. Michael Stevens purchased a lot on the southerly side of Free street, not far from Oak street, Portland, where he was burned out. He was a joiner and resided at several places, once on a farm at Minot or vicinity, but last on Oak street, Portland, southerly of Free. He died in the month of March 1856 aged 68 years; she died at No. 30, Oak street, Nov. 14, 1888, aged 94 years and 11 months, thus showing she was born 1794.

CHILDREN:
1 Lucy Ann, married.
2 Margaret, married Abial T. Noyes of Portland.
3 Smith Cobb, married and resided in Minot.
4 Lucretia, went to California where she married.

It was in 1828 that Michael Stevens sold the Henry Webb house to David Burnham of Scarboro, for the small sum of $200.

7 David Stevens born Apr. 11, 1789, married March 12, 1819, Sophia Peaks. She was the daughter of Mary Peaks who became the second wife of Col. James Webb, Nov. 19, 1809. This Mary was a widow when Col. Webb married with her, and her maiden name was Mary Thomes of Libby's Corner. She was a sister to Capt. Sam'l. Thomes, whose wife was Phebe Fickett of Stroudwater, noticed in the News Nov. 16, 1895, also to the wife of Zenas Pratt who owned at one time the State Reform school farm, and who was drowned in Portland harbor 1818. Sophia (Peaks) Steven's sister married with Lemuel Stevens of Woodfords, noticed in the News Oct. 20, 1894. Isaac Thomes, brother to Mary (Thomes, Peaks) Webb died at Biddeford. Mrs. Mary Webb died very suddenly on the way home from Portland, June 24, 1841, while riding. David Steven's widow Sophia died at Stroudwater, Apr. 3, 1878 aged 85 years. They resided in the Col. James Webb house the last part of their lives, that stood next southerly of the residence of Henry Webb. He was noticed in the News of May 25, 1895.

In 1815 he resided upon the Patrick homestead and paid a tax on a valuation of $170, one-third of a barn $10, and one-half shop $20; while Samuel and Tristram, his brothers, paid a valuation of $700 upon the present Stevens mansion house; two-thirds of the barn, and two acres of land valued at $30.

8 And last, Charles born ——— 1791. He married at Portland Nov. 27, 1825, Eunice Marriner, whose parents resided at the foot of State street, that city. He was a joiner, resided at one time on the Patrick homestead, tore out the great chimney of the residence and otherwise changed the above, which came into the possession of Tristram, son of Tristram C. Stevens, by purchase, about the year 1840, who, about ten years later, sold to Seth Frazier, who renovated again and raised and put in the underpinning as now observed, Tristram building on "Stevens Court," Park street, Portland, but now residing, an aged and respected citizen, on Neal street, of that city. Charles finally removed from Portland with his farm to the "far west country."

Elizabeth, the fifth child of David Patrick, married with Richard Paine. He was a blacksmith and resided in Gorham, Me., or Windham, and in 1785 disposed of their interest in their father's estate to Tristram Stevens.

Mary, the sixth child of David Patrick, married Aug. 21, 1762, with Richard McDougal and had children named David, a joiner of Gorham, Me., and James, who died here. There may have been others. Their part of the estate was the present Stroudwater hall lot, the list of names of owners of which at different times is long, the first house upon it being built by Josiah Cox of Portland, an uncle to the venerable Hon. W. W. Thomas of that city and part of the dwelling or all of it at one time was used as a shop.

An extract from a deed relating to the premises dated 1791, reads as follows:

Josiah Cox to David Choate, consideration 170£, lawful money—"The dwelling house, shop and barn which I lately occupied, standing at Stroudwater landing, in Falmouth, upon land belonging to Mary Patrick, and which buildings are now improved by Gardner Goold as a tenant under me."

This David Choate was a baker, and came here from Wiscasset, then called Pownalboro. He built the house now standing at the head of Waldo street, next southerly of the Milliken house and now owned by Mr. Washington Tate. Two years later the property went back to Cox 10£ less than was paid by Choate, and a few years later he died leaving minor children.

This Gardner Goold at one time was a trader at Capisic.

Betsey, the seventh and last child of David Patrick did not marry. In 1815 she was living in Portland but when and where she departed this life, and age, I cannot ascertain.

This closes my notice of the Patrick name.

THE DEERING NEWS.

Saturday, January 11, 1896.

GRANDPA'S SCRAP BOOK

[Under this head historical and genealogical memoranda will be furnished the readers of the News that appears worthy of preservation, particularly of remote periods in our history within the city limits and immediate vicinity.]

In the News of Aug. 10, of last year and subsequent numbers I presented the date of the organization of the Third Parish church of Falmouth, now Deering, and many facts connected with the Parish.

The Third Parish Book of Records Since the Year of our Lord one thousand Seven Hundred & Sixty four September ye tenth.

```
The THIRD
Parish
BOOK OF RECORDS
Since September the Tenth
Annoque Dominie
1764.
```

The above is a *factum simile* of the first page of the old Parish book of records, now, before me as I write, which is in size by actual measurement 13 inches long, 8 inches wide, 1 5-8 inches thick and in excellent state of preservation considering its age, but it must be bore in mind this is the Parish record, the church, being an independent organization, whose record book was destroyed at the time of the burning of Dea. Hiram H. Dow's shop at Brighton Corner some years since.

Dea. John Bailey, who spent his last days on earth in the house now occupied by Miss Helen M. Bailey, Congress street, near Libby's Corner, which was then one story, when he died, March, 1770, was the first clerk, Mr. Daniel D. Chenery being the last whose name appears in the old book, though the Parish has at this time a legal Parish organization. The records comprise 256 pages, and the last entry was made Feb. 25, 1871. Deacon Bailey who was noticed briefly in the News of Sept. 7, last year, was continued as clerk till 1770, when Joseph Riggs was elected his successor, who was continued three years, during which time the book now before me evidently was obtained, and the records from a smaller book transferred to it.

The record after the title page reads as follows:

Page first of the forth Parish Book in falmouth in the County of Cumberland Sep tenth 1764 The Said Parish by a Legall Worning Mett at mr Joseph Riggs and agreed to Settell the Gospell among them, in the first they Chose Mr. Jno. Johnson their moderator

2d They Chose John Bayley their Parish Clerk

3d Voted a Commity and Chose them Namely Mr James Merrill Mr. William Slemons & Mr Joseph Riggs to gitt the Parish incorporated into a Regulation by applying to the great and General Court for a Conforming Said Parish as a forth Parish

4 Voted that Mr Joseph Riggs goo See if He Can Gitt a good Gospell Minister to Preach unto them as Soon as Convainly will alow of Said Riggs. To agree with Minister to Preach for Sometime in order for tryall in Said Parish. October the third 1764 the Revraud Thomas Browne Came to Preach to the above Said Parish or peopell and the Next Lords Day He preached unto them —and Monday the Eight Day following the Parish mett att Mr Jeremiah Riggs And Voted an addition to the former Comity Namely Cptr Samuel Skillings,— and Mr Anthony Morss to be impowred with the other Commity to agree With the Revd Thomas Browne to Preach three or five Months & Like Wise to agree With Said Minister for His Bourding.—Voted Likewise Said Comity to gitt a frame forty feet Long & thirty feett wide one Story High to be Slit Near where the meeting house is to be Bult Near the County Road above Mr anthony Brackett Jun House to Be for the Meting House for the Pressent

The foregoing is a *facsimile* of the first page of the Parish records as it appears in the old book which compreses some over three-fourths of a page in copy.

The house for worship for which provision was made as above indicated stood where the present so called Bradley meeting house, which is the third building erected on the site for the same purpos, is seen today.

I would be pleased to continue here the record as found in the old book, but too much space would be required, so will content myself by saying that trouble immediately arose with reference to the parish territorial boundary lines, and the matter carried to the halls of the State Legislature more than once, where I find records and a plan.

In 1773, in compliance with a resolve of the Legislature, the matter of running the line was referred to a committee of three of the parish, consisting of William Slemons who resided where Fred A. Johnson now resides in the original Slemons house, though renovated and repaired, located a little westerly of Stroudwater, Joseph Riggs, who resided at Bradley's Corner, and John Brackett, a civil engineer, then residing at Saccarappa, who died at Ipswich, Mass., while a captain in the war of the Revolution, which committee reported April, 27 of year 1773.

In the record the "Back Cove bridge" that stood south westerly of the James Deering mansion house is alluded to, now Grove street, Portland, where the land is "high and dry," as well as a tree on the south east side of Presumpscot river "about 15 rods below Joshua Brackett and John Robinson dividing fence, and is on said Brackett's land," where the running was stopped.

The adoption of the State Constitution was an act that was very damaging for a while to the prosperity of the Congregational church which was supported by a tax upon the pole of the voter and estates of all.

On page 131 of the old record I find the following:

To Randall Johnson, Clerk of the Congregational society of Westbrook:

We, the subscribers, hereby notify the Parish that we do not wish to be classed with said Parish, or society, and hereby declare ourselves exempt from, and not liable to pay any part of any future expense, which may be incurred by said society. Westbrook, April 14, 1821:

James Means	Nathl. Waldron
Tyng Smith	James Barber
John Porterfield	Rufus Huston
James Porterfield	Stephen Knight
Jonathan Smith	Robert Ilsley
Amos P. Knox	David Smith
Wm. Slemons	Jeremiah Clement
Charles Ferguson	Thomas Riggs
Samuel Stevens	Daniel Conant
Tristram C. Stevens	Thomas Starbird
Robert Bartlett	Amos Winslow

CONTINUED!

Thomas Smith
David Stevens
Henry Pratt
Chas Bartlett
William Bartlett
Noah Jordan
Nathaniel Libby
John Knight, Jr.
Will Trickey
Silas Hamilton
Randall Johnson
Roland Knight
Silas Broad
Samuel Bailey
Jesse Green
Joseph Cox
James Johnson
Benj. Waterhouse
Joshua H. Marean
Henry Sawyer
Frederick Marble
Thomas Broad
Henry Blake
Benjamine Roberts
Daniel Trickey
Brackett Sawyer
Timothy Galvin
John Stevens
Enoch Freeman
Andrew P. Frost
Nathl. Haskell, Jr.
William Hicks
Nathaniel Stevens
William Stevens
James P. Bailey
Berilla Buckley
Joseph M. Sawyer
Samuel Goold
David Trickey
Zich. Brackett
Levi Starbird
Samuel Lamb
Rufus Fluent
Peter Pride
James Barber, Jr.
Mrs. Charity Thomes
Nathl. Thomes
Joshua Thomes
Joshua Porter
Enoch Preble
Benj. Burnham
George Tukey, Jr.
Isaac Fly
Charles Stevens
George Tukey
F. A. Bailey
Samuel Dalton
Job Thomes
Wm. Libby
Alexander Babb
James Webb
Dexter Brewer
Wm. Goold
Joseph Copps
Asa Knight
Simon Cutter
Benj. B. Foster
Wm. Valentine
John Jordan
Daniel Lombard
Jeremiah Bailey
Bela Shaw
Samuel Ray & Son
Francis Hicks
George Jones
Wm. Copps
George Haskell
Nathl. Wakefield
Moses Stiles
Major Plumer
Henry Jackson
Jeremiah Johnson
Wm. Emery
Wm. Siemons, Jr.
James B. Tucker
Peter T. Clark
John Stiles
Samuel Mason
Wm. Pride, Jr.
Rufus Road
Josiah Maxfield
Simon Gilmore
Gardner Walker
Anthony Nutter
Joseph Libby
Joseph W. Haskell
Nathan Sawyer

At this date Westbrook and Deering were one town.

The withdrawal from the parish as indicated by the foregoing did not interfere with the individual's membership of the same.

The Saccarappa Congregational Society is an off-shoot of what is now the First of Deering over which Rev. Joseph Searl was installed Apr. 3, 1833.

A movement in the winter of 1871 to repair the so-called Bradley meeting-house accelerated the contemplated departure of the Woodfords Corner part of the society, and in the fragmentary church record left by the late Dea. Hiram H. Dow may be seen as follows:

July 21, 1872, eight members and Aug. 11 three more left the society to join the Congregational church about to be formed at Woodfords Corner as follows: Mrs. H. B. Read, Mrs. Jane B. Read, Mrs. Miriam Felton, Mrs. S. B. Hopkins, Mrs. Mary E. Chenery, Mrs. H. B. Woodford, Mr. Isaac Bailey, Mr. John J. Chenery, Mr. Wm. H. Scott, Miss Mary A. Newman and Mrs. Harriet Sawyer.

THE DEERING NEWS.

Saturday, January 18, 1896.

GRANDPA'S SCRAP BOOK

[Under this head historical and genealogical memoranda will be furnished the readers of the News that appears worthy of preservation, particularly of remote periods in our history within the city limits and immediate vicinity.]

THOMAS CLOISE AND CHARLES FROST.

NAMES OF OFFSPRING AND SOME OF THE EVENTS CONNECTED WITH THEIR LIVES.

Soon after the time peace was declared with the Indians here at Casco which was Apr. 12, 1678, the inhabitants began to return and occupy their former places of abode at Back Cove, Stroudwater, etc.

In the year 1680 President Danforth came down from Boston and in the month of September, that year, held a court in the fort that stood at the foot of India street, Portland. He took the matter of granting land titles into his own hands. Some of his proceedings in this particular are recorded at Alfred, York county. "It is granted," the record reads, "to Mr. Gedney, George Ingalls, and John Ingalls that instead of sixty acres apiece accommodation on some of the islands they shall be allowed the like quantity in the place where George Ingalls corn mill standeth." The like grant is made to Francis Nicholls, Thomas Mason, Joseph Ingalls, St. George Ingalls, Samuel Ingalls and John Welden.

It is beyond question that the mill built by the Ingalls' at the time of which I now write stood on the Stroudwater river. In fact the present title to the privilege is readily traceable to that period in time as are other land titles hereabouts. And here I wish to introduce an old paper containing several truths of a local historical nature, as well as of a genealogical character of much value. This paper has never been printed; it is in its original form, and is before me as I write.

On the 27th of July 1657, certain Indian representatives deeded to one Francis Small an indefinite number of acres of upland and marsh at Capisic which title came into the possession of George Munjoy, and under which the land in front of the so-called Bradley church, this city, is held; easterly to the rear line of the lot of Mr. John B. Curtis, upon which he now resides, and westerly to the water of the mill pond, and southerly to Fore river.

In 1674, Thomas Cloise settled on a part of this and the site of his dwelling is supposed to be the site of the Brewer House that was used so many years as an inn, which was destroyed by fire a few years ago, but the large cellar remains on the southerly side of Congress street, and easterly bank of Fore river—opposite Stroudwater village.

When the town of Falmouth was last settled the heirs of former real estate owners were recognized in 1730 by the court as the lawful owners of the soil and in many cases there were so many claimants, possession was difficult.

In the Cloise case Thomas Haskell, shipwright, purchased a right. In 1736 he purchased sixteen acres of Thomas Westbrook who had bought one or more of the Cloise heirs. The deed refers to a "new bridge" which had been erected over the creek about two rods northerly of the present Frost street, which would now be at the rear end of the Arthur Milliken lot, the road then from Stroudwater to Portland Neck, passing that way, thence along the bank over the gully and in front of the Riggs house at Bradley's Corner, soon to be removed by Mr. Daniel D. Chenery, which stands adjacent his new house at the northeasterly corner.

A deed of a hundred acre lot made by one Benjamin Ingalls of North Yarmouth, March 19, 1734, in favor of Col. Thomas Westbrook, refers to the new house of Thomas Haskell, as it does to the "new bridge," before mentioned, over against the house of Thomas Westbrook, Westbrook living where Walter Fickett does in Stroudwater, and Haskell on the top of the bank south easterly of the present residence of Mr. John Nelson on Frost street. In this deed is recorded the fact that the creek over which the bridge had been built, in 1734 which is now the one passing to the westerly side of Nelson's house, "ran down on the back side of the place where the former dwelling house of Thomas Claice formerly stood"

A record on file at Alfred of a road surveyed in 1751 between the bridge below the paper mill at Stroudwater and North Yarmouth refers to the "bridge" here alluded to then "up the hill as now trod, then south 58 degrees 30 minutes east 63¼ rods to a white oak tree marked, then south 65 degrees east 32 rods to a steak near the middle of Haskells old cellar," etc.

This Haskell referred to is the one who went to Windham and whose descendants reside now at Saccarappa. The cellar hole is still visible.

In the year 1730 this Thomas Haskell, shipwright, supposed to be a brother-in-law to Jeremiah Riggs who built the house to be removed by Mr. Chenery, for a consideration of 500£ sold to Charles Frost, Esq., the two certain parcels of

Saturday, January 25, 1896.

GRANDPA'S SCRAP BOOK

[Under this head historical and genealogical memoranda will be furnished the readers of the News that appears worthy of preservation, particularly of remote periods in our history within the city Limits and Immediate vicinity.]

CHARLES FROST.

HIS ANCESTRY AND SOME OF THE EVENTS CONNECTED WITH HIS LIFE.
Continued From Last Week.

Nicholas Frost came to Piscataquis about the year 1636 and settled at Sturgeon Creek, now Eliot, this state, which was formerly a part of Kittery and called the Upper Parish till 1810. He died July 20, 1663, aged about 74 years, and left five children, the eldest of whom was named Charles, and was killed by the Indians, July 4, 1697 This Charles was born in Tiverton, England, July 50, 1631, and married Mary Boles of Wells, this state. He is known in history as Major Chas. Frost.

Maj. Frost and wife Mary had nine children, the second of whom, born May 1, 1681, was named John, married Mary a sister to Sir William Pepperell, Sep. 4, 1702. He died Feb. 25, 1732. He was a prominent citizen, commander of a ship of war, representative and councillor in State matters. His wife survived him and after marrying twice, died. Apr. 18, 1766, aged 80 years. This John is known in history as "Honorable John Frost," and had six children, the third one of whom was named Charles. He was born Aug. 27, 1710, married first Sarah 2nd, Joanna Jackson of Kittery, the publishment being recorded in the Old Falmouth records, which is positive proof of her maiden name, Sep. 17 1738. Of him can say but little, not having made any special effort to look up his record. He first appears here as clerk to Col. Thomas Westbrook at Stroudwater from whom he received "power of attorney" to act for the Colonel, and was a Justice of the Peace. He must have been a man of ability and influence. Whether or not he or his son Andrew P. Frost built the original part of the Brewer House does not appear, by records thus far examined, but his residence was protected by a Garrison. He was apparently a religious man. Parson Smith visited him often. In 1741-2 a great religious excitement visited here, and Jan. 29, 1742, Parson Smith says: "I rode with my wife and preached a lecture at Mr. Frost's where the work broke out.

Soon after Frost's advent to Stroudwater apprehensions of an Indian raid were communand Esquire Frost addressed the authorities at Boston as follows.

CONTINUED:

land, lying and being in Falmouth, etc., containing about 60 acres, "with the dwelling house, barn and all other buildings."

Under date of April 30, 1740, Parson Smith's journal printed edition of 1849, reads: "Mr. (Charles) Frost made known also that he is offended with me for some passages in a sermon which he thought reflected on his taking Haskell's house, etc." Then the compiler of the work in a foot note presents a few facts relative to Mr. Frost.

But a careful investigation fails to produce anything "crooked" in the business transaction between Messrs. Haskell and Frost. The name of the wife of Mr. Frost was "Joanna" it appears from the document before me, but Willis says it was Hannah Jackson, but as all other records say it was Joanna, even her grave memorial, Joanna must be correct.

The documents to which allusion has been made reads as follows:

York, ss GEORGE the SECOND, by the Grace of God, of Great Britain.

FRANCE and Ireland, KING, Defendee of the Faith, &c.

To the Sheriff of Our County of York, his Under-Sheriff of Deputy Greeting.

We Command you that you summon Joanna Frost if she may be found in your Precinct to appear before Our Justices of Our Inferior Court of Common Pleas to be Holden at Falmouth within and for Our said County of York, on the First Tuesday of October next: Then and there in Our said Court to Answer unto Mary Waters of Sturbridge in the County of Worcester, in our Province of the Massachusetts Bay, widow, action of ejectment wherein she demands one-third part of sixty acres of land more or less in said Falmouth the whole of which bounded as follows: viz., southerly and south westerly by Fore river, so-called, south easterly by Ingalls' cove on the north east by land of Jeremiah Riggs and on the northerly and north westerly by a large gully in part and a certain creek below the (Capisic) Falls, so-called, in part, being the same tract of land which was formerly sold by George Munjoy to Thomas Claise by the following bounds, and description, viz:

"A certain piece of land lying and "being on the river over against the mill "of George Ingersoll, being a neck of "land bounded on the northeasterly "with a certain creek lying between the "falls and that and so down the river "about the point with a certain marsh "of the said Munjoy as it's now fenced "in and so to a certain creek between "that meadow and the house of Joseph "Ingalls and so up in the woods between "the two creeks to the bounds of said "Munjoy's," with one third part of all the buildings thereon, and the appurtenances thereunto belonging which third part of said premises the plaintiff claims as her right and inheritance in fee and says that Thomas Cloise aforesaid, lot of Falmouth, her father deceased, was in his lifetime seized of said sixty acres, more or less, with the appurtenance and in or about the year 1687 died so seized thereof intestate, leaving Thomas Cloise his son and heir to whom the same by law descended in fee and afterwards, viz: In or about the year of our Lord 1717 the said Thomas not having entered into said premises nor disposed of his right to the same died intestate without lawful issue, leaving the plaintiff and Hannah Cloise his sister and George Cloise his brother and next of kin to whom the interest and property of said premises by virtue of law of our said Province in such cases provided vested and come in fee, viz: one third part thereof to each of them by force whereof, the plaintiff is well entitled to the premises demanded, and ought to recover possession thereof accordingly, yet the defendant has entered and unjustly withholds the same.

To the damage of the said Mary as she says the sum of Five Hundred Pounds which shall then and there be made to appear with other due damages? And have you there this Writ, with your doings thereon. Witness, Sir Wm. Pepperell, Baronet, at York the 1st day of July. In the 31st Year of our Reign Annoque Domini 1757.

JNO. FROST.

The record on the back of the writ shows it was duly served.

Accompanying this paper is another in the original, now before me, as follows:

We, Joseph Knight of Middleton in the County of Essex, Massachusetts Bay, yeoman, and Benjamin Knight of Middleton, aforesaid, aged between sixty and seventy, years do testify and say that we well knew Susannah Cloise aforesaid of Salem in the county aforesaid widow of Thomas Cloise, formerly of Casco Bay, in the County of York, and we always understood that the said Thomas Cloise was killed by the Indians at Casco Bay aforesaid when it was destroyed and likewise that we well knew Mary, Hannah, Thomas and George, children of the above named Thomas and Susannah Cloise and that Thomas was the eldest son, and we always understood that the said Thomas, their son, died without having any children, and that he has been dead more than forty years from this time, and that the above named Mary Cloise married one Daniel Waters, then of Topsfield, in the county of Essex aforesaid, Middleton, Apr. 3, 1758.

GEORGE KNIGHT, BENJAMIN KNIGHT.

The above named statement, the back of the paper shows, was sworn to before Benj. Jones, Jus. Peace, by the parties named

CONTINUED:

Although we have got a parcel of brave young fellows—we shall, if the Indians ae incline, be knocked in ye head like fools for want of proper care for ye chief officers here will neither hang nor Gee.

This copy is made from the original now filed in the Massachusetts archives.

On the 10th day of June, 1746, it is recorded that "an Indian was seen and fired at three times from Mr. Frost's garrison."

He served as selectman two years. His commission as Justice of the Peace made him a member of the Court of Sessions, and at the time of his death he was a Representative to the Great and General Court of Massachusetts.

Jan. 4, Sunday, 1756, Parson Smith makes the following record: "I was in the evening called to Justa Frost, who, going from meeting was seized with a fit, but before I got to him he was dead."

In the old Stroudwater cemetery stand two memorial stones inscribed as follows:

Here lyes Buried
the Body of
CHARLES FROST, Esq;
Who Departed this Life,
Janry. 4th, A. D., 1756, in
ye 46th Year of His Age.

In
memory of
MRS. JOANNA FROST,
Relict of the late
Charles Frost, Esq.,
of Falmouth, who died
Jan. ye 7th, 1796;
Aged 80 years.

THE DEERING NEWS.

Saturday, February 1, 1896.

GRANDPA'S SCRAP BOOK

[Under this head historical and genealogical memoranda will be furnished the readers of the News that appears worthy of preservation, particularly of remote periods in our history within the city limits and immediate vicinity.]

CHARLES FROST.

HIS ANCESTRY AND SOME OF THE EVENTS CONNECTED WITH HIS LIFE.

Continued From Last Week.

Before me as I write, and from which I propose to make some extracts, is the original account book of Nathaniel Knight, who resided and died at Stroudwater Falls, near the residence of the late Edward Chapman, where the cellar hole of the house is now plainly visible, which was a two story, nice building, and was destroyed by fire Sept. 4, 1729. Nathaniel Knight's wife was Priscilla Berry, but her parents' names and place of birth I cannot name at this time. He was a nephew to Col. Thomas Westbrook, his mother's maiden name being Mary, and a sister to the Colonel. Their first born was baptized at Scarboro, Aug. 25, 1728, and it was soon there after that he settled at Stroudwater Falls—a mile southerly of Saccarappa. Concerning him I have much memoranda.

The old account book is sixteen inches long and two inches thick. His account commences with "Charles Frost, Esq.," March 29, 1741, and covers a page and half, and relates largely to lumbering transactions. It seems Knights kept shop, or articles of merchandise for sale, though he had six oxen and teamsters, a slave, and worked himself. And here I will present a few extracts from the old book.

to 1½ bushel wheat	£2	5	0
to ye land I sold you in Gorhamtown,	50	0	0
to 1 day work myself	0	10	0
to 2 narrow ax polls and steel	1	0	0
to ye one half of a cart and harrow	3	0	0
to 4 days hauling masts	2	8	0
to one half of a set of iron, work for a saw mill	21	5	0
to 700 red oak hogs'd staves	5	0	0
to 2000 feet white pine Match boards	8	0	0
to ye half of 15,000 boards hall'd for you from Sacarap to Embencongon	5	12	6
to my part of twitching ye boards at ye falls, rosting and bring down	0	16	0
to one days work myself taking care of ye lumber above Stroudwater Falls	1	10	0
to a hind quarter of wheel (veal) 14 lbs	1	14	6
to ye half of a barle of Syder.	1	5	0

The account shows that Mr. Charles Frost of troudwater was a stirring man, something more than a mere clerk to Col. Westbrook, and since Mrs. Jane E. Quinby, widow of the late Thomas Quinby, of Stroudwater, who is a great grand child of Charles Frost, her grandfather being Andrew P. Frost informs me that when her father, Capt. Dexter Brewer, whose wife was a daughter of Andrew P., went to live in the Andrew P. Frost house in about the year, 1830, and she was ten years of age, and the house had a very ancient appearance and it was traditional that the building was near a century in age, it must be admitted that Charles Frost was the builder of the original great two story edifice with gambrel roof, to which Capt. Dexter Brewer added a story as many of us remember it when it was burned, Jan. 80, 1882, in the forenoon, an account of which appearing in the Portland Press the following day. And right here let me say that a cut of the house appeared in a supplement to the Press, with a graphic sketch of the house and girlhood recollections by Mrs. Jane E Quinby, now a resident of this city, as it appeared before the additional story, Sep. 7, 1895.

There were six children born to Chas. Frost Esq., and wife Joanna, and they were named respectively as follows: 1—Joanna; 2—Abigail; 3—Charles; 4—William; 5—Jane; 6 and last—Andrew Pepperell.

Joanna. Her memorial grave stone may be seen in the old Stroudwater cemetery, the inscription of which, as near as can be made is as follows. It is the oldest stone in the enclosure.

HERE LYES Ye
BODY OF JOAN-
NA. DAUGHTER
tO CHARLES
FROSt ESq &
MRS JOANNA
FROSt. OBt Ye 6th
NOUr 1739 ÆtAtIS
SeU En W & 3 D.

Abigail, born Aug. 26, 1744, married Oct. 20 1781, Daniel Epes.

A Mr. Epps is alluded to by Parson Dean in his diary Nov. 8, 1784, and Willis says "he probably was Daniel Epps who married Abagail Frost; was a graduate of Howard college, came here from Danvers, went into trade at Stroudwater, became an insurance broker in Portland after the war of the Revolution and died in May, 1799, aged 60 years, leaving a daughter 10 years old."

At a parish meeting Daniel Epes was chosen clerk, Apr. 8, 1788. Instead of a "p" he used an "e" in his name as shown above, copied from the original record he made of the event which is now before me as I write. His penmanship was good and spelling correct, but his signature is peculiar. The "D" is made with a flourish stroke of the pen but all the rest of the letters are of one size and all joined together. The first e in Epes however is made different from the second e used in the name. He served as clerk till spring of 1791, filling up eight pages of the record book. Among the names of the persons to whom license was granted at his time in life as retailers of liquors appears his name. His daughter, Abigail Epes Jr., dressmaker, appears on record, but of the end of her wordly career I have no knowledge, nor that of her father.

In the first volume of records of the doings of the old court of sessions which court was composed of fifteen justices of the peace, appears something that is quite amusing when compared with the freedom of the present time. The judges of this court when in one sense a grand jury. The record commences

CONTINUED:

with the allegation that.

"Samuel Waldo, Esq , and Sarah his wife; Edward Watts, physician, and wife Mary; Daniel Epes, Merchant; * * * * Abigail Frost and Jane Frost and * * * * did on the 6th day of December, 1765, at Falmouth, aforesaid, dance in the house of Joshua Freeman, of Falmouth, innholder the same house then being a tavern, and a public licensed house, against the peace of our Sovereign Lord the King, in the evil example to others and against the Law of the Province."

The respondents appeared by counsel and showed that the parties had leased the room for a term of three months, hence was not a part of the inn; and all were discharged, the county paying £46-17-7 expense.

This was a party of the elite of the town, the names of all I would give, did time and space allow. The names of the two Frost girls were daughters of Chas. Frost Esq. The inn stood where the First National bank stands in Portland, corner Exchange and Middle streets.

TO BE CONTINUED.

Saturday, February 8, 1896.

GRANDPA'S SCRAP BOOK

[Under this head historical and genealogical memoranda will be furnished the readers of the News that appears worthy of preservation, particularly of remote periods in our history within the city limits and immediate vicinity.]

Continued from last week.

Jan. 12, 1765 Rev. Samuel Dean of Portland says: "Snow is about two feet deep on a level, and we hear it is four feet deep in Boston."

Jan. 28 Rode to Mrs. Frost's and spent the evening. 29. Rode to Windham and dined there. At sundown, Mr. P. Smith, Miss Nabby Frost, Mr. Browne and myself set out for Gorham.

This Nabby Frost, unquestionably, was later Mrs. Abigal Epes, daughter of Chas. Frost, to whom allusion was made last week as the wife of Daniel Epes. Mr. Browne was the Rev. Thomas Browne of the Stroudwater parish who, later, resided at Woodford's Corner, and of whom something was told in the News of August 24 and 31st last year. The Mr. Lombard noticed farther along in this article was Rev. Solomon Lombard of Gorham. Rev. Mr. Dean was a single man at that time and officiated on the site of the old stone church, Portland, but was married Apr. 3, of the following year.

The narration of the journey to Gorham in which Miss Frost acted a part continues as follows:

Met several teams, and passed them with difficulty; went over the place called Horse Beef, a mile and a half beyond the Fort; then we had three miles and a half to go by moonshine, under great uncertainty about the way, and amidst a variety of paths that branched out on both sides. In this way we met with a mast sled by itself lying in the highway, which we could not pass, till with our united strength we had tumbled it into the snow. The night was one of the coldest I ever knew, and I was under sad apprehension that one of my toes was frozen. At length we arrived at Mr. Steward's, where I expected we should have been invited, part of us, to lodge; but we were turned off with a dose of flip. The next stage was Mr. Lombard's, but neither he nor his wife was at home. We let the son understand that we came to pay his father a visit, and should be glad to have our horses sheltered, as they were sweaty; to which he answered, they had no room where they could put them. Then we desired he would turn out some of the cattle to make room. I was so astonished at the impudence and churlishness of the answer, that I have almost forgotten it; but the sense of it was, that he would not turn them out of his barn for the best men's horses in the world. I then went to Capt. Phinney's, and Mr. Smith to the Elder's. I rapt at the door and found nobody at home. I returned to Mr. Lombard's, and found that Mr. Browne had gone more than a quarter of a mile to water his horse, and that there was a new, well finished barn, of thirty feet square, entirely empty. I desired my young friend to get some hay laid, and went to water my horse; but when I came to the place, there was no coming at the water; then I returned, tied my horse, though the young man endeavored to prevent me, by saying that Capt. Phinney had been over to invite me to his house, and said he would turn out his cattle rather than not accommodate my horse. I then found Mr. Lombard in the house and told him my difficulties; but he showed no regret, nor did he offer to send anybody to water my horse at the well, as he might have done. Our supper was tea at ten o'clock, though we had drank tea before, reinforced with pea porridge. Mr. Browne requested a little more of the porridge, after he had swallowed his mess, to which the lady answered, she had no more in the house. The next morning, having lodged at Capt. Phinney's, I was up early and went to Mr. Lombard's before he arose, and found his wife warming up a mess of pea porridge, which she gave to her grandchildren to eat for breakfast, and her memory was so good that she called it by its name before me and Mr. Smith. She asserted that all her cows happened to be dry, and they had neither butter nor cheese in the house; so we breakfasted on tea and johnny cake, without butter, and fled for our lives.

Mrs. Quinby remembers a Nabby Epes, and says she died in the old brick Frost house located northerly of Allen's Corner. She must have been "Abijail Jr."

In the old Stroudwater cemetery stands one Epes memorial stone inscribed as follows:

Sacred to the memory of
Mrs. Abijail, widow of
Daniel Epes Esq,
died Mar 10, 1826,
Æt. 81.

TO BE CONTINUED.

Saturday, February 15, 1896.

GRANDPA'S SCRAP BOOK

[Under this head historical and genealogical memoranda will be furnished the readers of the News that appears worthy of preservation, particularly of remote periods in our history within the city limits and immediate vicinity.]

CHARLES FROST.

HIS DESCENDANTS AND SOME OF THE EVENTS CONNECTED WITH THEIR LIVES.

Continued from last week.

3 Charles, born 1746, and in the old Stroudwater cemetery may be seen a memorial stone inscribed as follows:

Charles Frost, Son of Charles Frost; Esqr. & Mrs. Joanna his Wife, Died Janry. 8.h, 1747, Aged 14 Months.

4 William, born Aug. 20, 1748. Of his career and characteristics I have but little knowledge. In the year of 1771 he was licensed a retailer of liquors which continued to be renewed yearly till 1790. He took part in the war of the Revolution as a defender of his country, being a second lieutenant in Captain Wild's company, 18th Reg, Col. Phinney's Co., 1776. For this fact I am indebted to Nathan Goold of Portland, writer of Revolutionary war articles for the Portland Daily Press. March 16, of that year, he was made parish clerk, and the old book of records, alluded to in the News of Jan. 11, ult., is before me as I write. The position he held five years, and his records are among the best. His chirography was good, spelling correct in the whole sixteen pages of his work, excepting the word "committee" which he spelled with one "e". In the spring of 1776, the record shows he was absent, Samuel Knight was dead, and Capt. John Brackett of Saccarappa was absent or dead. The three constituted the committee for calling parish meetings, and one was held each year notwithstanding the war. He did not marry. July 7, 1778, his mother, Joanna, widow, and sister Abigail made him an agent to take possession of one-sixth part of a sawmill located at Horse Beef falls, a place on Presumpscot river, which sixth was obtained by a mortgage to Charles Frost, 1752, by Wm. Knight then deceased, also land in the town that was reckoned by hundreds of acres. And this record, or the introduction of it here, brings up the outcome of the lawsuit between Joanna Frost and Mary (Clois) Waters that was presented by the News, Jan. 18, which was that Joanna Frost should pay, by mutual agreement, Mary Waters one-twelfth the value of the land without the buildings, (the house now supposed to be the original part of the late Brewer House) and the court appointed William Buckman of (now Falmouth Foreside), Capt. Saml. Skillin, (Long Creek, C. E.,), and Lieut. Andrew Libby of Scarboro, who, on the 1st of Dec., 1761, fixed the award to Mary Waters of 22£ 18s 4d lawful money, who, through Capt. Ebenezer Mayew acknowledges its payment.

The record before me in its original form must convince those who see it, and compare it with the times in which it was made, that Wm. Frost was above the average in intelligence of those of his surroundings, and it is with sadness I record the fact that so few of his tracks upon the "sands of time" can be found.

To the memory of his name there stands at Stroudwater a memorial stone inscribed as follows:

Mr. William Frost,

Died Janr. 23d,

1—7, 9—1,

Aged 43 years.

5 Jane, born Aug. 15, 1750; died unmarried. "The Eastern Herald," of July 2, 1792, published in what is now Portland contains a brief notice of her demise. A stone inscribed to her memory and standing at Stroudwater reads as follows:

Miss Jane Frost,

Died June 23d,

1 7 9 2

In the 42d year

of her age.

Epitaphs were very common in the days of which I write, hardly a gravestone being reared without one, yet none none appear on the Frost stones.

TO BE CONTINUED.

THE DEERING NEWS.

Saturday, February 22, 1896.

GRANDPA'S SCRAP BOOK

[Under this head historical and genealogical memoranda will be furnished the readers of the News that appears worthy of preservation, particularly of remote periods in our history within the city limits and immediate vicinity.]

CHARLES FROST.

HIS DESCENDANTS AND SOME OF THE EVENTS CONNECTED WITH THEIR LIVES.

Continued from last week.

6 Andrew Pepperell Frost was born 1752, and married with Eleanor Siemons, (now spelled with a double "m") Nov. 7, 1782, she a daughter of William Siemons of Stroudwater who married, Sept. 10, 1744, with Catharen Pote-field.

Of his career I have comparatively little data hence but slight knowledge of his career. He evidently came into the Frost homestead mansion at the time of the division of his father's estate, but as the Probate court records were destroyed at the time of the great fire in Portland in 1866, I cannot state dates or make quotations from the division record of real estate among the heirs. In the year of 1779, when prices were greatly inflated in consequence of the war with England then raging, he sold for a consideration of £2500 one fourth of the so-called "Bonington Patent" consisting of 800 acres and one fourth of a double sawmill located within the bounds of the Patent lot located on the Nonesuch river, in Scarboro, which he had received by the division of the estate of his father. And as grantor and grantee, he appears on the Cumberland Co. registry sixty three times. His signature also appears which is very good, also that of his mother, Joanna, and two or her pieces.

His children were seven in number, as follows:

1 Nancy, married June 13, 1799, with Capt. Thomas Seal and resided at Cipisic, then Falmouth, now Deering.
2 William did not marry and died in 1810.
3 Catherinne, married, Dec. 15, 1811, with John Mahan, resided 1st. at Stroudwater, 2nd. at Portland.
4 Eleanor, married, May 25, 1805, Peter T. Clark, resided 1st. at Stroudwater, 2nd. westerly of Bradley's Corner, a few rods easterly of the Ogdensburg railroad crossing.
5 Andrew Pepperell, died unmarried in New York.
6 Joseph, died unmarried, with the Society of Shakers.
7. Jane, married, Jan. 24, 1818, Capt. Dexter Brewer, of Framingham, Mass., and retained the Charles Frost, Esq., homestead.

When the news reached here, April 21, 1775, of the battle of Lexington, Andrew P. Fost was one of the party of "Minute Men" who left immediately under the command of Capt. John Brackett, of Saccarappa, and traveled to Wells before they were turned back.

He was 2nd. sergt. in Capt. Jesse Partridge's Co., in Col. John Greaton's Reg. and served from Apr. 1, to Nov. 1, 1778. He joined Washington's army, and was at White Plains, N. Y., in August. (See Portland Press, Apr. 6, '95.

His estate was one of considerable size but I cannot find a description of it. It was not taxed in 1815 in the name of the heirs. I was told some years ago by a person who if now alive would be 90 years of age that one Burnham used the house as an inn in her girlhood and that she once attended a picnic there. And there is a tradition connected with the house, that one of the upstair rooms was haunted, that when it was opened a large back bear would make his appearance and so the room was kept closed.

Upon the first valuation book of Westbrook, made in 1815, I find the following, which, probably, applies to the place:

Joseph Burnham—one house $800; two barns $80; one stable $60; three outhouses $60.

In the old cemetery at Stroudwater stand a pair of memorial stones inscribed as follows:

To the Memory

of Mrs. ELEANOR FROST,

Wife to

ANDw. PEPP. FROST,

Who departed this Life

on the 6th of Octr. 1795.

Aged 37 Years.

Gentle of manners, to her friends sincere,
A tender Mother,
To her Children's memory Dear.

In memory of

Mr. ANDREW P. FROST,

who died

May 24, 1805:

Æt. 52.

TO BE CONTINUED.

Saturday, February 29, 1896

GRANDPA'S SCRAP BOOK

[Under this head historical and genealogical memoranda will be furnished the readers of the News that appears worthy of preservation, particularly of remote periods in our history within the city limits and immediate vicinity.]

CHARLES FROST.

HIS DESCENDANTS AND SOME OF THE EVENTS CONNECTED WITH THEIR LIVES.

Continued from last week.

Since my last article under this head I have been exceedingly fortunate in my search for Frost family memoranda and can now present a copy of the division of the real estate of Charles Frost Esq., among his four children. An accompanying paper, which bears upon the matter, is dated Falmouth, Feb. 13, 1775, and as the youngest child became of lawful age at that period it is reasonable to suppose that the division was made then, but no allusion is made to the "widow's thirds." Accompanying this paper are others, with family records, in the original forms, valuable as relics of historical data, which will be used in chronological order. The first paper I shall here present is as follows:

DIVISION OF THE REAL ESTATE OF CHAS. FROST, ESQ DECEASED.

To Abigail Frost:

1 Right in Canterbury 300 acres	£180-0-0
11 Acres & 107 rods, Also 70 acres land in Scarbo., adjoining George Knight	163-6-8
64 Acres & 11 rods land, part of John Darling's 104 acres	43-2-6
100 Acres land in Gorham, near Zeph. Harding's, No. 59	80-0-0
20 Acres land in Windham, adjoining Caleb Graffams	24-0-0
100 Acres land in Windham, No.—	6-0-0
	£550-9-0

To Jane Frost:

50 Acres land laid in Scarbo., bot. of Nath. Knight	£20-0-0
½ of 10 acres in Scarbo., above Bragdon's Mill	10-0-0
38 Acres & 20 rods part of James Irish 80 acre lot	38-2-6
52 Acres land, ½ execution's, 104 acre lot	104-0-0
200 land in Brunswick, called the Garnet near Mericoug	160-0-0
100 Acres land in Gorham, No. 18	80-0-0
100 Acres land adj. Sol. Lombard Jr.	120-0-0
2 Acres land adj. the Round Marsh, Falmouth,	8-0-0
	£540-0-0

To Andrew Peppl. Frost:

200 Acres land in Scarbo., ½ part of a double Saw mill	£180-0-0
11 Acres land bot. of Elipha Cobb	34-0-0
30 Acres land in Gorham, adj. Eboor. Hall's	40-0-0
70 Acres land in Gorham, above Gambo	37-6-8
70 Acres in Gorham, called the Hour-glass lot	28-0-0
70 Acres in Gorham, called the Triangle lot	28-0-0
70 Acres in Gorham on the upper plain	18-13-4
235 Acres & 30 rods of land adj. the road from Winslow's Bridge to New Boston	156-13-4
1 Pew in the Stroudwater meeting house	14-18-8
	£543-5-4

To Chas. Frost:

1 Right 200 acres land in Epsom	£180-0-0
10 Acres Meadow near Andrew Gibb's	20-0-0
173 Acres & 26 rods of land at Presumpscot	340-0-0
	£540-0-0

The Abigail, Jane and Andrew P. Frost, who received land as above indicated have been noticed in previous articles of the News.

The original deed of gift of the Epsom lot from Mary (Pepperell) Frost, widow of Hon. John Frost, dated at New Castle, N. H., March 22, 1736, to her son Charles Frost Esq., is before me as I write which contains the signature of Mary.

In my article under this heading in the News of Feb. 1, I state there were six children in the family of Chas. Frost Esq., when in fact there were seven, and the seventh and last, born July 6 1755 was named Charles, who grew to manhood, but his youthful days, in the absence of records can only be imagined. Upon the 173 acre lot he erected the large brick two story house now seen a mile, or thereabouts, distant in a north easterly direction from Allen's Corner, in this city, then the town of Falmouth, the highway of that day now being known as Summit street.

Before me as I write is a pocket memoranda of his, and though not what I wish it was it contains records of great value to the student of genealogical research:

In the war of the Revolution he enlisted under Capt. John Brackett of Saccarappa and was made 1st., corporal of the company. Mr. Nathan Goold of Portland gives the date of enlistment as May 21, 1775, and continued till Dec. 31. According to Parson Smith's Journal the company left here July 8, of that year

chives, announce.
Argus, Apr. 23, 1889.

The book before me is 4x6 inches, a half inch thick, and in front is a printed page as follows:

THE

NEW ENGLAND

MEMORANDUM BOOK,

OR

COMPLEAT POCKET JOURNAL.

BOSTON:

PRINTED AND SOLD BY W. M ALPINS AND J. FLEEMING IN MARLBOROUGH STREET,

M, L, C C, L X V

At the top of this page is written Charles Frost's Book 1775"

He had a quaint way of entry, so much so that but very little of his memoranda is of use.

He records the number of his watch and by whom made

July 3, 1775 Josiah Peabody is charged with a knapsack, 2s 8d, and on the same date, John Blair with a "bullet pouch, 6s."

And here is a copy of a note of hand.

CAMBRIDGE, Aug. 17, 1775.

For value received I promise to pay to Charles Frost or order ten shillings and eight pence lawful money.

Witness my hand."

(The signature is cut out.)

At the bottom of the page is this entry:

"Bought my land of Amos Harris Feb. 28, 1776.

This entry has reference to a 20 acre lot purchased at that time for a consideration of £23-6, at Presumpscot adjoining land of Jonanna Frost, with "dwelling house thereon standing," and became a part of the 173 acres of land obtained in the division of the Chas. Frost Esq., estate, and later known by the name of the Frost farm, "Frost's woods" being for many years a familiar local name.

But it is the Chas. Frost family record of births of thirteen children, deaths, time of birth of his wife, maiden name and marriage. written in ink of almost as many colors as dates of occurrences that gives the little book its real value.

TO BE CONTINUED.

THE DEERING NEWS.

Saturday, March 7, 1896.

GRANDPA'S SCRAP BOOK

[Under this head historical and genealogical memoranda will be furnished the readers of the News that appears worthy of preservation, particularly of remote periods in our history within the city limits and immediate vicinity.]

CHARLES FROST.

HIS DESCENDANTS AND SOME OF THE EVENTS CONNECTED WITH THEIR LIVES.

Continued from last week.

It is traditional that Charles Frost who built the large brick house now standing a mile northeasterly of Allen's Corner commenced work on his land immediately after coming into possession of it. He was betrothed but the object of his affections who was a kin, was not in the opinion of somebody of sufficient age to don the bridal attire, so he waited and tarried with a neighbor till 1782. And here I will insert an item of a manuscript record now before me:

"Charles Frost, born July 6, 1755, (at Stroudwater); married Oct. 20, 1782, to Abigail Frost, Daughter of Timothy Frost, Esq., and Hannah his wife, Born in Kittery, County of York, Sep. 8, 1763, died Apr. 6, 1841, aged 74 and 11 mo. Charles Frost died April 6, 1841, aged 85 and 9 mo."

As Chas. Frost, Esq., married a woman by the name of Jackson and as the wife of Chas. Frost, Jr., was a Frost by name there was more relationship between the last Charles and his wife than I am able to state at this time.

Before me now are two sheets of paper folded in the middle, covered with brown colored paper, held together by linen thread, so as to make leaflets 4x6 inches, and all bearing the evidence of mature age. In one part is the date, Feb. 13, 1775, so I will take it for granted in the absence of positive proof that the personal property of the estate of Charles Frost, Esq, was divided at that time and Charles Jr., came into possession of his share as follows: "One cow and calf and 2 sheep belonging to me from the rest before the division."

	£	s	d
One cow that goes by the name of Colly,	30	0	0
One bull,	20	0	0
3 stear calves,	24	0	0
2 barrows,	15	0	0
8 sheep,	32	0	0
	£121	0	0

Sheep pointed on the left ear.

	£	s	d
1 Tin Kettle,	0	2	0
1 Iron dripping pan,	2	5	0
1 Branding iron C. F.,	0	10	0
1 Chese,	5	0	0

* This "wall piece" evidently refers to an oil painting which will be noticed later.

After this follows abstract descriptions of the real estate which the writer says "is the real estate belonging to me, Charles Frost of Falmouth."

Then in pencil is the following: "Memd. The within was Old Tenor 45 to $s."

From the foregoing one can learn the comparative values at the time this record was made, and form an idea of the size and value of the personal property of Chas. Frost Esq.

At that time a gig was called a chair, hence where the terms "old chair wheels" and "old saddle for do," appears in the foregoing, a gig and backsaddle to a harness is meant.

THE DEERING NEWS.

Saturday, March 14, 1896.

GRANDPA'S SCRAP BOOK

[Under this head historical and genealogical memoranda will be furnished the readers of the News that appears worthy of preservation, particularly of remote periods in our history within the city limits and immediate vicinity.]

CHARLES FROST.

HIS DESCENDANTS AND SOME OF THE EVENTS CONNECTED WITH THEIR LIVES.

Continued from last week.

Before me is a well preserved paper 13x14 inches. The middle is printed; upon each side is a margin nearly three inches wide; in the left hand top corner, as the paper lays before me, a seal. It reads thus:

STATE OF
MASSACHUSETTS BAY.

The HONORABLE

HENRY GARDNER, ESQ.;

Treasurer and Receiver General of the said State.

To Charles Frost Constable or Collector of Falmouth.—Greetings, Etc:—

By Virtue of an act of the Great and General Court or Assembly of the State of Massachusetts-Bay in New England, begun and holden in Boston, in the County of Suffolk, on Wednesday the Twenty Eighth Day of May 1777 * * * * An act for apportioning and assessing a Tax of Two hundred and fifty-four Thousand, Seven hundred and eighteen pounds, upon the several towns, and other places of this State, for defraying the Public Charge."

* * * * * *

The portion set down for the town of Falmouth to meet was £311, 4, 10, and the paper before me, dated April 25, 1778,

and signed H. Gardner, is the evidence that Charles Frost, son of Chas. Frost Esq., was selected to collect the amount. Whether or not he held other offices, I cannot state, but in the absence of proof, I will imagine him a farmer, and an industrious, careful, prudent man, letting religious, political and other public matters alone. To him and wife were born thirteen children as follows:

	NAME	DATE.
*1	Joanna,	Jan. 7, 1784
*2	George,	Jan 6, 1785
3	Sophia,	Oct. 21, 1786,
	Died Nov. 5, Same year.	
*4	Harry,	Mar. 10, 1789
5	Polly,	Dec. 4, 1790
	Died Dec. 12, same year	
*6	Charles,	Nov. 17, 1791
7	John,	Nov. 18, 1793
	Died Jan. 22, 1802.	
*8	William,	Nov. 14, 1795
9	Eliza,	Sep. 26, 1797
	Died Jan 24, 1798.	
*10	(Nabby,) Abigail,	Nov. 8, 1798
*11	Eliza,	Mar. 22, 1802
12	John,	Aug. 20, 1805
	Died next month.	
*13	John, June 12, 1807, in the large two story brick house, hip roof, with an addition of one story on the southerly end, there chimneys two on the northerly side next to the wall, one in the center of the southerly half much larger than the other two, the whole standing on the easterly side of the highway, fronting westerly, the walls said to be unusually thick because the builder claimed that he should return to earth a thousand years after death and desired that the building should then be standing, which was built the year before the birth John last named.	

In 1833 there was printed a list of the members of the Stroudwater Congregational church and among the names of those "admitted by profession" prior to 1795 appear the names of Jane Frost and Daniel Epes, both noticed in previous articles, and in the list of 1833, which comprises the names of all the church appears the name of Abigail (Frost) Epes, both of which women were sisters to Chas. Frost now being noticed, but the names of no other Frosts appear.

CONTINUED:

1 Large blunderbus,	4	0	0
1 Spader,	0	10	0
1 Scouring rod,	0	10	0
2 Blocks for a takle	1	15	0
1 Writing desk and chair	6	0	0
1 Gugging rod	2	5	0
1 Sliding Gunter	0	10	0
1 Pocket Compass	0	15	0
1 Pair Dividers	0	12	0
1 Pair small scales	0	18	0
1 Pair pack pistols	4	10	0
1 Scale	0	10	0
1 Iron stake	2	5	0
2 Beetle rings and iron wedge	1	10	0
1 Old plow and irons	5	0	0
1 Iron shovel	0	10	0
1 Hoe	1	5	0
1 Hand saw	4	0	0
1 2 inch auger	2	5	0
1 1 1 2 inch do	1	10	0
1 1 1-4 inch do	2	5	0
1 1 inch-do	1	15	0
1 7-8 inch do	0	10	0
1 3 4 inch do	1	0	0
1 Drawing knife	0	12	0
1 Gouge	0	10	0
1 Chisel	0	10	0
1 Old chair wheels	6	0	0
1 Old saddle for do	2	5	0
2 Pitch forks	1	10	0
2 Sickles	0	15	0
1 Stub scythe	0	15	0
1 Jointer	0	15	0
1 Hollowing plain	0	5	0
1 Bang borer	0	10	0
2 Waled homespun blankets	9	10	0
2 Coverlets	15	0	0
1 Bed and pine bedstead	44	0	0
1 Pair sheep shears	0	7	6
1 Pair pruning shears	0	7	6
1 Hand vice	1	5	0
1 Small pine desk	1	0	0
1 Carbine gun	1	10	0
1 Pruning hook	0	10	0
1 Spy glass	1	10	0
1 Gun	6	15	0
*1 Wall piece	5	5	0
1 Iron crane	2	5	0
1 Cane head	2	2	0
1 Stock buckle	2	5	0
1 Pair knee buckles	1	10	0
Total, including stock	283	15	0

When the first valuation of the town of Westbrook was made in 1815 the name of Frost appears as follows:

Charles Frost. One house $700; one barn $40; one out house $10; twenty-five acres mowing land at $20 per acre; thirty-five acres of pasturing at $0 per acre; one hundred and twenty acres unimproved at $7 per acre; 4 oxen, $80; 4 cows, $56; 1 horse, $40; 3 swine, $15, and 2 two yr. olds, $10.

George Frost. One horse, $40; money, $250.

Harry Frost. Cash, $300.

Joseph Frost. Twenty-three acres of land at $12 per acre; add money at interest, $500.

Andrew P. and William Frost pole tax each. These three last were sons of Andrew Pepperell Frost. Joseph who lived at one time at Nason's Corner was noticed in the News of April 27, last year, but not in the Scrap Book article.

A passage reads as follows:

Joseph (Frost) became enamored with a Miss Nancy Hall, a school teacher of the town of Windham, and Capt. Thomas Seal built for him the small dwelling as now seen, though in its originality it was plastered on the outside with lime mortar and painted with a bright yellow colored paint. But the courtship, however, blew over, etc.

In the extracts from Rev. Caleb Bradley's journal, printed last week in the News, appears the following:

July 27, 1831. It is said Thomas Jones is married this day to Mary Hall.

*1 Joanna, born at time above indicated, resided under the parental roof and died there Oct. 31, 1869, unmarried.

*2 George, born as above indicated, and I presume he was the one who was taxed in 1815 for a horse and cash amounting to $250. In 1827 he was a voter of the town.

In 1836 his father gave him a note for $10,000, and the next year one to "Abigail Frost, Jr.," for $500. The father gave other notes. In the District court holden in Portland March of 1841 George obtained judgment against the Charles Frost estate for $13,580, having previously purchased the claims held by his sisters, and took possession of the farm, estimated at 179 acres with buildings appraised at $7,600, as well as certain property located in Portland, received by will from his father's sister, Abigail (Frost) Epes, which will is before me as I write, and dated April 6, 1825, which says that Mrs. Epes' house and lot upon which it stands joins that of Mrs. Merriam Lord's lot, Mrs. Epes making the home of her brother Charles her last abiding place for a period of more than a dozen of years.

The note for $10,000 may have been in lieu of a will; any way the claim was not contested, and the latchstring of the door of the homestead was ever on the outerside to sisters and brothers where generous hospitality was freely offered not only to those of near kin but all who chose to visit the habitation.

Upon the same side of the unfrequented highway, particularly in the winter season, where stands the ancient Frost abode now gone from the possessionship of the Frost family, at a point a few rods northerly, may be seen a sturdy oak tree, and close adjicent to the eastward a small lot in square form surrounded by the arborvitae fully twenty feet high. When I reigned my steed, a few weeks since, from the one track way, the air was chilly and in motion, and as it passed through the arborvitae surrounding of the little lot and I gazed within the enclosure upon the half score of unnamed graves scattered upon which was but a slight sprinkling of snow, seemingly to make the place less cool and more inviting than the outside world, the wind's requiem, with the sight of the unmarked worldly resting places gave the place a gloom which has not yet been expunged from the mind of the writer, and the question then suggested "What is man?" still lingers. But one memorial stone adorns the enclosure the inscription of which I transferred to my note book and it reads thus:

GEORGE FROST,
BORN JAN. 6, 1785,
DIED AUG. 13, 1865.

Among the records of the probate court of this county is a copy of his will bearing date of July 18, 1859, which paper contains the names of quite a number of relatives.

He did not marry.

TO BE CONTINUED.

THE DEERING NEWS.

Saturday, March 21, 1896.

GRANDPA'S SCRAP BOOK

[Under this head historical and genealogical matter will be furnished the readers of the News that appears worthy of preservation, particularly of remote periods in our history within the city limits and immediate vicinity.]

CHARLES FROST.

HIS DESCENDANTS AND SOME OF THE EVENTS CONNECTED WITH THEIR LIVES.

* 4 Harry (Henry) Frost, born as indicated in the News of last week was a traveling peddler. Before me as I write is a bill made to him by Robert Gedney & Co., 413 Pearl street, New York, for 200 dozen combs amounting to $238 87, bearing date of April 12, 1815. The paper is in appearance as clean and new as though it was but a day old, with a very curious heading. It is traditional that he was lost at sea, but upon a more close research it is ascertained that in the year 1820 he started overland for Texas with $1000 in goods and cash, and no direct tidings of him have ever been received.

*6 Charles. By occupation was a hatter. He died unmarried under the parental roof, August 4, 1858.

*8 William. He resided at home, and vicinity, and died on the homestead, Dec. 11, 1848.

*10 Nabby, or Abigail as she was known in the last years of her life, resided under the parental roof most of the time and died there, April 20 1880. She made her will Feb. 14, 1871, which is on file at the Probate court office.

*11 Eliza. Resided at home and died there Oct. 24, 1846.

*13 and last. John. Like the rest of the family he resided under the parental roof but unlike them in one respect, he united in marriage, July 9, 1854, with Phebe C., widow of William A. Hayes, whose maiden name was Phebe C. Hamilton of North Yarmouth. He died Oct. 13, 1872. For times of birth of all here noticed, see the News of last week.

In former numbers of the News I gave fragmentary dates relating to the times of birth of the children of Charles Frost, Esq., since which I have found a manuscript record which is evidently full and correct and I will here give it.

Charles Frost, Esq., son of John and Mary (Pepperell) Frost, born at New Castle on the first day of the week, being the 27th day of August, 1710.

Nov. 9, 1738 was married to Joanna Jackson, the daughter of George and Joanna Jackson, born at Kittery in the county of York on the fifth day of the week, being the 14th day of June 1716

1 Joanna born on the first day of the week about 4 o'clock in the afternoon, being the 23rd of Sept. 1739, and died 6th day of Nov. 1739 about 10 o'clock in the morning being 6 weeks and 3 days old.

2 Abigail born on the first day of the week about 8 o'clock in the morning 1g the 26 day of August 1744.

Charles born on Wednesday about o'clock at night on Nov. 5 1746, and d on Friday, 8th Jan. 1747 about 12 lock at night.

William born 20th day of August 748.

5 Jane born August 20 1750.

6 Andrew Pepperell born Oct. —1752

7 Charles born 6 July 1755.

After this follows the date of marriage etc., of Charles Frost, son of Charles Frost, Esq, and names of children etc, all of which record has been presented to the readers of the News.

Where it says "wall piece £ 5-5" in the list of articles received by Charles Frost in the division of his father's personal property, I said in the News of the 7th inst. that I would notice the matter later. The following interesting note from Mrs. Quinby in reference to a painting in the old Frost house refers to the "Wall piece" estimated at the time of the unquestionable division at £ 5-5

WOODFORDS, ME. Feb. 9, 1896.

To THE EDITOR OF THE NEWS:—If the following bit of girlhood's recollections interests you I shall be pleased, if you use it.

Aunt Epes as she was called, occupied room in the old brick farm house which still stands, belonging to my great uncle, Charles Frost, and where she died.

On the periodical visits to the family the younger members thereof were allowed to call at aunt Epes room and regale themselves with gazing on the marvelous beauty of the picture of a young girl who stands admiring a flower that she holds in her graceful fingers.

The portrait was more than half length and painted by Copley, that celebrated artist of ancient days. I regret that in our admiration of the picture we neglected to secure the name. It was presumably a representation of some far off connection of the family. At length it fell to the care of Miss Joanna Frost, who, knowing that we all wanted it, solved the difficulty by selling it to a New York gentleman, a distant relative, for five hundred dollars, and whose walls it probably now adorns. She informed us later that with the money she purchased a muff and a gold watch and chain, luxuries that she had perhaps coveted for years, and the transaction was an excellent way out of the difficulty.

I also remember attending the funeral of my aunt Frost, a mild blue eyed lady quite the reverse of her husband, who, while waiting the hour of service, enlightened the minister by relating in an audible voice, some of the events of their lives.

On returning from the burial, "hot toddy" as it was called, was liberally served. Some adjourned to the orchard among the ancient trees the trunks of which were filled with holes showing the ravages of time. A sprightly lady present, the wife of a well known physician in the neighborhood, on being questioned as to the cause of the holes, replied that it was where the old bachelors picked them, one of whom there being four in the family stood by her side.

Yours respectfully,
JANE E. QUINBY.

THE DEERING NEWS.

Saturday, March 28, 1896.

GRANDPA'S SCRAP BOOK

[Under this head historical and genealogical memoranda will be furnished the readers of the News that appears worthy of preservation, particularly of remote periods in our history within the city limits and immediate vicinity.]

STROUDWATER PARISH.

NAMES OF THOSE WHO PAID A TAX TO SUPPORT THE CONGREGATIONAL CHURCH IN 1765.

Jan. 11th, of this year, there was printed in the News a *factum simile* of the first and second pages of the old Stroudwater Parish record book, which Parish comprised territorially the westerly part of the present city of Deering, the northeasterly corner of what is now Cape Elizabeth, and the whole of what is now the city of Westbrook, to which we now refer the reader who is interested in the general history of the part of Falmouth to which we now write, as well as the commencement of the Stroudwater Parish as an independent ecclesiastical organization, because the article of Jan. 11 shows the time of organization of the Parish, and who were its first officers.

At the meeting held March 16, 1765 the old record shows that the following votes were passed and recorded as follows:

Fifthly Voted John Johnson Jr. Chase Parish Colector for the present year.

Sixthly Voted Willm Slemons, James Merrell & Solomon Haskill parish Sessors.

Seventhly Voted that a meeting House is to be built and Erectted att the Place agread being Prefixed above Anthony Brackett Jun. adjoining. The County Road Near the Corner of the Road that Leads to Sacarappy. The North Side of Said Road Said house to bee bulded as Soon as may bee.

The site chosen is the present site of the so-called Bradley meeting house as now seen standing on Church street. Anthony Brackett, Jr., lived where the Nathan Tibbett's house stands.

The Saccarappa Congregational Society as well as the Woodfords are off shoots of this old Stroudwater parish, and the history of the old Stroudwater parish is the early history of the two in common till the time of their departure.

The "parish Sessors," as the clerk wrote it, lived as follows:

William Slemons—westerly edge of Stroudwater village where Fred A. Johnson now resides; James Merrill—northerly side of Presumpscot Falls; Solomon Haskell—Saccarappa; John Johnson, Jr. —a mile westerly of Stroudwater where Mr. George Johnson now resides, the dwelling then standing on the opposite side of the highway. To the last named, rather to his nieces, the two daughters of his brother Joseph who died some years since in Portland, the public, and the writer hereof in particular, are indebted for the manuscript record of the tax payers of the Parish at the time of incorporation. With other papers of historical value it was found in the attic of the John Johnson house, in an excellent state of preservation. At the time the assessment was made Quakers and Episcopalians were exempt from taxation if they so requested, so the list I am about to present does not cover the entire tax payers of the region, but very nearly, so much so the list is one of great local historical value—a booklet of 16 pages of written matter in the hand of William Slemons, 3¼x6 inches, without cover, and is arranged in several compartments: 1st, names and number of poles, for the owner of a slave was obliged evidently to pay a tax on him; 2nd, "real estate"; 3d, "personal and faculty," and 4th, "sum total."

The amount of poll tax was eight shillings so where the figure "1" or figure "2" appears opposite a name here presented, it must be understood that one or two slaves was owned by the person the name represents. Then the word "faculty" means ability to subsist beyond manual labor, that is, if a person was a professional, or had an income from a slave or money at interest, he was obliged to pay for the privilege.

In some cases the spelling of names would be misleading should I allow them to be printed as written, so I have made the name correspond with the person or family represented. Thus: Merrill is spelled "Marel".

The "sum total" of the individual tax I omit here as unimportant for historical purposes. The numbers af the left of the names are placed by the writer which do not appear in the original, but here place for future reference marks:

The list of names of owners of mills is one of special historical value and a matter that admits of study.

Perhaps it would be well here to state for the second time since the publication of these articles were commenced that the easterly territorial boundry line of the Parish commenced at the bridge near the James Deering place and extended in a northerly direction, but persons living easterly of the line had the privilege of being taxed in the Stroudwater Parish, and attend ing services at the Stroudwater meeting house.

Following is an exact copy of the first written page of the booklet as I can make.

"Falmouth, Dembr the 26: 1765
The foloing List is the originel
Tax or assessment on the
in nabetents of the fourth Parish
in Sd town for D fraing the
Parish Charges for Said yere
Containing forten Pages
amounting to one hundred and
fifty five Pound nineteen
Shillings and Seven Pence Laful
money which we have
Comited to John Johnson Jr.
Colecter to Colect all which
Colectons he is to Complete at
one or be fore the List day of
march next and Deliver in to
mr. Joseph Rigs Trasurer of
Sd Parish or his Sucksaser in Said
Office.

William Slemons } Assessors for the fourth
Solomon Haskell } Parish in Falmouth"

TO BE CONTINUED.

NOTE. Where the word "five" appears in the contribution of Mrs. Quinby last week it should read, to correspond with the copy, "one." The pen picture from her which appears below and words of cheer contained in a private note are indeed acceptable and the picture of Joanna Frost in her quaint garb will be appreciated by those who remember her and see the News. Joanna's place in family record will be found in the list published two weeks since, as eldest child of Charles Frost of the old brick house fame.

CHARACTERISTICS OF JOANNA FROST.

Miss Joanna Frost, or "Cousin Joan," as she was familiarly called, was a person of more than ordinary intelligence, with unmistakable Frost features, blue eyes and fair skin. A strong Universalist, but no disputant, and partaking in a great degree, the hospitable nature of her family. Her periodical visits to her relatives was a signal for a rummaging of closets for remnants of the finest wall-paper and cast away pictures, which, with scissors and paste-brush she converted into band boxes of all shapes and sizes, which were doubtless as much admired by the younger members of the families where she visited as is many a work of art of the present day by older persons. Her style of dress was somewhat peculiar. Short ringlets depended from either side of her head, on which was a close cap sparsely trimmed with straw-colored satin ribbon, which in its quaintness, looked as if especially invented for the wearer, and an immaculate muslin under handkerchief with a standup collar on the edge of which was a ruffle most carefully crimped, all of which appeared as designed for her alone. She was perfectly erect as if protection of the backbone had entered largely into her education and let the fashions be what they might, the close fitting skirt, cap and kerchief were always the same. At her request she was laid in her last sleep, by direction of her cousin whom she favor-

Saturday, April 4, 1896.

GRANDPA'S SCRAP BOOK

[Under this head historical and genealogical memoranda will be furnished the readers of the News that appears worthy of preservation, particularly of remote periods in our history within the city limits and immediate vicinity.]

STROUDWATER PARISH.

NAMES OF THOSE WHO PAID A TAX TO SUPPORT THE CONGREGATIONAL CHURCH IN 1765.

(Continued from last week.)

It appears from a little careful consideration of the following tax list taken in connection with my knowledge of persons and real estate at the time the list was made, the amount of land a person owned was not considered—buildings almost wholly, and that the tax on a two story house was about fifteen shillings.

	REAL ESTATE	PERSONAL & FACULTY
	£. s. d	£. s. d
Babb William,	0 0 0	0 0 0
Babb Peter,	0 18 5	0 7 6
Bryant James,	0 9 8	0 5 1
Brackett Thomas, (Morrill's Corner)	0 10 3	0 14 6
Brackett John,	0 3 5	0 16 9
Brackett Anthony, Jr., (Bradley's Corner)	0 15 8	0 3 8
Baker Josiah,	0 2 5	0 3 2
Bailey John, 2 (Libby's Corner)	0 12 8	0 12 1
Bailey John, Jr., (Spring Street)	0 4 0	0 2 5
Bailey David, (Later at Saccarappa)	0 0 0	0 0 0
Barbor John,	0 11 7	0 5 8
Barbor Hugh, 2	0 18 5	0 5 7
Brackett Zichariah, (Stevens Plains)	0 10 0	0 4 10
Barbor John, Jr.,	0 3 0	0 3 4
Brackett Joshua,	0 5 10	0 5 11
Cradiford Nath'l,	0 5 10	0 5 11
Conant Joseph, (Saccarappa)	0 2 3	0 1 11
Chapman Edward, (Buxton road)	1 2 5	0 7 3
Conant Samuel,	0 5 8	0 1 3
Chick Nathan, (Bet. Stroudwater & Saccarappa)	0 14 4	0 7 4
Crockett John Jr., (Stroudwater Falls)	0 0 0	0 0 0
Danty Thomas, 2	0 17 10	0 4 5
Elder Nathaniel,	0 0 0	0 0 0
Fickett Jonathan, (Stroudwater)	0 0 0	0 0 2
Frost Joanna, (Stroudwater)	1 18 7	0 19 3
Goold Aaron,	0 18 10	0 2 1
Gilman Edward, (Cumberland Mills)	0 9 0	0 2 1
Gibs Andrew,	1 3 11	0 3 2
Gibs William,	0 0 0	0 2 3
Hardy Isaac,	0 0 0	0 0 0
Gilman Edward, Jr.,	0 0 0	0 0 0
Hobbs Daniel,	0 15 1	0 2 2
Hill John,	0 0 0	0 0 0
Haskell Solomon, 2 (Saccarappa)	0 0 0	0 11 10
Haskell Thomas, (Saccarappa)	0 13 19	0 3 11
Haskell Benj., (Saccarappa)	0 0 0	0 15 11
Hicks Samuel, (Morrill's Corner)	0 7 10	0 7 11
Huston Geo.,	0 15 11	0 3 7
Huston Paul,	0 13 9	0 7 10
Hall Joseph,	0 0 11	0 1 0
Hobbs Jeremiah,	1 8 4	0 5 0
Hopkins Nathan,	0 0 0	0 0 0
Johnson John,	0 15 4	0 9 7
Johnson Geo.,	0 11 11	0 11 5
Johnson James, Jr.,	0 19 6	0 10 6
Johnson Robert,	0 16 7	0 9 7
Johnson John, Jr.,	1 3 8	0 11 9
Patridge Jesse, (Saccarappa)	0 0 0	0 4 10
Knights Richard,	0 0 0	0 0 0
Knights Mark,	0 10 11	0 5 9
Knights Samuel, 2	1 7 0	0 14 9
Knights Moses, 3	0 9 8	0 0 2
Knights Henry, Jr.,	1 2 1	0 2 1
Knights Nath'l, Jr.,	1 8 0	0 1 3
Knights Henry,	0 0 0	0 0 0
Knights Nath'l, 2 (Stroudwater Falls)	2 4 1	1 0 0
Knights George 3rd,	0 0 0	0 1 3
Knights Joshua,	0 5 11	0 4 11
Low John,	0 0 0	0 0 0
Lamb William, 3 (Near Congin)	1 10 4	0 12 9
Merrill James, 2 (Presumpscot Falls)	1 2 11	0 7 11
Merrill Nathan,	0 0 0	0 2 1
Morse Anthony, (Easterly Allen's Corner)	0 16 8	0 11 8
Mons Niles,	0 0 0	0 0 0
Mann Thomas,	0 0 0	0 0 0
Noyes Joseph,	0 0 0	0 0 0
Noble Nathan,	0 0 0	0 0 0
Nason Jonathan,	0 0 0	0 5 3
Nason Richard, Jr.,	0 0 0	0 0 11
Nason Isaac,	0 0 0	0 8 9
Patridge Preserved, 2	1 8 9	0 7 5
Patridge Nathan,	0 0 0	0 8 6
Pennel Clement, 2 (Capisic)	0 2 10	0 2 6
Pride William,	0 0 0	0 0 10
Proctor John,	0 16 9	0 2 11
Patrick Charles, (Stroudwater)	0 0 0	0 1 0
Poterfield William, (Westerly of Stroudwater)	0 18 1	0 19 3
Poterfield Robert,	0 0 0	0 2 0
Proctor William,	1 8 8	0 4 8
Pride Joseph, (Bradley's Corner)	0 14 10	0 4 7
Riggs Joseph,	0 16 0	0 14 6
Riggs Jeremiah, (Bradley's Corner)	0 8 0	0 17 0
Riggs Stephen (Westerly Nason's Corner)	0 17 0	0 10 6
Swett Stephen,	0 1 10	0 0 11
Skillin Isaac, (Southerly Woodfords)	0 17 8	0 14 0
Slemons William, 2	2 0 7	1 2 1
Strout John,	0 0 0	0 0 0
Small Joseph, (Stroudwater. The Quinby farm)	0 10 10	0 1 6
Small Daniel,	0 18 5	0 0 4
Smith Niles, 2	0 0 0	0 1 1
Starbird Jathro,	0 0 0	0 0 0

TO BE CONTINUED.

Saturday, April 11, 1896.

GRANDPA'S SCRAP BOOK

[Under this head historical and genealogical memoranda will be furnished the readers of the News that appears worthy of preservation, particularly of remote periods in our history within the city limits and immediate vicinity.]

STROUDWATER PARISH.

NAMES OF THOSE WHO PAID A TAX TO SUPPORT THE CONGREGATIONAL CHURCH IN 1765.

(Continued from last week.)

	REAL ESTATE	PERSONAL & FACULTY
	£. s. d	£. s. d
Small James,	0 0 0	0 1 2
Small Thomas,	0 0 0	0 0 2
*Thomes John, 2,	1 16 9	0 18 1
Thomes John, Jr., Libby's Corner.	0 14 0	0 3 8
Thompson James,	0 9 1	0 9 1
Trickey Zebulon, Saco road C. E.,	0 16 10	0 12 2
Trickey David, Saco road.	0 9 0	0 4 10
Thompson Nicholas,	0 0 0	0 0 0
Thompson Niles,	0 0 0	0 0 0
Thompson Bartholmew 2, Saccarappa.	0 6 8	0 3 8
Wilson John, 2,	0 10 5	0 2 4
Wilson Nath'l.	6 5 8	0 5 1
Walker George,	0 4 11	0 4 4
Warren John, 2, Sac. and Stroudwater road	0 3 1	0 2 9
Wiggins Chas.	0 0 0	0 0 0
Mathews John,	0 6 1	0 0 11
Epes Daniel, trader at Stroudwater	0 0 0	0 14 6
Sanborn John,	0 8 5	0 1 3
Grey John,	0 0 0	0 0 0
Chatben,	0 0 0	0 0 0
Douty Jonathan,	0 0 0	0 2 0
Douty Geo,	0 0 0	0 2 3
Douty James Jr.,	0 7 3	0 4 3
Humphrey William,	0 0 0	0 0 0
Douty James,	0 0 0	0 0 0
Thomes Benj.,	0 0 0	0 0 0
Freeman Enoch	0 11 2	0 4 5

MILLS.

Fulghia Nathaniel, Stroudwater Falls.	½	0 7 3
Bailey John, Mill at Saccarappa, he resided at Libbytown,	½	0 7 3
Chick Nathan, He resided bet. Sac. and Stroudwater.	1-8	
Lord Chas. Saccarappa.	1 8	0 3 7
Johnson Robert,	1-4	0 7 3
Trickey Zebulon,	½	0 7 3
Slemons William, Saw mill Stroudwater.	½	0 2 11
Johnson Geo.	1-8	0 1 5
Johnson John,	1-8	0 1 5
Trickey Zebulon,	½	0 2 11
Brackett John, Saccarappa.	½	0 7 3
Bailey Joseph,	½	0 7 3
Waldo Samuel,	1-2	0 16 7
Wayte Benj,	1-2	0 16 7
Mayo Elonezo,	1-2	0 16 7
Moody Enoch,	1 2	0 16 7
Webb David,	½	0 7 3
Jackson Thomas,	1-4	0 7 3
Freeman Enoch,	1	0 18 7

GRIST MILLS.

Haskell Thomas,	0 11 11
Jackson Thomas,	0 6 0
Conant Sam'l.	5 16 0

VESSELS.

Thames John, 50,	1 6 0
Thames Benjamin, 15,	0 7 10
Bailey John, 30,	0 16 8
Trickey Zebulon, 20,	0 10 8

ADDITIONAL LIST.

(But the record does not show on what account the addition was made.)

Noyes Josiah,	0 4 4
Starbird John,	0 2 9
Merrill John,	0 3 9
Thompson Miles,	0 3 9
Chapman Edward,	0 6 7
More Robert,	0 8 0

*John Thames kept an inn at Libby's Corner. The house stood close to the westerly end of the present brick house, and was two-story front, and one-story back. It was purchased by George Libby, Esq., deceased, who erected the present house, the only brick building of the locality. This can be used as a guide in imagining the values of other residences, of names of persons here appearing.

THE DEERING NEWS.

Saturday, April 18, 1896.

GRANDPA'S SCRAP BOOK

[Under this head historical and genealogical memoranda will be furnished the readers of the News that appears worthy of preservation, particularly of remote periods in our history within the city limits and immediate vicinity.]

RECORD OF THE FIRST UNIVERSALIST SOCIETY IN WESTBROOK, (ME.)

(Organized July 31, 1829.)

The above is a copy of the inscription written upon the fly leaf of a record book loaned me by Mr. Walter F. Goodrich of Stevens Plains whose father was the first clerk of the Universalist society that built the meeting house situated as now seen at Brighton Corner, this city. The book which is well preserved and was used till Sep. 6, 1851, is 6x7 inches square and 3-4 inch thick. As an historical relic it is of considerable importance and like all other books of similar character should find the way to the fire proof vault of our Maine Historical society. Considered alone the recorded facts contained within its covers are somewhat monotonous, but viewed in connection with other events, events particularly of an ecclesiastic character as recorded by the Rev. Caleb Bradley who, as an expounder of divine law, from a Puritanical point of observation, held almost unlimited sway hereabouts for a period of thirty years but whose term of active service terminated with the advent of organized Universalism as a religous belief, the records before me became a matter of importance to those interested in our local history. At that time beliefs of Puritanical Congregationalism and Universalism carried the question not only into the conversation of everyday life but the parish meeting for the election of officers and even into the municipal election, and though the representatives of Universalism were out sanctioned in the Parish meeting, they had their own way in the town meeting according to Parson Bradley's diary.

After the inscription as above presented in the record book above noticed then comes the following:

To Moses Quinby of Westbrook, one of the Justices of the Peace in and for the County of Cumberland:

The undersigned request that you issue your warrant under your hand & seal authorizing some one of your applicants to notify & warn your subscribers to meet at such time & place as shall be designated in your warrant to organize themselves as a religious society & to act upon such other matters as shall be set forth in your warrant. Westbrook, May 25, 1829.

NAMES.

Benjamin Quinby. S.   Amos Fobes. A.
Cushing Pratt. S.   Thomas Howard.
Cushing Pratt Jr. S.   George Bishop. M.
Levi Starbird. N.   Nathaniel Walden. M.
James Riggs. N.   Francis Hicks M.
Stephen Riggs. N.   Philo Hall. M.
Samuel Harper. N.   Thomas Seal. C.
Job Thorn. A.   Zachariah B. Stevens.
Levi Morrill. M.   S. P.
Sam'l B. Stevens. S. P.   Isaac Mason. B.
Elisha Higgins Jr. H.   John Jones. B.
Randall Johnson W.S.   Wm. Slemons Jr. W. S.
James Means. S. V.   John Porterfield. W. S.
Jonathan Smith. S. V.   Isaac Walker. S.
Silas Broad. S. V.   Henry Pratt. S.
Chas. Bartlett. S. V.   Oliver Buckley. S. P.
Wm. Perterfield. W. S.   Alfred Stevens. S. P.
John Babb. W. S.   Walter B. Goodrich.
Charles Quinby. S.   S. P.
Moses Stiles. S.   Joseph Chenery. B.
Chas. Pratt. S.   Thomas Jones. B.
Levi Tole. S.   Isaac Johnson. W. S.
Nathan Harris.   Henry Babb. S.
William Valentine. S.   Arron Winslow. C. M.
Otis Valentine. S.   Thomas Merrill.
Rufus Morrill. M.   John Jorian. S. V.

The letter or letters at the end of the name indicates the place of residence at the time the record was commenced.

A—Allens Corner.
B.—Bradleys Corner.
C.—Capisic.
C. M.—Cumberland Mills.
H.—Higgins Corner.
M.—Morrills Corner.
N.—Nasons Corner.
S.—Saccarappa.
S. P.—Stevens Plains.
S. V.—Stroudwater Village.

TO BE CONTINUED.

THE DEERING NEWS.

Saturday, April 25, 1896.

GRANDPA'S SCRAP BOOK

[Under this head historical and genealogical memoranda will be furnished the readers of the News that appears worthy of preservation, particularly of remote periods in our history within the city limits and immediate vicinity.]

RECORD OF THE FIRST UNIVERSALIST SOCIETY IN WESTBROOK, (ME.)
(Organized July, 31 1829.)
CONTINUED FROM LAST WEEK.

CUMBERLAND SS:

To Silas Broad, one of the above named applicants, GREETING:

Pursuant to the foregoing application to me directed, these are to notify and warn the aforenamed applicants to meet at the school house, near the meeting house at Stroudwater, on Friday the thirty-first day of July instant, at two o'clock in the afternoon to act on the following articles, viz: (There follows a list of twelve parts.)

Silas Broad kept a public house a fourth of a mile southerly of Stroudwater, and the school house stood near the so called Bradley meeting house of today in which the original Universalist church society of what is now Westbrook and Deering was born.

The Old school house was sold Monday afternoon, Aug. 11, 1851, to Chesley D. Nason for $33, he being allowed seven days in which to move it off, which was done and placed on a lot opposite the present residence of Mr. A. P. Chapman, Nason's Corner, a story added and has since been used as a dwelling house.

At the meeting for organization the following named officers were chosen:
Moderator—Capt. Thomas Seal.
Clerk—Walter B. Goodrich.
Standing Committee—Randall Johnson, Oliver Buckley, Benjamin Quinby Esq. Amasa Fobes and Isaac Walker.

Under the seventh article it was voted that this society be called The First Universalist society in Westbrook.

At a meeting holden Sept. 5th and at intervening meetings the following named persons were made members of the society.

Joseph Cox.   Moses Quinby, Esq.
Stephen Bacon.   Isaac W. Bailey.
Nathan Freeman.   G. A. Longfellow.
Andrew Limington.   Thomas Gould.
Abiel Cutter.   Robert Warren.
Simeon Mabury.   F. T. Cutter.
Chas. Raymond.   Isaac G. Walker.
          James Parker.

Samuel B. Stevens and Charles Bartlett were added to the standing committee, and Josiah Knight, Silas Dinsmore, and William Stevens were admitted as new members.

REPORT.

WESTBROOK, Apr. 3, 1830.

The committee appointed by The First Universalist Society in Westbrook to select a spot of ground on which to erect a meeting house have met for the purpose and taken into consideration the various circumstances relative to the subject ask leave to report that in their opinion the spot offered by John Jones, Esq., is the most suitable one.

Signed,
BENJ. QUINBY,
ISAAC WALKER,
S. B. STEVENS,   } Society Com.
CHAS. BARTLETT,
CHAS. PRATT,

3d, Voted to choose a committee to receive proposals for building a meeting house.

Moses Quinby, Esq., Oliver Buckley Esq., and Benjamin Quinby, Esq., were chosen.

Various notes were passed, but the records only show that the house was built by contract, and a committee of seven were chosen, of which Oliver Buckley, Esq., was chairman to superintend the building.

On the 26th of August Samuel B. Stevens (1) was chosen "to request some suitable person to prepare a sermon to be delivered at the dedication of The Universalist Chapel," and Isaac Mason (2) and Joseph Cox (3) were chosen to superintend the singing.

On the 18th of Sept., the following recorded votes were passed:

"That this society thank the Rev. W. I. Reese (4) for his service on the day of dedication of The Universalist Chapel, and for the purpose Capt. Thomas Seal, Samuel B. Stevens and Oliver Buckley were chosen. It was also voted that the committee request a copy of the sermon and the address delivered by him on that day. Joseph Cox and Isaac Mason were requested to return thanks of the society to Wm. Wood and all other singers who favored the choir."

The plain, well built structure now standing upon the elevated ledge at what is now known as Brighton Corner and owned by the city and used for a storehouse is the "Cradle for Universalism" then constructed.

1—Samuel B. Stevens has been noticed in these Scrap Book articles—place of residence and family connections given. Nov. 17 1834, he sent the society a letter which reads as follows:

To the Clerk of The First Universalist Society in Westbrook:

As the state of religion is such in said society that the business of it is the last and least felt, and instead of being treated as a privilege, a blessing and a duty that should be cheerfully performed, an irksome task, and believing as I do that a society in such a state had better be extinct, are reasons for my requesting you to strike my name from the list [of membership.] I shall cheerfully pay all my subscriptions and proportion of back arrearages

Respectfully Yours,
S. B. STEVENS.

WESTBROOK, Nov. 17, 1834.

After this he attended the Unitarian society of Portland.

2—Isaac Mason was son of Moses Mason, born July 24, 1764, at Watertown, Mass., and was a soldier in the war of the Revolution. Isaac was born there Sept. 6, 1787, married July 14, 1814, Sarah, daughter of James Riggs of Nasons Corner, this city. He was a tanner and resided in the house opposite Bradley's, Bradley's Corner, since transformed. He was usually called "Major" Mason on account of his connection with the State military. They had no children. She died in the Portland home for aged women.

In the Evergreen cemetery next to the southerly side of Pine Grove cemetery stand two memorial stones inscribed as follows:

Uncle,
ISAAC MASON,
Sept. 5, 1787.
June 5, 1847.

Aunt,
SALLY RIGGS.
wife of
Isaac Mason
March 23, 1788,
Feb. 11, 1881.

3—Joseph Cox was undoubtedly a son of Enoch Cox and grandson of Captain Joseph Cox of Portland. Enoch departing this life while his son Joseph was a minor, who became a comb maker, and united in marriage, Jan. 3, 1816, with Charlotte Sawyer, daughter of "Collector," alias, Isaac Sawyer who resided where the late Isaac Bailey resided so many years, on Ocean street, Woodford's district,—a sister to Lucy Sawyer who became, Nov. 17, 1800, the wife of Elisha Higgins, Jr., and Peggy Sawyer, another sister, the mother of our venerable Wm. Woodford, etc., etc.

CHILDREN OF JOSEPH COX. AND WIFE CHARLOTTE.

1—Enoch born Aug. 5, 1816.
2—Susannah S. born June 5, 1818.
3—Lemuel, born Sept. 17, 1820.
4.—Charles Edward, born June 25, 1825.
6—Jane Stevens, born Dec. 31, 1827.

Mr. Cox lived during the last days of his life in the house at this time that is second northerly from the Westbrook Seminary grounds on Stevens Plains avenue, the lot of which he purchased in 1838, his son and heirs disposing of the same to Rufus Dunham in 1854, for $476.

Upon a lot located on the easterly side of Pine Grove cemetery stands a marble monument inscribed on one side as follows:

JOSEPH COX

Died March 28, 1843,
Aged 50 years and 7 months.

Happy in the Savior's love, he was willing to go and be with Christ above.

CONTINUED:

CHARLOTTE,

His widow, died at Sturbridge, Mass., Aug. 14, 1852, aged 58 years.

"Thy spirit seeks beyond the tomb
A brighter and a better home."

There are other inscriptions on the monument.

4—Rev. Wm. I. Reese was settled over the Portland Universalist society Sept. 28, 1829. He was a man of marked goodness. By him the Widow's Wood society was organized which has done good work ever since. He remained but two years and two months in Portland.

In the old cemetery on Congress street, Portland, at the corner of the main avenue leading in from Congress street and the one from Mountfort street stands a handsome monument of marble, the inscriptions on which tell the interesting story of its erection and purpose.

On the east side are these words: "Erected Dec. 1, 1859, by donation for the purpose from the Hon. F. O. J. Smith, etc.

The west side reads: "This friend of mankind was born in Charlestown, Montgomery county, N. Y., on Dec. 25, 1798, and died in the city of Buffalo, N. Y., Sept. 6, 1834, a self-sacrifice to his charitable nature in devoting himself to the sick, dying and dead, during the eminently terrific prevalence of the cholera in that city, from which fatal disease and its victims others fled for safety, while he remained a Samaritan and a martyr. In his love of mankind he was faithful to God."

The other two sides are inscribed also.

In 1824 Jonathan Smith, the father of Hon. F. O. J. Smith, kept a public house that stood at Woodfords where Saunders street joins Stevens Plains avenue, and F. O. J. S. lived most of his life and died in what is now Deering.

TO BE CONTINUED.

THE DEERING NEWS.

Saturday, May 2, 1896.

GRANDPA'S SCRAP BOOK

[Under this head historical and genealogical memoranda will be furnished the readers of the News that appears worthy of preservation, particularly of remote periods in our history within the city limits and immediate vicinity.]

RECORD OF THE FIRST UNIVERSALIST SOCIETY IN WESTBROOK, (ME.)
(Organized July, 31 1829.)

CONTINUED FROM LAST WEEK.

After Portland Neck was made a municipality, which was in the year of 1786, the town meetings were held in the Stroudwater Parish meeting house that stood where the present so-called Bradley meeting house now stands in which the voters of what is Falmouth, Westbrook and Deering assembled to elect town, county and state official and transact municipal business. The building was large, side to street, two story, a two story porch on each end containing stairs, a door in the center of the front side, over which was a roof supported by two posts, and a door in the front of each porch so as to make three entrances. A broad aisle lead from the front door to the pulpit, and there was an aisle at each end connected with the end doors with a double row of pews between the aisles. A gallery ran round three sides, under which was a row of windows and thus making the building appear two story outside. The building was not plastered only under the galleries. There was a half circle window over each of the three outside doors, and there was a gable on the portico, or porch, next to the street. The front door hinges are in the possession of the writer.

It was what was called a "proprietors building," that is, a certain number of individuals took it upon themselves to cause the building to be constructed and sold the pews to liquidate the demands for building, then put the care of the structure under the parish organization, which furnished the preacher for the church society. The peculiar situation is readily seen. This state of affairs is found today in many societies.

In Portland the orthodox Puritanical element withdrew from the old First Parish and the parish committee met with no opposition in employing a Unitarian preacher. But here the orthodox element was not so ready to yield their claim. Evidently the meeting house was looked upon as a prize worth contending for, and the Universalists as well as the other side pushed their respective claims.

June 28, 1824 Rev. Caleb Bradley notified the parish by letter that he did not want any more money raised for his support by taxation.

Aug. 6, 1827 it was voted "9 no's" to "7 yea's" that the "Pastoral connexion between the Rev. Caleb Bradley and the Parish be dissolved."

But the parish was in debt to the reverend gentleman, and as there was manifest slowness in procuring a settlement and his successor, on the first day of Jan. 1829 he informed the parish that unless his successor was provided he should continue to officiate as his agreement made many years before allowed him to do so.

Under date of Jan. 1, 1829 he says in his diary:

This is the commencement of a new era in my life. In the evening attended the bible class at Back Cove—interesting time. After the exercise was over, at 8 o'clock, the church met in the same house (the brick school house on Ocean street). I made a communication to them stating that I had been the pastor of the church nearly thirty years, and then requested my connection be dissolved in twelve months. The church then voted unanimously, thirteen members being present, to give (Rev.) Mr. H. C. Jewett an invitation to take the charge of the church for five years, and voted to call a Parish meeting to see if the Parish would concur with the church. Came home in a snowstorm.

Jan. 9. Attended Parish meeting. The Parish voted to dismiss the article relative to the settling of Mr. Jewett. Quite an excitement—a full meeting—but everything calm.

On the 21st of February the parish record shows that it was voted "that the Rev. Henry C. Jewett be the minister of the Parish." In reference to the matter Rev. Mr. Bradley says:

A violent snowstorm through the night. It continues at the present time—11 a. m. very uncomfortable. 2 o'clock p. m. Parish meeting to give Mr. Jewett a call. Notwithstanding the storm and drifts of snow a number attended. Sixteen were in favor of concurring with the church and six opposed, namely: (Dr.) Jacob Hunt, Joseph Broad, (Capt.) John Jones, Moses Quinby, (Esq.) John Jordan and apt.) Thomas Seal. I think of those who are in favor of order and religion I be blessed if they pray and persevere. They must go forward. He who endures unto the end the same shall be saved. At 3 o'clock p. m. one Morgan of Portland killed his wife and stabbed himself with the same knife. O, what will not men do when left to themselves! Who can say the heart of man is not deceitful above all things and desperately wicked? How necessary the change of heart should take place of which our Saviour speaks. Except a man be born again he cannot see the kingdom of God.

This last action of the parish was distasteful to many, and a meeting was called with the view of reconsidering the vote to invite the Rev. Mr. Jewett to become the pastor of the parish and on the 3d of March 1829 the following votes are recorded:

That the list of those present who had joined other societies previous to March 1821 and the list of those who have polled off from said Parish since that time and the list of those who have become members of said Parish since that time be read in this meeting.

That those who are not members of the Parish seat themselves in some separate part of the meeting house apart from the members of the Parish.

Voted, To dismiss the article.

Voted, To choose a committee to wait on the Rev. Henry C. Jewett in concurrence with the committee of the church, and Mr. Solomon Allen, Thomas Blake and John M. Wilson were chosen said committee.

Capt. Thomas Seal was moderator and John M. Wilson, clerk, who wrote a very fine business hand.

CONTINUED:

On the 3d of March Rev. Mr. Bradley makes this entry in his diary:

Let it be remembered, this day was held a Parish meeting to undo what was done at the last. The enemies of religion and their friends met in solid column and such a collection never before was together in this place on a similar occasion, but the friends of good order and religion prevailed—43 to 32. This meeting terminating so favorably must be owing to the watchful and superintending providence of a good and gracious God—forcibly impressing the truth. If He be for us who can be against us. He says to the church go forward.

TO BE CONTINUED.

NOTE. Where it says in my last article that Jonathan Smith's public house stood where Saunders street joins Stevens Plains avenue, it should be Forest Avenue.

In my article of two weeks ago, "W. S.," at the end of a name means westerly of Stroudwater.

THE DEERING NEWS.

Saturday, May 9, 1896.

GRANDPA'S SCRAP BOOK

[Under this head historical and genealogical memoranda will be furnished the readers of the News that appears worthy of preservation, particularly of remote periods in our history within the city limits and immediate vicinity.]

RECORD OF THE FIRST UNIVERSALIST SOCIETY IN WESTBROOK, (ME.)

(Organized July, 31 1829.)

CONTINUED FROM LAST WEEK.

TO BE CONTINUED.

March 16, 1829, Rev. Mr. Bradley makes this entry in his diary;

Town meeting; all bluster at the meeting house. (The reader will remember that the meeting house was used for municipal elections.) A mixed multitude new set of selectmen—all Universalists. O when will the inhabitants become correct in principles and practice? God has the time.

The names of those elected selectmen that year were as follows; Oliver Buckley, Stevens Plains; Charles Bartlett, Stroudwater; Benjamin Quinby, Saccarappa.

April 10 he writes,

Church meeting this evening at Back Cove. Agreed on a day for ordination. Agreed on a council. Ordination to be on the 29th inst. Everything harmonious and pleasant. Hope it will continue so. While we are very were much pleased others are vexed, but there is union in the church.

13th. (Rev.) Mr. Jewett here writing the letter missive. Dined here. At 2 o'clock p. m. letter finished and he has gone home.

20th. I spent the day in the house writing my charge for ordination—no calling to-day.

28th. At home till 4 (o'clock) p. m. Took tea at Mr. Marean's (Joshua H. Marean, who lived———and was deacon of the church. The deacons in 1833 were Archelaus Lewis, Joshua H. Marean and Pereze H. Eldridge.) Council met at 6 o'clock p. m. Papers were read relative to my request. It was unanimously granted. All the papers were read relative to the ordination of Mr. Jewett, and all was right. The council being organized adjourned to the school house (The one that stood near the meeting house) Examined Mr. J. Voted to proceed with the ordination tomorrow at 11 o'clock a. m. and then adjourned to meet at my house at 1-2 past 10 in the morning. At 1-2 past 9 at home.

29th. Ordination to-day. The council to be here at 1-2 past 10. At 11 went to the meeting house—large assembly, everything still and pleasant. I gave the charge and delivered all up to Mr. Jewett. Eight dined here (with me.) A good time, long to be remembered.

May 3rd. Sabbath. Communion. Mr. Jewett took the pulpit, and officiated at the table for the first time. Very well very solemn. Went to Saccarappa to attend the Bible class. Very rainy before I returned home.

24th. Sabbath. The Universalists set out to occupy the meeting house but did not succeed. I preached and had a good day. Was wonderfully supported. Mr. J. (Rev. Mr. Jewett) preached at Falmouth, and Mr. Miltimore (Rev. Mr. Miltimore who was settled over the old Falmouth Congregational Society) at Saccarappa. (Rev.) Mr. Blake here at 5 p. m.

The record of the struggle between the friends of the Puritanical Congregational form of worship and Universalism as made at the time I now write for supremacy, is an interesting feature of our local history. In both factions were the best men of the day, and Westbrook had a reputation as wide as the State of Maine, on account of the industry and intelligence of its inhabitants.

It seems that at the time of the dedication of the Universalist chapel a meeting of the "Association of Universalists" was holden at the same place, which was the 8th and 9th days of September 1830, Moses Quinby, Esq., Isaac Mason and Amasa Fobes acting as a delegation to request the admission of the new Westbrook society to the Association.

Of the dedication Rev. Mr. Bradley says:

Sept. 8th 1830. Still rainy. The Universalist Chapel to be dedicated (today) so it is said and to whom is it to be dedicated? If to the only living and true God I hope those who meet there to worship will be true worshippers of this living and true God, and great multitudes will be born there unto the kingdom, and it will be a place where God's honor shall dwell; and may all the assembly be under the consecrating influence of the holy spirit. One half past 11 a. m.—very rainy. People have met in the new house. O, that I might hear on their return, (the cry), Men and brethren, what shall we do (to be saved)? I wish it might be a Pentecost and that many there might be brought to their senses like the prodigal and resolve as he did to repent and return to their Heavenly Father. But they think they shall go to Heaven. They have no idea that any will fall short of there. No matter how they live, how they conduct, and what they believe. They are sure of Heaven at last.

Now, can it be true let us live as we list, do as we will and believe what we may that we shall all at last belong to one great congregation? It may be so, and if we believe this what need of denying ourselves, what need of remembering the Sabbath day to keep it holy, what need of so much fuss about meeting houses and ministers.

9th. Very rainy—meeting all day at the Universalist Chapel.

11th. The week is now closed. Much excitement on politics and Universalism —they will do to go together.

13th. Monday. Governor's day. (I) voted for Governor and Senators for the first time in my life.

P. M. My workmen all gone to town meeting—all bustle at the meeting house (where the election was held.)

14th. Foggy morning. A.M. at home. Meranda Jones married this morning p. m. went to Saccarappa by the way of Deacon (Benjamin) Bailey's, (who lived on the Windham road and whose family record has been presented in these Scrap Book articles,) Mrs. B(radley) with me. Having heard that Dea. Bailey and wife had become Universalists, I conversed with them on the subject and found the report to be altogether false. He had of late been repeatedly visited by that class of people whose object appeared to be to persuade them to give up their former belief, but said he had never altered his sentiments and could see no reason why he should; that he more and more confirmed in his belief. The deacon and wife appeared to have no disposition to conceal their sentiments. They are now as they ever have been since they made a profession of religion and hope they ever will be enabled to hold out. They are both of them hard of hearing and in consequence of this may have said "yes" to a falsehood when they would have said "no" had they not been deceived as to questions propounded. Mrs. Bradley and myself felt satisfied with each of them. Went from deacon B's to Saccarappa, visited G. Babb, prayed with him. Took tea with Mr. Hays and then came home. Mrs. B. stayed all night."

There are a large number of descendents of deacon Bailey in this and other places.

15th. Mrs. B. at Saccarappa, I must go after her. We called to see G. Babb. Dined at Mr. Akers. P. M. Set out for home. Called at Maj. Valentines. at Mr. Lamb's, and at Mr. Larrabee's where we took tea and had rather a pleasant time. I called to see a girl sick of fever, Sally Millions by name. Prayed with her. At home at sunset. All well. The day is closed and I do not know how much good or hurt I have done. The political excitement has been very great but seems to be subsiding. I believe that officers and office seeking will destroy our country or rather we shall lose our boasted republic. Each party are taking every unjustifiable means to carry their points. God reigns let the earth rejoice."

THE DEERING NEWS.

Saturday, May 16, 1896.

GRANDPA'S SCRAP BOOK

[Under this head historical and genealogical memoranda will be furnished the readers of the News that appears worthy of preservation, particularly of remote periods in our history within the city limits and immediate vicinity.]

RECORD OF THE FIRST UNIVERSALIST SOCIETY IN WESTBROOK, (ME.)

(Organized July, 31 1829.)

CONTINUED FROM LAST WEEK.

On the 30th day of May, 1830, the lease from John Jones, Esq., to the Universalist society, recorded in vol. 126, p. 8, of the Cumberland County Registry of Deeds was made of a half acre lot where the old meeting house then built as now seen stands, the considerations of which was, that the society pay one cent per year to Mr. Jones or heirs and fence the lot so long as the same should be used for meeting house or church purposes. When the society sold the building to the town of Westbrook the town purchased the lot of the Jones' heirs.

Oct. 4, 1830, it was voted that the standing committee be authorized to employ the Rev. Samuel Brimblecom as a preacher to this society for one year with a salary not to exceed four hundred dollars.

4th. Voted to raise the money on the poles and estates of the members of the society according to the town valuation.

The building having been built as now seen, and blinds for two sides secured of Samuel Harper who resided westerly of Nasons corner, a vote passed not to sell pews in the future to persons not members of the society, everything was in shape for Sunday services.

On the 8th of Oct. 1831 it was voted that the Society offer the Rev. Samuel Brimblecom $450 provided he continue another year.

The next year it was voted that it be expressly understood that Rev. Mr. Brimblecom will preach at Saccarrappa in proportion as the inhabitants of that village, i. e., all north westerly of George Tate's and John Porterfield and westerly of Benjamin Larrabee's may subscribe under the direction of the superintending committee.

Oct. 6, 1832. It was voted to employ Rev. Samuel Brimblecom three-fourths of the year.

Then followed on Apr. 10, of the next year the real draw back to the society, and the following copy explains the situations:

To Samuel B. Stevens, Clerk of the First Universalist Society of Westbrook.

We, the undersigned, hereby give notice that we wish to withdraw from said society, being about to join another which is soon to be organized in our immediate vicinity, (Saccarappa) Westbrook, Apr. 10,1833.

BENJAMIN QUINBY,
ISAAC WALKER,
HENRY BABB,
WILLIAM BABB,
MOSES STILES.

All these resided at Saccarappa.

Sep. 15, 1833. Voted that we have preaching a part, or all the time as our funds will admit, and of the 18 ballots cast Rev. Mr. Brimblecom received 15 to 3 in opposition.

At a meeting held a week later a resolve of which the following is a copy was passed:

Resolved. That the thanks of this society be presented to Miss Elizabeth Jones for her generous donation of an elegant Bible for the pulpit of the First Universalist society.

On the 7th day of Jan. 1836 a meeting was called to see what the society would do to support preaching, and to see if the society would unite with the Universalists at Saccarappa in the hire of a minister to preach alternately with the two societies.

Feb. 6th, the committee of conference consisting of Messrs. Moses Quinby, of Stroudwater, Amasa Fobes of Allen's Corner, and Isaac Mason of Bradley's Corner, recommended that Rev. John G. Adams of West Rumney, N. H., be employed; but May 4th voted to employ Rev. Mr. Bates; and May 23, voted to employ Rev. D. J. Mandell

At an adjourned meeting it was voted to employ Rev. D. J. Mandall for the term of six months, commencing on the 4th Sunday in June 1837, not to exceed $250 for 6 months.

At a meeting holden Jan. 12 1839. Voted to employ Rev. Zenas Thompson to preach half of the time.

May 19, 1839, a contribution amounting to $16.84 was taken for the purpose of purchasing a bass viol.

Apr. 22, 1844 a resolve was passed of which the following is a copy:

That the thanks of this society are due and hereby presented Miss Almena M. Stevens for her generous, devoted and very able service as organist during the present year; also to the other individuals composing the choir.

Rev. Joseph P. Atkinson was then employed to commence June 1844 on a salary of $450.

Apr. 1, 1848, it was voted to confer with the Westbrook and Falmouth society relative to employing a minister, and the name of Rev. F. Foster was suggested, but no arrangement was entered into.

Then Rev. L. Hussey was employed to preach half of the time, to commence his labors about the middle of June 1848.

At a meeting holden March 16, 1851 Rev. Mr. Hussey asked to be discharged when the old record book was closed.

Following are the names of members written on the last page of the record:

Benjamin Quinby, Cushing Pratt, Chas. Pratt, Jr., Levi Starbird, James Riggs, Stephen Riggs, Samuel Harper, Rufus Morrill, Ama Fobes, Thomas Howard, Silas Broad, Wm. Porterfield, Chas. Quinby, Levi Towle, Wm. Valentine, Thomas Seal, Isaac Mason, Wm. Slemons, Jr., Isaac Walker, Oliver Buckley, W. B. Goodrich, Thomas Jones, Isaac Johnson, Henry Babb, Moses Quinby, Stephen Bacon, Isaac W. Bailey, Nathan Freeman, G. A. Longfellow, Andrew Simington, Thomas Gould, Abial Cutter, Robert Warren, Simeon Mabury, F. F. Cutter, Charles Raymond, Isaac G. Walker, Daniel Lombard, Josiah Knight, Silas Dinsmore, T. B. Thompson, Alpheus Bailey, Arthur Milliken, John Dore, Sam'l H. Lunt, B. W. Ballard.

Alexander Blake, Henry P. Starbird, Freeman Foster, N. K. Sawyer, George Bishop, Nathaniel Walden, Philo Hall, Job Thorn, Levi Morrill, S. B. Stevens, Elisha Higgins, Jr., Randall Johnson, James Mains, Jonathan Smith, Chas. Bartlett, John Babb, Moses Stiles, Nathan Harris, Otis Valentine, Zach. B. Stevens, John Jones, John Porterfield, Henry Pratt, Alfred Stevens, Joseph Chenery, A. Winslow, Thomas Merrill, John Jordan, Joseph Cox, William Stevens, Enoch Burnham, J. A. Thompson, George Sawyer, Charles Stevens, Chandler Rackleff, Gerry Cook, Rufus Dunham, Jeremiah Beedle, Geo. Libby, C. C. Tobie, C. S. Buckley, Henry Blake, Amos Abbott, Orin Buckley, Francis Hicks, Geo. M. Stevens,

TO BE CONTINUED.

THE DEERING NEWS.

Saturday, May 23, 1896.

GRANDPA'S SCRAP BOOK

[Under this head historical and genealogical memoranda will be furnished the readers of the News that appears worthy of preservation, particularly of remote periods in our history within the city limits and immediate vicinity.]

THE RELIGIOUS REVIVAL OF SIXTY YEARS AGO.

WHAT THE REV. CALEB BRADLEY SAYS OF IT IN HIS JOURNAL.

It is traditional that many years ago this place was visited by a great religious excitement. Rev. Caleb Bradley at the close of the year 1830 alludes to the matter in his journal at follows:

The year in this town has been very boisterous. A set of men calling themselves Universalists have built a meeting house and have someone to talk to them on the Sabbath whom they call a preacher. The parish has refused the town the use of the meetinghouse for town meetings. The town is all in an uproar—can't agree on a spot to place the Town house—almost equally divided on this subject. Matters are as gloomy as the weather, (which he describes.) Nothing will bring the inhabitants of the town to their senses but the power of Omnipotence. The religious appear to be disposed to come to an understanding, but the ungodly are self-willed and selfish, and seem inclined to be determined on their own way. Another revival of religion would have a wonderful effect towards bringing order out of confusion, good out of evil, and light out of darkness. The unhappy discord which seems to exist with regard to location of the town house seems to come from that class who were so much opposed to the revival of religion in 1827, 1828 and 1829. So long as self will and madness inhabit the bosom, so long there will be uncomfortable members of society.

Referring to the parish record of Sep. 17, 1830, it says:

Voted to instruct the standing committee to notify the selectmen of the town of Westbrook that the parish can no longer allow the town to hold their meetings or do their business in the meetinghouse of said parish.

Referring again to the journal Parson Bradley says:

In the autumn of 1826 there was a remarkable attention in our public meetings and especially in the Bible class; and it was the opinion of visiting ministers that God was about to visit our people by the outpouring of His spirit. The attention continued to increase. People attended the Bible class instructions and the public worship of God in crowds. In January, of 1827, the Cumberland conference met in this place and appearances were more than usually flattering. In the month of February more than forty were asking—"What shall we do to be saved?" Careless sinners were awakened, and the devil awoke and set his agents to work. In proportion as the work of grace advanced the opposition to the gospel increased. In the course of the year there were about eighty who united with the church, hopefully converted, and it is believed about fifty to other churches. In 1828 there was a solemn attention. Meetings frequent and frequent additions to the church; but the enemies of religion were up and doing. They introduced one Wood who called himself a Universalist, who preached or rather held a meeting one Sabbath in four in each of the meetinghouses here and at Saccarappa.

The journalist then devotes four pages of the book now before me to a notice of some sort of an insult bestowed upon him at Saccarappa "at the hearing of which transaction," he says, "all heaven must be astonished and the devil himself, upon cool reflection, blush and be ashamed to think himself outdone in wickedness."

After a storm, then comes a calm. A storm of persecution commenced on the 11th day of December, 1828 at Saccarappa village. The devil seemed to be doubly infuriated and came into that place in great wrath.

The description of the affair that follows is written in parables and only parts of names given, but it seems the Reverend gentleman's enemies, (such he considered them) sent a letter to him asking for a conference—that "an awful silence prevailed which David to a Son of Jacob read the communication" in reply to the one sent Parson Bradley.

He closes the volume and the description of the Sacarappa affair as follows:

O that they may return and confess their sins and forsake them, and live lives of obedience is the fervent prayer of
C. B.

On the 20th day of March, 1831, he says: "Townhouse raised today." It stood on the easterly side of the highway opposite the old Universalist meetinghouse.

The town purchased the lot of Susan Bailey, widow, Dover, N. H., for a consideration of $65, which was 9 rods in front and ran back easterly 18 rods to the Bradley estate, and is now the Ackley house lot.

THE DEERING NEWS.

Saturday, May 30, 1896.

GRANDPA'S SCRAP BOOK

[Under this head historical and genealogical memoranda will be furnished the readers of this News that appears worthy of preservation, particularly of remote periods in our history within the city limits and immediate vicinity.]

THE SACCARAPPA CHURCH SOCIETY AND THE STROUDWATER MEETINGHOUSE.

Rev. Caleb Bradley records in his diary as follows:

Jan. 3, 1832. A very cold snow storm. A. M. Went to Saccarappa meetinghouse with a view of meeting a council for the purpose of organizing a church. The storm was so violent only part of the council met and then adjourned for two weeks.

17. Mrs. B. and myself went to Saccarappa. The council called for the purpose of organizing a church met at the meetinghouse at 10 o'clock a. m. Ministers present, Dr. Gillet, Mr. Chesley and Hobard. Attended to the preliminaries. At 2 o'clock p. m. The persons to be organized were examined. At 6 o'clock attended to the public exercises. Dr. Gillet preached. Dr. Hobard made the consecrating prayer. (Rev.) Mr. Chapley the fellowship of the church. (Rev.) Mr. Bradley the introductory prayer, and (Rev.) Mr. Jewett the concluding prayer. A solemn and interesting day. Returned home at 9 o'clock.

18. The meeting at Saccarappa continues. Mr. Hobard preached a. m. and Mr. Tenney p. m., and Mr. Jewett in the evening.

19. No help today, but Mr. Tenney. Exercises as yesterday—solemn and interesting. Stayed at night with Mr. Akers.

20. This is the last day of the feast. (Rev.) Mr. Gamthew and Tenney here—a solemn and interesting day, The meeting closed this evening about 8 o'clock. Deep impressions seem to have been made upon a full congregation. Six remained as enquirers. Many we expect are wounded, but can be healed by the blood of the Saviour. Sleighing bad, Lord bless the religious exercises of the week.

This Saccarapp church, which is now in existence, was a branch of the Stroudwater Congregational society.

June 5th Sabbath, This afternoon preached at Saccarappa and administered the communion service. Five received into the church—four baptized. Nath'l and Mary Johnson, Jane Vaugh Bixby and Abigail Brown and the wife of John Bixby.

April 3, 1833. Attended the installation of (Rev.) Mr. Searl, (but the journalist fails to state where,) (I) gave the charge, Mr. Jewett the right hand.

In another part of his diary he says Rev. Joseph Searl was installed over the church at Saccarappa, Apr. 3, 1833, "which was a branch of the old church (at Stroudwater) and the first at that place."

From September 8th 1830 till the 3d of April 1834 there were no parish meetings holden, so nothing appears on the parish record with reference to the Saccarappa branch.

The exact time Wm. Graves came to Westbrook I cannot state. He lived on the Mr. John B. Curtis lot near Bradley's Corner, in a house moved to the corner of Spring and High streets. He was a tanner and active in the church. He agitated for a new meetinghouse, and April 7, 1825 a parish meeting was holden that passed the following votes:

That we sell the old meetinghouse, take down or remove and erect a new one on the same spot lot.

Voted—That Wm. Graves, Christopher S. Davis and Joseph Chenery be a committee to sell take down or remove the old house and contract for and superintend the building of a new meetinghouse.

Voted—That Addison P. Woodford. John Merrill and Moses Dole be a committee to make arrangements with the pew owners of the old house either by purchase, giving an equivalent in the new house or otherwise.

Voted—that Royal Lincoln, Hosea Ilsley, Nathaniel Ilsley be a committee to appraise the old meetinghouse and the several pews in the same.

At an adjourned meeting Nathaniel Ilsley was excused from acting on the committee and Ezera T. Beal substituted.

Thomas D. Woodford was parish clerk, but the records are very imperfect; in fact nothing of importance is shown by them. Nothing is said as to cost of building, or who purchased the pews, or to whom the old house was sold. To other sources of information the seeker for facts must look.

On Oct. 24, 1835, it was voted at parish meeting that the building committee be authorized to furnish the new meetinghouse with carpets, lamps, settee, chairs and table: and E. D. Woodford, Dr. Soloman Allen, Joseph Chenery, Perez E. Eldridge, and Nathan Holden were chosen a committee to appraise the pews in the new meetinghouse, but no report is recorded.

Joshua H. Marean, Wm. Graves and Henry W. Stevens were authorized to sell the pews and Joshua H. Marean to sign the deeds of the same. Here is what Rev. Mr. Bradley records:

January 2, 1835. Took tea and spent the evening at Mr. Graves. Mr. (Rev.) Lane and wife, Mrs. Foy and Philip Woodford and wife there. Pleasant time. Talked about building a meetinghouse, and some other things of not too much profit. The company was pleasant and agreeable, and sociable and we parted with good feelings. Thus closes the second day of the year (with me) O, how swiftly time passes. Sager of Gardiner was executed for poisoning his wife today.

8th. Evening at a meeting at Back Cove relative to building a meetinghouse. Talked about it, and chose a committee to prepare a plan, another from out-of-town to designate the place where it shall be placed, (consisting of) Royal Lincoln, Clement Dyer and Rev. Thomas Jameson. Adjourned to meet at the same place two weeks.

17th. The committee to locate the meetinghouse met here at 9 o'clock a. m. Mr. Jameson, Mr. Dyer and Royal Lincoln. Took a view all around. Dined at Mr. Woodfords. 3 p. m. at home.

22nd. Went to Back Cove in the evening to hear the report of the (meetinghouse) locating committee, who recommended the place for the house to be opposite Mr. (Elisha) Higgins, the elder. This was a strange report, but the very best of men sometimes differ very much in their judgment. The report was accepted—a plan of a meetinghouse was accepted—a committee chosen to receive proposals, one to obtain funds, then the meeting adjourned to meet in two weeks.

27th. Like summer—the snow dissolving very fast. Evening at (Rev.) Mr. Lane's. Mr. E. D. W(oodford), Mr. Eldridge and Mr. Graves there. Conversed about building the new meetinghouse and agreed that it was best to have it (set) up on the old lot.

THE DEERING NEWS.

Saturday, June 6, 1896.

GRANDPA'S SCRAP BOOK

[Under this head historical and genealogical memoranda will be furnished the readers of the News that appears worthy of preservation, particularly of remote periods in our history within the city limits and immediate vicinity.]

THE FIRST CONGREGATIONAL MEETING HOUSE.

ITS ERECTION, DEDICATION, INSTALLATION AND OTHER FACTS CONNECTED THEREWITH.

CONTINUED FROM LAST WEEK.

Rev. Caleb Bradley records in his Journal as follows:

June 7, 1835, Sabbath. Expect to preach here. The Lord assist me and help me through with the services of the day, 4 o'clock p. m. Have preached twice. Felt assisted—felt a pardon. Preached in the town house. Good number at meeting, the first preaching ever in that house. Thomas Woodford and wife here, took tea and sang. Mr. Blake here, played on the bass viol.

15th. Deacon Holden began the meeting house.

20th. Sent for to go to the old meeting house and advise with regard to the location of the new.

July 2nd. The meeting house raised to day—no one hurt—no noise—no confusion—no rum. I attempted to lead in prayer before raising. Four hours in accomplishing the object.

Aug. 26th. A church meeting at the town house—7 church members present. Mr. Graves, Moses Dole, and myself. Mrs. Bradley, Mrs. Dole, Mrs. Johnson. How gloomy and distressing to see so little attention paid to the subject of religion.

Sept. 9th. A great convention of the Universalists.

10th. The Universalist meeting continues today.

October 29th. Fine day. The meeting house in this place dedicated. I introduced the services by asking a blessing. Read the 84 Psalm, and then a hymn was sung. Mr. Pomeroy made the first prayer. Mr. Loring preached. I made the dedicatory prayer. Mr. Kellogg made the address to the congregation, sang an anthem. Closing prayer by Mr. Searl. Benediction by myself. Everything was done decently but not in order. I spent the evening at Deacon Holdens.

Nov. 1st. Sabbath. Commenced today, the first Sabbath of the month, services in the new meeting house. Mr. Loring preached. An interesting day.

7th. The pews of the new meeting house were sold today, and they answered our most sanguine expectations. Three pews to me.

8th. Sabbath. The people occupied their own pews. Mr. Loring preached—full meeting. Preached in the evening at Back Cove. All very well. Laus Deo.

9th. Church meeting at the brick school house, District No. 3. Mr. Bradley moderator, after prayer by him, voted unanimously to invite the Rev. Caleb F. Page of Bridgton to become pastor of this church. (He did not accept.)

15th. Mr. Loring preached three times today in the meetinghouse. Full meetings.

21st. Some of the people in this town are mad and this day commenced to move the town house, but not very good luck."

It is stated above by the journalist that meetings were holden in the town house; this was because the old meetinghouse had been sold and taken down. It was disposed of by auction sale and was purchased by John Haskell for Capt. Dexter Brewer who used it in constructing the third story to the old "Chas. Frost, Esq.," house, which was converted into a public house and given the name of "Brewer House," and stood opposite Stroudwater village on the bank of Fore river, which house has been noticed in these articles.

Nov. 4. The journalist continues: "Went to the city with Mrs. W. and daughter to assist in some business—silk and cloth made by themselves, and sold to good advantage—the first silk thread ever brought to this market for sale. At noon at home and Mrs. W. and daughter gone."

Who this "Mrs. W. and daughter" was I have no knowledge." At about this date I notice that domestic silk was on exhibition at a cattle show and fair, which "attracted much attention."

At 3 o'clock of this date, the journalist states, "there was a lecture preparatory to the communion preached by (Rev.) Mr. Vaile from the words, Only let your conversation be as becometh the gospel," at which time a church meeting gave, or rather voted to give Rev. Joseph Lane a call to settle here as a minister to the gospel; present Ebenezer D. Woodford, Thomas Woodford, Isaac Bailey, Christopher S. Davis, Moses Dole, Wm. Graves, Thomas Sawyer, Anson Woodford (probably meaning Addison P. Woodford) and (Rev.) Caleb Bradley—an unanimous vote.

Dec. 20th. Fine morning. Installation today. Council to meet at the meetinghouse at 9 o'clock a. m. Examination was over at 11 o'clock. Dined at 12 M. Messrs. Pomeroy, Sheldon, Brown and Lane dined here. (These were all clergymen.) At half past one the public exercises began. Mr. Jameson made the first prayer, Mr. Dwight preached, I. G. Merrill made the consecrating prayer, Mr. Bradley gave the charge, and Mr. Searl the right hand of fellowship; Mr. Vaile the charge to the people, Mr. Pomeroy the concluding prayer, and Mr. Lane the benediction. Everything was done decently and in order. A fine day, and everything pleasant—very agreeable. Laus Deo."

And thus the meetinghouse as now seen, but closed, was dedicated according to the account or the affair made by the Rev. Caleb Bradley.

THE DEERING NEWS.

Saturday, June 27, 1896.

GRANDPA'S SCRAP BOOK

[Under this head historical and genealogical memoranda will be furnished the readers of the News that appears worthy of preservation, particularly of remote periods in our history within the city limits and immediate vicinity.]

WESTBROOK SEMINARY

THE OLDEST UNCHANGED PUBLIC BUILDING WITHIN THE LIMITS OF THE CITY.

The grounds of this old institution of learning are very pleasantly situated on Stevens Plains Avenue. At the rear end of the lot the old seminary building—the only public building now within the territorial limits of this city that has not had its exterior altered—may be seen today standing on rising ground as approached from the avenue, fronting easterly, the avenue shaded by majestic trees and skirted by dwellings of modern and ancient style of architecture, in excellent repair with neatly kept surroundings, which lot is dotted with transplanted forest trees of two score years since the event, beneath the shadows of which are neatly kept drives and paths. Of all Deering highways Stevens Plains avenue is by far the finest in point of artificial endowments, the old institution of learning giving the town of Westbrook and a part of the town now Deering both since the division having become cities as relates to municipal government, a more than local reputation, and adding very materially to the attractions of the avenue.

Who conceived the thought and who formed the same into dennable and definite materialization of erecting the building, the fine cut thereof which we present to the public in this issue of the News, records that are obtainable, do not show but many facts during a protracted research have been found, some of which we now propose to present. I have given in these Scrap Book articles the time as July 31, 1829, when the Westbrook Universalist religious society was organized, the place and many facts connected therewith, and it is presumed that the Seminary enterprise was a result of the activity displayed by the Universalists of that period.

"An act to establish a Literary Institution in Westbrook" was approved March 4, 1831, by Samuel E. Smith, Governor of Maine. The second section provides that James C. Churchill, Francis O. J. Smith, Daniel Winslow, Nathan Nutter of Portland; Wm. Slemmons and Moses Quinby of Westbrook; Josiah Dunn of Poland; William A. Drew of Augusta; D. McCobb of Waldoboro; G. W. Tucker of Bowdoinham and Alfred Prince of Greene; be, and they hereby are appointed Trustees of said Seminary and are hereby incorporated into a body politic, by the name of "Westbrook Seminary."

James C. Churchill was made president of the board, who served nineteen years; Daniel Winslow vice president who served seven years; Francis F. O. J Smith, treasurer, who served eleven years, and Daniel Winslow secretary, who served ten years. Samuel R. Stevens then succeeded Winslow and served till the time of his death. And here comes in a sad part—namely: On the 11th day of April 1842 the place of business of Samuel B. Stevens was destroyed by fire and all the seminary record books belonging to the secretcy perished. Again, in 1872, at the time of a fire in Portland when Charles S. Fobes was treasurer, his books belonging to the institution were destroyed, so that all now obtainable of the early history of the ancient institution is simply scraps.

The first purchase of land that is recorded occurred Jan. 12, 1832: Oliver Buckley to Frances O. J. Smith, treasurer of Westbrook seminary, four acres and twenty square rods of land "if the contemplated seminary building should not be built the $200 to be refunded." James Hicks conveyed to the same for $120, one hundred and twenty-one square rods; and Zachariah B. Stevens for $113 two acres and seventy-three square rods.

By whom the building was built and the amount paid, there is nothing obtainable I know of at this time.

It is claimed the school was opened the first time in 1834. A notice in the Christian Pilot, a Universalist paper published in Portland settles conclusively the date and is as follows:

WESTBROOK SEMINARY.

The Westbrook Seminary will open on the 9th of June. Its friends are requested to exert themselves to procure scholars at the commencement of the school. The terms are $3 common English studies; $4 for higher branches.

In 1837 the building was mortgaged to James Huse of Portland, and 1839 it was sold at public auction by the sheriff to Asa H. Carter of Portland, but in 1840 the trustees received back the building and land.

Rev. Samuel Brimblecom was the first principal; but of him I cannot speak with accuracy so will say but little. He was school town committee with the two Congregational ministers, pastor of the Universalist society and assistant editor of the Pilot. In 1833 he purchased of Levi Morrill a three acre lot located on the easterly side of Stevens Plains avenue, agreeing to pay for the same $250 and build a brick house evidently for students as well as for himself and family. In 1836 he made an assignment of the property which later came into the possession of the seminary. The following notice taken from a copy of the Portland Transcript of 1842 tells of its fate. It stood where the only brick building on the easterly side of the avenue stands today:

The brick house on Stevens Plains built by Rev. Samuel Brimblecom, and owned by Samuel Whitten was consumed by fire on Sunday evening. The furniture was saved.

His connection with the school was but two years when he was succeeded by James Furbish. In 1840 John K. True became principal, and in 1843 Moses B. Walker and Geo. W. True. Concerning John K. True I find the following notice dated Apr. 22, 1842:

Rev. John K. True of the Westbrook Seminary has taken the charge of the 'Eastern Rose Bud,' a Sabbath school paper published by S. H. Colesworthy of Portland. The work has been enlarged and is published semi-annually at fifty cents per year.

After Messrs. Walker and True come, in 1844, E. P. Hinds; Geo. R Bradford 1846; and Rev. L. L. Record, 1849.

In 1850 a half township grant of land was received from the State, and a vote of thanks was extended by the trustees to Hon. Samuel Jordan (Woodfords) for the care, vigilance and ability with which he sustained successfully in the Legislature, the petition of the trustees for the grant."

In 1851 Nathaniel Hatch, a Congregationalist minister acted as principal.

It was the year before this that the "Union Speaking School" petition the trustees for the "stage room" of the building, but a vote was soon passed to "restrict the use of the building to the exclusive purpose of education in regular course of instruction."

The "Union Speaking School" was a local theatrical party so common nowadays.

Up to this date no examinations of the scholars were had at the closing of the terms. Strange as it may seem, Rev. Caleb Bradley does not notice the Seminary even once in his diary.

The employment of Rev. Mr. Hatch evidently opened wider the eyes of the friends of the Universalists of the State, and a new impetus given the old institution; but it was not till 1853, I think, that the "Maine Universalist Society came into existence," or a "basis of union" was found "on the plan of making the Seminary a first class and permanent school in connection with the Universalist denomination of Maine," the number of Trustees to be raised to thirteen from "men of high reputation in the Universalist denomination of this State."

Among the articles of stipulation was this: "The trustees of the Educational Society shall have the right and the power of nominating the principal of the

CONTINUED:

Seminary and professors also."

In the year 1853 Rev. I. P. Weston was given the place of chief tutorship and a $100 voted him to repair the building and liberty to place trees upon the ground before which time the whole lot was a barren waste.

From the time of the advent of Rev. Mr. Weston the course of the old Institution has been onward and upward with incidents too numerous to be noticed in this article.

At one time in the early life of the Seminary the management promulgated the following declarations which I understand to be in force at this day though the institution has the fostering care of the State Universalist denomination:

"This Seminary is designed and pledged to the public by its founders for the education of young men to the various professions and pursuits of mankind, free from all religious bias and prejudices, and under the influence of such religious doctrines and opinions only as each may elect for himself and sanctioned by the dictates of his own conscience."

Since then the charter has been amended which was in 1863 and a "Ladies' collegiate department added."

Saturday, June 13, 1896.

GRANDPA'S SCRAP BOOK

[Under this head historical and genealogical memoranda will be furnished the readers of the News that appears worthy of preservation, particularly of remote periods in our history within the city limits and immediate vicinity.]

REV. JOSEPH LANE.

HIS DISMISSAL FROM CHURCH AND PARISH AND DEPARTURE IN 1838.

CONTINUED FROM LAST WEEK.

A copy of a notice for a parish meeting dated Oct. 17, 1838, is recorded in the old Congregational parish book of this city as follows:

To see if the parish will appoint some person as a committee to act with a committee of the church on the subject of dissolving the connection of the Rev. Joseph Lane with the church and parish in Westbrook.

(Deering then being a part of that town) and it was voted that (Dr.) Solomon Allen be a committee.

This is all the parish record shows relative to the matter of Mr. Lane's closing his engagement with the church and parish. Dr. Allen lived at Allen's Corner in the large old-fashioned house now standing in the northeasterly corner made by the crossing of the highways, but the journal of Rev. Mr. Bradley furnishes a good deal of interesting information as follows:

Oct. 16, 1838. A meeting of the church at the brick schoolhouse, (Ocean street, Woodfords district) to agree with Mr. Lane for a council for his dismission from this people and church. A full meeting of the church which complied with his request. Mr. Lane was exceedingly affected and cried heartily.

(I will put in an entry here that does not relate to church matters directly.)

17th. This has been a day of confusion confounded—a cattle show at Brewer's, all classes and color met to see and hear. Drunkenness and gambling and every evil work was the order of the day. David Hayes and wife and Noah Nason and wife here (from Saccarappa) and William C. Bradley (his son) and wife and child to dine and at supper. I was not very much distressed when the day closed.

18th. 2 o'clock p. m., the church met at the meetinghouse and held a season of prayer. Mr. Lane had many things to say by way of advice as he expects to be dismissed next week.

The journalist then goes on to state the substance of Mr. Lane's reasons for leaving.

20th. Evening meeting at Mr. Lane's, the usual number present. Mr. Lane much affected and overcome, who gave up the lead of the meeting to me.

Mr. Lane when he came to this place boarded with Mr. Bradley, then he kept house in the vicinity, but I cannot state positively the house.

24th. This has been a day long to be remembered, and will be remembered long by the church and people of the First Congregational society in Westbrook. The Rev. Joseph Lane became pastor of this church and minister of this people Dec. 29, 1836. Oct. 24, 1838, the connection was dissolved by mutual council convened to consider the matter. The council consisted of Messrs. Dwight, Chickering and Condit, ministers of Portland with their delegates, Rev. Mr. Stevens of Falmouth and his delegates two representing the church at Saccarappa, and (Rev.) Mr. Bradley. The council met in the meetinghouse at 2 o'clock p. m., and was organized by the choosing of Mr. Dwight, moderator, and Mr. Stevens scribe. The throne of grace was addressed by the moderator. After hearing what the church and parish had done, Mr. Lane made a statement of some length of his difficulties, and the reasons why he wishes to be dismissed. Questions were asked. The council went into a thorough examination, and endeavored to make themselves fully acquainted with the whole matter; then the council was left alone, and after due deliberation voted unanimously with one exception, that the connection be dissolved. Thus Mr. Lane was dismissed, after having sustained the pastoral office one year and ten months.

The journalist then goes on to state the reasons given by Rev. Mr. Lane for:

Providence had provided a field of labor which appeared to be more agreeable, for which he thought himself more suitable, and it would be better for his health to become an agent for the Bible society, and hence more useful than being a minister in a country parish.

25th. Things religiously and politically wear a gloomy aspect, everything is dark, but God reigns and He can easily bring light out of darkness, order out of confusion, and good out of evil. We had a meeting this evening at the brick schoolhouse. Only two male members from the corner; three from this quarter and a few females. I had to take the lead of the meeting and endeavored to make it solemn and interesting. Read a chapter beginning thus: Let not your heart be troubled, believe in God, believe also in me.

26th. There is a gloom hanging over the religious society of this place. The candlestick has been removed from its place. To live without preaching, no, we can't; we shall die if we don't have preaching.

27th. Mr. Lane getting in his garden sauce and preparing to leave, full of anxiety, all excited. He thinks Providence has made it his duty to engage in another field of labor. He can't set down to study and write sermons; he never used himself to do this, and at this period of life with his wandering habits he can't do it and be contented.

Nov. 2. What an awful day will that day be when God will by the blast of his trumpet call the world to judgment. What must be the distress, the anguish, the honor of those who shall then be found without a wedding garment! O God may not this be my lot, but prepared for the momentous period when a world shall be judged.

24th. This day Mr. Lane wound up his labors among this people—farewell. Mr. Graves and myself into Mr. Lane's and held the monthly concert, a very agreeable time.

5th. Mr. Lane has been rather a moving character. He has never remained very long in one place; been a settled minister twice; spent between one and two years upon hire in Franklin, N. H. He has been a missionary to an Indian tribe near Buffalo, N. Y.; been an agent of a Bible society for the states of New Hampshire and Maine, preached here six months, had a call to settle here, but negatived the call, and went in the employ of the D. M. S. to Kentucky. He had another call to come and settle here in Nov. 1836, which he accepted. He now enters the employ of the A. B. S. for New Hampshire, Vermont and Maine. This is an outline of Mr. Lane's labors since he entered the ministry; but few have had so many changes as he.

26th. Mr. Lane loading his goods and expects to leave for Gilmantown. Mr. Berry goes with one load.

27th. Mr. Lane's goods all loaded. Mr. Berry not ready—proposes to be ready at 10 o'clock a. m. The time arrives, but Mr. Berry not ready. Mr. Lane begins to grow impatient. Noon. Dinner. Will start in half an hour. The half hour comes about—not ready, but will be ready in one hour. One hour passes, not ready. Three o'clock p. m., begins to spit snow. Mr. Lane and Mr. Berry begin to move slowly, and will probably reach Scarboro tonight. Farewell. He has got his pay for preaching one year and ten months—$1016 00. No minister was ever better paid in the country.

THE DEERING NEWS.

Saturday, July 4, 1896.

GRANDPA'S SCRAP BOOK

[Under this head historical and genealogical memoranda will be furnished the readers of the News that appears worthy of preservation, particularly of remote periods in our history within the city limits and immediate vicinity.]

WILLIAM GRAVES.

HIS CONNECTION WITH THE FIRST CONGREGATIONAL CHURCH AND PARISH.

Nathaniel Graves died at Waterford, Vt., Apr. 18, 1801, aged 53 years. Mercy, his wife, died there Jan. 29, 1841, aged 87 years.

Capt. Barnabas Baker was born Aug. 6, 1762. Ruth, his wife, born Oct. 18, 1768. She died at St. Johnsbury, Vt., May 2, 1845, aged 76½ years; he died at Newport, Vt., Feb. 28, 1846, aged 83½ years.

A daughter of this couple became the wife of one Fairbanks, the founder of the Fairbanks Scale Company of St. Johnsbury.

A son named John was at one time a blacksmith in Portland, who engaged in hotel keeping at Bangor and other places; he finally went to New York.

William Graves, son of the preceding, was born at Athol, Mass., Apr. 17, 1789. Sarah Brown Barker, daughter of the preceding, born at St. Johnsbury, Vt., Feb. 13, 1793. This couple were married at the last named place by Luther Clark, Esq., Jan. 5, 1813, and settled in Craftsbury, Vt., about 30 miles from St. Johnsbury, where he engaged in tanning, and where three children were born: 1—Sarah Maria; 2—William Wallace; 3—Horace Porter.

March 5, 1831 he with his family arrived at Westbrook, and commenced house keeping in a two-story dwelling that stood where Mr. John B. Curtis resides on Stevens Plains avenue Bradley's Corner district: There was a tanyard on the place all of which he purchased of George Warren, the house being built about 1808 by one William Homes, it appears.

Mr Graves on arriving at Westbrook commenced immediately in church work, and through his labors in part the old meeting house was removed and the present one built.

Rev. Caleb Bradley does not allude to his advent in his diary, but does July 31 of that year as follows:

Sabbath. Preached for Mr. Millimord, (Falmouth, now the First Congregational Society) three times. A very solemn and interesting occasion. Mrs. B. with me. Sunset at home. Mr Graves took the lead in the Bible class. This is as it should be.

April 12, 1834 Mr. Graves was chosen with Joshua H. Marean and (Dr.) Solomon Allen parish committee. When he was made a member the records, which are very brief, do not state.

The parson's diary shows that he, Mr. Graves, and the Rev. Mr Lane held frequent meetings for prayer for the conversion of their children.

Feb. 17, 1835 this entry was made.

Nothing done or talked about, but a wedding to be at Mr. Graves tomorrow. 18. Fine day—good sleighing—all hands preparing for the wedding tonight. Sarah Mariah Graves married by Mr. Dwight (Rev.) Mr. Lane and myself having no invertation. O tempora, O mores. Mirabile dictu mirabile vesu!

Mr. Graves business adventures were a failure, and as Rev. Mr. Bradley and Dea. E. D. Woodford were his endorsers they came into possession of the property, but I can allude to but one entry in reference to the matter:

Nov. 6, 1840. Went into the city, (Portland) and called on Mr. Graves. Met with Capt. Prince and his son. Sold to them the Graves place for $2,500, $500 to be paid when the deed is made, the rest with interest annually in installments. This has taken a very great burden from my mind, and I am in hopes of getting along now without a great deal more of trouble. This has been a perplexing business to me. It has taken the flesh off my very bones. It is an awful temporal calamity.

Five days before this date it appears as a matter of record that Mr. Graves asked for a dismissal for himself, wife and son William Wallace that they might join the 3rd church of Portland.

Under the firm name of Wm. Graves & Son, Mr. Graves engaged in the business of leather currying on Union street, Portland, on leaving Westbrook, which was continued till 1849, when the establishment was destroyed by fire. Mr. Graves and wife then removed to St. Johnsbury, Vt., where she died June 6, 1865, aged 72 years. After her death he came back to Portland and died Dec. 10, 1870, aged 81 years and 8 mos. Both buried in St. Johnsbury.

CHILDREN.

1 Sarah Mariah, as noticed above, was born Nov. 7, 1813, at Craftsburg, Vt., where all the children were born. She married at Portland Nov. 14, 1839, Ebenzea P. Burbank and there was born to them Frances Mariah, Sep. 17, 1839, and Nov. 14 of that year the mother died. The daughter married in the state of Michigan and removed to California where she died Feb. 28, 1882. He in company with the late Moses G. Dow of this city kept a grocery store corner of Congress and Preble streets Portland; and married 2nd in Portland and removed to New York where he died.

2 William Wallace Groves, born at Craftsburg, Vt., June 24, 1817. While a student at the Gorham, Me. Seminary in company with the late John J. Chenery of Woodfords, born in the old Riggs house just removed at Bradley's Corner, where his parents resided they both joined the First Congregational church, and as before stated engaged in business with his father in Portland. Oct. 16, 1848 at Portland, Rev. W. T. Dwight performed the marriage ceremony between him and Miss Eliza Waite Bartol, who was reared by an aunt. In 1861 Mr. Graves went into the Portland P. O. under Postmaster. Dole, and remained eight years; then he was postal clerk between Portland and Boston. His wife died Feb. 1889, aged 71 years. They resided on Lincoln street. He is a well known character on the streets of Portland—tall slim, straight, full head of hair, gray or well whitened side whiskers, mustache, easy in conversation and an inmate of the inestimable retreat for the worthy—"The Home for Aged Men."

CHILDREN.

1 William Henry, born March 7, 1845 died same month.
2 Maria Louise, March 1, 1846, died Apr. 22, 1849
3 Samuel Bartol, Apr. 29, 1848, learned the druggist business, married, and now resides at Brunswick as a groceryman.
4 Mary Chandler, Feb. 19, 1851, died Apr. 11, 1854.
5 Charlotte Harwood, March 4, 1853, died Sep. 6, 1861.
6 Dwight Cushing, Apr. 2, died same month.
7 Annie Thayer, Feb. 26. 1856, died March 17 same year.
8 Hattie Eliza, March 22, 1857, died Oct. 8, 1862.

3. Horace P. Graves, third and last child, born same place as the other two, Oct. 29, 1819, married in New York city, Sarah Ann Gurling, June 14, 1848. She died in Lynn, Mass., where Horace P. engaged as a morocco finisher. He married 2nd at Chicago, Ill., Feb. 15, 1860, Zilpha A. Dent. This Mr. Graves has been for 25 years a commercial traveler for a boot and shoe firm and resides at Detroit, Mich.

THE DEERING NEWS.

Saturday, July 11, 1896.

GRANDPA'S SCRAP BOOK

[Under this head historical and genealogical memoranda will be furnished the readers of the News that appears worthy of preservation, particularly of remote periods in our history within the city limits and immediate vicinity.]

ROBERT BAYLEY.

THE FIRST SCHOOL MASTER OF PORTLAND AND FAMILY.

This department of the News is in receipt of a communication which throws light upon schoolmaster Bayley, and which, though not intended for publication, I cheerfully lay before the readers of the News, with the hope that additional light may be reflected upon the career of an old time public character and a record of his ancestors obtained. Mr. Archie L. Talbot, the writer, is general agent of this state for the "Provident Life and Trust Company," with an office at Lewiston. Learning that the residence of Mr. Bayley was only temporary here, I regret to say, that what allusions I have met relating to him I have passed without making a single note.

Mr. Talbot's communication is as follows:

In the history of Portland by Willis, chap. xiv.—"Education," etc., it appears that Robert Bayley in 1733 was the first schoolmaster in that part of Falmouth that is now Portland, and the town records of Scarboro show that Robert Bayley was the first schoolmaster there in 1737. In a foot note to the chapter on education in the Willis history it is stated that "Robert Bayley was admitted a proprietor of Falmouth on payment of £10, August 17, 1727, and in February following a house lot was granted him, and the south side of Middle street where Plum street has since been laid out. He probably came from Newbury, Mass., where the Bayley family settled about 1642. . . . In 1745 Robert Bailey and his wife Martha were dismissed from the church of Falmouth to join the church of North Yarmouth. The town records of North Yarmouth show that the said Robert Bayley was town clerk of that town in 1749 and 1750 and while town clerk he made the following record of his family—viz:

CHILDREN OF ROBERT AND MARTHA BAYLEY.

1, Bethsheba, born at Biddeford March 14, 1727.
2, Judith, Falmouth Sept. 14, 1730, died Apr. 25, 1731.
3, Hannah, Falmouth, May 13, 1732.
4, Mary Clark, Falmouth, March 10, 1734.
5, Robert Jr., Falmouth Jan. 15, 1736.
6, Martha, Falmouth, Feb. 8, 1740.
7, Naomi, North Yarmouth, June 12, 1742.
8, Achsa, North Yarmouth, Apr. 5, 1748.

The history of Newbury, Mass., gives a statement of the Bayley family and says Joseph, son of John Jr., removed to Arundel, Me., and then gives children of Joseph and Priscilla Bayley as follows:

1, Rebecca, born 25th Oct. 1675.
2, Priscilla, born 31st Oct. 1676.
3, John, born 16th Sept. 1678.
4, Joseph, born 28th Jan. 1681.
5, Hannah, born 9th Sept. 1683.
6, Daniel, born 10th Jan. 1686.
7, Mary, born 9th Jan. 1688.
8, Judith, born 11th Feb. 1690.
9, Lydia, born 25th Nov. 1695.
10, Sebah, born 14th Feb. 1698.

Bradbury's history of Kennebunkport (Arundel) p. 226 says John Bayley came from Chippanham, Wiltshire, England, cast away at Pemaquid 1639, died 1651, and that his son John settled in Newbury. Joseph the 4th son of John Jr., born Apr. 4, 1648, bought land of Nicholas Morey 1700, and lived in Arundel until it was destroyed in 1703—returned 1714, was selectman in 1719—killed by Indians in 1723 at the age of 75 years.*

The history of Saco and Biddeford show a John Bailey as one of the early settlers.

I am a descendant of this Robert Bayley. His daughter Mary Clark Bayley married, Nov. 28, 1754, Ambrose Talbot who settled in the part of North Yarmouth that is now Freeport. I have been trying some time to trace the ancestry of Robert Bayley. If he was a schoolmaster in 1733 he must have been about 20 years of age then, or I should say would make his birth 1713 or thereabouts. He was probably a grandson of Joseph Bayley of Arundel. But where can I find the family record of this Joseph? . . . The records of North Yarmouth show that the town clerk of 1749-'50 always wrote his name Robert Bayley, which also show the way of spelling the family name at that time.

Yours very truly,
ARCHIE LEE TALBOT.

CONTINUED ON PAGE 11.

[*Book X, York Deeds, p 194, shows that on the 18th day of May 1720 Joseph Bailey of Arundel (Cape Porpoise), sold a hundred acres of land to George Biggsbee of Salem village, beginning bounds "at a turn in the Kennebunk river above the interval point where John Purington did formerly dwell and so up the river to James Mussey's line," etc., and at the same time he sold fifty acres adjoining to Israel Josslin of the same place, in both cases he spelled his name "Bailey."

Concerning Dea. John Bailey whose first child was born at Newbury, Mass., Oct. 30, 1722 and who was admitted a citizen of Falmouth, Dec. 14, 1727, and who died at Libby's Corner. I will say, I have much material; the same also concerning his brother Joseph whose first child was born at Newbury, Nov. 5, 1727, and who came to Falmouth and died near Saccarappa. Dea. James Bailey, born Aug. 1, 1749 at Long Creek, C. E. has been written up in the *News*.

COMPILER SCRAP BOOK ARTICLES.]

THE DEERING NEWS.

Saturday, July 18, 1896.

GRANDPA'S SCRAP BOOK

[Under this head, historical and genealogical memoranda will be furnished the readers of the News that appears worthy of preservation, particularly of remote periods in our history within the city limits and immediate vicinity.]

THE GREAT BRIDGE.

A STRUCTURE AT STROUDWATER BUILT BY COLONEL WESTBROOK IN 1734.

The original name for the arm of the sea now known as Fore river was Casco. The change of name was produced in consequence of a protracted dispute as to the correct boundary line between the Spurwink plantation occupied by one Jordan and Casco occupied by Cleaves whose home was on Portland Neck, Cleaves claiming the first or Fore river to be the westerly boundary line of his plantation, while Jordan claimed the second or Presumpscott, from his point of view, to be Cleaves' true boundary. In this way the name of "Casco" was dropped and that of "Fore" substituted.

Upon the resettlement of Falmouth in the year 1718 the emigration by land was from a south westerly direction and along a path adjacent the shore of the salt water, "Casco" or Fore river being a source of great difficuty in reaching the Neck which was the centre of attraction.

The privilege of keeping a ferry over "old Casco river"—I here use the words of the record—was "granted unto Mr. John Prichard for 7 years on condition it bedone at said Prichard own charge," and "by reason of the difficulty of calling over the river" it was voted that "the privilege of the ferry on the Papooduck side be given to John Sawyer to keep a good cannoe for the accommodation of the passengers." This was in 1719.

When Col. Thomas Westbrook settled at Stroudwater, in 1728, he proposed a bridge at that place which he built where the so-called long bridge now stands, the record being found in the Massachusetts State archives after a protracted research.

In view of the past as presented by the records the inhabitants did not over rate the structure when they called it "great," or "The Great Bridge." The present one is comparatively small and insignificant now, but the enterprise of that day was great—great for several years in the eyes of the inhabitants, and how to keep the thing in repair was an all absorbing question of vast importance. In the year 1749, Moses Pearson, Esq., was paid £2-14 for answering to an indictment for not keeping it in a passable condition, at the same time the inhabitants voting at town meeting "that the selectmen of Falmouth for the time being prefer a petition to the Great and General Court to take into their wise consideration the Extraordinary charge sd town is annually at in maintaining the Great Bridge over fore river and order a toll on sd Bridge, or some other way Ease sd town of the Extraordinary Expense of sd Bridge as they in their wisdom think best."

The town had previously presented the matter to the Court of Sessions but failed to obtain the kind of notice the town desired. Following is a copy of the petition:

PROVINCE OF }
MASSACHUSETTS BAY. }

To his Excellency William Shirley Esq., Commander in chief of his Majesty's Province of the Massachusetts Bay. The Honorable, his Majesty's Council, and the Honorable House of Representatives In General Court Assembled. May 1749:

The Petition of the subscribers, selectmen of The Town of Falmouth, Humbly Showeth, That In about the year 1734, By the Interest of Thomas Westbrook Esq., late of Falmouth, deceasd, there was a bridge erected over fore River In Said Town, In length 640 feet with a caseway at each end of said bridge In length 70 feet, on or about ye year 1738, by the force of The tide and Ice a great part of sd. Bridge was Broken up, the Repairs of which amounted to upwards of 300 Pounds old Tenor, and In the several years since the Repairs have amounted to upwards of 300 Pounds, old Tenor. Said Town have made application to the Court of General Sessions of the Peace for the County of York for their assistance In the Repairs and maintainance of said Bridge. But have had no Relief, other charges of sd. Town Being at least Equal In Proportion to any other Town. In this government, there being a great Number of large expensive Bridges in the town exclusive of sd Bridge, being equal to ff not the most expensive Bridge In the government, the Inhabitants of sd. Town are not able any longer to bare up under said Burthen, therefore your Petitioners Humbly pray your Excellency and Honors, to take the same Into your Wise Consideration and order the County of York to Repair and Maintain the same or order a toll on sd. Bridge or otherwise Relieve your Petitioners as In your wisdom shall see meet, and your Petitioners as In duty Shall ever Pray:

Ezekil Cushing }
John Snow } Selectmen
Joseph Thompson } For
William Cotton } Falmouth.
Christa Strout }

The memorandas and Order by the Senate and House of Representatives endorsed upon the documents, I omit as unimportant.

To the foregoing petition the Court of Sessions made a reply which will be presented next week.

THE DEERING NEWS.

Saturday, July 25, 1896.

GRANDPA'S SCRAP BOOK

[Under this head historical and genealogical memoranda will be furnished the readers of the News that appears worthy of preservation, particularly of remote periods in our history within the city limits and immediate vicinity.]

THE GREAT BRIDGE.

A Structure at Stroudwater built by Colonel Westbrook in 1734.

To the Court of General sessions of the Peace held at Falmouth within and for the County of York on the first Tuesday of. October 1749 in Answer to the Petition of the Selectmen of Said Town of Falmouth and ' in Obedience to the Order of the Honorable Council and House of Representatives dated the 14th and 15th of August 1749:

Say that the Said Court of General Sessions of the Peace having considered the circumstances of the town are of the opinion that the County ought not to be charged with the repairing and maintaining the Said Bridge, for, as the Petitioners show, that In or about the year 1734 the same Bridge was built by the Interest of Thos. Westbrook Esq., late Deceased (which should be remembered to the Honor of that Gentleman) and if the work was so great, and performed by the Interest of one man for the good of the Town, they ought not to complain of the Cost of Keeping the same in repair, and more especially since there are now four times ye Inhabitants belonging to Said Town than there were when said Bridge was built, and therefore so much better able to repair and maintain the Same, but their showing forth in their Petition that in the year 1738 the tide and sea carried away a great part of Said bridge, the repairs of which cost upwards of three hundred pounds, old tenor, and the several repairs since have amounted to upwards of Two Hundred Pounds, old tenor, but the Petitioners do not show how this charge arose, whether they let out the work or reckoned wages for men that stood Idle as is sometimes the case in mending Highways.

The Petitioners, reckoning Ten or Twelve Years repairing all in a lump, to look great, may possibly lead Some into a mistake, for the several Towns in the County, or most of them, at their own Cost and Charge, support and maintain as many great Bridges in their respective Towns, and at great expense, and if an account was kept of the charge it would appear to amount to as much as the Town of Falmouth pays to their ways and Bridges.

As to their other Bridges they maintain they are not equal to the Bridges in most other towns in the County for Charges and the Court are of the opinion if the Town of Falmouth would follow the method of other Towns in the County of mending their ways (not by a Tax) but by warning ye Inhabitants to Work—by that means less than a fifth part of the Inhabitants of Falmouth would repair the Said Bridge in a day, a much easier way than imposing a tax.

There is not one in five hundred of the Inhabitants of Said County that ever pass over said bridge, or ever receive any benefit thereby, why then should the County be compelled to pay towards the support of Said Bridge?

And Further, since said Bridge has been built, Falmouth has neglected the Ferry over the said Fore River to the Town which is of great convenience, not only to the Publick in General, but especially such as travel East no farther than Falmouth and to the Second Parish on the South side of the River.

Nextly, this Court are assured that the Cost of repairing and maintaining this and several other large Bridges erected over Rivers and Creeks, and divers more proposed to be erected, which, with as much reason, should be maintained by the County, will be an Insupportable burthen, especially at a time when the bills of publick Credit are to be called in and Sunk, and no certainty of other mediams whereby an extraordinary Tax may be paid.

The Justices of said Court do not oppose a Toll to be set until further order, or until the way laid out formerly above the head of Fore River, which is more direct for a County Road, be cleared and made fit for travelling.

Furthermore, this Court are of the opinion that Falmouth is not at greater Cost in mending this and all other of their highways than any of the Towns in this County are, according to their ability, and that they ought still to support and maintain the same or procure the Road to be turned or altered to a more convenient place.

Wherefore, said Court pray ye said Petition may be dismist,

All of which is humbly submitted to Your Honors by order of Court,

JNO. FROST,
Clerk.

TO BE CONTINUED.

Saturday, Aug. 1, 1896.

GRANDPA'S SCRAP BOOK

[Under this head historical and genealogical memoranda will be furnished the readers of the News that appears worthy of preservation, particularly of remote periods in our history within the city limits and immediate vicinity.]

THE GREAT BRIDGE.

A STRUCTURE AT STROUDWATER BUILT BY COLONEL WESTBROOK IN 1734.

Continued From Last Week.

With reference to the petition by the selectmen of Falmouth, a copy of which was presented two weeks since in the *News*, under this head, the legislative committee reported as follows:

The com'tee on the part of Ezekil Cushing and other Selectmen of Falmouth have considered the same and are hereby of the opinion that the Bridge mentioned in the Peti. be repaired at the Charge of the town of Falmouth only, and that the Town be empowered by this Hon. bl. Court to Receive a Toll from all persons and Carriages that pass over sd. Bridge at these Rates, Vizt: (The copy here presented is as near as I could make from the original found in the Massachusetts archives. It appears that the report of the committee was amended as indicated by the letters.)

For every Person one penny, for every man and Horse (A) two pence, for every horse and Chaise or Horse and Chair (B) three pence, (C——D) all of which is humbly submitted pr, John Wilder. (Z) during the Term of five years (D) provided at that time said Town of Falmouth shall within 12 months cause to be built sufficient Bridges across the river and above the Bridge refer'd to in the Petition on such part of said River as shall be approved by the court of sessions for the County,

A Three Pence

B four pence

C For each horse or oxen six pence and for each sleadand Slay three pence provided nevertheless that the Inhabitants of Falmouth be exempt from paying the Toll aforesaid.

In Council, April 11, 1750. Read and concured with the further amendment at D and Z.

SAML. HOLBROOK,
Dep. Sc.

It is plain to the present beholder that the location of the bridge was not changed as then contemplated, which would have caused the road to have gone up over the present farm of Mr. Daniel Dole.

This same year, 1750, the parish of Cape Elizabeth was made a township but required to "pay its proportional part of the expense of the repairs of the Great Bridge till further orders of the Court, in case the toll does not prove sufficient for the purpose."

In 1751 there was objection to loading vessels with lumber from the bridge, but the town did not take foral action in the matter till the year 1757 when it was

Voted, "that all vessells Loading and unloading at Stroudwater Bridge pay 8 pence p. Day each Day they lay there, the Person collecting to have a quarter part for collecting, and that Mr. John Bailey be the Person to collect it."

In 1760 a special town meeting was holden "to see what method the town will take to repair the long Bridge at Stroudwater which is greatly damaged by the late storm."

Forty-two pounds lawful money was voted.

In the year 1786 Portland Neck was set apart from Falmouth and encorporated as a town with the provision in the act of separation "that the inhabitants of Portland shall amend and repair the great bridge on Fore river, so called, although the same be not within the limits of Portland aforesaid."

In 1800, and again in 1809 the inhabitants of Portland were indicted for not keeping the structure in repair, particularly for allowing the bridge to be without a railing.

The visit of President Monroe to Maine after the war of 1812-15 was over, was an event of great moment to the inhabitants of the state, and although suffering from the effects of the war, particularly the embargo, the citizens of Stroudwater were not behind in furnishing evidence of their loyalty to country and respect to the President. From the Eastern Argus of July 22, 1817 the following is taken:

"The President, under an escort of cavalry commanded by Major Trowbridge, arrived at the village of Stroudwater in Westbrook, about 6 o'clock Tuesday evening. The citizens had for two or three days before busily employed themselves in decorating the bridge over which the President was to pass, as an expression of their respect for the first majestrate of the nation. Nineteen arches were thrown over it, dressed with evergreen and roses tastefully festooned, and connected by an evergreen wreath, one for each State, with the name of the State in large letters on the top of the arch.

A twentieth was erected as symbolical of the nation. Surmounting this arch was another of a shorter chord and deeper curve, the base resting upon it, dressed like the first in evergreen and was imblazoned in front with nineteen brilliant stars. From the brow of the hill before the bridge to some distance beyond, were planted ranges of small white pines, spruce, larch, etc., upon each side of the way, exhibiting to the eye the appearance of a flourishing green hedge, and forming a beautiful mall for the distance of nearly a quarter of a mile. The whole producing a most pleasing and picturesque effect.

As the President arrived at the brow of the hill he alighted from the carriage, descended the declivity, and passed the bridge on foot. As he was passing under the Arch a national salute was fired from the hill above.

A LIVING EAGLE, a native of our own forest, and the symbol of our material prowess perched on the summit of the twentieth arch, and under the canopy of Stars by which it was surmounted, apparently watching with intense curiosi-and surpvise, the concourse of people passing under him, heightened in the bosom of every beholder, the interest of the lively spectacle. It was a delightful sight to behold this haughty monarch of the feathered tribe, the pride of the forest, encircled by the blaze of stars he loves, stifling for a moment his untamed spirit of liberty, and gracefully spreading his pinions as the chief of the nation passed, which had chosen him from the whole range of animated nature, as the emblem of its glory and strength.

The President having passed the bridge reentered his carriage. The cavalcade that accompanied him to the city was a mile and a half in length, and was much the most numerous ever witnessed in the District of Maine."

There are many record incidents connected with the bridge but I cannot allude to but one, namely: The attempt in the winter of 1886, when Chas. J. Chapman was Mayor of Portland, to annul the ancient agreement between Falmouth and Portland for Portland to keep the bridge in repair for all time, and only to refer to the newspapers of that day for particulars.

THE DEERING NEWS.

Saturday, Aug. 8, 1896.

GRANDPA'S SCRAP BOOK

[Under this head historical and genealogical memoranda will be furnished the readers of the News that appears worthy of preservation, particularly of remote periods in our history within the city limits and immediate vicinity.]

ANTHONY BRACKETT, JR.

THE SITE OF HIS ABODE AND FACTS CONNECTED WITH IT.

The origin of land titles hereabouts and records of attempts to dispossess claimants and occupants in ye olden times with incidental facts therewith connected are in many cases very interesting studies to the student of history.

Of the list of those that were ill treated I place the name of Anthony Brackett at the head of this article. The site of his worldly place of abode was the eastly side of Stevens Plains avenue, Bradley's Corner district, but the place of his sepulchered ashes is not known to me.

December 9, 1774, Rev. Samuel Dean says in his diary as printed, "I prayed with Anthony Brackett, at Joshua Brackett's." And a foot note says,

Anthony was the son of Zachariah, who was the son of Capt. Anthony, killed by the indians on the farm now occupied by Mr. (James) Deering (located within the city of Deering.) He was born in Hampton, Aug. 25, 1712; married Abigail Chapman, who lived at the foot of Bramhall's hill, in 1734, by whom he had three sons, Jeremiah, David and John his second wife was Abigail daughter of Joshua Brackett, who lived at what is now north westerly corner of Congress and High streets, and widow of Job Lunt to whom he was married in 1764, and by whom he had Abigail, born February 1766, married to Daniel Green of Portland."

The name David Brackett in the foregoing should be Daniel to correspond with the record of signers to the deed from Anthony's heirs.

In the News of November 3, 1894 appeared a valuable record of the family of Zachariah Brackett, father of Anthony whose name I have placed at the head of this article and to it I now refer, in which it is stated that Anthony, Jr., was born Aug. 25, 1712, and married Abigail Chapman whose parents resided near the present Union Railroad Station located on the corner of Congress and St. John's streets, Portland.

The father of this Abigail Chapman was named Edward, born at Kittery. The descent being as follows;

Edward was in Ipswick, Mass., 1643. He had two wives and died there April 18, 1678. His son Nathaniel married at about the age of 40, and probably the second time, Dec. 30, 1674, Mary Wilborn, after several children were born he moved to Kittery where Edward the father of Abigail was born April 14, 1702 and who married Oct. 24, 1725 Abigail Broughton of Portsmouth, N. H. In the year 1725, July 5, "for divers good causes and parental affection" his father, Nathaniel gave him his estate in Kittery which he sold after his father's demise, and in the year 1737 he purchased at or near Saco Falls in Biddeford a hundred acre lot, where he was a member of the church and where his wife died and where he married a second time. Seven years later he sold in Biddeford and Aug. 19, 1746 came to Falmouth and located as before stated, about where the Fred Clark house stands near the Union Depot, but not being satisfied there he commenced to clear a farm northerly of where Mr. James Babb resides at the present time near the Buxton road, two miles westerly of Stroudwater, where the old well and cellar hole may be seen.

With him in a separate house lived his sister Abigail, whose husband was named Joseph Muzzett. In the year 1750—1 he made his will and provided for his daughter who became the wife of Anthony Brackett, Jr., as follows:

One good feather bed, two pillows and bolster with other suitable bedding for the same, one looking-glass, one desk, one oval table, six black chairs, one two-armed ditto, four pewter dishes, two pewter plates, and all other suitables to furnish one room, which I leave to the discretion of my sole executor to be raised and levied out of my estate, on the day of her marriage, two good milch cows, and clothing for her, which I also leave to the discretion of my sole executor.

His son Edward, evidently with his sister Abigail were the only surviving children at the time of the death of their father.

April 6, 1751, this Edward Chapman married with Eleanor Small of Stroudwater, who resided with her parents on the Quinby farm now occupied by Hon. Andrew Hawes.

After the death of Edward, the executor of the will of 1751, his widow married Jan. 8, 1779, James Frost of Gorham.

In the year 1769 this James Frost purchased a fourth of an acre of land, where Warren Harmon's cooper shop stands at Capisic, and built a two-story dwelling where he kept a public house a few years and where Capt. Thomas Seal commenced married life.

On the 19th of March, 1734, Benjamin Ingalls of North Yarmouth for a consideration of "£300 current and passable money to me in hand well and truly paid" by Col. Thomas Westbrook conveyed to him one hundred acres of land in Falmouth" near the new dwelling house of Thomas Haskell which is over against the house of Col. Westbrook at a place called Stroudwater; the said one hundred acres of land being butted and bounded as follows:

Beginning bounds at a cross path at a pitch pine tree wich is marked T. W. standing about thirty rods from Haskell's house on the road that runs to Falmouth meeting house (Portland) on the north side of Fore river, thence running east, one hundred and thirty rods to a white oak marked, and thence north eighty rods to a stake; thence west two hundred and thirty-two rods to a pitch pine tree standing by the water about fourteen or fifteen rods northward of the creek that runs down on the back side of the place where the former dwelling house of Thomas Cloyce was, etc.

The "pitch pine" tree stood near the old Fowler house that stood on Congress street, Bradley's Corner district, removed three or four years since, and Haskell's house was on the bank towards John Nelson's house on Frost street, where the cellar hole may be seen, the "white oak" towards Portland from Bradley's Corner, on Congress street, and the northerly line running westerly passed in front of the present meetinghouse site of Capisic mill and the Cloyce house stood two hundred years ago where the Brewer house stood, easterly side of Congress street, opposite Stroudwater, which was burned a few years since. All these points have been alluded to in former articles but not in a connected manner as now.

TO BE CONTINUED.

THE DEERING NEWS.

Saturday, Aug. 15, 1896.

GRANDPA'S SCRAP BOOK

[Under this head historical and genealogical memoranda will be furnished the readers of the News that appears worthy of preservation, particularly of remote periods in our history within the city limits and immediate vicinity.]

ANTHONY BRACKETT, JR.

THE SITE OF HIS ABODE AND FACTS CONNECTED WITH IT.

CONTINUED FROM LAST WEEK.

Of the 76 acre land purchase made in the year 1734 by Col. Thomas Westbrook of Benjamin Ingalls of North Yarmouth the easterly part comprising 46 acres was the next year conveyed to Anthony Brackett, Jr., for a consideration of £156-10, current money, bounded as follows;

"Commencing at a white Oak tree marked and then running west eighty-four rods to a stake and thence from the afore named white oak tree north eighty rods to a stake and thence west one hundred rods toa stake and thence a straight course eighty rods to first bounds mentioned."

Vol. 19 p. 235, York Deeds.

This lot was located upon the northerly side of what is now Congress street and included therein the southerly side part of the present Parson Bradley homestead lot adjoining Congress street to the amount of twenty-five acres. The westerly side line was located about where Stevens Plains avenue is now found.

Upon this forty-six acre lot Anthony Brackett Jr., erected his two-story house, end to the highway, in the then forest. The brook as now seen, and the spring recently noticed in the Portland newspapers as containing water of valuable medicinal qualities, furnished water in abundance for cattle and culinary purposes. The site selected and upon which the dwelling was built was the site of the Nathan Tibbetts house noticed in the News, June 1st 1895. The Ingalls title to the lot conveyed to Westbrook commenced with the Indian grant made to Francis Small, the 27 of July 1657, at "Capissicke" and recorded on page 83 of Vol. 1, York Deeds two years after the transaction was concluded.

In Vol. 1, page 222, date Nov. 25, 1728, of the proprietors of the "Common and undivided lands of Falmouth," may be seen a record that reads as follows;

"Granted and laid out a certain tract of land containing forty acres lying and being in the Township of Falmouth and is bounded as follows;

It Being the fifth lot In number and begins at a white oak tree marked (the owl more than probable before noticed in this article and the one last week) on four sides;adjoining on (Rev.) Mr.Smith's lot (who sold it to Deacon John Bailey) and thence fronting forty Rod on ye Highway that goes up into the country, said forty acres to be for a thirty acre lot and a ten acre lot, according to the Draughts of ye Town for the ministerial lots (church or parish lot) to the town, said lots to run back Into the woods Eighty score Rod till the forty acres be completed."

This grant included, it appears by court records to be presented herewith, 25 acres of the Anthony Brackett, Jr. purchase becoming, i. e. the forty acres, the Bradley farm, a half of which Mr. Wm. L. Bradley of Portland, grandchild of the reverend, now owns; thus showing that the south easterly corner of the Brackett purchase is the south easterly corner of the Wm. L. Bradley lot, minus a house lot.

Of the characteristic of Anthony Brackett, Jr. I cannot speak only to say he endeavored to protect the land he had purchased but with poor success.

In 1764 a writ of ejectment was issued against him on complaint of Jeremiah Riggs who lived in the house recently removed by Mr. Daniel D. Chenery adjacent his new house and Riggs recovered judgment for an acre and a half of land.

In the year 1767 the town commenced an action against him by indictment for fencing in a strip of land "10 rods in length and 2 rods in width of the road leading from Joseph Riggs' brick kiln to and by the house of Zachariah Brackett" (his brother residing on Stevens Plains) and he was fined 6 shillings from which he appealed to a jury trial, but the jury sustained the verdict.

On page 320 of Rev. Saml. Dean's journal of July 7, 1769, appears this entry: "My case with Brackett tried."

This was a claim, as the court records show, for twenty-five acres of the 46 he had purchased, the Rev. Mr. Dean and Rev. Thomas Smith appearing for the First Parish of Falmouth, and the parish recovered.

A little later the same persons commenced an action of trespass against him for entering upon the premises between July, 1769, and March 21st, 1770, and taking therefrom twenty cords of maple, birch and oak wood to the value of £60, and Dean and Smith recovered against him. He appealed to a higher court.

Dec. 9, 1774 this same Rev. Samuel Dean according to his journal prayed with him as was shown in my last article, and it is supposed he died at about that date, leaving four children as follows: 1—Jeremiah; 2—Daniel; 3—John and (by his second wife) 4—Abigail.

NOTE:—It is stated at the close of my last article that the Brewer house stood on the "easterly" side of Congress street. It should have been "southerly" side opposite Stroudwater village.

TO BE CONTINUED.

THE DEERING NEWS.

Saturday, Aug. 22, 1896.

GRANDPA'S SCRAP BOOK

[Under this head historical and genealogical memoranda will be furnished the readers of the News that appears worthy of preservation, particularly of remote periods in our history within the city limits and immediate vicinity.]

ANTHONY BRACKETT, JR.

THE SITE OF HIS ABODE AND FACTS CONNECTED WITH IT.

CONTINUED FROM LAST WEEK.

Respecting the demise of the last wife of Anthony Brackett, Jr. who was widow Lunt, I have no knowledge. Her first intention of marriage with Job Lunt was recorded Oct. 8, 1740, and for her immediate relation, see Smith and Deans' journal, page 365. The first intention of Anthony, Jr. with Abigail Chapman, noticed in my first article under this heading, was filed Sep. 14, 1751, and then Anthony, Jr. married second Abigail (Brackett) Lunt, August 29, 1764.

In the year 1787 Jeremiah Brackett, Daniel Brackett and John Brackett all of Falmouth for a consideration of £70 conveyed to John Kimball four undivided fifth parts of 9¼ acres of land (the Anthony Brackett homestead,) it being our shares of said 9¼ acres descended to us from our father Anthony Brackett, deceased. In 1795 this John Kimball conveyed the premises to Enoch Knight of North Yarmouth for a consideration of £140, and the same year Knight, cordwainer, conveyed to William Homes the same premises for $500, "purchased of John Kimball March 7, 1793, together with buildings thereon."

Dec. 25, 1795, Abigail Brackett, spinster, for a consideration of $50, conveyed to Homes her 5th part, "being the same that devised to me by heirship from my honored father, Anthony Brackett of Falmouth, deceased."

There was a time in our history when the oldest son received two shares of an estate, and this may have been the time, otherwise I cannot account for the third son's selling the four shares as noticed above.

In 1802 Homes sold the southerly point of the lot containing 90 square rods of land to Rev. Caleb Bradley for $100, as now observed, at the junction of Stevens Plains Avenue and Congress street. The same year he sold a lot containing 135 square rods to John Chenery, wheelwright, where the Tuttle house, recently built may be seen, but Chenery never occupied it. He was a great uncle to Mr. Daniel D. Chenery, our county treasurer.

In 1803 Homes sold Peleg Mitchell an acre for $200; and 1806 two acres to Jonathan Sparrow, father to Mr. William Sparrow, now of Woodfords, for $500, which constitutes the southerly side of the present John B. Curtis lot. But Jonathan Sparrow, who was at the time a very active man, residing at Stroudwater where the cellar hole may now be seen on Westbrook street, westerly side, where Waldo street intersects, never occupied his purchase. In 1809 Homes alludes to the spot where the Curtis house stands as "the land whereon I now dwell," and a little later to himself as a resident of Scarboro. He also made a sale from the premises containing five acres to Peleg Mitchell for a consideration of $15. It was just before this date that the house then upon the lot was erected which was at the building of the John B. Curtis house by Thomas O'Brion, in 1862, removed to the opposite side of what is now Stevens Plains avenue, then by the late Edward Newman to near the corner of Spring and High streets, adjacent to which point on Spring street Mr. Newman lived. The final end of the old Anthony Brackett, Jr., dwelling has been noticed in former articles and needs no further attention, which stood where the Nathan Tibbetts house since was built.

TO BE CONTINUED.

THE DEERING NEWS.

Saturday, Aug. 29, 1896.

GRANDPA'S SCRAP BOOK

[Under this head historical and genealogical memoranda will be furnished the readers of the News that appears worthy of preservation, particularly of remote periods in our history within the city limits and immediate vicinity.]

ANTHONY BRACKETT, JR.

HIS SON JOHN, THE REVOLUTIONARY SOLDIER, AND OTHER DESCENDANTS.

Continued from Last Week.

In the News of August 15th I stated that the children of Anthony Brackett, Jr., were named respectively as follows:
1—Jeremiah; 2—Daniel (not David, as appears in Smith and Dean's journal); 3—John; 4—(by second wife) Abigail.

1.—Jeremiah. May 31, 1787, a Jeremiah Brackett purchased a farm lot in North Yarmouth. In the year 1826 a Jeremiah Brackett of Cumberland sold the same lot to John Brackett for a consideration of $1,900, both of Cumberland, and as the town of Cumberland was taken from North Yarmouth in 1821, I am of the opinion that Jeremiah of Falmouth and Jeremiah of North Yarmouth and later town of Cumberland, represent the same individual.

Since the foregoing was put in type I have come into possession of many facts relative to the descendants of Jeremiah Brackett and will here state that the Jeremiah alluded to above was the eldest child of Anthony Jr. His farm was located in the centre of the northerly part of Cumberland not far from the Gray town line. The point of location may be seen by referring to the county map of 1857. And it is the opinion of my informant that his grave stone as well as that of his wife may be seen in the old Methodist church yard of that region.

CHILDREN:

1 Jeremiah, married, and settled in the town of Naples.
2 Anthony, married Eunice Estes, and settled in the town of Naples not far from the foot of Long Pond.
3 Nathaniel, married Maria Mabury, and settled in Naples not far from his brother Anthony.
4 John, retained the homestead as noted in the foregoing where he died. He did not marry.
5 Mary, resided at home with her brother John. Did not marry. After his death, went to Naples and resided with a brother.
6 Reuben, married Elizabeth Morrell and came into possession of the Morrell homestead located on the road from Saccarappa to Piscataqua, in Westbrook, near the Falmouth town line, not far from Presumpscot river. On the farm he lived, had a family of twelve children, and departed this life. In the year 1815 he was taxed as follows:

"One house $60; one barn $25; nine acres mowing land at $18 per acre; fifteen pasturing at $8; nine unimproved at $6; two cows $28."

A few years ago the house was burned which stood at the easterly end of the barn, and immediately thereafter the present 1½ story dwelling built at the westerly end of the barn, and is now occupied by Lionel O. Brackett and wife the 10th and only surviving child of Reuben. Some four years ago he had a paralytic shock since which he has not walked and with much difficulty speaks. When asked a few days since by the writer to name his grandfather said: "Jeremiah," and "his place of residence," said I, to which he replied, "Cumberland."

Southeasterly of the dwelling, distant about twenty rods is an enclosure by stone posts and chains shaped like the segment of a circle within which is a monument of granite constructed by Jeremiah Webber to the memory of his wife and children who married Margaret E., daughter of Reuben Brackett, since which he has died, but his name has not been engraved on the memorial. Within this enclosure are fully a score of nameless mounds and two white marble memorial slabs one of which is inscribed as follows:

REUBEN BRACKETT,
Died June 21, 1848,
Aged 69 years.

CONTINUED:
ELIZABETH MORRELL,
Wife of Reuben Brackett,
Died June 1860,
Aged 79 years.

Children of Reuben and Elizabeth:
1. William Plummer, married Laura Parker and settled in Peru.
2. Alma Maria married James Jordan, settled in Poland.
3. Jeremiah Chapman, married Sophrona Lunt, and resided a half mile westerly of his father in Westbrook where a daughter still lives who married a McDonald.
4. Jacob Morrell, died young.
5. Stephen Moulton, married Lucy Cobb of Windham, the mother of Mrs. George W. Furlong of South street, Woodfords district, Deering, to whom I am indebted for many items here presented. Her mother died when she was but two years of age and she was reared by her grandmother Elizabeth (Morrill) Brackett. Her father married 2nd Mary Cole.
6. Margaret Elizabeth married Jeremiah Webber. (See grave memorial.
7. Sarah Jane married Ezra Thomes of Gorham.
8. Esther Plummer died unmarried, June 2, 1885 aged 69 years. (See grave memorial.)
9. Mary Ann died unmarried, Oct. 2, 1884, Aged 67 years. (See grave memorial, though it is claimed there are errors in these dates.)
10. Samuel Mountfort (twin) married Harriet Russell, widow of Gardner Sturdivant.
11. Reuben, twin to preceeding, married Aurelia Leighton. Settled near Cobb Lane, Deering.
12. Lionlen married Adriand Sherman of Wiscaset, and resides on the homestead of his father.

2—Daniel. When the first valuation of Westbrook was made, in 1815, the name of Daniel Brackett appears as a poll tax payer, but in no other way do I find a recognition. He was not a real estate owner in this county.

4.—John, born April 11, 1761. He enlisted in the War of the Revolution and served three years as a private, being a soldier at the close of the war.

On the 3d of November, 1783 the army was disbanded by general order of congress.

In the year 1787, as shown last week, this John disposed of his interest in his father's estate, which estate consisted of 9¼ acres and buildings thereon in Falmouth, now Deering, Bradley's Corner district.

He united in marriage with Mary, alias Molly Walker, whose parents resided between Pride's Bridge and Duck Pond, now in the city of Westbrook. It is traditional she was a sister to Deacon Walker's father, whoever he may have been.

May 5, 1802, the George Walker farm was disposed of—George, the father of Mary, alias Molly. The record is of value as a genealogical guide board, as follows:

We, John Walker of Gorham, yeoman, and Elizabeth his wife;
George Walker of Otisfield, yeoman;
John Brackett of Falmouth, yeoman, and Molly his wife, in her right;
John Campbell, of Poland, cooper, Rebecca his wife, in her right; all of Cumberland County, in consideration of $400 paid by "William Walker & Charles Walker, of Falmouth, yeomen, all our right in the estate we have of a certain piece of land in Falmouth containing about eighty acres, being the homestead of our deceased father, George Walker, late of Falmouth, together with the buildings thereon, bounded southeasterly on Presumpscot river, northeasterly on land of William Brackett, northwesterly on Underwitted road, so called, southerly on land of William Lunt on the county road and land of Joseph Pride."

October 2, 1811, John Brackett, for a consideration of $2,500, purchased land and buildings of one John Lowell, housewright, located in the town of Harrison, and at the same time sold to the same John Lowell his own homestead for $2,300, consisting of "fifty-five acres with house, barn and other buildings thereon standing," located in Falmouth, bounds

Commencing at the most westerly corner of my land which is my homestead, running northeast 63 rods; southeast 134 rods; southwest 16 rods to Duck Pond brook; down the brook 65 rods; North 42 degrees west 34 rods, etc.
Signed—
JOHN BRACKETT,
MARY BRACKETT."

This evidently was an exchange of farms between Brackett and Lowell.

Edward Chapman, who settled westerly of the present abode of Mr. James Babb, who resides on the Buxton road, two miles westerly of Stroudwater, had, besides two sons, Nathaniel, a Revolutionary soldier, buried on the old farm (no stone), and Simon, who married Polly Jose, May 17, 1798, and was the father of Edward—and nine other children—born Nov. 11, 1814, who died two or three years since, had also three daughters: Ruth, married Sept. 25, 1790, William Conant of Saccarappa; Mary married Aug. 16, 1778, John Lowell; and another, who married Samuel March of Standish. This John Lowell was evidently the one who married as above stated Mary Chapman, a cousin to John Brackett.

In 1815 there were two Lowells in Westbrook, John and James, who were taxed as follows:

One house, $150; one barn, $40; one outhouse, $12; fifty acres of land, 2 oxen, 6 cows, one horse and 3 swine.

There were no other Lowells at that time in Westbrook who paid a tax.

And Edward told me a year before his death that he once had an aunt who lived on the road between Pride's Bridge and the Duck Pond, he not knowing at the time that I was aware of the relationship. He also stated that she married a man by the name of Lowell and they were "very nice people," "who have descendants still residing there."

In 1827 there were two Lowell voters in Westbrook—John and William, no more.

It is traditional that Brackett was a captain in the state militia and was a land surveyor. He died in Harrison February 22, 1844.

Mary Brackett, wife of Capt. John Brackett, born August 11, 1765, died there September 18, 1843.

A friend of mine residing in Portland, and interested in historical research, inform me that a short time since he stood by the memorial grave stones erected in that town.

TO BE CONTINUED

Saturday, Sept. 5, 1896.

GRANDPA'S SCRAP BOOK

[Under this head historical and genealogical memoranda will be furnished the readers of the News that appears worthy of preservation, particularly of remote periods in our history within the city limits and immediate vicinity.]

ANTHONY BRACKETT, JR.

HIS SON JOHN, THE REVOLUTIONARY SOLDIER, AND OTHER DESCENDANTS.

Continued from Last Week.

CHILDREN, ALL BORN IN WESTBROOK:

1.—George Brackett, born September 26, 1787; died October 21, 1814.
2.—William, born August 25, 1789.
3.—Abigail, born September 12, 1791; died January 18, 1816.
4.—Enoch, born July 27, 1793.
5.—Walker, born April 7, 1796; married Calista Wight of Raymond. He died October 16, 1871.
6.—Elizabeth, born December 2, 1799.
7.—John, Jr., born June 2, 1804; died June, 1885.
8.—Chapman, born Aug. 21, 1808.

This last one was evidently named for the first wife of Anthony Brackett, Jr.

Concerning Capt. John Brackett, the Revolutionary soldier, his grandson, Rev. Silas B. Brackett, wrote on the twenty-eighth day of February, 1888, then a resident of Chicago, Ill., now deceased, as follows:

The last time I saw the house from which my grandparents removed, to the town of Harrison, it was in good repair, which stood in the town of Westbrook, where all their children were born. When they lived there the place was called Falmouth.

"Immediately after the war," continues Mr. Brackett, "in which he was a soldier, grandfather was made a captain of a military company, and ever after was called 'Captain Brackett.' He died shouting 'Victory over death, the grave and hell!' Through Christ Jesus he was a conqueror. 'In the morning, I will see him in a land in which there is no death.'

"Yes, I shall then see him. There he will not be lame and gray, for there he will be young as when a worldly soldier boy."

September 6, 1894, at Chicago, this reverend gentleman wrote as follows:

I lived in the family of my grandfather at Harrison (Rev. Mr. Brackett was born Nov. 11, 1818, in that town) from the day I was nine years old till I was twenty-one, so I am prepared to say some things in regard to his history which can be relied on as true. He was born April 11, 1761, and died in his adopted town February 22, 1844 * * * He was in the army of the Revolution the last three years of the struggle. He was not a captain there but was made one immediately of the state militia at the close of the war. His father's name was Anthony, and according to the best of my recollection, my grandfather had two brothers, (he had three, as has been shown,) and one half sister, whose name was Abigail. She married a Mr. (Daniel) Green and lived in Portland. Captain John received a pension the last years of his life. He went to Portland for his pension money, and as he lived some thirty-seven miles from that city he would spend the night with her whom he called Nabby. Captain John (my grandfather) was some way connected with the Chapman name and so called one of his children "Chapman Brackett." (I have explained the relationship.)

April 21, 1775, the news of the Battle of Lexington reached here, and as Capt. John Brackett of Saccarappa immediately started off with his "minute men," I doubted family tradition, that Capt. John of Harrison held a commission, hence the foregoing from Rev. Mr. Brackett.

April 23, 1889, there appeared in the Eastern Argus, printed in Portland, a notice of the departure of the "minute men," with a list of their names, prepared by the compiler hereof.

Captain John Brackett of Saccarappa and Anthony, Jr., the father of Capt. John of Harrison, were cousins.

Capt. John Brackett, of Harrison, and wife, Molly, or Mary (Walker), had born to them, all in Westbrook, eight children, as follows: 1, George; 2, William; 3, Abigail; 4, Enoch; 5, Walker; 6, Elizabeth; 7, John, Jr.; 8, Chapman.

1—George, born Sept. 26, 1787; died October 21, 1814.
2—William, born August 25, 1789; married Sarah Hobbs, October 1, 1811. She was born July 6, 1792. They settled in the "Brackett Neighborhood of Harrison, and reared eleven children. He died Feb. 7, 1865. She died July 31, 1856.

CHILDREN:

I—Daniel H., born June 3, 1813; married Hannah Bennett of Cumberland, and lives in Freeport.
II—Mary, born July 3, 1814; married James Fogg; resides in Gorham, Maine.
III—Sybel S., born July 23, 1816; married George Pearsons.
IV—George W., born May 5, 1818; married Rebecca Bailey of Bridgton May 17, 1842. She was born October 21, 1818. Settled on the homestead. Seven children. Pamelia, the 3d child, born August 24, 1851; married George A. Hall; reside in this city, (Deering Ctr).
V—Louis P., born Nov. 26, 1819; married William Perley of Harrison.
VI—Jonathan H., born Feb. 19, 1821; married Elizabeth Bennett of Cumberland.
VII—Sarah, born April 14, 1824; married Artemus Mason of West Bethel. Both are dead. Charles C. Merrell of that place married a daughter and resides there.
VIII—Ann M., born Sept. 26, 1825; married Woodsom Mason of Bethel.
IX—Lucretia, born April 7, 1828; married Moses Cobb of Westbrook.
X—Ellen, born February 20, 1830; married Leander Barker of Bethel. He has been town clerk twenty years. No issue.
XI—Emeline, born December 22, 1833; married —— Dunn of Bethel. He died. She married 2d; resides in Washington, D. C.

The above copy is made from a record twenty years old. Forty years ago the Misses Brackett of Bethel kept a millinery establishment on Bethel Hill, and the compiler hereof well recollects a "surprise party" holden at their domicile over the millinery parlors as a very enjoyable affair.

4—Enoch, born July 27, 1793; married Arminta Caswell of Harrison, Sept. 21, 1818, and settled near Brackett's Corner in Harrison. They had four children, who married.
5—Walker, father to Rev. Silas, to be noticed further along.
6—Elizabeth, born Dec. 2, 1799; married John P. Lowell of Harrison, Jan. 27, 1824.
7—John, Jr., born June 2, 1804; married Martha Ann, daughter of Edward Lowell, Sr., of Harrison; settled on the Bolster's Mill road. He married second, Sanborn; third, Stevens. Five children.
8—Chapman, born August 21, 1808; married Amanda Wight. Settled in Casco. Five children.

TO BE CONTINUED.

THE DEERING NEWS.

Saturday, Sept. 12, 1896.

GRANDPA'S SCRAP BOOK

[Under this head historical and genealogical memoranda will be furnished the readers of the News that appears worthy of preservation, particularly of remote periods in our history within the city limits and immediate vicinity.]

ANTHONY BRACKETT, JR.

HIS GRANDSON REV. SILAS BLAKE, AND OTHER DESCENDANTS.

[Error. The list of names at the commencement of my last article should have been left out and down as far as where it says—"Concerning Capt. John Brackett, etc." Then in the next column where it reads—"4—Enoch," above this should be: 3—Abigail, born Sep. 12, 1791, died Jan. 18, 1816.]

Walter Brackett noticed in my last article as the fifth child of William, and grandson of Capt. John Brackett, born at Harrison, Apr. 7, 1796, married Calista Wight of Raymond. She was born Oct. 26, 1794; they settled in the "Brackett Neighborhood" where he died Oct. 16, 1871; she, Feb. 19, 1878. They had ten children as follows:

1 —(Rev.) Silas Blake Brackett, to be noticed later.
2 —Polly W., born Aug. 15, 1820, married Seth Pike of Norway, May 23, 1844. Died there June, 1895.
3 —Nancy C., born Nov. 19, 1822, married Alfred Noyes Nov. 7, 1844.
4 —Walter, Jr., born Nov. 24, 1824, married Eliza Leach of Casco, 2nd Jennie Hackett of Salem, Me., 3d a widow.
5 —Roxanna, born Feb. 27, 1827, died June 30, 1842.
6 —Harriet W., born Jan. 11, 1829, married Tristram Noyes, Nov. 8, 1849. Twenty years ago they resided in Harrison.
7 —Elbridge O., born Oct. 4, 1830, married Mary Hunt of Avon, and removed to Minnesota, in 1876.
8 —Betsey Walker, born May 20, 1833, married O'Neal R. Mills of Bethel, and 20 years ago resided in Harrison.
9 —Charles H., born Feb. 24, married Lois Talbot, of Avon and 20 years ago lived at Vinalhaven, now California.
10—Sophrona S., and last, born May 23, 1840, married Robert S. Lamb of Harrison, 2nd George Shead of Norway.

Willard.

Mr. and Mrs. Frank Libby are in town attending the funeral of Mr. Libby's father, B. F. Libby, who passed away at his residence in South Portland last Thursday night.

Capt. T. C. Thompson of Boston spent Sunday with friends in this place.

Mr. Clarence Graffam of Oxford visited a few days with Mrs. J. Berry.

Miss Annie Thompson who has been spending the summer in this place has returned to her home in New Hampshire.

Mr. Edwin D. Thompson of Boston is visiting his sister, Mrs. Freeman Willard.

Wednesday morning this village was startled to hear of the death of Mr. Wm. Farrington of Portland who for several years past has spent the summer here in his cottage on Loveitt's hill. The deceased was found dead in the mill where he was employed, with a severe wound in his throat, which caused his death. It is thought that temporary aberation was the cause of the deed as Mr. Farrington was always a well known and highly respected citizen, and up to the time of his death was of perfectly sound mind. The deceased was a deacon in the Bethel church of Portland. He was 68 years old, and leaves a wife and four sons to mourn his untimely death.

THE DEERING NEWS.

Saturday, Sept. 19, 1896.

GRANDPA'S SCRAP BOOK

[Under this head historical and genealogical memoranda will be furnished the readers of the News that appears worthy of preservation, particularly of remote periods in our history within the city limits and immediate vicinity.]

ANTHONY BRACKETT, JR.

HIS GREAT-GRANDSON, REV. SILAS BLAKE BRACKETT, THE METHODIST CLERGYMAN.

Continued from Last Week.

Rev. Silas Blake Brackett was born in the town of Harrison Nov. 11, 1818, and Sarah Ann Burnham of that town was born Apr. 12, 1821. They were married July 10, 1845. She died at Dwight, Ill., Apr. 18, 1889. He died at Chicago, Ill., Dec. 15, 1895, in the 76th year of his age. A short time previous to his death while residing at Chicago by request he made a short sketch of himself which I here present nearly as he wrote it as follows:

After attending in the Bolster's Mill district at Harrison, Me., what was termed a High school, first under the tutorship of a Quaker named Stephen Hall, then Dr. A. A. Mann and Rev. Mark R. Hopkins, I was a student in the North Bridgton academy for three terms.

The first school of which I was teacher was at Randolph, N. H., and that was before I was twenty-one. The day I became twenty-one my father went with me to Conway, N. H., where I was teacher of a district school for one term, boarding with a Daniel Chase, a shoemaker and a devoted Methodist, and after this and before I was twenty-one I taught three terms, one in Otisfield, one in South Bridgton and one in Paris. When I was 23 years, 9 months and 3 days old, I said farewell to my praying mother and left town for Northfield and Wesley wherein to do the work of a Methodist minister. The assignment to this field was made by the conference of the M. E. church into which I had just been received.

The distance from Harrison to Northfield was 200 miles which distance I rode in a single seated gig, and after being on the way five days I arrived at my place of destination and passed the night in the house and home of Rev. B. D. Eastman who had been a member of the Maine Conference.

The residents of the town were lumbermen, yet, somehow, managed to raise their potatoes and hay but were not farmers. In Wesley I preached in the Town house, in Northfield a schoolhouse and in Crawford I preached sometimes in a church building owned by the Baptists. And at other times the assembly I addressed occupied a schoolhouse. Every three Sundays I preached at one of these places.

On this circuit I received but very little money. So to partly supply myself with what I needed I taught school one term in Wesley and was hired to figure out the Wesley town tax for the assessors.

On the first day of April of this conference year the snow was five feet deep in the forests where I was—so deep that a man on snow shoes could run down a deer and some Indians ran down a large timber wolf and killed him. This was April, 1843.

I left this circuit a short time before conference and went home, or to the home of my parents, and from there went to Bath with Rev. Benjamin Foster who was in charge of Bolster Mills circuit, to attend the Maine annual conference of the M. E. church, and by this conference was sent to preach in Orland and East Buckfield. I enjoyed this field of labor much, but more especially the Orland part. I become acquainted with some persons I shall never forget whom I trust I shall meet in heaven.

The next conference met in Bangor which I attended and at which I was ordained deacon by Bishop Hedding, and he gave me the pastorate of a church in Trenton. In this town there were many seafaring men, Capt. Stevens, one of our members, was one of brother Haynes' sons, 12 or 14 years of age, and all the crew, save one, were lost, and it became my painful duty to inform sister Haynes. The survivor of the crew said the last time he saw the youth he was on part of the lumber with which the vessel was loaded and being carried out to sea.

When I looked over this field of labor on my arrival there, I saw a frame of a church building had been raised and left without a single board on it. After a while I commenced to solicit subscriptions to finish it, and work was commenced but was not finished at the end of the conference year, when I left the charge. There I had many friends. A short time before the close of that conference my marriage was solemnized with Sarah A. Burnham of Harrison, July 10, 1845, by Rev. W. D. Jones, who was pastor of the Methodist Church, So. Harrison.

On Wednesday morning of the next week, after my marriage, the annual conference of the Methodist E. C. commenced its session in Portland, and I was sent to the Farmington and Vienna circuit to which my wife and I went in a wagon, and on the first Sunday after our arrival, I preached in Vienna. Three Sundays out of four I preached at Farmington; the fourth at Vienna.

At the next annual conference I was continued on this circuit, and at which I was ordained an elder by Beverly Waugh who was the presiding bishop of the conference. And near the conference year, on the 14th of August, 1846, our first born, a son, came to us. We resided in an old parsonage that had been occupied as a home by many Methodist ministers who preceeded us as pastors of the church. On this circuit we made many friends, and after we had served as pastor two conference years we went to Industry and there also we found friends and a parsonage into which we entered and resided for two years. On the 27th of September, 1847, we saw our second son.

TO BE CONTINUED.

THE DEERING NEWS.

111

Saturday, Sept. 26, 1896.

GRANDPA'S SCRAP BOOK

[Under this head historical and genealogical memoranda will be furnished the readers of the News that appears worthy of preservation, particularly of remote periods in our history within the city limits and immediate vicinity.]

ANTHONY BRACKETT, JR.

HIS GREAT-GRANDSON, REV. SILAS BLAKE BRACKETT, THE METHODIST CLERGYMAN.

Continued from Last Week.

"I preached in Industry and Stark, and part of the time in New Vineyard. In Industry township, after a protracted meeting had closed, at which were several conversions, I baptized, I do not know how many, in a pond in mid winter, the ice having been cut and removed for the occasion. In this field we also found many good friends; and here our third son was born.

"Finishing our two years' work we went to Fairfield, where we remained two conference years. Here we resided in a parsonage. The places for Sunday services were Fairfield and Kendall's Mills—a large village located on the Kennebec river, the place being in Fairfield township. At this circuit we witnessed a revival. Some who professed, I baptized in the waters of the Kennebec. Our fourth son came to us at the parsonage here. The name of the attending physician, Dr. Henry Campbell, we gave to the boy. While now writing these lines how the names of the good people rush into my mind. How rapidly years have passed since I preached my farewell sermon to them, and can it be so long since I with my dear Annie and our four little boys on a pleasant summer day said good bye to that house which had sheltered us so faithfully during our pastorate, and started for Solon whose people we were by order of the conference to serve as pastor? At this place we did not find a house owned by the church society, but one rented. And it was a house with which my wife was much pleased, being the best occupied since our marriage. Some months later I started a subscription for a house that was for sale and succeeded in my effort to raise the money. On the first of Jan. after our arrival in Solon our fifth son came to us. The village in which we resided was beautifully situated on the banks of the Kennebec river. Our preaching places were Solon, Madison, and Bingham. In April, near the close our sixth son came to us. I named him Robert Peel, but my wife desired to change the name to Peel Bodwell as she was under the care

CONTINUED:

of a physician by the name of Bodwell, but when he was baptized he was called Robert Peel.

"Our next appointment was for Phillips circuit. At this place our first daughter came to us in the parsonage. And near the close of the second year of our work on this charge I purchased a farm nearly a mile from where we then lived and moved onto it. At the next annual conference, at my request, I was dismissed from the travelling circuit, but at this conference Phillips was left to be supplied, and so the presiding elder reappointed me for the place, and there I remained three years.

TO BE CONTINUED.

THE DEERING NEWS.

Saturday, Oct. 3, 1896.

GRANDPA'S SCRAP BOOK

[Under this head historical and genealogical memoranda will be furnished the readers of the News that appears worthy of preservation, particularly of remote periods in our history within the city limits and immediate vicinity.]

ANTHONY BRACKETT, JR.

HIS GREAT-GRANDSON, REV. SILAS BLAKE BRACKETT, THE METHODIST CLERGYMAN.

Continued from Last Week.

"The farm I purchased was called the Wells farm. In that farm house our second daughter was born to us. And when we had lived on the farm less than two years I sold it and purchased one in the town of Avon, known as the Haynes farm. While living there I taught school two winters in that district and one in Sylvester Hill district. We moved onto the farm in February of 1857. While residing there a son and two daughters were born to us. From there I moved onto a farm I had of Robert Walker which he deeded me March 31, 1860. While residing there I filled the offices of Town Clerk and Superintending school committee, and preached in several places. While on that farm two sons and three daughters came to us, and there we buried our little Oliver.

"August 31, 1864, Abner Toothaker gave me a deed of a farm in Rangeley, known as the Kimball farm. There I taught one term of district school, and after harvesting two crops I sold it to James W. Badger and moved to a farm on the north side of Mooselookmeg (now known as Rangeley Lake) called the Smith farm. While in Rangeley I served as superintending school committee. In the fall of 1866 we went to Norway onto a farm and I taught a term of school there.

"In Jan. 1869, we packed our goods for the state of Illinois, but when the day arrived one of our children was taken sick and in two weeks we buried our little Gilbert Mariner. I shall never forget his words, when he took me by the hand and said:'Good-by father;God bless father.

"On the 15th day of Feb. 1869, we bid farewell to friends in Norway and started on the journey to the West and on the morning of Feb. 19, we reached the town of Dwight, Ill., where we were met by Nathaniel Burnham who conducted us to his residence."

[This Mr. Burnham was the sixth child in the family of Nathaniel Burnham of Harrison, born Feb. 12, 1812, married first Mary Mustard of Bowdoin; 2nd Olive Sawyer of Madison. He was for some years a stage driver in the Eastern part of this state, but went to Dwight Ill., where he died, Apr. 8, 1870, leaving a widow. Rev. Mr. Brackett's wife was his sister. Ed. News.]

"From Dwight we went to Broughton onto a farm where we raised four crops of corn, the crop of 1871 amounting to 5,000 bushels, 2,000 of which went to the land owner as rental. In the spring of 1873 we left there, moved into a house at Dwight built for us. The lot contained three acres for which I paid $250. I was employed at various kinds of work.

'In 1882 I went to Dakota to labor as a missionary, and Ellendale and Keystone was the field. Both of these places are in North Dakota. While there I built a cabin on a ¼ section of United States land near Keystone village upon which I intended to reside with my family but in June of 1883 I changed my mind and transferred what interest I had in the 160 acres lot and improvements to a stranger whose name I have forgotten, and in July of that year left the mission for Dwight, Ill., where I found Jennie sick, who, the next April passed over to the other shore. Here the health of my wife failed, and on the 21st day of Oct, 1886, she experienced a paralytic shock from which she never recovered so as to stand without aid, and Apr. 18, 1889 the harbenger of death called her away. The greater part of that summer I remained alone in the dwelling she left. Nov. 29 I left Dwight for Chicago, and to this day, May 22, 1895, I have been here.

"I somewhat fear that what I have written will not prove to be what you desire.

"I should have said that in the months of Nov. and Dec. 1870, typhoid fever entered our family abode from which five suffered, Josephine and Sumner being taken from the family circle, whose bon s are interred in the cemetery at Broughton, Ill., sixteen miles southeast of Dwight."

SILAS B. BRACKETT.

[Error: In my article of Sep. 12, *Walter* Brackett should be *Walker* Brackett.

Where it says Walter Brackett fifth child of *William*, it should be Walker, fifth child of Capt. *John* Brackett.]

TO BE CONTINUED.

THE DEERING NEWS.

Saturday, Oct. 10, 1896.

GRANDPA'S SCRAP BOOK

[Under this head historical and genealogical memoranda will be furnished the readers of the News that appears worthy of preservation, particularly of remote periods in our history within the city limits and immediate vicinity.]

ANTHONY BRACKETT, JR.

HIS GREAT-GRANDSON, REV. SILAS BLAKE BRACKETT, THE METHODIST CLERGYMAN.

Continued from Last Week.

Rev. Silas B. Brackett and wife had fifteen children as follows:

1—Silas Frederick, born Aug. 14, 1846, now a hunter and trapper, Bock, Minn. Not married. (For places of births of the fifteen children, consult the sketch of the life of Rev. Mr. Brackett, appearing in the last few numbers of the *News*.)
2—Franklin Pierce, born Sept. 27, 1847. Roofing business, Chicago, Ill. Not married.
3—Alpheus Lowell, born at Industry, Jan. 16, 1849, married Jan. 25, 1881, Annie L. Ditman of Somerville, Mass., born Sept. 25, 1857. He is employed as baggage master, and U. S. Mail agent, with the International Steamship company, between Boston and the Provinces, where he has been 18 years, residing at Everett, Mass.

CHILDREN:

I—Annie May, born Nov. 13, 1881.
II—Alice Burnham, born Sep. 9, 1884, died Aug. 10, 1885.
III—Alpheus Ditman, born Dec. 8, 1885.
VI—Arthur Hamilton, born Feb. 14, 1888.
V—Anthony Howard, born March 15, 1890.
IV—Abigail Helen, born Feb. 23, 1895.

4—Henry Campbell, born July 29, 1850, married, has five children and resides in Youngstown, Ohio.
5—Virgil Neal, born Jan. 1st, 1852, married Clara Spencer, born in Rochester, N. Y., Apr. 27, 1868. Roofing business, and resides in Chicago, Ill. One child.
6—Peel Bodwell, born April 11, 1853. Head inspector of Armour canned meat company, Chicago, Ill., eleven years. Married and has three children.
7—Velzora Eastman, born July 8, 1854. Married Thomas Woodward, and resides in Denver, Colorado. They have five children.
8—Josephine Mariah, born Dec. 11, 1855, died at Broughton, Ill., Nov. 22, 1870.
9—Gilbert Mariner, born May 13, 1857, died at Norway, this state, Feb. 5, 1869.
10—Mary Geneve, born July 28, 1858, died at Dwight, Ill., Apr. 13, 1884.
11—Lavinia Downing, born Sep. 19, 1859, married, resides at Chicago, Ill., and has two children.
12—Sumner Burnham, born Sept. 27, 1860, died at Broughton, Ill., Nov. 4, 1870.
13—Calesta, born March 26, 1862, resides at Chicago, Ill.; not married.
14—Olive Stevens, born March 16, 1863; died at Avon, this state, May 24th, 1863.
15—Abbie Ann, born June 13, 1865, resides at Denver, Colorado; not married.

In a former number of these Brackett articles I stated that I had no knowledge of the time of death of Abigail Brackett, widow of Job Lunt, who became the second wife of Anthony Brackett, Jr., being born a Brackett, married Lunt and died a Brackett, as shown above, but since then I have fortunately found her grave stone in the Eastern cemetery in Portland with those of her daughter Abigail and husband Daniel Green, standing in Section I. & J., a few rods southwesterly of Mountfort street entrance. The inscription is as follows:

In memory of

MRS. ABIGAIL BRACKETT,

Widow of

Mr. Anthony Brackett,

who died Feb. 1, 1805.

Æ. t. 77.

This closes all I have to say relative to Anthony Brackett, jr., and descendants, excepting Abigail, the only daughter of Anthony, jr., who married Daniel Green of Portland.

THE DEERING NEWS.

Saturday, Oct. 17, 1896.

GRANDPA'S SCRAP BOOK

[Under this head historical and genealogical memoranda will be furnished the readers of the News that appears worthy of preservation, particularly of remote periods in our history within the city limits and immediate vicinity.]

REV. CALEB BRADLEY'S JOURNAL.

WHAT HE WROTE RELATIVE TO POLITICAL PARTIES IN 1830.

Jan. 6, 1830. Election day. The house not organized—great excitement. Parties almost equally divided. Spent the day in town.

7th. Went down to Back Cove, passed over the bridge into town. The house not organized. The excitement as great or greater than yesterday.

8th. A speaker was chosen half past nine. Mr. Goodnough had 73 and Mr. Ruggles 71 votes. The senate has balloted almost 20 times for a president. Neither party are willing to give up the contest, but it is party and nothing else but party, and if such a spirit continues to prevail we shall be a ruined nation, and the privileges we value so highly we may expect to see taken from us and given by the Governor of nations to those who will improve them better.

18th. The Jacksonites and Adamites are nearly equally divided. Expect the committee will report tomorrow relative to the vote for governor. Our situation as a state is really deplorable. There is but very little among the members of the two branches that looks like patriotism. I am sick of hearing men plead for their country when their conduct gives the lie to their pleadings.

22nd. The Jackson senators appear to be determined to stop the wheels of government. If the whole collection of this pestilental mass could go home it is very probable it would be a saving of thousands to the state.

25th. The legislature continues setting, but makes no progress. Next Wednesday will make the third week, and it is to be hoped by that day something will be brought forth, for a hen will hatch her eggs in that time.

29th. Went to town. Attended court a little while and heard much nonsense, and saw two great parties as much divided as two armies fighting for their respective people, exercising all the ingenuity to deceive each other and carry their points; pleading the rights of the people and the constitution, but I believe they have only a little regard for the constitution and less for the people. The senate is equally divided—8 and 8—and voted fifty times before they elected a president. In the house there is a Republican majority of 4 or 5. I prophesy the downfall of our republic before many years, for it can't be otherwise if things continue as at present. Yes, officers and office seekers will ruin the country. The people generally choose the most illiterate and unworthy and I may add the most unprincipaled and corrupt to fill places of honor, but there is not much honor attending an office at the present time. The most worthy, the most respectable, remain in the background; and all they do is to look on and lament the state of affairs and pray. Unless the invisible Ruler of the universe shall turn the hearts of the people as the waves of the ocean are turned we must, according to the natural course of things be a ruined nation.

Feb. 2nd. This day will be remembered in the state of Maine. Eight senators—one-half of the whole number—met in convention with the house to fill up the vacancies in the senate and the minority of the house took their hats and left—the best thing they could do; by this step the house was purged for a little time, and the work of filling up the senate was done without any difficulty.

8th. Went to town with Mr. Butterfield—spent the day chiefly in the senate chamber, and there I saw and heard much folly. The senators to meet tomorrow in convention with the house to choose the council, secretary and treasurer.

17th. Went to town, looked in upon the senate a few minutes, and then returned home.

19th. Went to town. Called at the house of representatives at 11 o'clock. Both houses were in convention. The councillors were introduced. Dined at Mr. Atwood's with 20 representatives.

20th. Walked to town and went to court which dissolved *sine die*, and I am glad. They have had a long session and rather a quarrelsome time—the parties almost equally divided, and, I think, much corruption and wickedness both in the house and senate.

We have a good country, but there are many hungry office seekers, we are kely to be devoured, and like other nations, either placed under the control of an absolute despot or a limited monarchy. If we are willing and are an obedient people, regarding the laws of God and man, we shall be blessed of heaven and prospered by an All-Wise providence; but I do now most seriously predict, that if we go on as we have done, we shall bring down the vengeance of heaven upon ourselves and deservingly so; but God is able to turn the hearts of men as the rivers of waters are turned. Lord save us from tyranny and oppression—save us from external and internal foes, save us from ourselves, for we are in more danger of self-destruction than by being destroyed by others. If we are united we shall stand, but if we are divided we shall fall, as all other republics have. O, my countrymen! Take warning, beware of flattery. Judas betrayed with a kiss, and you may be deprived of all you hold dear, when you are doing all you think you can in your power to save yourselves and country. I warn you not to be deceived by those who kiss only to destroy. Think, think and then act. Now is the day of salvation. Today hear my voice and take warning. Flee to the mountains, escape this mighty and formidable enemy who seeks to build on your ruin. Amen.

THE DEERING NEWS.

Saturday, Oct. 24, 1896.

GRANDPA'S SCRAP BOOK

[Under this head historical and genealogical memoranda will be furnished the readers of the News that appears worthy of preservation, particularly of remote periods in our history within the city limits and immediate vicinity.]

MAJOR JOHN SMALL.

WHAT "L. W. S.," THE PORTLAND ARGUS CORRESPONDENT SAYS OF HIM AND HIS WIFE.

Sometime during the publication in the columns of the *News* of the articles entitled "History of Westbrook," the compiler alluded to certain records of surveys and plans made by one John Small, and then expressed a desire to learn something of him.

He was a descendant of the fifth generation from Frances Small, the fisherman and trader who, in the year 1657, purchased of the Indians, Capisic mill privilege, and an unbounded amount of land located in Falmouth, now Deering, the name Capisic still being retained, and the titles of some two hundred acres of land located in front of the Bradley Corner meeting house being traceable to the transaction between Small and the Indians of 1657.

Mr. Lauriston Ward Small, who claims to be of the eighth generation from Frances, the adventurer, is now a citizen of Brooklyn, N. Y., and generally known hereabouts as a correspondent of the Portland Argus, read an article before the Maine Historical Society, which appears in the Collections, published in 1893.

The article is written in "L. W. S.'s" breezy newspaper style and the abstract here presented is evidently more replete with "flights of fancy" than facts, and must be received with many grains of salt.

But Major John Small was not a mythical character.

An original plan made in 1757 by him of certain lands where the shoe factory of Mr. Lorenzo P. Hawkins stands at Back Cove, in this city, is in the possession of the compiler of these Scrap Book articles, which shows the location of the old Ilsley house at that time.

The plan will be shown any one who calls at the *News* office, Portland, to see it, which contains the autographs of John Snow and James Merrill as were as John Small, and Christopher Strout, Justice of the Peace.

Following is the abstract from the printed article of "L. W. S..

Major John Small, son of Deacon Samuel and Anna was born in Scarborough Jan. 10, 1722. In that town April 1,

Continued:

1748, he married Sarah Atkins—In Falmouth, October 12, 1752, he married the gay and beautiful fairy-born Mary McKenney. He was an officer in the English army and also a land surveyor (however that may have been) and made several important surveys now on record at Alfred and Portland. In 1762 he was sent to survey a military road from the waters of the Kennebec to Quebec, and was shot while making that survey. One day when his command had halted for dinner the major retired a short distance to write up his notes and while doing it one of his men who did not know he was there, caught a glimpse of his military hat and thinking it the nose of a bear fired a hasty shot and killed him instantly.

Major John is the first member of the family of whose personal appearance we have much knowledge. He was large, dark complexioned, stately, courtly and exceeding handsome withal—indeed it is wholly safe to say that he was the finest-looking Small of the American wing of the family. His desk, chest and commission as captain (Commission now in rooms of Maine Historical Society,) are yet preserved in the family and I trust will be for many years to come, for he who honors not his ancestors will never do anything for which his descendants will honor him. "Honor thy father and thy mother" is a command which extends back beyond a single generation.

Major John's second wife, Mary McKinny, (Now spelled McKenney,) deserves more attention than I can here give her, but her story in brief runs in this wise.

In those primitive days the leaders of society were those who could dance the longest and with most vigor, and drink the most rum and molasses without giddiness. My great-great-grandmother McKenney was a big, elephantine woman who could dance but little, and as she was as poor a drinker as dancer she was not highly regarded in the polite society of the time. One evening after her return from a party whereat she had been a wall-flower because of her inability to drink or dance very much, she breathed an audible earnest wish that she might have a daughter who could outdance the whole world. Instantly, she heard tiny shouts and merry peals of laughter, and straightway myriads of fairies in gala dresses, with beautiful Queen Mab at their head, came trooping into the room singing, dancing, laughing and playing leapfrog over each other like the jolly little elves they were. The queen seated herself upon a thimble, and looked on for awhile with the eyes of delight, after which she raised her magic wand and all was still. Then turning to my great-great-grandmother she sang a little song to the effect that her spoken wish would be gratified; at the conclusion of which, the merry little fairies went their happy way. Her next child was my great-grandmother Mary McKenney, who in after years became the wife of Major John Small. In those good old days witches and fairies were as plentiful as pea blossoms in summer, but as Queen Mab was not often seen by mortals, the story of her visit created a profound sensation in the colony, for aside from her magic power she was the most beautiful creature ever seen on earth.

Now whether Mary was a "changeling" or was simply endowed with fairy gifts, was a matter of doubt; but all the old women of the town who were of course the best judges of such matters favored the changeling theory, partly because of her matchless beauty, but mainly because she was erratic and eccentric, and always did the unexpected and incomprehensible—a trait of character, God wot, which died not with her.

When the fairy-born Mary had grown to womanhood and was

Standing with reluctant feet,
Where the brook and river meet,

she was the most beautiful girl ever seen by her townspeople, and her dancing was so light, graceful and bewitching withal the good folks never tired with seeing her dance, nor did dancing tire her. So faithfully had Queen Mab kept her promise, that after a hard day's work at spindle or loom she could and did dance all night without a moment's rest and leap a gate higher than her head without touching hand or foot on her way home after daylight in the morning. The fame of her fairy-given beauty, grace and tirelessness in dancing spread from old Fort Popham to Plymouth, and on one occasion a party went all the way from Salem to see her, which was no light journey in those days.

The fairies had placed their mark of a mole on her right cheek where the edge of the beard would have been had she been a man, and that mark reappeared upon her son Henry, as also upon me her great-grandson Lauriston.

In those good old days witches were troublesome, and when neither the parson with his open Bible and leaf turned down at the verse "thou shalt not suffer a witch to live," nor the blacksmith with his leather apron could relieve a witch-burdened family, Mary was sent for, and when she entered the house every witch took to her heels or broomsticks, for they were in mortal fear of fairies.

After Major John's death she married a Haskins and had a daughter Sally, but her last years were spent with her son Henry in Limington. When nearing the grave she was flighty at times, whereupon all the old ladies said she was communing with her own people, the fairies. On one never to be forgotten occasion while three nice old ladies were sipping molasses with a little hot rum in it, they saw thousands of fairies around her, and were so frightened by the sight that they fell to the floor in an insensible condition and for an hour or more were unable to speak distinctly.

Such in brief is the story of Mary McKenney, wife of Major John Small, and if any hardened infidel doubts it, I can show him her skull in the family tomb at Limington. Doubtless this story was believed by a majority of the people with whom she associated, and she herself always believed that there was something supernatural about her birth.

Major John's children were: 1 John, 2 Edward, 3 Zacheus, 4 Francis, 5 Henry, 6 Daniel, 7 Rachel, 8 Dorcas, of whom John and Edward were of the first wife, and Daniel and Rachel were twins.

115

Saturday, Oct. 31, 1896.

GRANDPA'S SCRAP BOOK

PARSON BRADLEY'S JOURNAL.

WORK AGAINST THE DRINK HABIT IN 1829.

July 26, 1829. Mr. Meader preached at Saccarappa, a. m., on drunkenness and at Stroudwater, p. m., on the same subject—Text: "The way of the transgressor is hard." Full meeting at both places. Mr. Meader is an agent of the temperance society. I think much good will come in consequence of the delivery of the sermon. O, how important that there be a general reform in regard to temperance. If we don't reform we are a ruined people. God give success to temperance work.

27th. Walked with the boys on the bank of the canal to the cotton factory in Gorham; My men hauled in six loads of hay which finishes my haying; and let it be remembered that no ardent spirits were drank. Eleven days in getting forty-five tons of hay. No noise, no accident, no sickness, no rum.

28th. Charles and my men went to the cotton factory in Gorham—made several calls in Saccarappa. Took tea at Daniel Pierce's with Mr. Meader, agent of the temperance society. Had a meeting in the evening at the meeting house on the subject of intemperance. Full meeting, and 32 signed the constitution. To meet again next Tuesday. Mrs. Hillard signed.

August 4th. Went to Portland. Dined at Daniel Foxes'. In the evening at Saccarappa and helped organize a temperance society. Some prospect of good. Hope we shall not be disappointed. O, if Saccarappa could be reformed as respects intemperance, I have no doubt it would be a respectable village. A similar society formed at Stroudwater meeting house.

9th. Mr. Jameson preached. Two good sermons. "If the gospel be hid it is hid to those that are lost."

14th. Finished working on the highways. $63.04. Too much; too bad.

20th. Went to Gray with the little boy. Agreed to have them schooled and taken care of at Mr. Weston's at seven shillings per week. Rode to Sebago Pond; stayed all night at Mark Wites—bid welcome—never there before. Called at Wescott's falls, at Great falls, and dined with Mr. Gregg, the minister at Windham.

26th. Went to town. Dined at Wittiers. Rode home by the way of Mr. Woodfords. Chaise broke—went back to town—left the chaise to be mended.

27th. Mr. Pierce called and paid a note of $84.46. Expect to start out for Penobscot (Bangor). All for the best our chaise broke. The chaise mended and we now start.

Under date of Jan. 17th, 1830 in reference to the fact that he preached at Saccarappa he says: "Mr. Hillard closed with prayer after making some remarks," so Mrs. Hillard, who signed the pledge, was probably the wife of a clergyman.—Ed. News.

THE DEERING NEWS.

Saturday, Nov. 7, 1896.

GRANDPA'S SCRAP BOOK

[Under this head historical and genealogical memoranda will be furnished the readers of the News that appears worthy of preservation, particularly of remote periods in our history within the city limits and immediate vicinity.]

GEORGE LIBBY.

RECORDS AND RECOLLECTIONS OF ONE OF DEERING'S WORTHY CITIZENS.

At a point, according to the compiler of the Libby family genealogy, where the waters of the Nonesuch unite with the stream called Libby river in Scarboro, John Libby built his house who was the first by the name of Libby in this region.

Jan. 1663 he received record title to the land upon which he resided and was denominated a planter. In the year 1675 hostile Indians appeared in warlike attire with gun and torch and with others he fled from Black Point, but returned. He died at the age of 80 years making bequests to his children in his will dated Feb. 9th, 1682. The compiler of the family memorial credits him with twelve children, the tenth of whom was born at Scarboro 1657, and was named David, and he married Eleanor ———. "When the town was deserted, in 1690, he went to Portsmouth where he lived about ten years." In 1690 he purchased in the town of Kittery, (the part now known as Elliott), land where he built a two story dwelling which stood till after the year 1807. Upon the farm are buried with him representatives of five generations. He is credited with nine children, and David, the first child, married Esther Hanscom of Kittery, who lived on part of his father's homestead in what is now Elliott, till about the year 1731. From Kittery he moved to Scottow's Hill, Scarboro, and there settled on a farm. His house was a garrison. He died 1765. They are credited by the compiler of the Libby memorial with eight children David being the sixth.

This David—Captain David—of the fourth generation of the name born in Elliot about the year 1727 married first Dec. 13, 1750 Dorcas Means; she died, he married second in 1766, the widow Joanna (Joan) Page of Scarboro, by whom he had six children; by third wife four, David being the first child by second wife. His life was eventful.

The last named David, born about 1770 in Scarboro, married Jan. 14, 1790 Elizabeth (Betsey) McKenney, also of Scarboro, who became the mother of ten children, George, the subject of this article, being the fifth child, and Abraham, born March 2, 1808, who was noticed in the *News* some weeks since and who married Hannah Hancock, sister to John Hancock, who once flourished in Deering, being the ninth child.

Of this David of the fifth generation (also known as Captain David) C. Thornton Libby, Esq, compiler of the memoir says:

"He was carried by his father to Providence, R. I., and either there or elsewhere, was bound out to a carpenter. He, however, ran away to sea, and was ever afterward a mariner, rising to master. He returned to his native town where he at length married. About 1794 he was captured at sea by the French, and was five years a prisoner. He afterward followed the sea till 1814, when he settled on a farm in Newry, but being discouraged by severe frost which cut off his crops, sold, and moved his family to Chebeague Island, (Casco Bay). He continued to follow the sea until Apr. 26, 1818. His widow moved the family back to Saco. She died with a daughter in Standish, Apr. 20, 1848."

In Pine Grove cemetery situated adjacent Evergreen cemetery, this city near the southerly line that divides the former from the latter; within the enclosure of his son George, which will be further noticed, stands a marble grave memorial inscribed as follows:

DAVID LIBBY.
Died April 26, 1818,
Aged 48 Years.

BETSEY,
his wife,
died Apr. 20, 1848,
Aged 74 years.

Thus the descent of the name of John Libby from about the year 1630, at Scarboro, to George who settled in the year 1826 in the part of Deering that perpetuates his name—by its own—Libby's Corner—but here I part ways with my friend, the compiler, before noticed, and in the *News* of next week I hope to continue this notice of one whose name deserves a record more general and extended in circulation than has been accorded it.

Saturday, Nov. 14, 1896.

GRANDPA'S SCRAP BOOK

[Under this head historical and genealogical memoranda will be furnished the readers of the News that appears worthy of preservation, particularly of remote periods in our history within the city limits and immediate vicinity.]

GEORGE LIBBY.

RECORDS AND RECOLLECTIONS OF ONE OF DEERING'S WORTHY CITIZENS.

George Libby, fifth child of Capt. David Libby and wife Elizabeth, (or Betsey) McKenney, noticed in my article of last week, was born at Saco, May 22, 1800. Of his youthful days I can say but little. A few years before his death, (1878) I had some conversation with him relative to his lameness, and the place of his nativity, and he informed me that when a boy he dropped a chisel upon one of his great toes, that an Indian doctor was employed, but the injury caused a sore upon one of his legs which was very troublesome. While in this condition, and while a resident of Chebeague Island, during a winter of his boyhood he, a large boy, with others of the same mind constructed an iceboat by digging out a log, and upon the snow crust their first slide resulted in an overturn that so affected his lame leg that when he was able to stand he found a bone protruding from the skin, which, being removed, the affected part ceased to bother him. In this lame condition, and while a large boy he became part or whole owner in a sloop, gathered paving stones among the Islands of Casco Bay and sold them to the town of Portland.

In 1826 he was at that part of Westbrook which now commemorates his name, Libby's Corner, Deering, at which time, as appears by records, he leased real estate in the locality. What induced him to come to Westbrook I cannot say. There were but one or two houses between the Portland line and the house now occupied by Mr. Edward M. Thomes, Portland street, had not then been constructed, but the matter was seriously agitated.

Feb. 5, 1826, he was united in marriage with Fannie Prescott, daughter of Stephen and Elizabeth Prescott of Buxton.

The sawmills on the Saco at Buxton at that time furnished large quantities of boards and the teamsters made the region of what is now Libby's Corner a stopping place to feed on their return trip from Portland; and this, with the fact that the Oxford and Cumberland canal project promised to open up a wood, lumber, and shuck region which would make the "Bason" that would be formed in consequence at what is now Libby's Corner a depot for wood and bark as well as to furnish material for coopers, one of which the subject of this notice had become, evidently induced him to locate his home as he did at the time of his marriage.

The John Thomes house, a large, square building, two story in front and one at the rear, concerning which and its occupants I have much data, known at the time of the advent of George Libby and his bride, as the Huntress house, Huntress having married a Thomes, erected by George in after years which now stands, the Thomes house being used many years by John Thomes as a public house. In this Thomes house Mr. Libby commenced his married life as inn keeper and cooper.

Prosperity smiled on him and the old Thomes inn which sheltered "man and beast" as early as 1760 and was known to the travelling public by the sign of the "Golden Cow" soon gave way to the erection of the wooden dwelling now seen next westerly of the brick building at the "Corner," both of which were constructed by Mr. Libby and were attached and formed his dwelling place during his last days on earth, having been separated since his death.

To the Thomes—Huntress property he added other parcels of real estate, not only at the "Corner," but other parts of the town, so that in the course of a few years he became forehanded, and with pecuniary prosperity came political influence, and in this I desire to notice him more particularly than in any other consideration.

Upon his land at the "Corner" he built small dwelling houses, and on his other lots he caused by cultivation two or more spears of grass to grow where but one or none grew before. This required large barn room which he provided. And in addition to being an inn keeper, a cooper, a farmer, he quarried stone. About the year of 1850 he in company with Daniel Fowler built the stone walls to the bridge over Fore river at Stroudwater.

As a politician he came into public notice in 1845 when he was elected selectman of Westbrook, and being earnest and honest was re-elected in '46-'47-'48-'50 and '52. This last was the time of the enactment of the so-called Maine Liquor Law when members of the Democratic party became estranged to each other; and what is true of the Democratic party in this particular is also true of the Whig party. And Mr. Libby by giving his approval to the law lost the esteem of a majority of his party who declined to support him further. Then the friends of the law composed of both the old parties united and elected him to a seat in the House of Representatives of the Maine Legislature.

TO BE CONTINUED.

THE DEERING NEWS.

Saturday, Nov. 21, 1896.

GRANDPA'S SCRAP BOOK

[Under this head historical and genealogical memoranda will be furnished the readers of the News that appears worthy of preservation, particularly of remote periods in our history within the city limits and immediate vicinity.]

GEORGE LIBBY.

RECORDS AND RECOLLECTIONS OF ONE OF DEERING'S WORTHY CITIZENS.

(Continued from last Week.)

The socalled Maine Liquor Law which received a passage by the state legislature in 1852 exerted an aggravating influence upon the voting public, because the enforcement fell upon municipal officers, and the friends of the measure and those opposed to it separated politically and in many instances socially. There was in consequence a breaking up of old parties and the formation of new. The antislavery faction was a unit for the law, while a large percentage of the Whig party favored the enactment. They united and with the "Independent" element of the Democratic party organized the Republican party. The political history of Westbrook at the time, of which town Deering was a part, is indeed interesting.

George Libby was a Democratic, a local office holding Democrat, but had ceased to be an inn holder. As an innkeeper I do not remember him, only as a local politician, and a member of the Universalist church society that held meetings in the great building now seen at Brighton Corner, built by the society in 1830. Fortune and fame of a local nature smiled upon him, but the exact time he built the brick dwelling for himself as now seen I have no means of knowing, but the date 1840 is chiseled into the granite capstan over the brick store door, built by him adjacent his last abode, hence I will fix the date at about that time.

Mr. Libby's public approval of the "Maine Law" caused a chasm between himself and old Democratic party friends and the consequence was that in making up the ticket by the Democrats for municipal officers he was ignored; but as a testimonial of respect to his political independence and rebuke to others the Maine Law advocates and Antislavery voters nominated and then elected him to a seat in the State legislature where he distinguished himself as one of the most active, honest, and useful of the entire organization.

General John J. Perry as a politician was then in the zenith of success, and made the welkin ring as a stump-speaker for the cause of political temperance and antislavery. With his thick fleece of hair, round face, blue coat with brass buttons, white vest, and rounded periods in speech, he was a character that left a salutary influence upon the susceptible mind of that period, the influences of which exist to this very day.

Mr. Perry has more than passed the 84th mile stone in life's journey, but as a lawyer is still in active practice in Portland, and just before the appearance of the first of these articles, the writer waited on him and requested an outline description by his pen of Mr. Libby as he observed him in the legislature, who a day later handed me the following, with an expression of regret that he did not have time to prepare something more acceptable.

"The late George Libby of Westbrook was a politician of the old school—a Democrat of the Jacksonian stamp—honest and reliable and a hater of all shams, conscientious in politics as well as business.

He was one of the founders of the Republican party and was in 1853 elected a representative to the Maine legislature by the combined temperance and antislavery friends of all political parties in his town. He was one of less than a dozen members of the house who were that year elected as "Independent Democrats" having supported Anson P. Morrill for Governor.

These Morrill or Independent Democrats, held the balance power in the house in 1854, between the Whig and Democratic parties, and by a combination with the Whigs elected John J. Perry, Independent Democratic and Noah Smith, Whig, speaker.

Throughout the entire session of that legislature Mr. Libby was one of the leaders among the Independent Democrats. He knew how to plan and equally well how to execute. He was independent, bold and fearless in whatever he believed to be right. Another thing, he held to no theories which would not in his opinion work out good practical results.

After Anson P. Morrill was defeated for governor by the Whigs, many of the Independent Democrats were so much offended they declared they would not vote for Wm. Pitt Fessenden, for U. S. Senator, and without their votes it was apparent he could not be elected.

Mr. Libby carefully examined the whole situation, became satisfied that the best interest of the country required the election of Mr Fessenden, and from that moment privately assumed a bold front and labored zealously among the little band of Independents who, finally, to the surprise of all, elected that distinguished gentleman to the U. S. Senate. Mr. Libby was largely instrumental in the result.

Mr. Libby never claimed to be a public speaker, but as a shrewd party manager of that day he had but few equals.

In the legislature of 1854 he was an influential, popular member, highly respected by members of all parties both for his ability and honesty of purpose.

JOHN J. PERRY"

With Mr. Libby's retirement from the legislature his labors as a politician did not cease. He desired to wear the harness and be continued in office to which his friends agreed.

TO BE CONTINUED.

THE DEERING NEWS.

Saturday, Nov. 28, 1896.

GRANDPA'S SCRAP BOOK

[Under this head historical and genealogical memoranda will be furnished the readers of the News that appears worthy of preservation, particularly of remote periods in our history within the city limits and immediate vicinity.]

GEORGE LIBBY.

RECORDS AND RECOLLECTIONS OF ONE OF DEERING'S WORTHY CITIZENS.

(Continued from last Week.)

Jan. 6, 1857, Mr. Libby took the oath of office as a member of the board of county commissioners to which office he had been elected the previous autumn by the "Republicans" of the county. And right here, as Mr. Libby was an active figure in the political transformation of that period, I desire and will here insert an article that appears upon the outside page of the Weekly Lewiston Journal of today—Nov. 10, '96—as showing the claim made by that journal, whether it is correct or not, to the origin of the Republican party, as follows:

Just at this time, when the echoes of the jubilee of McKinley and Republicanism are ringing through the land, it is timely to recall a forgotten and almost unrecorded bit of history. Few people of the present generation know that the republican party had its birth in Maine, from whence it spread throughout the Union. Such, however, is the fact.

The man whose portrait heads this article bears the unique distinction of being the first man who was ever asked to join the republican party. Mr. Boothby was living in Paris, Oxford county, back in the early fifties. Politically he was quite a power in the anti-slavery party known as the "Free-soilers" and liked nothing better than a chance to get a whack at the "democrats" and "whigs."

One day in the year 1853 he was going down Main street, Paris, when Rufus B. Stevens, a born-and-bred-in-the-bone democrat, approached him with this question:

"What would you fellows say to joining hands and organizing a temperance party?"

As quick as the question, came back the answer:

"We'll do it!"

Without more ado the two linked arms and marched into the apothecary store of Dr. W. A. Rust. Dr. Rust was a son-in-law of Rufus K. Goodenow, formerly a member of Congress for the whig party, and one of the leaders of the local whig faction.

"Doctor," said the two in union, "will you join a new party on the temperance issue if we will?"

"By George!" exclaimed Rust in his high nasal key, bringing his fist down on the counter with a jar which upset a couple of bottles. "I'll go you!"

From there the three lost no time in reaching the office of the Oxford Democrat, where Editor Brown was let into

Next week the news was pushed through the State by faithful emissaries, and in due time a convention was held at which Anson P. Morrill was nominated for governor.

That year he polled 11,026 votes. Next year he swept the State and won hands down with a vote of over 44,000. From this spread the movement which elected Lincoln, saved the Union and will place McKinley in the presidential chair next March.

Mr. L. T. Boothby is now an esteemed resident of Waterville, where he has built up one of the largest insurance businesses in the state. He is a veritable encyclopedia of early political lore, and his memory on facts and figures is as reliable as the Maine Register. He also enjoys the distinction of having attended republican conventions for 31 years and in that period never failed to have his candidate receive the nomination.

In 1858 he signed with the other two members of the board entered into by the county, and the city of Portland to build the

COUNTY AND CITY BUILDINGS

as now observed in Portland, though the buildings were destroyed by fire in 1866, yet the front is the same that was then erected.

Jan. 4, 1859 he became chairman of the board; and the report then currently circulated that he was one of the best for the county that had held the office is still remembered by the compiler hereof.

After the election of Abraham Lincoln, the first Republican candidate to the office of Chief Magistrate of the nation, Mr. Libby felt that he should receive a political reward for steadfastness to what he conceived to be his duty and became a candidate for the first position in the Portland post office, Wm. Pitt Fessenden, whom Mr. Libby had helped more than any other person could, being then a member of Congress, whose assistance he relied upon, but Mr. Fessenden failed to compensate for "value received," and recommended Andrew T. Dole, born at Stroudwater, chairman of the Portland Republican city committee, and an anti-Maine Law member of the party, who received the appointment. But the unmerited treatment did not dampen the political ardor of Mr. Libby. None were more steadfast than he to the Union's cause during the Rebellion that followed Abraham Lincoln's election to the Presidential chair.

At this point in the career of Mr. Libby he reached the zenith of his political ambition.

TO BE CONTINUED.

THE DEERING NEWS.

Saturday, Dec. 5, 1896.

GRANDPA'S SCRAP BOOK

[Under this head historical and genealogical memoranda will be furnished the readers of the News that appears worthy of preservation, particularly of remote periods in our history within the city limits and immediate vicinity.]

GEORGE LIBBY.

RECORDS AND RECOLLECTIONS OF ONE OF DEERING'S WORTHY CITIZENS.

Continued from Last Week.

Mr. Libby's early book education was limited but he could state a proposition at a "town meeting" as readily as one with a more polished tongue, and he could handle figures swiftly and correctly as an expert. He was an economist in the handling of his own money, and equally so with that belonging to those who elected him to office but not niggardly. The color of his dress was always black, and he ever wore a "tall hat," but generally appeared around his premises minus a coat and frequently with his shirt sleeves rolled up. He was a lame man and was never seen without a cane. In conversation he was earnest, interesting and was a man without the slightest appearance of ostentation. He was a despiser of shams of all kinds and opposed to electing lawyers to draft and enact state laws.

A good likeness of him appears on page 24 of the

LIBBY FAMILY GENEALOGY,
PRINTED IN PORTLAND—1882.

He died December 22, 1878, his wife, April 19, the following year.

HIS FAMILY.

1—Priscilla, only child, born at Westbrook, Nov. 15, 1820; died, June 21, 1848, unmarried.
2—George (adopted) born Apr. 8 (or thereabouts) 1849; died June 13, 1852.
3—George (adopted) born Oct. 23, 1852, married Rosanna H., daughter of Wm. and Fanny (Hodgdon) McNeily of Clinton.

He was educated at the town school and Westbrook Seminary, worked upon the farm, and at the decease of his father came into possession of nearly all his property. For a while he continued the farm as managed by his father, then entered the law office of Congressman Reed of Portland and read law. County Attorney Selders appointed him his assistant, and then they opened a law office which was continued about a year. This present fall he was elected County Attorney. To him and wife have been born:

1—Priscilla Grace, born July 13, 1876, married June 3, 1896, Albert Henry Hicks and resides in Portland.
2—Mary Kidder, born Dec. 16, 1878.
3—George, Jr., born June 24, 1881.
4—Fannie Margaret, born Dec. 28, 1883.

Mr. Libby resides at 20 Carleton street Portland, but retains the Deering property.

Prior to his death, George Libby procured a burial lot in Pine Grove cemetery which he enclosed with a fine granite curbing some three feet high, containing an iron gateway—a very solid and enduring piece of work, and in the center of the lot there stands a marble memorial inscribed as follows:

GEORGE LIBBY.
died Dec. 22, 1878,
aged 78 years, 7 mos.

FANNY
his wife
died April 19, 1879,
aged 74 yrs. 3 mos.

PRISCILLA P.,
daughter of
George and Fanny
Libby,
died June 21, 1848,
aged 21 years.

GEORGE,
an adopted son of
George and Fanny Libby,
died June 13, 1852,
aged 3 years.

The records of his father and mother appearing with the above were presented to the readers of the *News* in a former article.

THE DEERING NEWS.

Saturday, Dec. 12, 1896.

GRANDPA'S SCRAP BOOK

[Under this head historical and genealogical memoranda will be furnished the readers of the News that appears worthy of preservation, particularly of remote periods in our history within he city limits and immediate vicinity.]

STROUDWATER HALL.

A FEW FACTS RELATIVE TO THE COMPANY AND BUILDING.

The two story building standing on Congress, opposite the foot of Waldo street, has a history that would evidently interest the public in the future could it be written now and preserved. The fact that about a $1000 was raised by entertainments at the time the building was erected for which no "security" was given the public, not even a share of stock being granted, is interesting now as well as the fact that when the public uses the building for even "benevolent purposes" the public pays for the use as a general thing.

Following is a copy of the original petition:

To Moses G. Dow, Esq., Justice of the Peace for the County of Cumberland, State of Maine.

SIR: The undersigned desire to be incorporated as a society for benevolent purposes, and respectfully request you to issue your warrant directed to Albert Morton, of Stroudwater, in the town of Deering, requiring him to call a meeting of the applicants at such time and place as you may be pleased to appoint.

Dated at Stroudwater village, in the town of Deering, this twelfth day of January, A. D. 1875.

THOMAS QUINBY,
MOSES H. DOLE,
ALBERT MORTON,
E. MILTON JACOBS,
MICHAEL STEVENS,
ANDREW HAWES,
EDWARD C. O'BRION,
SAMUEL A. CHAPMAN,
WALTER FICKETT,
AUGUSTUS TATE.

The warrant was issued, and on February 6th, a meeting of the applicants was held at the schoolhouse.

Feb 13 "The corporation of the Stroudwater Hall company" met according to adjournment, and voted to organize under Chapter 55 of the Revised Statutes of the State of Maine, and adopted a charter consisting of four sections and by-laws of two sections. Article two of the constitution provided that the capital stock of the company should be not less than $2000 nor more than $25,000 divided into shares of $5 each. The officers of the company to be a secretary, treasurer and a board of directors consisting of five members, "the president of whom shall be the president of the company." The articles of the by-laws were subsequently increased to thirteen.

The first annual meeting of the company was held in their new hall Jan. 1st, A. D. 1876. Walter Fickett was chosen clerk; Andrew Hawes, treasurer, and Thomas Quinby, Andrew Hawes, Michael Stevens, Thomas Jackson and Moses H. Dole, directors. The directors chose Thomas Quinby president.

The building is now called "Quinby Hall."

THE DEERING NEWS.

Saturday, Dec. 19, 1896.

GRANDPA'S SCRAP BOOK

[Under this head historical and genealogical memoranda will be furnished the readers of the News that appears worthy of preservation, particularly of remote periods in our history within the city limits and immediate vicinity.]

THE ARMAMENT OF ANCIENT STROUDWATER.

WHAT THE PROBATE COURT RECORDS AT BOSTON, MASS., SHOW.

Some of the present residents of Strodwater Village remember the old, low posted barn that once stood just westerly of the Fickett mansion now seen on the site of Col. Thomas Westbrook's garrison house at the southwesterly angle of Bond and Westbrook streets, the site of the house in which the Colonel died in 1744. This barn was included within the palisade, it is believed, of the colonel's residence at Stroudwater. In the autumn of the year 1853 it was taken down. It was known at the time as Dr. Hunt's old barn. Dr. Henry Hunt had a couple of years previously commenced the great barn as now seen a little northerly of the junction of Congress and Bond streets, westerly of the village. With the corner of the old structure that contained a plank floor was, at the time of the removal, a tradition that the floor was made of plank because in the corner, in the days of the colonel cannon stood for the protection of the ancient hamlet in case of Indian invasion. Anyway some of the planks were used in the construction of the apartments in the top of the new barn where they now remain and may be seen in the frames of the slide doors although covered with paint.

Just before the death of the Colonel the "garrison house" alias "Harrow House" came into possession of Col. Samuel Waldo, who, later, received the distinction of general and later still his son was known as colonel. Waldo was a man of great wealth, a merchant in Boston but he had large land and mill interests in Falmouth and elsewhere in the District of Maine. His Falmouth residence stood where the Southworth printing house now stands in Portland. Many manuscript letters on file at the Boston state house I have read, comparatively but a small item in history, but somewhat of him may be found in "Portland in the Past" and concerning his family, but the compiler errs in stating he had a voting residence in Falmouth. Cumberland county was erected in 1760, and Waldo died previous to the event at ... this state, whither he had come after his land titles, hence the state of records, and then action of Cumberland County Court records in 1866 makes the obtaining facts pertaining to him more laborious, and in some a blank is found that cannot be

---

Saturday, Jan. 2, 1897.

GRANDPA'S SCRAP BOOK

AN OLD CORPORATION.

The Mill Dam Company at Strodwater.

The Mill Dam Company at Stroudwater is the oldest company within the city of Deering and perhaps the county. It was incorporated Jan. 20, 1832, and the corporate members were as follows:
Dr. Jacob Hunt
Capt. Thomas Seal
Moses Quinby, Esq.
Chas. Bartlett
Hon. Jonathan Smith
Dr. John M. Brewer
Silas Broad
Wm. H. Gardner

Capt. Thomas Seal was chosen president, Moses Quinby, Esq., clerk and Charles Bartlett treasurer. Hunt was the village doctor, Seal a retired sea captain residing at Capisic; Quinby, a graduate of Bowdoin college, Bartlett a ship builder, Smith a tanner and office holder all three of Stroudwater. Brewer a physician of Philadelphia, brother to Capt. Dexter Brewer of Stroudwater Brewer House fame; Broad of the famous Broad inn, and Gardner of Portland of whom I have but slight knowledge.

The dam and first mill were located on the notherly side of the bridge over Fore river and both were built before the act of incorporation was passed by the state legislature.

The stock was divided into eight parts a printed blank form being used, which papers are still in existance with all the books of the concern.

Dec. 13, 1833 it was voted to make an assessment of $300 upon each member.

In 1835 Messrs. Smith, Quinby, Seal, Broad and Gardner disposed of their stock to Oliver Everett and Nathaniel Stevens of Portland and Bailey Babb of Saccarappa appears on the records as a stockholder who soon died at Stroudwater in the ancient square built house standing at the head of Waldo street.

In 1836 the company voted to purchase the "Town Wharf" and pay $800, but the purchase was made for a much less sum. The wharf was located where the new mill hay scales stand at this date, and was built over a 100 years ago.

After the purchase of the wharf additional mills were built.

In the year 1847 Messrs. F. A. and W. H. Waldron of Portland came into possession of a majority of the stock, and strange to say both of these gentlemen are still alive.

Some years since Walter Fickett, Esq., purchased a majority of the shares of stock and is secretary and treasurer of the company.

During these many years annual meetings have been holden and at this time the corporation has a full set of officers, seal and complete record books.

THE DEERING NEWS.

Saturday, Jan. 23, 1897.

GRANDPA'S SCRAP BOOK
REV. SAMUEL BRIMLECOM.

FIRST INSTRUCTOR OF WESTBROOK SEMINARY—HIS FAMILY—OTHER FACTS.

April 18th of last year there was printed in the *News* an article relative to the First Universalist Society of Westbrook, compiled from original records, which was followed by four or five others, then three or four more relative to religious matters hereabouts sixty odd years ago.

June 27th, of last year, there was also printed in the *News* an historical article relative to Westbrook Seminary to all of which articles I now refer.

At the time the matter was prepared for publication I supposed that "Universal salvation" as a basis of religious belief was shaped hereabouts in 1829 when the records now in existence were commenced, but further research proves that I was in error because I have lately found two records as follows which explode the idea that the believers in Universal salvation of the soul of man did not organize till the year 1829.

The part of Falmouth now known as Westbrook and Deering was taken from Falmouth and incorporated by the name of Stroudwater, February 14, 1814, but on June of same year the name was changed to that of Westbrook.

Westbrook Apr. 22, 1815

This is to certify that Jeremiah Edes of Westbrook is admitted a member of the First Universal Society of Falmouth according to the provisions of the act of incorporation of said society.

AMASA FOBES, Clerk of said society, Recorded by Alpheus Shaw, Town Clerk.

This is to certify that at a legal meeting of the First Universal society of Falmouth began and holden at said Falmouth on Saturday the fifth day of April A. D. 1817, that Enoch Burnham and Rufus Huston having given previous notice according to the act of Incorporation were admitted members of said society.

Attest, AMASA FOBES,
Clerk of said society,
Westbrook, May 1, 1817.

All the persons here named resided in what is now territorially Deering. The family record of Capt Edes consisting of four children, and that of Capt. Huston, whose eldest child was born Nov. 8, 1790, probably the Rufus referred to, and ten other children, as well as that of Burnham consisting of ten children, are all before me as I write.

Now for the record of Col. Samuel Brimlecom.

SANTA CLARA, CALIFORNIA,
Nov. 23, 1896.

My Dear Sir:—It is with extreme regret I find your letter has been so long neglected. It has but just now come into my hands. Being at Boulder Creek, my nephew handed it to me with the request that I furnish the desired information as he had not the data.

I am more than glad to do what I can, and am sorry to be compelled to have some blanks. I am greatly interested in the part of Westbrook now known as Deering, and intensely enjoyed a few hours there in the fall of 1882 when I visited Maine for the first time, in company with my brother Charles. Our stay was brief, as his business engagements would not admit of a lengthy absence. I so admired the locality that I have ever since been led to regret that it had not been the permanent home of my family. We have wandered far, and our "lines have fallen in pleasant places," but none where influences and opportunities would excel those in and around Portland, Me.

I cannot account for the return of your letter to me as we never have any trouble about our mail. We hear from the post office three or four times a day, and there being no other family of our name in the State, there are no opportunities for mistakes. There is a Santa Clara in Colorado and our mail, if simply marked "Cal.," is liable to be sent there. Any papers you would send would be highly appreciated and I assure you *nothing* would give me *greater pleasure* than to receive the photo of the *"old meeting-house"* of which you speak. To me it is "sacred ground."

My brother Samuel's business was a sea captain. He went out from Boston and was for many years in Chinese waters. Charles was a lawyer; William a teacher. All the others were in business trading and farming.

With deep interest in everything pertaining to your vicinity,
I am most sincerely
LUCY A. BRIMLECOM.

P. S. I have written East for dates etc., and should I receive anything relating to the birth places of Col. Brimlecom and wife, I will forward it. Their home called "Brimlecom Hall" was on Western avenue, Lynn, Mass.

Col. Samuel Brimlecom b———Oct. 8 1768, d. Lynn, Mass., April 24, 1850. Occupation, shoe manufacturer, resided at Lynn, Mass.

Mary Mansfield, his wife, daughter of ———b. at———Jan. 5, 1770, d. at Lynn, Mass., Sept. 19, 1816.

Samuel Brimlecom, (4th child of the above) b. Lynn, Mass., Feb. 11, 1790. Married Oct. 22 1822 at Concord, Mass., d. in Mass., July 14, 1879.

Harriet Buttrick, his wife, b. at Concord, Mass., Aug. 27, 1798, d. at Santa Clara, Calif. Jan. 23, 1878.

She was the daughter of Col. Jonas Buttrick, and grand daughter of Maj. John Buttrick who led the Concord fight on April 19th 1775 and fired "The shot heard round the world" which is immortalized in Emerson's poem. She was born and reared on the battle ground, which has been in possession of her family since the first settlement in 1635. He was educated at Harvard college and graduated in the class of 1817. Following this he spent three years in Harvard Divinity school. Was ordained pastor of Unitarian church at Sharon, Mass., on Dec. 18, 1821. Removed to Norridgewock, Me., in 1826, where he left the Unitarian denomination and became a Universalist. Removed to Westbrook, Me., in 1830, to Danversport Mass., in 1836, to Barre, Mass., 1840, to Dudley, Mass., in 1845.

In 1847 he left the ministry, took up his residence on a farm in Worcester Co., Mass., and subsequently lived a quiet and retired life.

In the later years of his ministry he was very active in Anti Slavery and temperance work, which interfered with his ministerial success, as committees in those days were perhaps even slower than now to adopt progressive and philanthropic ideas. He had four brothers all of whom died in youth.

CHILDREN OF REV. SAMUEL AND HARRIET (BUTTRICK) BRIMLECOM.

1 Samuel A.—b—Sharon, Mass., Nov. 2, 1823. Married Miss Sarah Holden, Barre, Mass., June 6, 1850. Now living at Boulder Creek, California.
2 Charles b—Sharon, Mass., Fed. 10, 1825. Married Harriet C. Houghton, Barre, Mass., Dec. 25, 1850, died at Barre, Mass., Apr. 20, 1894, leaving a wife and one daughter, Mrs. Alexander Martin, 870 Beacon street, Boston, Mass.
3 Frederic b—Norridgewock, Me., Jan. 21, 1827. Married Miss A. L. Harrington, Oct. 1853 at Grafton, Mass. Now living at Woosung, Ogle Co., Illinois.
4 Francis Alden—b—Norridgewock, Me., Aug. 1, 1828. Unmarried. Now living at Santa Clara, Calif.
5 Edward —b—Norridgewock, Me., June 13, 1830. Unmarried. Died at Santa Clara, California, Jan. 14, 1891.
6 William—b—Westbrook, Me., Feb. 1, 1832. Married Miss Emily Gragg, at Bedford, Mass., Oct. 1854. Veteran of the War of the Rebellion. Now living in Ohio.
7 Henry—b—Westbrook, Me., Feb. 8, 1834. Married Miss Anna Huntington at Thetford, Vt., Jan. 1860. Graduated from Dartmouth College Class of 1860. Now living at Woosung, Ogle Co., Illinois.
8 James Stedman—b—Westbrook, Me., March 16, 1836. Died at Danversport, Mass., Oct. 6, 1837.
9 Albert Jonas—b—Danversport, Mass. Apr. 20, 1838. Married Miss Augusta Reynolds, Illinois, 1859. Veteran of the War of the Rebellion. Now living at Scotia, Neb.
10 Lucy Adeline, only daughter—b—Danversport, Mass., Jan. 23, 1840. Unmarried. Now living at Santa Clara, California.

In the Bibliography of Maine, vol. 1, p. 194, published last year by Hon. Jos. Williamson, I find a reference as follows:

Brimlecom. Samuel—Clergyman, Haverhill, Mass. The Parental Character of God. A discourse delivered before the Second Congregational Society in Norridgewock, Me., February 15, 1829. Published by request by Thomas J. Copeland, 1829, 12mo. pp. 22.

As stated in the Seminary Article of June 27. Mr. Brimlecom was assistant editor of the Pilot, a periodical printed in Portland devoted to Universalism, a

Continued:

few copies of which are deposited in the Portland Public Library, bound into book form. This is all I know at present of his literary work.

The old society record shows as follows:

Oct. 4, 1830—Voted that the standing committee be authorized to employ the Rev. Samuel Brimblecom as a preacher to this society for one year, with a salary not to exceed four hundred dollars.

The following is a transcript from the city clerk's records of Westbrook, 1834:

Superintending School Committee.

Samuel Brimblecom, Zenas Thompson and Henry C. Jewett.

The second was a Universalist preacher at Saccarappa Village, Westbrook, the last a Congregationalist in the old meeting house that stood where the so-called Bradley meeting house now stands on Church street.

Mr. Thompson was father to Zenas Thompson, the carriage manufacturer of Portland and member of the city government. He has other descendants here and in Portland.

The brick building erected by Mr. Brimblecom on the easterly side of Stevens Plains avenue, and north easterly of the Seminary evidently for a home for students, as noticed in the former article herein alluded to, and now standing, was valued and taxed with other property in 1834, as follows:

House, barn, lot, etc.,	$1400
Horse and chaise,	130
Cow,	15
	$1545

There are many of our citizens who still remember Mr. Brimblecom as he appeared in the pulpit,—compactly built, round faced, slow in speech but deep in thought.

It was not till Nov. 13, 1831, that there was a public recognition of the Universalist church in this place, when the right hand of fellowship was extended to four women by an authorized agent of the pledged believers in Universal salvation of the soul of mankind.

As a new register book has recently been provided for names of preachers and members of the society, ancient and modern, dates of births, deaths, and other facts, and placed in the hands of our esteemed citizen, Walter F. Goodrich, Esq , 93 Stevens Plains avenue, this city, the facts herein contained may tend to infuse "dry bones" of the community with activity that will materially aid Mr. Goodrich in the laudable work.

THE DEERING NEWS.

Saturday, Jan. 30, 1897.

GRANDPA'S SCRAP BOOK

[Under this head historical and genealogical memoranda will be furnished the readers of the News that appears worthy of preservation, particularly of remote periods in our history within he city limits and immediate vicinity.]

BENJAMIN REMICK.

The Site of His Dwelling at Stroudwater and Other Facts.

The fire a few weeks since, noticed by the News in the Stroudwater items which originated, it is now believed, by placing a heated fire poker in the kitchen wood box, of the residence of Mrs. Ella M. (Ames) Bates, sister to Mrs. L. M. N. Stevens, and son Fred, recently married, brings up the fact that the house was a story and a half structure, situated on the northerly side of what is now known as Congress street, and the third house from the iron bridge over Stroudwater river, in excellent repair, neatly furnished, and built a few years since by Mr. Henry J. Hunt, on the site of the Remick house.

Between the dates of the close of the war of the Revolution and the "embargo" Stroudwater received quite a business boom, and among the arrivals was Benjamin Remick, a blacksmith by occupation, and his wife, a small, high spirited, pretty woman, from Kittery, this state. Her maiden name I do not know, nor do I know anything of his family connections. When I knew him he was tall, rather slim, bald headed, without beard, Roman nose, and rather austere in demeanor. A glance at Kittery records show that persons by the name of Remick lived in that town two hundred years ago, but as before stated I know nothing of this Benjamin's family, never having made it a study.

In former numbers of the News I have alluded to the early occupants of the north westerly corner lot made by the crossing of Westbrook and Congress streets, concerning which I have the following record made in 1806:

Moses Dyer to Charles Pierce, trader, and Benjamin Remick, consideration $1600, *** that I, together with Joseph Delano, purchased of William Waterhouse, Jr , (he was son of Wm. Waterhouse senior, who resided where his great grandson Frederick now lives at the easterly terminus of Bond street,) Dec. 2, 1802, and the same that I purchased of Joseph H. Ingriham July 1, 1803; also a one-fourth acre on southerly side of Fresh (Stroudwater) river being the same I purchased of Wm. Slemons, May 18, 1805.

To this one-fourth acre lot Mr. Remick moved the building on the corner lot here noticed, that was built for a blacksmith's shop and converted it into a dwelling for himself. It was one story, and when completed had a basement story, or cellar kitchen, parlor in one westerly end, kitchen through the middle, and in the other end two bed rooms. There were several steps leading up to the front door and in front of the house were a black cherry and balm of gilead trees. And many hours the writer spent in picking from the ground the fallen fruit and the white down of the balm of gilead blossoms. At the westerly end of the house was the lane leading to Dr. Jacob Hunt's pasture. The gate and every knot hole of the fence I still remember. Back of the house the doctor's cows roamed at will, where stood the oak and a birch as now observed, but the pine, beneath which I watched the floating ice of the swift waters of the spring freshet, observed the funeral procession enter and depart from "God's half acre," and then listened to the unwelcome sound of the thwack of the cold, unrelenting earth upon the sepulchered dead, which pine long since became the prey of the axe. Then the jasmin impeded the way to the place of the choke-cherry and witch-hazel nut bush of the steep sloped tangle between the grand old pine adjacent the Remick lot and the waters of the Stroudwater, a place visited only by the courageous youth of fifty odd years ago.

Business becoming dull Mr. Remick moved to Portland and the house was let but the family returned soon after the year 1825, which consisted of two sons Benjamin and John and a daughter who died unmarried, before my remembrance, father and mother. The sons became blacksmiths, Benjamin settling in Boston, Mass., where he married, had a family and died. The wife of Benjamin, senior, fell about the year 1818, fractured a thigh bone, which caused permanent lameness. After her death her husband and John lived without a housekeeper and in the year 1862, I think, Benjamin died. John, who, within my remembrance never worked at his trade, took up his abode with Daniel Conant at Saccarappa, where he resided several years, making himself useful about the premises when, having a few hundred dollars, went to board at the alms-house where he died. The house went to decay gradually and finally became a total wreck. A short time before its collapse, twenty odd years since, I entered it and in a cupboard where there were quite a lot of papers and some books, the whole lot of which I should have taken, I secured but one paper which reads as follows:

Kittery Me., Dec. 25, 1802.
Dear Son;—

I take this opportunity to inform you that I received your letter and the chest that you put on board Randell

CONTINUED:

and have received no letter from you since. But I hope these lines will find you in good health as they leave me. Your mother is in good health and your Brothers and Sister enjoys the same Blessing· and desires to be remembered to you. I heard from you last Mond·y by David Lewis. Hannah is well. She was here about a week ago. She and Polly are at Kittery to work. Lewis told me that you did not know you should come up. Remember me to all our Relatives at Scarborough, and I should be glad to hear from you every opportunity. I am building a Schoner for Enoch Lewis at Spruce Creek which will take me the most part of the win er. Jacob is at work at Portsmouth, I expect and was at home this evening. You may think yourself happy that you Did not go with Capt.——for he has not arrived yet. The last news from the Captain the Negroes had took the town and the wites had fled on board the Amaracon vessels. I think of Nothing more at present. So I remain
Your affectionate father,
Benjamin Remick.

Polly Millin has been with us ever since I was at Portland. Jacob has Not got your money from Passy Estate yet, But I am in hopes you will get it as soon as the estate is Settled it is Supposed it will pay all the debts.

Capt. Kennard we hear has lost two hands. But who they are we do not hear. I should be glad if I could send your great cote, if you will write word it shall be left.

I closed this letter Saturday and brake open Sunday evening to let you Know the unhappy fate of Portsmouth. A fire broke out about four o'clock in the morning in the old bank and continued until half after one. It burnt the New Market and as far as the widow Henderson's and acrost as far as Capt Cutts store on Church hill the whole square both sides of the paved street. Jefferys row and all on Spring hill as far down as madam Whipple's to the amount of seventy houses.
B. R.

In 1815 Mr. Remick was taxed as follows:

1 house and lot	$180
1 barn	25
1 shop	25
1 cow	14

His and his wife's earthy remains fill unmarked, in fact, unknown graves in the old Stroudwater village cemetery. John's repose in the "Deering Stranger's Lot" at Evergreen. And with the statement that I recently found at our deserted town hall a paper showing the fact that though interred upon this lot his estate paid all demands against it, and expression of the often repeated sentiment—"Peace to his ashes, I drop the matter.

THE DEERING NEWS.

Saturday, Feb. 6, 1897.

GRANDPA'S SCRAP BOOK

[Under this head historical and genealogical memoranda will be furnished the readers of the News that appears worthy of preservation, particularly of remote periods in our history within he city limits and immediate vicinity.]

WILLIAM STEVENS.

A FEW FACTS RELATIVE TO HIS HOME ON STEVENS PLAINS.

November 10, 1894, after several articles referring to the Sawyer and Stevens name at Woodfords had appeared in the *News*, I commenced the publication of others relating to the Stevens name in the Stevens' Plains district of this city, bringing the name down to the 8th child in the family of Capt. Stevens and Sarah Brackett with whom he was united in marriage Nov. 24, 1709.

Jan. 26, 1895 there appeared in the *News* an article relating to Deacon James Bailey and family whose daughter the subject of this sketch married, to all of which I now refer as an aid to those who have been sufficiently interested in the publications to preserve the matter.

William Stevens was born Dec. 11, 1785, and was united in marriage Nov. 26, 1801 with Sally, eighth child of Dea. James Bailey, born July 8, 1788, on the westerly side of the Windham road, a mile northwesterly of Morrill's Corner, in this city. As a child and young man I have no knowledge of him. He was, I am told, of muscular formation of body, was taught the rudiments of the philosophy of Iron welding, his father being a blacksmith as well as tavern keeper. And living in the days of wayside-inns and succeeding his father in business,

"The taverner took me by the sleeve,
'Sir,' saith he, 'will you our wine assay?'
I answered 'that cannot much me grieve,
A penny can do no more than it may;'
I drink a pint, and for it did pay."

The main part of the tavern house stands today on the westerly side of Stevens Plains avenue, a well preserved structure, owned and occupied by a granddaughter of Capt. Stevens—a daughter of William. In the days of Capt. Isaac it was a resort of the military of the neighborhood as it was when occupied by William, the son. From the top of the Liberty pole floated the flag of the country. Long strings of teams lined the wayside in front while military and political matters were discussed over the mug of flip in the bar room, the unchanged room located in the southerly end of the mansion as now seen.

The great stable that sheltered the perspiring steed of the over wined Portland "buster" now stands, but the bowling alley has taken its departure. Father Time has indeed laid his weighty hand heavily upon the old tavern surroundings in several respects. The large ell that stood upon the southerly end of the present structure has been removed and one built on the westerly side. The huge chimney that stood in the center of the building has been taken down and a smaller one erected. But the exterior with its fresh coat of paint, its plant bedecked windows bespeak within cheerfulness and intelligence. Love for the things of ye olden time and knowledge of ancient hospitality that was once dispensed within the walls of the abode, I ventured to ascend the stone steps and touch the modern front door alarm—the electric button, and in less time than it takes to record the fact, I found myself ascending the winding stair, but not the kind of wind the spider built for the capture of the fly.

The paneled partition next to the chimney the wooden cornice, the great corner post of a century or thereabouts ago, still remain in the southerly side of the second story, the room being divided by a set of folding doors. In the palmy days of inn keeping this part of the house was used as dining-hall on great occasions, such as military musters, and the assembling of dancing parties, from a door of which the hall was reached, which, when first constructed, was only sufficiently wide to admit of one set of dancers, to which was added another strip equally as wide as the original part.

The relics of a continued occupancy for a period of a whole century by carefully disposed persons of a well constructed abode are numerous when means of procurement are ample. To say that this ancient abode possesses many is stating a fact only in a mild way, but an enumeration is out of consideration here. The attic is a storehouse wonderfully full, the value of which cannot be determined by a casual view of a few minutes duration. The perforated tin lantern and the warming pan occupy, like the frozen sparerib of a century ago, each a spike in the attic ridgepole, while "Aunt Brisco's" bureau, newly scraped and freshly varnished, "grandpa's" clock, the tall brass lamp, and the mute double barrel shooter, manufactured on the Plains, occupy conspicuous places in the living rooms.

The age of the dwelling is a question. It is traditional that the original structure was one story, and its obliqueness in location with the street is owing to a change of the highway. And this is more than probable.

TO BE CONTINUED.

THE DEERING NEWS.

Saturday, Feb. 13, 1897.

GRANDPA'S SCRAP BOOK

[Under this head historical and genealogical memoranda will be furnished the readers of the News that appears worthy of preservation, particularly of remote periods in our history within the city limits and immediate vicinity.]

WILLIAM STEVENS.

A FEW FACTS RELATIVE TO HIS HOME ON STEVENS PLAINS AND FAMILY.

Continued from Last Week.

Upon the first valuation books of Westbrook, made in 1815, the name of Capt. Isaac S. Stevens does not appear, but that of his son William does as follows:—

1 House, $650
2 Barns, 70
1 Stable, 100
7 Acres tillage land at $20 per acre.
40 Pasturing & unimproved at $9.
2 Oxen $40.
2 Horses $80.
3 Swine $15.

The house belonging to the Captain's son Isaac, recently removed by the electric railroad company to make room for the car house, was taxed for $300; that in which Mrs. Levi Q. Pierce now resides, then belonging to her father, Zach. B. Stevens, another son, $350; and the large square house, now standing, and is the second one southerly of the Wm. Stevens house, then owned by Josiah Stevens, another son, $350.

The position of all of these abodes are shown upon the court plan of Stevens Plains made in 1811, to which reference has been made in former articles, and which I hope to see copied into the NEWS.

During the time the house was used as an inn, the Plains was a place for horse racing, from a point where our High school building stands to Morrill's Corner, as well as for military parades. And one of the curious relics of way-side inns is an original paper now before me in the writing of George Bishop, who was a Westbrook town official so many years, dated Sept. 7, 1840, and contains a list of names of thirty-nine persons deemed intemperate, at which time Rufus Morrill, William Roberts and Isaac Johnson were selectmen, and George Bishop town clerk. When a person was licensed to sell intoxicating liquors in those days, the party receiving the license certificate was prohibited from selling persons who used the beverage to excess, hence the list of names as now before me. On the back of the list is written as follows:—

Wafer this in your account book in the Bar room. Also make peace with Mr. Haynes, which will be 50 cents. (I have been to see him.) You must go strict as there is likely to be trouble and your license will only clear you after its date of Jan. 21.

G. B.

To Wm. Stevens, Inholder.

Every person named on the list has rendered, it is believed, his final worldly account, and now the written charge of "intemperance" is, at this time, cast into the midst of a hot fire by the writer hereof, who sees it destroyed and here records the fact.

In 1832 there was not a dwelling-house on the easterly side of the Plains highway, at which time the land was divided by George Bishop, Walter B. Goodrich and Moses Quinby, among the heirs of Captain Isaac S. Stevens.

For a period of fifty-one years William and wife Sally occupied together the vacated last worldy abode of the hero of the Revolution, and twenty years after the closing of the abode as a public inn.

"Far hence be Bacchus' gifts (the chief rejoin'd)
Inflaming wine, pernicious to mankind,
Unnerves the limbs, and dulls the noble mind.
Let chiefs abstain, and spare the sacred juice
To sprinkle to the gods, its better use."

As with the last years of the "chief" of the Plains hamlet of Westbrook, so it is now with the Plains district of Deering:

"Far hence be Bacchus' gifts; Let chiefs abstain!"

Upon the easterly side of Pine Grove Cemetery may be seen two memorial stones inscribed as follows:—

FATHER.
WILLIAM STEVENS,
died
June 3, 1862.
Aet. 76 years.

MOTHER.
SALLY STEVENS,
died
Apr. 1, 1863,
Aet. 75 years.

To William Stevens and Sally Bailey, his wife, were born five children: 1—Louisa; 2—Laura Jane; 3—George Mead; 4—Irene; and 5—William Wallace.

1 Louisa, born Aug. 28, 1811, married Feb. 8, 1830, James A. Thompson of Bridgton, and settled in Augusta, this state, where he engaged in the tinware and stove trade. From there he removed to New York city where he opened a jewelry shop. The war of the Rebellion came on and he again removed with his family to St. Paul, Minn.

CHILDREN:

1 Louisa.
2 James W., married Jane Elizabeth, dau. of Hon. Samuel Jordan of this city. She was born at Woodfords, Jan. 17, 1840. They now reside in Los Angeles, California.
3 George Homer, m. and is reported as a Catholic Priest, Santa Fe, Cal.
4 Lyman S. m. daughter of Dr. Kimball of Bridgton and resides at the Sandwich Islands, where his father died, and where he is a practicing physician.
5 Nellie, unm. resides at Blaine, Washington State.
6 Carrie, m., died St. Paul, Minn.
7 Jesse Murdock m, resides San Francisco, Cal.
8 Frank B. m.
9 Archibald, unm, resides in California.
10 Jennie, wife of Dr. King, and resides at Blaine, Washington-state.

There were other children who died young.

2 Laura Jane, born Apr. 4, 1814, married Apr. 18, 1833, Capt. Charles Sumner Buckley 3d child of Oliver Buckley of Stevens Plains; born there Apr. 11, 1811. He removed to Augusta, this state and engaged in business with his brother-in-law, Thompson. From there they removed to Chicago, Ill., where he died March 15, 1864. She died at Augusta, Dec. 13, 1852. Notice of Buckley family later.

CHILDREN:

1 Laura deceased m. Edward Sampson of Bowdoinham.
2 Charles M. m. resided in Boston, Mass., now in State of N. H.
3 Henry died in New York, unm.
4 Sumner, died unm.
5 Herbert resides in Portland, Oregon, married.
6 Sarah, deceased; m. Wm. Roberts who resided in Portland.

Note.—I am informed that the family record of William Stevens shows that he was united in marriage in the year 1809 and *not* 1801 as my article of last week made it appear.

TO BE CONTINUED.

Saturday, Feb. 20, 1897.

GRANDPA'S SCRAP BOOK

[Under this head historical and genealogical memoranda will be furnished the readers of the News that appears worthy of preservation, particularly of remote periods in our history within he city limits and immediate vicinity.]

WILLIAM STEVENS.

A FEW FACTS RELATIVE TO HIS HOME ON STEVENS PLAINS AND FAMILY.

Continued from Last Week.

III. George Mead Stevens, born June 23, 1816, married, Apr. 21, 1838, Hannah, daughter of Capt. Jonathan and Thirzah (Emery) Chase, born at South Berwick, March 18, 1821.

Capt. Chase removed to Portsmouth, N. H., and went into trade in addition to his being a sea captain. Then he took his family, furniture and cattle on board his vessel and migrated to Jewell's Island, Casco Bay, where he ever after resided till near the close of his long life.

William M. Scammon of Morrill's Corner married a daughter of Capt. Chase, died March 23, 1881, aged 91 years; his wife Jan. 28, 1877, aged 83 years, and both are buried on easterly side of Pine Grove Cemetery, where memorial stones appear.

At early manhood Mr. Stevens went to Augusta, this state, and engaged in tin and stove work with his uncles; then went to Bath where he engaged in trade with his brother William W., and after selling his interest to his brother returned to the parental home. His present dwelling which stands between the old homestead of his father and that of his grandfather and that of his uncle Josiah, immediately back of which about five rods is the large old stable, and still further back westerly, the old dance hall, converted into dwelling houses, was made from Philo Hall's britannia ware shop that stood on the opposite side of the street, Mrs. Stevens, wife of George Mead, retaining a half dozen of the spoons manufactured in it more than fifty years ago.

After the decline of tin and britannia business on the Plains, Mr. Stevens engaged in agriculture which he has since followed. And to them have been born four children as follows:

1.—George Byron, born June 13, 1839, married Jennie Graham of Westbrook. They have had eight children of whom five survive—Jennie May; Helen P.; George William Isaac, (the three Stevens grandpas in rotation;) Graham Chase and Annie Irene. Mr. Stevens resided at Deering Center.
2.—John Appleton, born Aug. 17, 1842, married Olena, daughter of John Dunham. She died on the Plains, March 15, 1894, aged 47 years. One child, Alberta Appleton; who resides with her father.
3.—Irene Elmore, born July 7, 1844, married Richard H. Davis, a trader in Bridgton where she died Oct. 22, 1886; he Jan. 1883, leaving one child Stella May, who resides on the Plains with her parents (grand parents?
4.—Cora Bell, born and died young.
IV. Irene, resides on the homestead, married Rev. Lewis L. Record, to be noticed next week.
V. William Wallace, born June 18, 1826. At about the age of 17 he went to Augusta, this state, and engaged in the tin ware and stove business with his uncles Buckley and Thompson, where he remained seven years; he then went to Bath, stopped three years, then returned to Portland and went into an iron foundry. Since leaving the foundry has been engaged in several kinds of business, now engaged in the manufacturing of certain parts of harnesses, head of Middle street. While in Augusta he married Helen L. Pike, Oct. 18, 1853, daughter of Daniel Pike of that city who served thirty-three years as country treasurer, and at time of his death was cashier of the Freeman's Bank of that city.

CHILDREN:

1.—Helen Gertrude b. Augusta, March 14, 1857, died there Sep. 14, same year.
2.—Arthur W., born Sep. 22, 1860, died Aug. 5, 1861.
3.—Mary Elizabeth, born Nov. 25, 1863, resides, unmarried with her parents, 58 Gray street, Portland.
4.—Daniel Pike, born April 3, 1865, unmarried, and a commercial traveler for a New York city firm.

TO BE CONTINUED.

THE DEERING NEWS.

Saturday, Feb. 27, 1897.

GRANDPA'S SCRAP BOOK

[Under this head historical and genealogical memoranda will be furnished the readers of the News that appears worthy of preservation, particularly of remote periods in our history within the city limits and immediate vicinity.]

REV. LEWIS L. RECORD.
GRADUATE OF BOWDOIN COLLEGE, TEACHER AND ARMY CHAPLAIN

(Continued from Last Week.)

Thomas Record was a farmer whose lands lay in the valley not far from the Androscoggin river, in that part of Minot, which, in the year of 1842, became the town of Auburn, this state. His wife's maiden name was Lydia Chandler and she was of the same town.

Rev. Lewis Leonard Record, eldest son of the preceeding, was born there, Sept. 1, 1816. His early educational advantages were limited. At the age of ten he became the happy possessor of a copy of Murray's grammar; to him it then seemed a treasure house of wisdom and he never ceased to care for the ancient looking volume. By persevering labor he fitted for college and, as have so many other earnest lovers of knowledge before and since, earned his way through, and was graduated from Bowdoin in 1845. He married the same year, and located at once in Lowell, Mass., where he taught about three years. In 1848 he became principal of Westbrook seminary. In the month of September of the same year his wife died at her paternal home occupied by her sister Mrs. Thomas G. Record, where she was spending a few months.

In 1850 Mr. Record was ordained at Gray a minister of the gospel in the Universalist church. In 1851 he went to Houlton as principal of the academy there and pastor of the Universalist church.

In 1852 he married Miss Irene Stevens, by whom he had two sons. Later he held pastorates in Mass., for several years, but in 1862 his health being impaired he removed to Westbrook, now Deering, to the paternal home of his wife. During his residence in Massachusetts, he had been very active in the anti-slavery movement, a fearless abolitionist. In '64 Gov. Andrews recognized his services by commissioning him Chaplain of the 23rd Massachusetts Volunteers. The regiment was then in the field in Virginia and in the Virginia campaign of '64 it was in the forefront of the almost uninterrupted fighting which followed the landing at Bermuda Hundred. It gained the foremost ground held by the 18th corps at Cold Harbor and bore its full share of the dangers and privations of the early days of Petersburg. Mr. Record the chaplain, shared the dangers and privations of the rank and file. He did perilous duty in removing the wounded from the field. At Newberne, N. C., he was detailed to hold service for the victims of yellow fever. As the result he was forced to yield to the dread sickness, lying unconscious for days, without attendance save the hurried calls of the surgeon. He never fully recovered from this sickness and returned from the army in May '65 broken in health. When sufficiently recovered he engaged in secular business, was tax collector for Westbrook in '68 and '69, preaching during the summer season in Harpswell, Wells, Raymond, Biddeford and other neighboring towns. He took an active interest in all questions of morality and with Mr. McCollister, Principal of the Seminary and others helped to close the sale of liquor at Morrills Corner. In 1870 Counter to the advice of his physician, he removed to Marlboro, N. H., to take the pastorate of the Universalist Church there. "He labored earnestly and successfully until July 1871 when he was compelled to desist from labor, and from that date he steadily declined until his death."

"Mr. Record was scholarly in his tastes and fond of research. He was a successful teacher. He was clear strong, persuasive as a preacher. He was highly respected as a pastor."

FAMILY RECORD.

Lewis Leonard Record, born at Minot, Sept. 1, 1816, married first Sept. 4, 1845, Cynthia, sixth child of David Munroe and Ruth Niles his wife, of Minot, now Auburn. She died Sept. 24, 1848, and was buried in the cemetery there at the foot of the hill near lake Auburn within view of the dwelling in which she was born and died.

Mr. Record died in the ministry at Marlboro, N. H. for date of which event, see copy of memorial stone following:

CHILDREN:

1. Cynthia Munroe, born Sept. 15 1848. Mr. Record married second, June 3, 1852, Irene, fourth child of William and Sally (Bailey) Stevens, born Oct. 6, 1819, at Stevens Plains, Westbrook, now Deering, as before stated.
2. Lewis Miner.
3. Willie.

Mrs. Record with her husband's daughter, Cynthia M., reside beneath the roof of the ancient Stevens mansion house.

Upon the easterly side of Pine Grove cemetery, located in the rear of Westbrook seminary stand three memorial stones inscribed as follows:
Lewis Miner, son of L. L. and I. S. Record, born Nov. 20, 1855, died July 17, 1875.
Willie, son of L. L. and I. S. Record, born Jan. 24, 1861, died Oct. 5, 1861.

REV.
L. L. RECORD
Born
Sept. 1, 1816
Died
Dec. 7, 1871.
Death is the sublimity of life.

The reverse side is inscribed as follows:

CHAPLAIN OF 23d REGIMENT
MASSACHUSETTS VOLUNTEERS.

Note—The record of Elisha North will appear next to be followed by that of his brother Elijah.

In the third paragraph of my article of last week, to be correct, there should be a period mark after "daughter," and "of" struck out. Then at the close of the notice of the third child of George Mead Stevens, the word "grand" should be inserted in the last line.

THE DEERING NEWS.

Saturday, March 6, 1897.

GRANDPA'S SCRAP BOOK

[Under this head historical and genealogical memoranda will be furnished the readers of the News that appears worthy of preservation, particularly of remote periods in our history within the city limits and immediate vicinity.]

NORTH.

A FAMILY NAME ONCE FAMILIAR IN TOWN BUT NOW EXTINCT.

Elisha North, whose younger brother Elijah resided the last part of his life on the Windham road near Morrill's Corner in the house now standing, was born at Berlin, Conn., in the year 1785. What induced him to come hither and the year in which he came I cannot now state.

He united in marriage with Nabby, ninth and youngest child of Capt. Isaac Sawyer Stevens and Sarah Brackett, his wife. (For Capt. Steven's family see NEWS of Nov. 17, 1894.)

His mother's name was Lois, but her full maiden name I do not know, who resided with her son, was a member of the old Congregational church society and died here.

He, as well as his brother Elijah, was a tinplate maker and he seems to have commenced business on Stevens Plains avenue, and resided there just southerly of the Evergreen cemetery entrance in what was later known as the Brisco house, or it may be that this house grew out of the "one half of a house and lot" purchased by North for $150 in 1807. Oct. 1 of that year, however, the two brothers purchased for a consideration of $350 nine acres of land on the westerly side of Stevens Plains avenue at Higgin's Corner, and the same year purchased fifteen acres adjoining for a consideration of $700, so that, in 1815, he was taxed as follows:

1 House,	$500
1 Barn,	50
1 Shop,	100
1 Wood house,	15
7 Acres of tillage at $19 pr. acre.	
18 Acres pasturing at $7 pr. acre.	
2 Cows,	28
2 Horses,	80
Stock in trade,	100

His brother Elijah does not appear on record as a taxpayer at this date.

A year later he purchased a small lot at Brighton Corner and moved his shop to it and opened a store where he kept for sale tin ware, combs, etc., which place he sold to Benjamin G. Camel, from which the old Brighton Corner team tavern grew that was destroyed some years since by fire.

The house here noticed as being taxed on a valuation of $500 was a square, two story, well built structure, which became an inn when the Presumpscot Trotting Park Association was incorporated, and which was destroyed by fire about midnight on April 8, 1878, when occupied by Dr. Geo. H. Bailey, who now resides at Morrill's Corner, Mr. Bailey losing his entire personal effects, embracing valuable paintings of his own making. About two years after the park was opened to the public, the cellar hole of the house now to be seen surrounded by the dilapidated buildings and fences erected at the time of the construction of the race course, which was changed in name from Presumpscot to that of Woodfords, but the project was a failure from the start.

Mr. North was a stirring man and fortune smiled on him as the tax record shows. He not only manufactured tin ware and kept a shop at Brighton Corner but he sent into the country a half score of peddle carts that brought back various kinds of country produce obtained in exchange for the products of his own manufactory, but at this late day, in the absence of manuscript records, I cannot enter into details without the aid of imagination which I do not care to employ. After him in the possession of his homestead came his son Samuel, and among my earliest recollections is the fact that I attended a cattle show held on the premises.

His wife died in the prime of womanhood while he was in business upon the summit of prosperity, and he married second Nancy Bradbury of Fryburg.

In the old cemetery, located on the westerly side of Windham road, a mile northwesterly of Morrill's Corner, may be seen a memorial stone inscribed as follows:

In Memory of
ABIGAIL,
wife of
ELISHA NORTH,
who died
Jan. 30, 1825, Æt. 34.

How sweet she shone in social life,
As daughter, mother, friend and wife,
Now done with all below the sun,
She shines before the brighter throne;
Her race was swift, her rest is sweet,
Her views divine, her bliss complete.

TO BE CONTINUED.

THE DEERING NEWS.

Saturday, March 13, 1897.

GRANDPA'S SCRAP BOOK

[Under this head historical and genealogical memoranda will be furnished the readers of the News that appears worthy of preservation, particularly of remote periods in our history within the city limits and immediate vicinity.]

NORTH.

A FAMILY NAME ONCE FAMILIAR IN TOWN BUT NOW EXTINCT.

Continued from Last Week.

The autumnal day was drawing to a close—one of the Indian summerlike days—when I walked up Spring street, leisurely, a dozen years ago. The large doors of the ancient appearing barn, located on the northerly side of the public way, opposite High street, were wide open, and immediately in front of the opened doors was an ancient appearing farm wagon by the side of which stood the venerable appearing John Newman, without a coat, and shirt sleeves rolled up—a custom of his he always followed. His eyes were fixed upon the ground and a churchyard obelisk was never more motionless.

"What are you about, Mr. Newman?" I asked.

"I was thinking when I was a boy and these forward wheels were new," he rejoined.

Then he gave me the history of both pair. "The hind ones were old Sile Broads," he said, and "the forward, Mrs. North's. Both pair I had cut down to the size you observe." "You know," he continued. "Old Sile kept the Broad tavern over beyond Stroudwater and these wheels were his chaise wheels. I purchased them of Jimmy Creddiford, the tin-peddler. It was my association with the forward wheels I was thinking about when you appeared. You see, when I was a boy I lived with Elisha North, his wife was a Stevens, sister to Billy, and she was a smart, prudent, and I tell you, a good woman as I ever saw. I was born in the next house northerly of the North house, in the one story dwelling now standing, which my father built, and went over to Norths to learn the tinman's trade. It was the custom then for the young people to take a day and go over to the beach. Well, a party had made arrrangements for such a time, and I went to Portland for a team, but everything had been engaged, and I returned with a sad heart. Mrs. North observed my mind was troubled and inquired as to the cause, I said, 'nothin', but she replied: 'I know better.' Soon after that, she said, 'John are you going to the ride with the others?' I replied: 'Guess not.' Then, said she, why not?' 'The teams are all engaged in Portland,' said I, 'and none to be had.' 'I know of one that is not, and that one is mine which you can have for nothing.'

"You see," continued Mr. Newman, "Mrs. North was a very prudent woman, and withall, a good woman, and by saving little things, such as dirty wool scraps, iron, and other little things that usually go to waste, she had got enough money together to buy hers. If a chaise which had never been used, and Elisha had given her a house, so she had a nice team of her own, the use of which I accepted for the occasion, and I'll assure you, I had the best turnout of the party, and guess I felt bigger than any other one in it; any way it was a greater day to me than any one since."

Who was the young woman who accompanied Mr. Newman? The writer does not know. Does any one?

Mr. Newman was born Oct. 22, 1803, and died May 26, 1885.

Mercy Hamilton was born in Waterboro, this state. She came to Portland and worked in a spinning and weaving establishment. When Mr. North concluded to engage in the business, and the one-story low-posted building situated on Stevens Plains avenue, westerly side, and a few rods northealy of Higgins Corner, now the dwellinghouse of Wm. R. Foss, being fitted for the purpose, Miss Hamilton was engaged to take charge and teach the operatives. It was while there engaged she made the acquaintance of young Mr. Newman and became his wife, and in the year 1837, or thereabouts, went into the house connected with the barn before noticed, to live, which he then purchased, where she has since resided, and on June 7, of this year if she lives thus long, will have reached the ninety-first mile-post in life's journey. At this date, I am informed, she appears much younger than she really is; and residing in the vicinity are representatives of four generations of hers.

"They sigh and whisper she is very fair,
And bid her cease from every pining care."

TO BE CONTINUED.

THE DEERING NEWS.

Saturday, March 20, 1897.

GRANDPA'S SCRAP BOOK

[Under this head historical and genealogical memoranda will be furnished the readers of the News that appears worthy of preservation, particularly of remote periods in our history within the city limits and immediate vicinity.]

NORTH.

A FAMILY NAME ONCE FAMILIAR IN TOWN BUT NOW EXTINCT.

Continued from Last Week.

Elisha North married as has been stated, Nov. 8, 1807, Nabby, the 9th and youngest child of Capt. Isaac Sawyer Stevens of Stevens Plains, who died at the time shown in this connection, two weeks since. He married second, Nov. 8, 1825, Nancy Bradbury of Fryeburg to which place she removed after the death of Mr. North and died there. At the time of the death of Mr. North's wife Nabby, Miss Bradbury was a school teacher residing with the family. He died March 31st, 1845. His children were as follows:

1, Rosilla an adopted daughter; 2, Samuel; 3, Josiah Stevens. Then by 2nd wife: 4, Abbie S.; 5, Edward.

1 Rosilla, adopted when an infant, married a man by the name of Albion Page and resided in Fryeburg. They have but one surviving descendant, who is a practicing physician at Bridgewater, Mass.
2 Samuel, born Feb. 11, 1817, married 1st., June 27, 1844, Mary A., daughter of Joseph Winslow of Windham; 2nd, Abbie Larry of same town and sister to Mrs. P. C. Dole, editor of the Narragansett Sun, printed at the office of the News. He was first, of the firm of Messrs. North and Winslow, his brother in-law who kept a stove and tin shop at Saccarappa, then Webb and North of same place; Webb removing to Portland and he continuing the business with another partner. He served as captain of the Westbrook Light Infantry made up mostly of residents of Stevens Plains. In 1855 he was chairman of the board of selectmen. He died suddenly at Saccarappa.

In the old Windham road cemetery are memorial stones inscribed as follows:

MARY A. W.
wife of
SAMUEL NORTH,
Died Feb. 4, 1861 aged 39 years.
"With God and His Angels."

Another as follows:
"GONE HOME."
SAMUEL NORTH,
died
Oct. 6, 1862 aged 45 years.
"The Good and the True God will Bless."

And two others for the children of Samuel and Mary A. W., his wife.

HARRIET W.,
died
Sept. 19, 1848, aged 1 year, 5 days.
"Gone but not lost."

MARY EMMA,
died
Nov. 4, 1863, aged 6 years, 8 months

Samuel North had by second wife one child now Mrs. Fannie Baston of North Yarmouth.

3 Josiah Stevens North, born Jan. 22, 1818, married Susan B., youngest daughter of Capt. Benjamin Herrick of North Yarmouth. While a resident of Westbrook, now Deering, he drove a wholesale delivery comb wagon for Dea. E. D. Woodford, then for the Thorn Brothers who manufactured combs by water power at Capisic; then he engaged in the tin ware and stove trade with a Mr. Pratt at Yarmouth, finally engaged in agriculture and now resides in Durham minus a leg, which was amputated a couple years since.

CHILDREN.

I Charles A., b. March 28, 1846. He served in the War of the Rebellion as Commissary Serg't, was wounded twice. Enlisted second with the D. C. Cavalry, was transferred to the 1st Maine. He m. Amanda Blanchard of No. Yarmouth Nov. 14, 1867, resides at Malden, Mass. Contractor and builder. Children: Gertrude died young; Mabel b. Dec. 30, 1869; d. Nov. 1894. Harry C., b. Sep. 17, 1872.
II Abbie S., b. May 28, 1848, resides at Durham. She m. Wm. H. Parker, a farmer who was drowned May 17, 1881. Children: Edgar B., b. Oct. 28, 1879; Emma H.; Grace; Susie Louise; Willie Stevens; Hattie May, b. May 18, 1887.
III Emily Herrick, b. Oct. 22, 1849, was a school teacher at Auburn; died Dec. 7, 1875.
IV Sarah Louise, b. Oct. 4, 1851; m. John H. Chase Apr. 27, 1873, and resided in Gray where she died, July 8, ——, aged 37 years and 9 months. *Mr. Chase is now engaged in the hardware trade at Lewiston, and has one child living, Ethel May, b. March 21, 1875.
V Frank W. ——, m. first Ada Babcock of Lewiston, Dec. 25, 1878. Children: Charles D.; Edna May; Bernice Washington and Dora Ada. He m. 2nd Mrs. Mary Nash of Lewiston. Is a farmer and resides in Lewiston.
VI Emma S., b. June 8, 1859; m. Jan. 2, 1881, Martin T. Hendrick, carpenter and farmer of Turner. Children: Frank S. and Elmer T.
VII Annie who died in infancy.

4 Abbie S., daughter by second wife, b. in Westbrook Jan. 12, 1829, m. May 1, 1851 Dea. Nathaniel Brown, an insurance agent of Portland. No issue. She at last accounts resided in No. Bridgewater Mass., with a Doctor Shirley.
5 Edward, born Oct. 4, 1830; died Feb. 12, 1847.

Of Mr. North's religious views or political sentiments I have no knowledge. Jan. 6, 1828 he purchased a pew in Elder Samuel Rand's meeting house, Casco street, Portland, for which he paid $101. The society was called "Christian Connection," and one of the wives was a member.

Under date of Nov. 12, 1837, Rev Caleb says in his journal:

Sabbath. A very rainy day, but very few people at meeting; only one female in the a. m., Mrs. Nancy North.

*The following appeared in a Portland paper, relative to Sarah Louise (North. Chase, above noticed, the name of paper or date I do not know:

GRAY.

This week it becomes our painful duty to announce the death of a loved neighbor and friend, Mrs. Sarah Louise Chase, wife of John H. Chase, aged 37 years, 9 months. She attended the W. S. R. C. Convention at Rockland two weeks ago, and while there contracted a severe cold. On the last day of June she took her bed, from which she never rose again, leaving this weary world for the heavenly home, Sunday evening, July 8th. Our dear sister was a lady of many Christian virtues, and held in great esteem by all who knew her. Loving hands and hearts performed the last sad offices, and Mrs. Chase died as she lived, in earnest, humble Christian. The obsequies were held on Wednesday morning at ten o'clock. The floral offerings were beautiful, including a handsome lyre from G. F. Shepley Relief Corps of which she was Vice President, and a pillow from Pythian Relief in which she held the office of secretary. A loving husband and daughter, father and mother, brothers and sisters are left to mourn the loss of one so dear to them. To these we offer our heartfelt sympathy in their bereavement.

TO BE CONTINUED.

THE DEERING NEWS.

Saturday, March 27, 1897.

GRANDPA'S SCRAP BOOK

[Under this head historical and genealogical memoranda will be furnished the readers of the News that appears worthy of preservation, particularly of remote periods in our history within the city limits and immediate vicinity.]

NORTH.

A FAMILY NAME ONCE FAMILIAR IN TOWN BUT NOW EXTINCT.

Continued from Last Week.

Elijah North was not younger than his brother Elisha as stated in the News of March 6th, but two years or there about, his senior. He was born at Berlin, state of Connecticut, Dec. 14, 1781, and united in marriage May 2, 1805 with Martha Woodford, a sister to Dea. Ebeneza D. Woodford and Josiah Woodford of Woodford's Corner, and Chauncy Woodford of Morrill's Corner, the family records of all of whom have appeared in the News. They were married by Rev. Caleb Bradley who says Oliver Buckly and Sally Reed had the ceremony of marriage performed at the same time.

There is a tradition that Elijah and his wife were cousins, but I cannot verify it at this time. She was a member of the First Congregational church of Westbrook, now Deering. After a stay of some ten or twelve years here in company with his brother Elisha in business, he removed to Connecticut but came back, and on the 21st day of Oct. 1829, for a consideration of $185 purchased a half acre lot on the easterly side of the Windham road of Benj. Bailey, and erected the one story dwelling as now seen, which is the third house north westerly from the three story brick house on the corner, known as the Keeley Cure, originally built for a public house. On page 42 of the county atlas the building is marked James Hibbs, the present owner, a gentleman of easy manners, born in England, at present a tin-ware peddler.

The two story building next northerly, now used as a dwelling, was built by Mr. North as a work shop, he being a tinman. At one time it was used for dormitory purposes by students of the Westbrook Seminary when the weather beaten North sign board was removed from its place of many years of rest and placed upon the belfry of the seminary school building, but that was at a time when the art of belles-letters was not taught as now at the ancient institution, hence the act was more excusable.

In the old Windham road cemetery there may be seen a memorial stone that is inscribed as follows:

In
MEMORY
of
MRS. MARTHA NORTH
who died
Oct. 22, 1834, Æt. 51.

Still, still is the pulse and departed the breath.
And the form that is loving is shrouded in death,
Thou sleepest dear Mother, beneath the green sod
But thy spirit we trust has ascended to God.

This verse is not a transcript from the stone but from a memorial piece in possession of a descendant of the name.

Mr. North married the following year Sophia Warren of Gorham, this state, but before entering the journey of connubial life, she, Nov. 17, 1835, invested $500 in the North domicile and took one of the reins of domestic affairs, if not the whip into her own hands.

I remember them at what is now called the Bradley meeting house, and they were indeed characters. He, with his high coat collar and hat of many summers, she, with her heavy iron bowed spectacles, not caring how many were observing, never failed to look over the object of her affections (no children being born to them) for specks of lint upon his garments and when found, let the occasion and time be what it might were always removed.

Upon the 21st day of Jan. 1890, there appeared in the Portland Argus an article headed, "Records and Recollections of Persons and Events," filling a space of one and a fourth columns, from which I make the following extract:

It should here be stated that the parish and the church connected therewith are two distinct organizations in the denomination of professing Christians bearing the name of Congregationalists. The church can be very good and the parish not. The parish enjoys the preachers, the church listens; if it is not satisfied it can leave. The parish holds the reins and the whip. The First Parish of Portland, of which the First of Deering is a branch, was once Congregational; it is now Unitarian because the last outcome bored the first and took matters into their own hands.

In constructing the seats of the new school house, although the "educated" were consulted far and wide, the requirements of the prayer meeting was kept in view, as well as the comfort of the scholars, and the seats were made "large and airy," which have, since been removed.

The spiritual adviser of the parish in 1851 was Rev. Donatus Merrill, who now has a sister residing on Pleasant street, Deering, Mrs. Furbish. He was a young man, fresh from the Bangor Theological School, very circumspect in all his ways, but lacked in physical vigor, and after his experiences in the First Parish of what is now Deering—being Westbrook at the time—he did not live long. He was succeeded by Rev. Chas. Lord. Whence he came or whither he went I am unable to state correctly. He possessed a large head, a large heart, wore spectacles with massive gold bows, was fond of good victuals, and could see God in everything. Parson Bradley, who was then full of vigor, though an old man, was constantly praying for "a rattling of the dry bones of the church." Parson Lord desired the same, but proposed a different course of procedure from that long in vogue. He said the house of God ought to be made attractive in more ways than one. He obtained the bell, he obtained an organ, he planted trees by the roadway, and he boarded at a public resort. Then it was that the Morrill House was better patronized on Sunday than the meeting house. Brother North and his wife, both tall, thin in flesh and old fashioned in dress, but both exceedingly desirous of doing right, lived close to the great Morrill House where Parson Lord boarded; and Brother North had a frisky mare, that, when hitched to a sleigh and hearing the sound of bells behind, was full of speed and frolic. His sleigh was one of the narrow, tall back kind, just wide enough for two persons. He invited the parson to ride from the meeting house to his boarding house. The two had fairly got seated when along came sleigh loads of "busters" from the Brewer House, traveling at a high rate speed, and Brother North's mare started, and Sister North jumped into the bottom of the sleigh with feet hanging out at the side and away they sped over the Plains road with the busters close behind crying out for Brother North to "get out of the way." It is needness to say that the town had something to talk about for several days thereafter.

From the Morrill House Parson Lord moved to the Miss Jones' boarding house, corner of Park and Congress streets, Portland. In those times two sermons per day were demanded and Parson Lord was seen plodding the way on Sunday morning from Miss Jones' boarding house with a basket of good things hanging on his arm for his stomach, while in his pocket was a prepared discourse for the souls of others, spread out on paper in a scholarly manner. He lived in advance of the age; was born too early in the history of the world; his kind are more numerous now; then the Congregational Club was not thought of; a year's sojourn and he was dismissed. The bell he left; it hangs in the belfry; its peals and echoes are now heard each Sunday. One of the trees he planted stands to-day, lofty and firmly rooted. His name, strange to relate, does not appear on the parish book—heretofore written in sand but now rescued.

In 1855 it was voted "that we reciprocate the action of the church in desiring the Rev. John B. Wheelwright to become our pastor and cordially participate in the invitation to him;" and he accordingly became the spiritual adviser of the church and parish, and labored five years, when he went to Bethel.

CONTINUED:

To Mr. North and first wife were born eight children: 1—Mariah H.; 2—Lois; 3—Sophia; 4—Rhoda; 5—Silas, died; 6—Silas; 7—Emily; 8 and last, Orin.

I—Mariah, born Jan. 12, 1806, married Johua S. Knight, intention recorded Sep. 21, 1828. After working awhile here he engaged in stove and tinware business in Chelsea, Mass., where both and children died.

II—Lois, born Sep. 14, 1807, m October 10, 1861, John Gardner of Portland. She died at Deering Center Oct. 1, 1882.

III—Sophia, born March 9, 1808, died June 1, 1874, unmarried at Deering Center. She was a member of the 1st Congregational church.

IV—Rhoda, born Apr. 14, 1811, m. July 3, 1833, Eben Barton Sawyer, son of Isaac Sawyer, who resided on the westerly side of Stevens Plains avenue, a little northerly of Central avenue, in Isaac's time called the Blake road. The exact time Isaac located there I cannot now state. He was a son of Zachariah Sawyer who resided easterly of Lunt's Corner, and was a cousin to Hiram Sawyer of Morrill's Corner, whose family record appeared in the News of Dec. 22, 1894. There were six children in the family: Isaac, Mark, Ruth, Eben B., Alfred, and Charles S. March 20, 1837, Isaac conveyed the homestead with one acre and 135 square rods of land to his son Ebeneza B., and in 1845, Eben B. (he appears by two names) conveyed a fourth acre to his brother Charles S, who built the one story house as now seen opposite the head of Hardey Avenue. The original Isaac Sawyer house now stands on Stevens Plains avenue a little southerly of the Chas. S. house, the entrance to the Goddard green house passing between the two.

Ruth's intention of marriage with Moses Meador of Conway, N. H., was recorded Jan. 22, 1832, but in 1836 she appears as a widow, but married again.

Chas. S., married Mary Abbie Witham of Danville, and she died Aug. 15, 1849, when he married second her sister, Julia A. who died last fall—sisters to the wife of Mr. Artemas L. Richardson of Deering Center.

Eben B. Sawyer was born 1808. He was a tinsmith, and resided in the Isaac Sawyer house. She d. there June 3, 1879; he Apr. 7, 1884, aged 76 years, 4 months. They had one child that survived, named Ellen E., born Apr. 30, 1834, who m. Stephen E. Ilsley, a painter, son of Joseph Ilsley who lived on Forest avenue, near Oak street, and succeeded Rhoda and Eben in possession of the homestead; she d. Nov. 24, 1888. They had one child, Henry W. Ilsley b. Dec. 26, 1855, who resides at Deering Center.

V—Silas, b. Nov. 3, 1813, died during a journey from Connecticut.

VI—Silas 2nd, b. July 14, 1815, m. Eliza E. Sampson of Bowdoinham where he engaged in the stove and tinware trade. They had two daughters; the first died young; the 2nd, born. Nov. 14, 1842, named Maria A., died July 31, 1861. Mrs. North died in Nov. 1882; he Apr. 12, 1896.

VII—Emily, b. Berlin, Ct., May 24, 1824, m. in Gardiner, Oct. 25, 1840, Isaac D. Merrill, b. at Paris, this state, Jan. 9, 1819. He was a plumber in Portland, where he died July 17, 1885. His widow resides there.

CHILDREN:

1—Isaac D., b. Boston, Mass., Feb. 22, 1843.
2—Emily, b. Boston, Aug. 23, 1845.
3—Sophia N., b. Portland, Oct. 19, 1847, died Aug. 14, 1848.
4—John Edward, b. Portland, July 11, 1850.
5—Isaac D. jr., b. Portland, Jan. 4, 1855.

VIII—Orin B., b. Feb. 8, 1819, married Eunice Snow of Bowdoinham, June 7, 1840 Was a merchant in Boston, Mass.; died there, Sep. 7, 1883.

CHILDREN:

1—Martha J., b. Oct. 14, 1841, m. June 17, 1872, Dr. J. V. Smith, (deceased) After being burnt out at Bowdoinham they removed to Melrose Mass.
2—John H., b. Apr. 2, 1843, m. June 20, 1866, Annie C. Drew, a merchant residing in Boston.
3—Orin, b. Feb. 23, 1846, d. Dec. 11, same year.
4— { Frederick O.. }
5— { Frank A., } Twins.
born July 5, 1852. Frank died at the age of 11 years; Frederick m. Oct. 25, 1876, Grace Gorden Young. He is agent for the John L. Stoddard lectures and resides in Boston.

There was a Lois North here who married Oct. 12, 1828, a Capt. Clement J. Dyer of Cape Elizabeth, but of these I have no knowledge.

The end of the North record.

Saturday, April 3, 1897.

GRANDPA'S SCRAP BOOK

[Under this head historical and genealogical memoranda will be furnished the readers of the News that appears worthy of preservation, particularly of remote periods in our history within the city limits and immediate vicinity.]

NORTH.

A FEW MORE NOTICES RELATIVE TO THE OLD NAME.

THE FAMILY OF WHICH REV. CALEB BRADLEY WAS A MEMBER.

At the close of my last article these words appear: "The end of the North record." Since then I find I made certain omissions which I now present as follows:

FROM REV. CALEB BRADLEY'S JOURNAL.

Dec. 16, 1829. Attended the funeral of Mrs. North, aged 88 years. (Rev.) Mr. Rand (probably Rev. Samuel Rand of Portland) and (Rev.) Mr. Jewett (of the 1st Congregational church) present. Mr. Rand officiated. I took tea at the house of mourning. One generation passeth away and another cometh. How often we are addressed by this admonitory language: Be ye also ready; watch therefore for time is short. O Lord, so teach me to number my days that I may apply my heart unto wisdom.

Feb. 15, 1837. Went to Falmouth. Called on Rev. Mr. McGregor and Rev. Mr. Miltimore—neither at home. Took coffee at Mr. Lunt's (Lunt's Corner) Evening at Woodfords. Four persons presented themselves for examination for admission to the church—namely: Mrs. North, Charlotte Stevens, Edward Newman and Josiah S. North.

Jan 11, 1841. Walked over to Back Cove, via Mr. (Elisha) North's, at whose house I called; he is a poor, asthmatical invalid.

April 30, 1841. A church conference was appointed to be observed this day, and to commence at 10 o'clock a. m. at Frederick Sawyer's. (He resided in the house that stood where Capt. Benj. H. Lewis now lives, Spring street.) I was on the spot a half hour before the time, and 10½ o'clock Samuel North made his appearance and before 11 Addison Woodford and the two Mrs. Sawyers living in the house.

FROM THE PARISH RECORDS.

Nov. 20, 1830. Capt. Samuel North was chosen clerk of the First Congregational Parish. In 1841 his name appears as one of the parish committee. Oct. 31, 1842 it was voted to adjourn the meeting to Nov. 13, 1842 at which time Mr. North was serving as clerk and committee man, but no record meetings were holden till 1850, when a new parish order of things was presented.

THE BRIGHTON HOUSE.

The Brighton house that stood in the northwesterly corner where Stevens' Plains avenue crosses the old Brighton or Congin road which was burned some years since is remembered by very many during the time it was used as a public resort. In saying that it was first placed on the spot by Elisha North some are of the opinion I am in fault, but here are some facts:

July 16, 1818, for a consideration of $600 Elisha North sold the "80 square rods of land" to Benj. G. Campbill, the plane workman, and "buildings thereon."

Sept. 2, 1836 for $300 Campbell of Bangor and Charity, his wife, conveyed the premises to Gerry Cook of Westbrook.

In 1855 for $2,500 Betsey Walker conveyed to William Eldridge.

Before Eldridge's day one Levi Burnham kept a team tavern there.

The one-story house to which allusion has been made as the spinning and weaving establishment was sold for $300 in 1845 by Samuel North to his brother Josiah S. North, who, in 1850, for $610 sold it to Levi Burnham, above noticed.

The intention of marriage was made public May 9, 1830, between Gerry Cook of Westbrook and Mary Jane Hallsbury of Portland, and they went to live in what was afterwards known as the "Cattle Market" and later the "Brighton House" hotel. Of this place and Gerry Cook, who has a daughter living in the Western country, I hope to record more very soon. Mr. Cook was a very stirring man.

THE MASSACHUSETTS BRADLEY FAMILY.

Extract from the Rev. Caleb Bradley's journal:

June 16, 1838,—As I have not much matter on hand will record in this place the births in my father's family as taken from the old Bible by my brother Joseph and given me when last at Dracutt, Mass.

1—Amos, born May 30, 1758.
2—Joshua, b. Oct. 2, 1762.
3—Elizabeth, b. Feb. 25, 1766.
4—Hannah, b. March 1, 1768.
5—Joseph, b. Dec 22, 1769.
6—(Rev.) Caleb, b. March 12, 1772.
7—Martha, b. Jan. 13, 1774.
8—Ruth, b. May 21, 1775.
9—Nehemiah, b. Sept. 20, 1776.
10—Sarah, b. Nov. 21, 1777.
11—Rhoda, b. Oct. 18, 1779.

These are the names and dates of birth of the household of my father, four of whom have been called home to their Heavenly father.

April 5, 1838—This afternoon I was called by the notice of the death of my sister, Mrs. Kimball to be also ready, watching and waiting for the coming of the Son of Man. This sister was my eldest of the six to grow up. Her name was Betsey or Elizabeth, married to a Mr. Kimball and lived in Bradford, Mass., from the time of her marriage till her death, aged 72 years. Three sisters out of the six are sleeping in death.

There were five brothers; the two eldest have deceased—Amos and Joshua, three are living—Joseph, Caleb and Nehemiah. Joseph and Nehemiah in their native town of Dracutt; and Caleb in Westbrook, (now Deering) Sister Hannah Hovey is in Boston, Martha is in Cambridgeport, whose name is likewise Hovey, and Sarah Hildreth in Dayton, Ohio.

These are the children of Deacon Amos Bradley who died in the 75th year of his age. He was an officer in the Congregational church a long time and died heaving a glorious hope of immortality beyond the grave. These children of Amos Bradley were great grandchildren of Hannah Duston whose name is well known in history, and Miss Bradley, concerning whom it is recorded having scalded to death with boiling soap in Haverhill, Mass., two Indians, she being taken by the survivors and carried to Canada, who after having suffered much on her journey and while among the savages was restored to her family.

Sept. 1, 1841.—Took breakfast this morning at Dr. Pelig Bradley's then went over to Lowell, Mass., and took the stage at 9 o'clock at the old stand in Dracutt for Haverhill, arriving at Enoch Bradley's at 12 m. and took dinner and here spent the remainder of the day.

This Enoch Bradley is a kind of a cousin, his father and my father were half brothers and grand children of the Mrs. Bradley who scalded the Indians in Haverhill one hundred years since. This is well known to all who are acquainted with the history of New England.

I hardly think the descendants of this woman would do much toward Indians in these days. They have not been brought up this way. This Enoch Bradley is the son of Enos who has been dead some years. His wife is a daughter of the late Dr. Hildreth, once a physician in Methuen. He has rather a smart family of girls and boys who are able to cut their own fodder. He has a good farm and knows how to take care of it; a close calculator; snug and prudent and likes to see everybody else so; he has been a very great worker and his wife also. He has a good property and says he has no anxiety for more. He is one of those kind of men who wants no more cats than will catch mice.

We spent the evening in religious conversation.

APRIL 10, 1897.

SCRAP BOOK

[Historical and genealogical furnished the readers of the ... worthy of preservation, particular periods in our history within and immediate vicinity.]

ECCLESIASTICAL.

E THE THIRD, NOW FIRST CONGREGATIONAL PARISH OF FALMOUTH.

A FEW GLIMPSES OF THE PAST COMPILED FROM ORIGINAL RECORDS.

When the Rev. Caleb Bradley in 1799 came to Falmouth, and on the 15th day of March in that year "took lodgings," as he says, with Maj. Lewis who resided in the house at Stroudwater, a room of which is now used for the post office, he kept a journal on paper the size of one's vest pocket. After he became the settled pastor of the parish he enlarged it to the size of fools cap paper, but at the end of eight years, or thereabouts, he discontinued; but on the 1st day of Jan. 1829, he recommenced in book form filling some eighteen bound volumes and continued the work till the time of his death, June 2d, 1861, being then 89 years old.

Much of his labor on this line was a total waste, consisting largely of self-exhortation, condemnation, and reports of sermons he delivered, and those to which he listened.

Rev. William Miltimore became the pastor of the Third Parish, now the First of Falmouth, in 1802, and was continued till 1833. Between him and the Rev. Mr. Bradley there was a warm intimacy. Mr. Miltimore resided in the second dwelling easterly of the meeting house on the northerly side of the highway whose residence is at this time the parsonage of the First Congregational church and parish. The site is marked on a plan of the highway from Presumpscot Falls to Yarmouth made in 1819. And the site of other residences are marked. Between the Miltimore house and the meeting house is a site marked "Merrill." The site where the long, ancient appearing barn is now seen and owned by Mr. Frank Maston, next westerly of the burying ground both of which are westerly of the meeting house and on the opposite side of the highway, is marked "McGregor"—Rev. David Mc Gregor, who, in 1808, was a resident of Bradford, N. H., and on the 20th day of January of that year was united in marriage with Miss Rebecca Merrill of Falmouth, purchasing in 1809, of Adams Merrill, 160 acres of the old James Merrill farm, paying for the same $10,000, or this is the record price.

It was in 1811 that Rev. Mr. Miltimore made his first purchase of land of Reuben and Samuel Merrill—one acre and ninety-three square rods, for a consideration of $47, "being the same whereon William Miltimore's dwelling house now stands." In 1839, for a consideration of $550, Mr. Miltimore of Litchfield, N. H., conveyed the premises to one John Buckman and "one other lot adjoining, containing a half acre, with buildings on both lots."

In 1842 for $100 Mr. Miltimore and Mary O. Miltimore conveyed the same premises to Giles Merrill of Falmouth.

Mr. Miltimore was evidently a man of ability. The Bibliography of Maine, by Josiah Williamson, 1896, says: "He was born 1768, died 1848. He preached a discourse Feb. 22, 1811, in the meeting house erected by seamen near the water, which was printed. (Where was this meetinghouse located?)

A sermon preached by him March 18, 1812, at the installation of the Rev. Elijah Kellogg, chapel Congregational church, Portland, which was printed.

A sermon preached Nov. 6, 1814, on the death of his son, which was also printed.

A sermon on the occasion of the death of Mrs. Clarisa Webber, who died March 20, 1815, in the 31st year of her age and printed at the request of her husband, Capt. Aaron Webber."

The region of Presumpscot Falls and the site of meeting house to which I have alluded is a rich field for the trained historical gleaner. A record of the "Merrill Family" alone, a record unsurpassed in more excellence by few, if any, of other names would be sufficient to fill a good sized volume.

In referring to a brother clergyman Rev. Mr. Bradley never uses the title "Reverend" and "Brother" but a few times. Words and names enclosed by brackets I have added to the original.

1829.

June 14. I preached for Bro. Miltimore and helped organize a Bible class. Attended a funeral.

October 25, Sabbath. Spent the day at Falmouth. Mr. Pearsons, agent for the A. B. S., talked on the Bible all day, and $83 raised.

Oct. 29, Went to Falmouth to marry a couple. Dined at John Wilson's.

Nov. 1, Sabbath. I preached at Falmouth. Dorcas Cox died this morning. Thirty-six meals of victuals have been given away this week.

1830.

August 28. Went to Falmouth. Mrs. Miltimore very sick. Supposed to be in consumption. Dined at Mr. Petingills, took tea at Joshua Morrills.

Sept. 1. Commencement at Brunswick. Mrs. B. and myself visited Mr. Miltimore and spent the day. Mrs. Miltimore very sick—not much hope of her recovery.

(She was his second wife. His first died March 5, 1826, aged 55 years. He m. 2nd, Dorcas Noyes of Falmouth, Oct. 19, 1826, who d. Sept. 10, 1830, aged 31 years.)

May 29, Sabbath. Forenoon preached at Falmouth; p. m. Mr. Cressey preached. (Rev. Noah Cressey of North Yarmouth 1823). At 6 prayer meeting—a great congregation—a very solemn day.

1831.

June 1. Went to Falmouth. Attended a meeting; 16 anxious. Staid all night at Mr. Miltimores.

June 10. Laid abed too long this morning. Went to Falmouth. Made several visits to the anxious inquirers. At 5 attended an inquiry meeting in the meeting house—38. Mr. McGregor, E. Merrill, Mr. Miltimore and myself present. Lord give them a good hope in Christ.

July 13. Went to Falmouth. Attended an inquiry meeting. About twenty offered themselves for examination for admission to the church. Staid all night with Mr. Miltimore.

July 31. Have preached for Bro. Miltimore 3 times. A very solemn and interesting day.

Aug. 3. Went to Falmouth to attend the examination of Mr. McGregor's school. (Rev. David McGregor). Took tea at Mr. Miltimores. School appeared well.

Aug. 7, Sabbath. Preached at Falmouth. Very interesting day; twenty-nine were added to the church. Hope they will adorn their profession, and live agreeable to their professions.

Sep. 2. Three o'clock p. m. Mrs. B. and I went to Falmouth. Attended an examination meeting, 15 were questioned relative to their qualifications to join the church.

Oct. 2, Sabbath. Attended meeting at Falmouth. Assisted Bro. Miltimore—14 joined the church. An interesting day.

1832.

Feb. 29. This p. m. at Falmouth. Attended a church meeting. Chose two deacons.

March 9. Went to Falmouth and attended the funeral of Mrs. Pote, aged 94 years.

March 31. Went to Falmouth. At 2 o'clock p. m. preached—after the service consecrated two deacons, and introduced them to the church and gave them the charge.

Aug. 23d Went to Falmouth. Mr. Miltimore had a fast.

Sept. 2. Nine o'clock, rainy. Set out for Bro. Miltimore's—was there at dinner. P. M. called to see the boys, and (then) set out for dear home.

CONTINUED:

Sept. 23. Mrs. B. and I went to Falmouth. Attended an examination meeting. Fifteen were questioned relative to their church qualifications. Tarried with Mr. Miltimore.

Oct. 1. At 3 o'clock set out for Falmouth, rainy and muddy. Sunset, turned aside for the night at Ephraim Marston's. Kindly entertained.

1833.

May 2. Moved some furniture to Falmouth for the children to commence keeping house next Monday. (They went there to attend school.)

May 12th. Sabbath. Preached at Falmouth. Dined and took tea in my own hired house with my children.

May 19th. Sabbath. Attended meeting at Falmouth—sat in a pew all day and heard Bro. Miltimore. He preached very well.

June 1. Mrs. Bradley brought home Franklin who had been sick three weeks.

July 24. Met in council at Mr. Miltimore's for the purpose of dissolving the connection between him and his church. After mature deliberation voted that the connection be dissolved the next Sabbath at the close of the meeting.

July 28. Sabbath. This forenoon I preached for Bro. Miltimore. Afternoon he preached his farewell sermon—a very large congregation and he and the people much affected—a solemn and interesting day. Bro. Miltimore has made himself unhappy by leaving a people so much attached to him. He had better have lived and died with his people and been buried with them, but the work is done. Read the result of the council after the sermon—the people were solemn and sober. Every one retired with a sober feeling. Mrs. B. and I returned at sun set.

August 7. On our way home from Raymond stopped at Falmouth to see the children. Took tea at Mr. Maston's—lodged at the old house, on the floor where the children were—rather a hard bed.

Dec. 31. I went to Falmouth to unite in a council relative to the installation of Bro. Miltimore. The council spent the evening in examining papers. Voted that the papers were not satisfactory and that we could proceed no farther. Chose a committee to make out a result of council. Adjourned to meet tomorrow morning at 7 o'clock. This year is now closed—is no more forever—the year 1833.

1834.

January 1. Welcome the new year, at Falmouth, in council agreeable to adjournment at Bro. Miltimore's house and having agreed to the result, adjourned, sine die. Had a meeting in the meeting house at 11 o'clock a. m. After the result of council was read to the congregation we sang a hymn. I made the first prayer. Mr. Kellogg preached, Mr. Jewett made the concluding prayer. Dined at Bro. Miltimore's and then all returned to their respective homes.

(There must have been an attempt made to reinstate the reverend gentleman which failed.)

Sep. 27. Mrs. Bradley sick. Started for Freeport to preach for Mr. Kent. (Rev. Cephas H. Kent who died in Freeport, 1885), but stopped at Falmouth, and Mr. Miltimore went for me. Mr. Gregg called and spent the night here. (Rev. William Gregg of Cape Elizabeth.)

Oct. 2. Went to Falmouth and preached for Bro. Miltimore a lecture. Took tea there.

1835.

January 11. I preached at Falmouth. Full meeting. Much improved feeling in the church, still much contention and strife. Bro. Miltimore's enemies multiplying. He has some warm friends.

1836.

March 31. The last day of March. A summer-like day. Mrs. Bradley and I went to Falmouth in a sleigh—a very pleasant ride. Been quite good sleighing since the 23d day of November—4 months and 8 days—something very uncommon—such a winter for snow, cold and sleighing has not been known for a long course of years.

May 30. Heard of the death of Mr. Weston yesterday. (Rev. Daniel Weston of Gray.) Am sent for to attend the funeral. Lord may this death teach me so to number my days that I may apply my heart unto wisdom. Another classmate dead. My turn will presently come.

31st. Set out for Gray to attend the funeral of Mr. Weston. At 11 o'clock arrived at the house in company with Mr. Miltimore. At 1 o'clock p. m. attended the funeral exercises at the meetinghouse. Mr. Chapin preached, (Rev. Perez Chapin of Pownal.) Returned home after tea. Rode the last eight miles in one of the most violent showers, accompanied with thunder and lightning I was ever out in, and it continued to rain after I arrived home.

Oct. 28. This day attended the installation of Mr. Sheldon at Falmouth. (Rev. Anson W. Sheldon.) Took part in the service—the first prayer. On the whole rather a pleasant time. Mrs. Bradley with me. No tea in Falmouth. None seemed to be much interested.

TO BE CONTINUED.

THE DEERING NEWS.

Saturday, April 17, 1897.

GRANDPA'S SCRAP BOOK

[Under this head historical and genealogical memoranda will be furnished the readers of the News that appears worthy of preservation, particularly of remote periods in our history within the city limits and immediatevicinity.]

ECCLESIASTICAL.

ONCE THE THIRD, NOW FIRST CONGREGATIONAL PARISH OF FALMOUTH.

A FEW GLIMPSES OF THE PAST COMPILED FROM ORIGINAL RECORDS.

(*Continued from Last Week.*)

My article under this head last week closed as follows:

Oct. 28 This day attended the installation of Mr. Sheldon at Falmouth. (Rev. Anson W. Sheldon.) Took part in the service. (I made) the first prayer. On the whole rather a pleasant time. Mrs. Bradley with me. No tea at Falmouth. None seemed to be much interested.

The foregoing should have appeared under date of 1835 instead of 1836, for it was in the year of 1835, Oct. 28, Rev. Mr. Sheldon was installed over the people of the First Parish of Falmouth, but the pastorate lasted but a year and half a month, according to the journal.

1836.

Oct. 30. Sabbath. I preached in Falmouth for Mr. Sheldon (Rev. Anson W. Sheldon.) Everything in this church and society is in a snarl; so says Bro. Sheldon, and the more they try to unsnarl the more snarled things become because they don't know how to undo things they have done wrong. O, Falmouth! How has the gold become dim, and the most fine gold changed. Thou art fallen. * * * * * *

And it came to pass in those days when thou didst speak reproachfully of thy minister and because thou didst listen and believe what that woman Jezebel, who called herself a prophetess, did say, thy minister became unhappy and discontented, and because his feelings were quickly excited he invited to assemble a council at his house to learn what was best to be done in so trying a case. The council were composed of Thadeus, and Thomas and Joseph and Caleb and some others who agreed that William, the minister, (Rev. William Miltimore) should have no more to do with the people of Falmouth who were so full of bitterness and wrath and clamor and evil speaking against the minister William, that he should be free from them and the once tender tie should be severed. And it came to pass this tender tie was severed, and William made his pilgrimage to the West and after having wandered through deserts and over mountains and taken up his abode for a time in dens and caves of the earth he thought on his ways and retraced his steps. Here I leave Falmouth and their once minister William and those who happen to read this (page) may guess, if they can, what it means.

Nov. 15. I set out for Falmouth to meet in council to consider the expediency of dismissing Mr. Sheldon (Rev. Anson W. Sheldon) and dissolving the connection between him and the church. The council (M. D.) convened at Mr. Tuckesbury's—organized. Mr. Vaill moderator (Rev. Joseph Vaill) Mr. Searle (Rev. Joseph Searle) of Saccarappa, scribe, Mr. Hobert (Rev. Caleb Hobert) Mr. Gregg, (Rev. Wm. Gregg) Mr. Stone, (Rev. Nathaniel Stone) Rev. Caleb Bradley and Deacon Lincoln composed the council. After investigating the whole matter the council unanimously agreed to dissolve the connection. Mr. Bradley closed with prayer and the council adjourned

(And here I will make a digression to show where the Rev. Mr. Sheldon went when he left Falmouth. Under date of Jan. 30, 1838, Rev. Mr. Bradley says: Dea. Duren and wife called at 3 p. m. Heard a long story of church, parish and minister in that place. I should think they are in quite a snarl from the deacon's story—hope the difficulty will be settled without much confusion and noise. O, what trials, troubles and difficulties the ministers of the gospel meet with at the present time. Windham has been noted for ministerial trouble. A minister continues but a little time in that place. Mr. Shepard, their present minister, is the sixth since I became acquainted with the place and it seems he is not likely to remain with them much longer, and so things go on. After tea Deacon Duren and wife left for home—gave them my best advice *****.)

1837.

Feb. 11. Rev. Mr. Miltimore preached in the First Congregational meeting house, in what is now Deering, and Mr. Bradley presents an abstract of the discourse, and closes with these words; "Mr. Miltimore is very fond of figurative texts, and seems to have a wonderful faculty in handling them. This is rather popular and he has a popular way."

1838.

March 10. (Mr. Bradley returned from a visit to Brunswick. He says:) At 2 o'clock left this place for Westbrook, stopped at Yarmouth to oat my horse. Called at Mr. Howes'; left here a little before sunset. At 7 o'clock at Mr. Miltimore's. Here I was over-persuaded to spend the night and Sabbath. The day has been pleasant, the ride pleasant and now am in this house—Mr. Miltimore's. I see nothing unpleasant. Had a cup of tea and trimmings, but (things) are not here as they used to be in old times—the inward management perhaps a little better than formerly. The outward management—I mean things relating to the wood and barn—very much as usual, all heads and points, 'helter skelter.' Bro. Miltimore has no regard for this world, or rather he appears to care but little about it—not enough to make himself comfortable. He might have things in order, but he thinks it of no importance at all. 'Tomorrow shall be as this day and much more abundance,' but he appears to take no thought for tomorrow.

March 11. Sabbath. At Bro. Miltimore's. Here I attended meeting. Forenoon he preached, or talked, or exhorted from these words of the prophet Isaiah 66:6; "A voice of noise from the city, a voice from the temple, a voice from the Lord that rendereth recompense to his enemies."

The preacher enlarged upon these words, and told the people that a voice was constantly addressing them from different places—from families of mourning, from funeral ceremonies, from the bed of sickness, from the grave, from the pulpit—behold! I stand at the door and knock, then the voice of the Lord speaks and calls upon sinners to repent. Today if you will hear my voice now is the accepted time—this is the way, walk ye in it. In the afternoon I preached—text: Eph. 2:1, "You hath he quickened who were dead in trespass and sin." All men by nature are dead in sin and need to be quickened and raised to life. * * * * *

1838.

May 8. Went to Falmouth with Mrs. Graves, (wife of the Dea. of the 1st Con. church, Westbrook) and Mr. and Mrs. Lane, (Rev. Joseph Lane, pastor of the 1st Con. church of Westbrook, now Deering) to attend, a protracted meeting, this being the eighth day since the meetings commenced. The exercises were solemn. Afternoon Mr. Lane preached—text, Luke 10:9, *Appropinquevit in vos regnum Dei,* "The kingdom of God is come nigh unto you"; the kingdom of God has come nigh to this people to whom the gospel is sent; and what a deplorable state must those be in at last who reject the gospel when by the preaching of the gospel the kingdom of God has come nigh unto them. These sentiments were enforced by addresses, then the meeting was closed by prayer by Mr. Bradley. At 2 o'clock p. m. we met again. Mr. Parsons of Freeport (Rev. Eben G. Parsons) preached, text, Matt. 25:10, *Et clausa est janua,* "And the door was shut." In the great day the door of heaven will be shut against the rejecters of the gospel—the door was shut, yes, and the door will

CONTINUED:

be shut against every unpenitent sinner. "Lord, Lord, open," but the answer—"I know you not, depart, be gone." Let sinners fear and tremble, for the door will be shut, and no man can open. After some addresses I closed the meeting with prayer. Dined at Jere Merrill's, took tea at Albert (J.) Merrill's (who lived nearly opposite the meeting house.) Sun set at home.

It is a serious time among many in Falmouth; hope the result of these meetings will be happy. (The Association at Mr. Jamesons today, (Rev. Thomas Jameson of Scarboro), but Mr. Lane and Mr. Bradley not there.

May 9. Eight o'clock—not determined what to do, or which way to go, so many things to think of, and so much to do, hardly know what to do first.

Nine o'clock set out for Falmouth via Portland, and attended the place of worship. Mr. Pearsons preached—text: Rom. 8 9, "Si antem quis spiritum Christi no herlet hic non est ejus."

In the afternoon Mr. Chapin preached. (Rev. Perez Chapin of Pownal who died a year later.) Text, Hosea 11:12 About fifty appeared as enquirers. They were addressed, and the meeting closed with prayer by Mr. Richmond, a Methodist, who seems to be the Alpha and Omega of the meetings and was Mr. Miltimore's right hand man.

I preached at 6 o'clock at the school house near Capt. York's—good numbers —good attention and arrived home about 10 o'clock. This is the 9th day since these meetings commenced. Large numbers have attended.

Today the Methodist and Freewill Baptists took parts. Great seriousness prevailed in the congregation. From time to time many tears were shed, many enquiries made, many groans uttered, many ejaculations offered up, now what will all these nine days of religious excitement amount to? What will be the result? Will the consequences be happy? Will Christians be revived and become more engaged and more anxious for the salvation of their own souls and the souls of sinners around them? This would be very desirable. Will God bless this church and people. Are they being prepared for a blessing? Are they of one heart, one soul, one feeling and all their prayers one prayer, and their minister's heart one heart with them and this one heart and prayer speak and feel for the honor and glory of God and the upbuilding of the Redeemer's kingdom? This being so they may hope for a blessing upon themselves, and sinners will be converted and all this preaching, exhorting will not be in vain and the ministers will not have spent their strength for naught. Mr. Chapin (Rev. Perez Chapin of Pownal) will preach tomorrow which will make the tenth day. The Lord bless these religious exercises, and through this instrumentality may there be many added to the church of such as will be saved. Amen.

TO BE CONTINUED.

THE DEERING NEWS.

Saturday, April 24, 1897.

GRANDPA'S SCRAP BOOK

[Under this head historical and genealogical memoranda will be furnished the readers of the News that appears worthy of preservation, particularly of remote periods in our history within the city limits and immediate vicinity.]

ECCLESIASTICAL.

ONCE THE THIRD, NOW FIRST CONGREGATIONAL PARISH OF FALMOUTH.

A FEW GLIMPSES OF THE PAST COMPILED FROM ORIGINAL RECORDS.

(Continued from Last Week.)

1838.

May 25. I understand by Mrs. Marston there is likely to be trouble in Falmouth. The protracted meetings held there have caused much excitement and diversion among the people. Mr. Stevens (Rev. Joseph B. Stevens of West Falmouth in 1834) and Brother Miltimore will find it a bitter pill to be connected with the Free Will Baptist and Methodist. These have more zeal, more warmth, more activity, more life and more silly things to say and express more love for the people than the Congregational ministers who are more formal, more patient and more correct than the other denominations that have less discipline.

1839.

January 31. Cold morning. Set out for Pownal in a sleigh with Ruth Adams. Stopped at Falmouth on account of the bareness of the ground and took a chaise and Mr. Dame, (a candidate preaching in Falmouth, (Rev. Charles Dame) and left Ruth to take care of herself. Arrived at Pownal at 12 m., and dined at Mr. Newall's. At 1 o'clock the funeral solemnities of Mr. Chapen were attended at the meetinghouse. (Rev. Horace B. Chapin.) A solemn occasion. Mr. Hobert (Rev. Caleb Hobert) made the first prayer, after reading a select portion of the scriptures by Mr. Cummings (Rev. Asa Cummings) "Well done good and faithful servant." Mr. Pomeroy (Rev. Thaddeus Pomeroy) made the closing prayer. All the services were solemn. Returned to Falmouth, and to Mr. Dame's where I spent the night.

March 23. At 4 o'clock p. m., went to Falmouth with Ruth Adams. Very muddy.

Took tea at Joseph Colley's; lodged at Mr. McGregor's.

24th. Sabbath. Attended meeting here. Heard Mr. Dame the candidate for settlement. Liked him much. Subject a. m. "Men and brethren what shall we do?" Afternoon—"Repent." I made the first prayer. The probability is that Mr. Dame will be settled here as the minister, and the society will be built up. Wish it might. The Universalists had a meeting today. Mr. Thompson preached (Rev. Zenas Thompson.) (The volume of the journal covering the time between July 28th 1839 and August 19, 1840 is not among the lot in my possession.)

1840.

October 20. This a. m. went to Portland via Woodfords Corner, and there I met Brother Miltimore whom I had not seen for a long time; dined with him at Capt. Turner's and we had a very good dinner, and a very pleasant interview. Talked about old affairs and days gone by, for we lived neighbors for thirty years—both pastors of churches and no root of bitterness ever sprung up between us. Exchanged pulpits when we pleased and no one to say why doest thou thus or so, but those years are past and gone; he has left his parish and the town and has a farm in the state of New Hampshire where he resides, only when he is abroad preaching. I am here where I have been more than forty years enjoying the best of health, and ever have—preaching every Sabbath to the poor in Portland.

Mr. Miltimore has preached the past season in Canada, and lately returned from that region. He is here tonight with his youngest daughter, Susanna Dorcas Bradley (Miltimore)—quite a promising little girl.

July 23, Half an hour before sunrise and every appearance of rain. Have hauled in two loads of hay before breakfast. 8 o'clock—no rain—men hauling in hay. 9 o'clock, have concluded to go to Falmouth. Called at Mr. North's (in what is now Deering) a few minutes and then proceeded on to Mr. Dame's, (Rev. Charles Dame,) but he was not there. Called at Mr. McGregor's, (Rev. David McGregor,) and took dinner, and then left and called to see Mr. Stone a few minutes and then proceeded to the residence of Rev. Enos Merrill and spent a half hour with him. He lives on the homestead of his childhood, a farm founded upon a ledge of rocks, the very first look enough to discourage me from trying to live and he says he doesn't know what to do. He has been a settled minister twice, once at Freeport and once at Olney (Alna probably) but now

138

CONTINUED:

feeble in health and must leave preaching—hard case. A family to provide for and two maiden sisters. Left the rocky foundation and called at Isaac Adams' where I spent the night, this being quite a ministerial house—always glad to see ministers—thus they appear. One of the daughters called round with me to see a broken-boned woman—Mrs. Sweat, and then to the school house for the purpose of attending a lecture, but looking so likely to rain we returned immediately to Mr. Adams before quite dark, and I soon went to bed.

1841.

January 12, I slipped into the city today. (Portland) The Cumberland conference meet there in High street church Mr. Shapley of New Gloucester preached. Mr. Dame of Falmouth (Rev. Chas. Dame) made the introductory prayer. *** Took tea at Eben Steel's and Mr. Warren of Windham (Rev. William Warren) and Mr. Dame of Falmouth likewise—pleasant time.

March 30. Yesterday p. m. and last night about six inches of snow fell. Sleighs are moving about and it is one of the coldest and most uncomfortable days we have had for a long time. This p. m. took Charles (his son) and went to Falmouth in a sleigh to a wedding at Mr. Isaac Adams'; one of his daughters was married to a Mr. Dunham. Mr. Dame (Rev. Chas. Dame) married them. Mr. McGregor (Rev. David McGregor founder of the Falmouth Academy, died there Oct. 19, 1845.) and myself were present, (but) took no part. Quite a large company—well entertained—good time—everything was done decently and in order. The young couple have my best wishes. They have listed during life whether it be short or long, and very likely will experience many unpleasant days as well as pleasant. *** Between 9 and 10 o'clock the house was closed. I concluded to stay all night. There was one very pleasant occurrence. A young girl who had often heard the shakers sing and seen them dance undertook to show the company how they performed their devotions in this way.

September 29. Ruth (Adams) and self went over to Falmouth to the dedication of the new meeting house just finished. This house is in the modern style. The exercises were asking a blessing, singing, reading of the scriptures, prayers, then sermon on the occasion by Mr. Dame, the minister (Rev. Chas. Dame) Yarmouth (Rev. Caleb Hobert of the 3rd church of that town)

Afternoon. Prayers introductory by Rev. Enos Merrill (before noticed) sermon by Mr. Warren (Rev. Wm. Warren then another prayer by Mr. Sewal (Rev. Jotham Sewall of Westbrook, now Deering) and the forms prayer by Mr. Hobert of Windham) closing prayer by Mr. Bradley of Westbrook (now Deering.) Everything was conducted in a very proper manner. There was a crowded congregation, about 500. This house is calculated to seat this number or more; 80 pews, 6 in a pew besides the singing seats. The day has been rather rainy but not sufficiently so to prevent a large congregation from assembling. It has been an interesting day and one long to be remembered by the people of Falmouth. I dined and took tea with Mr. Tewksbury.

On my way home called on Mr. McGregor (Rev. David McGregor) He did not attend the dedication; he does not feel right in his mind about something, and does not attend meetings on the Sabbath very regularly.

THE DEERING NEWS.

Saturday, May 1, 1897.

GRANDPA'S SCRAP BOOK

[Under this head historical and genealogical memoranda will be furnished the readers of the News that appears worthy of preservation, particularly of remote periods in our history within the city limits and immediate vicinity.]

ALL SOULS CHURCH.

"LET YOUR LIGHT SO SHINE BEFORE MEN THEY MAY SEE YOUR GOOD WORKS."

"AND WHEN THE DAY OF PENTECOST WAS FULLY COME. THEY WERE ALL WITH ONE ACCORD IN ONE PLACE."

"AND WHEN THEY WERE COME IN, THEY WENT UP INTO AN UPPER ROOM, WHERE ABODE BOTH PETER AND JAMES AND JOHN AND ANDREW, PHILIP AND THOMAS, BARTHOLOMEW AND MATHEW, JAMES THE SON OF ALPHEUS AND SIMON ZELOTES, AND JUDAS THE BROTHER OF JAMES."

It was a new departure in the history of the work of All Souls' church, the assemblage in the vestry of the church edifice located in the south easterly corner of the old Westbrook Seminary grounds on Stevens Plains, of the several clans that are marching and counter-marching individually, in private and public life, with Sabbathday and other reunions, under the denominational church banner inscribed "Universal Salvation for the Souls of all Mankind," on Friday evening Apr. 23. The weather was fine and the assemblage was composed of the young, middle aged and veterans in church work, of both sexes, to the number of 152. The event inaugurated the putting into practice the new ordinance of the parish relating to annual meetings of the parish organizations, lately adopted, which it is claimed has come to stay and to be know as the Parish annual supper. The exercises consisted of a general interchange of friendly greetings, singing, the partaking of a much modernized Passover in fact, it was a banquet but without wine, the burning of incense, the killing of a lamb and the washing of the door posts with its blood as of old. The symbols consisted of toothsome viands, tea and coffee, after which the reading of reports and speeches that continued till 10 o'clock and all of a character to encourage each member of the brotherhood to press forward in high moral work of protection and a corresponding elevation in worldly life and finally a perpetual home of bliss "beyond the clouds."

The tables, decorated with numerous pot plants, extending the whole length of the large vestry, across the head of which was one for those who participated in the reading of reports and speech making, made a fine display. Judging from the large quantity of food that was disposed of it is believed by the writer that the rule imposed upon the ancient celebration of the Passover should now e practiced and nothing left uneaten on ch occasions.

Cyrus B. Varney, Esq., was made moderator for the evening, who, upon taking the chair, responded in an appropriate manner.

The programme was arranged as follows:
Prayer, Rev. F. T. Nelson
Singing by the choir led by Mr. John L. Shaw,
Parish History,
Prepared by Walter F. Goodrich, Esq., read by the Pastor—Rev. Mr. Nelson.
Report of Parish Treasurer,
Miss Helen Forbes
Report of church. Rev. Mr. Nelson
Report of Sunday school,
C. S. Varney, Esq.
Report of Treasurer and Librarian,
Walter F. Goodrich, Esq.
Solo, Miss Low Harding
Report of Ladies Circle, * *
Mrs. F. E. C. Robbins
Report of Circle Finances,
Mrs. C. B. Varney
Report of Young People's Christian Union, Miss Abbie Holden
Report of Treasurer Young People's Union, Miss Kate Knight
Solo, Mr. John L. Shaw
Report of Mission Circle,
Mrs. Samuel Burnes

These reports were all of an interesting character and it must be a surprise to the News readers that so much work is done by All Souls' church society, and here the regret is expressed that the News cannot print but two of the many reports.

Speeches being in order at this stage of proceedings Mr. Fred L. Tower of the Woodfords young and promising society was called upon who responded by presenting interesting statistics relative to

CONTINUED!

the new organization, stating that of the 53 scholars composing the Sabbath school but 4 of the number ever attended All Souls'.

Then followed Prof. Whitman of the Seminary; then Rev. W. W. Hooper, State Missionary, whose remarks served the purpose of crackers and cheese at the close of a more elaborate banquet, now referring to time of sitting. Then came Rev. Mr. Nelson who closed the speaking.

The whole affair was well arranged and every part was a success.

We would be pleased to go more into detail with our report but cannot.

---

*HISTORICAL SKETCH OF THE FIRST UNIVERSALIST CHURCH SOCIETY OF WESTBROOK, NOW KNOWN AS THE FIRST UNIVERSALIST SOCIETY OF DEERING.

This society was organized July 31, 1829, under a warrant issued by Moses Quinby, Esq., the request being signed by fifty persons living in different parts of the town. The first meeting was held in an old school house that formerly stood near the "Old South" or Bradley meeting-house on Church street, Capisic.

In 1830 a meeting-house was built on the corner of Stevens' Plains avenue and Brighton street, which was bought in 1866 by the town of Deering for a town house, and is still standing. It was dedicated Sept. 8th of the year it was built, Rev. Mr. Reese of Portland preaching the dedication sermon. In his journal Parson Bradley says of this dedication:

I wish it might be a Pentecost and that many there might be brought to their senses, like the prodigal and resolve, as he did, to repent and return to their Heavenly Father. But they think they shall go to Heaven. They have no idea that any will fall short of there. No matter how they live, how they conduct, and what they believe, they are sure of Heaven at last.

In the following month (Oct., 1830,) Rev. Samuel Brimblecom, who was one of the projectors and the first principal of Westbrook Seminary, was settled as pastor over the society at a salary of $400 per year. Judging by the records it was difficult to raise even this amount. Oct. 19, 1833, it was voted "That the society pay Rev. Mr. Brimblecom thirty-two dollars and give him the benefit of whatever he can obtain upon all tax bills and subscriptions which have been raised by the society for the support of the ministry since his engagement with us—he giving a full discharge to the society for his services to Oct. 19, 1833, and saving the society from cost."

Mr. Brimblecom continued to preach, however. April 13, 1835, it was voted "That the committee be instructed to give up the subscription papers to Rev. Mr. Brimblecom, provided he will give a receipt in full for his services to this time." It was about this date, probably, that he severed his connection with the society as pastor, as he left Westbrook for Massachusetts in 1836.

There is nothing in the records to show whether the pulpit was supplied during 1835 and '36 or not.

In 1837 Rev. David J. Mandell was engaged as pastor, his services commencing on the fourth Sunday in June. He was engaged to preach six months for $250. Sept. 1, 1838, it was voted "That the soliciting committee for 1836 and 1837 be authorized to settle with Rev. D. J. Mandell," so it is probable he preached a year at any rate, whether any longer is not stated. Those were hard times. Sept. 22, 1838, the committee reported that all the debts standing against the society amounted to about $19, and those present "subscribed enough to settle all demands."

Jan. 26, 1839, it was "Voted to employ the Rev. Zenas Thompson to preach one half the time for one year if he can be obtained for $300."

Now commenced an evident improvement in affairs. The old members waked up and new ones joined. A bass viol was purchased for the choir and quite an interest was created Father Thompson staid with them five years, preaching a part of the time in Saccarappa.

On the first Sunday in June, 1844, Rev. Joseph P. Atkinson commenced to preach at $450 a year with a month's vacation. Next, in June, 1848, came Rev. Leander Hussey, to preach half of the time for $250 per year. March 16, 1851 it was "Voted that the committee be authorized to tender to Bro. L. Hussey, in pay for his services, the balance due on last year's subscription that is collectable," he having asked for a discharge from the society. Rev. W. C. George was settled as pastor in May, 1851, and remained two years.

In the spring of 1856 Rev. James P. Weston came here and took charge of the seminary. He also preached in "the old church on the rock," but there is no record to tell how long. It would be interesting to know just when the last sermon was preached there. In an old journal kept by the writer, the last date of services held there is Jan. 27, 1856, when Rev. Mr. Lovejoy preached. Under date of Feb. 7th, the same year, is the following: "Meeting at the school house to see about moving the meeting house over here. Decided to build a new one, and committees were appointed to get subscriptions." $1,695 was subscribed, but nothing came of it.

Some time in 1856 the chapel at Allen's Corner, in which no services were held then, was moved over here on to the seminary grounds. This was done through the efforts of Dr. Weston, who wanted to have some place where his scholars could attend religious services. In 1858 a society was organized which took the name of the "3d Universalist Society in Westbrook," and a small amount was subscribed for preaching, but not enough to warrant the engagement of a regular pastor. This society was still in existence in 1864.

Rev. Benjamin Ames succeeded Dr. Weston as principal of the seminary and preached in the chapel, but not regularly, during his stay of two years. Rev. S. H. McCollister came as principal in 1863, and had a large and flourishing school. He preached pretty regularly for three years or more, mostly in the chapel, but during winter weather in the seminary building. His services were given gratuitously for the benefit of the school. Rev. L. L. Record preached some, also, during this time.

May 16, 1866, a corporation was formed under a warrant issued by Walter B. Goodrich, Justice of the Peace, for the purpose of building a church, or as the warrant has it, 'of erecting a meeting-house," and the present church was commenced soon afterward by that corporation and finished in 1867. The idea originated with Mrs. E. B. Dunham, who started the Ladies' Circle in 1865 for that object. The church was designed by Mr. Fassett, the architect, of Portland, and built by Mr. Joseph W. Thompson, of Stockton. Its entire cost, finished and furnished, was about $14,000, but how that amount was ever raised in this community is somewhat of a mystery, even to those who had a hand in it. Several hundred dollars were obtained from the sale of the old house. The Ladies' Circle helped very materially and a loan of $2,250 was procured from the trustees of the seminary. Mr. Rufus Dunham very generously paid for the pulpit and the expense of putting in the pews out of his own pocket, and others, among whom were Messrs. Grenville M. and Frank G. Stevens, subscribed liberally. Quite a sum was also realized from the sale of pews.

The church was dedicated Dec. 3, 1867, Dr. McCollister making the dedicatory prayer and Rev. E. C. Bolles preaching the sermon. A beautiful hymn was written for the occasion by Mrs. Dunham.

December 27 of the same year our present society was organized under the old name of the "First Universalist Society in Westbrook." This was changed, however, in 1874 to the "First Universalist Society in Deering," and in 1888 it was voted that the church be called

Continued:

and hereafter known as "All Souls' Church."

Rev. Mr. Bolles was the first preacher engaged. He was preacher only, being pastor of the Congress Square church, and preaching out here in the afternoon. He had $15 per Sunday and commenced preaching Jan. 5, 1868. In 1869 Rev. J. C. Snow, who had come here to serve as principal of the seminary, was engaged as pastor at $800 per year. His services commenced Oct. 1st and ended July 1st, 1872, when he left for Auburn. From that time until 1873 various preachers were engaged at so much per Sunday. In the spring of 1873 Rev. H. C. Leonard began his pastorate at $900 per year and served until July, 1875, when the society again fell back on the per diem system. Among these afternoon preachers were Rev. Messrs Bailey and Buck of the First Parish church, Portland, and Rev. Geo. W. Bicknell of the Church of the Messiah. Mr. Bicknell preached his last sermon Dec. 30, 1878, having had a call to Philadelphia. Rev. C. A. Hayden was then engaged by the Church of the Messiah, and preached out here in the afternoon. In 1880 he built the house on College street now known as the "Jordan house" and moved his family out in the fall. The following year he severed his connection with the Church of the Messiah and became pastor of All Souls' church. Doubtless all remember how the Auburn society stole him away. He preached for the last time Dec. 30, 1883, having been with us just five years.

Rev. F. M. Houghton succeeded him as pastor Jan. 6, 1884, and was installed Feb. 18, [Dr. Patterson preaching the sermon. He remained but one year, and after candidating until [May 3, 1885, Rev. Q. H. Shinn was settled as pastor at $1500 per year, the society at Saccarappa paying a part. His pastorate closed April 28, 1889, when, after candidating again until October, Dr. Safford commenced preaching on the 13th and remained, as Mr. Shinn did, just four years. Dec. 3, 1893, Rev. Mr. Hayden began his second pastorate, and in one year was stolen from us again, this time by Augusta.

Rev. F. T. Nelson's pastorate commenced Sept. 1, 1895. He was ordained and installed Oct. 25, and the writer will always remember it as a very solemn and impressive ceremony, especially the ordaining prayer by Rev. Dr. Atwood.

THE DEERING NEWS.

Saturday, May 22, 1897.

GRANDPA'S SCRAP BOOK

[Under this head historical and genealogical memoranda will be furnished the readers of the News that appears worthy of preservation, particularly of remote periods in our history within the city limits and immediate vicinity.]

INFORMATION WANTED.

EVERETT, MASS., May 18, 1897.

To the Editor of the News:—

I am desirous of obtaining information relative to the offspring of John Snow Brackett, son of Thomas and Mary Snow, his wife, born in Falmouth, the part that is now Deering, Nov. 23, 1749. It is traditional that he died and she married second, Joseph Cobb, and by both husbands became the mother of thirteen children.

If those in possession of the desired information will forward it to me a favor will be bestowed upon one who will readily pay the expense.

Very truly,
A. L. BRACKETT.

LETTER FROM MR. F. O. NORTH.

Messrs. Burditt and North of Boston, Mass., are managers of the Stoddard Lectures. From Mr. Fred O. North, grandson of Elijah North, whose family record appeared in the NEWS March 27th, sends the NEWS the following:

BOSTON, May 14, 1897.
MR. L. B. CHAHMAN,
Dear Sir:— I have received the papers and have been very much interested in your articles on the North family. I wish to correct two errors, however. Martha J. Smith, nee North, lived at Richmond, Me., not Bowdoinham, and after the fire moved to Melrose, Mass. I had no brother named Orin, as you state, but a sister named Alice, and her birth and death dates correspond to those given by you to Orin.

Thanking you for the excellent articles,
I am   Yours truly,
F. O. NORTH.

REV. GEO. WHITEFIELD.

The Rev. W. W. Hooper, the state missionary of the Universalist denomination of Christians, who resides in this city, in his first discourse at Lewis hall, some weeks since, alluded to Rev. Geo. Whitefield, which causes me to say that he was probably the greatest pulpit orator of his day and perhaps the greatest the world has seen. He was born in Gloucester, England, Dec. 16, 1714, and came to America the first time before he was twenty years of age. He made seven voyages to this country, and died at Newburyport, Mass., Sept. 30, 1770, preaching the day before his death. He was a Methodist, and originated out door preaching. During his thirty-four years of ministry he preached 18,000 sermons, an average of about eleven a week. Meetinghouses were too small for his hearers. Once he addressed 20,000 persons assembled on Boston Common. In 1741 he was expected to visit this locality.

Jan. 29, 1742, Rev. Thomas Smith says in his diary: "I rode with my wife and preached a lecture at Mr. Frost's, where the work broke out."

This reference was to Charles Frost, Esq., who resided where the Brewer House stood, opposite Stroudwater village. Many joined the church in consequence of the "religious fire" there kindled.

March 23, 1745, Mr. Smith says: "Mr. Whitefield preached in my pulpit. (Portland.) Multitudes flocked from Purpoordock and elsewhere."

He preached in Yarmouth and other places hereabouts. But there was strong opposition to his coming here and a resort to violence was expected, but the opposition subsided when he finally came.

The fact that one so celebrated as the Rev. Mr. Whitefield once stood upon the soil of what is now Deering and addressed the inhabitants is worthy of remembrance—hence this notice.

Saturday, May 15, 1897.

GRANDPA'S SCRAP BOOK

[Under this head historical and genealogical memoranda will be furnished the readers of the News that appears worthy of preservation, particularly of remote periods in our history within the city limits and immediate vicinity.]

AN OLD RECORD.

The 1823 Assessors Book of the First Congregational Parish.

I am in receipt of a valuable historical record from Mr. F. E. C. Robbins, superintendent of schools, who resides on Ocean street, near Woodfords, found in his dwelling, consisting of the original assessor's book of the First Congregational Parish of Westbrook, now Deering, made March 18, 1823, when (1) Hon. Archelaus Lewis, (2) Capt. John Jones and (3) Oliver Buckley were assessors, whose autographs appear. There are 177 names of residents appearing and 44 non-residents. Forty cents was the amount assessed upon the poll, and Hon. Arch Lewis paid the largest amount, which was $13.97.

The parish comprised what is now Deering and Westbrook. Ebenezer D. Woodford paid on the property, as now seen at Woodfords and owned by his daughter, Mrs. Moser, $6.45; Moses Quinby, Esq., paid upon the property, where Andrew Hawes, Esq., now re-

CONTINUED:

sides at Stroudwater, $4.19; Catherine Dole, on house and farm opposite the Quinby house, both of which now remain as then seen, $9.37; Oliver Buckley, Stevens Plains, $9.87, and Elisha Higgins, Jr., Higgins Corner, $2.06.

There were 43 non-residents, and the largest amount paid was by Josiah Pierce, on property at Saccarappa, $12.49. And on this list the kinds of property taxed are enumerated.

This levy was made only upon the property of those who supported the Congregational Parish, or method of taxing to support preaching. Quakers, Methodist, Universalists, and all other denominations, were exempted, provided the several members paid to support the kind of preaching they claimed to like best.

(1.) Hon. Archelaus Lewis was a Revolutionary soldier, and his grave memorial stands at Stroudwater. He built the house there, now the residence of the Milliken family, in which the post office is located, and went into trade. He purchased the Congin mill privilege and moved there. He had three wives and died Jan. 2, 1834, aged 81 years. He was a very active and useful citizen.

(2.) Capt. John Jones was a retired sea captain, residing in the Jeremiah Riggs house (his wife was a daughter of Riggs) that was taken down recently to ake room for a new one, now seen a ew rods westerly of the new dwelling .ouse of Mr. Daniel D. Chenery at Bradley's Corner. Capt. Jones purchased nearly all of the Riggs farm, and died August 22, 1897, aged 80 years. He had two wives, sisters. His memorial grave stone stands at Stroudwater.

(3.) Oliver Buckley came from Rockey Hill, Conn., and resided on Stevens' Plains in a house that stood where the waiting rooms of Evergreen cemetery are located at the main entrance to the grounds. He died March 9, 1872, aged 90 years. His grave memorial stands in Pine Grove Cemetery.

THE DEERING NEWS.

Saturday, May 8, 1897.

GRANDPA'S SCRAP BOOK

[Under this head historical and genealogical memoranda will be furnished the readers of the News that appears worthy of preservation, particularly of remote periods in our history within the city limits and immediate vicinity.]

CAPT. SAMUEL A. BRIMBLECOM.

DIED AT BOULDER CREEK, SANTA CRUZ CO., CALIFORNIA, SATURDAY, APRIL 10TH, 1897. CAPT. SAMUEL A. BRIMBLECOM, FORMERLY A RESIDENT OF MAINE, AGED 73 YEARS.

"At the close of day, at the hush of eve, a shadow came."

At quarter to eight, as shades were gathering among the mountain peaks,—enshrined in the hearts of the family gathered round about—he "fell asleep."

He was the son of Rev. Samuel and Harriet [Buttrick] Brimblecom, born at Sharon, Mass., Nov. 2nd, 1823.

Many of his earlier years were passed in Maine, where the family removed in 1826. He spent several years at school at Westbrook Seminary, of which his father was the first principal. These were among the most pleasurable years of his life, and memories of his schoolmates were carefully cherished.

After the family returned to Massachusetts in 1836, he was placed in the store of Mr. Osborn at Kennebunk, Me. As customary in those days, intoxicating liquors were dispensed in this store. One day he sold a man a glass of liquor, and the man died that night from the cumulative effects of hard drinking. This event affected the boy's mind deeply, and he resolved never again to be instrumental in such a tragedy. From that time Mr. Osborn permitted him to confine himself to other duties; but shortly, his mind thoroughly awakened on the subject, he became unwilling to remain where liquors were sold, and obtained permission to join his family in Massachusetts, where he resumed his studies.

At the age of sixteen he went to sea, making a voyage to Brazil on the brig "Palm." His second voyage was to India in the ship "Barnstable," being absent one year. After this he spent some time at home, once more pursuing his studies at Barre, Mass.

At the age of nineteen he sailed for China in the fine new barque "Antelope." After arduous service on the Chinese coast as seaman and mate on vessels belonging to Russell & Co. of Boston, he was promoted, at the age of twenty-three, to be captain of the fast schooner "Petrel," carrying four guns, the armament being made necessary by the swarming Chinese pirates of those perilous seas. After spending seven years in Chinese waters, he purchased a part interest in the "Petrel" and sailed for California, arriving at San Francisco in the summer of 1849. Here the "Petrel" was sold, and soon after the young captain took command of the store-ship "Panama," belonging to Macondray & Co.

During all these years in the distinguished English and American society gathered on the Chinese coast, he was true to the temperance principles imbibed in the honored old state of Maine, and in every company touched his glass of cold water to their wine.

In the spring of 1850 he resigned his position in San Francisco to return home to Massachusetts, via. the Isthmus of Panama. Here he finally abandoned the sea, and married Miss Sarah Ware Holden of Barre, Mass., and emigrated to the West, where, in company with other retired sea captains, he founded the town of Woosung, Ogle Co., Illinois.

In 1861 he removed to California, where he has since resided at San Francisco, Santa Clara and Boulder Creek. After suffering a very long and severe illness, he died at his home near the latter town.

The funeral took place from the residence on Monday at 10.30 a. m., Rev. Dr. Anthony of the M. E. church officiating, assisted by Rev. C. R. Nugent, pastor of the Presbyterian chapel. The burial took place at Santa Clara on the arrival of the 4.30 p. m. train the same day, th service conducted by Rev. Dr. Haskell of the Unitarian church, attended by many friends of the family.

Nature laid upon the scene her gentlest benediction. The blue above, the evening song of birds, the glint of dying sunlight across the western mountains, the soft breeze laden with the breath of ocean, all spoke the joy and beauty of omniscience.

The flowers, the friends grouped about the pendulous pepper trees, the spontaneous choir from out their midst softly chanting the music of hymn and psalm—while earth returned to earth—glorified the hour, and clothed it with memories saintly and beautiful.

A wife, two daughters and two sons are left to mourn his loss. Five brothers and one sister survive him.

THE DEERING NEWS

Saturday, July 17, 1897.

GRANDPA'S SCRAP BOOK

[Under this head historical and genealogical memoranda will be furnished the readers of the News that appears worthy of preservation, particularly of remote periods in our history within the city limits and immediate vicinity.]

WESTBROOK SEMINARY.

NAMES OF SOME OF ITS BENEFACTORS IN THE YEAR EIGHTEEN HUNDRED AND FORTY.

The News has printed considerable and thus preserved many items of history relative to this old and now much respected institution, but the whole story of its conception and early growth can never be known as both the clerk's and treasurer's books have been destroyed; but the News is in possession of a valuable relic that shows how the $1200 debt of 1840, or the most of it, was wiped out and who assisted in doing it; and the relic is a subscription book obtained of Walter F. Goodrich, Esq., of Stevens Plains, one of the fast friends to the Institution. The book in size is 6x8 inches and ¼ inch thick, well worn and commences as follows:

"In behalf of the Board of Trustees of the Westbrook Seminary, we the Subscribers, President and Secretary of said Board, would respectfully inform the Universalist public that there is an unpaid debt of twelve hundred Dollars, against said Institution which has been standing since 1834, the time of the completion of the Seminary; and that the time has come when said debt must be paid, or there is danger that the whole property will pass into other hands, entirely beyond the control of the Board of Trustees.

"Feeling full confidence in the zeal and liberality of our brethren in the State of Maine, and fully believing that they will, willingly, lend us their assistance in the relief of said Institution, the Board of Trustees, at its late annual meeting, holden in Westbrook on the 26th of August last, unanimously elected two agents, one for the Eastern, the other for the Western section of our State, to go forth and solicit donations of the friends of said Institution; which donations shall be, when received by the Treasurer of said Board, expended in the liquidation of said debt.

"We would further state that it is desired by the Board, that every man who may give us his assistance, place his name upon this book, together with the amount of his subscription, that a true & faithful account may be had of all funds received, and that we may now and hereafter, know who the friends of the Westbrook Seminary are.

"And in all cases, when it is possible for the Donator to pay at the time of his subscribing, it is very desirable and necessary that he should do it. If it is not, he will be called upon about the first of May next. If the sum of $1200 is not raised, the money will be refunded to those who may pay in at the time of their subscribing."

I. C. CHURCHILL, *President.*
S. B. STEVENS, *Secretary.*

Portland, Sept. 1, 1840.

"This may certify that G. W. Quinby, of North Yarmouth, has been duly appointed by the Board of Trustees of the Westbrook Seminary, and is hereby authorized and commissioned by said Board as their Agent to solicit funds of the Universalist public, in the Western part of the State of Maine, for the relief of said Institution.

"Our brethren, who may feel a desire and willingness to assist us in this time of need may; therefore, feel the fullest confidence in Bro. Quinby; as any business which he may do, in behalf of the Westbrook Seminary has the approbation of the Trustees, thereof."

Portland, Sept. 1, 1840.

I. C. CHURCHILL, *President.*
S. B. STEVENS, *Secretary.*

The following is a partial list of the contributors and amounts contributed, all of Portland:

NAME.	AM'T.
J and C Barbour,	25 00
Nathl. Shaw,	10 00
John Leavitt,	5 00
Danl. Winslow,	10 00
Chas, Fobes,	10 00
R G Green,	15 00
Wm H Purington,	5 00
S H Colesworthy,	5 00
J S Sargent,	5 00
Lemuel Dyer,	10 00
William Robinson,	10 00
Winslow H. Purington,	5 00
A W and C Clapp,	15 00
Horace Harres,	5 00
John M Chase,	5 00
Joshua Dunn,	5 00
D W Millett,	5 00
E E Beal,	10 00
Ammi Vining,	5 00
C F Safford,	3 00
Benj. Stevens,	2 00
Robert Howell,	1 00
Benj. Littlefield,	1 00
John W Small,	2 00
Samuel Clarke,	5 00
Capt. Joseph Walker,	5 00
J F Safford,	5 00
Chas. Blake,	5 00
J C Washburn,	2 00
Jacob Kimball,	2 00
Edward Hamblen,	2 00
Capt. A Winslow,	5 00
	$203 00
S H Colesworthy,	5 00
J W Mansfield,	2 00
Capt J F Safford,	2 00
Asa Clapp,	10 00
Isaac Ilsley,	5 00
J L Farmer,	10 00
James Churchill,	5 00
Alfred Dyer,	5 00
Daniel Green,	2 00
E P Burbank,	2 00
Henry Hunt,	2 00
Otis True,	1 00
T C Hursey,	5 00
Robbin Fletcher,	2 00
A J Sargent,	1 00
Geo. W Woodman,	2 00
Wilson & Jack,	2 50
I & C Barbour,	5 00
C T Pike,	1 00
J Daniels,	1 00
Edward Hamblin,	2 50
James Winslow,	5 00
Wm. Merritt,	1 00
Joseph L. Smith,	1 00
Both of these to be found at the depot,	
Mr. Sargent,	1 00
Wm. Richards,	50
Oren Ring,	50
James Bailey,	50
Wm. Bailey,	25
John Sweatt,	1 00
Daniel Winslow,	5 00
Moody F. Walker,	5 00
Jos. ——— (?)	1 00
Jas. H. Perley,	1 00
Wm H Purington,	2 00
Chas Fobes,	6 00
Joseph Dyer,	4 00
W H Purington,	2 00
Chas. P Winslow,	50
Hosea Harlow,	1 00
Geo. Knight, Jr.,	3 00
J P Safford,	1 00
John W Sweat, on steamboat,	1 00
C F Safford,	2 00
John Leavitt,	3 00
Jas. Siminton,	2 00
Wm. H Siminton,	1 00
J R Matthews,	1 00
Eli Webb,	1 00
John M Jordan,	50
John Cowell,	50
Jacob Kimball,	3 00
Chas. Blake	3.00
Nemiah Ryerson	1.00
Capt. Jos. Walker	5.00
Henry Dyer	1.00
Lemual York	3.00
Chas. H Greene	
Boat builder, Fore street	1.00
John W Smith	2.00
C C Tobie	1.00
W C Osborne	1.00
John J Davis	1.00
Geo. L Bradbury	3.00
Middle street No. 6	
Wm. Pearson	.50
Annie Vining	2.00
Joshua Dyer	1.00
Andrew Fuller, chaise repairer	1.00
Henry Knight	1.00
John Rounds	2.00
Sanborn & Carter	5.00
G S Barston	1.00
Samuel Clark	3.00
Capt. Coyle, steam boat	1.00
Elias Thomas, Exchange street	3.00
John C Baker	1.00
John Simonton	2.00
E Daniels	3.00
R F Green	1.00
Thos. W O'Brion	2.00
Asa Bailey, Cor Congress and Franklin streets	1.00
Wm. Noble, tailor	.25
Wm. Steel	1.00
E Winship	1.00
E Gammon	1.00
A W Clapp	5.00

CONTINUED:

Name	Amt.
J E Hodgkins	1.00
Samuel Haskell	2.00
I I Brown	1.00
Friend	1.00
John P Pike	1.00
C S Davis	1.00
Luther Fitch	1.00
Walter Corey	1.00
I O Bancroft	1.00
Joshua Dunn	1.00
S Warren	1.00
J T Gilman	1.00
Cash	3.00
Daniel Plummer	1.00
John Mussey	20.00
Sumner Cummings	5.00
P T Varnum	5.00
Wm. C Kimball	1.00
O P Thork	1.00
John Fox	5.00
Hezekiah Winslow	3.00
Chas. W Strout	1.00
Elbridge Bacon	1.00
Dr. Clark	1.00
Cash	1.00
Cash Paid—Israel Richardson	20.00
?	3.00
?	1.00
?	3.00
J P Boyd	3.00
John & W Chase	3.00
Jos. B Haskell	1.00
Arthur S Ricker, city market	1.00
Chas. E Boody	.50
Wm. Wallace	
Capt. Isaac Knight	5.00
Jas. F Roberts	.50
Chas. Atwell, quarter of a pew in Rev. L L Saddler's meeting house sold to C F Safford for	8.00
Oliver E Silsby	2.00
Wm. P Fessenden	3.00
Dr. Ichabod Nichols	5.00

This is all relative to what was subscribed in Portland, and the whole amount is $578.00.

TO BE CONTINUED.

Continued from Last Week.

WESTBROOK WHICH INCLUDED WHAT IS NOW THE TERRITORY OF DEERING.

NAME.	AMT.
Levi Morrill	$25.00
Rufus Morrill	20.00
Gerry Cook	10.00
Amasa Fober	10.00
Silas Broad	10.00
Jonathan Smith	10.00
Alfred Stevens	8.00
Jeremiah Beedle	5.00
Amos Abbott	5.00
James Deering	50.00
Samuel Jordan	15.00
Wm. B Goodrich	5.00
Rufus Dunham	5.00
S B Stevens	20.00
Andrew Cram	2.00
John B True	5.00
Chas. Bartlett	10.00
Randall Johnson	20.00
D C—?	5.00
Tristram C Stevens	.50
Cash	10.00
N L Woodbury	5.00
Freeman Porter	2.00
A G Fobes	5.00
Geo. Libby	100.00
E P Hinds	25.00
M B Walker	10.00
S B Stevens	5.00
Freeman Porter	
Oliver Buckley	10.00
Rufus Dunham	3.00
James Torrey	2.00
Rufus Morrill	10.00
Wm. B Goodrich	3.00
C S Buckley	3.00
Jos. P Atkinson	10.00
A Leach	3.00
E D Woodford	5.00
James Deering	20.00
Sam'l Jordan	5.00
Jonathan Smith	5.00
Cyrus Thurlow	1.00
Jas. Brackett	5.00
Chas. Bartlett	5.00
Silas Broad	3.00
John Jordan	1.00
Martin Hawes	1.00
David Torrey	2.00
Wm. Burnell	1.00
Josiah Woodford	1.00
Thomas J Riggs	2.00
Nathaniel Sawyer	1.00
Hiram Jordan	5.00
Eliza Thayer	1.00
Isaac Mason	1.00
Mrs. Miranda Fowler	1.00
Elizabeth Jones	1.00
Arthur Milliken	1.00
Geo. Libby	5.00
Capt. Arron Winslow	2.00
Geo. Frost	10.00
Wm. H Jewett (deceased)	1.00
Friend	.25
Wm. Bartlett	1.00
Hon. F O J Smith	20.00
J C Brackett	1.00
	$545.75

All of the foregoing resided in what is now Deering with perhaps two exceptions. Where the name appears the second time I suspect it is for what was not paid at time of subscribing.

BACCARAPPA VILLAGE, (IN WESTBROOK)

I G Walker	$10.00
Isaac Walker	5.00
(Dr.) E Stone	1.00
Dana Brigham	3.00
Simon Elder	3.00
Aaron Quinby	3.00
Cash	.50
R E Lyon	1.00
T B Edwards	1.00
Leander Valentine	3.00
Col. Geo. Small	3.00
J Walker Jr.	5.00
Levi Blaisdell	1.00
G W Lunt 2nd	.50
W P Babb	1.00
M Waterman	1.00
C W Quinby	.50
Isaac F Quinby	.50
I G Bailey	.50
C M Phinney	.50
Wm. Bixby	.50
Mrs. Pride Anderson	.50

Albert Webb	1.00
J R Andrews	1.00
D C—?	1.00
J H Watson	1.00
J E Brown	1.00
A S Harding	.50
F E W Bradbury (?)	1.00
Benj. Larrabee	1.00
Samuel Lamb	1.00
	$53.50

SUBSCRIPTION FOR LADIES.

Ruth Rust, Norway	$1.00
Jane Fogg, Brunswick	.50
H J Corbett, Lisbon	.50

MINISTERIAL SUBSCRIPTIONS.

G. W. Quinby No. Falmouth,	$5.00
Wm. R. French, Fryeburg,	5.00
O. H. Quinby, Bowdoinham,	3.00
Henry C. Baker, No. Yarmouth,	3.00
W. B. Werit, Freeport,	5.00

SUBSCRIPTIONS BY TOWNS.

Bowdoinham	$32.75
Minot,	6.75
Lewiston,	25.00
Danville,	5.00
West Livermore,	37.00
Readfield,	2.00
East Livermore,	8.00
Dixfield,	14.00
Wilton,	4.00
Bridgton,	23.00
Denmark,	10.00
Brownfield,	12.33
Lovell,	9.96
Sweden,	3.00
Paris,	9.00
Norway,	39.00
Hiram,	5.00
Waterford,	19.00
Harrison,	1.00
Raymond,	1.00
Brunswick,	62.00
Topsham,	10.00
Lisbon & Webster,	12.25
North Yarmouth,	68.00

Under the name of this town appears the following:

Donation from a sailor boy,	5.00
Donation from a land lubber,	5.00
Donation from a friend in Cumberland,	5.00
Donation from a lady Universalist,	5.00
East Turner,	20.25
Bath,	30.50
Freeport,	25.00
Pownal,	24.00
South Windham,	
Gorham,	

Saco & Biddeford, 2 1-2 pages of names from 25 cents to $1.00 each.

Gray,	$7.25
Falmouth,	2.25
New Gloucester,	
Pownal,	
Bangor, Collection taken in Universalist church,	27.87
Collection by Bro. Maglothlin,	7.50
Total for Bangor,	$72.87
Scarborough,	
Buxton,	
Cumberland,	
Lewiston Falls,	
Danville,	
Auburn,	

The names of the contributors in all these towns are given but lack of space in the News prevents giving them, and when footings are not given in the book I leave them out.

THE END.

THE DEERING NEWS.

Saturday, July 31, 1897.

GRANDPA'S SCRAP BOOK

[Under this head historical and genealogical memoranda will be furnished the readers of the News that appears worthy of preservation, particularly of remote periods in our history within the city limits and immediate vicinity.]

THIRTY YEARS.

THE MEMBERS OF ALLEN'S CORNER SABBATH SCHOOL AND FRIENDS CELEBRATE.

The Allen's Corner Sabbath school held its 30th anniversary celebration last Sunday afternoon and evening.

The building in which the school meets is located on the southerly side of Stevens Plains Avenue, a few steps easterly of Main street, formerly called Meadow road. The building is small but inside very cozy. In it many good times have been indulged in. It was originally a school house, but was purchased by the Sabbath school society.

Rev. W. H. Haskell of the Falmouth 2nd Congregational parish presided in the afternoon. Remarks were made by Mr. Henry Smith formerly of Portland and Miss Abbie Leavitt of that city who indulged in reminiscences when they performed missionary work in the locality. She was present when the "mission" was organized thirty years ago—came out to sing, and continued coming for a period of twelve years. Of the work at Allen's Corner the Free Church at Morrill's is an offspring—according to Miss Leavitt's statement.

The wife of Rev. W. H. Fultz who resides between Allen's Corner and Presumpscot Falls read a paper from which we are permitted to make extracts as follows:

"The number of houses in the district in 1864 were 27, now 68—an increase of 41.

"The religious preferences of the people then were: 27 Universalists, 7 Baptists, 4 Congregationalists, 2 Quakers, 1 Methodists, 15 Spiritualists.

"The rest were 'nothingtarious', and out of all these only about a dozen confessed they were trying to live a Christian life. There was no religious service of any kind and many of the children had never seen the inside of a Sunday school room.

"In 1864 I visited the parents of all the children and asked permission to open a Sabbath school. The encouragement was such that we opened a school with twenty members. This continued about six weeks, when the use of the key which opened the school house where we met was denied by the summer school teacher who was a Spiritualist, and the school agent also denied us.

"The district was about to repair the school house in front of which was a pile of lumber, so we seated the scholars on it and commenced the exercises, when a delegation from the Y. M. C. Association of Portland came along on their way to the Falls mission, and observing the situation rendered us assistance by stopping and joining us.

"That week I visited every home of the district and asked permission to use the school-house. All but two, the family of the school teacher and agent, gave consent. The agent did not refuse, but said he did not want to get the ill-will of the teacher he had hired. The key was at last obtained and the school was continued.

"For an assistant we obtained the aid of one George Kimball of Woodfords, who would address on the Sabbath day those who would come to the school house.

[Mr. Kimball was a house carpenter and resided on what is now High street near Prospect. The house now stands. Ed. News.] "This state of things continued about two years when I went from home, and the school went into decline. We had no lesson papers as now—we learned from the Bible and then commented and transmitted as much as we could.

"In 1867 the present school was organized with 67 scholars. The seed sown by the first school germinated. The wayside of life has been more beautiful to scores of people in consequence. The fruit we have tasted. We now behold it.

"From the school house the school removed to the hall of the brick building where $60 per year was paid for rent."

Mrs. [Hamblin] Fultz in closing said: "I have been absent from the place (excepting when I have visited here) twenty-three years, and return to find the Sabbath school of 30 years growth flourishing, preaching nearly every Sabbath, prayer meetings, a church at Morrill's Corner which is an outgrowth of the labors here, the little old school house purchased, renovated and enlarged into this pretty room, a temperance society, electric cars, tract society, and buildings going up all around us. By and by the Book of Records resting upon the great white Throne will be opened and there will be revealed what has come from the little beginning here, 'thirty odd years since.'"

Saturday, Aug. 7, 1897.

GRANDPA'S SCRAP BOOK

[Under this head historical and genealogical memoranda will be furnished the readers of the News that appears worthy of preservation, particularly of remote periods in our history within the city limits and immediate vicinity.]

THE WOODFORDS.

WILLIAM AND AN INTERESTING LETTER TO HIS UNCLE IN THE YEAR 1827.

Chauncey Woodford was the eldest of the three brothers who came to what is now Deering, and, undoubtedly was the pioneer of the name. He settled at Morrill's Corner and has been written up in the News.

His brothers, Josiah and Dea. Ebenezer D., (sometimes called Eben,) evidently came later. Both of these were written up in the News in the issue of August 18, 1894, and in the next number we gave the location of their respective places of abode, and of whom obtained.

William Woodford, who departed this life Friday evening at 7 o'clock at his home at Woodfords Corner, July 30th, at the great age of 92 years, was born there July 21, 1805, and was the eldest child in a family of eight children. He married, April 26, 1827, Nancy W., daughter of Benjamin and Charlotte (Webb) Stevens, born January 7, 1807; Charlotte Webb being the daughter of Capt. Henry Webb, born at Stroudwater in what was later known as the Benjamin Burnham house, corner of Westbrook and Bond streets, now gone. The residence in which the deceased died was that of his wife's father, in which his wife was born, and now wears the mantle of antiquity, standing on the northerly side of Ocean street.

Appropriate notices of his death appeared in the Portland morning papers. He left children. His wife died twenty years since.

In the years 1826-7 a great religious excitement passed over this place, and scores of converts joined the Congregational church, of which Rev. Caleb Bradley was pastor. He did not then keep a diary but did in after years, in which he alluded to the matter.

A few weeks since we found in the attic of the Samuel Jordan house at Woodfords, an old, well-worn manuscript letter, which would fill a column in this paper, bearing upon the Woodfords family and the religious revival of that period, and now propose to print it, in a condensed form, in connection with this brief notice of William's death, as follows:

"POMPEY, N. Y., May 28, 1827.
Dear Brothers:—

I received a letter from your minister yesterday, dated May 14, which gave me much joy. We are informed in the word of God there is joy in heaven over one sinner that repents; if there is joy throughout all heaven when one sinner returns to Christ, how it becomes us to rejoice and give glory to God when we hear of thousands flocking to Christ as the only ark of safety. Yes, dear brothers, I rejoice to hear of the glorious work going on among you, of the numbers that have been united to your church, among which our sister Polly, and your children being among the numbers, it ought to fill our hearts with gratitude to God. Tell your children and your converts that they have much remaining sin unsubdued; that they live in temptation; that the world, the flesh and the Devil will be great enemies to their religious improvement. * * * * I rejoice to hear that brother Eben is engaged in the cause of Christ—that he can pray and exhort in his family, also in the house of God before a congregation. Dear brothers, you must remember you were bought with a price, that you were once enemies to God, that you and your children are taken and others left.

"I am sorry to hear my brother Chauncey is not more awake in so glorious a cause. Awake, my brother; come up to the help of the Lord against the mighty; tell your children that they must repent or they cannot be saved; Tell sinners around you they must be born again or they will sink to hell. * *

"I will now give you a short account of the religious excitement in Pompey last year. I was requested by our minister in the spring to visit the village. Before this, however, there was some appearance of religious excitement I visited almost every house and found the minds very tender. When I pressed it upon them to repent and believe in the Saviour tears flowed. Our minister was supported by a young candidate from Utica. Our meetings were solemn and very full. * * * The number that joined our church was 150; 15 with the Baptist and a small number with the Methodists. The work here spread to various other towns. There was a great shaking among the dry bones, Universalists and some deists being made subjects of hope. * * * * *

"Of my own family my second daughter was a subject of the awakening. After some days she stated to her mother she felt that she wanted to fly to Christ. The most of my other children appear solemn, but with grief, I must tell you, they at present are stupid. O, my brothers, pray for them. * * * * Where I would do good evil is present with me. O, wretched man that I am, who shall deliver me from bondage? * * *

"I have received a letter from Rensalearville (?) informing me brother Eben visited our brothers there last fall and will again this fall. * * *

"Please give my respects to all, especially your minister.
ISRAEL WOODFORD.
To Chauncey & Ebenezer D. Woodford.

Saturday, Aug. 14, 1897.

GRANDPA'S SCRAP BOOK

[Under this head historical and genealogical memoranda will be furnished the readers of the News that appears worthy of preservation, particularly of remote periods in our history within the city limits and immediate vicinity.]

THE LATE ALPHEUS S. ALDEN.

The report of the church likewise grave Freemason service over the remains of the one whose name appears above prepared for the News, was crowded out of the last issue but we here insert a few extracts as follows: Rev. Frederick T. Nelson, pastor of the Universalist church said;

"The deceased has solved the mystery of death—the never ending circle of life and death he knows. All that is earthly of him we tenderly give a place in the dusty earth, but we have reason to believe that his soul continues to live.

"Death brings us sorrow and tears but it should bring us no fears.

"We see prophecy in the seed time and harvest. The mortal remains is not a fit temple for the soul. All through the ages man has struggled with the great question of 'what becomes of man after death?' I believe we grow after the event till we approach so near as to become a part of the Perfect Man.

"On an occasion like this it is wise for us to pause and consider the situation.

"The deceased was a constant attendant here. He was born and ever lived in this locality. He was not only hopeful but cheerful. He was faithful; he was good. Your presence on this occasion speaks in praise of him—speaks in more eulogistic terms than I can. He inspired us by his presence, his word and example."

Ebenezer D. Woodford, deacon of the First Congregational Church; Walter B. Gookrich, Samuel B. Stevens and Jesse D. Alden, father of the deceased, married sisters, all four of the wives coming from the State of Connecticut, and the remains of all are deposited in four adjoining lots in Pine Grove Cemetery. A monument to the latter is inscribed as follows:

JESSE DUNBAR ALLEN,

Died May 26, 1834,

ÆT 45 YEARS.

ISABEL,

wife of

JESSE D. ALDEN,

Died May 15, 1862,

AGED 65 YEARS.

THE DEERING NEWS.

Saturday, Aug. 21, 1897.

GRANDPA'S SCRAP BOOK

[Under this head historical and genealogical memoranda will be furnished the readers of the News that appears worthy of preservation, particularly of remote periods in our history within the city limits and immediate vicinity.]

HISTORICAL MEMORANDA.

July 21, 1818, married in Westbrook, by Rev. Caleb Bradley, Mr. Samuel Mountfort, aged 83, to Miss Esther Shaw, aged 25!—*Portland Argus*.

He resided on what was known a few years since as the old Town House road, in this city, westerly of Riverton Park. In 1816 he was taxed for a $200 house, $70 barn and a large and well stocked farm. We think the Minotts occupied the place after him, and still retain it.

Died in Gorham, Me., October 26, 1826. Eli Webb, aged 89 years. His wife died about three months since, after they had lived together 66 years. The deceased was a soldier in the Old French War, and likewise in the War of the Revolution. He was a kind parent, a good neighbor and is deeply lamented by all who was acquainted with him.—*Portland Argus*.

A LAND MARK GONE.

The old dwelling that stood on the southerly side of Middle St. near India, end to the street, with the large garden in front and high retaining street wall, in Portland, has been removed and Mr. Elbridge G. Johnson, contractor and builder, of Stroudwater, is erecting on the site a large wooden building for a boarding house. In the old house the two sons, Capt. Thomas and William, as well as several other descendants of Rev. Thomas Browne, the first Congregationalist minister of the Stroudwater parish of Falmouth, now Deering, closed their eyes to the scenes of earth.

Capt. Thomas B. was born March 24, 1769; died March 3, 1849. We have never been able to discover the maiden name of his wife. They had five children.

William was born March 1, 1779, and died 1861. His wife was Octavia Southgate, daughter of Dr. Robert Southgate of Scarboro, and she died January 9, 1813. aged 28 years. They had two sons, William, who graduated at Bowdoin College when very young, became a poet, lawyer and author, and died in Texas, having a son at West Point when the War of the Rebellion broke out, who became a Confederate general and was killed in battle. Frederick became a writer and assistant editor in Louisville, went to New Orleans, where, in 1860, he had his name changed to Southgate. He left quite a large family. From the South we have secured a copy of daguerreotype likeness of the elder William and a photo of the graduate of Bowdoin College.

Bishop Southgate, the Episcopalian clergyman, once settled in Portland, and we think the first minister of the State street cathedral, married a daughter of William Browne, senior. He was a graduate of Bowdoin and has a son in Maryland, who is a Roman Catholic priest.

Parson Browne's daughter Abigail, married March 23, 1789, Major Hugh McLellan; had a large family and resided in Portland. Their eldest child, Eunice, married Charles Fox, March 4, 1805; and their next, named Nabby, married, Nov. 1, 1805, Horation Southgate, Esq., many years connected with our Probate court, and died on the old Doctor Southgate homestead at Dunston, Scarboro.

Parson Browne's daughter, Elizabeth, became the second wife of Hon. Archalaus Lewis, a Revolutionary soldier. The house he built, and in which she died, is the large dwelling in Stroudwater at the head of Waldo street, a room of which is used for the post office.

Rebecca, the youngest child of Parson Browne, married June 13, 1802, Capt. John L. Lewis of Portland, and died two years later, and he married a second time. The Lewis house and the McLellan house both stand in Portland.

The grave memorial stone of Parson Browne may be seen in the old grave yard at Stroudwater. The graves of his sons are unmarked in Evergreen cemetery. Parson Browne resided close to the present residence of Dr. A. P. Topliff, Woodfords. He was the first vice-president of Bowdoin College.

Rev. Caleb Bradley married for his first wife Sally Crocker, Nov., 1801, an inmate of the Brown family. An obituary of whom, which may be found in the Christian Mirror of 1843, says she was born in Wrenham, Mass., and came here when sixteen years of age. Her grave is unmarked in the little Mitchell Hill grave yard.

Saturday, Aug. 28, 1897.

GRANDPA'S SCRAP BOOK

[Under this head historical and genealogical memoranda will be furnished the readers of the News that appears worthy of preservation, particularly of remote periods in our history within the city limits and immediate vicinity.]

THE STORER MANSION.

TIME OF ITS ERECTION AND FACTS THEREWITH CONNECTED.

Frost street, located in the year 1833, and church street, originally known as Capisic road, located in 1752, the starting point being a stake in the "most easterly corner of Charles Frosts Esq. land," unite in front of the First Congregational meeting house of this city, the society of which was organized in the year 1764, and the two join what is now known as Stevens Plains avenue, on the westerly side thereof, ten rods distant from the meeting house of our Bradley Corner district, the avenue being first located and called a highway in 1735, "beginning by the bridge at the paper mill at Stroudwater, thence"—etc. In the northwesterly corner lot, where Frost and Church streets join Stevens Plains avenue, stands a large, two-story dwelling, fronting southerly, or upon Church street, but entered from Stevens Plains avenue. The westerly wall is constructed of brick, the others wood. The ground floor, or story, is divided into four rooms, each being very large, and a hall-way through the middle. A like division is made of the second story. In each room is a large fire place, the building containing four stacks of chimneys, two upon each end. The front door has a brass handle and side lights, and arched finish over the top, and on each side of the door there are two windows. The clapboards have never been painted, and are now weather-worn to a thickness of about an eighth of an inch in many places. The air of antiquity envelopes the structure, particularly the barn, and the passer-by shrugs his shoulders and says "That's an old fellow; wonder who built it, and when?" and the oldest citizen of the neighborhood replies, "You must ask some one older than I am." So to the written records we must go, scattered here and there, and search and search. The work can't be done in a day, nor a month, nor a year, but in connection with other work of the same nature, making a note here and another there, and then uniting all, the blind are made to see. This we have done and now record the result.

The first record of a person by the name of Storer residing hereabouts is in the old Parish record book, and reads as follows:

Voted to give Mrs. Storer for 2-3 year past, 0, 16, 9.

The next vote passed at the meeting which was holden March 29, 1785, explains the foregoing, when it was

Voted to give Mrs. Storer for Current year for taking Care meeting house twenty Four Shillings.

The next year Mrs. Storer's account of £1-4 was voted and the namedi appears on the records.

In the year 1787 a Joseph Storer had a license to retail liquors in Falmouth, but we cannot find a place of residence of the name hereabouts at that date.

In the year 1797, for a consideration of $300, the title to a piece of flats land, located in Portland, was conveyed and the following names appear on record:

We, Joanna Storer, widow of Joseph Storer, housewright, Thomas Knight, housewright, Joanna, his wife, in her right, Thomas Pierce, bricklayer, and Betsey in her right, all of Falmouth, Jonathan Ellsworth of ——? Lincoln county and Esther, in her right, Miriam Storer, singlewoman and Joseph Storer, housewright, both of Falmouth, etc.

The foregoing, and other data, shows the offspring of Joseph Storer, senior, and Joanna ———, his wife to have been at that time and a little later, as follows:

1—Joanna, m. Thomas Knight, Dec. 29, 1789. On the sixth day of December it is recorded that he was living on what is Spring St., where Nevens street joins it.
2—Betsey, m. Thomas Pierce, born in Scarboro, October 26, 1763; son of Rev. Thomas Pierce, who died in that town. (More about this couple and descendants later.)
3—Esther, m. Jonathan Elsworth, who testified in 1811 that he was then living in the town of Avon, Kennebec county.; that he was then 47 years of age; that in 1792 he resided in the family of Joanna Frost, and worked for Andrew P. Frost (who lived where the Brewer house stood.)
4—Miriam Storer, unmarried in 1797.
5—Joseph, m., November 11, 1800, Charlotte Knight, and built the house we have described.

In the year 1799 this Joseph agreed to pay $4 toward the $400 promised Rev. Caleb Bradley, and Thomas Pierce $2, if the reverend gentleman would locate among the people and become their pastor.

In 1803 he purchased a pew in the meeting house, paying therefor $33, which he sold to Joseph Stevens.

In 1807, for a consideration of $2,150, he purchased of the heirs of Joseph Noyes, Esq., who resided on the place now known as the James Deering farm, forty-five acres of land, located on the northerly side of Capisic highway, thirty acres of which he immediately sold Pelig Mitchell—notice in back numbers of News in connection with the Maxfield family—who built the so-called Moses G. Dow House, as now seen, in an unchanged state as to the original design, standing next westerly of the meeting house, and then built for himself a dwelling on the site of the one herein described, the record of the fate of which is found in the following transcript from the Eastern Argus:

Jan. 17, 1812. The house of Joseph Storer, of Falmouth, was destroyed by fire with its contents. There were two families in the house, who, with difficulty, escaped from the flames.

TO BE CONTINUED.

GRANDPA'S SCRAP BOOK

[Under this head historical and genealogical memoranda will be furnished the readers of the News that appears worthy of preservation, particularly of remote periods in our history within he city limits and immediatelvicinity.]

MASON.

AN OLD NAME WITH BUT FEW REPRESENTATIVES HEREABOUTS.

Near the centre of the old cemetery at Stroudwater village, adjoining the highway, stands a well preserved memorial stone inscribed as follows:

In Memory of
DANIEL MASON, ESQ.
Formerly of Watertown, Mass.
Died Oct. 9, 1817.
Aged 60.

To the casual observer the slate slab expresses but little—no more than any of its kind—and the passerby moved on to the next, but to the one sufficiently aged to live in the past the invisible prompter in zephry voice whispered the word "halt" and I pause.

The Masons came to old Falmouth—the part that is now the city of Deering—from Watertown, Mass., as the memorial indicates, and those who desire to learn of the name in that town will find much that interests by consulting Bond's History of that municipality, but I have only room to say that—

Nehemiah Mason married March 28, 1755, Elizabeth Stone, and after her he had two other wives, and nine children: 1st, Daniel; 2d, Hugh; 5, Moses.

I here present these names because descendants can be traced to this place and in the case of Daniel descendants are still with us.

Daniel Mason, eldest child of Nehemiah, whose name the slate slab commemorates was born in Watertown, Mass., Aug 17, 1757. Of his boyhood and decline in life I have but little knowledge. By occupation he was a tanner and spent his last days in the house at the north westerly corner of Congress and Stevens Plains avenue, (Bradley's Corner district) which the late Edward Newman renovated and repaired some fifteen years since and left it as now seen and owned by the Widow Knight whose husband was of the tribe of the name descending from Nathaniel Knight of Stroudwater Falls (near Saccarappa.)

To the original house he added another, or an ell, which after the purchase of the premises by Joshua Richardson was moved to Cotton street, Portland, and there burned.

When Daniel located here I can not say. He was interested as an owner in what is now the sight of the John B. Curtis estate (the original house was removed to Spring street) located about fifty rods distant on the opposite side of Stevens Plains avenue where his son Daniel Mason, Jr., first resided while with Daniel senior, resided his son Samuel and some of his other children.

In the year 1810 Daniel Mason, Jr., was taxed for a house valued at $70; barn, $40; bark house and slaughter house, $200; store, $150, (store deducted); 4 1 2 acres of land; one cow, $14; two horses, $80; chaise, $80 and stock in trade $1000. Back of the present Curtis house was a tan yard.

Samuel Mason, brother to Daniel Jr., was taxed at the same time as follows: One house $500; one barn $40; 1-2 bark house and yard $100; 1 1 2 acre mowing and other land; house on wharf $125; one cow; two horses; one swine; one chaise $80; stock in trade $1000. Back of the Bradley Corner house was the old Riggs tan yard where Daniel senior and his son Samuel resided.

In the year 1819 Samuel Mason conveyed to his mother his interest in the Bradley Corner lot, and in 1829 he administered on the estate of his mother, Esther Mason.

Before me is a well preserved ancient appearing scrap of paper found among the few papers that have been kept pertaining to the Mason name hereabouts, the record upon which I now preserve by placing it here, excepting the name of the day of the week and hour the ten children of Daniel and Esther Mason originally of Watertown, Mass., were born as follows:

1 Nehemiah, b, Aug. 31, 1780. A Portland Argus record reads as follows: May 26, 1826. Died, Nehemiah Mason of Westbrook aged 46 years. Death occasioned by drinking cold water, the weather being excessively warm.
2 Daniel Jr., b. June 1, 1782. He last occupied and died in the old Storer residence discribed three weeks since in the News. (He and son Daniel to be further noticed in another article.)
3 Samuel b, June 8 1782. He died in the Means house at Stroudwater village. He and family to be noticed later.
4 Lewis, b, 27, 1785.
5 Azor b, Dec. 14, 1786.
6 Joel b, March 3, 1788.
7 Varlow b, March 3, 1790; d, Nov. 27, 1790, aged 18 mo., 26 days.
8 A daughter b, Sep. 15, and d, five days later.
9 Noble b, Feb. 9, 1793, at Chelsea, Mass., d, Aug. 2 1793.
10 Nancy, and last, b, Apr. 19, 1794. Nancy Mason died Dec. 31, 1814. Bradley journal. A memorial stone stands by the side of that of her father—no others.

Of the career and time of death of the above named I have no knowledge excepting Nehemiah, Daniel, Samuel and those who died young, having made no effort to discover their "foot-prints in the sands of time."

It is proposed to continue this Mason record in the next issue of the News to conclude with that of Col. James Means, of Stroudwater, the eight year Revolutionary soldier whose daughter Samuel Mason married.

THE DEERING NEWS.

Saturday, Sept. 18, 1897.

GRANDPA'S SCRAP BOOK

[Under this head historical and genealogical memoranda will be furnished the readers of the News that appears worthy of preservation, particularly of remote periods in our history within the city limits and immediate vicinity.]

MASON.

AN OLD NAME WITH BUT FEW REPRESENTATIVES HEREABOUTS.

(*Continued From Last Week.*)

Daniel Mason, Jr., son of Daniel senior, was born as stated last week, June 1, 1782. Mr. Elbridge G. Riggs born here Jan. 14, 1813, hence is now 84 years of age and has lived here about all his life, a man of excellent memory, says Daniel Jr., married before he came to this place a Miss Polly Monday and resided in the state of Rhode Island.

The amount of his possessions for which he was taxed in 1816 I gave in my last article, but I cannot place the dwelling for which he was taxed on a valuation of $70. His name does not appear on the list made in 1823 of those taxed to support preaching in the First Congregational meeting house, near which he lived, but the name of his wife, Mary appears on the church member list made in 1832. Samuel Mason, brother to Daniel Jr., was taxed to support preaching, in 1826, the sum of $4.22. The names of Mary and Samuel are the only names of Masons appearing on the church or parish records.

The widow of the third, or last Daniel has stored, she states, with her household goods a family Bible in which are recorded some Mason names, but is unable to find it at present.

It was July 16, 1832, for a consideration of $700 that the old Joseph Storer mansion, described in the *News* of August 28th, was sold to the Masons. Jan. 12, 1836, the lot upon which the Milliken family resides, between the old Storer lot and the meeting house lot was sold by the Masons to John Haskell and the Storer joiner shop moved onto it and converted into the dwelling as now seen, which event has been noticed but exact date not given till now

Daniel Mason and Mary Monday, his wife, had but one child whom they named Daniel. He resided with his parents and Phoebe Chenery of Falmouth became his wife. Her ancestors came from Watertown, Mass. They had no children. Rev. Caleb Bradly frequently alludes in his journal to calls upon the family and religious meetings being held in the house, and his stopping to take tea with them.

The last Daniel must have been rather a good appearing young man. He possessed a pleasant countenance; and was a constant attendant upon public worship. He never wore whiskers, and with his white vest and shiny tall hat, always appeared on public occasions otherways neatly attired. He kept a few cows and sold milk, then he engaged in trade in a small way in the small building as now seen upon the front of the lot. He took life carelessly, was pleasant to all, accommodating, and died without an enemy.

His wife died in 1840; his mother in 1866; and he married his house keeper, the widow Murphy with one child, by whom he had one, they named Herbert D., both of whom are deceased, but the widow survives; and Chas. F. Cowan occupies the premises on a five-year lease. The grave memorials standing in Evergreen cemetery, northerly of the soldiers monument, tells the rest of the story, as follows:

Daniel Mason died Aug. 23, 1864, aged 82 years, 3 months.

Mary, wife of the late Daniel Mason, died May 20, 1866, aged 84 years, 8 months.

Daniel Mason died May 10, 1887, aged 77 years, 5 months.
"Gone, but not forgotten."

Phebe, wife of Daniel Mason, jr., died April 13, 1840, aged 28 years.

Ellen F., (2d) wife of Daniel Mason.

Herbert D. Mason died Oct. 20, 1888, aged 17 years, 8 months, 2 days.
"Goodby, Mother."

TO BE CONTINUED.

THE DEERING NEWS.

Saturday, Oct. 2, 1897.

GRANDPA'S SCRAP BOOK

[Under this head historical and genealogical memoranda will be furnished the readers of the News that appears worthy of preservation, particularly of remote periods in our history within the city limits and immediate vicinity.]

MASON.

AN OLD NAME WITH BUT FEW REPRESENTATIVES HEREABOUTS.

(*Continued From Last Week.*)

Samuel Mason, third child of Daniel and Esther Mason, was born (it is supposed) at Watertown, Mass., Saturday morning, June 8, 1783, and married Nov. 14, 1816, in Falmouth, now Deering, Sopha Means born at Stroudwater, Jan. 12, 1797, sixth, and youngest child of Capt. James Means and wife Mary Cox, the last of Portland. He died Feb. 4, 1837, aged 54 years;* she died Jan. 3, 1890, aged 94 years. The house in which she first saw the light of day stood between the westerly end of the bridge over Four river and the shop of Andrew Hawes, esq., northerly side of the highway. I know nothing of the youthful days of Samuel. Besides being a tanner, in 1820 he was engaged in beef packing. Before me are several receipts from Joshua Richardson of that year for money received on account of beef. They are in an easy hand and as clear and fresh as of yesterday.

The date he removed from Bradley's Corner to the Means house at Stroudwater I cannot state. In addition to tanning and beef packing he had a large truck garden where the High school building stands—so Mr. Elbridge G. Riggs says. He died Feb. 4, 1837, Parson Bradley says, "at 2 o'clock Sunday morning." She died Jan. 3, 1890, aged 93 years, and was straight, and fair and smart to the last. The last time I saw her was a few months before her departure for the other world. Some work was being done in the old burying ground; the sun was nearing the western horizon and had divested itself of its intensity in brightness. In fact the halo partook strangely of a sable pall—a condition strictly in accord with the scene. On the cold piece of marble bearing the name of her son, who had died in the Union army during the war of the Southern Rebellion, and other names of the departed, she sat, and when I had approached to close speaking distance she said: "There are occasions when one is justified in using harsh language. For a period of two years I have been waiting to see this stone re-set—when it is done I am ready to die." I assured her that the neighborhood wanted to see her reach the hundredth mile post in life's journey, but the stone should be re-set in the morning of the coming day, which was done. In her utterance I felt the will power and determination of her father, who passed the whole period of eight years in the army of the war of the American Revolution.

CHILDREN OF SAMUEL AND SOPHA (MEANS) MASON:

1 James, b. Sept, 27, 1816, m. Jan. 13, 1840, Mary A. Bradbury of Buxton. He was a hatter, and died in Portland. Children: 1 Julia T., Henry A. Gray; 2 Martha I., m. Henry J. Humphrey; 3 James M., m. Nettie Brewer, who d. this spring. He, with his mother and a widowed sister reside at No. 45 Myrtle St. Portland.

150

CONTINUED:

Samuel, b. Oct. 3, 1818, m. Aug. 10, 1851, Eunice N. Winship of Portland. He occupied the Means homestead. She d. March 19, 1868, aged 51 years;* he d. June 2 1871, aged 52 years. They had one child, Frank W., m. and resides in the Means homestead.

3 Charles, b. Nov. 5, 1820, m. Sep. 19, 1847, Harriet Tolman of Tolman Place, Portland. Had one child, named Charles, who m. and had one child named Charles. The widow of Charles senior, m. 2d and resides in New York. He was a cooper.

4 Mary Ann, b. Nov. 25, 1822, m. June 17, 1846, Dea. Arthur Libby of Scarboro, now Gorham, a house carpenter, and resided on Atlantic street, Portland. She d. July 22, 1854, leaving five children. He m. 2d, Elizabeth A. Dresser and they had two children. He died Dec. 10, 1884. (For further particulars see Libby genealogy, p. 515.)

5 Sophaetta, born March 5, 1825—the day La Fayette was at Stroudwater and called at the Means house. She m. Nov. 15, 1846, Daniel A. Hinds, a painter and engineer, and resided in Portland. She d. June 14, 1853, aged 28 years; he m. 2d and went West.*

6 Caroline, b. Feb. 25. 1827, m. Dec. 11, 1848, John W. Gilbert of Waterville, b. April 1827, d. Aug. 24, 1825, leaving a daughter named Carrie L., b. Sept. 9, 1854., who m. Sept. 27, 1882, Samuel Thompson, Esq., a lawyer, residing in Boston, Mass., where he d. Apr. 12, 1893. The Widow Gilbert m. 2d; Feb. 15, 1862, at Biddeford, William Perkins, who d. Dec. 13, 1890, leaving one child, Charles P., b. Apr. 4, 1800. They all reside in Boston—the two widows at the Glenwood House, 49 Warren street.

7 George W., b. March 6, 1829, m. Dec. 19, 1849, Eliza Ann Pierce, dau. of Alden Pierce of Cape Elizabeth. He was by occupation a brick layer and resided on Bond street, Stroudwater, in the Capt. George Morton house which he purchased, since destroyed by fire. Both are deceased.

CHILDREN:

I Georgian, m. d. leaving a child.
II Alden P., m. d. leaving a child. (See Libby gen. p. 363.)
III William Frederick, b. Dec. 2, 1857, m. Myram P. Morton of Standish, dau. of Nelson Morton. Two children, Edith M. and Wilma N. They reside in Westbrook.
IV Albert H. m. d. His widow and son reside in Portland.

8 Pauline Adams, b. Oct. 22, 1831, d. young.

9 Emily Cox, b. Nov. 27, 1832, m. Benj. F. Dudley, b. at Lyman, son of Benjamin Dudley, Esq., who was reared by Capt. James Means at Stroudwater, and d. at Biddeford, Apr. 18, 1884, where she resides. He enlisted in the marine service during the war of the Rebellion and served on the U. S. Steamer Ossipee.

CHILDREN:

I Ellen S., b. Sept. 18, 1853, at Lyman, and resides unm, with her mother.
II Gilbert F., b. March 19, 1855, at Lyman, m. 1st, Mary F. Fellows, 2d, Ida Chenery of South Berwick.
III Clarabella, b. at Biddeford, July 10, 1857, m. Oct. 24, 1881, Otto W. Lousen of Lockport, N. Y., where she d., Nov. 10, 1887; he d. same year.
IV William P., b. Dec. 9, 1869, d. same year.
V George Edward, b. Feb. 19, 1872, resides with his mother, unm.

10 Edward, b. Nov. 29, 1834. He enlisted in the war of the Rebellion and d. in Mower Hospital, Phila., Pa., Nov. 14, 1864, aged 29 years.*

11 Elizabeth and last, b. Feb. 17, 1838, d. at home unm.* d. 1878

* Memorial stone at Stroudwater cemetery

THE DEERING NEWS.

Saturday, Oct. 9, 1897.

GRANDPA'S SCRAP BOOK

[Under this head historical and genealogical memoranda will be furnished the readers of the News that appears worthy of preservation, particularly of remote periods in our history within the city limits and immediate vicinity.]

CAPT. JAMES MEANS.

REVOLUTIONARY SOLDIER WHO SETTLE AT STROUDWATER VILLAGE.

Capt. James Means was a character of his generation. He lived in an eventful period whether viewed from a local or a national point of observation, but a connected story of his experiences does not exist, never having been made.

Of Irish lineage, born in the town of Biddeford, alias Saco—the part that is now known as Old Orchard, his ancestors residing near to the beach, as a soldier of the Revolution he was undaunted, and in civil life highly respected. Such in brief is the story of his existance, but a name so prominent as he made his by meritorious acts of loyalty to the American Republic in the dark days of its infancy, and confidence imposed in civil life in after years by his associates is entitled, and I hope to make a record at this time in a connected form, of some of the incidents of his life that will be as enduring as local and national archives. But I do not propose to resort to assertion or indulge in conjecture, but to connect chronologically the records I have found.

In volume 12, on page 143, York Records in the year of 1720, I find as follows :

Elizabeth Davis (alias Nickerson) formerly widow of Lawrence Davis who formerly dwelt at Casco Bay, more lately at Beverly where he died, for a consideration of £30, to Robert Means, 100 acres of land with 4 acres of marsh in Falmouth, Purpooduck side, her grandson, Jacob Davis, conveyed to her in 1700.

In the year 1735, he was taxed in Cape Elizabeth for land and personal property.

Volume 19, page 127, same records, as above indicated, 1738, consideration £377, division of a large lot among Robert Means, formerly of Falmouth and Ireland in Saco, alias Biddeford"—and others. (The beach mentioned.)

I will now turn to the Cumberland county history, 1879, page 384, and quote as follows :

The Willis Manuscripts, Book N, page 240, contains the following statement of James Means, of Stroudwater, in 1830.

I am seventy-seven years of age, grandson of Robert Means. Robert came here a young man from Ireland, by way of Massachusetts with John Armstrong. He married Armstrong's daughter. He lived five years upon the Neck, (Portland) one or two years in a log house near Stroudwater meeting house, then at the ferry at Purpooduck, about ten years. He then moved to Saco, where he died, with his wife who was aged about one hundred years, and my father. They came here in 1717, not direct from Ireland. Robert had two sons, John and Thomas. My father's name was John [John Means of Biddiford, married Eleanor Johnson, Dec. 25, 1748. Falmouth Records vol. 1, p 441.] Thomas lived at Freeport, he was killed by the Indians, [killed 1756,—Smith & Dean's journal page 165.] leaving one son. Armstrong was descended from the one that came here who moved to Pennsylvania. My grandfather Robert was fifteen or sixteen years of age when he came from Ireland. Before he moved to Falmouth he had married Miss Armstrong.

Then it is stated in the history, John Means died at Old Orchard Beach, March 16, 1776, leaving five sons, John, Robert, James, Thomas and George.

On page 60 of Smith & Dean's journal the compiler presents some facts, among others that Robert Means was one of the original members of the church organized in Portland in the year 1726, and states also he was one of the Scotch Irish immigrants bound for Londonderry, N. H., but with Barbour, and Armstrong stopped here.

In 1735, Simon or Simeon and John Armstrong were taxed in Cape Elizabeth.

The statement made by Capt. Means as quoted above, coincides with the extracts from the York Records. I present that Robert lived in what is now Cape Elizabeth prior to going to Old Orchard.

The log house in which Robert Means lived, stood opposite the Nathan Tibbetts house, Deering, Bradley's Corner district, on the land now owned by Mr. Edward C. O'Brion, located on the opposite side of the road from the Tibbetts house.

THE DEERING NEWS.

Saturday, Oct. 16, 1897.

GRANDPA'S SCRAP BOOK

[Under this head historical and genealogical memoranda will be furnished the readers of the News that appears worthy of preservation, particularly of remote periods in our history within he city limits and immediate vicinity.]

CAPT. JAMES MEANS.

A REVOLUTIONARY SOLDIER WHO SETTLED AT STROUDWATER VILLAGE.

(*Continued From Last Week.*)

March 25, 1728, "Laid out to Matthew Patten a thirty acre lot, next southwesterly of the parish lot."

The parish lot was purchased by Rev. Caleb Bradley. Under date of June 10, 1800, he records in his journal: "Bargained for Loring's place."

The York Records show that in 1732, Matthew Patten, a blacksmith of Biddeford, sold for £100 to Messrs. Waldo & Westbrook, the lot "whereon is a small dwelling house"

The small dwelling house here alluded to was evidently the log house in which Robert Means, grandfather to Col. James Means, lived at the time he states he lived in a log house.

Patten was voted a citizen of Falmouth in 1727.

A few years ago there stood between the beach and the Boston & Maine railroad station at Old Orchard. two memorial slate slabs inscribed as follows:

In Memory of
MR. ROBERT MEANS,
died Decem. 27th, 1769,
in the 80th year
of his Age.

In Memory of
MR. JOHN MEANS,
died March 16th, 1776,
in the 48th year
of his age.

They were in the carriage way, that is to say, carriages passed both sides of them, and so close that pieces had been knocked from the edges, in going to the beach from the hotels. Later I could not find them, but was informed that they had been placed supinely upon the graves they marked and were buried under the sod of the green plot southerly of the railroad station as now seen.

So the earthly remains of John Means, the father, and Robert Means, the grandfather of Capt. James Means, the subject of this article, are deposited under the green turf of the plot, as here noticed, between the railroad station and the rolling surf of Old Orchard beach.

What induced the Captain to come to the hamlet of Stroudwater I cannot state. There were but four two story dwellings and a saw mill, and prehaps a grist mill, three of the four large houses stand today and one of the smaller. He was accompanied by John K. Smith, later known as General John Kilby Smith, Capt. Jesse Partridge, (Colonel) James Webb, Archelaus Lewis (Hon Archelaus Lewis) all soldiers of the war of the Revolution and Joseph Cox, the last of Portland, whose sister Mary, Capt. Means married, April 4th, 1785. Smith engaged in trade in a small building on the easterly side of what is now named Waldo street, and Cox built the two story house on leased ground that stood where the Stroudwater alias Quinby hall stands today which house Andrew Hawes, Esq., removed some years since, but Cox soon returned to Portland, and Smith left for Thompson's Pond. (Partridge and Lewis to be noticed in another article.)

March 18, 1786, this trio of Means, Smith and Cox, "Gentlemen" for a consideration of £80 purchased the "triangular piece of land, about quarter of an acre, more or less" where the Means, alias Mason, house is now seen. Then came a local war when Capt. Means proposed to erect a dwelling house on the lot, originated probably by Lewis, Quinby and Tate who resided on the westerly side of the conveyed lot, claiming the lot was donated to the town of Falmouth as a public square or park by Col. Thomas Westbrook who used it in his day as a place for landing mast logs for shipment, and after him George Tate, the King's mast agent. But Capt. Means held the lot to which an addition from the "Public Landing" has since been made on the northerly side.

Many facts relative to General Smith as well as a copy of his family record are in my possession. Before the purchase of the "triangular" lot they purchased, Jan. 15th, 1875, the George Tate ware house and lot located between the end of the bridge over Fore river and the ancient appearing shop occupied by Andrew Hawes Esq., built by a son of the original George Tate, and in the ware house Capt. Means engaged in trade, and in it he went to housekeeping at the time of his marriage.

A paper contained in the package before me as I write, left by Capt. Means, bearing date of 1794, refers to the old Tate ware house as "the building in which I now live." And the Captain's daughter, Mrs. Sophia (Means) Mason told me a short time before her death that was the place of residence of her parents when they were first married and the Means house as now seen was built the year she was born which was was 1797, Jan. 12, thus showing the house to be one hundred years old at this date.

CHILDREN :

1—Mary, b. March 18, 1788, d, March 16, 1837, unmarried. She resided with her parents. Memorial stone at Stroudwater.
2—Charles, b. Nov. 12, 1789, d. Feb. 12, 1790.
3—Sopha, b. May 16, 1791, d. Nov. 4, 1792.
4—George, b. Jan. 6, 1793, d. Dec. 17, 1793.
5—James, b. Jan. 3, 1795 d. Oct. 29, 1796.
6—Sopha, b. Jan. 12, 1797 m. Samuel Mason, whose family record appeared in the News, Oct. 2nd, and d. Jan. 3, 1890, aged 94 years.

TO BE CONTINUED.

THE DEERING NEWS.

Saturday, Oct. 23, 1897.

GRANDPA'S SCRAP BOOK

[Under this head historical and genealogical memoranda will be furnished the readers of the News that appears worthy of preservation, particularly of remote periods in our history within the city limits and immediate vicinity.]

CAPT. JAMES MEANS.

A REVOLUTIONARY SOLDIER WHO SETTLED AT STROUDWATER VILLAGE.

(Continued From Last Week.)

Before me as I write is one of the Captain's account books, well preserved, 10x15 inches square and 2 1-2 inches thick, opened August 11th, 1791 and closed Oct. 30th, 1799. There is nothing very curious about it other than showing the great amount of intoxicating liquors consumed in those days, prices of merchandise, a few autographs, etc. It appears from it that in 1798 he was a selectman and there is a page of charges against the town of Falmouth.

The number of terms he was elected to office I cannot state. He was selectman, representative to the legislature, State Senator, and once ran for member of Congress on an independent ticket. He was also a custom house official. His grand daughter, Mrs. Emily Cox Dudley, Kossuth street, Biddeford has several of the certificates to office, while Mr. Will F. Mason, a great-grand-son, now of Cumberland Mills, Westbrook, has his army commission. Mrs. Caroline Perkins, a grand-daughter residing at 79 Warren street, Boston, has in her possession the portraits of the Captain and his wife, but the originals are so dark colored they cannot be photographed—so she writes.

Now for newspaper records;

[From the Eastern Argus, March 19, 1807.]

At a large and respectable meeting of the Republican delegates from the towns of Portland, **** assembled at Gray, March 17th, 1807 it was—

Resolved unanimously that they approve the nominations of and will support the Hon. James Sullivan *** for Governor at the ensuing election *** and Capt. James Means of Falmouth for Senator.

[From Eastern Argus, Apr. 2, 1807.]

Capt. James Means has been nominated by the citizens of this county as a candidate for senator at the ensuing election. He is too well known to his constituents from past services to require an enumeration of them, and from his faithfully discharging the duties of his situation with so much credit to himself and satisfaction of his fellow citizens, it is presumed they will all endeavor to secure his election. Capt. Means, for multiplicity of reasons, is most deservedly entitled to the suffrage of every honest and true friend of his country. He bore a commission in the Revolutionary War, which he supported with the heroism of a soldier and the firmness of a freeman, determined to die in the attempt, or by every possible exertion rescue his country from the thraldom of tyranny and render her free, independent and happy. In many battles did his robust and martial conduct render him particularly distinguished. He is a member of the honorable society of Revolutionary heroes, the Cincinnati, and ever through his whole life has been remarkable for his exemplary deportment.

He carried the county that year with the rest of the ticket by 400 majority.

This was an eventful period in our history both local and national. All Europe was at war. America was prospering and growing rich. Portland was flourishing and so was Stroudwater, when came the embargo act, an edict that required our shipping to stay at home. Fore river was full of dismantled vessels. Boston proposed to have the embargo act repealed and sent a circular letter to all the cities and towns of New England. Part of the reply from Falmouth I present as follows:

[Eastern Argus, Sept. 8, 1808.]

To the Selectmen of the Town of Boston:

GENTLEMEN:—The communication of the Selectmen of Boston addressed to the Selectmen of Falmouth on the subject of petitioning the President of the United States to suspend entirely or partially the operation of the laws laying an embargo, or to summon Congress to meet immediately for the purpose of a consideration thereof, was duly received by us.

The glory of our country and the prosperity and happiness of our fellow citizens are the first and fondest wishes of our hearts.

* * * * * * *

In Republican governments jealousy in the people is watchmen for the security of their liabilities; but we ought not and will not withhold merited confidence in the government; we trust in the patriotism and virtue of our rulers; and our best discretion approves their course.

In your personal and official characters, we tender to you, gentlemen, assurance of our most respectful consideration.

JAMES MEANS,   } Selectmen of
JOHN DOLE,   }   the town
SILAS HALL.   } of Falmouth.

Falmouth (Maine) September 5th, 1808.

The foregoing is a living witness to the loyalty of Capt. Means to both country and party in power.

TO BE CONTINUED.

THE DEERING NEWS.

Saturday, Oct. 30, 1897.

GRANDPA'S SCRAP BOOK

[Under this head historical and genealogical memoranda will be furnished the readers of the News that appears worthy of preservation, particularly of remote periods in our history within the city limits and immediate vicinity.]

CAPT. JAMES MEANS.

A REVOLUTIONARY SOLDIER WHO SETTLED AT STROUDWATER VILLAGE.

(Continued From Last Week.)

In the year of 1816 he was taxed as follows:

One house $900; one barn $20; one old house and barn $50; 25 acres mowing and tillage land $18 per acre; 15 pasturing at $9; 52 at $7; 1-2 wharf, $125; 2 oxen $40; 2 cows $28; 1 horse $40, and 1 chaise $40.

The house is the same as now seen, also the wharf in a dilapidated condition opposite the house, where the barn stood, which was removed about the year 1848, by Jeremiah Folsom, to what is now Bond street where Folsom then resided, and which fell to pieces from decay a few years since, but I have a photo of it. The farming land was located on the Saccarappa road, a mile from Stroudwater. The "old house" was probably part of the Tate ware house, in which the captain first commenced housekeeping at Stroudwater.

The following gives the date of his demise, as well as that of his wife and the obituary from the Eastern Argus (tri-weekly) of Oct. 22, 1832, presents some facts relative to his career:

Sacred
to the memory of
JAMES MEANS, ESQ.,
who died
Oct. 15, 1832,
Aged 79.
He was officer in the Revolution.

Sacred
to the memory of
MARY,
wife of James Means, Esq.,
who died
Nov. 27, 1831,
aged 77.

MARY,
daughter of James and Mary Means,
died May 16, 1837,
aged 48.

In the Tri-Weekly Argus of Oct. 22, 1832, appeared an obituary of which the following is a copy:

ANOTHER REVOLUTIONARY PATRIOT HAS GONE.

CONTINUED:

Died in Westbrook, on the 15th inst., James Means, Esq., aged 79 years. Mr. Means was a faithful soldier and officer during the Revolutionary war. He saw and experienced much of the hard service which was the price of our country's Independence. He entered the Massachusetts line, as a volunteer, in April, 1775. At the expiration of eight months he was made an ensign and went to Ticonderoga. In 1777 he received a lieutenant's commission, and in 1780 was commissioned captain. He was at the evacuation of New York and in the rear guard with Col. Francis on that occasion. He was likewise at Bemus Heights. He wintered with the troops at Valley Forge; was at the battle of Monmouth; the taking of Stony Point, and several other battles. He did not quit the military service of the country until the disbanding of the army.

Capt. Means was one of the early settlers of that part of Falmouth which is now Westbrook. Possessed of a strong and well informed mind, his townsmen soon selected him for their most important trusts; he was many years one of the Selectmen, and one of the Board of Assessors. He likewise successively represented his town in the House of Representatives, and then his county in the senate of the Legislature of Massachusetts for several years. He was in various other public offices anterior to the few last years of his life, and until disease admonished him to leave to others the care and responsibilities of public business. He was in religious sentiments an unwavering Universalist, and in politics a republican of the old school. He bore the many years of sickness to which he was subjected with patience and fortitude, and closed his connections with the world at last without a murmur.

To this the interested reader in local history, it seems, must say with the compiler thereof: "Brief, concise, precious words—as connected let them live long."

In the family of the captain dwelled a boy who was apprenticed, by the name of Benjamin Dudley, and he ran away. Then, as now, a story started by a waggish person was destined to live long; so it used to be said that when the boy left the Captain advertised him as having "walked away being too lazy to run," and offered as a reward for his return, one cent. The following tells the true story:

[From the Eastern Argus.]

TWENTY DOLLARS REWARD.

Ran away from the subscriber, an Indented apprentice, named Benjamin Dudley, aged 16 years, about five feet, two inches, brown complexion and an active boy. Whoever will return said apprentice shall have the above named reward. All persons are forbidden harboring or trusting said apprentice on penalty of the law.
JAMES MEANS.
Falmouth, Jan. 26, 1809.

Young Mr. Dudley, born 1792, m. 1st, August 30, 1817, Clarrisa Libby of Scarboro; b. there Oct 3, 1799, dau. of Capt Moses Libby (see Libby Gen. p. 115) who d. Aug. 31, 1831, and he m. 2d, June 23, 1832, Hannah W. Luch of Kennebunk, who d. 1893. He settled in the town of Lyman, where he was a useful citizen, engaging in trade, a Justice of the Peace, representing the town in the legislature and receiving many other testimonials of merited respect. It was his son, Benj. F. Dudley, who Miss Emily C. Mason, noticed in my Oct. 2d article, married.

The house Capt. Means built for himself at Stroudwater is a square building, two stories high, hip roof, fronting easterly, and towards Fore river, two ends made of brick, four square well finished rooms on each floor, hall through middle, with four stacks of chimneys, and in his day was well furnished, containing the first woolen floor carpet of the village, which cost $100 and which people came a long distance to see. Recently the house received a new front door, new sash, and a coat of straw colored paint, and the barn built by Samuel Mason, senior, removed. About thirty years ago the dormer window on the front roof and later the wooden ell on the back side were removed.

The school house, built in the year 1811, or 12, now gone, which stood adjacent, was two story, the second having some conveniences for public meetings, so travelling preachers, as well as the local, would frequently entertain the public in it, and nearly every time, the first thing on such occasions would be for a boy to run into Mrs. Mason's and borrow a chair for the minister and a Bible, the audience using benches as seats. The Bible thus loaned (or there may have been two) is now the property of Mrs. Emily C. (Mason) Dudley, of Biddeford.

[TO BE CONTINUED.]

Saturday, Nov. 6, 1897.

GRANDPA'S SCRAP BOOK

[Under this head historical and genealogical memoranda will be furnished the readers of the News that appears worthy of preservation, particularly of remote periods in our history within the city limits and immediate vicinity.]

CAPT. JAMES MEANS.

A REVOLUTIONARY SOLDIER WHO SETTLED AT STROUDWATER VILLAGE.

Continued from last week.

It was announced in the News some weeks since that Mr. Nathan Goold of Portland would present an article to the public through the columns of the Portland Daily Press upon the military records of Capt. Means which appeared in that paper Thursday morning, Oct. 7th, with a cut of the Captain's last earthly abiding place. The article does Mr Goold much credit as does all his articles appearing in print, and we propose to use a part of it and refer the readers of the News who are interested in these Scrap Book articles to the rest in the Press, the management of which paper having kindly loaned the News the cut which will appear in connection with this article

The article by Mr. Goold commences as follows:

"There died at Stroudwater, on Oct. 15th, 1832, at the age of seventy-nine years, a man of some note, in his time, who seems to be almost forgotten by the busy world. The memory of his life deserves well of us, for, as a citizen of Old Falmouth, he served us well and faithfully. He was Capt. James Means who came from that part of Saco now Old Orchard, to Stroudwater when a young man."

* * *

Then the compiler continues:

"Capt. Means was one of those men who first resisted the insults of England to the colonies, and on the receipt of the news of the battle of Lexington, on the morning of April 21, 1775, seized his gun and started that day in Capt. John Brackett's Co., for Cambridge, to assist his suffering countrymen. He was then about twenty-two years of age, and ranked as third corporal. The company was sent back after they arrived at Wells, and three weeks later he enlisted under the same captain in Col. Phinney's Regiment, and continued in the service, as will appear in his army record. After nearly eight and one-half years of service, he returned to Stroudwater and married Mary Cox, April 4, 1785. She was the daughter of John Cox, who left the country in the Revolution for Nova Scotia, where he died."

* * *

Through the courtesy of L. B. Chapman, Esq., of Stroudwater, we have been enabled to examine his account book, deeds and papers, which show him to have been a careful and methodical man of affairs. A paper of his time said of him, "Ever through his whole life has been remarkable for his exemplary deportment."

Mr. Chapman has prepared for the Deering News the story of Capt. Means as a citizen of Stroudwater, with an account of his civil services to his country, which is very interesting and instructive. This he also loaned us, and it is another one of those valuable contributions of his to the history of that ancient hamlet.

Capt. James Means was a brave patriot and one of those men who did not hesitate at the call of his country. His country's enemies were his enemies, and he never faltered until Washington disbanded the army

CONTINUED:

in 1783. The record of the services he rendered in the long Revolutionary war, are of lasting credit to him and the town where he lived.

James Means enlisted as a corporal in Capt. John Brackett's Company, in Col. Edmund Phinney's 31st Regiment of Foot, May 12, 1775, and served at Cambridge, under Gen. Washington, until Dec. 31. They were in Gen. Heath's Brigade, in Gen. Putnam's Division. Jan. 1, 1776, he enlisted as a sergeant in Capt. Hart Williams' Company, in Col. Phinney's 18th Continental Regiment, was promoted ensign, Aug. 3, and served until Dec. 31. In these regiments he served through the seige of Boston, and marched in August, 1776, to reinforce the northern army at Fort Ticonderoga; and was discharged at Fort George, Dec. 31. He was commissioned lieutenant to serve from Jan. 1, 1777, in Col. Samuel Brewer's 12th Mass. Regt., promoted to captain July 5, 1779, transferred to the Mass. Regt., Lieut. Col. Ebenezar Sprout; Jan. 1, 1781, and continued in the service until Nov. 3, 1783, when the army was dismissed.

"Capt. Means' regiment was in the battles of Stillwater and Saratoga, witnessed the surrender of Gen. Burgoyne, joined Washington's army near Philadelphia, marched to Valley Forge Dec. 19, 1777, where they passed that terrible winter, and he signed the oath of allegiance to his country there. The oath that he signed then is among the precious relics of the beginning of our country in possession of the government at Washington, and is as carefully cared for as the gold in the vaults of the Treasury. They left Valley Forge in June, fought the battle of Monmouth June 19th, where the army suffered terribly from the heat of the day, marched to Danbury, Conn., to guard the stores in August, returned to the Hudson river in December, and probably witnessed the execution of Andre in Oct., 1780. Jan. 1, 1781, the 12th Mass., Regt. was consolidated with the 2d Mass. Regt. and both were known as the latter.

"Capt. James Means was one of the original members of the society of the Cincinnati, formed at the close of the war, when each member deposited one month's wages towards a fund which still exists. His living representative in that honorable society is James Means Mason of Portland, who has his original certificate of membership signed by George Washington and Henry Knox The only other member of that society in Portland is Charles Edwards, who epresents his grandfather, Thomas Edwards, who was judge advocate general of the army. William H. Smith of Raymond, represents his grandfather, Capt. John K. Smith."

[The residence of Mr. Smith, the well known hotel keeper, was recently destroyed by fire, an account of which has appeared in the News.—Ed. News.]

"It is said that when Gen. Lafayette was here, in 1825, that on his way bock he called on Capt. Means to pay his compliments to an officer of the Revolution, which seemed to have been his custom everywhere.

"Among Capt. Means' papers were found two original muster rolls brought home by him from the army. One is dated at Fiskhill, N. Y., July 30th, 1780, when he was in the 12th Mass., Regt., under Col. Spout, who had superseded Col. Brewer, and then they were in Gen. John Nixon's Brigade. The other is dated at West Point, N. Y., Dec. 7, 1781, when they were in the 2nd Mass. Regt., under the same officer, but then were in Gen. John Patterson's Brigade. These rolls contain the autographs of those generals written at the front. The other commissioned officers of the companies were Lieut. John Whitney and Ensign Joshua Danforth.

During the later years of the war the question of locality did not enter into the formation of the companies and regiments. As the men left the service at the expiration of their terms of enlistments, those remaining were consolidated into companies, and they into regiments in the same manner. No places of residence are given on the following muster rolls, and the companies were probably composed of men from many towns in the Commonwealth. This shows the difficulty of ever obtaining anything like a complete list of the soldiers of the Revolution, who went from the Province of Maine. The colonel in command at the time these rolls were made was Ebenezer Sprout, and a short sketch of the officers may be of some interest.

The compiler then presents interesting notices of the several higher officers and closes with a list of the privates.

Saturday, Nov. 13, 1897.

MASON.

ADDITIONAL MEMORANDA RELATIVE TO AN OLD TOWN NAME.

Continued from last week.

My first article under the caption of "Mason" appeared in the issue of the News bearing date of September 18th, '97, which related to Daniel Mason, Esq., the first of the name who located here, and his immediate offspring.

This Daniel Mason, Esq.; as stated was the eldest child of Nehemiah Mason of Watertown, Mass. There were nine children in the family and Hugh was the name of the second child, born Dec. 29th, 1758, married June 20th, 1782 Elizabeth Clark.

Where Hugh resided or the names of his children I do not know. One was named Seth, born Nov. 24th, 1790, published Sept. 14th, 1817, and married Hannah Bryant that year, and settled in Portland. They had: 1st Margaret; 2d Seth; born Dec. 4th, 1820, married April 6th, 1843, Rebecca, daughter of Abraham and Rebecca Perley of Gray; 3d Joseph H.; died; 4th Joseph B.; 5th Sumner R.; 6th Hannah.

Into this family Dr. Rugg of Portland married. I am informed by an aged resident that Seth was by occupation a mason and removed to Massachusetts where he died.

The first child of Nehemiah, and brother to Daniel Mason, Esq., was born July 24th, 1764, named Moses, and married in Oct. 9th, 1786, Lucy Kingsbury, he a soldier of the 10th Massachusetts Reg., Continental army of the war of the Revolution. His eldest child was named Isaac, subject of this sketch, born Sep. 5th, 1787, married July 14th, 1811, Sarah, daughter of James Riggs of Nason's Corner, born there March 23d, 1788, and granddaughter of Stephen Riggs who resided a half mile westerly, on what is now known as the Anson C. Trask farm.

In the issue of the News of Sept. 14th, '95, is a short notice of the Riggs family and April 25th, 1896 one, of Isaar Mason giving the inscription of his grave memorial stone and that of his wife which may be seen in Evergreen at the southerly side of Pine Grove cemetery.

Isaac was a tanner like his uncles, Daniel and Samuel, but I know nothing of the first part of his married life. He engaged in beef speculation and July 27th, 1830 entered into an agreement for the James Riggs farm where he resided for a while but surrendered it and moved to Bradley's Corner where he prosecuted the business of tanning and where he died at time indicated by inscription on grave memorial. He was known as "Major Mason" because he held a major's commission in the state militia. His wife died in the Portland Home for Aged Women. They had no offspring.

He was elected as selectman of Westbrook in the year of 1832, also in '33, '34, '35, '36, '37, '38, '39 and again in '42. So he must have been a man of some ability and received respectful recognition from his party friends. He was active in the Universalist church according to the records.

THE DEERING NEWS.

Saturday, Nov. 20, 1897.

GRANDPA'S SCRAP BOOK

[Under this head historical and genealogical memoranda will be furnished the readers of the News that appears worthy of preservation, particularly of remote periods in our history within the city limits and immediate vicinity.]

STEPHEN RIGGS.

A NAME THAT DESERVES A PLACE IN WRITTEN HISTORY.

In our article prepared for last week's News we promised to say something this week about the Riggs name. Since then we have received a note from Henry C. Quinby, Esq., Attorney at Law, 52 Wall street, New York city, which we here insert with pleasure as follows:

In connection with your Riggs research these lines may amuse you.

Thomas Riggs (I) Gloucester, 1658, d. Feb. 26, 1722, aged 90 years; his daughter Mary Riggs (II) m. Benjamin Haskell Nov. 21, 1679, and had a son, Dea. Thomas Haskell (III) who came to Portland from Gloucester, d. 1785, aged 97 years. They had Mary Haskell (IV) m. Joseph Quinby, and they had Capt. John Quinby (V) who had Moses, (VI) who had Thomas, (VII) who had Henry Brewer Quinby, (VIII) who had Henry Cole Quinby, (IX)

In addition to the foregoing we will state that the cellar hole of the first dwelling erected by Dea. Benj. Haskell, (III) is still to be seen in the field owned by George Libby, Esq., now county attorney, located between Frost and Congress streets, this city; that Joseph Quinby was a ship carpenter residing near the south westerly corner of India and Middle streets, Portland, who removed to Saccarappa in 1775. after the burning of the city, and died there the next year; that we have fortunately found a copy of the record of the Joseph Quinby family containing dates of births and deaths of his children; that the house Capt. John Quinby built at Stroudwater now stands in Portland at the junction of Congress and Pine streets; that Moses Quinby, Esq., (VI) was one of the first class of graduates of Bowdoin college who lived and died at Stroudwater; and that Thomas Quinby, (VII) his son, was the much esteemed Thomas Quinby who died in this city a few years since, etc., etc.

Notices from time to time of the Riggs name have appeared in the News but the files of the paper, we regret to state, with some memoranda, are beyond our reach at this writing, but missing dates, etc., will appear later.

Jeremiah Riggs the first of the Riggs name of which there is record that came to Old Falmouth, removed from Portland and resided in the Bradley Corner district of our city, and Stephen Riggs was his son. In the possession of Mr. Samuel Riggs, residing on Brackett street, Portland, is the family record of this Stephen and Mr. Riggs allows us to copy it with such names of Stephen's decendants as appears on it.

It commences as follows:

JEREMIAH RIGGS. RACHEL HASKELL. WIFE OF JEREMIAH.

Stephen Riggs, their son, b. Oct. 9, 1735. Margaret Barbour, (his wife) b. Oct. 7, 1744. m. Dec 20, 1759.
James Barbour, father of Margaret, b.— d. Dec. 19, 1763 Margaret Nelson, wife of James Barbour, b.—— d. July 19, 1766.

[James Barbour settled on wild lands easterly of Lunt's Corner district, this city, about the time Stephen Riggs was born, at which time Jeremiah Riggs, his father, purchased the John Ingalls farm at Bradley's Corner.

Sept. 25, 1762, James Barbour gave by deed to each of his two daughters, one the wife of Stephen Riggs, the other the wife of his brother Jeremiah Riggs, Jr., certain lots of land situated in the town of Gorham, and to John Barbour, the same year, "land on which I now dwell, with buildings." This was the year previous, it will be observed, to the recorded year of the death of James Barbour.]

Stephen Riggs, subject of this article, lived in a two story, red colored house, destroyed by fire some years since, built by himself on land his father gave him, located westerly of Nason's Corner district, this city, now occupied by our aged citizen, Mr. Anson C. Trask, the new house of Mr. Trask occupying the site of the old Riggs mansion house. And Mr. Riggs was drowned in the month of December, 1800, while attempting to cross Back Cove creek on the ice, his horse escaping death, where Green street now crosses, there being no bridge then. Rev. Caleb Bradley notices his death in his journal.

The old Riggs record then read as follows:

CHILDREN OF STEPHEN RIGGS.

1—Stephen, b. Oct. 1, 1760.
2—James, b. July 27, 1762.
3—Rachel, b. July 19, 1764, d. Aug. 14, 1765.
4—Rachel, b. Dec. 16, 1766.
5—Sally, b. April 5, 1769.
6—Margaret, b. July 3, 1771.
7—Thomas, (and last) b. April 16, 1774, d. Sept. 16, 1776.

To Mr. Elbridge G. Riggs, noticed in our article of last week, b. Jan. 14, 1813, living on a part of the Stephen Riggs farm, who possesses an excellent memory, we are indebted for the following relating to Stephen's children, in addition to the record quoted, as follows:

1— Stephen Riggs, b. Oct. 1760, m. Susanna Jones, sister to Capt. John Jones, who m. two of the daughters of Jeremiah Riggs, Jr., Capt. Jones occupying and dying upon the parental homestead at Bradley's Corner, later known by the name of Fowler place, Daniel Fowler marrying a daughter of Capt. Jones.

CHILDREN:

I—Thomas, m. Hannah (Anderson) Jordan, a widow. He resided in Portland, where he lost an arm, and where he has descendants now living.
II—Stephen Jones Riggs, m. Ann Hall of Windham, and resided on what is now the Richard Rowe place, in the original Starbird dwelling house that stood where Mr. Edward D. Starbird now resides on Church St., the original house being one story, which was removed to its present site. No children.
III—Mary, m. Thomas Hall, of Windham, to which place he removed with the children after her demise. Her grave memorial stone stands in the Dea. John Bailey burying ground located on Mitchell's Hill, near Brighton street, this city. This Stephen Riggs, Jr., resided on the homestead of his father.

2—James*
4—Rache, b. 1766, m. Wm. Moody, lived on what is now India street. They had one child named Edward, who was lost at sea.
5—Sally, b. 1769, m. Joel Prince, of Cumberland, and they had several children.
6—Margaret, b. 1769, d. unmarried.

The record then continues as follows:

CHILDREN OF JAMES RIGGS.

1—Rebecca, b. Nov. 19, 1785 d. Sept. 10, 1797.
2—James } Twins, b. Jan. 11, 1786. James
3—Nancy } d. Dec. 5, 1786.
4—Sally, b. March 23, 1788, m. Isaac Mason. See News of last week,
5—James, b. Sept. 11, 1791, m. Ann Delano. He was in the war of 1812-15, and resided in Portland. Chas. J. Riggs, who m. Miss Nancy Morton of Stroudwater, and now resides in the state of Wisconsin, was their son, also Mr. Sumner Riggs, before noticed. James d. Feb. 21, 1864.
6—Jeremiah, } Twins, b. Sept. 13, 179 .
7—Stephen,   } Jeremiah m. Lydia Ingalson and resided in Windham. He d. there Sept. 8, 1869. They had four, children, all of whom are dead, Stephen d. Jan. 4, 1826, on the homestead unmarried.
8—George, b. June 21, 179: d. Oct. 9, 1798.
9—George, b. Sept. 29, 1799, m. Eveline Pike; was a shoe maker residing at Saccarappa village, where he d. May 22, 1872. They had three children
10—Charles, b. July 14, 1805, d. July 10, 1831, on the homestead, unmarried.

*This James was second child of Stephen, senior, born July 27, 1762, m. May 26, 1784, Rebecca Morse of the Morse family that resided near Stevens Plains avenue, easterly of Abbotts Corner district, this city.

THE DEERING NEWS.

Saturday, Nov. 27, 1897.

GRANDPA'S SCRAP BOOK

[Under this head historical and genealogical memoranda will be furnished the readers of the News that appears worthy of preservation, particularly of remote periods in our history within he city limits and immediate vicinity.]

THINGS AND PERSONS.

EXTRACTS FROM RECORDS MADE NEARLY NINETY YEARS SINCE.

CAPT. WILLIAM WEBSTER.

Died in the town of Gray on the 19th of October, 1808, Capt. Wm. Webster, aged 68 years. He was born in Cape Elizabeth and removed to Gray when it was a new settlement. A widow and four sons mourn the loss.

In the "Historical Sketch of Windham" that appeared in the News last week is an allusion to Widow Margaret Knight of that town. Following is a copy of the newspaper item referred to by the compiler. If the record could be found it would be a treasure indeed.

MARGARET KNIGHT.

[Portland Argus, Nov. 24, 1808.]

Died in Windham, (Me.) Widow Margaret Knight, aged 92 years. She practiced as a midwife for more than forty years; and kept an account of her being present at the births of three thousand and thirty-seven children.

FORT PREBLE.

[Portland Argus, Nov. 30, 1808.]

The Fort lately constructed on Spring Point, Portland harbor, under the direction of Henry A. S. Dearborn, Esq., was named Fort Preble in due form on Saturday last and was at the same time taken possession of by Capt. Chandler's company of U. S. Light Infantry. The style and excellence of the work does great credit to the engineer who superintended its erection. * * * *
An appropriate address was pronounced by D. W. Lincoln, Esq.

FORT SCAMMEL.

[Portland Argus, March 16, 1809.]

On the 4th of March inst. the fortification on House Island in Portland harbor, opposite Fort Preble, lately erected under the direction and superintendence of Henry A. S. Dearborn, Esq., was named Fort Scammel. The beauty and strength of the fortification while it furnished the highest encomiums of the skill, ability and fidelity of the laymen who conducted the work, inspired every beholder with confidence which was doubly assured by the martial appearance of the troops under the command of Lieut. Pitts. An elegant address was delivered to the soldiers by H. A. S. Dearborn, Esq. * * *

REV. TRISTRAM GILMAN.

[Portland Argus, April 20, 1809.]

On Saturday, the 5th inst. Rev. Tristram Gilman, A. M., pastor of the First Congregational church of North Yarmouth, departed this life. On Tuesday following his remains were entombed. Great respect was paid to his memory. Between one and two o'clock, p. m., the procession moved from his late dwelling house to the meeting house. His pall was supported by the Rev. Mr. Appleton, president of Bowdoin college, Rev. Mr. Eaton, Rev. Mr. Lancaster, Rev. Mr. Herrick, Rev. Mr. Kellogg and Rev. Mr. Mosley. The Rev. Messrs. Smith, Green, Bradley, Weston, Lyman, Milttimore and Dutton followed as mourners next to the family. After them the church of which Mr. Gilman was pastor; next to these the parish and then strangers, and members of other churches. The Rev. Mr. Appleton made the first prayer; Mr. Eaton preached an excellent sermon from Rev. 14:13, and Mr. Lancaster made the concluding prayer. Besides the usual singing, a funeral anthem was performed and at the grave Mr. Kellogg made an appropriate address to the mourners, bereaved church and congregation, and to the people at large. The numbers assembled were many. The procession was very extensive and the whole conducted with great solemnity.

THE DEERING NEWS.

Saturday, Dec. 4, 1897.

GRANDPA'S SCRAP BOOK

[Under this head historical and genealogical memoranda will be furnished the readers of the News that appears worthy of preservation, particularly of remote periods in our history within the city limits and immediate vicinity.]

MARRIAGE EVENTS.

COMPILED FROM THE DIARY OF THE REV. CALEB BRADLEY.

April 30th, 1840. I was at the Casco bank (Portland) before one o'clock, p. m. Called at Moses Norwell's and spent an hour he being an old acquaintance, both from the same town, (Dracut, Mass.); talked about the days gone by and events of our boyhood. At 4 o'clock p. m. left the city via Tukey's bridge for home. Called at Mr. Lunt's, (Lunt's Corner district, this city—the house now stands.) His daughter Jane to be married at 7 o'clock. I was urged to attend the wedding and concluded I would. Went to Seth Clark's and took tea, shaved, and then I carried Mrs. Clark in my chaise to the wedding. (He resided in what is now known as the John J. Frye house, built by Maj. Wm. Berry and son Obadiah, more than a hundred years since at Fall brook Ocean street.) There were a large number present. Rev. Mr. Condid (Portland) was the officiating clergyman. The gentleman who took Jame by the hand was named Witmore. Everything was pleasant and agreeable; the company sociable, with a good piece of wedding cake and a glass of lemonade or wine to wash it down. About 9 o'clock p. m. the company separated and I conveyed Mrs. Clark to her lodgings and then returned home.

DR. JOHN SLOAN.

Nov. 4th, 1839. Went over to Dr. (Caleb) Hunt's, (Stroudwater) about 3 o'clock and married John Sloan to Miss Caroline Hunt; good wedding; no company. Immediately after tea they left for Boston and so on as fast as steamboats and cars will carry them to New Albany, Indiana, where they expect to make the place their home, he being a regularly educated physician, and having already made a stand in that place and resided there about a year. They have my best wishes for their happiness and prosperity now, and may they be prepared for a better residence beyond the present scene of things.

How time passes. It seems but a few days since I married the parents of this couple, notwithstanding it is nearly thirty years since the event.

Dr. Jacob Hunt of Falmouth and Miss Sally Rea of Windham, married June 26, 1809.

Adam Sloan and Eunice Milliken, married May 8, 1815.

"Mr. Sloan gave me as a fee $2; and Dr. Hunt $3 which I made a present to his wife; and the young Dr. Sloan, whom I married today, gave me a fee of $3. My marriage fees have been various. I have received $20, $10, $5, $2 and so down—one couple nothing."

[Dr. Sloan made New Albany his home where both died without issue, she bequeathing her Deering property received from her father to a religious society of that place by whom a part is now held.

The Dr. Jacob Hunt residence, built by Dr. Jeremiah Barker nearly a hundred years ago who came here from Gorham, Me., and has the remains of three wives interred in the old Stroudwater cemetery, stands nearly as originally built.

The Sloans resided on the Buxton road, two miles westerly of Stroudwater (now Westbrook) where Mr. Moses Chapman resides.]

JOSEPH CHENERY.

"June 18, 1840. At 7 o'clock I and E. P. Smith (Mrs. Elizabeth P. Smith, Parson Bradley's daughter who resided in Calais, but at home on a visit) went over to Mrs. Dole's (the Widow Dole who resided at Stroudwater where her aged daughter and son Daniel now reside) to attend the marriage ceremony of Joseph Chenery and Mary Dole (the widow's daughter). Had a very decent and respectable wedding. ("Decent" and "respectable" being descriptive words very commonly used by the Parson.) About thirty present—family and all. The scene so far as the marriage is concerned is closed as it respects Joseph Chenery and Mary Dole. How long before death will dissolve the connection is beyond the foresight of mortals; of that day and hour no man, no, not the angels know; but it will be dissolved, death performing the ceremony. He destroys, he undoes. It is appointed unto us once to die. This is a decree of heaven—it is then fixed—it cannot be otherwise. The fatal darts cannot be turned from their course. They came from the quiver of the Almighty and go as directed and are to accomplish the object for which sent; and all must submit to the fatal decree."

[Mr. Joseph Chenery resided on the Chenery homestead at Bradley's Corner and both he and wife reached a ripe old age.

His father came here from Watertown, Mass., and was drowned at Stroudwater on the evening of a very stormy and dark night, on the way home.

He was born August 4, 1805; d. March 22, 1882, aged 79 years. Mary Dole, his wife, b. Jan. 12. 1805. She d. 3 or 4 years since, and was descended from Richard Dole who came from Bristol, Eng., in 1639 to Newbury, Mass. Her grandfather, Capt. Daniel Dole. m. Sarah, daughter of Moses Pearsons, Esq., of Portland, and built the mansion house as now seen at Stroudwater about the year 1771.

Joseph Chenery and wife had but one child, Daniel Dole Chenery, who is County Treasurer, residing at Bradley's Corner.

THE DEERING NEWS.

Saturday, Dec. 25, 1897.

GRANDPA'S SCRAP BOOK

[Under this head historical and genealogical memoranda will be furnished the readers of the News that appears worthy of preservation, particularly of remote periods in our history within the city limits and immediate vicinity.]

HISTORICAL MEMORANDA.

COMPILED FROM THE JOURNAL OF THE REV. CALEB BRADLEY.

In the notice of Stephen Riggs that appeared in the News a few weeks since, A. D. 1800 was presented as the year in which Mr. Riggs died, but Mr. Bradley has it a year earlier:

Dec. 22, 1799, Sunday. Stephen Riggs was drowned last night at Back Cove.

Dec. 24. Attended the funeral of Stephen Riggs.

Dec. 26. Attended the funeral of Mr. Proctors, aged 86. Took tea at James Blake's.

Jan. 7, 1800. Spent the day in Portland. Three volunteer companies undertook to bury Gen. Washington and such an irregular confusion and chaotic piece of business I believe no man ever saw before.

Feb. 22. Delivered an oration upon the death of Gen. Washington. Had a full assembly.

March 23. A wedding at Mrs. Storer's. (I am unable to learn where this woman resided.)

May 7. Attended upon Capt. Stevens. He died at 1-2 past five p. m. (He lived at Woodfords.)

May 9. Attended Capt. Stevens' funeral. A large number of people present.

June 10. Spent the day chiefly in my study. Bargained for Loring's place. (The socalled Bradley house as now observed.)

June 27. The fullest meeting I have seen in Stroudwater meeting house.

June 31. I preached a lecture at Deacon Bailey's and baptized 17 children. My horse went into the troop. Attended a wedding. (Deacon Bailey resided on the Windham road.)

Sept. 1, 1800. Attended the funeral of Isaac Bailey. (He was father to Isaac Bailey who died at Woodfords a few years since. Isaac senior resided near Saccarappa.)

Sept. 4. Henry Knight had my horse in the troop. (I think "troop" means cavalry.)

Sept. 18. Mrs. Patrick was burried. (Stroudwater.) My horse went into the troop.

Nov. 23. Eight members added to the church. Went to meeting in a sleigh for the first time.

Nov. 27. Thanksgiving. Preached. Married three couples—two at Cape Elizabeth. Baptized children for Mr. Robert Dyer by the name of Silas Gray, Enos H. (?) and John Hancock.

(Under this date, on the list of marriages solemnized by him I find the names of "Ebenezer Newman and Polly Dyer of C. E."; and "George Deak and Jerusha Dyer, both of Cape Elizabeth," the last named "aged 70 years.")

(Ebenezer Newman built the one story house southerly of the Deering Centre schoolhouse and was the ancestor of the Newmans of this city.)

Dec. 30. Samuel and Joseph Sawyer cut bushes for me in the forenoon and I paid one dollar. This makes $40 worth of work done on my place since I bought it.

Jan. 4, 1801. Attended the burial of Mrs. Titcomb. Dined at Pepp Frost's (Stroudwater.)

Jan. 5, 1801. Received $164 towards my last year's salary from Collector Stevens.

April 15. Made the fence between Capt. Jones and me. A hard days work—33 rods.

May 14. Lewis chosen representative to the very great mortification of John Waite. As much as he is depressed so much I am elated. *Invye ratis*. (Maj. Arch Lewis who resided at Stroudwater, Waite at Presumscot Bridge.)

May 30. Attended the funeral of John S. Knight.

June 3. The Association met at Rev. Thomas Lancaster's, Scarboro. Mr. Thompson preached. I was taken into the Association.

June 10. Forty men and six oxen worked for me in the afternoon.

June 16. Mr. Loring left my house and I moved in. Took coffee at Mr. Holmes. (He lived where the John B. Curtis house stands.)

June 28. Went to a wedding at Saccarappa. Somebody entered my house while I was away and turned many things upside down.

Sept. 20. Baptized 15 persons, 6 of whom were adults.

Oct. 16. A company of ladies to tea in the afternoon, who presented me with a cloak. (A list of names is in existence.)

Nov. 16. Rainy, very warm. Was married by Mr. Stone and moved home. (A college classmate of the Rev.)

Dec. 14. A villain, but a devilish coward, stuck his fist through my window, and my wife was dreadrully scared.

Feb. 11, 1802. Five hundred and thirty sleighs and teams passed by house today.

March 2, 1802. The people of Capisic came and shoveled the snow away from my door.

April 20, 1802. Set out my poplars. (The Lombardy poplars, the last of which disappeared a few years since.)

April 28. I visited Mr. Richards' school with the school committee.

May 3, 1802. Set out some of my apple trees. (Those now to be seen, probably.)

May 27. Went to Gray to marry D. Bailey.

June 2, 1802. Went to town, dined at Mr. Jewett's. Saw the rascals on the gallows.

June 3. Rained as though all the bottles of heaven were unstopped.

June 13. Attended a funeral and wedding. Rebecca Browne was married. (Daughter of Rev. Thomas Browne.)

July 22, 1802. Some person broke into my house this afternoon and took away a decanter part full of rum. Villain.

THE DEERING NEWS.

Saturday, Dec. 11, 1897.

GRANDPA'S SCRAP BOOK

[Under this head historical and genealogical memoranda will be furnished the readers of the News that appears worthy of preservation, particularly of remote periods in our history within the city limits and immediate vicinity.]

FALMOUTH IN 1838.

VIEW FROM REV. CALEB BRADLEY'S STANDPOINT.

April 25th, 1838. Rev. Caleb Bradley on this day closed his diary as follows:

Mr. Lane [Rev. Joseph Lane, who officiated at what is now known as the Bradley meeting house of this city] gone to Falmouth this p. m. to preach at the protracted meeting commenced there last week—2d parish. [The second parish meeting house as we understand the situation is the brick structure where Rev. W. H. Haskell preaches near the town house, who in the year 1867, was settled over the Parson Bradley parish but left the next year for Falmouth where he has since labored—a period of 30 years. October 12, 1868, the Bradley parish voted to raise a committee to "engage some one to read sermons," Mr. Haskell was the last settled minister at the Bradley meeting house.]

26th the diary continues:

Cold, cloudy, disagreeable morning—some spitting of snow. Finished writing a letter to Mr. and Mrs. Hadley, Sandusky, Ohio. (His daughter.) Mr. Lane returned from Falmouth this morning, who says there is some seriousness among the people, some attention and excitement. The meetings are to be continued. Let it be remembered the Freewill Baptists have had a part in these meetings and have been the primum mobile of the excitement. What the result will be is wisely concealed in the future.

[In the year of 1823, Mary, the wife of Capt. Jediah Leighton who was converted in 1802, with three other women, started a series of prayer meetings, and seven years later, at the Poppie Ridge school house, on May 6, 1829 a church of about 30 members was organized. On his 80th birthday, in midwinter, a hole was cut in the ice of Piscataquis brook and the captain was emersed. So the story goes.]

At 6 o'clock p. m. I have just returned from a meeting of the church (Bradley's Corner church). Eighteen present—cold and stupid. Christ seems to saying to this as he once said to the first church, "Sciotus opera, quid nequa pigidus es, neque calidus; itinam pigidus esses aut calidus; Sic qua tepidus es, et nec calidus, nec pigidus, futrus sum te exemore ex on meo." Now, what are we to expect if we do not wake up and be more engaged in the service of Christ? Will he not be sick of us? Does he not nauseate? If we should treat an earthly friend in this manner would he be pleased with us?

THE DEERING NEWS.

Saturday, Jan. 1, 1898.

GRANDPA'S SCRAP BOOK

[Under this head historical and genealogical memoranda will be furnished the readers of the News that appears worthy of preservation, particularly of remote periods in our history within the city limits and immediate vicinity.]

GLIMPSES OF THE PAST.

REV. CALEB BRADLEY'S DIARY WITH ANNOTATIONS.

Oct 31, 1802. The greatest South-east blow I have ever known. Pierce's frame blew over and my bee-house and much other damage was done.

Thomas Pierce, b. in Scarboro, Oct. 26, 1763, son of Rev. Thomas Pierce. The house in which he was born, built by his father, stands just as it was originally constructed, near Scarboro depot of B. and M. railroad. He m. Betsey Storer of Falmouth, was a brick mason, and his wife had eleven children. Thomas Knight, Jr., who was b. and lived at Woodfords, m. a daughter and reared a large family there. The Storer family was noticed in the News Aug. 20, '97. The Pierce house now stands on the westerly side of Stevens Plains avenue, between Frost street and Brighton Corner, but has been moved back up the hill, and a piece added.

Feb. 6, 1803. Preached at Saccarappa. Eat a piece of roast turkey at Dr. Bailey's.

David Bailey, son of Deacon John Bailey, was. b. Oct. 28, 1737. a half brother to Benjamin Bailey who built the tomb on Mitchell's Hill, and in 1766 went to live on land located opposite where the Stroudwater road enters Main street at Saccarappa, given him by his father. He had son Jesse who in 1809 was dead. He had a daughter Lucy who m. Chas. Babb, and Babb died May 23, 1821. Also a daughter who m. Capt. Joshua Swett of Gorham, and Rebecca who m. Oct. 13, 1805 Nathan Burnett of Poland. David was past 90 years of age when he died. He owned 1-4 of the Bailey saw mill at Saccarappa, 1-8 of which he received by heirship.

March 21. Pigeons remarkably plenty.

April 7. Funeral of Sally Lunt.

April 11. Funeral of Mrs. Paine, aged 85.

Oct. 12. The regiment met on Stevens Plains.

Oct. 25. Went to Gray with Esq. Lewis. Dined at Maj. Cobb's; took tea at James Dudley's and lodged at Mr. Greeley's. Rev. Mr. ——— was ordained.

After dinner, Esq. L. and myself went to Thompson's Pond. Lodged at Gen. Smith's.

Feb. 7, 1804. Had nine loads of slabs hauled gratis, except one load hauled by Mark Haskell (who lived at Saccarappa) The teams were Titcomb's, Dole's, Chick's, Porterfield's, (Stroudwater and vicinity,) Seal and Knight, (Capisic), Stephen Riggs (Nason's Corner) and D. Small.

June 14. Capt. Jones raised his barn. (He lived near Bradley's Corner.)

June 21. Conversed with Mr. Storer (Joseph) relative to his absenting himself from the sacrament.

After this date he built and lived in what is now known as the Daniel Mason house, near Bradley's Corner.

June 22. Funeral of Mr. Anthony Sawyer.

Resided at East Deering. Grave stone there, aged 69 years.

Sept. 22, 1804. Prayed with Zebulon Sawyer a few moments before he died.

Sept. 24. Attended the burial of an infant. Took tea at the house of mourning. (Mr. Henry Knight, jr., of Woodfords.)

Sept. 27. Capt. Waterhouse's company met at the meeting house.

Capt. John Waterhouse lived at the south easterly corner of the bridge over Mill Creek in Stroudwater, in a house that stood on the Town Landing, which house was moved to Portland. He was captain of the Stroudwater Light Infantry at the time the standard was presented the company by the ladies of that village, in the year 1805, which is now deposited in the archives of the Maine Historical Society. He was the son of William Waterhouse, the first of the name at Stroudwater, baptized at St. Paul's church, Portland, June 28, 1764, married 1784, Hannah Brooks. At Stroudwater he was a ship builder, from which place he removed.

THE DEERING NEWS.

Saturday, Jan. 8, 1898.

GRANDPA'S SCRAP BOOK

Under this head historical and genealogical memoranda will be furnished the readers of the News that appears worthy of preservation, particularly of remote periods in our history within the city limits and immediate vicinity.]

GLIMPSES OF THE PAST.

REV. CALEB BRADLEY'S DIARY WITH ANNOTATIONS.

Oct. 4, 1804. Regimental muster upon Stevens Plains where I spent most of the day.

May 2, 1805. Married two couples at the same time at Isaiah Woodford's.

Mr. Woodford resided at Morrill's Corner. The contracting parties were Elijah North and Martha Woodford; Oliver Buckley and Sally Reed. Each paid the Parson $1.55. A son of Mr. Buckly resides on Stevens Plains—Edward M. Buckly.

May 21, 1805. Attended the funeral of Mr. Waterhouse.

This was William Waterhouse, father to Capt. John Waterhouse, noticed last week. He built a house on the "Point" where his great grandson Frederick Waterhouse now resides at Stroudwater. It was in 1783 that he made his land purchase there. In 1795 he conveyed the premises to his son Robert, grandfather to the above named Frederick, and to his son Joseph Hote Waterhouse he conveyed the westerly part of the lot now occupied by Mr. Cypress Dill, upon which he (Joseph) constructed a one story, dwelling, to, which has been added another story. He removed to Portland thence to Gorham, this state and engaged in farming and then came back to Stroudwater, purchased the lot where Mr. Charles Fickett resides in Westbrook street and converted his boat house into a dwelling, he being a boat builder by occupation, where he soon died. He left six children as follows: Capt. John; Robert; Joseph H; William; Elizabeth; m. Nov. 8, 1774, Aaron Chamberlain, a saddler, Stroudwater, and grandfather to the wife of the late James Parker of Stroudwater and Sally who m. Dec. 7, 1783, Joseph Bailey, a blacksmith who was drowned at Lisbon; and Nov. 29, 1804, the widow m. Isaac Fly, and she was known as "Aunt Fly" residing where the late George Morton lived at Stroudwater. By first husband she had seven children, none by the last. Her fifth child m. Feb. 11, 1813. Joseph Quimby of Saccarappa, whose third child is Capt. Isaac Fly of that place

In the year 1851 when the last homestead of William Waterhouse was conveyed the heirs of Capt. John Waterhouse were as follows:

"John Cloudman and Mary his wife, Paul Cloudman and Eliza B. Cloudman, heirs at law of John Waterhouse, late of Saco, gentleman died, Hannah Waterhouse widow of Wm. Waterhouse, son of John Waterhouse, died, and Eliza, widow of Chas. Waterhouse, son of said John Waterhouse, died heirs of William Waterhouse."

In my next article I shall give out a copy of the presentation speech made by Miss Eunice Quimby and response on the occasion of the presentation of the banner to Capt. Waterhouse's company, Rev. Caleb Bradley delivering an oration.

[Note. Where "Dr. Bailey" appears in the article of last week the "r" should be omitted. D. Bailey was not a doctor.]

HE DEERING NEWS.

Saturday, Jan. 15, 1898.

GRANDPA'S SCRAP BOOK

[Under this head historical and genealogical matter will be furnished the readers of the News that appears worthy of preservation, particularly of remote periods in our history within city limits and immediate vicinity.]

GLIMPSES OF THE PAST.

(REV. CALEB BRADLEY'S DIARY WITH ANNOTATIONS.)

...4, 1805, I delivered an oration before ...ple of this place.

...is all the parson says relative ...at transpired on that day in ...cinity. From other sources I ...much.

...village of Stroudwater was ...in its zenith of prosperity; its ...of settlement being nearly co-stant with that of Portland. As ...ow, party feeling ran high at times, the name of "Republican" being applied to the Jeffersonian or what is now known as the Democratic, and Federal" to what was later known as the Whig and now the Republican ...arty.

...Rev. Caleb Bradley was an intense ...ederalist and he attempted to fix ...e name of "Federal Corner" to the ...istrict now known as Bradley's ...orner, but failed.

Capt. James Means and Thaddeus ...ad of Stroudwater, and Capt. ...n Wayte, the master ship builder ...t Presumpscot Falls were Republicans. Capt. John Quinby evidently ...as a Frederalist. The political ...eling of the individual then we now ...ehold cropping out of the descend-...nts. Military parades were the ...aramount pleasures of the time. ...troudwater and Stevens' Plains had ...s uniformed infantry, artillery and ...valry companies, but few remind-...of the military events however of ...commencing of the century, now ...wing to a close, remain.

...a copy of the Eastern Argus of ...11, 1804, I find as follows:

...correspondent who attended ...Review of Col. Merrill's Regi-...on Tuesday last, was much ...d at the appearance of the four ...med companies, and the new ...Infantry Company of Capt. ...Waterhouse (of Stroudwater) ...a correctness of discipline ...cial appearance not to be ...u from so new an establish-...This company, with that of ...radish. (Portland) exhibited ...ess of uniforms which we ...ll be imitated by all the in-...ompanies of the Regiment."

...can fix the date of the first ...ace of this company in uni-...1804, but the names of the ...composing the company at

...e I have not yet found out but ...a period ten years later.

...forenoon of July 4th, 1805—...ears ago—the company was ...d in line in front of the Capt. ...Quinby residence that stood ...the only brick residence now ...on Westbrook street, Stroud-...opposite the Means house, ...escribed in the News—the ...house being moved to Port-...here it now may be seen as ...lly constructed at the junction ...and Congress streets—for the ...se of receiving a banner from ...ies of the place, the record ...the time of the proceedings ...as the demonstration at ...tavern being as follows:

AT FALMOUTH.

...itizens of that Republican Town, ...ended celebrating our Independence, ...numerous, tha they found it neces-...order to be accommodated, that they ...meet in two distinct companies. The ...ng are the communications from each.

...Glorious Anniversary of our Inde ...ce was celebrated at Mr. *Broad's* in ...*th*, by a large number of the Repub-...f that and adjoining towns. After ...Capt. James Means as President, ...John Waite as Vice-President, and ...mittee of Arrangements, they with ...one hundred respectable Citizens, ...in procession to a Platform under a ...(erected in an Orchard for the pur-...here a short but comprehensive ...ON was delivered by the *Rev. Joab* ...isplaying the principles of American ...nce under the auspices of the pres-...istration. The Company then ...the Hall, where an elegant ...prepared for the festive occasion. ...er, the following *Toasts* were ...nr ied with acclamations of ...rom hearts sensible of the ...edom and Indedendence. ...company retired in good ...ng a joyful day in harmo-

...in number seventeen ...eleventh as follows:

May Freedom never be ...their breasts by the acts of

...rteenth:

...gy. May they be religious—not ...ecturers.

ARTY AT MAJOR WEBSTER'S.

...e Major Webster's public ...as located I cannot ascertain ...y at the head of Waldo street ...he cellar of the so-called Bart-...e may be seen.]

(TO BE CONTINUED.)

THE DEERING NEWS.

Saturday, Jan. 22, 1898.

GRANDPA'S SCRAP BOOK

[Under this head historical and genealogical memoranda will be furnished the readers of the News that appears worthy of preservation, particularly of remote periods in our history within the city limits and immediate vicinity.]

GLIMPSES OF THE PAST.

REV. CALEB BRADLEY'S DIARY WITH ANNOTATIONS.

Continued from last week.

"The day was ushered in by the discharge of cannon. At 8 o'clock the *Stroudwater Light Infantry Company*, commanded by Capt. *John Waterhouse*, paraded, and after performing a number of military manoeuvers, were joined by the *Falmouth Cavalry* under Capt. *William Brackett* and marched to Capt. *John Quinby's*, where were assembled the ladies of the village and vicinity, who displayed their patriotism by presenting the *Light Infantry* with an elegant standard accompanied by the following address of Miss Eunice Quinby:"

"The martial ardor which actuates the *Stroudwater Light Infantry*, affords a pleasing satisfaction, while the celerity, with which, from a state of ignorance, it has obtained an extensive knowledge of military discipline, is matter of surprise to every beholder,—you have begun the career of glory; and we trust that honor which is the soldiers sole reward, will amply compensate you, in whose breasts are implanted the love of liberty, of virtue and of your country, for all the toil, anxiety and danger, to which you are liable.— Ours is the land of Liberty, and happiness; we peculiarly enjoy the blessings of peace and prosperity; but these advantages are to be preserved only by the smiles of an over-ruling Providence, and the virtue and watchfulness of our citizens. On those of military capacity we depend for protection from foreign invasion and domestic usurpation; to effect which unremitted vigilance, patience of discipline and scorn of danger, are absolutely necessary. Being sensible that you are deeply impressed with the truth of this observation, I have the honor, in the name of the ladies of Falmouth, to offer this standard to your protection. Let it ever be the signal of Liberty. May that which is now entrusted to your heroism and magnanimity never be deferred; may the motto which is inscribed thereon, be indelibly imprinted on all your hearts—and may the spark of ambition, which at first warmed your breasts and which is now kindled into a flame, never,

never, be extinguished."

"The standard was received by Mr. Enoch Richards who made the following reply:"

"WITH the warmest emotions of gratitude do we receive from the virtuous fair of this town, an emblem of their devotion to the cause of Liberty and Independence. May this standard never be unfurled but in defence of its loved patroness, women whose external grace and internal virtues, inspire the noblest attachments to Freedom. Without her smiles victory would lose her exultation—without her presence domestic retirement would have no power to charm. But excited by her zeal, fighting her cause, under her banner what heart but must beat with the most ardent hatred of her foes. We acknowledge this present on this day, and at this time, far beyond our power to reward or ability to express. Accept our sincere thanks, our open, unequivocal declaration, that when the good of our country shall require it, we will on the erection of this signal assemble ourselves, and then patriotically sacrifice our lives to the cause of our country and its patriotic fair."

"The *Cavalry* and *Infantry* being again joined, received a large and respectable procession, whom they escorted to the meeting house, where an ORATION was delivered by the Rev. CALEB BRADLEY, in commemoration of the day, accompanied with music selected for the occasion. The procession was again formed and escorted to Maj. *Stephen Webster's* where they partook of a splendid dinner, which was concluded with the following toasts, accompanied with music, and discharge from a field piece:"

There were seventeen toasts drank, the copy of which I omit, and two volunteers, the volunteers reading as follows:

'*The Orator of the Day*. We tender him our hearty thanks for his exertion on this day, to animate us with true patriotism, by stamping afresh upon our memories the cause which roused us to action to obtain those rights and privileges which continue to be held sacred by every true American.'

'*The Stroudwater Light Infantry*. They have this day bound themselves in a perpetual covenant to aid the cause of Liberty and Indpendence; even to the sacrificing their lives if required; may they never forget their vows.'

"The companies again paraded and marched to Mr. Broads, when, after taking some refreshments which was generously provided by the citizens who had assembled there, they fired a salute, and were dismissed in the utmost harmony. * *

It is highly gratifying to see our citizens make such rapid progress in military acquirements and uncommon celerity with which the Stroudwater Light Infantry have pro-

gressed in military discipline, attaches the highest honor to the officers and soldiers composing the company."

THE DEERING NEWS.

Saturday, Jan. 29, 1898.

GRANDPA'S SCRAP BOOK

[Under this head historical and genealogical memoranda will be furnished the readers of the News that appears worthy of preservation, particularly of remote periods of our history within the city limits and immediate vicinity.]

GLIMPSES OF THE PAST.

REV. CALEB BRADLEY'S DIARY WITH ANNOTATIONS.

Continued from last week.

Miss Eunice Quinby, who presented the banner was born at Stroudwater and was the daughter of Capt. John Quinby and wife Eunice Freeman. (For Freemans, see p. 135, Smith & Dean's Diary; and for Capt. Quinby's grave memorial inscription, see p. 193, Maine Historical and Genealogical Recorder.) The Captain was the eighth child of Joseph Quinby and was born May 12, 1758.

Miss Quinby was united in marriage by Rev. Caleb Bradley, May 24, 1808, with Ezekiel Day, of Portland, and they resided where the Natural History building stands on Elm street, Portland.

Mr. Day had been married before to Hannah Smith who had a daughter that married Enoch Crocker of Oxford, Mr. Edward D. Crocker of Oakdale, this city; being a grandson. She died October 15, 1806, aged 30 years. He died March 22, 1842, aged 70 years, and Eunice, his last wife, May 9, 1862, aged 79 years, leaving an estate appraised at $23,-100. Their remains are deposited in a tomb in the Eastern cemetery, Portland.

CHILDREN BY LAST MARRIAGE.

1—John Q., born June 24, 1809. Married. Died, leaving children now residing in Portland.

2—Joseph, born May 30, 1811. Died in Portland, unmarried, July 28, 1851.

3—Lucretia, born February 1, 1813. Married Kiah B. Sewall, Esq., and was a lawyer at Mobile, La., at the commencement of the Civil War. Returning they settled at Freehold, N. J.

4—Henry Ezekiel, born December 17, 1822. Married, retired from business and resided in Gorham, this State.

TO BE CONTINUED.

Saturday, Feb. 5, 1898.

GRANDPA'S SCRAP BOOK

[Under this head historical and genealogical memoranda will be furnished to readers of the News that appears worthy of preservation, particularly of remote periods of our history within the city limits and immedia vicinity.]

GLIMPSES OF THE PAST.

REV. CALEB BRADLEY'S DIARY WITH ANNOTATIONS.

Continued from last week.

Of Enoch Richards I can learn but comparatively little. He was in trade somewhere hereabouts. In the year 1802 he purchased four acres of land situated on the northerly side of Congress street, this city, adjoining the south-easterly corner of the Parson Bradley farm and a year later sold half to Thomas Wiswell, a joiner, of Newton, and March 11, 1811. he and wife Mary and Wiswell sold the premises to Samuel Dalton of Parsonsfield, grandfather to Rev. Asa Dalton of Portland, for $2,000. During Wiswell's ownership it was a place of resort—a team tavern where rum was freely sold, a bowling alley maintained, and the amusements of the times freely indulged. One of the buildings, which was two story, containing a dance hall, was removed and now stands at Libby's Corner and is the third house westerly on Congress street, from the George Libby brick dwelling—the only brick house of the neighborhood. The Richards—Wiswell place with added land is now owned by the J. B. Brown heirs.

The oration by Rev. Joab Young was printed at the Augus office the week after it was delivered and was a document of twelve pages. I find it charged in Mr. Jonathan Sparrow's account book at 12½ cents per copy, and it is noticed in Williamson's Bibliography of Maine, printed in 1896, so the oration is to be seen somewhere.

During the month of June, 1880 the Broad house was thrown open to the public a week, which had been closed as an inn for nearly fifty years, and on the twenty-second day of that month a description of the premises appeared in the Portland Daily Press, and a notice in the Argus. The Press article contains a good description of the old banner now to be seen in the rooms of the Maine Historical Society, as follows:

Perhaps the most attractive feature to any one interested in military affairs was the white silk banner presented by the ladies of Stroudwater to the Stroudwater Light Infantry in 1805. The banner bears on the reverse the coat of arms of Massachusetts with the motto *Sub libertate quietem ense petit paleidam*. Above is the legend—Death or an Honorable life. Below—From the fair to the brave. On the obverse is the eagle grasping in his talons javelins and the olive branch, the same legands as the reverse and the inscription—To the Stroudwater Light Infantry.

From a report of a meeting of the Maine Historical Society found in the Portland Argus of Jan. 22, 1892 I now quote as follows:

A flag was presented by Miss Ann A. Broad of Stroudwater, in whose family it has been preserved many years. It is of heroic size made of heavy silk with gold bullion tassels, and fringe, and bears the lone Indian who represents Massachusetts in the list of state seals, with the motto 'Better Death than Dishonorable Life,' and 'From the Brave to the Fair.'

TO BE CONTINUED.

Saturday, Feb. 19, 1898.

GRANDPA'S SCRAP BOOK

[Under this head historical and genealogical memoranda will be furnished the readers of the News that appears worthy of preservation, particularly of remote periods in our history within the city limits and immediate vicinity.]

GLIMPSES OF THE PAST.

REV. CALEB BRADLEY'S DIARY WITH ANNOTATIONS.

Continued from two weeks since.

CHARLES PIERCE.

[NOTE. There was so much material on hand last week for the News that would not keep a week, the matter prepared for this department was necessarily left out.]

Considerable remains unsaid of the Stroudwater Light Infantry Company and persons and events connected with it.

The shop occupied and owned by Andrew Hawes, Esq., was erected in the year 1785 by one William Tate, son of George Tate, who was sent to Stroudwater by the English government to procure masts for the English navy and as it is traditional that the "loft," or second story of the building, as now called, was used as a military drill room in dull weather and public exhibitions, it is safe to suppose that this company used the upper part of this building as their armory.

Before me as I now write is a well preserved paper, 9x15 inches in size. It bears the seal of the Commonwealth of Massachusetts and the signature of James Sullivan and is addressed—

To Charles Pierce, Gentleman, Greeting:

You being elected Ensign of a company of Light Infantry annexed to the first Regiment in the Second Brigade, Sixth Division of the Military of this Commonwealth, Reposing special trust and confidence in your ability, courage and good conduct, I do, by these Presents, Commission you accordingly. * * * April 13, A. D. 1807.

The copy of the declaration and oath administered covers the whole back of the paper. The commission will be placed with the standard in the archives of the Maine Historical society, appropriately mounted.

In the News of February 16, 1895, appears a column notice of Ensign Pierce which also presents a record of his family and grave stone memorial at Stroudwater, and other facts. The following copied from the original lets in some light upon his relation and place of abode:

HAVERHILL, Sep. 7, 1801.

DEAR BROTHER: * * * * *

"As for the old gentleman he is more difficult and uneasy than ever he was."

MARY.

Before me also is a Ms. letter dated at Topsham. Me., Aug. 3, 1807, and was written by a gentleman who signs himself—Your Cousin, G. Rogers, from which I make an extract as follows:

I hear, by the by, that you are to be married; if this is the case for Heaven's sake give me an invitation to the wedding, for I should think myself at the highest pinnacle of honor and favor to be present at the wedding of so beautiful, amiable and virtuous a lady as my cousin. As for Mr. Pierce, I have never seen him but hope my curiosity may be gratified in September.

ATKINSON, March 12, 1802.

This may certify to whom it may concern that I, Rebecca Peirce do hereby appoint my son, Charles Peirce, to sell or dispose of a certain piece or Parcel of Land with half a house thereon, in Newbury Port, formerly the Estate of Joseph Peirce, late of Atkinson, in the State of Newhampshire and county of Rockingham, deceased, and I hereby impower him to sell or dispose of said Land and half the house above mentioned as he Shall think to the Best advantage for the heirs of deceased.

Witnesses,   REBEKAH PEIRCE.
* * * *   for herself and heirs.

He was married Oct, 11, 1807, to Peggy Porterfield, maternal aunt to Portland's esteemed citizen, John Sparrow of No. 126 Winter street, also to Wilham Sparrow of Pleasant street, this city, brother to John and Mrs. Nathan Fickett of Stroudwater, where he engaged in trade.

At Haverhill, N. H. March 12, 1803, Samuel Pierce writes his brother Charles at Stroudwater as follows:

I will inform you that my folks expect to live on the place formerly owned by Jacob Tyler and I am going to live with Maj. Moody where I lived last year.

HAVERHILL, Aug. 28, 1808,
BRO. CHARLES.   * * * * * *

I received your letter of the 3rd inst. in which you wrote that mamma wished to come home, and you wanted me to come down after her. I cannot well come but rather than have her come by water I will come. I want my chaise very much for I have had to borrow twice to go to Boston besides all other travel. If you do not come this way as I wish you would I shall come that way sometime next month. Remember me to mother and Peggy.

Yours,
SAM'L PEIRCE.

Saturday, Feb. 26, 1898.

GRANDPA'S SCRAP BOOK

[Under this head historical and genealogical memoranda will be furnished the readers of the News that appears worthy of preservation, particularly of remote periods in our history within the city limits and immediate vicinity.]

(Continued from last week.)

CHARLES PEIRCE AND THE QUINBY FAMILY.

At the February meeting of the Maine Historical Society, reported in the Portland Advertiser the 9th day of that month, 1888, a letter written by Charles Peirce to his brother Samuel of Haverhill, N. H., was presented the society by Dr. Chas. E. Clark, of Lynn, Mass., and is now deposited in the archives of the society. (The newspaper says Boston.) It reads as follows:

STROUDWATER, April 20th, 1814.

BROTHER:—

I will write a few lines to inform you that we are all well at present. I hope that you & all the (others are the) same. tell Mama the old Lady is well & harty. (1.) She can see & hear as well as any of us.

She is now in her 94th year of her age. Our Little family are well. Our Neighbour Stevens has lost three Children this winter with sickness. I received a line from you last March, 16th I found by that you were well. We have a report this morning the British are coming in ten days to Burn Portland but we do not believe the story. (2.) I have nothing of any use to write you. I wish you to write. as soon as you can conveantly & let me know how you are thear.

Yours &c. CHARLES PEIRCE.

(over)

We are now in Corporated into a Town by the name Stroudwater. (3.) it has been devided But I suppose it will be altered by the next General Court to the name of West brook as a great part of the town are dis satisfied with the present name.

At the Last Town Meeting they ware all but one in favour of the name of West brook. I Believe I was the Instigner of Giving it the name. it is named for Co Thomas Westbrook the first setler tha came from Stroudwater in England. (4.) he once ownd the Land I now live on & all the land in this Village. I find this by the old Cronoligee & old Law book that I Brout from Haverhill The other part is calleo Falmouth. (5.) Let me know what time you think you will be hear to see us.

Addressed—

Capt. SAMUEL PEIRCE,
Haverhill,
Mass.

(1) This has reference to Mary (Haskell) Quinby, Mr. Pierce's maternal grandmother, who was born Apr. 22 1722, (O. S.) died at Stroudwater, Apr. 12, 1815, which shows she was but 92 years at the time he wrote. She was the widow of Joseph Quinby.

(2) This country was at war with England at that time and Portland had 6000 volunteer troops quartered there. Goods were removed from the city in every direction.

(3) Westbrook when set off from Falmouth, Feb. 14, 1814, was named Stroudwater, but in June of the same year, the name caused so much confusion, was changed to Westbrook.

(4.) This is the only evidence I find how Westbrook got her name and is worth something being as it is a re corded assertion; but Col. Thomas Westbrook was not the first settler of the soil upon which the ancient village is located. Away back in 1680, Oct. 13, John and Geo. Ingalls obtained a deed from the Massachusetts General Court of the mill privilege and "land on both sides of the falls." It was not until 1727 that Westbrook was admitted a citizen of Falmouth, and 1728 he took up his abode at Stroudwater.

In the year of 1665 John Westbrook was in Portsmouth, N. H., and in 1697, according to Exeter, N. H., records, Thomas his son was appointed administrator of his father's estate. A record of all these facts may be found in the Portland Transcript, commencing Nov. 7, 1883, and running through three numbers. Westbrook named the village undoubtedly but where he got, or from what he made the name has never been fixed to a certainty.

(5.) When the part was set off that was named Stroudwater, then changed to Westbrook, Falmouth retained the original name of which town Cape Elizabeth was taken, (recently divided) and Portland, as well as what is now Westbrook and Deering.

Col. Thomas Westbrook died Feb. 11, 1744. The fact is recorded in a letter on file at Alfred, York county, probate court, written in Gen. Samuel Waldo's neat style; and as an officer was paid for keeping guard over his house after his demise, I do not think his wife was with him at the time, and his remains were removed to New Hampshire, vicinity of Portsmouth, where he had relatives, and the place of interment may yet be discovered.

QUINBY FAMILY.

Joseph Quinby was a ship-capenter residing southerly side of Middle, near India street, Portland, till the destruction of the place by Capt. Mowatt, Oct. 18, 1775, when he went to Saccarappa and bought into a mill privilege. He was born in ―― intention of marriage with Mary Haskell made public Sept 28, 1740, in Portland. He died at Saccarappa April 14, 1776. His wife was born April 22, 1722, (O. S.) and died at Stroudwater April 12, 1815. This is the one to whom Charles Peirce alludes in the foregoing letter as "the old lady who can see and hear as well as any of us."

The exact relationship between the Quinbys of Saccarappa and those of Stroudwater has not yet been dis covered. The paternal grandmother of the compiler hereof was Hannah Quinby who married Samuel Chapman and died Sept. 27, 1801. He was born at New Market, N. H., Jan. 13, 1762.)

CHILDREN OF JOSEPH QUINBY AND WIFE MARY.

Mary, b. Nov. 9, 1742, d. Oct. 15, 1750. (See Smith & Dean's journal, p. 145, edition of 1849.

Rebecca, b. April 9, 1744, d. May 15, 1816. She married Joseph Peirce, whose son Chas. settled in Stroudwater and was author of the foregoing letter.

Joseph Jr., b. May. 15, 1746; m. Dec. 3, 1772, Hannah Noise. (Smith & Dean's journal, p. 333.) He resided in Portland in a house his father gave him before he made his will. He died Dec 26, 1775, and the widow married a man by the name of Lunt and went to Brunswick to reside. In 1788 "Hannah Lunt, widow of Joseph Quinby" sold the Portland homestead to Jonathan Bryant. They had children

Sarah, b. May 9, 1748; d. July 12, 1772.

Eunice, b. Aug. 2, 1750; m. March 2, 1780, Brig. Gen. Wm. Cobb of Portland. She d. Jan. 23, 1795. They had children.

Thomas, b. Nov. 3, 1752; d. Dec. 27, 1781, and it is supposed unmarried.

Mary, b. Aug. 4, 1755, m. June 14, 1781 Wm. Slemons of Stroudwater; b. there April 15, 1755. Had three children. She died ―― 1828. He d. April 9, 1834. He built the house at the north westerly corner of Westbrook and Bond streets as now seen and owned the mill privilege adjoining. Had children.

John (Capt. John,) b. May 12, 1758; m. Oct. 31, 1782, Eunice Freeman of Portland b. there Jan. 19, 1762. He was ancestor of the Quinby's of Stroudwater.

Levi b. May 12, 1761; d. Oct. 14, 1784; and it is supposed, unmarried.

My next will contain further facts relative to the Stroudwater Light Infantry.

THE DEERING NEWS.

Saturday, March 12, 1898.

GRANDPA'S SCRAP BOOK

[Under this head historical and genealogical memoranda will be furnished the readers of the News that appears worthy of preservation, particularly of remote periods in our history within the city limits and immediate vicinity.]

CHARLES PEIRCE AND THE QUINBY FAMILY.

(Continued from last week.)

STROUDWATER LIGHT INFANTRY COMPANY.

This independent, uniformed company was attached to the 1st Regiment, 2nd Brigade and 12th Division of the Massachusetts militia. Its officers were, in 1811, as follows:
Thomas Slemons—Captain
Wm. Slemons—Lieutenant
William Kenney—Ensign
1812. Thomas Slemons promoted to Captain
William Kenney promoted to Lieutenant
Daniel Broad—Ensign

As Broad was the last ensign of the company this fact accounts for the banner being at the old Broad Tavern where it was so well perserved.

Thomas Slemons was son of William of Stroudwater noticed last week. William Slemons, the captain, was son of Robert who resided a mile and a half westerly of Stroudwater, and this William was father to George, still living on part of the homestead. Thomas and Wm. were cousins. William removed to Coryon, Ind.—See "Poets of Maine," p. 435.

William Kenney resided in the Morrills Corner district of our city and has been noticed in connection with the Stevens family.

Daniel Broad to be noticed further on.

Muster Roll of the Field and Staff of Lt. Josiah Hobb's Reg. of Mass. Militia in service at Portland from the 8th to the 20th of Sept. 1814. War of 1812-15:

First Reg. Second Brigade, Twelth Division.
Josiah Hobbs—Lt. Commanding, Falmouth.
*Thomas Slemons—Maj., Westbrook.
Ezekiel Dyer—Maj., C. Elizabeth.
Arthur Dyer—Adjutant, C. Elizabeth.
Peter Lunt—Adjutant, Westbrook.
*Joseph Chamberlain—Qr. Master, Westbrook.
*(Rev.) Caleb Bradley—Chaplain, Westbrook.
Wm. Sanborn—Surgeon, Falmouth.
*(Dr.) Jacob Hunt—Surgeon's Mate, Westbrook.
Josiah R. Clough—Sergt. Maj., Falmouth
*Hezekiah Slemons—Qr. Mas. Sergt., Westbrook.
*James Poterfield—Fife Maj., Westbrook.
Chas. Walker—Drum Maj., Westbrook.
*Stroudwater and vicinity.

Muster Roll of Capt. Wm. Slemon's Co. while on duty in Portland was as follows:
Wm. Slemons—Capt.
Wm. Kenney—Lieu.
Daniel Broad—Ensign.
Sergents—Josiah Stevens, *Benjamin Burnham, *John M. Millken, *David Stevens.
Musicians—David Knight, Samuel Kenney.
Privates—Henry Blake, James Blake Jr., Richard G. Bailey, Ephraim Broad (Bro. to Daniel,) Wm. Bell, George Cobb, Benjamin Choatt, Frederick Davis, *Isaac Flye, Wm. Hicks (Morrills Corner,) Nathaniel Haskell Jr. John Jordan, Henry Knight, Rowland Knight, Theopilus Knight, *Nicholas Eaton, Jonathan Ray, (East Deering,) Nathaniel Stevens, Steven's Plains, William Stevens, (Father to George Mead Stevens, G. P.)
Officer's waiters—Rufus Jeffords, George Strout.
The company disbanded Aug. 31, 1815.
*Stroudwater.

The cavalry company that took a part in the escort when the standard was presented was commissioned Aug. 12, 1799, with Daniel Lunt as captain, who resided near Pride's bridge.

The muster roll when the company was on duty in Portland in 1814 shows as follows:
Lieut.—Nathaniel Leighton.
Cornet—Wm. Thambs.
Sergeants—James Smith And. Leighton.
Corporals—John Phinney, Levi Wilson.
Privates—Zachariah Brackett, Adam Winslow, Nathaniel Abbott, Solomon Baker, Daniel Blake, Samuel Crockett, Jr., Timothy Cochran, David Chase, Joshua L. Dearing, Daniel Freeman, James Fry, John Fields, George Leighton, Joseph Libby, Harry Stevens, Benj. Pettingill, William Webb, Cyrus Wilson.

TO BE CONTINUED.

THE DEERING NEWS.

Saturday, March 19, 1898.

GRANDPA'S SCRAP BOOK

[Under this head historical and genealogical memoranda will be furnished the readers of the News that appears worthy of preservation, particularly of remote periods in our history within the city limits and immediate vicinity.]

STROUDWATER LIGHT INFANTRY AND THE FALMOUTH ARTILLERY.

(Continued from last week.)

I am now in possession of an original order for a meeting of the Stroudwater Light Infantry company received from Thomas Ferguson, Esq., born in the ancient village Apr. 18, 1830, and son of Chas. Ferguson and Mary Slemons, but is a resident of the part of Hollis now Dryton, to which place the family removed in 1836. His father was prominent in Stroudwater affairs many years a sketch of whom I propose to present very soon. He was a member of the Stroudwater military company in 1812.

The paper upon which the order appears is well perserved at the top of which is an impressive wood cut of an eagle then the printed form filled in with pen and ink as follows:

COMPANY ORDERS.

Mr. Charles Ferguson:

YOU being a Member of the Stroudwater Light Infantry are hereby ordered to appear at the house of Lieutenant Wm. Kenney on Thursday, the 11 day of June, at one o'clock, p. m., in Company Uniform, armed and equipped as the law directs for Military Discipline, and there await for further orders.

By order of the Captain.
Josiah Stevens, CLERK.

Falmouth, June 5, 1812.

Lieut. Wm. Kenney resided on the Windham road a mile or so northwesterly of Morrill's Corner; born in Portland, married Molly Stevens of Stevens Plains, sister to the above named Josiah. (See News of Dec. 29, 1894, for Kenney family.)

Josiah Stevens, clerk of the company, died Dec. 24, 1818, aged 34 years. His last earthly abiding place remains just as he left it—on Stevens Plains—a large, two-story, square house, retained by descendants.

(For a lengthy notice of him see News, June 8, 1895.)

This article finishes all I have to say relative to the old Stroudwater standard and company, excepting what I have to say about the Broad family, unless something more is discovered of public interest.

THE FALMOUTH ARTILLERY.

When Falmouth was divided in the year 1814, the part called Stroudwater and six months later Westbrook, was not, to use a slang phrase, "a spring chicken." In military matters she was well up to date—infantry and cavalry as I have shown she had and now her artillery company comes in for a notice.

In volume 86, page 432, Cumberland county Registry, is the record of a sale of land in Morrill's Corner district, "beginning bounds southwesterly corner of Henry Blake's homestead on the northeasterly side of the road leading through Stevens Plains, so called, by road, southwesterly sixteen rods to a stake adjoining the Artillery Gun house."

(Henry Blake married Nancy Barber, or the intention was published, April 27, 1816. The Blake house is now standing, and was taxed at the time on a valuation with two acres of land, $200 and $50 added.)

From the place here noticed, which must have been about where the Free church building is located, the Gun house was moved easterly to the westerly side of Forest avenue to a spot near the one story brick dwelling house as now seen. When the company was organized I can not state. It survived the war of 1812-15. In the month of Sept. 1814 its muster role was as follows:

Isaac Leighton—Capt.
Isaac Nason—Lieut.
Sergeants—Thomas Hudson, Nathaniel Merrill, Will Knight, Peter M. Knight.
Corporals—Jos. Quinby, David Barbour, John Batchelder, Robert Huston.
Musicians—Thadeus Leighton, Edward Leighton.
Privates—Alexander Knight, Richard Knight, Wm. G. Lord, Enoch Cobb, Nathaniel Morse, Isaac Cobb, Wm. Elder, Stephen Knight, Elijah Baker.

The following is copied from the Eastern Argus of July, 1818:

On Saturday, 4th inst., the Westbrook Artillery Company, under command of Capt. Daniel Knight, assembled on Stevens Plains, to receive an elegant standard, about to be presented by the patriotic young ladies of that town. The weather being favorable a large concourse of spectators assembled on the occasion—the company was drawn up in order—the young ladies to the number of about 40 were neatly and tastefully dressed in uniform. Miss Frost, after delivering the following pertinent address, presented the standard to Ensign Th. Broad.

ADDRESS.

Sir—In compliance with the request of the ladies of Westbrook, I present you, in their behalf, this Standard. May it ever be sacred to freedom and honor. Should any hostile power invade our peaceful shores, may it not tardily nor reluctantly be unfurled for the defence of our country. Under this standard, may you with coolness and intrepidity, with firmness and resolution, meet the foe, who dares to assail our rights or menace our liberties. May it guide you to victory and in the hour of triumph, may the circumstances under which you received it, remind you that humanity, not less the appropriate ornament of a soldier than valor.

JOANN FROST.

ANSWER.

Madame—In behalf of the Westbrook Company of Artillery, I receive with the utmost pleasure the very elegant Standard you have done us the honor to present. May it prove the standard of freedom and honor. In the event of war, were any other incentive than duty necessary to our exertion in defence of our country, this proof of your approbation would of itself, be a sufficient stimulous to animate our hearts with courage and *nerve* our arms with strength. Be assured that in time of danger, it shall never be tardy or reluctantly unfurled; it will ever prove our rallying point; with it we will conquer, or around it perish—*We are Americans.*

TH. BROAD.

Joann Frost was born Jan. 7, 1784, on what is now known as Summit street, northeasterly of Allen's Corner. Her father built the large brick house now standing out there. Her family connections were noticed in the News of March 14th, 1896. Before and after said date, appeared articles relating to the Frost name.

This notice of her presentation of the Standard has since been discovered. Some one who reads this, may be able to tell where the Standard is deposited, if in existence.

Thomas Broad, born in the "Broad Tavern", now standing a little southerly of Stroudwater, Aug. 15 1791, will appear in the proposed Broad family notice, probably next week.

TO BE CONTINUED.

THE DEERING NEWS.

Saturday, March 26, 1898.

GRANDPA'S SCRAP BOOK

[Under this head historical and genealogical memoranda will be furnished the readers of the News that appears worthy of preservation, particularly of remote periods in our history within the city limits and immediate vicinity.]

THE BROAD TAVERN.

AN OLD TIME FASHIONABLE RESORT, WITH A HISTORY.

The Broad Tavern was located a half mile southerly of Stroudwater village on the road that leads to the State Reform school, and for a period of fifty odd years was a place where more real good first class "sprees" were indulged in than all other places in or around Portland. It flourished till the close of stage travel between Portland and Boston and the advent of the Temperance Washingtonian movement. And though the house was closed to the public it stood with its out-buildings unmolested nearly fifty years with the exception of the removal of the two story addition joined to the northerly end of the main house which was used as a hall and dining-room for parties. Of late years there have been wonderful changes connected with the once famous resort. First in disappearance after the hall was the bowling alley, then the long shed, carrage house, and barn opposite. The remnant of the primeval forest of massive pines adjoining Fore river disappeared by sale some ten years since, when later the premises on the easterly side of the highway were disposed of and the main dwelling, a square, two story structure with chimney in the middle, portico over the front door and ell on the rear side was renovated and new front door and windows put in. So where once the chained bear was poked by the gentleman with the walking stick and he growled and showed his teeth, the village youth made ten cents or more in a half day by bringing to the door the customer's horse and other boys set up ten pins, the old year was danced out and the new in, and the "buster" during the time of the great land speculation lighted his cigar with a dollar bill, which good times were succeeded by public soup houses in Portland, money was so scarce, the Broad name has departed and quietude partaking of the grave abounds, but the centurial elm with its long arching branches remains, while Mr. Abner Goold who for a period of forty years was a "hied man" on the place is rich now because he husbaned his wages instead of a wife, makes periodical visits to the historic spot from Portland where he resides.

A true story of the place, particularly the military part would be amusing and instructive and sufficient in quantity to fill a good sized volume of library size, but I can in this Scrap Book article preserve but a little of it. When the contents of the attic was dumped, three or four years ago, I obtained a few articles, among which was a ball and pin of the alley board, and deposited them in the archives of the Maine Historical society. The arm to the sign post upon which is painted on a white surface in black letters—S. (ilas) BROAD, beneath which hung a board two and a half feet or more long, with edge cut and gilded to represent a bunch of grapes may be seen in the new house opposite, and from Miss Almira Ann Broad, a granddaughter, (see Portland city directory 1894, for address,) I have obtained a family record of births and names I propose to preserve by using it in connection with this article.

1.—Thaddeus Broad, son of Thaddeus and Eunice Broad born in Natick (Mass.) Dec. 12, 1744.
2.—Eunice, born July 31, 1746.
3.—Ephraim, born June 11, 1748.

This Ephraim I find, was once a resident of Portland. In 1783, he had a house he had built on leased land located on Middle street, and was an inn holder, having obtained a retailer's license. Meeting trouble with the authorities, he and wife Abigail left the place, and in 1793, they then being residents of Hillston, Mass., gave power of attorney to his brother Thaddeus of Falmouth, now Deering, to dispose of his interest in the Portland property, and at that date, the name disappears on the public records of this vicinity.

What became of the sister Eunice, I cannot state, nor do I know anything concerning the parents, other than what the copy of the above record shows.

The exact time Thaddeus Broad came here or what induced him to come, does not appear on record. It is traditional that he worked in a grist and saw mill at Long Creek, Cape Elizabeth, owned by Samuel Skillings, the ninth child of whom and wife, Rebecca Sawyer of Cape Elizabeth, Thaddeus Broad married. (See vol. 11, p. 106, Maine Historical and Genealogical Recorder for Skillings.)

At Long Creek, a few rods in a northwesterly course, unprotected in a pasture once owned by the Skillingses, is a burying place where I counted about a hundred graves, twelve years since, twelve of which having memorial stones, the inscriptions of which I copied.(See vol. IV, p. 227 of above named publication.)

Two of which inscriptions are as follows:

Here lyes Buried
the Body of Lieut
SAMUEL SKILLING
Who departed this Life
Jany the 2. 1754 in ye
80th year of His Age.

In memory of
CAPT. SAMUEL SKILLIN
Obt March 12
1799
Æt 93.

(For Capt. Skillin see Portland Argus, August 19, 1889; and Vol. III, p. 281, Collections Maine Historical society. He was a son of the Lieutenant.)

The last of the above shortened his name by leaving off the final "g."

It was the ninth and youngest child of the last named that Thaddeus married, and the record of marriage and births is as follows:

TO BE CONTINUED.

THE DEERING NEWS.

Saturday, March 26, 1898.

GRANDPA'S SCRAP BOOK

[Under this head historical and genealogical memoranda will be furnished the readers of the News that appears worthy of preservation, particularly of remote periods to our history within the city limits and immediate vicinity.]

THE BROAD TAVERN.

AN OLD TIME FASHIONABLE RESORT, WITH A HISTORY.

(Continued from last week.)

Thaddeus Broad was born at Natick, Mass., as stated last week, Dec. 12, 1744, married Jan. 24, 1771, Lucy, ninth and youngest child of Samuel and Rebecca (Sawyer) Skillings of Long Creek, Cape Elizabeth. She was a niece of Deborah Skillings, whose husband was Daniel Bailey from whom the Baileys of the Windham road district of this city have descended through Dea. James Bailey, the first of the name to settle there. The memorial stones in the old cemetery at Stroudwater are inscribed as follows:

Sacred
to the memory
of
Mr. Thaddeus Broad,
died June 9, 1824,
Æt 79.

In memory of
Mrs. LUCY,
widow of
Thaddeus Broad
who died Jan. 9, 1837
Æt. 84.

At the time of the death of Thaddeus, there was published in Portland an organ of the Universalist church, called the Christian Intelligencer, and in the issue of Saturday, June 19, 1824, there appeared an obituary that read as follows:

In Westbrook, (the part that is now Deering,) on the 9th inst., Mr. Thaddeus Broad, aged 79 years and 6 months; one of the most virtuous, exemplary and worthy men of the town. Having a very extensive and respectable circle of acquaintances, Mr. Broad was not only esteemed and beloved, but, for the unimpeachableness of his deportment, he was venerated as one of the excellent of the earth. As a lover of his family, his neighbors, his country, his fellow mortals, and his God, his course of life was commendable. His character need no panegyric but to be generally known. He had for many years been a professor of the doctrine of Imperial Benevolence, and when oppressed with the infirmities of age, contemplated with christian calmness an exchange of worlds. When attacked by his illness, Mr. Broad apprehended his departure was at hand, and having finished his course by keeping the faith, he resigned himself into the hands of his God with joy unspeakable and ful of glory. He left an affectionate bereaved widow, eleven children, and a large circle of relatives and friends to lament his death. Thus "man goeth to his long home, and the mourners go about the streets."

Before me as I write is a copy of a lease of land and a dwelling house made from the well preserved original in possession of Miss Ruth E. Knight of Auburn, which commenced as follows:

This Indenture of Lease made this Eighth Day of November, Anno Domoni 1746, By and between Samuel Waldo of Boston * * * on the one part and Nathaniel Knight in the County of York and Province aforesaid, Gentleman, on the other part Witnesseth: etc. * * * from the Eighth day of November until the fifteenth day of March next ensuing the Date hereof, a certain dwelling House standing near Fore River in Falmouth, aforesaid, and commonly known by the name of Salt Box in which House Henry Young of sd. Falmouth, Weaver, lately dwelt."

The price stipulated as rental money was £4 and upon the back of the lease in Gen. Waldo's hand writing is an endorsement of the amount.

Nathaniel Knight was a nephew to Col. Thomas Westbrook and settled on the northeasterly corner of the eight hundred acre lot sold by the town in 1732 to Gen. Waldo. (See Smith and Dean's journal, p. 78.) Knight's purchase included Stroudwater Falls, located a mile southerly of Saccarappa, where he built a mill and dwelling which the Indians destroyed, hence his appearance in "Salt Box" house. But he returned and died on his purchase. The farm is now known as the Edward Chapman farm and is owned by the city of Westbrook excepting the falls. The d'scent of the Knight's name of this branch is as follows: Nathan (1) of Dunstan Landing, Scarboro, 1720, who married Col. Westbrook's sister, Nathaniel (2), Nathaniel (3), John (4) and Ruth E. Knight (5) of Auburn, born on the Chapman farm, Aug. 30, 1818. An official copy of the will of Nathaniel 3d is before me. He owned a slave woman for whose support till her death he made provision. The first Nathaniel's brother, named George, married June 6, 1771, Elizabeth (Betsey) Slemons, from whom the clan of Knights on the Buxton road, including Capt. Chas. A. Plummer of Woodfords, descended. (For a more extended notice of Knights, see p. 390, vol. 7, Collections Maine Historical Society, 1896.)

Nathan Goold, the compiler of "Portland in the Past," published in 1886, says on page 267, "The Salt-Box farm is the Reform School farm," but from what I have shown, and propose to show, it seems Mr. Goold is mistaken.

It is traditional that Mr. Broad soon after his marriage till his death ever lived in one place, namely, the place where the Broad tavern house stands today.

In the possession of Miss Almira A. Broad, granddaughter of Thaddeus, is a well perserved lease, dated May 18, 1772, between Isaac Winslow of Roxbury, Mass., and Thaddeus Broad of the said Isaac's farm "at a place called Stroudwater containing about one hundred acres of land, bounded easterly by Fore river and on all other sides by land belonging to the hiers of Col. Waldo of Falmouth, together with the house there on, called Salt Box, and barn nearly opposite said house, but not the other barn on said farm, for a term of three years, * * * to keep and repair the fences, and to deliver half the hay in the barn, one half the after feed sold, one half the corn, flax, roots, grain, potatoes, other things raised and pay half the tax."

Winslow was Gen. Waldo's son-in-law and what I have presented from original documents must be received as proof positive that the farm now known as the Broad farm was the "Salt Box" farm.

The "Salt Box" house, it is traditional, was made of logs and stood close to the line of the highway, a few steps southerly of the present dwelling—say about where the ice receptacle stood, many of us still remember, which was a stoned pit in the earth with a roof over it, the eaves of the roof of which were close to the ground and the whole shaded by evergreen trees.

It was some ten years later than the date of the lease when Thaddeus purchased the premises which were then called the "Tavern," and a little later erected the dwelling as now observed, where he furnished accommodations for the way-farer, indulged in farming and reared a large family.

As a farm home and as a surburban retreat for city denizens in ye olden time—the whole way from Portland being by nature of a high order—the resort was one unexcelled. Even now the view from the highway a few rods northerly, or better still from the opposite western field from the indicated highway standpoint, is most charming and will well repay for the trouble of a visit by those favoring landscape views.

TO BE CONTINUED.

GRANDPA'S SCRAP BOOK

[Under this head historical and genealogical memoranda will be furnished the readers of the News that appears worthy of preservation, particularly of remote periods in our history within the city limits and immediate vicinity.]

THE BROAD TAVERN.

AN OLD TIME FASHIONABLE RESORT, WITH A HISTORY.

(Continued from last week.)

The children of Thaddeus Broad were born and named as follows:

1—William, March 3, 1772, died at home Aug. 6, 1846 unmarried
2—Ephraim, March 23, 1774, died Sept. 4, 1856
3—Eunice, Dec. 28, 1775, died at home, Oct. 6, 1777
4—Thaddeus, Dec. 3 1777, died at home May 28, 1807 unmarried
5—Eunice, Dec. 26, 1779, died at home Sept 10, 1856, unmarried.
6—Joseph, March 11, 1782, died at home, Dec. 1, 1854, unmarried
7—Daniel, Dec. 30, 1783, died Sept. 30, 1846
8—Amos, Sept. 11, 1785, died June 5, 1864
9—Margaret, June 11, 1787, died March 25, 1849
10—Lucy, July 1, 1789, died at home, Dec. 6, 1863, unmarried
11—Thomas, Aug. 15, 1791, died at home Oct. 13, 1865
12—Silas, Apr. 8, 1795, died at home, March 12, 1873, unmarried
13—Almira, March 10, 1797, died at home Sept. 10 1867, unmarried

1—William, the above noticed, was the last Ensign of the Stroudwater Light Infantry company hence it was that the banner of the company was found at the Broad house. He lived at home and was a very large man, his weight being somewhere about 350 pounds. During his day it was a common saying among the boys of the neighborhood in speaking of any thing large to say it was as large as Billy Broad.

2—Ephraim. He married Elizabeth Greene of Cape Elizabeth. He died Sept. 1, 1856 aged 82 years, and Elizabeth, his wife, May 20, 1865, aged 78 years

He purchased land and built the fine appearing two story, now ancient, dwelling standing on the southerly side of the highway passing the front of Reform school farm, and is the next building westerly on the land adjoining the State farm, where the great oak stands in the road and the barn on the opposite side of the highway, all in excellent repair considering age of the buildings. It is said his wife lived with her parents opposite the spot where Ephraim built and her father's land became part of the homestead There were five children as follows:

1—Mary Ann, who became the wife of Charles Chesley and resided after marriage on the Chesley farm, located next northwesterly from the old Thaddeus Broad farm, where his son, Albert A. Chesley, now resides She died May 9, 1867, aged 59 years, and was his third wife, married Oct. 5, 1855.
2—George B., died at home, Feb. 22, 1856, aged 44 years, unm.
3—Ephraim, born Aug. 20, 1817, m. Mary Skillin, 1854, and resides a little westerly on the opposite side of the highway from the residence of his boyhood. He was a stone mason, but late years a farmer.
4—Edward B., died June 7, 1872, aged 52 years; m. and resided upon the homestead. After his death the widow removed to Boston where she died in consequence of her clothes taking fire.
5—William F., died at home, Sep. 3, 1859, aged 35 years. unm. The whole family have memorial stones standing in the old Stroudwater cemetery.

7—Daniel. He married Elizabeth Jewett, was a farmer and had children: Caleb, Henry and Elizabeth. He resided in Gorham.

8—Amos, married Abigail, daughter of Ezra Carter of Fryeburg, and resided in Brownfield, where he was a farmer, and they had thirteen children: Thaddeus, Amos, William, b. Jan. 23, d. Jan. 10, 1883; Abigail Sarah, Almira Ann, b. Nov. 18, 1820, resides in South Portland; Eliza, Lucy Ann, Mary, Ezra, Silas, Thomas, Augustus and Sophia Augusta, who were twins. The last married Henry Rich of Northumberland, N. H., and had Henry A. who resides opposite the old Broad place, and Nellie, who married John H. Johnson of Deering with whom Almira Ann resides. All of the thirteen have deceased excepting Almira Ann and Ezra, the last residing at Thornton, N. H. Mr. Johnson resides westerly of Cash's Corner, So. Portland.

9—Margaret. She married with Capt. John Jones, Jr., Jan. 13, 1811, who was born in the Bradley Corner district, Deering, then Falmouth, and went to reside in the McCobb house recently removed in Portland to make room for the erection of the Young Men's Christian Association building, corner High and Free streets, Portland. He died at Martha's Vineyard, Mass., she in Portland, March 25, 1849.

CHILDREN.

1—Lucy Caroline b. Feb. 10, 1813, died in Portland.
2—Mary, b. Oct. 31, 1814, resides in Philadelphia, Pa.
3—Thaddeus B., b. Nov. 12, 1816. While a clerk at Bangor, m. Sept. 3, 1843, Harriet J. Winslow of Westbrook, and died in that place within a year thereafter. She resides now, (1898) at Bradley's Corner with her daughter Theodora B., who m. Thomas C. Hudson of Nason's Corner district, Deering. (See Deering News of March 27, 1897.)

After the death of her husband Mrs. John Jones opened a boarding house at the southwesterly corner of Park and Congress streets, Portland, and aided by her daughters it became famous as a first class resort. The house itself has an interesting history. A little less than a hundred years ago it was occupied and owned by Capt. Thomas Browne, son of the first minister of the Stroudwater parish. Two or three years since when it was moved up Congress street, the Portland Press printed a lengthy account of the place and presented a cut of the house and surroundings.

Thomas married Sophia, eldest child of Robert and Elizabeth (Fickett) Waterhouse, all of Stroudwater. It was he who made the Falmouth Artillery banner acceptance speech in 1814, noticed in the News of recent date. He was a ship carpenter and resided in New York city till about the year 1850, when he returned and erected a small house on a part of the homestead located close to the Cape Elizabeth town line on the northerly side of the highway, where he departed this life. He was of a happy disposition and a ready talker. His widow went to the town of Harmony, where she died

12.—Silas. He was of a portly build and carriage and stately air and easy manners. In 1817 he was elected Lieutenant of a military company of the First Regiment of Infantry; where he served until 1821 when he was promoted to be captain, but soon declined to hold the position.

We might if we had space use many newspaper references of military gatherings, cattle shows and the like in closing our notice of this family, but can insert only one from Rev. Caleb Bradley's diary as follows:

"April 21, 1840. I worked some after dinner, then went to Stroudwater with the intention of going to Saccarappa, but did not go. Mrs. Bartlett died about 3 o'clock, a few minutes before I called. [Elizabeth, wife of Caleb Bartlett, aged 81 years. He died Aug. 13, 1820, aged 63 years. Their son Charles married Elizabeth Sparrow, a sister to William of Pleasant street, this city, and became (what was termed fifty years ago) wealthy by ship building at Stroudwater.] Went up to Mr. Broad's where I spent some time; was kindly treated, a good cup of coffee and all the trimmings necessary. Let it be remembered that I have been cordially received and kindly treated in this family of the Broads more than forty years. The old gentleman and lady always seemed glad to see me whenever I called, notwithstanding Mr. Broad and I never agreed in religion or politics, yet we moved on very well together. So it is now, I like to go there occasionally and I believe they like to have me. Silas and Almira seem to have the care, and they express a good feeling towards me when I call

THE DEERING NEWS.

Saturday, April 23, 1898.

GRANDPA'S SCRAP BOOK

[Under this head historical and genealogical memoranda will be furnished the readers of the News that appears worthy of preservation, particularly of remote periods in our history within the city limits and immediate vicinity.]

DR. JEREMIAH BARKER.

A MAN WHO HAD FIVE WIVES.

This is anniversary month of the Maine Genealogical Society with headquarters at Portland that was launched upon the great unknown future fourteen years ago with eight corporate members which now possess a well stocked library, a creditable fund as to size, with a membership of 270 a year ago which has been increased to over 300.

The present board of officers now in the tenth year of services deserve meritorious mention for the untiring interest manifested to make the enterprise a success. The Librarian Mr. Joseph P. Thompson has been untiring, not only in building up, classifying and cataloguing the library, but has added a card catalogue of all family histories, published in this country, together with those in preparation as far as known. Hon. Marquis F. King is president, under whose editorship the records of the early publishments, marriages and deaths of the Mss volumes of the town of Gorham, this state, have appeared from week to week in the *Portland Evening Express*, and now in book form under the auspices of the society for a copy of which I now tender hearty thanks to the compiler. The book contains an interesting account of Hon. Wm. Gorham born in Barnstable, Mass., July 12, 1742 and settled in Gorham about 1770 according to the Introductory notice. The compiler then states that he was appointed in 1782 Judge of Probate and in 1787 Judge of the Court of Common Pleas of this county; that his first wife was widow Temperance White of Cituate, Mass., who died April 1788, aged 43 years; and that he married the next year Temperance daughter of Richard Garrett of Barnstable, who survived him and became the second wife of Dr. Jeremiah Barker of Falmouth, whose first wife was Judge Gorham's sister Abigail.

Away back in the time of Col. Thomas Westbrook there stood a building upon the site of the now called old Dr. Hunt house at Stroudwater alluded to in 1744 in the old records as "a cottage inhabited by one Westbrook Knight." And the old Dr. Caleb Hunt house stands on Westbrook street to-day, westerly side thereof and is the fourth house southerly on that side from Mill Creek bridge, and strange as it may seem, the three lots southerly of Bond street are the same as originally staked out a century ago, the first at the south westerly corner of Bond and Westbrook streets being the spot where Col. Westbrook closed his eyes in death to an active life February 11, 1744.

And what makes the records of the bounds of the Barker-Hunt lot peculiarly interesting is the fact that an "oak tree", then the stump thereof, standing "back of the residence of Col. Thomas Westbrook", was used to mark the north-westerly corner of the lot, thus showing the location of the Colonel's abode at Stroudwater.

During the war of the Revolution the Westbrook Knight cottage was inhabited by the Ilsleys of Portland, the fact being alluded to twice in Smith and Dean's Journal, first on page 129, second, on page 253.

The first house after crossing the bridge on a southerly course, is the William Slemans dwelling, built in 1786, or thereabouts, then comes Bond street, then on the southwesterly corner stood the Garrison House where the large Fickett house now stands, built a hundred years ago by Samuel Fickett, then the Small house, constructed from William Waterhouse's boathouse, where he died in 1807, then the Westbrook Knight house, the occupants of which removed to Scarboro, northerly of Dunstan Landing, where he purchased land and departed this life. He was a brother to Nathaniel Knight, noticed in my Broad article, and married, March 23, 1735, Abigail Munson and had baptized children as follows:

1—Jonathan, Dec. 11, 1737.
2—Nathan, March 18, 1739.
3—Thomas, June 14, 1740.

In the year of 1780, Dr. Jeremiah Barker of Barnstable, Mass., made his first purchase of real estate in the town of Gorham. In 1799 he purchased the Westbrook "cottage" and lot and erected on the site the large two story dwelling as now seen just as it was built, with the exception of a rebuilt chimney in the southerly end in a smaller size, and the replacement of the front door within a couple of years by one of modern style.

Dr. Barker had five wives of which I find records, to the memory of three of whom there may be seen in the old Stroudwater cemetery inscribed small slate slabs as follows:

ABIGAIL BARKER,*
1st wife of
Doct. Jeremiah Barker,
died June 29, 1790,
Æt. 40.

*She was Abigail Gorham, sister to Judge Gorham.

An intention of marriage was then recorded as follows:

Oct. 23, 1790, Doct. Jeremiah Barker of Falmouth with Susanna Garrett of Gorham.

They were married Dec. 17 of that year.

Grave memorial record as follows:

SUSANNA BARKER,*
2nd wife of
Doct. Jeremiah Barker,
died June 3, 1794.
Æt. 25.

* She was sister to Judge Gorham's wife.

EUNICE BARKER,
3rd wife of
Doct. Jeremiah Barker,
died Nov. 10, 1799.
Æ. 29.

It is a Riggs family tradition that Dr. Barker selected a Riggs for one of his wives, and as Capt. John Jones married two of the daughters of Jeremiah Riggs residing at Bradley's Corner, and named a child Eunice who married Col. Jeremiah Bailey, tradition in this case probably is correct.

July 2, 1802, the marriage intention of Doctor Jeremiah Barker of Falmouth and Mary Williams of Gorham was publicly announced.

Nov. 17, 1808, according to the *Portland Argus* of that date Doctor Jeremiah Barker and Temperence Gorham were united in marriage (Judge Gorham's widow.)

This was his *fifth* marriage adventure.

June 25, 1815, for a consideration of $1000 Dr. Barker transferred the premises at Stroudwater to Dr. Jacob Hunt who had been located in the village some seven or eight years. The record reads, "Dr. Jeremiah Barker of Gorham," and is signed by him and wife Temperance Gorham. He made no land purchase after this date.

A Benjamin Johnson of Portland married Oct. 5, 1800 Mary G. Barker of Falmouth and paid Parson Bradley a fee of $10 and kept a shop where Andrew Hawes, Esq., now keeps at Stroudwater, and removed to Portland, is all I know of the Doctor's descendants.

The Barker house was in 1815 taxed to Dr. Hunt on a valuation of $600 and barn $20.

The Slemons house $700, barn $60 (taken down last year) and the grist mill $300.

The Fickett house $540.

[NOTE. The Broad matter closed in the News two weeks ago. The appearance of the words—"To be continued" was in consequence of an oversight. Then where it reads that Nathan Goold compiled "Portland in the Past" it should be *William Goold*.]

THE DEERING NEWS.

Saturday, April 30, 1898.

GRANDPA'S SCRAP BOOK

[Under this head historical and genealogical memoranda will be furnished the readers of the News that appears worthy of preservation, particularly of remote periods in our history within the city limits and immediate vicinity.]

GLIMPSES OF THE PAST.

REV. CALEB BRADLEY'S DIARY WITH ANNOTATIONS.

It was the practice of clergymen of a hundred and more years ago to keep a diary and note current events. When Rev. Caleb Bradley started to come down here to the District of Maine a century ago, he fell into the course adopted by his brethren, but his labors in this direction were not of a praiseworthy character. He made a note every day, but mostly in so general a manner as to render unfit for public use at this day what he wrote, from 1798 to 1809, when he discontinued the practice and did not resume it again till 1829.

Last January the News commenced the publication of items as I deemed of public utility. The diary covered during the period here noted, but the *annotations* were so absorbing that I departed from the text, but have now returned and propose to finish the undertaking, with the single further remark that had names of persons been used and events fully chronicled, the work would have been one of much value.

1805.

Sep. 5. Paid a visit to Isaac Stevens. Baptised a child of his. (He lived where the electric power house stands on Stevens Plains.)

Oct. 5. Attended the funeral of Joseph Pride who was killed on Wednesday (by the wheel of a cart). Dined and took tea at N. Winslow's. (They lived in the vicinity of Pride's Bridge and Corner.)

Oct. 8. Attended the funeral of Nathan Pride. Dined at Joseph Pride's. Took tea at Wm. Pride's. Two children. (Same as above.)

Oct. 16 1805. Mrs. Browne, widow of Rev. Thomas B., buried. Very rainy. Rev. Mr. Lancester (of Scarboro) here. Rev. D. Dean prayed at the funeral. (They lived in a house that stood between the residence of Geo. Rackleff and Dr. A. P. Topleff, Woodfords district. Memorial stones at Stroudwater.)

Jan. 16 1806. Visited Mrs. Brisco, where I married a couple.

(Ebeneza D. Woodford and Mary Frances. The Brisco house stood on Stevens Plains, just southerly of the main entrance to Evergreen cemetery. Woodford has been noticed in the News.

1806.

Feb. 13. Married two couple. George Bishop and Thomas Sawyer, Jr.

(The Bishop house stands at Morrill's Corner district. He has been noticed in the News, and family.)

The heavy rains this past week were just what was needed to give nature an impetus; the grass is beginning to be green, the flowers are blooming, and violets were seen this week. People are making their gardens in spite of the cold weather and everything is looking quite springlike.

May 1. Attended funeral of Dolly Lancaster. (Daughter of Rev. Thomas Lancaster of Scarboro. The Lancaster house stands just as it was built, inside and out, in 1763, by Rev. Thomas Pierce, near Scarboro depot, B. & M. railroad.)

May 5. Town meeting. Chose four representatives, Means, Waite, Ilsley and Hobbs. O, shame to Falmouth to be under the influence of such a base and corrupt spirit.

May 13. Attended the funeral of Susannah Sawyer, widow of Simon Sawyer's, aged 29 years. (East Deering.)

May 21. Went to the Duck Pond and dined with James Gowen. (The Gowen house stands about a mile easterly of Duck Pond on the old road to Morrill's Corner. The inside of the house is the same now as then. Gowen was a stirring man. Levi Gowen, a great grandson, now occupies the premises.)

May 26. Mr. Dalton came for a recantation.

May 27. Mr. Dalton paid me $100 for disappointing me. (Whether it is $1.00 or $100 I can't determine. He was grand father to Rev. Asa Dalton of Portland.)

June 2. Attended the funeral of Capt. Blake, aged 82 years. (He resided westerly end of Central avenue.)

June 16. The sun almost totally eclipsed—stars to be seen.

THE DEERING NEWS.

Saturday, May 7, 1898.

GRANDPA'S SCRAP BOOK

[Under this head historical and genealogical memoranda will be furnished the readers of the News that appears worthy of preservation, particularly of remote periods in our history within the city limits and in u. ediate vicinity.]

GLIMPSES OF THE PAST.

REV. CALEB BRADLEY'S DIARY WITH ANNOTATIONS.

(Continued from last week.)

☞Last week's Scrap Book contained numerous typographical errors, some of which require correction, viz:

The diaries covering the period from 1798 to 1809 will now be completed in weekly installments.

Rev. D. Dean should read Rev. S. Dean.

The item about the weather, under date Feb. 13, 1806, was astray from our Woodfords column, April 30, 1898

The Gowen house stands about a mile southerly (not easterly) of Duck Pond

June 16, 1806.—The sun almost totally eclipsed—stars to be seen.
(In the Eastern Argus of June 19, of that year, I find as follows:

"On Monday last, the predicted eclipse of the sun was visible in this town, it being an uncommonly clear day. The eclipse was not total; apparently about nine-tenths of the sun was covered. The darkness was such, a few minutes past 11 a. m., as to render a number of stars visible. The atmosphere which was previously warm and sultry was changed to a chilly, damp air."

(The writer then states that another eclipse of the same sort would occur April 14, 1809, and on September 17, 1811, another.)

June 20, 1806, attended the funeral of Capt. Isaac Lobdell. Took tea with the family.

Capt. Lobdell was at Stroudwater in 1793 or 94. In 1795 he purchased the house and lot where Mr. Augustus Tate lives on the easterly side of Westbrook street, Stroudwater, a little southerly of the head of High street, where he engaged in trade in a building that stood nearly adjacent the northerly side of the present dwelling that was removed just over the line of the town into Cape Elizabeth, on the way to the State Reform school, where half a story was taken off and then used as a dwelling, as now seen standing opposite the residence of Mr. Edward K. Chapman. The Lobdell house came into the possession of Mr. George Tate, father to Augustus, in 1825, who moved the shop part to where it now stands. Capt. Lobdell—called captain because he was engaged in navigatoin as well as trade—was a man of some means and his family was prominent in society. The house, more ancient than appearances indicate, was, in 1735, owned by Richard Forder, an Englishman. During the time of the Revolutionary war one widow Mary Billings kept it open as an inn, and was evidently a good customer of the bar herself, as an old account book kept after the war shows her favorite beverage to have been brandy. Here is a specimen:

1795, March 24, To 2 qts. Brandy, 5 shillings.
" April 7, To 2 qts. Brandy, 5 shillings.
" April 14, To 2 qts. Brandy, 5 shillings.
" April 22, To 2 qts. Brandy, 5 shillings.

June 21. Set 200 cabbage plants.

June 27. The meeting house was opened to that disturber of the public peace, Elias Smith.

Elias Smith was a native of Lynn, Conn., where he was born 1769. At the age of sixteen he united with the Baptist church, at 21 he began to preach. Then he withdrew from the Baptist and labored with the Freewill Baptists, but did not join them, objection being made to his heretical views. He organized here and there Christian bands, and there were a sect in Falmouth and other places called "Christians." He composed in 1805 a hymn book which was published. In 1808 he commenced at Essex, Mass., the publication of a denominational paper. In 1817 he became a Universalist, and for ten years preached Universalism, or Imperial Benevolence. He then renounced these views. He was father to Mathew Hale Smith, long a correspondent to the Boston Journal under the nom de plume "Burleigh."

July 5. Hay $30 per ton.

Sept. 8. Went to Gorham to the introduction of Mr. Nason to the academy.

Nov. 6. Set the front of my land out with elms.

His lot comprised forty acres, extending from what is now Congress street nearly back to Brighton street, and easterly on Congress street to the lot now owned by the estate of J. B. Brown, where Samuel Dalton lived, then James Jack, now the J. B. Brown lot. Westerly the lot ran to what is now Stevens Plains avenue, the three corner piece, covering the gully and allowing the lot to extend to the avenue, being an addition purchase for which $100 was paid. There are now 12 or 14 of the trees, about twenty inches through the butts, which show how much elms will grow in clay soil in a period of 90 years. The elms of State street, Portland, were set the same time. Somebody barked them and the selectmen offered a $20 reward.

Dec. 31, 1807. Preached a lecture at Henry Knights.

He resided on what is now Ocean street, Woodfords district, where the street grade was raised two years since which caused so much discussion in the city council then, and again last year, and finally $1000 was paid to the heirs of Erastus Knight as damages. There were two houses, one where the Dotons reside next easterly of the Erastus Knight house, the Doton house then being one story.

Henry Knight, Senior, was born between Lunt's and Allen's corners, April 5, 1732, married Mahitable Sawyer, and died Oct. 17, 1817, aged 85 years. They were the parents of eight and may be nine children as follows:

1. Mark, born Dec. 8, 1759, died Jan. 20, 1835.
2. Thomas, born June 12, 1759, married, 1st., Dorcas Cox, born March 27, 1764, died May 1788; he married 2nd., Joanna Storer, born June 3, 1766. They had two children:
   I. Thomas Knight, Jr., born June 23, 1784, married Elizabeth Pierce Feb. 13, 1806. She was the eldest child of Thomas Pierce who resided on Stevens Plains avenue near the Bradley meeting house, (the residence now stands) and granddaughter of Rev. Thomas Pierce, whose place of abode in Scarboro was noticed last week. Rev. Thomas Pierce's wife who was Joanna Haskell of Gloucester, Mass., had five children, his son Thomas' wife eleven, and Thomas Knight's wife had twelve—descendants now residing at Woodfords district of our city.
   II. Mark, born July 1786, died unmarried, Isle of Barbadoes, Aug. 1, 1809.
3. Eunice, married —— Pennell.
4. Elizabeth, born Dec. 31, 1765, died May, 1836.
5. Edward, born May 18, 1767, married Doratha Haskell, born May 9, 1768. They had eight children. Resided in Paris, this state. See history of that town, p. 654.
6. Mehitable, born Aug. 20, 1774, married Isaac Stevens. She died Sept. 13, 1815. He and his family have been noticed in the News.
7. Zebulon.
8. Henry, Jr., born March 14, 1781, died Dec. 20, 1820.

This memoranda is inserted here as a foundation of future work upon the Pierce and Knights families.

TO BE CONTINUED.

THE DEERING NEWS.

Saturday, May 14, 1898.

GRANDPA'S SCRAP BOOK

[Under this head historical and genealogical memoranda will be furnished the readers of the News that appears worthy of preservation, particularly of remote periods in our history within the city limits and immediate vicinity.]

GLIMPSES OF THE PAST.

REV. CALEB BRADLEY'S DIARY WITH ANNOTATIONS.

(Continued from last week.)

1808.

Jan. 1, attended the funeral of Jas. Babb, who died suddenly, aged 23 years.

(The Babbs resided at Saccarappa and vicinity.)

Jan. 17, Memorable day. Haymarket row of buildings burned today. Went to town, Portland, in the morning to assist in extinguishing the fire. Rode from Portland to Saccarappa in 50 minutes. Preached at Saccarappa, a. m. and at Stroudwater p. m. Rather a day of confusion.

(A full account of the fire is given in the Portland Argus of Jan. 21, of that year, which was reprinted in that paper March 27, 1890. The block stood on the southerly side of Middle street opposite where the Soldiers and Sailors monument stands in Monument Square. It was rebuilt and two of the stores now stand. Jonathan Sparrow of Stroudwater, was one of the owners. The loss was estimated at between $15000 and $20,000. The building had been built but two years. The Argus office was removed to Jones' Row, No. 10 Fish, now Exchange street, near Fore.

Jan. 20. Attended the funeral of Parker who was killed by Drew at Saccarappa.

Jan. 21. Took tea at Peter Knight's, where I married a couple, William Knight and Lucy Knight. Fee, $1.25.

(Peter Knight, son of Moses Knight, resided on Quaker Lane near where it joins the county road at Allen's Corner, on what was after known as the Rev. Henry A. Hart farm. Peter occupied the easterly half of the lot till near his death in 1817, when his son-in-law, William Knight, purchased it, who at his death willed it to Andrew Winslow who sold it to Rev. Mr. Hart.

Jan. 25. Married George Bailey and Betsey Webb. Fee, $2.00.

(He was son of Thomas Bailey and built the house where his son, Mr. Chas. E. Bailey now resides. His wife was a daughter of Col. Jas. Webb of Stroudwater, a Revolutionary soldier. The Bailey house stands opposite the school house between Libbys Corner and Bradley,s Corner, on Congress street.

Jan. 26. Married Rev. David McGregor of Bedford, N. H., to Rebecca Merrill of Falmouth, Me. Fee, $5.00.

(On the easterly side of the highway leading from Presumpscot Falls, in the town of Falmouth, to Yarmouth, a mile or thereabouts distant, is a neglected burying ground, and a little further to the eastward on the high ground on the opposite side of the public way, stands the large Congregational meeting house, seen by all the surrounding country on account of its elevated site, with a history a little longer than that of the Stroudwater parish, because organized a little sooner than that of Stroudwater, which was in 1764.

To the south of the burying ground and meeting house stood, till recently, the abode of James Merrill, from whom so many have decended. Upon the northerly bank of the waters of the Presumpscot, southwesterly of the first Merrill abode in what is now a pasture where cattle roam at will during feeding time, within sound of the dashing waters of the river, a spot little known and seldom visited, repose the remains of many now unnamed, with only a rude, ledge stone to mark the resting place. The pine has reared itself on the spot, and the unmerciful contractions of winter and expansive forces of summer have thrown down and broken the lettered memorials, but two stand, the inscriptions of which I here present, for safe keeping, to those who are in search of the names of the heroes of the war of the Revolution:

MAJOR JAMES MERRILL,
died, Nov. 16, 1806.
Æt. 78.

ABIGAIL MERRILL,
Wife of
MAJOR JAMES MERRILL,
died Nov. 7, 1806.
Æt. 82.

The first minister of the parish, Rev. John Wiswell, became a tory and after the decease of Rev. Ebenezer Williams, his successor, in 1799, Rev. David McGregor preached a few times and then to the writer disappears on records till united in marriage to Rebecca Merrill as indicated in the foregoing, a granddaughter, probably to the James Merrill, the progenitor of the Merrill race in that locality.

In the year 1809, for a consideration of $10,000, the Rev. Mr. McGregor of Bradford, N. H., clerk, purchased of Adams Merrill 160 acres of the James Merrill homestead located on the southeasterly side of the highway, above located, and in the year 1810, he purchased for a consideration of $316, of Robert A. Merrill and Sarah his wife, brother to Adams Merrill, 10 acres with a tanyard located thereon, formerly a part of Adams' farm. But he did not locate on his purchase at that time. For a period of 24 years he labored in Bradford, N. H., as a clergyman. Then he came to Falmouth and his residence stood southwesterly of the burying ground noticed in the foregoing as being adjacent the highway, but was burned a few years since. The long barn however stands and a new house has been erected, and both owned by Mr. Frank Marston.

In his dwelling Mr. McGregor opened a school, and strange as it may seem there are three persons residing at Stroudwater who attended—Capt. Wm. Leavitt who resided with Dr. Allen at Allen's Corner, this city, walking the distance every morning and night, and Mr. Daniel Dole and sister Catherine. Then the Parson built an academy building opposite his own residence which now stands in the grove a little easterly and occupied by a secret society.

Oct. 19, 1845, he departed this life leaving a will, and Ervin N. Tuksbury was appointed executor. Two years later Tuksbury sold the farm of 160 acres at public auction to Rebecca, widow to the Rev. Mr. McGregor, for $2,600, "reserving proprietors rights in the Academy." In 1852 she sold the place to Chas. A. and M. G. Foster, both of Falmouth, for $5,000.

The monument inscription tells something of the man and his wife, as follows:

(Northerly on street side.)

A FATHER
TO THE
FATHERLESS.
McGREGOR.
REV. DAVID McGREGOR
Born in Londonderry, N. H.,
March 21, 1771.
Pastor of the Presbyterian Church of Bradford N. H., 40 years.
Departed this Life
Oct. 19, 1845,
Aged 74 years
Servant of God, well done!
REBECCA,
Wife of Rev. David McGregor,
Born Dec. 14, 1788,
Departed this Life
July 21, 1852,
Aged 64 years.
Beloved in Life, Lamented in Death.

West side.

UNCLE.

East side.

AUNT
HANNAH G. FOSTER.
1799—1884.

James Merrill made his will April 6, 1753, and it was probated Oct. 3, 1753, and may be seen in the printed copy of Maine Wills, also on p. 182, vol. III of the Maine Historical and Genealogical Records; but the Recorder is wrong when it says, James Merrill, Senior, died 1770. It must have been prior to 1757, when the will was probated.

THE DEERING NEWS.

Saturday, May 21, 1898.

GRANDPA'S SCRAP BOOK

[Under this head historical and genealogical memoranda will be furnished the readers of the News that appears worthy of preservation, particularly of remote periods in our history within the city limits and immediate vicinity.]

GLIMPSES OF THE PAST

REV. CALEB BRADLEY'S DAIRY WITH ANNOTATIONS.

(Continued from last week.)

1808.

Feb. 4. Attended a wedding at Back Cove—Robert Knight.
Feb. 23. Attended the examination of scholars at Gorham Academy.
March 4. Attended the funeral of Thankful Berry.

Maj. George Berry, the Indian fighter, and son Obediah built the large house in which Mr. John J. Frye lives, located at Fall Brook, Ocean street, northerly side of the highway. The original Berry house stood on the opposite side of the way a little south westerly where the cellar hole may now be seen. Berry built vessels with his brother-in-law, John Snow, who lived at the foot of George street. Berry died Feb. 22, 1776; his wife, Aug. 31, 1782. Maj. Berry and wife had four children:

1—George, m. Sarah Stickney.
*2—Josiah, b. 1736.
3—Obediah, b. Oct. 14, 1738, m. Lucy Torrey.
4—Elizabeth, m. Jeremiah Pote, b. Jan. 18, 1724, whose parents resided where Dr. A. P. Topliff lives, Woodfords district. Pote was a trader in Portland, became a tory, and went to the Provinces where he resided.

*Josiah Berry m. Thankful Butler and died Feb. 12, 1815, aged 79 years. Thankful, his widow, died Nov. 28, 1821, aged 78 years. They resided a little easterly of the Maj. Berry farm, on Ocean street. In 1815 she was assessed on bank stock and 2,000 at interest. Memorial stones in the old George street cemetery.

Thankful Berry, at whose funeral Rev. Mr. Bradley attended, was, according to the Portland Argus of March 10, 1808, 36 years of age when she died and beyond doubt a daughter of Josiah Berry. He had other daughters but no sons. One daughter became the wife of Zachariah Brackett Stevens of Stevens Plains. Her name was Miriam P. Berry, b. June 1, 1778, m. Nov. 8, 1798. (See News of Nov. 17, 1894, also Feb. 2, 1895.)

Nancy, another daughter of Josiah Berry, m. Jan. 18, 1798, Joseph Beels, and they resided in a house now gone that stood on Ocean street, easterly of the Maj. Berry house, same side of the way. One of the Beels children was the mother of our esteemed citizen, Mr. Alfred R. Huston, postmaster at Woodfords. The Huston homestead stands in the north easterly angle made by the intersection of Reed with Ocean street, but has been sold out of the name.

Mrs. Beals died, according to the George street grave memorial, July 3, 1855, aged 85 years. (See Portland Argus of Sept. 29, 1888, for an interesting notice of "God's half acre" where the ashes of the departed were not allowed to rest in peace, also Oct. 17, same year.)

March 12. My birthday,
March 24. Attended the funeral of Capt. Miles who died at sea. Aged 33 years. Took tea with the widow.

Many still remember a two story brick house that stood at Capisic where the cellar hole may be seen as well as the barn, standing on the southerly side of Church street. In the year 1806, for a consideration of $370, Wm. Miles purchased the lot. It comprised one and ⅞ acres, and he probably built the house concerning which and the Mills family there is much that is difficult to find.

April 2, 1821, according to Parson Bradley's notes, "Mrs. Miles died, aged 78 years," thus showing her to have been born in 1743, and Capt. Miles in 1775.

In a bundle of old papers I find a memoranda bearing upon the life experiences and death of the widow, as follows:

1817 May. To paid Thomas Merrill, Jr. Predemption of Widow Miles house $21 00
To paid the direct taxes for 2 years on the above as per Collector's receipt 5 60
Paid Asa Knight for supplies 22 88
Nov. 1817 paid Thomas Seal for supplies 47 41
1819 paid Asa Knight for supplies 8 20
Apr. 1821 paid Asa Knight for attendance in sickness 8 43
Paid Sam'l Mason for supplies 52 00
May 18, 1821 paid funeral expenses 8 75
$174 27

George Libby, Esq., of Portland, now owns the lot and barn.

NOTE.—On December 4, last year, there appeared a notice of Dr. John Sloan's marrage in this department of the News. Eliminated of two errors, for the appearance of which I have been very sorry ever since, the notice was as follows:

Nov. 4, 1839, Went over to Dr. (Caleb) Hunt's (Stroudwater) about 3 o'clock and married John Sloan to Miss Caroline Hunt; good wedding; no company. Immediately after tea they left for Boston and so on as fast as steamboats and cars will carry them to New Albany, Indiana, where they expect to make the place their home, he being a regularly educated physician, and having already made a stand in that place and resided there about a year. They have my best wishes for their happiness and prosperity now, and may they be prepared for a better residence beyond the present scene of things.

How time passes. It seems but a few days since I married the parents of this couple, notwithstanding it is nearly thirty years since the event.

Mr. Sloan gave me as a fee $2, and Dr. Hunt $3 which I made a present to his wife; and the young Dr. Sloan, whom I married today, gave me a fee of $3. My marriage fees have been various. I have received $20, $10, $5, $2 and so down—one couple nothing.

In earlier parts of the Parson's Diary I find as follows:

Dr. Jacob Hunt of Falmouth and Miss Sally Rea of Windham, married June 26, 1809.

Adam Sloan and Eunice Milliken, married May 8, 1815.

[The Sloans resided on the Buxton road, two miles westerly of Stroudwater (now Westbrook) where Mr. Moses Chapman resides.]

Recently an esteemed friend has sent to this department a clipping received from a Western paper, she says, minus the name of the paper in which the notice appears as well as the date, which reads as follows:

DR. SLOAN DEAD.

"Dr. John Sloan, the oldest medical practitioner of the city, died early this morning at his home, East Sixth and Main streets, of the infirmities incident to advanced age.

Dr. Sloan was born in Maine eighty-three years ago. When a very young man, over sixty years ago, he settled in this city, and he had resided here continuously ever since. He possessed great skill in his profession, and soon had a very large and lucrative practice, his services as a surgeon, in which branch of the profession he was particularly skillful, being in demand for many miles around the city. Over thirty years ago he retired from practice, and since that time he had been occupied with the care of his large estate and his studies, to which he applied himself as assiduously as when a young man, until a few weeks ago. Brusque in manner, Dr. Sloan had a kind heart and his benefactions were many and were given without ostentation freely to persons in every walk in life. His wife, the bride of his young manhood, died several years ago, since which time he had lived alone in his handsome residence, occupied with his books and comforted by the frequent visits of his only child, Mrs. Anna Bicknell, wife of Commander George A. Bicknell, of the United States navy. The funeral will be from the family residence Friday morning and the burial will be private. The family requests that no floral offerings be sent."

174

CONTINUED:

Two weeks since there appeared a lengthy notice in this department of the News of the Doctor Barker and Hunt house where Dr. Sloan wooed and wed, reference being made at the time of one Johnson who married one of Dr. Barker's daughters, since which I have discovered the following:

Oct. 13, 1800, at Stroudwater Mr. Daniel Johnson, merchant, of this town (Portland) was married to Miss May Barker, eldest daughter of Doctor Jeremiah Barker.

"The Blooming Fair,
The pride of all the country round; in her
The charms of virtue, taste and elegance combine
To form the matchless maid, congenial
With her soul, the Swain she loves
Who feels her worth; and Hymen sanctifies
Their mutual vows."

TO BE CONTINUED.

GRANDPA'S SCRAP BOOK

[Under this head historical and genealogical memoranda will be furnished the readers of the News that appears worthy of preservation, particularly of remote periods in our history within the city limits and immediate vicinity.]

GLIMPSES OF THE PAST.

REV. CALEB BRADLEY'S DAIRY WITH ANNOTATIONS.

(Continued from last week.)

1808.

April 1. Very rainy and only 20 at meeting. Joseph Storer among them

He resided near the meeting house where the widow of the late Daniel Mason resides, and has been written up in the News. He was a member of the Congregationalist church, but on the list of members of 1833 is marked as "absent from town." He went west during the time of the Ohio land fever.

April 23. Visited Mr. Peaks and prayed with him.
May 2. Visited Mr. Titcomb and Mr. Peaks and prayed with them. Town Meeting. Four representatives chosen.
May 8. A very full meeting. Communion. Attended the funeral of Mrs. Titcomb. Took tea there.

Her maiden name was Rebecca Bailey, daughter of John Bailey, who resided on Spring street, Woodfords district, in the John Newman house opposite High street where she was born, a granddaughter to Dea. John Bailey who last resided in the house where the late Capt. Francis H. Bailey lived, between Libby's Corner and Bradley's Corner. She married first, Capt. Jesse Partridge of Saccarappa; second, Andrew Titcomb, a widower with four daughters, a son having died young, named as follows: Sally, Ann, Mary, Almira and William Capt. Partridge was a Revolutionary soldier born at Saccarappa and at Stroudwater engaged in trade. He built the house Andrew Hawes, Esq., occupies.

Andrew Titcomb's first wife was Mary Dole, daughter of Capt. Daniel Dole, a sea captain who come here from Old Newbury, Mass. and purchased the 218 acre farm in 1770 and built immediately the house as now seen, located opposite the Partridge-Titcomb-Quinby Hawes house.

Both houses though having met with some slight alterations are now fine specimens of what good buildings were in ye olden time both now owned by descendants of original occupants, and both good for another 100 years. Titcomb was born in Portland, Jan. 28, 1754, and resided with his first wife at Saccarappa. (For further notice of his family see Smith and Dean's Journal.)

In the old Stroudwater grave yard may be seen memorial stones inscribed as follows:

Here lies the Remains
of CAPT. JESSE PARTRIDGE,
who departed this Life
Dec. 21st, 1795,
Aged 53.

Here lies the Remains
of MRS MARY TITCOMB,
Wife of
MR. ANDREW TITCOMB,
departed this life
August 30th, 1796,
In the 37th Year
of her Age.

In memory of
REBECCA TITCOMB
2nd wife of
Andrew Titcomb
who died
May 5, 1808,
Aged 58 years.

Tho' the pale corpse is in the grave confin'd
She leaves a pattern for her sex behind;
The sun of virtue never can decay;
It shines in time, and gives eternal day."

Here lies the remains of
ANDREW TITCOMB
who died
Nov. 19, 1818,
Aged 65 years.

May 10.—Visited Mr. Peaks. Took tea at Capt. Mean's. (Stroudwater.)
May 13. Doctor Kinsman died.
(Who this "Doctor" was I am unable to learn. I do not meet with his name in any other connection.)
May 24—Supreme court sets today. Attended Drew and Quinby who were indicted for murder.
May 26.—Attended the trial of Drew. Poor fellow, was convicted of murder at 10 o'clock.
May 27.—Attended the trial of Levi Quinby, who was indicted for murder and was acquited.
May 28.—Attended court and heard the sentence of death pronounced by Judge Parsons.
May 30.—Visited Mr. Drew in prison.
May 31.—Attended a funeral at Peter Brackett's. A daughter, 21 years.
June 1.—Visited Mr. Peaks and prayed with him. Paid several visits at Back Cove with Dr. (Jacob) Hunt.

(It was shown in my article of last week that Dr. Hunt and Miss Sally Rea were married June 26, 1809, but where the name Caleb Hunt appears it should be Jacob Hunt. Of the Doctor's parents and early life I have at this writing no knowledge. The exact time he came to Stroudwater I cannot state. Before me is a private paper, well preserved, endorsed as follows:

"Dr. Jacob Hunt's lease of house he now lives in, Feb: 20, 1811 to 1812."

The inside reads:

This Indenture of Case made this twenty-first day of February, Anno Dom. one thousand eight hundred and eleven and between Charles Pierce of Falmouth within the County of Cumberland on the one part, and Jacob Hunt, Physician, of said Falmouth on the other part, Witnesseth, that the said Pierce doth grant, demise and let to him, the said Hunt, the whole of that house of mine lately purchased of Benjamin Rhemic standing in Stroudwater (so called) and the whole of said Barn which stands north westerly from said house, and a piece of land near said house for a Garden, to have and to hold the premises with all the privileges and appurtenances to him the said Hunt for and during the term of one year.

The rental was $45. The house was built by William Waterhouse, Jr., and was two story and stood on the westerly side of what is now called Westbrook street, between Congress street and the public watering place, the distance between the two points being about five rods. Waterhouse made the purchase of the deed in 1795 of the land. From Stroudwater he removed to Portland. He was a son of William Waterhouse who came here in 1764. The house was taken down about 1845. In the year of 1815, Dr. Hunt purchased the Dr. Jeremiah Barker house as noticed in the News of April 23, where he after lived and departed this life.

Dr. Hunt built up a large practice as a physician and was a successful farmer. Besides the daughter Caroline noticed last week, he left a son named Henry, now deceased, who succeeded his father in business.

In Pine Grove cemetery, adjoining Evergreen, may be seen an earth mound sepulchre some eight feet high, surrounded by stone posts connected by chains on the southerly side of which is a small square granite monument inscribed as follows:

Dr.
J. HUNT,
Born
London, N. H.,
Feb. 3, 1778,
Died
Aug. 16, 1846.

TO BE CONTINUED.

'ANDPA'S SCRAP BOOK

[Under this head historical and genealogical memoranda will be furnished the readers of the News that appears worthy of preservation, particularly of remote periods in our history within the city limits and immediate vicinity.]

GLIMPSES OF THE PAST.

V. CALEB BRADLEY'S DIARY WITH ANNOTATIONS.

[Continued from last week.]

1808.

June 4. Visited Zachariah Sawyer and wife who think of joining the church.

Zachariah Sawyer whose father was named Zachariah and was at Lunt's corner as early as 1756. His son, Zachariah, married June 17, 1799, Sarah Thompson, and settled on the Windham road, Morrell's Corner district, where his son, Hiram, recently deceased, resided. On the printed list of members of the church made in 1833, appears the name of Zachariah and under it "Mrs. Sawyer." For a record of his family see NEWS of Dec. 22, 1894.

June 7. Attended the funeral of Mr. Peaks.

July 5. Visited David Sawyer and prayed in the family.

July 5. The solemn and awful day has arrived when Drew must die. Attended his execution—walked with him from the prison to the gallows. A vast multitude of people attended.

This and previous notices of Quinby, Parker and Drew had reference to an affair at Saccarappa in which the three persons were participants. Quinby was a blacksmith and had a shop in that village and upon an execution that had been issued on account of small debt was arrested by Deputy Sheriff Parker of Cape Elizabeth, who unwittingly allowed him to go at large after the transaction. It reached Quinby's ears that he could not be re-arrested on the same warrant, but Parker thought differently and went there for the purpose. Quinby was a jolly good fellow and when Parker came a boon companion of Quinby's was present by the name of Drew who fastened the doors of the shop and warned Parker against entering, but Parker was determined, and when he put his head into the shop Drew struck him with a piece of an arm of a carriage, the hold-back iron entering the skull in such a manner as to cause death. Drew, who was a young man belonging over in York county, was convicted, erroneously it is claimed, of murder, when it should have been manslaughter, and hanged in Portland, the execution causing great excitement, people coming in from a radius of 75 to 100 miles to observe the event.

July 24. Attended the funeral of Dorcas Sawyer.

Sept. 27. Attended the Regimental review at Mt. Stevens.

(Capt. Isaac S. Stevens, Stevens Plains, which was a resort for such reviews many years, the parson being chaplain a long time.)

Oct. 9, Sunday.—This day nine years ago I was ordained to the ministry. Preached on the occasion.

Dec. 1—Married three couples

(Their names were respectively, Joseph Phagins and Mary Whitney; Samuel Weeks and Eleanor West; Isaac Cox and Martha Quinby. In 1823, Joseph Phagins lived opposite where Mr. Augustus Tate resides at Stroudwater, and claimed the lot where Shaw's hat shop stood, or the old building occupied by Shaw which was a very rude affair and the title was nothing more than that of a squatter which he sold for $50.)

Dec. 6.—Samuel Pride killed last night. Aged 43 years.

Dec. 8.—Dined at Joseph Pride's Attended the funeral of Samuel Pride and Mr. Jordan.

Dec. 16.—Had a lecture at Mr. George Berry's. Took tea at Mr. Isaac Stevens.

(George Berry, Jr. He was the son of Maj. Geo. Berry, the Indian scout and ship builder, who with his son Obediah built the house where Mr. John J. Frye resides on Ocean street, Fall Brook district. He married Sarah, daughter of David and Mary Stickney, March 6, 1752, and resided on Stevens Plains avenue, a little easterly of Morrill's Corner, in a house that stood where the late David Torry resided, which was destroyed by fire about the year 1835. His farm was a part of the original Berry farm, which he vacated about the time the prayer meeting was holden, and removed to Denmark, this state, where he died, April 3, 1816.)

CHILDREN.

1. William, b. July 30, 1753; m. Joanna Done of Long Creek, Cape Elizabeth, August 4, 1774. There were eleven children, and from this union the late Dr. Wm. B. Lapham, the genealogist and historical writer was a descendant; also Hon. Leonard Swett, the greatest criminal lawyer of the west, whose mother was Remember Berry, b. Dec. 22, 1794, tenth child of William, m. John Swett of Turner. [See Portland Argus April 13, 1891.]
2. Josiah, b. May 12, 1754, m. May 10, 1781, Elizabeth Blackstone, and settled at Lisbon Falls, where he died April 24, 1840. There were twelve children.
3. Jeremiah, went to sea and never returned.
4. George, m. Jane Bowie and settled in Bowdoin, this state. There were six children.
5. Sally, m. Benjamin Haskell of Windham.
6. Samuel, m. Dorcas Shattock of Portland. He went to Denmark, this state, where he died April 19, 1834. His wife, b. Oct. 13, 1777, died, March 21, 1841. There were six children.
7. Joanna, m. Samuel Proctor (My Proctor notes are loaned.)
8. Abigail, m. Benjamin Pride of Pride's Bridge and was an early settler in Waterford. Six children.
9. Miriam, d. July 6, 1801, aged 32 years.
10. Rebecca, m. Ebeneza Hilton Sawyer, who build the one story, low posted dwelling, easterly side of Stevens Plains avenue, in the turn of the way at Morrill's Corner. (The record of this family has been presented in the NEWS.)
11. Eunice, b. Sept. 24, 1761, m. Dec. 26, 1782, and removed to Harrison about the year 1815. He was born Aug. 15, 1759, in the Duck Pond region of Westbrook, and they produced a family of six children: Samuel, the eldest child born Oct. 8 1783, married Hannah Hicks of Deering, and settled at Little's Bridge, Westbrook, subsequently owned by "Zac Brackett," but about the year 1816 removed to Harrison. Charles, the third child, born here in Deering, Oct. 1, 1787, m. Sally Barbour. He was deacon up there of the F. B. church, and was known as the "sweet singer of Israel."

Dec. 21. Visited Mrs. Stevens and Mrs. Webb and prayed with them.

1809.

Jan. 7. Mrs. Webb buried.

This was the wife of Col. James Webb, of Stroudwater, and this entry as well as the reference to "Mr. Peaks" under date of June 7, will be considered in my next. The widow Peaks became the second wife of Col. Webb. The article will include notices of Henry Webb and Gen. John K. Smith, who married a sister to the Webbs.

Jan. 14. Mrs. Stevens buried. Exceedingly cold.

Jan. 17. Ordination at Gorham.

Feb. 27 of that year the last entry was made in the diary, and the work was not resumed till 1829—a period of twenty years.

THE END.

[er this head historical and genealogical and a will be furnished the readers of the hat appears worthy of preservation, partly of remote periods in our history within y Limits and i n ediate vicinity.]

COL. JAMES WEBB.

A SOLDIER OF THE WAR OF THE REVOLUTION WHO SETTLED AT STROUDWATER.

The names of the parents of Col. James Webb, as well as the spot where his eyes were first exposed to the light of day, are secrets of the past which careful research failed to disclose. Hon. F. M. Ray of Saccarappa village, Westbrook, who has bestowed a good deal of labor upon the Webb name is of the opinion that he was a son of one John Webb of Falmouth who had a son John, that settled, in the year 1781, on the northerly side of the Buxton road about three miles westerly of Stroudwater, the dividing line between Westbrook and Scarboro passing through the lot, upon which in a pasture under the shadow of a large maple tree may be seeen six graves marked by large s stone, around three of which is a wall eighteen inches high and the enclosure filled with earth to the top of the wall, but no clue is furnished by a single letter or figure engraved upon the rude stones, so conjecture only takes the place of facts as one gazes upon the secluded spot some little distance from the travelled way. Not far off I am told, is the cellar hole of the John Webb, Jr., house, but being without a guide I failed to find the spot when I visited the place a year since. Mr. Ray gives the public in the DEERING NEWS of Sept. 14, 1895, the benefit of his labors on this branch of the Webb name as he does in other articles in an interesting manner both before and after the date above presented.

It is apparent that Col. Webb had a brother Henry, who was a mariner, and a sister, Sally, who became the wife, March 2, 1785, at Falmouth, of Gen. John Kilby Smith, a Revolutionary soldier, born in Boston, Mass., both of whom commenced married life in Stroudwater. Col. Webb's life first became a matter of public record when he enlisted in the cause of American freedom, but of his experiences as a soldier little is now known. His obituary consisting of less than a half score of lines in a Portland newspaper. Only a very few now remember him in tottering old age plodding the streets leaning upon two canes—one in each hand.

Col. Webb was born 1753. Of his demise the Portland Advertiser remarked, Sept. 6, 1825:

DIED. Col. James Webb of Falmouth, aged 72 years. He served through the whole of the Revolutionary war and as an ensign bore the standard at Manmouth, N. Y., in one of the most severe battles in the Revolutionary war.

He married, Falmouth, Nov. 7, 1782, Nancy Cony, said to have been the daughter of an English surgeon.

April 10, 1786, Col. Webb of Falmouth, trader, purchased a house lot located on the "southerly side of Mill Creek," Stroudwater, on the easterly side of the road that goes to the State Reform school farm, for which he paid £18 and thereon erected a dwelling house that was two story in front and one story back, two rooms wide. It stood back from the street some thirty feet. By the side of the walk to the front door the Colonel constructed lattice work of strips of wood the size of laths, some 2½ feet high with caps and base and 9 posts at ends, upon the sides of which he planted the forest evergreen tree and in front the elms now seen, so the premises compared very favorably with the then prosperous village. Where his shop was located I cannot determine. It is very doubtful if he had one; merely speculated in lumber, etc. He had a running account with Col. James Means commencing in 1793 when his name was entered with the prefix of "Captain," two years later as "Major," and 1799 when the book was full and closed as "Colonel." Oct. 17, 1792, he is charged three shillings wharfage on three tons of hay, and July 9, 1794, four pence wharfage on a hogshead of molasses, and July 10, 1795, wharfage and surveying on boards, £2-0-5.

When the embargo and then the war of 1812-15 came he suffered with the rest. A half of his house and a half of the front yard was set off for debt, and March 2, 1814, he gave Zebulon Trickey a mortgage deed of the rest for $150 which was never paid.

March 27, 1838, Trickey conveyed the place to William Bartlett. In a part of the house there was living at the time Peleg Mitchell, father to the wife of the late Chas. Maxfield of Stroudwater. Then Mary (Peaks) Webb, widow and second wife of James Webb sued for an allowance and recovered a life lease of a third of the place, and on the 8th of December of 1838, Bartlett sold the premises to Enoch Skillin of Cape Elizabeth, and in turn, March 12, 1841, Enoch to Nathan Skillin of that town, a ship carpenter, who moved onto the premises, but did not remain many years.

Enoch to Nathan Skillin of that town, a ship carpenter, who moved onto the premises, but did not remain many years.

March 2, 1867, the house having become untenantable and vacant from neglect, was sold to Mr. Andrew J. Parker, a young man and native of the place, for $260, paid by him to Nathan Skillin, then residing at the foot of Pleasant Hill. Cape Elizabeth, on the road from there to the B. and M. R. R. crossing, and Mr. Parker erected the neat appearing story-and-a-half house as now observed on the second lot from the southeasterly corner of Bond street, easterly side of Westbrook street, and now owned by Mr. Humphrey Hunscome, whose only child, a son and wife resides with him. On the right side of the front door as the house is approached, is a sign with gilt letters as follows:

A. LEROY HUNSCOME,
JUSTICE OF THE PEACE.

Capt. Webb's first wife died as indicated by Parson Bradley's diary, Jan. 5, 1809, and he married, second, Nov. 19, same year, Mary (Thomes) Peaks with two children, her husband having departed this life according to the diary noticed above, June 7, 1808. With reference to him records are reticent. The names of her parents and place of birth are also secrets of the past that careful research fail to disclose.

A sister of Mrs. Thomes (Peaks) Webb, by the name of Nancy, married Zenas Pratt, who lived after the event on the State Reform school farm, and was drowned in Portland in 1818, and Capt. Samuel Thomes married Phebe Fickett, who died at Stroudwater, Aug. 23, 1830, aged 42 years, leaving eight children, and Capt. Issac Thomes, who married in Scarboro, Aug. 20, 1801, Eleanor Tyler, and resided in Biddeford, Mrs. Chas. E. Somerby, residing at 149 Park street, Portland, being a granddaughter, whose father was Capt. Wm. Thomes, lost at sea.

Mrs. Mary (Thomes) Webb was a stout, round faced woman, and in youth must have been considered handsome—a woman of an exceedingly kind heart, who in her last days acted the part of the Good Samaritan in the neighborhood.

The following is from a copy of the Portland Argus of July 21, 1818:

DROWNED, In this harber, about 12 days since, Mr. Zenas Pratt of Westbrook, (should be Cape Elizabeth) aged 52 years. His body was found on Tuesday last. The decision of the jury in inquest was accidental death.

He went to Portland with a scow load of wood and while away in the evening the boat was moved and not being aware of the fact walked into the water on his return. He built the old two story brick house standing on the front of the Reform school farm, now out of the use.

Extract from Rev. Caleb Bradley's diary:

June 24, 1841. At 3 o'clock I attended the funeral of Mrs. Webb, the widow of Col. James Webb, aged 72 years, who died very suddenly while returning rom Portland with Mr. Chas. Bartlett in a wagon.

THE DEERING NEWS.

Saturday, June 18, 1898.

GRANDPA'S SCRAP BOOK

[Under this head historical and genealogical memoranda will be furnished the readers of the News that appears worthy of preservation, particularly of remote periods in our history within the city limits and immediate vicinity.]

COL. JAMES WEBB.

A SOLDIER OF THE WAR OF THE REVOLUTION WHO SETTLED AT STROUDWATER.

[Continued from last week.]

☞ The article of last week contained several errors.

In the word "consisting" that appears after the word obituary "ing" should be stricken out.

The letter Y after the name of Monmouth should be J.

Where it reads "9 posts," should be "a post."

The repetition consisting of three and a half lines near the bottom of the first column, commencing thus: "Enoch to Nathan Skillin" should be stricken out.

A. Leroy Hunscome should be A. Leon Hunscome.

Next under the foregoing where it reads "Capt." should be "Col." Webb.

COL. WEBB'S DESCENDANTS.

In the absence of the record of names and dates of births of a family that existed a century ago it is difficult putting together correctly the names of fragment members thereof. In this case this assertion is specially true.

On page 24 of a MSS. volume presented to the Maine Historical society by Mr. Z. K. Harmon, the deceased pension agent, Portland, is a statement that Col. Webb had two children and in the "Memorials of the Massachusetts society of the Cincinnati," is another error of a similar nature.

His first wife had six if not seven children, his last none by him, but two, as has been stated, by a former husband, as follows:

1. Thomas. It is a family tradition that he went to the state of Louisiana while young where some one took a fancy to him and he became a physician, but never returned to his native place.

2. Betsey alias Elizabeth, born March 4, 1785, married Jan. 24, 1805, George Bailey born March 31, 1783, son of Benjamin Bailey born 1746, died Sept. 26, 1812, whose wife was Mary Blake of Lunt's Corner, East Deering district, died Aug. 24, 1817, aged 62 yrs. 4m., having had 14 children, George, here noticed, being the fifth in number.

Vol. 30 p. 351. York Deeds, A. D. 1755. Jane Bailey, wife of (Deacon) John Bailey of Falmouth, late Jane Curtis, widow of John Curtis, late of Narragansett No. 7 (Gorham) deceased, and adm'x on his estate.

After eight children had been born to the Deacon, his wife died, and on Sept. 27, 1741, the intention of marriage between him and the Widow Curtis who had minor children was made public and then the "intention" was duly consummated, and she bore the Deacon one child whom they named Benjamin. The family lived in what is now known as the Miss Helen M. Bailey house, because she occupies it at the present time, located on the northerly side of Congress street, between Libby's and Bradley's Corner, which was then but one story. Helen's father was Col. Jeremiah Bailey, brother to George Bailey here noticed. Jeremiah married, January 14, 1818, Eunice, daughter of John Jones, Esq., who resided on the Riggs farm at Bradley's Corner.

March 8, 1805, George Bailey purchased an acre of land of his father where he had prior to his marriage built a house which I presume is the one that was reconstructed in outside finish some years since and stands an ornament to the locality directly opposite the schoolhouse, partly under the shade of the immense elm tree at the soutesnterly corner thereof. He was a wheelwright by trade. In 1834 he is represented on a public record as a sleigh maker. His shop stood at the westerly end of his dwelling. When the infatuating new form of treatment for bodily disease called "Thomsonian" came round he became a convert, and dedicated his house to the new belief and practice and hung out a large sign inscribed—

THOMSONIAN INFIRMARY.

Parson Bradley in his diary alludes to the new method of cure, states that he had been to a lecture, "but," says Mr. Bailey, "is not meeting with very good success." The notice reads as follows:

"April 14, 1841. This p. m. was buried George Bailey aged 58 years, asmatical consumption. He was a Tompsonian doctor, but not very successful. Mr. Brown the minister of Temple street (Portland) officiated. Six inches of snow today. Many have been to the city in sleighs."

In the reception room of the George Bailey mansion hangs an oil portrait of the original builder, a yard square, and one of his wife, Betsey Webb, painted, it is said, by Cloutman, when George Albert Bailey, their son, was six months old and he was born in 1820.

George Bailey died April 11, 1841; she Jan. 18, 1853. Memorial stones may be seen in Evergreen cemetery.

THEIR CHILDREN.

I. Walter Webb Bailey, born Nov. 12, 1803, married at Stroudwater, Dec. 27, 1835, Miriam Lincoln Hobert, daughter of Miles Hobert who lived on Westbrook street opposite the head of Waldo street where the post office is kept. She died Sept. 5, 1840, aged 29 years, 8 mo. 5 days; he, May 10, 1842, and was buried with military ceremony, leaving one child, Nancy Cony Winslow Bailey, born Oct. 11, 1837, married Oct. 27, 1859, Hiram Augustus Dow, and died Feb. 3, the following year.

II. Elizabeth Ann, born Jan. 12, 1812, lived and died under the parental roof, unmarried, Jan. 27, 1890.

III. John, born Nov. 7, 1813, married Sept. 25, 1838, Abby Nichols White of Freeport. He was clerk of the House of Representatives and connected with governmental matters at Washington, D. C., for a period of forty years, and died there March 11, 1897. Had three daughters:

Harriet White Bailey born at Freeport, July 14, 1839. She is the wife of Ex-Governor Seldon Connor, residing at Augusta, this state, otherwise known as Gen. Connor, who lost his leg in the war of the Rebellion.

Annah Elizabeth Nichols Bailey, born in Portland, Oct. 23, 1845. She is the wife of Dr. I. Alja Adams of Pittsfield, Mass.

Florence Cutler Bailey, born in Portland, Jan. 23, 1852. She is the wife of Rev. T. J. Kelley, a Presbyterian, officiating at Washington, D. C.

IV. Alpheus, born April 8, 1816, married Elizabeth B., daughter of Nathaniel Stevens who lived at Stroudwater at the time in a house now gone that stood next southerly of the Dr. Jacob Hunt's house. This Stevens was a son of Capt. Isaac S. Stevens of Stevens Plains. Alpheus Bailey was a wheelwright and worked with his father. He died under the parental roof, Aug. 11, 1853. His widow, who, after the death of her husband resided in Providence, R. I., and died Jan. 11, 1894, while visiting her sister, widow of Henry S. Jackson, of Cape Elizabeth, northerly part of the town. For a detailed notice of this Stevens family see Deering News of March 23, 1895.

V. George Albert, born Feb. 2, 1820. He was self-educated, could speak three languages with ease, a poet, a prose writer, and newspaper editor at Washington, D. C., for a period of twenty years, but died, unmarried, under the parental roof, Dec. 26, 1877. All like him deserve frequent public testimonials of appreciation by his townsmen that a course of self-schooling and persistency in a right and laudable purpose may be chosen by the young, so I propose to make my next article up of some of the pen productions of his young manhood.

VI. Charles Edward, born April 15, 1822, married Ann S. Noyes of Pownal Nov. 26, 1879, and resides upon the homestead.

Walter W. and Alpheus continued the mechanical calling of their father, so Charles E. joined with his brothers. Then after their demise small fruit growing and the art of horticulture became with him an enrapturing pursuit—not for profit so much as for pastime, the surroundings of his home representing at times a carpet of the gorgeous hues of nature, thus showing the many directions of inquiring thought in the original thinker.

TO BE CONTINUED.

GRANDPA'S SCRAP BOOK

[Under this head historical and genealogical memoranda will be furnished the readers of the News that appears worthy of preservation, particularly of remote periods in our history within the city limits and immediate vicinity.]

COL. JAMES WEBB.

A SOLDIER OF THE WAR OF THE REVOLUTION WHO SETTLED AT STROUDWATER.

The first poem of George Albert Bailey, a grandson of Col. Webb. appeared in print July 4, 1840, when Mr. Bailey was 20 years and 5 months old, as follow:

LINES.

From the Port Folio of an Invalid.

Original.

Darkness and light! No more
  Thy dusky fold or brilliant beam doth bring
To my sick heart relief.—Dark sorrow's wing
  Shadows me o'er.
                     C. P. I.

Oh, for those days of joy!
When in health and careless glee I roved,
Where soft winds sigh'd and wild flowers bloom'd,
  A free and robust boy;
Or listless laid me down to sleep,
Far in the green-wood shadows deep—
  Oh, for those days of joy!

Oh, for that joyous time,
When I could range the ocean's shore
And scan the varied beauties o'er,
  And list the waves low chime.—
See the proud flag and tapering mast
Of great ships dashing onward fast—
  Oh, for the joyous time!

For those old sports I sigh!—
The rod, the line, the gliding river,
The dog, the gun the bow and quiver,
  Seen now by mem'ry's eye,
'Mind me of joy, of youthful health—
Heaven's greatest boom, life's greatest wealth,
  And make me thus to sigh.

Such, such for me no more—
A wasted form, slow step and weak,
And fled the health-tinge from my cheek—
  The tinge that erst it wore;
A labored voice, faint, weak and low,
A feeble pulse with actions slow—
  No health for me! no more!
                     G. A.

Westbrook.

In the *Portland Tribune* of May, 1840, there appeared a poem by Mr. Bailey entitled—

IT IS NOT ALWAYS MAY.
                     Longfellow.

In December of 1845, Mr. D. C. Colesworthy, the prolific poetry and prose writer, then of Portland, in a lengthy article that appeared in the Baltimore Saturday Visitor, entitled "The Children of Portland," noticed Mr. Bailey as follows: Mr. George A. Bailey is a young man, and has written but comparatively little. If his whole attention should not be given to mercantile pursuits, he will be distinguished from a poem written on reading Longfellow's, "Not Always May,", we select what follows:

"By day one dense and watery cloud
  Shuts out the sun's glad light,
And chilling winds are mourning loud,
  Through all the night;

"From sun, nor moon, nor from a star,
  Comes one elevating ray—
Yet this sweet thought my heart shall cheer,
  "It is not always May."

Mr. Bailey is not over five and twenty years of age, and is doing business in Boston.

Mr. Bailey on leaving the parental roof went to Salem, Mass., where he remained in a dry goods store four years it seems. While there he wrote articles repeatedly, both of prose and poetry for various newspapers and periodicals.

From Salem he went to Boston, engaging in the same line of business; then he came to Portland and entered the book store of Joseph G. Bailey.

The following lines were evidently written upon leaving home for Salem:

TO A COUSIN.

I.

I must leave thee, sweet cousin, fain, fain
  would I stay,
But stern duty calls loudly, and bids me
  away;
Yes! I go—but ah! never in life to forget
The sunshine of gladness that has beamed
  where we've met.
What'er my lot is, or task, where'er I may
  me,
I shall be thinking, dearest cousin, on thee!

II.

Where the glade is besprat with its own
  fairest flowers,
Like a queen in her jewels, reclined in her
  bowers,
And the eye is entranced with the beauties
  it greets;
When the warm breath of summer comes
  laden with sweets,
And the song of the wood bird is heard
  from the tree,
I will high me again, dearest cousin, to thee!

III.

Then farewell my sweet cousin! fain, fain
  would I stay,
But stern duty calls loudly, and I must away;
Yes! I go—but oh! never in life to forget
The sunshine of gladness that has beamed
  where we've met.
What'er my lot is, or task, where'er I may be,
I shall, shall be thinking, dearest cousin, on
  thee!
                     B.
Westbrook.

Before me as I write are fifty-two samples of his poems and as many more prose articles nearly all of which contain more or less lines of poetry, original or selected, and in the book of Maine Poets may be found two of his productions. But it is a curious fact that in the "Bibliography of Maine" by Joseph Williamson of Belfast, Me., two volumes, containing nearly 700 pages of references, his name does not appear.

THE DEERING NEWS.

Saturday, July 2, 1898.

GRANDPA'S SCRAP BOOK

[Under this head historical and genealogical memoranda will be furnished the readers of the News that appears worthy of preservation, particularly of remote periods in our history within the city limits and immediate vicinity.]

COL JAMES WEBB.

A SOLDIER OF THE WAR OF THE REVOLUTION WHO SETTLED AT STROUDWATER.

[Continued from last week.]

As a prose writer Mr. Bailey was witty; he was sedate; he was a critic; he was just and he was to all appearances a despiser of shams.

To show that compositors made mistakes in his day, I will quote the first paragraph of a letter dated Westbrook, (now Deering) August, 1849—49 years ago—as follows:

As I have not written to you for a long time, it is quite too late to blow you up for causing me to say, in more than one instance in my last letter exactly the reverse of what I wrote. I am aware it is easier to make than to avoid errors in sticking type, and, perhaps, as far as my communications are concerned, it is of but little importance to your readers, how the matter is presented, but then I have a sneaking sort of a wish, etc. However, upon the whole, I have not much cause to complain, as the worst I have ever experienced at your hands, falls far short of what—in point of provoking ludicrousness—once occurred to a poem sent by a friend of mine to one of our best magazines. He had acted on Hood's advice in copying his effusion,—entitled, "The Last Brown Leaf;" when, therefore, it appeared in the beautiful print of—rechristened, "The Lost Brown Loaf." Poor fellow! It proved a crust that choked him badly,—for a week he did little else but wink and swallow. He has since got used to such things; and, moreover, the angularity of his vanity has become somewhat modified.

The communication appeared in the Boston Weekly Museum.

It seems Mr. Bailey edited in 1850 a paper published in Portland called the Literary Advertiser.

A newspaper clipping before me without date and name of paper, reads as follows:

ANOTHER HEAD RESTORED.

It will be gratifying to the humorous friends of Mr. John Bailey, to learn that he has received a lucrative appointment from Judge Young, the new clerk of the House of Representatives of the United States. Mr. Bailey is well known here as a Democrat—and for 4 years one of the clerks in the Portland post office, from which position he was removed for political reasons upon the coming in of the present postmaster. Mr. Bailey left for Washington on Wednesday last, carrying with him the good wishes and congratulations of many friends.

Another item reads as follows:

In Thompson, Conn., on the 27th inst., (August, 1848) by the Rev. Charles Willet, Mr. Alpheus Bailey and Miss Elizabeth B. Stevens, both of Westbrook.

The names of John and Alpheus Bailey appeared in last week's News.

In Evergreen cemetery stands a white marble slab at the foot end of a row bearing names of father, mother, sister and brothers, inscribed as follows:

GEORGE A. BAILEY
BORN
Feb. 2, 1820,
DIED
Dec. 26, 1877.

From a newspaper clipping, without date, I will make in closing an extract, or two, as follows:

He was for several years in the bookstore of J. S. Bailey under the old Exchange (post office lot.) His fine taste and unusual literary ability and discrimination made him a great favorite, and his genial manners and kindness of heart won him a warm place in the esteem of those whom his intelligence attracted. After a time he left this city for Washington where he entered the office of the Congressional Globe.

In the course of time Mr. Bailey became one of the owners and at the end of twenty years left the office with a respectable fortune as to size. The notice closes as follows:

With a literary taste and ability which had he allowed them scope, would have given him a good place among the honored names of the State, he permitted his talent to rest in obscurity, so that only a few of his old friends, who were blessed with exceptionally good memories, remember the really charming verse which he wrote, and which he was always capable of writing. His life was an upright and stainless one, and his memory will long be sacred.

TO BE CONTINUED.

THE DEERING NEWS.

Saturday, July 9, 1898.

GRANDPA'S SCRAP BOOK

[Under this head historical and genealogical memoranda will be furnished the readers of the News that appears worthy of preservation, particularly of remote periods in our history within the city limits and immediate vicinity.]

COL JAMES WEBB.

A SOLDIER OF THE WAR OF THE REVOLUTION WHO SETTLED AT STROUDWATER.

[Continued from last week.]

The third child of Col. Webb was named Sophia, born 1789; intention of marriage with Albert Winslow, "both of Westbrook," made public, August 29, 1808. He taught in town schools and had a private school in Portland, then he became a money broker, residing at the northwesterly corner of Cumberland and Elm streets.

In the northeasterly corner of Eastern cemetery, Portland, is a tomb on top of which is a small white marble monument inscribed on the northerly face as follows:

ALBERT WINSLOW,
DIED
April 3, 1863,
Æt. 78.

Upon the easterly face appears the name of Col. Webb's third child as follows:

SOPHIA, wife of
Albert Winslow,
died Feb. 27, 1861,
Æt. 72 years, 11 mo.

Mr. Winslow and wife had but two children;

I Nancy Carrie Winslow, killed at Stroudwater, Dec. 28, 1835, aged 26 years, 1 mo.

II William H., born Aug. 29, 1811, marrianth Cobb of Brooklyn, N. Y. He was a book-keeper there where he died Oct. 21, 1840. His remains were brought to Portland and being a member of a military company (Portland Rifle Corps, it is thought) was buried with military honors. His widow removed to Indianapolis, Ind., where she reunited in marriage with one Dr. Livingston Dunlap.

Connected with the death of Miss Winslow there was a marriage festival holden at the residence of Miles Hobert, a farmer, residing with a very respectable family on the westerly side of what is now Westbrook street, opposite the head of Waldo street, Stroudwater district, in the building where the post office sign is now displayed. He was a short, stout built man, with a large neck and a shirt binding much larger, who was not particular whether he called a grandchild a niece, or something else, but a very accommodating neighbor who removed fifty years ago to Hingham, Mass. Walter Webb Bailey, noticed June 18, '98, married Miss Miriam Lincoln Hobert, his daughter as has been stated, and it was at the close of the festival connected with the event when the participants were on their way to their respective homes that Miss Winslow lost her life.

Dec. 28, 1835, Rev. Caleb Bradley notices the affair as follows:

One of the most distressing of accidents occurred last evening. On returning from a wedding at Stroudwater village, the wedding of Walter (W.) Bailey, seven persons seated in a double sleigh, three males and four females drawn by a pair of high spirited horses ran down the hill, the sleigh slewing turned all the occupants out and all were considerably hurt—one young lady, Nancy (C.) Winslow, had her skull bone fractured and died this morning, leaving a father, mother and brother to lament her untimely end. "Put not off till tomorrow for thou knowest not what a day will bring forth. God's ways are not our ways."

CONTINUED:

deep affliction to her parents, and a most impressive lesson to youth and old age of the uncertainty of human life.)

Col. Webb's fourth child was named James (if the list I have made is correct) and he was a mariner, the time and place of whose death is unknown.

Fifth. Amelia, born 1793, married Feb. 3, 1823, Samuel Johnson, a book seller, doing business at No. 3, Merchants Row, Portland, (where the Falmouth hotel is located.) He died May 3, 1825, aged 38 years, 9 months; she died July 11, 1859, aged 64 years, making her home after the death of Mr. Johnson with her sister Winslow, having had one child, Samuel Johnson, born Nov. 27, 1823, who has been a book keeper till recently, now residing opposite the Union station, Portland, on St. John street, No. 269, with his family, to whom I am indebted for several items of information as well as the following reply to a note addressed to him:

My grandmother's maiden name was Hepsbath Norton, and was born at Ipswich, Mass., about the year of 1750, died 1848, aged 94 years; my grandfather, James Johnson, a few years before; who had been residents of Fitzmillianic, N. H., for several years. I never saw but one of the family as they married out South. My father married when he was 36 years of age and died two years later. I have the above from my uncle, who resided at New Orleans, who was a brother to my father. He sent me a list of names of relatives 50 years ago which I lost, and could not obtain a duplicate because my uncle was dead. The Johnson name is a common one hereabouts, but I know of no one bearing the name to whom I am related.

Mr. Johnson was a member of an orchestra in Portland for a period of over fifty years, playing the flute to perfection, and possessed a scrapbook containing more than 200 printed programs of entertainments where he played a part.

All the Johnsons' names may be seen on the Winslow monument with dates.

Sixth—Pauline, twin to Mrs. Johnson, married July 25, 1820, Stephen Huckins of Effingham, N. H.; Amelia, a daughter, died there April 19, 1830; a son resides in New Hampshire; a daughter, who is a widow, resides in Dorchester, Mass.; James Huckins, another son, was the originator of Huckins' Soup, by the manufacture of which in Boston, it is claimed, he became wealthy.

A few years ago I was informed by Mr. Chas. E. Bailey that he had an aunt who married a man by the name of Sennet, and upon Parson Bradley's list of marriages, under date of Oct. 11, 1801, I find the names of Nicholas Sennet and Suckey Webb. This would place her name at the head rather than at the foot of the Colonel's children.

My next article will be made of memoranda relating to Gen. John K. Smith, whose wife was a sister to Col. Webb.

A newspaper clipping dated Dec. 28, 1835, but without the name of the paper, reads as follows:

"SHOCKING ACCIDENT.

"We have just gathered the particulars of an accident that occurred last evening which has resulted in the death of an amiable and accomplished young lady and cast a gloom over the feelings of many of our citizens. A wedding was consummated at Stroudwater village last evening at the house of Mr. Hobert whose daughter was the bride. A party of friends from this city consisting of Mr. Albert Winslow, wife and daughter (Nancy C. Winslow), Mrs. Johnson, (sister to Mrs. Winslow), Mr. John Bailey and sister and A. W. Fletcher had been out to the wedding, and were returning at half past 9 o'clock in a two horse sleigh. They had proceeded barely a quarter of a mile from Mr. Hobart's house on the way to this city, when on descending a hill (Waldo street), the horses quickened their pace, and from some unexplained cause, but probably from striking their heels against the whiffletree, on reaching the bottom of the hill they quickened into a run and a cervation in the road caused the sleigh to slew so forcibly as to throw the whole party out. Miss Winslow's skull was fractured —she was taken up senseless—and never spoke afterwards. She was taken back to the house and circle where but a few minutes before she had left with a joyful heart, and there died this morning at 9 o'clock!

"Nearly all the those in the sleigh were seriously or slightly injured. Mrs. Johnson was so badly bruised as to be unable to rise from the bed this morning.

Miss Winslow was 26 years of age, and beloved by a large circle of friends.

THE DEERING NEWS.

Saturday, July 16, 1898.

GRANDPA'S SCRAP BOOK

[Under this head historical and genealogical memoranda will be furnished the readers of the News that appears worthy of preservation, particularly of remote periods in our history within the city limits and immediate vicinity.]

GEN. JOHN K. SMITH.

A HERO OF THE WAR OF THE REVOLUTION WHOSE WIFE WAS SALLY WEBB.

John Kilby Smith was born December 17, 1753, in Boston, Mass. Of his parents and youth I have no knowledge. He was a soldier of the Revolution and this entitles his name to perpetual public remembrance and the fact that he commenced married life at Stroudwater a recognition in this column of the Deering News.

January 15, 1785, with James Means, a Revolutionary soldier whose record has appeared in the News, he made his first purchase of and at the ancient village. The original deed is before me. The conveyance is by Jonathan Webb and wife Mary, Inn holder, of Falmouth, (Saccarappa village) and the amount paid two hundred and sixty pounds for "A small lot of Land at Stroudwater in said Falmouth, on the southerly side of Fore River and nigh unto the great Bridge built over the same and bounded—* * *, being part of the land I bought of George Tate the 26th of Nov. 1782, together with the Building and wharf thereon."

This has reference to the lot where the blacksmith shop now stands at the village end of the bridge made of the mill that stood on the wharf above alluded to, which was the first building built by the Stroudwater Mill Dam Company, and the "Building" referred to in the deed was the "ware house" of George Tate, the King's mast agent.

The deed refers to Smith and Means as "both of Falmouth, Merchants."

March 2, 1785, he and Sally Webb were united in marriage, and the record of the event filed in Portland.

On March 18, 1786, he and Means and Josiah Cox, "all of Falmouth, Gentlemen," (Mean's wife being a sister to Cox) for £80 lawful money, purchased "A triangular piece of land about a quarter of an acre lying in front of George Tate's house (the house the same as now seen, 1898) and between and bounded by the following roads, to wit:" etc.

The original record of this conveyance at the time is also before me as I write.

In Colonel Westbrook's day the lot was used and noticed in records as his "mast yard." When Tate made the purchase of his house lot it was bounded by the "mast yard" on the easterly side.

Smith's shop stood about half way up what is now known as Waldo street on the easterly side, on land purchased by Smith, Means and Cox, and he lived in the two story house that stood at the top of the hill, same side of the road, built by Zebulon Trickey, which house was taken down about the year 1850, removed to Brighton Corner district of our city and occupied after the rebuilding by Deacon Hiram H. Dow, and finally burned six or eight years ago. Smith did not remain long at Stroudwater. His shop was a small affair, and many stories are connected with the house in which he lived after his time of occupancy, as well as his shop.

In 1789 he became with two others of Stroudwater, the owner of

Continued:

1800 acres of wild land at Thompson's Pond, (Otisfield,) and four years later was a resident of New Gloucester, the proprietor of a public house with "Esq." attached to his name. his license as an innholder being a matter of record in Portland.

A paper dated April 3, 1799, "at Thompson's Pond, so called," contains his signature, which is now before me as I write.

The compiler of the history of New Gloucester on page 334 to be found in the history of Cumberland county makes it appear he was a native of that town, and states he enlisted in the war of the Revolution, June 12, 1775, and that he fought in the battle of Monmouth as commander of his regiment.

In the month of September, 1817, he was a resident of Portland, having sold part of his estate at Thompson's Pond to his son, John Kilby Smith, Jr., then a book seller in Boston, Mass., but the fact that he commanded a military company made up of men like himself so aged they were exempted from performing military service, when it was expected Portland was to be attacked by the British, when some 6000 soldiers were quartered in that city for a term of two weeks during the war of 1812-15, makes it appear that the General moved to Portland before the year 1817.

July 6, 1822 for "love and affection I have for my son, William Smith, a minor, as well as for $100 paid," Gen. Smith conveyed one half of 121 acres of land "improved and lived on as a farm in Thompson's Pond Plantation."

This same year, at a large fire on Congress street, Portland, opposite the head of Green street, his place of business as well as many others was consumed, he then being a dealer in potash, as well as inspector of the same including hops, being appointed to the position by the town government.

When Gen. Lafayette was in Portland in 1825, he presided at the banquet which was given at Union hall, Portland, and proceeding reported in the Advertiser June 24.

His last place of abode was on Oxford near Portland street.

On the easterly side of the Congress street entrance to the Portland Eastern cemetery, facing the nearest monument, some thirty feet distant, that is enclosed by a fence, and so close that one must enter the monument enclosure to read, may be seen his memorial grave stone as well as that of his wife inscribed as follows:

GEN. JOHN K. SMITH.
Died
August 7, 1842.
Æt. 89.

An officer in the Army of the Revolution.
SALLY,
Wife of John K. Smith,
Died
Feb. 2 1837,
Æt. 77.

There is also a head stone for a grandson—no more, and all of slate.

Under date of Aug. 8, 1842 the Portland Advertiser remarked under the heading of "Deaths" as follows:

In this city, on Sunday last Gen'l John K. Smith, aged 89. He was born in Boston, Dec. 17, 1753. Funeral tomorrow (Tuesday) from his late residence on Oxford street. Friends and relatives are invited to be present.

The weekly Argus of the 9th inst. contained as follows:

A REVOLUTIONARY HERO GONE.

Another link in the chain of existence of the officers and soldiers of the Revolutionary Army is severed! Gen. John K. Smith expired at his residence, in this city, on Sunday last, having nearly attained his 89 year. He was an officer of high standing in the army, and was conspicuous for his bravery and prudence. If we mistake not, he was at some period of that arduous struggle for our liberty aid to Gen. Lafayette. He was a member of the Massachusetts society of the Cincinnati and at their last annual meeting, he with 13 others was all there were known to be left of the original members. A few more years and they too will be gathered up and sleep with their families.
M.

A few years ago I addressed a note to the veteran pension agent, Mr. Z. K. Harmon then of Portland, since deceased, relative to the General's position in the army and the following is a copy of the reply:

GEN. JOHN KILBY SMITH.

John Kilby Smith was appointed adjutant at the organization of the Massachusetts Line in November, 1776, and was promoted to a captaincy in 1778, and subsequently promoted to a brigade major in Col. Benj. Tupper's regiment, General John Patterson's brigade, and remained in the service as inspector and major of brigade until June, 1783.

Under pension laws of 1818, Smith was placed on the pension roll as captain at $240 per annum and which pension was subsequently increased to pension of a staff officer.

Under the head of "Local Notes" there appeared in the Portland Transcript, April 24, 1895, a notice as follows:

On the 15th inst., Mr. William W. Smith died in Augusta, aged 93 years. He leaves an aged widow and three daughters. He was the youngest and last surviving child of Gen. John Kilby Smith, a revolutionary veteran; Gen. Smith was a lieutenant of continental infantry, in the regiment of Col. Asa Whitcomb, during the siege of Boston in 1776, marched to reinforce Fort Ticonderoga with the brigade of Gen. St. Clair, and arrived there early in September. He became 1st lieutenant and adjutant in the 13th Massachusetts regiment, Col. Edw. Wigglesworth, Jan. 1, 1777. He was made captain, Feb. 12, 1778, and transferred in 1781 to the 6th Massachusetts regiment, and to the 21st Massachusetts regiment in 1783. He not only served at the siege of Boston and Fort Ticonderoga, but in Sullivan's Rhode Island campaign, at the battle of Monmouth, and Yorktown. He was an aid to Gen. La Fayette, and was conspicuous for bravery and prudence. He commanded a company of exempts at Portland in 1814, and was chairman of the committee of arrangements for the reception of La Fayette on his visit to Portland, June 25, 1825. After the revolution he was a brigadier-general in the militia. He was born in Boston, Dec. 17, 1753, and died in Portland, Aug. 7, 1842. He was married to Sally Webb, in Falmouth, March 2, 1785. She died Feb. 2, 1837, aged 77. They had four sons and five daughters.
A. B. S.

☞ To the shame of the municipal government of Portland let it be said that just before the death of the General his home was sold for taxes, thus proving that two things in this world are sure—taxes and death.

TO BE CONTINUED.

GRANDPA'S SCRAP BOOK

Saturday, July 23, 1898.

[Under this head historical and genealogical memoranda will be furnished the readers of the News that appears worthy of preservation, particularly of remote periods in our history within the city limits and immediate vicinity.]

GEN. JOHN K. SMITH.

A HERO OF THE WAR OF THE REVOLUTION WHOSE WIFE WAS SALLY WEBB.

[Continued from last week.]

There were nine children born to the General and his wife Sally, and the names here presented and dates of birth, are taken from his family Bible by the writer:

1. Sally, born Nov. 22, 1785, married Daniel Walker, had children, only one of whom survives. She married Capt. Samuel A. Silsby of Portland who was lost at sea in brig Practice a few days out from Portland on her way to Cuba, leaving three children. She resides in Saco.
2. Elizabeth, born April 27, 1785, married Samuel Hodgdon, and resided in Portland. He died, she married 2nd.
3. Ebenezer, born Nov. 30, 1788, died unmarried, in the State of Alabama, it is said.
4. John K —— jr., born Sep. 4, 1791. He was noticed last week as a book seller in Boston, Mass. It is tradition that he was a smart business man who died unmarried "down south."
5. Henry, born Sep. 12, 1794, married Jane Hilton and they had nine children. 1, Mrs. Ezra Filker; 2, Mrs. Caroline Tillerson; 3, William Henry Smith who kept a public house 1st at Windham; 2nd at Raymond. To be further noticed at the bottom of this article. 4, Mrs. Cyrus Buck; 5, Mrs. Mary Plaisted; 6, Mrs. Edward Brooks, now residing at Concord, N. H.; 7, Mrs. Ezra Hawkes of Portland; 8, Mrs. Charles Sawyer; 9, and last, Alonzo died unmarried in the army, war of the Rebellion.
6. Polly, born March 22, 1796, married George Johnson of Poland and they had five children, one of whom, a daughter, Mrs. Mary Bigalow, is living at Chicago, Ill.
7. Nancy, twin to Polly married Alvan Cushman of Portland and had eight children; 1, Sarah died unmarried; 2, Charles died young; 3, Levi died unmarried; 4, George H., m. Susan E. Hasty of Portland; he died in Sioux Falls; 5, John S. m. Martha Downing of Kennebunk, resides in Portland; 6, Maria, m. Alexander B. Stephenson of Portland and resides at No. 121 State street; 7, Nancy S., died unmarried in Portland. One died young.
8. Rebecca, born Feb. 10, 1800, died unmarried.
9. William W., and last, born January 7, 1802, married Sarah Green of Portland. He removed to Augusta, this state, where he died according to the clipping from the Portland Transcript that appeared at the close of our article of last week. They had six children; 1, Mrs. Rebecca Dyer, Augusta, 2, John died in the Union army, war of the Rebellion; 3, William, died in same army; 4, Abbie married F. W. Hunt of Melrose, Mass.; 5. Mrs. Wm. F. Bussell of Augusta, this state; 9, Sarah Ellen died young.

On July 6, 1822, I showed in my article of last week, William W. Smith was a minor who received from his father one half of his father's farm, located in the Thompson Pond plantation. When he came to Portland to reside I cannot state, but when the first Portland general directory was made (about the year 1825) he was keeping a meat market in that town.

With his wife he obtained "riches" —thus the story goes, who owned all of Green street, and much more.

Rev. Samuel Dean, under date of Oct. 27, 1776, remarks his diary as printed on page 344:

I married Daniel Green, (to Mrs. Sarah Wood, daughter of Joshua Brackett.)

On page 365, edition of 1849, the compiler of the diary remarks on page 365 as follows:

The easterly part of his farm Joshua (Brackett) conveyed to Daniel Green and wife, his daughter, and Benjamin Larrabee.

The foregoing refers to certain land located on the northerly side of Congress, covering Green and extending easterly nearly to Brown street.

William Henry, the third child of Henry Smith, was married in Lewiston, 1848, to Miss Joan F. Moore and they immediately commenced to keep a public house in Windham where they resided several years. From there they went to Raymond and opened the Central House where they lived together 33 years, or till death claimed the wife Oct. 11, 1897. Their house was the most popular hostelry in the vicinity, the burning of which was the cause of the death of Mrs. Smith, which occurred but a few day before her demise, the general public lamenting the loss of the willing hands and large heart of the woman, who, as well as the proprietor, was ever ready to make their inn a real home to the wayfarer. The funeral was unusually large and the letters of condolence received were many.

My next will be made of memoranda relating to Henry Webb, who was a brother to Col. James Webb, and to the wife of Gen. Smith.

GRANDPA'S SCRAP BOOK

Saturday, July 30, 1898.

[Under this head historical and genealogical memoranda will be furnished the readers of the News that appears worthy of preservation, particularly of remote periods in our history within the city limits and immediate vicinity.]

CAPT. HENRY WEBB.

HIS HOME AND FAMILY AT STROUDWATER.

But little can be known of Capt. Henry Webb till the question, "Shall these dry bones live again?" is answered authoritively in the affirmative in a supernatural manner, and the sea gives up its dead.

He was a mariner, but this is all that is known of his vocation. An impenetrable veil hangs between his birthplace, parents and youth and the present day as it does between his brother, Col. James Webb, and sister, who was the wife of Gen. John K. Smith, both of whom have been noticed in recent issues of the News. March 20, 1780, he and Ann Riggs, who was born at Bradley's Corner in the Daniel Fowler alias Riggs house, taken down in 1892, were united in marriage.

According to Parson Dean's diary, (Smith and Dean's) page 331, January 9, 1772, John Wright and Miss Shore Chapman were united in marriage. He was a housewright. Nov. 15, 1773, he purchased of Sarah Waldo twenty-five acres of land at Stroudwater including thereon said "Harrow house," in which house Col. Thomas Westbrook died February 11, 1744. "Also seventy-six rods more of land." beginning bounds "at a stake by Fore river side just below the entrance thereto of Stroudwater river."

Upon this 76 rod lot the residences of Messrs. Frederick Waterhouse, Cypress Dill, Humphrey Hanscom (which is the Col. James Webb lot) and Fred H. Libby now stand.

May 15, 1776, Wright sold the two lots to Enoch Ilsley for £123-7-4; the same as he gave for them, Ilsley being a trader in Falmouth, probably at Stroudwater.

April 10, 1786, Ilsley sold what is now the Fred H. Libby lot, being four rods on front, and bounded northerly by the Town Landing, to Henry Webb for £18, extending easterly to the present Cypress Dill lot. On this lot, which is now the southeasterly corner lot where Bond crosses Westbrook street, Capt. Webb constructed his abode, which was a two-story wooden house, hip roof, fronting the "Landing," a door in the middle of the front side with portico, chimney in

CONTINUED:

the middle, one large room on each side of front door, with an open room on back side, which room was one story. It is doubtful if the outside of the house was ever painted. Between the end of the house and what is now Westbrook street was space for a small garden. The easterly end of the lot Capt. Webb sold to Benjamin Fickett immediately after he purchased it for £7-4, upon which a two-story house was built by Fickett.

In an old account book of his time the prefix of "Captain" appears in connection with his name, and another record presents at the end of it the word "mariner" hence the fact of his calling and position therewith. A correctly arranged list I cannot make of his children—the following is the best I can do at this time:

1—A son, who enlisted in naval service of the United States, went to sea and was never heard from.
2—In the desecrated George street ancient burial spot of this city may be seen two memorial slate slabs inscribed as follows:

BENJAMIN STEVENS, died Nov. 26, 1850 aged 72 years.
CHARLOTTE STEVENS, born Aug. 9, 1785, died Dec. 7, 1860, widow of Benjamin Stevens.

"Thou shalt quicken me again and shall bring me up from the depths of the earth." (See Portland Argus Sept. 29, 1888, also Oct. 17.)

The words of the quotation have proved true in one sense, and if the opinion of Rev. Caleb Bradley, who was a persistent believer in "hellfire" for the wicked, they will in the sense intended, by the use of the quotation, for he says: "She is is good enough to go to Heaven and will, though she has never made a profession of religion," in alluding in his diary to her neatly kept house and finely seasoned cooking, her last worldly abiding place being the old Wm. Woodford house.

Her maiden name was Charlotte Webb, daughter of Capt. Henry Webb.

During the year 1894 the News printed several notices of the Stevens' both of Stroudwater and Woodfords.

Oct. 20, it states that Benjamin Stevens married Jan. 9, 1801, Charlotte Webb, etc.

3—Lucy, married March 9, 1809 Daniel Cobb, Jr. He did not survive long after the event and she married 2nd, June 11, 1811, Michael Stevens, son of Tristram Stevens and wife Margaret Patrick of Stroudwater. Michael was born Nov. 30, 1787 and died in Portland in the month of March, 1856, aged 68 years. She died in same place, Nov. 14, 1888, aged 94 years. (See News Jan. 4, 1896, for further particulars.)

Nov. 1, 1809, Eunice Webb and William Toby were united in marriage.

Mrs. Submit C. Russell, wife of Mr. John H. Russell, residing at 55 India street, informed me three or four years ago that this Eunice Webb was a Stroudwater woman; that William Toby was born on Hampshire street, Portland; that he was a cooper, but removed to Pownal where he bought a farm and where he died. He was related to the wife of Jonathan Stevens.

This closes my notes on the Webbs of Stroudwater.

THE DEERING NEWS.

Saturday, Aug. 6, 1898.

GRANDPA'S SCRAP BOOK

[Under this head historical and genealogical memoranda will be furnished the readers of the News that appears worthy of preservation, particularly of remote periods in our history within the city limits and immediate vicinity.]

BENJAMIN BURNHAM.

ONE WHO WAS BORN IN SCARBORO, LIVED IN STROUDWATER AND DIED IN SACO.

The time the first Burnham came to Scarboro or where he located I have not endeavored to ascertain. There are but two Burnham wills recorded in this state prior to 1760. That of Mary of Kittery, probated 1734, and Job of Scarboro, probated in 1757, which the court would not allow. They spelled the name Burnam—not Burnham, as is now the case. Job alluded to Rebecca, widow of his son Daniel, deceased, and gives her the "improvement of 52 acres of land together with the house and barn standing on the same in Scarboro," "the same where and in which she now dwells, in order the better to enable her to bring up the children she bore to my son Daniel." He then mentions the name of his son, Job, Jr., and grandchildren, Daniel, Thomas, Robert Samuel, Job, Rebecca and Solomon, children of Daniel, and appoints his grandsons, Daniel and Thomas, executors, which, as before said, was disallowed May 17, 1757.

Job Burnham was admitted to the Scarboro church Aug. 11, 1728. His son Daniel, alluded to above, was "baptized into the church" Sept. 1, 1728; Rebecca and Samuel, Sept. 7, 1734; Robert, July 22, 1739; Job, Jan. 3, 1743; Solomon, Oct. 7, 1744.

There were others by the name in Scarboro at that time.

Nov. 13, 1729, Moses Burnham and Mercy Harmon were married and had children "baptized into the church."

Following is a list of the children of David and Olive Burnham of that town, but I do not now know the connections with the preceding names:

1. Eunice, born Dec. 17, 1771.
2. Olive, born April 24, 1773.
3. Moses, born Feb. 8, 1775.
4. David, born April 4, 1777.
5. Rebeckah, born April 3, 1779.
6. Joel, born Jan. 12, 1781.
7. *Benjamin*, born Oct. 13, 1782. (Another record says 1785.)
8. Jane, born Oct. 25, 1786.
9. Amos, born Aug. 27, 1789.

Benjamin was a character. He united in marriage with Miss Naomy Royals, born May 6, 1788. The Royals homestead may be seen as originally built in 1737, at Medford, Mass.

He was a tanner and May 9, 1807 purchased a house and lot located at Ferry village, between the ferry and Congregational meeting house; South Portland, but sold it two years later and came to the Bradley Corner district, of Deering, and resided in the house that stood on what is now Stevens Plains avenue where the large John B. Curtis' dwelling may be seen. While there his second child was born, May 2, 1810, whom they named George W. From there he removed to the Chas. Frost house that stood at the easterly end of the bridge over Fore river at Stroudwater, later known as the Brewer house, for many years kept as an inn which was destroyed by fire some odd years since, to the delight of the local public, its days of usefulness having passed.

The Capt. Henry Webb house, described in my article of last week, was sold by Michael Stevens and wife Lucy Webb, Jan. 19, 1828, to David Burnham, of Scarboro, trader, for $400. He was a brother to Benjamin, but the exact date Benjamin accepted the premises I cannot state, but it was not till Feb. 2, 1844, that David, then a trader in Saco, conveyed finally the place to his brother, Benjamin.

Continued!

Naomy Royals, wife of Benjamin, died very suddenly while on a visit to Bangor, August 30, 1849. It was a very sickly season, the epidemic partaking of the nature of the Asiatic cholera. He died in Saco May 25, 1873, aged 87. She was 61, and her remains were interred at Stroudwater.

As I have said, he was indeed a character—possessed of a natural flow of words, he was a man of great physical endurance, a good story teller, and as a shouter in a religious meeting he had no equals hereabouts. If not convincing in his illustrations he never failed to keep the boys awake when he spoke in meeting. He had a massive frame, short neck, bald head when we knew him, and the cause of the rainbow which he saw from his point of observation through the teaching of the Bible we still remember and smile as the thought comes up before us, though fifty years have passed since he and Brother Hill of Portland filled the double place of shoemaker and Freewill Baptist preacher, shouted Hosanna and indulged in song in the second story of the old Stroudwater schoolhouse and at private residences. The bandanna was then in use but Uncle Ben did not handle his in the graceful manner Beecher did the little white linen handkerchief; he made it into a wad and passed it from one hand to the other occasionally wiping his perspiring brow with a corner. His conversion was often told which was the result of a prayer in the deep gully where the Ogdensburg railroad crosses Congress street to which place he went one dark night on his return home from Portland, a supernatural power, as he claimed, directing his feet.

The schoolhouse room was used alike by all classes and there was no rental to pay. The benches were long and as hard as could be made of plank but they had backs. A two inch plank partition separated the stair-way from the small hall, constructed by grooving each edge of the planks and inserting a strip of white pine. The planks having shrunk a full half inch it was easy making a hole through the strips which the boys and men did with knives. So during meetings in the evening it was sometimes the case that every aperture in the partition had a claimant, but there was never any noise outside the partition, which extended from side to side of the room, the "pulpit" being in shape like half of an octagon and coming well up under the occupants arms, and placed opposite the door. The nasal melody of Brother Hill's—"Poor way-faring man of grief" and Uncle Ben's high pitched exhortation we hear now in imagination as we did then in reality.

Uncle Ben loved besides the prayer meeting the fox chase, his gun, dog and boat. "Nig", the partridge dog, yellow in color, with a tail curled the size of a large doughnut, was all ready to show his teeth when a finger was pointed at him with a serpent noise of the mouth, and many a boy of his day went home with no seat to his pants and a heel off a shoe for attempting to retreat posterior to the enemy after Nig had been aroused to resentful indignation by hisses and pointing a finger at his nose. But Uncle Ben, Brother Hill, the school house, Nig, gun and boat have all left us. The Reaper has done his work with these persons and things as he will with us and ours.

"Yes! the vacant chairs tell sadly we are going, going fast,
And the thought comes strangely o'er me,
Who will live to be the last?"

TO BE CONTINUED.

THE DEERING NEWS.

Saturday, Aug. 6, 1898.

GRANDPA'S SCRAP BOOK

[Under this head historical and genealogical memoranda will be furnished the readers of the News that appears worthy of preservation, particularly of remote periods in our history within the city limits and immediate vicinity.]

BENJAMIN BURNHAM.

ONE WHO WAS BORN IN SCARBORO, LIVED IN STROUDWATER AND DIED IN SACO.

(*Continued from last week.*)

Benjamin Burnham did not work at tanning all his days, but engaged in ship work, going to the forest for timber.

He was united in marriage with Miss Naomy Royals (Rials, of Portland, the Portland city records say), July 12, 1807.

Following is a copy of the record of his children's names, dates of births and some of his other descendants:

1. Angeline, born May 16, 1808. She married Sep. 20, 1830, Thomas B. Garland. The record says, "both of Portland." They resided in Bangor or vicinity.
2. George W., born May 2, 1810, near Bradley's Corner, as stated last week. (To be further noticed.)
3. Naomy Royals, born Dec. 17, 1812, married Benjamin Abbott. He was a shipwright and while a resident of Stroudwater resided in the Fickett house that stood "on the point" easterly of the Henry Webb house, from which place he moved to Saco. They had 1—Sarah; 2—William; 3—Miranda; 4—David and 5—Charles, who is a minister officiating at Gray and Cumberland. There may have been other children.
4. Mary A., born March 17, 1814, married Jonathan Londer. He was a sea captain, and they resided at Bangor. He died Jan. 1, 1873. The widow lives with a daughter in Somerville, Mass.
5. Royal R., born April 1, 1817, married Mary A. Nickery; he was a brick mason, now residing at Dover, N. H., with a son, where he has resided since marriage, spending the summers at Pine Point, Scarboro, of late, where he has a cottage.
6. Paul Dyer, born Dec. 17, 1820, married Miss Caroline Kennard, one of whose sisters married Mr. Hanson M. Clay, now residing at Woodfords, this city. She had one child who was adopted by Cyrus and Esther King of Saccarappa and died at the age of 20 years. Her name was Henrietta. The mother died Aug. 15, 1861; he married 2nd. Oct. 2, 1845, he purchased the square built house and lot situated on the westerly side of Westbrook street, Stroudwater, opposite the head of Waldo street, being the second house northerly from the old mill, which house he sold in 1853 to Mr. F. A. Waldron, who owned the tide mill, and resided in the next house northerly from the Burnham house, where the cellar hole may be seen at this time of the burned Waldron house. Mr. Burnham was then a resident of East Boston, Mass.
7. Benjamin, born Oct. 20, 1823. He was a brick mason, and united in marriage with Miss Mary Ann Foster. They had Charles with whom Benjamin and wife now reside on a farm at Rochester, N. H., and Ella J., who married George West and resides in Chicago, Ill. Mr. Burnham was many years a Portland policeman, residing at the West End.
8. William D., born April 11, 1826, married Roxanna Richards. He was a brick mason, learning the trade in Bangor; lived in Livermore, but removed to Saco where he died. Had children.
9. Stephen A., who was the youngest of the family, born Oct. 17, 1828. When the California fever was on he went to the gold digging country; returning, married Miss Henretta Kelley, Feb. 16, 1854. His father gave him his house, lot and "household furniture of every description," which house and lot he sold to Robert Waterhouse, Oct. 13, 1866, for $400, being then a resident of Saco. Like his father and mother he became a prayer meeting exhorter but far less demonstrative than his father. At Saco he was a stevedore, becoming instantly and violently insane from over exertion and died in consequence, leaving children.

CONTINUED:

2—GEORGE W. BURNHAM.

He married, Oct. 15, 1829, Miss Olevia Y. (alias Olive) Libby, of Gray, born Oct. 12, 1806. She was, as we remember her, more than fifty years ago, a stout built women, with a full round face—a real Libby face, as we saw them when coming from Scarboro on their way to Portland via Stroudwater. To her the Burnham family of this region as well as the readers of these articles in the NEWS are indebted for many of the dates here presented, she having preserved them. She says:

Went to Westbrook, 1830; experienced religion, 1840; removed to Portland, (West End), 1845.

While residing in Westbrook (which was at Stroudwater) they occupied the two story house that stood on the Town landing at the southeasterly corner of the bridge over the fresh water river below the mill. He was an active man. When the tide mills were built at Stroudwater he was a member of the "Harpswell Soapstone company," organized for the manufacture of fire-place frames from Harpswell Soapstone. When the Portland and Oxford canel was opened he built two canel boats near his home, and at one time he manufactured brick near the canal opposite the Brewer house.

In 1846 he purchased land in the West End district of Portland, went to the California gold diggers regions, returned, built houses for himself, engaged in brick making and ice cutting.

The history of the Libby family gives on page 101-2 some interesting facts which we here present:

"Asa Libby was born in Scarboro in 1737; married April 15, 1759, Abigail Coolbroth, of Scarboro. He was a farmer and moved to Falmouth a few years after marriage, and thence, probably a short time before the Revolutionary war, to Gray. He served in the Continental army eight months. He and John Nash went to Gray about the same time and both lived with Daniel Libby until they had built houses and cleared some land. Asa Libby settled about two miles west of Gray Corner. His house stood some distance southerly of the road leading to Windham. There he lived until old age, and then went to live with his son Asa, in Belgrade. There he died, Nov. 5, 1828."

Their second son, born Nov. 6, 1762, in Scarboro, married Mehitable Nash. This the Libby family history also says, also that his brother Asa was a Baptist minister who preached many years in Gray and was settled finally in Belgrade where he died in 1810.

Mrs. William Richards, a daughter of Geo. W. and Olevia J. (Libby) Burnham residing at Libby's Corner this city, has a record, made with ink and paint for a wall decoration to a room, evidently very ancient, which reads:

JOHN NASH, born May 7, 1732.
ELIZABETH ANDREWS, born Oct. 13, 1739.
MARRIED Nov. 1, 1759.

They were the parents of Mehitable Nash who became the wife of Joel Libby. Joel was stung to death, according to the Libby book, at Gray, July 5, 1820. The widow died with her daughter, Mrs Burnham, at Stroudwater, Aug, 13, 1843.

TO BE CONTINUED.

Saturday, Aug. 20, 1898.

(Continued from last week.)

BENJAMIN BURNHAM.

ONE WHO WAS BORN IN SCARBORO, LIVED IN STROUDWATER AND DIED IN SACO.

Joel Libby, born in Scarboro, Nov. 9, 1762, who married Mehitable Nash, had nine children, a record of whom, Olevia J., the youngest of the family, preserved, which may also be found on page 223 of the Libby book with the names of the persons to whom the whole nine were severally united in marriage, added by the compiler as follows:

1. Eleanor, b. June 15, 1786; m. 1st, Oct. 15, 1805, Wm. Delano; 2d, Samuel Jones
2. Ann, b. Feb. 2, 1788; m. Alexander Jellison of York.
3. Andrew, b. Apr. 15, 1790; m. Nancy J. Pulsifer of Sumner.
4. Eunice, b. June 28, 1792; m. 1st, July 3, 1816, James Weymouth; 2d, Wm. Moore.
5. Elijah, b. Aug. 20, 1794; m. Lydia Howe.
6. Ebenezer, b. June 2, 1796; m. Louisa Winslow.
7. Abigail, b. Sept. 21, 1798; m. Isaac Carson.
8 and last, Olevia J., b. Oct. 12, 1806.

Joel Libby, according to the Libby book, was a farmer and mechanic, and lived about a mile from his father's on the road from Gray Corner to West Gray.

George W. Burnham united in marriage July 1st, as was stated last week.

Oct. 14, 1880, an intention of marriage between Mr. Burnham and Miss Mary Ann Hamilton of Portland was filed, and the ceremony was performed accordingly.

CHILDREN all by FIRST WIFE:

I. George Collins, born July 28, 1830, in Stroudwater.
II. Eliza A., b. in S., March 3, 1833.
III. Harriet D., in S., Jan. 12, 1836.
IV. Royal R., b. in S., March 5, 1838.

I. George C. Burnham united in marriage with Miss Olive B. Foss of Hollis. He was a brick mason and resided at West End, Portland, a few years, then went to California, and it is supposed was robbed and killed by Indians in the gold diggings. His widow died last month. The following is copied from the Portland Express of July 29:

OLIVE B. BURNHAM.

Mrs. Olive B., widow of the late George C. Burnham of this city, died Thursday morning at the home of her daughter, Mrs. Chas. A. Stuart, Saco. Mrs. Burnham also left two sons, Fred L. and Frank P. Burnham, both of Portland, a sister, Mrs. Emily A. Burnham, of Portland, and a brother, Charles A. Foss, of Fitchburg, Mass.

Mr. Chas. A. Stuart alluded to is a son of the late Solomon Stuart, Esq., who held office so long in this place, a fitting notice of whom appeared in the Portland Argus May 13, 1889, a few days after his demise.

II. Eliza Burnham was united in marriage April 19, 1846, with William Richards, of Scarboro, a cooper, residing at the end of Liberty street, Libby Corner district of our city, who has spent nearly a score of winters in Cuba. They have children: George William, Harriet Elizabeth, Albion Royal, now in the employ of the U. S. marine service and stationed on board the monitor in Portland harbor, and Annie Olevia.

III. Harriet D. united January 1, 1856, in marriage with Frinces Foss, brother, to the wife of George C. Burnham who was a blacksmith, and they resided at the West End where he died July 24, 1859.

She married 2nd Capt. James Jellison and accompanied him several voyages on the sea. It is said she can handle a ship on the water as well as a man. She is now a widow, residing at No. 413, Main street, Charlestown, Mass., with a daughter.

A few years since, after an illness of long standing, she had a "presentment" in her sleep following the direction of which she soon recovered her health and is now the manufacturer of "HARRIETT'S DISCOVERY," which she sells at $1 per bottle, meeting with success.

IV.—Royal R., united in marriage Jan. 1, 1857, with Mary E. Foss, sister to the wife of his brother, Geo. C. Burnham. He engaged in the ice business, making it a success, residing on Congress street, West End, Portland, where his wife died March 4, 1864, aged 24 years. He married 2nd, her sister, Emily Augusta, who now occupies the homestead. He died Nov. 12, 1896, aged 58 years, a much respected citizen, the newspapers of the time furnishing fitting notices of his demise. He left children.

These Fosses were children of Albert and Mary Foss of Hollis. He died Jan. 7, 1871, aged 70 years.

A memorial monument may be seen in Evergreen cemecery and several slabs. From the monument we copied the following:

GEO. W. BURNHAM.
died
May 19, 1886, Æt. 79.

His wife,
OLIVIA J.,
July 1, 1880, Æt. 83.

THE DEERING NEWS.

Saturday, Aug. 27, 1898.

GRANDPA'S SCRAP BOOK

[Under this head historical and genealogical memoranda will be furnished the readers of the News that appears worthy of preservation, particularly of remote periods in our history within the city limits and immediate vicinity.]

"GRANDFATHER'S CLOCK."

THE MAN WHO MADE THEM ON STEVENS PLAINS.

Three-fourths of a century ago the part of the town of Westbrook that is now the city of Deering possessed many industries of which the present generation have only a slight or no knowledge whatever. The change that has taken place in the meantime is wonderful.

The long-cased, eight day brass clock was manufactured on Stevens Plains though in a small way—a way in which most business was performed at that time. The name of the proprietor of the clock establishment was Enoch Burnham, born in Dunbarton, N. H., March 26, 1784, united, Feb. 16, 1808 in marriage with Judith Virgin, born in the town of Concord, that State, Jan. 27, 1790. He first established himself in business in the town of Paris, Me., this state, where he built a house and shop at Paris Hill which he sold Feb. 12, 1816, to Nathaniel W. Green for $650, and which house now stands though it has been moved. Augustus Bemis was an apprentice. Many of his clocks it is said are still in use at this place. From Paris Hill he removed to Rumford, then to Stevens Plains, and lived in the Brisco alias Ballard house that stood on the southerly side of the main entrance to Evergreen cemetery in the rear of which was his shop, the house being removed to High street, to make room for the "Stevens twin houses," one of which was burned five or six years since while owned by Mr. W. P. Goss.

Mr. Burnham's work here was of a superior character, several specimens still being in existance on the Plains.

CHILDREN.

1. Alexis, b. Paris, Me., Feb. 23, 1809.
2. Jennette, b. Paris, Me., Nov. 5, 1810.
3. Brittania, b. Paris, Me., Sept. 1, 1812.
4. Elbridge Gerry, b. Paris, Me., Nov. 30, 1814, died at Westbrook, (Stevens Plains district (Sept. 3, 1818(?)
5. Emily Ann, b. Paris, Me., July 1, 1817.
6. Vista, b. Paris, Me., April 11, 1820, died Aug. 24, same year.
7. Enoch Lincoln, b. Paris, Me., June 3, 1822.
8. Elbridge Gerry, b. Rumford, Sept. 30, 1824, died July 23, 1826.
9. Cymene, b. Westbrook, (Stevens Plains district) April 6, 1828.
10. Patrick Henry, b. Westbrook, Sept. 26, 1832.

This is a very odd lot of names. From here he removed to Massachusetts, but we have no knowledge of the place he stopped.

PRESUMPSCOT FALLS.

For a period of a hundred years the Falls district of Old Falmouth was a busy place, a place of industry. A little has been done, a very little comparatively, on its history but much that should now be done probably will not be. Following is an interesting item gleaned from a copy of the Eastern Argus of July 14, 1808:

AT FALMOUTH (ME.)

The anniversary of the auspicious Day, on which the United States assumed rank as an indipendent nation, was honored at the rising of the sun by a federal salute, and displaying of colors. At 9 o'clock the military Companies paraded, under the command of Major Hobbs, consisting of Capt. Leighton's Cavalry, and Capts. March and Merrills Infantry, with appropriate Music, and agreeable to previous arrangement, escorted the Procession in the following order: Orator and Clergy,—Committee of arrangements—Military officers—Citizens. Having arrived at the meeting house, the Throne of Grace was addressed by the Rev. Wm Miltimore, in a Prayer well adapted to the occasion—to which (after the intival of an Anthem by a select choir) succeeded an ORATION, by Mr. Enos Merrill, which, from the correctness of judgment, elegence of taste, brilliancy of imagination and candor of mind displayed, gave favorable omen of future distinction. The solemnities being closed by an appropriate Ode, (in the performance of which, the power of music; vocal and instrumental, were happily executed and sensibly felt by a numerous audience of both sexes) the procession returned to James Merrills, jun's, and partook of a handsome entertainment at which Dr. Wm. Sanborn presided, and Mr. Christopher Graves officiated as Vice President. After the cloth was removed, the following Toasts were drunk accompanied with discharge of a field piece, and enlivened with music and appropriate songs.

(The seventeen toasts reported we here omit.)

Enos Merrill was born in Falmouth, graduated from Bowdoin college Sept. 15, 1808, when he delivered the class oration and received the degree of Bachelor of Arts. He became a Congregational minister and in 1816 was settled in Freeport where he labored with the church and people till 1831. He died in that town in 1861.

THE DEERING NEWS.

Saturday, Sept. 10, 1898.

GRANDPA'S SCRAP BOOK

[Under this head historical and genealogical memoranda will be furnished the readers of the News that appears worthy of preservation, particularly of remote periods in our history within the city limits and immediate vicinity.]

OLIVER BUCKLEY.

AN EARLY RESIDENT UPON STEVENS PLAINS AND DESCENDANTS.

Whether viewed from an historical point of observation, or through the eyes of one who admires evidences of a harmonious blending of old and new in the arrangement of residences, neatness of surroundings, contentment in enjoyment of what is, Stevens Plains district is unsurpassed by any other of our city.

For a period of ninety years the name of Buckley has been prominent. Outside of this city, however, or in the State of Connecticut, the name is, we are told, spelled "Bulkley."

In Pine Grove cemetery located back of the seminary buildings may be seen a stone slab inscribed as follows:

MARTHA,
wife of
SOLOMON BUCKLEY,
DIED
Sep. 15, 1839,
Æt. 78.

Mother sleepeth.

Oliver Buckley, son of Solomon and Martha Buckley, was born at Rocky Hill, township of Wethersfield, eight miles from Hartford, Ct., Aug. 22, 1782. By occupation he was a tinsmith.

Referring to the marriage record of Rev. Caleb Bradley we find as follows:

May 2, 1805. Elijah North to Martha Woodford—fee, $1.55. Oliver Buckley to Sally Read—fee, $1.55. These four were married at one and the same time.

(The family records of both of these families have been given in the News.)

Upon the early Read name the curtain of obscurity is almost impenetrable. Sally, the wife of Oliver Buckley, was born July 9, 1789, and one William Read, it is said, was her father, and after his death the widow married second a man by the name of Holden. Mrs. Read had a son William, so it is said, who married a woman by the name of Whitman; Lydia, who married Reuben Humphrey of Yarmouth; Rebecca, who married a man by the name of Mabury of Yarmouth; Nabby, who married a man by the name of Young and lived in Yarmouth, and May 6, 1818, an intention of marriage between Ann Read (or Reed) and Abizer Howard, Jr., was made public, who, we understand, was the son of Abizer that died Feb. 20, 1834, aged 70 years, and Sally, his wife, Apr. 28, 1848, aged 82 years—grandparents of Oliver Buckley Howard, our aged and much respected citizen now residing at Morrill's Corner, this city, whose daughter became the first wife of Rev. Geo. W. Bicknell, the able Universalist preacher, and then with the Goodrich family the Buckley's are connected.

Barzillea Buckley, who lived awhile on the Plains was Solomon's son.

March 28, 1807, Oliver Buckley made his first purchase of land—an acre and a half, located on the northerly side of the old entrance to Evergreen cemetery, which entrance is now included in the enlarged main entrance as well as Mr. Buckley's 1807 purchase of Capt. Isaac S. Stevens. In 1713 he made another small purchase of Capt. Stevens alluding to the first "as my homestead." And here we wish to remark that any one who desires to learn how the old entrance appeared can do so by referring to "John Neal's Illustrated Portland," p. 91, published in 1874.

In 1815 when the first valuation of Westbrook was made Mr. Buckley was assessed as follows:

1 house,	$500 00
(This was the house removed to widen the entrance.)	
1 barn,	40 00
1 shop,	100 00
1 and one-half acre land,	22 00
25 acres of unimproved land.	
1 cow,	14 00
1 horse,	40 00
1 chaise,	60 00
Stock in trade,	300 00

In 1834 he was assessed as follows:

New house and buildings,	1,100 00
(This is the one-story house on the opposite side of the avenue where his son Edward M. Buckley resides.)	
Old one story house,	100 00
(This we understand was the house purchased by Charles Maxfield, removed to Stroudwater, enlarged and now stands there on Congress street.)	
51 tons navigation at $17, and 16 acres Plains land,	1,187 00
16 acres Gower lot, $320, and 31 acres at $10 per acre.	630 00
9 acres mowing land at $38 per acre, and 2 chairs, $160,	520 00
2 cows $30; 1 horse $75, 2 swine,	1,15 00
8 shares of bank stock,	784 00
	$4,418 00
Oliver and Charles G. Buckley (his son). House, chaise and wood house, and one acre of land,	$1,200 00
Old barn, shop and truck,	400 00
Stock in trade,	1,000 00
Cow,	15 00
	$2,615 00

When Oliver Buckley came to Falmouth, of which town Deering was then a part, there was a religious excitement passing over the country. From the preaching and writings of the eloquent and gifted Elder Elias Smith, a new sect was forming, opposed to supporting preaching by direct taxation of property, to the rule of Kings and Bishops, to calling preachers "Reverend", to the Trinity, infant baptism and creeds in general. If baptism was necessary, they claimed, it should be done in the water and not by sprinkling. God, they claimed, is the only Creator—Christ a law giver. Arguments were held "eight hours long" were hooted, windows smashed in some cases in public buildings where the new sect met who called themselves "The Christian Church," using the New Testament as their only rule in religious matters. Then everybody was assessed and taxed in proportion to their property to support the Congregational church who did not pay to support some other, and there being no other hereabouts, everybody paid to support Rev. Caleb Bradley, at the time of which we write, or were sent to jail.

In the year 1815 the Parish voted $522 "to defray parish charges, including the salary of the Rev. Caleb Bradley" and to allow the collector six per cent on all collections, the assessors to receive $12 of this amount and Mr. Thomas Pierce $8 for caring for the meeting house. The parish included territorially the present city of Westbrook and Deering.

Thomas Pierce was a son of the Rev. Thomas Pierce of Scarboro, whose last worldly abiding place was a large two story house, standing near the Scarboro depot of the B. & M. railroad, which may be seen just as it was built, in every particular, in 1763. Thomas, the son, was a mason by occupation and resided in a house that stood on Stevens Plains avenue, about 50 rods northerly of Frost street, since moved part way up the hill in the rear where it may be seen with a room added to the front side. Thomas, the mason, it is said, never failed to wear seven days in a week a leather apron and a tall white hat.

The Quakers held the region of Cobb and Quaker Lanes; the Methodists had "deluged" Saccarappa, but the rest of the town was open for the coming of the "Christian" clans and the "converts" moved more it is presumed to prevent personal taxation than acquiescence to devout and holy thought were quite numerous on Stevens Plains and vicinity, so in 1814 they appeared in organized form.

CONTINUED:

May 27, 1814 the prudental committee was made up as follows:

Zachariah B. Stevens.
Oliver Buckley
Joseph Storer

Mr. Storer built and resided in what is now know as the Daniel Mason house. He was a member of the Parson Bradley church and at that time moved to Ohio when his place on the committee was filled by William Kenney the family records of both of whom have been presented in the News.

The subscribers to the new and liberal religious belief so far as we have obtained them were as follows:

George Bishop,   Zachariah Brackett
Capt. Aaron Wilson,   Francis Blake
Benjamin Stevens,   Elijah North
Andrew Mitchell,   Henry Knight
John Blake,   Benjamin Bailey
Henry Wilson,   Nathaniel Thombs
Samuel Dalton,   John Clark
William Read,   Isaac Stevens
Zachariah Sawyer, Jr.,
              Capt. Isaac S. Stevens*
Daniel S. Jones,   Lemuel Stevens
Joseph Beals,   John Collens
Stephen Riggs,   Josiah Stevens
Isaac Sawyer, Jr.,   Simeon Howard
William Blake,   Albion Howard
Artemas Prentiss,   Samuel Hicks
              John Barber

Capt. Isaac S. Stevens was a Revolutionary soldier, a member of the Parson Bradley's church and built the two-story dwelling as now seen on the Plains, occupied late years by his granddaughter, Mrs. Record, lately deceased, the meetings of the "Christians" being held in the hall that was attached to the southerly end of the dwelling, removed, and converted into a double tenement, standing on the lane near by, in a south westerly direction.

TO BE CONTINUED.

THE DEERING NEWS.

Saturday, Sept. 17, 1898.

GRANDPA'S SCRAP BOOK

[Under this head historical and genealogical memoranda will be furnished the readers of the News that appears worthy of preservation, particularly of remote periods in our history within the city limits and immediate vicinity.]

OLIVER BUCKLEY.

AN EARLY RESIDENT UPON STEVENS PLAINS AND DESCENDANTS.

(Continued from last week.)

On Feb. 1, 1810, John Gray was ordained in the town of Gray who immediately started out to do missionary work as a "Christian" and a little later he published a letter showing how he was opposed by the Methodists down in the State of Georgia, but he adds, "my congregations consist of from one to two thousand and I sometimes speak in the open air from three to four hours." At this date this new sect had fifty elders at work in New England.

A letter addressed to Elder Elias Smith at Portsmouth, N. H., relative to religious matters, reads as follows:

PORTLAND, ME., July 20, 1814.
BELOVED BROTHER:—

As to the state of religion in these parts, it is very encouraging; the Brethren have been quite revived of late. Lord's day before last I spake three times, broke bread, and Baptized two; it was a good heavenly time; the meeting house was crowded with solemn, attentive listeners, while a number spoke of the goodness of God to their souls.

In Falmouth, (or rather a part of it now called by another name) the Lord is moving wonderfully on the minds of the people. I was with them last Lord's day, and we had a wonderful time; it may be said the Lord was there of a truth. I spoke in Mr. Steven's Hall on the Plains, but the hall does not hold much more than half of the people. They come from nine to eighteen miles to attend these meetings. There is a number much awakened who appear to be seeking Jesus sorrowingly; in fact they appear to be inquiring as they did under the preaching of Peter, "What shall we do to be saved?"

I lately visited Gorham and found a great desire to hear the word and the Brethren striving to press forward, in Scarborough also there is a great cry for preaching.

Dear Brother, there never was such an open door in these parts for preaching as at the present time. We may say it is great, it is needful that some preacher should come this way and we should be glad if you could find it your duty to come soon for the harvest is great but the laborers are few. The old formalities are greatly alarmed—they find their craft in danger. Not long since I had an appointment to preach in a school house at New Casco,* but when I got there they had so much of the Pharisee religion they would not let me go into the house, but they did not prevent us having a meeting, for there was an house near by and the doors were opened to receive me and the people. May the Lord hasten the day when such as these shall know the truth that makes free.

Yours,
SAMUEL RAND.

E. SMITH.

*"New Casco" is now known as Falmouth Foreside.

A "Christian" society was organized in Portland Jan. 11, 1810, with Elder Elias Smith as leader, but a year later Elder Samuel Rand took Elder Smith's place. From this beginning grew the Casco street meeting house society, with which Elder Rand remained till his death, Oct. 10, 1839.

The duration of the "Stevens Hall" meetings we cannot state, reliable data not being obtainable.

Commencing April 18, 1896, the News presented several articles in succession relating to the formation of the Universalist society, composed of citizens of Saccarappa and hereabouts, but whether or not this society which has been continued from 1829 to the present is a lineal offspring of the "Christian" society we cannot state.

Among the petitioners for the latter we find the name of Oliver Buckley and several others connected with the former. In belief we can discover no difference between the two.

The number of civil offices Mr. Buckley held we cannot state correctly at this time. We notice he served two terms as selectman, was a member of the order of Masons, and his name appears frequently on lists of committee men. His son Charles was captain of the Westbrook Light Infantry, hence his title of captain.

His memorial stone as well as that of his wife in Pine Grove cemetery tell a meager story as follows:

FATHER.
OLIVER BUCKLEY.
1782—1872.

MOTHER.
SALLY BUCKLEY.
1789—1828.

The names and ages of the children of Oliver and Sally were as follows:

1. Nancy G., b. Feb. 22, 1806, m. Oct. 27, 1826 Alfred Stevens, b. Sept. 3, 1801, son of Zachariah B. Stevens. He d. Sept. 9, 1884. (For his place on the Stevens family record see News of Feb. 2, 1895 and other members.) On the 23d of August of the year he was united in marriage he purchased of James L. Bailey, and Caroline his wife, the Josiah Stevens house and three acre lot, the house then appearing as now seen on the westerly side of Stevens Plains avenue—a two story building, containing four large rooms upon each floor, with a one story ell—for which he paid $800. Upon this lot he manufactured tinware, and sent out many peddler carts, to sell the same or exchange for rags and country produce. It is but a few years since the long building, where rags were assorted and carts housed, was pulled down, and the last "cart" destroyed, and thus disappeared the last relic of a once flourishing industry on the Plains.

The widow of Alfred survives him in the 92 year of her life, is up first in the morning, and last to retire, seeks and peruses with avidity the morning paper, writes with a steady hand and takes as lively an interest in current events as any of the young, calling frequently upon her sister, Mrs. Porter, who resides a few rods distance and who, at 90, is equally as smart and bright as Mrs. Stevens. In this Stevens family there are six children as follows:

I Sarah Buckley, b. June 24, 1828, m. George Henry Ballard, of he Plains. He d., the widow resides there. Three children.

II Oren Buckley, b. May 28, 1820, m. Emeline Treadwell. (See monument inscription to follow.) Two children—Alfred and Mary Louisa.

III Miriam Frances, b. June 18, 1834, m. Andrew J. Forbes, who came from

CONTINUED:

the State of Connecticut, and after her death which occurred Feb. 16, 1861, he went to Massachusetts. One child that died in infancy.

IV Alfred Augustus, b. Dec.—1836, m. Lottie Turner. He resides on the plains. Two children.

V William Pitt, b. Jan. 31, 1839, m. Ella Eliza Woodford, dau. of Joseph and sister to the wife of Mr. Edward M. Buckley who resides on the Plains, in the residence last ocupied by Oliver Buckley, his father. (For this Woodford family see News of May 18, 1895.

VI and last. Edward Clifton, b. Oct. 21, 1844, m. Maria D. Moses. (See monument inscription to follow.) Two children--Henry C. and Hattie Bell.

TO BE CONTINUED. Pg. 190

THE DEERING NEWS.

Saturday, Oct. 1, 1898.

GRANDPA'S SCRAP BOOK

[Under this head historical and genealogical memoranda will be furnished the readers of the News that appears worthy of preservation, particularly of remote periods in our history within the city limits and immediate vicinity.]

ABIZER HOWARD.

AN OLD AND RESPECTED NAME AT MORRILL'S CORNER.

Abizer Howard was born in the town of Randolph, Norfolk County, Mass., 1764. Of his parents or youth we have no knowledge. Mr. Arthur P. Howard, of Portland, it is said, is collecting names and dates for a Howard genealogy. He may be able to supply the omissions we make.

Oct. 9, 1789, Mr. Howard, "gentleman," purchased fifty acres of land located in the town of Buckfield, this State, for which he paid $421.67. As his second child was born in 1791, July 25, it is reasonable to suppose he was a man with a family of two small children when he went to Buckfield. In Buckfield he remained nineteen years, when, in 1810, he came to what is now known as the Morrill's Corner district of our city, retaining the record appellation of "gentleman."

There was but one house then at what is now known as Morrill's which stood on the northerly side of Stevens Plains avenue a very little southerly of the Portland and Rochester railroad crossing; but the house has no record history other than that of a brief notice; its history is that of tradition.

It appears that on the 6th day of May, 1811, a highway was laid out, "beginning near Widow Bishop's house at a point in the middle of the road," thence running south, etc., to a small bridge between Morse's (he kept a public house where Saunders street joins Forest avenue) and Woodfords. (A bridge a little southerly of Saunders street, at this date, would be a curious sight; yet it seems there was one.) Capt. Isaac S. Stevens and his son, Zachariah B. Stevens, being dissatisfied petitioned for a sherriff's jury to consider the award for land damage, and the jury met in the month of August, 1813, at the residence of Bela Shaw, who reported the road "inexpedient and ought to be discontinued."

Bela Shaw married June 30, 1811, with Hannah Doughty of Allen's Corner and was a cousin (we think) of Alpheus Shaw, who came here from Paris, this state, and married with Jane Doughty, sister to Hannah, Alpheus keeping shop at Allen's and Bela at Morrill's Corner, who built and resided in the two-story house now standing in the point made by the junction of Forest with Stevens Plains avenue, where the late Dr. Alexander M. Parker resided, his shop standing in front of the dwelling, removed to the westerly side of Forest avenue next southerly of the engine house and now known as Bailey's paint shop.

In the year 1798, Joshua Racklyf of Newburyport, shipwright, and his brother Benjamin, of the the same place, rigger, owned 105 acres of land fronting on the westerly side of Stevens Plains and Forest avenues which they state they received from their father who obtained it of Phineas Jones by deed dated May 15, 1738. The northerly part of this 105 acre lot went to Zachariah Sawyer, who built the dwelling as now observed on Forest avenue, a little northwesterly of the "Corner," standing back from the road. So in the absence of record proof we will settle down to the belief that the Widow Bishop lived in the Racklyf house. Connected with her advent is a tradition that at the time of the burning of Portland by Mowatt, Oct. 18, 1775, she came here bringing her effects on a wheelbarrow and took possession of the empty house—the only house of the place—the residence of George Berry, Jr., being the nearest, who resided on the southerly side of Stevens Plains avenue, easterly of the "Corner," where the late David Torrey resided.

Nov. 29, 1792 one George Walker (supposed by us to have been born northwesterly of Prides' bridge, Westbrook) was united in marriage with Elizabeth Bailey born Dec. 19, 1773, daughter of Dea. James Bailey, who resided on Forest avenue, northerly of the "Corner." (See News of Jan. 26, 1895.)

Ebenezer Hilton Sawyer, who was a shoe maker, married with Rebecca, daughter of Geo. Berry, Jr., and had two children, Jeremiah, the eldest, becoming the father to our aged and much esteemed citizen, Mr. Nathaniel K. Sawyer, residing now on the Plains. The husband of Rebecca died as did the wife of Ebenezer H. and then Ebenezer H. Sawyer united in marriage with the Widow Walker and removed to Otisfield where six more children were born.

Mr. Sawyer built a one story, low posted, large house, four rooms on the ground, with a large chimney in the center, and a shoe maker's shop on the land of his wife's father as now seen, minus the chimney and shop, with a two story ell added, situated where it was originally built on the southeasterly side of the curve made by Stevens Plains avenue at the "Corner."

In the year of 1799 for the small sum of $186 Geo. Berry, Jr., conveyed 18½ acres of land where the house stood to his brother-in-law, Ebenezer H. Sawyer, and in 1809 for $92 nine acres additional. This same year Sawyer sold thirty acres of land, dwelling house and other buildings to Zach. B. Stevens for $1,300—hence his objection to the location of the road from Morrill's and Woodford's as noticed in the foregoing.

In 1810, Abizer Howard of Buckfield came to the part of Falmouth now the Morrill's Corner district of Deering, and purchased of Mr. Stevens nineteen acres of the Sawyer property, with buildings, and paid $1,200.

Upon this lot Mr. Howard prosecuted the vacation of a farmer and speculated in land and other ways. For a "shop" he was in 1815 taxed on a valuation of $15—evidently Mr. Sawyer's shoemaker's shop, and a house on a valuation of $250.

So Mr. Abizer Howard is entitled, so far as we are able to learn from records, to the title of "pioneer" as refers to Morrill's Corner and its immediate surroundings.

In the rear part of the old cemetery located between Morrill's Corner and Riverton, may be seen two large slate memorial slabs inscribed as follows:

ABIZER HOWARD,
Died
Feb. 20, 1834,
Æt. 70 years.

SALLY,
Wife of
ABIZER HOWARD.
Died
April 28, 1848,
Æt. 82 years.

TO BE CONTINUED.

THE DEERING NEWS.

Saturday, Sept. 24, 1898.

GRANDPA'S SCRAP BOOK

[Under this head historical and genealogical memoranda will be furnished the readers of the News that appears worthy of preservation, particularly of remote periods in our history within the city limits and immediate vicinity.]

OLIVER BUCKLEY.

AN EARLY RESIDENT UPON STEVENS PLAINS AND DESCENDANTS.

(Continued from last week.)

Near the middle of the westerly side of Pine Grove cemetery is a white marble monument inscribed as follows:

ALFRED STEVENS
Sept. 3, 1801.
Sept. 9, 1884.

LIEUT. ORIN B. STEVENS,
Co. F 5th Regt. Me. Vols., wounded in battle at Spotsylvania, May 12, died at Fredricksburg, Va., May 17. 1861.
Æ 34

Writing home he said: If I die it is in a good cause. I do not think it matters whether the blossom be rudely blown from the tree or simply withers and falls—the fruit followeth in due season.

EMELINE,
wife of
Lieut. O. B. Stevens
died July 28, 1856,
Æ 22.
Affectionate and kind.

MARIA D. MOSES,
wife of
E. C. Stevens,
March 30, 1843.
Feb. 13, 1889

MINNIE F.,
wife of
Andrew J. Forbes,
Died Feb. 16, 1861,
Aged 26 years.

EMMA.

2—Mary Ann, b. June 2. 1808, m. Oct. 18, 1826, William Partridge, b. Oct. 2, 1800, d. Sept. 28, 1829, One child, b. May 14, 1828, d. Dec. 25, same year. Mr. Partridge was a tinman and resided on the Plains.

The widow m. second, July 1, 1835, Freeman Porter, b. Colebrook, N. H., July 9, 1808; went from there to Stratford, then came to the part of Falmouth now known as Stevens Plains. He was a tinman, engaging largely in the manufacture, and was a much respected citizen. His business history is the same as all the manufacturers of the tin business of the Plains.

The widow now occupies the homestead of her first husband which became that of her second, situated on the westerly side of the main avenue of the locality, and is the first residence northerly of the cemetery main entrance, but has been considerably enlarged

CHILDREN:

I—Thressa Ellen, b. June 28, 1836, d. Jan. 19, 1846.
II—Samuel B., b. Apr. 16, 1840, d. Sep. 2, 1868.

3—Capt. Charles Sumner, b. Apr. 11, 1811, m. Apr. 18, 1833, Laura Jane Stevens, second child of William Stevens and wife Sally Bailey, the family record of both of whom having appeared in the News. She was b. Apr. 4, 1814, d. Dec. 13, 1852 at Augusta, this State, where he was in the tin ware and stove trade. From Augusta he removed after the death of his wife to Chicago, Ill., and there departed this life,

I—Laura A., b. Apr. 23, 1834, d. Oct. 29 1880. Married Edward Sampson.
II—Charles M., m. resided first in Boston, now in the State of N. H.
III—Henry, died in N. Y. unmarried.
IV—Charles Lawrence, Jr., d. unmarried.
V—Frederick H., d. Apr. 8, 1844, aged 4 m.

CHILDREN.

1—Frederick J. Stevens, b, Sept. 1866 Traveling Salesman for St. Louis Stamping Co., married in 1892. Leontine, daughter of C. J. Farrington, Esq., of Woodfords.
2—Philip H. Stevens, b, March 1868., Jeweler, resides at Bristol, Conn., m, in 1893, Hallie, daughter of Hon. Henry L. Beach of that place.
3—Ervin G. Stevens, b, August, 1871; is in employ of Maine Central R. R., Union Station, Portland. Resides at Portland.
4—Martha G. Stevens, b. Dec. 1874. Resides at Portland.
II—Frank Melvin, b, Nov. 25, 1846. m, in the Western country, d, at Augusta, this state, 1888. Memorial stone in Pine Grove cemetery. No issue.

5.—Edward William, b. Jan. 11, 1816, d. Oct. 23. 1824.

6 and last—Edward Melvin, b. Dec. 20, 1825, m. April 1848, Adeline B. Woodford, b. in Morrill's Corner district, Aug. 29, 1826. daughter of Joseph Woodford and wife Eliza Knight. She is a sister to the wife of Mr. Wm. Pitt Stevens, whose name appeared in the News of last week. (For an extended notice of this Woodford family see News of May 18, 1895.)

He resides in the homestead of his father that is located on the easterly side of Stevens Plains avenue, opposite the main entrance to Evergreen cemetery. Retired from active business.

CHILDREN.

I—Alice C., b. Nov. 12, 1848, m. Edward A. Bernell, son of the late Ferdinand Bernell of Woodfords district, who died suddenly while holding the office of town clerk.
II—Mary A., b. Sept. 13, 1853, m. as shown above.
III—Ralph, b. Nov. 13, 1859, m. ——. Resides at Leeds.
IV—Gertrude, b. Oct. 12, 1865, m. Henry W. Hackett. Resides on Old Town house road, Westbrook.
V—Ernest Lynn, b. Apr. 7, 1867. Resides with his parents.
VI—Herbert, resides in Oregon, married.
VII—Sarah J. m. March 5, 1885, William H. Roberts, res. in Portland where she died.
VIII—Ralph E. d. Sep. 5, 1851, aged 7 mo.

4—Oren, b. Feb. 13, 1814, m. March 29, 1834, Martha Ann, dau. of William Hicks. He d. Feb. 19, 1852. Her memorial stone in Pine Grove says: "1816-1870." Two children—Sophia Alberteen and Frank Melvin.

I—Sophia Alberteen, b, Feb. 22, 1844, m., July 27, 1863; Frank G. Stevens, b, Dec.25, 1840.

(For his place in the Stevens family see Deering News, Feb. 9, 1895.)

He enlisted in the Union Army in the spring of 1862, in Co. E, Capt. Elisha Newcomb, 25th Maine Regt., Col. Fessenden, promoted to 2nd Lieut. in December, 1862, mustered out in fall of 1863.

Engaged in business with his brothers Augustus E. and Granville M. (A. E. Stevens & Co.) Portland, until 1875, then he entered the employ of the New York & New England R. R. as traveling agent. Elected Register of Deeds for County of Cumberland, in fall of 1877 for five years; returned to the railroad business in employ of Maine Central R. R., where he now holds position in office of Wm. W. Colby, General Auditor.

THE DEERING NEWS.

Saturday, Oct. 8, 1898.

GRANDPA'S SCRAP BOOK

[Under this head historical and genealogical memoranda will be furnished the readers of the News that appears worthy of preservation, particularly of remote periods in our history within the city limits and immediate vicinity.]

ABIZER HOWARD.

AN OLD AND RESPECTED NAME AT MORRILL'S CORNER.

(Continued from last week.)

Abizer Howard and wife Sally had one daughter and seven sons born to them, but in the absence of a record of dates of births we do not claim that the following is correct as to time in arrangement. The names were as follows: 1—Sally; 2—Simeon; 3—Thomas; 4—Abner; 5—Hiram; 6—Zebulon; 7—Chas.

1—Sally, d. young.

2—Simeon, b. July 25, 1791; m. Jan. 18, 1811, Tryphosa Bowker, b. in Paris, this state, August 18, 1790, second child of James Bowker, a Swede, who settled in that town about 1787, and Judith Chase, his wife. They had twelve children. (See history of that town.)

Simeon was a shoemaker and after residing a year in Paris, came to Morrill's Corner, and in 1828 built a house on the easterly side of Forest avenue—now opposite the hose house—where his son-in-law, Mr. Francis O. J. Bodge and family resides, the house having undergone some changes by Mr. Bodge. They were an industrious, frugal couple and the parents of nine children. She d. Feb. 22, 1861; he, March 17, 1870. Monument and memorial stones in Pine Grove cemetery.

CHILDREN.

I. Rosetta J., b. March 16, 1812, m. Sept. 16, 1834, Wm. R. Humphrey. His mother was a sister to the wife of Oliver Buckley and also to the wife of Abizer Howard, Jr. They had three sons. She d. in Yarmouth April 15, 1852, where he was born and where they resided.

II. Sarah, b. Nov. 22, 1838, m. Wm. H. Small

THE SMALL FAMILY.

Atkins Small was born on Cape Cod, Mass., Nov. 7, 1784. Martha, his wife, was born Oct. 30, 1788. He came to Cape Elizabeth and resided where the Cape Cottage was afterwards built. From there he removed to Dutton district of the town of Gray. June 20, 1807, Elisha Small of Gray conveyed land to Atkins Small of that town.

CHILDREN.

1 George, b. Oct. 16, 1808, d. June 4, 1828.
2 Nathaniel, b. Apr. 8, 1810, d. Apr. 29, 1836.
3 William H. b. Sept. 24, 1813. At Morrill's Corner he acquired the vocation of a tanner. Sept. 18, 1837, he purchased the large two story brick house standing at East Deering which is the first house on the westerly side of Main street as it is entered upon from the bridge that connects with Portland, for which he paid $1,075. Nov. 13, 1838, he united in marriage with Miss Sarah Howard, noticed above as born March 22, 1814, and with his bride commenced housekeeping in the brick house where he has ever since resided. On the opposite side of the highway, a little northerly of Veranda street, he purchased land and started a tannery of his own, at the same time converting his dwelling into an inn, the large building in the rear of the house as now seen being built for a stable. At the opening of the Atlantic and St. Lawrence railroad the house was closed as an inn.

Atkins Small sold his place in Gray and moved here and was "lock tender" where the Portland & Oxford canal passed through Dole's woods near Stroudwater, making his home winters with his son Wm. H. Small. The compiler with other boys of the village were often chased by Atkins and his assistants for changing the flow of water, and the last deed of vandalism of which we recollect was the rolling down the embankment of a small building into the canal called a "shanty," located about a fourth of a mile westerly of the main "shanty" where Atkins resided. It took several fence rails to accomplish the enterprise and six or seven lads on the ends of the rails when in position. The building stood on land owned by Samuel Mason.

Wm. H.'s is deceased. Memorial stones in Pine Grove cemetery.

CHILDREN OF WM. H. SMALL.

a Mary Ellen, b. Aug. 9, 1839, d. Sept. 12, 1864.
b Lucinda P., b. Feb. 14, 1841, d. May— 1846.
c William H., Jr., b. Sept. 14, 1847, m. and resides under the parental roof.
d Benjamin F. &
 Emma J., b. Jan. 4, 1850, twins. He d. 1850. She d. Feb. 11, 1878.

III Charles Howard, b. May 9, 1815, m. April 21, 1839, Caroline Weeks of Standish, and had ten children, one of whom died Sept. 10, 1847, aged 2 yr., 3 m., has a memorial grave stone in the cemetery northwesterly of Morrill's corner. He d. a fourth of a mile northerly of Woodfords, by occupation a mason, Sept. 1, 1866.

IV Mary A. b., Feb. 21, 1820 m. March 26, 1844, John L. Lovell of North Yarmouth. He d.; She m. 2nd Benj. Chadsey, resides next to the Free church building Steven's Plains avenue. No issue

V James B., b. May 9, 1824, went to California, and is supposed by his relatives to have left the world unmarried.

VI Maria F., b. August 14, 1827, m. Jan. 7, 1848, James E. Day of Woburn, Mass., where he d.; she at Morrill's Corner.

VII William H., b. Sept. 30, 1830, m. March 25, 1854, Mary J. H., dau. of Gardner Bacon of Westbrook. Two

SONS.

VIII Martha E. and.
IX Franklin S., b. Jan. 9, 1832, twins. Franklin d. young; Martha E., m. Jan. 7, 1848, Francis O. J. Bodge (sometimes called Franklin) of Windham.

THE BODGE FAMILY.

Thomas Bodge, Jr., was b. on Canada Hill, Windham, July 11, 1812, son of Thomas Bodge and Abigail Nason his wife, b. Great Falls, Gorham, Nov. 2, 1809, daughter of Joseph Nason. He d. Windham, Feb. 20, 1890, she Feb. 27, 1892, Westbrook, while visiting a daughter.

CHILDREN.

I Frances F. O. J. Bodge, b. Feb. 10, 1835. m. as above indicated.
II Joseph G., May 22, 1836.
III Louisa M., Aug. 11, 1838.
IV William A., March 10, 1839.
V Elbridge S., Feb. 19, 1840.
VI Elizabeth Ellen, Jan. 9, 1843.
VII Emily Jane, May 22, 1845.
VIII Abbie M., June 16, 1847.
IX James A. Feb. 1, 1848.
X Aurelia A., Nov. 9, 1849.
XI Andrew T., Oct. 13, 1851.
XII and last—Dayton, Oct. 1, 1853.

3 Abizer Jr., b. March 9, 1793, m. July 1, 1818, Ann Reed, b. Sept. 5, 1795, a sister to the wife of Oliver Buckley, recently noticed in three issues of the News. He resided under the parental roof and at the decease of his father came into possession of the homestead. He engaged in comb manufacturing and farm work and speculated somewhat in real estate.

In the old cemetery located northwesterly of Morrill's Corner may be seen two slate memorial slabs inscribed as follows:

ABIZER HOWARD.
Died
Feb. 16, 1846,
Æt. 53.

Long shall his memory be revered,
By those who knew his worth,
By those to whom he was endeared,
By strongest ties of earth.

ANNA
Wife of
ABIZER HOWARD
Died Nov. 29, 1844,
Æt. 51.

Dearest wife thou hast left us,
Here thy loss we deeply feel,
But 'tis God that hath bereft us
He can all our sorrows heal.

TO BE CONTINUED.

THE DEERING NEWS.

Saturday, Oct. 15, 1898.

GRANDPA'S SCRAP BOOK

[Under this head historical and genealogical memoranda will be furnished the readers of the News that appears worthy of preservation, particularly of remote periods in our history within the city limits and immediate vicinity.]

ABIZER HOWARD.

AN OLD AND RESPECTED NAME AT MORRILL'S CORNER.

(Continued from last week.)

Abizer Howard, Junior, son of Abizer and Sally Howard, had but two children, as follows:

I—Oliver Buckley Howard, b. May 14, 1819, m. Miss Ellen Moore, reared in a family in the town of Falmouth, residing near the First Congregational meeting house where Moses H. Merrill was a member. She d. Oct. 25, 1868, aged 48 years.

They had but one child, named Ellen. When Rev. Geo. W. Bicknell was a student at Westbrook Seminary he boarded in the family of Mr. Howard, and "friendship, love and marriage" was one of the outcomes. She died Jan. 14, 1865, aged 23 years and 24 days, whose death was much lamented by a large circle of friends. She left two children, one died young, the other, named George Edward, is married and resides in Lynn, Mass., who tips the beam with the pea at the 275 notch. The Rev. has his third wife, and is one of the ablest pulpit orators of the New England Universalist denomination.

At the death of his father Oliver B. Howard come into possession of the homestead and still resides under the parental roof—a roof that has afforded shelter more than a century. He has led a quiet life, though an active man. Commencing manhood as a shoemaker he soon thereafter engaged in trade as a groceryman in a shop standing near his house which was burned some thirty years since, and connected with his shop was a lumber yard. Then he started a successful razor strop manufactory which was closed only a short time since on account of the advanced age of the proprietor.

II—Louisa S., b. Oct. 29, 1821, m. Sept. 28, 1843, Moses H. Merrill alluded to in the foregoing. She died April 17, 1844, aged 22 years and 6 months. He went to Lowell, Mass., where he married the second time. By the side of those of her father and mother stands a memorial slate slab inscribed as follows, the sentiment of the quotation, it is claimed, being correct in every particular:

LOUISA S.,
wife of
MOSES H. MERRILL,
Died
Apr. 17, 1844,
Æt. 22 yrs. 6 mo.

Her life was gentle, and serene, her mind,
Her morals pure, and every action just;
A wife most dear, a friend, a daughter kind,
As such she lies lamented in the dust.

4—Thomas, m. Dec. 29, 1825, Mary Ann Ayers of Portland. He was a tinsmith and resided in the one-story house standing in the southeasterly angle made by the Portland and Rochester railroad crossing, Forest avenue, Morrills Corner. No children.

5—Abner, m. Ann Pomeroy of Falmouth. He was a tinsmith in Portland, where he had a shop and a good trade.

CHILDREN.

I—Sarah Ann, b. July 15, 1819.
II—Mary Elizabeth, Oct. 7, 1820.
III—Edward Buckley, Oct. 2, 1824.
IV—Clorendo, Oct. 7, 1827.
V—John Lane, June 29, 1830.
VI—Abner Franklin, Aug. 30, 1834.
VII—William Runnels, June 7, 1842.

The first was born in Saco, the rest in Portland. There may have been others born after the last recorded.

6—Hiram H., m. Leonora McDonald of the eastern part of Maine; was a tinsmith and engaged in business with his brother Abner. In 1848 he purchased of James Creddiford the small house that fronted on the Brighton road at Brighton Corner district, being next easterly from the Nelson Leighton house in which Mr. Sumner Libby now resides, which Hiram H. sold, July 9, 1866, to Mrs. Sarah M. Bridges of Lubec for $1,100, where she and a daughter kept shop several years in a building that stood in front of the dwelling house. Mrs. Howard died in Falmouth, May 10, 1873, aged 63 years; he died at Morrill's Corner, Dec. 7, 1889, aged 83 years, 10 m. Memorial stones in Pine Grove cemetery.

CHILDREN.

I—George B., b. March 14, 1830, d. Dec. 10, 1850
II—Sarah E., Apr. 6, 1833.
III—Emeline G., Dec. 15, 1834.
IV—Leonard, July 3, 1836.
V—Thomas H., Sept. 29, 1838.
VI—Albert S., July 4, 1840.
VII—Augustus, April 12, 1843.

These were born in Portland, and there may have been others after the last named. Three of the sons, we are told, married three sisters by the name of Roberts of Cape Elizabeth.

7—Zebulon, m. Lucy Allen and resided at Cape Cod, Mass. In 1823 he paid a tax of forty cents, the amount assessed upon the poll of every voter in the town, towards supporting preaching in the First Congregational meeting house located near Bradley's Corner, and there is no record evidence that he "kicked."

8 and last—Charles, died young.

The old Sawyer-Howard house has had sometime in late years, a large two story ell added, and is now successfully used as an inn, Mrs. Fred Boucher, proprietor, assisted by her daughters, who also conduct a first class livery stable. In the house the Deering News may be found on file.

Under the roof of his father and that of his grandfather Mr. Oliver B. Howard still resides and is kindly cared for, having nearly reached the 80th milestone in life's journey. And—

"Now let the merriest tales be told,
And let the sweetest songs be sung
That ever makes the old heart young."

[CORRECTIONS. In the closing part of the first paragraph of my article of last week, which commences thus: "The names were as follows: The name of Abizer Howard, Jr., which should have occupied the third place, was by an oversight left out, hence the numbers in the paragraph are wrong, which, to be correct, should be as follows: 1—Sally; 2—Simeon; 3—Abizer, Jr.; 4—Thomas; 5—Abner; 6—Hiram; 7—Zebulon; 8 and last—Charles.

Where it is stated that Sarah, daughter of Simeon Howard, was born "Nov. 22, 1838," and married Wm. H. Small, the year is wrong; it should be 1813.

At the close of the notice of Wm. H. Small, where it says—"Wm. H.'s is decreased," it should read, Wm. H.'s wife is deceased. He is hale and hearty in his 85th year.

In this connection we desire to state, in answer to a question, that the residence of Mr. Small was built in the year 1796 by Thomas Sawyer, son of Anthony. He was a mariner, and was born easterly of Lunt's Corner. Of this ancient abode, the oldest of East Deering, we propose to speak in the near future.]

THE DEERING NEWS.

Saturday, Oct. 22, 1898.

GRANDPA'S SCRAP BOOK

[Under this head historical and genealogical memoranda will be furnished the readers of the News that appears worthy of preservation, particularly of remote periods in our history within the city limits and immediate vicinity.]

PAUL REVERE, SENIOR.

NAMES OF SOME OF HIS DESCENDANTS HERE AND ELSEWHERE.

BY LEONARD B. CHAPMAN.

Paul Revere (Rivoire in French) was born in St. Foy, France, Nov. 5, 1702, and was united in marriage, June 19, 1729, with Deborah Hichborn, born in Boston, Jan. 25, 1704, to which place he had emigrated and established himself in business as a silversmith and engraver. He died July 22, 1754.

CHILDREN:

1—John, b Jan. 10, 1729, and died young.
2—Deborah, Feb. 21, 1731.
3—*Paul, Jr.*, Dec 21, 1734.
4—Francis, Jan., 19. 1736.
5—Twins—died young.
6—Thomas, Jan. 10, 1739.
7—John, Oct. 2, 1741.
8—Twins—*Mary* and Elizabeth, July 10, 1743, Elizabeth d. 20th same month.
9 and last—Elizabeth, b. Jan. 10, 1745.

PAUL REVERE, JR.

"There are plenty to pause and wait,
But here was a man who set his feet
Sometimes in advance of fate."

Who Paul Revere, Jr., married, we cannot here state. He was a man of energy and one upon whom the confidence of the community was bestowed. He was a patriotic night rider at the commencement of the Revolutionary war in which struggle he played an important part. Our Longfellow has assisted in immortalizing his name in a poem of great merit. The story of his hanging the lantern in the meeting house tower is a familiar story. He was one of the 1773 "Boston Tea Party." He engraved the plates, having adopted the calling of his father, from which the first Continental money, now so highly prized by holders, was made. He manufactured powder for the American Patriots. When the purpose of the British to destroy stores at Concord and Lexington was discovered he was chosen as one to carry the information to those places and to advise the people by the wayside to resist. Upon the return of peace he enlarged his business by establishing at Canton, Mass., buildings where cannon were made, church bells cast and copper rolled into sheets. He died in Boston May. 10, 1818, aged 83 years. Among us are many descendants of the elder Paul, one of whom is our much esteemed Walter F. Goodrich, who has a much worn and highly prized heavy silver table spoon made by his ancestor which bears upon the back of the handle in plain letters the word REVERE, and on the front the monogram AMB.

To Mr. Goodrich we are indebted for much of the valuable records we present. Besides the family of his father, Walter B. Goodrich, the Dea. Ebeneza D. Woodford, Samuel B. Stevens and Jesse D. Alden families are branches of the Revere "genealogical tree," members of all of which are still residing among us, and most truly they have played important parts in the drama of life upon the Plains and Woodfords districts of our town.

Mary Revere (No. 8 in the foregoing) twin, who was born July 10, 1743, united in marriage with Edward Rose, an Englishman.

CHILDREN.

I.—Mary, b Dec. 21, 1765, m Caleb Frances.
II.—Sarah, b 1772, m Thomas Brisco, who settled on what is now "a jewelled elm tree avenue" of our city. (He and wife to be noticed later on.)
III.—Philip, printer, d in Boston, Mass., March, 1800, aged 28 years. There may have been and undoubtedly were other children.

Mrs. Mary (Revere) Rose m second, Alexander Baker of Boston, Mass., hence the monogram on the Revere spoon.

In the Copp's Hill cemetery of Boston were standing at last advices memorial stones inscribed as follows:

In memory of Mr. Alexander Baker, who died May 22, 1801, aged 72 years; born March 1, 1729.

In memory of Mrs. Mary Baker, who died Dec. 27, 1801, aged 59 years.

Caleb Frances* was born March 3, 1766, and the memoranda from which we copy, says: "came to Sterling, Mass., to live Oct. 25. 1787,"—married Mary Rose, May 10, 1789, daughter of Edward Rose, the Englishman. She d Sept. 20, 1804, aged 38 years, 9 mo.

*[Caleb Frances was son of Nathaniel and Phebe Francis. He d Feb. 16, 1812, aged 80 years; She, Dec. 28, 1806, aged 75 years.]

CHILDREN.

I.—Mary Frances, b Dec. 20, 1789, m Jan 16, 1805. Dea. Ebeneza D. Woodford. (For his family record see News of August 18, 1894.)
II.—Harriet, b Feb. 24, 1795, died Oct. 12, 1887. She made her home in the family of Samuel B. Stevens.
III—Isabel, b. May 22, 1797, m. May 8, 1820, Jesse Dunbar Alden. (To be noticed later on.)
IV—Sally, b. Nov. 11, 1799, m. Oct. 17, 1821, Samuel B. Stevens. (For his record see News of Feb. 9, 1895, also News of Sept. 17, 1898.)
V—Maria, b. Aug. 25, 1804, m. May 24. 1828, Walter B. Goodrich. (To be noticed later on.)

When the mother of these, five daughters departed this life the youngest was less than a month old and it is traditional that Miss Mary Frances and young Mr. Ebenezer D. Woodford met for the first time on the stage coach plying between the state of Connecticut and Falmouth, now Deering, on the way hither and there weighed each other's love in

God's balance watched over by angels.

He became successful in business and a deacon of the First Congregational church here and she the mother of a large family of Woodfords. The house in which they spent their married lives is the one that was raised from the ground last year the height of a story and one of brick added, on Woodford street.

But we cannot speak individually of these five sisters, removed from the parental roof to that of their Aunt Brisco, where they, as fast as they ripened into young womanhood, displayed the characteristics of their ancestor, Revere, as designers with pencil and brush upon the merchandise of their uncle Brisco, which was japaned tinware which he sold from a peddle cart, specimens of their work in youth and of more elaborate work in old age still being in existence. In one row they sleep the sleep in Pine Grove cemetery that knows no awakening.

TO BE CONTINUED,

THE DEERING NEWS.

Saturday, Oct. 29, 1898.

GRANDPA'S SCRAP BOOK

[Under this head historical and genealogical memoranda will be furnished the readers of the News that appears worthy of preservation, particularly of remote periods in our history within the city limits and immediate vicinity.]

PAUL REVERE, SENIOR,

NAMES OF SOME OF HIS DESCENDANTS HERE AND ELSEWHERE.

BY LEONARD B. CHAPMAN.

(Continued from last week.)

Thomas Brisco who married Sarah Rose, referred to in our first article under this caption, is noticed in his business relationship upon the first record we find of him hereabouts as a "merchant." What brought him hither from the state of Connecticut to the Plains district of our city does not appear. He was a peddler and the driver of his own horse and cart. His goods consisted of Japanned tin ware, japanned and ornamented by his wife, aided later by the five orphan nieces who have been noticed. Undoubtedly he was the first tin-ware manufacturer and peddler of the Plains. The exact time of his coming does not appear. Of business qualifications his wife was the superior. July 31, 1803, he is noticed for the first time as having bought of Capt. Isaac S. Stevens 1 1-4 acres of land where his house is alluded to for the first time, for which he paid $75. He may have built it or the North Brothers may have done so, which we can't say.

In 1815 he was taxed on a valuation as follows:
1 House $250.00.
1 Barn $20.00.
1 1-4 Mowing and tillage land, $22.00.
2 Unimproved acres at $7 per acre.
1 Cow $14.00.
1 Horse $40.00.

May 7, 1819 he conveyed the lot "on which I now live" and buildings to Ebenezer D. Woodford, his brother-in-law, for $800 paid who turned all over to Sally Brisco, wife of Thomas for the same sum.

In the Windham road cemetery stands a memorial slate slab inscribed as follows:

IN MEMORY OF
MRS SALLY BRISCO
who died Aug. 1, 1822,
Æt. 50.

Thine honor shall forever be
The business of our days,
Forever, shall our thankful tongues
Speak thy deserved praise.

From the Portland Argus of August 6. 1822 we copy the following:

"In Westbrook (now Deering) the 1st inst., Mrs. Sally Brisco, aged 50. In the death of Mrs. Brisco a husband is left to mourn the loss of a kind and faithful wife, five adopted children a tender and indulgent parent relatives, neighbors and acquaintances a true and worthy friend. The poor and distressed smiled at her approach—the friendless and the orphan found an asylum with her, for, on all occasions, she done unto others as she would that others should do unto her. Wherever she was known she was universally beloved and esteemed. It truly may be said of her that for industry and punctuality, economy and frugality none surpassed her."

But wher's the passage to the skies?
The road through death's black valley lies,
O, do not shudder at the tale
Though dark the way yet straight the vale.

Tradition indicates that the words of the obituary are fitting and it affords us pleasure to reproduce them, and so place that they may be more generally known and their total loss prevented

Of Thomas we have no more memoranda than we have presented in the foregoing. The time of his departure from earth we have not learned.

The Brisco house was a two story building, hipped roof and stood upon land now used as a part of the ornamental grounds of the main entrance to Evergreen cemetery—southerly side thereof.

The place was sold to a son of Enoch Burnham, whose son was a cabinet maker, Enoch being noticed some weeks since in the News as a clock maker, but he failed to pay for the place.

Then an attempt was made to make it the parsonage of the Universalist society of the town, and on the 5th day of May, 1841, the heirs of Mrs. Brisco for a consideration of $500 to be paid in shares of $10 to $20 each conveyed the property to

Rufus Dunham,
Jeremiah Bedell,
Rufus Merrill,
Zach. B. Stevens,
Amos Abbott,
Amos Fobes,
Geo. Libby,
Isaac Johnson,
Samuel Jordan,
Wm. P. Walker,
J. C. Brackett,

Rev. Zenas Thompson then occupied the place, but the bottom fell out of the scheme and the place went back to the original owners, or heirs to Mrs. Brisco.

May 3, 1857, the heirs sold it to Benj. W. Ballard for $500. In 1863, Walter B. Goodrich, acting in the capacity of administrator upon the estate of Mr. Ballard, deceased, sold it to Mr. Granville M. Stevens for $1,975, and he and brother Frank G. built the "twin houses"—one of which now stands—which buildings for some years were the "pride of the town."

To make room for the Stevens' houses the Brisco domicile was sold to Mr. Edward Newman who removed the structure to High street where it may now be seen on the westerly side thereof and the first from the corner house on Spring street.

The church circle of the "parsonage" time has not only been severed but annihilated; the home gatherings at the Brisco residence none remember, and,

"We turn the pages that they read,
Their written words we linger o'er,
But in the sun they cast no shade
No voice is heard, no sigh is made."

TO BE CONTINUED.

Saturday, Nov. 5, 1898.

GRANDPA'S SCRAP BOOK

[Under this head historical and genealogical memoranda will be furnished the readers of the News that appears worthy of preservation, particularly of remote periods in our history within the city limits and immediate vicinity.]

PAUL REVERE, SENIOR.

NAMES OF SOME OF HIS DESCENDANTS HERE AND ELSEWHERE.

BY LEONARD B. CHAPMAN.

CONTINUED FROM LAST WEEK.

Of the place of birth, early life, or what induced Jesse Dunbar Alden (later known as Major because he was an officer in the militia) to come to the Plains district of our city I have no knowledge. In the year 1815 Messrs. Shaw and Alden were taxed on a valuation as follows: One house and store, $450; one shed, $20; one and one-fourth acres of land, $50; stock in trade. $350; one horse, $40; one cow, $14 and one chaise, $30.

In the possession of his grandson, Mr. Geo. F. Alden, is a memorandum that reads as follows:

I—John Alden,   } Came over in the
   Priscilla Mullins. } May Flower in 1620.
II—Joseph Alden, }
    Mary Simmons. }
III—John Alden, }
     Hannah White. }
IV—David Alden, }
    Judith Paddeford. }
V—Dea. David Alden, }
   Rhoda Leach. }
VI—Caleb Alden, }
    Susannah Dunbar. }
VII—Major Jesse D. Alden, }
     Isabella B. Frances. }
VIII—Alpheus S. Alden, }
      Elizabeth E. Stevens. }
IX—George F. Alden.

This paper was prepared by Alpheus S. Alden, who departed this life a year or more ago, but his sources of information is not known to us.

Whatever else may be said of the Major he was slack in making records or his work is placed beyond recovery. His sword, an account book, and one of Enoch Burnham's "long clocks" and a few other minor articles are all that remains in the homestead residence of his personal effects, which is located on the westerly side of Stevens Plains avenue, the first building southerly of the entrance to the Morrill's Corner grammar school building and which is a one-story structure.

The earliest dates in the old account book are in the spring time of 1819. We will give a sample of what one family subsisted upon at that time on the Plains:

Sept. 11, 1819. To 1 gal. rum,
3 1-2 lbs. cheese, $1.69

" 14. To 1 qt. rum, 3 1, lb. sugar, 1-4 lb. tea,   0.79
" 16. To 1 gal. molasses, 1 lb. sugar,   0.67
" 18. To 1-2 gal. rum,   0.63
" 20. To 22 lbs. flour, 1-2 gal. rum,   1.63
" 21. To 22 lbs. flour, 1 1-2 gal. rum,   2.87
" 23. To 1-4 Hyson tea, 31c, 1 lb. coffee,   0.65
" 25. To 2 lbs. sugar, 1-2 gal. rum, 1 qt. oil,   1.22
" 26. To 1 qt. rum,   0.31
" 28. To 22 lbs flour,   1.00
" 30. To rum, sugar and tea,   1.13
Oct. 4. To 2 doz. edge plates,   1.50
" " To 22 lbs. flour,   1.00
" 5. To Sundry goods training day,   13.32

At the time Major Alden was in trade intoxicants were common articles of traffic and of common use, every shop keeping a supply. We present the foregoing to show the difference then and now in the traffic, and the change as regards the use.

The "goods" went to a house that stood on the Plains, and the foregoing is just as the account runs.

The Major was a trader and his shop stood, after he left Shaw, where the building stands which is the third one from the Portland and Rochester railroad track, southerly, and easterly side of Stevens Plains avenue at Morrills, which was removed about the year 1870. Three dollars were paid then for 1/2 ton of hay, 75 cents per day for a man, man and yoke of oxen $1.50 per day.

Jesse Dunbar Alden was of a military turn of mind. While dressed in his regimentals and mounted on a prancing steed at Woodfords he was observed by his prospective wife, who was visiting then her sister Woodford. It was a case of love and languishment at first sight, and on the 8th day of May 1820, Miss Isabel Frances and Maj. Alden were united in marriage by Parson Bradley. And—

"They lived a true poetry."

He was born in 1790; she May 22, 1799, as we have shown in a previous article. He died May 26, 1835, aged 45 years; she died May 15, 1862, aged 65 years. Walter B. Goodrich administered on the estate.

CHILDREN.

1—Sarah Rose, b. Aug. 9, 1822, m. George William Merrill, b. in the Parson Bradley house at Bradley's Corner, July 6, 1824. He d. Nov. 4, 1879; she d. Jan. 5, 1895. He was a merchant in Boston, Mass.

CHILDREN:

I—Franklin Thayer, b. Dec. 14, 1848, m. Miss Jessie Aldrich, b Feb. 19, 1856. Three children, Alden, Paul and Royal.
II—Clara Alden, b. Aug. 5, 1851.
III—Emma Louise, b. Nov. 6, 1856.
IV—George Arthur, b Nov. 25, 1859.
V—Mary Bliss, b. March 2, 1862.
   b. 1821, d. Jan. 21, 1837.
3—Sarah Dunlap, b. 1824, d. May 13, 1842
4—John Q. Adams, b 1827, d. April 12, 1828.

5—Alpheus S., b. Jan. 14, 1830, m. Feb. 28, 1854, Miss Elizabeth Ellen Stevens, b. June 8, 1829, in the two story brick house standing on westerly side of Forest avenue, between Saunders and Pleasant streets, and to the highway, fronting southerly, Woodfords district. This house was built for Henry Webb Stevens by his father, Benjamin Stevens, who resided in the large and now ancient appearing house situated a few rods distant—say forty—on the northerly side of Ocean street where the late William Woodford resided and died—a very aged citizen, and son-in-law to Benjamin. Henry Webb Stevens was b. July 12, 1802, m. Feb. 9, 1825, Jane L. Noyes, reared in the family of Rev. Caleb Bradley. His daughter, Elizabeth Ellen, was the second child in a family of nine children.

Alpheus S. Alden was a bookkeeper for a period of more than thirty years in the Stevens iron store on Commercial street, Portland. He d. July 30, 1897. (See obituary in the News of that period.)

CHILDREN:

I—Walter Franklin, b. June 16, 1856, d. Sep. 20, same year.
II—Isabel Frances, b. Jan. 25, 1858, d. May 31, 1875.
III—Henry Shaw, b. Dec. 8, 1861, d. Sep. 16, same year.
IV—George Forest, b. Jan. 8, 1865

6—Jesse Franklin, b. 1835, d 1882, in Boston, Mass., very sudden, unmarried. He was in the wholesale boot and shoe trade.

Memorial monument and slabs in Pine Grove cemetery.

TO BE CONTINUED.

THE DEERING NEWS.

Saturday, Nov. 12, 1898.

GRANDPA'S SCRAP BOOK

[Under this head historical and genealogical memoranda will be furnished the readers of the News that appears worthy of preservation, particularly of remote periods in our history within the city limits and immediate vicinity.]

PAUL REVERE, SENIOR.

NAMES OF SOME OF HIS DESCENDANTS HERE AND ELSEWHERE.

BY LEONARD B. CHAPMAN.

CONTINUED FROM LAST WEEK.

Joshua Goodrich was born in Withersfield, Conn., July 21, 1775, Nancy Bulkley, his wife, daughter of Solomon Bulkley, born September 28, 1779. He died at Rocky Hill, Co.,n., April 11, 1839; she died there Jan. 23, 1857. (Here in Deering the name is spelled uBekley.)

CHILDREN:

1. Walter B. b. May 19, 1802.
2. Oliver B., Nov. 4, 1803, went from home and never heard from.
3. George W., b. Feb. 2, 1806, d. Hartford, Conn., May 16, 1833
4. Martha E., Oct. 18, 1808. Mrs. Martha E. Corey d. Apr. 30, 1851.
5. Eli, b. Feb. 20, 1811, d Rocky Hill, Conn., May 24, 1882
6. and last, Jerusha H., Jan. 21, 1814, m. Edward P. Elmer, Dec. 17, 1844. Went to Elkhart, Ind., where both died.

Walter B. Goodrich (No. 1 in the foregoing) came to the Plains district of our city

Upon the inside cover of a book used later as the record book of the Universalist church society of Westbrook now Deering, we find a record of three important events connected with his life— namely: "Arrived in Westbrook, Jan. 26, 1824. Commenced business for myself April 2, 1825. Built house 1828 and 1829." He was a tinsmith and was united in marriage the year he commenced his house. Where did the house stand?

In the year 1809, for $105, Capt. Isaac S. Stevens conveyed to Zachariah Brackett a house lot as follows:

"Begin at a steak on the westerly side of the road on a course south 14 degrees west 49 rods and 18 links distant from the front door of my dwelling house, thence south 14 degrees west 8 rods," etc.

Capt. Isaac S. Stevens resided in the house occupied by the late Mrs. Irene (Stevens) Record, her father, William Stevens, keeping an inn which, for several years after the war of the Revolution, was famous as a resort. Capt. Isaac being succeeded by his son William as inn holder, all of which has been noticed in the News.

Upon the Brackett lot, now the site of the Martin W. Best house standing next to the southerly side of, Evergreen cemetery where it joins Stevens Plains avenue, Mr. Goodrich built his residence—a two story brick building fronting the street. Upon going to Augusta, this state, to engage in the tin ware and stove trade, he sold, Nov. 14, 1836, for $2,000, to Hon. F. O. J. Smith the property, "reserving the shop on the premises."

It was at this house Rev. Zenas Thompson, the Universalist preacher, resided awhile, and there in the parlor our now venerable citizen, George Mead Stevens, son of William above noticed, and Miss Hannah E. Chase were united in marriage in 1838 as well as many others. The house was destroyed by fire several years ago.

Returning from Augusta Mr. Goodrich constructed the two story wooden house as now seen standing on the easterly side of Stevens Plains avenue a little northerly of the seminary grounds and to street and fronting southerly where his descendants reside. On the County Atlas of 1871, the location of the spot is marked "Mrs. Goodrich." It was May 1, 1841, he purchased the lot of the North brothers, paying $100 for the same, and the house was erected immediately after the purchase of the lot.

Mr. Goodrich went to Augusta about the time of the departure of the "tin kitchen" from the list of household utensils which brought largely into disrepute in its advent the fireplace as a means of cooking, which "kitchen" was displaced by the cook stove, thus losing to the Plains in the tinware industry one of its chief articles of manufacture. In later years many a miniature duel was fought by the boys in house attics where the kitchens were stored, using the "spits" for swords, which were flat strips of iron, three-fourths of an inch wide, pointed at one end while the other contained a crank-shaped handle, used for piercing meat and fowl and revolving the same in the kitchen before the open fire of the fire place.

Mr. Goodrich was a very estimable citizen, taking a position in the forefront of every good work.

FAMILY RECORD

Walter B. Goodrich and Maria Frances married June 11, 1829.

CHILDREN.

I—Caroline Maria, b. May 19, 1830.
II—Walter Franklin, Apr. 6, 1834.

Walter B. Goodrich died May 4, 1869; his wife, May 29, 1891. Memorial stones in Pine Grove cemetery

The children reside unmarried on the Plains under the parental roof of their ancestors; both active members in good work and in the church of the Universalist denomination of the neighborhood.

——He never brought
His conscience to the public mart
But lived himself the truth he taught.

NOTE. In 1891 a work in two volumes entitled The Life of Paul Revere, profusely illustrated and edited by E. H. Goss, was published in Boston, Mass., but the memoranda presented in the News has been secured wholly outside the contents of the Revere memorial.

TO BE CONTINUED.

THE DEERING NEWS.

Saturday, Nov. 19, 1898.

GRANDPA'S SCRAP BOOK

[Under this head historical and genealogical memoranda will be furnished the readers of the News that appears worthy of preservation, particularly of remote periods in our history within the city limits and immediate vicinity.]

BARBOUR.

A FEW FACTS RELATIVE TO THE NAME HERE AND ELSEWHERE,

BY MRS. CARRIE T. BARBOUR OF PORTLAND.

John Barbour the eldest son of "Father Barbour" mentioned by Willis came here a few years in advance of his father and brother James. He was one of the fifteen men who made up the population of the town in 1716. He and his wife Mary were living as late as 1757. They had six children but we have records of but one named Hugh who was probably born in York, Me. He married in 1736 Mary Bean, daughter of Joseph and Joanna Barbour. Joseph Bean was born in York in 1676, but came to Fort Casco 1709 as he was a man feared by the Indians. (A cut of the fort appears in the October number of the "Quarterly" published by the Maine Historical Society.) His daughter Mary was born in Falmouth 1710. Hugh and Mary settled on a farm about a mile from Stevens Plains towards Allen's Corner, and there they dispensed the hospitality which characterized them during their entire lives. At that place their children were born and in the old burying ground near, their remains were placed. Their four sons were Joseph Bean, b. 1737, John, 1739, Robert, 1742, and Adam, 1748.

Joseph Bean Barbour and Robert both served in the war of the Revolution and then Robert settled in North Yarmouth.

Joseph Bean married Elizabeth Goodridge of Old York and was the father of seven children. Two daughters Ann and Hannah were wives of Mark Walton. Betsey married Zaccariah Nowell who was in the battle of Valley Forge. Mary married Andrew son of Walter Scott of Paisley, Scotland, and a descendant was her grandson Capt. Robert Boyd, N. S. N., who died in Brooklyn, N. Y., 1890.

Elizabeth was another daughter married to Nathaniel Hatch of Bangor. One of her children was Brevet Brig. Gen. Edward Hatch of Fort Robinson, Neb., died 1889.

Joseph the only son of Joseph Bean Barbour died in Gorham 1854. He was three times married. (1) Lucy, daughter of Judge Potter, Kensington, N. H. One son by this marriage was Henry who married Harriet, daughter of Elias Merrill of Portland and whose grandson now living in Chicago is the only known living descendant of Joseph Bean son of Hugh Barbour. Joseph second wife wrs Judith Stevens of Portland and his third marriage was to Agnes (Archer) widow of Eben Preble of Salem, Mass. Joseph and his family lie side by side in the Eastern cemetery.

JOHN SON OF HUGH.

John the son of Hugh was married Aug. 18, 1764 to Susanna Wilson and in a short time after removed to Gray where he took a farm and built his house on an eminence near Gray village known as Barbour's Hill. The place now occupied by Mr. Henry Hunt. Here he lived and died in 1787. By his first wife he had ten children and by a second wife, Lucy Tenney he had one.

The first of the ten was Joanna who married Nehemiah Porter of North Yarmouth and some of their descendants are here today.

2 Miriam, m. Joseph Merrill a prominent citizen of Gray and their descendants are still there and some in Portland.

3 Esther, m. Moses Bartlett of Bethel and fourth Dorcas, her sister, married Moses' brother Stephen.

5 Eunice, m. Mr. Lane of Bethel.
6 Susan, m. Jonas Willis who came to Bethel early, in life from Sudbury, Mass. Charles was born, lived and died in Gray and was twice married. 1st Betsey Lowe by whom he had seven children. One of these was Mary, who m. Capt. Charles B. Hamilton and lived and died here. Capt. H. d. in 1843.

Charles Barbour's second marriage was to Joanna (Cobb) Cummings widow of Jonathan Cummings of Norway. She was the mother of two daughters. One is the wife of Mr. Wm. P. Merrill of Falmouth, and the other married Wm. Deering, (formerly of Deering & Milliken) now of Chicago, who died in 1856.

Wm. son of John married Mary Porter of Scituate, Mass., and among his descendants are Capt. Wm. Leavitt, Portland, and Miss Mary S. Morrill, Missionary to Turkey.

John another son of John died at sea unmarried. Robert son of John was born in 1780 but came back to his father's birthplace and opened a shop on Exchange street in 1801 where for some years he manufactured boots and shoes. He married Jane, daughter of Capt. Joshua Robinson of Kennebunkport and had two sons, John and Charles to succeed him in bussiness when he died in 1832. The original location of his place of business on Exchange street is occupied by his grandson, Edward Russell Barbour, the last of the name in that line, as Charles died without issue. (His wife was Clementine Dennett.)

After the marriage of John to Lucy Tenney he lived but a short time but had one daughter who became the wife of Abel Quimby of Saccarappa.

NOTES BY L. B. C.

In the year 1731 there was laid out to John Barbour of Falmouth a sixty acre lot beginning the bounds at a "Pitch Pine tree marked J. B. that stands on the westerly corner of James Doughty's sixty acre lot" which tree stood near the southeasterly corner of the old burial place located on the easterly side of the highway leading from the Morrill's Corner district to the Allen's Corner district of our city. The burial place occupies the south easterly corner of the lot. About three-fourths of the lot lies on the northly side of what is now Stevens Plains avenue.

Sept. 3. 1744, John Barbour a weaver of Portland "in consideration of love, good will and affection which I have towards my loving son, Hugh Barbour, husbandman, give, grant and sell sixty acres of land to him situated in Falmouth," etc., etc.

On the northerly side of the highway where the large, square and somewhat ancient appearing residence of the late Storer S. Knight now stands, on the lot which is occupied at the present time by his widow, Mrs. Helen E. Knight, Hugh Barbour built his log cabin and resided therein fifty years.

Adam Barbour who built the ancient appearing two story dwelling now seen standing on the easterly side of the road leading from Duck Pond mills in Westbrook to the Morrill's Corner district of our city was a son of Hugh, and that there might be no dispute about his age he cut the date thereof into a stone post in the year 1809 which date he also chiseled, and there it now stands as then erected as follows:

A. B.
B—1748,
June
22.

His wife was Betty Knight, reared on the Rev. Henry A. Hart place, who was killed some years since at the time of the Haverhill railroad smashup, situated on Quaker Lane, a short distance northerly.]

James Barbour, a brother to John, settled on wild lands a little easterly of Lunt's Corner, his abode standing where James S. Knowles, Esq., resides. Descendants reside among us.]

THE DEERING NEWS.

Saturday, Nov. 26, 1898.

GRANDPA'S SCRAP BOOK

[Under this head historical and genealogical memoranda will be furnished the readers of the News that appears worthy of preservation, particularly of remote periods in our history within the city limits and immediate vicinity.]

STROUDWATER.

ITS NAME AND EARLY LAND TITLES COMPILED FROM ORIGINAL RECORDS.

BY LEONARD B. CHAPMAN.

The earliest reference to the land upon which the village of Stroudwater is located that we find on record was recorded the 20th day of February 1652. George Cleeves of Casco (now Portland) was in England and received record possession of one thousand acres including therein the present site of the ancient village. The deed which is recorded in Vol. I, p. 14, York Deeds, to which reference is made on page 117 of Vol. I of the Collections of the Maine Historical Society, was made by Edward Rigby, Esq., President of the Province of Lygonia, New England, in America, on the one part, and George Cleeves on the other. The description says:

"Beginning at the little falls in Casco River [Capisic falls, where the grist mill now stands, 1898], and running westwardly three hundred and twenty pools and five hundred pools southwardly, together with all and all manner of woods, underwoods, timber and trees"—etc.

Mr. Cleeves on the 18th day of July, 1658, conveyed the whole grant to Richard Tucker, his partner, but we cannot learn that any part of the grant was ever occupied by order of Tucker or sold by him; and the region remained a wood-clad Indian hunting ground in common with other lands till 1680, when Thomas Danforth was appointed President of the Province of Maine, and the stream at what is now called Stroudwater was granted to Lt. George Ingalls for a corn mill, the land on the westerly of the village to John Wheelden, and that located to the south and north to other members of the Ingalls family.

Willis, particularly on page 321 of the first volume of the Collections of the Maine Historical society, mixes the Ingalls name up with Capisic Falls occupancy, but they were never residents of that locality as we hope to show in the near future, the falls with a mile square of land being granted to other persons.

To follow the descent of title to the land on the northerly side of Stroudwater has required much labor, but we have accomplished the task at last. We could find that Gen. Samuel Waldo sold prior to 1744 the so called Quinby farm to the Small's, though the deed is not a matter of record, and they occupied the premises many years, and the Waldo heirs the 200 acre farm to Capt. Daniel Dole, in the hands of whose descendants most of it still remains, but how Waldo got hold of the titles was a stumbling block, his land possessions being so large, but—

"Knowledge never learned at schools" came to our assistance, and we discovered the right way.

On the 19th day of June, 1720, "I, Samuel Ingalls, (then spelled Ingersoll), of Gloucester, Province of Massachusetts Bay, Shipwright, (and Juda, his wife), for and in consideration of the sum of fifty pounds money in hand well and truly paid by Mary Sargent, of aforesaid Town, Innholders, as also a deed of sale of about two acres of land situated in Gloucester with a small dwelling house thereon give and grant and sell One certain Tract of land situated in the town of Falmouth in New England containing two hundred acres, being that which was granted my father, George Ingalls, formerly of said Falmouth, deceased, and deeded by my father to me, May 20, 1689, said land adjoining to Casco River (now Fore river 1898) at one end Seven score poles or rods, part by said marsh and so running up ye Great Sawmill River [the Stroudwater, 1898.] Ye same breadth till one hundred acres be made up, the other hundred Acres adjoining above, running up still further from the great River and up by the aforesaid Sawmill River to an old white pine stump at the upper end on the other side, bounded with a great Pitch pine, Marked, the whole Containing Two hundred acres, also Two small lots of land on Old Casco side, [Portland 1898,] so called," etc.

Jan. 6, 1731, for £200 paid, Epes Sargent of Gloucester conveyed the premises to Gen. Samuel Waldo of Boston, Mass.

A tract of land which my honored mother, Mrs. Mary Sargent, bought of Samuel Ingalls of Gloucester, * * * said land adjoins to Casco river at one end, seven score poles!

(140 rods on the now Fore river mill pond) etc. This deed in the original reads same as the preceding.

The grant of the Stroudwater river for a "corn mill" in the year 1680 then called Mill river with three acres of land on the northerly side thereof where the village is located came by purchase into the hands of Messrs. Waldo and Westbrook who immediately commanded the erection of a saw mill that stood about forty rods above the highway now leading from the village to the State Reform School farm in Cape Elizabeth.

One of the deeds may be seen recorded in vol. 12, p. 198, York County records, dated Dec. 13, 1727, in which the name STROUDWATER appears the first time among records. Later Col. Thomas Westbrook constructed *on his own account* a small mill for the manufacture of paper six or eight rods above the present way to the Reform School farm noticed in the preceeding.

That Lieutenant George Ingalls and Sons constructed a "corn mill" in the year 1680 where Messrs. Waldo and Westbrook, rebuilt what the Indians destroyed, there is an abundance of documentary proof. Page 88 of vol. 35 of the Massachusetts Archives shown by Joseph Prout's letter, dated Falmouth 1689, that soldiers were sent up from Fort Loyal located in Portland "to guard the mill while corn is grinding."

Passages in one of the deeds to Messrs. Waldo and Westbrook read as follows:

"Also a town grant to George and John Ingalls, Junr for the stream of water called Stroud Waterish—privilege of timber and land for an accommodation of mills—the above named Philips & Co. purchased the moiety of said Ingalls the 13th of March 1684, with outlands for an accommodation—Also at the place called Nonesuch Marshes, the moiety of twenty-five acres of marsh purchased of George Ingalls, Jr. for an accommodation of Stroudwater mills."

As we have stated at other times, when Col. Thomas Westbrook removed his residence from Dunston Landing in Scarboro during the year 1727 the site of the present Stroudwater village was a howling wilderness and had been for more than twenty-five years, the Indian and the wild beast roaming at will unmolested by the white man. It was at the date, 1727, the name of Stroudwater appears and the name of "Mill river" changed to that of the present. These record facts *explode* the story of the origin of the name as presented by "McK" in the News of the 5th of this month, for when the locality was given the name it still retains, beast only occupied and Indians frequented it.

Another record recorded on page 267 of vol. 24, of York Deeds reads as follows:

THE DEERING NEWS.

Saturday, Dec. 3, 1898.

GRANDPA'S SCRAP BOOK

[Under this head historical and genealogical memoranda will be furnished the readers of the News that appears worthy of preservation, particularly of remote periods in our history within the city limits and immediate vicinity.]

STROUDWATER.

ITS NAME AND EARLY LAND TITLES COMPILED FROM ORIGINAL RECORDS.

BY LEONARD B. CHAPMAN.

CONTINUED FROM LAST WEEK.

Province of Maine. At a meeting of the Selectmen of the town of Falmouth in Casco Bay this 30th of August, 1681:

"It is granted unto Mrs. Mary Munjoy all her marsh which was formerly possessed by Mr. George Munjoy, Sen., or his Order, which marsh lies on both sides Capisick River, and that Long marsh adjoining to Thomas Cloyce. (He lived where the Brewer House recently stood easterly of Stroudwater, on the opposite side of Fore river, then called Casco river.)

"It is granted unto Mrs. Mary Munjoy, formerly the wife of Mr. Geo. Munjoy, Sen., five hundred acres of upland to begin next to Samuel Ingalls land and to run in breadth on the West side of Capisick river to a Little falls and so into the woods till five hundred acres be completed, byways excepted out of this grant.

Varia Copia,
Anthony Brackett.

July 24, 1686."

The "Little falls" alluded to were those located westerly of what is now known as the Nason Corner district of our city where there is quite a charming spot where the water flows freely after a heavy rain and particularly so in the spring time.

Back in the year 1730, when adventures were numerous hereabouts, Joseph Conant, from Beverly, Mass., received a grant of land surrounding the falls which he was obliged to vacate because it was shown that the grant was located upon an older conveyance. After this he went to Saccarappa and erected a small house on the northerly side of the Presumpscot river which caused him and others much "vexation of spirit," the early history of which building will soon appear in the Quarterly published by the Maine Historical society, the facts being derived from depositions made and recorded a few years after the construction of the house.

Another record reads as follows:

Granted and laid out to Col. Thomas Westbrook, Esq., assignee to Benjamin Wright, late of Falmouth, deceased, thirteen acres of land lying between the Fore river and the Stroudwater river, bounded as follows: Beginning at a point of rocks where said rivers meet (southeasterly side of Mill Creek where Mr. Frederick Waterhouse resides, 1898, and where persons of the name have resided more than a hundred years) thence west ten degrees, north twenty-five rods; (up the creek) thence north ten degrees east ten rods to the stake; thence west sixteen degrees north thirty rods to a stake; thence north forty-seven degrees west twenty-six rods to the northwest part of a large flat rock, (Stevens rock known better to the boys of the place fifty years ago than now, adjoining Stroudwater river westerly of the Stevens mansion house) thence north forty-five degrees east three rods to a stake; thence north fifty-three degrees west eight rods—the southeasterly corner of the old cemetery lot—thence north forty-five degrees east sixty-four rods to ye Fore river—Dole's spring 1898—thence by ye Fore river as it runs to ye first bounds, allowance made for the county road going through which is for thirteen acres of the sixty acre lot belonging to the proprietor's right of ye aforesaid Benj. Wright, deceased.

JOSHUA MOODY,) Proprietor's Com-
STEPHEN JONES, } mittee for laying
JOHN BAILEY,   ) out lands

Falmouth, June 12, 1740.

Nothing came out of this grant that we find recorded. Three years prior to the date of this proceeding Waldo had taken from Westbrook by the force of an execution the land southerly of a line running from the public drinking fountain of the present day, southwesterly, between the old George Tate and Stevens lots as now situated, to Stroudwater river.

It is apparent that Col. Thomas Westbrook had more than one abiding place in the town of Falmouth, but the first evidently was erected in the center of the present village of Stroudwater at the head of what is now Waldo street, easterly side, where it joins Westbrook street and where, till very recently, the cellar hole was plainly seen. Many still remember the structure. It was two-story, fronting the west, with one room each side the front door with board shutters to the lower story windows to keep the Indians from entering. The site must have been charming at the time of the erection. The saw mill was located in a westerly direction at the foot of the lot now occupied by the Francis F. Milliken family where the post office sign is hung out—a dwelling erected more than a hundred years ago by Hon. Aarch Lewis; the "mast yard" was at the foot of the hill extending westerly; the view of Fore river being unobstructed. But the lot was without a natural flow of water for domestic purposes and so another dwelling, one story, was constructed at what is now the southwesterly corner of Westbrook and Bond streets; a large barn built and the whole protected by a stockade and cannon (noticed in the inventory of the estate of Gen. Waldo at the time of his decease). At this place Col. Westbrook closed his eyes to a busy and eventful life February 11th of the year 1744. (See Portland Transcript of Nov. 7, 1883.

[TO BE CONTINUED.]

Saturday, Dec. 10, 1898.

GRANDPA'S SCRAP BOOK

(Under this head historical and genealogical memoranda will be furnished the readers of the News that appears worthy of preservation, particularly of remote periods in our history within the city limits and immediate vicinity.)

STROUDWATER.

ITS NAME AND EARLY LAND TITLES COMPILED FROM ORIGINAL RECORDS.

BY LEONARD B. CHAPMAN.

CONTINUED FROM LAST WEEK.

Col. Westbrook received the title to the land upon which he erected the house in which he died, noticed at the close of our article of last week, from General Waldo. The deed runs as follows:

One half part of sixty acres of land granted by the general court of the Province aforesaid to George Ingersol, late of Falmouth, deceased, the 13th day of October 1680, situated in the town of Falmouth and on the southerly side of the river Stroudwater and lays either near the House and Barn of the said Thos Westbrook and Samuel Waldo, or whereon they stand, and on the northeast, of one hundred acres of land granted by said town of Falmouth to said Ingersol the 19th day of May 1720, or however otherwise the said sixty acres may be butted and bounded which said premises I lately purchased of Daniel Ingersol, of Boston, shipwright.

A later written document says "the lot was anciently granted to Bartholomel Gidney and by measurement consisted of sixty-nine acres and 55 rods within which bounds is included the dwelling house called Harrow House and outhouses near adjoining thereto and a garrison round said Harrow House and outhouses, also a cottage inhabited by Westbrook Knight and two other small cottages."

In our article of last week we stated that the land situated southerly of a line running from the public drinking fountain to Stroudwater river between the Tate house and Stevens lot was taken from Westbrook by the force of an execution. The document states that the line commences at the "southwesterly corner of the Great Bridge over Fore River and thence south 37 degrees west 46 rods to Stroudwater river, also from the first mentioned stake a course along the shore, south 30 degrees east, 15 rods to Zebulan Trickey's N. E. corner," etc., "on which said four acres and 47 rods and 261¼ feet is erected a paper mill, a dwelling house with some conveniences for paper makers now inhabited by one John Wilson and a cottage near adjoining lying unimproved, the whole being held in common and undivided between Col. Thomas Westbrook and Samuel Waldo, the whole valued at £111-11-4.

Gen. Samuel Waldo was an exceedingly active man—a merchant prince in Boston, and a land king in the Province of Maine. Many letters written by him we have examined. While in Europe he would induce mechanics and others to come to this country, and there is more than one court record showing he did not do here as he agreed there.

A millwright by trade, an Englishman by nationality, by the name of James Forder he induced to come to Stroudwater. In 1735 he was taxed here on real estate two shillings and on personal property two shillings and eight pence.

He commenced proceedings in court in Boston against Waldo which were taken from court and left to referees for settlement who decided that Waldo should pay Forder "five hundred, forty-seven pounds and five shillings within two months, balance due on account—then we award the contract made in England between said parties in 1731 shall be utterly void." (York Deeds.)

Sept. 17, 1734, Messrs. Waldo and Westbrook conveyed for a consideration of £40 "passable paper paid by James Forder of Falmouth, millwright," "a small Tract or Parcel of Land lying in the Township of Falmouth and on the North Easterly side of Stroudwater Stream, the same being the same whereon the said James Forder's House now stands and containing eight thousand, eight hundred and twenty-two Feet and is butted and bounded as follows: Viz;"—etc.. Samuel Waldo signed the deed but Col. Westbrook did not. (An official copy of the instrument made from the original in 1803 is before us as we write.)

This was the first land conveyance by Waldo & Westbrook at Stroudwater we find on record.

James Forder, the Englishman who built the house in which Augustus Tate, Esq., resides at this time (whose father, Geo. Tate, purchased the premises in 1824) sold the place in the year 1737 for a consideration of £300 paid by James Gibson of Boston, merchant, an abstract of the deed reading as follows:

With the buildings on the North easterly side of Stroudwater stream, the same being the place whereon said Forder's houses now stand.

The second house built by Forder was a shop and was joined to the northerly side of the house now standing on the lot, and it is reasonable to suppose that Forder went into trade in the second building erected by him, and obtained goods of Gibson, securing him upon his buildings and lot. Seven years later Gibson sold the place to John Buck "being the same [lot] James Forder bought of Messrs Waldo and Westbrook," with two houses built thereon."

Here the name of James Forder disappears from the records. His departure is more mysterious than his advent. The fact that he built the residence of Mr. Tate and still another building on the lot which was removed to Cape Elizabeth where it now stands, with half of the upper story taken off by one Samuel Pratt, a house carpenter, who occupied it as a dwelling, is established by records and tradition beyond a doubt.

The somewhat elevated land above its surroundings crossed by the highway leading from Stroudwater to Saccarappa where the way makes a curve to the westward a fourth of a mile northwesterly of Stroudwater is called and has been known these many years as "Forder's hill," and the question has often been asked from whence came the name? As no one ever resided there by the name of whom there is record it is reasonable to suppose that during the troublesome relationship with the Indians when the inhabitants were driven from Saccarappa during the war which commenced in the spring of 1744, the mill at Stroudwater Falls and Long Creek being burned and the inhabitants of Purpuddock driven to Portland, a garrison was maintained at the point, as was the case and a log house built where the Buxton and Saco roads separate a half mile westerly of Stroudwater where the well used is still to be seen, hence the corruption of the name "Fort hill" and consequently the use of Forders or Forters as a term of designation for the locailty.

[TO BE CONTINUED]

THE DEERING NEWS.

Saturday, Dec. 17, 1898.

GRANDPA'S SCRAP BOOK

[Under this head historical and genealogical memoranda will be furnished the readers of the News that appears worthy of preservation, particularly of remote periods in our history within the city limits and immediate vicinity.]

STROUDWATER.

ITS NAME AND EARLY LAND TITLES COMPILED FROM ORIGINAL RECORDS.

BY LEONARD B. CHAPMAN.

TO BE CONTINUED.

May 12, 1735, Messrs. Waldo & Westbrook conveyed to Zebulon Trickey for a consideration of £180 of Bills of credit on the Province, one acre and a half of land "located on the northerly side of Stroudwater river, together with the House and Fence yeon Standing," commencing bounds at a "stake standing ten rods and ten feet. North and by west from the northerly end of the Bridge over Stroudwater river (the bridge then over Mill creek, where the bridge now may be seen, 1898,) below the lower mills standing thereon—" etc.

This was the first homestead lot and abiding place of Col. Westbrook in Stroudwater before he built "Harrow House," noticed in our article of last week which was a one story structure.

Francis Trickey was at Kittery, this state, before 1659. He died Apr. 11, 1682, at which time an inventory of his estate was made and recorded among the York deeds. Zebulon was there in 1725.

In 1733 for a consideration of £100 Messrs. Waldo & Westbrook conveyed to Zebulon a fifty acre lot "lying on the northerly side of Lieut. Samuel Skillings new lot which land lies on each side the mast road to Dunstan, together with all and singular of ye buildings."

This lot was located about three-fourths of a mile westerly of Stroudwater and less than a fourth of a mile from where the block house stood in the fork of the roads, and the "mast road" of that day is Saco street now, the two-story house he erected standing end to road and fronting westerly, having been swung half round, half of the lower story taken off by the late James Johnson, father to George Woodbury Johnson, recently deceased, son of James, the heirs of the latter occupying the premises, where the old Trickey residence is now used as a wood and carriage shelter, and some fifty odd years since the change was made, and the new house built by James Johnson.

Mr. Trickey purchased the farm lot before he did the Stroudwater lot being a farmer as well as a bridge builder and mill wright he probably had use for both places.

The Stroudwater purchase was the second sale made in what is now the village by Waldo & Westbrook. In 1735 Trickey was taxed for a "bondman," (meaning a slave,) 5 shillings and 10 pence; on real estate 3 shillings; and on personal property 2 shillings.

On p. 252, of the Cumberland County History, published in 1880, may be seen some notes upon the Trickey family and a portrait of a great grandson of Zebulon of Stroudwater, and in the Westbrook Globe-Star of April 7, 1898, some notes by Mr. Nathan Goold of Portland and in the Portland Argus of Jan. 5, 1891, an obituary; and before us memoranda pertaining to the name sufficient to make more than one long article for the NEWS.

We will now copy from the Libby Genealogy, p. 50, a wonderfully correct book, but the compiler made a slight mistake in the location of the residence of Zebulon.

Eleanor Libby, born in Kittery, Me. 21 June, 1705; married 1727 Zebulon Trickey. They moved at once to Scarboro, and settled at Black Point, but a few years after removed to that part of Falmouth which is now Cape Elizabeth. There he died and she married second, 1757, Lieutenant Andrew Libby.

Lieut. Libby was an extensive, and in those times, a wealthy farmer in Scarboro, whose first wife had 11 children.

There were six children born to them of whom there is record. The three eldest, daughters, died young as did Thomas, the fifth child.

Zebulon, Jr., was the fourth child, born July 20, 1736, at Stroudwater, married Rebecca Skillings, daughter of the very stirring Indian scout of Long Creek, Cape Elizabeth, saw mill tender and inn keeper of that region, who leased the City Hall lot in Portland, concerning which there was so much newspaper discussion a few years since.

David Trickey was the sixth and youngest child of the family, born 1741, married Mary Hobbs, born 1745. They had eight children. He died April 5, 1814; Mary, his wife, died Aug. 7, 1799.

Memorial slabs for David and wife may be seen in the old Stroudwater cemetery.

Eleanor (Libby) Trickey married well the second time as she did the first, so well that she relinquished all claim to her husband's estate to her two sons, Zebulon and David—to David upon conditions. An abstract reads as follows:

Aug. 5, 1757. I Eleanor Trickey, of Falmouth, in consideration of £20 paid by my two sons, Zebulon and David (minor) as well also for the love, goodwill and affection which I have for them, give, grant and sell about eighty-three acres of land in Falmouth upon which I now dwell, bounded northerly by the road that goes from Stroudwater past the house of Frances Jacksons, deceased, to Dunston to be divided between my two sons in equal halves, Zebulon to have the half whereon the house and barn standeth, also half of the lot at Stroudwater, the half upon which the house and barn is standing, in which my late husband, Zebulon Trickey, formerly dwelt, the said land is bounded as followeth, etc. Provided, however, the said David lives with and serves faithfuly Zebulon till he is 21 years of age, otherwise he is to have nothing, and Zebulon is to have the whole.

It was further provided that David should have a yoke of oxen and two cows, if he continued to live with his brother.

I also sell unto my two sons about twenty acres of common and undivided land in the township of Berwick which devised to me as one of the heirs of my father, David Libby, late of Kittery, deceased.

On the 8th of Dec. 1783, Zebulon Trickey sold to his brother David for £133—6 his half of the 83 acres of land, "which our mother, Eleanor Trickey conveyed to me and my brother David, also the Stroudwater lot."

The intention of marriage between Zebulon Trickey and Rebecca Skillings was made public Aug. 10, 1758; that of David and Mary Hobbs, Sep. 1, 1768.

Of this David Trickey there are many descendants hereabouts. A son Daniel settled in Westbrook, southwestly of Saccarappa, and Enoch resided opposite the State Reform school farm where his son, Mr. Charles Pratt Trickey resides, occupying the homestead buildings. The large farm of David was divided in 1819 among his children.

David's brother Zebulon resided the last of his life a half mile westerly of his father's farm where the fine modern built and equipped Trickey residence may be seen. They had four children.

[TO BE CONTINUED.]

THE DEERING NEWS.

Saturday, Dec. 24, 1898.

GRANDPA'S SCRAP BOOK

[Under this head historical and genealogical memoranda will be furnished the readers of the News that appears worthy of preservation, particularly of remote periods in our history within the city limits and immediate vicinity.]

STROUDWATER.

ITS NAME AND EARLY LAND TITLES COMPILED FROM ORIGINAL RECORDS.

BY LEONARD B. CHAPMAN.

CONTINUED FROM LAST WEEK.

In 1735 Gowen Wilson was taxed eleven shillings and eight pence in Falmouth which was the amount of two poll taxes, thus indicating that he owned a slave or bondman; on real estate one shilling, eight pence; and on personal property one shilling and six pence. He came from Kittery, this state, to Stroudwater, and was a millwright. Among us are many of his descendants, including Rev. E. P. Wilson, the Congregational church pastor of Woodfords, his brother, Rev. Gowen Wilson, home missionary, of the same place Virgil C. Wilson and Scott Wilson, Esqs., Atty's at law, Portland, the former born in what is now Deering and the latter being a resident at the present time.

It was on the 28th day of December, 1736, that Mr. Wilson received the title to the lot for which he was taxed 1735, and it was the third land record transfer made by Messrs. Waldo & Westbrook at Stroudwater. An abstract of the deed reads thus:

Begin bounds at a stump standing two rods and three feet from the corner of the House sd Wilson now dwells in thence running southwest and be west one hundred and thirty rods to a stake, then north thirty-three degrees, eighty rods to a stake—etc., containing fifty-one acres.

Wilson did not retain the premises long; he sold to Josiah Plummer of Falmouth, who, on the 16th day of March, 1742, for a consideration of £100 sold to Robert Slemons, husbandman, a Scotch-Irish emigrant, who made the Wilson domicile his place of abode.

The house stood about four rods from the southerly side of what is Congress street, and about eight rods westerly of Stroudwater river, on land now owned by the heirs of the late Henry Chapman who purchased it of one Charles Furgerson fifty odd years since whose wife was a descendant of Robert Slemons—children of Furgerson now residing in the town of Dayton, York county.

The view from the site of the Wilson–Plummer–Slemons residence was a pleasing one. From it one could look down upon the saw-mill of Waldo & Westbrook, and out over the residence of Col. Westbrook, Fore river and the floating mast logs of the Stroudwater, but it must have been a place difficult to reach, the deep gully at the southward making the way one of fatigue.

Included with the bounds of the fifty-one acre lot are at this time the Fred A. Johanson residence, built by a son of Robert Slemons, the Charles Maxfield residence, Henry Chapman residence, Dr. Henry Hunt residence; and the Mrs. Ella M. Bates residence.

The tracks of Gowen Wilson after he left Stroudwater are somewhat difficult to follow. He had grants of land easterly of Allen's Corner. The proprietor's records of the common and undivided lands show that on the 30th day of March, 1737, he had a sixty acre lot laid out to him in that vicinity, adjoining 100 acres of land he purchased of Nath'l Locke. It is more than probable, however, that he went to reside at Presumpscot Falls. A record relating to him as a ferryman reads as follows, which shows that the school master did not come this way to stop very often:

Whereas I The subscriber at this Presen Court of Generall sessons of the Peace Held at Falmouth was Lycenced To Keep a Ferry over Pezumpscott River near the Great works.

I therefore Hereby Promise and oblige myself my Heirs Executors and administers To Pay or cause to be Paid unto the Treasurer of ye Town or His successor in said office Ten shillings P annum for Rent of the same and as an acknowledgement of Their Right in and unto the same Ferry.

Witness my Hand
this ——— Day of Oct. 1740
Gowin Wilson
Recorded P Sam'l Moody,
Town Clerk.

The "great works" alluded to were the saw mills erected by Waldo & Westbrook at the Falls, dam, block and other houses.

Upon the records of marriage publishments in Falmouth we find as follows:

July 23, 1738, Mary Wilson and Zacariah Field.

August 27, 1739, Sarah Wilson and Elisha Baker of North Yarmouth.

Oct. 31, 1739, Gowen Wilson, Jr., and Martha Sargent, both of Falmouth.

Sept. 13, 1750, Joseph Wilson and Mary Scott.

This was a son of the original Gowen and brother to Gowen Wilson, jr. He was a mariner and resided down in Lincoln county, at a place called Pleasant river.

April 20, 1759, Eunice Wilson and Richard Nason, both of Falmouth.

April 3, 1862, Nathaniel Wilson and Ann Huston.

The Major Nathaniel Wilson was born Nov. 28, 1740; his wife died and he married second Ann March, of Scarboro who lived to be 103 years of age. By the first wife he had nine children and by the second one son M. Wilson, Esq., who was the originator of the Atlantic & St. Lawrence railroad scheme. The Major resided easterly of Allen's Corner in the house destroyed by fire a year ago last spring that stood in the northeasterly angle made by Stevens Plains avenue and Summit street.

A monument erected to his memory stands upon the southerly side of the avenue about ten rods distant. He was a patriot of the war of the Revolution, and his grave deserves a better treatment than it receives. With unspent funds in the city treasury saised for the care of burial place the very apparent neglect displayed is not excusable in those chosen to care for such things. When the homestead farm was sold in 1831, consisting of 141 acres a reservation of the burial lot was made. Following is a public list of the Wilson marriages we find recorded:

Nov. 26, 1764, Gowen Wilson and Mary Gibbs They went off to reside with Alfred Shakers.

Oct. 15, 1767, Charles Wilson and Experience Wood.

March 3, 1767, Mehitabel Wilson and John Hill

Feb. 10, 1764, Peter Graffam and Mary Wilson, Windham.

Dec. 2, 1773, Mark Wilson and Olive Huston

Feb 2, 1778, Martha Wilson and Thomas Doughty.

May 12, 1778, Ichabod Wilson and Ruth Huston.

June 21, 1786, Martha Wilson and John Shepard.

Oct. 9, 1788, Rachel Wilson and John Maybury.

Jan. 27, 1789, Nathaniel Wilson, Jr, and Sally Pride. (He was the eldest son of Major Nathaniel Wilson and grandson of Gowen Wilson, Jr, who married Martha Sargent. Nathaniel Jr. resided in North Yarmouth

June 21, 1790, Alice Wilson of New Gloucester and John Craig.

Dec. 13, 1792, Hannah Wilson and Joseph Leighton.

Jan. 7, 1793, Polly Wilson and Theophilis Hilton.

In the near future we hope to give this Wilson family record more in detail. The foregoing memorial is presented with the view of inducing those who are in possession of reliable dates of a private nature to present it to the public.

TO BE CONTINUED.

THE DEERING NEWS.

Saturday, Dec. 31, 1898.

GRANDPA'S SCRAP BOOK

[Under this head historical and genealogical memoranda will be furnished the readers of the News that appears worthy of preservation, particularly of remote periods in our history within the city limits and immediate vicinity.]

STROUDWATER.

ITS NAME AND EARLY LAND TITLES COMPILED FROM ORIGINAL RECORDS.

BY LEONARD B. CHAPMAN.

CONTINUED FROM LAST WEEK.

Nov. 30, 1895 THE NEWS presented a Scrap book article entitled David Patrick which was continued through several issues of the journal. He made the *fourth* land purchase in Stroudwater in 1743, consisting of two lots, one contained "a fourth of an acre adjoining a cottage lately inhabited by one William Libby;" the other containing "three acres and twelve perches, lying on the southerly side of Fore river nigh unto the Great Bridge built over the same."

Upon the first named lot, located in the south westerly angle made by Westbrook street where it crosses Congress street, stands the one story Patrick house in which Mary, the widow of David Patrick departed this life August 6, 1806, aged 95 years, to which lot was added the land where the Tristram Stevens residence stands, extending southerly by the road so far as the ancient George Tate house lot. The title to the Stevens part of the lot is still held by descendants of Mr. Patrick, Tristram Stevens marrying a daughter of David, named Margaret, who was born August 17, 1754, the day upon which the chimney as now seen above the roof of the Tate mansion was fashioned by David himself.

The major part of the other lot is still retained by descendants of David, upon which the connected row of ancient appearing shops stand, now occupied and owned by Andrew Hawes, Esq., the Stroudwater hall, Walker house and blacksmith shop the last constructed of the first tide water mill of the locality, the northerly boundry line of the lot then established now exists between the lot in question and the Dole farm.

About the time David Patrick made his land purchase Joseph Small made one also of Gen. Samuel Waldo which was the FIFTH land conveyance made by Messrs. Waldo and Westbrook at Stroudwater.

FRANCIS SMALL.

Considerable has been written and presented to the public relative to this character in a disjoined manner, April 6, 1685, he testified he was then fifty-six years of age at which time he was residing at Kittery. He was an adventurer, a fisherman and a trader with the Indians. Notwithstanding Cleeves and Tucker held the title of all the land from what is now Portland westerly to Fore river Small purchased of the Indians the land at Capisic within the defined limits of the Cleeves & Tucker grant. The instrument is dated, Casco Bay, July 27, 1657, and is recorded in the York records of deeds, vol. 1, p. 83. It runs thus:

Be it known unto all men that I, Sitterygusset, of Casco Bay, Sagamore, do hereby firmly covenent, grant and sell unto Francis Small of the said Casco Bay, fisherman, his heirs, etc., all the upland and marshes at Capisic, lying up along the northern side of the river, unto the head thereof, and so to reach and extend unto the riverside of Ammoncongin.

The consideration for the conveyance was one trading coat a year for Capisic and a gallon of rum a year for Ammoncongin.

Ammoncongin was the chief, and Capisic his wife, of the tribe of Indians dwelling hereabouts, with their hunting grounds extending east as far as the Presumpscot and westerly to the Saco river, with planting grounds at Cumberland Mills.

Small speculated too extensively, got into debt, and was obliged to dispose of part of the lot to John Philips of Boston, whose son-in-law, Geo. Munjoy, purchased the remainder.

Silvanus Davis having obtained a grant of a mile square of land including Capisic Pond a conflict arose between Davis and Robert Lawrence who had married Munjoy's widow, with reference to titles to the Capisic property. Lawrence complained to the government that Davis had taken possession of his land, and represented that Davis had erected a saw mill at Capisic "on a small brook that was dry half of the time for no other purpose than to deprive Lawrence of his marsh," and if Davis' claim should be allowed, Lawrence would have to starve his cattle for such a person who seeks nothing but the ruin and destruction of his neighbors as is well know to the inhabitants." Lawrence attempt to remove the grass Davis had cut, when Davis had him arrested for stealing his thatch and in a heated discussion Lawrence called Tyng, the Justice of the Peace "a hypocritical rogue.'

Lawrence resided near the foot of India street, Portland, in a stone house and perished at the hands of the Indians in 1690, Davis resided a little easterly of Lawrence's residence. He was captured by the Indians and upon his release went to Nantasket, Mass. where he died. Plans of his Portland home, and his "mile square' land grant at Capisic we have found in the Massachusetts archives, and in the Portland Public Library is an order in the original from Governor Andras relating to the Lawrence—Davis Capisic grass dispute, which bears the date of 1687.

In 1668, while residing in Kittery, Francis Small received another Indian deed of land located between the Great and Little Ossipee rivers upon which are located the towns of Limington, Limerick, Newfield, Parsonsfield and Cornish. The deed was not recorded till 1773—105 years after it was made. He died at Cape Cod in 1713, or thereabouts. The writer hereof traces the title to his three acre house lot at Capisic to the Indian sale to Small as well as some two hundred acres more of land located between his residence and Fore river, via Bradley's Corner, including the lot upon which the residence of the late John B. Curtis stands as well as that of Nathan Tibbetts, the Brewer house and other residences, but, strange as it may seem, the land held under this Indian grant extends directly opposite to the course called for in the deed.

Joseph Small was a descendant of Francis Small but the line of descent or place of birth we cannot give with absolute certainty. Mr. Lauriston W. Small of Brooklyn, N. Y., states in a paper that may be seen in Vol. IV, p. 364, of the Maine Historical Society Collections, 1893, that Francis Small had six children —Edward, Francis, *Samuel*, Benjamin, Daniel and Elizabeth; that *Samuel* had Elizabeth, Samuel and *Joseph*.

The compiler of the LIBBY GENEALOGY, on page 32, refers to Frances Small and first generation of descendants. He says:

Joseph Small, son of Samuel, and grandson of Francis, was born Dec. 3, 1702, and married April 12, 1722, Mary Libby, daughter of David Libby of Kittery. The Genealogy was printed in 1882, the paper of L. W. Small 1893. The Genealogy contains other valuable Small data.

In Nathaniel Knight's ledger is an account which reads as follows:

MR. JOSEPH SMALL.   DR.

CONTINUED!

October, 1744, to 1 pair boys shoes, £ 0-19
to 10 lbs. salt fish, " 0-19
to one gall rum, " 0-16
to my draft on Capt. Jno. Wayte which you got excepted, " 4-0
to 3 pecks of Indian corn, " 0-13-6
to ½ bushel corn and peck meal, " 0-1-0
to 1 hal " 4-0-0
to 1-4 bbl. mackerel, " 2-0-0

Another account reads as follows:
MR JOSEPH SMALL, JUN. DR.
1745, to 1 gun, £9-10
to 1 load English hay, " 6-0
to mending chaise, " 0-4
to 4 lbs. tobacco, " 0-8
to pasturing steers last fall, " 1-0
to 500 feet boards, " 2-10
to pasturing your oxen and your father's, " 1-10

In the month of January, 1756, an account with Joseph Small "Junier" and one with Joseph Small "Seignor" was opened by Mr. Knights, who resided westerly of Stroudwater. The junior is charged with worsted stockings, a beaver hat, four yards broadcloth, shalloon, skeins of mohair and silk, buttons, tape, buckram, etc., etc.

The names upon a deed show that the name of the wife of Joseph Small, senior, was Mary.

May 30, 1752, an intention of marriage between Joseph Small of Falmouth and Mary Fogg of Scarboro was made public; and Dec. 4, 1752, Joseph Small and "Mrs." Mary Fogg were united in marriage.

This, seemingly, was a son of Joseph, Sen., and Joseph, Sen., married, according to the Libby Genealogy, Mary Libby, April 12, 1722.

The exact date Joseph Small located permanently at Stroudwater we cannot give, but it was not far from 1743, and whatever else may be said of him he had a love for the picturesque in nature's landscape, for a more pleasing location for a house could not be found than the one he selected. The rising and setting sun, Fore river, Capisic Falls, the floating mast logs, the mast yard, the lumber ladened vessel, the site of what is now the city of Portland were all his to look upon. His selection of 40 acres for a farm was covered by a heavy pine growth. Everything was inspiring to action. The bounds of his lot commencing at a stake on the westerly side of the road near the northerly line of the grave yard and adjacent the spot whereon the socalled Quinby dwelling stands which is owned and occupied by the heirs of the late Moses Quinby, Esq.,

Week of Jan. 3 6, 1900.

WESTBROOK.

NAMES OF THE SELECTMEN AND REPRESENTATIVES TO THE LEGISLATURE.

BY LEONARD B. CHAPMAN

Continued from last week

Hon. Francis O. J. Smith was the first treasurer of the Westbrook Seminary association and the first purchases of land in the Stevens Plains district upon which the Seminary buildings are situated appear upon record in his name.

In 1830 he represented with other members the citizens of Portland in the lower branch of the State Legislature. The vote stood as follows:

Democratic—Mark Harris, 1001
Nath'l Mitchell, 1009
F. O. J. Smith, 995
Whig—Andrew L. Emerson, 921
Eliphalet Greeley, 903
Thomas Hammond, 900

In 1833 he served as President of the Senate.

In 1833, 1835 and 1837 he served in the House of Representatives at Washington, D. C.

What he accomplished for his district we cannot now state. The establishment of the Marine Hospital at East Deering was through his labors.

He built or purchased a large wooden building in Gorham, this state, intended for a "Water-cure hospital" which, proving a failure was taken down and removed to the northwesterly corner of his "Forest Home" lot where a cellar was built, now overgrown by weeds and bushes, but the building was never reconstructed.

About fifteen rods back from the highway now known as Stevens Plains avenue, which way defines the westerly side line of the "Forest Home" lot, and a few rods southerly of the northerly line of the enclosure—the cellar hole appearing in the northwesterly angle of the two lines—he built a three story brick building with granite trimmings which building he claimed was designed as a Home for indigent mothers but like most of his projects it was never completed for occupancy. In the rear of the building he constructed a Smith family tomb of the Grecian style of architecture.

The Goodrich house which we noticed last week was a brick structure and stood directly opposite the "Forest Home" gate-way on Stevens Plains avenue; it was destroyed by fire some years since. On page 42 of the 1871 County Atlas the house is marked "W. Wilson." The tomb lot back of the home for indigent women is marked "Cemetery."

Next northerly of the Goodrich house, and adjoining the same, Mr. Smith arranged for a public burial place and gave the enclosure the name of Magdalene Cemetery, but the lot was never used as Mr. Smith intended. Portland now owns it, the front part of which is vacant; the rest is used for burial purposes.

Over the entrance to the sepulchre we have noticed closed by a marble slab, but open when we visited the place, the letters F. O. J. S. were fashioned when the granite was fashioned, and upon the marble door an inscription as follows:

NATURE
teaches that
All Flesh Must Die.
RELIGION
inspires Hope that all
Spiritual Beings will
live forever, in spheres
and forms to which they
are fitted.
Believe in
GOD,
and fear not to leave wholly
to Him the Great Future.
His plans for Heaven
as for Earth must be
All-wise, Benevolent
and
Inimitable.
All men can know of future life.

One of Mr. Smith's many projects which failed was to supply Portland with Sebago Lake water through a pipe laid in the Oxford and Cumberland Canal channel which canal he purchased after it had outlived its usefulness.

Another was to dam Presumpscot river just above the Grand Trunk railroad bridge in Falmouth and by canal conduct the water to the seashore where he proposed to build wharves and large mills. Much stone and many logs were landed for the dam, and the canal was partly constructed and left as now seen. The water scheme occurred about 1860, the Presumpscot river dam and canal a little later.

Among his possessions was a three story building constructed of wood situated on Congress, between Exchange and Market streets, Portland, which was used as an inn and known by the name of International House and which was destroyed by the great fire of 1866.

The will of Mr. Smith is a curious document. It covers forty-one pages of paper, letter sheet size, and contains XXIII divisions. It commences as follows:

"The last Will and Testament of Frances O. J. Smith, written by his own hand February 8, 1876, at Forest Home in the town of Deering." It is witnessed by Samuel H. Tewksbury, who was a physician residing on Ocean street, westerly of Lunt's Corner, Deering, Charles H. Bray, a student of Tewksbury, then a business partner, now a physician residing on Free street, Portland, and Fred C. Stephenson, then a collector, boarding at 17 Brown street. (For Tewksbury see page 121, History of Cumberland Co., 1880; and for Bray, page 323, same book.)

Week of Jan. 10-13, 1900.

WESTBROOK.

NAMES OF THE SELECTMEN AND REPRESENTATIVES TO THE LEGISLATURE.

BY LEONARD B. CHAPMAN

(Continued from last week.

We made a mistake two weeks since in saying that the name of Hon. Frances O. J. Smith appears on the Cumberland county records of real estate titles as grantee or grantor 212 times; it should have been 366, and after his decease 27 times; then where the name of Eleanor appears in connection with the name of Mr. Smith's second wife it should be Ellen.

Mr. Smith's first wife, whose maiden name was Junie, or Julia Loretta Bartlett, a woman of culture and many virtues, died very suddenly while making a call at the residence of Samuel B. Stevens on the Plains, August 15, 1849.

Mr. Smith died at his "Forest Home" residence Oct. 14, 1876. He made a request in his will that none but makes witness the depositing of his remains in the tomb he had prepared.

His will was probated January 1, 1877. The executors named by him declined to act, so Charles W. Goddard —an ex-judge of our Superior court and an ex-postmaster of Portland; John A. Waterman—an ex-judge of our Probate court, a resident of Gorham, and Daniel W. Fessenden—an ex-clerk of courts of Portland, all now deceased, were appointed, who accepted the trust imposed.

It appears that Magdalene cemetery alluded to in our last article was incorporated under the general laws of the state of Maine and that the following named persons comprised the board of trustees, all of Portland:

Ezra Carter, Samuel L. Carleton, Edward Mason, George Waterhouse, John W. Lane.

April 27, 1880, for a consideration of $200 the trustees conveyed the cemetery lot received of Mr. Smith, consisting of fourteen acres, to a member of the board of trustees of Evergreen cemetery. Two months later a transfer of the lot to the city of Portland was made by the trustee.

The following is copied from the Portland Transcript of October 21, the year Mr. Smith departed this life:

Francis Ormand Jonathan Smith, so well known throughout Maine as a lawyer, journalist, railroad and telegraph projector, died at Forest Home in Deering last Saturday night at the age of seventy. He was born in Brentwood, N. H., Nov. 23, 1806; was educated at Phillips Academy, Exeter; studied law with Ichabod Bartlett at Portsmouth, N. H., and with Fessenden & Debiois of Portland; was admitted to the bar at the age of nineteen years; was elected to the Maine Legislature in 1831, and was President of the Senate in 1833; represented this district in Congress six years from 1833 to 1839; became interested in Morse's telegraph invention and built the first line to this city; was active in the building of the York & Cumberland railroad and started gas works in Portland. He was a man of rare abilities, genial in manner, of extraordinary activity, an able lawyer, an eloquent speaker, of large reading, full of projects which he seldom completed, a politician always at war with his party, a journalist who killed more newspapers than any other man of his time, and a litigant who was seldom without a law suit on his hands and rarely lost a case. Had his moral integrity been equal to his ambition he might have attained the highest position in the gift of the people; as it was he failed in most of his endeavors, and his record serves as a warning rather than an example.

Later, Edward H. Elwell, editor of the Transcript, who resided many years on the northerly side of Pleasant street, Deering, printed a very denunciatory editorial of the man, giving a description of Forest Home, which called out a reply from the deceased gentleman's widow.

We cannot state the number or produce the names of the journals Mr. Smith edited and the Transcript says "killed."

January 1, 1861, Mr. Smith purchased the old Portland Advertiser, which had been Whig in its politics, then Republican, with a history of a century, one of whose proprietors and editors was in 1826 Jacob Hill, born in East Bridgwater, Mass., 1784, graduated at Brown University, 1807, admitted to the bar in old Plymouth county, Mass., after reading law with Judge Mitchell of Boston; united in marriage by Rev. Caleb Bradley of what is now Deering, Nov. 21, 1816, with Miss Marcia Lobdell of Stroudwater village, Deering. He died May 17, 1852, and was interred at New Gloucester, where memorial slabs of himself, wife and a son may be seen as well as her sister Nancy who was the wife of Rev. Elisha Moseley.

Another son of Mr. Hill resides summers in this state, winters in California.

Mr. Smith seated in the chair editorial Eliphalet Case, an old line Democrat, who died in the winter of 1862-3. The Portland Daily Press was started as a Republican party organ in June of 1862, and after the great fire of 1866, the Advertiser ceased as a daily, but continued as a weekly till 1868 when it was revived and started under a different management as an evening daily but independent in politics, and thus has remained ever since having been ably managed.

How much of Mr. Smith's literary work in printed form has been saved, and the extent of the records of his political labors that are in existence in our private and public archives we have no means of knowing. The Bibliography of Maine published in 1896, contains a list of twenty-five notices, which may be found on page 440 of Vol. II.

TO BE CONTINUED.

A Correction.

We wish to make a correction in our last paper on the Elder Family, Ruth, daughter of Samuel and Nancy (Mosher) Elder, married 2d, Jacob Baker of Gorham instead of Jonas as printed last week.

S. T. DOLE.

Week of Jan. 17-20, 1900.

WESTBROOK.

NAMES OF THE SELECTMEN AND REPRESENTATIVES TO THE LEGISLATURE.

BY LEONARD B. CHAPMAN.

(Continued from last week.)

A few years ago, in a large two story ancient appearing dwelling house, with a long addition and barn attached situated in "Egypt"—a name given to a certain section of the rear part of the town of Nobleboro, this state—we found, after receiving permission to enter, though one of the outside doors was not fastened, several valuable historical relics (valuable to the historical student) both printed and in manuscript, with several pieces of homemade furniture with which a memorial marble slab inscribed as follows:

JOSEPH CHAPMAN.
died Dec. 16, 1847,
Aged 76 yrs.

He was the original occupant of the house and grandson of Anthony Chapman who went in 1749 from Ipswich. Mass., to the plantation of Walpole, now Nobleboro. Joseph's father was named Joseph, born May 18, of the year above stated. Joseph, the elder, resided almost within speaking distance of his son in a large one story house now standing unchanged in the barn of which enclosure the first religious meetings of the neighborhood were holden from which grew the first church organization of the region, now in existance with a comfortable meeting house.

Among the manuscripts was the clerk's records of a Washingtonian Temperance organization, first meeting holden Dec. 2, 1841, covering 13 pages of letter sheet size of paper including fifty-one signatures to the pledge, all the names in the original hand, twenty-seven of which being Chapmans.

The cover of the record sheets is made of a part of a newspaper named and printed as follows:

THE PEOPLE'S PRESS.
"God and the People."
Bangor, Me., Sept. 3, 1836,
Vol. I. NO. 24.

At the head of the editorial column is a list of the

DEMOCRATIC REPUBLICAN NOMINATIONS.

This brings to our attention the fact that the class opposed to imposing a high rate of duties upon imported goods a century or so ago and keeping the supreme power of the people to rule, in the hands of the people, with as little law as possible, were known by the name of Republican, while their opponents were organized under the name of Federalist, the former changing their party name over to that of Democrat, hence the name of "Democratic Republican" as used in 1836 as appears by the above, the Federalist party assuming in 1830, or thereabouts, the name of Whig which continued as a party name till the gathering in of the several political clans and organizations in 1853 of the present Republican party which adopted the name discarded by the new Democratic party.

Upon the 1836 list before us appears the "Republican Democratic" names of candidates for President, Governor, Members of Congress, Electors and State Senators.

For M. C. for Cumberland County appears the name of Hon. Francis O. J. Smith.

SENATORS.
Rosco G. Greene
Rufus Soule
Nathaniel L. Woodbury
Nathaniel S. Littlefield.

Mr. Woodbury resided at one time on the easterly side of the highway leading from Morrill's Corner to Riverton Park, about half way, on the farm later owned by Liberty B. Dennett, Esq., now a lawyer in Portland.

As a representative of the citizens of Minot Mr. Woodbury appeared in the lower house at Augusta in 1837 and 1838.

He was post master of Portland, his term commencing April 2, 1845, ending May 4, 1849; re-commencing April 1, 1853, ending March 31, 1857. He departed this life Oct. 2, 1880. A marble monument erected to his memory may be seen in our Deering Pine Grove cemetery.

Hon. Jonathan Smith, the candidate for Presidential elector of that year appearing on the list before us was a native of Bridgton, but the part of Westbrook now known as Deering contained the home of his adoption at Stroudwater village. He has been briefly noticed heretofore.

As a public speaker Hon. Francis O. J. Smith had few if any peers hereabouts.

In the old Chapman house we secured a seventy-six page pamphlet containing the arguments made in 1856 by Messrs. Henry W. Paine, Rufus Choate and Francis O. J. Smith on, the proposed removal of Judge Woodbury Davis from his seat upon the Supreme court bench of the state. The attempt succeeded, but it was a piece of Democratic political tyranny that produced quack party punishment. The facts had somewhat faded from our memory but a perusal of the very able arguments as printed brings up for review the neighborhood talk, newspaper discussions and final act by the Democratic legislature in a drama well calculated to arouse the people at large against the party then in power which it did. Forty-four years having elapsed since the exciting event both actors and spectators of the revolutionary period are now quite scarce who can rehearse from personal recollections the story of the party mistake of that period.

TO BE CONTINUED.

GRANDPA'S SCRAP BOOK

Week of Jan. 24-27, 1900.

[The Westbrook matter will be continued next week.]

DR. CALEB REA AND DR. JACOB HUNT.

BY LEONARD B. CHAPMAN

Read before the Maine Historical Society, January 18, 1900.

Dr. Caleb Rea, Jr., who was the first physician of Windham, this State, was a son of Dr. Caleb Rea of Danvers, Mass., according to the printed statements of his great-grandson, Hon. F. M. Ray of Westbrook.

Dr. Caleb Rea entered, it is claimed, as a surgeon at the age of seventeen years, the colonial navy of the war of the Revolution. He was born March 8, 1758, and united in marriage Oct. 4, 1781 with Sarah, daughter of Capt. John and Abigail (Blaney) White of Salem, Mass. He was a man who stood six feet in his stockings and weighed 250 pounds. Four sons and two daughters were born to them when he fell a victim to the hardships of the practice of his profession, Dec. 29, 1796. Sally, the second child, was born at Windham Sept. 27, 1785, and was united in marriage with Dr. Jacob Hunt June 26, 1809, Rev. Caleb Bradley performing the ceremony.

A hundred years ago, just, Dr. Jeremiah Barker came from Gorham, this state, to Stroudwater village, three miles from Portland, and erected a good two story house, which may now be seen as originally constructed, excepting a replaced front door and a chimney. Dr. Barker had five wives three of whom were inetrred at Stroudwater where memorial slabs may be seen. Dr. Hunt purchased the Barker property and was the only physician for the region many years. And he was a successful farmer as well as physician. They had two children—Caroline who united in marriage with Dr. John Sloan of Westbrook and removed to the Western country and Henry who became a practicing physician in Portland and the neighboring towns. He was united in marriage with Emeline, daughter of Capt. Dexter Brewer. She resides, a widow, at Swampscott, Mass., with a son who is a physician.

Dr. Rea's widow resided a number of years with her daughter—Mrs. Sally Hunt, at Stroudwater. She died January 22, 1836.

By special request of Mrs. Emeline Hunt, I now present to this society the articles now on exhibition before us.

Mrs. Hunt writes:—"Most of the antique articles I desire to present, if acceptable, to The Maine Historical Society were the property of Mrs. Sarah Rea who came with her husband, Dr. Caleb Rea, to Windham in 1781."

The list is as follows:

A seal skin trunk, with the letters J. H. on the top of the cover—the property of Dr. Jacob Hunt.
A key, or hook, for extracting teeth.
A "perpetual almanac" or chart published by G. Goold at Portland Jan. 1, 1805.
A foot stove.
A pair of spurs.
Seven pieces of crockery and earthen ware.
A very ancient appearing box, probably made by Indians.
A very ancient tea-pot.
A skillet and steelyards.
A coffee mill and balances.
A pair of hand cards.
A wedding bonnet and two calashes.
A woman's pocket and two bags.
Two silk or thread holders.
Snuff and other boxes.
Two wine glasses.
A silver tea spoon marked H, a wooden spoon and wooden needle.
A boy's waist.
A pair of bellows and candle moulds (more modern.)
A pair of small red curtains used in the Second Parish church of Portland front of the singers.

Upon my own account I now present a specimen of Dr. Jacob Hunt's penmanship of 1814, the paper having been made when the doctor was acting as Serg. Mate in military matters and is countersigned by Jeremiah Bailey and Josiah Hobbs, Lieut. Colonel, the first residing in what is now Deering, the latter in Falmouth.

GRANDPA'S SCRAP BOOK

Week of Jan. 31-Feb. 3, 1900.

WESTBROOK.

NAMES OF THE SELECTMEN AND REPRESENTATIVES TO THE LEGISLATURE.

BY LEONARD B. CHAPMAN

(*Continued from two weeks since.*)

In the last paragraph of our article of two weeks ago the compositor substituted the word "quack" from design or otherwise, for the word quick, so the sentence read: "The attempt succeeded, but it was a piece of Democratic political tyranny that produced quack party punishment."

The word quack can be made very elastic. Rev. Caleb Bradley in referring to the several kinds of quacks of the "learned professions" in his time of life remarked in his diary—"Yes there are quack ministers of the gospel of Christ." The parson was a radical Federalist and gave the name of Federal Corner to the part of the town where he resided, but common usage changed the name to Bradley's Corner by which the locality is known and will probably remain until some office seekers or spirits it away but little now remaining of the locality other than mud, imported coal ashes, a high rate of taxation, and Sum Libby's quarry at Brighton Corner from which waste stone, in some instances pieces as large as tea-kettles, are dumped in heaps upon the surface of our highways.

Yes, quack and quarry are synonymous terms in modern road building in the locality to which we refer in Deering under annexation rule and an Australian ballot system in local elections. Pardon the digression.

The editor of the Portland Transcript remarked in the article which we have quoted that Francis J. O. J. Smith was a "politician always at war with his party."

In the matter of removal of Judge Davis from his seat upon the bench of the Supreme Court of the State, Mr. Smith took decided grounds against the Democratic Governor and proposed action of the Legislature, to Mr. Smith's everlasting credit be it said, whatever else of an objectionable character may be charged against him.

We would like to make extended quotations from the time-stained pamphlet containing Mr. Smith's argument with the other two to which we have alluded but can make but one, as follows:

"If a man be an honest man, when he goes into a caucus room, it matters not what transpires there, he will come out an honest man."

What a grand text for the advocate of independent political action and political party when the politician or office seeker attempts to coerce the individual when a packed caucus puts before the public incompetent nominees by using the argument that the nomination is the result of caucus action hence all of the party are bound.

The people voted in 1855 to amend the State constitution so as to take from the Chief Executive the power of appointing sheriffs and took it into their own hands to elect such officials. When January 1st, 1856 came around Governor Wells had appointed and commissioned one Daniel C. Emery as sheriff of Cumberland county in place of Seward M. Baker who claimed the right under the amended constitution to be continued in office as sheriff till his successor had been elected by the people as provided by the amended constitution. With force Mr. Emery entered the jail, but Judge Davis declined to recognize Mr. Emery's claims in open court, though defended by such men as ex-Judge Howard and Lawyer Clifford who became a Judge of the U. S. Supreme court at Washington, D. C., and Samuel J. Anderson who, like Gen. Washington, would not tell a lie for party purposes, and became a general in the war against the Southern Rebellion, now a resident of Portland, as he was then.

But the Legislature proceeded to remove arbitrarily the Judge thus making the judicial power of the State subordinate not only to the Legislative branch of the popular government but to the political party in power—a doctrine and proceeding of the most dangerous character.

It was in the month of April of 1856 the Judge's seat was declared vacant by the Democratic party in power.

but Feb. 25, 1857, he was reinstated, resigning in 1865 to become post master of Portland, for which place he was commissioned Dec. 9, 1865, as successor of Andrew T. Dole, the first Republican occupant of the position who was a native of ancient Stroudwater.

Mr. Davis died while in office Aug. 13, 1871, Judge Chas. W. Goddard becoming his successor Oct. 7, 1871, Portland having had from Oct. 5, 1775 down to Aug. 13, 1890, twenty-one post masters.

Judge Davis erected while in office the first brick dwelling situated corner of Mellen and Congress streets, Portland.

BE CONTINUED.

GRANDPA'S SCRAP BOOK

Week of Feb. 7-10, 1900.

WESTBROOK.

NAMES OF THE SELECTMEN AND REPRESENTATIVES TO THE LEGISLATURE.

BY LEONARD B. CHAPMAN

(Continued from last week.)

The compositor makes us say in the closing paragraph of our last article that Judge Davis erected the first brick dwelling situated corner of Mellen and Congress streets, Portland. We wrote "fine". If we make the correction now it will save some one else the trouble a week, or a year, or perhaps a hundred years later, of trying to do so.

The year Judge Davis' seat upon the Supreme Court bench was declared vacant, which was 1856, the Cumberland County delegation in the Senate was composed of the following persons:

    Phinehas Barnes,
    Abner B. Thompson,
    Josiah Blaisdell,
    Horatio J. Swasyey.

The House of Representatives from Cumberland county thus:

* Baldwin—James Norton.
* Bridgton—Samuel Andrews, 2nd.
  Brunswick—Samuel S. Wing.
* Cape Elizabeth—James Trickey.
* Falmouth—William Prince.
  Freeport—William Gregg.
* Gorham—Jacob C Baker.
* Naples—John G. Connell.
  North Yarmouth—Adams True.
* Otisfield—Johnson W. Knight.
  Poland—William Stanton.
* Portland—James S. Little, Speaker.
* Portland—Sylvanus R. Lyman.
* Portland—James Todd.
  Pownal—Jeremiah Mitchell
  Raymond—James M. Leach.
  Westbrook—Daniel Winslow.
* Windham—Ezra Brown.
* Yarmouth—Sylvanus C. Blanchard

Marked thus * voted YES, or to remove the Judge.

April 6 a protest against the removal was filed in the house signed by fifty-seven members of that branch among which we find the name of

DANIEL WINSLOW.

Westbrook and Deering were one town then and he was the Representative whose name has appeared in these articles. Among the remonstrants from this country we find also the names of James M. Leach of Raymond and William Gregg of Freeport. The name of Charles P. Walton—Judge Walton who, recently, as a citizen of Deering, passed beyond the veil, to the great unknown, appears.

Where William Stanton of Poland and Adams True of North Yarmouth were we have no means of knowing. We have now, and find all along the wayside, political straddlers and dodgers.

In his speech against the proposed removal Mr. Smith said:

"I would like to see the man who would be bold enough to return to his constituents and say: 'I voted for the removal of Judge Davis, because he would not be humbly subordinate to the will of the executive!' Do that, and there is not a voter in the State of Maine, within three leagues of a schoolhouse, who would not say: 'You never shall represent me again as a legislator!'"

He was removed and lo! according to Mr. Smith's predictions, not one of the Cumberland county delegation in the Legislative body of 1856 was returned the following year according to printed records and our own recollections of the situation.

Daniel Webster said: "It is wise us to refer to the history of our ancestors. Those who are regardless of them do not perform their duty to the world."

And Macauly said: "All human beings, not utterly savage, long for some information about past times."

Mr. Smith possessed a most magnificent library, probably the finest in the state. It was carted to Portland and sold by an auctioneer. Several boxes of his private papers, injured by the dampness of the place where they were stored in his house, were deposited in the cellar of the Maine Historical Society, where they have remained undisturbed to this day.

Upon the walls of the Society hangs an oil painting of the library side of Mr. Smith's residence made and presented by Harry Brown, Portland's most famous artist.

To satisfy a judgment obtained by some person through Hon. Josiah H. Drummond a certain part of the real estate of the "Forest Home" lot was sold before Mr. Smith's demise, now owned by Hon. J. P. Baxter, and the premises are in reality a real forest. The magnitude of numbers and greatness in size of pines and oaks and density of the under herbage surprised us a few weeks since when we passed through the enclosure. To make it into a public garden and park would be more in accord with the public purse than the million dollar proposed outlay with a century of time to redeem Back Bay and make it a representative of ancient Eden with sin left out.

In 1888 a fine plan of Forest Home lot was gotten up showing the several lots purchased by Mr. Smith, location of dwelling house, drives, cemetery walls and tomb. We made a rough tracing of the outlines.

The several purchases of the Stevens heirs extend on Stevens Plains avenue from Oak street southerly to nearly half way from the street entrance in the middle of Forest Home lot to Pleasant street, or nearly to the present residence of Isaac H. Johnson, of unequal rearage length The Nathaniel Stevens lot in the corner next to Oak street had 10 rods of front, marked No. 1; on plan No. 2, William Stevens, 10 rods; Isaac Stevens, 8 rods; (we omit the fractions.) heirs of Josiah Stevens as follows: Samuel R. Bailey, Catherine Bailey, Mary Stevens and Nancy B. Stevens, 8 rods; Chauncy Woodford, whose wife was a sister to the preceding, 10 rods; William Kenney, whose wife was also a sister, 13 rods; Nathaniel Haskell, whose wife was a sister 7 rods, which brings us to the gateway; then the Zach. B. Stevens, the distance not being made plain by the plan-maker. The above are names of the sons and son's wives of the original Capt. Isaac S. Stevens, the Revolutionary soldier, the first of the name on Stevens Plains, whose last place of worldly abode is now one of the best of the locality.

TO BE CONTINUED.

GRANDPA'S SCRAP BOOK

Week of Feb. 14-17, 1900.

WESTBROOK.

NAMES OF THE SELECTMEN AND REPRESENTATIVES TO THE LEGISLATURE.

BY LEONARD B. CHAPMAN

(Continued from last week.)

On the twenty-seventh day of July, 1881,

    Charles W. Goddard of Portland,
    John A. Waterman of Gorham,
    Daniel W. Fessenden of Portland,

as executors of the will of Mr. Smith, for a consideration of $3,700 conveyed to James Augustine Healy of Portland, Bishop of the Diocese, the north-westerly corner of the "Forest Home" lot, the account of the transaction calling for 203 lineal feet on Stevens Plains avenue, thence easterly 441 feet to the westerly corner of the "Cemetery wall built by said deceased," (Smith) thence 209 and a half feet along the outside of the wall to the easterly corner thereof, thence northerly by the outside line of the wall, 202 and a half feet, thence by the wall 209 and a half feet, thence 465 feet to the highway (or Stevens Plains avenue,)

"Reserving, excepting and excluding from the conveyed, a lot 60 and a half feet square enclosed within the outer corners of four granite posts set in the ground by said deceased (meaning Smith) said reserved lot being near the center of the enclosure, surrounded by the cemetery wall aforesaid and containing in the middle thereof the tomb built by said deceased wherein his body and the body of his parents, children and wives now repose, also reserving a suitable and sufficient right of way to and from said tomb over said granted premises from and to said county road (Stevens Plains avenue) through one of the two entrances left in the westerly wall of said Cemetery for the lineal descendants of said deceased and all other persons who are or hereafter shall be entitled to visit said Cemetery or tomb for burial or other lawful purposes so long as said tomb shall continue within said Cemetery."

The deed further provides that the walls of the Cemetery shall be maintained by the grantee so long as the tomb remains, also the enclosure shall not, or any part thereof, be sown or planted for crops or ploughed or in any way cultivated or used for agricultural purposes, and that no buildings shall be erected thereon so long as the tomb shall continue thereon.

Within the bounds as recorded was the three story brick building erected by Mr. Smith, designed as he claimed, for a home for indigent widows, which we have briefly noticed and which he attempted to make permanent and useful by State legislative action when there arose a tearful newspaper howl from Mr. Smith's political opponents, and the building as now seen (with an ell added) remained empty till after Mr. Smith's demise.

On the twenty-ninth day of April, 1882, for "one dollar and other valuable considerations," James Augustine Healy of Portland, Me., conveyed by deed to "The Saint James Conventry and Hospital, a corporation organized under the laws of the State of Maine, with a place of business at Deering, Me.," the property which he (Mr. Healy) had purchased nine months before of the executors of the Smith will. The recorded record of the transfer contains the same described reservations as the one running to Mr. Healy, our Roman Catholic priest.

To the lot the trustees of the hospital and school attached removed the wooden building that was erected by a handful of Methodists that stood where the imposing Methodist church edifice may now be seen at the northerly corner made by Forest avenue and Pleasant street and in it established a Roman church altar and lighted incense candles which never ceased to burn (we are told) till the building and altar were partially destroyed by fire a few months since.

Today, the Roman Catholic church hospital-school-lot, surrounded by the evergreen Norway Spruce and Arborvitae hedge, over the avenue aperture of which appears in golden letters on a black ground arranged in semi-circle form the words ST. JOSEPH'S ACADEMY, though the lawns and herbage are clad with the white habiliments of mid-winter, affords one of the finest places in Deering to look upon, made so by art and Nature combined.

Let us enter:

"Stand, stranger stand. The castle gate
  Through which you pass to fairy land
Is mine to guard. What happy fate
  Bids you within its border? Stand!"

"Let me pass. Oh stern faced warden,
  Through the wonderous castle gate,
Let me walk within the garden
  Led by fancy and by fate."

"Pass, stranger pass, the olden time
  Was full of song and mirth and cheer;
Sing any song that suits your rhyme
  And let it echo round the year."

"Where, warden, O, where is the 'reservation'—the sepulcher?"

A West wind, in doleful tongue, replies—"Here! Come bard, come historian both local and national, come moralist, come hither, come see and listen"—

"I number the sands, I measure the sea,
  What's hidden to others is known to me.
The lamb and the turtle are simmering slow,
  With brass above them and brass below."

TO BE CONTINUED.

GRANDPA'S SCRAP BOOK

Week of Feb. 21-24, 1900.

WESTBROOK.

NAMES OF THE SELECTMEN AND REPRESENTATIVES TO THE LEGISLATURE.

BY LEONARD B. CHAPMAN

(Continued from last week.)
FRANCIS O. J. SMITH'S TOMB.

The title to the lot given by the executors of the will of Hon. Francis O. J. Smith upon which the tomb was situated was not a clear title; there was an incumbency upon it in the tomb itself and the grantee could not in consequence of the stipulations imposed come into full legal possesion of the whole premises so long as the tomb remained. The title to the tomb was by the executors vested in the persons having legal rights in the tomb and their names may be found in the will itself. The reservation clause evinces the possession of wisdom on the part of the executors, and the bringing to light of day at this time the fact that such a reservation was made lifts from the names of the executors a cloud, for it has been repeatedly alleged they caused the removal.

It appears from the memoranda obtained at the Evergreen cemetery office that on the 19th day of June, 1884, Rev. James A. Healy of the Catholic church of Portland obtained in the name of Mr. Smith the use of the lot to which the tomb was removed, and that on the 17th day of October, 1887, he transferred the title to the lot to the name of Mrs. Harriet M. Sadler, a sister to Mr. Smith.

It will be remembered that we have stated that the will provides for the entombing of this sister's remains and that of her husband in Mr. Smith's "family vault," also of another sister, Mrs. Olivia E. S. Frink, and we think still another by the name of Adeline A. Munroe and her husband.

Mrs. Frink's husband was Dr. John N. Frink, a dentist in Portland, who died Oct. 11, 1846, aged 36 years; she, Aug. 19, 1876; and the husband of Mrs. Sadler was Rev. Levi L. Sadler, an able preacher of the Universalist persuasion, and it is recorded that "under his efficient ministry from 1842 to 1847, the First Universalist society of Portland prospered." Mr. Sadler died at Williamsburg, N. Y., Oct. 29, 1854, aged 57 years.

When we visited the tomb a few months since the wall each side the door that contains the quaint inscription reminded us of a monastery a thousand years of age with the heads of evil-eyed miniature reptiles protruding with rapacious natures burrowing in the seams between the stones when it was discovered by a closer inspection that what appeared to be the heads of reptiles with numerous eyes was newspaper waste used for mortar, heads, protruding parts; eyes, printer's ink, the or joints having once been covered by a thin coating of cement which had fallen out, thus leaving the paper exposed as we here state.

Having obtained consent of the reported custodian of the tomb, outside the cemetery management, who very readily gave it in a cheerful manner with the statement that he would be pleased to have our object in view accomplished—to wit: The door containing the inscription opened sufficiently long for us to compare our memoranda with the names and dates upon the tablets required to be placed upon the closed compartments of the tomb by a clause of Mr. Smith's will, and to obtain what we had not found outside records of, we address a note to the chairman of the cemetery trustees who are only in their office servants of the voters of Portland and the reply received is as follows:

Portland, Me., Sept. 27, 1899.
Mr. L. B. Chapman,
Portland, Me.

Dear Sir: I am in receipt of yours of the 23d which just came to hand, as I have been out of town for several days, and in reply would say that as far as I am concerned I could not grant you the privilege you ask for without consulting the other trustees. I am, however, of the opinion that we haven't the right to open a private tomb for the inspection of the public without the consent of the owners of the tomb or the trustees of the estate. I expect to see the other trustees soon, and as soon as I see them I will reply to you again.
Yours very truly

L. M. Cousins
Trustee Evergreen Cemetery.

About five months have passed and we haven't yet received the second reply.

This whole matter has its serious and ludicrous and its ridiculous sides "from a to Izard." And from a financial point of view the Evergreen cemetery management has another.

We bestow now very briefly our consideration upon Mr. Cousins as a trustee, and say that his letter compared with the facts reminds us of the days of epitaph writing when the fellow went to the church yard and prepared as follows for his use:

"Here I lie snug as a bug in a rug."

After his demise a chum of his feeling that life was with him drawing to a close went to the same place and upon the same errand. Espying what his chum had done he prepared for his own use, after death by his friends as follows:

"Here I lie snugger than that tother bugger."

Mrs. Harriet M. Sadler did not accept the bequeathed privilege in her brother's "family vault;" being a widow of means she has erected a tomb of her own. She resided at No. 55 Neal street, Portland, in a three-story brick house that was appraised at $6,000. The entire estate was appraised at $27,000. The will was probated July 8, 1889. One item provides for "perpetual care of my two lots in Evergreen cemetery and to keep in repair forever the tombs on said lots."

All the provisions of the will, both public and private, it is alleged, have been complied with by the executor excepting the latter, our informant, however, not knowing whether Jonathan Smith's and his son Francis O. J. Smith's "full length portraits" have been turned over to Exeter (N. H.) Academy or not as the will provides "they having been both educated there."

Under the circumstances, and we have stated the facts, who owns today the so-called Francis O. J. Smith tomb and who shall say when and to whom the outside door shall be opened? And can the Sadler will be stretched so as to pay for putting mortar where newspaper waste was used as a substitute?

TO BE CONTINUED.

GRANDPA'S SCRAP BOOK

Week of Feb 28 - Mar. 3, 1900.

WESTBROOK.

NAMES OF THE SELECTMEN AND REPRESENTATIVES TO THE LEGISLATURE.

BY LEONARD B. CHAPMAN

(Continued from last week.)

1863. SELECTMEN.
    Jonas Raymond,
      (Saccarappa district.)
    Henry B. Boody,
      (Morrill's Corner dist.)
    Charles B. Stevens,
      (Stroudwater dist.)
Rep. Francis O. J. Smith.

Smith received 540 votes and George Warren of Saccarappa district 524. Smith took but little interest that year in what was done at the Legislature, seldom being seen in his seat.

In 1807, July 16, Henry H. Boody and Jane Winslow were joined in marriage by the Rev. Caleb Bradley—fee $4. She was a daughter of Nathan Winslow who resided some rods back southerly from the road that leads from Pride's Bridge to Saccarappa village, upon the northerly side of the Presumpscot river about a mile and a half above the bridge, in a large two story house, now to be seen, in excellent repair, as originally constructed.

In 1815, Nathan Winslow and Benjamin Boody (no "H" in the name at this or later dates) were taxed jointly upon a valuation as follows:

One house,	$700
(This amount indicates one of the best houses in the town.)	
Two barns,	100
One out house,	25

Thirty-five acres mowing land at $19 per acre.
Thirty pasturing at $8 per acre.
One hundred and seventy unimproved at $7 per acre.
Six oxen; 8 cows; 2, "two year olds;" 4, "one year olds;" 2 horses; 4 swine and a chaise.

These figures indicate quite an estate for the period in this section.

On the twenty-fourth day of second month," 1820, Nathan Winslow in the presence of Noah Read, Edward Cobb and Archelaus declared and signed his last will.

After making ample provision for his wife Mary, the Fourth provision of the will read as follows:

"I give and bequeath unto my son and daughter Benjamin and Jane Boody one-half of my homestead, stock and farming utensils, together with my watch and all my outlands and other estate not otherwise disposed of; and also at the decease of my wife the remaining half of my homestead, stock and farming utensils."

He named in addition to daughter Jane (Mrs. Benjamin Boody) other children as follows:

Son and daughter John and Fanny Winslow, sons Richard, Jonathan, Aaron and Hezekiah and daughter Eleanor Harper; and named his wife Mary and son-in-law Benjamin Boody as executors of his will.

Benjamin and Jane had an interesting family of children who took as a general thing very kindly to books. For a period of several years scarcely one passed when a Boody name did not appear upon the school board, and we venture the assertion without fear of contradiction that more than twice as many addresses were made by the Boody brothers to the scholars on "closing day" than by persons of any other name.

Upon the town list of intentions of marriage for June 7, 1840, we find the name of Henry B. Boody and Ann Maria Proctor, and under the shadow of a monument of an afternoon's sun, a monument inscribed with the name of Henry H. Boody, in Pine Grove cemetery, we notice the name of one of the selectmen of Westbrook of the year 1863—one of the years of shedding of blood when the general government was contending with the South for an undivided territorial existence, for the perpetuation of which in an unbroken form Henry B. Boody gave a son—a mere boy!

HENRY B. BOODY
died
Dec. 31, 1880,
Aged 63 yrs. 9 mo.

There is rest in Heaven.

The Proctor name flourished many years upon a farm lot located between Pride's Bridge and the Winslow-Boody homestead, which Proctor farm came into the possession of Nathan W. Boody, a son of the original Benjamin, the Brackett name having existed there also upon a farm since 1744, situated between the farms of Winslow and Proctor, but of the connection between the wife of Henry B. Boody and the original Proctor family we cannot now discourse.

The widow of Henry B. Boody married a man by the name of Martin; and the inscription upon the headstone by the side of that of her first husband is somewhat misleading to those who do not know the facts—as follows:

ANN M. B. MARTIN,
died April 1, 1886.
Aged 66 years.
Asleep in Jesus.

The inscription on the head stone of the son is also misleading—as follows:

GEORGE DANA,
died at Arlington Heights,
Va., March 9, 1863, aged 17 years, 8 mos.

Mr. Boody resided in several places in town; at one time in the low-posted, large, ancient appearing, one story house situated southerly of the Windham road cemetery; at another time near the Stevens Plains avenue railroad crossing of the Maine Central at Morrill's Corner district, and at another, Deering's Bridge district.

Under the caption of David Patrick of Stroudwater, The News commenced a series of articles Nov. 30, 1895, which were terminated Jan. 4, '96.

Tristram Stevens, who came from Newburyport, married into the Patrick family.

Shadrach Chapman, born March 6, 1764, came from New Market, N. H. and married Lydia Starbird, born in the Riggs house, near Bradley's Corner, which has been noticed in The News. The Starbird house now seen situated on the Stroudwater road in Westbrook was built by her ancestors the year Lydia was born which was 1768, March 6.

Shadrach's daughter Nancy, born at Stroudwater Nov. 18, 1791, became, Oct. 25, 1810, the second wife of Tristram C. Stevens, who was born there Nov. 6, 1779. They had nine children: Tristram, who now resides in Portland; Henry; David; Ann Maria; (Mrs. George W. Morton of Stroudwater, lately deceased.) Henry; Lydia Maria; (Mrs. George Siemons, lately deceased,) Charles Bartlett; Olive J. (Mrs. Nicholas Hanson) and Michael, (the husband of Mrs. Lillian M. N. (Ames) Stevens, of the Woman's C. T. U. national renown,) the last three named residing at Stroudwater village.

The whole Stevens family grew to maturity, excepting one, all married except Charles B., he remained at home and engaged in trade in the westerly half of the building Andrew Hawes, Esq., uses for the storage of grain which was built in 1807 by Hon. Archelaus Lewis and Jonathan Sparrow.

Charles B. Stevens served the town as selectman four years in succession and as representative in 1867, being defeated the next year by George H. Hammond, agent of the Cumberland Mills Warren Paper Manufacturing Company. He died a Democrat as he ever was in politics, at Stroudwater and his remains were interred at the village cemetery.

TO BE CONTINUED.

GRANDPA'S SCRAP BOOK

Week of March 7-10, 1900.

WESTBROOK.

NAMES OF THE SELECTMEN AND REPRESENTATIVES TO THE LEGISLATURE.

BY LEONARD B. CHAPMAN

(Continued from last week.)

After "Archelaus" there should have appeared "Lewis" in the article of last week, then the name of the third person who witnessed the signing of the will of Nathan Winslow would have appeared as Archelaus Lewis and consequently correct. Lewis built and resided after the war of the Revolution in the house in which the post office is located at Stroudwater, head of Waldo, on Westbrook street, westerly side, district of Deering, in which war he took an active part as he did in the Stroudwater church being a deacon, and town matters generally, building the brick house on the northerly side of the falls at Cumberland Mills, Westbrook, and removing his family hither from Stroudwater, having purchased there the mill privilege. His remains with three wives are deposited in the old village cemetery where there are grave memorials.

1864—SELECTMEN.
  Henry B. Boody
  Jonas Raymond
  Charles B. Stevens.
Rep. Edward Payson.
1865—Henry B. Boody
  Jonas Raymond
  Charles B. Stevens.
Rep. Edward Payson.
1866—Henry B. Boody
  Jonas Raymond
  Charles B. Stevens.
Rep. Clement Phinney.

All the foregoing named were Democrats excepting Phinney.

It seems to us that a few way-side allusions at this time to "party politics" of the long ago can here be made without offense to any one—a few statements of facts pertaining to the political situation in Westbrook as we saw then and now record for those who come after us—Westbrook and Deering being one town from 1814 to 1870 when the territory of Westbrook was divided by an edict of the State Legislature.

At the time of our earliest recollection, and records long before that show, our citizens disagreed upon the matter of governmental protection of home industries. The Democrats (or by whatever other name called) opposed protection, yet Westbrook was a manufacturing town. The soil being good there were, it is true, many thrifty farmers. Unquestionably the Democrats could truly "point with pride" to the ship building industry, but all over the town were little manufactories now gone. The ship building industry—ships being required for a carrying trade—was comparatively unremunerative, mechanics working twelve and fourteen hours per day for the small sum of one and one dollar and a quarter per day, a large percentage of the small amount of wages going to the till of the person who sold intoxicants. Under such a state is it a wonder children died from neglect and want and others grew up to use an X in place of their own signature? Then a few thought for the many though the few were not always men of letters, but men born with brains who were destined by the natural course of events to become celebrated in some way, whether or not they saw the inside of a schoolhouse during their minority. We might allude to many individual instances in proof of our assertions none being more striking than the case of the first Governor of our State of Maine, but it is our purpose at this time to deal with local political rulers of long ago and present records of local events in connection with assertions deduced from personal observations of the period of which we write. Going back in thought to the good old Democratic times of our daddies the immensity of our recollections of a cent as then seen was wonderful! And then arises before us the image of the political ruler or dignitary—the man then of brain force, the days when the Democratic party was in control and the few ruled the many, days when cotton cloth was too expensive to be cut into handkerchiefs and flour bread was a luxury in many families! Then the political boss towered far above the average citizen and of all the "Westbrook Democratic Junto" performed a most domineering part in our local if not State politics, but the record does not stand out against the honesty of purpose and action of those who engineered the party in its success, it only shows what has been, reflects today, and foretells what will be continued. "Juntos" and Junto" proceedings being now shielded to a considerable extent by State legislative enactments, the caucus proceeding taking the place of the popular vote, the latter being subordinated to the former to a degree that causes apprehension of future evil.

This brings us to the introduction of the fact that we are in receipt of a communication from one who has lived long and observed sharply the course of politicians among us which we here present, as follows:

I am much interested in the historical articles you publish. I read every one. I have been especially interested in your references to F. O. J. Smith, whom I knew so well and with whom I was so much associated. He was a most wonderful man. I have said repeatedly, that in my opinion, if he had taken proper care of himself, let all his vagaries and moonshine operations have gone to the winds, and confined himself studiously to the law, he would have been second to no lawyer in the United States. But he not only threw away a large fortune, but threw away himself with it. But I write you for the purpose of calling up the recollection of the "Westbrook Junto," a term well defined and clearly understood throughout the whole State for many years. This "Junto" consisted of N. L. Woodbury, Jonathan Smith, Levi Morrill and Samuel Jordan. This "Junto," not unlike others, had its eyes out on personal considerations and so some of its members and generally all were in office. The ablest man of the four was Woodbury, the most sagacious politician was Smith, while Morrill and Jordan were very close seconds. This "Junto" flourished in the palmy days of the Maine Democracy, and had pretty general control. It was consulted on all occasions; it absolutely dominated the town of Westbrook (and of course Deering) and very largely the city of Portland and the county of Cumberland, while throughout the whole State scarcely any political scheme was started without its consent, and none was expected to succeed without its indorsement first having been received.

We hear much said nowadays about bosses and boss rule, but there never was in this State a boss or an aggregation of bosses that could for a single moment compare with the "Westbrook Junto."

In after years political changes considerably impeded the efficiency and weakened the power of this "Junto," but it was only finally dissolved by the death of its members.

TO BE CONTINUED.

ANDPA'S SCRAP BOOK

Week of March 14-17, 1900.

WESTBROOK.

NAMES OF THE SELECTMEN AND REPRESENTATIVES TO THE LEGISLATURE.

BY LEONARD B. CHAPMAN

(*Continued from last week.*)

THE PAYSONS.

A monument inscription in our Portland Evergreen cemetery is as follows:

EDWARD PAYSON, D. D.
Born in Ridge, N. H.,
July 25, 1783.
Ordained Pastor of the
Second Congregational Church in
Portland, Dec. 16, 1807.
Died Oct. 22, 1827.
His record is on high.

The causes that lead to the formation of the Second Congregational church are many; the whole story if printed would be very interesting reading. The act of incorporation was granted by the General Court in March, 1788. The church edifice was erected on the southerly side of Middle, next westerly of Deer street, and in outside finish was barn-like, i.e., resembled the old Universalist chapel building situated at Brighton Corner in Deering, which was used by the citizens of Deering as a Town House, and now to be seen as originally built, and used for storage purposes by the city street department. A flag-staff was placed upon the front end of the Portland structure and for some years the novel way of notifying the public of church service by hoisting the flag of the country was indulged in. Then a belfry was added and the city presented the society with a clock which was placed above the bell, the house enlarged and finish added.

The Rev. Edward Payson was a son of Rev. Seth Payson of Ridge, N. H. He was a graduate of Harvard college, received his degree in 1803 and very soon thereafter came hither to become preceptor of the Portland Academy, which position by agreement he was to hold three years. At the end of the time he was ordained as indicated by the monument inscription, and became a saintly, dogmatical theologian of more than local fame. He was a man of wit as well as Bible wisdom. July 4, 1806, he delivered an oration in Portland which was full of thrusts at the national administration and individual references that caused great merriment for the listeners. he being a "high toned Federalist," a counter meeting being held by the opposition party.

From the close of the war of the Revolution till the time of the ordination of Rev. Mr. Payson Portland, in common with the rest of the country, had enjoyed a season of great prosperity. For several years in consequence of foreign wars this country had the carrying trade. Many people had become rich; the forests were devastated to a great extent, and the lumber exchanged for molasses and West India rum,the former distilled here and New England rum manufactured, rum then being comparatively the cheapest article on sale and the most common in use.

When Payson, the academy preceptor, changed to the saintly scholar and expounder of what he understood in 1807 to be Divine law,he found the season of prosperity terminated, vessels tied up to wharves and Back Bay and Fore River full of them, all disrobed, and the President's proclamation of non-intercourse in full force; idleness in place of activity, poverty in place of growing riches; the people ready to receive the new advocate using a new style of delivery, yet one in belief of the old school, being so exceedingly dogmatical in his way of looking upon what he conceived to be the Bible truths that he would not extend the right hand of fellowship to the learned Parson Nichols, pastor of the First Congregational church of Portland. To hear the new man the people gathered in flocks and as many of them had nothing else to think of an impression was made upon those who listened of a wonderful nature. His sermons and notices of him were printed not only in this country but reproduced in foreign, notwithstanding Rev. Asa Cummings states in the preface of his Memoir, comprising three volumes, published in 1856, that but little of the teachings of Rev. Mr. Payson had been preserved by printing. He last lived and died in a house that stood at the northeasterly corner of Franklin and Middle streets, Portland, which he purchased not long before his demise. His remains were deposited in the church vault in the Eastern cemetery but with the monument removed to Evergreen.

The maiden name of Rev. Dr. Payson's wife was Ann Louise Shipman, who passed beyond this life Nov. 17, 1848.

CHILDREN:

1—Louisa Shipman b. Feb. 12, 1812.
2—Edward b. Sept. 14, 1813.
3—Caroline Shipman b. Feb. 13, 1815, died May 5, 1816.
4—Charles Henry b. Dec. 1, 1816, died May 1, 1819.
5—Elizabeth b. Oct. 26, 1818.
6—Henry M. b. Oct. 13, 1821.
7—George b. May 26, 1824.
8—Charles b. Sept. 3, 1826.

The three last became brokers and bankers in Portland.

Edward Payson, the son, had a muscular frame, dark complexion, black hair, black eyes and a lofty air—a man of eccentric parts and withal, to the casual acquaintance, stoical nature. He was a graduate of Bowdoin college, and spent some ten or fifteen years after graduation in our Southern country, where he read and practiced law, teaching a part of the time, but for the law he had little love. Upon returning to the place of his nativity he gave up his profession and June 15, 1847, purchased for a consideration of $5,000 sixty-two acres of the old Ilsley farm, situated on the southerly side of Ocean and a few rods westerly of Main streets, in Westbrook, now Deering, but he retained only part of the original purchase.

October 3, 1848, he was united in marriage with Miss Penelope A. Martin of Portland, and went to reside upon the land he had purchased in Westbrook where he had concluded to indulge in farming, which practice he continued to the time of his death, July 21, 1890, aged 76 years, 10 mos.

Upon his farm he displayed his eccentric nature. The first half of his dwelling was constructed from clay blocks moulded from clay mortar and chopped straw mixed, dried in the sun, then covered with mastic mortar after placing them in position for his house walls. The second half, built later, was constructed of brick, and the walls coated with mastic mortar so the whole, as now observed, presents a pleasing object to look upon, the situation being one of the finest in the whole town, the history of the locality being sufficient to make. if compactly compiled, a volume of fair size of interesting reading.

TO BE CONTINUED.

214
RANDPA'S SCRAP BOOK

Week of March 21-24, 1900.

WESTBROOK.

NAMES OF THE SELECTMEN AND REPRESENTATIVES TO THE LEGISLATURE.

BY LEONARD B. CHAPMAN

(*Continued from last week.*)

[We regret to say that we are compelled to defer for the present notices of Jonas Raymond and Clement Phinney, having neglected to supply in season missing memoranda.]

1867—SELECTMEN.

Daniel Dole
    Stroudwater.
George C. Cloudman
    Woodfords.
William L. Pennell
    Saccarappa.
Rep.—Charles B. Stevens
    Stroudwater.

All Republicans excepting Stevens.

THE DOLES.

In 1760, one Richard Dole, a cabinet maker, resided on the easterly side of what is now India street, Portland. The location is marked on one if not all plans made since 1775 that show the situation in Portland of buildings at the time of the bombardment and destruction by Mowat, Oct. 18, of that year.

In 1773, John Dole, a housewright, was living on India street. In 1776 he enlisted and took up the musket in the cause of the Colonies. In 1788 he became a charter member of the Portland Second Parish. In 1791 he purchased of Elijah Pope, a farmer and edge-tool maker, whose farm and shop were located on the easterly side of Quaker Lane, northerly of Allen's Corner, Deering, the Pope residence, used in 1771 as a landmark when Quaker Lane was surveyed, and as £360 were paid for the forty-six acres of land "with buildings" it is quite probable the two story dwelling now observed is the one then standing. Pope, whose wife was named "Phebe," first appeared there in 1769. Upon selling Pope removed to Windham and purchased of Josepha Hutcherson fifty-six acres of land, "house, barn and part of a saw mill" and part of lot No. 140 on Pleasant river. A descendant, an aged man, possessed of an ecclesiastical voice and demeanor made periodical visits a few years since to Deering and sold butter from a wagon, but his name we have forgotten or we would further immortalize by insertion here.

The section of Deering where Pope resided is replete with historical incidents as is the town generally. A little to the northward James, the first of the Winslows hereabouts, resided and kept an inn on the easterly side of the highway, but to the visitor of today nothing remains to show the location and the truth has never been told in print, though recorded in the Massachusetts archives that just prior to the war of the Revolution a county convention of citizens was holden at the WINSLOW INN to take into account the warlike appearances of things in general hereabouts and elsewhere.

In 1815 the Dole property on Quaker Lane was taxed on a valuation as follows:

JOHN & JOHN DOLE, JR.

One house, $700.00
Two outhouses,   30.00
Twenty-five acres mowing land at $20 per acre; thirty-five acres pasturing at $9; thirty unimproved at $7; 4-oxen; 5-cows; 2-two year olds; 1-one year old; 1-horse; 1-swine and 1-chaise.

The camera centurial hunter will most assuredly find a worthy subject in the Quaker Lane Dole mansion house, but the facts of modern history as found in the late built schoolhouse, located near by, are more startling—equaled only by the $70,000 High school building at Deering Center.

In what way, if any, Daniel Dole, who was elected selectman in 1867, was connected by the ties of kinship to the Portland clan of the name we cannot state, not knowing.

Richard Dole came from Bristol, England, in 1639, to what is now known as Old Newbury, Mass. He was born in December of 1622, and died July 26, 1705. His son, William Dole, was born April 11, 1660, and died Jan. 29, 1718.

William Dole, grandson of William Dole the emigrant, was born 1684 and died Aug. 8, 1752. His wife was Rebeckah Pearsons of Rowley, Mass. Their son, Daniel Dole, was born Sept. 28, 1717.

William Titcomb came from Newbury, England, in 1634. His son William, born August 14, 1659, married Ann, a daughter of William Cottle, who was a son of Edward Cottle. Moses Pearsons married Sarah, a daughter of the second William Titcomb. When married Mr. Pearsons was a house joiner. He came to Portland in 1728 with a family of four daughters to which two more were added, all of whom married.

Mr. Pearsons was a very stirring man, and obtained fame and fortune. He was at the time of his death not only rich in honors conferred but possessed a great estate. He owned the land from Libby's Corner northerly and passing over what is now Brighton street—nearly two hundred acres. As Parson Dean of the First Parish church of Portland married a daughter of Capt. Pearsons. Moses Pearsons and desired the tract to be all in Portland the proposed division line was changed to please the Parson, hence the crookedness of the inherited dividing line between the old town of Deering and Portland. He died June 5, 1778. The story of his career in detail if ever told in print will prove interesting reading and supply a long felt want among those who are interested in the preservation of our local history.

Sarah, the fourth child of Moses Pearsons was born Nov. 28, 1728, in Old Newbury, Mass.; and Daniel Dole was born there as we have stated, Sept. 28, 1717, and they were united in marriage March 8, 1753.

Mrs. Mary (Dole) Chenery, who resided at the Bradley Corner district of Deering, a sister to Daniel Dole, the selectman of 1867, had in her possession at the time of her demise a Bible three hundred (more or less) years old; and aside from the fact that the book contains the usual amount of subjects for contemplation found in such volumes and is valuable on account of its great age the book is otherwise interesting because it contains records written upon its once blank leaves that lead in thought if not in fact to places and events of the past that are dark as is usually the case, but places of amusement and instruction where descriptive records are obtainable.

The first inscription in the old Bible reads thus:

> This Bible is the gift of Capt. Abraham Lawrence to Jeremiah Pearsons, Jr., March, 1733.

SECOND.

> This Bible is the gift of Jeremiah Pearsons to Sarah Dole, Jr., 1753.

When the date of marriage and last record of presentation are compared it is not a stretch of the imagination to say that the Bible was a marriage gift, the last time, to the bride.

TO BE CONTINUED.

GRANDPA'S SCRAP BOOK

Week of March 28-31, 1900.

WESTBROOK.

NAMES OF THE SELECTMEN AND REPRESENTATIVES TO THE LEGISLATURE.

BY LEONARD B. CHAPMAN.

(Continued from last week.)

[Where the name of George C. Cloudman appears at the top of our article of last week it should be Geo. C. Codman.]

Daniel Dole was thirty-six years of age when he was united in marriage at Old Newbury, Mass., with Miss Sarah Pearsons. He was by occupation a mariner and became master of his calling or so much so as to become "Captain" of the vessels in which he went down upon the seas to do business. He made the place of his birth the place of his home till he came hither to reside.

Children.

1—Moses, b. Nov. 25, 1753; d. June 2, 1754.
2—Daniel, Jr., b. Aug. 26, 1757.
3—Mary, b. March 22, 1760.
4—Moses, b. May 20, 1766.

In 1770 Capt. Dole purchased of Samuel Waldo what is now known as the Dole farm situated on the northerly side of Stroudwater village, district of Deering, which contained 185 acres of upland and 27 acres of marsh. Soon after 6 acres of the Small farm was added making a total of 218 acres, most of which was heavily wooded, the cleared part being of a rich clay loam, undulating, but very productive of grass at that time.

What induced Captain Dole to come hither can readily be imagined. He evidently had become tired of sea-going life, being then fifty-three years of age. His wife's father, Captain Moses Pearsons, was a rich man and was in his dotage. In 1771 he gave each of his six daughters a hundred acre lot on account of love and affection he bore them. Parson Dean, Capt. Dole's brother-in-law, of the First Parish church of Portland, was upon the top wave of popularity and prosperity in the pulpit and out. He could write a novel; he could make an almanac; he could graft an apple tree, and he could act the part of the cow boy and drive his cows to pasture at Bradley's Corner and put them into the Parish lot, (which he never owned as has been stated in print) and he could write and deliver a sermon in a manner that would keep his hearers warm without the aid of a stove fire in the dead of winter, though he evidently did not believe half he preached, but was wise enough to keep the other half to himself, preaching then by many college graduates being a matter of business, he going out of the world leaving his confidential friends in a mystery as to his views upon several points connected with themes of pulpit discussions.

Upon his land purchase Capt. Dole immediately erected one of the most commodious dwelling houses in Falmouth not excepting Portland Neck, upon one of the pleasantest sites in the whole town. Indeed for history and as a picturesque point of observation and for suggestiveness, particularly the point a little easterly of the dwelling, though erected a hundred and thirty years ago, it even now is in a better condition to endure the wear of shower and sunshine than most of our modern built residences. Really, the view is most charming and so full of varied history of persons and events, covering a period pretty well known by a few of nearly two hundred and fifty years! When the "sea is in," for the water of the ocean comes to within a few paces of the Dole house, there is no point of observation like it hereabouts. This, however, may be imagined, for it is well known to the careful observer that a sea captain seldom builds upon retiring from active service where he cannot look out upon the water and snuff the sea-charged air though the water be ever tranquil. From the point of observation we suggest, the admirer of commingled water, trees, hills and dales, church steeples, great buildings and vessels masts in the distance, puffing locomotives attached to long trains of cars, ruins of the Oxford and Cumberland canal, with the imaginary slow moving boats, mills and grave yard monuments, the modern trolley car passing over a bridge that disgraces the contemplation of sublimity in art and nature, aqueduct pipes and telephone wires, will find all we have pointed out. At the base of the point of observation we suggest is a living spring of a prodigious flow of crystal water, and from whence it comes in such a quantity is a question that staggers the most learned when elucidation is attempted. Standing at the point here noticed it requires no unnatural stretch of imagination for those who have learned the facts to see on the 27th day of July, 1657, Sitteryguessett, an Indian Sagamore, barter his birth right in the lands at "Capisic" to Francis Small, a fisherman and adventurer, for the small stipend of a jug of rum and fighting jacket annually delivered, later Ammoncongin and Capisic, with other Sachems and squaws, bivouacing at the falls of Capisic stream, indulging in boastful shouts after the torch had been applied to the mill; then nearer in time, and perhaps upon the very spot we refer to, General Waldo, who at one time owned nearly all the land hereabouts, with parchment in hand, (which we had in our own not long since) trying to persuade the few people of the region in 1744, that it was for their interest to lease of him the Dole farm and erect on it a large garrison house, and pay him a liberal rental fee.

At that period the Charles Frost, alias Justice Frost's residence was standing, later known as the Brewer house, because Capt. Dexter Brewer married a granddaughter of Justice Frost and kept it as an inn as did the Frosts before him, the cellar hole and stones still remaining, the embankments forming a speck of the view to which we have referred. And again by the aid of imagination we can see in the month of June, (recorded on the 10th) 1746, an Indian skulking about the Frost house and fired at three times, the house being protected by a garrison.

The Dole house is a facsimile of the Frost house, only the Frost house had a long ell attached to the southerly end which contained a hall, both two story, square on the ground, gambrel-roofed, 30,000 bricks being required to construct the two stacks of chimneys in the Dole house.

Upon the ruins of the Frost house the dust of antiquity lies in a thick layer. Before the third story was added by Capt. Brewer in 1834 a painting was made of it by a traveling Englishman, a photo of which it is our fortune to be possessed.

TO BE CONTINUED.

GRANDPA'S SCRAP BOOK

Week of April 4-7, 1900.

WESTBROOK.

NAMES OF THE SELECTMEN AND REPRESENTATIVES TO THE LEGISLATURE.

BY LEONARD B. CHAPMAN.

(Continued from last week.)

[The name of Capt. Daniel Dole's father-in-law was Moses Pearson, not Pearsons, as we had it last week and the week before.]

When the Captain came to Stroudwater in 1770 there were, in addition to the Charles Frost house, three others that were two stories high, namely: The one in which Messrs. Washington and Augustus Tate reside, built in 1735 by one Richard Forder, an Englishman, who was a millwright, but didn't stop long; the house that was removed to Brighton Corner district of Deering about 1850 and occupied by Deacon Hiram H. Dow, and destroyed by fire some eight years since, which was built by Col. Thomas Westbrook and sold to Zebulon Trickey, in 1735, containing till its departure from Stroudwater the board shutters to the lower windows, placed during the Indian troubles of 1745 and later to keep the savages out; and the time-stained dwelling, containing the mammoth chimney, and known as the Old Tate House, because it was, in 1754, built by Capt. George Tate, who came to this country to procure masts for the English navy, situated in the heart of the village, which he occupied till he reached the end of life's journey at a ripe old age. And here, for the purpose of settling the question discussed years ago by Messrs. Willis and Goold, then our local historians, whether it was the father, Capt. George Tate, or the son George, who became famous as an Admiral in the Russian navy, that commanded the first frigate of that country, we here introduce an item found in the Eastern Herald, printed in Portland, Aug. 23, 1794, as follows:

"DIED in Falmouth, on Wednesday last, Capt. George Tate. He was born in England in the year of 1700 and was a seaman on board the first frigate built in Russia in the reign of Peter the Great."

Capt. Tate has a memorial slab in Stroudwater cemetery in addition to the dwelling he built. The son George did not accompany his father to this country, but after he became famous as a seaman and the commander of fleets of armed vessels and had received conferred honors from many nations he came, at the close of his eventful career laden with medals, as a visitor to his relatives, then returned.

Seven years after Capt. Dole constructed his residence, there were in Falmouth, which then included territorially what is now Deering, Westbrook and Portland, as well as the present town of Falmouth, only "709 males; 64 Quakers; 12 negroes and 1 molatta." We copy from official manuscript records found in the Massachusetts archives.

It was lawful then, which practice continued till the adoption of the Federal Constitution by Massachusetts, which was in 1780, to own slaves hereabouts or "bondmen" as such persons were then called, one of such making an item upon the schedule of personal property of Capt. Dole, known by the name of Leondon Dole.

In 1779 there was in Falmouth as follows, and the items are copied from the manuscript official paper:

Voters,		669
434 Buildings estimated at £30 each,		£13,020
Acres of mowing land,	3,945	
Acres of pasture,	4,175	
Acres of woodland,	15,297	
10 Wharves,		£450
11 Mills,		792
Money on hand and at interest,		6,089
Goods and merchandise,		5,460
Vessels of all sorts,		1,041
Ounces of silver plate,		76
291 Horses,		2,037
649 Oxen,		3,247
1039 Cows,		3,108
4729 Sheep,	4,729	1,413
Swine,		576
460 Carriages of all sorts,		347
Doomed,		2,516

These are the taxable rates; to obtain the real, add one-fourth of the taxable value.

Prior to 1787 Captain Dole served as selectmen three terms; after that date it is difficult telling what was done as the Falmouth Town Clerk's records have been destroyed by fire, and many of the town papers that have been preserved are without dates and official signatures.

The Parish records throw, however, some light upon the period of which we write. At the meeting holden March 8, 1773, Capt. Dole was chosen Parish Treasurer and re-elected a half-score of times, to which was added the offices of prudential committeeman and assessor, and at that date we find recorded as follows:

"Voted Said Dole two Dollars for his fee (as treasurer) for the Current Year."

During the whole period of the war of the Revolution the Parish meetings were kept up, though the meeting house was without the intended windows, the entries without floors and doors without steps, it being in process of construction when the war commenced.

June 12, 1780, it was voted as follows:

That £100 be raised for the Rev. Thomas Browne's salary the current year, to be paid in the following Articles, namely: "Indian corn at five shillings per bushel; rye at six shillings per bushel; wheat at eight shillings per bushel; wood delivered at the House in Back Cove (where Dr. A. P. Topliff lives) at ten shillings per cord; beef at two pence three farthings per pound, Spanish mill'd dollars at six shillings each, or in paper currency at the exchange of forty-five paper dollars for one Spanish milled dollar."

"Voted to raise sixty dollars in paper currency in lieu of every bushel of corn due to the Rev. Thomas Browne for the year 1779."

Capt. Dole can be imagined living in his large, new house, with marble topped tables and solid mahogany furniture, (which the house now contains) carrying bags of grain and pockets stuffed with depreciated currency, accompanied by his gentleman of color, for the honors of the office, for, certainly, it could not have been for the $2 cash salary; but the farmers didn't deliver according to votes passed and so Captain Dole didn't pay any more than he received, and then Parson Browne invoked the lower courts—the courts of man—and the Parish brought an action against the Captain for the small amount due and other actions against citizens for not attending public meetings held for worship—every person being required by law to attend at least one service in the course of each three months of a year.

Capt. Dole wrote a very fine hand and his Parish book is one of neatness. Matters in dispute were finally taken from court and settled privately, but the law requiring people to attend public meetings was enforced till the District of Maine became a state.

In 1795 Capt. Dole was taxed on a valuation as follows:

One house,	$1,000
Two barns,	300
40 acres mowing land,	600
27 acres salt marsh,	375
50 acres pasturing,	400
100 acres unimproved,	300
Secured notes,	600
20 ounces of silver plate,	22
1 horse,	40
4 oxen,	80
8 cows, 2 steers,	160
2 swine,	20

The house and two barns then taxed are the same as now observed, with their heavy oak frames, and large fire places in the attic of the house.

In the old burying yard, but a few paces off, may be seen in a long row two slate slabs inscribed as follows:

Here lies
the Body of
MRS. SARAH DOLE
wife of
Mr. Daniel Dole
who departed this life
July 11th, 1784,
in the 61st year
of her Age.

In memory of
Capt. Daniel Dole
who died
March 30, 1803,
in the 86th year
of his age.

TO BE CONTINUED.

GRANDPA'S SCRAP BOOK

Week of April 11-14, 1900.

WESTBROOK.

NAMES OF THE SELECTMEN AND REPRESENTATIVES TO THE LEGISLATURE.

BY LEONARD B. CHAPMAN.

(Continued from last week.)

Daniel Dole, Jr., born at Old Newbury, August 26, 1757, was thirteen years of age when his parents removed to Stroudwater, yet his penmanship was a model of neatness, and by it if no other a kinship may be established between him and Richard Dole of Windham, who displayed so much ability with the pen while he was town clerk of the inland settlement.

It is a family tradition that young Daniel never went to school a day after coming to Stroudwater, yet his records are clean and neat, spelling good, and punctuation marks correctly placed.

He served several years as town clerk, but we have no means of naming dates in this particular. On the 3d day of April, 1792, he was chosen clerk of the Parish and every year thereafter till the date of his death—a term of thirteen years—to which office was added that of Parish Treasurer.

In 1803, Daniel Dole, Jr., found himself the only surviving member of his father's family.

The exact date the Partridge name made its appearance at the village of Saccarappa we cannot now state, but in the year of 1803 there were several persons of the name who had departed from Saccarappa for Stroudwater.

There was the buxom Rhoda Partridge, with rooms at Sparrow's inn, that stood where the cellar may now be seen, at the head of Waldo and westerly side of Westbrook street, who, later, built herself a residence at the southwesterly corner of the iron bridge at Stroudwater, who would have been more than pleased had she became the second wife of Andrew Titcomb, Daniel Dole's brother-in-law; then there was Ann Partridge, who was the housekeeper of Daniel Dole, Jr., and her daughter, Katharine, the former being Mr. Dole's senior by six years, the latter his junior by twenty-eight.

Cupid was then on the alert as now. Such prizes as Messrs. Dole and Titcomb were worth the effort of an "aching heart." Upon the pages of the diary of Rev. Caleb Bradley we find as follows:

August 12, 1804. "I married Daniel Dole and Miss Katharine Partridge. Fee—$5."

This explains part of what happened. Rhoda remained in maidenhood; the bill of sale of her house is before us as we write, and the house is at Stroudwater, but removed from its original foundation.

March 2, 1815, the Portland Argus refers to the general illumination of the town "on Wednesday last," ringing of bells, and discharge of cannon at intervals in consequence of the ratification of the signing of the Treaty of Peace by reresentatives of our country and England. The inhabitants of Stroudwater joined in the demonstration. The schoolhouse was lighted by a candle at each pane of glass. Some of the tin candle sticks with points for the purpose of attaching to the sashes are still in existence at one of the village residences.

From injuries received in handling a log the spirit of Daniel Dole, Jr., in the evening of the day of general rejoicing, which was February 23, 1815, when there was special mirth and dancing at Broad's inn, but a mile away, departed for

"The mystery of unfolding life."

Behind was left a young widow and five small children, she proving herself equal to the saddening scenes of her household. The children all grew to maturity, all were physically strong, all surviving beyond the average age and all resided hereabouts—two passed the 80th mile stone in life's journey; one still remains with us and

"He has done the work of a true man."

It must have been fifty-five years ago when we attended a general muster of the military at Saccarappa, when the present Mr. Daniel Dole, Sr., was a staff officer—a Major. He was the only person in uniform we knew upon the muster field. The martingale of his prancing steed, bedecked with what seemed to us as "apples of gold," we now behold, and we well remember the desire to fill our elastic trousers' pocket with them. Our dinner of a single "bun" that cost a cent, which was only a bit of baked dough raised and sweetened, with a raisin in the center and the top coated with a brown colored susbtance, we have not forgotten.

In Rev. Caleb Bradley's diary we find as follows:

"September 4, 1839. Fine day for commencement, a. m. in the city, p. m. at Stroudwater—sent for to visit Mrs. Partridge—very sick. Took tea at Mr. Foys. Mr. Bragdon died.

"5th"—Went to Mrs. Doles to see Mrs. Partridge—very sick—very old—87 years. Mr. Bragdon buried—Mr. Lincoln tended the funeral. I was present. Took tea with Mr. Hanson. Leonard returned from Brunswick with Nathaniel and Franklin."

Mr. Bradley married for his second wife a Widow Partridge of Saccarappa with two children named respectively as above. Leonard was the Parson's son, who had returned from Brunswick, where the two Partridge boys were attending college.

"8th—Town meeting—Democracy reigns triumphant. I cast my vote for the Whig ticket. Thus far—so good.

"10th—This a. m. went into the city. The news from every quarter so far as heard—the Democracy has increased. Oppression is popular among the mobocrats and ignorance increases; they are pleased when merchants are distressed and the banks fail. Sunset. Went to Mrs. Doles with Mrs. Bradley. She is to tarry all night to watch with Mrs. Partridge, she being nigh unto death."

The Parson makes no further mention of Mrs. Partridge. She was the mother to the wife of Daniel Dole, Jr., who departed this life in 1815.

Three memorial slabs in the old cemetery at Stroudwater are inscribed as follows:

DANIEL DOLE, Jr.

Died Feb. 23, 1815.

Aged 58 years, 6 mo.

An honest man is the noblest work of God.

In Memory of

MRS. ANN PARTRIDGE

who died

Sept. 15, 1839.

Aged 87 years.

Katharine Dole

wife of

DANIEL DOLE, JR.,

died Jan. 10, 1861.

aged 76 yrs. 6 mo.

The victory is now obtained,
Mother's gone her Redeemer to see;
Her wishes, now fully are gained
She's where she long has panted to be.

Blessed are the dead who die in the Lord.

TO BE CONTINUED.

GRANDPA'S SCRAP BOOK

Week of April 18-21, 1900.

WESTBROOK.

NAMES OF THE SELECTMEN AND REPRESENTATIVES TO THE LEGISLATURE.

BY LEONARD B. CHAPMAN.

(*Continued from last week.*)

London Dole, a man of color, died, according to an entry in Parson Bradley's diary, February 7, 1812. No age given.

The sword Daniel Dole wore on the occasion to which we alluded last week is in the possession of his son Daniel who resides but a few rods away from the ancient Dole residence.

Westbrook was incorporated February 14, 1814; Daniel Dole, Jr., died one year and nine days later. Katharine Dole, his widow, was taxed in 1815 on a valuation as follows:

One house $900
Two barns 80
Two outhouses 40
30 acres mowing at $21 per acre; 45 acres of pasturing at $9 per acre; 15 acres of salt marsh, $20 per acre; 4 oxen, $20 each; 6 cows, $14 each; two 3 yr. olds, $10 each; three 2 yr. olds, $7 each; three yearlings, $5 each; one horse, $40, and 3 swine $5 each.

The salt marsh land it appears was considered equal, or nearly so, in value to good upland; now, should a farmer feed the hay of salt marsh land to milch cows he would be proceeded against by the officers of the law, but milk, though it be rank in taste from that feeding is not so abominable as the "doctored" stuff delivered in Portland.

We have shown that the maiden name of the widow of Daniel Dole, Jr., was Katharine Partridge—Katharine being spelled in some instances Catharine and Partridge with one "r", in others even by inmates of the same family. But the names of Partridge tax payers were not numerous in Westbrook in 1815, there being but two, Joseph, the name of one, Nathaniel the other.

Daniel Dole, Jr., was, as we have shown in a previous article the second child in his father's family.

CHILDREN OF DANIEL DOLE, Jr.

1—Mary T., b. June 12, 1805, m. Joseph Chenery.
2—Moses, b. June 8, 1807, m. Catharine M. Chenery, sister to Joseph.
3—Andrew T., b. Aug. 9, 1809, m. Mrs. Sophiah Mitchell Fosdick, a widow.
4—Catharine, b. Sept. 19, 1811, d. Sept. 15, 1898. She did not marry and always resided under the parental roof.
5—Daniel, b. Sept. 15, 1813,m. Mary Foster.

1—Mary T. Dole, b. June 12, 1805, m. June 18, 1840, Joseph Chenery, b. at Bradley's Corner district of Deering, August 4, 1803; he d. there March 22, 1882; she died Oct. 25, 1893.

He was a son of Joseph Chenery who was b. at Watertown, Mass., m. Feb. 24, 1801, Rebecca Johnson, b. March 14, 1773, a mile westerly of Stroudwater, district of Deering, daughter of Richard and Eunice (Trickey) Johnson.

Joseph Chenery, Jr., was the eldest in a family of six children; the father, in company with Capt. John Jones, who was a near neighbor, on the evening of Dec. 24, 1817, it being very dark and stormy walked through a gap in the railing of the bridge over Fore river at Stroudwater (the same gap in the railing being continued to this day.) Capt. Jones was rescued or he rescued himself having been a mariner, while Mr. Chenery perished, aged 48 years, leaving six children. A Portland paper dated Dec. 2, 1817, refers to the incident and states that the "violence of the storm and extreme darkness" was the cause.

The Chenery family resided in the Bradley's Corner district of Deering, where his grandson Daniel Dole Chenery resides upon the parental soil but in a new house.

June 6, 1798, in company with Peleg Mitchell and Jonas Hamilton Mr. Chenery purchased five acres of the Rigg's property upon which was a dwelling, pottery and tannery and commenced business but the co-partnership was of short duration, Chenery purchasing the interest of the others; he was by trade a tanner. The locality is full to overflowing of incidents worth recording, a few of which we have saved by printing, but we must move on, knowing well that we have already wandered far from the indications furnished by the heading of our article.

Joseph Chenery, Jr., was a house carpenter but worked with his brother Edward on the homestead acres at wagon building—his brother being a wheelwright—wagons constructed by them were for use, not beauty, from real pasture oak, each piece being examined many times before it was used. Their work, or productions in the vehicle line, was considered stylish in their day of manufacturing. The thills were long and body without dash-boards, but they introduced hereabouts, the side thoroughbrace spring for the body which was a wonderful innovation upon the old link system, which produced for their work ready sales.

Joseph Jr., was a man of easy manners, and many must still remember him as a tax collector; his wife a woman of stately demeanor, believing firmly in the probational state for general society as well as the church, both being exceedingly loyal to the Article of Faith of the Congregational church creed.

Around the old Chenery residence situated some four rods from the highway two storied, low posted, painted white with green blinds, numerous shade trees and flower-beds there was ever an air of neatness that always attracted our attention in passing as it must have the attention of the general public, but all is now changed.

In the diary of the Rev. Caleb Bradley we find as follows under date of June 18, 1840.

"At 7 o'clock p. m. Mrs. Elizabeth P. Smith (his daughter now residing in the State of Ohio) and I went over to Mrs. Dole's to attend the marriage ceremony of Joseph Chenery and Miss Mary Dole. (The record of this event does not appear in the printed list.) Had a very decent and respectable wedding, ('decent' and 'respectable' being common words of the Parson in his illustrations.) About thirty present, family and others. The scene so far as the ceremony goes is closed. How long before death will dissolve the union is beyond the foresight of mortals— of that hour and day knoweth no man, no, not the angels of Heaven. But it will be dissolved, and Death will perform the ceremony—he undoes, he destroys. It is appointed unto man once to die; this is a decree of heaven— it is fixed, it cannot be otherwise. The fatal dart cannot be turned from its course. It comes from the quiver of the Almighty God and will go as directed and accomplish the purpose for which it is sent, and all must submit to the fatal decree.

They had but one child,
Daniel Dole Chenery,
now deputy city marshal of Portland.
To be Continued.

GRANDPA'S SCRAP BOOK

Week of April 25-28, 1900.

WESTBROOK.

NAMES OF THE SELECTMEN AND REPRESENTATIVES TO THE LEGISLATURE.

BY LEONARD B. CHAPMAN.

(Continued from last week.)

2—Moses Dole, b. June 8, 1807, m. June 14, 1836, Catharine M. Chenery, daughter of Joseph Chenery, noticed last week. He d. Jan. 19, 1875, aged 68 years; she died July 15, same year, aged 63 years, 4 mos. They had but one child, named Moses H. Dole, who is married and resides in Portland.

It was the wish of the mother that Moses might become a clergyman and he was placed at school with the object in view but he preferred a farm life and received a goodly share of the original land purchase of his grandfather, now owned by the great grandson, Moses H. He resided in a good, two storied house, situated some fifty rods northerly of the homestead, which was constructed about the time of the marriage event in accordance with his own notions of a residence. The carriage house was moved from the home lot one afternoon in winter when there were far more boys present than teamsters, one of whom can now hear the "whoa-hush" pronounced in a loud voice by the "master-carter" when a chain would break, as well as the preparatory exclamations, "all-ready," "put your cattle- to-the-bows," "now she goes:"

Notwithstanding Moses was a deacon of the Congregational church he was a live man, quick in speech and quick in act and when he took the goad stick in hand his steers knew they were to choose between a quick step or a brad.

We presume the extract here presented from Parson Bradley's diary applies to the "other house," as follows:

February 14, 1839. "I attended the funeral of a child of Thomas Knights, aged six years; one of twelve children. No death in the family before this."

[Knights resided in the next house easterly of the Ocean street schoolhouse.]

"A meeting in the evening at the [Stroudwater] school house, but few of the church at the party—part at the of the church at party—part at the meeting. This is a melancholy truth, and an awful truth, that the church of Christ should prefer an evening frolic to a meeting of the church."

Wonder what the Parson would say today were he among us and observe the frolics and feasts and no fasting by his church?

3—Andrew Titcomb Dole, b. Aug. 9, 1809, m. Sept. 17, 1862, Sophia Mitchell Fosdick. He d. in Portland Aug. 6, 1866; she d. at Germantown, Pa., July 25, 1875, where she was residing with a daughter, aged 63 years.

He left home to take a clerkship with Ira T. Woodbury, who kept shop, corner of Portland and Green street, then he had an establishment of his own. He loved the military parade and political excitement, was known as Major Dole and when the Republican party was proposed he was placed at the head to organize and drill the converts and as "to the victors belong the spoils," when Abraham Lincoln was elected President, he was made a standard bearer by giving him the management of the Portland post office, which gift he accepted April 8, 1861.

It was a year and a half later that he became a party to the marriage ceremony, upon which occasion the Portland Advertiser, then the Portland organ of Republicanism, printed as follows:

MATRIMONIAL.

"After many years of patient waiting, and while the war cloud is hanging over our government and country Maj. Dole, our courteous, polite and symmetrical postmaster, was married yesterday in St. Lukes church, in presence of a large congregation. The fair bride was Mrs. Sophia Mitchell Fosdick, of this city. Although we have received neither cake nor wine, yet we cannot let the joyous event pass without making a record of it. We congratulate the happy bridegroom, and wish him and his partner a long and prosperous life. Thrice i- the Major exempt from a draft—1st. office; 2nd age; 3d the statute of Moses which says:

"'When a man has taken a new wife, he shall not go out to war, neither shall he be charged with any business; but he shall be free at home one year, and shall cheer up his wife which he has taken.'"

In consequence of physical disabilities, hastened by exposure at a fire on Exchange street, where he rendered the firemen assistance, Maj. Dole resigned his office as postmaster to Judge Woodbury Davis, who was appointed to the position Dec. 9, 1865; and at the age of 57 years Maj. Dole relinquished all claim to the scenes of earth.

5—Daniel Dole was united in marriage with Miss Mary Foster, daughter of Benjamin B. Foster of Saccarappa district of Westbrook. They have occupied the Dole mansion house where they still reside with Louise, an unmarried daughter. They celebrated a golden wedding a few years since which was duly noticed by The News. She was a school teacher before marriage and was employed three seasons at Stroudwater. The writer was a pupil.

We might write several columns upon the methods then and before in general use to punish pupils some of which were far more ridiculous than wise, and should some practices now be indulged in then in use the State militia would be called out if preventation could not be otherwise stopped. One little affair we well remember. The sleeve at the hand part of our jacket was pinned to the white apron of the teacher and

"Every where that Mary went
The lamb was sure to go."

For the time being we were in duress vile.

Moses Dole, born May 20, 1766, and died Sept. 4, 1788, in consequence of a disease contracted from bathing in the river when the water was too cold, was a silversmith, and had a shop in his father's house. He did marry. A memorial slab may be seen at Stroudwater.

Week of May 2-5, 1900.

WESTBROOK.

NAMES OF THE SELECTMEN AND REPRESENTATIVES TO THE LEGISLATURE.

BY LEONARD B. CHAPMAN.

(Continued from last week.)

The quotation from Parson Bradley's diary should have appeared in our article of last week as follows:

"A meeting in the evening at the schoolhouse, (Stroudwater) but few present, A party at Mrs. Dole's. A part of the church at the party—a part at the meeting. This is a melancholy truth and an awful truth that the church of Christ should prefer an evening frolic to a meeting of the church."

Sophia Mitchell Fosdic was a widow when she was united in marriage with Maj. Andrew T. Dole.

At the close of the article where it says, "He did marry," it should have been, "He did not marry," where allusion is made to Moses Dole, the silversmith.

Capt. Dole did not finish the southeasterly corner room of his dwelling and used it as a shop, his son Moses serving as a clerk and conducting his vocation in the same room. Several of his implements are still retained in the house. Then eyes were soldered to silver coins, which were used for buttons on men's garments. It would be a curious sight now to see a man in public with buttons made of twenty-five cent coins; then there was but little American silver in circulation, it being almost wholly of English design.

The frame of the building referred to last week that was removed is the frame of the house that was on the premises in 1770, when Capt. Dole made the purchase. The building may now be seen as it appeared when removed over fifty years ago. It stood originally in the back door yard of the present house, and was for some years the domicile of the persons of color owned by the captain, the more trusty one having an apartment in the attic of the main house which remains unchanged.

Upon the southeasterly slope of the bluff situated at the westerly side of Saccarappa village may be seen a large two story dwelling, containing two stacks of large chimneys, with windows boarded over, and a drive way of a serpentine character leading to it from the main road. The eminence is known by the unmusical name of "Pork Hill"—a name derived undoubtedly from the stubborn ways of a former owner. If the oldest citizen of the place is consulted relative to its history he will shrug his shoulders and refer you to some one older if such a person can be found. If "tradition" is referred to you will be informed that the house was built by a person named Conant with a present unknown Christian name. If the Conant genealogy is considered nothing will be found and the newspaper history as it appeared in The News is reticent; in short, the compiler of the News articles frankly confesses he had learned nothing definite relative to the date of construction or of the original owner.

The gateway being thus ajar to the general gleaner of historical memoranda we enter upon the grounds and wipe from the tablet stones the accumulated dust of ages and from the records themselves here tell the story in brief.

Joseph and Samuel Conant were brothers, the latter some sixteen years the junior; the former, born in Beverly, Mass., Nov. 9, 1701. Joseph had a wife and child when he came. Several of the names of other children born hereabouts are recorded as well as the "publishments" of Samuel, the 1st February 26, 1740, with Hannah Worcester, "both of Falmouth;" the 2d, March 29, 1743, with Mary Peabody, she of Middletown, Mass.

The story of the first European occupancy of Saccarappa, as we have told it from official records including the disposition made of the first house Joseph Conant built there may be found in the July number of the collections of the Maine Historical society of 1899.

Upon a deed bearing date of August 28, 1744, when a conveyance was made by Capt. Moses Pearson to Daniel Godfrey we find Joseph's name as follows:

"Twenty acres of land lying near and adjoining Sackrapy Falls on the southwest side of the Presumpscot river, excepting where Joseph Conant and said Godfrey are now erecting a Block House.

The Block House was upon or adjacent the site of the Conant house on Pork Hill, and was built when the Indians were about with scalping knives and lighted torches, who destroyed the mill on the Stroudwater river, a mile from Saccarappa and took William Knights and sons captives at the last named place, the event being recorded by Parson Smith, April 14, 1747. Whether or not the mills were destroyed we cannot state.

The funeral services of Joseph was attended by Parson Dean, January 2, 1765. He left sons:

1—Bartholomew Conant, intention of marriage with Miss Hannah Frink, made public Feb. 15, 1760.
2—Joseph Conant, Jr., intention of marriage May 22, 1762, with Ann Schofield.

And there were daughters and other sons who did not mature.

In the Deering News' Conant article of June 8, 1895, is a statement made by the compiler that Ann, a daughter of Joseph Conant, Jr., married Nathan Partridge. This appears to be an error.

Family of Samuel Conant.

1—William, b. 1754, m. Sept. 23, 1779, Ruth Chapman. His funeral services were attended by Parson Bradley, Nov. 18, 1804. (See Deering News Feb. 4, 1899.)
2—Elizabeth, b. 1755, m. William Babb, b. on the original Babb farm, located a few rods northerly of Stroudwater Falls about a mile from Saccarappa, the cellar hole still remaining, a part of which is in the highway.
3—Mary, m. David Partridge, who was a farmer and resided at West Poland, this state, a granddaughter and family now occupying the ancestral acres. Mary had seven children. Another granddaughter resides in Portland, with a brother, at No. 61 Oxford street, children of Samuel Partridge.
4—Daniel, b. 1760, m. Oct. 26, 1780, Ann Haskell. He d. a half mile westerly of Saccarappa, on the Capt. John Brackett place, aged 93 years; the only one of the old stock of Conants who has a grave stone in Saccarappa.
5—Ann, b. 1761, m. Nov. 1, 1781, Nathan Partridge, a brother to David Partridge, the preceding, and a brother to Capt. Jesse Partridge, who d. in Stroudwater. There were ten children in this Partridge family who grew to maturity, nine of whom married. Nathan died previous to 1797, and his widow died at Stroudwater as has been stated in a former article.

Samuel evidently had other children, as we find marriage records we cannot place.

Children of Nathan and Ann (Conant) Partridge.

1—Nancy, m. Feb. 21, 1802, in what is now Deering, Josiah Moxfield, and removed to the part of Raymond that is now Casco, where he was a farmer, and where descendants reside. He was an uncle to Chas. Moxfield of Stroudwater.
2—Katharine, m. Aug. 12, 1804, Daniel Dole, Jr., who has been noticed in these articles.
3—Joseph, m. Jan. 14, 1808, Lydia Quinby.

In the village cemetery at Saccarappa are two white marble slab scribed as follows:

Lydia Q.,
wife of
Capt. Joseph Partridge,
died Sept. 29, 1882,
aged 93 yrs. 6 mo.

Blessed are the dead which die in the Lord.

Capt. Joseph Partridge
died Sept. 27, 1856,
aged 71 yrs.

I will both lay me down in peace, and sleep, for thou, Lord, makest me dwell in safety.

To Be Continued.

NBPA'S SCRAP BOOK

Week of May 9-12, 1900.

WESTBROOK.

NAMES OF THE SELECTMEN AND REPRESENTATIVES TO THE LEGISLATURE.

BY LEONARD B. CHAPMAN.

(Continued from last week).

[Where the name of Moxfield appears in our article of last week it should be Maxfield.]

We cannot establish the place of abode at Saccarappa of Nathan and Ann (Conant) Partridge nor the kind of labor he performed. They had but three children whose names have been presented.

Joseph, the youngest child, built the large house as now seen situated on the westerly side of the old canal in which Mr. Frank Partridge resides, opposite the Lewis P. Warren mansion, but the house has had a new roof placed upon it. He was then engaged in lumber speculations; then he removed into a smaller house, situated south easterly of the Pork Hill mansion, where he remained till called to the other side of life.

Children:

1—Ann, b. January 4, 1809, m. George Haskell and they resided in Saccarappa many years.
2—Joseph P. b. Nov. 30, 1811, m. Mary Rich of Harrison.
3—Benjamin Q. b. Jan. 11, 1813, m. Phebe Berry of Bridgton.
4—George W. b. March 31, 1815, m. May 6, 1839, Nancy Proctor; m. 2nd her sister Isabel; m. 3d. Rose Knight.
5—Caroline P. b. May 22, 1817, m. Aaron Shackley. She died Oct. 11, 1867. Memorial slab at Saccarappa.
6—Nathan b. July 5, 1819, m. Sarah B. Ayer. "She lived 49 years, 11 months and one day and then left us to mourn our loss the 26 of January, 1885." Thus the grave memorial at Saccarappa. He resides at Portland, Oregon.
7—Albion K. P. b. Nov. 11, 1821, m. Jan. 8, 1853, Sarah P. Hawkes. Reside in Windham on a farm.
8—Charles L. b. Aug. 31, 1824, m. Louise Cloudman. Reside on Saco road, Saccarappa.
9—Mary C. b. February 9, 1827, m. Gibeon Elden of Gorham. He is deceased; she resides in Portland.
10—Andrew J. b. March 15, 1829, m. Nov. 7, 1851, Harriet N. Snow, sister to Mr. Temple Snow of Saccarappa, who is in the stove and tinware trade.
11—John W. b. Aug. 12, 1831, m. Adeline Quinby, dau. of Aaron Quinby, Esq.; m. 2nd Hannah Farnum of Bridgton. Reside in Cornish.
12—Lydia Ellen b. March 6, 1834, m. Dec. 25, 1884, Joseph W. Nelson. Reside in Portland.

It is seldom that a family of twelve children all mature and all marry as in this case. Of the Partridges we propose to speak more fully later on.

We will now roll the curtain a little higher and exhibit the Pork Hill mansion in a clearer atmosphere than has been done and thus dispel the uncertainty as to the time it was built and the Christian name of the Conant who constructed it.

In 1794 Bartholomew Conant and Joseph Conant convey to Daniel and William Conant a mill, privilege, etc., referring to the property as that of "our father, Joseph Conant, deceased, who owned the privilege, etc., in comowtnih m P dinu, mon with John Bailey and others."

Daniel and William were, as we have shown, children of Samuel Conant, hence cousins to Bartholomew and Joseph Conant, the legal successors to their father, the original Joseph Conant; and thus the origin of Daniel Conant's title to Pork Hill and mill privilege adjoining.

Before us is one of the ledger account books of Col. James Means of Stroudwater which was opened in 1791 and closed ten years later. It is fifteen inches long and nearly ten inches wide. He was in trade in Stroudwater. August 10, 1791, Daniel Conant commenced an account with the Colonel, which was continued to the end of 1799, covering eleven of the long pages with three or four articles named on a line, when Conant gave Means his note for a balance of £45, both affixing their signatures to the settlement page as witnesses to the transaction. And the account of lumber furnished is as long as the other which shows that merchantable boards were delivered at Stroudwater at $6 and clear at $11 per 1000. Means' charges against Conant amounted to £639—0—1.

During the summer months of 1795 there are unusual large charges made against Conant for salt fish, meat, and other articles of household consumption. Rum and molasses were purchased in barrel quantities. He is charged for glass, nails, thumb latches, clothes hooks, H L hinges and butts. Nails were then sold by count.

By order of the Court of Common Pleas of this county there was made in 1811 a levy amounting to $991 and costs in favor of John Gordon upon Daniel Conant and one-half of his Pork Hill house taken.

In 1813 there was another levy for $500 and the other half taken. And thus passed from Daniel his title to the Pork Hill mansion erected, very evidently, in 1795, the same as now seen. These claims were for money loaned Conant, the note made in the hand of Conant, which is above the average in penmanship appearing in the papers on file in the case we have examined.

In 1814 for the sum of $218 Conant deeded, with the incumbency upon it, not only the Pork Hill house and lot, but the passage way from Main street to it, including the mail privilege, and the "Falmouth Canal Proprietor's right," to John Gordon and retired to the Capt. John Brackett residence, a few rods northwesterly, where he resided till his death. In the village cemetery is a marble slab inscribed as follows:

Daniel Conant
died
Dec. 16, 1853,
Aged 92 yrs. 10 mo.

Ann,
Wife of
Daniel Conant,
died
Sept. 21, 1844,
Aged 79 yrs.

John Gordon's first appearance upon public records is dated Sept. 6, 1803, when he purchased the old George Tate warehouse, at Stroudwater, where Capt. Jesse Partridge kept shop, and went into trade. It is traditional that his average sale of rum while at Stroudwater was a hogshead per day. In 1809 he paid $2,500 for the Archelaus Lewis house now used at Stroudwater in part for a post office, which is in as good repair as then apparently, but worth only half as much now.

The Conant property at Saccarappa Gordon improved by building a saw mill, all of which he sold Dec. 9, 1817, to John and Nathaniel Warren of Saccarappa for $5,000.

Gordon was an unmarried man and very peculiar. Stetson Lobdell, whose parents resided where Augustus Tate lives at Stroudwater, married Gordon's sister and removed to Philadelphia, Pa. Stetson's brother Isaac resided upon the State Reform school farm, where, in his last years, Gordon raised a few vegetables for his own consumption, dwelling in the cave of a sand bank not far off.

The site of the Pork Hill house is commanding. The general view is extensive and pleasing to the observer. Out upon the roofs of the village residences, down upon the streets, the noble Presumpscot with its waterfalls and debris of departed industries with others inclined in the same direction; the site of "Holy Land," where a century ago the mildew of depravity was spread in a thick layer and the little Universalist chapel, the roof now nearer Heaven than it was fifty odd years since—another story having been placed under it—where Rev. Zenas Thompson made a hotter place on earth for his Orthodox brethren than the Orthodox Congregationalist made the imaginary one for the Universalist in the hereafter; the valley laying to the westward, caused by a mammoth landslide, where for decades the valorous militia soldier exhibited his dexterity in handling the musket;—upon Pork Hill, we say, all this may be seen, nay, the great elm tree, with a top as flat as the head of the non-believer in supernatural things, which tree is fully a hundred feet in spread; then the Daniel Conant Mansion itself, large on the ground, each story containing four large, square rooms, designed for two families, bereft outside of paint, serving in 1837 as a factory boarding house, clapboard nails protruding, windows boarded over, doors spiked, yet open to professional world plodders, the property now of S. D. Warren & Co. of Congin Paper Mill fame.

Such a spot, with such surroundings, and such a history should have been dotted when the ancient place was, a few years since, in its zenith of prosperity, with costly residences.

A week since we peered through a small aperture of the deserted mansion and

"In the stern monk's place,
We saw the shining of an angel's face!"

(To be continued.)

The Mitchell Family.

Probably no family name figures so prominently or so often in the annals of old North Yarmouth as that of Mitchell. Seven of the 27 deacons of the First Parish church have borne that honored name.

Mr. Frederic L. Mitchell of this place who has spent much time in tracing the genealogy of the Mitchell family has established a clear line of descent from Experience Mitchell, who was born either in Amsterdam or Leyden in 1609.

In 1623 this Experience Mitchell, then but a youth of 14 years, came to America in the ship Ann. He shared in the first division of lots in Plymouth and for some years lived at Spring Hill, Plymouth. In 1631 he removed to Duxbury and later to Bridgewater.

Experience Mitchell married for his first wife, Jane, daughter of Francis Cook, who came to this country in the Mayflower. She died in 1689, aged 80 years. The children of Experience Mitchell and Jane Cook were these: Thomas, John, Jacob, Edward, Elizabeth, Mary, Sarah, Hannah.

Jacob Mithchell married Susannah Pope in 1666 and settled at Dartmouth. At the breaking out of King Philips war in 1670, Jacob and his wife took their children to a garrison for safety. They were both killed by Indians, while seeking to reach the stronghold.

The three orphans in the garrison were named Jacob, Thomas and Mary. They were taken to Bridgewater and there brought up by their uncle Edward.

One day in the year 1696 a very remarkable event happened in the Mitchell family. On that day the three children of the Jacob Mitchell, who was killed by the Indians, were all married into the same family, that of John Kingman.

Jacob's wife was Deliverance Kingman. In the process of time a son was born to them, a Jacob too, who afterwards became the first deacon Jacob Mitchell of the First Parish church.

Thomas married Eliza Kingman and Mary married Samuel Kingman.

Deliverance Kingman Mitchell died soon after the birth of her son Jacob. The elder Jacob returned to Kingston, Mass., and there married Rebecca Cushman, daughter of Isaac Cushman.

Of Jacob and Rebecca these children were born:

1. Susannah, Jan. 15, 1702.
2. Rebecca, October 19, 1704.
3. Seth, March 16, 1705.
4. Mary, March 7, 1707.
5. Lydia, Jan. 2, 1710.
6. Noah, September 16, 1712.
7. Isaac, Jan. 20, 1714.
8. Sarah, April 29, 1717.
9. Elizabeth, April 27, 1722.

January 17, 1728, Jacob, the son of Jacob and Deliverance, removed to North Yarmouth. He was received into the First Parish church in 1730, was chosen deacon in 1737, and died Dec. 21, 1744.

Deborah, daughter of the Seth Mitchell (3) mentioned above, was married Dec. 10, 1758, to Solomon Mitchell, the great grandfather of Mr. Frederic Mitchell. Solomon died in 1802, aged 64. His wife Deborah lived until 1821, dying at the advanced age of 82. In this line of descent came the second deacon Jacob Mitchell of the First Parish church.

Not only is Mr. Frederic Mitchell interested in preserving the genealogy of the historic Mitchell family, but he also has a fine collection of rare old documents and coins. Noticeable among them is a sergeants commission, granted to a relative of his, Hiram Hatch, by name, Aug. 27, 1805. This commission appoints Hiram Hatch, Third Sergeant of a Light Infantry Company in the Second Regiment, Second Brigade and Sixth Division of the Militia of Massachusetts. It is signed at Brunswick by Charles Thomas, Lieut. Col. Commandant, and Alfred Richardson, captain.

His collection also includes the finest specimen of old-fashioned needle work we have ever seen. It is a memorial piece, worked in memory of David Greenleaf Hatch, born May 21, 1806, died Aug. 4, 1808.

A Spanish fourpence of 1748 and a $3 bill issued in 1818 on a bank at Castine were among the oddities noticed in Mr. Mitchell's coin collection.

NDPA'S SCRAP BOOK

Week of May 16-19, 1900.

WESTBROOK.

NAMES OF THE SELECTMEN AND REPRESENTATIVES TO THE LEGISLATURE.

BY LEONARD B. CHAPMAN.

(Continued from last week.)

[Where the typographical errors appear in the first column of our article of last week the passage should read as follows:

In 1794 Bartholomew Conant and Joseph Conant convey to Daniel and William Conant a mill. privilege, etc., referring to the property as that of "our father, Joseph Conant, deceased, who owned the privilege, etc., in common with John Bailey and others."]

Benjamin Titcomb came from Old Newbury, Mass., to Portland in 1746, after the capture of Lewisburg, of which expedition he was a member. Though but nineteen years of age he was by trade a blacksmith, and engaged successfully in the employment in Portland after the defeat of the expedition. In 1753 he united in marriage with Ann Pearson, a daughter of Capt. Moses Pearson and a sister to Capt. Daniel Dole's wife. He became a church deacon, selectman, and Representative to the General Court—meaning by this the State Legislature. His wife bore him twelve children. Andrew was the name of the eldest. Willis, Portland's historian, refers to him as Andrew Phillips Titcomb, but in no other instance do we find the name of Phillips used. Deacon Titcomb left to be divided among seven children an estate appraised at fifty-one thousand, four hundred and fifty dollars. We copy this from an official record; and Willis says his wife left $12,000. The Deacon died Oct. 15, 1798; his widow, July 8, 1800, each aged 72 years respectively.

Parson Bradley records under the date of Jan. 4, 1801, that he attended the funeral service of Mrs. Titcomb, aged 81. Who she was we cannot tell.

Under date of Jan. 25, 1799, Parson Dean records that "Mrs. Wise died"—widow of Joseph Wise and daughter of Capt. Moses Pearson.

Her Christian name was Elizabeth and she was a sister to the wife of Capt. Dole, and was born Feb. 20, 1722. She married Joseph Wise in 1749, being the widow of Joseph Binney, and resided in a large house a half mile northwesterly of Saccarappa that was burned a few years since. It stood near where the canal crossed the old Gorham road, upon the northerly side of the way.

On account of "love and parental affection," Capt. Pearson must have given his daughter Sarah, wife of Capt. Dole, real estate in Saccarappa, being "nine rods wide," located on the northerly side of Main street and running westerly, commencing at the bounds of what is now the Lewis W. Edwards' brick shop lot, corner of Bridge street, which is located upon a remnant of the Haskell property, the Simpson ten acre grant, which went to Capt. Pearson, and the John Tyng hundred acre lot, which went to the Haskells, coming together at the point here designated, the westerly side line of the Edwards shop, giving the course of the union line of the original lots of Simpson and Tyng, the Simpson lot lying westerly and the Tyng lot easterly of the line. We give now the location of the Sarah (Pearson) Dole lot because we shall have occasion to refer to it later on, and because the Edwards shop has been located in newspaper history upon the wrong lot.

Andrew Titcomb was born in Portland Jan. 28, 1754, m. Dec. 5, 1782, Mary, daughter of Capt. Daniel Dole of Stroudwater, b. Old Newbury, Mass., March 22, 1766. They were first cousins and had five children as follows:

1—Sarah, b. Aug. 25, 1783; d. May 5, 1840, at Stroudwater.
2—William, b. June 2, 1786; d. April 16, 1787.
3—Ann, b. June 17, 1789; m. Dec. 10, 1809, Moses Quinby, Esq., of Stroudwater.
4—Mary, b. Aug. 19, 1791; m. Nov 24, 1811, Levi Quinby, brother to the preceding.
5—Almira, b. Aug. 9, 1795; m Luther Fitch, Esq., of Groton, Mass., who was judge of the Portland Municipal court 29 years.

Capt. Dole, as we have shown, engaged in trade in a room in his residence, aided by his son Moses, the silversmith, who died Sept. 4, 1788. It is quite apparent that Andrew Titcomb attempted to carry on the business after the death of Moses in a shop of his own located somewhere on Capt. Dole's land, for, when the Captain gave his son Daniel in 1790 the homestead farm he exempted the shop of his son-in-law, Andrew Titcomb, to whom he gave the privilege of removal. A little later we find him a resident of Saccarappa where his father held land and mill interests, and where we believe he engaged in trade, and it may be he removed the shop building as well as the goods to that place from Stroudwater.

His residence was a large one story house that was situated a little easterly of the old Universalist chapel on Main street and a little back from the street line, adjacent the southerly side of "Holy Land."

In 1795 he was taxed on a valuation as follows:

1 house and barn,	$500.
20 ounces silver plate,	6.
12 acres mowing land,	180.
25 pasturing,	200.
25 unimproved,	50.
1 saw mill,	500.

One horse $40; two oxen, $80; two cows, $28 and three swine $15.

He owned later (perhaps then) the finest block of stores in Portland, upon which lot a part of the Falmouth hotel is located.
rf up rr uStroudwater

In the old cemetery at Stroudwater is a slate slab inscribed as follows:

Here lies the Remains
of Mrs. MARY TITCOMB,
wife of Mr. Andrew Titcomb
who departed this life
August 30, 1796.
In the 37th, Year
of her Age.

In the Capt. Jesse Partridge residence, opposite the Capt. Dole mansion, resided at the time of Mary's death Mrs. Rebecca Partridge, widow of the deceased Captain, of Revolutionary war fame, the residence still to be seen, having undergone but slilit changes—one of the best of Colonial days and occupied by descendants of the Titcombs. The maiden name of widow Partridge was Rebecca Bailey, daughter of John Bailey, Jr., who resided and died in the year 1776 in the one story house on Spring, opposite High street, Deering, the residence many years of John Newman, now deceased. In the same house where Capt. Jesse Partridge obtained his wife Jotham Partridge, a brother to the Captain, found his, named Mary; and the youngest member of the Bailey family, of which there were more than half a score, Lydia, born April 15, 1776 a month after her father's demise, became the wife of Daniel Maxfield, who was the father of Charles and other children of Stroudwater, all of whom have been noticed in The News.

Jotham had no permanent abiding place that we can find. One of his sons, if our calculations are correctly made, was Capt. Nathaniel Partridge who married the second wife of Jonathan Webb of Saccarappa, and then Rev. Caleb Bradley married for his second wife the widow of Capt. Nathaniel Partridge, she died and the Parson married again.

Rebecca (Bailey—Titcomb) Partridge was a most amiable woman, and her husband seems to have been a man of valor who performed a grand service for the cause of the Colonies, but like many others of his generation his patriotic acts are unnumbered upon public records. The site and residence he constructed upon it at Stroudwater are high testimonials of his ability to judge between the substance and the shadow, but he did not live long to enjoy the fruition of hope in his new home. In the old cemetery at Stroudwater may be seen a slate slab inscribed as follows:

Here lies the Remains
of Capt. Jesse Partridge
who departed this life
Dec. 21, 1795
Aged 53.

CONTINUED:

At the age of 21 he purchased a half acre lot of land located upon Main street at Saccarappa and engaged in trade, then an inn keeper. The war over he removed his residence to Stroudwater, but the Saccarappa inn building still survives. His wife bore him no children.

About a year after the death of the Captain, the widow became the second wife of Andrew Titcomb, Titcomb removing from Saccarappa to Stroudwater, then a flourishing place with bright prospects, where Titcomb engaged in trade, occupying the Capt. Partridge mansion, into the possession of which he came by purchase, and not by his wife's inheritance, upon the inner walls of which have hung an oil painting, bust size of Andrew as well as his wife Mary ever since their demise, and in the adjacent cemetery may be seen two slate slabs inscribed as follows:

Here lies the remains of
Andrew Titcomb,
who died
Nov. 19, 1818:
aged 65 years.

In memory of
Rebecca Titcomb,
2nd wife of
Andrew Titcomb,
who died
May 5, 1808:
Aged 58 years.

"Tho' the pale corpse is in the grave confin'd,
She leaves a pattern of her sex behind,
The sun of virtue never can decay,
It shines in time, and gives eternal day."

At this point in the history of Capt. Daniel Dole and his descendants we drop the consideration of the matter for the present, having already strayed too far from the course indicated by our head lines.

To be Continued.

BPA'S SCRAP BOOK

ek of May 30 – June 2, 1900

WESTBROOK

NAMES OF THE SELECTMEN AND REPRESENTATIVES TO THE LEGISLATURE.

BY LEONARD B. CHAPMAN.

(Continued from last week).

WILLIAM L. PENNELL.

[Where it reads as follows at the close of our article of last week "$50" should have been $500.

"Mem. It is $50 to each of the persons named, Chas. E. George, D. Donister, Emily M. B. Cadwell."]

Everybody of today in Deering knows the location of "Capisic Pond," and everybody belonging to the sporting fraternity of the days of the Southern rebellion knew of the "Capisic Pond House," which house was built by Andrew P. Frost and given to his daughter Ann, who married Thomas Seal, a sea captain, they occupying the premises where quite a large family of Seals were raised, the cellar hole now marking the spot; the "Capisic Pond House" being none other than the original Frost-Seal residence, which, as a public resort, was of short duration, it being visited by the all-cleansing element of fire that left nothing but the cellar hole and cellar walls that still remain; and, as Parson Bradley used to say, "let it be known" the location of the highway through Capisic is the same, with a few crooks taken out, as the King's highway of two centuries and more ago, and the first road into the country proposed at the last settlement of Falmouth was to the "head of Fore river"—meaning "Capisic." The old Indian name is now officially recognized in the late applications or change of street names hereabouts. And the modern spelling of the name "Kapissick" of two centuries and more ago is now officially in use as a street name, and probably will remain.

In our Frost family notes that appeared in The News a year and a little over ago we used a very little of the large amount of historical memoranda obtainable pertaining to this very interesting spot, but to do the place justice many lengthy articles in The News would be required. We cannot, however, refrain from presenting in this connection a little glimmer of light found in a record of nearly a hundred years old, showing vaguely the "Village of Capisic" at that period, as follows:

TO LET.

The pleasant and valuable stand for business in Capisic (Falmouth) now occupied by the subscriber. The premises consists of a large, commodious dwelling-house, out houses and store, together with ten acres of land and a good garden. It is an excellent stand for a public house, or for a trader.

ALSO TO LET.

A small dwelling house in the above named village, with from ten to twenty acres of land and an excellent Grist-mill with two sets of stones and a bolting mill.

LIKEWISE, FOR SALE.

A good stand near Presumpscot Mills, consisting of a new two story house, partly finished, about thirty acres of land and five sixteenths of a saw mill, being a valuable situation for a trader, mechanic or tavern keeper. For particulars apply to
Samuel Butts.
Capisic, Oct. 24, 1803.

The Presumpscot mills were located on Presumpscot Falls, where the new brick electric power house may be seen, a little westerly of the old covered bridge.

Butts was a character; we hope to live to give his name an extended notice.

In 1735 Thomas Pennell was in Portland and by occupation a ship carpenter. His intention of marriage with Rachel Riggs was filed Jan. 16, 1735; that of Clement Pennell, a supposed brother, with Ruth Riggs, June 10, 1741.

In 1735 Thomas Pennell purchased at Capisic sixty acres of land—the year Messrs. Waldo and Westbrook built a saw mill and grist mill there, the grist to use the water of the saw mill.

When Pennell purchased the land it was under attachment in a case of Waldo vs. Westbrook. The "village" then consisted of "two mills, three houses and two barns."

At the Falmouth town meeting, spring of 1742, Pennell procured a vote to keep a gate by his house in the road that leads from Saccarappa to "Kapissick."

In 1750 Clement Pennell purchased an acre of land of Thomas Pennell.

In 1758 Waldo got out a writ of ejectment against Thomas Pennell and recovered the sixty acres of land, but the jury brought in that Waldo should pay Pennell for improvements the sum of eleven hundred and seventeen pounds. After this transaction Thomas purchased a farm in Windham, from which place he removed to Harpswell. Persons at Harpswell by the name of Pennell are his descendants, as well as ex-County Treasurer Thomas Pennell of Portland.

May 2, 1766, Clement purchased of Waldo a quarter of an acre of land and in 1769 a half quarter, the residence of the late Warren Harmon, built by Levi Russell Starbird, opposite the Seal house cellar, is now standing on the lot at Capisic.

In 1766 Clement Pennell purchased also of Waldo a ten-acre lot located next westerly of the residence of the late Edward D. Starbird, whose father, Levi, and whose grandfather, Thomas, also, occupied the Edward D. house before Edward's day, located between Capisic and Nason's Corner, to which ten acres five were added of the adjoining land.

Clement was a charter, or original member of the Stroudwater church, instituted April 8, 1765, to which his wife Ruth, as well as Rachel, wife of Thomas, were admitted by letters from another church—probably the First Parish of Portland.

Upon the ten acre land purchase Clement built a long, one story house with two front doors, where the cellar hole of a later built house may be seen, and where he, or his widow, kept an inn.

August 8, 1781, Ruth was a widow, and sole executor of the last will and testament of her husband. Of her children we find Abigail (Pennell) Adams; Molly (Pennell) Fickett; Clement Pennell, Jr.; Eunice (Pennell) Goold and Thomas Pennell, the last locating in the town of Gray—the Pennell branch from which the subject of this sketch originated.

CONTINUED:

Clement Pennell was appointed in 1769 to care for the meeting house upon a salary of eighteen shillings per year, which position he held till 1779, when it went to Ruth Pennell and the salary raised to thirty shillings. In 1784 the salary was reduced to eighteen shillings. In 1785 the salary was raised to twenty-four shillings and the position given to "Mrs. Storer," whose son Joseph built the ancient appearing "Daniel Mason" house as now seen near the Bradley meeting house.

Under date of Oct. 11, 1800, Parson Bradley says:

Joseph Storer and Charlotte Knight married.

March 8, 1836. At home today. Nothing special except Mrs. Storer, aged 99 years and one month, was buried. Services in the meeting house I performed. Every thing was very decent. Wonderful old age. Her remains were here last night and conveyed from this house [Parson B.'s house] to the meeting house, and from there to the grave. [She died in Portland.]

Levi Starbird married March 18, 1809, Nancy Pennell, born in the "Inn," but I am not sufficiently informed now to state her parents' names.

In our old cemeteries not a slab appears inscribed with the name of Pennell and but once does the name appear on the list Parson Bradley made of the funeral services he attended, namely: Nov. 15, 1808, Mrs. Pennell, aged 43 years.

NBPA'S SCRAP BOOK

Week of May 23-26, 1900.

WESTBROOK.

NAMES OF THE SELECTMEN AND REPRESENTATIVES TO THE LEGISLATURE.

BY LEONARD B. CHAPMAN.

(Continued from last week).

GEORGE CALVIN CODMAN.

We have stated that the selectmen for the year of 1867 were Daniel Dole, George C. Codman and William L. Pennell. Richard Codman was born in Charlestown, Mass., in 1730. His father was poisoned to death by negro domestics in 1755. Soon after the event Richard came to Portland Neck and engaged in trade. July 10, 1758, he married Ann Jones, daughter of Phineas Jones, by whom he had Richard and Ann; the wife died March 31, 1761, aged 19; then, in 1763, he married Sarah, the seventh child of Rev. Thomas Smith, by whom he had William, Sarah, Catherine and Mary, who matured, and perhaps others. Sarah (Smith) Codman was born in Portland, Nov. 14, 1740.

June 21, 1787, Rev. Thomas Smith deeded on account of "love, good will and affection which I have for my grandson, William Codman, son of Richard Codman, of Portland, Esq., a house lot located on Queen street, adjoining lot of my son-in-law, Thomas Saunders, Esq., and Lucy (Smith) his wife"—she a daughter of the Parson.

Richard Codman, Sen., was a merchant on the corner of Exchange and Middle streets. His dwelling was a large wooden structure, located on the easterly corner of Temple and Middle streets. He was deacon of the Episcopal church more than a half score of years and served as selectman.

Richard Codman, son by first wife of Richard Codman, Sen., married a daughter of General Preble, and Ann, the other child by first wife, married James Fosdick.

William Codman, the eldest child of Richard Codman, Sen., by the second marriage of his father with Parson Smith's daughter, engaged in mercantile life in Portland. His intention of marriage with Lucretia Smith of Windham was recorded Dec. 22, 1805, she a daughter of Rev. Peter Thatcher Smith of Windham, hence granddaughter of Rev. Thomas Smith, but among the eleven names of children of Rev. Peter, born between the years of 1766 and 1783, we fail to find on the printed list that of "Lucretia."

William and Lucretia had, it appears, but two children:

1—William Henry, b. Sept. 23, 1806, who became a lawyer and located at Camden, this state.
2—George Calvin, b. April 8, 1823— the subject of this sketch—m. Harriet Louisa Bradstreet, b. Oct. 3, 1819, in Gardiner, daughter of Simon Bradstreet, b. in Biddeford, and wife Lydia Nichols of Boston, Mass. Bradstreet was a merchant. She d. Sept. 3, 1892, in Deering; he d. same place, (Woodfords district) April 9, 1898.

Names and dates in this case are somewhat conflicting.

William Codman died in Portland, Nov. 12, 1828, aged 57 years. His remains are deposited in a tomb in the Portland Eastern cemetery.

Upon a lot in Evergreen cemetery may be seen three memorial slabs, one for George C., one for his wife and one inscribed as follows:

LUCRETIA,
widow of
William Codman
of Portland,
died Jan., 30,
1853.

There is no date of age of deceased appearing; and upon the stone of George C.'s wife "Harriet" is left off. It reads—Louisa Bradstreet, wife of George C. Codman, etc.

We might have known more of the subject of this sketch, and when too late to make amends express our feelings of sorrow that we know so 'tle.

Mr. Codman was a very affable man, ever ready to communicate, yet a quiet and unobtrusive man. He was a reader; possessed rare books and family keepsakes, but he did not make any public demonstrations of his acquisitions deposited in the storehouse of his mind or library shelves. He performed labor upon the genealogy of the Codman and Smith names, the results of which should be secured by our Portland Genealogical Society, as he was a member. The extent of his labors in this direction we have no means of telling. Under date of April 13, 1893 he writes us: "I have been hunting some time for something in regard to Joshua Moody, who was published to Mary Codman April 5, 1763," etc., and then solicits help.

He was of medium height, somewhat corpulent the last of his life; red, round face, full, long white beard; bald head, which was above the average in size; wore a slouch black hat, but always shapely.

He was educated in the Portland public schools and when quite a young man became the agent and cashier of the Westbrook Manufacturing Company with mills at Saccarappa village. Nearly forty years ago he purchased the large, two story, ancient Benjamin Stevens residence and lot located opposite the brick school house on Ocean street, Woodfords district of Deering, by far the most ancient residence of the locality, Stevens making his will April 19, 1758, at which time the residence was in existence, naming as children—Benjamin, Martha, Joshua, Isaac Sawyer, (ancestor of the Stevens Plains branch of the name,) Sarah and widow Martha, whose maiden name was Martha Sawyer, whose parents were the first to locate at Woodfords at the last settlement in 1727, who resided where the late Isaac Bailey lived a little to the eastward, on the northerly side of the way. In 1815 the house, barn and lot were taxed to Lemuel Stevens on a $400 valuation, when the clapboards of the house played in the wind being held by one nail while some were entirely gone—a period when everybody drank rum.

The soil of the neighborhood is hard to work—a clay loam—but Mr. Codman made his house surroundings produce blossoms. From early spring till late in fall the blossoms of trees, shrubs and plants were perpetual. To the passer-by the house was almost enveloped in foliage and bloom. In the rear of and attached to his residence was his green house where he produced his plants and generated heat for the house, but so quiet was he that one would never suspect that he was such an admirer of the mysteries of Nature. But few men live to themselves as Mr. Codman did.

After leaving Saccarappa Mr. Codman was employed as an expert accountant, having an office in Portland, assisting banks to adjust their accounts.

He was town clerk several years but his penmanship was ill adapted to the position being fine and of a peculiar mould which rendered it difficult to be read easily.

He was an Episcopalian and the funeral ceremony was performed in the little chapel not far off.

Continued:

His will was peculiarly written when he was in his dotage and is as follows dated Dec. 13, 1894:

1—To Charles E., George D., Louisa children of my nephew John E. Isa children of my nephew John E. Codman $500 each.

2—To Emily wife of my nephew John $500.

3—To Mary B. Chadwell if living $500, and any articles of her family value that I may possess. I mean Bradstreets.

4—I give the diamond ring to the wife of the first son of John E. who is married.

5—I give to Don Codman, dau. of John any silver I may have.

6—I give to John E. or his heirs of Philadelphia all the rest of my property both real and personal and appoint him executor of this will without bonds.

Witness   Geo. C. Codman.
names.

"Dec. 15, 1894. I give to Mr. John Sawyer $250.
  Geo. C. Codman."

"Mem. It is $50 to each of the persons named, Chas. E. George D. Donister Emily M. B. Cadwell."

There is a large lot of land connected with the premises, but Old Antiquary is laying his hand heavily upon the buildings and immediate surroundings, general neglect and decay being very observable.

To be Continued.

GRANDPA'S SCRAP BOOK

Week of June 6-9, 1900.

WESTBROOK.

NAMES OF THE SELECTMEN AND REPRESENTATIVES TO THE LEGISLATURE.

BY LEONARD B. CHAPMAN.

(Continued from last week.)

During the week just passed we have revised the list of names of children of Clement Pennell and wife Ruth and now present the following:

1—Eunice m. John Goold, and resided westerly of Nason's Corner. (Memoranda has appeared in The News.)

2—Joseph m. July 18, 1773, Hannah Ward and finally located in what is now the town of Gray. They had eight children. Joseph, father to William L. Pennell, subject of this sketch, was the second child. The wife died and Joseph was married second at Gray, June 25, 1789, by Samuel Perley, Esq., to Eunice Nash. (Another record says Charlotte Nash.) By this union there were born eight children—sixteen in all. He then m. third the Widow Bucha. By this marriage there were no children.

3—Abigail (Pennell) Adams.

4—Molly (Pennell) Fickett. They resided upon the land now used for cemetery purposes by the City of Westbrook, located upon the Stroudwater road; and have appeared in The News.

5—Clement, Jr.

6—Samuel m. 1786, Mary Goold, then disappears from all records after signing away his interest in his father's estate.

7—Thomas, m. March 5, 1789, Eunice Knight, and retained the homestead or "inn" located between Capisic and Nason's Corner.

Ruth (Riggs) Pennell, the mother of the foregoing named, was licensed in 1773 as a retailer and not as an innholder, so her "inn" was not by the records much of an "inn." The license was renewed each year for some time.

Joseph Pennell, the second child of Joseph and Hannah (Ward) Pennell m. Oct. 29, 1779, Elizabeth Stone of Kennebunk. He was a shoemaker, or, as then called, a "cordwainer," because a man who could make shoe and understood also the art of mr u-facturing leather was known as a cordwainer.

The exact time Joseph Pennell removed with his family to what is now the Town of Gray we cannot state. He purchased of the heirs the little home place of his father that was located where the Warren Harmon house now stands at Capisic, and evidently resided there a short time, then sold it for £60 to Andrew P. Frost.

The following copy of a letter written in 1767 will prove interesting reading we feel to those who are interested in the history of the Town of Gray. What is now Gray was then known as the Plantation of New Boston—incorporated as a town June 19, 1778.

Boston, Mass., July 13, 1767.
Sr. Mr. Moses Twitchell informs me you are settled on my settlement lot No. 7, containing sixty acres, and upon the recommendation he gave me of you I promise and oblige myself and heirs to give you a Deed of the same, you obliging yourself and heirs to perform all the conditions of settlement the Province has obliged me to do to save me harmless from the Province, the said lot is in the Township commonly called New Boston back of North Yarmouth.

I am, Sr, your humble serv't,
  John Hill.
To Mr. John Wilson at
New Boston.

Cumberland, ss. Gray.
  Feb. 12, 1783.

This Day personally appeared before us the above named John Wilson and acknowledged the above obligation to be Joseph Pennell's, his Heirs, Executors and assigns forever, as witness our Hands.

  Jediah Cobb, David Hunt,
  Selectmen of Gray.

The first time the name of Joseph Pennell appeared on public records it was recorded as that of one who was a citizen of Gray, which was in 1783, he then acting as collector and constable, the only office he held of which we find a notice. His residence was located some three miles southerly of Gray Corner, on the road to Portland. The house was burned a few years since, while owned by Thomas Carey.

CHILDREN OF JAMES AND ELIZABETH (STONE) PENNELL.

1—Dixie S., m. in Gray, was a shoemaker and d. on the way to California.

2—Susannah, m. Benjamin Cole of North Yarmouth, where she died.

3—Jeremiah, Jr., m. in Gray, Irene Maxwell.

4—Robert B., d. young.

5—Hannah W., d. in Saccarappa, while residing there with her brother, William L. Pennell. Memorial stone at Saccarappa village cemetery.

6—Luther, m. Susan S. Smith, second, Judith Merrill, and resided in Freeport.

7—James, b. July 4, 1818, is alive and resides at Saccarappa.

8—William L., b. April 15, 1821, m. Sophia J. Pennell.

9—Luther d. unmarried in California.

March 26, 1806, Joseph Pennell deeded to Joseph Pennell, Jr., who was also a cordwainer and father to William L. Pennell, "one half of my home farm that I now live on being a part of three lots in the whole, with all the privileges and appurtenances, excepting the house I now live in and the land said house stands on and the orchard as the fence stands I reserving these to myself, and likewise a quarter of an acre of land where the school house stands in the town of Gray, in the whole of said farm about one hundred and ten acres."

Joseph Pennell, Jr., first lived in Minot, where the first five of his children were born; then in Gray, where he died in March of 1826; his wife in June of 1828. Joseph, senior, surviving both.

GRANDPA'S SCRAP BOOK

Week of June 13-16, 1900.

WESTBROOK.

NAMES OF THE SELECTMEN AND REPRESENTATIVES TO THE LEGISLATURE.

BY LEONARD B. CHAPMAN.

THE PENNELLS AND OTHERS.

(*Continued from last week.*)

It is a family tradition that the Pennells of Capisic came from the Isle of Jersey and there were three of them—three brothers—of whom Thomas and Clement, who were both ship carpenters, married. Mill building probably attracted them to the region of Capisic and they may have contracted in Europe to come to this country as it was the custom of General Waldo when there to influence mechanics to come over here and then fail to comply with his obligations. Several cases of this sort are on record.

When trouble was apprehended with the Indians in 1757, Samuel Skillings of Long Creek, Cape Elizabeth, acted as Captain of a military, composed of eighty-seven privates. Upon the roll of membership we find the names of Clement Pennell, Thomas Pennell and John Pennell, Jr. The list of names may be seen in volume three, page 289, of the Collections of the Maine Historical Society, Series II.

Imagine a line drawn from Woodfords in Deering up round Saccarappa village, thence southerly, including the region of Long Creek, thence to Woodfords, including Libby's Corner and a great majority, if not all the persons named, resided upon the horseshoe shaped piece of land inclosed as above indicated.

Capt. John Brackett was a land surveyor as well as a mill hand and resided on the northerly side of what is now called the old road from Saccarappa to Gorham, a half mile westerly of Saccarappa, where the Conant family resided later. Before the break of day, April 21, 1775, the almost breathless bareback rider informed the public hereabouts of the battle at Lexington with the British and before the sun disappeared on that day Capt. Brackett had his company, composed of thirty-four members, off for the seat of war, and they were thirty miles away when "counter orders were rec'd to return home."

James Johnson, who erected the large dwelling house which may now be seen, in all its Colonial simplicity, situated upon the southerly side of the Stroudwater road a mile southeasterly of Saccarappa village, and known as the Pratt house, was Capt. Brackett's First Lieutenant and Jesse Partridge his second, the last having been briefly noticed in these articles.

Then Capt. Brackett bestirred himself to organize a company for the war which consisted of sixty members when it was ready for service.

The names of two of the privates were as follows:

JEREMIAH PENNELL. Enlisted May 10, 1775.

JOSEPH PENNELL. Enlisted May 14, 1775.

[The above is taken from the Mass. Archives, Manuscript Vol. 2, No. 56, page 215.]

Capt. Brackett's service in the army was short. He died Sept. 24, 1775, at Ipswich, Mass., on the way home, leaving a widow and children at Saccarappa.

Lieut. Johnson, son of the first James Johnson—James who lived and died where the late George Johnson resided, a mile westerly of Stroudwater, married Elizabeth Porterfield, daughter of the original William Porterfield, whose son John, brother to Elizabeth, was one of Capt. Brackett's company, the Porterfield farm being situated next westerly of the James Johnson, Sen., farm and now known as the Boothby farm. Lieut. Johnson, after selling his house and farm to Samuel Butts, removed to Poland, this state, where he died June 16, 1851, aged ninety-six years, leaving a large number of descendants.

Lieut. Partridge had with him as companions two brothers, David and Nathan, noticed in former articles. And Lieut. Johnson had for a companion his brother George. To go through the list and notice all would take much space; but we cannot pass the matter without referring to Sergt. Joshua Stevens of Woodfords district of Deering, who died there May 7, 1800, whose remains fill an unknown grave in the much desecrated George street burying place. Though his children reared to his name a memorial stone interlopers displaced it with others and threw all into a slough two miles off.

At Woodfords, district of Deering—

"Gone are the barons bold,
Gone are the knights and squires,
Gone the abbot stern and cold,
And the brotherhood of friars;
    Not a name
    Remains to fame,
From those mouldering days of old!"

There, in the George street ancient burying place, "Death is (not) rest and peace."

Capt. Joshua Stevens was a son of Benjamin Stevens, the first of the name at Woodfords, born Oct. 28, 1743, in the house recently noticed in The News as the last residence of the late George C. Codman. The Captain built the venerable appearing two story residence as now seen situated opposite the Codman house, many years the home of the late William Woodford, who married a descendant. The Captain married Feb. 5, 1763, Susannah Sawyer, born at Woodfords April 3, 1743, who died there August 1, 1830, aged 87 years. Her memorial stone was one that was rescued and may be seen in the short row of stones at George street. They had twelve children. (For family record see News of Oct. 13, 1894.) The present Mayor of Portland as well as ex-City Solicitor Chapman are descendants.

Capt. Joshua Stevens, it will be remembered, was Sergt. Stevens, who enlisted in 1775 under Capt. Brackett. And Sergt. Stevens was a brother to Isaac S. (awyer) Stevens, the progenitor of the Stevens Plains Stevenses, who returned from the battlefields of the Revolution with a real Captain's commission, which is still in existence, while his remains repose in peaceful sleep in the Windham road cemetery, but there is not an indication on the stone that he went through the eventful period, or was stationed upon the coast easterly of Portland Neck in his regimental costume before active service commenced.

To be continued.

Week of June 20—23, 1900

WESTBROOK.

NAMES OF THE SELECTMEN AND REPRESENTATIVES TO THE LEGISLATURE.

BY LEONARD B. CHAPMAN.

THE PENNELLS.

(Continued from last week.)

Eunice Pennell, who married John Goold and resided in the Nason Corner district of Deering, had a son named Clement Goold. Of him we know but little. He engaged in trade at Capisic and later at Stroudwater, then he removed to Limington, where he was residing in 1834. He united in marriage with Miss Mary Miles, whose father, Capt. William Miles, built the two story brick house at Capisic which was taken down some forty years ago, the barn standing till last year when it was burned in the night. Before us as we write are several original papers relating to the brick house, one in the hand of Randolph A. L. Codman, Esq., at one time a celebrated criminal lawyer at Portland, which contains the signatures of Codman, Clement Goold, wife Mary (Miles) Goold and John Goold, the father to Clement. Concerning John Goold Parson Bradley says:

"June 25, 1840. This forenoon went into the city (Portland) and made calls at this place and at that and met with one another with whom I conversed, sometimes on religion and sometimes on politics—upon the times and season—prospects of crops—the drought, for it is very dry and the grass on poor land is drying up. At home to dinner. At 4 o'clock P. M. Mrs. Bradley and myself, Frances Hayes and Leonard (the Parson's son) went up the Congen road (now Capisic street) in a wagon—Leonard to gather strawberries—the rest intending to stop at Mr. John Goold's, where we took tea, he being in his ninty-fifth year and able to be about. His two children take care of him—one an old bacheldor, the other an old maid. Samuel, the son, is a curiosity—none such. Has some property, works hard and so does his sister. Hope they take good care of their father. He, the father, says he is well cared for, and he knows if anyone does. Returned home at sunset, Leonard with his strawberries. Had rather a pleasant time. I prayed with Mr. Goold at his request. I told him he had nothing to do but watch and pray. He said he done both, or as well as he knew how. This Mr. Goold is the oldest person among us. Mrs. Porterfield (of Stroudwater) is about the same age. May their so number their days as to apply their hearts unto wisdom."

The town of Westbrook made claim to the brick house noticed above and sold it and lot at auction, making a long story in detail, which was redeemed by Clement Goold, the town paying him for rent, and he paying the town for aid rendered one Samuel Miles. The cellar hole only now remains of the house.

Only yesterday we learned that Ruth Adams, a daughter of Abigail (Pennell) Adams married Uriah Paine and they resided upon the easterly shore of Watchic Pond, town of Standish, where representatives of the name still reside.

Molly Pennell who has been noticed as Molly Fickett, married June 25, 1765, Nathaniel Fickett. The remains of both probably slumber in the private burial place, now included in the Saccarappa cemetery purchased where we counted twenty graves without a lettered slab, a few years since, when an attempt was made at obliteration with the plow in the hands of interlopers, notwithstanding the existence of recorded reservations by original owners of the sacred lot. Loud threats only of quick retribution both verbal and written, with quotations from records, backed by an "opinion" of one of the best lawyers of Portland precented the threatened invasion. Now that the city of Westbrook owns the surroundings of the "reservation" future proceedings are looked forward to with considerable solicitude by those having relatives interred there.

Nov. 20, 1800, Soloman Strout of Limington married Patience Fickett, a daughter of Nathaniel and Molly (Pennell) Fickett, and they had a son named Clement and daughters.

We now come to Thomas Pennell, the youngest of the seven children of Clement Pennell—all we can find—who, by purchase of the rights of the heirs, retained the homestead or "Inn," located next westerly of the Levi Starbird lot on Capisic street which went to Levi's son Edward D. Starbird, recently deceased. He married as has been stated, March 5, 1789, Eunice Knight, and commenced house keeping in the "inn," but in saying that the cellar hole of the building remains, as we have, we made a mistake for it has been filled, and the second and much smaller house that succeeded the "inn" converted into a hay barn, and removed some rods from the original site.

Upon the rear part of the lot Thomas Pennell commenced the manufacture of bricks. Then brick making was a slow proceeding. A small, round enclosure was made, the clay, sand and water placed in it, and the barn yard stock turned in which was kept moving, thus preparing the clay for moulding, which was placed upon a table then put into the forms, and carried to the drying yard.

In Col. James Mean's store book is an account with Thomas Pennell which was commenced June 23, 1797, and is in length that of one's arm.

These old accounts are curious appearing. It is surprising how much rum one's skin was made to hold a hundred years ago. "As much rum drank now as then"—bah!

A few prices then may interest.

1 gallon molasses   3 shillings, 4 pence
1 gallan W. I. rum,   6 shillings, 8 pence
1 gallon new rum, 4 shillings, 4 pence
½ quintle fish,   16 shillings, 6 pence
1 bushel of corn,   7 shillings.
2 pounds coffee.   3 shillings, 4 pence
1 pound candles,   1 shilling, 3 pence
¼ pound tea,   1 shilling, 6 pence
1 peck salt,   1 shilling, 3 pence.
¼ barrel flour,   9 shilling, 6 pence.

Col. Means' house as now seen at Stroudwater is one half brick, that is, two sides are constructed of brick and the other two of wood, the house being a square one, two stories high.

August 9, 1797, Mr. Pennell is credited with 3500 brick at twenty shillings per 1000, total £4-14. Then brick were worth less than $3.50 per 1000, now about $10.

Evidently the brick credited to Mr. Pennell are now in the two walls of the Col. Means' house.

[To be continued.]

RANDPA'S SCRAP BOOK

Week of June 27–30, 1900.

WESTBROOK.

NAMES OF THE SELECTMEN AND REPRESENTATIVES TO THE LEGISLATURE.

BY LEONARD B. CHAPMAN.

THE PENNELLS.

(Continued from last week.)

Eunice (Knight) Pennell, the wife of Thomas Pennell, with whom she was united in marriage Feb. 1, 1791, who was son of Clement Pennell, after having given birth to three children died at Thomas' home, located near the Nason's Corner district of Deering, Nov. 15, 1808, which has been noticed, and Parson Bradley, who attended her funeral, states that she was 43 years of age. Her remains fill an unknown grave.

Thomas Pennell married second, April 28, 1809, Sally Jones of Standish. Not finding a meeting congenial to her religious views near her new home, she being a Methodist, prevailed upon her husband to dispose of the premises, which he did in 1809 to Peleg Mitchell for $1300 and they removed to "Methodist Corner," Buxton, where eight children were born and where descendants still reside upon the parental acres.

April 3, 1827, seventy-five persons purchased a parcel of land located in Saccarappa village, comprising something over an acre, for cemetery purposes and divided the same among the purchasers, but there is no obtainable record of proceedings till 1850, when a plan of the plot was made, lots numbered and names of owners written under the numbers. Upon the paper we find the name of Jones Pennell, a son of Thomas and Sally Pennell, and upon the lot two white marble slabs inscribed as follows:

Thomas Pennell died March 2, 1848, aged 81 years.

"Blessed are the peace makers."

Sarah, wife of Thomas Pennell, died Nov. 30, 1862, aged 81 years.

"The Lord doeth all things well."

Ten of the children were named respectively as follows:

1—Nancy, b. Feb. 1, 1791, m. March 18, 1810, Levi Starbird, who resided next easterly of the Clement Pennell homestead.

2—Henry, m. Eunice Thomes. He was a farmer and shoemaker, and resided upon the Buxton homestead. They had Thomas and Alexander, who succeeded the parents.

3—Almira. She did not marry and spent much of her life with her cousin, the wife of Chesley D. Nason, a daughter of Levi Starbird. Nason was a shop keeper at Nason's Corner, the building now remaining.

Children by second wife:

4—Thomas. He d. at home unmarried.

5—Jones. M. and his last days on earth were spent at 125 Oxford street, Portland, where he died January 18, 1895, aged 87 years, 5 mo. His remains were interred a few rods southerly of the office building in Evergreen cemetery. His wife is also deceased. They had no children. He was a dealer in cooper's heading and lumber. Just before his death he was interesting himself in the history of the Pennells, but we have never seen the result of his labors on this line.

6—Charles. He emigrated to the Eastern part of Maine, from which he never returned and was never heard from.

7—George, who died in Buxton, aged about twenty.

8—Sophia J. b. March 10, 1821, m. William L. Pennell.

9—John P. m. Mary A. Norton of the State of Connecticut. They resided many years at No. 37, Spring street, Saccarappa village. He was a tinsmith, and died there Feb. 18, 1897, aged 77 years, 11 mo. The widow and a daughter reside upon the homestead. The burial lot is located adjacent the westerly side of the "Soldiers' Lot," Evergreen cemetery, in Deering.

10—Ephraim, m. Clorinda Small; 2nd, Mrs. Sarah Sterns. Reside at No. 41 Spring street, Saccarappa.

A child by the last wife died young, making eleven in all.

William L. Pennell, b. April 15, 1821, at Gray, son of Joseph, was great grandson of Clement Pennell of Capisic, and Sophia Y. Pennell, b. in Buxton, March 10, 1821, who appears as number eight in the foregoing, was a granddaughter of Clement, and they were united in marriage May 25, 1848.

At the age of twenty-one William L. started out into the world on his own account, having lived till that time upon the homestead. He had $15 in his pocket and was in debt $5. He worked that summer in a brick yard in Massachusetts at $15 per month, returning to Gray in the fall, where he worked on a farm two years, appearing in Saccarappa in 1844, where he engaged in brickmaking with his brothers, James and Luther. Then he engaged there with his brother James in the manufacture of cooper's heading, which copartnership was continued till 1854, from which date till 1867, he, in company with Leander Valentine, engaged in the grocery and dry goods traffic at Saccarappa, the firm name appearing in the State Directory of 1861 as "Valentine, Hardy & Co.;" and it was a common saying then that the "concern" dominated the politics of the region, which became strongly Republican and on account of the rapid and overshadowing growth of Republicanism in Saccarappa, Westbrook was territorially divided in 1870. In politics William L. was originally a Whig, but when Republicanism made its appearance he was one of the first converts.

In 1861-62 he was town clerk and treasurer. He filled the office of selectman two years.

In 1867 he was appointed deputy sheriff, which office he held five years.

In 1872 he was elected sheriff of the county, hence jailer. In 1874 he was re-elected.

The enforcement of the Prohibitory liquor law during his first term was mild, but the second was one of the most severe the opponents to the law ever encountered; and he retired from office with his hat full of laurel and his purse full of gold eagles—honestly earned.

In the spring of 1878 he purchased the William Gilmore store and residence at Cumberland Mills district of Westbrook, engaged in the grocery trade, and drove a span of 2.40 clip, but soon thereafter retired from active labor and with his wife went to reside with Mrs. Boody, a daughter, at number eleven, Clark street, Deering.

Children:

1—Sarah F., b. Feb. 9, 1849, d. June 21, 1853.

2—Joseph Henry, b. July 27, 1852, d. Sept. 29, 1870.

3—Addie Louisa, b. Dec. 11, 1853, m. Jan. 27, 1876, Frank Hale Boody. They reside as above noted.

4—Jones, b. Sept. 7, 1855, m. May 14, 1879, Addie F. Quinby.

5—Hattie Jane, b. July 21, 1857, d. June 22, 1863.

6—Nettie S———, b. Nov. 11, 1859, m. Erwin B. Newcomb, manager of the Electrical works at Saccarappa, where they resided and where she died March 2, 1885, and he married again and now resides.

William L. Pennell died Dec. 17, 1886; his widow, July 25, 1891.

Upon the westerly side of the Saccarappa village cemetery may be seen two low blocks of stone, one inscribed "Father, 1821—1886;" the other: "Mother, 1821—1891." A clue to the names of the tenants is furnished by an examination of the adjacent slabs bearing the Pennell name.

William L. Pennell was an extremely kind hearted man and as liberal with the contents of his purse as he was kind.

To be continued.

GRANDPA'S SCRAP BOOK

Week of July 4–7, 1900.

WESTBROOK.

NAMES OF THE SELECTMEN AND REPRESENTATIVES TO THE LEGISLATURE.

BY LEONARD B. CHAPMAN.

JAMES PENNELL.

(Continued from last week.)

James Pennell, brother to William L. Pennell, noticed last week, was born in the town of Gray, July 4, 1818. He was an active boy, and has been a live man. And here we desire to correct an error or two.

Where it reads in our article of June 6-9, "children of James and Elizabeth (Stone Pennell)," James should be Joseph; and the name of the first born should be spelled Dixey, not Dixie. The last name on the same list should be Joseph, not Luther. We refer to number nine. The real Luther of the family appears as number six. Persons owning a "Cumberland County History" of 1880 would do well by making a change of the name of Luther to Joseph.

In my article of last week the letter "M." appearing after Jones (No. 5) should be erased.

Dixey S. Pennell, who died on the way to California, was in Gray a shoemaker. His wife was Abigail Small, and they had five children. Their son, Charles Thayer Pennell, occupies the homestead at Gray Corner.

With Dixey Stone Pennell, James Pennell, the subject of this article, at the age of fifteen went to reside, for the purpose of becoming a knight of the last and lapstone.

In 1838 James opened a boot and shoe store in New Gloucester, in which town he was united in marriage.

In 1843 he sold in New Gloucester his business and removed with his family to Saccarappa village where, as has been stated in a previous article, he engaged with his brother, William L., in the manufacture of bricks. Then he traveled through New England as an agent for a patent spring for carriages. Then for a period of two years he manufactured patent loom harnesses at Saccarappa, when a copartnership was entered into with Henry Smith, George and Lewis P. Warren and the business continued under the firm name of Warren, Pennell & Co. Then for some twelve years Mr. Pennell, in company with the Warren Brothers, manufactured wire. In 1875 he purchased the Brackett stove business, where he personally superintended the sale of stoves and tinware till 1892, when he disposed of the entire stock and closed the store.

In politics Mr. Pennell was a Whig, but became an original Republican, and has been elected to various town offices by the party.

He was from 1866 to 1869 County Commissioner.

He was opposed to the territorial division of Westbrook, but when the time of separation came he was appointed commissioner with Samuel T. Raymond, on the part of his adopted town, to adjust with commissioners from the new town of Deering the various matters claiming attention, growing out of the division.

When the Westbrook Trust Co. was formed in January of 1890, with a capital of $50,000, he was made a director, and upon the death of the president, Hon. Leander Valentine, in 1895, he was called to the chair vacated by President Valentine, a position he now fills, though in the 82nd year of his age.

Mr. Pennell's religious affiliations have been with the Congregational church, and he is a member in good standing of nearly all the secret organizations that have a record.

He has occupied his present two storied residence some forty-five years, located in a quiet part of the village, upon the northerly side of the Presumpscot river, with the river and river banks beyond, forming a picturesque view, but soon to be changed in consequence of the erection of a large mill building made of brick.

The view from Mr. Pennell's residence is replete with incidents, carrying the mind of those who have studied the record facts back a hundred and seventy odd years.

Referring to Parson Smith's diary, under date of April 30, 1740, we find as follows:

"I rode to Stroudwater to talk with Mr. Siemons who is offended with my sermon to the Irish. Mr. Frost also made known that he is offended with me for some passages in a sermon which he thought reflected on his taking Haskell's house &c."

Charles Frost, Esq., resided where the Brewer House stood, on the opposite side of the river, easterly of Stroudwater village, whose residence was made into a three storied building in 1834, from the material obtained by removing the Stroudwater parish meeting house, then converting it into an Inn, the pulpit being used in its changed location in the service of the devil as well as the Lord in its original, saying nothing about the wine of both places. The cellar hole of the Haskell house still exists and may be seen situated between Congress and Frost streets, notwithstanding so many years have elapsed.

In the vicinity of the residence of James Pennell Joseph Conant built his Saccarappa cabin and then bridged the river to get to it, there being no obtainable land on the southerly side. It was in the month of May of 1739 that Conant built his mill, just ten years after the first occupancy of the falls by others for mill purposes. Dec. 18, 1739, being the day he commenced his cabin. Thomas Haskell helped him, who was living then in the vicinity.

A while after this, when news came from Gorham that all the inhabitants of the town had been killed by the Indians, and Conant, Haskell and the rest of the men of the place started out to bury the dead, Mrs. Haskell moved into Conant's house, and "upon Enquiring into the Cause of so extraordinary a Proceeding She told him twas best to be all together in Time of War and that said deponants House was a good place for a Garrison." She "promised to dress his Victuals for him," "but he received such Treatment from said Haskell's Wife his life was soon made miserable."

Haskell became the "doctor" of the place and the fact is recorded on the grave memorial of the vicinity. It was this Conant's son who built the "Pork Hill" house that has been noticed in these articles, plainly visible from the residence of James Pennell.

From the woman who took matters into her own hands a 160 years ago, pertaining to her own safety, and who assured the public that she could "dress victuals," the present wife of Mr. Pennell is descended, as well as scores of others.

To be continued.

GRANDPA'S SCRAP BOOK

Week of July 11—14, 1900

WESTBROOK.

NAMES OF THE SELECTMEN AND REPRESENTATIVES TO THE LEGISLATURE.

BY LEONARD B. CHAPMAN.
JAMES PENNELL.

(Continued from last week.)

James Pennell was twice united in marriage, first, in New Gloucester with Miss Abigail Taylor, daughter of William and Mary Taylor; she died in 1852, having borne him three children.

The Larrabee name is an old name hereabouts, persons bearing it having been in this section continuously nearly two hundred years. The one who attempts to prepare a history of the family engages upon a large work. One of the several Benjamins went out from Portland and settled upon the unimproved land easterly of Congin Falls, a place now known as Cumberland Mills upon the Presumpscot river in Westbrook. His second residence was very pleasantly situated upon the northerly side of the highway, commodious, facing the south, and protected on the north by rising ground, as now observed, covered by an orchard. The land was good, and the occupant flourished. Even to this day it is believed there are pots of money buried upon the premises though none has ever been discovered. After the sale of the premises the house during the time of the war of the Rebellion was converted into a public resort and known by the name of The White House, but its life as an inn was short. It was removed to the Cumberland Mills district of Westbrook and converted into a boarding house but of late the name of White House has been restored and it is in fact again an inn, and in its new coat of paint its appearance is sufficiently charming to induce the best to call.

Benjamin Larrabee married first, Jane Cobby of Windham; she died April 29, 1824, aged 46 years. He married second Sept. 12, 1824, Sarah Lamb, daughter of a neighbor. She died Oct. 29, 1847, aged 57 years. Benjamin Larrabee died July 8, 1832, aged 64 years.

At the foot of the elevation in the rear of the site of the original house, or the one converted to an inn, the elevation that is covered with ancient apple trees, may be seen an oak with an immense trunk—the largest oak tree trunk we ever saw. Beneath the wide spreading branches may be seen the graves of Benjamin and his two wives and a few others, around which has recently been placed curbing stones of dressed granite enclosing a lot about fifty feet square

John Cobby died just a hundred years ago, June 25, a brother to Benjamin's first wife, whose memorial grave slab may be seen within the enclosure to which reference has been made.

Benjamin had quite a large family; a son now residing near the State Reform School farm in what is now South Portland.

In 1814 Benjamin Larrabee was taxed for a house valued at $550; two barns; woodhouse; 220 acres of land; four oxen; four cows; young cattle; swine; a horse and chaise.

We don't learn that he indulged in town or church matters and the only clue we have to his make up is found in the epitaph upon his grave memorial, as follows:

As high as heaven its arch extends
Above this little lot of clay,
So did his love excel.
The small respect we can pay.
As far as it's from East to West,
As far from us he is removed,
Kind husband, father, brother, friend,
Securely rest till time shall be no more.

Benjamin Larrabee's daughter Jane, by the first union was united in marriage February 27, 1831, with Edmund Haskell, the Rev. Caleb Bradley performing the ceremony as he did at the last marriage of Benjamin, the father to Jane.

Edmund built a good two storied residence corner of Spring and Main streets, Saccarappa, where he died Sept. 28, 1852, aged 52 years, leaving a widow, five daughters and a son; the son went to California where he died unmarried. The original house was removed some few years ago and placed upon a lot located northerly of Main street upon the southerly bank of the Presumpscot and easterly of Spring street where it may now be seen with the roof burned off which event occurred last spring. A fine brick residence occupies the original site and is the home of Mr. John Knights and family whose wife is a daughter of Edmund Haskell. Emma S., the eldest child, who was in trade several years died a year ago. Sarah C., who was also in trade and a school teacher, born March 2, 1836, died Aug. 19, 1865 Mary E. is the wife of Mr. Geo. F. Marriner, a trader, all of Saccarappa. Jane M. became the second wife of James Pennell, the subject of this sketch.

Children of James Pennell and his two wives:

Mary E. h. P. Osborne How. He
4—Susan; all deceased.

Mary E. m. P. Osborn How. He d. February 24, 1870, aged 28 yrs. Memorial slab at Saccarappa.

Frank Beverly Libby, son of Luther and Hannah (Libby) Libby, b. South Gorham, July 4, 1834, m. Mary E. Tounge of Dayton; she d. He m. 2nd. Dec. 17, 1874, Mrs. Mary E. How; she d. Sept. 6, 1877, aged 36 yrs. Joseph H. died April 21, 1851, aged 10 mo.; George died in New Gloucester. Susan d. Sept. 8, 1846, aged 2 yrs. 3 mo.

BY SECOND WIFE:
5—Frank H. employed in paper mill of S. D. Warren & Co.
6—Annie S. m. June 27, 1881, Frank B. Libby whose second wife was Mary E. Pennell a half sister to Annie S. He joined the union forces against the Rebellion and served three years. In 1871 he became turnkey at the jail and settled in Portland. From 1873 to 1881 he was a deputy sheriff of Cumberland County. Then he engaged in the boot and shoe trade occupying the Bell establishment easterly of City hall on Congress street, Portland. Now he is proprietor of "The Joselyn," the largest public house on Prouts' Neck, in Scarboro.

7—Jane F. a school teacher in Massachusetts.

8—Marcia, b. Nov. 29, 1866, d. July 2, 1883.

9—Bertha M. She is the wife of Harry D. Brooks of Westbrook.

10—Mary E. a teacher residing at home.

March 28, 1743, a Thomas Pennell and Hannah Brooks were married in Biddeford "Both of Biddeford."

April 12, 1748, David Martin and Hannah Pennell, "Both of Biddeford."

Sept. 1,0 1778, Parson Dean makes an entry in his diary as follows: "Married Pennell."

The compiler tells us that the names of the contracting parties were Mathew Pennell and Ann Tuckey, and were the parents of John, Josiah and Charles "now living here" (Portland) and that he was a caulker and came from Brunswick and lived on Franklin street, adjoining the Tukey estate.

Mathew evidently was a son of Thomas Pennell of Capisic.

Nov. 7, 1784, Clement Pennell and Esther Kinningham were united in marriage in Cape Elizabeth by the Rev. Mr. Clark, "He of Falmouth;" and evidently son of Clement of Capisic.

There were Pennells in Buxton before Thomas went there from Nason's Corner, Deering. The intention of marriage of Molly – as recorded July Mathew Pennell and Ann Tukey, and 1801.

This is all we have to record now relative to the Pennell name.

To be Continued.

GRANDPA'S SCRAP BOOK
Week of July 18–21, 1900.

WESTBROOK.

NAMES OF THE SELECTMEN AND REPRESENTATIVES TO THE LEGISLATURE.

BY LEONARD B. CHAPMAN.
JAMES PENNELL.

(Continued from last week.)

[Corrections.—James Pennell's children by his first wife were Mary E., George, Joseph H. and Susan, all deceased. Mary E., the eldest, married first, P. Osborn How, who died Feb. 24, 1870; second, Frank B. Libby.

The Pennells whose intentions of marriage were early recorded in Buxton are Molly, July 26, 1794, and Ephraim, March 3, 1801.]

1868—SELECTMEN.

The board of the previous year was relected and was as follows:

Daniel Dole, Stroudwater.

George C. Codman, Woodfords.

William L. Pennell, Saccarappa.

Rep., George W. Hammond, Cumberland Mills.

All Republicans, and the selectmen have been noticed in these articles.

Mr. Hammond was born in Grafton, Mass., April 4, 1833, son of Josiar Hovey Hammond; he born Oct. 15, 1806, on the old Hammond farm situated near Hammond's Pond in the town of Newton; a descendant of Thomas Hammond who made his first land purchase there in 1650 to which he made additions in 1656.

Mr. Hammond came to the Cumberland Mills district of Westbrook in the month of April, 1854, to take charge of the business of the paper mills, residing most of the time in the house now occupied by Charles Goodell, near the mills, the remainder in the ancient two storied brick house built by Hon. Archelaus Lewis, who was born in the town of Berwick, this state, settled in Saccarappa where he was by trade a tailor, removed to Stroudwater, built the large house there in which the postoffice is located, then purchased a part of what is now called the Cumberland Mills water privilege and removed to that place. The events connected with his name fill a large place in our local history. His remains as well as his three wives' were interred at Stroudwater where memorial slabs may be seen.

Mr. Hammond interested himself in local affairs at Cumberland Mills making quite a number of purchases of real estate; serving a couple of years as selectman of Westbrook after the town was birded.

A wonderful change in the appearance of the place has occurred since the advent of Mr. Hammond, then called Congin.

In 1815 Archelaus Lewis was taxed for a house valued at $950; barn $100; a saw mill $300; a "new saw mill $900"; 200 acres of land besides oxen, cows, horse and chaise.

It was about the year of 1808 that Lewis removed to Congin. His mills were located upon the northerly side of the river; between his residence there and the mills was a dwelling for mill men, and on the westerly side of the highway, adjoining the river, was a house for mill hands. This was all the buildings there were on the side of the river.

M. P. Sawyer had a saw mill opposite the Lewis mill, the Sawyer mill standing on the southerly side of the Presumpscot river where there is a fall of twenty feet.

Capt. Aaron Winslow resided in the Gilman house as now seen with the great elm tree in front where the Windham road joins the Portland road. Winslow being taxed in 1815 for the house on a valuation of $900. The place is now known as the Samuel T. Raymond property.

Westerly of the Winslow house upon the southerly side of the road leading to Saccarappa, stood the Gardner Walker house who was taxed for it in 1815 on a valuation of $600. a "store $35. stock in trade, $200." 83 acres of land, etc. The site of the house was later occupied by Mr. S. A. Cadwell, who, in 1861, was foreman in the paper mills.

John Stevens resided upon the northerly side of a little street that ran from a point westerly of the Gardner Walker house, easterly, to the Windham road. He came from Gorham, this state, and was taxed for a house in 1815 on a valuation of $30, barn $10 and saw mill $900.

The residences here noticed are all there were at Congin about eighty years ago. namely: six dwellings and four saw mills.

Next westerly on the way to Saccarappa was the residence of Maj. William Valentine, whose nail shop was opposite; next Charles Quinby; next school house and next the residence of David Bailey which stood opposite the head of Stroudwater street. David was a son of Deacon John Bailey who spent the last days of his life near Libby's Corner in Deering. David lived to be very aged.

The Valentine and Quinby houses stand today as built; Valentine's was taxed in 1815 on a valuation of $130, nail shop $20.

The "seaport" of Congin was Capisic where there was a landing place to which the Congin lumber was transported, one end upon a pair of wheels, the other trailing in the mud, and at Capisic rafted to Portland. It took a hundred years to raise Congin to a hamlet of six or seven houses.

We have presented a copy of an advertisement of Samuel Butts when he wanted to sell his place, who kept the only shop at Capisic, and here present a copy from the original of one of his ads. a hundred and seven years since, as follows:

SAMUEL BUTTS

Informs the public that he has opened a Store at Capissick, near the landing, where he has for sale, on the lowest terms for Cash

A well chosen assortment of English and Hard Ware

GOODS.

Among which are the following:

Best German Steel Plated Mill Cross cut and Tennon Saws, Iron and Steel; 4 d. 6 d, , and 20 d. Nails, 6 by 8. 7 by 9 and 8 by 10. Window Glass——ALSO—— W. I. & N. E. Rum, Brandy, Holland Ginn, Port, Sherry and Malaga Wines, Loaf and Brown Sugar, Molasses, Tea, Coffee, Chocolate, Cotton, Wool, Flax, Pepper, Ginger, Allspice, Nutmegs, Cinnamon——LIKEWISE:——Pork, Flour, Rice, Tobacco, Cod and Scale Fish—— Men's, Women's and Children's Shoes, Fur and Wool Hats.

FALMOUTH, APRIL 24, 1797.

N. B. CASH, or any one of the above artilces will be given for Lumber or Country Products.

Sixty-five years ago an attempt was made to boom Congin but the attempt failed. Quite an elaborate drawing was made of the land upon the southerly side of the Presumpscot. The paper contains a heading as follows: "Plan of mill sites on the Congin Falls. Surveyed and planned for N. Winslow, Nov. 1835, by F. A. Beard, Civil Engineer."

It seems the design provided for five mills; the water to be taken from a point above the falls and conducted by an open canal and let off below the falls. Provisions were made for nine boarding houses, lots, yards and streets which were named respectively as follows: Canal, Middle, Winslow, Back, Lincoln, Cumberland, Gorham and Congin.

From the year Samuel D. Warren & Co. purchased the Day and Lyon Paper Mill, Congin has expanded itself. The mills there are now among the largest of the world, and Congin is only known in history. Cumberland Mills takes the place of Congin in name.

In the month of November of 1875, Geo. W. Hammond and Samuel D. Warren of Waltham, Mass., paid $25,000 for the "Forest Paper Company" works at Yarmouth and Mr. Warren has the finest residence and best grounds in that town. He is now making a tour of Europe.

To be continued,

GRANDPA'S SCRAP BOOK

Week of July 25—28, 1900.

WESTBROOK.

NAMES OF THE SELECTMEN AND REPRESENTATIVES TO THE LEGISLATURE.

BY LEONARD B. CHAPMAN.

(Continued from last week)

1868—SELECTMEN.

Henry B. Walker,
 Pride's Corner.

Jonas Raymond,
 Saccarappa.

Freeman Porter,
 Stevens Plains.

Rep.—Geo. W. Hammond,
 Cumberland Mills.

Edward S. Walker was born in Fryeburg, this state, in 1775. Prior to the year 1800 he went to Charlestown, Mass., and with Miss Persis Phipps was united in marriage where he remained, his wife bearing him nine children, Henry B., the subject of this sketch being the eighth. Edward S., the father was a brick maker. At Charlestown both father and mother departed this life.

Henry B. attended the common school also Dodge's Academy of that place, and at the age of eighteen entered the U. S. Navy as carpenter's yeoman. After a year's service in that capacity he became assistant paymaster. His first service was upon the Mediterranean station. In 1846 he was transferred to the Gulf of Mexico squadron. The sloop-of-war "Boston" upon which he sailed as a passenger for the Gulf was wrecked on the island Eleuthera, one of the Bahama group Nov. 16, of that year. He subsequently joined the warship "Potomac," then one of the blocking squadron off Vera Cruz. There he remained a year, his naval service then coming to an end, when he returned to Charlestown, where he engaged in the provision trade, and was married April 22, 1847, to Miss Mary A. Lunt, daughter of George W. Lunt of Pride's Corner district of Westbrook. (For Lunts see Deering News, Oct. 19, 1895.) Two years later in January, he took the "gold fever" and sailed for California via Cape Horn. From San Francisco with a half score of others' with a boat carried from Massachusetts, the party went to Stocton, a hundred and more miles distant, but owing to illness of his wife, he started for his Northern home, arriving in January of 1851. His wife died May 6, 1851, and a few years since we copied her gravestone inscription on the Lunt farm in Westbrook where she was interred. In June of that year he returned to the gold regions and spent two years in the mines.

May 11, 1854, he was again married to Zella A. Lunt, a sister to his first wife. She was born May 13, 1825. The year he married last he purchased of his wife's father the Pride's Corner Lunt farm and ever after resided upon it, excepting 1861-62 when he visited Oregon, Washington and Idaho Territories.

At Pride's Corner he engaged in farming and brick-making, erecting upon the premises a fine set of brick buildings.

By careful observation while traveling and at various places of residence coupled with much reading, and being endowed with direct gifts, Mr. Walker was a very useful man in his adopted town. He was in politics a Democrat but this did not prevent his holding office in his Republican town. He was a Justice of the Peace, town auditor of accounts, assessor and selectman many terms of office after Westbrook was territorialy divided and Deering created. None were better acquainted with town matters than he and none while in office was more devoted to party friends and the real interest of all citizens than he. His second wife died Sept. 30, 1899; he, Feb. 22, 1900.

Children by Second Wife:

1—Calvin S., b. Sept. 28, 1855.
2—Edward S., b. Aug. 12, 1857.
3—Henry Percy, b. Nov. 17, 1859.
4—Charles B., b. Jan. 6, 1864.
5—Ernest W., b. April 17, 1866.

The last two were drowned in the Presumpscot river March 30, 1872. By the first marriage there was one child that died young.

John Raymond, son of Samuel Raymond, who maried Polly Smith, had at Lyman, this state, where he resided, Jonas, born 1812, and Samuel Tarbox, born 1815. Jonas married Mary R. Johnson of Boston in 1839, and had Geo. H., in 1841; and Hattie E., born 1845.

Samuel Tarbox Raymond, engaged in trade in Charlestown, Mass., where he was united in marriage in 1841 with Miss Elizabeth Andrews and had Helen M., born 1842; King S., 1844 and Addie M., 1848.

May 14, 1842, Jonas was a resident of Westbrook, and Samuel T. of Charlestown, when they closed with Capt. Aaron Winslow Winslow for the farm at Congin, noticed last week as the Gilman farm, where stands the immense elm tree in front of the ancient two story house, the price fixed being $5000, where both resided some years, speculating and farming very successfully, when Jonas removed to the old Joseph Bailey farm, located between Congin and Saccarappa about a mile northerly of the Presumpscot river. They were undeviating Democrats—Samuel T. very much so—both bright minded, with an eye ever open for a good trade. Both are deceased, and both have descendants residing in Westbrook. One of Samuel T.'s daughters is the wife of Hanno W. Gage, Esq., one of Maine's successful has the law partner of S. C. Strout, lawyers with an office in Portland, who was the law partner of S. C. Strout, Esq., till Strout was raised to the office of Judge of the Supreme Judicial court.

A notice of Freeman Porter appeared in the News of Sept. 24, 1898, under the heading of Oliver Buckley. Mr. Porter married Mary Ann (Buckley) Partridge, widow of William Partridge. Porter came from Colebrook, N. H., where he was born July 9, 1808, and was married by the Rev. Samuel Brimblecom July 1, 1835. He was a tinsmith and resided in the first house northerly of the main entrance to the cemetery on Stevens Plains avenue. He, his widow and the two children have passed away—the widow quite recently.

To be Continued.

WESTBROOK.

NAMES OF THE SELECTMEN AND REPRESENTATIVES TO THE LEGISLATURE.

BY LEONARD B. CHAPMAN.

(Continued from last week.)

1870—SELECTMEN.

Henry B. Walker, Pride's Corner.
Jonas Raymond, Saccarappa.
John R. Sawyer, Woodfords.

All Democrats; the largest number of ballots for a single candidate was 565; Republican 495.

The election was pronounced illegal and another meeting was ordered when the following named persons were elected:

Andrew Hawes, Stroudwater.
Nathaniel K. Sawyer, Morrills' Corner.
David Torrey, Morrill's Corner.

The first upon the list is still in trade at Stroudwater as he was then—a Republican.

Nathaniel K. Sawyer, a Democrat, a notice of whose ancestors has appeared in the Deering News, resided on Stevens Plains.

David Torrey, a Republican, now deceased, a notice of some considerable length having appeared a year since, was the nearest neighbor of Mr. Sawyer, Dr. George H. Bailey now occupying the Sawyer residence while Mr. Sawyer occupies the Dr. Eben Stone residence on the Plains which was built by Dr. Stone who is deceased.

In the last contest the highest number on the Republican ticket was 480—Democratic 424.

REPRESENTATIVE.

In the contest to Representative to the Legislature local politics were ignored, the question of dividing the town being the paramount issue and two Republicans were put in nomination, namely:

Joseph S. Ricker, the largest taxpayer of the town, residing half way between Woodfords and Deering's bridge, on the easterly side of the highway, where he may still be found, with his tannery on the Portland side of the bridge; and Fabins M. Ray, Esq., a college graduate, lawyer, prose and verse writer, residing at Saccarappa, bitterly opposed to the division of Westbrook while Mr. Ricker favored the project, the vote standing as recorded 648 for Ray and 487 for Ricker. A riotous meeting holden in the Town House at Bridgton Corner to discuss the question of division precipitated action, and the State Legislature of that winter created the town of Dering.

The meeting to which we refer was holdn Dec. 29, 1869. The whole number of votes cast for moderator were 879. Hon. Leander Valentine of Saccarappa, an opponent to division, had 557 and David Torrey had 322,—both were Republicans.

The resolution offered by F. M. Ray, Esq., read as follows:

"That the legal voters of Westbrook are opposed to a division of the town."

Mr. Ray was chairman of the committtee chosen at the spring town meeting to oppose division, at which meeting Hon. Samuel Jordan offered an amendment but was ruled out of order by the Hon. Jonathan Smith, who was moderator—both being Democrats, and "old time" friends. At the riotous meeting called by the town committee, Mr. Jordan had his substitute ready but for more than three hours the meeting was so noisy that business could not be transacted when it adjourned without day. Imagine 1000 voters packed into the old building on the ledge at Brighton Corner as now seen and three-fourths yelling and stamping every time a divisionist opened his mouth and an idea of the situation may be obtained.

At the first election after division, the newly created town of Deering threw 268 votes for Joseph S. Ricker, the Republican-division candidate for the Legislature to 320 for Solomon Stuart the Democratic-ant-divisionist residing at Libby's Corner district.

Mr. Stuart was born in Scarboro, near Dunstan Corner, now a part of Saco, Feb. 29, 1820; son of Solomon Stuart of that place, who was a farmer, civil engineer and office holder. Asa Stuart, who identified himself with the Washingtonian Temperance movement in 1844, and obtained considerable notoriety in consequence, used to take apparent delight in the statement that he (Stuart) was the only representative from the town heard from while the legislature was in session, and he was heard from because he got drunk in Augusta, fell, broke a leg, and sent home for money.

Solomon Stuart's first adventure in business was in shopkeeping in the town of Hiram, then brick making in summer and school keeping in winter. Five consecutive terms he taught in Dunstan. For several years he had charge of the "Steam Brick-making" business, that was transacted between Bradley's Corner and Stroudwater in Deering where the tall chimney and mounds of earth may now be seen.

He then engaged in politics, being elected repeatedly as selectman, Representative to the Legislature and County commissioner. He was, to the lasting praise of his name be it said an economist with the public's money as he was with his own.

His first wife was Miss Emma Haines of Saco, who bore him two children—Mary Elizabeth and Charles A. Stuart. He then married the widow of Baubridge Coffiin of Freeport who died in California. Her maiden name was Richards, and born in Saco. Mr. Stuart died in the month of May 1889, an obituary appearing in the Portland Argus. The widow died quite recently, leaving a son at Libby Corner, by the first marriage.

To the petition for division of Westbrook dated November, 1870, are attached seven reasons which document was prepared by Liberty B. Dennett, Esq., a lawyer, who resided westerly of Morrill's Corner, now of Portland, which reads as follows:

"First. The size of the town, the number of its inhabitants, (now nearly seven thousand,) its large valuation, the character and extent of its highways, make it unwieldly under a town organization, while from its situation and diversity of interests, a City Charter is impracticable.

"Second. On account of the large number of votes, our town meetings have become unwieldy assemblies, often exposing our citizens to great discomfort and inconvenience, detaining them unreasonably at the polls, and subjecting them to great loss of time. And this is but a small part of the evil, for the town business is often hastily and inconsiderately disposed of in the necessary confusion and tumult of such an assembly.

"Third. There is too much business to be done at our annual meetings. As many as fifty distinct articles have been contained in one warrant for an annual town meeting, many of them calling for appropriations of considerable sums of money, for repairs and improvements, and these matters of business have related to localities scattered over sixty-eight miles of road, and thirty-three square miles of territory, many of which in each section were totally unknown to the citizens of the other, and about which they were as indifferent as with the affairs of another town, except to get rid of liability and expense. And we have suffered, and are suffering under heavy suits for damages to indemnify persons who have sustained injuries in consequence of the indifferent manner of transacting our town business necessarily attendant upon its enormous extent.

"Fourth. The town as a whole has no centre, either business, social or municipal, but is composed of two sections, between which the proposed line makes the natural division, leaving on either side two villages or communities of nearly equal size; each with outlying farming country, and each having interests and aims of its own, which are different from those of the other—and as a consequence of this diversity, each community, naturally regarding the affairs of the other with indifference, and in many cases with jealously there has arisen between the two sections, an illfeeling, which has been of late increasing, and we can see no possible relief from this evil, except by a division of the town, and we believe that this will cause no conceivable injury to either section, for each will make a town among the largest in the State, in respect to wealth and population.

"Fifth. Our public schools are naturally divided in like manner with the other affairs of the town, and those of each section we believe should be superintended by the citizens of that part of the town to which they belong.

"Sixth. We do not wish to share with the people of the Western section the duties and responsibilities, incident to the management of their local concerns, but prefer to be a distinct community, and discharge the duties which our own affairs impose upon us, untrammelled by the opinions or wishes of the other section.

Continued:

"Seventh. And for proof of the allegations above submitted, we need only refer to the history of our town affairs. Our town house was located only after a long and angry sectional contest between the same sections now contending for and against division.

"And recently, when we petitioned the last Legislature for relief from the difficulties oppressing us, we were met not in the spirit which citizens of the same town should meet each other, but at the very first meeting, by the most extraordinary conduct, they forever rent asunder and divided the citizens of the two sections from each other. And this fact has been apparent at every town meeting held since that time. We were misrepresented at the Legislature, and members of that honorable body were led to believe by those misrepresentations that the movement to divide the town, was the project of a few designing men for purely selfish purposes, and that the great majority of the petitioners were indifferent about the matter, and were not sincerely seeking relief from evils, and endeavoring to bring about much needed reforms. This compels us now to reiterate all we said in our former petition, and to assure the Honorable Senate and House Representatives that we again present ourselves, sincerely believing it to be just and expedient and consistent with the interest and prosperity of the inhabitants of both sections of the town that our prayers be granted."

ANBPA'S SCRAP BOOK

Week of Aug. 8-11, 1900.

MAJOR ARCHELAUS LEWIS.

BY LEONARD B. CHAPMAN.

PART FIRST.

The subject of this article was born at Berwick, this state, February 15, 1753, baptized according to the South Berwick church records, March 11 of the same year. The church records show also that he was the younger of twelve children. His son, the last of his children to depart this life, told us that his grandfather (the father to Major Lewis came from Wales and was a sea captain; that upon the breaking out of the war of the Revolution two uncles who were residing in Falmouth, (brothers to Maj. Lewis) left the town for Nova Scotia where they ever after till death remained, leaving a large number of descendants in that region where it is said the name of Lewis is a common one; two aunts (sisters to Maj. Lewis) marrying in Berwick two brothers, by the name of Morrill each having eleven children some of whom distinguished themselves, one as a member of Congress representing a district of another state.

As a boy we have no means of knowing anything of the Major; as a man he had a massive frame, measuring over six feet in height in his stockings with a brain and a disposition to do right in keeping with his physical make up. He had a limited book education but as complete as the majority of the youth of his day. He learned the trade of a tailor but what induced him to come to Falmouth is as much of a mystery as what became of the ponderous amount of manuscript papers he left, a journal kept by him at one time while a Revolutionary soldier being the only document obtainable, but never having been printed to our knowledge.

Where he first resided upon coming to Falmouth whether at Stroudwater, Saccarappa or Gorham, we cannot state, but as it was a practice for tailors to travel from house to house as work required their presence it is more than probable that young Mr. Lewis had no permanent abiding place before he was married. He was anti-English in mental make up. When the report reached here that active hostilities had commenced between the British and Americans at Lexington he buckled on the armor and had proceeded as far as the town of Wells when orders came to counter march and await orders for which service commencing April 21, 1775, he received five days' pay as the records show; Capt. John Brackett of Saccarappa being commander.

July 3, 1775, he marched in Capt. John Brackett's company, Edmund Phinney of Gorham, Colonel of the 31st Reg. of Foot, serving at Cambridge till Dec. 31, of that year, ranking as a sergeant under Capt. James Johnson, (after the death of Capt. Brackett)—Johnson who built the Cushing Pratt house, noticed in a former article as standing now as built a mile southeasterly of Saccarappa, in Westbrook.

He reenlisted Jan. 1,1776, as sergeant in Col. Edmund Phinney's 18th Continental Reg.; promoted to Ensign Feb. 1, of that year, and April 18 was again promoted to Lieut. serving a year from date of enlistment.

From Jan. 1, 1777, to Feb. 20, 1779, he served as Lieut. and Adj. in Col. Voses 1st Mass. Reg.

For these military minutes from original records we are indebted to Mr. Nathan Goold of Portland who has made the records of that period a special study.

Maj. Lewis' time of service in the army covered a period of nearly five years, incidents as related by him being very entertaining as told to us by those now departed this life particularly by his son Archelaus.

Col. Phinney had surrendered his commission, and thoughts of the bliss of matrimony undoubtedly caused the Major to retire to civil life, having passed through five years of active service in the army and on the 14th day of March of 1779, he went out to Gorham, this state, where the marriage ceremony was performed by Col. Edmund Phinney between the Major and Rebeckah Hubbard, a widow, whose maiden name was Mayo, a record of the event being entered upon the town books of Gorham. Not long after this occurrence a child was adopted by them and named Sally Lewis who became the wife of one Joseph Adams and bore him two children.

Upon the 3d of August, 1780, the Major made his first purchase of real estate. It was situated on Main street, northerly side, and 49 feet westerly of the westerly side of Bridge street, Saccarappa village, in Westbrook, then Falmouth. Edwards' brick block now covers the whole of the "49 feet" lot. Commencing at the westerly corner of the Edwards lot the Lewis purchase extended westerly on Main street nine rods. He paid Daniel and Sarah (Pearson) Dole, of Stroudwater, £34.4 for the premises which extended back northerly to the river. This Dole-Lewis lot was located in the north easterly corner of the original James Simpson grant. We are entering into details for the purpose of establishing in an enduring manner land marks at Saccarappa as well as relationship pertaining to Major Lewis.

Near the center of this lot was a two story dwelling though no mention is made, which was not necessary, in the conveyance from Dole to Lewis.

In Chapter VII of the History of Westbrook by "R." appearing in the News of July 27, 1895, and in other ways it appears that Samuel Conant was born in Beverly, Mass., Nov. 18, 1717. "R." says:

"In 1760 Samuel Conant received one of the licenses from the municipal officers of Falmouth to keep a public house and sell spiritous liquors. It would be interesting at this day to know just where he lived at the keeping of a public house."

It is more than probable that Samuel Conant's inn was situated on the Dole-Lewis lot, the lot having been leased for the purpose, and Archelaus Lewis and his bride occupied a part of the Conant house during their short residence in Saccarappa, Conant and Lewis making a trade relative to land and house of which there is no obtainable record. The house contained two rooms below and two above, this the records disclose, and the back of the building was seventeen feet from the river's edge; so if pilgrims containing Lewis blood in their veins enter the public passage way created in 1833 which is thirteen feet wide and fifty-three feet westerly of the Edwards brick shop, proceed to the bottom, face westerly, the site of the Conant-Lewis domicile will be before their eyes.

Whether the Major was a trader in his two rooms or one in another building we cannot state, not knowing He received a license as a retailer of spiritous liquors in 1781 which was renewed in '82-'83 and '84, and as he sold in 1803 "one half of a small piece of land in Saccarappa, one half of a dwelling house, one half of a small shop and one half of a barn," the bounds of the lot being the same as given in the record of the purchase, "owned in common with Daniel Conant," who obtained his title in 1782 from Samuel Conant, it is more than probable, as we have said, part of the Conant house became the abiding place of the Major, and he entered into trade in a building he found or erected on the premises for the purpose.

In the year 1782 Samuel Conant for a consideration of £10 conveyed to Daniel Conant "the house I now live in," no mention being made of land.

wkPelb theingr

to the warmest supporters of the occa- to the tttttttttttttttee

Daniel Conant lost his half of the Lewis house and lot in 1810 in a law suit with Samuel Freeman. The house was finally destroyed by fire about

CONTINUED:

1845. Much history is connected with the premises we hope to see in print.

Francis Waldo, son of General Samuel Waldo, Samuel the great land king, hereabouts at one time, was a Tory, went to London, died there, and his real estate was confiscated by order of the Massachusetts State government in common with the property of others entertaining like views who evinced them by leaving the country.

Francis owned three small lots in Stroudwater when he fled his country. His father, General Waldo, resided in Boston, but had a summer home where the printing house block of Southworth Brothers is located on Middle street, Portland, while his only brother Samuel, a resident of Portland, and office holder had his summer home upon the State Reform School farm, which farm was a marriage gift from his father, containing about 400 acres. The dwelling stood upon the part of the farm now owned by Mr. Charles P. Trickey, and some 25 rods northerly of Mr. Trickey's residence. Francis Waldo was a bachelor.

A hundred years ago and more there was built by Josiah Cox of Portland upon the lot where the Quinby Hall building is seen, opposite the foot of Waldo street, in the Stroudwater district of Deering, a two story dwelling house, end to road, facing westerly, two rooms below, two above, ell on the northerly end of main house, and a building for a shop. Josiah Cox was a brother-in-law to Col. James Means. Means having appeared in the News, also to Samuel Butts who has been incidentally presented and Josiah engaged in trade on the premises, the shop becoming the blacksmith shop of Benjamin Remick and son "Dunk," the house which was taken down about 25 years ago, shop and "Dunk" being well preserved in the recollections of the eldest part of the community, though thirty odd years have passed since the shop disappeared. Cox's stay was short; he was succeeded by Capt. John Quinby and in 1791 the premises were in the possession of Gardiner Goold who went over from Capisic, Quinby occupying a house of his own but relative to his shop we are in darkness.

Abstract of a Record:

"I, Enoch Freeman of Falmouth, for a consideration of £45-7-2, paid by John Quinby, merchant, and Archelaus Lewis, gentleman, hereby convey a certain lot or parcel of land situated at a place called Stroudwater, in Falmouth, late belonging to the estate of Francis Waldo, an absentee, containing one acre and three quarters of an acre, and bounded as follows: Northeast by the county road (Westbrook street) northwesterly by the land of Geo. Tate, (the old Tate house lot) and on all other parts by Stroudwater river and mill privilege, being the lot conveyed to me and others, by the committee for selling absentee' estates in the county aforesaid. March 29, 1783."

For a consideration of £100 the lot was divided on the street line into five equal parts of four rods and three feet each, and were received as follows:

1—John Quinby, merchant at Stroudwater.
2—Archelaus Lewis, gentleman, in trade at Saccarappa.
3—Benjamin Bailey, son of Dea. John Bailey, by second wife, who was the widow Curtis of Gorham, this state, the widow Curtis of Gorham, this state, Bailey residing upon the ancient Deacon Bailey place located between Libby's Corner and Bradley's Corner.
4—Rev. Thomas Brown, the first clergyman of the place, filling the position 30 years and residing at Woodfords.
5—Jabez Jones who sold it as did Bailey and Browne, Messrs. Quinby and Lewis improving their lots by building substantial houses.

(To be continued.)

GRANDPA'S SCRAP BOOK

Week of Aug. 15—18, 1900.

MAJOR ARCHELAUS LEWIS.

BY LEONARD B. CHAPMAN.

PART SECOND.

Capt. John Quinby who built the house on lot No. 1, noticed last week as adjoining the old Tate house lot on the southerly side, at Stroudwater district of Deering, was a son of Joseph Quinby and wife, Mary Haskell of Portland, born there May 12, 1760, married Oct. 31, 1782, Eunice, daughter of Joshua Freeman, Jr., of Portland and wife Lois who was a daughter of Moses Pearson, hence, Mrs. Quinby was a niece to the wife of Capt. Daniel Dole, a record of whom has appeared in the News, Capt. Dole and wife influencing, probably, the determination of Capt. Quinby to settle at Stroudwater where Capt. Dole had located. It was but five months after the marriage event when Capt. Quinby purchased his Stroudwater lot and he was but 23 years of age. It is reasonable to suppose that he and Archelaus Lewis commenced the construction of their prospective dwellings upon her respective lots immediately after the purchase,—both two story, square, well finished buildings, the Quinby structure having been removed to Portland where it may now be seen at the east corner of State and Pine streets, while the Lewis mansion remains upon its original foundation, having though gone through several changes both inside and out, containing at present the post office, and owned as it has been for nearly fifty years by the Milliken family.

At the time of the advent of Messrs. Quinby and Lewis the Falmouth town authorities (including what is now Portland) had established a public landing place, and a wharf upon it, the wharf extending from the present public drinking fountain (there is but one) easterly to the channel of tide water. We do not know whether Messrs. Lewis and Quinby were in company in business but they received a permit by a vote of the town to erect a building upon the "town wharf" and occupy it twenty years free of taxation which building was built. It was two storied, with outside stairs, and remained intact till about 1845 when it was removed to the junction of what is now Frost and Congress streets (Brewer House hill) and fitted for a shop and dwelling by Capt. Dexter Brewer; it was then removed to Portland where it remains and is used for a dwelling house on Tate street.

At Stroudwater Maj. Lewis' name commenced to grow in public favor in civil matters. He was selected as guardian for minor children, executor of wills and administrator upon estates. In disputes in town county and church matters he was called on as an arbitrator frequently.

In 1790 the General Government of Massachusetts chose him one of a committee of three to inforce upon Falmouth the payment of a tax of £733 growing out of the expense of the war, £325 of which was set off later to Portland, the town of Falmouth having been divided, and Portland created.

In 1796 we find him a member of the Portland lodge of Free and Accepted Masons.

The time he became a member of the Stroudwater church does not appear as the church records are not in existence, but in 1833 he was one of the deacons, and frequently a parish assessor.

In 1796 he was chosen to represent the town in the General Court. In 1797-'99-1800-'01-'02-'03-'04 and '05, he was reelected. In 1817-18 he was elected to the State senate.

May 1, 1801, Rev. Caleb Bradley in his diary remarks: "Lewis chosen Representative to the very great mortification of John Waite. As much as he (Waite) is depressed so much I am elated." Lewis like Bradley was a Federalist.

In company with Jonathan Sparrow he built the two storied wooden building now used for storage purposes by Andrew Hawes, Esq., at Stroudwater, designed originally, and used many years by various persons for shops, but never occupied by Lewis, and from the appearance of Col. James Mean's account book one would think that Maj. Lewis was never in trade at Stroudwater but was a speculator. The largest charge of Means' for labor as a surveyor is on May 9, 1799. "19 shillings and 10 pence for surveying 33,000 boards, joist and timber." The charges for rum and brandy correspond with other accounts against other persons of the period. The autograph of the Maj. appears several times when settlements were made.

March 27, 1799, Parson Bradley who had kept school in Bether, this state, had kept school in Bethel, this state, records in his diary as follows:

"Rhode from Windham to Falmouth, nine miles and took lodgings with Maj. Lewis.

CONTINUED:

"28. This was a cold day, in the forenoon of which it snowed. Spent the day in reading.

"29. This was somewhat of a pleasant day which I spent in reading.

"30. This was a cloudy day which I spent in reading.

"31. This was a warm day, preached and some considerable of hearers—very bad travelling.

"April 1. This was a pleasant day. Rode to Portland—3 miles. Returned to my lodgings. Dined with Dr. Dean, (Rev. Samuel Dean of Portland.)

"2. This was not a very pleasant day—spent it in my study—Messrs. Lewis, (Isaac) Sawyer and (Capt. Isaac S.) Stevens engaged me to supply the desk in Stroudwater two months—It begins to storm very severely—rain and hail."

These entries were made in the diary in the house where the post office sign now appears at Stroudwater, and the "desk" was in the meeting house that stood upon the site of the present one.

Although Stroudwater was a comparatively lively place the business evidently was too limited for the Major's active nature and in 1804 he purchased of Gen. Henry Knox of Thomaston for a consideration of $2000 a part of the "Cooper Claim" containing originally a thousand acres of land—

"Confiscated property of Thomas Fluker" (when Lewis made the purchase) he a son-in-law to Gen. Samuel Waldo, and a Tory like Francis Waldo, situated at Congin, now known as Cumberland Mills district of Westbrook, and upon the northerly side of the falls he constructed a large brick mansion and other buildings where the latch string was never pulled in, the old soldier and civilian ever receiving hospitality in abundance.

Capt. John Quinby departed this life Sept. 27,1806, aged 48 years—then called "old", now comparatively young at 48. The pitaph upon his memorial slab at Stroudwater reads: "That life is long that answers life's great end."

In 1809 Maj. Lewis sold his Stroudwater residence to John Gordon for $2,500 who occupied it upon whom President James Monroe called when visiting this section of the country on account of the visible manifestation of the peculiarities of Mr. Gordon.

Maj. Lewis was three times married:

1st. With Rebeckah Hubbard, a widow, at Gorham, March 14, 1779, she born Feb. 18, 1753, died at Stroudwater, Dec. 17, 1788.

2nd. With Elizabeth Browne, daughter of Rev. Thomas Browne, pastor of the Stroudwater Congregational church 30 odd years, Sept. 18, 1791; she died Sept. 13, 1804, at Stroudwater, aged 37 years.

3d. With Frances Angier, a widow of Boston, Oct. 10, 1807, who died at Congin Nov. 5, 1815, aged 41 years. Her maiden name was McClink.

His memorial slab at Stroudwater is inscribed as follows:

In memory of
HON. ARCHELAUS LEWIS,
who died
Jan. 2, 1834
Aged 81.

We have used his military title by which he was generally known instead of the civil.

May 11, 1832, Parson Bradley records in his diary: "Esq. Lewis was taken bleeding last night."

"Jan. 6, 1834. Prayer meeting today at the meeting house for the conversion of the world. This afternoon attended the funeral of Esq. Lewis aged 81 years world. This afternoon attended the funeral of Esq. Lewis aged 81 years who died the 2nd inst. Saw his body committed to the grave. Made a short addressed to a few young men who attended on the occasion."

This entry in itself alone is misleading. From one who was present we learn the house was filled to overflowing of acquaintances and relatives; the weather was bitter cold—so cold the cemetery at Stroudwater could not be reached, or it was thought best not to try, and a grave was in consequence made near the house, from which the remains were removed in the spring, and the parson's notice had reference to a service held at the grave.

At Stroudwater appear the memorial slabs of the three wives and some children who died young, all in an excellent state of preservation.

GRANDPA'S SCRAP BOOK

Week of Aug. 29—Sept. 1, 1900.

MAJOR. ARCHELAUS LEWIS.

BY LEONARD B. CHAPMAN.
PART FOURTH.

(Where it is stated in our article of last week that Augusta Fox resides with her sister Elizabeth L. it should be Harriet L. Fox resides with Elizabeth L.; and where it states that the name of the 6th child of Daniel Fox was named Augusta, Augusta should be Augustus.)

(5) Eveline Lewis, dau. of Maj. Archelaus Lewis, b. at Stroudwater Nov. 13, 1795, was united in marriage by Rev. Caleb Bradley with Josiah Pierce, Esq., of Gorham, Sept. 0, 1825, he b. in Baldwin, August 15, 1792.

The original grant of land upon which the town of Baldwin is located was made February 8, 1774. The conditions were not complied with by the occupants so in 1780 an extension of six years was made when Josiah Pierce, Sen., of Woburn, Mass., took hold of the work of settlement and became a large proprietor and through his labors a sufficient number of persons were induced to become residents of the plantation called Flintstown to warrant the granting of a town organization, or government, and the place was incorporated June 23, 1802.

Mr. Pierce commenced the construction of his residence in 1785 which he finished two years later. It is now seen nearly the same as originally built in about the center of the town, is owned by a grandson and occupied at last advices by descendants. He erected three saw mills; the one on Quaker brook was purchased by Isaac Dyer. Mr. Pierce was a Justice of the Peace and performed the first marriage ceremony of the place Dec. 15, 1795 Miss Elizabeth Thorn was the bride. the proprietor of the Thorn name in this county was an Englishman who settled in Gorham, this state, but Gorham becoming too numerously settled. as he thought, he left the place and went back to what is now Baldwin and reared a large family. Greenlief Thorn whose widow resides in the Capisic district of Deering, Wm. J. who resided in Westbrook the last of his life, and Jobe, who built the brick house between Morrill's Corner and Allen's Corner, where the late Col. Moore resided were brothers and were descendants. Edward G. Thorn of Portland is a son of Greenlief.

Mr. Pierce had the first, and for quite a while, the only store in the town of Baldwin.

In 1803 he was elected a selectman; again in 1813-14-15-16 and 17. Reelected 1819. He was town clerk in 1806 and continued till 1819. He died Jan. 23, 1830, and his remains rest in the family burying place located on the farm near the house. His mother's remains deposited in 1795, also repose upon in the grove shaded cemetery. And his mother, the mother also of Count Rumford (Benjamin Thompson)

Continued:

lies interred by the side of her husband.

"Count Rumford, an inventor and natural philosopher was born in Woburn, Mass., 1753. At the outbreak of the American Revolution he favored the royal cause," that is, he became a Tory, "and displayed such ability as a bearer of dispatches that in 1780 he was made under-secretary-of-state. He afterward became chamberlain to the Prince of Bavaria, major-general, minister of war, and Count of the Holy Roman Empire. He planned the Royal Institute of London, made many discoveries in science, and was a political economist of the first rank. He died near Paris 1814, after making important bequests to the Royal Society of London, the American Academy of Science, and Harvard University."

Josiah Pierce, Jr., who married Eveline Lewis, was a nephew of Count Rumford. He graduated at Bowdoin college in 1818, and after studying law with Stephen Longfellow, Esq., of Portland, opened an office in Gorham In politics he was a Democrat.

After serving in the lower branch of the State Legislature he was three times elected to the Senate, acting as president of the body in 1835-36.

In 1837-38 he served as selectman of Gorham.

In 1846 he was elected to the office of Judge of Probate and held the position ten years.

He was a trustee of Bowdoin College several years and a live member of the Maine Historical Society. He may have filled other positions but these are all we find records of.

His Literary Work.

An address delivered on the 27th of May, 1836—entitled "The centennial anniversary of the settlement of Gorham."

"Information concerning Count Rumford," 1827.

"A History of the town of Gorham." 1802.

He died in Gorham, June 25, 1866.

His Family:

1—Josiah, 3d. b. June 14, 1827; a lawyer, resides abroad. In 1865 the Emperor of Russia made him a Knight of St. Ann. It is he who owns the original homestead at Baldwin.

2—Archelaus L., b. Aug. 25, 1828, d. Dec. 11, 1829.

3—Eveline L., b. June 3, 1830, m. John Anderson Waterman, Esq., of Gorham, d. Aug. 17, 1881.

4—Lewis, b. April 15, 1832, is a lawyer 'n Portland.

5—Nancy. b. April 7, 1834, m. Edwin N. Whittier, M. D., of Boston; died. Feb. 19, 1893.

6—George Washington, b. July 1, 1836; resides in Baldwin.

7—Eliza L., b. Aug. 4, 1838, d. April 13, 1879.

(10.) Frances E. Lewis b. April 2, 1809, at Congin, (now called Cumberland Mills,) Westbrook, m. Daniel Thompson Pierce, he a brother to the preceding, b. in Baldwin, March 15, trict of Westbrook where he was 1803; resided in the Saccarappa district of Westbrook where he was prominent in the lumber business, and held high military commands in the State Militia. Then he removed to Michigan, but returned to his native town where he died March 15, 1856.

Children.

1—An infant b. June, 1828, d. young.
2—Harriet, b. Nov. 19, 1829.
Susan, b. Aug. 15, 1831, d. Aug. 12, 1845.
4—Frances, b. April 20, 1833.
5—Daniel Thompson, Jr., b. May 15, 1835, d. Aug. 1895.
6—George Anne, b. June 23, 1836.
7—Richard Skinner, b. Aug. 1839, d. young.
8—Charles French, b. Oct. 14, 1840.
9—Arthur Dorr, b. Mar. 4, 1846, enlisted in the Union Army, war of the Rebellion, and was killed in the battle.

(11) Harriet Angier Lewis, b. at Congin, Nov. 15, 1810, a sister to the preceding, m. William C. Bradley, son of Rev. Caleb Bradley, of Bradley's Corner district, now Deering. He was tens infront, the jaunty black silk tie a widower. His first wife was Mary Alden of Portland and the marriage ceremony was performed at St. Stephen's church, Sept. 14, 1826. She d. Sept. 1,1827, aged 20 years and was interred in the Portland Eastern cemetery. He m. second as indicated above published Nov. 17,1832; the widow died, Oct. 4, 1884, aged 74 years. A son and daughter survive and reside in Portland, named respectively Harriet L. and William L. There were other children who died young.

Of Mr. Bradley's early life we have no knowledge. The house in which he was born remains unchanged but has passed from the Bradely ownership.

The story of the mills upon the fresh water stream at Stroudwater cover a period of two hundred and twenty years. The present ruin, old stone dam and adjacent bridge are charming subjects for the artist and camera and probably receive more attention than any others in the vicinity of Portland.

May 26, 1829, for $2,700 Charles Ferguson sold his new mill to John D. Gardner with the mill privilege.

April 5, 1831, Gardner sold to William Cammet a half of the privilege "excepting the grist mill which was burned January 21, 1831—" a very curious reservation, the record of which can be seen at the office of Registry of Deeds for this county.

Aug. 1, 1832, William C. Bradley, merchant, paid $3,000 for a half of the new mill, now seen in a dilapidated state.

Mr. Bradley in 1853 was a resident of Portland at 158 Cumberland street, having his place of business at the head of Long wharf where he dealt largely in grain. Prior to this he resided at Stroudwater on the southwesterly corner of what is now Westbrook and Bond streets, the name of last lately changed to Garrison street.

January 8, 1838, Rev. Caleb Bradley records in his diary as follows:

"Now that we have water we don't expect much grinding for this reason: A steam mill with two pair of stones commenced running in the city (Portland) for the purpose of grinding corn. What effect this will have time only can tell, but for the present, no doubt, it will keep much custom from coming as formerly. People will generally do that which they think will be for their interest. If it be for the interest of the city traders to have their corn steamed they most assuredly will send it there, and not to blame. I should do the same myself."

The steam mill was built by Jonathan Sparrow and Sons, John and William, both of whom are alive, residing hereabouts. It stood on Fore street, south easterly corner of Union, and was soon destroyed by fire.

(12) Archelaus Lewis, Jr., b. April 19, 1813, m., and resided for a spell upon the homestead at Congin, then between that place and Saccarappa upon the northerly side of Presumpscot river, then with his son Thaddeus M. Lewis at North Falmouth, where they owned a small mill, and where the father died, and where the son still resides as a farmer.

Jan. 21, 1895, an obituary appeared in the Portland Daily Press as follows:

WESTBROOK.

FUNERAL OF ARCHELAUS LEWIS.

A large number from this city attended the funeral services of the late Archelaus Lewis at his late home in North Falmouth Sunday. The deceased was born in this city 83 years ago, and resided here for many years. He was farmer and real estate owner, and was widely known. His parents were among the early settlers of Westbrook, being driven from Salem, Mass., it is stated, at the time the illusion of witchcraft prevailed in that city. At one time the father of the deceased owned the land now in the possession of S. D. Warren & Co., at the east end. The deceased was the father of six children, one Mrs. Howard Small, being a resident here."

Our next article will relate to the descendants of the Rev. Thomas Browne.

GRANDPA'S SCRAP BOOK

Week of Sept. 5—8, 1900.

The Descendants of
REV. THOMAS BROWNE.

BY LEONARD B. CHAPMAN.

PART FIRST.

In the News of Aug. 24, 1895, we presented some memoranda relative to Rev. Thomas Browne, also in the two following issues of the journal which contained a pen-picture made of the Reverend at the time of his demise, which was on the 18th day of October, 1797. He was the first clergyman of the Stroudwater parish and was installed Aug. 21, 1765, a church having been organized on the 8th day of April of that year, composed of the following named persons: Dea. John Bailey, Thomas Haskell, Nathaniel Knight, Henry Knight, James Johnson, John Johnson, Jeremiah Riggs, Joseph Riggs, James Merrill, Clement Pennell, Anthony Morse, Solomon Haskell and Benjamin Haskell. The names of the female members were not recorded. He continued in the service till his death as given above. His grave memorial may be seen at the ancient Stroudwater village cemetery. The present church edifice, seen on Capisic street, is the third upon the original site. He owned a farm at Woodfords, district of Deering, upon which he resided, and Spring street forms the northerly boundery line. It extended from the water of Back Bay, westerly, nearly to what is now High street. With an Episcopal church edifice and rapidly growing prospects of a Universalist in the near future located upon the acres he cultivated, the "spirit" of Parson Browne must feel uncomfortable, particularly in view of the fact that the heaven-pointing steeple of the now unoccupied building on the site of his old meeting house must soon fall as a result of decay.

Rev. Thomas Browne was a son of Rev. John Browne. John's wife had ten children; Rev. Thomas Browne, Jr., who came here, being the 9th name on the list, born in Haverhill, Mass., May 17, 1734, graduated at Harvard College in 1752, married Mrs. Lydia Howard (or Hammond), a widow of Mansfield, Mass., Feb. 7, 1763, and was installed over the Fourth Parish of Falmouth, now the First of Deering, as indicated above. His widow died Oct. 13, 1805, aged 69 years, and her remains were deposited at Stroudwater, the inscription of both memorial slabs having appeared in the News.

Their residence at Woodfords built by Capt. William Pote and first occupied by him disappeared some fifty years ago. The spot is memorable in more ways than one. It was in May, the 28th day, 1788, that

Rev. Samuel Dean, Portland,
Rev. Ephraim Clarke, Cape Elizabeth,
Rev. Ebenezer Williams, New Casco, (now Falmouth),
Rev. Tristram Gilman, North Yarmouth,
Rev. Thomas Lancaster, Scarboro,
Rev. Benjamin Chadwick, Scarboro,

and
Rev. Caleb Jewett, Gorham,

met and voted that "Messrs. Browne, Deane, Clark, Lancaster, Gilman, Williams, Chadwick and Jewett be formed into an association for the purposes of edification, which are the useful designs of such establishments."

This was the birth meeting of the "Cumberland Association of Congregational Ministers" that is alive today and not infirm in consequence of fullness in number of years since the event.

There were born to Rev. Thomas Browne and wife five children of whom we find records, as follows:

1.—Elizabeth, b. 1764, m. Sept. 18, 1791, Maj. Archelaus Lewis, noticed in our five last articles.
2.—Abigail, m. Hugh McLellen.
3.—Thomas, b. March 24, 1769, m. Ann ——.
4.—Rebecca, b. Feb., 1777, m. John L. Lewis.
5.—William, b. March 1, 1779, m. Octavia Southgate.

(2.) Abigail Browne born, ——, m. March 23, 1783, Hugh McLellan, a merchant of Portland. This marriage event we have already noticed in our Maj. Lewis articles, but for a more extended notice we refer the reader to the printed copy of Smith and Dean's Journal, edition of 1849, p. 233-34. The compiler's note reads in part as follows: Stephen was also Joseph's [McLellan's] son and with his brother Hugh built the large brick houses on High street in 1801, which, for several years, were the great attractions of the place, and are now [1849] more elegant and expensive than most modern buildings. Stephen's is now used by the 'Cumberland Club,' Hugh's is at the corner of High and Spring streets, where it may be seen just as it was built a century since, and first occupied by Hugh and Abigail (Browne) McLellan. He died Feb. 7, 1823. Under the name of William Browne the McLellans will receive in a quoted obituary further notice.

Children of Hugh and Abigail (Browne) McLellan:

I—Eunice, b. July 10, 1784, m. March 24, 1805, Charles Fox, who has been briefly noticed, but will receive further attention.
II—Nabby, b. Dec. 31, 1785, m. Horatio Southgate of Scarboro.
III—Mary, b. Jan. 25, 1788.
IV—Joseph, b. July 31, 1787.
V—Jane, b. April 29, 1791.
VI—Caroline, b. March 17, 1793.
VII—Stephen, b. Dec. 17, 1794, d. 1795.
VII—Hugh, b. June 23, 1796, d. same year.
IX—Caroline, b. July 20, 1797, m. Joseph Pope of Windham.

(3—) Thomas, son of Rev. Thomas Browne, born March 24, 1769, m. Ann —, but the rest of her maiden name we are unable to learn. The early part of his life was spent as a mariner, and he appears on record with the title of "Captain." He resided several years in the wooden house that stood on the southwesterly corner of Congress and Park streets,—Congress first known as Main street, laid out in 1729, and Park as Ann.

From an article prepared by Hon. Wm. Goold that appeared in the Portland Daily Press of Oct. 26, 1888, we will here quote as follows:

"The third in the venture, and by no means an obscure one, was the famous Salem merchant, Wm. Gray, Jr., ("Billy Gray the world over.) He had served his time with Richard Derby, of Salem, brother of Elias Hasket Derby, who was the pioneer in the India trade from New England. From his small savings, besides assisting his parents, Gray purchased a share in one of his employer's vessels in the China trade and finally became the largest shipping merchant in New England, owning and loading on his own account more than 40 ships at one time. He was originally a Federalist but became a Democrat and was elected Lieutenant Governor of Massachusetts on the ticket with Elbridge Gerry in 1810. After becoming wealthy he removed to Boston to enjoy it. But for him the frigate Constitution would not have been sent to sea when launched.

Capt. Thomas Browne's wife of Portland was a relative of Gray's which with some other interest often brought him here. In 1798 he purchased of Col. John May the large vacant lot on the southwest side of Ann, now Park street, reaching from Congress nearly to Danforth street. On this lot Gray built a large rope walk, and went extensively into manufacturing of cordage with Capt. Browne as agent. Gray's ships brought cargoes of hemp direct from Russia, which was stored in a large hemp house on the lot. His own ships required large quantities of cordage, and the rigging for the new ships came undoubtedly from his own factory."

The house in which Capt. Browne resided was later known as the Jones boarding house, and became famous as a temporary home of the refined, learned and wealthy of society. A few years since it was removed westerly a few paces, faced to the north, renovated, repaired and left as now observed in a new dress of paint.

Capt. Browne was a fine specimen of Colonial days of simplicity. We were told some years since—by one who remembered him well that he was often seen riding from his residence in his ancient appearing chaise to his down town place of business with a bundle of hay and sometimes a pail hanging out over the dasher of the vehicle.

Week of Sept. 12-15, 1900.

The Descendants of
REV. THOMAS BROWNE.

BY LEONARD B. CHAPMAN.

PART SECOND.

In the Portland City Directory, compiled in 1827, Capt. Thomas Browne appears as a merchant at No. 12 Long wharf, house corner of Ann and Main streets; (Park and Congress.) Thomas Browne, his son, at William Haskell's shop and William Browne (Capt. Thomas Browne's brother) "with Thomas Browne, Long wharf, at Morse's lime." The residence of Thomas Browne, Jr., was put down as Congress street. We think that what is now known as Congress street was, in name, in three parts—namely: "Mount Joy," "Congress," from India to Monument Square, and from that point westerly into the country was "Main street."

After a persistent search we are able to present the following record relative to the earthly resting place of Capt. Browne and wife:

Burial. "March 5, 1849. Capt. Thomas Browne, 79 years, 11mo. Old age. Eastern Cemetery, north side. In his tomb."

June 29, 1859. Ann, widow of Thomas Browne, 78 years, 8 mo. Old age. In his tomb."

Capt. Thomas Browne's children:

1—Mary Ann, b. July 1, 1803, resided with her parents. She did not marry, d. 1864.

2—Thomas, b. Dec. 14, 1808. He is reported as a lame man, and at one time as a bank accountant, but the Browne name is so mixed with the "Brown" on the records we don't dare to state only what we actually know to be true.

Oct. 13, 1823, a Thomas Brown and Esther W. Lane were united in marriage.

Capt. Browne's son Thomas died in Portland, of paralysis, March 15, 1866, and was, it is said, interred upon the lot No. 357, range F., Evergreen cemetery, but there are no memorial slabs—only sunken graves. He left two sons, John Cotton Browne, who died in New York city, leaving a son and four daughters, and T. Quincy Browne, who, at last advices was a widower with four sons, one married, the father in Europe on a business tour.

In 1891 Capt. Isaac Knight then residing at No. 154 Franklin street, Portland, made a statement to us as follows:

"I was born in Portland near Clay Cove, and at the time of the great fire in 1866, while residing upon Fore street, I was burned out. The Browne house being vacant I purchased of T. Quincy Browne, then residing in Boston, the household goods, hired the premises and moved in. The papers and old books of which there were a large lot in the attic, I sold with considerable old furniture I did not need. I was a sea captain in my young days and Thomas Browne went a voyage to Europe with me as a passenger."

3—John Cotton, b. Sept. 27, 1806, d. unmarried.

4—Merrill Cutting, b. Nov. 7, 1803, d. Sept. 17, 1828.

5—Abigail, b. March 13, 1810, d. May 1, 1810, "aged 28 days." Memorial slab in Eastern cemetery.

(4—) Rebecca Browne b. Feb. 1777, m. June 13, 1807, Capt. John L. Lewis. A note accompanying the death announcement of Rebecca in Jenk's Portland Gazette says: "The youngest daughter of Rev. Thomas Browne." She died Dec. 9, 1804, aged 27 years, 10 mo., and her grave may be seen marked by a brown sand-stone slab with inscription nearly obsolete in section F., of the Portland Eastern cemetery, a few paces southerly of the wide path running east and west from the eastern side entrance. She left one child named William Lewis who was alive in 1814, but after this we have no data of him. At the same place in the cemetery may be seen the worldly resting place of the remains of Capt. Lewis who died June 21, 1825, aged 52 years, memorial slab of white sand-stone with inscription now so effaced that it cannot be read. By close scrutiny the Free Mason sign of square and compass may be made out, but we should not have noticed this had not the man in charge called our attention to the fact with the statement that some recently aged visitors told him that Capt. Lewis' parents have memorial slabs in Nova Scotia and that the Captain was a high-up Mason and his funeral was one that was numerously attended, but our informant failed to learn the visitors names, much to our regret.

Capt. Lewis married second, June 19, 1806, Mary Bryant who died in 1844, aged 63 years. Of her we know nothing.

The Portland Transcript under date of March 25, 1891, and heading of "Queries and Replies," presents as follows:

(Note to 21.) "We have made some effort to obtain an answer to the inquiry made in the Transcript of Feb. 4th in regard to the house of George R. Davis, on Congress street, at the head of Park street, in Portland. We find that the land on which the house stands was sold, March 1, 1803, by Capt. Arthur McLellan to Zachariah Marston, a ropemaker. No mention is made in the deed of any building upon it. On the 27th of July, 1804, Marston sold the lot with a building upon it to John L. Lewis of Falmouth, mariner. The probability is that this building was erected by Marston in 1803, and is the building now standing on the lot. The timbers are of the size of those put into large buildings about a century ago. It was three stories in height from the first. But the French roof was added by Mr. Davis a few years ago. In 1819, Mr. Lewis sold the house to Nathaniel Crockett, a trader, for $950. In 1837, Crockett sold the house to Robert S. Randall, who in 1844 transferred it to the trustees of Bowdoin College. In each of the early deeds the lot is described as being nearly opposite the rope-walk of William Gray, (the famously wealthy Billy Gray, of Boston.) This rope-walk, built in 1794, extended from Congress street (then Main street) to Gray street, parallel with and a little above Park street (then Ann street.) It was about 1000 feet in length. It was cut in two when Spring street was extended to State street, in 1811. A short section of it still remains, and until lately has been occupied as a grocery store on Spring street, next below the engine house. The remainder of it was removed about 60 years ago."

The statement of the Transcript that March 1, 1803, Capt. Arthur McLellan sold to Zachariah Marston, a rope-maker, a lot of land and on the 27th of July 1804 Marston sold to John L. Lewis, mariner, is correct, but the statement that the lot was located opposite the head of Park street and Mr. George R. Davis now resides in the same is all wrong.

The facts are:

In 1803 for a consideration of $650 "Arthur McLellan, merchant, Union wharf, house corner pleasant and High streets" conveyed to Zachariah Marston, Jr., rope maker, a lot four rods wide on Main (Congress) street.

On the 27th day of July, 1804, Marston conveyed the lot to Capt. John L. Lewis for a consideration of $1,500 "with building,—" Sarah Marston joining with her husband in the conveyance, who appears to have been at the time of marriage widow Baker.

CONTINUED:

The building here referred to is the old appearing, hip-roof, two story, low posted, wooden building on its original foundation, a few rods westerly of Park street, northerly side of Congress, with roof and upper story as originally constructed, 96 years since, with a shop now in the first story, and is the first building next easterly of the odd appearing Grover brick building which occupies the westerly half of the original Marston lot. Capt. Lewis' purchase was two years after the marriage event, his wife's brother, Capt. Thomas Browne residing at the corner of Park and Congress streets.

In 1819 for $950 Capt. Lewis sold the premises to Nathaniel Crockett, and in 1835 Crockett sold to Amos Grover, brick layer, seventh child of Eli Grover of Bethel, Me., born there July 13, 1801, m. Susan Tyler Gould, part of the lot who built the present odd appearing house, died in it Aug. 1, 1883, where descendants may now be found.

Crockett sold the house to Robert S. Randall, and in 1851, the Trustees of Bowdoin College having received satisfaction relinquished all claim to the heirs of Randall.

Capt. Lewis resided next at the corner of Lime and Middle streets in a two story house that was moved to the southeasterly corner of Cumberland and Preble streets where it may now be seen.

Now about the George R. Davis house where he resides.

In 1803 Arthur McLellan sold to Daniel Creasey, of Portland, merchant, for $850, the lot upon which the large Davis house may be seen directly opposite the head of Park street.

In 1807 Creasey for a consideration of $7,000 conveyed the premises to Zachariah Marston, Jr., which is very good proof that Creasy built the present house noticed by the Transcript.

In 1817, Asa Clapp, as executor of the last will of Marston sold to Sally Marston "the house where the deceased last dwelled with land." In 1843 there was a division of the premises between the heirs, and in 1854 Hon. John M. Wood, Member of Congress, owner of the Portland Advertiser, etc., etc., on payment of $6,500, received the property, who sold to the venerable Mr. George R. Davis the present occupant; and is used as a boarding house of a high order of excellence.

GRANDPA'S SCRAP BOOK

Week of Sept. 19–22, 1900.

The Descendants of

REV. THOMAS BROWNE.

BY LEONARD B. CHAPMAN.

PART THIRD.

(5—) William Browne the youngest child of Rev. Thomas Browne, b. in the Woodfords district of Deering, March 1, 1779, m. Nov. 28, 1805, Octavia Southgate, daughter of Dr. Robert Southgate of Dunstan Corner, Scarboro, born there Sept 13, 1786.

When William Browne entered upon his business career the future was bright. While with his cousin, Stephen McLellan, for a business partner, and a young woman of position, and many personal charms, for a wife, he purchased a lot and erected, or commenced, a dwelling on State street, now by far the finest street in Portland if not the entire state, upon which site, or adjacent the imposing Roman Catholic church edifice, where stood till recently the wooden building constructed by the Catholics in 1829-30, and dedicated Aug. 11, 1833, may now be seen. A copy of a daguerreotype of Mr. Browne taken when he was aged, evidently when a wan countenance and a carelessness in dress had overtaken him, it is our good fortune to possess, obtained from Washington, D. C.; and from the state of Texas a photograph of William's son William, one of the youngest in graduation at Bowdoin College—lawyer, Methodist preacher, poet and editor who died in Texas, but we will forego for the present our own observations and present a copy of an article fortunately found in the Portland Advertiser of Nov. 16, 1861, by Hon. Wm. Willis, one of Portland's historians, entitled—

WILLIAM BROWNE.

"The injury received by Mr. Browne a day or two ago, in crossing the street, terminated fatally on Thursday morning. He died in his 83d year. We shall really miss Mr. Browne, for we scarcely ever passed through the thoroughfares of our city without meeting this aged and genial citizen.

"Mr. Browne was born in Westbrook, [the part that is now Deering] March 1, 1779, and was the youngest son, and last surviving child of Rev. Thomas Browne, the first minister of Stroudwater parish, who was installed in 1765, and died in the pastorate, Oct. 18, 1797. His other children were Capt. Thomas Browne, long an active and influential citizen of Portland, who died in 1849; Abigail, who married Maj. Hugh McLellan in 1782; Elizabeth married Archelaus Lewis, of Westbrook, and Rebecca, who married Capt. John L. Lewis of this city in 1802.

"The subject of this notice first went to school to a stern old fellow named McMahon, who kept at Woodfords Corner, during the desolate condition of the Neck [Portland] after its destruction by the British. A number of boys were sent out there to him and boarded with Mr. Browne, some of these were Thomas Robinson, John Deering and a son of Thomas Cummings. Young Browne afterwards went to school to Master Long, who kept in a building opposite the 2nd Parish church, owned by Samuel Freeman; the post office was also there. All his companions in these schools with the teachers, have long passed away, and this the youngest of their number frail and feeble always, has lingered til now, and has at last last been carried off by an untimely injury.

"When a boy he was put into the store of Joseph McLellan & Son, which stood on Congress street, just below where Blake's bake house ds [No. 532 Congress street.]

They kept, as was the custom of the day, a general assortment of everything that would sell, and received in barter whatever was produced in the country. They kept there, doing a profitable business, which was already extending into shipping and foreign voyages, until about 1798, when they established themselves on Union wharf just then built, and were extensively concerned in navigation, having large ships employed in the European trade. They built a ship about every year. The father, Joseph, came from Gorham, [Me.] and built in 1755 the house, a part of which is now standing on the same lot and the first built in this part of the town; he was also County Treasurer many years. The son Hugh was a most industrious man, being always a rival of the sun at his post of duty. He and his brother Stephen built in 1801, the large houses on High street, one now owned and occupied by Messrs. Wingate, built by Hugh, the other, owned and occupied by M. Noyes and M. Jose.

"Mr. Browne in 1801 formed a business connection with Stephen McLellan, and they were the first occupants of the store in Jones' Row, on the corner of Fore and Exchange streets. He went to England the same year and purchased goods to the amount of $50,000; and so prosperous was the trade here, they were rapidly sold out, and he went abroad again, partly to purchase goods and partly for his health, traveling on the continent. They soon moved to a larger store in the new block, which was built by Isaac Ilsley, and occupied partly for a Custom House, that being in the same room as now occupied by the Bank of Cumberland. To make way for this then elegant block, the house of Col. John Waite, sheriff of the county, was moved off, and now stands in a dilapidated condition, a third story added opposite Mr. Browne's sugar house; it was originally gambrel roofed.

"In that place, they went down in the general crash of 1807, which overwhelmed all the principal merchants of the town—McLellan & Son, Taber & Son, Weeks & Tucker, Webster, Ingraham, Storers, etc. From the disaster Mr. Browne never recovered, and being a permanent invalid, he has been a wanderer after health and found it not, and has had but little profitable employment since that time; so that he has had many years of struggle through his long pilgrimage, in narrow circumstances, but always to his commendation be it spoken with a submissive, nav, cheerful spirit. He was ever a strictly conscientious, upright man, and a sincere Christian professor; his life gave token to his profession.

241

CONTINUED:

"In 1805, Mr. Browne married Octavia, daughter of Dr. Robert Southgate of Scarboro, who gave a grace and charm to society wherever they moved, some sixty years ago. She bore him five children, two sons and three daughters; the sons only survive, and they have long lived far away, where their society and sympathy have failed to touch the parental bosom. One daughter married her cousin, Bishop Southgate. The death of his wife, the sweet and cherished companion of his early years, coming with other sorrows, seemed to leave the widowed husband in utter loneliness; still he waited patiently for his own time, which he always trusted would be in God's good time. It has come a welcome messenger; saying "come up higher."

"In these reminiscences, we have wandered as it were, among the dry bones of the catacombs. Many of the names we have reviewed, are wholly unknown and unheard of by the generation now busy on the stage; but we know them and looked up to them in youthful days, with wonder, it may be to the work they did, and the notoriety they achieved in town; now the places that knew them know them no more; the memory of hardly one of them is preserved out side the immediate family circle. How severe a comment this upon the sharp rivalries, the ambitious struggles for place, the harsh animosities of contending parties, which occupied so much of the time and thoughts, and so embittered the lives of that receding generation, of which we have been briefly speaking. The world's work is to be done, and happy are they who can come out of it, with unstained hands and unsoiled garments and can lay down their burdens at the grave's mouth with the cheering reflection, that at last, the world is no worse for their having passed through it."

GRANDPA'S SCRAP BOOK

Week of Sept. 26-29, 1900.

The Descendants of

REV. THOMAS BROWNE.

BY LEONARD B. CHAPMAN.
PART FOURTH AND LAST.

The remains of William Browne, who was noticed in our article of last week, as the youngest child of Rev. Thomas Browne, were not interred by the side of his wife, whose remains lie near those of Capt. John L. Lewis, noticed in our article of two weeks since, but upon the southerly side of the Eastern cemetery, where no memorial slab can be found, the spot not even being known.

Octavia (Southgate) Browne, wife of William Brown, son of Rev. Thomas Browne, died Jan. 9, 1815, aged 28 years. And here we remark as we have before, the memorial slab not being of a compact texture, but of a white sand-stone, the name is obsolete, but the epitaph, protected by herbage of summer and snows of winter is still legible and reads as follows:

Faith, Hope and Charity
were hers thro grace.
May patience, submission and consolation in Christ be ours till time and sorrow shall give place to eternal joy.

Children of William and Octavia (Southgate) Browne.

1. William Gray, to which he prefixed "George," b. in Portland, 1806, m. Sarah Gillespie; 2d Julia Chapman.
2. Frederic Southgate, m. Cynthia Eliza Denny.
3. Harriet, d. in Philadelphia, Pa. Her Bible was sent to the daughter of Bishop Southgate who married her sister Elizabeth, with a fly-leaf inscribed as follows:

Harriet Augusta Southgate.
The dying gift of her
Aunt Harriet,
June 6, 1845.

Bishop Southgate said of her: "She had the finest mind of any woman I ever saw."

4. Octavia S., b. 1813, d. April 28, 1829, aged 16 years, 9 mos. Memorial slab near that of her mother with inscription obsolete.
5. Elizabeth S., b. May, 1814, m. Bishop Southgate.

(To be further noticed in our proposed Southgate articles.)
She was his first wife.

(1.) William Gray Browne, son of William, and grandson of Rev. Thomas Browne, graduated from Bowdoin college in 1806, at the age of sixteen or thereabouts. He was remarkably smart as a scholar. Finding that his health was failing, at the age of nineteen, he went to Washington, D. C., and found employment as a clerk but not relief for his declining health.

From there he went to the southwestern part of the state of Virginia, started a school and engaged also in mountain horseback riding. The air and exercise brought relief to his lungs, and he was ever after a well man.

In 1826 he was clerk of Tazwell Co., Va., courts and where he engaged in other kinds of business, a student always and writing when at leisure for periodicals. A retentive memory being a direct gift he possessed, in consequence, a large storehouse of useful knowledge, but so modest and retiring was he in his ways that only those best acquainted with him knew the depth and compass of his intuitive knowledge of persons and causes. From Virginia he removed to Texas where he died at Dallas June, 1879, having served as clerk of courts in that state and where he lost his accumulation of property through the war of the Rebellion. The following is taken from the Southern Christian Advocate.

OBITUARY.

Rev. George W. G. Browne was born in Portland, Me., in 1806. He was educated at Bowdoin college and graduated with great credit at sixteen years of age. He won for himself an enviable place in a class composed of such men as Franklin Pierce, and Henry Longfellow. He moved to Tazwell County, Va., in 1826. There the energy and good character of the New England boy soon secured him permanent business. He was for a time editor of the Southwestern Advocate. He was married in 1835 to Miss Sarah Gillespie of Tazwell County and after the death of his wife, some ten years later, he married Miss Julia Chapman of Giles County. He raised a large family of children. In 1840 Mr. Browne, who had up to that time lived an unreligious life was converted, joined the Methodist Episcopal church South, and was soon licensed to preach the gospel of Christ, which he did till his death in all its beautiful simplicity, with spirit and power. He, like many another wayward boy, owed his conversion to his mother's prayers and home teachings. He said that when his mother came to die, she asked him to promise her that he would read the Bible every day. He gave the promise, which no doubt sent a thrill of joy to that dying mother, and, best of all, he kept the promise. God's word was ever a lamp to his feet and a light to his path. He moved to San Antonia, Texas, in 1857, and thence to Austin in 1862. A short time before he died he was out of employment, but he was not much disturbed. His trust in God was as simple and beautiful as that of a little child. The church and the Sabbath school have sustained an irreparable loss in his death. He illustrated in his life the beauties of the religion which he taught. He died in Dallas, Texas, June 20, 1879. A short time before his demise he said: "It's all right with me whether I live or die; I leave myself in my Master's hands." Again, in answer to the question whether Jesus was precious to him, he said: "Yes, very precious, and I feel He is very near me."

By his first marriage he had one daughter and two sons as follows:

1. Ellen Octavia, m. James Witten of Virginia, who d. leaving her with a son George and daughters Mary and Sadie, all of whom married. The widow married William Whitten, cousin to her first husband. She was highly educated.
2. William Henry. He was a West Point cadet of much promise, but left and joined the Confederates and was shot and mortally wounded while leading a regiment in a charge against the Union forces, the second year of the war—aged 22 years.
3. David McComas was educated at Lexington, Va. He was reading law when he died at San Antonia, Texas, aged 19 years.

The second wife, Julia Chapman, had two sons and four daughters, as follows:

4. Tennie, m. Joe Young; had three daughters, all pupils in the Methodist college at Dallas, Texas. The mother a bookkeeper. (This was 15 years ago.)

Continued:

5. Frederick Edward, d. aged three years.
6. Hannie, m. J. S. Burton of Dallas, Texas, manager of the Western-Union Telegraph of that place. She died 1879 without issue.
7. Kizzie C., m. in 1879, at Austin, S. Y. Swenson, a Swede by birth. He was first a banker in New York city, but removed to Texas, with the view of regaining his health and engaging in stock raising, but he soon died leaving a widow and one child, five years old, named William Gray. She, our correspondent, some years since. Before marriage she was a teacher in the blind asylum, then in a graded school at Austin.
8. Bettie. She a public school teacher in Austin.
9—and last. George Southgate. Residing on a stock ranch in Jones County, Texas.

The last wife of Rev. Mr. Browne died in April of 1874—"a quiet, modest, lovely, Christian woman," after an illness of eight years. The Reverend was engaged in writing a novel at the time of his death. A photo of him is now before us.

(2.) Of the descendants of Frederic S. Browne, second child of William and Octovia (Southgate) Browne and grandson of Rev. Thomas Browne we know but little. Frederic married in Louisville, Ky., Miss Cynthia Eliza Denny, daughter of Maj. James Wilkinson Denny, an officer in the Mexican war and a lawyer afterward of note, who died in early manhood while filling the office of Attorney General for the state. For a period of nineteen years he held the position of bookkeeper for the Louisville Journal when George D. Prentiss was editor. He was a man of modesty and retiring manners and delicate in health. In 1850 his wife died leaving six children when he removed to New Orleans where he held till his death a similar position on the Delta as that at Louisville, and where his health was improved.

During the war of the Rebellion, for reasons growing out of it, by an act of the State Legislature, upon his petition, the surname of his father was dropped and that of his mother adopted. A son resides in Washington, D. C., while other children dwell in Louisville, Ky.

RANDPA'S SCRAP BOOK

Week of Oct. 3-6, 1900.

DUNSTAN.

The Ancient Hamlet in the Town of Scarboro.

BY LEONARD B. CHAPMAN.

In Two Parts—Part First.

The town of Scarboro is often derisively alluded to as a place of salt marshes and clam beds, but as we survey the field we marvel at the richness in display of intellect that has been produced by one little place within the town limits.

Truly, much has been done to preserve in collected form the general history of the town, which is exciting even in a general unfolding, but in detail—tracing the descent of the foot-prints upon the "sands of time" of the descendants of the pioneers, more particularly the many ramifications of the last settlers and preserving in print the results, much remains to be done. We refer to "Dunstan," "the third principal settlement of Scarboro," made in 1651, by Andrew and Arthur Alger, brothers, which settlement they gave the name appearing above after Dunstan in England. Indeed the story, or the material for it, of the re-settlement, is more difficult in obtainment because the chain of years is longer and the settlers more numerous since, than before, the evacuation caused by blood-seeking Indians, and the desolation in consequence.

The Alger brothers received the title to their tract of land from the Indians and it comprised a thousand acres.

"Arthur, in the division of the estate, took the northern part, which was the highest English settlement in the region; it was separated from his brother's by a creek or brook; he died without issue. Andrew had six children; three sons: John, Andrew and Mathew, and three daughters: Elizabeth, married to John Palmer; Joanna married first Elias Oakman and second John Mills who dwelt in Boston, Mass., where she died, and the third married John Austin. John, son of Andrew, had several daughters, one of whom, named Elizabeth, married John Milliken, first of Boston, then of Scarboro, housewright. After the two brothers were killed, and their houses, barns and crops destroyed, the family moved to Boston. Andrew, Jr., was master of a vessel and was killed in Falmouth in 1690, leaving one daughter, wife of Mathew Collins. Mathew Alger was master of one of the transports in Sir William Phipp's expeditions to Canada, and died of the fleet fever soon after his return; he was the last surviving male of that race, and the name in this branch is extinct in this country. The widow of the first Andrew married Samuel Walker. Several of Andrew's children had married and were settled near him; first John, second Palmer, the others following, their dwellings fronting the marsh in the neighborhood of where the Dr. Southgate house is seen which farm is a part of the Alger estate."

[Maine His. So. Collections, Vol I., p. 213. A. D. 1865.]

The foregoing furnishes a comprehensive idea of the original occupancy of Dunstan. It was in the month of October, 1675, that the deed of murder and destruction of property was performed. The force consisted of ten white men and sixty to one hundred Indians. Of the Alger settlement there were seven houses and twenty-four years had intervened since the starting of the enterprise.

Of the Alger title the following copied from York Deeds, Vol II., p. 114, furnishes a good idea of the locality, and presents the names of the Indian claimants of the soil of the region at the time of advent of the Algers.

"The 19th of September, 1659."

"The declaration of Jane the Indian of Scarboro concerning land.

"This aforesaid Jane, alias Uphanum, doth declare that her mother, namely, Naguasqua, the wife of Wickwarrawaske, Sagamore, and her brother, namely, Ugagoyuskitt and herself, namely Uphanum, co-equally hath sold unto Andrew Alger, and to his brother Arthur Alger a Tract of land, beginning at the mouth of the river called Blue Point river where the river doth part and so bounded up along with the river called Oawascoage in Indian, and so up three score poles above the falls, on the one side and on the other side bounded up along with the northermost river that turneth by the great hill of Abram Jocelyn's and goeth northward, bounding from the head of the river south west and so to the aforesaid bounds, namely, three score poles above the falls. This aforesaid Uphanum doth declare that her mother and brother and she hath already in hand received full satisfaction of the aforesaid Algers for the aforesaid land from the beginning of the world to this day, provided, on conditions that for time to come, from year to year, yearly, the aforesaid Algers shall peaceably suffer Uphanum and her mother Neguasqua doth both live, and also one bushel of corn for acknowledgement every year so long as they both shall live. Uphanum doth declare that the bargain was made in the year 1651 unto which she doth subscribe.

The mark of Uphanum (X).

"In the presence of Robert Cooke the day and date above written."

The quotation we first present in this connection shows that the numerous Milliken family of Scarboro originates with John Milliken of Boston, Mass., whose wife was Elizabeth Alger, daughter of John and granddaughter of Andrew Alger, who was killed at Dunstan, Andrew Alger's residence standing near the Dr. Robert Southgate brick mansion as now observed, and that John Milliken removed to Dunstan, but the exact time we cannot state. On June 26, 1728, the First Church was gathered and we here present a few extracts from the church record of names "admitted into full Communion with the church of Scarboro since the first establishment."

243

CONTINUED:

Sept. 8, 1728, Thomas Westbrook, Esq.

Sept. 12, 1731, Nathan Knight.

Sept. 17, 1732, Samuel Milliken and Nathaniel Milliken, "dismissed from a church in Boston."

Oct. 31, 1736, Edward Milliken.

May 29, 1729, Edward and Abigail Milliken had a son Joseph baptized. June 17, 1733, Nathaniel and Sarah Milliken had son Jonathan baptized. April 25, 1734, Samuel and Martha Milliken had daughter Jemima baptized.

Col. Westbrook's stay at Dunstan was temporary. It is traditional that he erected a saw mill there, and records show that religious meetings were holden at his abode, but we cannot find that he owned real estate in that locality. The mill stood easterly of Dunstan Corner.

Nathan Knight, whose wife Mary was a sister to Col. Westbrook, purchased a house lot in Dunstan in 1720, where Richard King resided thirty years later, and raised the family of which some of the members became very celebrated. A part of the house may now be seen on the road to the "Landing."

The original account book of Nathaniel Knight, son of Nathan and Mary (Westbrook) Knight, is before us as we write. Nathaniel's wife was Priscilla Berry and they fill unmarked graves near Stroudwater Falls, a mile southerly of Saccarappa village. Their daughter Sarah was baptized in Scarboro Aug. 25, 1728. He was an active man, and we propose to speak of him in detail later on. A few extracts, however, from the ancient account book we will here present:

1728. to Dyating [boarding] ye men when hewing [masts] at Dunstan,	£77-4-10
to making Walter Hinds trousers,	5-6
to one day carrying things to Stroudwater,	8-0
to sundry times my horse and boy to Stroudwater	3-0-0
to 32 days hewing masts at Dunstan 9@pr. day,	14-8-0
to driving hogs to Stroudwater,	8-0

These charges with numerous others are against Col. Westbrook, but only in a few cases dates of months are given anywhere. Evidently Mr. Knight kept a pocket or some other sort of a memoranda and occasionally some one who wrote a better hand than himself copied onto the pages of the book before us.

In 1760 the "pound," or place of confinement for roving cattle was located on the southwesterly corner made by the main highway and, road to the Landing, and Morris Obryan had his residence and tailor establishment next westerly. Edward Milliken was a saddler and another by the name of Milliken was a cordwainer.

In 1764, John Milliken states in a recorded deed, that John Alger was his grandfather, and, in 1773, that Samuel Carle, Jr., and Joseph Hodgdon were his grandchildren, who were mariners, and for "love and affection" he bore them gave them a piece of land located between the main highway and the Richard King's residence—easterly side of road to the Landing.

In 1770 it seems that the matter of bounds of the Alger claim was a matter of discussion when a deposition was taken and recorded as follows:

The deposition of James Springer of Georgetown, in the County of Lincoln, aged seventy-two years, testifies and says, that he came to Scarboro in 1728, and that he lived there about ten years, and that he was well acquainted with the tract of land called Alger's Claim, and that Edward Milliken, Samuel Milliken and Nathaniel Milliken lived on said Tract of Land at that time, and in the year 1730, he, the Deponent, was with Mr. John Jones, Surveyor, when he ran out said land, and he began at the Head of said Claim which was at the Crotch on the Nonesuch River, above the bridge, near the great hill called Joslin's Hill, and that he, the said Jones, run from the aforesaid Crotch south west and came out about sixty rods above the uppermost Falls on Dunstan River, so called, and that he always understood by the general Talk of the people there that the aforesaid Line was the Head Line of Said claim, and that he has seen the tide flow up to the said Crotch and has carry'd pine timber down said river from above the bridge where it now stands, about thirty-feet long and from 12 to 17 inches square, and the said Millikens claimed the said Land as theirs and descendants of the said Algers at that time and that about the same time, he, the Deponant, helped to build a bridge over said River where it now stands in the road leading over said great Hill called Joslin's.

James Springer.

Falmouth, July 13, 1770.

To be continued.

NBPA'S SCRAP BOOK

Week of Oct. 10-13, 1900.

DUNSTAN.

The Ancient Hamlet in the Town of Scarboro.

BY LEONARD B. CHAPMAN.

In Two Parts—Part Second.

In 1782 the Millikens and other heirs to the Alger estate at Dunstan became dissatisfied among themselves and they entered into an agreement to petition the Supreme Judicial Court for a commission to rearrange and finally settle all matters in dispute—all the heirs signing. The commission was appointed accordingly, Capt. Daniel Dole of Stroudwater being one of the board, which reported two years later, or, in 1784, with a plan attached, the original papers filed in Boston, where they may be seen if not purloined.

A little westerly of the road that turns northerly from the way from Stroudwater to Dunstan and easterly of Dunstan Corner, "Jona" Milliken's residence—a one story building—appears on the plan and is placed on the northerly side of the road.

A little westerly of "Stickey Meadow Brook," on the northerly side of the same way, going westerly, appears a two story residence marked Nathaniel Milliken. Continuing in the same course westerly appears a two story house marked Edward Milliken.

In the southeasterly corner made by the main way and the way to the Landing appears a one story house marked Samuel Milliken.

On the westerly side of the Landing, on the westerly side of the river, fronting easterly, appears a dwelling marked Joseph Milliken, with a two story front and a one story back—the Landing appearing on both sides of the river with a bridge below, or southerly of the Landing. He was many years an inn keeper.

The Congregational meeting house, two storied, appears in the northwesterly corner made by the road to the Landing crossing the main way through Dunstan, and the lot comprised a half acre and twenty square rods.

The burying ground as now seen, comprising one acre and eight square rods.

A little westerly of the burying ground appears the "Parsonage lot," comprising an acre and a half.

Between the burying ground lot and the Parsonage lot two and a half acres are represented as assigned to Edward Milliken, this last lot extending back to the rear of the Parsonage lot and back of the burying lot.

The present appearance of Dunstan does not indicate that vessels were once built there, that mast-logs a hundred and more feet long were procured and sent off, that it was a place of much traffic, that it has produced from an adopted child a President for Harvard College, statesmen, a state Governor, clergymen, doctors and lawyers, but what we indicate is true and though now bereft of its pristine glory the hamlet will repay for a journey of some miles to view the situation as it appears today compared with what it has been, with its Congregational meeting house gone, parsonage gone, those to recite its true story gone, mast trees gone, cattle pound gone, military training gone, flip-drinking habit gone, but a harmonious blending in appearance of moderately aged and new residences and a neatly kept burying place of comparative great magnitude.

Continued:

ECCLESIASTICAL HISTORY.

In the month of September, 1730, the Rev. Samuel Willard was installed in Biddeford, but while on a visit at Eliot was taken ill in the pulpit and died two days later, which was in the month of October, 1740, leaving a widow and five children, of whom Eunice was born in 1733 and Joseph, Jan. 9, 1738, both in Biddeford. The father, Rev. Samuel Willard, was born in 1705, a descendant of Rev. Samuel Willard, pastor of the Old South church, Boston, Mass., born 1639, a copy of a painting of whom may be seen in the Memorial volume by Miss Ann A. Gordon, 1898, dedicated to the name of Miss Frances E. Willard, the female apostle of moral suasion for the fallen and legal prohibition for the liquor traffic, who, it is claimed, was also a descendant of Rev. Samuel Willard of Boston.

Richard Elvins was born in 1716, and by trade was a baker and employed at Salem, Mass. He was a man without book education, but became converted by listening to the enchanting words and pulpit oratory of Rev. George Whitefield, concluded to become a clergyman. In 1744 he was settled over the Dunstan society, and Nov. 13, 1744, he and Abigail Willard, widow of Rev. Samuel Willard, deceased, were united in marriage and went to reside at Dunstan. He did not preach from notes but extempore, being gifted in speech. A sermon, however, of his, preached July 26, 1747, at Dunstan, was printed. But it was not till 1758 that the second or Dunstan Parish of Scarboro was incorporated, and fifteen males and fifteen females were dismissed from the First to form a church society for the Second. Elvins died at Dunstan, August 12, 1776, after having officiated there 30 years, but his grave, if he was interred at Dunstan, has no head stone. His widow removed to Massachusetts.

Of the five Willard children we have traced but two.

Rev. Benjamin Chadwick graduated at Harvard College in the class of 1770, and December 19, 1776, was made a pastor of the Dunstan church. He was one of the original members who founded, May 28, 1788, at the residence of Rev. Thomas Browne, Woodfords district of Deering, the "Cumberland County Association of Congregational Ministers," noticed in the News of September 5-8, which has been continued to the present day. Chadwick was continued in the pastorate eighteen years, but becoming feeble in health and partially blind, in 1795, he was dismissed, when his health was restored to a great extent. In December of 1800 he was succeeded by Rev. Nathan Tilton.

Mr. Samuel Libby, a clerk in the coal office at 70 Exchange street, possesses one of Rev. Mr. Chadwick's sermons in manuscript. The paper upon which it is written is six inches long and there are forty-seven lines on a page. The letters are so small that scarcely a word can be read without study. A call and a perusal will repay. Mr. Libby will be pleased to show the document. There are others of the same sort of construction in existence.

In 1799 Rev. Mr. Chadwick purchased thirty acres of land located on the southerly side of the highway upon which highway the hamlet of Dunstan is located. He built—we venture the assertion without positive proof—the one-story, low posted, good sized dwelling house, as now seen, painted white, on the premises, nearly opposite the cemetery, next, at this time, to the easterly side of the schoolhouse, in which dwelling house his family resided and where all departed this life. For the thirty acres of land he paid $500.

Nearly a century has passed since the Methodists of Dunstan put themselves into an organized society. June 20, 1803, the Board of trustees consisted of the following named persons: George Harmon, Thomas Thurston, Wentworth Dresser, Moses Waterhouse and Richard Waterhouse; and the board at that time received for the use of the Methodist Society from the Rev. Benjamin Chadwick and wife Eunice (Willard) a meeting house lot, located upon which is the low posted building, which is in good repair and used by the Methodists as a place of worship, with ample shelter in the rear for vehicles.

Children of Rev. Mr. Chadwick:
1—Abigail, b. July 29, 1778.
2—Mary, b. April 6, 1781.
3—Sopiah, b. Jan. 17, 1783.

The above are all the names we find on the Scarboro town records.

August 31, 1857, Mary and Sopiah having sold the land received of their father, excepting an acre and the buildings on it, estimated at $600, and invested the money in Portland city bonds, and having become too aged to transact business and care for their personal wants, chose Amos Hight, Esq., their agent, with full power to act for them, but the two sisters did not survive long after the transaction, and the following transcript of the inscriptions from the small white marble monument tell the rest of our Chadwick family story as we know it from the records.

Rev.
BENJAMIN CHADWICK
died
Nov. 3, 1819, aged 75.

Eunice, his wife,
died Feb. 18, 1831,
aged 88.

Abigail Chadwick died Nov. 14, 1846, aged 68.

Sophiah Chadwick died January 13, 1866, aged 79.

Mary Chadwick, died January 20, 1861, aged 80.

"These all died in faith."

PROF. JOSEPH WILLARD.

Joseph Willard was born in Biddeford Jan. 9, 1738. He was six years of age when his widowed mother married the Rev. Richard Elvins and went to reside at Dunstan, where he was a bare footed boy, his stepfather residing a few rods westerly of the cemetery which has since been enlarged so as to make the parsonage lot join that of the cemetery. And it requires but a little stretch of the imagination to see him piling wood upon the "Landing" and unloading goods from vessels, for he made several trips as a sailor in a coaster, but the evidences of intellectual merit appearing in such a convincing manner friends advised a college course and tendered assistance, so that, in the graduating class of 1765, at Harvard we find his name, and a year later a tutor at the institution where he continued till 1772 when he was ordained at Beverly, Mass., as a Congregationalist clergyman, Nov. 25, of that year.

In 1781 he was elected President of Harvard College. Some of his literary work was printed, but not much. He is set down as a sound Greek scholar and had prepared a Greek grammar, which he left in manuscript. He held his position till death, which was at New Bedford, Sept. 25, 1804.

The End.

Week of Oct. 17-20, 1900

DR. ROBERT SOUTHGATE.

Of Dunstan, Scarboro, Ancestors and Descendants.

BY LEONARD B. CHAPMAN.

Part First.

Rev. William Scott Southgate who compiled the history of Scarboro performed some labor on the genealogy of the branch of the family to which he belonged. He departed this life on Sunday, May 21, 1899, at Annapolis, Md., where he had been Rector of St. Ann's church for thirty years, leaving his genealogical collection with his niece, Mrs. Harriet A. (Southgate) Graham residing at West End, Va., from whom we have obtained the loan, and, having made additions to the original, now present the whole to the public.

John Southgate of Coombs, Suffolk County, England, was united in marriage with Elizabeth ———, of the same place.

James Southgate, a son, came to New England and settled in Leicester, Mass., where he died, leaving no male issue.

Another son of John was named Richard. He was born in Coombs, Eng., March, 1671, and married there Oct. 17, 1700, Elizabeth, daughter of William and Elizabeth Steward of Bridley. Eng., b. June 11, 1677. In 1715, Richard came to this country with Daniel Denny, arriving in Boston, Sept. 12. June 7, 1716, he returned to England, but came back the next year with Rev. Thomas Pierce, arriving in Boston, July 20th. In 1718 he settled in Leicester, Mass., where he died April 1, 1758; his wife, Nov. 3, 1751.

[For a notice of Denny and Pierce, see Vol. I, page 187, Maine Historical and Genealogical Recorder. L. B. C.]

Children of Richard and Elizabeth (Steward) Southgate all born in Coombs, England.

1—Steward, Sept. 8, 1703. m. Elizabeth Scott; 2d, Elizabeth Potter.
2—Elizabeth, March 23, 1705, d. 1791.
3—Richard, Aug. 3, 1708, d. Aug. 24, 1708.
4—Hannah, Dec. 10, 1709. m. Nathaniel Waite, d. March 30, 1754.
5—Mary, June 9, 1712, m. Daniel Livermore.
6—Richard, July 23, 1714. m. Eunice Brown Jan. 20, 1741. Descendants residing in Vermont.

(1.—Steward, eldest child of Richard and Elizabeth (Steward) Southgate, b. in Coombs, Eng., Sept. 8, 1703, m. March 28, 1735, Sarah, 3d daughter of William and Sarah Scott of Palmer, Mass. She d. Sept. 19, 1748; he m. second, at the Quaker monthly meeting, Oct. 26, 1749, Elizabeth, dau. of Nathaniel and Rebecca Potter of Smithfield, Mass. They resided at Leicester, Mass., until 1730 when they removed to the "Elbows" (now Palmer) in the county of Hampshire, Mass. He d. at Leicester, Dec. 1764.

Children of Steward and Sarah (Scott) Southgate:
1—Elizabeth, b. Jan. 26, 1735, d. Jan. 28, 1738.
2—John, b. Jan. 13, 1737, d. Sept. 23, 1748.
3—William, b. Aug. 29, 1739, d. Sept. 25, 1748.
4—ROBERT, (doctor), b. Oct. 26, 1741, m. Mary King of Dunstan, Scarboro, Me.
5—Margaret, b. July 17, 1743, d. same day.
6—Sarah, b. June 18, 1744.
7—Mary, b. Oct. 16, 1746, d. May 13, 1756.
8—Steward, b. Sept. 10, 1748.

By second wife.

9—Sou, b. Oct. 21, 1750, d. same day.
10—Amos, b. Dec. 3, 1751, d. Sept. 30, 1775.
11—Rebecca, b. Aug. 23, 1754, d. Oct. 14, 1756.
12—Sou, b. March 11, 1757, d. same day.
13—Ruth, b. Dec. 3, 1758, d. Oct. 16, 1777.
14—Moses, b. July 19, 1761, d. Sept. 1777.

(4.) DR. ROBERT SOUTHGATE.

It is a family tradition that Dr. Southgate arrived at Dunstan June 21, 1771, who was then thirty years of age lacking three months, born at Leicester, Mass., Oct. 26, 1741, son of Steward and Sarah (Scott) Southgate, coming on horseback, his saddle-bags containing his entire personal outfit. What induced the Doctor to come hither is among the hidden things of the past. That no records of his career in early manhood were left to the public is a matter of regret. That the compiler of the history of Scarboro did not say more relative to his ancestors and insert more genealogical notes in his work is, at this date, a source of wonderment, but such things were not so much in demand as now, and people were then less inclined to pay for printing.

It is apparent that Dr. Southgate upon arriving here engaged in trade of some sort; this the records show. Every shop and inn keeper then held a license to sell alcoholic liquors. In 1771 his application was granted and renewed yearly till 1785. He was in company with one Samuel Southgate, but no records have yet been found showing the family relationship between the two. Prior to the year of 1774, however, Samuel Southgate had departed this life and Dr. Southgate was appointed and commenced actions in court as administrator against those indebted to Samuel's estate. Following is a copy of one record:

"Whereas, Robert Southgate of Scarboro, in Our County of Cumberland, Physician, and surviving Partner of the late Company of Robert & Samuel Southgate the said Samuel now deceased; by the consideration of our Justices of Our Inferior Court of Common Pleas holden at Falmouth within and for Our County of Cumberland, aforesaid, on the last Tuesday of March, 1774, recovered judment against John Milliken of Scarboro' aforesaid, Saddler, for the sum of Twenty-nine pounds," etc.

In settlement the Doctor received an acre and half of land which was the first he received at Dunstan.

Nov. 15, 1748, "Richard King of Scarboro, gentleman," purchased the Nathan Knight house lot at Dunstan, (Nathan Knight, who was noticed in our Dunstan articles), located on the easterly side of the road leading to the "Landing." The career of Richard and his descendants are full of events, many of which have been described in print. A part of the King house may even now be seen on its original foundation, which is the ell to the main house. Mary, the second child of Richard King in a family of nine children by two wives, became the wife of Dr. Southgate. One son of Richard King, named William, became Governor of Maine, and two others were statesmen.

The exact time Dr. Southgate left the practice of medicine and adopted that of farming and became also a counsellor at law we cannot state.

In 1800 he was appointed a Judge of the Court of Common Pleas which position he held ten years.

In the years of 1807-8-9 he erected "Dunstan Abbey," located a little easterly of the parting of the highway leading to Portland from Dunstan Corner—a large, brick, two story dwelling, long ell, large barn and all the other buildings necessary to make complete a not only first class farm house but at that time a genteel appearing residence. But it seems the house was in the prospective quite a while before it was commenced. In the work entitled "A Girl's Life Eighty Years Ago," made of letters of Eliza (Southgate) Bowne, a daughter of the Doctor, under date of New York, July 8, 1803, an allusion is made as follows: "How comes on the new house? We are to come as soon as ever that is finished. If you choose to send so far, I will purchase any kind of furniture you wish, perhaps cheaper and better than you can get elsewhere." At another time she writes her parents she is ashamed of the old house. Our authority for the assertion it was commenced in 1807, is a statement made by Hon. Seth Scammon. It now remains as originally constructed and in its history a wonderment to the stranger who passes, and ten years ago, or thereabouts, when we first visited the premises, they were owned by Mr. Scammon, who had occupied the "Abbey" since 1864 when he and Ezra Carter, the first of Saco, the last of Portland, purchased the home farm and seven other pieces of real estate of the heirs of Horatio Southgate, who received the property by will from the Doctor, who was the father of Horatio, paying $18,000—the homestead of Horatio Southgate at Portland not being included in the $18,000 sale.

It was in front of or adjacent the "Abbey" that Andrew Alger resided when he was murdered by the Indians two hundred and twenty-six years ago.

Looking southward from the front of the "Abbey" countless acres of marsh land appear, a belt of English grass land intervening; beyond, the ocean; while both sides, the scene is skirted by woodlands. Looking towards the southwest in the direction of the site of the King house, the land is undulating, and all, independent of the marsh, of a rich quality in fertility, the marsh prized higher by the first settlers than the up-land. But it was the northerly view, at the rear of the "Abbey," and much nearer, and far less

Continued:

in magnitude as to the question of number of acres, that attracted our special attention outside the historical consideration, where lofty evergreens had by the hand of Nature been placed, earth embankments, water-jets, rills, surface table rocks containing sculptured names of those whose "strife is past and triumph won"—reflections of Nature in all its miniature beauty by placid water, with stepping stones naturally arranged, paths carpeted by the waste of trees, all canopied by outstretching boughs of lofty specimens of monarchs of the forest. But a few years later when we again visited the scene—Alas! the venerable, long, white bearded Saco school master, like the builder of the "Abbey" had been called—obeyed—and the woodsman axe in hand, had come and felled the trees; so where natural beauty once abounded and there were expressions of glee in the early history of the Abbey and its surroundings and echoes from the lofty tree-domes, the evil spirit of the Indian of two centuries had appeared and permeated the minds of the lords of the land in the manner we here indicate. And now—

"We search the world for truth, we call
The good, the pure, the beautiful
From grave-stone and written scroll,
From all old flower-fields of the Soul."

and here present the record as we see it.

Hark! The voice of the Indian or something else. Do you hear it?

"Who wants recorded family records?" "Let the dead bury the dead." "Who wants eternal sunshine or shower?" "Who would fix forever the loveliest cloud-work of an autumnal sunset, or hang over the earth an everlasting moonlight?"

The echo—two hundred years earlier—"Give us desolation!"

For us let there be Nature's landscape perpetually displayed, rational glee and its echo—in realization "the dream that lovers dream," for Nature's path leads up higher in thought, and rational thought has made man what he is in his improved estate.

"Earnest words must needs be spoken;
When the warm heart bleeds or burns
With its scorn of wrong or pity."

(To Be Continued.)

GRANDPA'S SCRAP BOOK

Week of Oct 24-27, 1900.

DR. ROBERT SOUTHGATE.

Of Dunstan, Scarboro, Ancestors and Descendants.

BY LEONARD B. CHAPMAN.

Part Second.

FIRST GENERATION IN MAINE.

Within the cemetery enclosure at Dunstan, Scarboro, may be seen a tall, thick, white marble slab that discloses the date of the demise of Dr. Robert Southgate and wife Mary (King) Southgate, but his name is without a title. To other sources of information the cemetery visitor must look to ascertain what he was as regards his occupation. The face inscription is as follows:

ROBERT SOUTHGATE,
died
Nov. 2, 1833.
Aged 92 years.

MARY SOUTHGATE,
died
March 30, 1824,
Aged 68 years.

The back of the slab points to another story—a story with many branches—the story of ten children whose names are inscribed, time of demise and ages, but there were twelve, two that did not receive names before they were called away.

Clustering around the parental record stone are five others bearing the name of Southgate—then the long row of Horatio's wives and children in another place.

SECOND GENERATION.

Children of Dr. Robert and Mary (King) Southgate.

"There were six daughters, all remarkable for great personal beauty."

1—Mary King, b. Sept. 4, 1775, d. unmarried, June 22, 1795.
2—Daughter b. and d. Jan, 9, 1777.
3—Son, b. and d. Nov. 7, 1777.
*4—Isabella, b. March 29, 1779, m. Joseph C. Boyd of. Portland.
*5—Horatio, b. Aug. 9, 1781, m. 1st, Abigail McLellan; 2d, Mary Webster; 3d, Eliza Neal.
*6—Eliza, b. Sept. 24, 1783, m. Walter Bowne.
*7—Octavia, b. Sept. 13, 1786, m. William Browne, son of Rev. Thomas Browne who has been noticed in previous issues of the Deering News. She d. Jan. 9, 1815.
8—Miranda, b. Feb. 15, 1786, d. unmarried July 17, 1816.
*9—Frederick, b. August 9, 1791, d. unmarried May 29, 1813.
*10—Arixene, b. Sept. 17, 1793, m. Henry Smith.
11—Robert, b. Oct. 14, 1796, d. July 6, 1799.
*12—Mary King, b. May 6, 1799, m. Grenville Mellen.

* This sign indicates the name will be further noticed.

ISABELLA SOUTHGATE.

4.—Isabella Southgate (Boyd), b. March 29, 1779, daughter of Dr. Robert and Mary (King) Southgate, m. Jan. 24, 1796, Joseph Coffin Boyd; b. at Newburyport, Mass., 1760, son of James Boyd of Boston, Mass. His mother was a sister to the Rev. Paul Coffin of Buxton. James C. and brothers were all brought up to mercantile pursuits, and all left home young. One became a clergyman; one went to India, where he joined the English army, upon returning he engaged in the cause of his country and became a Brigadier in the war of 1812-15.

Robert came to Portland first, then Joseph C., and they engaged in trade on the corner of Exchange and Middle streets, where the "Boyd Block" appears.

Joseph C. first resided on Pleasant street, where the first children were born, in a house that Dr. John Merrill sold as guardian to the Boyd children in 1833 to Joseph Adams for $1,600; he resided second in the large three story residence numbered 65 situated on the northerly side of Spring street which he built where Dr. John Merrill later resided whose heirs still retain and occupy the premises.

In 1800 Joseph C. went to France where he remained a year and a half. Upon his return he became a Notary Public. In 1812 we find him as clerk of the court of Common Pleas.

In 1820 he became State Treasurer, which position he held at the time of his death.

Miss Isabella Southgate was a pupil in 1793 at Leicester, (Mass.) Academy. From on address delivered in 1847 by Rev. Dr. Pierce of Brookline, Mass., who had been an assistant, we extract the following:

"Miss Isabella Southgate, from Scarboro, Maine, was a youth of transcendant beauty and accomplishments. Though in my class which I instructed at the university were Dr. Channing, Judge Story, and other respectable scholars, yet I have been in the habit of remarking, I never knew one male or female, of a more extraordinary mind than was evinced by that gifted young lady."

She d. Jan. 28, 1821, aged 42 years; he, May 12, 1823, aged 63 years.

Children of Joseph Coffin Boyd and Isabella (Southgate) Boyd.

*1—Mary Southgate, b. Jan. 20, 1797, m. Dr. John Merrill.
2—James Joseph, b. July 25, 1798. Intention of m. recorded Oct. 15, 1825, with Miss Harriet Dummer of Hallowell. They resided in the Boyd Spring street residence, where he d. April 30, 1829, and the widow returned home. One child that died in infancy.
3—Charles Orlando, b. March 6, 1799, d. Dec. 12, 1821, unmarried.
4—Isabella Susanna, b. Dec. 28, 1801, d. North Conway, N. H., to which place she went hoping to recover lost health, July 17, 1825. She did not marry.
*5—Robert Southgate, b. Aug. 24, 1804, m. Margaret A. Hall.
*6—Samuel Stillman, b. May 27, 1807, m. Catharine C. Wilkins.
7—Frances Greenleaf, b. Nov. 25, 1808, d. Dec. 11, 1824, unmarried.
8—Horatio Erald, b. April 17, 1810, d. March 11, 1833, unmarried.
9—Walter Bowne, b. April 21, 1811. A farmer at Andover, this state, but removed to St. Paul, Minn., where he continued the calling, and where he resides unmarried.
10—Miranda Elizabeth, b. Dec. 24,

1812, d. May 31, 1830.
*11—Frederick William (Reverend), b. March 15, 1815, m. Mary Eliza Railey.
12—Octavia Caroline, b. March 15, 1815, d. April 6, 1826.
13—Edward Augustus, b. June 10, 1816, m. Sarah Farrington of Andover, this state, and settled in St. Paul, Minn., where he was first a farmer than a doctor.
14—Ellen Almira, b. Aug. 8, 1817, d. April 6, 1826.
15—Augusta Murray, b. Jan., 1819, intention of m. with Lloyd Tilghman of Baltimore, Md. He was a civil engineer; was in the Mexican war; took the side of the South in the war of the Rebellion, and was killed at Champion Hills while serving as a General. The widow died in New York city Feb. 1, 1898, where descendants reside.

HORATIO SOUTHGATE.

5.—Horatio Southgate, b. Aug. 9, 1781, son of Dr. Robert and Mary (King) Southgate, at the age of thirteen was placed at school at Exeter (N. H.) Academy with Henry Wadsworth; Joseph S. Buckminister, Augustine and Bushrod Washington from Virginia; Daniel Webster and others as companions. From there he went to the law office of Salmon Chase of Portland.

At the October term of court holden in New Gloucester in 1802 at the age of 21 years and two months he was admitted to the Cumberland bar as a practitioner with an office where the Canal Bank building is located in Portland, and one at Dunstan Corner in Scarboro.

In 1806 he purchased of Joseph Dillans a two story dwelling house and lot, which was his first venture in real estate, for which he paid $2,700, where he ever after resided while a citizen of Portland. The property was located on the southerly side of Pleasant street, is now owned and occupied by Moses H. Foster, proprietor of the Preble street dye-house and is numbered 124. The front door was originally in the end but Mr. Southgate had it changed to the side as now observed. In it fifteen of the sixteen Southgate children were born—the other at Dunstan.

In 1809 he was a trustee of the Portland Academy.

In 1814 he was appointed County Treasurer.

In 1815 he became register of the Probate Court for Cumberland County and held the office twenty-one years.

In 1818 he was one of the founders of the Portland Benevolent Society, and a member of the Board of Foreign Missions.

In 1821 he was a member of the board of overseers of the Portland House of Correction.

In 1830 he prepared the "Probate Manual," a work of much merit.

In 1840 he was the Portland Democratic candidate for mayor. The vote stood:

Greeley, (Whig),..................497
Cutter, (Whig)....................509
Southgate, (Democrat)............702
Scattering........................9

Total 1717

Under date of April 17, 1840, Rev. Caleb Bradley records in his diary as follows:

"Election in Portland, but no choice of mayor. Four candidates—two in each of the political parties. Whig candidates, Levi Cutter and Eliphalet Greeley; Tory [Democrat] Horatio Southgate and C. B. Smith. Thus they are divided in the city and so through the nation and a nation divided against itself cannot stand, and unless we become better united as a people our ruin is inevitable; there is no help for it; nothing can save us but the blessed influence of an overruling Providence. Lord turn the hearts of the people. O, save us with an everlasting salvation! These are days of calamities; we have brought down judgments, and more judgments are in reserve unless prevented by repentance. We are a wicked nation and have forgotten God and what He has done for us and our fathers—how He drove out the heathen, or suffered them to be subdued in order to make a way for our European fathers. We seem to have forgotten how He appeared for us in our struggles for independence. Now, God seems to be saying: 'Shall not my soul be avenged on such a nation?'"

In 1841 Horatio Southgate Esq., was again run and received 680 votes; Churchill, 710; scattering, 137; total, 1527, and Southgate, "the Tory-Democrat" (according to Parson Bradley,) was beaten by the Whigs.

(To be Continued.)

GRANDPA'S SCRAP BOOK

Week of Oct 31–Nov 3, 1900.

DR. ROBERT SOUTHGATE.

Of Dunstan, Scarboro, Ancestors and Descendants.

BY LEONARD B. CHAPMAN.

Part Third.

Horatio Southgate, Esq., was three times married as follows:

First— With Nabby McLellan, Nov. 1, 1805, dau. of Hugh and Abigail (Browne) McLellan, she b. Dec. 31, 1785, d. August 28, 1816.

Second—With Mary Webster, May 10, 1818, b. Jan. 7, 1799, d. Feb. 28 1819, dau. of Noah Webster, the compiler of Webster's Dictionary.

Dr. Webster d. June 25, 1847, aged 82 years; his wife survived him, having had one son and six daughters who grew to maturity. The third child of Dr. Webster m. for her first husband Edward Cobb of Portland. Mary was the fourth.

Third—With Eliza Neal, Oct. 14, 1821, dau. of James and Abigail C. Neal of Portland. She d. Feb. 21, 1865, aged 66 years.

After the death of his father (Nov. 2, 1833,) Horatio Southgate, Esq., removed from Portland to Scarboro and occupied "Dunstan Abbey," where he died Aug. 7, 1864, leaving a will that was destroyed in the Portland great fire of 1866.

In the Dunstan cemetery is a row of Southgate white marble head-stones, including the monument of brown color, that is fourteen paces long. There are thirteen of them and all of a size. The inscription upon the face side of the monument is as follows

In
memory of
HORATIO SOUTHGATE
and the members
of his family who
are here interred.

The south side contains a record of his own birth and time of death as it does his three wives, whose names we have presented. The other two sides are devoted to a record of his offspring.

Children of
Horatio Southgate, Esq., and his three wives, all born in Portland but the last who was born in Dunstan.

1—Robert, b. Sept. 4, 1806, d. July 27, 1807.
*2—Robert, (Reverend) b. Jan. 27, 1807, m. Mary Frances Swan.
*3—Abigail Browne, b. Oct 28, 1809, m. Dr. John Barrett.
*4—Horatio, Jr., (Reverend) b. July 5, 1812, m. first, Elizabeth Browne, second in New York, 1864, Sarah Elizabeth Hutchinson.
*5—Frederick, (Reverend) b. Oct. 23, 1814, m. Mary Moore, of Gardiner.

By Second Wife:

6—Mary Webster, b. Feb. 5, 1819. She was adopted by Dr. Noah Webster, m. Henry Trowbridge, Jr., Esq., of New Haven, Ct.

By Third Wife:

7—Richard, b. Jan. 27, 1822, d. Nov. 1852, aged 30 years.
8—Elizabeth, b. Juply 20, 1823, d. Dec. 17, 1862, unmarried, aged 39 years.
9—Emily, b. Nov. 13, 1824, d. Oct. 8, 1837.

CONTINUED:

10—Julia, b. Feb, 5, 1826, d. Oct. 1837.
11—Edward Payson, b. Sept. 27, 1827, d. Jan. 26, 1846.
12—Ellen, b. May 7, 1829, d. Nov. 26, 1852, aged 23 years.
*13—William Scott, (Reverend)b. April 10, 1831, m. Harriet Randolph Talcot.
*14—John Barrett, b. July 25, 1833, d. Feb. 7, 1862, unmarried, aged 29 years.
15—Henry Martin, b. Aug. 4, 1835, d. Dec. 30, 1852.
16—Julia Abby, b. in Scarboro, Jan. 25, 1838, m. Thomas Winslow of Gardiner, this state. She d. Jan. 23, 1883, at Brooklyn N. Y.; he d. a month earlier same place.

ELIZA SOUTHGATE.

6.—Eliza Southgate (Bowne), b Sept. 24, 1783, dau. of Robert and Mary (King) Southgate, was christened by the name of "Elizabeth" and "Elizabeth" appears upon the back of her father's memorial at Dunstan cemetery, but the name appears in print as Eliza and her letters are signed Eliza so we will refer to her as Eliza, but of her natural and acquired accomplishments we cannot speak in a manner the subject demands.

In 1888, Charles Scribner's Sons of New York, printed selections of her correspondence in book form with an introduction, portraits and views, entitled "A Girl's Life Eighty Years Ago."

Her minature as well as her writings represent her as a most charming young woman, who, like most of her name hereabouts, filled an early made grave. Of the ten pages of introduction we can make but one brief extract as follows:

"Love and friendship followed her wherever she went in her too brief span of life, and fortune heaped her girlish lap with all good things; but she showed herself worthy of her blessings and kept herself unspotted from the world."

The book contains a fine minature of Walter Bowne which, with her description, present him as a charming man, who became her husband. He was a merchant doing business in New York city, and his people were Quakers. They met the first time in the month of September of 1802, while both were making a pleasure tour of the state and each became at sight enamored with the other.

At Boston, Mass., May 30, 1803, she wrote her sister, Octavia (Southgate) Browne, from which letter we here make an extract:

But I have not told you how General Knox found us out at Newburyport. [The place of interment of Gen. Knox's remains is marked at Thomaston cemetery, this state, by a sunken grave, a small, inclining monument, enclosed by a rusty, tumble-down fence.] We always kept to ourselves, but in passing the entry Gen. Knox, who had just come in the stage, met Mr. Bowne and asked where he was from; he told him from the Eastward. Alone? No. Who is with you? Mrs. Bowne. So plump a question he could not evade, so the General insisted on being introduced to the bride. I was walking the room and reading, perfectly unsuspicious, when the opening of the door and Mr. Bowne's voice—'General Knox, my love,' quite roused me; he came up, took my hand very gracefully, pres't it to his lips and begged leave to congratulate me on the event that had lately taken place. After a few minutes of conversation—'And pray, sir,' said he, turning to Mr. Bowne—'when did this happy event take place?" I felt my face glow, but Mr. Bowne, always delicate and collected, said—"Tis not a fortnight since, sir.' The stage drove up to the door, and after hoping to see us at Mrs. Carter's he took his leave, and this morning I found him waiting in the breakfast room to see me. He introduced me to General Pickney and his family from Carolina,—General Pickney, they say, is to be our next President. 'Mr. Bowne,' said General Knox to General Pickney, 'has done us the honor to come to the District of Maine for a bud to transport to New York.' He was very polite and said 'he must find us out in New York.' Only think, I never thought of the wedding cake when I was in Salem. You would laugh to hear 'Mrs. Bowne' and 'Miss Southgate' all in a breath—'How do you do, Miss Southgate?—I beg pardon, Mrs. Bowne,' and do it on purpose I believe; when I hear an old acquaintance call me 'Mrs. Bowne' it really makes me start at first, it sounds so very odd. Mr. Bowne will be in, in a minute—and if I don't seal my letter, he will insist on seeing it, so love to all.

In a letter to her mother dated Aug. 9, 1803, she says: "Only think, 'tis just a year today since we first saw each other, and here we are, married, happy, and enjoying ourselves in Bethlehem. Memorable day!" (Bethlehem, Pa., to which they had gone on account of yellow fever in N. Y.)

As Mrs. Bowne's health was failing in 1808, it was thought best that she spend the winter in Charlestown, S. C., to which place she went with Mr. William Browne and wife Octavia (Southgate) Browne, who was a sister to Mrs. Eliza Bowne, making the journey by water.

From the last letter written by her, dated Charlestown, S. C., Jan. 28, 1809, we present an extract as follows:

"How are my dear little ones? I hope not too troublesome. Octavia is in fine health and grows quite fat for her. Frederick has been unusually troublesome. My dear little Walter! I hardly trust myself to think of them, —precious children—how they bind me to life! Adieu."

It appears that Mrs. Bowne had two children.
1—Walter, Jr., b. 1806.
2—Mary, b. July, 1808, who became the wife of John W. Lawrence.

In Archdale Church yard, Archdale street, Charlestown, S. C., may be seen a monument with an inscription as follows:

Sacred
to the memory of
ELIZA S. BOWNE,
Wife of Walter Bowne of New York. Daughter of Robert Southgate, Esq., of Scarborough, District of Maine, who departed this life on the 19th day of February, 1809, aged 25 years.

(To be Continued.)

Bishop Southgate.

In the pains-taking historical articles by L. B. Chapman in your last issue reference is made to Bishop Southgate, one of the numerous children, and namesake of Judge Horatio Southgate.

The writer remembers hearing the bishop preach in the Methodist church at Dunstan in the early sixties, and readily recalls the bishop as a small, slight man of an easy, graceful pulpit manner, but a very scholarly man of the positive order of mind, and the spirit that seemed to breathe through his discourse was that "You are accustomed to listen to Methodist, Baptist, Bullockite, Advent and Millerite sermons, which are all well enough until your moral, intellectual and spiritual development leads you to higher grounds, but you are now listening to the highest expression of religious truth, by one of the divinely accredited

GRANDPA'S SCRAP BOOK

Week of Nov 7-10, 1900.

DR. ROBERT SOUTHGATE.

Of Dunstan, Scarboro, Ancestors and Descendants.

BY LEONARD B. CHAPMAN.

OCTAVIA SOUTHGATE.

7.—Octavia Southgate (Browne), b. Sept. 13, 1786, daughter of Dr. Robert and Mary (King) Southgate, has been noticed in our Browne articles in the News as the wife of William Browne, son of Rev. Thomas Browne of the Stroudwater, or 4th Parish of Falmouth, now the First of Deering.

Several of Octavia's letters appear in the book entitled "A Girl's Life Eighty Years Ago," which show her as a woman of culture. William Browne and his wife Octavia accompanied Mrs. Eliza (Southgate) Bowne on her fatal sea voyage to Charleston, S. C., and the contents of his first letter addressed to Mr. and Mrs. Southgate of Scarboro, dated at Charleston, Jan. 1, 1809, we will present, as follows:

Our Most Esteemed Friends:

We have now been in the city a week. We find that Eliza has gained a little strength since she arrived, and her cough is not quite so distressing as before leaving New York. She complains of no pain, but her fever and night sweats continue to trouble her every other day and night, as was the case before. She can walk about her room with ease; and she rides when the weather is fine, which she is much pleased with, and no doubt it is of great service to her. The streets are entirely of sand, as smooth as possible, no pavements, not a stone to be seen, which renders it very easy riding for her. It is as warm as our first of May, (if not the middle), and when the weather is fine, the air is clear, very mild and refreshing. The change is so great between this and New York that I cannot help thinking it must have a great and good effect on Eliza. I find as to myself that my cough is done away entirely, and I had a little of it most of the time at home in the winter. Octavia has certainly grown fat, and our little Frederick is certainly very well indeed. Eliza eats hominy, rice and milk, eggs and oysters cooked in various ways, vegetables, too, which we find in great perfection here; fruit is plenty of almost every description. The oranges raised here are not sweet but are very large. The olives, grapes and figs are excellent. The meats and fish are not so good as ours. Their poultry is fine; a great plenty of venison, wild duck and small sea-fowl; green peas we shall have in about a month, so that, besides the change of climate, we have many of the luxuries of a Northern summer. Uncle King gave us letters to Gen. C. C. Pickney and his brother Maj. Thomas Pickney,—both of them being out of town on their plantations, their sister, Mrs. Hovey, received the letters and has been very attentive and kind to us all. She is a widow, about fifty-five, I should judge, of the finest respectability, and appears a very respectable and pleasant, amiable and cheerful old lady. She sends some nice things to Eliza almost every day. Her daughter, Mrs. Ruthlege, two Miss Pickneys (daughters of the General), Mrs. Gilchrist and daughter, Mr. and Mrs. Mannigault, Mrs. Middleton, Mr. and Mrs. Izard, Mr. and Mrs. Dessault and Mr. Heyard make an extensive acquaintance for us. They all seem very kind and hospitable, plain and open in their manners, and yet of the most genteel and easy. Eliza has seen only Mrs. Hovey, Mrs. Ruthlege, and the two Miss Pickneys, but she thinks in a few days to be able to receive short visits from her friends, and even thinks it may be of consequence to enliven her. She rides whenever the weather is fine, and is very much pleased with the appearance of everything growing in the gardens here like our June. We have had one visit from the physician only; he thinks taking a little blood from her will be of service, but she has not yet consented. He approved of her diet and of the Iceland Moss tea which was recommended at New York, and which is said here to have had a great effect in removing complaints of a cough. Mrs. Mannigault told us yesterday she found immediate relief from it after she had been sick a long time. We expect Mr. Bowne in the course of a fortnight, and then I shall return towards Scarborough immediately. We hope to hear from you in a few days; not a word have we yet from New York since we arrived. Our darling boy we think we see every day playing about us, without thinking who is admiring him at the distance of 1100 miles.

Our best wishes attend you always.
Affectionately,
W. Browne.

The author of the foregoing interesting letter was born in a house that stood a few feet northerly of where Dr. Albion P. Topliff resides at Woodfords district of Deering, (taken down some fifty years ago), and written at a period when foolish physicians vomited and bled their patients, thus aiding untimely death. What would the public do today with the doctor that vomited and bled a consumptive? The practice was as bad as "voting straight" now when clowns are put in nomination for an elective office, as is often the case, but the fallacy of voting "straight" when incompetents and tricksters are held up for office is on the decline hereabouts for a time at least, and like the practice of vomiting and bleeding the consumptive to effect a cure which practice has long since been abandoned, we hope voting "straight" for objectionable candidates may share the same fate.

FREDERICK SOUTHGATE.

9.—Frederick Southgate, b. August 9, 1791, son of Dr. Robert and Mary (King) Southgate, graduated from Bowdoin College, class of 1810, and while reading law in Portland the earnest preaching of Rev. Edward Payson, to whom he listened, so changed his plans that he concluded to prepare for the ministry, and at once commenced preaching himself, at the same time studying divinity with Rev. Mr. Payson, when he was chosen a tutor of Bowdoin College, but his days of usefulness were few in numbers. Quick consumption seized him and he died under the parental roof.

His memorial slab at Dunstan is inscribed as follows:

The
Remains
of
FREDERICK SOUTHGATE,
son of
Hon. Robert Southgate
Born Aug. 9, 1791.
Graduated
at Bowdoin College
1810,
Died May 29, 1816.

ARIXENE SOUTHGATE.

10.—The marriage intention between Miss Arixene Southgate and Henry Smith, she b. Sept. 17, 1793, daughter of Dr. Robert and Mary (King) Southgate, was recorded in Portland, Jan. 31, 1813.

John Smith was born in Plainfield, Connecticut, where he was united, June 25, 1699, in marriage with Miss Susanna Hall, daughter of Stephen Hall. Their son Lemuel was born there February 25, 1711, who married in 1736, Martha Coit, daughter of Rev. Joseph and Experience (Wheeler) Coit. Their son, named John, born at Sterling, (another record says Stonington,) Conn., March 7, 1749, graduated from Princeton College, 1770, and became a clergyman. He married July 3, (or 8), 1773, Alice Andrews, daughter of Elbanah and Alice (Beals) Andrews.

Rev. John Smith was for many years pastor of the Congregational church in Dighton, Mass., where a large family of both sons and daughters were born. In 1802 he removed to Canandaigua, N. Y., from there to the state of Pennsylvania, thence to Kentucky.

One of the sons of Rev. John Smith, named Isaac, a clergyman, made a first home for himself in Gilmanton, N. H., where he resided twenty years. Another son was Judge Smith of Plainfield, N. H., for some years a trustee of Dartmouth College. The other children of Rev. John Smith made homes in Kentucky and Illinois, excepting Henry, born in the town of Dighton, Mass., Dec. 10, 1783, who came to Portland and engaged in trade but failed in business. He then became superintendent of a cotton mill at Sacarrappa village, a village situated in the town of Westbrook, seven miles from Portland, where he took an active part in municipal and church matters, exerting a salutary influence for good in both respects.

His wife died Dec. 6, 1820, aged 27 years.

(To Be Continued.)

Revolutionary Pensions in the Town of Gray in the Year 1840.

	Age	Residence
Samuel Swett,	76	Samuel Swett,
Amavriah Dilanoe,	82,	Amavriah Dilanoe.
ames Welch,	76,	Abel Black.
John Merrill,	81,	Edward Harmon.
Joseph Allen,	81,	Emery Allen.

Where was S. Swett's residence?
S. P. Mayberry.

GRANDPA'S SCRAP BOOK

Week of Nov 14-17, 1900.

Dr. ROBERT SOUTHGATE,

Of Dunstan, Scarboro, Ancestors and Descendants.

BY LEONARD B. CHAPMAN.

Part Fifth.

Prior to April 18, 1819, John Maynard had departed this life leaving five children, two of age and three minors. His family last resided in the town of Scarboro, in the Vaughan mansion house, constructed of great oak timber, that was situated upon the southerly side of the highway leading from Dunstan to Portland via Oak Hill, about a third of the way from the Hill going towards Dunstan. It is traditional the house at the time was the oldest in the town, and was used as a garrison, where many children were born during the troublesome Indian times. The residence of the Warren brothers now occupies the site of the Vaughan mansion, and the frame of the residence of the Warrens' is constructed of that of the ancient abode.

[Elliot Vaughan, becoming tired of sea life, he being a mariner, removed from Portsmouth in 1742 to Scarboro, and located upon a large and valuable tract of land he inherited from Robert Elliot who was his grandfather, Elliot making a will in 1718. (See Maine Wills, page 255.)

Elliot Vaughan was a son of Lieut.-Gov. George Vaughan of Portsmouth, N. H.

The administrator upon the Elliot Vaughan estate sold the Dunstan property in 1759 to William Vaughan. William removed from there to Portland.]

In the month of April, 1819, Andrew Retchie, Esq., a lawyer of Boston, appointed Capt. Thomas Browne, a merchant of Portland, who has been noticed in the News, as his attorney to act in his stead in order to make sale of certain real estate located in Scarboro, "being the same lately improved by John Maynard, deceased, and which was devised by Cornelius Durant of Boston, Mass., deceased, to the use of said Maynard for life, then to his five children." Retchie was the guardian to the three children under age, named respectively as follows: William L., —though the "L." does not appear,— Edward and Maria Caroline. The two children having arrived at lawful age were named Sally and Thomas. Sally became the second wife of Henry Smith, and Maria Caroline the wife of Gen. Neal Dow of Portland.

The sale was made by Capt. Browne for $2,500 to Seth Storer, Jr. Esq., a lawyer of Biddeford and Ichabod Jordon, consisting of "400 acres of marsh and upland known as Vaughan's Neck, 120 acres marsh and upland known as the Vaughan home farm, 'being the same Cornelius Durant purchased of Vaughan Sept. 9, 1797; also 64 acres of upland and marsh, being the homestead of the late Capt. Nathaniel Harmon."

Upon the "Vaughan home farm" in the "garrison house" John Maynard, his wife, and five children resided, Sally, the daughter, having been born on the Island of St. Croix, all removing from there to Boston, Mass., thence to Scarboro.

The eldest of the three living children of Henry Smith was nine years old when Sally Maynard became the stepmother of the Smith children. She proved to be a woman of sagacity and well adapted to the training of children; she was, withal, a woman of culture.

"The Reminiscences of Gen. Neal Dow," published in 1898, lets in, on page 82, some light upon the Maynard family in addition to what we present above. We make a condensed abstract, as follows:

"When not quite twenty-six years of age," writes Gen. Neal Dow, the apostle of total prohibition for the liquor traffic by legislative restraint, "I married Maria Cornelia, [previously noticed as Maria Caroline] Durant Maynard, on the 20th of Jan, 1830. My wife's father, John Maynard, was born in Framingham, Mass., in 1766, where the family had lived two or three generations, the first John Maynard having come from England about 1660. My wife's father went to St. Croix when a youth, there met, and, in 1789, married her mother, Mary Durant, born on the Island of St. Croix in 1771, who was a daughter of Thomas Durant, then in business in St. Croix. They remained there till 1800 when they came to Boston, Mass., where the youngest child Cornelia Durant Maynard was born, June 18, 1808. At the age of four her mother died, and she went to Boston to reside with an aunt. After the marriage event of Sally Maynard with Henry Smith, Cornelia went to reside with her, being Mrs. Smith's junior by thirteen years."

After the death of Henry Smith the widow removed to Portland and resided in a one story house that stood on the westerly side of Dow street at next in the rear of the Neal Dow residence, the Smith house standing originally, we are told, on Exchange street, and was used as an insurance office. It had projecting eaves supported by pillars and was painted white the blinds green, forming as a whole an attraction to the passer-by in consequence of its uniqueness, the house having been removed since the death of the widow. Of its appearance on Exchange street or where it was situated we have no knowledge.

In the village cemetery at Saccarappa may be seen a small sized white marble monument inscribed as follows:

HENRY SMITH,
born in Dighton, Mass.,
died July 20, 1853,
aged 70 years.

Blessed are the dead who die in the Lord.

ARIXENE,
his wife,
died Dec. 6, 1820,
aged 27 years.

SALLY M.,
his second wife,
died March 6, 1887,
aged 92 years.

Children of Henry and Arixene (Southgate) Smith:

1—Frederick Southgate, b. in Portland, d. Feb. 14, 1814, aged 8 weeks.
*2—Henry Boynton, (Reverend), b. in Portland, Nov. 21, 1815, m. Elizabeth Lee Allen.
*3—Frederick Southgate, b. in Portland, Jan. 26, 1817, m. Emma Pike.
4—John Coit, d. Feb. 14, 1820, aged 14 months.
*5—Horatio Southgate, b. in Portland, July 28, 1820, m. Susan D. Munroe.

By the last marriage there were no children.

(To be Continued.)

GRANDPA'S SCRAP BOOK

Week of Nov 21-24, 1900.

Dr. ROBERT SOUTHGATE,

Of Dunstan, Scarboro, Ancestors and Descendants.

BY LEONARD B. CHAPMAN.

Part Sixth.

MARY K. SOUTHGATE.

12—Mary King Southgate, born May 6, 1799, daughter of Dr. Robert and Mary (King) Southgate, became, Sept. 9, 1824, the wife of the gifted Grenville Mellen, son of Prentiss Mellen, the first Chief Justice of the Supreme Court of Maine.

Justice Mellen was born in Sterling, Mass., read law, came to Biddeford, then to Portland. In 1817 he represented the State of Massachusetts in the United States Senate at Washington, D. C. His wife was Sally Hudson of Hartford, Conn. He built, in the year of 1807, the large three story house as now seen on the westerly side of State street, Portland, where William Pitt Fessenden, U. S. Senator and U. S. Treasurer resided—a fine, airy specimen of ye olden time with large, neatly kept grounds, now occupied and owned by U. S. District Judge—the Hon. William L. Putnam. Judge Mellen died in 1841, but not in the large house he had constructed, nor in the smaller one on the opposite side of the way, but in Mrs. Jones' celebrated boarding house that stood on the southwesterly corner of Park and Congress streets, which we exhibited in a former article in connection with the name of Capt. Thomas Browne, who occupied the premises a hundred years since.

Grenville Mellen was born in Biddeford June 19, 1799, graduated from Harvard college in 1818, resided in Portland in 1823, removed to North Yarmouth where he remained five years. He was a remarkably bright young man and was the intimate of the first literary men of the country, and his writings had a wide circulation. He was author of many odes, lyrics and books of prose—"Two Hundred Years Ago" being considered his best poem. (See "The Poets of Maine," published in 1888.) We find the following titles to his printed work:

- 1821—"An address delivered before the Maine Charitable Mechanic's Association for the benefit of the Apprentice's Library."
- 1825—"Ode for the celebration of the Battle of Bunker Hill at the monumental stone," June 25, of that year.
- 1825—"Address delivered before the citizens of North Yarmouth on the Anniversary of American Independence." July 4.
- 1826—"The Rest of the Nation"—a poem.
- 1826—"Our Chronicle"—a poem.
- 1828—"Sad Tales, and Good Tales."
- 1828—"The Red Rover."
- 1831—"Ode Sung at North Yarmouth."
- 1832—"The Martyr's Triumph," "Buried Valley" and other poems—300 pages.
- 1836—"The Ruin of a Night"—an ode.
- 1839—"Thoughts on viewing the mansion of Gen. Knox."

Gen. Knox, Washington's Secretary of War, spent his last days on earth and died at Thomaston, this State. The brick building he constructed for his servants is now used as a waiting room by the Knox and Lincoln railroad. We recently visited the spot. The residence stood a few rods southeasterly.

Young Mr. Mellen, it appears, was most deeply devoted to his wife and at her decease and that of her child, so early in life—May 13,1829—three years after the marriage event, a cloud of melancholy came over him from which, it is said, he never fully emerged. He went to New York city, where he died Sept. 6, 1841. His remains were placed in a tomb of St. Mark's church yard, and later in the same year they were removed to the Steward vault under St. Luke's church; and in 1890 were forwarded to Portland by his nephew, Mr. A. H. Gilman, care of Henry Deering, Esq., and were interred by Mr. S. S. Rich, undertaker, in the presence of Mr. Deering and others, in the family lot in the Western cemetery of Portland, where there is a large monument.

The memorial slab of the wife of Grenville Mellen and child may be seen at Dunstan, Scarboro, Inscribed as follows:

The Remains
of
MARY KING SOUTHGATE
MELLEN,
wife of Grenville Mellen,
who died 13th May, A. D., 1829,
aged 30 years.
And of
their infant,
Octavia Grenville Mellen,
who died 23d Sept., A. D., 1828.
Aged 11 months.

The flower and the bud were both beautiful—and they were borne from earth to Heaven before decay had marred either the promise or the bloom.

The monument of Judge Mellen is inscribed as follows:

ERECTED
By the Bar of Maine,
To the memory of
PRENTISS MELLEN,
First Chief Justice of the Supreme Judicial Court of this State.

The east side is inscribed as follows:

Hon. Prentiss Mellen, LL. D.,
Born at Sterling, Massachusetts,
Oct. 11, 1764,
Graduated at Harvard College,
Senator of the United States,
Appointed Chief Justice 1820,
Died Dec. 31, 1840.

Back side:

GRENVILLE MELLEN,
son of
Hon. Prentiss Mellen,
June 19, 1799,
Sept. 6, 1841.

The enclosure is neglected. The iron fence is covered with rust, and three head-stones lie flat. The very apparent neglect everywhere seen throughout the cemetery, while taxpayers's money is so lavishingly spent, if not squandered, on another cemetery of the city is a perpetual reproach upon the city government of Portland, and we hope to see the unfeeling neglect obviated in the near future, and the rules of economy adopted.

(To be Continued.)

Land Marks in the Town of Gray.

April 18, 1809, Samuel Clark, sadler of Gray, father of the late Jacob Clark, sold a lot of land adjoining the Paris road, between the house of the late James Ford and the schoolhouse, extending back the same width now occupied by Mr. Latimer and a one story house now standing and also a sadler shop, then on lot of land now occupied by Mr. Osgood to Michael S. Damon (sadler). October 12, 1815, Mr. Damon conveyed the above described real estate to Merrill Berry, tinsmith. Mr. Berry moved the shop to his home lot and carried on the tin business for many years. The shop was a low one story wood building with a roof projecting in front about 18 inches; under it was a door, also a window. In front of this window Mr. Berry had his work bench. On part of this lot Daniel Berry, his son, built a two story brick house, now occupied by Mr. Latimer.

The schoolhouse referred to was a one story square, wood building, with a four faced roof. It was heated by a wood fire in a fire place on the southern end, and also a box stove within ten feet of the northern end. What became of Mr. Damon I am unable to learn.

S. P. Mayberry.

GRANDPA'S SCRAP BOOK

Week of Nov 28 Dec. 1, 1900.

Dr. ROBERT SOUTHGATE,

Of Dunstan, Scarboro, Ancestors and Descendants.

BY LEONARD B. CHAPMAN.

Part Seventh.

THIRD GENERATION.

1.—Mary Southgate Boyd, b. in Portland, Jan. 20, 1797, eldest child of Joseph C. and Isabella (Southgate) Boyd and a granddaughter of Dr. Robert Southgate, m. Sept. 26, 1820, Dr. John Merrill, b. in Conway, N. H., son of Thomas Merrill and his fourth wife, who was a widow, Elizabeth (Abbott) Cummings. Benjamin Merrill, brother of Dr. John, was a lawyer in Salem, Mass., where he died unmarried. Thomas, the father, seems to have been of a roving nature and died in the autumn of 1789, aged 65 years. [See p. 178, vol. 3, Me. His. and Gen. Recorder.]

Dr. Merrill fitted for college at Exeter Academy, graduated at Harvard, studied medicine under Dr. Warren of Boston and graduated from Harvard Medical school in 1807, and was a member of the Massachusetts Medical Society.

He was appointed guardian of the minor children of Joseph C. Boyd (father to his wife) and occupied the Spring street Boyd residence, the title to which is still in the Merrill name. He was senior warden to St. Luke's church—the only office of which we find a record that he filled. His name appears as one of the founders in 1851.

He d. May 27, 1855, aged 73 yrs., 6 mos. She d. April, 1861, aged 64 years.

The Merrill burial place is in Evergreen cemetery, the lot enclosed by an Arborvitae hedge, within which are various designs, sizes and patterns of lettering memorial stones.

The epitaph on Dr. Merrill's is as follows:

I look for the Resurrection of the dead and the Life of the world to come.

That of his wife, as follows:

Having the testimony of a good conscience in the communion of the Catholic church: in the confidence of a certain faith: in the comfort of a reasonable, religious, and holy home, in favor with thee our God, and in perfect charity with thy word.

Children of Dr. John and Mary S. (Boyd) Merrill.

1—Isabella Southgate, b. July 3, 1823, d. Feb. 6, 1871. She did not marry.
2—A daughter that died young.
*3—Charles Benjamin, (Colonel) b. April 14, 1827, m. Abba Isabella Little.
*4—John Cummings, (doctor) b. Nov. 3, 1831, m. Clara Brooks.
5—Mary Boyd, resides in New York city, unmarried.
5—Robert Southgate Boyd, b. in Portland, August 24, 1804—a brother to the preceding—m. Margaret Ann Hall, int. of m. Oct., 1831, dau. of Joel Hall, a merchant of Portland, and sister to the wife of John Neal, Esq., he a lawyer, editor, author, poet and critic of Portland, also to wife of a Dr. Cummings of Portland. They resided at No. 45 Park street. He d. in Portland Dec. 1, 1877, aged 73 years, 3 mos.; she, May 1, 1881, aged 70 yrs., 4 mos.

We find recorded the names of four children of Robert S. and Margaret A. (Hall) Boyd, as follows:

1—Joel Hall, b. Dec. 9, 1836. Intention of marriage with Frances W. Whitmore recorded Jan. 24, 1862. They resided at No. 45 Park street. He d. Jan. 15, 1894. They had no children. He was a Custom House official several years.
*2—Samuel Stillman, b. May 6, 1838, m. Harriet E. Churchill.
3—Robert Southgate Boyd, b. Dec. 11, 1842. He resided in Boston; m. Elizabeth Wilson, and was burned to death March 17, 1887, in Buffalo, N. Y.
4—William Edward, b. June 4, 1844, d. May 31, 1845.
6—Samuel Stillman Boyd, b. March 27, 1807, son of Joseph C. and Isabella (Southgate) Boyd (and bro. to No. 5, next above) graduated from Bowdoin College in the class of 1826. His name stands at the head of the roll of that year. He then went to Cincinnati where his cousin, Bellamy Storer, was in practice and read law with him two years, from which place he went to Mississippi. In his first case in court he introduced points of law the court had not heard of which the judge sustained thus making him famous in that region. He grew in public favor rapidly, so that, in 1832, at the age of twenty-five, the office of Attorney General was tendered him, but he declined the offer. In 1837 he became a citizen of Natchez, and held for a while a seat on the Supreme court bench of the state. He often met in the forum his classmate at college, Sargent S. Prentiss, one of the most gifted orators Maine has produced, who was born at Gorham, this state. In the knowledge of law, by direct gift, and studious study, in deep reasoning and flights of speech, he was Prentiss' peer. He was in politics a Whig, and in 1852 President Fillmore urged his name for a seat upon the U. S. Supreme court bench. In 1837 he was united in marriage with Miss Catharine Charlotte Wilkins, daughter of Col. James C. Wilkins. He performed a large amount of legal work, retired from active business with a fortune. Indulged in literary pursuits and the pleasures of a large circle of children. A photo of him in the history of Bowdoin College shows a face of finely cut features.

11—Rev. Frederick William Boyd, D. D., b. March 15, 1815, son of Joseph Coffin Boyd and wife Isabella (Southgate) Boyd, and brother to the preceding, entered Bowdoin College, but did not graduate. He went South and Jan. 4, 1844, at Natez, Mo., was united in marriage with Miss Eliza Railey. Just before or during the war of the Rebellion he went abroad and for a while had a parish in Scotland. Returning, he went to the State of Wisconsin, where he was settled at Waukesha as an Episcopalian clergyman. He d. there 188—. They had nine children of whom we have a record of five, as follows:

1—James Railey, D. D., b. Aug. 13, 1836.
2—Frederick William, b. March 4, 1848, m. Oct. 12, 1871, d. Nov. 6, same year.
3—Charles Mayo, b. Dec. 15, 1856.
4—Walter Stewart, b. March 9, 1859.
5—Lloyd Tilghman, b. Dec. 19, 1861.

ROBERT SOUTHGATE.

2.—Rev. Robert Southgate, b. in Portland, January 27, 1807, son of Horatio and Nabby (McLellan) Southgate, and grandson of Dr. Robert Southgate, graduated from Bowdoin College class of 1826; then he attended the Theological Seminary at Andover three years; studied theology a year under Dr. Taylor at New Haven, Conn.; accepted the pastorate of a Congregational church in Woodstock, Vt.; then went to Wethersfield, Conn., where he was settled. From there he removed to Monroe, Michigan, then came back to Ipswich, Mass., where he officiated.

In 1832 he was united in marriage with Miss Mary Frances Swan, dau. of Benjamin Swan of Woodstock, Vt., where he died suddenly while on a visit, February 6, 1873, leaving three living children. The wife died Oct. 2, 1868.

Children of Rev. Robert and Mary Frances (Swan) Southgate:

1—Robert Swan, b. August 7, 1834, m. Dec. 13, 1865, Caroline Louisa Anderson.
2—Horatio, b. Aug. 24, 1836, d. Jan. 30, 1842.
3—Francis Swan, b. May 14, 1843, m. Edward Dana of Boston, Mass., June 6, 1870.
4—Charles McLellan, b. Nov. 18, 1845, m. Elizabeth Virginia Anderson, Nov. 30, 1870. A graduate of Yale College, and a Congregational clergyman at Dedham, Mass., in 1871, where Hugh McLellan Southgate was born Sept. 3, 1871.
4—Frederick Charter, b. January 25, 1852, m. Oct. 31, 1877, Ann French of Woodstock, Vt.

GRANDPA'S SCRAP BOOK

Week of Dec. 5—Dec. 8, 1900.

Dr. ROBERT SOUTHGATE,

Of Dunstan, Scarboro, Ancestors and Descendants.

BY LEONARD B. CHAPMAN.

Part Eighth.

ABIGAIL B. SOUTHGATE.

3.—Abigail Browne Southgate, b. in Portland, Oct. 28, 1809, dau. of Horatio and Abigail (McLellan) Southgate, and granddaughter of Dr. Robert Southgate, m. Jan. 19, 1831, John Barrett, M. D., of Portland.

Dr. Barrett was born in Northfield, Mass., Feb. 21, 1802, and was a son of John Barrett, Esq., and wife Martha Dickinson of that town. Esquire Barrett was a graduate of Harvard College, and became a lawyer.

John Barrett, Jr., graduated from Bowdoin College, class of 1821, and studied medicine under Dr. John Merrill of Portland and Dr. Geo. C. Shattuck of Boston, Mass., then commenced practicing in Portland which was continued till near the time of his death. He resided in the two story house, as now observed, with end to street, unchanged in outward appearances since it was vacated by the doctor, and is the next building southerly of the Methodist meeting house situated upon the easterly side of Chestnut street, Portland.

He was a man of superior ability, social, benevolent and liberal in every respect. When he visited Broad's inn—the fashionable resort of the time —the boy who hitched his horse or set up the pins in the bowling alley was always sure of pay for services rendered. Though sixty years and more have passed since the tamed bear was killed, the bar-room closed, and the latch string of the inn pulled in, there are a few men now who were boys then and who still remember some of the scenes at Broad's. Not long since we listened to a description of a few. The person who related them was a participant. He spoke particularly of Dr. Barrett and said: "He came out once with a small gunning party and invited another boy and me to accompany him to the woods. Soon he fired and a crow fell. We brought him to the doctor who found that the crow had previously lost a foot and the wound had healed. The doctor remarked that while it required a good marksman to bring down a crow it was no credit to a gunner to kill a disabled one, and to obviate the difficulty and so 'beat the crowd' he took out his pocket knife and performed an amputation, gave the boys a ninepence, first charging them not to tell, and thus received the cheers of the party as the champion marksman."

His wife died May 19, 1834; he, April 20, 1842, of consumption, at the residence of his brother in Portland— Charles E. Barrett. They left one child, named Abby Southgate Barrett, who was cared for by her aunt, Mary (Barrett) Storer, a sister to her father. She resides at No. 7 Deering street, Portland, unmarried.

HORATIO SOUTHGATE, Jr.

4.—Rt. Rev. Horatio Southgate, D. D., Jr., b. in Portland, July 5, 1812, son of Horatio and Nabby (McLellan) Southgate, and brother to the preceding, graduated from Bowdoin college, class of 1832, and from Andover Theological seminary in 1836, was ordained as an Episcopal clergyman, which church sent him on a tour of exploration among the Mohammedans of Turkey and Persia, where he spent three years investigating the state of the Oriental churches. Returning he published in 1839 an interesting book of his experiences entitled "A Tour Through Armenia, Kurdistan, etc.," and was ordained priest in New York.

In 1840 he was returned to Constantinople by the Episcopal church and given charge of a large mission, the object of which was to reform the Eastern churches, whose creed is similar to the Episcopalian of this land. Returning in 1844 he was consecrated in St. Peter's church, Philadelphia, Pa., missionary priest for the dependances of the Sultan and returned to the field of his former labors.

In 1846 he received the degree of D. D. from Columbia College, N. Y.

In 1849 he again returned to his home and abandoned missionary work in consequence of the illness of his wife.

He was chosen bishop of the State of California, but declined to accept.

While he was residing in Portland in 1851, and after the death of his wife who was as active in church work as himself, on the 19th day of April, thirteen citizens met in Recabite hall, where the city and county building is seen at this time, for the purpose of forming a Second Protestant Episcopal church. The names were as follows: James McCobb, Henry W. Hersey, Dr. John Merrill, Reuben Ordway, Hon. Josiah S. Little, Edward P. Gerrish, Charles B. Merrill, (son of Dr. John), Edward E. Upham, John T Smith, Ezra C. Andrews, N. Putman Richardson, Frederick Davis, and J. Ambrose Merrill.

At this meeting the parish of St. Luke's was organized with Dr. John Merrill as senior warden. Union hall, entrance on Free street, extending back to Congress, and near the junction of the two streets, in which many jolly good times were participated in by the citizens of Portland and vicinity in ye olden time, was hired and the work of collecting and organizing a church was given Bishop Southgate. He labored a year—the foundation was well laid. He resigned his charge May 1, 1852.

The corner stone of the St. Luke's Cathedral was laid on State street, Aug. 7, 1854, and on July 10, 1855, the building was consecrated. The society is one of the most flourishing in Portland.

The year Bishop Southgate resigned his trust in Portland he was called to the "Church of the Advent" in Boston, where he labored seven years, when he was elected Rector of Zion's church of New York city, where he remained thirteen years, devoting himself in the meantime to literary labors as well as that of the church; retiring from active church work in 1872.

Of his books we find as follows:
    1845. "A Visit to the Syrian Church of Mesopotamia."
    1856. "The War in the East."
    1859. "Practical Directions for Lent."
    1878. "The Cross Above the Crescent," a romance founded on fact.

Numerous sermons, pamphlets, contributions to different religious periodicals, etc.

(To be Continued)

GRANDPA'S SCRAP BOOK

Week of Dec. 19—22, 1900.

Dr. ROBERT SOUTHGATE,

Of Dunstan, Scarboro, Ancestors and Descendants.

BY LEONARD B. CHAPMAN.

Part Tenth.

HENRY B. SMITH.

2.—Rev. Henry Boynton Smith, D.D., LL. D., b. in Portland, Nov. 21, 1815, son of Henry and Arixene (Southgate) Smith, she a granddaughter of Dr. Robert and Mary (King) Southgate, was, from childhood, an invalid, yet he performed a masterly amount of labor. He was, in short, a wonderful man—a graduate of Bowdoin College, tutor, foreign traveler, country parson, newspaper contributor, then editor, book compiler, lecturer, church historian, philosopher, theologian, college Professor, a companion of the most learned of his generation, and yet, his name is seldom heard in the city of his birth or in Westbrook, the town in which his father, with his step-mother, resided, the inscription upon whose monument in the village cemetery at Saccarappa we have presented in a former article.

And why is this state of forgetfulness so complete hereabouts? The youth is told that if he engages in the cause of his country and falls upon the battle field his name will be revered. Where is the "Hall of Fame" for such hereabouts? Are there even official records of names?

In education, where is the record of the deserving? Where is the "Hall of Fame" located?

The trumpet of fame over the name of Prof. Henry Boynton Smith is so seldom heard now-a-days that the name almost sleeps the sleep of utter forgetfulness, but it may yet be reclaimed, and Westbrook, as a municipality, can perform no wiser act than to cause the erection of a statue in front of the Public Library building as an object lesson of a public character of a worthy citizen of whom in original thought and literary labor few only are his peers. His printed sermons, essays, lectures, newspaper editorials and books compiled by him, and all while in feeble health, are too numerous for us to notice only in a general way,—a reference only to a few of the most salient points in

Continued:

his career can we give.

When a mere child, and before his parents were aware of the fact, he could read with wonderful accuracy. His perceptions were quick, and his memory extremely retentive. At the age of thirteen he had assigned him for a composition the subject:—

"Which has the most influence in society, wealth or knowledge?"

John Neal, Esq., was present when the composition was read, and so struck was he with the ability displayed that Mr. Neal called at the lad's home and accused the parents of assisting but was assured that the lad performed the whole labor unaided, and furthermore, it was the original, and not a copy of the draft, that was read.

At the age of fourteen he kept a journal of his personal experiences, and in it is an account of his admission to Bowdoin College, then under fifteen years of age, and on the 23d day of July, 1830, he writes: "Here I am up at five o'clock, sitting at my desk in my chamber, writing a preface to it—[his journal.]

It appears his father was in religious belief a Unitarian who attended Rev. Ichabod Nichols' meeting at the Portland First Parish and young Smith viewed as irrational the doctrines of total depravity and spiritual change, but a "revival" in college, while a student there, changed his views upon theological matters and he not only accepted the light of the "revival" but presented criticisms for publication upon "Scientific Tracts," entitled—"Moral Reform," which were accepted, approved and praised by the radical Orthodox of the Congregational church, Dr. Cummings inviting him to contribute to the "Christian Mirror," the Congregational paper of the state. His college graduation part was entitled—"The Power of the Gospel," which was declared a masterly production.

In the month of October, 1834, he entered the Theological Seminary at Andover, in order to prepare himself for the ministry, but commencing study at six in the morning and continuing till eleven at night soon produced a prostrating illness which required him to leave Andover, but he resumed study at Bangor.

Finishing at Bangor he became a tutor in Greek and Librarian at Bowdoin, aged but twenty.

In 1837, in May, he was a visitor at Philadelphia, and witnessed the scenes of rupture in the Presbyterian Church General Assembly, the healing of which division he was more instrumental than any other person in producing, thirty years later, in the same city and in the same church edifice.

At Bowdoin College, March 4, 1837, he wrote, in referring to a seven weeks' vacation spent "at home" [Saccarappa] as follows:

"I enjoyed myself in reading, writing, talking, laughing—and preaching —for [Rev.] Mr. Searle was part of the time disabled, and I filled his place. [Rev. Mr. Searle was the Congregational clergyman at Saccarappa.] I like such extemporaneous trials for myself. I think the discipline does me good, and keeps my heart warm in the great work to which I have devoted myself wholly," etc.

Then he spent a period of two or three years in Europe, the state of his health forbidding a continuance of his theological studies in this country, returning and arriving July 1, 1840.

The following is from his diary:
Walnut Hill, [North Yarmouth,]
Me., Sept. 11, 1840.

"Father was quite urgent that I should attend the Association [of Congregational ministers] and get a license, so I went to work on my sermon, and in about five hours had written one that I thought might do, for, though in point of style it had many defects, yet it was sound in doctrine, scriptural, presented the grand reconciling truths of our dispensation; the text, I Cor. 1. 30, —'For of Him are ye in Christ Jesus, who of God is made unto us wisdom, and righteousness, and sanctification, and redemption.'

"Well, on Tuesday morning I went to New Gloucester, [Me.] where the Association met. The examination came on after dinner. They found me orthodox and gave me my commission. More than twenty ministers were present."

It appears that he had kept school at Walnut Hill and was there to preach to the people when he wrote the above, and added as follows:

"I had four invitations to preach this Sunday and five for the next but have refused all, for this I came here. I know the people. A beautiful new church is here."

Dec. 29, 1842, he was ordained as a Congregational minister at West Amesbury, Mass., and assumed the pastoral duties of the position. Of the examination one who was present remarked: "It seemed rather doubtful whether he was before the council or the council before him."

Oct. 10, 1847, he preached his farewell sermon at West Amesbury. During the time he was there he not only interested himself in local improvements of the neighborhood, but delivered many college lectures before college and other societies.

In 1850, at the age of 36, the chair of Church history was tendered him by the Union Theological Seminary of New York city, which, after much deliberation, he accepted. His first lecture in that institution "commanded the admiration of Christians throughout the land."

In 1853 there was added to his labors in the Seminary the chair of Systematic Theology, the duties of the two positions he performed till June, 1855.

In 1858 the editorship of the Presbyterian Quarterly Review published in Philadelphia, was tendered him, he having become a Presbyterian, which position he accepted in addition to his school cares—and he made a lively denominational paper.

In 1859 he again visited Europe, landing in New York on the return trip, Sept. 27, of that year.

His "Tables of Church History" were now printed, a work of great magnitude, containing more than thirty thousand references, and he smiled over a rich harvest of public approval of his labors on this branch of his work. One critic wrote: "The Tables are extraordinarily rich. It indeed has been a most laborious task, requiring a great deal of reflection, to present a general view of the rich contents of history, sacred and profane, you have done."

Of his writings during the War of the Rebellion in favor of the cause of the Union, George Bancroft, the historian, said: "I read nothing in our contest more instructive and more satisfactory."

Of an oration delivered at a Middletown, [Ct..] commencement, the New York Tribune said: "Profundity altogether too deep for a popular audience;" to which he added—"so much for trying to enlighten people!"

"Amid all his work in the Seminary and in the church his literary labors were manifold. His pen was never idle. He was constantly at work on translations, reviews of books, sometimes elaborate articles for different periodicals."

(To be continued.)

256 GRANDPA'S SCRAP BOOK

Week of Dec. 12—15, 1900.

Dr. ROBERT SOUTHGATE,
Of Dunstan, Scarboro, Ancestors and Descendants.

BY LEONARD B. CHAPMAN.

Part Ninth.

Rt. Rev. Horatio Southgate was twice united in marrige, first, January 30, 1839, with Miss Elizabeth S. Browne, dau. of William and Octavia (Southgate) Browne, he a son of Rev. Thomas Browne of Stroudwater Parish, she, dau. of Dr. Robert Southgate.

Hugh McLellan's wife was a daughter of Rev. Thomas Browne, and Horatio Southgate, Esq., the father of Rt. Rev. Horatio Southgate, Jr., and son of Dr. Southgate, married for his first wife Hugh McLellan's daughter. All of this, however, has appeared in former articles.

The Rev. Mr. Southgate's first wife, b. in Portland, May, 1814, d. in Portland August 10, 1850, aged 36 years. Her memorial slab may be seen in the Dunstan cemetery. He m. second in New York city, Dec. 28, 1864, Sarah Elizabeth Hutchinson, dau. of Hiram and Mary Ann Hutchinson of that place. He d. at Astoria, Long Island, N. Y., April 12, 1894, aged 85 years.

Children of Rt. Rev. Horatio, Jr., and Elizabeth S. (Browne) Southgate, all born in Constantinople, Turkey:

1—Horatio, April 1, 1841, d. Jan. 29, 1854.
*2—Harriet Augusta, Oct. 19, 1842, m. Nell Ferguson Graham, M. D.
3—Clara Sophia, b. Feb. 28, 1844, d. Jan. 26, 1849.
4—Edward, April 18, 1846, graduated from ———— Theological Seminary, entered Church of Rome 1873, now a Priest in charge of St. Mary's Parish, Brianton, Md.
5—Octavia, b. Jan. 1, 1848, "Sister Octavia," St. Gabriel's school, Peekskill-on-Hudson, N. Y.
6—Frederic, July 29, 1850, m. Renie Caroline Hutchinson.

Children by second wife:

7—Hiram Horatio, b. in New York, Oct. 25, 1865.
8—Richard King, b. in Astoria, April 29, 1867.
9—Henry, b. in Nyac, Oct. 23, 1868.
10—William, b. Locust Grove, Long Island, N. Y., June 27, 1870.
11—Hutchinson, b. Morrisonia, N. Y., Jan. 10, 1872.
12—Mariam Agnes, b. Harlem, Sept. 9, 1873.
13—Charles Joseph, b. Feb. 29, 1875, d. Falls Church, Va., Feb. 17, 1878.

FREDERIC SOUTHGATE.

5.—Rev. Frederic Southgate, b. in Portland, Oct. 23, 1814, son of Horatio and Nabby (McLellan) Southgate and brother to the preceding. graduated from Bowdoin College, class of 1835. It is said of him that he was not a brilliant man but a man of solid sense and a practical thinker. He studied medicine and having taken his degree went to Texas. In 1841 he settled in Burlington, Iowa Territory. Then he changed his calling for that of the ministry and went to the southern part of Illinois. His next move was to take charge of an Episcopal Parish at Edwardsville, and died at Quincy, Ill., Feb. 29, 1844, aged but 30 years. He was united but a few months before in marriage with Miss Mary, dau. of Eleazer Moore, of Gardiner, this state. The widow survived till this year—a period of 56 years—all the while clinging fondly to the name of her departed husband, even her last request being that his name might be coupled with hers in the opening paragraph of her obituary She died in Muscatine, Iowa.

The inscription upon the cross, marking her grave, is as follows:

MARY M. SOUTHGATE.
wife of
Rev. Frederic Southgate,
Born Jan. 10, 1817,
Died Apr. 7, 1900.

WILLIAM S. SOUTHGATE.

13.—Rev. William Scott Southgate, b. in Portland, Apr. 10, 1831, son of Horatio and Elizabeth (Neal) Southgate, and brother to the preceding. graduated from Bowdoin College, class of 1851, grad. Theological seminary 1855, ordained Deacon at Portland same year; ordained Priest at Portland 1856; Assistant, church of the Advent, Boston, Mass., Sept. '55 to Oct. 27, 1856; Rector St. Michael's church, Brattleboro, Vt., Nov. '56 to April 1860; Rector St. Michel's Litchfield, Conn., Nov. 1, 1860 to Dec. 27, 1863. From Jan. 1864 to Sept. 1869, traveled and sojourned in various parts of England, Mexico and the United States. Oct. 3, 1869, became Rector of St. Ann's, Annapolis, Md.

While a citizen of Maine the record of the literary productions of Rev. Scott Southgate, D. D. is as follows:

1850. Two works of fiction.
1853. "History of Scarboro, Maine."
1855. "Church in the Catacombs."

He m. Nov. 1, 1858, Miss Harriet Randolph Talcott, dau. of Andrew and Harriet Talcott, b. in Philadelphia, Pa., Nov. 9, 1835, d. Annapolis, Md., Aug. 13, 1886.

He departed this life at Annapolis, Md., on Whit Sunday, (May 21) 1899. The newspapers of the place contained long obituaries. The stores closed, bells were rung, and a large concourse of people of all classes attended his obsequies.

Children of Rev. William S. and Harriet R. (Talcott) Southgate:

1—Randolph, b. Aug. 10, 1860, at Brattleboro, Vt., civil engineer.
2—William Scott, b. Jan. 2, 1862.
3—Mary King, twin, at Litchfield, Conn.; she d. May 8, 1863; he a sailor in the British merchant service.
4—Grace Helen, b. June 19, 1863, at Litchfield, Vt., m. June 21, 1883, Abram V. Zane, 1st. ass't Engineer U. S. Navy.
5—Frances, b. Feb. 14, 1865, at Tancenbagy, Mexico.
6—Henry Talcott, b. June 19, 1868, at Brattleboro, Vt., d. Feb. 9, 1869, at Fernandina, Fla.
7—Eleanor, b. July 18, 1869, at Washington, D. C., d. Aug. 10, same year.
8—Anita Mary, b. June 18, 1871, at Annapolis, Md.
9—Grace Talcott, b. July 25, 1873, at Annapolis, Md.
10—Frederic Charles, b. Sept. 15, 1879, d. June 20, 1883., Annapolis, Md.

JOHN B. SOUTHGATE.

14.—Rev. John Barrett Southgate, b. in Portland, July 25, 1833, son of Horatio and Elizabeth (Neal) Southgate and brother to the preceding. graduated from Bowdoin College, 1853, at the head of his class, and delivered the English oration at the commencement of 1856 as a candidate for the degree of A. M. A year later he graduated from the Theological School at New York, with great credit—"the most learned and finished writer and thinker of the school." He was ordained at Portland, July 8, of that year, as Deacon. In 1857 he was Rector of Trinity Parish, Lewiston, this state. March 20, 1859, he was ordained at Portland by Bishop Burgess to the Priesthood and took charge of St. John's Church at Wheeling, Va. His health failed, he returned to his father's home in Scarboro, officiating a part of the time at Trinity Church, Saco. He died of consumption February 7, 1862, aged 28 years. Obituary notices of considerable length appeared in the New York Church Journal, the Boston Christian Witness and other religious journals.

A poem of his may be seen in the volume of poems printed in 1888 at Portland, page 487, which volume is entitled "The Poets of Maine."

His memorial slab may be seen at Dunstan.

To be continued.

GRANDPA'S SCRAP BOOK

Week of Dec. 26-29, 1900

Dr. ROBERT SOUTHGATE

Of Dunstan, Scarboro, Ancestors and Descendants.

BY LEONARD B. CHAPMAN.

Part Eleventh.

Prof. Smith, in the spring of 1854, purchased the residence numbered thirty-four, East 25th street, New York city where he ever after resided till his death. In 1864, George Bancroft, the historian, proposed a donation to pay off the mortgage, saying he would contribute $500, and June 16th, of that year, a bank check of $5,100 was sent the Professor. Mr. Bancroft pronouncing publicly, Prof. Smith "the most learned man in his line ever produced."

At Hudson, Ohio, July 14, the same year, Prof. Smith wrote: "This college made me LL. D. yesterday!"

Of notices of him recorded the previous year we select the following:

After preaching in Portland, he went out on Monday to Prout's Neck, Scarboro, a favorite resort of his, ten miles distant. "He took his family one day, to the old home of his grandfather where his uncle, Hon. Horatio Southgate, still resided. (We have noticed the place.) With the eager delight of a boy he went round with them, up stairs and down, and into the large barn, to the garden and orchard, to the fir-grove (hemlock) and the clear, flowing brook, and above it the picturesque ledge of rock cut with the initials of many a household name. After the death of his uncle, the following year, all these passed into the hands of strangers."

In 1869, accompanied by his wife and son, on the 24th of February, in extreme feebleness he again sailed for Europe, returning, landed in New York, Oct. 14, 1870.

He took special pleasure in fitting up the library and study of his New York home. Of it Rev. Marion R. Vincent, D. D., wrote as follows:

"Ah! those hours in the library! Who that has enjoyed them can ever lose their fragrance? Who can forget that room, walled and doubled walled with books, the baize-covered desk in the corner by the window, loaded with the fresh philosophic and theologic treasures of the European pens, and the little figure in the long gray wrapper seated there, the figure so frail and slight that, as one of his friends remarked, it seems as though it would not be much of a change for him to take on a spiritual body; the beautifully moulded brow, crowned with its thick, wavy, sharply-parted iron gray hair, the strong, aquiline profile, the restless shifting in his chair, the nervous pulling of the hand at the mustache, as the stream of talk widened and deepened, the occasional start from his seat to pull down a book or to search for a pamphlet, how inseparably these memories twine themselves with those of high debate and golden speech and converse on the themes of Christian philosophy and Christian experience."

Prof. Henry Boynton Smith m. Jan. 5, 1843, Elizabeth Lee Allen, born at Hanover, N. H., Sept. 3, 1817, dau. of William Allen, D. D., who served as President of Dartmouth and Bowdoin Colleges and who finally settled and died at Northampton, Mass., Aug. 16, 1868, and where his remains were interred. Prof. Smith died at his New York residence February 7, 1877; she, in Lakewood, N. J., Dec. 5, 1898, at the home of their daughter—the wife of Rev. Charles H. McLellan, D. D.

Of the much that was said at his funeral exercises which were holden on the 9th of February in the New York Madison Square Presbyterian Church we can present but a few lines from the addresses of Rev. Dr. Prentiss as follows:

"Should the story of his noble career ever be fully told, his name will be enrolled, by general consent, among those of the most useful and most remarkable men of his generation * * * * Our country has produced no theologian who combined in a higher degree the best learning, literary and philosophical culture, wise, discriminating thought, and absolute devotion to Christ and His kingdom."

In the ancient Northampton, Mass., cemetery may be seen upon a dark stone transported from his native State of Maine, an inscription that read as follows:

In Pace Domini.
Sacred to the Dear and
Honored Memory of
HENRY BOYNTON SMITH, D. D.,
LL. D.,
1815—1877.

"In Christ Jesus who of God is made unto us Wisdom and Righteousness and Sanctification and Redemption."

The epitaph is from 1 Cor. 1. 30,—the text of his first sermon, which was delivered in 1840, at Walnut Hill, North Yarmouth.

Children of Prof. Henry B. and Elizabeth E. (Allen) Smith:

* *1—Arixene Southgate (Smith,) b. in New York, Nov. 2, 1843, m. Col. Charles W. Woolsey.
* *2—Maria Malleville Wheelock (Smith,) b. Dec. 15, 1845, m. Rev. Charles H. McLellan.
* *3—William Allen (Smith,) b. August 16, 1848, m. Zilpha I. W. Cutter.
* *4—Henry Goodwin (Smith,) b. January 8, 1860, m. Helen R. Larman.

FREDERICK S. SMITH.

3.—Frederick Southgate Smith, b. in Portland January 26, 1817, son of Henry and Arixene (Southgate) Smith, a brother to the preceding and grandson of Dr. Robert Southgate. m. Emma Pike. He was a civil engineer, held office in the Patent Office at Washington, D. C., but resigned on account of ill health and died at the home of his wife's family in Northern Pennsylvania Oct. 17, 1861, of consumption, and his remains "lie in a little wood-sheltered nook of the farm on the border of the wood—a beautiful spot. The bearers carried him there relieving each other on the way. At the grave they sang a resurrection hymn." He is alluded to as a college-room companion of his brother, Henry B., at Bowdoin College. He left a son.

HORATIO S. SMITH.

5.—Horatio Southgate Smith, M. D., b. in Portland July 28, 1820, a brother to the preceding and child of Henry and Arixene (Southgate) Smith, was a graduate of Dartmouth College in 1840, and from Bowdoin Medical School of 1843. He was a practicing physician in Brooklyn, N. Y. He married in Boston, Mass., May 16, 1849, Miss Susan Dwight Munroe, dau. of Edmund and Sophia (Sewall) Wood. He died in Brooklyn, N. Y., April 26, 1876. The widow resides on Appleton street, Cambridge, Mass.

Children, born in Brooklyn, N. Y.:

* *1—Henry Maynard (Smith,) b. March 25, 1850, m. Alice M. Brown.
* *2—Edmund Munroe (Smith,) b. Dec. 8, 1854, m. Gertrude Hinde-Roper.
* 3—Alice Durant (Smith,) Dec. 6, 1859.
* 4—Susan Elizabeth (Smith,) Oct. 9, 1863.
* *5—Sophia Munroe (Smith,) Oct. 17, 1865.

(To be continued.)

GRANDPA'S SCRAP BOOK

Week of Jan. 2 5, 1901.

Dr. ROBERT SOUTHGATE,

Of Dunstan, Scarboro, Ancestors and Descendants.

BY LEONARD B. CHAPMAN.

Part Twelfth.

FOURTH GENERATION.

Col. Charles Benjamin Merrill, A. M., LL. D., b. in Portland, April 14, 1827, third child of Dr. John and Mary (Boyd) Merrill, and great-grandson of Dr. Robert Southgate, m. Sept. 24, 1856, Miss Abba Isabella Little, dau. of Hon. Josiah S. Little, a lawyer and politician of Portland. He graduated from Bowdoin College, class of 1847, and from Harvard law school in 1849, when he located in Portland as a lawyer. He was in politics a radical Democrat, but enlisted in the Union army and served in the 17th Maine Regiment as Lt. Colonel.

After the war he resumed his practice of law in his native city, engaging also in manufactory, his family residing in the town of Gorham, this state, from which place he removed to the Boyd residence on Spring street, Portland. He was a member of the city government, a school committeeman, also warden of St. Luke's church. He was a man of fine physique, neat in dress, social and benevolent.

He d. April 5, 1891, she, same year.

The representatives of the Grand Army of the Republic place each year the miniature flag at his grave in the Dr. John Merrill enclosure at Evergreen cemetery. Nothing upon his cemetery monument indicates his rank in the army.

Children:

1—Josiah Little, b. Feb. 6, 1859, d. August 24, 1859.
2—Mary Southgate, b. April 8, 1861, d. August 29, 1861.
3—Isabella Little, b. April 5, 1862, d. May 25, 1894.
4—Charles Putnam, b. Sept. 18, 1864.
5—John Fuller Appleton, b. February 10, 1866. He graduated at Andover in 1855; at Yale in 1889; studied law in the office of Hon. Wm. L. Putnam, Portland, two years, spent a year at the Harvard Law school and was admitted to the Cumberland County bar in 1892; is now a lawyer in Portland. He was a member of the City Council in 1896, and an Alderman in 1898-99. He is now a member of the school committee from Ward four.
6—Daniel Chamberlain, b. January 11, 1868, d. April 20, 1868.
7—Alec Boyd, b. Feb. 19, 1869, d. June 22, 1869.
8—Richard King, b. June 21, 1871, d. July 28, 1872.

JOHN C. MERRILL.

John Cummings Merrill, M. D., b. in Portland Nov. 3, 1831, son of Dr. John and Mary (Boyd) Merrill and bro. to the preceding, graduated at Bowdoin College, class of 1851, studied medicine and received his diploma in 1854 at College of Physicians and Surgeons, of New York.

When the war of the Rebellion came on he was located in the South and served as a surgeon in the Confederate army. Returning to Portland at the close of hostilities, October 18, 1886, he was united in marriage with Miss Clara Brooks. He d. Aug. 8, 1900, and was interred on the burial lot of his father. Two children:

Mary Boyd, b. June 15, 1887, d. Nov. 13, 1887.

SAMUEL S. BOYD.

Samuel Stillman Boyd, Esq., b. May 6, 1838, second child of Robert Southgate and wife, Margaret Ann (Hall) Boyd, and grandson of Joseph C. and Isabella (Southgate) Boyd, graduated from Bowdoin College, class of 1860, read law in the office of Judge Shepley of Portland and settled in St. Louis, Mo. He m. Oct. 5, 1863, Miss Harriet E. Churchill of Portland. He was a lawyer and died in St. Louis, March 5, 1883. The widow removed to Portland, where she resides.

Children of Samuel S. and Harriet E. (Churchill) Boyd, born in St. Louis, Mo:

1—Louie, b. May 12, 1865—resides in Portland.
2—Margaret, b. Feb. 13, 1868—resides in Portland.
3—James, b. Aug. 19, 1871—a civil engineer in Boston, Mass.
4—Samuel Stillman, b. Feb. 12, 1874 is with the Boston Elevated railroad company.
5—Alice Stillman, b. Sept. 9, 1875—resides in Portland.
6—Robert Southgate, b. May 6, 1879—a clerk in Boston, Mass.

HARRIET A. SOUTHGATE.

Harriet Augusta Southgate (Graham,) b. in Constantinople, Turkey, Oct. 19, 1842, second child of Rt. Rev. Horatio and Elizabeth S. (Browne) Southgate, Jr., and great granddaughter of Dr. Robert Southgate, engaged as a hospital nurse in the Union army, war of the rebellion, where she met Neil Ferguson Graham, M. D., who was acting as a surgeon. They were married in the month of April, 1865.

Dr. Graham by birth is a Scotch-Canadian, who received his medical education in Cleveland, Ohio. He was, first, connected with the Ohio 12th Regiment of volunteers, then served as a hospital surgeon at Harper's Ferry, Va. After the marriage event he went to the state of Virginia and settled at West End. He is in practice in Washington, D. C.; a Professor in Surgery in Howard University and a member of the Examining Board for pension applicants.

Children:

1—Elizabeth Browne, b. March 2, 1867, m. June 20, 1899, Olaf Sangstad.
2—Mary Du Bois, b. May 18, 1871, m. Sept. 8, 1900, Silas Henry Kingsley.
3—Neil Duncan, b. Sept. 22, 1874.
4—Clara Octavia, b. April 2, 1878.
5—Harriet Ferguson, b. June 27, 1880.
6—Horatio Southgate, b. Oct. 30, 1882, d. Sept. 5, 1883.

Children of PROF. HENRY B. SMITH.

1.—Arixene Southgate Smith, b. in New York, Dec. 15, 1845, a granddaughter of Henry and Arixene (Southgate) Smith and great granddaughter of Dr. Robert Southgate, m. April 25, 1857, Col. Charles William Woosley of New York, now residing at Ashville, N. C. He went in the Union army, through the war of the Rebellion, at one time was a staff officer. Since his marriage he has spent, with his family, most of the time abroad.

2.—Maria Mallevia Wheelock Smith, b. Dec. 15, 1845, a sister to the preceding, m. June 18, 1874, Rev. Charles H. McLellan, D. D., of Wheeling, Va., now residing at Lakewood, N. J. He is a graduate of Princeton University.

3.—William Allen Smith, b. Aug. 16, 1848, a brother to the preceding, m. Dec. 31, 1874, Zilpha Ingraham Williams Cutter, dau. of Hon. J. C. Cutter, and granddaughter of Hon. Reuel Williams, both of Augusta, this state. Mr. Williams represented his state in the U. S. Senate from 1837 to 1843, as a Democrat, when he resigned. Mr. Williams' dau., Helen A., m. Aug. 24, 1837, John Tyler Gilman, M. D., a much esteemed and successful practitioner of Portland, who was born in Exeter, N. H.

William Allen Smith, graduated from the New York School of Mines, and devoted his life to mining interests. He d. in New York city, March 24, 1899.

4.—Henry Goodwin Smith, D. D., b. January 8, 1860, bro. to the preceding, and youngest child of Prof. Henry B. Smith, m. Helen Randolph Farman, dau. of Dr. Samuel R. Farman of Jersey City Heights. He graduated from Amherst College and Union Theological Seminary, and is a Professor of Systematic Theology in Lane Seminary, Cincinnati, Ohio.

Children of DR. HORATIO SOUTHGATE SMITH.

(A brother to Prof. Henry Boynton Smith.)

1.—Prof. Henry Maynard Smith, b. in Brooklyn, N. Y., March 25, 1850, in 1872 assumed the name of Munroe, his mother's maiden name. He m. at Chester Hill, Philadelphia, Pa., Sept. 12, 1882, Alice M. Brown, dau. of John E. and Jane Emeline (Farmer) Smith. He is a dean in the Scientific school of Columbia University, New York.

CONTINUED:

Children:

a—Eleanor Roberts Munroe Smith, b. at Pelham, N. Y., Aug. 22, 1883.

b—Robert Malcolm Munroe Smith, b. at Litchfield, Ct., Aug. 3, 1894.

2.—Edmund Munroe Smith, b. in Brooklyn, N. Y., Dec. 8, 1854, (son of Dr. Horatio S. Smith,) m. in Philadelphia, Pa., April 17, 1890, Gertrude Hindekoper, dau. of Gen. H. T. Hindekoper. They have one dau. b. at Easthampton, Long Island, N. Y., June 6, 1891. He is a Professor with his brother, Henry Maynard Smith, at Columbia University, New York.

5.—Sophia Munroe Smith, b. in Brooklyn, N. Y., Oct. 17, 1865, a sister to the preceding, m. at Cambridge, Mass., Dec. 19, 1887, William Coombs Codman, Jr.

Children:

1—William Coombs, 3d, b. Dec. 19, 1888.

2—Constance, b. Feb. 7, 1891.

3—Horatio Southgate, b.; d. young.

(To be continued.)

(Flushing is reached by ferry boats over East river at the foot of 34th street and railroad. It is situated upon the southerly end of Long Island and six miles distant from New York. It is a farming and residence district, and its buildings are constructed almost wholly of wood. It has no shipping, being inland. It possesses many fine Colonial buildings, the Quaker meeting and Bowne house near by being each over two hundred years of age. Nearly all the shops are located upon one side of Main street, which is some six rods wide. L. B. C.)

GRANDPA'S SCRAP BOOK

Week of Jan. 9-12, 1901

Dr. ROBERT SOUTHGATE.

Of Dunstan, Scarboro, Ancestors and Descendants.

BY LEONARD B. CHAPMAN.

A continuation of Part Third of Oct. 31—Nov. 3, 1900.

WALTER BOWNE.

(Whose wife was Eliza Southgate.)

Mayor in 1828-'29-'30-'31-'32.

From Valentine's "Manual of the Corporation of the City of New York, 1863."—Contains also a portrait of Bowne. Contributed to this paper by Victor H. Pallsits, Ass't Librarian, Lenox Library, New York city.

The first of the name of Bowne, in this country, was John Bowne, a native of Mattock, in Derbyshire, England, who emigrated to Boston in 1649, in the twenty-second year of his age. His origin was humble, his habits plain, and his manners unaffected. He was endowed with a strong mind and sound judgment, whilst his avocations as a farmer tended to add to his physical powers of endurance. Having removed to Flushing, Long Island, he attended, at first from curiosity, some of the Quaker meetings in that town. Struck with the simplicity of their worship he invited them to his home, and next became, in the course of the year 1662, a member of their society. His house, thenceforth, became the headquarters of their sect. Information of this fact being communicated to Governor Stuyvesant, who, in common with many of the other sects of Christians, was violently inimical to the Quakers, he ordered Bowne to be arrested, and fined him twenty-five pounds, to be committed until that sum was paid. Bowne suffered himself to be committed to prison, as his conscience prevented his paying a penalty, however trifling, for exercising the form of worship which he considered a duty. Continuing his resistance to the demands of the authorities, he was warned that he would be sent across the seas if he did not submit. This threat did not, however, prevail with him, and he was accordingly shipped for Holland, whither Stuyvesant wrote in strong terms complaining of the obstinacy of the man, as a disturber of the peace and a contumacious subject, who was thus banished, in the hope that others in the same course might be discouraged. On his arrival in Holland, Bowne made his case known to the West India Company, and found there a more charitable disposition towards the sect. They refused to recognize the justice of Stuyvesant's course; and, on the contrary, dispatched a missive to Stuyvesant, severely censuring the course pursued by him, advising him that, in the youth of the colony, its rulers ought rather to encourage than check the population of the country; the consciences of men ought to be unshackled, so long as they continue moderate, peaceable, inoffensive, and not hostile to the government. The persecutions of the Quakers ceased from this time but the affections of that people were alienated from the Dutch Government of the colony after that period. From this individual were descended numerous families of that name, inhabiting Long Island and the neighborhood.

From James Bowne, a farmer at Flushing, was descended the subject of this sketch, who was born in the year 1770. Upon arriving at years of maturity, he engaged in the hardware business in this city, which he followed with success for a number of years, at the corner of Burling slip and Water street, in company with Richard T. Hallet. Mr. Bowne, upon his retirement from business, became a prominent politician of the Democratic party. He represented this city in the state senate for three successive terms, and was appointed Mayor by the Common Council in the year 1827, continuing for the four succeeding years. Mr. Bowne was one of the Commissioners appointed by Congress for the erection of the Custom-house, which, we believe, was the last public duty of importance performed by him. He was noted in public and private for scrupulous and exact dealings, descending to the smallest details; and, by his successful business operations, acquired a large estate. Mr. Bowne died at his residence in Beekman street, in this city, on the 31st day of August, 1846, in the seventy-sixth year of his age.

In the time of his mayoralty the city contained about 200,000 inhabitants.

GRANDPA'S SCRAP BOOK

Week of Jan. 16-19, 1901

NINETY-FOUR YEARS AGO.

A School-boy's Life in the Town of Gorham, Me.

BY LEONARD B. CHAPMAN.

(Through failure to receive material of which to construct the last part of our Walter Bowne article, which appeared last week, and which will close the Dr. Southgate series to be followed by two or three on the King family of Dunstan, S arboro, we are compelled to substitute this week. And in this connection we will state that it is proposed to reprint at the conclusion the whole in pamphlet form with as many halftone cuts as can be obtained.)

John Siemons, whose name appears at the foot of the copy of the ancient document here presented, was born September 10, 1787, in the two story dwelling house situated upon the southerly side of the so-called Buxton road, in Westbrook, some over a mile from Stroudwater village, which is now owned by and is the residence of Mr. Elmer E. Cummings of the Portland firm of Cummings Brothers. The house has recently been renovated and thoroughly repaired and a saw mill constructed on the farm where stood a cloth-finishing mill a century ago.

John Siemons was the second child of Robert and Sally (Rounds) Siemons, he, of Stroudwater, she, of Providence, R. I. The parents were married Sept. 10, 1784. The son lacked two days of being nineteen years of age when he copied in a neat, round hand the "strait-jacket" rules of the Congregational church school, which paper has been with others of historical value saved by the Siemons family. The student of 1806 at Gorham became a member of the merchant marine and rapidly rose in rank till he became a commander, filling, however, an untimely grave Feb. 16, 1811, at Demarara, in consequence of the ravages of yellow fever. Verily, school life has changed since then.

LAWS AND REGULATIONS OF GORHAM ACADEMY.

Qualifications for Admittance.

No person shall become a member of Gorham Academy without sufficient evidence that he is of a good moral character. No student shall be admitted for a less term than one quarter, the price of tuition for which shall be paid in advance. No student shall be admitted under ten years of age, none without being able to write joining hand, and read English correctly.

COURSE STUDIES.

Students in this institution will receive instruction in any or all the following Branches viz: reading, writing, arithmetic, English grammar and composition, speaking, geography, the use of the Globes, mathematics and the Latin and Greek Languages. The Preceptor will also instruct them weekly in the doctrines and precepts of the christian religion.

In teaching the above branches the following Books shall be used together with such others as the Trustees, together with the Preceptor, shall see fit to introduce viz: the Bible which shall be read daily previous to morning and evening prayers, beauties of the bible. Columbian Orator, Enfields Speaker, Walshe's Arithemetic, Murray's grammar and Exercises, Blair abridged, Morris' Geography, Webber's Mathematics, Moor's Navigator Adams' Latin and the Gloucester Greek grammar, the Lattin primmer, Bigalow's introduction to making Lattin together with such classical authors in both Languages, as required for admission into any of the neighboring Colleges, the Worcester catechism, and Mason on self knowledge.

HOUR OF ATTENDANCE.

From the first of April to the first of October from six to half pas seven, and from nine to twelve A. M. and from three to six P. M. During the remaining part of the year from half past eight to half twelve A. M. and from two to five P. M.

VACATIONS.

There shall be three vacations annually viz: the first, of three weeks, commencing the Wednesday previous to the third Wednesday in August; the second, of three, from the first Wednesday in January; and the third, of two weeks, from the last Wednesday in May. If any student shall fail to return punctually at the close of the vacation, he shall, if a minor produce a written certificate from those who have the charge of his education specifying the reasons of his absence.

No student whose connections do not reside in Town shall on any pretence leave Town or absent himself from any stated exercises of this institution without leave first obtained of the Preceptor. When any student whose connections do reside in Town is detained from attendance in the Academy he shall bring a written excuse from his Parent or Guardian with the reason of his non-attendance.

When any student shall come into the Academy after the exercises have begun he shall be considered as tardy. At the tolling of the Bell every student shall repair to his seat, which he shall not quit, without permission from the preceptor. Silence and strict attention are required of every student during the hours of study, and especially in presence of the Trustees and during religious exercise.

To prevent noise and confusion, it is expected that every student be provided with everything necessary to the advantagious prosecution of his studies.

That the minds of the students may not be diverted from those pursuits, which ought during the hours of study engage their individual attention, no prints, playthings, Books of Amusement, &c, shall be brought into the Academy under penalty of forfeiture.

If any student shall wantonly, carelessly, or maliciously injure the buildings or property of the Academy or the property of his fellow students, he shall make such compensation as the Preceptor shall deem adequate.

It is strictly enjoined upon the students to abstain from all insulting or abusive language, and every thing which may tend to disturb the peace and harmony which ought ever to be found among those who are engaged in similar pursuits. On the contrary it is earnestly recommended to the members of this institution to cultivate a spirit of harmony and unanimity and to consider one another as brothers of the same common family, remembering "To do to others as you would have others do to you."

The behaviour of the students as they pass the streets to and from the Academy, and all other times shall be decent and orderly without noise or confusion; especially on the Sabbath, when every appearance of mirth or levity is strictly forbidden.

It is particularly enjoined upon the students to remember the Sabbath day to keep it holy by attending public worship on both parts of the day with proper reverence and attention, and by spending the remainder of the day at their lodgings in a manner suitable to the character of christians. All walking or assembling for amusement or trifling conversation is most positively forbidden.

All gaming and intemperance and all profanities and indecency of language or behavior will be considered as a gross violation of the laws of this institution, and will be censured and punished accordingly; and no student shall spend his time in any Tavern, or other place of public resort of a similar kind.

Every member of this institution is most positively forbidden as character highly criminal in itself, and utterly inconsistent with the characters of young Gentlemen—to take

Continued:

fruit of any kind from the orchards, gardens or other enclosures of the Town without leave first obtained of the proprietors.

It is considered the indispensable duty of the students of this academy on all occasions to treat the inhabitants of the Town and all strangers passing through it, with civility and respect and carefully abstain from everything which might afford them just cause of complaint.

Strict attention shall be paid by the students to the orders and regulations of the families in which they board, and particular care must be taken not to incommode them by staying out late in the evening.

There shall be a monitor appointed from time to time whose duty it shall be to note those who are absent or tardy at any exercise of this institution or who are irregular in their attendance on public worship.

If any member of this institution after repeated admonitions and discipline obstinat'ly persists in a course of negligence and inattention to his studies so that the purposes of the institution, as it respects him are like to be frustrated; or if he be generally irregular in his deportment or corrupt in his morals, as to endanger others by his example, after all proper methods to reclaim him have failed, he shall be privately removed, or publicly expelled, in presence and with consent of one or more of the trustees, as the nature and circumstance of the case may require; and his name be blotted from the Books of the institution.

Enacted Sept. 6th, 1806.
A True Copy. Attest,
John Siemons.
Rev. Reuben Nason, Preceptor.
Mr Joseph Osgood, Assist.

GRANDPA'S SCRAP BOOK

Week of Jan. 23-26, 1901.

PAPERMAKING.

The Manufactury at Stroudwater Village—1734.

BY LEONARD B. CHAPMAN.

The art of papermaking is very ancient. The soft part of certain kinds of trees and a picked pointed instrument for writing was first used. From China the practice was carried to other countries, England being slow to adopt what other countries were doing in this respect, but there is no authentic record of the first manufactury in this country.

Upon page 184 of volume XI of the records of the court of General Sessions for the District of Maine, depositions in the archives of York county, dated 1738, we find a tangible record then made reflecting light upon the mooted question of a real existence of a paper mill in Falmouth, the town then including within its territorial limits the hamlet of Stroudwater, as well as Presumpscot Falls, as it does now the latter, as follows:

"Thomas Westbrook and Samuel Waldo vs. Richard Fry of Boston. In 1734 Fry leased the paper mill with five mortars situated on the river Stroudwater, in Falmouth, for a term of twenty-one years at a yearly rent of forty pounds sterling money of Great Britain, yet, in 1736, but forty reams of paper had been furnished, Fry now being in arrears seventy pounds." The jury brought in a verdict for Westbrook and Waldo.

Another action at the same time was brought by James Plummer, a millwright, residing at Stroudwater, who claimed Fry owed him £100 for a year's work.

Fry was an Englishman and a papermaker, who was persuaded to come to this country as other mechanics were by inducements held out by General Samuel Waldo, who would fail to comply with his obligations after his men arriving here.

The original plan was to build a paper mill at Presumpscot Falls, but, though saw mills were built, the paper mill scheme failed to mature. As late as 1736, when "articles of agreement were entered into" by these two dignitaries the improvements at Presumpscot Falls were referred to as "not yet finished." In the Portland Transcript of 1883 we went over this Presumpscot Falls matter pretty thoroughly so will say no more here.

Richard Fry was a queer compound. We next meet him on the records a prisoner in Boston jail where the officers of the law had placed him for alleged non compliance with court mandates, relating to the Westbrook and Waldo demands.

We have seen and examined several of his specimens of writing in the originals. He wrote a most excellent hand, and though we have felt that he drew largely upon his imagination in his statements are now of the opinion that in the matter of dispute here referred to he was largely in the truth. His intellectual capacity was far in excess of the general criminal, if not the average citizen, as indicated by obtainable specimens of his writings while in the Boston jail. He claimed the officers of the law robbed him of his personal property at Stroudwater, and appropriated it to their own use. He presented the court with a long list of articles carried away, which is very curious when looked upon at this day, he going into details with reference to papers recorded in England bestowing a life annuity upon his wife at the date of marriage. And all this upon the soil of Stroudwater—paper manufacturing and official robbery—a hundred and sixty-six years ago, and we see the very proceedings through the records then made!

In his petition to the Governor of the Commonwealth and the Legislature, Mr. Fry states he is imprisoned "under color of an execution from Samuel Waldo" enforced by Abraham Tyler an under sheriff." Then he goes on to say that Waldo agreed in London in 1731, to build within ten months after arriving in New England a paper mill, that he waited after arriving, four years, planning mills at Presumpscot Falls, which were built and let to one John Collier of England whom he, Richard Fry, influenced to come here and lease the mills at £200 sterling per annum for a period of twenty-one years. "Your petitioner was to pay sixty-four pounds sterling per annum for twenty-one years for the paper mill;" and Collier finding what sort of men he had to deal with sold Westbrook and Waldo his lease for £600. The said Westbrook and Waldo offered your humble petitioner £500 for his lease, but he would not comply with the most unreasonable and unjust request; so they entered into combination with Sheriff Tyler under cover of an execution and violently entered my mill, converted my substance to their own use and committed my body to the Boston jail."

It seems by the petition that Fry had had a son born in this country whom he had named James Brook Fry, and suggested that a piece of unimproved land in Falmouth be given him, as the improvements he had been the means of causing had greatly enhanced all land in the town of Falmouth.

While in jail at Boston Mr. Fry claimed to have invented a "banking scheme," which he advertised, and which he laid before the Governor, claiming that if adopted the threatened "darkness in financial matters would be dispelled and in less than a year there would be a general jubilee, the balance of trade being in favor of the Colonies from all parts of the world." "I have proved," he goes on to state, "my scheme by the mathematics, and all mankind well know, figures won't lie. It is plain to a demonstration, by the just schemes of Peter the Great, the late Czar of Muscovy in the run of a few years arrived to such a pitch of glory, whose empire makes as grand appearance as any Empire on earth, which Empire for improvement, is no ways to be compared with his Royal Majesties domains in America." "They had their rough material to produce from other countries—we have them all within ourselves." The scheme was: "The use of a paper currency tile such a time as by industry and frugality silver and gold to pass as a medium."

So the currency question is not a new one among us. A hundred and sixty-five years ago there was at least one "currency reformer." The results of Mr. Fry's scheme we have no means of knowing.

In another paper Mr. Fry states that at the end of four years, in which he spent a good sum in coming to this country, "and there is no member of this Honorable House but must know the keeping of a family in a pretty genteel manner four years must

CONTINUED:

amount to a large sum." Waldo purchased a mill of one James Forder for me and agreed with me that upon my surrendering up my sterling agreement for £400 I should pay no rent for the mill till said Waldo should build me a dwelling house and that the mill should be completely finished. The house was framed, but never raised to this day. Said Waldo gave me a promisory note for the same, which was carefully locked up in my desk. The sheriff in my absence broke open my desk, and appropriated the instrument to his own use, with all my other papers of great value. Then finding I was robbed of my papers I was sued in York county."

In the first contest in the Boston courts the jury found for Fry but in the second for Waldo and Tyler, Fry being kept in jail all the while, but his keeper got an order from the Governor, to whom he petitioned, to bestow better care on him and the other prisoners.

Richard Forder was an English millwright, induced by Waldo to come to this country, who sued in court and recovered damage against Waldo, because Waldo failed to do as he agreed in London.

Strange as it may seem,Forder built the two story house in which Mr. Augustus Tate and family resides at Stroudwater, and occupied it a short time, then sold and moved away.

The paper mill "with some convenience for paper making." a long, low posted one story building, stood where the store-house stands in which the "Canal Club" keep their boats, westerly of the old fresh water mill. The saw mill, with double saws, stood at the first turn in the river, some thirty rods above. Several records give clues to the existence of mills as we place them, but none furnish the proof definitely pertaining to the Stroudwater paper mill as our presentment and the actors names connected with the enterprises, and what transpired in connection.

As there were five mortars in the mill, the rags from which the paper was made must have been pounded to atoms. Fry states he had several tons he had imported taken from him.

The life of th papermaking enterprise was short. We find no records of its being revived after the departure of Richard Fry from Stroudwater.

Col. Thomas Westbrook died at Stroudwater Feb. 11, 1744.

Gen. Samuel Waldo resided in Boston, but he had a branch residence in Portland, where the Southworth printing house establishment may be seen on Middle street. He fell dead May 23, 1759, while viewing a newly built fort at the mouth of the Penobscot river in company with the Governor of Massachusetts, aged 63 years, a great land owner, and industrious merchant of Boston.

GRANDPA'S SCRAP BOOK

Week of Jan. 30 - Feb. 2, 1901

BLACK POINT FERRY.

Scarboro—1740.

BY LEONARD B. CHAPMAN.

There is a tradition in the Johnson family, residing a mile westerly of Stroudwater village, in Deering, that the immigrant, James Johnson, came over from Ireland in 1733, and that he, with father and brothers,went from Scotland to that place. The Cumberland Co. History of 1880 states on page 393 that James Johnson, the ancestor, settled in Scarboro, or Cape Elizabeth, and his occupation was a ferryman over Spurwink river, afterwards between Old Orchard and Prout's Neck beaches; that he was the ancestor of James and John brothers, who settled as we have stated, and died in 1740, the farm of James still remaining in the family name.

The records of the Court of General Sessions, October term, 1740, vol. 10, p. 279, deposited in the York Co. archives disclose as follows:

"Petition of Timothy Prout of Boston, merchant, that James Johnson of Scarboro, husbandman and Tenant to said Timothy, be licensed to keep a Ferry over Black Point River by the Harbours Mouth in said Scarboro," which was granted. The price of toll was fixed at fifteen pence for every horse and six pence for every person. He was required to give a bond in the sum of fifty pounds and Timothy Prout and Samuel Milliken were his securities. Later the license was renewed and the rates reduced to four pence for a horse and two pence for a person.

This is pretty conclusive that it was James Johnson, the Scarboro ferryman, who settled on the wild land westerly of Stroudwater. The Scarboro town records reveal nothing,other than a James Johnson was elected a tithingman, during the time James was a resident of that town. John, who settled next easterly of James was James' brother.

Nor do the Cape Elizabeth town records show anything relative to this particular Johnson family, but at the October term of the court to which we have here referred, holden in 1743, a license was granted to one Benjamin Haskell to keep a ferry over Spurwink river; he to keep good and sufficient boats and give a bond for ten pounds, which he did with Bryce McLellan and William Watson as his securities.

Lots of people are now making historical and genealogical scrap-books. Custodians of many libraries are doing so. The librarian of the library at the State House in Boston, Mass., prides himself upon what has been done in this direction. Some months since he asked for the dates of the deaths of the Representatives to the State Legislature of Massachusetts from Falmouth from the time of the close of the war of the Revolution to 1820, when the District of Maine became an independent state, with facts pertaining to the several names.

Isaac Stevens was one, evidently of Stevens Plains district of Deering, then Falmouth, but father and son had such a way of signing their names it cannot be learned which it was that was Representative. The senior was a Revolutionary soldier. Sometimes he appears on record as simple Isaac Stevens, again as Capt Isaac Stevens, again as Isaac Sawyer Stevens, which was his real legal name. "Isaac S. Stevens" is upon his grave memorial. His son appears as Isaac Stevens, and as Isaac Stevens, Jr. It seems the father was the Representative, but there is no telling for sure. Isaac Stevens, Jr., lost his wife, then removed to New Gloucester. Then, as now, political wounds were not always deep, and scars were not lasting.

JOSEPH HOBBS.

Born in Falmouth Oct. 29, 1762.

In 1848 Joseph Hobbs, residing in a brick house near the Gray road, on the northerly side of Presumpscot river, where the Maine Central railroad crosses, now called West Falmouth, under oath "deposed and said:"

I am now nearly eighty-six years of age, was born in Falmouth, October 29, 1762. I was a soldier in the war of the Revolution. I enlisted in the fall of 1779 in Capt. William Cobb's company, Col. Mitchell's Regiment and was stationed at Falmouth Neck. (Portland.)

Mr. Hobbs continues at some considerable length, giving the military situation, with location of the three forts in Portland, but we do not know his parents' names nor the place where he was born. He states the company were nearly all from Falmouth and he had been acquainted with nearly all of them from boyhood.

March 27, 1788, he and Mary Kilpatrick were united in marriage by Rev. Ebeneza Williams of Falmouth, and then he bought land and settled down to farm life at the place we have pointed out.

The war of the Revolution over, he married and settled down on good soil of a productive nature, we know of but two events in his long life, exclusive of what his grave memorial indicates, namely: He was elected in 1806 to represent Falmouth in the Massachusetts state Legislature and again in 1812, the delegation in 1806 consisting of the following named persons:

Josiah Hobbs—West Falmouth.
George Ilsley—East Deering or Lunt's Corner. He lived in both places.

CONTINUED:

Col. James Means—Stroudwater.
John Walt—Presumpscot Falls.

These towns sent as many representatives as they wanted, the towns paying expenses.

IN 1812.

Josiah Hobbs.
James Merrill—Presumpscot Falls.
Capt. John Porterfield—a mile westerly of Stroudwater, d. Sept. 22, 1837, aged 80 years. A Revolutionary soldier.
Jonathan Sparrow—Stroudwater, b. Eastham, Cape Cod, Dec. 25, 1768, d. Portland, Aug. 20, 1843. Buried at Stroudwater.

A little distance northerly of the West Falmouth depot on the easterly side of the highway, where the land is productive all around, may be seen a small burial place, containing modern made memorial slabs, and three or more obelisks, two of which are erected to two practitioners of medicine, the whole enclosed by a substantial fence but of late converted into a horse pasture! with bushes claiming rights as well as the horse that grooms himself by rubbing against the obelisks and calling the attention of the passer-by to the superiority of the brute by clinking his shoes in climbing over the fallen slabs.

The inscription upon one of the obelisks is as follows:

In Memoriam.
COL. JOSIAH HOBBS.
A Soldier of the Revolution.
Died Oct. 29, 1849,
Aged 87 years.

Mary, his wife, died,
Jan. 13, 1852,
Aged 83 years.

Blessed are the dead who die in the Lord.

Another side reads as follows:
In Memoriam. Jeremiah Hobbs, died May 8, 1879, aged 82 years. Joanna, his wife, died, Dec. 3, 1871, aged 70 years. "At rest in Jesus." He was a son of Col. Hobbs, and resided at Blackstrap.

The signers to a transfer of real estate made in 1850 to Mary Hobbs of "land of which Josiah Hobbs died seized" were as follows:
Miriam Hall, wife of Amos, in her right,
Adeline Maston, wife of Ebeneza, in her right.
Emily Jane Knight, wife of Mark, in her right,
Josiah Hobbs, Jeremiah Hobbs and Daniel Hobbs, 2nd, children and heirs-at-law of Josiah Hobbs, late of Falmouth, deceased.

GRANDPA'S SCRAP BOOK

Week of Feb. 6-9, 1901

MATRIMONIAL.

Records of Marriage Events Solemnized in the Part of Westbrook Now Deering.

1814—1842.

BY LEONARD B. CHAPMAN.

Rev. Caleb Bradley performed by far the larger part of the marriage ceremonies in what is now known as Westbrook and Deering during his "settlement," which commenced in 1799 and ended in 1829. His list of names copied from his diary has been printed in the "Maine Historical and Genealogical Recorder." What we here present may quite correctly be called "fugitive records." A few persons who answer to the roll call still remain among us, who were married by Rev. Mr. Bremblecome or Rev. Zenas Thompson.

BY ALPHEUS SHAW, ESQ.

[Mr. Shaw was born in the town of Bridgewater, Mass., Dec. 1784. His father was Solomon Shaw, who removed to Paris, Maine, about 1795. Solomon was b. there July 25, 1749. He had b. in Paris six children. Alpheus was the eldest child. He m. Oct. 4, 1807, Jane Doughty of Allen's Corner, Deering. She was a daughter of Joseph and Hannah (Hicks) Doughty of that place. He was a Revolutionary soldier and has a grave stone at Allen's Corner. He built the "Dr. Allen" house as now observed. His wife was b. Sept. 29, 1784. (Another record says Dec. 15.) They had eight children, but to tell the whole story of this man's career or that of Dr. Allen would require too much space just now. He sold his residence built soon after he was married to Dr. Solomon Allen in 1824 for $2,000. The house and actors all have interesting records. Capt. Shaw died July 25, 1869. He was a brother to Bela Shaw, who settled at what is now Morrill's Corner; and they married sisters. Both were in trade.
Westbrook was incorporated in 1814. Where the town is not named the inference is they were residents of Westbrook.]

1814. June 4. Crispus Graves and Isabella Hutchinson of Portland.
July 15. William Brackett, Jr., and Dorothy Bailey.
Sept. 30. Thomas Harmon of Buxton and Joanna Skillin of Cape Elizabeth.
Oct. 9. Joseph Marrow of Standish and Isabella Hutchson.
Nov. 24. Samuel Libby of Portland and Phebe Webb.
Nov. 29. Charles Ferguson and Mary Slemons. [They owned Stroudwater Mill.]
Dec. 1. Elijah Allen and Olive I. (or J.) Higgins.
Dec. 3. Peter Pride and Margaret Baker.
Dec. 13. Charles Pratt and Ann Porterfield. [They resided at Saccarappa.]
Dec. 18. Thomas Hanson of Windham and Hannah Gowen.
Dec. 21. John Clark and Sally Hicks.
1815. March 30. Thomas Riggs and Hannah Jordan.

BY SILAS ESTES.

He has been written up in the News He was a Quaker, and resided where Mr. Charles F. Cram lives between Morrill's Corner and Allen's Corner.

1816. April 17. Isaac Stevens and Hannah Wier. His second marriage. He was noticed briefly last week. His residence stood where the Electric rail road car depot stands on Stevens Plains.
May 15. Samuel Kenney an Sopiah Wormell.
1817. Jan. 19. Nathaniel L. Morril and Mary Hall. Both o Falmouth.
April 17. James Riggs, Jr., an Ann Delano.
Oct. 12. William Elder of Falmouth and Judith Leighton.
1818. Feb. 22. Edward Leighton and Hannah Hicks. Both of Falmouth.

BY MOSES QUINBY, ESQ.

He was a lawyer who resided at Stroudwater, and was a member of the first graduating class of Bowdoin College.

1817. April 5. John Parker and Sally Kennard.

BY PETER MORRILL, ESQ.

He resided in the Blackstrap region of the town.

1817. Oct. 21. Enoch Cobb and Betsey Brackett.
1519. April 1. George Cobb and Charity Brackett.

BY LUTHER FITCH, ESQ.

He was a lawyer at Saccarappa, who removed to Portland.

1818. Feb. 22. Charles Pratt and Elizabeth Woodbury

BY SAMUEL BREMBLECOME.

He was the first Universalist clergyman of the town who came from Massachusetts, and was also the first teacher at the Seminary. He returned to his native state. He has been written up in the News. He preached in what is now known as the Deering Town House" at Brighton district of Deering, built by the Universalists for a meeting house.

CONTINUED:

1835. Jan. 4. Naham Fickett and Elizabeth Larrabee. A notice of her death appeared in the News two weeks since. She was in her 92nd year.

Jan. 4. Charles Bartlett and Eleanor E. Sparrow, of Portland. He became a wealthy ship builder at Stroudwater. She was a cousin to Elizabeth (Larrabee) Fickett.

March 19. Henry S. Burgess and Eliza W. Montgomery.

May 24. Carlile Whipple of Boston, Mass., and Sarah W. Bunker of Gorham.

April 30. Ebeneza P. Dunning of Lynn, Mass., and Sarah Martin.

July 1. Freeman Porter and Mary Ann Partridge. This was her second marriage. Her maiden name was Buckley. They have appeared in the News. She died but recently.

July 5. Eli McDonald and Catharine Bishop. She was a dau. of George and Nancy (Stevens) Bishop, the father of Morrill's Corner, the mother of Woodfords. Catharine b. Oct. 17, 1808, d. Oct. 15, 1842.

Aug. 25. James S. Waite and Sarah M. Paine. Both of Portland.

Sept. 10. George Morton and Mary Ann Purington of Falmouth. He was a son of Capt. George Morton, a mariner, who spent his last days at Stroudwater. His wife was a sister to Charles Bartlett. Ann Purington was a School teacher. They, with several children, "went West," where the children are well-to-do farmers.

Sept. 20. Ann Waite and Betsey Bacheldor, both of Falmouth.

Dec. 31. Cyrus Skillings and Eunice Doan, both of Portland.

1836. Feb. 21. Rufus Morrill and Sally Webb. This was the father of Miss Mary Morrill, the missionary to China, who was killed there by the natives the last year, concerning whose tragic death so much has been said. Mr. Morrill resided at Morrill's Corner, where his son Rufus resides. He had two wives.

March 3. Joseph H. Watson and Marie Howe.

Rev. Mr. Bremblecome was a deep thinker and a powerful reasoner. He resided opposite the electric railroad car house on Stevens Plains in one of the two brick houses he built, which were destroyed by fire, but rebuilt on the original foundation, after the first plan. The foregoing contains all the records of marriage we find solemnized by him.

GRANDPA'S SCRAP BOOK

Week of Feb. 13— 1901.

BIRTHDAY-BOOK.

A Stevens Plains Monographical Family Puzzle.

BY LEONARD B. CHAPMAN.

"The past and the future meet and blend."

The birthday event is usually of a nature to be easily remembered after the story has been told, but recorded evidence if not always beneficial, to quicken the memory of the one most interested. is often instructive to one's friends, and when placed in a monographical combination that serves to make the time of the evening caller glide rapidly in an attempted elucidation or the presence of "gammer," with her carefully wiped spectacles, necessary to dispell the darkness at the "afternoon tea" relative to neighborhood kinship, the words of the frequently repeated injunction, "Know Thyself," becomes a matter of adoration.

We know of but one birthday-book on the Plains, and it required considerable effort to find it. If we knew the name of the originator we would here present it hit or miss After the next issue of the Deering News there will be many copies of the fifty-six names the little work contains, which "fifty-six" will live as long as fireproof archives in this and other states survive, if in no other way.

The eclipses of the moon and the sun come, are seen, the record made and depart, but the name of the one who first foretold the event is lost to the public. There was no birthday-book then.

BIRTHS.

Jan. 7, 1861, Jennie Starr.
" 8, 1865, George Forest Alden.
" 9, 1862, Fanny Revere Stevens.
" 14, 1830, Alpheus S. Alden, d. July 30, 1897.
" 19, 1865, Carrie Wm. Stevens.
" 25 1858, Isabel Frances Alden, d. May 31, 1875.
" 28, 1861, Mary Fletcher Stevens.
" 31, 1833, Granville Mellen Stevens.
Feb. 19, 1856, Jesse Alden Merrill.
" 20, 1844, Alvertene Buckley Stevens.
" 24, 1795, Harriett Revere Frances.

d. Oct. 12, 1889.
" 25, 1857, Charles Granville Starr.
March 2, 1862, Mary Bliss Merrill.
" 3, 1766, Caleb Frances. Oct. 25, 1787, went to Sterling, Mass., to live; m. Mary Rose May 10 1789.
" 25, 1869, Philip Herman Stevens.
April 6, 1834, Walter Franklin Goodrich.
" 20, 1823, Almena Maria Starr, d. May 29, 1887.
May 4, 1849, Mary Maling Stevens.
" 15, 1824, Charles Richard Starr.
" 19, 1802, Walter Buckley Goodrich, d. Aug. 4, 1869.
" 21, 1852, Samuel Augustus Stevens.
" 22, 1797, Isabel Frances Alden, d. May 15, 1862.
—— 1790, Jesse D. Alden, d. May 26, 1835, aged 45.
" 29, 1856, Henry Frances Stevens.
June 8, 1829, Elizabeth E. (Stevens) Alden.
" 16, — died Walter Franklin Alden.
" 26, 1873, Granville Mellen Stevens, Jr.
" 27, 1857, Hattie Frances Stevens, d. March 4, 1866.
July 6, 1824, George Wm. Merrill, at Bradley's Corner, d. Nov. 4, 1879.
" 10, 1743, Mary Revere Rose Baker, d. Dec. 27, 1801.
" 13, 1827, Samuel Henry Stevens.
" 15, 1834, Emily Sargent Stevens.
Aug. 5, 1851, Clara Alden Merrill.
" 9, 1822, Sarah Rose Merrill, d. Jan. 5, 1895.
" 22, 1863, Walter Starr Buchanan.
" 24, 1863, Lizzie Tyler Stevens.
" 24, 1871, Ervin Greenwood Stevens.
" 25, 1804, Maria Frances Goodrich, d. May 27, 1891.
Sept. 10, 1866, Fred Jarvus Stevens.
" 20, 1825, Augustus Ervin Stevens, d. Nov. 10, 1882. Was Mayor of Portland.
" 25, 1855, Almena Stevens.
Oct. 5, 1881, Alden Merrill.
——1702, At St. Foy, France, Apollas Rivorie, d. in Boston, Mass., July 22, 1754.
Nov. 6, 1856, Emma Louise Merrill.
" 11, 1799, Sally (Stevens) Brisco.
" (A Sally Brisco, d. Aug. 1, 1822, aged 50. L. B. C.)
" 11, 1828, Jennie Tyler Stevens, d. Jan. 6, 1869.
" 25, 1859, George Arthur Merrill.
Dec. 5, 1832, Sarah Knight Stevens, Dudley, Mass.
" 5, 1888, Paul Aldrich Merrill, d. Dec. 26, 1891.
" 8,—died Henry Shaw Alden, born

CONTINUED:
June 6.—
" 14, 1848, Frank Thayer Merrill.
" 18, 1874, Martha Gordon Stevens.
" 20, 1765, Mary Rose Frances, d. in Sterling, Mass., Sept. 20, 1804.
" 20, 1769, Mary (Frances) Woodford, d. Oct. 12, 1871, wife of Dea. Ebeneza D. Woodford.
" 20, 1830, Caroline Maria Goodrich.
" 25, 1840, Frances Greenwood Stevens.

From the Portland Argus of Oct. 31, 1826:

Married.—In Turner, on the 1st inst., Zenas Thompson to Miss Leonora Leavitt, (dau. of Maj. Isaac Leavitt of Turner).

He departed this life at Woodfords, Nov. 17, 1882, aged 77 yrs., 10 mo.; his wife at the same place. Memorial stones may be seen standing in the northeasterly corner of Evergreen cemetery, Deering district of Portland; also one for George W. Thompson, a son, who was killed in the Union army.

Children of Rev. Zenas and Leonora (Leavitt) Thompson: Leonora; Mary Jane; Louise M.; Abba Valentine—deceased; Zenas; George W.—deceased; Julia S. and Frederick H.

Zenas and Frederick H. are the well known carriage manufacturers in Portland whose work for style, durability, completeness in workmanship stands at the head of the list in this state.

GRANDPA'S SCRAP BOOK

Week of Feb. 20—23, 1901

MATRIMONIAL.

Records of Marriage Events Solemnized in the Part of Westbrook Now Deering. 1814—1842.

BY LEONARD B. CHAPMAN.

(Continued from Week of Feb. 6-9.)

In our first article under this heading our reference to Messrs. Doughty and Shaw was not made plain in all respects. James Doughty was a Revolutionary soldier and has a gravestone in the Allen's Corner cemetery upon which the fact is stated. And it was Alpheus Shaw who built the so-called Dr. Allen house at Allen's Corner, not Joseph Doughty.

Another correction we desire to make: Miss Mary S. Morrill, the missionary to China who was killed by the natives, was a granddaughter of Rufus Morrill and Sally Webb, who were married Feb. 21, 1836. Rufus, Jr., the son of Rufus and Sally, being the father of the missionary.

Rufus Morrill, Sr., married first, Mary Webb, daughter of Edward C. Webb, who resided near the powder mills in Gorham, this state. She was the mother of Edmund N. Morrill, ex-governor and ex-M. C. of Kansas. She died; he married second, her sister, Sally. They were sisters to Eli Webb, who died in Portland, who was father to Judge Nathan Webb of the U. S. District court of this state.

Rufus Morrill, Jr., now residing in the homestead at Morrill's Corner, married Lizzie Barbour Allen, born Nov. 13, 1837, the fourth and youngest child of Dr. Solomon Allen. Mary S. Morrill was their daughter.

Dr. Allen was born at New Gloucester, March 29, 1785, and a son of James Allen, who was b. Oct. 4, 1758. Dr. Allen's wife was Mary Leavitt, a widow, and mother to Capt. William Leavitt, now a resident of the Stroudwater district of Portland.

REV. ZENAS THOMPSON.

He was born in Auburn, this state, Dec. 4, 1804. He was of Scotch-Irish lineage; his first American ancestor, Archibald Thompson, coming to America in 1724 and settling at Bridgewater, Mass. Capt. John Thompson, the grandfather of Zenas, married Jeanette Allen and removed to Buckfield. Archibald Thompson was a mechanic —a wheel-maker. Capt. John Thompson followed the same calling.

The father of Zenas was Hannibal, son of Capt. John, and his mother was a Dillingham, of Auburn. Zenas graduated from Hebron Academy. Possessed of large reasoning faculties and a natural command of language, he applied the law of the square, compass and plummet to every-day conduct of mankind, particularly to the evils of the liquor traffic, the slave pen of the South, and to the belief in a future place of punishment beyond the grave for the soul of man. having espoused the cause of "Universalism," and began to explain, when quite young, the Bible as he understood it, but an inherited mechanical genius never departed from him. He was skilled in wood carving. He made in his little work room, attached to his residence, elegant fly-rods and rifles, and he could handle both to perfection. His knowledge in every department of the useful and ornamental in arts was intuitive in him. And he was possessed of social qualities of a high order, and was ever an agreeable man to meet, but in the pulpit he was aggressive and destructive in the use of words to that in which he did not believe as he was kind and sympathetic in the social circle. He was "at home" in the farmhouse barn as he was in the costly church edifice of the city—as entertaining in one as in the other. We see him now in our mind's eye as we did nearly fifty years ago with a red, roundish face, much bald crown, white whiskers, a turban-like fur cap, fur collar, fur mittens, gold-bowed spectacles, up in Oxford county, seated behind a little "two-forty stepper" on the way from his headquarters at Bethel Hill to some meeting house ten miles distant from his own immediate society, with the mercury twenty degrees below zero. After the delivery of his discourse the public always had something to talk about, whatever the nature of the subject. And when Parson Bradley heard him at a funeral or at a military "muster," where Parson Thompson officiated, Parson Bradley had something to write about in his diary in denunciation, Parson Bradley representing the real "Orthodox" Congregationalists in what is now Deering.

The date Father Thompson commenced his labors with the Universalist denomination we cannot state, or the location of his first settlement. He labored in Chicopee and other places in Massachusetts, Newmarket, N. H., at Farmington, Frankfort, Bridgton and Saccarappa village in Westbrook, at which time he was a corresponding editor of the Universalist paper, printed in Portland, called the Christian Pilot, and edited by Rev. Samuel Brimblecom, incomplete files of which are now in existence. From Saccarappa he came to what is now Deering, and succeeded Rev. Mr. Brimblecom, who had retired from the pulpit of the society that had built in 1830 the chapel as now seen at Brighton Corner and known as the old Town House; who had retired also from the Westbrook Seminary as its principal, Father Thompson residing on the Plains.

In 1847 eight persons formed and caused to be incorporated a Universalist society in the town of Bethel. The creed was short, to wit: "We believe in the Truth." In 1853 a church edifice was erected there at a cost of $2,000, and in June of 1854 dedicated with Father Thompson acting as pastor. Whether he went direct from Deering we cannot state, but think not. He remained five years after the meeting house was dedicated, accomplishing much for the society and the general public, the society being now, according to reports, strong and influential. A couple of years ago, according to newspaper reports, Col. Clark S. Edwards, a veteran of the Union army, war of the Rebellion, an original member, presenting the society with a fine portrait of the first pastor.

In April, 1860, a movement was begun to establish a second Universalist society in Portland, and the following May Father Thompson commenced to preach in Union hall, but in June, next following, the society moved into Mechanic's hall. At the end of a year's service he retired, and engaged as a chaplain in the sixth Maine Regiment. The war over he had other settlements in other places —at West Waterville and at Mechanic Falls, returning to Deering, where he erected a good two story house on the northerly side of Lincoln, near Grant street, Woodfords district.

Father Thompson usually delivered his pulpit orations without the aid of notes. He was very slow in speech at first, but would become very animated as he proceeded, particularly in denouncing slavery and intemperance.

He did not print much, at least we can't find much. A sermon entitled "Religious Prosperity," delivered at Augusta, Oct. 27, 1850, and one delivered at the same place, 1879, entitled —"The Judgment of the World; or, its subjugation to God through the reign of Christ," is all we find in the

CONTINUED:

public archives.

Following is a list of all records of marriages we find solemnized during his first sojourn hereabouts:

1839.

April 21, George M. Stevens and Hannah E. Chase.
May 4, Hezekiah Winslow of Bangor and Jane C. B. Winslow. (?)
" 29, Joel Murray and Nancy Stevens.
June 18, George M. Morton and Ant. Maria Morton.
" 20, Joshua D. Roberts and Ellen Babb.
July 23, Thomas Wilcox and Susan Lang of Portland.
Oct. 23, William M. Scammon and Adah E. Chase.
Dec. 4, Claredon Waters of Lawrence and Sophronia Quinby.

1841.

June 27, Wm. Parker and Abigail Fessenden, both of Portland.
July 18, Josiah Knight and Sarah Bangs.
Aug. 1, John A. Montgomery and Mary Dennison, both of Portland.
Oct. 23, Sewall V. Walker and Eunice G. Whitten.
Nov. 30, Smith C. Goold and Catharine Starbird.
Dec. 2, Jeremiah B. Sampson and Mary W. Knight.
" 19, Daniel C. Cloudman and Esther B. Quinby.
Nov. 26, William T. Chadbourn and Elizabeth Wescott, both of Standish.

1842.

March, Samuel L. Babb and Lucy Libby.
March 23, Frank B. Wiley and Susan B. Pratt.
April 28, Arthur Milliken and Caroline Lowell.

GRANDPA'S SCRAP BOOK

Week of Feb. 27—Mar. 2, 1901

OLD WESTBROOK.

The Town a Battlefield of Church Clans. 1830—1840.

BY LEONARD B. CHAPMAN.

In two parts.—Part first.

Sixty to seventy years ago the town of Westbrook, including the part now known as Deering district of Portland, was the battle-ground of church clans, speaking more particularly, the battle-ground between the "orthodox" Congregationalists and the Universalists. Why it was that Westbrook became the field of encounter we cannot state, unless it was the territorial discrimination of the people.

But before the advent of the Universalists there were manifestations of discontent among the people. In fact there never was perfect harmony hereabouts upon the question of church creeds. When the Stroudwater parish was granted permission by the Great and General Court to leave the Portland parish a day of fasting and prayer was appointed by the Portland church.

Then there were further manifestations of discontent, and the Stroudwater Parish, on March 24, 1787, voted to "clear the 'Independent Society' of paying parish taxes by the request of Job Knight for the whole."

The names of those excused were as follows: Job Knight, Nathaniel Hale, John Hurley, Moses Knight, Richard Knight, Enoch Knight, Merrill Knight, Peter Knight, William Gibbs, Adam Barbour, John Husting and Moses Knight, Jr.

The nature of the "Articles of Faith" of the Independents we cannot here state, but think the most of the persons represented by the names here presented resided between Pride's Corner and the Duck Pond region of the town.

Rev. Caleb Bradley was the pastor of the Stroudwater Paris from 1799 to 1828. Before us is the original partition of twenty-two persons residing in Saccarappa to be set off from the Stroudwater Parish, but the paper is without date. It must however, have been prior to 1814, for it refers to the Second, or Stroudwater Parish, as located in Falmouth. It reads as follows:

To the Second Parish in the Town of Falmouth. Gentlemen:

As it appears to be a matter of the Greatest importance as well as the real duty of Christians to do all they Can for the Glory and honor of God and the good of their own Souls and as we the Subscribers inhabience of the district of Saccarappa are in providence so situated that we Cannot neither indeed do we attend the Publick worship of God at the meeting house of the Revd. Mr. Bradley, we therefore under these Considerations beg leave to withdraw our Selves from the Parish and Still wishing to incorring all that love and friendship which becomes Christians hope that you will peacefully Discharge us in Order that we may form and incorrige a Religious Society in Saccarappa for the Publick worship of God in testimony where of we have here unto Set our names. James Grant, Josiah Bailey, Nathaniel Hatch, A. R. Wise, Daniel Small, Edward March, Saml. D. Pike, Samuel Lary, Frederick Quinby, Miles Winslow, Jeremiah Johnson, Joseph Small, Daniel Babb, Joseph Babb, Joseph Adams, Dean Frye, Job Winslow, Jr., Zachariah Small, Johathan Newbegin, Wm. Babb, Jr. Timothy Pike, John Elder

When civil government was established in this country none but "Freemen" were allowed to vote.

"To become a freeman, each person was legally required to be a respectable member of some Congregational church. Persons were made freemen by the General Court of the colony, and also by the quarterly courts of the counties. None but freemen could hold office or vote for rulers. The regulation was so far modified by Royal edict in 1664, as to allow individuals to be made freemen, who could obtain certificates of their being correct in doctrine and conduct from clergymen acquainted with them."

In the older towns of Massachusetts the form of oath is spread out upon the town clerk's books with a list of names of those who were freemen. An extract from that of Ipwich, Mass., reads as follows:

"And therefore [I] do here swear by the great and dreadful name of the everlasting God, that I will be true and faithful to the same, and will accordingly yield assistance and support thereunto, with my person and estate, as in equity I am bound."

The Legislature of the state created the parish, and the parish officers levied the tax for the support of the Congregational church.

Harvard College was of the Congregational order, and New England was flooded with Congregational clergymen. They now go to China or some other far off place.

Thus is was as we state till 1820, when the State of Maine was created and the property and church disability were removed by provisions of the adopted state Constitution.

Nine years after the adoption of the Constitution the first Universalist society was formed in Westbrook in the old schoolhouse that stood a few rods westerly of the meeting house on Capisic street, the pulpit of which meeting house had been occupied for a period of thirty years by Rev. Caleb Bradley, who vacated the year the Universalist society was formed, the liberal, or Universalist, element of the town having made an effort to outvote the "Orthodox" but failed. For a place of worship the Universalists then built the meeting house as now seen, but owned at this date by the city, located at Brighton Corner. The skirmish line was at that time formed between the clans, and the battle raged several years. Parson Bradley was then fifty-three years of age, not an eloquent speaker but an outside agitator.

April 29, 1829, Rev. Henry C. Jewett was formally conducted to the seat vacated by Parson Bradley, but he could not hold the "Orthodox" forces together, and on April 3, 1833, Rev. Joseph Lane was put in charge of a newly organized "Orthodox" society at Saccarappa.

Last week we presented a sketch

Continued:

of Rev. Zenas Thompson. From Norway, Me., Oct. 7, 1826, he wrote to a Portland paper that he had just arrived there from Turner for the purpose of preaching "tomorrow." He was then twenty-two years of age.

A public notice dated Sept. 20, 1832, states that Bro. Zenas Thompson is expected to preach at Saccarappa, Sunday the 23d.

The Universalists were proselyting; their numbers were growing; a building on Stevens Plains for a school had been started Jan. 24, 1833, the Cumberland county conference of Congregational churches made a report, the part referring to Westbrook being as follows:

"Ours is the task of exhibiting facts which show a melancholy reverse in the situation and prosperity of the churches. O, let us weep in view of the melancholy condition and search out the cause! But one member has been added by letter, 2 deaths, 2 dismissed, whole number of members 93, baptized, 19. The interesting feature in connection with the matter is the organization of a second church in the village of Saccarappa."

It appears that the new "Orthodox" Society at Saccarappa endeavored to start a "revival" in that locality, making unusual exertions during the spring of 1833, to stop the march of the Universal clan, and at our time an attempt was made to inflict mob violence upon Parson Bradley.

The official report by the Universalist scribe, dated May 3, 1833, and headed as follows is interesting reading:

SECOND UNIVERSALIST SOCIETY IN WESTBROOK.

A new society has recently been formed in this village, (Saccarappa) bearing the above name. The circumstances attending its organization, and the pleasing prospects in view of its members, assure them that this Religious Association will not be unproductive of much good, by destroying "the covering cast over all people, and the veil that is spread over all nations."

The first meeting of this Society was holden on the nineteenth day of April. The meeting was called to order by Capt. Isaac Walker, and the following named officers were chosen: J. G. Read—Moderator; J. T. Gilman—Clerk; Charles Pratt—Collector and Treasurer. Benjamin Quinby, Esq., Moses Stiles and Stephen Bacon were chosen a committee to superintend the secular officers of the Society. Messrs. J. H. Curtis, J. G. Read and Benjamin Quinby, Esq., were chosen to draft a Constitution, which they accordingly did; and, at a subsequent meeting of the Society, Mr. Curtis presented said Constitution, which was unanimously adopted. Benj. Quinby, Esq., was likewise chosen Corresponding Secretary, to correspond with the Rev. Zenas Thompson of Farmington, concerning his becoming Pastor of this Society. This was considered a very important part of the business transacted in relation to the Society. I hope and trust the negotiation with Mr. Thompson will have a favorable and satisfactory issue.

And now, what is it, I inquire, that has given this new and sudden impulse to Universalism in this vicinity? Is it the fruit of the late fourteen days meetings? Or is it the "copious shower" that was so often predicted during that meeting, which would succeed the few drops that fell (by the wayside) during said meetings? But what is it, I again inquire, that has induced forty-three among the most respectable citizens of Saccarappa village to combine and organize themselves into a Christian Society and who, at this early hour, have a fund of nearly three hundred dollars contributed for the glorious purpose of supporting the public ministration of the word of Universal grace and Eternal Life? In a few words, I will endeavor to assign a rational cause for this long needed resolution and exertion. The fact is simply this: Our good citizens have silently observed the Fire, the Earthquake and the Whirlwind passing by, but, praise be the Eternal King of Heaven, the "still small voice" is now speaking to their hearts and telling them to awake from their slumbers, and behold the danger to which they are exposed, not the danger of an eternal Hell—a future state, of an endless burning in liquid fire and brimstone, but the danger of bigotry, superstition and Priestcraft inundating our free and independent Republic, and preventing the Gospel of Jesus, the glorious character of religious liberty, and of man's salvation.

Now, is this not a praiseworthy example of our good citizens? To all those who acknowledge this to be a good sign of the times and who have not yet combined their forces, we would say, "Go and do likewise;" and our fervent wishes and devout supplication for your success and prosperi ever accompany your exertions.   T. J. Gilman,.
    Clerk.

To be continued.

GANDPA'S SCRAP BOOK

Week of Mar. 6-9, 1901.

OLD WESTBROOK.

The Town a Battlefield of Church Clans. 1830—1840.

BY LEONARD B. CHAPMAN.

In two parts.—Part second.

After the incorporation of Portland as an independent town, Falmouth held her town meetings in the Stroudwater meeting house; then Westbrook did the same till the advent of Universalism, when, on the 17th day of September, 1830, a vote of the parish was passed as follows:

"The standing committee to notify the selectmen of the town of Westbrook that the town can no longer hold meetings or do business in the meeting house of the parish."

This vote antagonized much of the liberal element of the parish and turned it towards Universalism and the hastening of a church division, the Saccarappa part of the society contending that a division of church and parish would tend to thwart the march of Universalism in that section.

We will here copy from the diary of Rev. Caleb Bradley:

Jan. 17, 1832. I went to Saccarappa. The council called for the purpose of organizing a church met at the meeting house at 10 o'clock. [This house was a free house that was located on Saco street, where the schoolhouse may now be seen and was used by all denominations. It was rudely constructed about the year 1800, and finally destroyed by fire, supposed to have been the work of boys.] Mr. Bradley continues: Ministers present—Dr. Gillet, Messrs. Chickley (?) and Hobert. [Rev. Caleb Hobert of North Yarmouth.] Organization attended to. At 2 o'clock the persons to be organized were examined. At 6 o'clock attended to the public exercises. Dr. Gillet preached. Mr. Hobert made the consecrating prayer; Mr. Shepley the fellowship of the church; Mr. Bradley the introductory prayer and Mr. [Henry C.] Jewett [of the Stroudwater church] the concluding prayer. A solemn and interesting day.

"18th. The meeting at Saccarappa continued. Mr. Hobert preached; in the afternoon Mr. Tenney; in the evening, Mr. Jewett.

"19th. No help but Mr. Tenney; exercises same as yesterday—interesting and solemn.

"20th. Meetings closed this evening. Deep impressions seem to have been made. Six remained as inquirers. May we hope all were wounded for they can be healed by the blood of the Savior."

Whether the references contained in the notice of the organization of the Universalist society presented last week were intended for the "revival" noticed as above, or some other, we have no means of knowing.

But the building of a meeting house by the Universalists was not so rapid as indications displayed by Mr. Gilman in his communication, quoted last week, would indicate. In Rev. Mr. Bradley's diary we find as follows:

Dec. 23, 1840. Leonard [the Parson's son] and Franklin [Partridge, son of the Parson's second wife,] gone to Saccarappa, the Universalist meeting house to be dedicated in that place. Some parade about it. Universal salvation to all the sons and daughters of Adam to be preached in the house. Blessed doctrine! And so considered by many in this town who evince no disposition to submit to the requirements of the gospel as I believe. All who repent and believe will be saved; those who do not will be damned, the Bible says. I leave the Universalists to dispute with the Bible.

Five years before the date of the above, Parson Bradley made a record as follows:

Went to Saccarappa and was present at the funeral service of Mrs. Harris. Mr. Thompson [Rev. Zenas Thompson] preached a Universalist discourse. He made all fair weather—a great encouragement to wickedness. He said nothing about sin, only death was not caused by sin—nothing about repentance. And he did not tell his hearers that he had ever heard that there was a Holy Ghost. All that seems necessary is to have a strong faith and all will go to heaven, and all will, all right, and no doubt, in his mind. I don't know but he believes according to his preaching. If he is right, all is right, but the Bible says the wicked shall go away into everlasting punishment and the righteous into life eternal.

June 20, 1833, there appeared in the Universalist organ "The Pilot," a notice that read as follows:

"Br. Zenas Thompson having removed to Saccarappa village requests all letters, papers, etc., intended for him in future, to be directed to that place."

Our article last week pointed to the field of labor as at Farmington of Bro. Thompson at the date of Mr. Gilman's communication in the "Pilot;" the above fixes the date of his location at Saccarappa, and Parson Bradley exposes the grounds of dispute.

Rev. Samuel Brimblecom was a man of letters, a deep thinker and a powerful reasoner, but not an eloquent pulpit orator. He sowed the seed while "Br. Thompson" threshed the harvest. Mr. Brimblecom's pulpit was then in what is now the old "Town house." He was literary—a teacher, and wanted a schoolhouse; the "Westbrook Seminary" building was started. He was a writer—therefore he was assistant editor of "The Pilot." Following is from his pen and the first notice of the Westbrook Seminary we find, which appeared May 25, 1833.

WESTBROOK SEMINARY.

Our brethren will rejoice to learn that the contemplated Westbrook Seminary is in progress. The energy with which the project was first undertaken has never subsided, and it will now be carried through as rapidly as circumstances will allow. If there has been a delay in the undertaking there have been reasons for it which have satisfied the Trustees that a little delay was better than precipitation. The public may rest assured that the duty of carrying this Institution into operation is committed to men who will not slight the responsibility which has been laid on them, nor fail through want of firmness or perseverance.

The building is to be of brick 37 by 70 feet, two stories high, with cupola. It is precisely such a building as we believe the Institution will require, which will furnish large, airy and healthy rooms. The expense of erecting such a building must be considerable, and the friends of the Institution, who have not contributed to it, are earnestly requested to lend a helping hand at this time. Assistance at the outset of such an enterprise is often of greater importance than the donor is ready to believe. In due time we doubt not that the Institution will meet with liberal patronage, and we hope it will prove to be, as it is meant, worthy of distinguishing favor.

The Institution is of no private or local character, but is general in its design and object, and we hope that no principle of private or local interest will prevent any one from the exercise of liberality towards it.

Continued:

The first Universalist Society built their meeting house upon an eminence at Brighton Corner, now within the Deering district of Portland, with a rock for a foundation, as observed at this time, the lot being a donation to the society, but the Saccarappa society placed theirs in a slum, a part of the village derisivly known by the name of "holy ground," where the denizens resided in slab huts and where rum drinking and attendant evils were the rule, which building may now be seen, but elevated a story and used as a machine shop, the society having built and removed to enlarged accommodations, the Congregationalists still occupying their original selection of a lot on Main street, but with an enlarged and modernized building.

Then the Democratic party was in power (excepting when the Universalists changed the issue and voted themselves into office,) and it was claimed that poverty and self-government were preferable conditions to abundance possessed by a few and the people governed by rich Lords of the Whig political pattern, which would be the case should protection to manufactures be adopted.

Between that period and this there has been a great change politically and religiously, particularly as regards creeds. Then the sun shown upon all and we had a low rate of taxation and farmers with wood-lots, who raised wool and mutton and potatoes, but there was no money circulating. But we had schools and schoolhouses, now we have school palaces, with such a ridiculous system of "forcing" we are bothered to find a candidate sufficiently mature to make a Chief Magistrate for a small place like Portland, Deering ceasing to exist as an independent municipality on this account.

Now, the "good deacon" is said to visit the ball room, and the only fear talked about is fear by the poor man of the tax-gatherer, the bills of the trained nurse, the doctor and the undertaker.

To be continued.

GRANDPA'S SCRAP BOOK

Week of Mar. 13-16, 1901.

OLD WESTBROOK.

The Town a Battlefield of Church Clans. 1830—1840.

BY LEONARD B. CHAPMAN.

In two parts.—Part second concluded.

Not a single meeting of the members of the Stroudwater parish was holden from the September meeting of 1830 till April 12, 1834, when Dea. Joshua H. Marean, William Graves and Dr. Solomon Allen were chosen a Parish Committee, with Thomas D. Woodford, who acted as clerk.

Mr. Graves was a new importation, a tanner by occupation, from the state of Vermont, and resided in a two story house that was situated where the residence of the late John B. Curtis may be seen, on Stevens Plains avenue, nearly opposite Capisic street. Like the invited guest to the family or society feast or the "new recruit" in the political caucus, Mr. Graves was given the right hand of fellowship and the head in church and parish matters. He stood not for traditions regarding the meeting house, but for renovation and innovations, so much so, the ancient meeting house, the second on the site, on account of its great size and inattractiveness was pulled down, it being also urged that the erection of a smaller house of a neat pattern would tend in a degree to overcome by its appearance the public drift towards Universalism, but the scheme was a dismal failure as was Mr. Graves' business venture, who removed to Portland and there engaged in a sort of city religious Missionary work for some of the churches of that place, where a son now resides at the "Home for Aged Men." A sketch of Mr. Graves and family has appeared in the News. The meeting house then erected is the one now seen on Capisic street, northerly side, about twelve rods from Stevens Plains avenue, so out of repair that it is not fit for use; then there are not a half-score of persons who would be regular attendants were there regular services holden. The last male member of the church was Dea. Hiram H. Dow. The church organization is now dead, only one or two women being left. The old church book was destroyed by fire when a shop was burned at Brighton Corner some forty years ago. A substitute record was made by Deacon Dow from memory and the names of the younger members recorded, which is in possession of Mr. James N. Read, who resides at Woodfords. A parish organization exists, and holds annual meetings. The parish record book is in existence but it discloses but a few facts. Under date of Sept. 25, 1865, an entry was made by Henry S. Jackson, Parish Clerk, as follows:

"Voted to instruct the Parish Committee to fulfill and make good the agreement with Mr. Haskell that the former Parish Committee made, that is, six hundred dollars a year commencing the 16th of last July."

This had reference to Rev. William H. Haskell, who was then settled over the society, though the entry quoted is the only one that throws light upon his connections with the society.

Under date of Oct. 12, 1868, another entry reads as follows:

"Voted that the Parish Committee engage some one to read Sermons."

From the last entry it is inferred that Rev. Mr. Haskell had closed his labors which he had done.

He was immediately after settled over the Second, or West Fulmouth, Congregational parish, where he has ever since been—a period of more than thirty years, a much respected person, both in and out of the church pulpit.

The Woodfords Congregational society is an offshoot of the Stroudwater, went unceremoniously without "purse or scrip," not even taking hymn books or pew cushions, and July 21, 1872, eight persons, who, on August 11, were joined by three more, left the church to organize one at Woodfords; their names were as follows: Mrs. H. B. Read; Mrs. Jane B. Read; Mrs. Miriam Felton; Mrs. S. I. Hopkins; Mrs. Mary E. Chenery; Mrs. H. B. Woodford; Mr. Isaac Bailey; Mr. John J. Chenery; Mr. William H. Scott; Miss Mary I. Newman and Mrs. Harriet Sawyer.

Here the importance of complete names in record-making is observable.

Deacon Dow in making his report to state officials in 1874, said: "Our condition and prospects are discouraging; the church numbers four males and twelve females."

The Woodfords church reported in 1887: "In the fourteen years of our history this church has had a membership of two hundred and thirty-seven, and I venture to affirm that during the year upon which we are to enter many of those lifeless and 'dead in trespasses and in sin,' will awaken to a realization of the great, bright continent of which they may become citizens."

As the Woodfords society is strong in numbers, not only out of debt but wealthy, perhaps, if invited, it might shingle the old house "just for the looks of the thing," if nothing else, and then make an occasional pilgrimage to the shrine of their ancestors. The stone used for horse-back mounting before the days of carriages remains—that's worth seeing; the Bible, but not the most ancient one, is in the dwelling near by, two organs are within—both said to be in tune; a good bell occupies the belfry; the communion set is at Bradley's Corner, the publishment box at Stroudwater, a contribution box and the large hinges of the front door of the old house are with the writer, which are three feet long.

With uncovered head we approach the structure, the spire nods and sways:

"Let us alone. * * * *
All things are taken from us, and become
Portions and parcels of the dreadful Past,
Let us alone. What pleasure can we have
To war with evil? Is there any peace
In ever climbing up the climbing wave?
All things have rest, and ripen toward the grave
In silence; ripen, fall and cease:
Give us long rest or death, dark death, or dreamful ease!"

A season of general business prosperity surrounded the building of the meeting house as was the case also with the Seminary building, which is now known as the "days of land speculation," and which was followed by great business depression. In the month of May, 1837, specie payment was suspended, the prices of necessities of life were doubled, public indignation meetings holden, and measures taken to reduce the prices of bread stuff held by speculators.

This business depression had a ten-

CONTINUED:

nancy to depress the ardor of the clans of creeds.

The patrons of the Seminary were few, and in 1836 the Rev. Mr. Brimblecom had closed his labors hereabouts, and returned to Massachusetts.

Nov. 18, 1838, Rev. Mr. Bradley records as follows:

"No meeting in the meeting house last Sabbath nor today. This is something new. The gosel of Christ having been preached in this place nearly seventy years and now no preaching. 'How is the gold become dim! how is the most fine gold changed!' Will this church scatter? Will she give up the meeting house; give up the preaching of the gospel of Christ; give up all that is worth having? No, it must not be; the meeting house must be opened; the Sabbath day must be remembered, the gospel of Christ must be preached and people must attend and be more engaged. And I have no doubt but there will be better attention after we are waked up to the subject.

"'Awake, my soul, stretch every nerve,

And press with vigor on.'

"Nov. 22, 1838. A meeting this evening at the brick schoolhouse; [Woodfords] about 20 present. I gave some plain truths to the church members.

"Dec. 13, 1838. I called at five banks to get a small note discounted —less than a $100—good note—good endorsers, but could not be accommodated. At 6 o'clock p. m. obtained my wish. The banks are poor and do but little business. They pay no dividends having met with great losses. Times are troublesome."

At the commencement of the year 1839, "Father Thompson was engaged to take charge of both the Universalists societies, a bass vial was purchased; a choir formed; the old members were awakened; new ones came in and a new interest created"—so the records declare.

Then came the "winter of discontent" and discord in the First Universalist society which culminated in a division of members upon trivial questions of a local character; and on June 16, 1845, "Hon. Francis O. J. Smith, on account of good will and respect for the men and the cause hereinafter mentioned, and payment of one dollar by the committee of George Bishop and Jeremiah Beedel of the 'Westbrook and Falmouth Universalist Society' conveyed a lot of land located at Allen's Corner, containing 999 square feet for the purpose of erecting a meeting house."

The house was built, but the life of the new society was short. The building then erected may now be seen in the rear of the Seminary on the Plains.

In the part of Westbrook, now known as Deering, there are at this date two flourishing Universalist societies, and Congregationalists, Quakers, Methodist, Universalists, Baptists and Episcopalians, all having places of worship, are dwelling together in brotherly love.

A paragraph in a late periodical reads as follows:

"Study the history of your church, particularly the biographies of her sainted dead; acquaint yourself with her doctrines and policy; breathe her spirit; imitate her holy and righteous example, and reproduce her life. The ideals to contend for are a pure heart, a consecrated life, the art of bringing things to pass, and God's approval."

The recommendations contained in the foregoing all clans and believers in creeds can approve. In short, it is a general creed that is growing in public favor.

We listen to the discourses delivered from the pulpit of the Congregationalist, from the Universalist, from the Methodist, from the Episcopalian, and from the Free church with an attentive ear and can detect no difference in the doctrine presented. The heat of argument between the Congregationalist and Universalist and the consequent clashing of sixty to seventy years ago hereabouts seems to have subsided wholly, while scientific investigations produce a higher theology that is overcoming the dogma of the Holy Ghost.

GRANDPA'S SCRAP BOOK

Week of Mar. 20–23, 1901.

REV. CALEB BRADLEY.

A few extracts from his diary.

No. One.

BY LEONARD B. CHAPMAN.

We have presented a good many interesting items from Parson Bradley's diary and a good many remain.

He commenced his first work in this regard upon leaving college, according to the custom of graduates, and continued till 1808, when he stopped, and did not resume till some twenty years later.

"Jan. 28, 1829. At 7 o'clock p. m. went to Cape Elizabeth and met at Mr. Dyer's in counsel for the purpose of examining [Rev.] Isaac Estis. At 8 o'clock adjourned to 10½ o'clock tomorrow. Lodged at Capt. Jordan's.

"29th. Met according to adjournment. Voted to proceed to ordination. Bro. Miltimore [of Falmouth] implored a blessing and read the scriptures. Mr. Bradley [Rev. Caleb Bradley] made the introductory prayer. Bro. Jenkins [Rev. Charles Jenkins of the 3d parish of Portland, who died in 1831] preached. Bro. Pomeroy [Rev. Thaddeus Pomeroy of Gorham who died in 1858] made the consecrating prayer. Bro. Tyler [Rev. Bennett Tyler, 2nd parish of Portland] gave the charge. Bro. Weston [Rev. Daniel Weston of Gray] extended the right hand of fellowship. Bro. Jameson [Rev. Thomas Jameson of Scarboro] addressed the people. Bro. Sawyer [Rev. Moses Sawyer of Scarboro 2nd church] made the concluding prayer. A solemnity pervaded the congregation—a day long to be remembered. I dined at Capt. Jordan's. May Mr. Estis be a faithful minister, do much good, find much happiness, be well supported and free from those embarrassments common to ministers."

[The meeting house in which the ceremonies were performed had an oak frame, cut near the site, or south stood on the southerly side, or south westerly corner of the cemetery lot on Sawyer's Hill, westerly of Point Village.

Hon. William Goold states in his book entitled "Portland in the Past," on page 285, that the frame of the present house, which was erected the year after the parish was incorporated, which incorporation act was obtained in 1733. In this Mr. Goold is mistaken.

The old house was taken away wholly, including the frame. The old records were destroyed by fire. The present records were commenced in 1801, at which time Rev. William Gregg was pastor. He was also parish clerk and and wrote a most excellent hand.

The present house, which was renovated, improved and moved to the other side of the highway a few years since, was built by Dea. Holden, after the pattern of the Saccarappa and Stroudwater Congregational houses, all of which were built nearly at the same time. Messrs. Eli Webb, Rufus Beal and Deacon Holden were the committee to appraise the old Cape Elizabeth house.

When the late changes of the Cape Elizabeth house were in progress we visited the place and examined every part; the frame we found was of soft wood, roughly hewn, and the whole work was performed in the cheapest manner by the builder.

From whence came Dea. Holden or whither he went we cannot state. The last we find of him was when Parson Bradley visited him when he was engaged in conducting farm operations between Saccarappa and Gorham, where Mr. J. Henry Rines, the Portland dry goods man, now resides.

Could the true history of the early days be written of this Cape Elizabeth church and parish it would be exciting reading.

There were continuous clashings for years, first between the Presbyterians and Congregationalists, then between the friends of education and ignorance, followed by refusals to pay parish taxes which finally culminated in court proceedings after an ordination was performed outside the church edifice and under an ap-

CONTINUED:

ple tree, the ordaining party being protected by loaded shot guns, but Rev. Ephriam Clark proved a very worthy man, who died Dec. 11, 1797, aged 75 years.

"Feb. 5, 1829. I attended a wedding at the Point at Mrs. Tabith Sawyer's. Seventy present. Uncomfortable time, too full house, etc. [East Deering, but the Parson does not record a marriage event corresponding in dates.]

"March 6th. A violent snow storm through the night, now as violent as ever. Not such a storm since 1802, the 25th of February. Then Mr. W. and wife were here and here now. [This was Rev. Daniel Weston of Gray.] Not one solitary sleigh or sled has passed thus far. Now, at 4 o'clock p. m. all hands shoveling snow. Not such a block for 27 years.

"16th. The weather has become more calm. 10 o'clock a. m. Rev. Mr. Gregg gone. [Rev. Wm. Gregg who died in Cape Elizabeth in 1856.] Mr. William Akers called. [He resided at Saccarappa, and was a church deacon also father to Paul Akers the sculptor.] Town meeting. All bustle at the meeting house. [We have explained that elections were holden at the meeting house and we think this was the last one.] A mixed multitude. New set of selectmen chosen. All of a sort—all Universalists. O, when will our inhabitants became correct in principle and practice. God hasten the time.

[The selectmen chosen in 1829-30-31, were Oliver Buckley, of Stevens Plains, Charles Bartlett, Stroudwater, Benjamin Quinby, all of whom have been noticed in the News.]

"2nd. This day completes 30 years since I first preached in this place. 'O, time, how swift thy flight.'

"April 4. The river rose very high last night at Saccarappa. The boom broke and seven hundred logs lost—went over the falls.

"26th. Visited an old lady aged 90 years—Mrs. Skillin. Attended a wedding— Eleanor Trickey. A pleasant time. Took tea there. Richard Loring of North Yarmouth and Eleanor Trickey of Westbrook were the couple —the former 62 and the latter nearly 50 years of age."

[Zebulon Trickey was among the first to locate at Stroudwater at the last settlement. He is noticed in the Libby Genealogy on page 50. He was residing at the time of his death a mile westerly of Stroudwater on his farm land adjoining the Saco road. He died prior to 1757.

Zebulon, his son, was born July 20, 1736, and cleared a farm a little westerly of that of his father's. With the death of Robert Trickey, a couple of years since, the farm went from the name, when the Trickey monument, located there, was removed to Evergreen cemetery.

David, the other child who survived, born 1741, retained the homestead. The mother born June 24, 1705, seems to have been a most thoughtful and excellent woman. She married second, 1757, Lieut. Andrew Libby of Scarboro. and went with him to reside, deeding before her marriage all the property to her two children. Her maiden name was Eleanor Libby.

David married Sept. 1, 1768, Mary Hobbs, but of her parentage we know nothing. Both have memorial slabs in the ancient Stroudwater cemetery. He erected a good two story house, now used for the protection of carriages and storage purposes.

They had seven children.

1.—Eunice, m. Richard Johnson, who resided on the Buxton road, some two miles westerly of Stroudwater, whose son, James Johnson,Esq..purchased the David Johnson homestead and part of the farm where descendants still reside.

2.—Mary, m. Zebulon Wescott. He was a shoemaker, etc., and they resided at one time at Stroudwater. She died prior to 1819, leaving as children: Wm. Wescott, Zebulon, Jr., David and Elizabeth. Of them we know nothing.

3.—Daniel, m. Sally Johnson, and resided a mile southerly of Saccarappa. He d. April 26, 1863, aged 92 years.

4.—David, m. Sylvia Barbour of Gray; they resided in North Yarmouth.

5.—Enoch, b. June 24, 1783, m. Nancy Pratt. He d. June 30, 1864, aged 82 years. They resided opposite the entrance to the State Reform School. Charles P. Trickey occupies the homestead.

6.—Eleanor, m. as above, Richard Loring, when both were well along in years.

7.—and last, William, m. Statira Skillin. He resided a half mile westerly of Stroudwater in the two story house he built, now known as the Otis Trickey house. He d. July 8, 1825, aged 38 years, of blood poisoning, leaving two children. The widow m. second, Wm. W. Burnham. Both husbands were tanners.

If there was an eighth child named Statira Trickey it must have died young.

James Johnson, Esq., purchased the David Trickey premises in 1837. We have much data pertaining to these names we are obliged to defer.]

"Sept. 23, 1829. Charles and Moses went to a corn husking last night which continued till 3 o'clock in the morning. I was very much grieved. Hope they will never do it again. I believe they are ashamed of it."

GRANDPA'S SCRAP BOOK

Week of Mar. 27-30, 1901.

REV. CALEB BRADLEY.

A few extracts from his diary.

No. Two.

BY LEONARD B. CHAPMAN.

"January 14, 1830. I was awakened last night about 10 o'cl by the ringing of bells for fire. Moses and I went to town [Portland] and a tremendous fire there was in a cluster of wooden buildings in the center of which was Alpheus Shaw's establishment. [We noticed him briefly in the News of March 23d. He removed from Allen's Corner to Portland.]

[A condensed newspaper accoun of the affair we have made is as follows:

"Wednesday night, about 10 o'clock, fire broke out in or near a saddler's shop occupied by Mr. James Shaw, in the block of wooden buildings on Middle street, known as Main Row. Before the fire was discovered it had made such progress as to preclude the possibility of saving any part of the building. * * * The fire extended to a building on Federal street, which was a double tenement, occupied by four families, and consumed that, together with the wooden addition to a house occupied by Mr. Stephen Swett. The greater part of the property was taken out of the Main Row and saved by the activity of a part of the citizens, whose exertions, together with those of the engine men and volunteer firemen, deserves all praise. We regret however to state there were present those who seemed to consider a little labor as too much for them to bestow for the relief of their suffering fellow citizens.

"All of the wooden block on Middle street was burned. The sufferers are James Shaw, who had no insurance; Paine and Meserve, grocers; Burbank and Hanson; Alpheus Shaw, who was insured $8000 on stock and $1000 on building; David Griffin, apothecary, insured $2,500; W. Harris, insured $2,500. Besides the above the block was occupied by W. P. Smith, John Morgan, Andrew L. Emerson; R. A. L. Codman, Esq.; Adams & Cummings, Attornies: and by N. G. Jewett, lottery office. It is understood these gentlemen saved their papers."

[The firemen held a mass meeting at the "brick engine house on Market street" and passed resolution denouncing citizens who appeared in kid gloves and silk hats at fires and declined to assist when called upon by firemen, and recommended that a law be enacted and enforced to punish such persons.]

"Feb. 6, 1833. I attended the installation of Rev. Josiah G. Merrill at Cape Elizabeth [who died at Otisfield, 1872.] Rev. Henry C. Jewett of the Westbrook. now Deering, society asked a blessing and read a chapter of the Scriptures. I made the introductory prayer; Rev. Mr. Merrill, of Biddeford, preached; Rev. Thomas Jameson, of Scarboro, made the concluding prayer; Rev. Elijah Kellogg, of the Portland 2nd parish, gave the charge; Rev. Mr. ——— of Norway gave the right hand of fellowship; Dr. Tyler, [Bennett Tyler, D. D., President of Dartmouth, who was called to the 2nd church of Portland in 1829,] gave the charge to the people; and Rev. William T. Dwight, [of the Portland 3d parish,] made the concluding prayer. A good degree of solemnity manifested, concluding with a violent snow storm.

"July 9. Married Eveline Mitchell and John W. Dunn."

[She was a daughter of Peleg Mitchell, and sister to the wife of the late Charles Maxfield of Stroudwater. He was a Methodist clergyman. They removed to the Western country.]

"January 15. 1831. Very cold. At 11 o'clock, Rev. Mr. Jewett and I went to Scarboro to attend the funeral of Rev. Thomas Lancaster, aged 87 years,—services at the meeting house at 12.30 o'clock. Rev. Mr. Jewett made an introductory prayer, Rev. Mr. William Miltimore, [of the Falmouth 1st parish] preached. I made the funeral prayer. We went to Mr. Lancaster's house and conveyed the remains to the tomb. Pall bearers—Messrs. Miltimore, Jewett, Tilton and myself. No other clergymen present. Returning to the house we took refreshments. Mr. Tilton prayed and then we returned home. Called at Mr. Jameson's—left there at dark, amid a most violent blow and very cold. Called at Mr. Skillins to warm ourselves and arrived home at 8 o'clock p. m. A more uncomfortable ride I never had, but God took care of us, and I was glad when I was seated before a good fire at home with my family, and Mrs. B. appeared to be exceedingly glad."

[From an obituary we have compiled the following:

Rev. Thomas Lancaster was born in Beverly, Mass., and graduated from Harvard College in 1764 For some years he was employed at school keeping in Beverly and vicinity, where he was united in marriage with [Lydia Jones.] Feeling called by God to the work of the Christian ministry he prepared himself for the labor and accepted a call, in 1775, from the First Church of Scarboro to become its pastor. He had an excellent voice and delivered his discourses with a good degree of earnestness. He was early in life antique in his manners and was of a positive temperament, hence sometimes was abrupt, so much so, that he would call his parishioners by name in pulpit discourses when he thought they were sinning. His salary never exceeded $266. He outlived all his children, and his first wife. He continued in the ministry till he was four score in years and was greatly enfeebled, but his parishioners would not set him aside but employed a colleague He fell asleep at the age of 87, somewhat suddenly and in the 56th of his ministry in the same church.

In the old cemetery located upon the easterly side of the highway leading from the Boston and Maine depot to Prout's Neck, and not far from the depot, may be seen two memorial slabs inscribed as follows:

In memory of
MRS. LYDIA LANCASTER
wife of the
Rev. Thomas Lancaster
who slept in Jesus
Nov. 11, 1815,
In the 70th year
of her age.

Are these the forms that moulder in the dust,
Or the transcendant glories of the just.

In Memory of
REV. THOS. LANCASTER
who died
January 12, 1831,
in the 87th year of his age
and 56th of his ministry.

He, like his Master was by some despised;
Like Him, by many others loved and prized:
But theirs shall be the everlasting crown
Not whom the world, but Jesus Christ will own.

Upon another slab is recorded the fact that Miss Dorothy Lancaster, a daughter of the above named, was born Oct. 18, 1781, died April 29, 1806. Epitaph.

Virtue, not length of years the mind matures,
That life is long that answers life's great end

CONTINUED:

[Rev. Thomas Pierce of Newbury and Ann Haskell of Gloucester, Mass., were united in marriage Nov. 30, 1762. He was a Harvard College graduate and a Presbyterian, but he was settled over the First Congregational church of Scarboro.

The next year he purchased two to three acres of land located on the easterly side of the highway from the present Boston and Maine railroad depot to Prout's Neck, and between the depot and the old cemetery. Upon the lot he built the large, two story house as now seen with the parlor unfinished, to which and from which house, it is said, not a nail has been added or taken since the construction. He died in 1775 and was succeeded both in the ministry and the possession of the house by Rev. Thomas Lancaster.

Rev. Thomas Pierce left a widow and several children, one of whom was an odd character, who resided and died in what is now the Deering district of Portland, where there are many descendants. Of him we can make at this time only this brief allusion.

Parson Lancaster was settled over the Scarboro 1st Parish Nov. 8, 1775.

We find records of children as follows:

1—Sewall, b. July 5, 1776.
2—Thomas, b. March 25, 1778.
3—Sewall, b. July 1, 1779.
4—Dorothy, b. Oct. 18, 1781.
5—Thomas, b. April 2, 1784.
6—John, b. April 30, 1786.

Under date of Dec. 26, 1812, Rev. Samuel Dean records—"Major Lancaster's funeral," and adds: "Sewall, son of Rev. Mr. L., of Scarboro, aged 33."

Sewall Lancaster's remains were interred in the Portland Western cemetery, where there is a memorial slab.

At the funeral service of Sewall Lancaster, which was holden Nov. 25, —31 days earlier than Parson Dean has it—there was read, by Sewall's request, which he had prepared, a farewell address to Ancient Land Mark Lodge, which was printed. His wife had two children who died young.

Parson Lancaster's wife had two children before coming to Scarboro—Sarah, who m. June 1, 1788, John McLellan of Portland, and Mary, who m. June 18, 1797, Samuel Tompson, Esq., he b. in Standish, Oct. 11, 1773, but of the Scarboro stock. She d. Feb. 11, 1813 after having had ten children, and he m. 2nd Hannah Fogg.

Esther Libby, b. in Scarboro, Nov. 2, 1767, dau. of Edward Libby, m. 1st, July 14, 1875, Matthias Libby of that town, he b. Jan. 5, 1762. He was a farmer occupying a part of his father's farm. He was industrious, and became well-to-do. They were members of the church where Parson Lancaster officiated. He d. April 9th, 1807. The widow m. 2nd July 11, 1816, Rev. Thomas Lancaster. She d. Oct. 13, 1840.

Esther, the 4th child of Esther and Matthias Libby, b. Dec. 25, 1794, m. May 23, 1819, George Tate of Stroudwater, where two sons, named Washington and Augustus Tate, respectively, reside.

William Tate, b. in London, England, Nov. 15, 1740, and died there in 1833, was the father of George Tate. William had two wives, first, Eleanor Patrick, who died at Stroudwater in 1784, aged 38 years, and he m. second, June 29, 1794, the fifth child of Jethro Libby of Scarboro. She was named Hannah. William Tate built the block of two stores, in 1784, at Stroudwater, now occupied by Andrew Hawes, Esq., where William Tate was in trade before going to London, where he also engaged in trade, and where he died.

In the Eastern Herald, published in Portland, Aug. 23, 1794, is a notice that reads as follows:

"Died in Falmouth [Stroudwater] on Wednesday last Capt. George Tate. He was born in England in the year 1700 and was a seaman on board the first frigate ever built in Russia in the reign of Peter the Great."

This was the grandfather of George Tate who married Esther Libby, the stepdaughter of Parson Lancaster.

Capt. George Tate came here to procure mast trees for the English navy, acting in the capacity of agent for that country. He built in 1755 the two story house at Stroudwater with the gambrel roof and huge chimney, still remaining. He had two wives, the first he brought with him, the second he obtained here. He has a memorial slab at Stroudwater.

The story of the Tates if truly told in print would read like a romance. Should we ascend the parent stalk as the squirrel does the sturdy oak and examine the branches we should find many names connected by direct genealogical descent and by marriage ties that are illustrious—the eldest son of the American ancestor, fifty years a naval commander, under the Russian Government, his garments all bedecked at the close of life with befitting badges for meritorious acts in battle, who not only became a First Admiral, but a member of the Imperial Senate of that country; a granddaughter, who was the wife of the originator of State street, Portland, and the grandmother of ex-Mayor Ingraham of the same city; Admiral Alden being of another branch and a grandson—one of Portland's illustrious citizens: Timothy S. Arthur, with a world-wide fame as a writer and publisher of fiction on moral subjects, whose wife was a descendant; then the wife of the late Joseph Walker, both of whose names will live as long as records endure.]

273

CAPT. GEORGE TATE.

A Record of a Few of the Events Together with Some of the Names of His Descendants.

BY LEONARD B. CHAPMAN.

In our article of last week we made allusion to the Tate family.

Capt. George Tate came to Stroudwater, as we stated, from England as an agent for the procurement of masts for the English navy. Commencing on page 390, vol. VII, of 1896, may be seen a record of many facts connected with the industry.

At the northwesterly corner of the bridge over Fore river, Capt. Tate erected a large warehouse, and a residence for himself as now seen upon the lot he purchased in 1753, now in the center of the village, which was by far the finest residence outside of the limits of Portland. His penmanship was of the first order and he lived "English" as an ancient account book before us plainly shows where turkeys and mutton legs are charged to him by the half-score. His wife died Sept. 30, 1770, aged 60 years. A finely executed likeness in colors in a gold locket shows her to have been a woman of comeliness, which is one of the few articles of the household that has been saved at Stroudwater with the Bible, now bereft of the cover, which contains the names and dates of births of five children, as follows:

1—Samuel, b. Aug. 3, 1734. He had two wives.
2—William, b. Nov. 15, 1740, d. in London, England, Aug., 1833. He had two wives.
3—George, Jr., b. Nov. 7, 1741, d. young.
4—George, Jr., (the Russian Admiral), b. June 14, 1746, d. at St. Petersburg, 1824, making this country a visit in 1820. Of his personal effects nothing is known hereabouts. He did not marry.
5—Robert, b. Jan. 3, 1751, d. at Berbrice, 1804. His wife was Martha Slemons of Stroudwater.

Capt. Tate was a member of the Rotherhithe Parish of London, where he has a record. His daughter, Mary, was baptized there April 24, 1748, aged 28 days, whose burial is recorded there Sept. 5, 1749, which shows Capt. Tate and family were in London at the time of the last date.

Following is a transcript of the grave stone record of Capt. Tate and his first wife:

To
the memory of
GEORGE TATE,
who departed this life
in the year 1794,
aged 93 years, and
nine months.

To
The memory of
MARY TATE,
wife of the above George Tate,
who departed this life
in the year 1770,
Aged 60.

Capt. Tate was married in England and all his children were born there and the few relics of their school work show them as scholarly and in the matter of penmanship far above the average of the present day hereabouts.

He became "American" immediately on arriving here, and in the records of the organizations to meet the Indians at the last encounter with them his name appears in the vanguard. Then when the war of the Revolution came on his name is found among those who contributed much to aid the Colonies, but in church matters he was "English" and served in Portland as church Warden; but his son Samuel kept in touch with the Tories, though we find no record that he took up arms against the Colonies.

Capt. Tate married, second, April 15, 1779, (when nearly 80 years old) Mrs. Mary Coverly, a widow, in Falmouth.

At Gorham, this state, there was born in a certain family by the name of Webb a child that received the Christian name of Jonathan, and he appears on record as Jonathan Webb. In early manhood he was employed about the mills at Saccarappa, then he became a stockholder in mill property, kept shop, built the largest and best house on Main street—now the public house of the place—with a story added, his name still being recalled by the villagers.

March 4, 1781, Jonathan Webb and Miss Mary Coverly—a daughter of Mrs. Mary Coverly, the last becoming, as we have shown, the second wife of Capt. George Tate—were united in marriage.

Capt. George's son William took himself a wife home to the house of his father, Robert, the youngest son, resided on the road to Saccarappa, as we will show, and Mary Coverly, nee Webb, at Saccarappa, Mrs. Capt. Tate resided alternately; and to even up property matters, Capt. Tate gave Jonathan Webb, who had an open eye for good things, the Stroudwater warehouse and lot. The records show, however, a sale, but "tradition," a gift. But Jonathan did not get peaceful possession of the premises, for, with "force and arms against the laws and peace of the King," the Patrick clan, as former owners, aided by those who were united to the name by marriage ties, came from near and from afar and removed the ancient bounds and then declared "war" upon the new claimant when the matter of the dispute was heard in court.

Oct. 20, 1804. Parson Bradley states he attended the funeral of Mrs. Tate, which was probably that of Capt. Tate's second wife, both of whose Christian names seem to have been Mary.

After Mrs. Mary (Coverly) Webb had given birth to five children, whose names, etc., appear in the Deering News of Aug. 31, 1895, she departed this life, and on Dec. 23, 1803, at the age of 36, Parson Bradley says he attended her funeral.

Jonathan Webb married second, July 1, 1804, Miss Susannah Smith, born in Stoughton, Mass.—one of twelve daughters.

In the old cemetery located northwesterly of Saccarappa, now so deserted that it reflects discredit upon the City of Westbrook, towering above the three or four others, and hid by bushes, may be seen a slate memorial slab inscribed as follows:

Sacred
to the memory of
MR. JONATHAN WEBB,
who was born in Gorham
Nov. 25, 1755, & died
April 8, 1810, Aged 55.

JESUS, I give my spirit up,
And trust it in thy hand.
And dying flesh shall rest in hope,
And rise at thy command.

Now I renounce my carnal hope,
My fond desire recall,
I give my worldly interest up
And make my GOD my all.

March 10, 1816, Mrs. Susanna (Smith) Webb, widow of Jonathan, was united in marriage with Capt. Nathaniel Partridge, and he went to reside with her in the Webb mansion.

Capt. Partridge died, and Nov. 1, 1827, the widow became the second wife of Rev. Caleb Bradley and went with him, taking her two sons, to reside at Bradley's Corner, now in the Deering district of Portland. While at Bowdoin College the Parson went there often to see them and his observations on "modern" college life is quite interesting.

We will make just three extracts from his diary, as follows:

"Sept. 7, 1837. At 9 o'clock a. m. left home for Brunswick, with Mrs. Bradley, Nathaniel and Franklin. Dined at Freeport; at 5 p. m. at Brunswick. Put up at Elliots.

"8th. The two Partridges admitted into college. At 3 p. m. set out for home. Three miles from Brunswick the stage upset, the horses with front wheels ran against my carriage, broke the axletree, but no one hurt. Wonderful escape! The good providence of God took care of us, the neighbors being kind.

"9th. The carriage carried to Brunswick—mended—cost $3.75, stage agent paid it, then set out for home, arriving at 7 o'clock."

CONTINUED:

Nov. 3, 1843, Mrs. Susanna Smith—Webb—Bradley died, and Parson Bradley took as his third wife, Dec. 26, 1844, Mrs. Abigail (Loring) Codman, the second wife of and widow of Capt. James Codman of Gorham, and went home with her to reside. She was born in Halifax, Mass., July 23, 1779, and was a daughter of Ignatius Loring, who built, in 1797, the Bradley house as now seen, the frame being shipped from that town, or it may be that Ignatius, who built the house, was a brother. She died Aug. 17, 1854, and the Parson returned to his former home at Bradley's Corner, where he died June 6, 1861, aged 86 years.

His first wife was Sarah Crocker daughter of a Massachusetts clergyman, whom he found in the Browne family at Woodfords when he came here to locate, going to the Widow Browne's to board. They were married Nov. 16, 1801; she d. April 27, 1821, and was interred in the Mitchell's Hill cemetery, near Brighton Corner; the second wife at Saccarappa, the third, at Gorham; he, at Pine Grove, back of the Westbrook Seminary. Following is a transcript of the white marble memorial slab:

REV. CALEB BRADLEY
died
June 2, 1861,
aged 89.
Pastor of the Con. Ch.
in Westbrook from
1799 to 1829.
Sarah Crocker
his wife
died April 27, 1821
Aged 41.
To be continued.

GRANDPA'S SCRAP BOOK

Week of April 10-13, 1901.

CAPT. GEORGE TATE.

A Record of a Few of the Events, Together with Some of the Names of His Descendants.

BY LEONARD B. CHAPMAN.

(Continued from last week.)

(1.)—Capt. Samuel Tate, b. Aug. 3, 1734, in Rotherhith Parish, London, England, son of Capt. George and Mary Tate, was employed by the English government as a captain of ships for the transporting of masts from this to that country. Parson Smith notices his coming, loading and sailing. During the time of the war of the Revolution he had a stronger love for that country than this, but we find no records of overt acts.

He married his first wife (it is presumed) in that country—she died in this. In the Stroudwater cemetery may be seen a memorial slab inscribed as follows:

Here lies the body of Mrs.
Elizabeth Tate,
Wife of Capt. Samuel Tate,
Who died July 26, 1769,
Aged 29 years.

He had no record as the owner of real estate in this country. In London he resided in Algas Parish. They had born there Mary Ann in 1761, and Sarah Maria in 1763, who died young. In this country, and somewhere hereabouts, they had Ann, b. March 18, 1767. She was less than ten years of age when her mother died. Then there was one who was named William Major Tate, who was but a month old when his mother died and both were taken to London by the father, where Mary was liberally educated. Upon her return to Portland she became the second wife of Joseph Holt Ingraham—he prosperous—she beautiful. Mr. Ingraham was a selectman many years, and representative to the General Court, and a man of forethought and great liberality. She bore him a large number of children.

William Major Tate returned also to this country, and Dec. 7, 1797, was united in marriage with Mary Trickey seventh and youngest child of Zebulon and Rebecca Skillings, his wife, the Trickeys residing on the Saco road, a couple of miles westerly of Stroudwater. This Mr. Tate was a mariner.

May 24, 1805, Eleanor Frost, the 4th child of Andrew P. Frost and Eleanor Slemmons, his wife, all of Stroudwater, became the wife of Peter T. Clark, a tailor and fiddler, and Mr. Clark built a two story house on leased land on the northerly side of Congress street opposite the school house where the great elm tree may now be seen, which stood at the south westerly corner of the dwelling. Mr. Clark hung out his sign as a tailor and fiddled while others danced, the old hamlet then being in its zenith of prosperity, but the house soon went from the possession of Mr. Clark on a foreclosed mortgage to the Trickeys, and Clark removed his sign, and fiddle and tailor business towards Bradley's Corner to his wife's inherited estate, where Mrs. Clark died Oct. 3, 1853, having had eight children. The Clark story is a long one or we would tell more of it.

In this Clark house Mrs. Mary (Trickey) resided till enfeebled by age when she was removed to the home of her brother and nephew, both named Zebulon, when the house was taken down, and the boards and timber made into firewood. We remember the transaction.

In Parson Bardley's diary we find as follows:

"Sept. 30, 1840. Set out for Dunstan Corner in Scarboro, with Mrs. Bradley with me. * * * * Upon our return called at Zebulon Trickey's where we took tea and where we were kindly treated. They are a pleasant family but have nothing to do with religious matters. They don't go to meeting, so it is said. Mrs. Tate, an old lady, sister to Mr. Trickey, very sick there, seemed to be glad to see me, said she had been praying that I might call. I conversed and prayed with her, and she expressed a wish that I call again.

"Oct. 15, 1840. I went over to Zebulon Trickey's where I took tea. Prayed with Mrs. Tate and the family. Mr. Trickey had a sister die this morning in Scarboro, aged 80 years—a sister to Mrs. Tate. [Zebulon Trickey, father to Mrs. Tate, and his wife had seven children and Mary (Tate) Trickey was the youngest.] Mrs. Lancaster was buried this p. m., widow of the late Parson Lancaster, he having been dead a number of years, she his second wife, [and widow of Matthias Libby. Another record says she died Oct. 13, 1840. Her remains were interred on the farm and by the side of her first husband. Her name was Esther Libby.]

"February 5, 1841. I set out on foot to attend the funeral of Mrs. [Mary Trickey] Tate at Zebulon Trickey's, she an aunt to him. Mr. Trickey and wife have six children, five of whom are grown, and all are very industrious, and all what the world calls sharpers or money catchers. If they were as much engaged for heaven and salvation they no doubt would go there."

We think she had no children.

Capt. Samuel Tate, father to the husband of Mrs. Mary (Trickey) Tate, married in Portland, second, Eunice Graffam, intention of m. recorded August 21, 1808.

In the Portland Argus we find as follows under date of Sept. 28, 1809:

Died, Mrs. Eunice Tate, wife of [Capt.] Samuel Tate, and daughter of Caleb Graffam, aged 21 years. Funeral from her father's residence, Main street.

Capt. Samuel Tate spent his last days in Portland in the Ingraham family where he died April 2, 1814, aged 77 years. His remains were deposited in the Ingraham tomb.

(To be continued.)

275

GRANDPA'S SCRAP BOOK

Week of April 17-20, 1901.

CAPT. GEORGE TATE.

A Record of a Few of the Events, Together with Some of the Names of His Descendants.

BY LEONARD B. CHAPMAN.

(Continued from last week.)

(2.) William Tate, b. Nov. 15, 1740, in London, England, son of Capt. George Tate, the mast agent, did not take kindly to the water as did his brothers, but on the 23d day of April, 1785, purchased the lot for £27, and built the building where Andrew Hawes, Esq., trades at Stroudwater, in Deering, then used himself a part of it for mercantile purposes as we have before stated. He was, however, in trade before this date.

Among those who came from "over the water" to stay at the time of the last settlement of the hamlet was David Patrick. The date he departed this life does not appear but Mary, his widow, lived to the ripe age of 95 years, departing Aug. 6, 1806, leaving seven children, or seven heirs. He has no memorial slab nor has anyone by the name, but the mammoth chimney in the ancient Tate house, and the one story dwelling at the southwesterly angle made by the crossing of Congress over Westbrook street where the Patricks last resided are reminders of the name. It was in this one-story house that William Tate wooed and wed Eleanor, evidently the third child, born to David and wife Mary, but she was not long of the world after the marriage ceremony.

In the old village cemetery may be seen a reminder of the events we now chronicle, the inscription of which reads as follows:

In Memory of
MRS. ELEANOR TATE
wife of Mr. William Tate,
who Departed this Life
Nov. 20th, 1784,
aged 38 years.
Also of Samuel late son of
the above Eleanor and
Wm. Tate
who died Nov. 22d, 1776,
aged 3 years & 8 months.

Jethro Libby of Scarboro, a farmer, married second, March 5, 1761, Hannah (Woodbury) Moody, widow of Daniel Moody and daughter of Israel Woodbury of Cape Elizabeth. Their second child, named Jethro, was born in 1763; their fourth, named Charles, April 8, 1767; between the dates of these two events Hannah Libby was born. We find no record of her birth, but she became, January 28, 1794, the second wife of William Tate.

Charles Libby resided the last part of his long life in the Beech Ridge region of Scarboro, where he died on the Shute farm, May 14, 1850. He was always clean shaved, had a round, full face, smiling countenance, long, white hair, slouch hat, was thick set—in short, in outward appearance a real Libby. He was the Stephen Gerard of the region, though his fame as a money lender covered a much larger area than that of Beech Ridge, but in his composition, socially, a far different man from Gerard, the Philadelphia millionaire, but "Uncle Charlie's" horse partook strongly of Gerard's nature, and we boys of fifty-odd years ago kept ourselves from his mouth, not caring to go home minus an ear. Charles' son, John, succeeded his father, and departed this life May 19, 1869—a tall, slim man of few words. Though a half century has passed since the demise of "Uncle Charley Libby," the wagon he used, may, perhaps, still be seen in use on the premises, not having been washed since its construction.

Mrs. Tate spent her last days with her brother, Charles Libby.

Children of William Tate and his two wives:

1—Samuel, b. July, 1773, and died young, according to grave stone record of the mother presented above.

2—William, b. Feb. 9, 1775. He became a mariner, and we find him in London, England, in 1801, when he signed away his claim to his mother's share in the Patrick estate at Stroudwater which was "one-seventh part." This is the only intelligence we have of him.

Children of second wife:

3—George, b. Nov. 3, 1796, m. Esther Libby.

4—Eleanor, b. Aug. 17, 1801, m. Nathaniel Jordan.

5—John, b. 1803. He was a mariner and died of an epidemic in the Southern country. He did not marry.

We find names of other children, but as dates are conflicting or missing and they died young we omit as unimportant.

William Tate resided in the original Tate house as now observed. It was he who changed the original construction of the front roof, which disposed of the balcony at the top of the second story, by continuing the roof down over the third, thereby covering the third story windows, which may now be seen by entering the attic where the boys gathered more than once, when the house was empty, fifty years ago, to obtain lead from the roof-closed window holes from which to manufacture shot gun bullets.

From the now concealed balcony the view at the time of construction of the house must have been all-inspiring, particularly at the closing hours of the day, with the "mast yard" in front filled with mammoth mast-logs; vessels loading with lumber from the bridge, others awaiting their turn; Capisic falls, saw and grist mill, one up the stream from the other; the Charles Frost garrison house, known many years later as the "Brew House;" the awaiting escort to accompany the "court" from York to the "Neck"—now Portland, but we have never seen it stated but once that a cannon was discharged when the "court" arrived at the bridge that the fact of the approach might be known at the "Neck" in advance. Then the knee breeches and cocked hat were worn by the denizen of the hamlet, the raftsman's song was heard, as well as the din of the mill saws on the Stroudwater immediately back of the Tate house—all conspiring to make the view and situation a charming one. We see the landscape now in our imagination as it was then. A few years later, at the close of the war of the Revolution we observed a changed scene, hunters for boundary land marks, the Means house going up as now observed, commotion, neighbors divided in opinions, the view from the Tate house balcony obstructed, the town authorities appealed to, town meetings holden, the courts invoked, then tranquility coming out of chaos; and now, a century and over later, the Tate house still defying the storm tempest, the Means house occupying the "mast yard," standing upon its original foundation, but the knee-buckle, the cocked hat, the actors in the ancient drama all gone, only a footprint here and there remaining.

A century from now who will tell the story of official neglect in the care—or no care—of our highways since we were annexed territorially to Portland, and never before within the memory of the oldest citizen, and no written record can be found of the fact, that brick-yard clay was ever used as surface dressing for highways and a mixture of coal-cinders, many as large as a man's fist, and broken glass ware from Portland hotels for sidewalks!

A story is told that recently an anti-annexationest visited the old Stroudwater cemetery and shouted—

"And wilt thou not one moment raise
Thy weary head, awhile to see
The later sports of earthly days—
How Unlike what once enchanted thee?"

The reply was as follows—

"O, not like thee would I remain.
And o'er the sidewalks ashes strew;
But municipal liberty regain,
Compelling - Street - Commissioner-In Fernal(d) - to - return - Robert C. Hawkes to-the-farm-and-make-repairs on-the-roads-that-will-stand-rain!"

To be continued.

GRANDPA'S SCRAP BOOK

Week of April 24-27, 1901.

CAPT. GEORGE TATE.

A Record of a Few of the Events, Together with Some of the Names of His Descendants.

BY LEONARD B. CHAPMAN.

(Continued from last week.)

(2)—William Tate, second son of Capt. George Tate, the mast agent, seems to have possessed the qualities of a business man. He wrote an excellent business letter. He owned shipping, and in 1799 his brother Robert was in his employment as Captain of a brig, but an adverse wind overtook him in business affairs and he saw his house and his shops and his goods go to meet the demands of creditors; then he went to London, Eng., where the business tide turned in his favor and where he built residences upon a public thoroughfare he named "Westbrook" street.

It was in 1803 that Samuel Parkman of Boston took possession of the Capt. Tate house to satisfy a claim of $4,895, who in 1805 transferred it to Dr. Calvin Thomas of Tyngsborough, Mass., for $2,500. This shows the value of real estate a hundred years ago hereabouts.

In 1810 one Charles Barker, a shipwright, was residing upon the premises.

William Tate never returned to this country, but sent considerable money to relatives from time to time; the date of his demise we have not obtained.

3—George Tate, b. Nov. 3, 1796, son of William and his second wife, named Hannah Libby, whose name we number three on the margin, because he was the third of his father's children who matured, added, when he became of lawful age, the distinguishing mark of "Jr.," that the name might be known on the records from that of his cousin George, son of his uncle, Robert Tate.

George Tate, Jr., m. Jan. 22, 1819, Esther Libby, b. Dec. 25, 1794, dau. of Matthias and Esther (Libby) Libby, she the 4th child named on the family records.

They commenced housekeeping in Scarboro, but his father purchasing for him the house at Stroudwater where two of his children still reside, in the house once occupied by Capt. Isaac Lobdell, who owned the first carpet of the place, George, Jr., removing to Stroudwater, where he hauled the surplus part of the house, which was two story, and used as a shop by Lobdell, to the place where it may now be seen, with a story taken off, the first house northeasterly of the State Reform School farm, engaged in trade and built vessels, but as in the case of his father, an adverse wind stranded his business career and he died Oct. 7, 1841, aged 45 years. His remains repose in the family lot in Evergreen cemetery, located on Spruce avenue, which commences a few rods in front of the Main entrances and passes to the left.

Children of George Jr., and Esther (Libby) Tate:

1—Dorothy, b. Nov. 24, 1819, m. Sewall Cloudman, and they resided in Gorham, this State.

2—William, b. May 19, 1821, d. April 26, 1862, aged 41 years, 5 months.

3—George, m., resided in Biddeford, where there are descendants.

4—John S., m. Julia Hicks. She has appeared in the Stevens articles of Stevens Plains. He d. at Stroudwater, March 5, 1861, aged 38 years, 7 months. The widow m. Joseph C. Parker and resides at Stroudwater.

5—Samuel, m. Caroline Emery of Limington, resided at Stroudwater. A daughter only remains of the family, who m. and resides in Gorham.

6—Sarah Maria, b. Jan., 1830, d. unmarried, April 2, 1848, at home, aged 18 yrs. 9 mo.

7—Charles, b. Jan., 1831, m. d. recently in Waltham, Mass. No children.

8—Washington, b. Feb. 22, 1833, resides at home, unm.

9—Augustus, b. April 3, 1835, m. Sarah McDonald of Gorham. Resides at Stroudwater, under the parental roof. No children.

10—Henry, b. Jan., 1837, d. Sept. 5, 1859, aged 22 yrs.

William Tate of this family was the only member who indulged in the calling and traditions of his ancestors, he engaging in whale-fishery, sailing from New Bedford, Mass., and was one of the most accurate with the harpoon and best managers of a boat's crew who sailed from that port. The others, all being genealogically more than three-fourths Libby, sought land employments.

Eleanor Tate, sister to the preceding, b. Aug. 17, 1801, m. in Cape Elizabeth Feb. 14, 1821, Nathaniel Jordan, he b. Nov. 1, 1793, and d. at Poland, this state, Feb. 12, 1873, upon a farm William Tate, her father, purchased for her. They had nine children, who produced a score and a half of grandchildren. After his death the widow removed to a farm in Gorham, this state, located upon the road from Saccarappa to Little Falls. We met with her when she had passed the 80th mile stone in life, when she displayed every evidence of having been a woman of keen wit, who had and was then, the possessor of a bright intellect and a mind replete with incidents of the long ago, and evidences of personal beauty in youth, even then, at that late day in life, possessing a fair countenance.

George Tate, Jr., and his sister, Eleanor, were the only children of their father's family who married.

To be continued.

GRANDPA'S SCRAP BOOK

Week of May 1-4, 1901.

CAPT. GEORGE TATE.

A Record of a Few of the Events, Together with Some of the Names of His Descendants.

BY LEONARD B. CHAPMAN.

(Continued from last week.)

(4) In our allusion April 3 to George Tate, Jr., the Russian Admiral, b. June 14, 1746, fourth child of Capt. George Tate, the Mast Agent, departing this life after an eventful career, in 1824, at St. Petersburg, we remarked: Of his personal effects nothing is known hereabouts.

It appears that he followed the custom at school of the bright, smart boys of ye olden time, performing every sum in the arithmetic, and in a very neat appearing hand copied the work into a blank book, which is still in existence at Stroudwater in a good state of preservation, as is also a copy of the Admiral's will, which we are allowed to preserve by printing. It is an interesting document and lets in upon the Admiral's career a little light that richly deserves recognition. We understand there is also in existence a manuscript letter of his in which he expresses a desire to be informed of the date he was born, as he had been so absorbed in the numerous events of his life he had actually forgotten the time of the greatest event of all.

Following is a copy of his will, but it must be understood that he did not marry:

IN THE NAME OF GOD, AMEN.

I, George Tate, Admiral, in the service of His Imperial Majesty, of all the Russians, and at present residing in St. Petersburgh, being of sound and disposing mind and memory, do make and ordain this my last will and testament in the manner and form following, that is to say:

First: I will that my debts, if any, (which I know of none) and funeral charges be paid and discharged by my executor hereinafter named.

I give and bequeath to my brother, William Tate, at present residing in Great Britain, all my stock in the Bank of England consisting of two thousand six hundred and eighty-eight pounds, eleven shillings and a penny in the B per cent loan Annuities, and in case of his death to his children.

To my niece, Ann Ingraham, wife of Joseph Holt Ingraham, residing at Portland, Casco Bay, in the United States of North America, the whole of the money I have in the Imperial Loan Bank at St. Petersburgh, Russia, consisting of the sum of Forty Thousand, six hundred and forty *rubles with the interest due thereon, after her death to her children by the said Joseph Holt Ingraham.

To the two sons of my late brother, Robert Tate, George and Robert, [Robert should be Samuel. L. B. C.] the remainder of the money I have in the Imperial Lombardy, consisting of the sum of nine thousand rubles, with the interest due upon the whole sum of twenty-four thousand rubles.

To my Godson, Edward Simpson, son of Dr. Robert Simpson, residing at St. Petersburgh, the sum of ten thousand rubles from the money I have in the Imperial Lombardy. In case of his death before he becomes of age, it will then go to the above said Dr. Robert Simpson, to dispose of to the rest of his children as he may think proper.

To my Godson, James Booker, son of John and Isabella Booker, now residing at Cronstadt, Russia, the sum of five thousand rubles, to be taken from the money which I have in the Imperial Lombardy, which money is to remain at interest until he comes of age. In case of his death to any of his children, the above named John Booker.

To my brother, William Tate, all my silver in a small trunk sealed up, and covered with canvas; in case of his death, I then bequeath it to my before named Ann Ingraham, my niece.

To Mr. John Simpson, son of Mr. Robert Simpson, the fourteen of fifteen volumes of Encyclopedia Londonnical. I bequeath to him likewise to Mr. Joseph Simpson all the rest of my books that are in his father's house in St. Petersburgh.

To Dr. Robert Simpson I bequeath my large bear skin shako, likewise a table service of Queen's ware packed up in a large cask in a cellar of Vice Admiral George's house in Cronstadt, with all the therein packed in the round cask.

To Mrs. Isabella Booker, wife of the aforesaid John Booker, my blue table service lying in the cellar of the house of Vice Admiral George in Cronstadt.

To Vice Admiral George, all the wine and other liquors belonging to me, lying in his cellar in his house in Cronstadt.

The money I have left to my two nephews, Robert [error, should be Samuel. L. B. C.] and George Tate, sons of the late Brother Robert Tate, who at present reside at Falmouth, Casco Bay, in the Massachusetts State, is to be divided equally between them, capital and interest.

To my brother, William Tate, before mentioned, I bequeath my gold sword, which is lying in the large trunk, and which was given me by His Majesty, the King of Great Britain.

All the rest of my things, as carriages, clothes, linen, furniture and every other article to be sold and the sum they amount to I bequeath to my brother, William Tate.

I request the kindness of Mr. John Simpson to act as executor with the advice of his father and for the trouble he may be at to make a regular charge and pay himself from the money from the things sold. What sum may be over he will pay to my brother, William Tate, as above mentioned.

I have furniture and other things at Mr. Booker's, at Vice Admiral George's house at Cronstadt, likewise at Dr. Robert Simpson's in St. Petersburgh, and a chariot at Mr. William Booker's with all belonging to it.

St. Petersburgh, June 14, one thousand eight hundred and eighteen (1818.

George Tate, L. S.

Witness:
George Montague Hamilton,
Charles Baird,
Archd. Ingles.

I, Thomas Bishop, his Imperial Majesty's Notary Public, do hereby certify unto all whom it may concern that the above and foregoing is a duplicate, or true copy of an original last will and testament made, signed and sealed by the late Admiral George Tate and duly witnessed as above, as exhibited unto me this day, for the purpose of transcribing the same. In testimony whereof I have hereunto set my hand and seal of office in St. Petersburgh, this third day of March, 1821.

Thomas Bishop,
Not. Pub.

Proved at London, April 26, 1821, before the worshipful John Danbury, D. of Laws, etc., etc.

---

*A ruble is a Russian silver coin of the value of about seventy-five cents.

(To be continued.)

GRANDPA'S SCRAP BOOK

Week of May 8—11, 1901.

CAPT. GEORGE TATE.

A Record of a Few of the Events, Together with Some of the Names of His Descendants.

BY LEONARD B. CHAPMAN.

(5.) Capt. Robert Tate, born Jan. 23, 1751, the fifth and youngest child of Capt. George Tate, the mast agent, was, in one respect, like his brothers —he worked out the examples of the school arithmetic and transferred the results to a copy book, which is now in existence, running through the entire work, of which every few leaves, he made with his pen a finely executed representation of a ship, thus exhibiting the inclination of his mind.

Dec. 25, 1770, he was united in marriage with Martha Slemons, born 1750, at Stroudwater, dau. of William and Catharine (Porterfield) Slemons, who were married Sept. 16, 1744, and who built the large house a little westerly of the village and died in it, where Fred A. Johnson and family now reside.

Robert purchased, March 18, 1779, of his father, a farm lot located on the northerly side of the highway leading from Stroudwater to Saccarappa, a little nearer Saccarappa than Stroudwater, upon which he built a good two story house that fronted the east and was end to the road. We remember it well, with its yellow paint, front garden enclosed with a slat fence as was the custom, within which was the cinnamon rose, hateful tansy bush, a sprig of which stuff every aged lady carried to funerals sixty-odd years ago, and there were also a row of great fir trees in the yard, but all have been displaced by buildings more attractive, but the good quality of the soil still remains, the farm being one of the best.

At one time Capt. Tate was in command of a vessel belonging to his brother, William, as we have shown, and this is all we know of his business career. The name of the vessel appearing upon an ancient paper we cannot decipher.

In the Stroudwater cemetery is a memorial slab inscribed as follows:

In Memory of
MARTHA TATE,
widow of
Capt. Robert Tate
who died
April 3, 1822,
aged 71.

Capt. ROBERT TATE,
died at Berbice,
June 24, 1804,
Aged 53.

His name also appears upon the headstone of his daughter, Elizabeth (Tate) Alden, in the Portland Eastern cemetery, under the shadow of the Admiral Alden monument.

Children of Capt. Robert and Martha (Slemons) Tate:

1—George, b. 1771.
2—Mary, b. 1775, m. William Libby.
3—Ann, b. Oct. 23, 1778, m. Charles Johnson.
4—Catharine, b. 1780, d. Sept. 6, 1818, at home, unm. Grave memorial at Stroudwater.
5—Elizabeth, b. 1783, m. James Alden.
6—Eleanor, m. Gardner Walker, who, in 1807, was a merchant in Portland.
7—Samuel, in 1807 a merchant in Portland; can learn nothing more of him.

1—George Tate, b. 1771, son of Capt. Robert and Martha (Slemons) Tate, was first a merchant in Windham, then resided upon the homestead. He was taxed in 1814 for a $500 house; 120 acres of land, 4 oxen; 4 cows; horse and chaise, young stock, swine, etc.—as much as the best had. He was a round faced, dark complexioned, dark haired man, and seldom spoke to any one. We frequently saw him in the chaise on the road. He died Oct. 31, 1847, aged 77, and has a memorial slab at Stroudwater.

2—Mary Tate, sister to the preceding, became, May 16, 1824, the wife of William Libby of Scarboro. Rev. Caleb Bradley performed the ceremony. She has a memorial slab at Stroudwater. He died March, 1854, having outlived her 14 years. He was a practical farmer though he never had a farm of his own.

3—Ann Tate, born Oct. 23, 1778, a sister to the preceding, m. Dec. 25, 1805, Charles Johnson, b. May 18, 1777, son of Major James Johnson, a Revolutionary soldier, who built the so-called Cushing Pratt house—a large, two story structure, now to be seen as originally constructed, opposite where the Capt. Robert Tate house stood, the location of which we have pointed out. Mr. Johnson was the tenth child in a family of eleven children.

In 1780 Maj. Johnson, in company with Aaron Chamberlain and Capt. Jesse Partridge, both of Stroudwater, purchased eighteen hundred acres of land located in Thomson Pond plantation, now Poland, and Chamberlain and Maj. Johnson both went there to reside; Chamberlain, who, it seems, had a second wife, named Bethiah in 1795, removed to Portland, his first wife being Elizabeth Waterhouse, dau. of William, to whom he was m. Nov. 8, 1774. He was a saddler, his shop standing at the southeasterly corner of Mill creek bridge, Stroudwater village, a very small building standing over the creek and supported by posts; he was also a retailer, as many good people were. We have a list of five of Chamberlain's children. He was the maternal ancestor of the Parker family of Stroudwater.

Charles Johnson was a farmer on Windham Hill, and known as 'Squire Johnson. He died there Feb. 23, 1865, aged 88 years; she, April 30, 1863.

Their children were as follows:

1—Martha Tate (Johnson) b. Dec 1806, d. Nov. 27, 1818.
2—Elizabeth (Johnson), b. June 22, 1808, m. Oct. 21, 1838, Dr. Maddison J. Bray of Evansville, Ill.
3—Ann (Johnson), b. Jan. 24, 1810, m. Feb. 13, 1834, Joseph Walker, the man who became very wealthy. She was his second wife.
4—George Tate (Johnson) b. Jan. 14, 1812, m. and died in Louisiana Oct. 22, 1853.
5—Margaret (Johnson), b. Aug 20, 1813, d. May 20, 1814
6—Charles Pope (Johnson), b. Jan. 1, 1814.
7—Samuel Tate (Johnson), b. March 27, 1819.

The last named m. first, Olive Coombs, and second, Lucinda Trull. He was the father of nine children. He served as First Lieutenant in the 25th Maine Reg. and later was Asst. Prov. Marshal. His son, George Tate Johnson, served in Co. K. 4th Maine Reg., was wounded at Gettysburg and died there. The father died in Nov. 1888 and has a memorial slab at Windham Hill. For the record of this Johnson family the public are indebted to Nathan Goold.

To be continued.

GRANDPA'S SCRAP BOOK

Week of May 15-18, 1901.

CAPT. GEORGE TATE.

A Record of a Few of the Events, Together with Some of the Names of His Descendants.

BY LEONARD B. CHAPMAN.

(Continued from last week.)

Elizabeth Tate, b. 1783, a mile and a half southerly of Saccarappa village, at a point represented by the name of "G. Skillings" on the County Atlas of 1871, she a daughter of Capt. Robert and granddaughter of Capt. George Tate, the Mast Agent, became, Dec. 25, 1803, the wife of Capt. James Alden, Rev. Caleb Bradley receiving a fee of $5 for performing the ceremony. Upon the records of that time the name appears as Betsey Tate—Elizabeth and Betsey being synonymous.

Upon a manuscript record we find the following, which shows, when taken in connection with other presentations here made, the difficulty in many instances of obtaining the truth. Capt. Alden's wife was, as appears from the following, named Eliza Tate, and the Admiral was named James Madison Alden.

Robert Tate Alden, son of James and Eliza, his wife, born February 19, 1805.

Mary Alden, daughter of James and Eliza, his wife, was born Oct. 8, 1807.

James Madison Alden, son of James and Eliza, his wife, was born March 31, 1810.

Capt. Alden was a Portland man and resided upon the easterly side of Hampshire and northerly of Federal street, the site of the house now making part of Lincoln Park. He attended the Episcopalian meeting; March 10, 1813, entered Portland Lodge, No. 1, Free and Accepted Masons; June 19 was admitted to membership; was S. Deacon (whatever this means) from 1838 to 1848, and died May 29, 1863, his memorial slab appearing beneath the shadow of the monument of Rear Admiral James Alden, his son, in the Portland Eastern cemetery, as does that of Mary, first wife of William C. Bradley, he a son of Rev. Caleb Bradley, she departing this life Sept. 1, 1827, aged 20 years, some memoranda appearing in the News last August, relative to William's second wife, who was Harriet L. Lewis, a daughter of Deacon Arch. Lewis of Stroudwater.

Elizabeth (Tate) Alden died Aug. 8, 1824, aged 41 years, and Capt. Alden m. second, March 13, 1825, Parmelia P. Phillips, daughter of Dea. John Phillips. She was the widow of Joshua Shirley. She died in York, this state, 1853, aged 78 years, where she was interred. He was descended from David Alden of Duxbury, who came to Falmouth in 1750, as a descendant of Capt. John Alden of the May-Flower.

James Alden, son of Capt. James and Elizabeth (Tate) Alden, b. in Portland, became famous when a boy as a leader of bat and ball players and in snow ball gangs, the excitement often culminating in close encounters. Upon reaching mature manhood he became famous in his country's navy. Many words of praise have been written and spoken of him. His monument in our Eastern cemetery, to which we have alluded, made of polished red granite, and erected by his executor, at his request, with a medallion likeness of the Admiral's face in bronze, tells, through the inscriptions, the story in brief of his career, a transcript being as follows:

Real Admiral
JAMES ALDEN
Born in Portland
March 31, 1810,
Died in San Francisco,
Feb. 6, 1877.
Entered the Navy
April 1, 1828.
Commissioned
Rear Admiral,
June 19, 1871.

MEXICAN WAR.
NEW ORLEANS.
PORT HUDSON.
MOBILE BAY.
FORT FISHER.
INTREPID EXPLORER.
SKILFUL HYDROGRAPHER.
CATROGRAPHER of
WEST COAST of
UNITED STATES.

James Alden was but eighteen years of age when he entered the Naval service at Boston. In 1832-3 he served in the Mediterranean, in 1835 was assigned to the Charlestown Navy Yard. From 1839 to 1842 he was engaged in an exploring expedition. His next service was in an East India squadron.

He took an active part in the Mexican war, being present at the capture of Vera Cruz, Tuspan and Tobasco.

Then he served twelve years upon the coast survey.

In 1855 he was made commander and at Puget Sound served against the Indians.

At the commencement of the war of the States he was in command of the steamer South Carolina, and took part in the engagement at Galveston, Texas. He then took command of the steam-sloop Richmond and with Farragut passed Forts Jackson and St. Philip and took a part in the capture of New Orleans, in April of 1862. He ran twice past the famous Vicksburg Batteries and was present at the capture of Mobile bay. In the same vessel he was present at both attacks on Fort Fisher. As a commander he had in the war of the States but few equals, and saw, it is claimed, more real service than any other commander.

July 25, 1866, he was commissioned as Commodore, and the next year he went on a special cruise. In 1866-7 he was in command of the frigate Minnesota, when she took the senior class of naval cadets on the special cruise to the Continent. Upon his return he was put in command of Mare Island Navy Yard, Cal. In 1871 he was assigned to the command of the European squadron.

He was one, or the only one, of our American Navy commanders who dined with Queen Victoria.

He was a man of fine presence, of medium size, dark brown hair, kind and generous, but a man replete with determination as the monument medallion presents him.

His wife was Sarah Thompson, daughter of Dr. Thompson of Charlestown, Mass. She died about a week in advance of him. They had no children.

Thus the boyhood, thus the manhood, and thus the demise of a great grandson of Capt. George Tate of Stroudwater, who became truly famous.

His remains, on arriving here, were laid in state in the City Building, Feb. 23, 1877, and viewed by the public for a period of twenty-four hours. The room was appropriately fitted for the occasion, a squad of soldiers forming a guard over the remains, which were in citizen's dress, and finally interred with military display. The weather was extremely unfavorable, but hundreds bestowed the respect due by their presence.

"And the stately ships go on
To their haven under the hill;
But, oh, for the touch of a vanished hand,
And the sound of a voice that is still!"

To be continued.

GRANDPA'S SCRAP BOOK

Week of May 22-25, 1901.

CAPT. GEORGE TATE.

A Record of a Few of the Events, Together with Some of the Names of His Descendants.

BY LEONARD B. CHAPMAN.

(Continued from last week.)

We know comparatively little of Gardner Walker, whose intention of marriage with Eleanor Tate, daughter of Capt. Robert, and granddaughter of Capt. George Tate, the Mast Agent of Stroudwater, was made public, March 1, 1807, at which time he was a merchant in Portland. He had a daughter Maria, a daughter Catharine, who, April 17, 1832, was united in marriage with John H. Trowbridge, Parson Bradley performing the ceremony, and a son Peter H. Walker, all of whom were alive in 1848, the latter residing in Boston, Mass. Gardner Walker was then residing in Salem, Mass., and may have had other children than these whose names we here present.

May 12, 1846, Eleanor Walker, "widow of Gardner Walker," died in East Boston, Mass., and was interred in the Portland Western cemetery. The statement that she was the "widow" of Gardner must be erroneous, for, in 1848, he was alive, and a resident of Salem, as we have stated. His parents we cannot locate nor the place of his birth. Dec. 29, 1808, he purchased a house and lot on the southerly side of Main street at Saccarappa village, and two years later he sold and removed to Cumberland Mills, locating where C. A. Cadwell resided later, which place is shown on the County Atlas of 1871 as the second house from the steam railroad, southerly side of the way from Saccarappa to Portland. While a resident of that locality he was a Deputy Sheriff and handled considerable real estate.

In 1814 he paid a town tax on a house valued at $600; barn, $50; outhouse, $100; eighty-three acres of land; store, $35; 2 oxen; 4 cows; 1 horse; 1 chaise; 3 swine, and stock in trade $200.

When Gardner Walker resided at Cumberland Mills—then called Congen—there were but two other families residing upon the southerly side of the river—namely: Capt. Aaron Winslow and John Stevens.

As in the case of Gardner Walker, so in that of the parentage of Joseph Walker, who married Feb. 13, 1834, Ann Johnson, born on Windham Hill Jan. 24, 1810, she a granddaughter of Capt. Robert Tate, we know but very little. The story of his career when told in full, particularly that of the distribution of his great estate will not fail to please if correctly presented to the public. The Westbrook Library is an outgrowth of one of the bequests of his will, as are others of a like nature.

Upon the westerly side of Evergreen Circle in Evergreen cemetery, Portland, may be seen a block of granite with a polished pillar of darker stone at each corner, resting on a base of the same material of which the block is made, and the base inscribed—

WALKER.

Upon the face of the block an inscription appears as follows:
JOSEPH WALKER.
1800—1890.
EUNICE P. CARTER,
1796—1825.
ANN JOHNSON,
1810—1890.

We find a record of Eunice Walker who died in Portland July 21, 1826, aged 21 years, and was interred in the Eastern cemetery. We understand this has reference to his first wife.

Joseph Walker, for whom the monument here noticed was erected, died in Portland June 6, 1891, aged 91 yrs., 4 mo. We, or somebody, has made mistakes in dates.

Joseph Walker, senior, came from Denmark, this state, to the region of Pride's Bridge, Westbrook, in 1814. Pride's Bridge, Westbrook, in 1814, and purchased of Jonah and Mary Pride, his wife, their farm, paying $3,000. Joseph was a "gentleman."

The name of Walker had been in existence in the vicinity for a period of fifty-odd years when Joseph came in 1814. George Walker was there, whose wife was Elizabeth Snow, cleared and occupied the farm next northerly on the same side of the way to Pride's Corner—a mile or two distant, where he reared quite a large family, which was at our latest advices owned by Abner T. Smith, the ex-Street Commissioner of Deering.

Joseph Walker, sen., kept a public house at Pride's Bridge, but removed to Portland and located on the corner of what is now known as Walker and Congress streets, and resided in the brick two story house as now seen in its ill shape—the first house westerly of the Gen. Neal Dow residence, where Joseph, sen. engaged in trade, retailing rum and other liquors, the door in the Congress street brick wall being now closed, but the marks of which are still to be seen by the careful observer.

"Capt. Joseph Walker" died in Portland Jan. 6, 1861, aged 86, and a tomb in the Western cemetery is marked "J. Walker." He had two wives. The records here quoted refer to the father of the late Joseph Walker. Oct. 3, 1832, Joseph, sen. conveyed his farm at Pride's Bridge to Joseph Walker, Jr., which he states he purchased in 1814. Joseph, sen., was taxed the year he made the purchase on a house valued at $700, which shows it as one of the best in the town; two barns, eighty-five acres of land; stable; six oxen; four cows; a horse and swine.

William Phipps Walker, b. at Charlestown, Mass., March 14, 1807, who died in 1892, a son of Edward S. Walker, who was born in Fryeburg, this state, in 1776, and a brother to Henry B. Walker, Esq., of Pride's Corner, recently deceased, purchased in 1849 the Joseph Walker, sen. residence and farm at Pride's Bridge, where his wife bore him thirteen children, seven sons surviving the father.

From the obituary of Wm. P. Walker, which appeared March 7, 1892, in the Portland Daily Press, we will here make an extract as follows:

In 1849 he bought the Joseph Walker farm, and moved upon it, where he lived till his death. This farm is the first farm after passing Pride's Bridge, on the Presumpscot river, a beautiful locality made famous by the paintings of Harry Brown, and other artists.

Joseph Walker, Jr., had brothers, and resided at one time at Saccarappa, finally in Portland, in the house next southerly of the Universalist meeting house, beneath the shadow of the steeple, which was the torment of his life, living constantly in fear of being crushed by its fall. It was removed last winter, but none too soon, for it was a sham from the day of its construction and our wonder is that the wind allowed it to remain as it did.

Mrs. Ann (Johnson) Walker, wife of Joseph Walker, Jr., gave Windham Hill church $5,000 and from Joseph's estate Windham Center received a $400 library.

Charles Pope Johnson b. Jan. 1, 1814, retained the homestead at Windham—the homestead of Charles and Ann (Tate) Johnson. He m. Nov. 19, 1848, Harriet Rogers Berry of Denmark, this state. She was b. March 6, 1815, and was the fifth child of Samuel and Dorcas (Shattuck) Berry—she of Portland. Samuel went from Morrill's Corner, Deering, in 1808, to Denmark, where he d. April 19, 1834. While at Morrill's Corner he resided with his father. George Berry, Jr., the house standing upon the southerly side of what is now known as Allen avenue, where the late David Torrey, Esq., lived. George Berry, Jr., m. March 6, 1753, Mary Stickney of Portland. He was a son of Capt. George Berry of the Fall Brook region of Ocean street, Deering, whose second residence is now owned and occupied by John J. Frye, Esq. George Berry, Jr., accompanied his son Samuel to Denmark, where he d. April 3, 1816, his wife having had eleven children. Capt. George Berry came from Kittery, this state. He was an active man and his descendants are numerous, many residing here in Deering, known by other names.

Continued:

In 1848 the heirs of Capt. Robert Tate were as follows:

1—Delia Henderson, wife of——
2—Timothy S. Arthur, publisher, Philadelphia, Pa., and Eliza Arthur, his wife (in her own right.)
3—John H. Trowbridge, Portland, and Catharine T. Trowbridge, his wife (in her own right.)
4—B. F. Pratt, Portland, and Ellen Pratt, his wife.
5—Charles Johnson, Windham, and Ann Johnson, his wife, (in her own right.)
6—James Alden, (the Admiral), Sarah A. Alden.
7—Peter H. Walker, Boston, Mass.
8—Gardner Walker, Salem, Mass.
9—Robert T. Alden.
10—Sarah B. Alden.
11—Maria Alden.
12—Henry Henderson, Baltimore, Md.

Timothy S. Arthur died in Philadelphia, Pa., March 6, 1885. He was born at Newbury, N. Y., in 1809. He m. in 1836 Miss Eliza Alden, daughter of Capt. James Alden, and sister to Admiral James Alden, noticed last week. She died in Philadelphia, Pa., in 1876. A portrait of him appears in Hill's Album, published in 1888, at Chicago Ill. In his youth he was apprenticed to a trade at Baltimore, Md., then served as a clerk, became a Journalist, and compiled and published a host of stories on moral subjects, giving his name a world-wide fame. Besides publishing pamphlets by the hundreds he printed books, and a monthly magazine. Among his most popular works was, probably, his "Ten Nights in a Bar Room."
The End.

GRANDPA'S SCRAP BOOK

Week of May 29–June 1, 1901.

Dr. ROBERT SOUTHGATE.

Of Dunstan, Scarboro, Ancestors and Descendants.

BY LEONARD B. CHAPMAN.

(Continued from January 9—12.)

WALTER BOWNE, JR.

1—Walter Bowne, Jr., b. in New York city June 18, 1806, only son of Walter and Eliza (Southgate) Bowne, Sen., and grandson of Dr. Robert Southgate, m. Eliza Rapalye, b. New Lots, Long Island, N. Y., Nov. 8, 1808, dau. of Simon and Helen Rapalye. They resided at "The Clifford," where the father spent the summer months, and where Walter, Jr. was a "gentleman farmer," the farm lot said to have contained five hundred acres. An aged and much respected citizen of Flushing writes us: "I knew personally Walter Bowne, Jr., and his father well. Walter was a careful man and left a larger estate than his father." Walter, senior, we are informed, left a round $1,000,000, but another authority says: "Reduce the amount a half," but rich and as popular as he may have been the Flushing historian fails to mention his name in his printed work.

Walter Bowne, Jr., died at the Buckingham Hotel, New York city, Oct. 30, 1877. The widow purchased the ancient Bowne residence, where she died July 27, 1885. Both were interred in the Flushing cemetery.

Children of Walter and Eliza (Rapalye) Bowne, Jr.:

*1—Eliza Southgate (Bowne), b. Aug. 21, 1827, m. Spencer Henry Smith, a brother to Emma.
*2—Simon Rapalye (Bowne), b. Oct. 18, 1828, m. Emma Smith, a sister to Spencer Henry Smith.
3—Walter (Bowne), 3r, b. Sept. 16, 1830, d. unmarried, Nov. 27, 1855.
*4—Helen (Bowne), b April 12, 1832, m. Sylvanus Smith Ricker.
*5—Frederic (Bowne), b. Aug. 15, 1834, m. Adelaide Huntington.
6—Horatio (Bowne), b. June 9, 1836, d. Oct. 9, 1837.
7—Caroline, (Bowne), b. Aug. 7, 1838, resides, unm., Buckingham Hotel, New York city.
*8—Mary Ann (Bowne), b. April 17, 1841, m. James T. Murray.
*9—Robert Southgate (Bowne), b. Sept. 18, 1841, m. Jessie Draper.

MARY BOWNE.

2—Miss Mary Bowne, b. July 25, 1808, (to whose name somebody added that of King), only sister to the preceding, m. Dec. 5, 1826, Hon. John Watson Lawrence, b. in Flushing, Long Island, N. Y., Aug. 19, 1800. His father was Effingham Lawrence, b. June 6, 1760, who m. Elizabeth, dau. of Thomas Watson. The name is easily traced to John Lawrence, 1664, one of the incorporators of Hempstead, L. I., and to Flushing a few years later, as one of the eighteen granteers of the town which then received the name by which it has ever since been known. He was a man of influence who had brothers settle at Flushing. He d. in 1699.

Effingham Lawrence was a stirring man. He built and resided in the large two story, hip-roofed house, with pillars on the front and extending from the stoop to the projecting gable, with a conservatory at the opposite end of the hallway, which hallway extends the entire length of the residence, the residence fronting northerly, before which is a vast area of salt marsh, like that of Dunstan, Scarboro, between which and the residence passes the highway to New York city and the sluggish waters of the little stream that rises and falls with the flow and ebb of the tide water of the ocean. The conditions of a century ago are the conditions of today relative to the situation. The residence is reached from the rear street, by a serpentine, flagged walk, the appearance of the dwelling not having undergone a change since the first construction.

It was to this place John Watson Lawrence took his bride, who was possessed of many of the charms of her mother, where she displayed her tact and talents in entertaining, performing at the same time a leading part in society circles. This was the place where the letters of Eliza (Southgate) Bowne were kept and read till they were worse than threadbare by use that now form the major part of the book entitled "A Girl's Life Eighty Years Ago."

Hon. John Watson Lawrence was an active and much respected man. At the age of sixteen he was placed in a counting-house in New York city. At the age of twenty-one he formed a copartnership under the firm name of Howland & Lawrence, as Commission Merchants. For a series of years he was president of Queens County Savings Bank, and for a number of years President of the Seventh Ward Bank of New York. For fifteen years he was President of the Village Corporation of Flushing, and many years warden of St. George's Episcopal church.

In politics he was a Democrat, and was elected to the State Legislature, and in 1845 he was a member of the House of Representatives at Washington, D. C., but declined to accept a renomination as he did the nomination for the office of Lieutenant-Governor of the state of New York.

He d. Dec. 20, 1888, at his residence where his father died about the time he was born, in the residence as now seen, and known as "William Bank." His wife died there August 3, 1874. Both were interred at Flushing cemetery.

Children of Hon. John W. and Mary (Bowne) Lawrence:

*1—Caroline Bowne (Lawrence), b. Sept. 17, 1827, m. Hon. Henry Bedinger.
*2—Eliza Southgate (Lawrence), b. Nov. 6, 1828, m. Armistead Tomson Mason Rust
*3—Mary Bowne (Lawrence), b. Sept. 28, 1830, m. Henry A. Bogert, Esq.
*4—Emily (Lawrence), b. August 20, 1832, m. Charles Hamilton Shepard.
*5—Ann Louise (Lawrence), b. Aug. 20, 1832, m. Rt. Rev. Thomas A. Jagger.
*6—Walter Bowne (Lawrence), b. Oct. 31, 1839, m. Annie Townsend.
7—Rebecca (Lawrence), b. Sept. 8, 1841, d. Jan. 10, 1848.
*8—Isabella (Lawrence), b. Oct. 16, 1846, m. Lemuel Pendleton Dandridge.
*9—Frances (Lawrence), b. Aug. 10, 1849, m. Rev. Frederick Brewerton Carter.
*10—Robert Bowne (Lawrence), b. Dec. 1, 1852, m. Eliza H. Clements.

To be continued.

GRANDPA'S SCRAP BOOK

Week of June 6-8, 1901.

Dr. ROBERT SOUTHGATE.

Of Dunstan, Scarboro, Ancestors and Descendants.

BY LEONARD B. CHAPMAN.

(Continued from last week.)

Descendants of WALTER BOWNE, Jr. Only son of Walter Bowne, Sen.

Eliza Southgate Bowne, b. Aug. 21, 1827, granddaughter of Walter and Eliza (Southgate) Bowne, Sen. and great granddaughter of Dr. Robert Southgate, m. April 9, 1851, Spencer Henry Smith, b. in New York city, March 4, 1827, son of Isaac and Jane (Beadle) Smith. He was a manufacturer of umbrellas, later President of the Flushing branch of the Long Island railroad; then he became a New York Wall street broker, but now retired from active business.

His wife d. at San Gabriel, California, May 6, 1892, but her remains were interred in the Flushing cemetery. Two children: Caroline Bowne and Frances.

1—Caroline Bowne (Smith), b. New York city, Jan. 29, 1852, m. Oct. 16, 1879, Charles Whitney Carpenter, formerly of Albany, N. Y., now a resident of New York city. He is a member of the firm of "R. Hoe & Co.," printing press manufacturers of New York and London, Eng. Children:
  (a)—Lillian (Carpenter) b. April 11, 1881.
  (b)—George Washington (Carpenter) b. August 23, 1882.
  (c)—Florence (Carpenter) b. Nov. 2, 1883.
  (d)—Charles Whitney (Carpenter) Jr., b. Dec. 23, 1884.
  (e)—Adele (Carpenter) b. May 4, 1886.
  (f)—Beatrice (Carpenter) b. July 15, 1887.
  (g)—Jessie (Carpenter) b. Dec. 18, 1888, d. Jan. 10, 1891.
  (h)—Arthur (Carpenter) b. Dec. 16, 1891, d. Sept. 7, 1892.

2—Frances Smith b. Sept. 4, 1858, dau. of Spencer Henry Smith, m. June 2, 1881, Samuel Freeman of New York, formerly of Portland, Me.; was a member of the New York Exchange, but now President of "The Morristown, N. J. Trust Company." Children:
  (a)—Samuel Harold (Freeman) b. Aug. 15, 1882.
  (b)—Mabel (Freeman) b. Nov. 28, 1883.
  (c)—Louise (Freeman) b. Jan. 2, 1885.
  (d)—Southgate Bowne (Freeman) b. March 1, 1888.
  (e)—Spencer Smith (Freeman) b. May 13, 1890, d. May 23, same year.
  (f)—Leonard Chester (Freeman) b. Oct. 18, 1895.

2—Simon Rapalge Bowne, b. Oct. 18, 1828, brother to the preceding, m. Emma Smith, a sister to Spencer Henry Smith. They resided at "The Clifford," where he was a "gentleman farmer."

From the history of Flushing we take the following:

"The second Fair was holden in Flushing Sept. 22, 1858. The invited guests, in a carriage, to which was attached fifty-six oxen, accompanied by a brass band, was drawn through the principal streets and fully seven thousand persons witnessed the scene. Simon R. Bowne exhibited twenty of his fine horses." Children:

1—Emma Bowne b. January 17, 1853, m. Sept. 21, 1876, Charles Francis Beebe. Reside Portland Heights, Oregon. Children:
  (a) Walter Bowne (Beebe) b. Sept. 25, 1877.
  (b) Gerald Edwin (Beebe) b. Feb. 8, 1882.
  (c) Kenneth (Beebe) b. Nov. 16, 1883.

2—Walter (Bowne) b. Aug. 25, 1854, m. Oct. 27, 1880, m. Ida Sutton; res. New York city.

3—Spencer Frederic (Bowne) b. Sept. 28, 1855, m. Lizzie McAdams, d. Nov. 15, 1883.

4—Edward Randolph (Bowne) b. June 29, 1857, m. Emily Embury; res. in New York city.

5—Helen (Bowne) b. Oct. 6, 1858, m. April 19, 1881, Allen M. Sutton—a bro. to Ida; res. Berkeley, California.

6—James Bruce (Bowne) b. April 27, 1860, m. Agnes Burchard.

7—Clarence Southgate (Bowne) b. June 21, 1861, d. unm., Flushing, Oct. 21, 1889.
m. W. H. Hix, 1 child, d. W. H. Hix, 1 child, d. m. 2nd Dr. Pope; m. 3d. —— Sutton, bro. to Ida, also to Allen M. Sutton; res. Paris, France.

9—William (Bowne) b. Nov. 30, 1865, m. Millie Garfield, a niece of President Garfield; res. New York city.

3—Walter Bowne, 3d b. and d. as above stated, and a bro. to the preceding.

4—Helen Bowne, b. April 21, 1832, a sister to the preceding, m. Sylvanus Smith Ricker, 1857; she d. Feb. 3, 1889; he d. some years later. Both interred in Woodlawn cemetery.

5—Frederic Bowne, b. Aug. 15, 1834, a brother to the preceding, m., 1861, Adelaide Huntington, widow, with a dau. four years of age, Adelaide, a dau. of William Stebbins. They, resided in Flushing, where he was a "gentleman farmer." He d. June 20, 1877. Children:
  (a)—Lillie (Bowne) b. Nov. 15, 1861, d. March 31, 1876.
  (b)—Frederic (Bowne) b. Dec. 10, 1862, m. Alice Holbrook; res. Flushing.
  (c)—Clifford (Bowne) b. Feb. 26, 1864, d. April 11, 1868.

7—Caroline Bowne, b. Aug. 7, 1838, a sister to the preceding; res. Buckingham Hotel, New York city, unmarried.

8—Mary Ann Bowne, b. Aug. 17, 1841, a sister to the preceding, m. 1871, James T. Murray. He d. March 1 1894, and was interred at Woodlawn cemetery. No children. The widow resides at the Buckingham Hotel, New York city.

9 and last—Robert Southgate Bowne, b. Sept. 18, 1842, brother the preceding, m. Jessie Draper, da of William B. Draper. He was merchant, and d. Sept. 20, 1896, his summer home—"Clifford by t Sea," East Hampton, Long Island, Y. The widow resides in Flushin Children:
  (a)—Elizabeth H. (Bowne b. Dec. 4, 1866, m. Harr Duncomb Colt of New Yor
  (b)—Francis D. (Bowne) July 21, 1868, m. Gertru Travers.
  (c)—Walter (Bowne,) 2d, b. April 2, 1870, m. Katharine Guild.
  (d) Marion Southgate (Bowne) b. Feb. 3, 1872, m J. C. Crosby.

To be continued.

TOWN OF GRAY. 1901

Historical memoranda pertaining to some of her citizens.

By Leonard B. Chapman.

From the diary of Rev. Caleb Bradley:

"Oct. 15, 1839. This p. m. left home with Mrs. Bradley for the Gray cattle show. Spent the night at Benjamin Marston's in Falmouth. Appeared glad to se us—well entertained.

"Oct. 16. After breakfast I started for Gray, Mrs. B. remaining at Mr. Marston's. After all not much to be seen. A few oxen—a few cows—some swine—butter, cheese, rugs and many manufactured articles. At noon an address by William P. Fessenden, which was very good. A prayer by a Free-willer." (Freewill Baptist.) I dined with the Society at the hotel, and nothing to pay; this was the best part of it; a good dinner and nothing to pay. At 3 p. m. returned to Mr. Marston's, he having gone with me, where I staid all night."

The first religious society of Gray was of the Presbyterian order and was organized in the month of August of 1774. A house of worship was commenced but never finished. It was sold in 1790 for four pounds.

In 1803 a council was called, but two male members only could be found, who proceeded to organize a Congregational society. The Rev. Mr. Weston was called and became pastor, who remained as such till 1825. The present church edifice was dedicated in 1828, when Rev. Samuel H. Peckham was pastor, who served till 1831.

John Humphrey was deacon from 1803 till near the close of his life in 1833.

An obituary copied from a Christian Mirror:

"Died in Gray, June 15, 1834, Miss Emma Carleton Weston, dau. of Rev. Daniel Weston, in the 22nd year of her age. Her sister, Caroline K. Weston, died Sept. 30, 1832, at about the same age of her sister Emma.

"Within 8 or 9 months past four members have been removed from this church by death. The two first, Des. John Humphrey, (who has been noticed), and Mrs. Miriam Merrill, aged 67 years, relict of the late Joseph Merrill, who died last autumn, Mr. David Briggs, who died at Buckfield about the same time with the subject of this notice, aged 83 years."

From the diary of Rev. Caleb Bradley:

"February 23, 1838. We started for Gray. Called at Dr. Allen's, and Benjamin Marston's where at 3 o'clock we took tea, arriving at Mrs. Weston's at sunset. Cordially received by the family, consisting of Mrs. Weston; Mr. Pennell and wife; William Weston and sister. This is a pleasant family. Rev. Mr. Weston was a classmate of mine, graduating from Harvard college in 1795. He was a minister in the town of Gray a number of years and was dismissed from the ministry some years since for want of support. Since he was dismissed there have been three settled ministers there, but all dismissed for want of support. The one now there takes what the people please to give. My opinion is he will come short of bread, but it may be otherwise. The people may do more for his support than they would were they under a legal obligation, but I think in all cases a bargain should be made by the parties—a contract entered into and the parties should each conscientiously fulfill the obligation."

From the diary of Rev. Caleb Bradley of May 30, 1837:

"Went to Portland with Mrs. Bradley shopping. Heard of the death of Rev. Mr. Weston. Am sent for to attend his funeral. Another classmate deceased. My turn will probably come soon. Lord, may this death cause me so to number my days as to apply my heart unto wisdom.

"May 31. Set out for Gray, to attend the funeral of Rev. Daniel Weston. Eleven o'clock arrived at the house in company with Rev. Br. Miltimore. At one o'clock attended the funeral exercises at the meeting house. Rev. Mr. Chapin preached. Returned home after tea. Rode the last 8 miles in one of the most violent showers, accompanied with lightning and thunder. I was ever out in."

The "Mr. Pennell" refered to by Parson Bradley was Henry Pennell, who was an adopted child of Stephen Pennell, the Pennells of Gray being descendants of the Pennells who resided in the Capisic Pond district of Deering many years ago.

Henry Pennell was born, according to the family Bible, in Danville, January 6, 1803.

His foster father was a ship carpenter, who did not reside all of his life in one place, but moved as his occupation required. Henry's chances of obtaining book learning were slim but he succeeded, and to him the people of Gray are indebted for the "Pennell Institute," which stands as a living monument to the name of the donor.. The maiden name of his wife was Mary Susan Weston, eldest daughter of Rev. Daniel Weston and wife, Susan Buxton.

Henry Pennell's wife died in Gray, August 23, 1881, aged 73 years, 11 mo. 25 days. He then removed to Portland, where he died June 8, 1884, aged 81 years, 5 mo., 2 days.

He held the office of a deputy, then that of sheriff of Cumberland County, represented his town in the State Legislature, then was a Senator

Augusta M. Weston, the youngest child in the Parson Weston family, became the wife of Henry P. Humphrey. She died in 1853. Henry Pennell and wife having no children they adopted Susan Augusta Humphrey, a child left by Augusta M. (Weston) Humphrey, who, October 31, 1869, became the wife of Melvin Porter Frank, Esq. The family reside in Portland. He was born in Gray, Dec. 29, 1841, graduated from Tufts College, read law in the Portland office of Shepley & Strout, and was admitted to practice in 1868. He is a ready speaker, of pleasing manners and indulges considerably in politics as a Democrat. He has represented Portland in the State Legislature, served as speaker of the house in 1870, and in 1890 was candidate for congress from this district. He is a trustee of Westbrook Seminary and the Pennell Institute. A good half-tone cut of him may be found in "Portland Past and Present," a book printed in 1899.

GRANDPA'S SCRAP BOOK

Week of Oct., 17—19, 1901.

WESTBROOK SEMINARY.

Some of the First Principles of the Old Institution.

By Leonard B. Chapman.

The first school was opened June 9, 1834. Regarding its records the institution has been unfortunate. The secretary's books were destroyed by fire on Stevens Plains; then the treasurer's books were burned at the time of the fire on a wharf at noon day in Portland about thirty years ago, so anything of a written or printed nature relating to the early history of the institution is of public interest.

The first principal, Rev. Samuel Brimblecom, edited a paper devoted to the school and the cause of Universalism, which was printed in Portland and from which we copy the following that appeared August 15, 1833:

"A tribute of respect is due the founders of this institution for their determination to exclude sectarianism from its proceedings and government, and to make it, what every Literary Institution ought to be, the abode of science and a resort for every lover of knowledge without respect to persons. The By-laws, which have been adopted by the Board of Trustees, contain expressions of their views on the subject, which will be satisfactory to the liberal and candid of all denominations. We are indulged the privilege of making the following extracts:"

ART. XVII. As this Seminary is designed and pledged to the public by its founders, for the education of young men to various professions and pursuits of manhood, free from all religious bias and prejudices, and under the influences of such religious doctrines and opinions only as each may elect for himself and sanction by the dictates of his own conscience;

Therefore, it shall be deemed repugnant to the spirit, principles and designs of the Charter and Constitution of the Seminary, for any Trustee to introduce into the proceedings of the Trustees or before the Board, any measure, motion or topic partaking of a sectarian religion, or tending in any way to the subordination or preference of any religious sect or denomination to another; "nor shall any religious test be required as a qualification for any office or trust" in the Seminary, nor of any student or other candidate for the privileges of the Seminary.

ART. XVIII. A Library shall be formed as soon as it can be effected. The books to be purchased, shall be such as may be ordered by the Board of Trustees. Yet books upon religious and all other subjects, which may be presented to the Seminary, shall be deposited in the Library, without regard to their peculiar tenets. The titles of all books presented, with the name of the donors, shall be entered on the records of the Secretary.

"Such are the views of the Board of Trustees, exhibited in the regulations which they have adopted, and by which they are to be governed. If any irregularities should arise in the management of the Institution, there is remedy wisely provided in the charter, (which we published last week,) by an appeal to the authority of the State. B."

GRANDPA'S SCRAP BOOK

Week of Oct., 24—26, 1901.

"Died at Gray, Sept. 24, 1833, Dea. John Humphrey, aged 90 years. Soon after the organization of the Congregational church, in 1803, he was made deacon. He came from Waymouth, Mass."

"Died in Portland July, 1834, Capt. Samuel Drinkwater, aged 92 years. He was a soldier of the war of the Revolution, and pilot on board the schooner Enterprise at the time of her engagement with the British brig Boxer which she captured near this port."

*"Died in Gorham, Oct. 18, 1834, Mr. James Phinney, aged 94 years. He was born April 13, 1741. At the age of seventeen years he experienced religion. He was married Jan. 12, 1762 to (*) Miss Martha Hamblen, who died Sept. 3, 1816, (aged 76 years). He married second Miss Jane Cross Aug. 30, 1816. His first and only child was born August 30, 1821, when her father was a little over eighty years of age; at this time both widow and child are living."

*Have grave memorial slabs.

The following extract is taken from the report of the state of religion at a conference of the Congregational churches held at Falmouth June 11, 1834:

"Rev. Joseph B. Stevens was installed pastor of the Second Congregational church in Falmouth Feb. 9, 1834. Since the organization of the church, Sept. 1830, there have been regular meetings and the gospel has been supported with little foreign aid. A house for religious worship has been erected, and much done towards liquidating the debt thereby incurred. A protracted meeting was holden with the church in February and a few hopefully converted. The Sabbath school numbers 133 scholars. A female mission society has been operated since 1832, the collections amounting from $15 to $50, annually. A tract society was organized in March last. The monthly concert and preparatory lectures are regularly holden. In temperance work the churches have united. The present number on the pledge is 750."

I understand that the brick building now used by the society is the one to which reference is made in the foregoing as having been built in 1834.

Rev. Mr. Stevens was made a member of the Cumberland Association of Congregational ministers that was organized in 1788 at Woodfords, Deering, (then Falmouth) which "still lives." He served as scribe from 1836 to 1840. He died in 1860, but I do not know where.

Rev. John Gunnison of West Falmouth church was made a member of the Association in 1842, who died in 1861.

After leaving West Falmouth he officiated for small pay—about $100 a year—at the Bradley meeting house in Deering, working as a brass finisher in Portland though he was a college graduate. He was an able speaker.

Rev. John Wild of West Falmouth joined the Association in 1846 and died in 1868.

Rev. Isaac Carleton was at West Falmouth in 1853, coming from Oxford, Me., where he officiated many years, returning to that town where he died in 1858. He has two daughters, now residing at the northeasterly corner of Congress and St. John street, Portland; a married daughter and a son residing in the far West.

Rev. Joseph Loring of West Falmouth joined the Association in 1858, who in 1888 was residing at East Otisfield, Me.

Rev. Thomas S. Roble of West Falmouth joined in 1864, who in 1888 was residing at South Plymouth, Mass.

Rev. Edward C. Miles of West Falmouth was admitted in 1866 and in 1888 was residing at Mountclair, N. J.

Rev. William H. Haskell was a merchant in Portland, but concluded to study theology. He was settled first over the First Con. Parish of Deering, where I find his name in the parish records in 1865, but he did not tarry long. He soon removed to West Falmouth, where he now officiates. He did not, however, unite with the Association 1885. He was the last settled minister of the Deering First Parish; the house is now closed, and rapidly going to decay.

"All within is dark as night:
In the windows is no light;
And no murmur at the door,
So frequent on its hinge before.

* * * * *

"Come away; for Life and Thought
Here no longer dwell;
But in a city glorious—
A great and distant city—have bought
A mansion incorruptible.
Would they could have stayed with us."

GRANDPA'S SCRAP BOOK

Week of Oct. 31–Nov. 2, 1901.

SMALL POX.

[From Jenk's Portland Gazette, August 25, 1800.]

"All persons who wish to have small pox may be inoculated in the Hospital on the Waldo Farm, near Stroudwater village, the first Monday in September, or either of the following days in the same week, where every necessary attention will be paid them by Doctors Hillard and Barker.

"The patients may be supplied with every thing they need by Mr. Pratt on the premises."

The farm then known as the "Waldo Farm" is now the State Reform School farm. It originally consisted of 400 acres. Zenas Pratt then owned what is now owned by the state. He erected and resided in the brick house recently demolished.

The small pox was much feared. In 1721 it raged in Boston, Mass., where it made great havoc, when inoculation was recommended by Rev. Cotton Matha, but all declined it, excepting Dr. Zabdiel Boylston, who was hooted at and members of his family insulted upon the streets.

In 1752 the disease again appeared in Boston which then had but 17,500 inhabitants, of whom 5,544 had it, 514 dying.

Under date of Dec. 8, 1760, Parson Smith says:

"The people upon the Neck (Portland) are in a sad toss about Dr. Coffin's having the small pox, which it is thought he took of a man at New Casco (Falmouth Foreside), of whom many there have taken it. It is also at Stroudwater.

"Dec. 9. The uproar is quieted by the removal of Dr. Coffin to Nolce's farm.

"March 7, 1764. The people of Boston are all inoculated at the Castle and at Shirley's Point with marvellous success, in the new method of mercury, etc.

"March 8. The guards at infected houses in Boston are removed, the people finding they can stop the spreading no longer.

"March 27. Capt. Gooding and Milk added to the selectmen [of Portland] because of the small pox."

[Jenks' Portland Gazette, June 14, 1802.]

"Capt. Levi Morrill of this town, and a young lad of about 12 years old, set off for Freeport on the 4th inst. in a small boat and have not been heard of since. The wind blowing fresh, and the boat being pretty deeply loaded with ballast, it is supposed she filled with water and sank. Their bodies have not yet been found, notwithstanding most diligent search for several days."

Under date of April 23, 1898, the News printed some memoranda relating to Dr. Jeremiah Barker who had five wives, three of whom have memorial slabs at Stroudwater village cemetery, Deering.

In the Portland Gazette of May 6, 1811, I find as follows:

"Lost at sea, on the 19th of Dec., 1810, Mr. Jeremiah C. Barker of Falmouth (Stroudwater village), Maine, aged 32 years, eldest son of Dr. Jeremiah Barker of that town, and has left sorrowing parents, a brother and sisters to lament the loss of a dutiful son and affectionate brother."

"Nov., 1833. Died in Bath, Me., at the almshouse, Nathaniel Spingent, aged 103 years. He was a native of the north of Europe and came to this country before the Revolution and resided in Portland, where he lost his property when the place was destroyed by Mowat. He went to Bath soon after peace was declared. He was a rigger."

[I find his name on the list of Portland Revolutionary soldiers.]

[From the Christian Mirror.]

"August, 1834. Died in North Yarmouth Mrs. Rachel Mitchell, aged 86 years, the last of the children of Rev Dr. Loring, an early minister of North Yarmouth."

Under date of August 2, 1763, Parson Smith says: "I rode to North Yarmouth and attended the funeral of Mr. Loring."

He was the second minister of North Yarmouth, born at Hull, Mass., and was 52 years of age when he departed this life. His wife was Mary Richmond of Tiverton, R. I., who died Sept. 15, 1803, aged 90 years. Of him Judge Williamson says:

"With an olive leaf plucked off, and in his mouth, he came to his charge, the messenger of peace. His excellence was like a star that never shines of borrowed light, and his life like a lily which no sunbeam had freckled."

The remains of Frank Richardson of Greenbush, who was lost in the woods near Edinburg in March, 1900, were found in the woods last Sunday. There was nothing but the bones left and the only way they knew that they were those of young Richardson was the finding of his snow shoes beside him. The remains were found within half a mile of the road and if he had but kept on for that distance he would have escaped death. The discovery clears up a mystery. It was a year ago last March that Richardson in company with two men started into the woods for the day. The young man wandered away from his comrades and was lost in the woods. The snow was deep and the whole party was on snow shoes. A thorough search was made for him at the time and it was kept up for more than three months.

GRANDPA'S SCRAP BOOK

Week of Nov. 7–9, 1901.

CAPISIC.

A few facts connected with the ancient name.

By Leonard B. Chapman.

In consequence of the territorial annexation of Deering to Portland a change of names of several streets became necessary, and the ancient highway, called Church street, leading from a point on Stevens avenue in Deering, along by the First Congregational meeting house over Capisic bridge to Nason's Corner is now known as Capisic street.

Nearly two hundred and fifty years have come and gone since the name was first recorded upon public records, and connected with the locality appears many names of persons whose descendants are still with us, not alluding here in detail to events which should be preserved in a connected form as forming an important part of our local history.

Primarily the name represents and perpetuates an Indian who resided hereabouts, then it was applied by European settlers to the locality of the little pond and waterfall at the head of Fore river, first called Casco river, but changed to that of Fore river in consequence of a long discussion relative of the true dividing line between Casco and Spurwink.

July 27, 1657, Scitterqusett, (spelled in various ways) Sagamore of Casco Bay, sold to Francis Small, a fisherman and trader with the Indians, the land upon which the pond and falls are located with an indefinite number of acres in connection, extending to what is now known as Cumberland Mills, in Westbrook, the stipulated price being an annual payment during the lifetime of Scitterqusett of "one trading coat for Capisic and one gallon of liquor for Ammoncongin."

Francis Small commenced a clearing and George Cleeves commenced a suit at law against him for trespass. Small got into debt and then disposed of his interest in the venture to George Munjoy. Munjoy was killed by the Indians, then his son-in-law claimed the premises, and Munjoy's widow was granted twenty acres of Marsh land, now known as the "Round-a-bout." Attempts of possession lead to the exchange of harsh words and law suits, but about two hundred acres of land are now held, located between the meeting house and Fore river, under the Indian sale to Small.

Continued:

Sylvanus Davis was a stirring man. In 1659 he was engaged in large land speculations at Damariscotta, and vicinity; was pursued by four Indians, his partner, named Thomas Lake, being killed in the month of August, 1676, and Davis barely escaping in a wounded condition, when he came to Portland Neck.

In 1680 Lt. Governor Danforth came here to resettle Falmouth, and Davis soon obtained the confidence of the Governor. He and others obtained a land grant of a "mile square" at Capisic, the pond and falls being located in the southwesterly corner of the same, the location of what is now Central avenue forming the northerly boundary line of the grant. In the northwesterly corner John Blake of East Deering purchased a farm lot, where he lived and died, Central avenue being known many years as the Blake road, and should today be known as "Blake Avenue.' A small piece, three cornered in shape, of the mile square grant lies upon the easterly side of Stevens avenue.

Easterly of India street, on Portland Neck, fronting 'Thames street," now called Fore street, Sylvanus Davis built his abode upon a two and half acre land grant, a copy of a plan of which, as well as a copy of a plan of the mile square grant, the originals of which being made in 1735, are now before us as we write, both found in the Massachusetts archives. Davis' house was one of the best of the period; and upon the lot he had a shop; and being an official high in command he had also upon his premises a jail, which is marked upon the plan "Ward house."

April 8, 1685, the mill privilege was leased for five years for saw mill purposes to Joseph Ingalls and Robert Morrill, at five pounds per year, who, it seems, built a mill, which was soon destroyed by the Indians. The facts are found among "papers on file" at Alfred in connection with a law suit some years later. The cellar hole of the Ingalls house still remains.

Soon after the appearance of Col. Thomas Westbrook at Stroudwater in 1728, he and Gen. Samuel Waldo purchased the "mile square" lot and built mills and houses and barns upon it. When, in the case of Waldo vs. Westbrook, the property was taken by Waldo upon an execution, there were located upon the lot a "saw mill, a grist mill, three dwelling houses, and two barns," which were named in the return upon the writ.

Notwithstanding the attachment Westbrook sold the mills in 1739 to Samuel Cobb, carpenter, and son, Chipman Cobb. In 1762 the Cobbs and others located near the mills were ejected by the Waldo heirs, who paid by order of the courts for improvements. One of the barns still stands, but removed to the premises of the late Edward D. Starbird.

In 1762, one James Frost, purchased a lot, built a two story house, and opened an inn. Capisic had then become the seaport of what is now Cumberland Mills, in Westbrook. In 1775 Gen. Jedediah Preble purchased the Frost house, in which he made his last home, where he died—not in Portland as is stated.

James Frost, with his family, removed to Limington, Me., where his son, Wingate Frost, built a brick house, which now stands and is occupied by descendants.

In the year 1800 little, funny Samuel Butts, whose wife was a sister to the mother of Hon. W. W. Thomas; as well as to that of Col. James Means of Stroudwater, was owner of Capisic mill, and resided in the Frost house, and one of his advertisements, copied from Jenk's Portland Gazette, I will here present:

"VALUABLE COUNTRY STAND TO LET.

"That pleasant and valuable stand for business in Capisic, Falmouth, now occupied by the subscriber. The premises consist of a large, commodious dwelling-house, out houses and a store, together with ten acres of land and a good garden. It is an excellent stand for a public house, or for a trader.

"Also to let a small dwelling house in the above named village with from ten to twenty acres of land, and an excellent grist mill with two sets of stones and a bolting mill.

"Likewise for sale, a good stand near Presumpscot Mills, consisting of a new two story house, partly finished, about thirty acres of land, and five-sixteenths of a saw mill, being a valuable situation for a trader, mechanic, or tavern keeper. For particulars apply to

SAMUEL BUTTS.
Capisic, October 24, 1803."

In 1810 Jonathan Sparrow, father to John Sparrow, Esq., of Portland, purchased the mill, Butts being a bookseller in Portland. After this it was claimed the Frost house was haunted and was taken down. The mill was destroyed by fire about forty years ago, but another was built which is intact at the present time, and used for grinding corn.

Samuel Butts' remains were deposited at the time of his death in a tomb in the Portland Eastern cemetery and "Capisic village" is as quiet as are his remains.

GRANDPA'S SCRAP BOOK

Week of Nov. 14 - 16 1901.

THE STROUDWATER PARISH.

Records Over a Century Old Recently Found.

By Leonard B. Chapman.

Originally the Stroudwater parish comprised territorially what is now Falmouth, Westbrook and Deering, and was incorporated in 1764.

As we have stated a Congregational church parish of ye olden time was of a very peculiar composition—a thing of three parts—the parish, the church and the meeting house proprietors, each acting independent of the other, yet one and each having a record of its own making. In the case of this Stroudwater parish, the parish record book, which is very incomplete, is safe, but the church record was destroyed by fire about fifty years ago, when the shop of Dea. Hiram H. Dow was burned at Brighton Corner, the Proprietor's records with papers covering the important period from 1773 to 1793 having recently come to light and been presented to the writer by Lewis Pierce, Esq., of Portland, all unworn and as clean as well-preserved records of far more recent dates.

By whom the first meeting house of the parish was built, or what became of the first nine years of records we cannot state. The book before us is home-made, 6x7 inches square and contains forty-eight written pages. The twenty-three papers accompanying the record book aid materially in presenting the numerous obstacles then in the way of meeting house building in the Stroudwater parish, the difficulty in collecting funds, and the long period the house was in process of construction. Though in an excellent state of repair, having been thoroughly built, the house was sold in 1834 for $200, and removed. A very few now remember its appearance. In it town as well as other public meetings were held till the advent of Universalism, when a strong and determined effort was made by the Universalists to obtain possession by out-voting at parish meetings the real owners.

The book to which we refer is indorsed on the outside as follows:

Minutes of the Proceedings of the Subscribers for building a Meeting House in the Third Parish in Falmouth, December 10, 1773.

The inside commences as follows:

Falmouth, December 10, 1773. Att a meeting duly warned of the Subscribers for building a Meeting House in the third Parish in said Falmouth, Voted—

1st—William Frost Clerk of said Meeting.
2nd.—That three Men be chosen as a Committee to demand and receive of each Subscriber the particular Sum he has subscribed, and for laying out the same in building said House and to call Future Meetings of sd. Subscribers.
3d.—That Mr. Nathaniel Wilson, Capt. Daniel Dole and Mr. John Brackett are chosen a Committee for the purpose aforesaid.

Atts. Wm. Frost, Clerk.

[Nathaniel Wilson became a Revolutionary soldier, lived and died at North Deering, where a memorial monument may be seen in a field at that place. He has many descendants. Capt. Daniel Dole, was a retired sea captain, built the large house at Stroudwater, which still remains, where he died. John Brackett was a land surveyor, resided at Saccarappa, raised a company for the war, but died at Ipswich, Mass., before seeing active service, leaving a widow and children at Saccarappa. Wm. Frost wrote an excellent hand, was son of Charles Frost, Esq., of Stroudwater; William was a Revolutionary soldier, who has a memorial slab at the place of his birth.]

Falmouth, Dec. 10, 1773.

We the Subscribers do hereby severally oblige ourselves to pay towards erecting and completing a decent House for public Worship in the third Parish in said Falmouth, the said house to be fifty-seven feet in length, and fifty feet in width, to have a Porch at each end of said House, the sum, or sums affixed to our Names respectively, or the Value thereof in our Labor or material for building said House, the one-half of said Sums to be paid within six months & the other half of said sums to be paid in twelve months from the Date hereof, the whole of said Sums to be paid to a Committee chosen and appointed by us for the purpose of building said House—

The said House to be erected where the present One now stands—

Joseph Riggs,	£13
Daniel Dole,	20
William Frost,	20
John Johnson,	10
Benjamin Bailey,	14
Solomon Haskell,	12
Thomas Browne, (Rev.),	13
Nathaniel Fickett,	13
Nathaniel Wilson,	10
Robert Josnson,	10
John Brackett,	10
Joseph Pride,	10
Samuel Knight,	10
Mark Knight,	10
Isaac Sawyer,	5
Daniel Lunt,	8
John Snow Brackett,	5
David Bailey,	10
Henry Knight,	5
Andrew Gibbs,	8
Daniel Bailey,	5
Wm. Lamb, Jr.,	10
Mark Wilson,	10
Joseph Quinby, Jr.,	10
John Starbird,	10
Thomas Starbird,	6
George Knight, 3d,	10
Nath'l Knight,	15
John Sawyer,	5
Jonathan Sawyer,	5
Anthony Morse,	13
John Barbour,	12
William Gibbs,	5
Lemuel Hicks,	10
Thomas Brackett,	12
Geo. Walker,	6
Jesse Partridge,	10
Miles Thompson,	12
Samuel Dunn,	5
Wm. Proctor,	8
Wm. Brackett,	5
William Siemons,	13
Peter Babb,	10
Robert Siemons,	8
Joanna Frost,	7
Isaac Sawyer Stevens,	8
Joseph Pennell,	6
Benjamin Haskell,	12
Stephen Riggs,	12
Jeremiah Riggs,	12
Edmund Merrill,	10
John Thomes,	13

Notice is hereby given to the Subscribers of the Meeting House in the 3d Parish in Falmouth to meet at the meeting House in said Parish on the Second monday in April at 2 o'clock.

1st—To see if they will go on with the Meeting House or not.
2nd—To add one to the Committee in the Room of Capt. John Brackett, [deceased].
3d—To take any Methods to go on with the House they shall think best.

Falmouth, March 29, 1777.
Nath'l Wilson,
Daniel Dole,
Committee.

A true copy of the warning,
Atts. Wm. Frost, Clerk.

Falmouth, April 14, 1777.
The Subscribers met & chose Daniel Dole Moderator. Voted—

1st—To finish the Meeting House as as far as the Committee think proper.
2nd—Wm. Frost, a Committee Man in room of Capt. John Brackett, deceased.
3d—That the Committee, or any two of them be, and they are hereby impowered to call on all the delinquent Subscribers to see if they will pay their Respective subscriptions, which if they decline, the said Committee to admit other Persons in their Room.

"The foregoing is a Minute of the proceedings of the Subscribers for building a meeting House in the 3d parish in Falmouth.

Atts. Wm. Frost, Clerk."

(To be continued.)

GRANDPA'S SCRAP BOOK

Week of Nov. 21-23, 1901.

THE STROUDWATER PARISH.

Records Over a Century Old Recently Found.

By Leonard B. Chapman.

NO. 2.

[I committed an error last week in stating that the Third parish of Falmouth comprised the territory of what is now Falmouth, Westbrook and Deering. The Third comprised what is now known as Westbrook and Deering only. When Portland Neck was made a town, in 1787, then the Second of Falmouth became the First of Falmouth and the Stroudwater, or Third, became the Second, and the First of the original Falmouth became the First of Portland, but it required special State legislation to fix the dividing parish line between the Falmouth and Westbrook parishes.]

Now I will go on with the Stroudwater, or Third parish Proprietors' record.

"This is to warn the Proprietors or Subscribers of the new meeting house in the 3d Parish in Falmouth to meet at the House of (*) Capt. Joseph Riggs, Innholder, in said Parish, on Monday the 5th day of Feb'y., next, at One O'Clock in the afternoon to act on the following Articles—Viz.

1st—To choose a Moderator.
2nd—To admit Proprietors or Subscribers in lieu of those Subscribers that have not advanced anything towards building said House, and who still decline.
3d—To receive the account of disbursements on said meeting House.
4th—To see what methods the Proprietors or Subscribers will take to finish said House.
  Daniel Dole,
  Nath'l Wilson,
  Wm. Frost,
   Proprietors Committee.
Falmouth, Jan. 22, 1781."

* Capt. Joseph Riggs, Innholder, resided at Bradley's Corner in the dwelling house recently removed by Mr. Daniel D. Chenery, to make room for Mr. Chenery's new house.

"Cumberland, ss., Falmouth, Feb'y 5th, 1781.
Persuant to the within, we have warned the Proprietors and Subscribers to meet at Time & place within named.
  Wm. Frost,
  Nath'l. Wilson.
The foregoing is a true copy from the original.
  Atts. Wm. Frost, Clerk.

Feb'y 5th, 1781. The aforenamed met & acted as follows, Viz.

1st—Chose Capt. Jo. Riggs Moderator.
2d—Voted in the affirmative.
4th—Voted that the Committee, or any two of them, be & they hereby are directed to admit proprietors sufficient to take up what pews are not already subscribed for.
  Atts. Wm. Frost, Clerk."

"This is to warn the Proprietors of the new meeting House in the third Parish in Falmouth to meet at the house of Capt. Joseph Riggs, Innholder in said Parish, on Monday, the twenty-fourth day of February, current at two O'Clock in the afternoon, to act on the following articles, Viz.

1st—To choose a Moderator.
2d—To see if the Proprietors will take any different methods than what has been heretofore used by the Committee to finish said house either in part or in whole, and to act thereon.
  Wm. Frost,
  Daniel Dole,
  Nath'l. Wilson,
   Committee.
A true copy from the ye original.
  Atts. Wm. Frost, Clerk.

Feb'y 24, 1783, the aforenamed Proprietors agreeable to the afore recited Warning met & acted as follows, Viz.

1st—Chose Anthony Morse Moderator.
2d—Voted. In order to finish the new meetinghouse in the third Parish, aforesaid, in Falmouth, that the Proprietors' Committee be and they hereby are impowered & directed to advance a new subscription in the manner following, viz., Each new subscriber to subscribe fifty dollars, or a sum equal to the cost of a Pew on the lower floor after said house is finished, and each & every Person so subscribing, except those Persons who have been heretofore Subscribers, and have already advanced to the Proprietors' Committee aforesaid, and by them rec'd any money, labor or materials towards building said house, which money, labor and materials so advanced and received by said Committee, shall be deducted from each of those Proprietors aforesaid, on or before the tenth day of July next.—Then the meeting was adjourned to the Day the Parish meet in March.
  Atts. Wm. Frost, Clerk."

This is to warn the Proprietor of the new meetinghouse in the third Parish in Falmouth, to assemble at the old (*) meetinghouse in said Parish on Monday, the 7th day of July next, at 3 O'Clock in the afternoon, to act on the following articles, viz:

1st—To choose a Moderator.
2d—To prolong the time ordered for the Committee to bring forward a new Subscription by a vote passed the 24th day of February, last.
3d—To see if the Proprietors will pass a vote for their Committee to sell to the highest bidder who has heretofore belonged to the said third Parish, or any Person residing to the westward of the divisional line between the first and second Parishes in said Falmouth but within the bounds of said Falmouth, excepting those Persons who live on Falmouth Neck, so called, the Rights of those Proprietors who have neglected to pay unto said Committee the sums by them severally subscribed and who have refused to comply with the vote noted in the second article hereof and shall continue so to do, after a day to be set agreeable to said second article hereof.
  Wm. Frost,
  Daniel Dole,
  Nath'l. Wilson,
   Committee.
Falmouth, June 28, 1783.
A true copy, attest, Wm. Frost, Clerk."

[* The old and new houses both stood where the so called Bradley meetinghouse stands in Deering.]

July 7th, 1783. The aforesaid Proprietors met and acted as follows, viz.

1st—Chose Solomon Haskell Moderator.
2d—Voted to prolong the time for the delinquent Proprietors to pay in their respective subscriptions until the 3d Monday in September, next, also to adjourn this meeting to that time, then to meet at this place at 3 O'Clock in the afternoon.
  Atts. Wm. Frost, Clerk.

Cumberland, ss., Falm. 3d Parish, 15th of Sept., 1783. Then the aforementioned Proprietors met & adjourned to the 3d Monday in October next, then to meet at 3 O'Clock in the afternoon at the meetinghouse in said Parish.
  Atts. Wm. Frost, Clerk.
Oct. 20th, 1783.

The aforesaid Proprietors met and passed the vote following, viz.:

That the Committee be impowered to sell or dispose of to any Person whatever, such or so many Pews, or the rights of such Proprietors as have not, or shall not upon application of the sd. Committee, or either of them, pay their respective subscriptions, as will enable said Committee to fulfill their contracts and finish said meetinghouse.
  Atts. Wm. Frost, Clerk."
(To be Continued.)

GRANDPA'S SCRAP BOOK

Week of Nov. 28-30, 1901.

THE STROUDWATER PARISH.

Records Over a Century Old Recently Found.

By Leonard B. Chapman.

NO. III.

"This is to warn the Proprietors of the new meeting house in the 3d Parish in Falmouth, to meet on Monday the 16th day of Feb'y, current, at One O'Clock in the afternoon, at the dwelling house of Capt. Riggs, Innholder, in said Falmouth, to act on the following articles,—viz—

1st—to choose a Moderator.
2—to choose one or more Men to act as a Committee with the present One.
3d—to see what allowance they will make to those Proprietor who advanced materials and Cash for said house before the year 1775.
4th—to see what method they will take to set of the Pews to the respective Proprietors.

    Wm. Frost,
    Daniel Dole,
    Nathl. Wilson,
        Committee.

Falmouth, Feb. 12, 1784.
A true Copy of the original.
    Atts. Wm. Frost, Clerk.

[The proceedings in connection with the warrant as recorded as above do not appear among the records.]

"This is to warn the Proprietors of the new meeting house in the 3d Parish in Falmouth to assemble at said House, on Monday the 15th day March, current, to act on the following articles—viz—

1st—to choose a Moderator.
2nd—to see if the Proprietors will reconsider a clause in the 4th article voted in their meeting of the 16th of February, viz., "Cause to be drawn by a general lot the Pews on the lower floor," and direct some other method.
3d—to see if the Proprietors will direct that no Pew be delivered unto any Proprietor until said Proprietor has fully paid unto their Committee the price of said Pew, and in case any Proprietor does not before the 20th day of June next, pay unto their Committee, the price of said Pew, direct the said Committee to sell said Proprietors Pew, and return him the amount of his act, against said meeting house, first deducting the charges arising on the sale of said Pew.

Falmouth, 6th March, 1784.
    Daniel Dole,
    Enoch Ilsley,
    Wm. Frost,
        Proprietors Committee.

True Copy of the original.
    Atts. Wm. Frost, Clerk.

"Falmouth, 3d Parish, Monday the 16th day of Feb'y. 1784.
The aforesaid Proprietors met and voted as follows—viz.—

1st—chose Solomon Haskell Moderator.
2nd—chose Enoch Ilsley a committee Man.
3d—voted to allow twenty-five per cent to the Proprietors who advanced Articles prior to the year 1775.
4th—voted that the Committee, or the major part thereof, be & hereby are impowered to Number, appraise & cause to be drawn by a general Lot the Pews on the lower floor and each Proprietor respectively shall receive said Pews according to appraisment.
    Atts. Wm. Frost, Clerk.

"Falmouth 3d Parish, 15th March, 1784. The Proprietors agreeable to the warning the 6th current met and acted as follows—viz.—

["The warning" is not a matter of record.]

1st—Chose Enoch Ilsley Moderator. (*).
2nd—voted in the affirmative and agreed that the Proprietors shall draw for choice.
3d—voted in the affirmative except the last clause, viz., "first deducting the charges on the sale of said Pews" which was not agreed to.

[* When Mowat bombarded Portland Neck Enoch Ilsley removed to the Garrison House that stood at the southwesterly angle made by what are now called Westbrook and Garrison streets, Stroudwater village. I have stated that he resided where Dr. Barker lived—later Dr. Jacob Hunt, a few rods southerly of the Garrison, but recent disclosures place his residence in the Garrison house, built by Col. Thomas Westbrook. While at Stroudwater Ilsley's wife died, who, it is supposed, fills an unmarked grave in the old Stroudwater cemetery, much to the regret of descendants.]

"The aforesaid Proprietors at the meeting house aforesaid, proceeded to draw for choice of Pews, and each drew as follows—viz—

"MENS NAMES.

No. 1. Robert Johnson,	£20:0:0	
No. 2. Miles Thompson,	" 21	
No. 3. Daniel Dole, Jr.,	" 21	
No. 4. Peter Noyes, Esq.,	" 19	
No. 5. David Bailey,	" 18	
No. 6. Josiah Cox,	" 18:12	
No. 7. Jonathan Fickett,	"19:16	
No. 8. Wm. Porterfield, Jr.,	" 14:12	
No. 9. James Johnson,	" 15:10	
No. 10. James Pride,	" 17:10	
No. 11. Joshua Knight,	" 16	
No. 12. David Trickey,	" 16	
No. 13. Samuel Knight,	" 15	
No. 14. George Walker,	" 18	
No. 15. Jacob Adams and Joshua Stevens,	" 16	
No. 16. Enoch Ilsley,	" 16	
No. 17. PARISH.		
No. 18. [Capt.] John Quinby,	" 22	
No. 19. Thomas Brackett,	" 21	
No. 20. Mark Wilson and [Capt.] Isaac S. Stevens,	" 16	
No. 21. Benjamin Haskell,	" 16	
No. 22. Solomon Haskell,	" 17:10	
No. 23. Js. Bailey,	" 15:10	
No. 24. Andrew P. Frost,	" 14:12	
No. 25. John Starbird,	" 19:16	
No. 26. John Johnson, Jr.,	" 18:12	
No. 27. Peltiah March,	" 18	
No. 28. Wm. Slemons, Jr.,	" 16	
No. 29. Wm. Slemons,	" 21	
No. 30. Nathl. Knight, Jr.,	" 21	
No. 31. John Thomes,	" 20	
No. 32. Benj. Bailey,	" 21	
No. 33. Joseph Riggs,	" 20:10	
No. 34. Daniel Ilsley,	" 20	
No. 35. Isaac Sawyer,	" 17:10	
No. 36. Wm. Frost,	" 18	
No. 37. Josiah and Obadiah Berry,	" 17	
No. 38. Zach. and Anthony Sawyer,	" 16	
No. 39. Anthony Morse,	" 17	
No. 40. Mark and Amos Knight,	" 17	
No. 41. Jesse Partridge,	" 17	
No. 42. Daniel Dole,	" 17:10	
No. 43. Saml. Hix,	" 19	
No. 44. Henry Knight,	" 21	
No. 45. Wm. Lamb, Jr.,	" 20:10	
No. 46. Archelaus Lewis,	" 20	
No. 47. John Porterfield,	" 17:10	
No. 48. James Webb,	" 18	
No. 49. Jeremiah Riggs,	" 17	
No. 50. John Barbour,	" 16	
No. 51. Stephen Riggs,	" 17	
No. 52. Andrew Gibbs and Josiah Baker,	" 17	
No. 53. Daniel Lunt,	" 17	
No. 54. Nathl. Wilson,	" 17:10	
No. 55. Rev. Thomas Browne,	" 19	
	£977.	

"This is to notify the Proprietors of the new meeting house in their parish in Falmouth to meet in said house on Monday the 14th day of March, current, at two O'Clock in the afternoon to act on the following articles—viz.—

1st—to choose a Moderator.
2nd—to choose a committee to examine the former Committees & all other acts. [accounts.]
3d—to receive accts. against said house, and to do any other business which may appear neccessary.

Falmouth, March 7th, 1785.
    Wm. Frost,
    Daniel Dole,
    Enoch Ilsley,
        Committee.
    Atts. Wm. Frost, Clerk.

"In Persuance to the within, We have warned the Proprietors to meet at the time & place for the purpose within mentioned. March 14, 1785.
    Daniel Dole,
    Wm. Frost,
    Nathl. Wilson,
        Proprietors Committee.

"Same day the Proprietors aforesaid met & chose Anthony Morse Moderator.
Then adjourned to Monday next, then to meet at the aforesaid House at the hour of 10 in the forenoon.
At the adjournment on said day, Voted on Article 2nd, to choose a Committee of three & James Frost [Capt.], John Quinby and Archelaus Lewis [Esq.], were chosen for said purpose, then adjourned to 29th, current, to meet at the meeting house aforesaid at the hour of One in the afternoon.

GRANDPA'S SCRAP BOOK

Week of Dec. 5-7, 1901.

THE STROUDWATER PARISH.

Records Over a Century Old Recently Found.

By Leonard B. Chapman.

No. IV.

The papers accompanying the Meeting house Proprietor's record book reflect considerable light upon parish matters the book does not. They give the prices of building materials, prices of labor, prices of some kinds of provisions, prices of board, prices of intoxicants, methods of doing business, from which one can obtain a tolerable good idea of the state of society, popular education and particularly the appearance of the meeting house both inside and out, and who were the leading men of the period in public matters. Then, as now, there was crookedness in public proceedings, investigations, reports and changes in office holding.

The records do not show who the Treasurer was of the Meeting house Proprietors, but I surmise it was Capt. Daniel Dole. His bill is a comparatively long one, to the acceptance of which many obligations were made, requiring a long time in settlement, ending in court action, he finally taking a note from the parish examining committee, which is before me as I write as well as notice of payment.

In my article of last week I gave a copy of the report of the first examining committee from the original not recorded in the record book, when James Frost was chairman, but to Archelaus Lewis, Esq., more than to any other one, the credit of working out the real status of the Meeting house Proprietors, the credit belongs. A sketch of him the News has given to the public through its columns. His original bill for services is before me as follows:

The Proprietors of the New Meeting house, Dr.
1785, August. To 2 days as Committee for Examinin Accounts 6s, 12d.
1791, Nov. To 3 days do., @ 6s., 18d.
£1:10.

ARCH. LEWIS.

I will now present a few extracts from bills in the original, as follows:

Dr. The new Meeting House, 3d Parish in Fal., to Wm. Frost.
1774, March 19. To 4 oak Principal Rafters, 34 feet long, 8x12 inches, £2: 0:0
My time drawing plans, giving bills, &c., 1:16:0
July 26, 16,700 shingles @ 10 shil, 8 p. 8:18:1
Sept. 500 Clapboards, 1:10:0
Sept. 29, Cordage, 14:8
Oct. — 5. Gal. W. I. Rum @ 4s. 2 lbs. sugar, 1: 1:0
Myself one day, 4:0
1775, June 17. 2 Gal. W. I. Rum @ 5s. for Engine Men & others to stop fire. (*), 10:0
Advance @ 25 per cent per vote Proprietors, Feb. 16. 4:16:1
£21:10:4

A two story wooden building with rafters made of 8x12 inch oak would be a curiosity at th's date, but of such was the 3d parish meeting house.

(*). If Smith and Dean's diaries are referred to it will be seen that the fact that the engine was carried from Portland to the 3d parish meeting house, when it came near being destroyed by fire, was recorded which explains the above where the price of two gallons of W. I. rum is charged for "Engine Men & others to stop fire." The nature of the fire I cannot learn; it may have been the old house was stroved.

In 1787 the account was continued but no dates of months appear; some of the items are as follows:

2 Gal. Molasses @ at 12 s., 12 lbs. sugar @ 10 d. £ 16:0
6 lbs. pork, 1 s. 3 d.,
2 lbs. hogs lard, 2 s. 8 d., 10:2
50 lbs. lamb & mutton @ 4 d., 16:8
2 gal. N. E. Rum @ 4 s. 6 d. 9:
1½ bush. meal @ 6 s., 9:
24 lbs. corned cusk @ 2 d. 4:
3 pecks potatoes, 3:
1000 6 d nails @ 6 s. 6 d. & 1000 4 d. 17:2
1340 feet best clear seasoned pine boards, 4:16:6
Time as a committee Man, 10 days @ 6 s. 3: 0:0
Pd. Enoch Riggs for paint pots, 1: 9:8
To paid Mrs. Ann Moody her balance in full, 2:10:7

Andrew P. Frost was a brother to William Frost, and both children of Mrs. Joanna Frost, whose name appears among the pew owners, she widow of Chas. Frost, Esq., and all resided where the cellar of the late "Brewer House" may be seen on Congress street, near Fore river, a daughter of Andrew P. Frost becoming the wife of Capt. Dexter Brewer, who purchased the Frost mansion and converted it into an inn, hence the name, using the meeting house at the time of sale for the purpose of constructing the third story of the Brewer House— thus appearing at the time of its destruction by fire some twenty odd years ago.

Dr. New Meeting House 3d Parish, in Fal. to A. P. Frost.
1774. To 4 pine sills, 27 tons @ 10 s. £1: 5
1 yoke Oxen 1 day, 2:8
pd. John Bailey for one day, 4:0
37½ days framing @ 4 s., 5: 8:4
1776, June. pd. Huchin Moody 5 days clapboarding, 1: 0:0
Boarding H. Moody 5 days, 0: 6:8
Advance of 25 per cent. per vote, Feb'y. 16, 1784, 2: 7:5
1783, Sept. 16. 1 Gal. Brandy @ 7 s., 0: 7:0
Sept. 22. 1 Gal. do., 0: 7:0
Sept. 25. 1 Gal. do., 0: 7:0
Sept. 30. 1 Gal. do., delivered (*) Mrs. Storer's son, 0: 7 0
Oct. 11. Paid Richard Dole for 2 Pillars, 0:16:0
"The above account settled in Book, June 1784."

There are other items but the above are all that are important.

(*). Mrs. Storer was a character. Her maiden name was Joanna Graves; her husband was a Revolutionary soldier who died in the service of his country. At the time of her demise she lacked but a few days of being a hundred years of age. One of her sons built the ancient apparing residence as now seen occupying the northwesterly angle made by Stevens avenue and Capisic street, Deering district of Portland, which attracts so much attention by strangers. A more lengthy notice of her and descendants than has been given is nearly ready for publication.

A bill, evidently in the hand of Capt. Daniel Dole, containing over fifty items of charge commences as follows:

Dr. New Meeting house To Daniel Dole, his Second account.—The first allowed.
1784, June 19. To cash paid Mr. Ingraham for one barrel of flour, £3:10:0
To 175 maple gice.
May 29. "(*). To pine Piece for Pulpit, By Mr. Stephens & fixen ye Canniper," 0: 7:6
June 17. "To maple plank & Gice, 353 feet," 1:15:9
June 25. To lock & hinge for Door under Pulpit, and maple plank, 1: 4:5
To 56 Pounds of whiten & 4 pairs of hinges for pews, 0:16:8
To paid for 4 boxes glass, 14:08:0
To cash paid James Bailey to By Oyl & Whiten, 1: 08:0

CONTINUED:

1785. July 2. To paid Mr.
John Kimbal (**) for
work Done on the new
meeting house to the
above date pr. act,   51: 0:0
To Paid Mr. John Bagley (or Bayley) for
turning of 21 Banisters
for meeting house,   0:18:0
To Paid Nathaniel
Moody Painting Pulpit,   2:17:0
To Paid Mrs. Storer for
Dressing of Vitals for
the joiners, 1783,   10:10:0
To furnishing 3 men
Breakfast & Dinner 13
weeks @ 6 s. 8 d.   13:00:0
To my borden 3 joiners the first week, 1:16:0
To one water Pail &
earthern Mugg for joiners,   0: 2:5
To Rum Delivered the
joiners sundry times, 12
gallons @ 5 s. 6 d.,   3:06:0
To Sugar Delivered the
joiners, 21 lbs.,   0:14:0
To bread and fish for
their Luncheons,   0: 8:9
To going to Town for
Painters & coming back,   0:13:0
To Brass hinges & braces for Pulpit door, 0:18:0
To hinges to hang Communion Table,   0:02:8

The foregoing transcript comprises but a few of the 50 odd items which are the most instructive at this time.

(*). The "Canniper" evidently was the sounding board placed over the pulpit.

(**). John Kimball's last residence was on South street in Portland, which was the first house built in that locality. He was an architect and master builder—many buildings still standing in Portland to his memory as a designer, but unknown to the public. His first residence was on Fore street, opposite the Portland machine works. He was grandfather to Wm. G. Kimball, who was selectman of Westbrook some forty years ago, residing at Woodfords, who has been noticed in the News.

(To be continued.)

GRANDPA'S SCRAP BOOK

Week of Dec. 12-14, 1901.

THE STROUDWATER PARISH.

Records Over a Century Old Recently Found.

By Leonard B. Chapman.

No. V.

The sum total of Capt. Daniel Dole's bill was £199:6:1. This amount seems to have caused the committee of investigation a good deal of figuring, if not vexation of spirit, the committee reporting there was due him £95:19, after many corrections in his account and charging him with two pews at £19:5 each.

Written upon one slip of paper before me is a memoranda that reads as follows:

"1784. Capt. Dole for Inspecting Cimball, [Kimball's work]. £10:19.
Amount of Boarding
Cimble & men   £42:9:10
Cimble account against
ye Meeting house,   £51."

One of the bills in the original hand of Solomon Haskell of Saccarappa is among the package of meeting house papers, who was one of the leading spirits of the saw mill hamlet a century and a quarter since, and is dated July 6, 1774, the amount of which is £16:11:11, mostly for lumber.

The investigating committee finding that the Proprietors of the meeting house seemed to be in debt about £125, at an adjourned meeting, held March 29th, 1785, voted as indicated by the following transcript from records:

"To raise one hundred & fifty pounds, to be assessed by the former Committee on pews according to their Value heretofore set on said Pews, to be demanded by & paid unto the said Committee for the payment of debts due from the proprietors of said house.
Voted. To adjourn this meeting to the last Tuesday in April next, then to meet at said meeting house at the hour of two in the afternoon.
Attest. Wm. Frost, Clerk.
"Falmo. 3 Parish, Tuesday, April 25th, 1785.
Voted. On the adjournment further to adjourn to the third Monday in June next, then to meet at said meeting house at three O'Clock in the afternoon.
Atts. Wm. Frost, Clerk.
"Falmo. 3d Parish, Monday, June 20th, 1785.
Voted. That the former & latter Committees are desired to confer together respecting the accounts, and that this meeting be further adjourned to the 3d Monday in July next, then to meet at the meeting house in said parish at three O'Clock in the afternoon.
Atts. Wm. Frost, Clerk.

"Falmo. 3d. Parish, Augst. 8th, 1785. The Proprietors met agreeable to Adjournment & voted to receive the Committee's report, which is as follows, viz.. Money due from several Proprietors of said House, viz.,

Isaac Sawyer,   £1: 8:9
Wm. Lamb, Jr.,   10: 0:3
Mark Wilson,   5: 6:5
Isaac Sawyer,   £ 1: 8:9
Isaac Sawyer Stevens,   3: 5:5
Peter Noyes, Esq.,   4: 0:0
Joshua Stevens,   2: 1:6
Mark & Amos Knight,   0:13:8
Wm. Slemons,   0:14:4
Henry Knight,   7:17:3
Joseph Cox,   4: 7:11
                         £39:15:6
Due to the Proprietors, viz.,
Andrew P. Frost,   £ 2: 3: 8
Wm. Frost,   1:13: 7
Nathaniel Wilson,   3:17:10
Jeremiah Riggs,   1: 7: 1
Joshua Knight,   7: 9: 6
Daniel Dole,   95:19: 0
Anthony Morse,   0:15: 0
Wm. Harper,   6:15: 0
Daniel Ilsley,   0:12: 6
Solomon Haskell,   1:13: 5
                         £123: 7:1

Voted—To reconsider a vote passed on the 3d Article of this meeting held by adjournment on the 2 8th day of last March respect.g raising One hundred & fifty pounds for the payment of debts due from the proprietors of the Meeting House & voted to raise in lieu thereof ninety-seven pounds and fourteen shillings, to be assessed & demanded as is expressed in the Vote passed on the 29th day of March aforesaid, said sum to be appropriated for the payment of said Debts & for the finishing the Porch at the West End of said meeting house.

Voted—To choose a Man to finish & dispose of the two front Pews on each side the broad Alley & James Frost is chosen for said Purpose.

Voted—To adjourn this meeting to the 2nd Monday in November next at the meeting House at 2 O'Clock in the afternoon.
Atts. Wm. Frost, Clerk."

In the package of papers, to which reference has been made, I find two bills that read as follows:

"Falmouth, April 3d, 1792. Daniel Dole, William Frost & Nathaniel Wilson, Proprietors Committee, Dr.

To Mark Wilson.
To finishing one pew on
the left hand of the
Broad aley In [Rev.]
Mr. [Thomas] Browne's
meeting house,   £1: 4:0
To paid James Frost
for 6 clear boards,   0: 5:0
                        £1: 9:0

A true copy.
Atest Mark Wilson."

"Falmouth, April 3d, 1792. Proprietors of the 3d Parish meeting house to Isaac Sawyer,   Dr.
To finishing the front
Pew on the Right hand
Side of the Broad Alley
in Mr. Brownes meeting
house,   £1: 4:0
Recd Payment.
Isaac Sawyer."

GRANDPA'S SCRAP BOOK

Week of Dec. 19-21, 1901.

THE STROUDWATER PARISH.

Records Over a Century Old Recently Found.

By Leonard B. Chapman.

NO. VI.

The record book of the doings of the Proprietors at their public meetings does not show that a single meeting was held from Sept. 4, 1786, to May 30th, 1791, and it is doubtful if there was one. It appears that all that was done at the last meetings reported was to meet and adjourn. Every effort made to put matters in order relative to arrearages, it seems, was by vote negatived, but after the lapse of a period of five years a recorded effort was made, headed by Capt. Daniel Dole, to bring order out of chaos among the Proprietors. A petition was then prepared and sent to a Justice of the Peace, which read as follows:

"TO Samuel Freeman, Esq., one of Justices of the Peace within the county of Cumberland:

"Whereas the new meeting house in the second Parish of Falmouth is at present an undivided propriety, belonging in common with others to the subscribers,—We therefore request you would issue your warrant to call a meeting of the proprietors of said meeting house on Tuesday the sixth day of April, next, at 3 O'Clock, P. M. at the said meeting house.

To choose a Clerk, Treasurer, & such other officers as they may judge necessary.

Also to agree on a method of calling meetings in future. Falmo. 20th March, 1790.

    Daniel Dole
    Josiah Cox
    Wm. Frost
    Archs. Lewis
    And. P. Frost.

The warrant was issued duly, but the report and copy of the warrant does not appear in the regular record book, but alone on what appears to have been a new home-made book, used but once, and for the meeting now under notice. It reads as follows:

"At a meeting of the Proprietors of the new meeting house, agreeable to the notice—Wm. Frost being chosen moderator—they proceeded as follows —Viz—

Wm. Frost was chosen Clerk, the oath of office being administered by Joseph Noyse, Esq.

Wm. Frost was chosen Treasurer.

Isaac Sawyer was chosen Collector.

Nathaniel Wilson, John Quinby & Archelaus Lewis were chosen a Committee.

Voted—That the Clerk be directed to call future meetings whenever any five of the proprietors, in writing, apply therefor, by posting up the warning for said meetings on said meeting house door at least fourteen days before any such meeting is held.

The above is a true record of the doings of the said Proprietors.

  Atts. Wm. Frost, Clerk.

The petition for the next meeting is dated May 14, 1791, is addressed to Joseph Noyse, Esq., and signed as follows:

    John Quinby,
    Archelaus Lewis,
    Andrew P. Frost,
    James Webb,
    Benjamin Bailey.

The meeting was held at the meeting house May 30, 1791, and the record reads as follows:

"1st—Chose Andrew P. Frost Clerk and Treasurer, who was sworn by Joseph Noyse, Esq.

2nd—That Nathaniel Wilson, Archelaus & John Quinby be a Committee.

3d—That the Clerk is Authorized to call Meetings in future by application from any five of the Proprietors, and in case of Death or Removal of said Clerk the Committee is to Call meetings same as the clerk.

  Attest. A. P. Frost, Clerk.

The petition for the next meeting is dated June 16, 1791, for purposes as follows:

1st—To Chose a Moderator.
2—To Chose a Collector.
3—To see what method the proprietors will take to raise money to pay the Ballances due Sundry proprietors.
4—To See if the proprietors will impower their Committee to dispose of the pews belonging to the Proprietors.

  [Signed] James Webb
    Jesse Partridge
    Daniel Dole
    John Quinby
    Archelaus Lewis
    Josiah Cox

The meeting, it seems by the records, was duly called and assembled July 4, 1791, and the record relating to it reads as follows:

1st—Chose Capt. Nathl. Wilson moderator.
2d—Chose Isaac Sawyer Collector.
3d—Voted that the Committee be Directed to take all accounts & papers belonging to the proprietors into their possession and to Settle accounts as soon as possible.
4th—Voted that the Committee Sell the pews Not Disposed of
5th—Voted to adjourn to the first Monday in Oct. next at 2 O'Clock.

  Atts. A. P. Frost, Clerk.

"Oct. 3, 1791, the proprietors Met according to Adjournment and chose Joshua Knight Moderator.

Voted to Adjourn to the first Monday in November at 3 o'clock P. M.

  A. P. Frost, Clerk.

The next meeting was held the 3d day of April, 1792, to act on the following named articles:

"1st—To chose a Moderator.
2nd—To see what Sum of money the Proprietors will raise to Finish the gallery Pews and to paint the outside of the Meeting House and act on any other Business they shall see Cause, said sum not to Exceed Three Hundred Pounds for that and to pay the Ballances Due to Sundry proprietors.

  Atts. A. P. Frost, Clerk.

"Falmo. April 3d, 1792.

The Proprietors of sd. Meeting House met at the time & place and acted as Follows,

Viz—1st—Chose Archelaus Lewis Moderator.

2d—Voted to accept of Proprietors Committees report Concerning the Ballances Due to and from Sundry Proprietors of said House [*] Voted to sell enough of undivided property in said meeting house so as to pay the Ballances Due to Sundry proprietors.

3d—Voted to choose a Committee to sell sd. proprietors undivided property in sd. meeting house.

4th—Chose John Quinby Archelaus & James Webb a Committee to sell at public vendue sd. property.

5th—Voted the Committee be Impowered to call on all the deficient persons from which there is Ballances Due to the Proprietors and if not paid to prosecute to final Judgment.

Voted—a Committee to finish the gallery pews, & number them, & the money arising from the sale to pay Capt. Daniel Dole.

  Atts. A. P. Frost, Clerk.

[*] The package of papers, to which reference has been made, contains a paper that reads as follows:

"Ballances Due to ———— & from the proprietors of the Meeting house of the 2d parish in Falmouth. (This is the second appearance of the term '2d parish in Falmouth.')" Nov. 4, 1791.

to A. P. Frost	£	2: 3: 8
to Wm. Frost		10: 3
to Nathl. Wilson		3:17:10
to Joshua Knight		1: 0: 6
to Enoch Ilsley		7: 9: 6
to Willm. Lamb		1:11: 0
to John Barber		1: 4
to Solomon Haskell		1:13: 5
to Anthony Mors		1:17: 0

THE KING FAMILY OF SCARBORO.

WILLIAM KING.

The First Governor of Maine.

By Leonard B. Chapman.

NO. LXIX.

VAUGHN'S BRIDGE.

I cannot discover that any of the King family were interested in the movement to establish a bridge over Fore river at Portland, nor the exact time when the discussion commenced, can I state. Chroniclers are silent. The history of Portland lets in no light upon the matter which, a hundred years ago, both before and since, was an exciting theme of discussion, and the agitation has not yet ceased.

June 11, 1792, in compliance with a petition of Thomas Robinson and others the General Court of Massachusetts passed a resolve authorizing "Ichabod Goodwin, Josiah Thatcher and William Widgery, Esquires, to be a committee, by agreement of the parties, to view the harbor and river with the place proposed for building said bridge and report at the next session of the court."

The "place proposed for building said bridge" was from the end of Robinson's wharf to Cape Elizabeth, the wharf being located at the foot of what is now known as Park street, Portland—originally called Ann street—where Robinson resided, upon the westerly side of the way, where he had not only a wharf but large conveniences for piling and shipping lumber and the manufacture of rum that was retailed in large quantities at the public house that stood at the corner of Park and Congress streets, still in existance, but removed from its original foundation to a point "around the corner" on Congress street, now three story, formerly but two.

Before me as I write is a well preserved certificate of inspection of a thirty-two ¾ gallon barrel of "Old Stock Rum" destilled from "foreign materials in Portland" and "marked as per margin, August 8, 1719, Daniel Epes, Collector."

Mr. Epes was a Harvard college graduate whose wife was a Stroudwater village girl—daughter of Charles Frost, Esq.

An attempt was then being made to "boom" the west end of Portland, but the bridge project of Robinson and his co-partners failing

The Robinson scheme having exploded a new move was made by others to bridge the river at another point, and—

"William Vaughn, Portland,
"Capt. Jesse Partridge, Stroudwater,
"Col. James Webb,   "
"Maj. Archelaus Lewis,   "
"Capt. John Quinby,   "
"Pelig Wardsworth, Portland,
"Tristram Jordan,
"Thomas Cutts, Saco,
"Richworth Jordan, Jr.,
"Samuel Calef,
"Joseph McLellan, Portland,
"Joshua Fayben, Scarboro,
"Jeremiah Hill,
"Samuel Scammon, Saco,
"Nathaniel Scammon, Saco,
"Mathias Rice,
"Joshiah Libby,
"Seth Libby,
"Domicus Goodwin and
"Isaac Skillin, Cape Elizabeth,
"be and are constituted a corporation," by the General Court, "for the purpose of building a toll bridge over Fore river between Portland and Cape Elizabeth," upon the location of the present bridge, soon to be replaced by an expensive stone structure. The charter stipulated that each single share holder should be entitled to one vote at corporation meetings, but no stock holder should cast more than ten votes. The rate of tolls was also established, and a draw to be twenty-eight feet wide was provided for, which tends to show the size of the numerous sailing crafts built at Stroudwater village.

March 4, 1800, the name of "Portland Bridge"—given the proposed structure by the General Court— was exchanged for that of "Vaughn's Bridge," by which the structure, that was made free to travel by the county commissioners in 1854, has ever since been known. It is "twenty-five hundred and sixty-four feet long."

Before the establishment of the Turnpike and Vaughn's bridge the mails were carried on horseback from Dunstan over Scottow's Hill, crossing the present electric railway where the way from Scottow's joins it, near Storer's brook, thence on easterly near Pleasant Hill in Scarboro, where the town fairs are held, to Ferry village in Cape Elizabeth, (now South Portland), over the river by boat to Portland.

I have never seen a list of the original, or any list of the stockholders' names of the ancient bridge, but Lieut. Gov. William Gray, of Salem, Mass., was one. He was interested in the West End "boom" of Portland, where he built a long rope-walk on the south-westerly side of Park street, and was a partner in ship building. Other interests called him here and to the eastward of Portland, so it was natural for him to interest himself in making the way to Portland as easy and as short as possible. Then he had a relative residing here who was the wife of Capt. Thomas Browne, and Capt. Browne was a brother to William Browne whose wife was a daughter of Dr. Robert Southgate, both being sons of Rev. Thomas Browne of the Stroudwater parish of Falmouth, but the exact relationship between Gov. Gray and Capt. Browne's wife I have not established.

Between William King and William Gray, (the Lieut. Governor), there was evidently a strong social, business, and after Mr. Gray had become a Democrat—otherwise called Republican— political friendship existing.

Before me are several of Mr. Gray's manuscript letters, paid up notes of William King, and other memoranda of business dealings, the paper as clean and fresh, nearly, as of yesterday, though eighty years, yes, ninety-three in one case and a hundred and one in another, have come and gone since the hand made the records to which I now refer as being before me, some of which I propose to preserve by printing, as follows:

"Salem, April 29, 1802.

"Messrs. King & Porter, Gentlemen."

"Mr. Hammet, the bearer hereof, goes to Bath to carry on Rope-making in the Walk which I have lately purchased. I have taken the liberty to recommend Mr. Hammet, who, I find, is a very decent & reputable young Gentleman from his general character. I have no doubt you will find him worthy your attention, and that he will be a very useful mechanic in your growing place. Any advice, or assistance, that you may be pleased to offer him will be gratefully received by him & will be acknowledged as a favor conferred upon a Gentleman.

"Your most Ob't Ser.

"Wm. Gray."

"Camden, Aug. 8, 1810.
"Hon. William King,
Bath."

"Dear Sir: I have no acquaintance with His Honor, Lieut. Gov. Gray & he, having no personal acquaintance with any gentleman of this place, I am therefore under the necessity of requesting you to name me to His Honor by letter. My object is to obtain from Mr. Gray sails & rigging for a brig which I am building and shall have off in September. It is true you are not personally acquainted with me, but I believe Erastus Foote, Esq., Dr. Stere(?) or any other gentleman of this place would satisfy you or any other gentleman as to my situation in life. I shall insure the vessel as soon as she is launched, therefore there can be no great risk in furnishing sails and rigging for her on credit. In getting my sails of His Honor I have two objects in view: first—to be connected in business with a good man, the other— I expect to build a large vessel every year, (or as long as there is any prospect of doing anything with vessels), and being connections with such a man as His Honor, William Gray, Esq., I conceive it may be of great service to me. I have His Honor's letter under date of the 3rd inst. wherein he says: 'Mr. King's introduction will be quite sufficient.' Should you conclude to give me a letter to His Honor, William Gray, Esq., please to inclose it in a letter to me by return mail, as I expect to go from here soon by water to Boston.

"Friend Stere(?) is with us, & I find, as far as I am able to judge, he is the correct Physician, Politician and gentleman & nothing on his friend's part will be lacking to insure him success. This however cannot be done immediately. It is to be done with moderation to insure permanent support.

"Your Ob't. servt,
"Farnham Hall."

To be continued.

GRANDPA'S SCRAP BOOK

Week of July 2-4, 1903.

THE KING FAMILY OF SCARBORO.

WILLIAM KING.

The First Governor of Maine.

By Leonard B. Chapman.

NO. LXXI.

JOSEPH EMERSON AGAIN.

I find that in my notice of Joseph Emerson I did not say all I might. On Nov. 7, 1809, at Scarboro, he addressed a letter to "Hon. William King, Esq.," informing him that he had bought into a certain brig and asked advice of Mr. King relative to wages of sea captains.

At Scarboro, June 2, 1813, he again writes "Gen. William King, Esq.," informing him that—

"I am about to remove from this place [Dunstan] to Limerick, about twenty-four miles from here, in the interior of the county, and have for sale an excellent tract of land of about nine acres which will pasture three cows and so adjoins your lot of sixty acres as would render your property far more valuable and saleable by connecting it with a delightful front, inclosed with a good post fence on the county road just beyond Lemuel Coolbroth's, and it would furnish an elegant and very pleasant situation for a dwelling house and store. I gave $200 for the lot, put up the fence, cleared an acre and a half—overrun with bushes—which has added much to the value of the lot. As your front is very far from the great county road, I think it would add to your lot at least five dollars per acre by annexing my lot to yours, and the whole would command thereby a very ready sale. My price is $250 for the lot but would not take less than $300 were I to continue in the place.

"Please address me at Portland.
"Your Ob't Servt,
"Jos. Emerson."

From Scarboro, June 26, 1815, the Rev. Nathan Tilton sent William King a "Bill of Exchange" for collection to the amount of $157.56.

The parson states in closing his letter as follows:" Our sister at Gandeloupe informs us that she has sent us a piece of cambric muslin which has not been received."

July 11, 1815, the parson informs Mr. King he has receipted for some money from him. The postage between Dunstan and Bath was fifteen cents on a letter. He wrote a very easy and lady-like hand.

From Scarboro, Oct. 13, 1815, George Height informed William King that he thought more of Mr. King's verbal promise to pay than he did of twenty notes of some persons.

From Scarboro, July 9, 1821, Robert Hasty addressed "His Excellency, William King of Bath," in reference to a claim held by Hasty and others for a vessel condemned by order of the French government. She was, it seems, a brigantine, named "Freemason," and was captured by the French in July of 1797, carried into Pampall. (?)

"She sailed from Baltimore, Md., with a freight for Bermuda and had no contraband goods on board as you can inform yourself by seeing Hon. Bernard Smith, senator in Congress of the U. S., who was one of the freighters. [Bernard Smith, a Representative from New Jersey, is the nearest I can come to the name. L. B. C.] Mr. Whitman* informs me that all the spoliation made on commerce is released to the French by the Lousiana treaty. If this is the case can such a good government as ours take private property to pay for public land?

"In 1799 our government called on those who had met with losses to send in their papers and claims which we did. I suppose they are now in the office of the Secretary of the General Government.

"She was a new brigantine, built in Scarboro, Capt. George Bunker was master, and she had been one voyage to Liverpool. Where captured her bills were between eleven and twelve thousand dollars, [for freight on board.]

"I write you now as an old friend and neighbor although your station in life is now far above mine.

"From this loss I am reduced from affluence to indigent circumstance.

"The owners with me in the brigantine were Joseph Emerson, Jonathan Libby and Jeremiah Plummer.

"A close with sentiments of esteem.
"Robert Hasty."

*Ezekiel Whitman, lawyer, Portland, Representative in Congress 1821.

From Scarboro, April 9, 1823, Ephraim Rice wrote William King, who was then at Washington, D. C., that he had "purchased the part of the Knight farm that was set off to William King's brother Cyrus from Mr. Bridge of Augusta [who married Hon. Cyrus King's daughter,] and requested that division lines be run, and fences divided as Dr. Southgate was disinclined to do anything but threatened to 'lay the lot common, which you know cannot be done at this season of the year.'"

COMMISSION PAPERS.

Several papers bearing official seals and signatures informing William King of his election to office are before me, as follows:

1807, May 11. Senator from Lincoln, Hancock and Washington counties.
Caleb Strong—Gov.
John L. Austin—Sec.
1808, May 9. Senator from the same counties as the preceding.
James Sullivan—Gov.
James L. Austin—Sec.
1818, May 11. Senator from the same counties as the preceding.
J. Brooks—Gov.
Alden Bradford—Sec.
1816, June 28. A notice that he had been elected a member of "The Maine Missionary Society."
D. Thurston, Ass't Sec.
1829, Sept. 29. Receipt for a $1 annual dues as a member of the Maine Historical Society.
P. Mellen, Treas.
(Prentess Mellen, Judge of the Supreme court of Maine.)
1829, Jan. 31. Justice of the Peace.
Edward Russell—Sect. of State.
1829, April 21. Collector of the Port of Bath.

This paper contains the signature of "Andrew Jackson, President of the United States of America," and S. D. Ingham—Secretary of the Treasury, with the Seal of the Treasury Department.

The record made upon the back of the paper that the usual oath of office was administered is in the hand of William King and signed by David Shaw, Justice of the Peace.

FREE MASONRY.

I have heard it remarked that William King was up high in degrees in the order of Free-Masonry, but I fail to find anything showing his standing. The following scraps of information may interest somebody.

"Boston, May 19, 1800.
"Mr. King. Sir. Agreeable to promise I will now inform you there will be a special Meeting of the St. Andrew's Royal Arch Chapter tomorrow Evening at the Green Dragon, and if you are desirous of being proposed as a candidate by any of the Members it is necessary to fill and present the within petition addressed to the Officers & Members.
"I am respectfully,
Your humble serv't,
"Jas. Harrison."

The following may be in "regular style" of Masonry, but whether it is or not, it is gotten up in quite a lively manner.

"Bucksport, Dec. 1, 1821.
"To the Grand Master, Grand Wardens, Other officers & Members of the Grand Lodge of Maine.
"Greeting:
"Whereas, a number of respectable brethren residing near Union River in Surry & Ellsworth in the State of Maine, have petitioned the Grand Lodge for a Charter to empower them to assemble in said Surry, near said Union River, as a regular lodge under the name and designation of 'Lygonia Lodge' to Institute Apprentices, pass Fellow crafts & raise Masters Masons, also to do & perform all the duties & enjoy all the privileges belonging to all regular lodges agreeable to the laws & regulations of the said Grand Lodge & Ancient Usages; considering the remote distance from any regular lodge, the number & respectability of the petitioners and that the granting of the prayer of said petition would conduce to their convenience, the good of the craft & the advancement of Masonry generally, readily add my assent and approbation to the petition & recommend that the prayer be granted.
"Manly Hardy, D. D. G. M.
"5th Mason Dis. of Maine."

To be continued

Grandpa's Scrap Book

Week of July 9-11, 1903.

THE KING FAMILY OF SCARBORO.

WILLIAM KING.

The First Governor of Maine.

By Leonard B Chapman.

NO. LXXII.

"Solar Lodge" of Masons of Bath the adopted home place of William King, was organized in 1804.

In 1820, when the District of Maine was made into a State there were thirty-one Masonic lodges with Boston, Mass., as the nearest place where authority for organizing a local lodge could be obtained.

Vessels at that period and long before carried sometimes large amounts of specie which was required in trading. At the office of Asa R Reed, Esq., of Waldoboro, a descendant of a successful sea captain of a century ago, may be seen a strong iron chest then used.

Among pirates there were Freemasons though plunderers of the ocean and as a precautionary measure of self-protection many sea captains became members of the Freemason craft, and as William King was largely engaged in navigation and having in his employ many sea captains it is readily seen one reason why he became a member of the order for the captain of a trading merchantman who fell into the hands of a pirate, fared much better if both were members of the same brotherhood.

Politicians, too, were Freemasons and as the most distant lodge of Maine was three hundred and seventy five miles from Boston, and the politicians were unusually active in 1820 an additional evidence to what I have presented is observable why there was an early move made for a Grand Lodge of Freemasons hereabouts when the District became a State. For the purpose of forming such an organization a circular letter was circulated Augus 13, 1819, suggesting a meeting in Portland. The meeting was held Oct. 14, at which twenty-five lodges were represented by forty-four delegates.

June 1, 1820, twenty-five lodges by delegates met in convention with "William King in the chair who made a short speech," and proceeded to organize a Grand Lodge, June 24, the officers were installed at the meeting-house of Rev. Edward Payson. Prayer was offered by Mr. King's friend, Prof. Allen of Bowdoin college, and the consecration prayer was by the Rev. Mr. Tilton of Scarboro, whom I have briefly noticed.

William King, then Governor of Maine, was made Grand Master of the Grand Lodge of the new state, not so much on account of his "degrees," or labors for the success of the order, but for his high political, social and business rating. John Hannibal Sheppard of Wiscasset, A. M. and A. B., a graduate of Harvard college and honorary member of Bowdoin, class of 1820, delivered the oration.

The duties of Mr. King being so numerous, Deputy Grand Master, Simon Greenleaf, Esq., was chosen Grand Master at the meeting of January, 1822.

AN HISTORICAL LETTER.

I looked many times upon the Island of Grand Menan from Quaddy Head, while spending a summer in the town of Lubec, but I know nothing from a personal examination of the place other than that obtained from the high rocky shores of Lubec, opposite, where the waves lash the stern rocks most furiously during a southeasterly blow.

Between the island and the main land steamboats pass but vessels are cautious, at low water in a blow. Forty odd years ago when I was so situated as to look out upon the Island, the whole northern surface was a mass of scrub spruce without a house or wharf in sight. Why it is a British possession I cannot state.

William King had the Island in his mind in 1817, but his purpose I do not know. The manuscript letter before me which I propose to preserve by printing was penned in the winter of 1817 for "General William King, Bath." Of the writer I know nothing, but it must have been a person above the average in book education. It reads as follows:

"St. David, Jan. 20, 1817.
"My Dear Sir.

"With peculiar pleasure I embrace this opportunity to write you a few lines. I enjoy comfortable health and hope you and your family possess the same. Agreeable to promise I will now give you what information I have received respecting Grand Menan. The Island was first settled by three families who went from Machias during the time of the Revolutionary war. The Indians opposed the settlement and made complaint against them to the British government, and threatened to destroy their property, upon which the chief commander of the military then stationed at Machias advised them to leave the Island. They left it accordingly and did not return. The next settlers were refugees with a family from Scotland. These remained upon the Island and held their property under the British protection from then till the present. Some of them say that if ever Grand Menan should be ceded to the States they shall leave the Island. Many of them, however, are friendly to our country. The Island now contains about seventy-five families besides ten or twelve families on the Island adjacent. It is problematical whether England itself contains so much hostility against the States as appears in this Province of Brunswick.

"That wars may cease and piety and philanthropy harmonize the nations is the prayer of yours in lively sentiments of esteem.

"Abram Cummings."

"P. S. My special regards to Mrs King and the family whose kindness I remember. A. C.
"To General King."

A RUM DISTILL.

Joseph Wingate, Jr., who died in Portland, and whom I have noticed as a postmaster of the town from Feb. 20, 1805, till Aug. 8, of the same year, when he resigned, had a brother named James F. Wingate who was appointed immediately, and who served till May 31, 1815, a period of nearly ten years. From Bath, January 31, 1811, where his brother Joseph was then residing who was the collector of the port, James F., wrote "Hon. William King, Member of the Senate, Boston, Mass.," a letter, the closing part of which reads as follows:

"What you name in regard to Rum Distilling induced me to obtain what information I could respecting the profits, etc., etc., of an establishment of this kind and I am convinced that there is no business in which capital can be employed to so much advantage. A distillery that would cost 8000 dollars may safely be calculated upon to clear itself in sixteen or eighteen months if properly managed. I would therefore observe that if upon further enquiry you feel disposed to interest yourself in one I shall be pleased to take a third part or a half with you. It would probably take four or five months to get one in operation, as I am informed it takes nearly three months to make the Still.

"I enclose you a copy of a communication respecting Domestic Manufacturies penned by me a few days since, and altho' you may not approve of my anti- commercial disposition, I hope you will confess the principle correct. So little having been said in the newspapers respecting the importance of Domestic Manufacturies I wish if possible to bring the matter into discussion. With the assurance of the most respectful regards in which my brother and Mrs. Wingate join towards yourself and Mrs. King,
"I am, Sir, most sincerely,
"Jos. F. Wingate."
"Hon. Wm. King,
"Boston."

I find nothing more relative to "Rum Distilling" participated in by Mr. King.
To be continued.

RANDPA'S SCRAP BOOK

Week of July 16--18, 1903.

THE KING FAMILY OF SCARBORO.

WILLIAM KING.

The First Governor of Maine.

By Leonard B Chapman.

NO. LXXIII.

POLITICAL LETTERS.

Fifty years ago when the Whig and Democrat parties were broken, the members of the Whig party dispersed, the Democrat party reorganized upon a rum and slavery basis and the Republican party created from several factions in opposition to the Democrat party, it was a common assertion—"Politics were never before so corrupt as now." The saying of that time is now used. One hears it daily but comparing the present with my knowledge of what transpired fifty years ago that came under my personal observation, and the present with what was done seventy-five and a hundred years ago—a knowledge gained from printed records, but more particularly from MSS letters, now before me, that have not seen the light of day for a period of many years—I must declare for the present as occupying a higher plane of political virtue.

Rev. Samuel Foxcroft was the first pastor of the First Congregational church of New Gloucester where he was settled in church work Jan. 16, 1765. He was a Harvard college graduate of 1754. Rev. Thomas Smith and Rev. Samuel Dean both notice the event in their diaries. Mr. Smith states "It was a jolly ordination; we lost sight of decorum. Mr. L. [Stephen Longfellow] kept us alert and merry." This character was the grandfather of the poet.

Joseph E. Foxcroft, his son, was born in New Gloucester March 10, 1773. The father was made an Overseer of Bowdoin college in 1794, serving till 1797, and Hon. Joseph Ellery Foxcroft, the same, by Gov. William King, in 1821, who served till 1834.

Joseph E. commenced his business career early. He purchased one of the five townships of land granted Bowdoin college by the Commonwealth of Massachusetts, one of the conditions imposed by the college being that young Foxcroft should make a settlement of twenty-four families upon the lot within a stated period. The Town of Foxcroft, incorporated in 1812, located upon the purchase of ground by Foxcroft, is one of the enduring monuments to his name.

He was appointed postmaster of New Gloucester in 1806 and held the position till 1841.

In 1807 he was chosen to represent his town in the General Court at Boston, and was repeatedly elected to both the house and senate.

He was a delegate to the convention to prepare a State Constitution, and was appointed the first sheriff of Cumberland county when the District of Maine became a State. A biographer states that "he was ever genial and courteous and ever bore about him a halo of joyousness that reflected the sunshine of a happy disposition wherever he went." The expression upon the face of the cut of him which may be seen on page 334 of the History of Cumberland county of 1879, furnishes proof of the correctness of the quotation here used. His father built the first two story house in New Gloucester which may be seen today and occupied by descendants.

Before me are several of Joseph E. Foxcroft's productions in the form of manuscript letters, addressed to William King, upon which appear the same low of cheerfulness that characterizes the picture and biographical notice to which I have called attention, and the first is as follows:

"New Gloucester, August 12, 1805.
"Wm. King, Esq."

"Sir. Knowing your attachment to Republicanism, I am of the opinion you will not be affronted if I trouble you with a few lines. I think the season of flattery in this quarter is over, and I am not without hope that our harvest in April next [spring elections] will be such as shall promote the interest of our Commonwealth. Esquire Prince of North Yarmouth is now engaged. I trust the great O—— Dr. Mitchell—will not hereafter have so much to crack about. Lewiston, I think, will do well another year. Mr. Read has never liked the arbitrary measures of the Junto. The calumny & abuse with which Judge Sullivan has been loaded has had a good effect on him, though prudence, I think, prohibits our speaking of him at present. He may give Col. Thompson a little surprise by telling him he had seen things in Federalists he did not expect—that it appears their leaders are after a Monarchal Government. He is now enjoying the pleasures of contemplation, and doubtless inquiring in his mind for the evidences that they were pursuing measures which tend to wrench sovereignty from the hands of the people. A cloud of witnesses might be offered, but as people who have not been conversant with public men, nor measures, they are sometimes put to it to adduce such evidences of the fact as they would be glad to obtain, so that, I have sometimes thought an epistle sent to some people is preferable to personal conversation because it places arguments before their minds which, by reading, they will remember, when, by conversation, they would forget. I hope, sir, you will be able to get Col. Thompson ardently engaged, for, in such a way there can be no doubt of Lewiston. I think Esquire Herrick will eventually favor Republicanism. In Pejepscot [Brunswick] I think there will be a very handsome majority. You will think, perhaps, sir, a more general attention should be paid to the subject; that one part of the Commonwealth is as important as another, but my means of observation are feeble and limited—yours are extensive and doubtless will continue to be well improved. Please to honor me with an Epistle.

"From your friend and servant,
"Joseph E. Foxcroft."

"New Gloucester, July 25, 1811.
"Hon. William King.

"Dear Sir. The 10th of Aug. is near at hand when the several appointments in the Commonwealth are to be made, and as my friends depend wholly on you I hope you will excuse my troubling you. There has been a county meeting here but I am informed there was division manifested and dissolution was the result without coming to an understanding only the voters of the county should petition for whom they please, and my friends are circulating petitions pretty generally. There is one in Brunswick, but I cannot anticipate the result as Doct. Page is zealous for Mr. Daas Doct. Page is zealous for Mr. David Green of Portland. Messrs. Mazzy & Jewett of Portland told my neighbor, Capt. Johnson, that if Mr. G [Green] should obtain the name of every man in Portland the Governor would not appoint him, that he had failed in business & that his affairs remained too unsettled. This much I have said because I tho't you would like to know how things are going on here.

"We all feel the importance of the several appointments to be made so as shall best cement and strengthen the cause of our country. As respects the Court of Sessions I think it would be wise to have Jonathan Stone, Esq, one of the number, Col. Parsons, Chief Justice, and Major Hasty, Associate. Doct. Page is trying to make a little party with Butts & perhaps one or two more in your tow. I think his appointment would animate him and put the opposition down. I have talked with him in regard to the part Mr. Tolman has taken and he is opposed to him though he was importuned to join with him. I would like to have him see that all his friends are against Tolman. Mr. Stone can have much influence in Brunswick, Harpswell and Durham if he has a mind to put it into operation. Now, all things considered, whither more advantage will not result to the public good from his appointment than any other gentleman, is a question I submit to your better judgment.

"I shall not mention this communication to you to any one but if it meets your approbation no doubt but he will learn you are in his interest.

"With the highest esteem
I am your cordial Friend."
(No name attached.)

"New Gloucester, Aug. 2, 1811.
"Hon. William King.

"Dear Sir. The bearer hereof is Francis Eaton, Esq., who is in the practice of law in this town. He studied with our friend Dana. I asked the favor of him to take a line to your honor.

"Office or no office, you know, is now the question, and each man wants one, and each man is the best, and all must be considered. You must have the strength of a Samson and the wisdom of a Solomon to bear the accumulating load, for every one seems to put on his ton, and then looks to you for direction.

Week of July 23-25, 1903

THE KING FAMILY OF SCARBORO

WILLIAM KING.

The First Governor of Maine.

By Leonard B. Chapman.

No. LXXIV.

"New Gloucester, Dec. 12, 1812.
"Hon. William King.

"Dear Sir. Please accept my thanks, my dear sir, for your favor of the 5th inst. I have no doubt that when business becomes brisk again land will be higher than it ever has been. What I propose selling is about half of what I have on my hands as my creditors are solicitous for payment. I see no way I can get along without selling a part; and believing that important events are before us I feel anxious to become unembarrassed that I may take some part in serving my friends and country. It is probable Maine will shortly become a State of the Union and I am willing to make any sacrifice to be free and active. When you see the gentleman I named if you will contrive some plan so I can sell at some price so as to pay the two colleges so that you shall never have occasion to say that you lost money by the purchase, nor of upbraiding me for forgetting the favor of 1812.

"An 'honest settlement' with G. B. [Great Britain] is most ardently to be wished, and I am happy you can see prospects of its near approach.

"With great esteem and respect, I am, Honored Sir, your obliging friend and most humb. servant,
"Joseph E. Foxcroft."

"New Gloucester, May 10, 1821.
"Governor King.

"Dear Sir. On my way home yesterday I was musing on the subject of Roads, etc., and was thinking that if you send or take with you a copy of the Resolves & state that the Executive of this State had made arrangements to advance the money on the part of Maine for making the one & laying out & making the other road as far as the Government of Massachusetts shall make similar advances on her part, that you might think it necessary to name some person who had been appointed by the Executive of this State on her part to carry the objects of the Resolves into effect so far as relates to the Roads, and in doing thus will the Governor permit me to recommend Gen. Irish. I am sensible there is a possibility that Massachusetts may not make the appropriation of the money & proceed on her part, but even if she does not the appointment would probably prove very acceptable to him [Gen. Irish] and his friends, and do no injury to the State nor to our county elections. I pray you, give him this appointment if it does not militate your arrangements.

"While the Governor is in Boston I have no doubt you will be interrogated about Col. H.: may not your answers be very easy. You tried all in your power to save him and you got along very well with your own political friends, but the other side finding that he was likely to be retained came forward with such mighty power from all parts of the country that there was not a man in the Universe who could have longer withstood their united forces.

"I send this in a way to go safe to your hands and I will thank the Governor to burn it and believe me one among the many of his most obedient and very, very humble servants.
"Joseph E. Foxcroft."

This communication was addressed to—
"William King, Esq.,
"Gov. of the State of Maine,
"now at
"Portland."

It seems that Gov. King violated the request of his "very, very humble servant" in not destroying this "confidential" letter, and now, after the lapse of eighty-odd years, it is brought before the public.

Not long ago I stood by the graves of the Foxcrofts in the old cemetery at New Gloucester and read upon the stone tables names and epitaphs but I did not have at my command the necessary time to copy.

The town of Lewiston has been alluded to which was incorporated Feb. 18, 1795.

William King visited the place in 1810 but for what purpose does not appear. He may have made a political speech as certain people were "thunder-struck after the meeting he attended" there. It seems the place was a miniature political battle ground and the object of William King may have been to restore peace. The following lets on a light:

"Lewiston, May 17, 1810.
"Hon. William King, Esq.

"Sir. Having lately read that the Marshals are to take the census in this District, I now write to say, I should like to be appointed an assistant to take this part of the County of Lincoln to the west of the Kennebec river. You will therefore excuse me for requesting you to use your influence in my behalf with the Marshal so far as you conscientiously can, provided you are not engaged by some other person.

"At our meeting here for the choice of a candidate for Representative we were more prosperous than we have been for several years before although not so much so as I wish. As soon as the meeting was opened the Feds moved to dismiss the nomination and aided by some doubting Republicans carried the vote.

"They have appeared quite thunderstruck since the meeting you attended here and altho' that increased the rage of a few yet I think in the course of another year their numbers will be small.

"I am, Sir, respectfully your obedient Servant,
"Oliver Herrick."

I know but little relative to Peleg Tallman other than the fact that he was a sea captain, was a Republican alias Democratic politician, and a very large owner in navigation.

May 19, 1804, at Woolwich he and seven others authorized William King to vote for them at the proposed meeting of the stockholders of the Hallowell & Augusta bank.

Feb. 8, 1811, at Bath, he informed William King that Dr. Jonathan Page "has a Demand on the Kennebec Insurance office for the total loss of the brig 'Isaac' amounting to $2,021.77." He continues: "I have paid one half of the demand, and will you have the goodness to make him up the other half?
(Signed) "Peleg Tallman."

At Boston, Mass., March 4, 1811, which seems to have been an exciting political year, he addressed William King a lengthy political letter as others did in the same strain of denunciation, Mr. King being in Boston, also, as follows:

"Hon. William King, Esq.

"Sir. I had the honor to address you on the 2nd inst. since which I have received your favor of the 1st. which is now before me, to which you request an answer. You say you have been waited on by a respectable Committee requesting you to stand as a candidate at the next senatorial election, and that your answer was in the affirmative, for which I must beg leave to express my regret, for it was generally understood that tho' named you would decline. If you persist you will probably be elected. Excuse me when I tell you that many of your friends have now altogether lost confidence in you and however painful it may be yet candor compells me to say that I am one of the number. 'I regret,' you say, 'that Mr. Carleton should hesitate to name to me he had wished to stand as a candidate; that he never wished so, nor do I believe that he ever named it to any one.' Some of Mr. Carleton's friends requested me to name it to him and his language was consistent with his character, which has been so long and justly respected. You express a regret 'that our enemies should be successful in wrecking the Bonds of Friendship between us.' In this you are mistaken for it is mostly from my own observation & from a thorough conviction of your political instability, your ambitions, overbearing & selfishness that has induced me to believe it a duty I owe the public and myself thus freely to say and to declare to you that if our hitherto friendship would induce me my conscience will not suffer me to second the views of any man whose political integrity & public patriotism I have so much and so many reasons to doubt. I profess to be a Republican from principal and hope I shall in danger as well as in sunshine be found so. You name the subject of rivalship, but how it rests with you I am not prepared to say, and believe me, it is ungenerous in you to apply it to me, for I believe no man has wished to do more in times past than I have to aid you, and if I am not mistaken it would have been only to have consented and to have filled the public places that you have and now hold, you would have been beaten.

GRANDPA'S SCRAP BOOK

Week of July 30—Aug. 1, 1903.

THE KING FAMILY OF SCARBORO
WILLIAM KING.

The First Governor of Maine.

By Leonard B. Chapman.

NO. LXXV.

Comparatively but little is known of the early career of William Widgery. He was born in 1753, in the state of Pennsylvania, and was a sailor. Sometime during the war of the Revolution he was a privateersman, sailed from Portland, and served as a lieutenant. He first appears on record as a real estate owner in New Gloucester in 1777, with a wife, "Elizabeth," obtained, it is conjectured, at Lewiston, or Poland, which is not far off, then called Bakerstown. In 1781 it appears he was a citizen of the last named place when he paid four hundred "Spanish milled dollars" for more land in New Gloucester.

In 1787 he was elected to a seat in the Massachusetts General Court and was re-elected several times as representative and senator.

In 1788 he was commissioned a Justice of the Peace and commenced the practice of law in spite of the provisions of law itself and bar rules, was appointed a judge and succeeded in having a court house built and courts held at New Gloucester. Besides a lawyer he was a merchant and politician, but the country town was too slow for his expanding views of public policy and he removed to Portland, and in 1811 was sent as a Representative to Congress.

In bank matters and in political schemes he was William King's advising friend though friendly to the war of 1812-15, to which King was hostile.

Before me are two of Widgery's letters, clean and fresh in appearances. His views then on political party management are good today.

The first, dated at Portland, June 30, 1802, informs Mr. King that "the subscribers of the Maine Bank are determined to get under weigh with all possible speed, that advertisements will appear in tomorrow's issue of papers and it [the bank] appears to have many friends." The next, dated at Portland, April 16, 1809—a political letter—I give in full, as follows:

"Portland, April 16, 1809.
"Hon. William King.
"Bath.

"Dear Sir. The Federalists calculate on a gain of Representatives from your quarter this spring. Several towns have changed & it is thought they will be able to prevent others from sending. [Representatives.] The only way to prevent this is to write to every Republican town. Long speeches is of little consequence. Let the committees of each town have a meeting of their Republican friends previous to the May meeting. Choose committees to see that the Republicans attend elections and have ballots written beforehand. Unless this is attended to immediately we may lose our vote in the House of Representatives. I have received several letters from gentlemen to the westward and they say if we do our duty they are sure of the House. Let not a single town escape notice! Do what you can in Kennebec. I would spare no time, pen nor paper.

"I remain with friendship and esteem, Sir, your most obedient
"William Widgery."

This William Widgery was the ancestor of Hon. William Widgery Thomas of Portland, now U. S. Minister at Sweden, half-tone cuts of whom with the Crown Prince, shaking hands, have lately been received by mail by the general public with "greetings."

Rev. Thurston Whiting, born 1752, died 1829, was a clergyman at Warren. Following is a copy of a breezy letter of his addressed to Gen. William King:

"Warren, July 15, 1811.
"Gen. King.

"Sir. I think it proper to premise that I now address you by desire of some of our Republican brethren, my own obscurity & insignificance precluding a personal right to protrude my opinion upon your notice.

"Republicanism having happily, after a long and arduous struggle, gained an ascendancy in the councils of the State it becomes the policy & duty of the friends of order & national union to preserve it—a temporary triumph would only render a subsequent defeat more mortifying in itself & more disastrous in its consequences & perhaps as great vigilance, activity and good management are necessary now to preserve as was required to gain our present station.

"Popular opinion which gives stability & efficiency to any form of government is, in democracies especially, very delicate, susceptible, irritable, fluctuating, by which, I mean, not to insinuate that the people are incompetent for self government, but it can't be denied that public sentiment is liable to be control'd by a thousand adventitious circumstances concerning which no human sagacity can make any positive calculations or even probable conjecture. Whether Republicanism shall become stationary in our State government depends upon European transactions & events—the state of commerce— the acts of Congress—the doings of our General Court—executive appointments—the official acts of public men—etc., etc.

"I am not aware the General Court in its late interesting sessions has passed any acts that will prejudice the good old cause,' or [Lt.] Gov. [William] Gray's banking will be questioned. The religious toleration act is popular and will have an effect. I conceive it to be perfectly consonant with the spirit & letter of the constitution and I am not trembling for our 'Ark' on this account—I mean the honor of religion & the respectability and standing of a learned clergy.

"Time & experience can only test the merits of the new system of courts; much, however, obviously depends on the selection of justices. The tenor & provisions of the law would lead us to contemplate them as on a higher grade, 'a size larger,' & 'some inches taller' than the old judges of the Common Pleas. Their extended districts, frequent terms and liberal emoluments of office point them out as men of cultured minds, possessing a very considerable share of Law—Knowledge, who are to detach themselves from all other occupations & devote their attentions to the duties of the station, that they may command the respect and confidence of the people.

"In the district to which we belong I don't know who are the most eligible characters but should it be deemed expedient to retain one of the two Federal justices of the late court of Common Pleas for this county there is no uncertainty in my mind as to which of them would best comport with the sentiments & wishes of Republicans in this quarter. I know not what are Judge Hill's scientific and jurisprudential qualifications. It is suggested that his politics will not be offensive in future, & so fair is his moral and religious character—such the smoothness of his exterior, his 'suaviter in modo,' as will render him very acceptable to the people. They view him as their friend & feel safe in committing their concerns & disputes to his care & decision. The reverse of this holds true with regard to Judge L. [Silas Lee, Esq. of Wiscasset.] He is believed to be an Aristocrat—ingrain & his blood to have been corrupted by the attainder of his family in the time of the Revolutionary war. He is suspected of being in heart averse and unfriendly to a government under which he holds an honorable and lucrative appointment, & are we to be restrained & gagged by the appointment of one of the most violent abusers of the powers that be?' His name to many is very forbidding & he is too apt to conceive & betray strong partialities which ought to be concealed and stifled.

"Be advised, Sir, that I am not divulging my own private sentiments. The Judge is my friend & I am under great obligations to him & I respect his abilities. I am only stating a popular prejudice which neither you nor I nor the subject of it can at once [if ever] do away, & if this prejudice is so deep-rooted and violent why his appointment? Under the present administration and existing circumstances his appointment would be received by true Republicans as a betrayal and abandonment of their cause & you, Sir, by aiding his appointment will be stigmatized and denounced. Will it be wise and prudent that it shall take place?

"Your influence in the political councils of the state is confessedly great & it is generally confessed that hitherto it has uniformly been employed 'pro bono publico.' Political enemies you undoubtedly have for eminence always attracts envy & vents itself in calumny. This is a kind of involuntary, indirect homage with which little minds pay merit which trancends their capacity of emulating. Popularity and extensive influence is to be considered as an enlargement of the sphere of usefulness & the real patriot feels high responsibility to his God, his country and his conscience for the use he makes of it,—and he will not lightly or without unavoidable necessity risk the loss or diminuition of it.

CONTINUED:

"You will certainly risk much by patronizing the gentleman in question as a Justice of the ancient court. There are those among us who wish to see the Ostracism of ancient Athens revived and exercised among us.

"When a community has been long struggling against an opposition & are at length relieved from common danger, which united them they are very exposed & prone to fall out among themselves in the language of Scripture—'to bite and devour one another.' Something like this (& there can be nothing worse) is to be apprehended by the friends of popular government at this juncture.

"There is not a perfect unison and cordiality among the members of our political community in your part of the county—Bath, Wiscasset, etc. I enter not into these little animosities & cavils, neither know I 'who and who' are of a side or who is the 'shibboleth' of destination, but enough has transpired & is daily circulated to convince me there is 'something rotten in the State of Denmark.' You, Sir, must be sensible of the importance of speedy extinguisument of these petty feuds & jealousies & from the station you hold you can do much towards affecting so desirable an object. A chasm in our political church would be fatal to our cause. When our phalanxes are once broken & their weapons turned against each other I shall despair of ever seeing them again rallied and reunited.

"Suffice me to address you in the style of the commission that was given by the Senate and people of Rome to a Dictator appointed in a great emergency: 'See that the Commonwealth receives no damage!'

"When you act as a dictator in quelling disturbances & keeping peace & good order in the political camp I shall be willing to officiate as your 'master of the house,' or in any other way you may please to assign me, i. e. I shall ever be ready to concur with you in my humble sphere in promoting the public welfare.

"I have now discharged an obligation which I suffered myself to be laid under by some patriotic friends. I need not tell you that if the contents of this letter is disagreeable to you burn it & forget it was ever written.

"With great respect, your humble servant,
"Thurston Whiting."
To be continued.

GRANDPA'S SCRAP BOOK

Week of Aug. 6–8, 1903.

THE KING FAMILY OF SCARBORO

WILLIAM KING.

The First Governor of Maine.

By Leonard B. Chapman.

NO LXXVII.

The name of the author of the following is not attached, and the manuscript is without date, but was written undoubtedly in 1821. During political campaigns, in common with the reading public, I have seen the same style of argument as is here used. I think the ideas expressed were those of Hon. Mark L. Hill, a character whom I have located at Philipsburg, a merchant, and one of the first Representatives to Congress after the adoption of the State Constitution. I have noticed him at considerable length in former chapters. It was to him Rev. Thurston Whiting referred, whose interesting letter to William King has been presented. Messrs. King and Hill were warm political friends and Mr. Hill evidently placed his draft of a newspaper article in Mr. King's hands for inspection, who did not return it, which is now publicly used.

"The Policy of the South is to give their members a political education and keep them in their places long enough to become acquainted with the offices, with the several members of the committees, the officers of the government, and with the routine of business, the consequence of which is these persons are placed at the heads of all important committees, and hence, have an influence no new members can obtain let their talents and standing be what they may.

"As agriculture, commerce, manufacturing and fisheries are inseperably connected, and as Commerce is the great active agent of all the others, it is peculiarly for our interest to send a practical farmer and merchant from this District which is the most commercial of any in the state (but one,) made up of a parrelogram comprising an important sea coast and at the extremes, the mouths of two of the longest rivers in New England, being owned between the same nearly seventy thousand tons of shipping and from which is made a large proportion of exports from the State.

"A universal sentiment has been expressed in favor of shorter sessions of Congress, fewer long speeches and more activity in business transactions. How is this to be brought about? To send more pressional men? or by sending more practical men? The present House of Representatives consists of 186 members of whom 100 are practicing lawyers; 62 farmers and planters, 33 of these having had a law education, but do not now practice; 9 merchants; 2 mechanics and 13 physicians.

"Commerce between the United States and England and France is now peculiarly connected. Care for agricultural and mechanical interests in Congress ought to be increased instead of being diminished.

"It might be stated without fear of contradiction that some if not all the members from Maine have been continually at their post, that a regular correspondence has been kept up with the principal merchants of the country from Maine to Georgia on the subject of foreign relations particularly with reference to England and France, that the standing of the Maine delegation with the Executive Department has been good, that particular attention has been paid to all individuals in Maine who have had private business to transact in Washington, and local affairs such as mails and post roads and lighthouses have not been neglected."

In a letter dated at Camden, Aug. 8 1810, and written by Farnham Hall to William King, which has been presented, a name was used as follows—"Dr. Stere (?)." The letter as presented closed as follows:

"Friend Stere(?) is with us, & I find, as far as I am able to judge, he is the correct Physician, Politician and gentleman & nothing on his friend's part will be lacking to insure him success. This however cannot be done immediately. It is to be done with moderation to insure permanent support.

"Your Obt. servt.
"Farnham Hall."

The following shows that it was William Sterne who was the "correct Physician, Politician and gentleman," and he was at work for the location of a custom house at Camden which would afford the "Physician" an office:

"Camden. Jan. 15, 1811
"Gen. King.
"Sir. Esq. [Farnham] Hall will take the liberty to hand you a copy of a petition to Congress for the establishment of a new District and Port of Entry, in support of which, in behalf of the petitioners, and at their request, he will ask your aid.

"You will at once see upon calling to mind the local situation of the section of the country which the petition embraces that it is a subject of much interest to the commercial part of the citizens, and they have a just claim to the attention of the government as set forth in the prayer of it.

"The original is in the hand of Mr. Cook (or will be before this reaches you), and should it pass, I shall put in a claim for the Collectorship. I shall then have your influence to ask in my own behalf which you have taught me to expect by the favors you have already conferred on me.

"I remain, respectfully,
your Obliged Servant,
"William Sterne."

GEN. JAMES IRISH.

I have presented the copy of a proposition made by Joseph E. Foxcroft of New Gloucester to William King to have Gen. Irish— Gen. James Irish of Gorham—appointed to an office. That was in 1821 when the District of Maine had become a state.

Before me are two manuscript letters written by the General himself in 1812 and 1818, and in the most excellent history of the Town of Gorham, recently presented to the public, may be seen a half-tone cut of the General with thirteen others of the Irish family and a seven page notice of a genealogical character. The letters run as follows:

"Gorham, Feb. 19, 1812.
"Hon. William King, Esq.
"Dear Sir. I have once had the honor of seeing you and at the same time was introduced, which I am sensible is a very small acquaintance, but however, I feel safe in communicating the following—viz: the subject of Eastern Lands. I really believe the opening of a sale in the manner contemplated to be of the greatest importance to the District of Maine. I have been in the habit of surveying for a number of years which has caused me to explore a considerable part of the district; and I am well ac-

CONTINUED:

quainted about the Schoodic waters and St. Johns, up as far as Roostic. [Aroostook] and it is a most excellent country. I also know there are a great number of young men who will settle there. The personal view I have before me in writing your honor is that should a bill pass for the purposes above indicated which would render the appointment of a Surveyer Master General necessary that you would procure the office for me. Whatever information you want of my ability to discharge the duties of such an office you can obtain from the Senators of Cumberland, Oxford and York counties and an examination of my returns and plans to be found in the Land Office. If it should be thought necessary that such an office should be kept further to the Eastward than where I reside [Gorham] I would very readily move to that section. I have understood that such an office is to be opened during pleasure but I think it ought to be for a certain number of years because this state may have a Federal Governor when the Legislature is not so, and then a man would like to have the office permanently,—however this is only my opinion.

"Now, if you think this communication worthy of attention I wish you would send me a letter by the first stage. If not, pray pardon my imprudence.

"I have the satisfaction to state to your honor that the nomination [of yourself] for Lieut. Governor will be very popular in this section of the Commonwealth, and I rejoice that I am situated so I can do so much for the cause.

"Anything respecting myself, from any point of view, I wish you to inquire of Mr. Ripley.

"I am Respectfully yours,
"James Irish, Jun."

Another letter from Mr. Irish reads as follows:

"Portland, May 17, 1818.
"Hon. William King, Esq.

"Dear Sir. In order to give an answer to the question so often asked: 'When is the separation question coming up again?'* I have concluded to drop a line to your hon'r requesting your opinion on the subject and more especially as I am going into the Eastern Country to spend the season, and shall very probably see many persons who are very anxious about the thing. My opinion is that it is gaining friends very fast in this quarter of the country and that the subject ought to be brought before the State Legislature next winter so that before taking the next census we can have the thing settled.

"As I expect to start off by the middle of next week I shall be pleased to receive a line previous to that time.

"I am respectfully yours,
"James Irish."

*Territorial separation between the State of Massachusetts and the District of Maine.

To be continued.

GRANDPA'S SCRAP BOOK

Week of Aug. 13—15, 1903.

THE KING FAMILY OF SCARBORO.

WILLIAM KING.

The First Governor of Maine.

By Leonard B. Chapman.

NO. LXXVII.

[The number last week should have been LXXVI.]

A letter addressed upon the outside, "Free. Joseph E. Foxcroft, Esq., P. M., New Gloucester," and signed upon the inside, "William King," reads as follows:

"Bath, April 27, 1821.
"Dear Sir. Your letter under date of the 3d inst. received this day. I thank you for it; the views are such as I have been thinking of, and they confirm me in the opinion which I have been forming.

"I think some employment for Gen. Irish in the way you suggest will be well, and a postponement of the appointment of a Surveyer General well.

"I have a list made out of the persons to be nominated Overseers of the College [Bowdoin] which embraces your own as well as Dr. Page's.* I should like very much to extend it further at Brunswick, but find it difficult to do so, as we have to look to the Counties of York, Penobscot, Hancock, etc.—to these, as well as in the Counties more immediate in this section, to select the best men.

"I shall be in Portland on the third of May and shall then endeavor to finish as much of the business as the Council and the people are at this time prepared for.

"I am, Sir, respectfully,
your Obt. Servt,
"William King."

*The nomination of Dr. Jonathan Page as an overseer of Bowdoin college by Gov. King in 1821 was confirmed and he served till 1842. He was born in Conway, N. H., in the month of October, 1777, and located in Brunswick. In 1836 he made an honorary member of the college. He died Nov. 18, 1842.

Hon. Silas Lee, to whom frequent and further notice will be made, the date of whose death I have given, was a son of Dr. Joseph Lee of Concord, Mass., born there, July 23, 1760, and a graduate of Harvard college, class of 1784. He read law at Biddeford, and in 1789 commenced practice in Wiscasset—the first lawyer of the locality—the town then, and some years later, holding a high rank as a business place, possessing at this time objects of attraction and an interesting unwritten history—containing the county archives since 1760, a hotel more than a hundred years old, and one of the best kept in the State, a fort adjacent, a century of age, a court house, built in 1824, jail that cannot be described, a toll-bridge, said to be the longest and most rotten of any other in the world, and a harbor that has no equal in New England, for depth of water and natural protection for shipping. Its burying place of early date—Oh, my!—graves full of water as well as human bones, a worse place for such a purpose would be difficult to find.

In 1799, "Hon. Silas Lee, A. M." was elected a trustee of Bowdoin college and served till 1814—the date of his death.

In 1799 he was elected also as a Federalist to a seat in the House of Representatives at Washington.

In 1801 President Jefferson appointed him U. S. District Attorney for Maine.

In 1804 he was elected Judge of Probate, which position he held till his death.

In 1810 he was Chief Justice of the court of Common Pleas, at which time, by a change of the State laws, he was thrown out of employment as a Judge.

It is apparent that he was tinctured with Toryism to such a degree that criticism, particularly with reference to his career as District Attorney, hastened the day of his death. He possessed natural talents, but as a pleader at the bar was exceedingly slow in speech and monotonous. He died childless and poor.

Before me are several letters of Judge Lee, the first is dated at Wiscasset, Feb. 17, 1805, and is addressed upon the outside to "William King, Member of the General Court, now at Boston," written upon a very large sheet of paper upon which is drawn a plan of a proposed two story brick building at Wiscasset for a bank and insurance building with a detailed description. The description commences as follows:

"My dear sir. It becomes necessary to know something of the plan of our Bank & Insurance building in order to agree for the material and work and as there is only Col. Payson here besides myself and a full board of Directors are now in Boston, I have sketched a rough plan to convey to your mind my ideas and have to request that you write me as soon as possible how far you and the other gentlemen approve of it.

"Major Wood suggests there had better be an entry-way in the east corner for the insurance office rather than have the stairs out-of-doors.

* * * * * *

"The building to stand so as to have the vaults next to the new street which passes my residence.

"With great esteem, etc.
"Silas Lee."

If the building was erected according to the design it was one that would reflect, for convenience, credit upon an architect of the present day.

Judge Lee seemingly took an interest in military affairs. March 22, 1808, he addressed a letter to William King that commences as follows:

"In consequence of the late arrangements of our militia some appointments are to be made by you, and will you permit me to name to you our friend, Mr. Moses Carleton, Jr., as one of your aids?"

The Judge then offers other names of persons for military appointments with suggestions.

A month before the date of the foregoing the Judge addressed Mr.

Continued:

King a letter couched in language of great gratitude for favors received of Mr. King at the same time evincing considerable spite towards his political assailants, as follows:

"I thank you, My Dear Friend, for your favor of the 21st, which came to hand on Thursday evening last. On the next evening I presume you received a letter addressed to you from me upon the same subject. The Friendship exhibited by you and my other friends alluded to in our other letters can only be equaled by the confidence I have ever felt in the sincerity of your friendship. I had no doubt but you would do precisely as you have, if you were made acquainted with measures taken against me, & fearing that you might not know the plans on foot induced me to write you. I now feel highly flattered with the notice friendship displayed by Gov. Lincoln & shall certainly never forget his attention to my interest. I should like however to know the manner in which the petition against me is received, and shall consider it as an additional act of your friendship to inform me. Pray accept my thanks and believe me to be your obliged and affectionate friend.
"Silas Lee."

"P. S. I notice Mr. Thomas' motion upon the old subject of old Copeland. I was sorry to see it, for it is thought to savor of persecution. Copeland went home much pleased with the impartiality of the senate and I have no doubt really feels grateful for the treatment he received & considers it as owing much to you and Gen. Ulmer. I am convinced you will use all endeavor that is right and should be done, but the malice of a Wellington is in my mind. S. L."

In 1810 Silas Lee was a Major in the State militia. A petition addressed to him on the 7th day of May, though the name of the town is not given, is of interest as showing how military business was sometimes done, as follows:

"The undersigned, members of an Independent company of Cavalry in the Second Brigade, Eleventh Division, beg leave to represent that on Tuesday, the first day of May, said company was assembled by order of the Capt.—Thomas McCrate—for the purpose of review & to fill a vacancy by the resignation of Lieut. Geo. R. Freeman. Lieut. James Marr commanded & presided at the ballot in the absence of Capt. McCrate and permitted the following named grievances and innovations:—

"1st—He allowed minors to vote in the choice of a Lieutenant and of a Cornet to fill the vacancy occasioned by the promotion of the former Cornet.

"2nd—He permitted those not belonging to the company who were never members to vote in the choice of the officers above mentioned.

"Against this innovation, prostration of the law & dangerous precident we beg leave to remonstrate, & to request your interference that we may obtain a redress of grievances & retain our military character unsullied by a now pliant submission to new & dangerous proceedings.

John Chism.   Daniel Weatherby.
Sam'l. Growin.   Edward Austin.
Nathan Call.   John Mayse.
Joseph Johnson.   Sutton Foye.
Chas. Houdlet.   Ephram Smith.
John Bigford.   Chas. Rundlet.
   James Hodge."

This cavalry company was attached to Maj. Gen. King's command. Copies of the orders for its formation are now before me.

(To be continued.)

RANDPA'S SCRAP BOOK

Week of Aug. 20—22, 1903.

WATERHOUSE.

By Leonard B. Chapman.

Departed this life, at an early hour, Monday morning, the 11th inst., at Stroudwater Village, suddenly, Fred Waterhouse, born August 20, 1837.

The following editorial by L. B. Dennett, Esq., appeared in the Portland Press of August 12, relative to the deceased:

"In our beautiful rural suburb, historic Stroudwater, in a little one story cottage having a little sunset piazza, and standing very near the bank of Fore river, and in a place of such quietude and seclusions, and yet in full sight of the beautiful homes of happy families with their troops of children, that it seems like the abode of one of nature's high priests and guardians, and we approach it with a certain sense of awe, and when we are once within its nature painted brown gate, the only entrance to or exit from this natural rural enchantment, we feel that we have stepped beyond the bounderies of the busy, throbbing world into the solitude of nature, there lived a philosophic man for many a year alone with nature, a man whose soul was as cheerful as the summer sunshine which made the garden about his cottage blossom with flowers.

"This philosophic man was Fred Waterhouse. He was born within six rods of the cottage where he died and always dwelt within these narrow boundaries. He was as familiar with every tree, bush, knoll and slope as a child with its mother's face. He seemed to have an affection for them, and even their silence had its intelligent significance to him. He was least alone when alone with nature. His lips were truth itself. The trees and flowers never lied to him, and he never found it necessary to lie to man or woman either. He was never married. His intelligent industry supplied all his needs, and he wanted nothing which he did not need. Neither foolish pride, ambition nor avarice gave him spur. He cared not 'how money heeds,' nor sought he a 'larger trough and wider sty.'

"He had no eccentricities. Although he lived alone in his little cottage, yet he mingled with his fellow citizens and had just as many friends as acquaintances. His devotion to his principles was steadfast and undeviating. He never swerved when public clamor took the other side. A distinguished citizen of Stroudwater, who had always known him, for they had been boys and men together, told me that Fred Waterhouse had the greatest amount and the best quality of common sense of any man he ever knew; and that his honesty and good citizenship commanded the respect of all who knew him."

In 1764 William Waterhouse appeared in court as a witness, and the same year was elected at a town meeting to an unimportant office, held in Portland.

At St. Paul's church, June 28, 1768, John, a son, born May 13 of that year, was baptized. I find nothing further concerning him worthy of note till 1783, when he purchased a small lot of land located at the easterly end of the Town Landing, which was located on the southerly side of Mill creek, where the creek joins Fore river. The Landing extended westerly to the county road, a distance of about fifteen rods, which was used in Col. Thomas Westbrook's day, who died in 1744, as a place for landing mast logs, the whole length of the Landing on the northerly side joining the creek. At that time, and long before, the mill privilege having now been in use two hundred and twenty-five years, was in use, and "Waterhouse's Point" must have been possessed of many pleasing, natural environments.

Upon his purchase at Stroudwater, William Waterhouse erected a two story dwelling, out-buildings and boat-shop. He was then well advanced in years and had a family of six children consisting of four sons and two daughters.

In 1795 he conveyed the premises to his son Robert, excepting the westerly end of the lot, which he conveyed to his son Joseph Hatch Waterhouse, who built upon it a one story house, to which a story was added a few years since, and may now be seen in good repair.

From Stroudwater Mr. Waterhouse removed to Gorham where he had purchased land, but his stay there was short. Returning to Stroudwater he purchased a quarter-acre lot, where Mr. Charles Fickett now resides, removed his boat-shop to it, which he converted into a residence, that now remains as then placed. The Portland Eastern Argus notices his death, March 5th, 1805. The obituary consists of three words—"An honest man."

The Argus of Tuesday, Feb. 19, 1822, notices also the death of William's widow, as follows:

"Died on Saturday Mrs. Elizabeth Waterhouse, aged 86 years. Funeral from the residence of the late William Waterhouse." [Jr.]

Children of William Waterhouse, Senior:

I. Elizabeth, m. Aaron Chamberlain.
II. William, Jr., b. 1765, m. Hannah Pierce.
III. John, b. May 13, 1768, m. Martha Brooks.
IV. Robert, b. Nov. 15, 1769, m. Elizabeth or Polly Fickett.
V. Joseph Hatch, m. Esther Fogg.
VI. Sally, m. Joseph Bailey, Jr., 2nd, Isaac Fly.

GRANDPA'S SCRAP BOOK

Week of Aug. 27—29, 1903.

WATERHOUSE.

By Leonard B. Chapman.

(Continued from last week.)

As I have intimated, William Waterhouse was a boat builder, and his last earthly abiding place was in his boat shop, which was moved, converted into a dwelling house, and is now the second house on the westerly side of Westbrook street going southerly from Garrison street, in Stroudwater village. The bounds of the lot have not been changed since the time of purchase by Mr. Waterhouse a hundred years since. In establishing the bounds the "stump of a tree that stood back ot the residence of Col. Thomas Westbrook," is referred to, which is one of many evidences that Westbrook's "Garrison House," alias "Harrow House," occupied the southwesterly corner made by Garrison crossing Westbrook street.

The Landing extended, as now seen, from Westbrook street easterly to Fore river, Mill creek forming the northerly boundary line—a ragged line of ledge rock fifteen or twenty feet above high water mark.

The Landing was never donated for public use, nor has there ever been a way legally laid out to "Waterhouse's Point." Mr. Waterhouse's lot joined Fore river on the east and on the north, fronting on the Landing. Next to his residence on the west side, his son, William, built a one story house, upon a part of his father's purchase, to which allusion has been made, and to which Cypress L. Dill a few years since added a story, between the time of Messrs. Waterhouse and Dill the premises having several owners.

Next westerly of the William Waterhouse, Jr., residence Benjamin Fickett erected a two story dwelling which was moved to Portland, and next westerly to him Henry Webb, a mariner, put up a two story, hip-roof house which went to Benjamin Burnham. "Uncle Ben" was a religious character of the Freewill Baptist order, or of no order when becoming excited in the prayer meeting, who furnished us boys of that period much amusement in the manner he used his yard-square bandana in exhortations, usually held in the second story of the village school house. If there really is such a thing as escape, sanctification and redemption from the devil's mortgage upon the soul the site of Uncle Ben's worldly residence at the Stroudwater Landing must still contain the dust of unalloyed contrition. About thirty-five years ago Robert Waterhouse, a great-grandson of William Waterhouse, Sen., purchased the premises, removed the Webb-Burnham house and erected the one now seen, with some changes since made, on the corner of the Landing lane and Garrison street, which was used in Uncle Ben's day as a garden spot. All of these residences fronted on the Landing.

"As with the father, so with the son." Like himself, William Waterhouse's sons were all boat or vessel builders at Stroudwater, and all flourished for awhile, or till vessel building met with an adverse wind. But the Waterhouses were not alone in the avocation. Jonathan Fickett came over from Barren Hill, Cape Elizabeth, and leased the point of land on the northerly side of Mill creek, erected a one story house, the cellar hole of which remains, and engaged in the avocation. He reared a large family who have been noticed in the News, commencing with the issue of Oct. 12, 1895.

(1.) Elizabeth Waterhouse, the eldest child of William Waterhouse, Sen., m. Nov. 8, 1774, Aaron Chamberlain. Of his parents or place of birth I can learn nothing. He was a saddler by occupation, and his place of business was in a small building located upon the northwesterly corner of the Landing, and southeasterly corner of the bridge over Mill creek, and he may have resided there. The building extended out over the creek and was supported by long posts. After him the premises were occupied by William Maxfield as a family residence.

In 1789, Mr. Chamberlain, with others, purchased eighteen hundred acres of land adjacent Thompson's Pond, now in the town of Poland, and, I think, went there to reside.

June 6, 1790, he mortgaged his shop at Stroudwater for £35:17 shillings.

Aug. 21, 1793, the 1800 acre land purchase was divided, he receiving three shares.

In 1795 he was a resident of Portland, and in 1798 he sold his entire land interest to Gen. John K. Smith, then a trader at Stroudwater, who went there to reside. Gen. Smith was Revolutionary soldier.

this date Mr. Chamberlain had a s nd wife. Her maiden name was thiah Pearson, but when or where born I have no knowledge.

Upon the westerly side of the Congress street entrance to the Portland Eastern cemetery, a few paces off from the receiving tomb, may be seen two white memorial slabs inscribed as follows:

Sacred
to the memory of
AARON CHAMBERLAIN
who died Sept. 11,
1834,
Aged 79 yrs. 6 mo.
An honest man.

Sacred
to the memory of
BETHIAH CHAMBERLAIN
who died June 25,
1837,
Aged 81 yrs.
Blessed are the peace makers.

Children of Aaron Chamberlain:

1. Mary, b. 1776, m. Jacob Yeaton Intention of marriage recorded Dec. 29, 1798. Rev. Caleb Bradley says in his diary, Nov. 17, 1835, "I attended the funeral of Jacob Yeaton, aged 59." In 1825 the names of Jacob and Aaron Yeaton were upon the voting list.
2. Joseph, b. Dec. 25, 1779, m. Abigail Jordan.
3. Aaron, d. unmarried.
4. Eliza, m. George Tukey, Jr., May 9, 1825. They resided in the town of Gardiner.
5. Lydia, m. Leonard Merrill, Nov. 6, 1833. "He of Gardiner; she of Westbrook." (Bradley's Diary.)

(2.) Joseph Chamberlain, second child of Aaron and Elizabeth (Waterhouse) Chamberlain, b. in Stroudwater Dec. 25 1779, m. Jan. 7, 1801, Abigail Jordan of Cape Elizabeth, b. there Jan. 10, 1780. He was a boat or vessel builder, or both.

In 1808, Capt. John Waterhouse (Captain of the Stroudwater Light Infantry company, a history of which having appeared in print may be seen in scrap book form, also the company's standard at the library rooms of the Maine Historical Society rooms,) received a mortgage for a consideration of $700, an abstract of which writing is as follows:

"John Waterhouse, gentleman, to Joseph Chamberlain, a certain two story dwelling house adjoining the southerly end of the short bridge, said house standing on land belonging to the town of Falmouth, together with the barn and other buildings being the same in which I now live."

(Signed) "John Waterhouse."

Capt. Waterhouse was a son of William Waterhouse, Senior, who will be noticed later on.

In a Falmouth town valuation book, without date, but made prior to 1814, I learn as follows:

"Joseph Chamberlain—a house valued at $300; barn $25; building yard and work-shop $200; cow $14; horse $40; chaise $100; stock in trade $120 and six scholars."

In 1814, when the first valuation book of Westbrook was made, Mr. Chamberlain's house and barn were taxed to Jacob Yeaton. He had evidently at that date, in common with other vessel builders, encountered an adverse wind in his business career, and had been wrecked.

His wife died Feb. 21, 1816, aged 36. A memorial slab may be seen in the Stroudwater cemetery. He died in the month of June, 1821, in St. Louis, Mo., aged 42 years.

Children:

1. Eliza Chamberlain, b. Aug. 3, 1801, m. Thomas Smith, May 15, 1823. He was a clothier at Stroudwater at the time, but returned to Windham where there are descendants. He taught school winters and wrote a history of the town.
2. Emeline D. Chamberlain, b. June 29, 1803, m. May 25, 1828, William H. Robbins of Boston, Mass., where they resided.
3. Abigail Chamberlain, b. March 10, 1805, m. James Parker.
4. Mary Ann Chamberlain, b. May 7, 1807, m. William Budd. He kept an eating house in Portland. She d. July 31, 1839.

   Children:

   a. Bethiah Ann Budd, b. Cape Elizabeth, June 22, 1831.
   b. Eliza Smith Budd, b. Portland, March 15, 1834.
   c. Mary Jane Alexander Budd, b. July 3, 1836.

CONTINUED:

   d. Willia:: Edward Budd, b. Dec. 7, 1837.
   e. George Bailey Budd, b. March 12, 1838, d. May 5, 1838.
   f. George Bailey Budd, 2d, b. July 3, 1836, d. Aug. 31, 1839.
5. Martha Chamberlain, b. June 11, 1809, d. May 26, 1811, aged 2 yrs., 4 mo.
6. Joseph Chamberlain, b. Oct. 16, 1810; d. Sept. 16, 1811, aged 11 mo.

To be continued.

GRANDPA'S SCRAP BOOK

Week of Sept. 10—12, 1903.

WATERHOUSE.

By Leonard B. Chapman.

(Continued from last week.)

(III) Capt. John Waterhouse, b. in Portland, May, 13, 1768, third son of William Waterhouse, Sen., m. Martha Brooks, b. Aug. 15, 1769. Of her I know nothing. .

He was a boat and vessel builder at Stroudwater. His residence I have noticed as standing on the Landing, also the fact that he was Captain of the Stroudwater Light Infantry company when the standard was presented by the ladies of the village. From Stroudwater he moved to Saco where his last two children were born, the first of the two, June 24, 1810. He made a small purchase of real estate and died March 16, 1816. June 14 the widow was appointed administratrix, when a minute inventory was made of the estate which was small. One item returned was as follows:

"House and lot of land, situated on the southeasterly side of the wharf, proprietor's first purchase, and being a part of said purchase, which he bought of Jonathan Tucker, being under mortgage—nothing."

This was located in Saco. The Stroudwater house was moved to Portland more than fifty years ago, and the site is now a grass plot and the grass is kept short by a cow.

Children of Capt. John and Martha (Brooks) Waterhouse, b. in Stroudwater:

1—William, [3d.] March 10, 1790. Intention of marriage filed in Saco, with Hannah Chase of Limington, Feb. 5, 1810.
   Children b. in Saco:
   a—Chas. Wm., Dec." 27,1810.
   b—Geo. Hight, Feb. 17, 1813. d. March 2, same year.
   c—Catherine, Jan. 12, 1814.
   d—Lucinda, May 27, 1816.
2—John, Feb., 10, 1791.
3—Martha, Dec. 12, 1791, d. young
4—John 2d, Oct. 25, 1792.
   (See above for John.]
5—Samuel B., Feb. 8, 1795.
6—Charles, Jan. 8. 1797; died young.
7—Martha, Sept. 6, 1798. Intention of m. with James Coffin of Deerfield, N. H., Jan. 8, 1815.
8 Charles, 2d Sept. 16, 1800. Elizabeth, his widow, alive in 1850.
9—Naylor, July 28, 1802, m. July 12, 1825, Charlotte Kendrick, b. May 17, 1797. They resided in Saco. Children o. there:
   a—Adelaide Lorinda, May 17, 1828.
   b—George Warren, May 24, 1831.
10—Mary Ann, July 15, 1804; died young.
11—Thomas, June 13, 1806.
12—Mary Ann, Dec. 31, 1807, int. of m. filed Dec. 1, 1827 with John T. Cloutman of Gorham. He b. there Nov. 24, 1805. He died in Westbrook, Jan. 15, 1852. (See History of Gorham, p. 435 where it states John T. Cloutman m. Mary "G." Waterhouse. The old way of spelling the name has been changed.)

Heirs of Mary Ann (Waterhouse) Cloutman in 1850: John [T.] Cloutman, Jr., Mary, his wife Paul and Elizabeth Cloutman. John [T.] Jr., was born in Saco, July 4, 1829.
13—Eliza B., b. in Saco, June 22, 1810. d. June 11. 1811.
14—Eliza B. 2d, June 11, 1811 m. May 4, 1832, Paul Cloutman of Gorham. He died April 23, 1864. (History of Gorham, p. 436.)

The two Cloutmans who married the two Waterhouses were cousins and were cousins to Sewall Cloutman of Gorham, who m. Dorothy L. Tate of Stroudwater, March 30, 1842, and resided on the road from Gorham to Little Falls.

(IV) Robert Waterhouse, b. Nov. 15, 1769, son of William Waterhouse, Sen., m. Sept. 16, 1792, Elizabeth alias Polly, dau. of Jonathan Fickett who resided on the point of land northerly of Mill creek, to which I have alluded. (See Deering News articles, commencing Oct. 12, 1895, for Fickett family records.) Mr. Waterhouse built at Stroudwater boats, or vessels, or both, residing in the house his father erected, which, for a consideration of £150, in 1795, he conveyed to Robert,referring to him in the conveyance as a boat builder and a son. He d. Aug. 7, 1808, aged 38 years. The Portland Eastern Argus said of him Aug. 25, as follows:

"Died, in Falmouth, Robert Waterhouse,shipwright, aged 38 years. An honest and influential citizen who lived beloved and died universally lamented. He has left a wife and seven children to lament the loss of an affectionate husband and kind father."

When the first valuation book of Westbrook was made (1814) Elizabeth, widow of Robert, was taxed for two cows valued at $9 each; four oxen, $20 each; a horse, $40; a house, $350, and a barn, $20. The family owned also land in Cape Elizabeth. She was a member of the Stroudwater Congregational church and died in New York City, Aug. 13, 1829, aged 56 years. Both have memorial slabs at Stroudwater.

Children of Robert and Elizabeth (Fickett) Waterhouse, b. in Stroudwater:

1—Sopha, b. March 29. 1792. m Thomas Broad of Stroudwater son of Thaddeus, the inn keeper. They resided in New York where he was a ship carpenter, but finally returned and resided upon a part of his father's farm in a house he built. He was in conversation a jolly soul. No children. (See Deering News of Jan. 15, 1898, for Broad family.)
2—Betsey, b. Nov. 28, m. June 15, 1836, Moses Hanson of Windham. She was his second wife. Robert, Jr., b. Jan. 6, 1797 I know nothing of him.
4.—Frederick, b. March 16, 1799, m. Sarah J. Mange, of West End, Portland, Aug. 17, 1823.
5.—Almira, b. March 18, 1801, m. William Roberts of Westbrook, (Sacarappa) int. filed Aug. 14, 1825. They "went to Harrison.".
6.—Charlotte, b. July 16, 1803. She did not marry. Resided in the interior of the state.
7—Alpheus, b. Sept. 15, 1805. m. 1st. in New York City, one child; Celia 2nd, Hanson, dau. of Moses Hanson.

(2) Ichabod Hanson, b. Sept. 22, 1741, son of Timothy and Sarah (Chesley) Hanson, m. Abigail Hayes, b. Dover, N. H., May 9, 1742.

Ichabod was reared a Quaker and settled in Windham prior to 1765. where he was a farmer. He was a Revolutionary soldier, selectman of Windham, etc. In 1800 it was recorded that he was the ancestor of eleven children, twenty grandchildren, and "had never lost any." (Rev. Paul Coffin's diary.)

Ichabod's seventh child, Sally, b. Oct. 7, 1775, m. Dr. John Converse of Durham where he d. Dec. 5, 1815, aged 45 years. Upon his grave memorial may be seen as follows:

"Thousands of miles night and day
I've traveled weary all the way,
To heal the sick, but now I'm gone
A journey never to return."

Ichabod's tenth child was named Moses, b. January 10, 1780, m. 1st, January 22, 1801, Sally Lowell, dau. of Capt. Abner and Mercy (Paine) Lowell, b. Aug. 7, 1772, d. May 28, 1832, and he m. 2nd, June 13, 1836, Betsey, dau. of Robert Waterhouse as above noticed Moses lived on the Saywood farm near Windham Center; 2nd at Gambo, performing farm work.

Moses Hanson's second wife was a sister to Alpheus Waterhouse and Alpheus second wife was Moses Hanson's daughter, hence Moses by marriage was the grandfather to Alpheus' children and also an uncle.

After the second marriage of Moses he removed to Stroudwater and resided with Alpheus under the roof of the William Waterhouse, Sen., house till the chimney fell carrying a part of the roof of the house along with it to the cellar, when they all moved into the Uncle Ben Burnham house which was about the year of 1850, where he d. Apr. 17, 1858, aged 78 years, and was buried by the side of his first wife at Windham. His second wife died at Stroudwater, Jan. 29, 1873, aged 67 years.

Moses Hanson, according to tradition, was in his young manhood, physically, a powerful man. In his sear old

Continued:

age he was a character. In youth a Quaker, in old age a home-made doctor, quiet and meek. With the going out of his life his formulas for the manufacture of bitters were lost. Tall, clean shaven, erect, plug hat worn upon the back of his head, overcoat and cowhide boots, both worn in summer and winter alike, walking stick held by the hand a foot from the top which he never placed to the ground; the freezing winter wind and the hottest air of summer failing to change his street locomotion—I see him now!— a friend to all, an enemy to none.

Children of Moses Hanson by first wife, born in Windham—none by second:

1. Daniel Lowell Hanson, b. May 3, 1803, m. Mary E. Sawyer.
2. Celia Lowell Hanson, b. May 11, 1805, m. Alpheus Waterhouse, as has been stated.
3. Lewis Hanson, b. Nov. 6, 1806, m. Nov. 18, 1833, Rebecca Swett of Gorham. She was a descendant of Dea. John Bailey of the Stroudwater parish. They lived at Gambo. No children. (See History of Gorham, p. 785.)
4. George Hanson, b. May 10, 1808, d. Feb. 5, 1821.
5. Mary Ann Hanson, b. April 15, 1810, d. Dec. 18, 1834.
6. John Lowell Hanson, b. Feb. 15, 1813, m. 1st. Charlotte E. Kelley of Saco; 2nd. Rowena P. Hillard of Kennebunk.
7. Moses Hanson, Jr., b. Jan. 28, 1816, m. Frances Kelley of Saco. He resided in Boston and died soon after the marriage event. No children.

To be Continued.

GRANDPA'S SCRAP BOOK

Week of Sept. 17—19, 1903.

WATERHOUSE.

By Leonard B. Chapman.

(Continued from last week.)

Daniel Lowell Hanson, born at Windham, May 3, 1803, eldest child of Moses and Sally (Lowell) Hanson, who united in marriage with Mary, daughter of Thomas Sawyer that resided on Ocean street, northwesterly side, in the first house easterly of the brick schoolhouse, Deering district of Portland, taught school winters and ran a peddler's cart the rest of the time. They were both members of the Stroudwater Congregational church, and were both alive in 1833 when a printed record of the members was made. In a Sabbath school diary commenced in 1830, and continued for a period of five years, I find the name of Daniel Hanson frequently mentioned as opening the school with prayer. He died in Oldtown while making a business tour of that region. His wife ever lived under the parental roof where she died. They had three children:

1.—Alonzo, m. has children, resides in the Deering district of Portland, a number of years a manufacturer of heavy tinware in Portland, Congress, corner of Oak streets.
2.—Alfred L., resides in the West.
3.—Mary Ann, d. young.

Dr. Moses Hanson's youngest brother, and youngest child of their parents, b. at Windham, Oct. 18, 1781, was a practitioner of medicine. He studied with Dr. Converse of Durham, and Dr. David Hasack of New York. In 1809 he was in Windham; 1812, North Yarmouth, and in 1814 at Middlebury college; in 1821 preceptor of an academy in Stroudsburg, Pa. In 1827 he was in western New York, and finally died, Nov. 1, 1858, in Medena county, Ohio, aged 77 years, leaving four children.

The Hansons here referred to were connected with the Waterhouse name only by marriage of Moses Hanson and are referred to only incidentally; and it is but just to say in this connection that the public are indebted to Mr. Nathan Goold, now of Portland, for much of the public record concerning this Hanson name.

(7) Alpheus Waterhouse, b. Stroudwater, Sept. 15, 1805, son of Robert and Polly (Fickett) Waterhouse, was, like the rest of his name, a ship carpenter, understanding the occupation so well that he could fashion a model and make molds therefrom for the finest vessels constructed in his day, but he never rose to the eminence in the art he was from natural ability entitled, contenting himself with a secondary position. He resided under the roof of the residence constructed by his grandfather on Waterhouse's Point. The name of his second wife I have given, not knowing the first, the marriage ceremony being performed July 20, 1836 by the Rev. Caleb Bradley. He d. at Stroudwater, July 3, 1863.

Children born in Stroudwater:

1.—Fred, christened Frederick and thus called till of late, born, lived and departed this life as noticed at the head of these articles.*
2.—Robert, b. Feb. 23, 1839, m. Addie J. Curtis of Portland, she being deceased. He erected the two story house on the southeasterly corner made by Westbrook crossing Garrison street a little after the year of 1870. He owned horses and carts and done a large amount of trucking for the Stroudwater mills. He died August 28, the present year in the cottage made vacant on the death of his only brother short time previous, leaving married daughter in New York and a son in Stroudwater.
3.—Charlotte, b. March 16, 1842, m Humphrey Hanscom, son of William and grandson of John Westbrook. (See Libby Ge. and History of Gorham). S is deceased; he is engaged farming, residing with the on child at Stroudwater.
4.—Celia F., b. July 5, 1845, who h departed this life.

*From the Portland Daily Press of ugust 13:

The funeral of Fred Waterhouse was held yesterday morning at 119 Westbrook street in Stroudwater. The house was filled with a large number of his old friends, and the floral tributes were present in equal profusion, a tribute to the man who had raised so many flowers for the service of others. Rev. Francis Southworth conducted the services. The pall bearers were Daniel Doe, Samuel A. Chapman, Elias M. Jacobs and Walton Fickett. The interment was at the cemetery at Stroudwater.

The pass bearers who served in the first instance served also in the second, Rev. Mr. Southworth officiating at oth.

(V) Joseph Hatch Waterhouse, son of William Waterhouse, Sen., b. ———, m. Sept. 13, 1795, Esther, dau. of Jeremiah Fogg, of Gorham, Jeremiah being born in Scarboro, June 11, 1744. (See History of Gorham, p. 497). .sther (Fogg) Waterhouse was b. Feb. , 1775, d. April 26, 1826, but I do not now the place nor have I found here or when Joseph H., her husand, took his departure from Stroudter or this world. He was a vesl builder at Stroudwater and soon ter the marriage event commenced usekeeping in the lower part of the use now seen situated upon the terly end of the landing place and this date by the heirs of Cyich reference has crowning his efforts he desired a larger place of abode and therefore made a change.

In the division of the large Waldo estate the piece of land lying between Westbrook street and the Stroudwater fresh water stream extending from the mill northerly to the old Tate house, as now seen, fell, with very much other land, to Gen. Samuel Waldo's son Francis, who proved himself a Tory and went to London where he died, and his property hereabouts was confiscated by order of the Massachusetts General Court. He was collector of the port of Portland when he left here and died there May 9, 1784. The committee making the sale consisted of Samuel Freeman of Portland, Samuel Small of Scarboro and John Lewis of North Yarmouth. The purchasers, Capt. John Quinby and Hon. Archelaus Lewis, "gentlemen and merchants of Saccarappa," paying £45 for the puurchase, divided it into five lots, each measuring four rods and three feet upon the highway, both constructing good two story houses upon the two northerly end lots, both buildings now to be seen, one in Portland at the junction of Pine and Congress streets, the other, owned by the Milliken family, where the last U. S. postoffice sign of the village was exhibited to the public, both houses being at this time in an excellent state of preservation.

The lot located upon the mill end of the purchase went to Jabez Jones, from Jones to Josiah Cox who was in trade at the village where the Stroudwater or "Quinby Hall" is seen at this time.

Continued:

In 1797, John Brooks, a shipwright, owned the lot who built some sort of a house upon it and who conveyed it to Messrs. William Shaw and William Bisby of Gorham, traders, for $433.33 and a few months later Bisby sold to Shaw for $150, then William Shaw mortgaged to Joseph Sewall of Marblehead and Rufus Bigelow of Boston, Mass., merchants, for $731.86. In 1802 these gentlemen sold the premises to one Joshua Shaw for $600, and three years later Joshua Shaw purchased of Oaks Sampson, a ship carpenter, "six-hundred and sixty square feet" of the southeasterly corner of his lot, which was the next northerly lot, which Sampson had obtained by purchase. With this one change the original bounds of the five adjoining lots, situated as here described, remain as fixed in 1784—a period of nearly one hundred and twenty years—excepting the addition of a small lot, without bonds, added to the Shaw lot, after the Messrs. Shaw's time, coming through "squatter sovereignty" and purchased of "Old Fagen" for $50, containing a "house" in which Fagen stayed.

From an old account book it appears that William Shaw done a large trade in lumber, shingles, hay, etc., selling flour to the man living upon the Sampson lot, as well as molasses, and purchasing "biscuits" and gingerbread" of the man who ran a bakery on the Sampson lot in the very house as now seen upon the premises.

(To be continued.)

Week of Sept. 24—26, 1903.

WATERHOUSE.

By Leonard B. Chapman.

(Continued from last week)

Attending the advent of Joshua Shaw is an impenetrable mystery that persistant inquiry fails to penetrate. By occupation he was a hatter. August 22, 1803—just a hundred years ago—he was united in marriage with Mary G. Lobdell, Rev. Caleb Bradley performing the ceremony, fee, $2.36—thus the parson records. Captain Isaac Lobdell, father of the bride, was a new comer to the village with a family of five children, who purchased the residence situated upon the opposite side of the road as now seen. Upon the parlor floor of the Lobdell residence the first carpet of the village was put down which cost an even $100. This family and other people who have occupied the premises form an interesting chapter of local history.

Joshua Shaw upon coming into possession of the premises constructed the two story residence as now seen, and upon the southerly side of his hat manufactory, upon the southerly side of which was the "Old Fagens" fifty dollar homestead, built undoubtedly in Col. Westbrook's day, and next southerly Col. Westbrook's paper mill a long, low-posted structure which, with the Fagens place was known a hundred years ago as "Pollster's Row," the mill "having some conveniences for paper making, with a room fitted for paper makers," in which building Col. Westbrook at the time of his death (1744) had some furniture stored, and in which David Patrick resided. These facts are shown by original records.

Joseph Fagens, alias, "Old Fagens" and Mary Whiting were united in marriage by the Rev. Caleb Bradley Dec. 1, 1808.

Happening that way soon after the birth of a child the parson was invited "to see the baby"—so the story runs—and was asked what he thought of the new comer, the parson replying that "I should under the circumstance have preferred a barrel of flour."

Joshua Shaw did not remain long in Stroudwater. He moved to Portland where he had organized a hat manufacturing company, and before me are two certificate papers of stock issued and dated Sept. 8, 1810, Daniel How, treasurer. Accompanying these are receipts pinned onto the stock papers for money paid as assessments. One is numbered 69, the other 70.

The year the "Portland Hat Company" was organized (1810) the Joshua Shaw house was sold to Joseph H. Waterhouse for $2310, but the war of 1812-15 brought business reverses to such a degree to Mr. Waterhouse that the sheriff was obliged to enforce upon his home several mandates of the courts which so crippled him in business that he finally disposed of all rights in the establishment to John Jordan, not, however, till he had sold to Dr. Jacob Hunt for one hundred and twenty dollars the Shaw hat building, the original bill of sale, dated Dec. 23, 1814, being now before me, which states that the building was erected by Joshua Shaw "for a hatter's shop." It was removed to Cumberland Mills.

John Jordan of Cape Elizabeth and Susan Bartlett of Stroudwater were married Dec. 17, 1820. By an enforced execution and purchases of pieces he came into possession of the Shaw-Waterhouse residence where he resided the remaindr of his life, three daughters and a son being born to him. He was a master vessel builder.

In 1823 Phagens sold for $50 to Abiel Hamilton the lot "together with the dwelling house in which I now live," and in 1825 Hamilton sold to John Jordan the premises for $23. Benjamin Remick purchased the Fagen "house" thinking to convert it into a barn, and with this view put shoes under it and invited a lot of teamsters to the "hauling." All knowing the building to be worthless the teamsters agreed that upon arriving at the "parting of the parting of the ways," where Congress street crosses Westbrook street, one string of cattle should take one road and the other string the other way which was done and the old building fell.

Shaw's Portland Hat Manufactury was a failure and he moved to Philadelphia where he was more successful, and where descendants now reside.

In the absence of records it is impossible to arrange correctly a list of the children of Joseph H. and Esther (Fogg) Waterhous. There were:

1.—Ezekiel.
2.—Benjamin.
3.—Joseph.
4.—James W.

(VI.) Sally Waterhouse, b. ——, dau. of William Waterhouse, Sen., m. Dec. 7, 1783, Joseph Bailey, Jr., (another record says Joseph Bailey, 3d, because he had a great uncle named Joseph.) Joseph, Jr., was a son of John Bailey, Jr., who resided in the one story house, removed a couple of years since, that was situated on the northerly side of Spring street, opposite High street, in Deering, that was erected prior to 1750, a half-tone cut of which appeared in the Portland Sunday Times of March 8, 1903. John Bailey, Jr., was a son of Dea. John Bailey, who resided during the last years of his life between Libby's Corner and Bradley's Corner, northerly side of Congress street, in the house now occupied by Miss Helen M. Bailey which was when occupied by the deacon, but one story, his land extending northerly so as to include the fifty acres where the house of John, Jr., stood which John, Sen., gave his son on the occasion of his son's marriage. John, Jr., was born in Newbury, Mass., Oct. 30, 1722, and died in March, 1776, leaving a large family of children, the youngest less than a year old, who became the mother of Mr. Charles Maxfield of Stroudwater.

Joseph Bailey, Jr., by occupation a blacksmith, was drowned in crossing a river upon the ice in the town of Lisbon while visiting relatives there, leaving seven children, all of whom arrived at the period of lawful age and all married, including the widow, which was Nov. 29, 1804, with Isaac Fly, who was evidently a widower; and they went to reside in a house presumably built by Col. Thomas Westbrook for mill-hand purposes, which was painted red inside and out, standing now upon the original site at Stroudwater, a few rods northerly from the northeasterly corner of the bridge over Mill creek, it having been turned so as to front the street, a story added and an ell also. As originally constructed it faced upon "Shipyard Point," which was a busy part of the village most of the time from the date of Westbrook's advent (1727) till near 1850 when vessel building ceased wholly. Within my own recollection there was built at the same time two vessels between the Fly house and the creek, which creek forms the southerly boundery of the "Point."

When Fly commenced the exercise of "squatter sovereignty" in the "red house" there stood a shop a few feet northerly of the Fly house upon the lot "thirty feet square" which was used for private schools and religious purposes, and at one time was known as "Aunt Fly's meeting house," and at another as "Mrs. Thoms' residence,"

Continued:

she being a sister to Uncle Ben Burnham whose religious peculiarities I have noticed. Then between Aunt Fly's residence and Fore river there was a breastwork where trading schooners put off casks of rum and other kinds of merchandise and took on boards any other products of the region about.

Tradition has it that Aunt Fly was a woman with a great heart who was ever acting the part of the Good Samaritan. She never passed on the opposite side of the way where there was hunger or pain, the latch string of the door of her humble home ever remaining upon the outside.

Upon the 7th day of April, 1830, Isaac Fly, in consideration of $175 paid by Charles Bartlett, a vessel builder of the village, conveyed the premises to him, and retired. It is supposed to the town of Baldwin, where he had formerly lived, and where, it is reported, both have memorial slabs.

From Bartlett the premises went to the Morton family who added a strip of "Shipyard Point" to the southerly side of the Fly lot—all now being occupied by a Morton descendant.

To be continued

GRANDPA'S SCRAP BOOK

Week of Oct. 1—3, 1903.

WATERHOUSE.

By Leonard B. Chapman.

(Continued from last week.)

The name of Fly is an uncommon one hereabouts and ever has been. With us, however, there are a very few persons by the name of Flye. For a period of a hundred and twenty years the name of Fly appears as grantor and grantee but twenty times upon the Cumberland county registry of deeds.

On the 12th day of Oct. 1759, John Bryant made his will. He says:

"Being very Sensible that I can't continue long in this Life by Reason of a Hurt I have received in my Body this Day, but in perfect Mind & Memory, etc.

"I give to my Grandson James Fly five shillings."

"I give to my Granddaughter Dorcas Fly five shillings."

"I give to my Granddaughter Mary Fly five shillings."

"I give to my Granddaughter Elizabeth Fly five shillings."

There were other grandchildren known by other names.

John Fly was evidently the father to the Bryant grandchildren by the name of Fly, Fly residing adjacent Bryant, but in 1766 John Fly was dead when, by order of the court, his homestead was sold to the Bryant family.

An intention of marriage between James Fly of Scarboro and Jerusha Freeman of Portland was announced Nov. 21, 1761. They went to Gorham to reside where they had born and recorded eleven children, as follows:

1—Hannah (Fly) b. Nov. 24, 1762.
2—ISAAC, July 7, 1764, whose intention of m. was made public June 10, 1786, with Joanna Libby of Scarboro, who, it is more than probable, became the second husband of the widow of Joseph Bailey, Jr., as I have stated.
3—Mary, April 5, 1766.
4—Lucy, May 7, 1768, m. Rufus Kimball of Scarboro.
5—Elizabeth, Jan. 6, 1771, m. Oct. 11, 1792, Jacob Clark of Gorham, and moved to Baldwin. He was a son of Morris Clark of Windham.
6—Dorcas, April 5, 1773.
7—James, March 26, 1775.
8—Sarah, Dec. 7, 1776.
9—Susannah, Dec. 5, 1779.
10—John, March 8, 1782.
11—Eleanor, Dec. 22, 1786.

James Fly did not own real estate in Gorham though he resided there some twenty-five or more years, nor does his name appear in any manner in the history of the town recently published; he did, however, own a lot in Flintstown, (now Baldwin), in 1797, at which time he was a resident "of a place called Hiram" in York county.

It must be remembered in order to have a clear conception of the situation, that this Fly family has no blood connection with the Waterhouse name but is placed here more particularly for the purpose of making perpetual the preservation of the Fly family record, the connection of the two names being through the marriage of Isaac Fly with the widow Sally (Waterhouse) Bailey.

Children of Joseph, Jr., and Sally (Waterhouse) Bailey, whose last husband was Isaac Fly:

1—Sarah Bailey, m. a man by the name of Tibbetts, he d., m. 2d, a man named Thomas A. Ryland and went to Ohio, with whom she was living, May 16, 1826, in Hamilton county of that State.
2—Jane Bailey, b. 1784, m. May 26, 1808, David Webb, b. Saccarappa, Nov. 30, 1786, son of Jonathan Webb, and Jonathan was one of the most active business men of the place in his day, b. in Gorham, whose remains fill a very neglected grave in the very neglected "Conant Cemetery. One child, d. Oct. 7, 1812, aged 3 years. He d. in May of 1817. (For Webb see Deering News, Aug. 31, 1895.)
3—Rebecca Bailey, m. March 2, 1806, John Brawn, a mariner, lost at sea. They resided at one time in the small house where William Waterhouse, Sen., died. There were three daughters, Eliza, Jane, Mary, and son Charles who had his name changed to Stevens. The widow Brawn moved prior to 1850 to Winchester, and from there to Woburn, Mass., where all the children married and where descendants now reside.
4—Eliza Bailey, b. Oct. 17, 1792, m. Feb. 11, 1813, Joseph Quinby, Jr., son of Joseph and Azuba (Partridge) Bailey, he b. March 12, 1791, d. April 28, 1838. She d. May 5, 1874. An excellent photo of her may be seen with her granddaughter, Mrs. Charles E. Quinby, Saccarappa, and a monument at the village cemetery. They had six children, as follows:

1—Joseph B. (Quinby) b. Jan. 14, 1814, d. Oct 23, 1822.
2—Martha C. Quinby, b. Dec. 6, 1815, m. Joseph Knight of Worcester, Mass., resided in Biddeford.

Children:

a—Sarah Eliza Knight, b. 1836, d. 1852.
b—Edward Franklin Knight, b. 1838, d. 1861.
c—Martha Adelaide Knight, b. 1844, m. John Linscott, resides in New York City.
d—Maria Frances Knight, m. John Harmon of Bar Mills. Resides at Kingston, N. H. Martha C., her mother, resides with her. (1903).
e—George Joseph Knight.
3—Capt. Isaac F. (Quinby) b. May 26, 1818, m. in 1844, Catherine G. Brown of Parsonsfield. (To be further noticed).
4—Eliza Ann (Quinby) b. Jan. 31, 1820, m. Joseph Eastman of Buxton. She d. Jan. 1876.
5—Charlotte A (Quinby) b. Dec. 17, 1821, d. Feb. 15, 1822.
6—Joseph B. Quinby, b. March 14, 1823, m. Annie Laurie. At the time of the commencement of the war of the States in 1861, Joseph B. Quinby was residing in New Orleans, La., where he kept a book store. Being opposed to "Secession" he left the South and served in the Northern army. He edited the Cincinnatti Times, of Ohio, and the Newport Leader of Kentucky.

Children:

a—Sylfio Laurie Quinby, who is dead.
b—Sylphia Laura Quinby, who is dead.
c—Emanuel Swedenburg Quinby, who went to California where he died.
d—Isaac Franklin Quinby.
e—Joseph Bailey Quinby.
f—John Laurie Quinby.
g—Annie Laurie Quinby, who is dead.
h—Josiah Kilby Quinby.
i—Henry Quinby, who is dead.
5—Joseph Bailey, a hatter, settled in Portsmouth, N. H., A son, John H. Bailey, was mayor of the city in 1864 or 1865 or thereabouts. There was a daughter. The father b. 1796, d. 1824. The son was b. Nov. 12, 1823, d. Oct. 23, 1879.
6—John Bailey, b. April 12, 1796, m. Olive Brackett. He resided with his uncle, Benjamin Bailey, on the Windham road when young; then he was a tinsmith; then a house joiner, residing a fourth of

CONTINUED:

a mile southerly from the residence of his uncle. He d. Aug. 4, 1870, aged 74 years. She d. July 22, 1872, aged 74 years. Memorial slabs may be seen in the Windham road cemetery not far from Riverton. She was a daughter of Peter Brackett, who resided on the L. B. Dennett farm, and a brother to Zachariah, who resided in the low posted, one story, small window house recently removed that stood near the northerly corner of Forest avenue and Warren streets.

Children born in the Deering district, then a part of Westbrook:

1—Joseph Bailey, b. May 19, 1821, d. 1829.
2—Peter Brackett Bailey, b. Nov. 30, 1822, m. Mary Haggett. He d. 1855, on the way to California. She d. Aug. 8, 1849, aged 22. Memorial slab in the burial lot of his parents.

"Like a fresh rose some hand has torn,
When opening to the morning sky,
Such was the fate of her we mourn,
One who was called early to die."

3—Charles A. Bailey, b. June 7, 1825, m. Abbie A. Winslow of Falmouth. She d. Feb. 24, 1825. They resided at Cumberland Mills in Westbrook. He d. there Aug. 1, 1901. (See obituary).

Children:

a—Winslow Bailey, b. Feb. 25, 1847, d. 1849.
b—Mary A. Bailey, b. Dec. 27, 1849, m. George H. Sawyer, a carriage maker at Cumberland Mills, Westbrook, with whom her parents resided.
c—Charles C. Bailey, b. July 29, 1851, m. Louisa Clark, he an engineer at the paper mills, Westbrook.
d—Emma L. Bailey, b. June 4, 1853, m. David H. Watson, treas., "Foster Dye House," Portland. Two children.
e—Annie Bailey, m. Ellery Starbird, firm of Starbird & Bailey, grocerymen, Morrill's corner, Deering. He was a son of Howard Starbird of Gray.

*From the Portland Daily Press, Aug. 2, 1901:

"Mr. Charles A. Bailey died yesterday afternoon about three o'clock after an illness of two years and a half as a result of Bright's disease. The deceased has made his home with his daughter, the wife of Mr. George H. Sawyer, Haskell street. He was 76 years of age and was born at Morrill's Corner, now a part of Portland, but at that time a part of the town of Westbrook. Mr. Bailey has been a great sufferer and death comes as a relief. The deceased was for one year, some twenty-five years ago, road commissioner of the old town of Westbrook. Aside from this Mr. Bailey never held any public office. He was a member of Temple lodge of Masons of Westbrook, and of Portland Commandery, Knights Templar, of Portland. Mr Bailey is survived by a widow, Mrs. Abigail Bailey, and the following children: Mr. Charles C. Bailey, engineer at the S. D. Warren paper mills; Mrs. Mary, wife of Mr. George H. Sawyer of this city, and Mrs. Watson, the wife of Mr. David H. Watson of Portland, and a daughter, the wife of Mr. Ellery Starbird of Morrill's corner. He is also survived by a brother, Mr. Edward Bailey, and two sisters, all residents of Morrill's corner, Mrs. Leon Burnham and Mrs. Joshua Roberts."

To be continued.

GRANDPA'S SCRAP BOOK

Week of Oct. 8—10, 1903.

WATERHOUSE.

By Leonard B. Chapman.

(Continued from last week.)

[Correction. Where it reads in my last (No. 4) Eliza Bailey, b. Oct. 17, 1792, m. Feb. 11, 1813, Joseph Bailey, Jr., son of Joseph and Azubah (Partridge) Bailey, "Bailey" should be Quinby.]

4—Susan M. Bailey, b. June 5, 1827, m. Joshua S. Roberts of Biddeford who was born in the town of Lyman, York county, resided on a farm some years situated in Cobb Lane, Deering district of Portland, which he sold to J. Winslow Jones and purchased one in South Windham where he remained over thirty years, then, some five years since, returned to the locality of his wife's birth where both are now hale and hearty in Deering, near Morrill's Corner.

Of their children the following are alive:

a. James W. C. Roberts, Deering Center, a groceryman, b. on the Cobb Lane farm Dec. 2, 1856, m. Oct. 12, 1881, Nellie F. Sanborn of Fryeburg, b. May 20, 1856, and have children named, Percy L., Ina M., Philip C, and Clyde S. Roberts.
b. Olive L. Roberts, m. Robert B. Lowe, b. Walnut Hill, No. Yarmouth, reside in the 9th ward, which he has represented in the City government, and is now representative in the State Legislature.

They have three boys and he is a carpenter and builder.

c. Emeline A. Roberts, m. Henry Leighton of Windham, where he is a farmer.
d. Gilbert F. Roberts, m. Lillian Jackson of Windham, a farmer, where they reside with three children.

5—Emeline Bailey, b. Feb. 7, 1829, m. Leonard C. Burnham of Biddeford. No children. He was a contractor and builder, retired, and resides near his wife's parents'.

6—Marcena Bailey, b. Aug. 4, 1831 m. Ambrose Sheldon of Camden, one son, named Ralph, Frank d. young.

7—Joseph Edward Bailey, b. May 25, 1834, m. Lucy E. Atkins of Woodfords Corner, Deering. Four children: Alice, Herbert, Walter and Leon C. He occupies the residence of his parents in Deering.

7—William Bailey, a ship carpenter, who in 1825, with wife, Jane M. (Bailey), were residents of Medford, Mass. He was the youngest of the Joseph Jr. and Sally (Waterhouse) Bailey children.

The name of Partridge is traceable back to "Partridge the Norman" who migrated to England during the reign of Stephen, (1135—1154) but the name has undergone changes in construction from time to time.

Preserved Partridge was born in Medway, Mass., March 13, 1709. He was the eldest of the eleven children of Benoni and Mehetable (Wheelock) Partridge, and was a great-grandson of John Partridge, who settled about the year of 1650 in Dedham, Mass. He married Nov. 10, 1735 Catharine Armstrong and soon thereafter settled in Holliston, Mass., where five of their ten children were born. He may then have moved to Milford, as in 1754 there was a man there by his name.

In 1761 the name of Nathan Partridge, Preserved's eldest child, appears on our Cumberland county record of deeds as having received a title to land in New Boston, (Gray) and made a clearing there.

Upon the little, old, Stroudwater parish assessors' book, dated December 26 1765, appear the names of "Presavued Patradg" and "Natheu Patradg"—father and son. "Presavued" was assessed for two polls, thereby indicating that he owned a bondman or slave, and sixteen shillings on real estate—total tax, £2:13:2; that of Nathan sixteen shillings and six pence on personal property, no other.

Continued:

The real estate upon which the church, or parish tax was assessed, was located at Capisic, then in Falmouth, now in Portland in consequence of territorial annexation. The residence was situated upon the westerly side of the highway, close to the site of the residence of the late Warren Harmon, and nearly opposite the cellar hole of the residence which was Capt. Thomas Seal's, who has been dead many years, located on the opposite side of the highway which fire consumed. Preserved Partridge's title to the real estate was of the "squatter" nature. His name does not appear on the York county records nor does it on the Cumberland county. He was ejected from the premises by the enforcement of an edict of the court, from the date of which event to the present, the name does not again appear. His demise and place of interment are not known.

Children of Preserved and Catharine (Armstrong) Partridge.

1—Nathan, b. Holliston, Mass., Aug. 3, 1738, m. Nov. 1, 1781, Ann Conant, dau. of Samuel and Mary (Peabody) Conant. They resided at Saccarappa.
2—Bathsheba, b. Holliston, Mass., Aug. 19, 1740, m. Uriah Nason, int. of m. made public Oct. 16, 1762. (Not the Uriah Nason of Gorham.) Resided a mile westerly of Stroudwater on Saco road. Removed to Poland. Graves on the farm lot in Poland. Cellar hole on the Stroudwater farm.
3—Capt. Jesse, b. Holliston, Mass., Aug. 29, 1742, m. Rebecca Bailey, dau. of John Bailey, Jr. He d. Dec. 21, 1795, at Stroudwater. The widow m. Andrew Titcomb. Resided there.
4—Catharine, b. Holliston, Mass., Aug. 26, 1744, m. Timothy Cloutman of Gorham, July 24, 1766. Resided at Gorham. Eleven children recorded there.
5—David, b. Holliston, Mass., January 26, 1747, m. Mary Conant of Saccarappa. Settled in Otisfield, (Thompson's Pond region.)
6—Jotham, b. 1750, m. Mary Bailey, dau. of John Bailey, Jr. Resided at Saccarappa. He died there Oct. 28, 1800. She m., 2d, Solomon Haskell, Jr.
7—Azubah, b. 1752, m. Joseph Quinby, a Revolutionary soldier and grandfather of Capt. Isaac F. Quinby of Saccarappa. Joseph Quinby resided on Capisic street, Deering, at date of his death, in a house that stood between the present residences of Mr. Albion P. Chapman and Edward L. Goold. He died prior to 1797. She married Col. John Harvey, a soldier of the Revolution. He d. May, 1812, and the widow removed to Portland. Their son, Joseph Quinby, Jr., m. Feb. 13, 1813, Elizabeth Bailey, dau. of Joseph Bailey, Jr., the blacksmith, who m. Dec. 7, 1783, Sally Waterhouse of Stroudwater, and 2d, Isaac Fly. The wives of Capt. Jesse and Jotham Partridge were sisters to Joseph Bailey, Jr., who m. Sally Waterhouse.
8—Rosina, m. May 2, 1779, Nathan Quinby of Saccarappa; he m. 2d, Widow Achers. They resided upon the "holy ground" district of the village.
9—Zipporah, m. Eliphalet Watson, Jr., of Gorham, int. of m. filed July 22, 1780. They have a record in that town.
10—Rhoda. She did not marry. Upon a blank leaf of one of the account books of Jonathan Sparrow the following is recorded: "Rhoda Partridge came to board with me July 13, 1804, at nine shillings per week, also took one of my chambers, May 2, 1804, at $15 per year. Left the chamber Oct. 8, 1805, which is 17 months & 6 days." Sparrow kept shop in Stroudwater, and resided at the head of Waldo street, where the cellar hole appears on the west side of Westbrook street. Rhoda built a one story house on the southwesterly corner of the present iron bridge, now in existence, but removed from the original site and known as the Walker house.

To be continued.

GRANDPA'S SCRAP BOOK

Week of Oct. 15—17, 1903.

WATERHOUSE.

By Leonard B. Chapman.

(Continued from last week.)

The Quinby clan at Saccarappa village in Westbrook, which place was a part of Falmouth until 1814, requires more attention than I am able to bestow just now, if detailed and correct statements are made. The name has been noticed in the Scrap Book from time to time, and I will here refer the reader to the issue of April 27, 1895, and May 4, same year; to Aug. 12, and Oct. 14, 1899; also to the history of Gorham by Katharine B. Lewis, p. 436.

Benjamin Quinby, born in Somersworth, N. H., was the first of the name to locate at Saccarappa, which was Sept. 11, 1770, when he purchased a right to use water from the Presumpscot river for the purpose of running "a fulling mill and carrying on a clothier's business." His residence was, more than probable, upon the island where the mill was located. In 1775 he was reinforced by the presence of his brother, Joseph Quinby, whose intention of marriage with Mary Haskell, dau. of Thomas Haskell, the first of the name, who came to Falmouth, was made public Sept. 28, 1740. Joseph was a ship carpenter and resided upon the southerly side of Middle street, near India, then known as King street, where they had born to them nine children, a record of whom appeared in the Scrap Book, Feb. 26, 1898, and where they resided until Mowatt's bombardment of Portland, Oct. 18, 1775, when they retired to Saccarappa, as above indicated, and where he died April 14, 1776, having purchased a part of his brother's mill May 6, 1775. The widow died at Stroudwater, April 12, 1815, where they have a memorial slab, and where descendants still reside.

Benjamin Quinby and wife had children born in Somersworth, N. H., but in the absence of records I cannot state the number. In coming to Saccarappa they left behind grown-up offspring. He acknowledged here, and it is a matter of record, children named Simeon; Benjamin, Jr., born 1746, died in Saccarappa Nov. 6, 1810, aged 64 years; Moses, born 1758, died at Saccarappa in 1840. There was a Jacob, born in 1743, died Nov. 27, 1805, aged 62 years, but whether or not he was a son I cannot state. Then there was Nathan, a son, who married Rosina Partridge, and Joseph, the Revolutionary soldier, who married Rosina's next older sister, named Azubah, the seventh child of the Partridge family.

Benjamin Quinby had two wives if no more. His second was Eleanor Starbird, whom he married May 6, 1779, and in 1799, Benjamin Quinby, Jr., of Somersworth, clothier, enters into an agreement to maintain, for a consideration, Benjamin Quinby and wife, Eleanor.

Prior to this transaction, which was in 1792, Moses Quinby, Joseph's son, purchased of his father and wife Eleanor, a fourth part of a grist mill where, as Benjamin says, "my saw mill now stands, and has for many years, being on the northeasterly side of the privilege sold my son, Benjamin Quinby, Jr."

In 1806, Moses purshased of his father the "dye-house, fulling mill, etc." all of which, including a paper mill, on the 24th day of Sept. 1813, was destroyed by fire, the Quinby clan with others losing heavily, the whole loss amounting to $20,000.

It appears nearly all the members were mechanics and possessed a mania for mills, not only at Saccarappa but other places.

Benjamin, senior, "the king of the clan," must have died in 1806 or 7, for Nov. 5, 1807, Thomas Haskell's son Solomon was united in marriage with "Mrs. Eleanor Quinby, she seventy-three, he eighty-four years of age." She was his second wife.

[Mr. and Mrs. in many cases are written exactly alike in Parson Bradley's diary. Under date of Feb. 26, 1807, he records that Mr. or Mrs. Quinby died, aged 92 years. I have once printed it as "Mrs." but it must have been Mr. Benjamin Quinby, who died at the date given by Parson Bradley—born, 1715.]

The following transcript is from the Parson's diary:

"Died Aug. 1822, Deacon Haskell's widow, aged 90."

The deacon and his first wife have memorial slabs in the village cemetery but Eleanor has none.

Of all the Quinby clan at Saccarappa, in the old Conant cemetery there is but one memorial slab; two monuments in the village cemetery, and a row of six slate slabs, as follows:

1—"Mr. Benjamin Quinby, son of Mr. Benjamin Quinby, died Nov. 6, 1810, aged 64 years." Born 1746, son of Benjamin, sen., who agreed to maintain his father, and Eleanor, his step-mother.

2—"Benjamin Quinby, born in Somersworth, N. H., July 13, 1786, died in Saccarappa, April 19, 1854." He was aged 68, and a grandson of Benj., sen.

3—"Elizabeth, wife of Benjamin Quinby, died Oct. 27, 1821, aged 34 years."

4—"Sarah, 2nd wife of Benjamin Quinby, 3d., died Aug. 2, 1850, aged 58 years."

5—Two slabs for 1st and 3d daughters of Benjamin and wife, Elizabeth Quinby—one aged 8, the other 14 years.

Joseph Quinby, son of Benjamin Quinby, sen., of Saccarappa, married Azubah Partridge, as has been stated. He was a Revolutionary soldier. His wife, in her own capacity, March 30, 1797, as "Zuba Quinby, wife of Joseph Quinby," purchased land on each side of the highway between Saccarappa and Cumberland Mills, where the school house is located, about half way between the two places, paying therefor $424, but May 2nd of the same year she sold the same, "Zuba Quinby, widow," did—whose real name was "Azubah"—to Samuel Butts, then a trader at Capsic, for $246. Elbridge G. Riggs, some years ago, informed me that it was an exchange of titles between Azubah and Samuel, but it does not appear thus on our Cumberland records, but more than probable Mr. Riggs' statement was true, for Azubah with "Colonel" John Harvey resided in the "low-posted residence, facing the south, with very small glass," located as I have represented, near Nason's Corner, in Deering, where Mr. Harvey worked for Mr. Butts in his mill at Capisic, and in which house Mr. Harvey died, according to Parson Bradley's diary, in February of 1812, as I have before stated.

It is traditional that Joseph Quinby, Jr., son of the Revolutionary soldier, and grandson of Benjamin Quinby, Sen., "king of the Quinby clan" at Saccarappa, was born upon the site of the school house in Westbrook, as I have located it, and the cemetery memorial gives the date as March 12, 1791. This being true, Joseph Quinby, Jr., was but six years of age when his father departed this life.

June 24, 1799, Parson Bradley records that John Harvey subscribed two dollars towards the parson's "settlement fee," thus indicating that Mr. Harvey was hereabout at that date.

Mr. Harvey was a widower at the time he married the widow of Joseph Quinby and set up housekeeping at Nason's Corner, the indentation of the residence still appearing on the northeasterly corner of the residence of the late Edward L. Goold.

June 26, 1819, an agent of the United States government sold the house and an acre of land to satisfy a demand growing out of a special tax on account of the war of 1812-15, the demand being against Joseph Quinby, the Revolutionary soldier, whose son John, residing at Minot, redeemed, March 14, 1820, but the title, I think, was worthless.

Joseph Copps was the next occupant of the house with a much larger lot.

John Harvey has a good war record. He was an ensign and quartermaster, and a careful observer of events. He kept a diary a part of the time while a soldier—commencing at Eastern Pennsylvania, June 18, 1779, till January 5, 1781. He evidently was a New Hampshire man and born in the town of Northwood, Rockingham county, though he fails to give the slightest statement as to his birthplace, but evidently was sixty-seven years old at the time of his death, which was in 1812, at which time he presented his step-son, Joseph Quinby, Jr., his diary as a keepsake—in fact, Joseph, in the month of January, 1812, so states upon a fly-leaf.

In the same hand, upon another page, is a record, of which the following is a transcript:

The age of my Father & Mother.
John Harvey was Born March 29, 1719. and Died August 18, 1756.

Mary Harvey was Born June 22, 1722 and Died Nov. ——

The Age of my Self & my wife.
John Harvey was Born August 4, 1745.
Sarah Harvey was born Dec. 5, 1747.

Continued:

The age of our Children.
Joseph Harvey was born Apr. 28, 1772.
He Died Nov. 30 1782.
John Harvey was born Apr. 16, 1774.
Sally Harvey was born May 5, 1785.
Joseph Harvey born Oct. 13, 1787.

Joseph Quinby, Jr., b. March 12, 1791, to whom Mr. Harvey presented his diary, who married Feb. 11, 1813, Eliza Bailey, dau. of Joseph Bailey, Jr., was a house carpenter and seems to have been a sort of rolling stone.

March 17, 1817, he purchased what is known as the Nicholas Hanson place located in North Scarboro, which, after he sold to Hanson, became notorious as an inn, and which now remains

In 1823 he was residing at the corner of Essex and Congress streets, Portland.

His family record has already appeared.

To be continued.

GRANDPA'S SCRAP BOOK

Week of Oct. 22—24, 1903.

WATERHOUSE.

By Leonard B. Chapman.

(Continued from last week.)

[Correction. Where the name of "Joseph" appears in the second line of the fifth paragraph from the top in the Scrap Book article of last week "Joseph" should have been Benjamin.]

In the "Biographical Review of Leading Citizens of Cumberland County," this state, published in 1896, page 328, may be seen a half-tone cut of Capt. Isaac F. Quinby with a notice of the first possessors of the name hereabouts which contains some expressions of extravagance in the attempt to state facts. The compiler says that Capt. Isaac F.'s great-grandfather "held a commission issued by the King of Great Britain to take any tree suitable for a mast for any vessel of the King's navy no matter where found."

Col. Thomas Westbrook was the first to engage in the mast industry hereabouts; he died in 1744, and George Tate was sent over to prosecute the business who located at Stroudwater where he erected a residence, now standing, nearly the same as originally constructed, and where he died and where he has a memorial slab and descendants.

Capt. Isaac F. Quinby's grandfather, Joseph Quinby, senior, son of Benjamin, the clothier, enlisted in the cause of the Colonies May 10, 1775, under Capt. John Brackett, a land surveyor, residing at Saccarappa, who commenced to obtain recruits April 24, of that year. The entire company, with five exceptions, was made of citizens of the parts of Falmouth, now known as Westbrook and Deering, including all the officers. Joseph Quinby, senior, was a private, and I cannot learn that he ever ranked higher. (Mass. Archives Vol. 56, page 215.) His name appears also upon the Falmouth town books as a soldier. If he ever bore the title of "Colonel" it must have been honorary and homemade. It is traditional that he located after the war in the town of Gray where he worked at shook making, and once, provisions being so scarce and transportation so very limited, he walked to Saccarappa and returned with a bushel of meal which he carried all the way to keep actual starvation from entering the abode of his family. The "Biographical Review" states also that he died in 1806, but Azubah (Partridge) Quinby, his wife, was a widow on the second day of May, 1793, when she sold her land located between Saccarappa and Cumberland Mills where it is traditional Joseph Quinby, Jr., was born who chose Eliza Bailey for his wife. (Vol. 218, page 106, Cum. Co. Deeds.) The "Review" states also that Capt. Isaac F. Quinby was born in Westbrook, May 26, 1818, but it is a family tradition that he was born at Coal Kiln Corner in Scarboro in what is now known as the Nicholas Hanson residence, which became an inn.

Like many of the Quinby clan, Isaac F., adopted the calling of his father— a house carpenter— and in Saccarappa in 1844 he was united in marriage with Miss Catherine G. Brown of Parsonsfield, York Co.

July 2, 1845, he purchased a house lot at Saccarappa, located upon the easterly side of Brown street next northerly of the steam railway crossing, where he erected a large dwelling to which a piece has been added to the rear end, higher and wider, the whole attracting the attention of the passer-by only by its magnitude, now arranged for four tenements.

In spiritual matters, Capt. Quinby espoused early in life the cause of the Universal Father and supported with a liberal hand the Universalist church. In politics he was an original Republican and 1860 was elected County Treasurer and re-elected the following year, but vacated the office to take up arms for the preservation of the Union, recruited a company of 103 men, was made a captain of company E. and placed in the 13th Regiment of Maine Voluteers, commanded by Col. Neal Dow, which was assigned to Gen. Benjamin F. Butler's expedition against New Orleans, La.; but the climate there was too severe for his constitution, and he was obliged to return physically exhausted, a state from which he never fully recovered, but he performed a large amount of business in the town of his adoption as a conveyancer, land speculator and builder, the appearance of many residences now proving his good taste as a designer.

He was not an enthusiast, rather slow in thought and expression, but he possessed an intuitive knowledge of man which made him a safe counselor not only for himself but for others.

His spirit was called away Wednesday, April 7, 1898; that of his wife, Catherine G., (Brown) Quinby, June 19, 1896, that first saw the light of day. February 2, 1822.

A monument of enduring material marks in the village cemetery the place of deposit of the worldly remains of both.

Capt. Quinby and wife left the only two children born to them, Mary, the wife of Charles E. Quinby of Saccarappa, (Benjamin, Moses, Aaron, Charles E.) who reside on Mechanic street, and Ella C., the wife of Henry H. Hawes, who occupy the last homestead of their parents that is located upon the westerly side of the same street, nearly opposite that of Mr. Chas. E. Quinby.

The "Westbrook Chronicle" of April 8 and 15, 1898, contain full accounts of the death and funeral services.

CONCLUSION.

After the destruction of Portland Neck by Mowatt, Oct. 18, 1775, the town chose a committee to make a canvass of the losses sustained by its citizens "for inspection by Congress," of which Peter Noyes was chairman. (Willis History of Portland, page 900. Names not indexed.) The following are extracts:

"William Waterhouse, sen., the first of the name at Stroudwater, £480:00:0.
"Joseph Quinby, sen., brother to Benjamin of Saccarappa, £413:00:0.
"Joseph Quinby, Jr., £310:00:0."

This last Joseph, Jr., married Hannah Noyes; he died in Portland and the widow married Amos Lunt and went with her children; and there was Joseph, Henry, Franklin, etc. Mr. Lunt wrote a very correct and neat appearing letter. Henry engaged in trade there and was postmaster. Several of his manuscript letters are before me in one of which he states he is about to start for Washington, with a patent. Joseph who was a millwright bought into the Brunswick water power, but in 1821, Nov. 3rd, with a wife named Mary C. (Quinby), was a citizen of Fryeburg.

In 1753, Joseph Quinby, sen., of Portland purchased land and mill privilege in Gorham, and Oct. 2, 1764, raised the frame to a mill, which was at Stephen's bridge on Little river.

The residence of William Waterhouse, Jr., was located upon one of the corners of Congress and Montgomery streets, Portland. In 1827 John P. Waterhouse, son of William, Jr., sold his interest to Nathaniel Montgomery who was his brother-in-law.

The End.

GRANDPA'S SCRAP BOOK

Week of Oct. 29—31, 1903.

THE KING FAMILY OF SCARBORO

RICHARD KING, JR.

An Interesting Letter From a Descendant.

[Joshua Scottow was a merchant in Boston, Mass. Henry Jocelyn became indebted to him and July 6, 1666, Jocelyn conveyed to Scottow the large tract of land he had received in Scarboro by marrying Gorges' widow. Scottow immediately occupied his purchase and, in 1671, engaged in trade and was a licensed retailer of liquors when there was but one person in trade on Portland Neck, and Black Point, in Scarboro, had more houses than Casco contained which was about fifty. Scottow spelled his name as I have here. On the county map made in 1859, and the atlas made in 1871, it is spelled as I have used it. "Scottoway" is only a corruption of the correct spelling. L. B. C.]

To the Editor: I have been following, with interest, your record of the King Family of Scarboro and I see your historian speaks of Scottow Hill, but my grandmother, who was born in the house built by Richard King, Jr., always spoke of it as "Scottoway Hill," and that it was known by that name is shown by a record in the account book of Richard King, Jr., where, under date of Feb. 3rd, appears the following record:

"Feb. 3rd. 1802. Moved to Scottoway Hill," while the date of the erection of the new house is proved conclusively by the following:

"Sept. 12, 1805. Moved into my New Hous." The spelling is Richard King's, not mine.

"Feb. 3rd. 1802. Moved to Scottoway Hill. Paid Doct. Robt. Southgate Esq. for his wife's share, Mary,	$389
"July, 1802. Paid Silas King for his share,	100
"July 1802. Paid Mr. Joseph Leland for his wife's share, Dorcas.	70
	40
	100
"Paid Doct. Aaron Porter for his wife's share Paulina	100
"Paid Doctor Benjamin J. Porter for his wife's share Elizabeth."	

I find an answer to his sister Pauline's letter asking William to help her brother Richard, who has just built a house, in the following entry:

"Money received by me of my Brother Rufus King, Esq. New York, Jan. 1805, transmitted to me via. Cyrus King as a present. (Added afterwards as the ink shows.) $400

"Sept. 1805. Recd. of Doct. Benj. J. Porter as a present $45

"Money Recd. by me of my Brother William King, Bath, (as a present) $300

"Sept. 1805. Recd. of pr. Dt. $200
Recd. pr. Dt. $1000
___
$1500

In relation to the schooner the following may be of interest:

"Nov. 1802. Bought the Sloop Betsey $250.

"Sept. 5th. 1809 Sloop Federal to Richard King, Dr. myself with work at $1.25 per day.
(This account ends Dec. 16.)
"Sloop Federal Cyrus King Dr. Sept. 5th, 1809, at $1.10 Day.
"Sloop Fedr. to Willm. King Dr. Sept. 5th, 1809 at 80 Cents.

The two accounts of Cyrus and William, sons to Richard, Sen., end Dec. 6.

Then follows pages about the calking, rigging and workmen's wages for the vessel, and lumber, bolts, rum and other supplies for same; also a store account with Joseph Emerson, but nothing about the disposal of the vessel.

Under a later date I find:

"Went to Saco on Board Sloop Pythagorus Aug. 2nd. 1812. Sailed Augt. 4th.; taken by the British Augt. 9th. Put in Halifax Prison Augt 17th. Exchanged Sept. 10, 1812. Got home October 17th. In a Cartel with 515 Prisoners.

Is there anything known about the 'Pythagorus,' whether the vessel belonged to Richard King, or was he merely going to Saco on business? I find no further referece to the affair.

My grandmother was Hannah Larrabee King, so the name is written in her father's account book, in his own hand, afterward changed to Fidelia Hannah King (Hawkes).

Hannah Larrabee King, wife of Richard, Jr., was born June 22, 1771, died May 23, 1845.

Cyrus King, their son, married May 7, 1815, died Feb. 1, 1847.

Hannah (Carter) King, his wife, died July 23, 1875.

The following corrections I am sure are correct as I make them from the account book where they are recorded in Richard King's hand.

"Mary King, born Oct. 12, 1791.
"Benjamin Samuel Black King, born Jan. 11, 1803.

Then in another hand:

"Mary King, died Nov. 10, 1834.

Among my records I find that Eliza King Austin was married Jan. 25, 1829, died June 17, 1864.

William Austin, her husband, died Sept. 8, 1876.

My mother states that Joseph Leland King did not die as stated at Eliza Austin's, but at the house of Fidelia King Hawkes, in Windham, also Miranda Southgate King, who married Philip Gammon, April 15th, 1834, did not live in Windham, but West Falmouth, near Blackstrap Observatory, where she died. Her husband moved to Raymond, being previously remarried, and then to Naples where he died.

Fidelia Hannah King (Hawkes) died Dec. 18, 1893, in Vineland, N. J., at the home of her daughter, Mary E. (Hawkes) McDavitt.

Aaron Hawkes, husband of Fidella (King) Hawkes, died June 27, 1866 at Windham, Maine.

Margaret Ann (Hawkes) Craig died June 13, 1901.

It is William H. Hawkes instead of D.

In the account book of Richard King, Jr. are copied the births of all his children, and the death of those who died in infancy, in his own hand. The other records are taken from the same source where another hand has written them, and also from slips cut from newspapers and pasted in.

My mother has in her possession many relics from the King family, among them a silver teaspoon and a pair of sugar tongs, a glass decanter, mahogany stand and a large mirror, all of which came from the house of Richard King, Senior, and were given to Richard King, Jr., upon his marriage.

I could supply the records of Fidella Hannah (King) Hawkes' grandchildren if desired.

Yours very truly,
Ina Lord McDavitt.
Vineland, N. J., P. O. Box 397.

CONTINUED:
GRANDPA'S SCRAP BOOK

Week of Nov. 5—7, 1903.

CAPT. JOHN L. LEWIS.

A Son-in-law of the Rev. Thomas Browne.

By Leonard B. Chapman.

Aug. 24, 1895, I made an extended allusion to the Rev. Thomas Browne, who officiated from April 8, 1765, as a clergyman, upon the site of the Mary Brown Home in the Deering district of Portland, then known as the Fourth, or Stroudwater parish of Falmouth, till near the close of his life, which was Oct. 18, 1797. In the Scrap Book for week ending Sept. 12-15, 1900, I alluded to his youngest daughter, Rebecca Browne, born, Woodfords, Feb. 1777. Jenk's Portland Gazette states she died Dec. 9, 1804, aged 27 years, 10 months—"the youngest daughter of Rev. Thomas Browne." They resided in a house he owned, now standing upon its original foundation, with second story same as built, nearly opposite the head of Park street. They had one child named William who was alive in 1814. Capt. Lewis was a mariner, and it is stated on page 352 of Smith and Dean's Diary that Polly, dau. of Dr. Edward Watts, born, Portland, Dec. 4, 1782, married Capt. John L. Lewis and died May 8, 1844. Another record which I perused stated that Capt. Lewis married second June 19, 1806, Mary Bryant. Dr. Watts resided in a house he owned, now standing on the southwesterly corner of Cumberland and Preble streets. As Capt. Lewis sold in 1819 his Congress street house and built, or inherited, a house near Dr. Watts' which was moved to the southeasterly corner of Cumberland and Preble streets, it is more than probable that Capt. Lewis' second wife was Dr. Watts' daughter. Capt. Lewis died June 21, 1825, aged 52 years, and the widow married. His sandstone memorial slab in the Eastern cemetery is worn out but enough remains to indicate that he was a Free Mason. Dec. 18, 1804, he was admitted to the Portland Marine society, and while the British fleet was blocking the Portland harbor in August of 1814 he was put in command of the company composed of ship captains and mates.

A resident of Washington, D. C., contributes the following interesting item:

John Lewis, a custom house official at Boston, residing in Lynn, Mass., m. Sept. 25, 1764, Sarah Lindsey. In 1776 he removed to New York with other refugees and remained there until 1783, when he left with his children for Halifax, N. S. Sarah, his wife, died in New York, Oct. 6, 1780, aged 36, and was buried in Trinity church yard. John Lewis died in Halifax, Nov. 26, 1789, aged 53 years.

GRANDPA'S SCRAP BOOK

Week of Jan. 1—3, 1903.

A KING FAMILY OF SCARBORO.

WILLIAM KING.

By Leonard B. Chapman.

NO. XLVI.

A letter from Mrs. William King to her husband prior to the Presidential election of 1824 reads as follows:

"Bath, Dec. 8, 1823.
"My Dear Husband:
"Yours of the 30th I received in due time. It quite revives me to find you in such good spirits about the residential business. It is very strange that the people here should be so sanguine that they are to be uccessful. [The Adams supporters.] You certainly have better opportunities of knowing the sentiment of the public than they have. I most sincerely hope you are not deceived; but you must not give me credit of being much of a Crawfordite as my anxiety for his success would lead you to suppose I am, for it is to put down the opposition that is so outrageously abusive that I am so desirous he may be the fortunate candidate.

"I heard yesterday that it is reported in town that you are abandoning Mr. Crawford and trying to get round the Adams people, likewise you and Mr. Holmes have quarreled, [Hon. John Holmes, M. C.] and other reports too ridiculous to mention, which so vexes me that I cannot keep my temper.

"I hope you will write your friends here as I think some of them need encouragement as well as myself.

"Our darling children are [both[well. Mary E. went to Miss Eaton's school today. She is very much pleased with it and already begins to put on the appearances of a young lady. Cyrus did not like going without his sister. I do not think he learns anything, so I cannot feel easy to have him there. Think I shall instruct him myself at home this winter.

"Mr. Edgcomb has cut his wood out of the ice and delivered it to us. Gorham (?) is still at work on the farm.

"I have nothing further to tell you only the Doctor is published. I expect Olive will be obliged to stay here till sleighing. I am rejoiced to learn you will return in January. Are you attending to the Massachusetts claim business?

"When I last wrote I forgot to mention the death of Charlotte Lithgrow (?); it was sudden. I was always attached to her and feel it exceedingly.

"I hope you will continue in being punctual in writing. Tell me every thing that is going on.
"Very truly yours,
"Ann N. King."

Copy of a letter to William King from Hon. John Holmes after the election of John Quincy Adams as president.

"Washington, [D. C.,] Jan. 15, 1826.
"Dear Sir:
"It is difficult to answer your questions in regard to the political aspect here. We hear little of Crawford, Jackson, Calhoun or Adams men. The probability is, however, if these gentlemen were now candidates Mr. Crawford would count about one-half and Mr. Adams a fourth, but most of the friends of Mr. Crawford, now the contest is over, will be disposed to try the administration by its acts—support it where they can and oppose it where they must.

"Some of the Adams regular supporters are not, or affect not to be entirely satisfied with the aspect of affairs. They appear to be alarmed that certain Federal [party] gentlemen should be his private counsellors. What ground there is for fear I do not pretend to know. Our course is, however, very plain. Swanton's nomination lays on the table. As we hear nothing from Maine against him, and as we presume it is not expected the Senators are to look up evidence, I presume the opposition to his appointment is withdrawn. We shall probably be obliged to act on it this week. We have a great executive question pending and one which will elicit much discussion in secret session. You can GUESS what it is.

"Write me what is doing and to be done in Maine. Will there be a general amalgamation? Write me.
"Yours respectfully,
"J. Holmes."
To be continued.

314

GRANDPA'S SCRAP BOOK

Week of Jan. 8-10, 1903.

THE KING FAMILY OF SCARBORO.

WILLIAM KING.

By Leonard B. Chapman.

NO. XLVII.

The following is a copy of a letter relating to the death of Mrs. Mary (King) Southgate, who was the wife of Robert Southgate and a half-sister to Gov. William King. Joseph C. Boyd's wife was a daughter of Dr. and Mary (King) Southgate, as has been shown in the Southgate memoranda:

"Portland, March 31, 1824.

"My dear Uncle: I have just returned from Scarborough whither I went last evening expecting to see my Grandmother again, but it had pleased GOD to call her hence a short time before my arrival there. At the request of Grandfather I write to inform you of the event which, tho' it be unto us cause of mourning and grief, is unto your dear sister an event of unspeakable joy. Her heart has been for some months so fixed by faith in Christ that she has endured the most excruciating agony in quiet resignation and calmness; and her last hours were witness of the truth of the scripture which saith: 'Nothing shall separate us from the love of Christ.' Her faith triumphed over sufferings of body which cannot be conceived so that in the anguish of dissolving nature she could say—

"'Jesus, lover of my soul,
Let me to thy bosom fly.'"

"Grandfather appears calm and tranquil tho' he suffers.

"May we not pray that this event may be sanctified of GOD unto us all who are connected with our dear Friend, that we may be prepared to follow her hence and 'to dwell forever with the Lord.'

"With a deep interest in the loss which you, my dear uncle, have met permit me heartily to sympathize with you and to subscribe myself—

"In affliction,
"Your nephew,
"James J. Boyd.

"P. S.—The funeral will be at 1 o'clock on Friday, 2nd April. J. J. B.
"Hon. William King,
"Bath."

The following copy contains data worthy of preservation:

"To the Honorable, The President of The Senate of The United States;

"James J. Boyd of Portland, in the State of Maine, administrator on the estate of Joseph C. Boyd, late District Paymaster of the Army of the United States, deceased, respectfully showeth: That on the fifth day of April, 1822, a Bill of Relief of the said Joseph C. Boyd passed the Senate of the U. S., and was sent to the House for concurrence; that it was there referred to the Military Committee who reported the Bill without amendment, on the 7th day of May—the day before the close of the Senate—when it was laid on the Table.

"Your Memorialist would therefore respectfully request that the subject on which the Bill was predicated may be again examined and such Order taken thereon as may appear to the Honorable the Senate, in justice, proper and requisite.

"As in duty bound your memorialist will ever pray,
"James J. Boyd,
"Administrator on the estate of Joseph C. Boyd, late District Paymaster U. S. Army, deceased."

To be continued.

GRANDPA'S SCRAP BOOK

Week of Jan. 15-17, 1903.

THE KING FAMILY OF SCARBORO.

WILLIAM KING.

The First Governor of Maine.

By Leonard B. Chapman.

NO. XLVIII.

In the Portland Sunday Telegram of Feb. 10, 1901, in connection with an article entitled the "Portland Federal Volunteers," appeared a half-tone cut of Joseph Coffin Boyd made from an oil painting, of which company he was, in 1798, the first Captain.

In my Southgate articles I have noticed Capt. Boyd and his family.

In the Portland (Maine) Daily Press of Feb. 3, 1898, I find as follows:

"MISHAP TO GEN. TILGHMAN'S WIDOW.

"She Falls, Breaking Her Thigh—Recovery Problematical Owing to Her Age—She Was a Portland Girl.

"Mrs. Augusta M. Tilghman, widow of the late Gen. Lloyd Tilghman, met with a serious accident a short time ago, and is now in a critical condition at her home, 929 Madison avenue, New York. On Thanksgiving day Mrs. Tilghman fell as she was leaving her bed and broke her thigh. Her age made recovery difficult, and, instead of improving, Mrs. Tilghman is at present very low.

"Mrs. Tilghman was born on January 10, 1819, in Portland. She was the youngest of the fifteen children of Joseph C. Boyd, first treasurer of the State of Maine. Her grandmother was Mary King, sister of the Hon. Rufus King, first United States Minister to the court of St. James, and Mrs. Tilghman was in this way cousin of John A. King, governor of the state of New York from 1856 to 1858. Her mother was Isabella Southgate, whose sister, Eliza Southgate, married Walter Bowne, Mayor of New York, in 1833. When she was a young girl Mrs. Tilghman visited Mayor Bowne at his residence in Beekman street, and there she often met Martin Van Buren, with whom she was a favorite.

"Mrs. Tilghman was named for Miss Augusta Murray, or 'Lady Augusta,' as she was called by her friends. The Murrays then lived on St. John's Park, and at their house and at their farm on Murray Hill Mrs. Tilghman was a frequent visitor. In 1843 she married Lloyd Tilghman, who afterwards became a General in the Confederate army, and who was killed in the battle of Champion Hill. Her eldest son, Lloyd Tilghman, Jr., was killed in August, 1863, near Selma, Ala.

"Mrs. Tilghman has lived in New York since the war. Of her eight children only two are now living, Frederick B. and Sidell, both of whom are members of the Stock Exchange."

A notice of the Tilghmans of Maryland will appear in my forthcoming work on the Southgate and King families commencing on page twenty-nine.

The following is a copy of another interesting letter addressed to "William King, Esq., Bath, Me.," by James J. Boyd, the second child of Capt. Boyd, and brother to Mrs. Augusta Murray Boyd (Tilghman.)

"Portland, Oct. 13, 1826.

"My dear sir: Owing to an affection of a pulmonary nature which has troubled me for a few months, I am about leaving here for Jamaica, to remain until about the first of January; and it will gratify me to be able to afford any assistance in my power to you the transaction of any business it may be your wish to confide to my care; and I shall esteem it a favor to be named to any of your friends who may have unfinished business on the Island as an agent who will attend to interest which they may entrust me. If it be necessary I will remain longer on the Island than the period I have here named. Letters addressed to me at Kingston, or by the way of Montego Bay, care of John Apthop Vaugh, Esq., I shall receive and attend to their requirements. I anticipate much benefit to my health, by my proposed voyage, and have made such arrangements at my office as will permit me to be absent until spring.

"I am sensible of my indebtedness to you for your influence in procuring the situation which has afforded subsistance to my family and I cannot doubt the continuance of that interest in our condition you have so frequently manifested, nor can I doubt that your kindness to us as a family will remain though I am called away for a season from its head. My Brother Merrill [Dr. John Merrill, who married the eldest child of the Boyd family] will take the House with the remains of our large family and continue with it until my return.

I look with confidence, sir, as one of the chief of my friends on whom I may depend for the influence necessary to obtain a renewal of my Commission which expires in March of 1827, and shall consider that you have laid me under increased obligations personally as a member of a family you have so often and so generously befriended.

"It may gratify you to know that my Brother Stillman has been invited and has accepted the invitation of Bellamy Storer, Esq., of Cincinnati, Ohio, to come into the family and into his office until he is prepared to practice as an Attorney at Law. He left us this morning for that place.

Continued:

"I beg to be affectionately remembered to aunt and to my cousin Joanna, who is, I believe, still with you; and I pray you, my dear sir, to acept my acknowledgements for your past favors, and the assurance of my regard and esteem as your relative.
"James J. Boyd."

Whose daughter James J. Boyd's cousin Joanna" was I have not learned. She seems to have been a "star" in Gov. King's family, yet I fail to establish the exact relationship. The Governor was from home much, possessed a large residence at Bath and it seems it was seldom one or more of his nieces were not the guests of the Governor's wife. After the death of the Governor's brother Cyrus, in 1817, Cyrus daughter Caroline went there to reside. To whom the writer of the letter of which the following is a copy referred I cannot tell. It is addressed to Gen. William King, Bath, Maine, and reads thus:

"Milford, (Conn.) November 11th, 1818.
"Sir: As I have not the honor of an acquaintance with Gen. King I fear I shall be thought presumptuous in writing this communication, but if I have taken an unwarrantable liberty, I hope he will pardon me, and pass it over in silence. The reputation of a young man just commencing his part in the world is dearer to him than life.

"My object in writing is to request your consent to a continued correspondence with Miss King.

"As to future prospects, my advantages are such as to warrant a confident hope of success at the Bar. With regard to the respectability of my Father's family, my own moral character, as well as literary and scientific attainments, I can rely for the amplest recommendation upon Dr. Day, President of Yale College. I mention him because there is no person in this vicinity with whom I am acquainted whose opinions would be better received. I could not, however, at present, request him to write, fearing Gen. King might view it as an intrusion; and not knowing that he would consent to a continuance of the correspondence, on this, or any other condition whatever.

"If it be not an impertinent request, I could wish the favor of hearing from you on the subject.
"Yours with greatest respect,
"Joseph Fowler."

A letter from Dr. John Merrill reads as follows:

"Portland, July 18, 1826.
"Gen. King.—
"Sir: Another daughter of the late Joseph C. Boyd is rapidly declining. She is at my house. Ripe fruit of all kinds is particularly aceptable to her. She is fond of cherries, but we can get none here (or scarcely any) except the common red kind Knowing you raise an abundance of nice ones, I take the liberty of requesting you to send her a few by steamboat conveyance.

"Mary [his wife] unites with me in presenting our best respects to Mrs. King.

"With sentiments of regard and esteem, I am your ob't servant,
"John Merrill."

GRANDPA'S SCRAP BOOK

Week of Jan. 22—24, 1903.

THE KING FAMILY OF SCARBORO.

WILLIAM KING.

The First Governor of Maine.

By Leonard B. Chapman.

NO. XLIX.

Another letter reads as follows:
"Portland, March 16th, 1829.
Gen'l Wm. King.
Bath.
Dear Sir: It was with much regret that I learned from you on the 4th inst that your stay in town was to be short, as circumstances rendered it impossible for me to ask personally from you a favour of great importance to me——My object in calling on you in company with Dr. Merrill on that evening was to solicit your friendly interest in my favour for the appointment of weigher and guager for this port, and supposing that you had gone to Boston I addressed a letter through the P. office) to you there. I have been informed today that you returned immediately home, and supposing that you cannot have received the letter I now repeat the request. I have received assurances of the influence of many of the leading Jackson men here—perhaps stronger assurances than I had a right to expect, yet there is no one, My dear Sir, whose influence I have any reason to suppose could be at all compared to yours, should you give it me. I can only repeat what I said in my letter before mentioned that the importance of your influence in this case, and the certainty which I should feel of success by obtaining it, would have deterred me from asking, had I not known how willingly you had always lent that influence in aid of our family—this was my apology then—I can offer no other now for troubling you in this matter.

"Gen. Chandler, the Collector elect, arrived in town last evening and leaves again in the morning for his home. Nothing definite as to his appointment can be known here until his return, which will be in about a week. If you should not see him while he is at the eastward and north drop a line to him stating my wishes; believe me, my dear sir, whether successful or not in my application, the favour you could do me would be held in grateful remembrance as long as I live.

"I have the honor to be
"Respectfully Yr. Nephew
& Mo. Ob. S't.,
"R. Southgate Boyd."

The writer of the foregoing was a son of Capt. Joseph Coffin Boyd.

From an original bill made by Dr. John Merrill, Jr., against Hon. William King amounting to $19.00, I here make a transcript as follows:

1804.—— To $10, advanced to Miss Octavia Southgate by request of Gen. King, she being on a visit to Mrs. Lee & when she first heard of the death of a relative.

A Silas Lee, (Judge Lee) a man with strong Federalistic and Tory proclivities resided at the time in Wisasset, but I am unable to locate a relative of hers who departed this life
1804. Miss Octavia S. was a daughter of Dr. Southgate, who became the wife of William Browne, as have shown.

When Rufus King was a Minister at the Court of St. James he wrote his brother William as follows:

"London, August 4, 1802.
"Dear Sir: As I presume there must have been a failure of our communication upon the subject of the enclosed letter, I do not know that I can better than to send it to you. I know nothing of the writer, and am equally ignorant of the transaction to which he refers.
"With compliments to your wife, although you did not inform me of it, I have heard that you are married to an amiable woman.
"I remain your affectionate
"Brother,
"Rufus King."
P. S. I have just resigned my mission and ask leave to return home next spring."
William King, Esq."

The following is a copy of a letter to James Gore King, the third child of Rufus King, while James G. was a student at Harvard college:

Cambridge, April 26, 1808.
My dear uncle: Having, during my stay of my brothers in Boston, by engaging in Parties with them, expended my annual receipts from New York, I do not now find it in my power to meet the payment of several bills. Having before this received many benefits through your bounty, I am again induced to trouble you to lend me have a hundred dollars which, you desire it), I will endeavor to remit as soon as I may be able. I would likewise beg of you not to disclose this, & by being good enough to reply you will greatly oblige, your affectionate nephew,
"James G. King.
P. S. My love, if you please, to ―* & rest of the family."

Young King was seventeen years one month of age when he addressed the "business" letter to his uncle, William King, of which the preceding is an exact copy, and all I confess that it was well done, whether or not it had the desired effect I cannot here state.

Nine years later he addressed his uncle William another letter upon a different line, but the real facts attending the matter I cannot give. The young man had evidently settled down to business pursuits. It is as follows:

"New York, Feb. 4, 1817.
William King, Esq.
Dear Sir: In answer to your letter respecting a steam engine, I have to inform you that Mr. McQueen, who is a manufacturer of steam engines in this city, & a man of very considerable intelligence & experience, gives me to understand that it would require for a boat of thirty tons burthen an engine of four or five horse power, and that it would cost, with an iron boiler, four thousand, and with

315

CONTINUED:

a copper boiler, five thousand dollars, complete and set up for operation in the boat. You will observe that in fresh water an iron boiler would be sufficient, but in salt water, a copper boiler would be required. As to draft of the boat, by increasing its beam, it need not draw more than fifteen inches of water.

"If the distance on which this contemplated boat is to ply be not over twenty-five miles, a horse-boat would probably answer every purpose, not costing more than half as much as a steam boat, either for first cost or for annual support. Many reasons besides might be urged why a horseboat should be preferred to a steamboat, one of which is the difficulty of repairing the machinery of a steam boat at your place. In any event be pleased to command my services, either in further inquiries or ordering the machinery to be made.

"Present me & my wife kindly to Mrs. King and all friends with you, & believe me,

"Truly yours,
"James G. King."

I learn from the history of Bath, recently published, that the first steamboat appeared in that place in 1818, that it was a small affair, side wheels and no deck, so it is safe to say that William King introduced the first steamboat to the waters of the Bath region of our State.

A letter to William King, Esq., from his nephew, James G. King, dated at New York Aug. 9, 1815, informs his uncle that his uncle's ship "Resolution" sailed on that day for Bath and one article on board of her is $2,000 in a keg, and that the receipts of the sale of sugar in New York amounting to some $5,000 was held subject to his (William King's) order.

Another letter dated Feb. 19, 1816, says: "Your vessels at Bath have been advertised several days but no application for them."

A letter dated Aug. 28, 1816, alludes to William King's vessel named "Ann" as on her way to Bath. Another dated at New York Aug. 17, 1816, and from his nephew, states that the "Ann" had arrived from Cork, and he had been obliged "to enter into Bonds, in your behalf, and in the penal sum of Twelve Thousand Dollars, that in case any of the aliens who came out in your Brig should become a charge, either themselves or their children to the Corporation of the City of New York within two years, you shall idemnify for the same."

Aug. 19, 1818. William King's nephew informs him that "In the course of a month I intend to embark for England, taking my family with me, having dissolved my business copartnership here and entered upon a new one with Archibald Gracie, Jr., my brother-in-law, for the conducting of a commission business solely at Liverpool &, New York, under the firm name of King & Gracie."

In January of the year 1821, Charles R. King, an elder brother of James G., acting under the advice of his uncle, William King, started in to secure the "Agency of the Spanish claims for New York and Philadelphia."

GRANDPA'S SCRAP BOOK

Week of Jan. 29-31, 1903.

THE KING FAMILY OF SCARBORO.

WILLIAM KING.

The First Governor of Maine.

By Leonard B. Chapman.

NO. L.

The last letter I find of James Gore King to his uncle, William King, reads as follows:

"New York, April 30, 1827.

"My Dear Sir: My father was last evening released from his protracted illness by death, and, as we trust, without suffering, for which, considering the utter hopelessness of his disease, we all feel grateful. He retained his intellect 'till within a few hours of his death and was sensible of the presence of all his children, except Edward, who is in Ohio.

"We all unite in affectionate remembrance to you and Mrs. King.

"I am always y'rs.,
"James G. King.

"The Hon. W. King."

Black sealing wax was used, and the embossment was a belt with a buckle upon which appears as follows:

"Recte Et Suaviter."

Within the belt the monogram, J. G. W., may be seen.

Red sealing wax was used by Hon. Rufus King as a seal to his letter to his brother William bearing date of August 4, 1802, at London, which I have quoted in full, and the stamp used contained a simple shield, shaped like the one that has been described by Marquis F. King, Esq., with a figure of a rampant lion but without a motto or other embellishments.

When James Gore King wrote his uncle William, February 4, 1817, relative to a steam boat boiler, which letter I have quoted, he used a stamp like the one used by William King on his finger ring. So it must be conceded that the "Coat of Arms" of the Kings of the district of Maine is a mere work of fancy rather than one of hereditary merit.

A COUSIN.

I have stated that William King appears to have had an uncle William King who was baptized in Boston, Mass., June 27, 1725, m. November 6, 1751, Mary Goldwait, he a mariner.

At Alfred, Me., December 21, 1826, there was mailed to "Hon. William King, Esq., Bath, Maine, a letter dated at Alfred November 29, and in substance as follows:

"Respected Sir: My circumstances and the cold season that is fast approaching plead my excuse for writing to you. I have often heard of your benevolent character and prosperity. I am a poor widow, advanced in years and my health is declining fast, so any assistance you may render me will be very acceptable. I have a room near the meeting house for which I have to pay rent and am obliged to buy my wood.

"I am the only surviving child of your Uncle William King. I feel the loss of your sister Southgate very much indeed, who was very kind to me.

(Signed). MARY SAWYER."

I cannot dispute the disclosure this old letter makes, and wish it contained more. If additional light is obtained I will again raise the curtain and exhibit the "find."

(A record of a family of which Miss Harriet Dummer, born at Hallowell, April 17, 1798, daughter of Jeremiah Dummer of Newburg, whose wife was Mehitable Moody of that place, may be seen on page 438, vol. VII, series II, Collections of the Maine Historical Society. Harriet became the wife of James Joseph Boyd, some of whose letters I have presented.)

TRADE PARTNERS.

William King's first business partner was his brother-in-law, Dr. Benjamin Jones Porter. The copartnership in mill and vessel building at Topsham continued till about the year of 1807. They engaged also in general mercantile affairs, exporting manufactured lumber of all sorts and importing all kinds of goods.

William King's next partners in business affairs were Peter H. Green and William Emerson, the last of Scarboro, and a son of Joseph Emerson, and a letter dated in that town June 26, 1806, and addressed to William King, lets in a little light upon the situation. It says in substance as follows:

"I learn you have it in contemplation to open a retail store in Bath, and express a desire to have my son William transact the business, and so receive a certain percentage of the profits. I have denied a flattering proposal from Mr. Kimball in his store as I need him in my own. Mr. Kimball is very much attached to my son, but for some special reasons I prefer that he go with you, as he is very much attached to Bath, and the inhabitants there express a favorable opinion of him."

(Signed). JOSEPH EMERSON."

October 4, 1813, the firm gave a large bond for import dues on goods from St. John.

The wording of the paper commences thus:

KNOW all men by these presents That we, William King, Peter H. Green and William Emerson, all of Bath, State of Massachusetts, Merchants, are held and firmly bound unto the United States of America in the sum of thirty thousand dollars, etc., etc., as the amount of duties ascertained as due on goods imported in the brig Margeutte."

A marginal memoranda declares the real value of the bond to be equal to $10,728.99.

Peter H. Green became a political lieutenant of William King's and played an important part in the politics of the town. William Emerson was there in 1829.

THE BATH CUSTOM HOUSE—1828.

John B. Swinton was collector of customs at Bath in 1828, and leased of William King for the "sole use of the

CONTINUED:

United States the southern room, or front of the lower story, of the long store on said King's wharf in Bath, being the same apartment heretofore leased to the United States for a Public Store, and to keep the same in good repair together with the adjoining wharf for the purose of reaching, storing and removing goods as specified in a former lease bearing date of June 1, 1825."

The consideration was seventy-five dollars, paid by the United States.

DOMESTIC AFFAIRS.

The following is a copy of a letter from the wife of William King to her husband, dated at Bath, March 17, 1823, and addressed to him at Washington, D. C:

"Yours, my dear husband, of the 9th inst., I received by this day's mail. All the week I am anticipating a letter from you and not to be disappointed when Sunday arrives is indeed a pleasure which your punctuality has of late afforded me.

"I am quite disappointed, however, in hearing you are not to return sooner than the first of April. Your absence already seems very long and as I have never been altogether reconciled to it, it is very hard to submit. I cannot relinquish the hope that you have miscalculated the time..

"Our darlings are quite well. I often take them out to ride, but do not let them go out of doors at any other time. Perhaps I shall make them too delicate, but I suffered so much when Cyrus W. was ill that I am unwilling to take any risk unless you are here to sanction what I do. Mary E. has been with me all day at meeting, behaved like a young lady, and improves in her appearance.

"Judge Hill called a few minutes on Friday. He had dined at Mr. Onnold's. Had I known your wishes I should have offered to have sent them home, but he observed they were in a great hurry, indeed, hardly gave me time to make an inquiry. Mrs. Hill did not call as it was storming badly.

"On Friday evening Mary, Joanna and myself attended a ball and supper at Col. Wingate's. It was very splendid. Perhaps you will think I had better have declined the invitation. I was some time deliberating but they were very urgent for me to come and requested the loan of many articles which I was pleased to lend. Indeed, my inclination decided the matter for I really wanted to see the customs of the fashionable world, but, although I am growing old and domesticated, I cannot forget that we have a daughter that in a few years will want to be introduced into society, and if I seclude myself now I shall at that time be totally incapable of performing the office. I hope you will tell me if I am wrong and what course I should pursue.

"Yours as ever
"Ann N. King."
(To be continued).

GRANDPA'S SCRAP BOOK

Week of Feb. 5-7, 1903.

THE KING FAMILY OF SCARBORO.

WILLIAM KING.

The First Governor of Maine.

By Leonard B. Chapman.

No. LI.

I am not able to state definitely the time William King located permanently in the town of Bath, but an original manuscript, now before me, of which the following is a copy, exhibits the earliest date thus far found:

"We have a Goose for Dinner on Thursday next, half-past Two and will You take a side Bone in Company with Mr. Greenwood, Mr. Davis &
"Your obliged very
"h'bl. Servant?
"Ja. Davidson.

"Tuesday Mor'g,
"26 November, 1799.
[To] "William King, Esq."

The chirography of the foregoing specimen is very feminine and neat in appearance.

Of the four characters appearing as above represented, Davis, King and Davidson, were business men, while Greenwood was a lawyer, of Bath, and James Davidson was, in 1790, of sufficient age to witness the signing of a will, and the following furnishes slight clues to their business careers:

"Bath, 5th Sept., 1803.
"For Value received, I promise to pay, Samuel Davis, or order, at the Lincoln & Kennebec Bank, in fifty-seven days, Thirteen hundred & fifty Dollars.
"Jas. Davidson.
"Dolls. 1350."

The mechanical part of the work of the foregoing is very neatly done by the same hand that prepared the written invitation I have quoted.

William King was president of the bank above noticed which was located at Wiscasset, where the note was paid.

Another paper accompanying those noticed above is as follows:

"Bath, April 2nd, 1807.
"William King, Esq.

"Sir: I now renew the assurance of a friendly disposition. It is far from my wish that further disagreements should exist between us and my only desire is that a fair and impartial distribution of the shares in the Insurance Company should take place. You cannot forget the conversation between us at the Theater in Boston; much less can you be unmindful of the solemn engagement made at your house since our return, that the business should be settled in a manner satisfactory to all concerned. From the conversation I have had with Mr. Wingate it seems to me that a plan has been made up that the assessment of the shares in the Insurance Company will be confined to the persons on your petition with those named by me as concerned in navigation & that no abatement of this decision will be made in favor of the other persons on my petition. It is necessary you should be explicit on this subject & that it should be in writing, in order that I may have no further uneasiness & be able to explain to those interested with me how they stand. I hope you will be disposed to act with candor. It is now too late to make any other arrangement than the one enclosed, which, if you approve of it, you will please to sign and return to me, otherwise I hold myself at liberty to take such steps as I may think proper.
"I have the honor to be with due respect, your most obt. h'ble St.
"A. Greenwood."

The paper Andrew Greenwood wanted William King to sign reads as follows, but as it is now before me minus the required signature, William King did not do as requested:

"Boston, Jan. 10, 1807.
"The subscribers having two several petitions for an Insurance Company in Bath, do agree to unite the same and that William King, Peter Tallman, [Dr.] Benjamin Jones Porter, Joshua Wingate, John Peterson, John Richardson, Mark L. Hill, Andrew Greenwood and James Davis be named in the act for incorporating said company, that the said Hill, Greenwood and Davis shall have the disposal of three hundred and thirty-three shares and the remaining six hundred and sixty-seven shall be at the disposal of the six gentlemen first mentioned."

As the town records of Bath, as I understand, the situation, were destroyed by fire, which town was incorporated Feb.-17, 1781, therefore, any item of history that has been saved is worth preserving in print, hence, I here present a copy of an official paper before me, as follows, which also exhibits the notice taken of William King:

"Bath, May 4, 1801.
"In Town meeting voted to Choose a Committee of fifteen to procure a preacher, when the following persons were Chosen, viz;
"William King, Esq.,
"Dummer Sewall, Esq.,
"David Trufant,
"Samuel Davis,
"David Ring,
"Jonathan H. Crocker,
"David Shaw,
"Joseph Hall,
"Edward H. Page, Esq.,
"Christopher Cushing,
"Laban Loring,
"John Ham,
"Dea. James Lemont,
"Thomas Crawford,
"Thomas Lemont.
"Attest, Christopher Cushing,
"Town Clerk."

The history of Bath informs the public that William King was united in marriage in 1802, with Ann N. Frazier, of Scarboro.

The William King Bible at Brunswick is silent upon the matter as it is upon the time Mrs. King was born. It gives the date of William's birth, but not that of his wife. It gives the dates of birth of their two children.

The Bath historian is in error.

William King was, according to the Boston, Mass., city records, united in marriage by the Rev. Peter Thatcher, October 1, 1800, with Miss Ann N. Frazier of Boston. Of the bride's rela-

CONTINUED:

tives I propose to refer later, as well as William King's family.

Before me is a communication, written in a bold hand, addressed on the outside to "Mrs. King, Bath, Kennebeck,"—"Bath, Kennebeck," being a common way of addressing letters to that place prior to the year of 1820. The letter is post marked at Boston, Jan. 15, but date of year is missing, and was fowarded by "SHIP," postage nineteen cents.

The inside reads as follows:

"Dear Madam.

"I beg leave to inform you that I have taken the liberty of sending under the care of Capt. Redman, a set of English Tea China, which I hope you will do me the honor to accept. They were chosen by Mrs. Logan, who, as well as myself, will be happy to hear that they meet your approbation.

"I remain,
Dear Madam,
Your Ob. Sr.,
"C. Logan."

INVITATIONS.

A few names of persons who invited and copies of styles of invitations I will present:

"Mr. Lenox presents compliments to Mr. King. Understanding he expects to pass through this place in a day or two would be glad to see him at 'Chadwick's Tavern' on business.

"Portland, Sept. 19, 1805."

A bill made on a piece of paper two inches square reads as follows:

"Portland, Aug. 8, 1808.
"Hon. William King, Dr.
"3 dinners, $1.26
"Children, .50
"Servant, .25
"Horse, .75
$2.76

Mr. and Mrs. King had no children of their own for quite a period after the marriage event, but they seem to have always had enough of some bodies to educate.

To be continued.

GRANDPA'S SCRAP BOOK

Week of Feb. 12-14, 1903.

THE KING FAMILY OF SCARBORO.

WILLIAM KING.

The First Governor of Maine.

By Leonard B. Chapman.

NO. LII.

Gov. Christopher Gore, of Massachusetts, had a peculiar way of signing his name—for "Christopher" he used the letter C, only, and for each letter required in "Gore," he used a capital. He was the Chief Executive of Massachusetts for one year, which was 1809, when he came to Maine to attend the fourth commencement exercises of Bowdoin college, and was the guest of William King. From his various offices held and law practice he had massed a great fortune. He was a rank Federalist, and his county seat was at Waltham. "He drove a coach and four with out riders in livery." His love for ostentation was disapproved at the ballot-box by the average citizen and at the second contest for the office of Governor he was defeated by Elbridge Gerry, one of the Massachusetts signers of the Declaration of Independence. The attentions showered upon Gov. Gore at Bath, Wiscasset, Brunswick and other places were numerous, William King, acting as Commander-in-Chief of the militia, ordering four regiments to parade at Brunswick. Two of Gov. Gore's communications in his own hand are before me as I write. (See Vol. V, Series II, page 71, Collections Me. His. So.)

John Brooks, LL. D., was Governor of Massachusetts from 1816 to 1823, and made a tour of the District of Maine in 1818, when he was a guest of William King. Following is a copy of a note of his in his own hand:

"Governor Brooks presents his very respectful compliments to General King & thanking him for his polite attention, will with pleasure submit himself to the disposal of the General while in Bath, on the single condition of being permitted to take quarters for the convenience of doing business the accommodation of his domestics.

"Medford, Aug. 27th, 1818."

A note from the Governor dated, "Council Chamber, Feb. 15, 1819," informs Gen. King that in consequence of bad weather "he, [Gov. Brooks] will defer the pleasure he anticipated from his company to some future opportunity."

Another note dated at Tremont St., Jan., 1820, is as follows:

The Lieut. Gov. requests the pleasure of Mr. King's Comp.' at dinner, on Friday 4th Feb'y next, at 3 o'clock. (No year given.)

"At a meeting of the citizens of Augusta held Aug. 9, 1821, Hon. Daniel Cony in the chair, and James L. Child acting as secretary, it was unanimously—

"Voted to unite in an invitation to the Hon. William King, the late worthy Chief Magistrate of this State, to partake of a public Dinner with the citizens of Augusta at Palmer's Hotel on Thursday, the 16th instant,—and Hon. Joshua Gage, John Davis, Henry W. Fuller, Robert C. Vose and Robert Howard, Esquires, were appointed a Committee to communicate with Governor King and signify to him the wishes of the citizens of Augusta."

The original paper contains the autographs of the entire committee, the secretary performing his part in a very creditable manner.

"Mr. and Mrs. Adams" [John Q. Adams] used generally an engraved steel plate in soliciting the company of Mr. King, dates of months appearing but not the years.

In the month of January, 1822, the "Gardiner Lyceum" was incorporated —a school "having for its purpose the giving to Farmers and Mechanics such a scientific education as will enable them to become skillful in the professions."

William King was a member of the Board of Trustees.

Oct. 1, 1823, one Mr. Gardiner invites him to come "up river," be present at a meeting, and "It would give us very great pleasure if you would take a bed at our house. Mrs. Gardiner hopes she shall have the pleasure of seeing Mrs. King."

Mrs. Gen. Brown, Mr. Hill, Mrs. Wirt, the wife of Hon. William H. Crawford, twice a candidate for the Presidency, and others extended invitations to dine.

Prof. William Allen, Pres. of Bowdoin college, often invited him to commencement exercises and to lodge and dine with the Professor, reminding Mr. King to "bring his wife, nieces and other ladies of his house."

Politically speaking Messrs. Allen and King were political bed-fellows, William King having but little use for persons who did not endorse his own political views, condemning every thing, always, he discovered, or even imagined, partaking of Federalism in the management of the college—even in the private walks of its professors.

In 1829, the excitement of the Presidential campaign was continued in the State, the two parties being both Republican-Democratic—one national, after Gen. Jackson—the other, sectional, after John Quincy Adams. William King espoused the half—for the party was that year in the state about evenly divided—with national views.

July 27, 1830, there appeared in the "Maine Inquirer," published at Bath, largely, if not wholly, under the control of William King, an article copied from the "Lincoln Intelligencer," published at Wiscasset, which fiercely assailed the Bowdoin college management for allowing one of its Professors liberty to go over to Wiscasset to atend a Hunton political meeting, because of its being of a sectional, or Adams-character—(Hunton being a candidate for Gov.)

"Knowing the institution has shared most liberally of the State's funds and that it is nurtured and sustained by the whole people."

Editorially the "Inquirer" approved of the article in the plainest of language.

Sept. 7, the "Inquirer" brought up the matter again and censured the "Brunswick Journal" for abusing the ' Inquirer," "Wiscasset Intelligencer" and "Portland Argus," particularly on account of placing the authorship of the article in question upon the shoulders of William King.

I have presented the reasons for Gov. King's coup de main in adding members to the Board of Trustees and Overseers of Bowdoin college. He seems in every act to have taken the necessary precaution to make his project a success.

GRANDPA'S SCRAP BOOK

Week of Feb. 19-21, 1903.

THE KING FAMILY OF SCARBORO.

WILLIAM KING.

The First Governor of Maine.

By Leonard B. Chapman.

No. LIII.

An invitation addressed "To the Hon. Wm. King, Bath," from the above named reads as follows:

"Gardiner, July 13, 1824.
"Dear Sir: The annual examination of the classes at the Lyceum will be held on Tuesday, the 20th. inst. at which time the Board of Trustees & Visitors will meet. We shall be much gratified if you can make it convenient to be present, and it will afford Caroline & Myself very great pleasure to have you for our guests while you are in town.

"You will please to present our respectful compliments to Mrs. King & accept assurances of the highest respect from

"Your very obt. servt,
"Benj. Hale."

"Caroline," Mr. Hale's wife, was a daughter of Hon. Cyrus King, hence, William King's niece, who resided in the family of her uncle William after the death of her father in 1817. She was christened by the name of Mary Caroline. The next in the Cyrus King family was named, Ann Frazier King, and she, too, resided with her uncle William. This was James J. Boyd's "cousin Joanna" whom I have not been able to locate till this hour. These are the names of the two Misses King that accompanied William King's wife to the Wingate ball. And it was evidently with one or the other of these two sisters that Joseph Fowler, a law student in the State of Connecticut, expressed, in 1818, a desire to correspond, whose letter I have presented. But as all these are to be noticed in detail later under the heading of CYRUS KING, I must here part company for the present.

By the will of Richard King, a third of his residence fell to the lot of his daughter Betsey (or Elizabeth) Lyden King who became the wife of Dr. Benjamin Jones Porter, and two-thirds to Cyrus King, his son.

The record of the disposition made of the house and lot by the grantees may be seen on page 506, vol. 111, Cumberland County Registry of Deeds, of Feb. 1, 1823. The consideration was $175—"Mary Caroline King, of Saco, to Lemuel Coolbroth of Scarboro, the same that was the homestead of Richard King, late of Scarboro, one third part of which I received [by purchase for $75] from Dr. Benjamin Jones Porter and Betsey (or Elizabeth) L., his wife, in her own right, and the other two-thirds part was assigned to me in the division of my late father, Cyrus King's estate."

On February 21st, of the same year, Coolbroth conveyed the premises to Asa Milliken on payment of $175; and in 1828, Milliken reconveyed to Solomon Harford for a consideration of $125, whose heirs retain the lot and the one story ell, the two story part having become much out of repair was taken down some fifteen years ago.

Over the name of the builder of both the one and two story parts and date of construction of the habitation where Richard King closed his eyes to the scenes of Dunstan Landing hangs an impenetrable veil, and the pilgrim finds but little of an ocular nature to compensate for a journey hither.

SHIPPING.

William King was twenty-five years of age when he built or made or purchased a vessel if the records are correct. This was in 1794.—a schooner of ninety-four tons burthen and she was built in the town of Brunswick. Her name was "Minerva." I say this was his first purchase because this is the earliest date his name appears upon the Bath custom house records. Other dates when his name appears there as owner of shipping are as follows:

1793—Sch. Minerva, 94 tons,
    Built at Brunswick.
1795—Ship Adrastus, 232 tons,
    Built at Topsham.
1795—Sch. Guardian, 124 tons,
    Built at Topsham.
1797—Brig Ferdinand, 155 tons,
    Built at Topsham.
1794—Brig Androscoggin, 133 tons,
    Built at Topsham.
1800—Ship Reunion, 281 tons,
    Built at Bath.
1801—Brig Valerius, 137 tons,
    Built at Bath.
1803—Ship United States, 301 tons,
    Built at Woolwich.
    In 1811, Richard King Porter, William King's nephew, was Captain.
1804—Ship Reserve, 394 tons.
    Built at Woolwich.
1806—Brig Huron, 173 tons,
    Built at Bath.
    Richard King Porter, Captain.
1807—Ship Resolution, 353 tons,
    Built at Bath.
1808—Brig Perseverance, 232 tons,
    Built at Topsham.
1808—Brig Harmony, 194 tons,
    Built at Topsham.
1810—Brig Ann, 266 tons.
    Built at Bath.
1815—Brig Visitor, 210 tons,
    Built at Bath.

In the year 1800 Messrs. William King, Dr. Benjamin Jones Porter, who was William King's brother-in-law, and John Richardson owned a schooner by the name of "Nancy," John Lane, Captain, who was long in the employ of William King and who at last on a bribery fee of $40 caused Mr. King much trouble, but of this I propose to speak later.

Before me is a clearance paper of the schooner "Nancy" dated at "Berbric, Oct. 4, in the fortieth year of His Majesty's Reign," which shows she was 106 tons burthen "mounted no guns" and "navigated with four men." Connected with this is a paper showing that on Dec. 4, 1800, goods to the amount of £96 were furnished "to enable the vessel to proceed on her way" and that £96 was then equal to "233 Spanish Dollars & 22 cents."

April 11. 1800, Dr. Porter writes William King that "on searching the Androscoggin' she is found very rotten in both planking and timbers" and advises her sale; that "at Grenardo boards are selling at 40 dollars, shingles 4.50, rum, 50cts." and "at Tobago vessels sell for 45;" and "at St. Vincent 55 dollars" [per ton.]

Feb. 7, 1800, the Doctor writes: "I am glad you have got some more insurance on the 'Orisis and Ferdinand.'" The Orisis I do not find on the Bath custom house list.

Again, April 24, 1800, "I am pleased to hear of the favorable market at which our ships have arrived." "The 'Nancy' cargo [of coffee] is landed." "The 'Ferdinand' is yet at Bath awaiting a favorable wind."

From Boston, Feb. 12, 1801, Dr. Porter writes: "The anchors for the new ship went from this place for Portland by Capt. Riggs. We have had some proposals for the ship from Mr. John Gore of this town. We asked him $13,000(?) Our friends think she would do extremely well at Baltimore."

Nov. 20, same year: "I congratulate you on the successful launch of the ship and safe arrival of the 'Reunion' at Liverpool, but I cannot do the same on the prospects of immediate peace between England and France for a great change will come to our carrying trade, I think."

At Topsham, Jan. 5, 1802, Dr. Porter again writes:

"I am advised of the safe arrival of the 'Confidence and Valerius.'"

"I stated to you in one of my last letters the sad misfortune to the 'Ferdinand.' Capt. Lane writes me from Trinidad, April 27, that he arrived there in 26 days from Wilmington, that the day after he sailed the brig sprang a leak which obliged him to keep both pumps going during the whole voyage, and was under the necessity of throwing off a part of the deck load, selling the remainder of her cargo for $250, the market being very poor at Trinidad. I hope you now have the 'Ferdinand' in Boston, where, I think it for our interests to sell her."

[To be continued.]

GRANDPA'S SCRAP BOOK

Week of Feb. 26-28, 1903.

THE KING FAMILY OF SCARBORO.

WILLIAM KING.

The First Governor of Maine.

By Leonard B. Chapman.

NO. LIV.

Under date of Dec. 29, 1804, Dr. Benjamin J. Porter writes: "I have sold the 'Ferdinand' for $3,500; that the report of her condition affected the brig, it was believed a crew for her could not be obtained; and Capt. Lane was so staggered at her condition he offered me $50 to be released from going to sea in her again."

At Boston, Nov. 6, 1807, Hon. Christopher Gore, who became Governor of Mass., as has been stated, writes William King how to proceed relative to a vessel of William King's that had been captured and confiscated—going into port, supposing the blockade to be off.

From Boston, Aug. 24, 1808, John B. Frazier writes to inform his brother-in-law, William King, of the arrival of the brig "Valerious" and sale of her cargo, at that port.

A "Bill of Lading" signed at Savannah, Ga., by Capt. Robert McKown, May 12, 1810, shows what was required for a load for the "good ship 'Resolution' " at that time and place, as follows:

"302 pitchpine logs.
"241 boards and plank.
"22,287 hogshead staves.
"1,907 headings.
"23,500 reeds, for the account and risk of Mr. William King of Bath, a nation citizen of the United States.

This load was for the Liverpool mart.

Oct. 7, 1813, William King purchased in Boston, Mass., a half of brig "Margarette" for which he agreed to pay the sum of $1,775, "now registered at the Port of Boston and Charleston."

It appears the vessel was built in 1808 at Newburyport and was registered by the name of "Latonia," that at the time of disposal the name was changed. She was a vessel with "two decks; two masts; seventy-seven feet and nine inches long; breadth twenty-three feet; depth eleven and one half feet; measured one hundred seventy-eight tons; a Brig; has a square stern; no galleries and no figurehead."

On the 29th of April, 1814, William King purchased a half of the brig "Henry built at Bowdoinham in 1811, for which he paid two thousand dollars. She was "87 feet long; breadth 24 feet; depth 10 feet and measured one hundred ninety tons."

As this memoranda is made from official papers, it can be relied on as showing correctly what vessels, comparatively new, sold for ninety odd years ago.

In 1816, the ship 'Resolution" was in commission, as was the "Huron" and "Reserve", and all standing on the Bath custom house records in the name of William King.

From a letter dated Savannah, Ga., Jan. 2, 1811, it appears that ship "United States" was at that port loading with lumber for Liverpool, "that the demand for lumber is the greatest I ever saw," "that the 'Resolution' is here, throwing out balast, that six of his men have deserted and the great number of ships here makes seamen scarce," "that timber is ready for her to begin upon."

"The 'Reserve' is here and taking on a load of cotton, but as laborers are scarce only our crew can be worked."

From Bermuda, March 5, 1811, a letter, of which the following is a copy, was written to William King. I present it entire. The author was Capt. Robert McKown.

"Gen. King.

"Sir: I have to inform you that we had misfortune to spring a leak on the 27th of February in lat. 34-27 and long. 71-36 We could not free her with both pumps. We cleared her decks but the leak still continued. On the first of March we began to clear her between decks, as we thought she would fill and the cotton would blow up the deck. We got out about one hundred bags of cotton, and on the 2nd of March came to anchor on the east end of this island and got eight hands to pump on the 3rd and 4th. We had then a heavy gale of wind which we rode out with both anchors ahead. This day we have got into the safety port of the town of St. George. If it is possible to find the leak without unloading we will get from here soon as possible. If we have to unload her God only knows when we shall get off from here. We have as much as we can do with eight hands besides our own men to keep her up. If we had not gotten her here the day we did we should have filled as the water had gained about 3½ feet with both pumps going all the time as hard as we could work them.

"I remain, Sir, Your
Humble St.
Rob. McKown."

I have shown that in 1811, Capt. McKown was commander of the "good ship Resolution."

These old letters and papers are mirrors that furnish true reflections of events of the long ago which if not recorded now will be lost. I wish my space and time admitted of more and longer extracts.

It appears that in 1799 coal was shipped from Liverpool to New York as follows:

"SHIPPED in good Order and Condition by John and Adam Lodge, in and upon the good Vessel, called the Orisis whereof Tristram Redman is Master for the present voyage, now lying in the Harbour of Liverpool, and bound for New York, viz:

"Twelve tons, six hundred weight of Coals, loose.

"One hundred, seventy-five tons white Salt.
"Sixty-four Crates of Earthernware.

"The same to be delivered to Messrs. Porter & King, nothing being owner's property.
"Liverpool, Nov. 23, 1799.."

The name of this vessel, as I have remarked, I do not find on the Bath custom house list, but I do find to the name of [Dr.] Benjamin Jones Porter as follows:

1806—Brig Mercutor, 162 tons,
Built at Topsham.
1811—Brig Criterion, 138 tons,
Built at Brunswick.

To the name of Peter H. Green, one of William King's business partners, and political Lieutenants, I also find as follows:

1815—Brig Huron, 246 tons.
1815—Radius, 156 tons,
Built at Bath.
1818—Brig Transit, 199 tons,
Built at Bath.

To be continued.

GRANDPA'S SCRAP BOOK

Week of March 5-7, 1903.

THE KING FAMILY OF SCARBORO.

WILLIAM KING.

The First Governor of Maine.

By Leonard B. Chapman.

NO. LV.

In December, 1808, congress decreed an embargo, the design of which was to call home all American vessels and sailors and keep them at home not only as a retaliative measure upon England and France but to prevent destruction of American property, but the measure was found to be ruinous to American commerce and the public became rebellious, so, in March, 1809, congress repealed it, but a year later, "non-intercourse" with Great Britain was again proclaimed by President Madison, and in June 1812, war with that country was declared by congress, and Great Britain pronounced all our ports as closed to the world, and stationed her war ships to enforce the decree.

The public has now nearly outgrown all traditional recollections of the events of that far off period, and written history refers to the scenes only in a general manner, so when anything is found reflecting light, though ancient, there is a freshness about it that is exhilarating to those sufficiently aged to live in the past.

Before me are several scores of letters written by sea-captains, merchants and others of many places between the years of 1800 and the autumn of 1814 when the treaty of peace between Great Britain and the United States was promulgated, that have not till now seen the light of day for half a century;—printed documents, too, exhibiting the manner politicians cut each other up, that is, their reputations,—men who were the best of the times; (outside of love for office) governors of states; congressmen; court judges; editors of newspapers; custom house officials, hurrying to Washington and there dealing in criminations! How this government has existed is indeed a mystery!

I should state, perhaps, in order to be exact and cause the foregoing paragraphs to be correctly understood that the proceedings of the period of 1800—1814 by some of William King's sea-captains was the foundation of his political troubles between the years of 1820 and 1830, when there was exciting and exasperating rivalry between individuals and combinations for political supremacy. That he was a live participant in the latter condition there can be no doubt, but of the former I am not so ready to advance an opinion. He was largely engaged in the carrying trade and a large owner in navigation, as I have shown; governmental edicts were numerous, some of which were difficult to be understood as the English "orders in council," and communication was slow. Vessels were caught from home when ports of entry were interdicted, and then the temptations to evade were great, and the "sin" looked upon as comparatively small. As the scene now presents itself at this far off point of observation, when the profit in handling merchandise was so large and the rates of carrying so great the owners of a vessel who did not improve the golden opportunity was a "sinner" against himself rather than the general public. Some had the courage to sail their vessels and the faculty of obtaining the necessary custom house papers that afforded protection to some degree in most cases, one of whom seems to have been William King, who, evidently, when called to an account, always seemed to have had a ready and convincing reason for his acts—convincing to his friends if not his political enemies.

A vile political weapon from 1820 to 1830, was a "deposition," which was an exparte statement made before a magistrate and sworn to—a most dangerous thing a century and less ago, when the average citizen was less informed than now, and when magistrates' commissions were furnished as political rewards for services rendered successful candidates for State governors, seven hundred of such, William King claimed, was issued by one Massachusetts governor in the course of a year.

Another weapon of attack was a political pamphlet containing a collection of copies of "depositions" arranged with much ingenuity and scattered broadcast. Some are now in existence; one is before me as I write; and the part relating to Mark L. Hill of Lincoln county, who became a Judge of a court of Judicature, a Member of Congress and collector of the port of Bath, reads like romance. He was the boon companion of William King. His residence still remains in the town of Philipsburg, where a monument covered with inscriptions may be seen, eight miles from Bath. A memorial of him should be prepared in detail.

Concerning anonymous political missives Judge Wm. Pitt Preble, while a Member of Congress, wrote Mr. King as follows:

"I never read these infernal pamphlets."

Perhaps I have presented enough to explain Mr. King's connections with mercantile life and magnitude of ownership in navigation, but so much remains unsaid that from my point of observation seems instructive that I cannot refrain from a little further presentation of extracts from business letters, as most seem interesting in a general way.

From Belfast, Ireland, under date of Nov. 4, 1800, one John Cunningham writes as follows:

"Owing to the two last crops in this country failing, our government has issued a Proclamation prohibiting all distilleries from working in this Kingdom, in consequence, spirits of all sorts have undergone an astonishing change in price, such a change I never could have had an idear of, so, on receipt of this, you can purchase two hundred puncheons of such Jamaica rum as that which was on board the 'Ferdinand,' provided it can be shipped free under one dollar per gallon. This you know is 33 cents more than the last lot. You will have it as strong as possible and of good flavor, as the weakest pays the same duty here as the strongest."

"Liverpool, Dec. 24, 1800.

"You, no doubt, before this, will be apprised of the advance that has taken place in all kinds of timber in consequence of the Emperor of Russia having declared war against this Country by which we are deprived of the principal source of supply for this article. The proceeding has caused a great advance in the price of all timber and all sorts of naval stores."

The contents of one paper commences as follows:

"Bath, Me., Dec. 11, 1801.

"An agreement between the Master, and seamen of the 'Brig Valerius'"—the year William King purchased her—, the captain being named Robert Harding, the crew consisting of a mate and six seamen.

Another as follows:

"Boston, Mass., Aug. 26, 1802.

"Ship 'Confidence' (standing in the name of Messrs. King and Porter,) in account with Eben L. Boyd," whose wife was a sister to William King's wife. Boyd was a commission merchant. The name of this vessel I do not find on the Bath custom house list.

To be continued.

GRANDPA'S SCRAP BOOK

Week of March 19-21, 1903.

THE KING FAMILY OF SCARBORO.

WILLIAM KING.

The First Governor of Maine.

By Leonard B. Chapman.

NO. LVI

In 1806 an insurance of $8,000 was put upon the ship "United States." The premium was $800 for a year.

In Cork, Ireland, April 7, 1807, Messrs. Lecky and Mark wrote as follows:

"We wish to appraise our American friends that by a late regulation our government seems determined to put the navigation laws in full force with respect to neutrals bringing goods to this country not the actual products of the country to which they belong; we therefore recommend our friends at your side not to ship any goods not the actual products of the United States as such goods in future will not be permitted to entry, but must be bonded for exportation."

"Norfolk, Va., April 9, 1807. "Your schooner 'Eagle,' Capt. Woodward, arrived here this day after a passage of thirty days."

The name of "Eagle" I do not find on the Bath custom house list.

May 7, 1807, ship "Vigilant," "drawing 12½ feet of water, Robert Bosworth, Captain, from Charleston, S. C.," was piloted "from Point Linas through the Rock Channel into the Port of Liverpool," for which service the sum of £6.11.3 was paid. The little well preserved paper containing the record is now before me.

The name of "Vigilant" as well as that of "Eagle" I do not find on the Bath list.

From Baltimore, Md., April 28, 1807, William King was informed by Capt. Robert Harding that for $5,500 he had sold at auction his ship, as she was too large for the West India and too small for the European trade, but Capt. Harding fails to disclose her name. The Captain continues: "I have set my heart on the new ship, but if she is gone before my return home and you should conclude to build another that will do. I think a ship of 280 to 300 tons of easy draught and an easy sailor that will take 800 bales of cotton, and will not draw over 13½ feet of water, the best."

A letter in William King's own hand, dated at Bath, Nov. 29, 1808, and addressed to Matthew Cobb of Portland reads as follows:

"Sir: The ship owners in this quarter of the District of Maine consider a meeting of those persons concerned in commerce desirable at this time for the purpose of consulting and advising as to the best mode of explaining to the Government the true situation of our commercial interest in this section of our country.

Such a proceeding is rendered more necessary at this time on account of the many propositions before congress, any one of which if adopted cannot but effect the persons engaged in the lumber business (in particular) very injuriously, as the business will neither pay the expense of a circuitous rout to a market nor of arming in defense.

"As it is intended that this meeting shall not be influenced by party considerations at all, it has been proposed that as many names from one of the political parties as the other shall be made use of in calling the meeting, which is suggested shall be held in Brunswick early in December, and it has been proposed that two gentlemen at Portland, two at Kennebec, two at Wiscasset two at Brunswick, two at Topsham and two at Bath shall be designated to call the meeting, and that the persons designated shall be of different political creeds at each place.

"Should you, sir, and your friends think favorably of the proposed meeting, will you permit your name to be made use of for the purpose of notifying the same with others to be hereafter named?

'Please let me have your answer as soon as convenient for should anything be done on this line no time should be lost.

I am, sir, respectfully
Your Obedient Servant.
"William King."

The outcome of Mr. King's proposition as above indicated I have no means of knowing.

From Portland, January 12, 1809, a petition signed by a committee consisting of seven of the leading merchants of the town was addressed to William King, which commences as follows:

"Sir: The undersigned in behalf of themselves and others beg leave to address you upon the subject of their misfortunes. Being involved in difficulties and embarrassments from which they cannot entertain the most distant hope of being extricated without the interference of the state Legislature of which you are a member, is the only apology for troubling you."

The petitioners continue at considerable length, and make their troubles known. They were ready to surrender every cent of their property, but they wished to retain unincumbered their credit, but what action was taken I cannot state.

A letter dated at Liverpool July 7, 1809, informs Mr. King that his ships "Vigilant" and "Huron" are ready to sail for Boston, and the "Reserve" and "Reunion" will also sail soon, and "we have put up the 'United States' for Norfolk, Va."

I have presented the family connections of Capt. R. King Porter (Richard K. Porter) and stated that was a nephew of William King.

I have stated also that in 1806 Capt. Porter was in command of the brig named "Huron," and that in 1811 he was in command of the ship named "United States." In 1806 he was twenty-two years of age, and there was indeed an air of smartness about him that time. He made repairs on his uncle's vessels when in foreign countries that his uncle would not in this which gave his uncle no little vexation of spirit on account of expense incurred. Before me are twenty letters he wrote beginning Feb. 8, 1807, and fifty-seven letters written and other documents prepared by Dr. Aaron Porter, his father, between the dates of June 23, 1799, at Biddeford, and Sept. 5, 1832, at Portland.

In one the doctor states that he is the administrator on his father's estate at Boxford, Mass., which tends to show the location of his native town.

Jan. 22, 1813, after the doctor had moved from Biddeford to Portland he made for William King, from whom he was expecting pecuniary aid, an inventory of his estate "as estimated in January of 1811," as follows:

"In Biddeford, lot, building, fruit trees and two acres of land,	$1,000.00
"Farm, 250 acres, @ $10,	2,500.00
"House and lot by Maxwell's,	1,500.00
"Nursery trees and chaise house,	500.00
"Ship yard,	1,000.00
"Carpenter's house and land,	400.00
"Wm. Perkins' house and lot,	500.00
"Stephen Perkins,	200.00
"Smith house and garden,	400.00
"Three acres salt marsh,	50.00
"Twenty dogs in two saw mills on Saco Falls, @ $100,	2,000.00
"Stacy house and garden,	100.00
	$10,000.00"

Then follows a long list of farms and buildings located in different places, including a half of the Boxford, Mass., farm, estimated at $3,000, and debts due him, amounting to a total of $85,964.00.

He then shows in detail that in 1811, before the war commenced, his rents amounted to $1,150 in Biddeford and his half of the Boxford farm $200 more, but in 1813, in consequence of the war there was general poverty, and he was circumscribed on every side, not being able to collect a cent from his practice, or sell a square foot of farm land.

To be continued.

GRANDAP'S SCRAP BOOK

Week of March 26-28, 1903.

THE KING FAMILY OF SCARBORO.

WILLIAM KING.

The First Governor of Maine.

By Leonard B. Chapman.

NO. LVII.

Capt. James Oliver writes William King from Liverpool July 8, 1809, as follows:

"I have had three men run away from the ship and one fall from the main top yard.

"On the morning of July 4 all the American ships in this port displayed their colors, and about one o'clock in the afternoon a mob hauled them all down, tore, carried away and dragged many of them in the streets. Luckily no American made any resistance or there would have been murder committed. In the evening the mayor called out his forces and cleared the streets of the rioters."

On March 16, 1810, Capt. Porter wrote:

"We have had a very severe gale of wind, and it lasted four days. About thirty sail of vessels were driven on shore which is in possession of the French and all were burned. There were eight Americans among them, the only one belonging to Kennebec was the ship named 'Commoner,' belonging to Hallowell, Capt. Colbourn. She was burnt.

(Signed) R. King Porter."

Again Capt. Porter writes William King as follows:

"Cadiz, Feb'y 4, 1810.

"Sir: It is now eighteen days since we arrived at this port, twelve of which we were in quarantine. Have not yet began to discharge. Everything is in such a fluctuating state it is impossible to do any business. The people are so alarmed at the reports that the French army is on the march to attack this place that there is nothing doing but preparing for a siege. Every lighter is in the employ of the government transporting troops, provisions, etc. There are at least twenty sail of American vessels in the same situation as my own. Many that have been unloaded ten days can get neither salt for a cargo or anything for ballast. The few last days we have reports that a part of the French army has advanced within thirty miles of this city, but I think it is a hundred away. There are a great many English merchants here and have large stocks of goods on hand, which they want to get away, but there are not vessels enough to carry what they want to get off.

"Your nephew,
"R. King Porter."

From a letter dated Cadiz, Feb'y 24, 1811, from the same to the same as the preceding, I have made a condensed extract, as follows:

"I have been here thirty-seven days and only a third of my cargo has been discharged. Government has purchased all the provisions in the place and so kept all the lighters employed. The French army has possession of all the country about here, and have command of the river. The army is only some three miles off—nothing but the Bay of Cadiz separates us. The army is said to be strong and every day increasing. King Joseph has been down and taken a peep of the situation. The place has been strongly fortified since I have been here, and may now be defended forever, if the inhabitants will consent to be cut off from the country which appears doubtful. As there is a strong English and Spanish fleet here there is no danger at present. There are now reports that Napoleon is advancing with powerful reinforcements, so think I shall get a good freight.

"Please inform my brothers in Bath that you have heard from me, if you receive this.

"R. King Porter."

The vessel it appears from further correspondence got away safely with a cargo of salt.

From Demerara, Aug. 8, 1810, Capt John Lane writes:

"I arrive here after a passage o forty-seven days. Sold my cows fo 72 dollars and took pay in rum and molasses. Sixty head of cows arrived before me and sold for 64 dollars each."

"Savannah, Jan. 10, 1811.

"The ship 'United States' has arrived here. Several freights have been offered but nothing that meets the approbation of Capt. Porter. The great number of English ships here and their extreme anxiety to get away before the first of February has caused the price of timber to advance to the enormous sum of $12½ per 1,000 feet and even at this price is scarce. I feel no anxiety for the ship on account of freight, as British vessels will not be admitted after the first of February, Americans will be wanted. It is settled that the existing law does not prevent the clearing for Great Britain after that period."

Thus writes a commission merchant at that place.

Under date of March 4, 1811, at Liverpool one of William King's captains, whose signature I cannot decipher writes him as follows:

"I arrived at this place after a disagreeable passage of fifty days and the loss of a man and a boat. There is more or less failures here every day, and I candidly believe if the non-intercourse law is carried out strictly, England must comply with our terms, for the merchants will all fail together. I should advise every American who has property here to make sure of it as fast as possible. There are now only wo or three persons whose credits are good."

A commission merchant at Liverpool March 9, 1811, informed William King of the arrival there of "your ship Reserve," but on acount of the enforcement of the 'orders in chambers' cannot state whether or not I can procure a return freight for her." He then expresses the hope that the "Ann" and "Reunion," two of William King's vessels then in port, "may be allowed to land their cargoes."

A few days later another shipping merchant sends out a circular letter from the same place, to his American friends, an extract of which reads as follows:

"Our Government has at last taken into consideration the distressed state of the commercial part of this country, and we have great pleasure in stating, a bill has just passed Parliament, granting six millions sterling to be distributed amongst those Houses who may require assistance. This liberal grant will be of the greatest service to the country, and in a very short time we shall undoubtedly see confidence restored and trade assume its former vigor."

On March 18, 1811, Henry Dearborn, (a well known character in history), then collector of the port of Boston, Mass., wrote William King as follows:

"Dear Sir: I have been informed that there are two respectable men who will, if required, testify that a large part of the cargo of your vessel was taken on board after the second of February; of course it will become necessary for me to seize the vessel.

"Youfs with esteem,
H. Dearborn."
"To Hon. William King."

This is the man who dominated the Federal party of Massachusetts, whose son-in-law, Joshua Wingate, Jr., wanted the office of governor of Maine in 1821 and again in 1822, or the father-in-law wanted it for him as the family of Dearborns held about all the monied offices of the state. It will be remembered that I have noticed Joshua Wingate, Jr., and may have occasion to do so again; and in passing I want to say there was the same love displayed seventy-five and a hundred years ago for office as now, or the evidences of a desire to succeed in the attempt was far more desperate then than now, and there was political bossism then as now, and the chief in this region was Willam King as early as 1811,—many facts to establish the truthfulness of the assertion being before me, only one of which I can use, as follows:

Abiel Wood, Jr., banker, politician and largest ship owner of his region of country, who was the grandfather to Joseph Wood, Esq., of Portland, editor of the "Maine Const Cottager," under date of Wiscasset, July 31, 1811, closes a political letter to William King as follows: "There should be more offices or less office seekers."

The extracts here presented, and many more I might present, furnish conclusive proof of the difficulty and hazard of doing a mercantile business during the "embargo", "non-intercourse," "orders in council" and during the time the war of 1812 to '15 was on. Much was left to the discretion of commanders of vessels, many of whom were very illiterate. The wisest under such a trying condition of unsettlement, laws and edicts made hastily, were liable to error.

Maine was largely interested in the ship building industry, having the men to construct, and material for use, near at hand and men to serve as sailors. William King's experiences were the experiences of the general public.

To be continued.

Week of April 2-4, 1903.

THE KING FAMILY OF SCARBORO

WILLIAM KING.

The First Governor of Maine.

By Leonard B. Chapman.

NO. LVIII.

It was January 25, 1795, when the petition of William King, Dr. Benjamin James Porter, who was his brother-in-law, and eighteen others for a bridge over the Androscoggin river at Brunswick, was approved by the state legislature. The act states that the structure must be "twenty-eight feet wide, beginning at the mill, called the Noyes' mill, in Brunswick, thence running to the middle rock of the river, and from said rock to the great rock, so called, below the great mill at Topsham." The proprietors were to collect toll of all patrons, a list of amounts to be collected accompanying the act of incorporation.

I have alluded to the fact that William King was chosen at an open town meeting at Bath, with others, soon after his location there, to procure a gospel minister.

A state legislative act establishing the Congregational society was approved February 13, 1804. I find but three names upon the petition, Dummer Sewall being the first. The name of William King does not appear.

A BELL FOR BATH.

Part of a business letter under date of November 10, 1805, written at Boston, Mass., by Messrs. Frazier, Savage & Co.—Frazier being a brother to Mr. King's wife—reads as follows:

"If Capt. Springer does not sail before tomorrow we shall send down a Bell for the meeting house, the weight of which is 1000 pounds. A larger one could not be obtained under three or four weeks, but we have agreed with Mr. (Paul) Revere that if the bell (altho' a good ton'd one) should not meet your wishes, he must receive it back again, and cast a larger one by your paying the expense of the same,"

"The first bell for Bath," the history of the town states, on page 469, "was placed upon the North church, and is now in use on City Hall." The bell shipped to Mr. King is more than probable the one to which the Bath historian alludes, and lacks a couple of years of being a century in age.

THE BATH ACADEMY.

March 16, 1805, the state legislative act incoporating the Bath academy was approved by the governor. The names of William King and Dr. Benjamin Jones Porter of Topsham appear with others. A condition was that $3,000 should be raised by subscription, then the state would appropriate a half township of land—a tract "three miles square."

The "Year Book" of 1831, page 77, states that the Bath academy had a land grant consisting of 11,500 acres, and the Female academy of the same place, incorporated in 1808, had another of the same size.

William King was a member of the Massachusetts State legislature when the boys' Bath academy was incorporated. A letter addressed to him reads as follows:

Bath, Feb'y 21, 1805.
"William King, Esq.

"Dear Sir: Your ship sailed this day. I left her abrest of Mr. Cobb's mills, under whole sail and a good wind. Clapp's went on Sunday; the tide was not very favorable and the Charterer having no confidence in the Pilot (Lunt), I went down with her myself. It was extremely cold.

"Col. Small has sent you the petition for the (Bath) Academy. It went on Monday last. I really hope it will obtain a handsome allowance from the Government. You may with safety pledge that the subscription hereabouts will amount to about $3,000. Here in Bath $1,000 will be received and in Georgetown and Woolwich the inhabitants are very fond of the movement, and will strain every nerve to accomplish the object.

"I am, Dr. Sir, your
"Ob't serv't,
"Peleg Tallman."

"N. B. I think if you were to write a subscription paper you might get considerable among your members.
P. T."

Peleg Tallman was a sea captain, who became one of the largest ship owners of the region, who dabbled in politics, being an ardent Republican—Democrat.

Another letter addressed to Hon. William King, October 9, 1818, "or to the Trustees of the Bath Academy," by the two gentlemen residing at Waterville, having in charge the Bath academy land grants, reads as follows:

"We have just returned from a visit to the Dead river and regret extremely to inform you that the timber there seems vastly different than it did at our former visit. Both in quality and quantity it falls exceedingly short. Of about forty trees cut by the appraisers and our men, many of them, the fairest which could be picked, not one proved sound, most of them being rotten both top and bottom. Though the land is marked 'first quality' by the surveyors, we feel confident we saw not over two hundred sound trees."

"Respectfully your ob't serv'ts,
"Asa Redington,
"Nath. Gilman."

(Asa Redington, L.L. D., was born February 4, 1789, at Vassalboro, and a graduate of Bowdoin college in 1811. He became Judge of the District court. residing at Augusta, and died at Lewiston, June 6, 1874, where he last resided.

AS A MANUFACTURER.

From Bath, November 30, 1809, a letter was sent William King, that read as follows:

"Sir: At the request of Dr. Porter, (Benjamin Jones Porter) I have been to Wiscasset to see Silas Lee, Esq., (a lawyer there) to learn if he would like to take a part with us in the Cotton Business, as there are about seven or eight shares not yet taken. He wish'd me to leave the Subscription paper with him until next Sunday and in the meantime he would see his friends in Wiscasset and endeavor to get it completed. He will be at your house on his way to Portland next Monday and leave it with you, and I will call for it on Tuesday. I was obliged to stay at Mr. Joseph Day's at the Ferry last night, owing to the river being so full of ice, and as he could not make change for my expense I left it unpaid. If he should call on you before Tuesday I will thank you to permit Mr. Emerson (Mr. King's clerk) to pay him the sum due, which is ninety cents for myself and horse.

"Yours most Respectfully,
"Jas. S. Simmons."

Following the preceding, next in order of the material before me, is my memoranda of the state legislative act of incorporation of the "Brunswick Cotton Manufacturing company, March 4, 1809."

The building erected, which was on the Brunswick side of the falls of the Androscoggin river, at that place was a wooden three story structure, where yarn only was manufactured from raw cotton for hand looms when weaving was a home industry, but according to tradition the enterprise was not a success in all respects, and the company was reorganized, and an application made to the state legislature for a new charter, which, was granted and approved by the governor October 24, 1812, the corporation adopting the name of the "Maine Cotton and Woolen Factory Company." The persons named in the act were Jonathan Page, Robert Eastman, Samuel Page, James Jones, Daniel Stone, Naham Haughton, David C. Magoon and John B. Swanton, the name of William King, for a wonder, not appearing, but the new company agreed to exchange with him a half share in the new for a whole share in the old corporation.

In addition to the letter presented in the foregoing, here is another dated at Brunswick, July 10, 1809—four months after the one I have presented, as follows:

"To Gen. William King:

"The Second assessment of 320 Dollars on your shares in the Brunswick Cotton Manufactory will become due on the 20th instant.

"Yours respectfully,
"Wm. Stanwood,
"Treasurer of B. C. M."

"P. S. A former assessment of 80 Dollars on your shares remains unpaid."

To be continued.

GRANDAP'S SCRAP BOOK

Week of April 9–11, 1903.

THE KING FAMILY OF SCARBORO.

WILLIAM KING.

The First Governor of Maine.

By Leonard B. Chapman.

NO. LIX.

The next letter I find is addressed to "Hon. William King, Merchant, Bath," and reads as follows:

"At an adjourned meeting of the Stock holders of the Brunswick Cotton Manufactory at Stoddard's Inn, Oct. 6, 1813—

"Voted—That this meeting be adjourned to meet at this place on Monday the 18th inst. at eleven O'clock before noon.
Nath. Poor, Clerk."

Sir: Above is a vote of the Stock holders of the B. C. M. at their last meeting.
"With considerations most respectful, your ob't humble servt,
Nath. Poor."

The following is a characteristic letter of William King, in his own hand. "Mr. Robinson" to whom reference is made below was Thomas D. Robinson, Mr. King's bank cashier and political lieutenant. The name of the person to whom addressed, the letter does not disclose.

"Bath, March 23, 1814.

"Sir: Mr. Robinson observes that he has repeatedly notified you to pay the note given on account of the Factory
" am confident unless more attention is paid to this business that no note will ever pass at this Bank with your name upon it—and further, I am confident that no one ever ought to.— A note was handed to the Directors the last discount day to take up your old one, and the ten per cent has not been paid. I think the Directors will take up the business this day and no doubt they should order the note to be sued, and I can only say they will not do their duty unless they do.
"Yours,
William King."

"Brunswick, August 30, 1815,
"I, the subscriber, hereby certify that William King has this day bought at public Auction One Share in the Brunswick Cotton Manufactory, numbered fifty-nine, for thirty-one dollars and fifty cents.
"Samuel Davis, Treasurer."

"Brunswick, Jan. 12, 1817.
"Received of William King Eleven hundred and twenty Dollars in full for an assessment on thirty-two shares in the Brunswick Cotton Manufactory." [The whole number was sixty and his numbers are given in the receipt.] "Said assessment laid Oct. 2d. last."
"Saml. Davis—Treas."

It appears by public records that William King sold, in 1821, his thirty-seven shares, which was the controlling part, to the "Maine Cotton and Woolen Factory Company," for $3,700.

The last notice served on Mr. King reads as follows:

"Brunswick, Aug. 10, 1824.
"Sir: You are hereby notified, that there will be a Statute Meeting of the Proprietors of the Maine Cotton and Woolen Factory Company, holden at their counting room in Brunswick, on the Tuesday preceding the Wednesday of September next, at 10 o'clock A. M., for the choice of officers for the ensuing year; also to transact any other business that may legally come before the meeting.
"By order of the Directors of said Company,
"A. Bourne,
Clerk of the Maine Cotton and Woolen Factory Company."

"GREAT FIRE IN BRUNSWICK."

(Portland Argus, Dec. 16, 1825.)
"An extra sheet from the Herald office at Brunswick of Tuesday last gives the following account," which was copied by the Argus:
"Thursday evening, Dec. 13, at eleven o'clock a. m., the fire broke out. It caught in the Cotton and Woolen mill, and in two hours the whole square from the factory to Demerits on the corner of Mill street was prostrate. The whole number of buildings burned were twenty-six, consisting of two factories, five dwelling houses occupied by eleven families, two stores, two saw mills, one grist mill, and a number of mechanic shops. Bath was applied to for assistance. The mercury was thirteen degrees below zero. The loss was $100,000."

I am unable to find a file of the "Brunswick Herald." It was short lived.

Of individual, or of William King's loss in particular, I have at present no means of knowing, but the mills were rebuilt, and are now in a flourishing condition though the water privilege is not half utilized, which is of the cascade order. Its appearance at times being of a sublime nature. And another thing that excites wonderment—is what induced the two young men, Messrs. King and Porter, to buy into the privilege and attempt such an immense structure as the toll-bridge must have been!

LAND SPECULATIONS.

Some two miles from Bath William King owned a tract of land called the "Rock House Farm," which he cultivated to quite an extent. The origin of the farm house, made of stones, or cause of its construction, is conjectural. I have been quite near but never close to it. One tradition is that the house was constructed by a club of Englishmen for a shooting gallery, but another and the more reasonable is that it was erected as a place of refuge during the war of 1812-15, should the town fall into the hands of the English. But I will not dwell on the matter and pass on to take up another matter equally as difficult to comprehend, as follows:

"Know all Men by these presents that I, W. King of Bath, in the County of Lincoln, Esquire, hereby constitute and appoint James White of Dorchester in the County of Norfolk, Esq., [no state named] my attorney for me and in my name to surrender to the Treasurer of the New England Mississippi Land Company, ten of the Scrip or Certificates of the Trustees of said Company, numbered from 1083 to 1092, both inclusive, for ten thousand acres each amounting in the whole to one hundred thousand acres of Land, with full power and authority to receive in lieu thereof all the Dividends of the United States Stock, called Mississippi Stock, which may be due thereon conformably to the decree of the Commissioners of the United States and the settlement of the affairs of the Company by the Directors thereof, sanctioned by said Company with power also to give release and discharge to said Treasurer, which may be necessary and usual * * * *
" In witness whereof* * * * *
this tenth day of June, 1816.
"W. King."

"Signed, sealed and delivered in presence of
M. J. F. Wingate,
W. R. Porter."

The document is in the hand of Mr. King. He seems to have had but little use for lawyers, doctors or ministers.

To be continued.

THE KING FAMILY OF SCARBORO.

WILLIAM KING.

The First Governor of Maine.

By Leonard B. Chapman.

NO. LX.

Whether or not William King originated the idea of his becoming a great land proprietor or simply came into a movement with the object in view as a second does not appear sufficiently plain from the data at hand for me to state definitely nor does the date appear when he and Messrs. Moses Carleton and Abiel Wood, "both of Wiscasset in the County of Lincoln; Samuel Dana, of Groton, County of Middlesex, and Commonwealth of Massachusetts, Esquires, and William King of Bath, in said County of Lincoln, Esquire," purchased "No. 3 Range I, Bingham's purchase," located in what is now Franklin county, this state, twenty miles northerly of Farmington, comprising territorially what is now known as the town of

KINGFIELD

and, perhaps, a part of Lexington and Concord; as Mr. King owned later a large amount of land in these two towns, the three towns comprising a line running East and West.

The four were business men of large practical experience.

1—Moses Carleton, Esq., was a lawyer at Wiscasset. He died there in 1857, aged 90 years; his wife died there a year before, aged 93 years.

2—Hon. Abiel Wood has been briefly noticed. He was born in Wiscasset, a son of Abiel Wood, who was a Brigadier General, 11th Div. 1st Brig. of Me. Militia. Abiel, Sr., died March 1st, 1814, aged 54. Abiel Jr., was a Federalist, represented Wiscasset in the Mass. Gen. Court in 1807-11-16. He was opposed to the war of 1812-15 and was sent to the U. S. House of Representatives in consequence in 1813, where he served one term. He was cashier of the Wiscasset bank, owning at one time over $20,000 in stock. He was a delegate to the convention that drafted the State Constitution, in 1819, and was appointed by Gov. William King as one of his councillors. He was a bank commissioner, and died at Belfast while on an official visit, Oct. 25, 1834, aged 62 years. (Another record says Nov. 2).

His residence, then unoccupied, was pointed out to me last year at Wiscasset.

3—Samuel Dana was born in Groten, Mass., June 26, 1767. His father was Rev. Samuel Dana of that town, a liberal Congregational clergyman, but meeting with trouble growing out of his views relative to the war of the Revolution he quit the pulpit, studied law and became a lawyer.

Samuel, Jr., became a lawyer also, and had a large practice in Groton and vicinity. Samuel Emerson Smith who became Governor of Maine, in 1831, was a law student of his in 1813, as was Luther Fitch of the Portland Municipal court.

Samuel Dana, Jr., held many offices. He was Chief Justice of the Circuit court of his district from 1811 till 1820; a member of the Mass. Legislature, both house and senate, member of Congress in 1814, Presidential Elector in 1820, and died at Charlestown, Mass., Nov. 20, 1835, to which place he had removed, after the death of his wife which was the year before, on May 11, there having appeared in the last years of his life a lack of fixedness of purpose in his business transactions.

Thus the associates of William King attempted to settle the inland tract of land the location of which I have alluded, but the following, which is a copy of an interesting original letter before me sheds additional light upon the nature and history of one of Mr. King's associates in the attempt to create a town in the wilderness of the District of Maine, as follows:

"Boston, Mass., July 15, 1811.

"My Dr. Sir—I was sorry that your affairs required you to leave this place so soon after the Legislature rose. I wanted one whole day with you free from interruptions. I wish I could refrain from reviewing the expressions of a sentiment with which I have too often troubled you, namely: my own future prospects as to property. I do not represent myself to you as an indigent or dependent man, far otherwise, but yet, looking forward, beholding around me a wife who from the disparity in our ages is likely to survive me, six children to whom I have given existence and must provide for, besides the pleasure which results from the contemplation, that I may be in a situation when I need not labor for my daily bread, is not (in my mind) a small care.

"Could I be dismissed from all public employment & left to work exclusively for myself six years, I believe that I should not fear for a future subsistence; but I am now told (excuse the vanity of the suggestion often made to me) that I must go into the newly created Court or it will wither & die, or pass into the hands of Federalists. If this is so, surely, as much as I may relent, I ought to go upon the Bench in which case my yearly earnings from all sources would not exceed $2,000.

"This day I have received from Mr. Gray, (Hon. William Gray, one of the rich men of Mass. and twice State Governor) as chairman of the committee a communication addressed to Messrs. Bond, Tuttle, Bridge, Varnum and myself authorizing us to obtain subscriptions to the State Bank to the amount of $200,000. You will probably have a similar one, but not having seen my associates I do not know what is to be done. Why I address you is to learn whether I cannot in an honorable, honest & correct manner derive some personal benefit from it or in some way make some money from the Bank. And I now ask your advice & direction. You will not think it more than I have a right to claim from our long & I can say very sincere and fervent friendship. You must be as particular as you may deem necessary for my understanding. And give me an answer as soon as your leisure will permit.

"As you are in weekly receipt of newspapers from this place you know all the news I have. Accounts from all parts of the commonwealth give the Legislature a most excellent character.

* * * * * * * *

"With the highest regard,
"I remain yr's,
"Samuel Dana."

The town of Kingfield is 5½x7 miles square. Through it, from North to South, runs the Carrabasset river, a stream of rapid moving water, sufficient in quantity to supply power for twenty mills. The forests at the time of settlement were of rock maple and other hard wood trees—of soft wood, mostly spruce and hemlock. Along the river the soil was good, but back from the river it was sandy and unproductive, the northerly part mountainous.

The settlers were adventurers without money. The first one I cannot name.

Mr. King seems to have been the "head center" in the enterprise. He held the "power of attorney." Bonds for land titles were given and notes received, the price agreed upon was from fifty cents to two dollars per acre, time for payment, five years, payments quarterly with interest.

Before me are ten of the original bonds, signed and dated at "Kingsfield" in 1815. When the first settler located I cannot say. The "State Year Book" states the town was settled about 1806, and was incorporated Jan. 24, 1816, when the letter "s" was left out of the name. Nathaniel Dudley seems to have been Mr. King's first agent. Some of Mr. King's letters to him with two sketches of the man are printed in the "Maine Historical and Genealogical Recorder," Vol. I, pages 95 to 106. The first from Mr. King is dated, Bath, February 24, 1813, at which time Mr. Dudley was building a mill.

Under date of March 18, 1816, Mr. King writes his agent a letter from which I here present an extract, as follows:

"I cannot refrain from stating to you the satisfaction I feel in common with the Republican-Democrats generally at the very great changes which have taken place since I last saw you.

"Vermont commenced by a thorough change of men. New Hampshire has now followed her example; it can truly be said that Federalism falls in the same proportion as the country rises. As there is not, perhaps, a nation in the world at the present day that has a higher standing than our own among the nations of the earth, we are, therefore, to conclude that we are to have very little more opposition from Federalism after the present year."

October 15, 1815, Joseph Knapp received a bond for the "easterly half of lot No. 2, in the sixth Range of Lots in said Kingsfield,for Knapp's promissory notes for $100, to be paid in quarterly yearly payments within five years with interest."

September 30th, 1819, Joseph Knapp conveyed his title for a "valuable consideration" to Rufus K. J. Porter, son of Dr. Benjamin Jones Porter, hence a nephew of William King.

(To be Continued.)

GRANDAP'S SCRAP BOOK

Week of April 13-25, 1903.

THE KING FAMILY OF SCARBORO

WILLIAM KING.

The First Governor of Maine.

By Leonard B. Chapman.

NO. LXI.

It was October 11th, 1817, that William King informed Nathaniel Dudley, his agent at Kingfield, that his nephew, Rufus K. J. Porter of Topsham, intended to engage in farming and was about to start for the wilderness of Kingfield for the purpose of selecting land, and then added: "As he is very little acquainted with the business of clearing wild land, I think, if you can obtain the improvements of a good piece reasonably, it would be better for him than to take a tract entirely new. A farm on the intervale would be, I think, most likely to please him. I wish you would look round with Mr. Porter and so let me know what improvements can be had and at what price."

Rufus K. J. Porter was, in 1817, when he went to Kingfield, eighteen years and one month of age. When Joseph Knapp conveyed his land and improvements to him, for "a valuable consideration," he was nineteen years and eleven days of age. In 1820, he was united in marriage with Miss Ruth, daughter of Joseph and Eunice (Carver) Knapp. For the half lot, located about a mile westerly of the village, improvements, and a story and half house, which was burned some years since, William King paid Joseph Knapp $500.

In addition to the cares of his own farm, young Mr. Porter seems to have been in the employ, as an agent, of his uncle, William King, and besides, he purchased the improvements on other tracts of land. With his uncle he had a long account who charged him, October 25, 1825—

"For 100 merino sheep,@ $10, $1,000
"For 50 merino lambs, @ $5, 250
"For 60 mixed, @ $5, 250
                                    _____
                                    $1,500

The sheep raising branch of farming there does not seem, from the data before me, to have been a success. Great results were expected from the merino breed, so much so that such men as Hon. Samuel Dana engaged in the enterprise, but only to meet with disappointment and loss.

Before me are several of young Mr. Porter's letters addressed to his uncle at Bath and marked "Free—" signed "Rufus K. J. Porter, P. M.," and forty-seven from other persons residing in Kingfield, together with a few from Anson and Lexington, the earliest dated 1815, the latest, 1834, from which I propose to present a few gleanings—the whole, if they could be printed, would be interesting reading for the residents of that region, if not the general public.

"Kingfield, Oct. 18, 1815."

It appears that at this date a mill had been built on the stream passing through lot "No. 3 in the Third range of lots," when the lot was conveyed to Solomon Stanley, Esq., with a half of the mill privilege, reserving for the proprietors the other half and "all the necessary accommodations on the shores on each side the Falls for mill conveniences, with the necessary road ways to the mill," for the sum of $100, $25 of which amount to be paid each year with interest.

"Kingfield, Dec. 28, 1816.
(From William King's agent.)
"Agreeable to your directions, I have attended to your business and have taken notes of settlers to the amount of $2,200, which will be forwarded the first opportunity. There are six or seven more I have not seen.

"Esquire Stanley, or as some term him, 'our Smuggled Justice'—a term for which I cannot account—says he 'cannot sell his claim on the mill privilege to advantage with your restrictions, but the inhabitants of the town generally want you to adhere to them.'
"Nathaniel Dudley."

"Kingfield, April 26, 1817.
"To William King, Esq.
"Necessity calls loud for your attention. Your neglect in sending the balance of your tax ($38.32) has caused me trouble. The town of Kingfield is laboring under many embarrassments which must be remedied. Our circumstances, on account of unforeseen expenses, as a town, are very distressing, and must so remain till after the harvest.
"Simeon Knapp, Collector."

"November 4, 1819.
"I am disappointed in receiving money so I cannot pay Esquire Stanley the $350 as I agreed to at this time for the mill, unless I get assistance, therefore I make this statement to you, as you have a large interest in the town, and now own the one half.

"The price was $500. I had $150, which I paid over, and have repaired the mill. Perhaps you can think of something that will answer the very thing I have mentioned.
"Thomas Butler."

September 11, 1819.
Thomas Fillebrown, blacksmith, for $130 transferred his claim to a certain lot of land located on the westerly side of 'Seven mile brook,' in Kingfield, to Esquire Stanley, Luther Hathaway and Tristram Norton, which, in 1822, went to William King for a "valuable consideration."

"Kingfield, Apr. 10, 1822.
(Young Mr. Porter to Wm. King.)
"Dear Uncle: The saw mill is now doing business and goes remarkably well, but there is an unaccountable want of calculation in Stanley's management. I called on him several times and named to him the necessity of the mill's being employed and he has often stated that he would commence sawing in a few days. The mill, however, has done but a very little till within a few days. Half of the logs might now have been sawed but seven-eighths remain untouched. The saw from Bath would not answer the purpose so got one from Anson.

"There are at the mill 250 pine logs besides numberless spruce and hemlock, nearly one hundred of which belong to me.

"The grist-mill remains in the same condition as when you were here last fall.

"I wrote you that about eighty acres of trees had been felled and got in readiness for fire, and I had discharged the hands.

"I find difficulty in obtaining seed—hay-seed in particular, and should more trees be felled, the difficulty will be increased. The trees adjoining the felled piece, should the fire get among them, would cost more to prepare for the fire, as the under brush would be burned as well as the hollow trees, and, when felled, the fire would go through the ground again.

"Hay-seed is so scarce that I am obliged to promise cash for 400 pounds at ten cents per pound. I am now employed in getting out fence stuff to secure the sheep but shall commence soon in jerking in the felled trees.

"The sheep are not doing well in consequence of being kept too close, and too many in a flock.

"The cotton cloth you name is in good demand, and if you could send some cheap broad-cloth twenty per cent could be made in paying off the help here.

"I am in need of two hogsheads of salt, two quintle of fish, a half barrel of molasses and an ox-cart. If you can send all to Waterville I can go there for them. I want for the saw-mill about forty pounds of board nails and the same amount of shingle nails.
"Your Nephew,
"Rufus K. J. Porter."

"Kingfield, July 24, 1822.
"I shall be unable to make arrangements with all the settlers respecting their crops. If you are here three weeks before the corn is disposed of you can manage matters as you please.

"I sowed on the burn 23 bushels of wheat, 3 of rye, 10 of oats, planted 80 bushels of potatoes, (seed ends) 2 bushels of corn and one of beans.

"I shall need an advance of $100 to pay off the help.
"The carding machine does very well, and Mr. Little is very well satisfied with the situation.
"Your Nephew,
Benjamin K. J. Porter."

Before me, next in order, is an agreement, signed May 28, 1823, between William King and Nathaniel B. Chadbourn, in the original writing by which it appears that William King agreed to "erect a Bark House, and prepare the necessary pits, with a Bark Mill, in a suitable place within the Town of Kingfield, and advance $600 for hides towards stocking the yard." Mr. King was to have six per cent for the investment, Chadbourn to do all the work, and the two to divide the profits.

GRANDPA'S SCRAP BOOK

Week of April 30—May 2, 1903.

THE KING FAMILY OF SCARBORO.

WILLIAM KING.

The First Governor of Maine.

By Leonard B. Chapman.

No. LXII.

"Kingfield, Sept. 24, 1827.
"Dear Uncle—The saw and grist mill are doing about the same as last year, Mr. Little says 'he shall have as much wool to card as he can handle the present season.' Mr. Chadbourn is atending to his tanning business and will finish some of his upper leather soon. I expect to finish clearing the dry land in my cut-down this fall; the remainder, which is wet, next spring.
"Affectionately, your Nephew,
"Rufus K. J. Porter."

"Kingfield, Nov. 28, 1828.
"Mr. Bradbury arrived at this place on the thirteenth. He left the lame ox at New Sharon. I am sorry that you did not send up a better team; there is not more than one yoke fit for logging.
"Lemuel Bartlett."

"Kingfield, March 25, 1829.
"I got through work in the woods the last day of February. The snow got so deep it was not profitable to stay longer.
"We got in 1137 logs which will make 606,039 feet of boards. Your team arrived here the 17th inst. The snow is now as deep as any time this winter.
"I called on Mr. Brooks according to your directions and he said 'he could not get the money.' I then called on Esquire Stanley and he said 'he had made arrangements with Esq. Norton to pay the note sometime this season.' So I did not get any money of either, therefore I must borrow some to meet expenses.
"Lemuel Bartlett."

"Kingfield, March 14, 1829.
"When you were last here at Kingfield you will recollect I gave you some account how your business had been managed.
"Now, as respects the proposition you made me to stop on your place, I will inform you that I would be pleased to stay if I could do it with safety to myself, but I find myself and property continually harrassed from a most inveterate enemy who regards neither principle nor the law. You know something of the injury I have suffered, and it is becoming worse and worse. A few days since my young horse was taken in the night time and all the hair was sheared from his neck and tail. What will be done next I cannot tell.
"If you do not come up soon I wish you to write me what business you want me to attend to, for Mr. P. is pretending that he had orders from you to manage your affairs.
"If you wish me to put up a barn on the farm as we talked last fall I wish to know it so I may get the frame before the snow is gone.
"Abraham Smith.

"Kingfield, Nov. 30, 1829.
"I think six shillings per day for a man to survey lumber high wages, but if you cannot get one less it must be paid.
"I have been to Farmington and purchased 1800 lbs of pork and 70 bushels of corn at six shillings per bushel, but can get no more at these prices. As I am obliged to pay money for our supplies I wish you to send me $50. If the weather should hold cold we shall go to the woods next week.
"Lemuel Bartlett."

Kingfield, Jan. 18, 1830.
"Your lumbering business at Spruce stream is lively and a success. Your neat stock is in good order and without loss of cattle, or sheep. It is very probable you will have hay enough too for your stock.
"Edward Dudley."

"Kingfield, February 20, 1830.
"Your teams at Spruce stream are to leave camp in one week from today by order of Col. Berry, your agent. They say they have cleared the lots there.
"One of your oxen came to his death in the supply team, which Bradley drove, by eating too much provinder at one of the camps.
"The stock under my care is well—no deaths or sickness among the sheep, thus far this season. Your Merino sheep at Otis' began to die off some time ago, and 'tis said they are very poor in flesh. When I write you again shall give you a more particular account of Tom Otis and his management in regard to your stock and farm he occupies if you wish it.
"Mr. Webster wants to know what you will do with him about the tanning business as soon as possible.
"Edward Dudley."

"Kingfield, June 30, 1830.
"Your directions about the hides came to hand duly and the team was sent according to directions.
"The wool was as follows: Merino and common, 540 lbs., 80 lbs. of which I received from Otis. Of the common, about 200 lbs, making four packets, sent to Augusta by team. I have three black fleeces and 17 pounds pulled wool which I can get worked at the halves.
"Your hemp seed I received and prepared six acres of the best tillage land and sowed in drills in due order, but unfortunately the seed has proved to be poor, or damaged, so not more than one in fifty came up. When I discovered the trouble I seeded the land to oats.
"The Porter farm is not yet disposed of. I have sowed five or six bushels of wheat there and nine bushels of oats, and planted an acre of potatoes and repaired the fences. The prospect there for hay is slim, the fields having been grazed so severely in the spring the last few years. Otis left there the 10th of May. I presume you have not heard of his keeping the products of the place and pretending the place did not raise anything, that he did not keep the buildings in repair and that he converted the fence stuff to his own use, etc., etc.
"Your receipts from the Granary, by me put up, is 133 bushels for the logging concern and some before I was employed.
"To boards sawed, according to Lane's account, ninety thousand.
"One-fourth of all the toll from the clover mill is six hundred pounds.
"Mr. Chipman, who is engaged here for you by the month at present, will take the Porter farm at halves, provided you will make some repairs on the buildings. He will take 100 or 150 of the sheep and a half-dozen of the cows, a yoke of oxen, some of the farming tools, pay half of the taxes, etc., according to the custom here. He has a family and appears to be a steady and fair minded person.
"I will inform you that I have put a man on my place at the halves and I have moved to the mills, so devote my whole time to your interest, with as much economy as I am capable.
"For labor I am paying one half in grain and the other half to go on the interest account of land purchases.
"Breadstuff from the mill, the product of the cows, and what can be gathered from the fields will go far towards boarding the farm help.
"Edward Dudley."

"Kingfield, June 30.
"I have gone on with your business according to your wishes. I have hired four men by the month and have cleared off the choppings, sowed thirty bushels of wheat, ten of oats, planted eight acres of corn and three of potatoes, all of which appear to be flourishing.
"We are now repairing the old barn, and next week expect to put up the new one.
"In consequence of managing the farm this way, I have been obliged to buy supplies and seed and now am under the necessity of asking you for $35.
"I would like two barrels of flour, twelve to fifteen bushels of corn, one barrel of mackerel, two hundred of dry fish, one barrel of molasses, and nails and irons for building what you may think necessary.
"Your affairs here in general are prosperous, and your land is selling fast. Nine or ten applicants for lots this spring.
"Abraham Smith."

"Kingfield, May 28, 1832.
"I have contracted for the floor plank and have them stuck for seasoning. Mr. French is preparing the hard wood.
"We have succeeded in repelling the assaults of the bears by trapping the ringleader and compelling his associates to flee to a more distant forest. Mr. Page, upon the Butler farm, is progressing. The young Blanchards are cutting bushes.
"Ed. Dudley."

"Kingfield, June 13, 1832.
"I have succeeded in finishing planting, which in a common season would be considered very late, and am now working out your road tax which is $60.
"I have sowed ninety bushels of seed and planted five acres of corn and potatoes, having spared no labor with the plow and harrow.
"There are ninety of the common sheep with twenty lambs. This flock has decreased less than any flock hereabouts.

GRANDPA'S SCRAP BOOK

Week of May 7-9, 1903.

THE KING FAMILY OF SCARBORO.

WILLIAM KING.

The First Governor of Maine.

By Leonard B Chapman.

NO. LXIII.

"Kingfield, September 18, 1832.
"Mr. Luce has been absent about a fortnight, during which time the channel through the ledge has been cut and abutments built. All the necessary preparation for the floom has been made and Mr. Luce has returned for putting in the same. 'Tis highly probable the mill will be started in about four weeks.

"I am engaged in harvesting the thirty acre piece, and am quite successful in obtaining laborers without paying much money in advance. The part requiring the sickle will be completed today.

"The two young Pullens wish to purchase some land on the usual terms. They would prefer a lot with a small house on it and something else done. Will you say what place they may have with price set?
"Ed. Dudley."

"Kingfield, Oct. 3, 1832.
"Since I wrote you last a trench has been cut to the pan, or ledge, and layers of timber put down backed by a thick, heavy wall from the abutment to the extent of seventy feet westerly, and planked sufficiently to prevent the water from flowing into the mill yard front of the mill in high freshets."

The account of what was being done on the mill was continued at considerable length, then a description of the farm work was indulged in, which I omit. The letter continues as follows:

"Mr. Brett is still solicitous to learn if you will let him have the Wing house, to be moved onto a spot where he can repair it to live in, while he is building one; if not he will be under the necessity of moving out of town as he has no place for his family. As he has furnished a considerable amount of timber and has quite a bill for blacksmith work done for the mills, and on farming utensils, there would be no risk in accommodating him. He is a good mechanic and has a promising family.

"Mr. Washington Pullen wishes to take half or all the place which J. Johnson is on. He can have Johnson's right for $25. There is no prospect of Johnson's ever paying you.

"Mr. Moses Mills wishes to purchase the hundred acres adjoining the Maston place, upon the northerly side. He wants it for a pasture, and is able to pay for it.

"Mr. George Peterson wishes to purchase the easterly half of the hundred acres which Ira Durell is upon and will pay down a pair of steers worth twenty-five or thirty dollars.

"Mr. Chas. Pike wishes to purchase the building spot adjoining himself, upon the bank westerly of his including the blacksmith shop which he owns upon your terms stated. He would like thirty or forty acres of land above Norton's, on the east side of the road.
"Edward Dudley."

"Kingfield, Oct. 18, 1832.
"Probably the corn mill will be started next week. A new cleanser was found to be necessary, which is being built. Mr. Brooks is repairing the fulling mill. Mr. Blanchard will commence repairing the clover mill next week. I found the abutments upon the east side gullied out by the great freshet and employed Mr. Judkins to make the repairs. The young Blanchards are making wall and have four of the working cattle, and Page has one yoke, which makes my team scant. Another yoke is absolutely necessary.
"Edward Dudley."

"Kingfield, Oct. 31, 1832.
"The mill is in operation and grinds with very great despatch. It is presumed that not a mill within the State of Maine can be found that can compete successfully with it. It grinds a bushel of old, hard corn in a little less than five minutes. The cleanser and bolter required more attention than I expected. The flour mill is not quite completed. The fulling mill is in operation.

"The work upon the farm progresses each day agreeable to your directions.

"The Messrs. Blanchard are making wall. Mr. Page upon the Butler place is not inclined to divide any part of the crop at present, and evidently not at all, excepting the hay, if he can prevent it.
"Edward Dudley."

"Kingfield, February 5, 1833.
"If my charge for labor for the days when I should have been at rest the past year is illegal, and my services unsatisfactory, surely, I am not entitled to reward, and cannot of course make another engagement, but if you think I have been faithful, and merit the pay received and due me then I will engage with you another year upon the following conditions—namely:

"'Independent of any restrictions imposed by any person excepting yourself, I will occasionally labor, and manage your stock and farming interest for the sum of twenty dollars per month (boarding myself) from the first day of April next till the following last day of November, with the privilege of boarding the laborers whom I employ to work with me at the rate of one bushel of wheat per week, or nine shillings in money. Your answer solicited within one month.'
"Edward Dudley."

"Kingfield, March 17, 1833.
"Dear Sir. I have not received a reply to my letter, nor anything whatever from you respecting my continuance in your service after the last day of this month. As you have the conditions stated in writing, 'twould be exceedingly interesting to me to know the determination to which you have arrived, that I may be at liberty to arrange my own affairs.

"I completed in due time all the thrashing of grain intended for marketing. The oats reserved for seed in the old barn I delayed a spell for the purpose of getting the new barn clear of straw, but the work will be done this week and the straw fed out to the cattle.

"The stock is in good plight. The sheep have gained in quality since winter commenced. You will have, 'tis probable, a good deal of hay to summer over.

"I did not think to make engagement with you for a little necessary supply of bread-stuff when you were here, if you can do it please write me at once.

"Probably among the many enquiries relative to affairs here in Kingfield you have been informed of an indictment issued against me by the Grand Jury on complaint of Tom Otis & B. Foster, for defending myself against an impudent and violent assault by Otis sometime last summer, at which time an examination was had before a Justice of the Peace selected by both parties when an acquittal was ordered.

"Last Thursday I attended at Norridgewock a session of the Court of Common Pleas and after a little plea was made by the county attorney and reply by the Def't the case was given to the jury who, after some time, reported 'not agreed,' but receiving some further instructions retired again, and after much discussion returned a verdict against the Def't, whom the Judge discharged with a fine of five dollars only. The jury were divided upon the question of personal defence, and decided that it would have been more proper on the occasion for the Def't to have used the Yankee fist, or the Irish Shillaly, than the dirk. It was made to appear before the court that Otis made an assault and battery upon myself in the street while I was engaged with a small knife in whittling, in consequence of which he got in some degree whittled himself before he could be induced to break his clinch and stand back a little.

"Respectfully, your humble serv't,
"Edward Dudley."
"To Gen. King."

I have alluded to Nathaniel Dudley, Esq., who acted as William King's agent at Kingfield. He went from Mt. Vernon to the Plantation of Kingfield, going from Raymond, N. H., to Mt. Vernon about the year 1800. The above noticed Edward Dudley was probably Nathaniel's son.

March 1, 1858, from Boston, Mass., Deane Dudley, born in Kingfield, a grandson of Nathaniel, Deane residing in Bath at the time of William King's death (1852) sent to the Franklin Patriot, at Farmington, a very interesting short article for publication. It may be seen on pages 95-98, vol. I, of the Maine Historical and Genealogical Recorder.

To be continued.

GRANDPA'S SCRAP BOOK

Week of May 14-16, 1903.

THE KING FAMILY OF SCARBORO.

WILLIAM KING.

The First Governor of Maine.

By Leonard B Chapman.

To be continued.

NO. LXIV.

"Kingfield, April 22, 1833.
"Mr. Peabody commenced plowing this morning the large field southerly of the barn, [which shows the season to have been very early that year.]
"The cows that Mr. Dudley had last year I have let out for a year at $5 each. I have hired C. B. Butler and Wm. K. Dudley to assist Mr. Peabody for nine months at $12 per month, most of the wages to be retained by you on account (of land rent.)
"Mr. Bourne wants to work for you at $13 per month and turn it in on his land notes. He wants to work on the place at the Mills.
"Mr. Johnson commenced on the mill on the 8th. It is now mostly framed, but will not be raised at present for fear of freshets.
"Samuel Usher."

These old letters give a lucid idea of life in the region of Kingfield at the time of writing them, and suggest the question, "Upon what did the laborer subsist when only $13 per month was received and the amount to go to pay for land notes?" Bad as Ireland.

Kingfield, May 13, 1833.
"The saw mill was raised the 30th of last month, and you have the best frame you ever had at this place.
"I have hired Mr. Abbott and Mr. Clough to work with Mr. Johnson for six shillings per day till the mill is finished. I cannot hire good men for such work for less money where they owe you.
"We have been visited with a heavy wind and many buildings are injured. Your tan-barn will require in consequence a new roof and shingled with short shingles.
Your barns will not hold half your hay this year as you have much left over.
"Mr. Gould has returned the second time from Canada and has not got any money. What will you have done with the oxen and cow he had of Mr. Thompson?
"I have hired Mr. Otis' second son for $10 per month and have it turned in on his notes.
"Samuel Usher."

From Kingfield, June 1st., 1833, Ira Blanchard informed "Mr. William King, Esq.," that Mr. Gould would not give up the oxen so he has purchased a fine pair of five-year-olds, measuring six feet and two inches, for $65.

"Kingfield, June 5, 1833.
"I can get a barn frame put up, 40x60, for $150. The timber must be hauled four to five miles and this is a busy part of the year, hence the extra cost. I will put it up for $130 provided I can have your carts as I have none of my own. The timber I should, at this price, cut on your own land where it can be found. I will turn one half on your land bills.
"The saw mill will be finished this month, and what will you have done with it?
"Will you let out any of your wool on shares as several persons have applied?
"Samuel Usher."

Kingfield, June 10, 1833.
"Everything is promising. The sheep have wintered well and have thirty lambs—Chipman's flock have thirty more. The old house Mr. Gower lived in I have taken down to get plank to plank the mill flume, for the walls were all covered with plank.
"Samuel Usher."

"Kingfield, July 25, 1833.
"I forwarded your letter to Stephen Landers but he does not conform to your requirements.
"Peabody commenced haying last Monday in the large field. The grass is all that can be made on the ground. Your barns will not hold more than half the hay and grain."
"Samuel Usher."

My supply of information relative to the settlement of Kingfield and what transpired there obtainable from old letters ceases at this date, but we will look at the town with Concord and Lexington added through a manuscript prepared by William King, and is in his own hand, but without date. It is a sort of inventory of his land possessions in the region of Kingfield, as follows:

"Valuation of land in Kingfield."
"5,030 acres unimproved.
"7,574   do   do
" 425   do owned by town.

"13,029 acres @ 50 cents, $6,514.50
"10,385 acres, (say) ———   3,000.00
                              ————
                             $9,514.50

"Valuation of Land in Concord, No. 1, 1st. Range."
"1,819 acres of wood Land.
" 911   "   unimproved.
"13,592   "   "
" 1,976   "   "

"18,298 @ 50 cents, $9,149
        Deduct,   1,000
                             ——————
                             $8,149

"Valuation of Land No. 2, 1st. Range."
" 1,053 acres unimproved.
" 515   "   "
" 1,280   "   "
"20,000   "   "

22,848 acres @ 50 cents, $11,424
            "Deduct, $2,000
                             ——————
                             $9,424

The town of Concord was incorporated Jan. 25, 1821.

The town of Lexington, March 4, 1833, but February 24, 1885, not being able to maintain a town organization returned to that of a plantation.

To be continued.

GRANDPA'S SCRAP BOOK

Week of May 21—23, 1903.

THE KING FAMILY OF SCARBORO.

WILLIAM KING.

The First Governor of Maine.

By Leonard B. Chapman.

NO. LXV.

Mr. King had also large land possesions in the town of Anson, located a little southerly of the towns I have mentioned but manuscript communications from these towns are less numerous than from Kingfield, but are equally or more interesting. The first is dated, Anson, Jan. 3, 1820, and is very long, from which I will present a few extracts.

"The last time you were here at Anson and Kingfield I expected to have seen you relative to some deeds of possession & Bonds I hold as collateral security for debts due me and wish your disposition more particularly now that there are various stories afloat about what you intend to do respecting your claims when the time of the Bonds expire, or, rather, perhaps I should say, what will be done. I will plainly state to you, Sir, the interest have in the persons in Kingfield, and wish you to have the goodness to inform me of what I must do, or how to manage so I may receive my pay, or be secure and your interest not injured. I have made a general rule, when parties owe me who cannot pay, and one great reason wry they owe me is on account of two cold seasons,) to take their land Bonds as collateral security and sometimes quit claim deeds, and unless a disposition to defraud is manifested, I wait in expectation of receiving my money sometime, but in no instance have I enforced my claims so as to compel settlers to quit the land.

"I am satisfied from what I know of the quality of the land in Kingfield that it will be in time the first farming town of the county and when the land is settled around in the adjoining wilderness that Kingfield will be a place of considerable business.

"I hope, Sir, you will excuse me for taking so much liberty in writing.

"I am, yours respectfully,
"James Dinsmore."
"Hon. Wm. King."

"Anson, May 18, 1823.
"I should like to have you notify me when you are coming to this place, as a number besides myself wish to see you upon business, particularly Capt. Rowe, the collector of Concord, who says he has been called upon two or three times, and has been obliged to borrow $20 on your account, while waiting for a remittance from you.

"I was at Kingfield a month since. The people there appeared very busy in getting in their crops. Mr. Porter was clearing land; your saw mill was going; your clothier was digging up stumps on the land southwesterly of Stanley's, and the worst I heard was that Stephen Wing's wife has another child born blind. Is there no way of helping these poor unfortunates? Why not propose to the State Legislature for aid as in cases of deaf and dumb?
"James Dinsmore."

"Anson, Oct. 23, 1824.
"I have just returned from Kingfield and Mr. Stanley wished me to write you concerning the mill, etc.
"There is considerable smutty wheat this season and the mill at Strong (Hunter's) has a smut cleaner and people are going there to have their wheat ground. Stanley suggests the propriety of getting one and making some other alterations to insure your share of custom, and wishes you to write him immediately. He has heard you do not intend to come up till the middle of November, and so is very anxious to know if you can oblige him with the money he talked about with you. His place is now under mortgage for $250 and he owes his brother's widow $900 for which she will take $250. One hundred dollars additional would clear him of debt and then he could mortgage the whole to you."

The foregoing is taken from a manuscript letter written by James Dinsmore to "Hon. William King." Mr. Dinsmore, after writing as above, launches into a "history of the politics of the county," as he terms it, but as he does not use the whole of the names of the persons to whom he alludes, the confidential exposures made are not of public interest, but the manner of conducting politics and assailing officeholders has not undergone much change in the eighty years last passed. Mr. Dinsmore closes as follows:

"I do not wish to resign the register's office unless I am sure of the clerk's. If I was only sure the Governor would nominate me if Gould is rejected I should feel safe in resigning. The Presidential question brightens even here in this dark region of [John Q.] Adamsites and there are daily additions to the Crawford party.
"Yours Respectfully,
"James Dinsmore."

"Anson, Jany 23, 1828.
Hon. Wm. King—
"Dear Sir: Capt. Rom called last Monday and informed me that Hilton and others had commenced taking lumber from your lands in Concord but he had not been up to see what they were doing. I considered on he subject a few moments and then took my horse and sleigh and proceeded forthwith to the scene of action where I arrived early on Tuesday morning I believe too early for Hilton, for the weather being extremely severe, he had not started with his team when I passed his house. When I arrived on your timber lands I found the roads excellent in every direction. I found Ebenezer C. Felkin and Cornelius Jackson near the line between lots No. 7 and in the 4th Range with four oxen and a good log on their sled which they had hauled about twelve rods when I met them; they proceeded about one hundred rods with the log after I passed them when they dropped it from their sled and left the woods with great haste taking their oxen and chains with them and I saw no more of them. I remained on the grounds four or five hours and according to my estimation saw about one hundred pine trees of the best quality which had been recently cut on lots No. 7 and good roads cleared to them. I put a private mark on each, although not particularly authorized from you so to do. I am informed that the Hiltons have purchased a public lot adjoining yours and that the lumber taken from your lands is to be hauled onto that belonging to the Hiltons and there left for the present. I saw 30 or 40 logs already placed there on which were evidently taken from your lands. I was also informed that a man by the name of Longly was engaged in taking lumber from your lands northward of No. 8 and hauling it to the Kennebec River. The Hiltons from Anson are again connected with Elisha—one of them went up to Concord with his team on Saturday last.
"Yours Respectfully
"E. Cobb."

"Lexington, June 10, 1833.
"There are a number of persons who are desirous of settling for their lands but I am not able to give out numbers for want of a Plan of the Town.
"I have sowed about fifty acres of wheat, and what I have sowed with oats and planted amounts to about fifty acres more.
"If I board your men I shall be under the necessity of having from you some supplies, which you had better send from Bath to Waterville, as you can purchase much cheaper than I can. I wish for three or four barrels of flour, twelve to fifteen bushels of corn, four or five hundred weight of dry fish, or some mackerel, and a small chest of tea.
"Our stock is doing extremely well. I am raising eleven calves.
"Abraham Smith."

"Lexington, June 29, 1833.
"I will inform you that the town has raised eight hundred dollars to be expended on highways. Your assessment amounts to two hundred and sixteen dollars, and mine to forty-five dollars.
"The town has accepted several new roads—one from Concord to Embden, one from here to Kingfield, one from the northwest part of the town to the county road, and one on the east side of Sandy stream, and your tax is divided among them.
"Respecting the farm, everything in general appears well.
"I have sold one lot of land in the northeast part of the town which begins a new settlement there.
"Abraham Smith."
To be continued.

Week of May 28-30, 1903.

THE KING FAMILY OF SCARBORO.

WILLIAM KING.

The First Governor of Maine.

By Leonard B. Chapman.

NO. LXVI.

I have alluded to a land grant made to the Bath Academy and presented some extracts from a letter addressed to the trustees of the school by Asa Redington, who had made a re-examination of the lot having in view its purchase, but his fact is not shown by the letter itself. His denunciation is so outspoken relative to the impressions he claimed he had received at the second examination plainly shows a "cat under the meal'" somewhere, but not visible without careful study.

It appears the lot was located on the Dead River, northerly of William King's Plantations.

Redington, otherwise known as Judge Redington, a Bowdoin college graduate of 1811, and LL. D., who died a rich man at Lewiston, was a schemer. For a period of two years he was the preceptor of Gorham Academy, commencing his labors there immediately after his graduation. Hon. Isaac Reed's first wife was his daughter. Mr. Reed was a shipbuilder at Waldoboro, and politician, whose name was used by the Whig party in 1854 as a candidate for state governor, when the united friends of the "Maine Law" and the "Know Nothing" party elected Hon. Anson P. Morrill and thus broke, in the State of Maine, the back bone of the Democratic party. Mr. Redington's second wife was the widow of Capt. Samuel Longfellow of Gorham, whose maiden name was Sophia Storer of Saco.

A letter from William King throws light upon the situation as follows:

"Bath, May 9, 1818.
"Nathaniel Dudley, Esq., Kingfield.

"Sir: The proprietors, or rather the trustees of the half township granted to the Bath Academy, have sold to Nathaniel Gilman and Asa Redington, Esqs., the half of said township. As these gentlemen are desirous of making a road to the land, and as it will be interesting to your town to have the road pass through your place, I hope you will aid these gentlemen in making the road, at least so far as to the extent of your town. And should you aid them a little farther, I have no doubt you will find it interesting to your settlement.

"Will you have the goodness to advise with your friends on this subject, so that such encouragement shall be given these gentlemen as will induce them to make the road through your place?

"I will thank you to name to these gentlemen a capable person to pilot their people in a route the best and most direct to the Academy lands.

"Respectfully your ob't servant,
"W. King."

Nathaniel Gilman's second wife was a niece of the wife of William King. Her maiden name was Miss Joanna Boyd. She resided in the King family at Bath. Mr. Gilman was a rich man who resided at Waterville and left a large family. He was intimately connected with the college there.

What became of Mr. King's great landed estate forms an interesting inquiry which I cannot with data at hand fully solve. When evidence appeared that his mind was yielding to the influences that produce mental dissolution in old age the management of his affairs was placed with Asa Redgton, LL. D., who, on the 5th day of November, 1851, at Hapgood & Brown's tavern at North Anson, sold at public auction thirty thousand acres of land located in the towns of Kingfield, Lexington and Concord. He was aided by Thomas D. Robinson, William King's bank cashier, political lieutenant and many years confidential friend.

When Messrs. Redington and Robinson made sales most of the Kingfield farm went to Mr. Amos E. Dolbier, whose wife is a grand niece of William King. Upon his purchase is located the village of the town—the village of Kingfield.

For a period of half a century Mr. Dolbier has been in trade in Kingfield and Farmington and on the 6th day of June next he and Mary Ann Porter, his wife, who is a granddaughter of Dr. Benjamin Jones Porter, will have spent fifty-eight years of married life together!

I have stated from information derived from printed reports that Kingfield seems to be, as regards population, on the decline, but from a statement just received which I cheerfully herewith present, am glad to learn the village is now more prosperous than ever before, as follows:

"KINGFIELD,
"Franklin County."

Twenty-two miles north of Farmington, at the terminus of the Franklin & Megantic R. R., on the direct route to the Dead River region, lies Kingfield.

Nestling at the foot of Mt. Abraham (3,587 feet high), on the banks of the Carrabassett River, and surrounded by limitless forests and fertile farms, it affords unsurpassed facilities for lumber manufacturing.

"The new Kingfield & Dead River R. R. makes easy communication with the famous sporting grounds of Dead River, and furnishes an outlet for the vast amount of white birch, of which this section surpasses that of any other part of the State of Maine, besides spruce and poplar in abundance.

"Already important industries have been established, giving employment to from one hundred to three hundred men. The Jenkins & Bogert Manufacturing Co. (capital stock, $50,000), manufacturing wooden novelties, have two mills, an enameling factory, blacksmith and machine shops, giving employment to nearly one hundred persons, and will immediately build an extension to their main building of two stories 56 feet long, making their main factory 36x141 feet.

"During the last two years the population has nearly doubled, several families having come from Massachusetts to make it their permanent home.

"There is a large hotel, four churches (two built in 1895), a good high school, a savings bank, located in the recently erected building of the Alhambra Building Co., in which is the law office of H. S. Wing, Agency of the Union Mutual Life Insurance Co., store, and K. of P. hall. A system of water works is proposed in the near future. Pure water is abundant, and the general health of the community excellent.

"One of the principal attractions to visitors is the old mansion of Ex-Gov. King, Maine's first Governor, erected in 1821, and is now in a remarkable state of preservation. The immediate vicinity of Kingfield furnishes a great variety of fish and game, being less frequented by sportsmen than the region beyond."

"POLITE ASSEMBLYS."

How far William King indulged in the pastime of dancing I cannot state. While a member of the Massachusetts Great and General Court at Boston, 1808, he received an invitation as follows:

Sir. The Managers of the Social Balls Request William King, Esq., to accept the enclosed.
Per Order,
Daniel Hastings, Sec.
Concert Hall, Feb. 16.

"The enclosed" is in print on paper 8x10 inches and reads as follows:

SOCIAL BALLS.

IMPRESSED with the necessity of the observance of order and propriety, in every polite assembly, the Managers of the Social Balls have adopted the following

REGULATIONS.

To which they request strict attention, viz.

1. Tickets, issued to Subscribers, are not, in any case, to be transferable;—and a gentleman will not be admitted before first producing a ticket.

2. Strangers may be admitted with the approbation of the Managers; but the subscriber who introduces a stranger, must pay to the Secretary five dollars for his ticket—and indorse the ticket. Strangers must be introduced to the Managers, in order that proper attention may be paid to them.

3. Drawing for places will commence precisely at 7 o'clock. The Lady drawing No. 1, First Set, will call the First Dance. The Lady drawing No. 2, Second Set, will call the Second Dance. Then a Voluntary by Ladies'· Numbers. After which the Drawing will recommence. The Lady drawing No. 1, Third Set, will call the First Dance;—the Lady drawing No. 2, Fourth Set, will call the Second Dance. Voluntaries by the Ladies' Numbers will succeed. A Lady will not be entitled to her place unless she produces her Number, if required by a Manager. Should a Number be wanting, the Lady producing the next Number will be entitled to the place. Should any Lady sit down before the dance is ended, she will be considered as infringing on these regulations.

GRANDPA'S SCRAP BOOK

Week of June 4-6, 1903.

THE KING FAMILY OF SCARBORO.

WILLIAM KING.

The First Governor of Maine.

By Leonard B. Chapman.

NO. LXVI.

THE SCARBORO TURNPIKE ROAD.

A hundred years ago the highway from Dunstan to Portland was very crooked and was located over hill and dale with a ferry at Fore river.

February 25, 1794, William Vaughn and others were constituted a corporation for the purpose of bridging Fore river. On March 4, 1800, the time was extended nine months by the General Court, the time specified for completing the bridge having expired.

True, Portland could be reached via Long Creek and Stroudwater village from Saco and Dunstan, and thus avoid the ferry, but the way was very crooked with many ups and downs with ledges and mire places for the traveler to encounter.

The King family took in the situation. In improvements to the way the family saw a paying investment. A petition was accordingly started, and June 24, 1802, a turnpike road corporation was established by the General Court which act was added to and amended February 18, 1803, and then it was declared that "Robert Southgate, Esq., William King, Cyrus King, Dr. Benjamin J. Porter, Joseph Leland, Ebeneza Libby, Mayor Joseph Libby, William Thompson, Esq., Reuben Libby, James March, John Watson, John M. Milliken and Samuel Milliken shall be a Corporation by the name of 'The First Cumberland Turnpike,' for the purpose of laying out, making and keeping in repair a turnpike road in Scarboro, to commence at the bridge near the dwelling house of Nathaniel Moses, from thence running across the upland and marsh in a southwesterly course, between the dwelling houses of Edward and Jeremiah Milliken until it meets the county road near Edward Milliken's dwelling." The rates of toll to be as follows: "For each phaeton, chariot and other four wheeled carriages, twenty cents; for cart or sled drawn by two oxen or horses six cents," etc., etc.

Various provisions were made in the act, one of which was that a copy of the expense, etc., of building the way should be filed with the Secretary of State. The western termini was at that part of Dunstan now known as the "Four Corners," a term derived from the fact that at that point the road to Dunstan Landing and the county road cross each other. The old Dr. Southgate residence stood in a southeasterly direction from the "Four Corners" in what is now an open field, which tradition tends to prove that the Landing road was then located some rods easterly of the present way, which tradition also tends to show that the old King house stood upon the westerly side of the Landing road and not upon the easterly side as the remaining part of the residence is now seen. Since the location of the turnpike road, which was a little over a mile in length, located mostly upon salt marsh, the Dr. Robert Southgate large brick house as now seen has been built. A little easterly of the brick house upon the southerly side of the turnpike road the toll house and gate were erected.

The building of Vaughn's bridge and the turnpike road created a good deal of uneasiness among the people of Stroudwater village because the enterprise took away the travel and changed the current of trade. And then there arose jealous feelings between the stockholders of the bridge and the road, and the owners of stage lines felt aggrieved on account of tolls required, ($75 annually), and permission was obtained to construct a new way from a point easterly of Scottow's Hill towards Stroudwater, making Portland a mile nearer to Dunstan, as it was claimed, than via the turnpike and Vaughn's bridge, the way then built taking the name of "Paine road," which name is still retained, Paine being interested in stage lines and a citizen of Portland where he was an innkeeper. This was in 1815.

Stowed away for protection by Mr. C. Thornton Libby in one of the safety deposit vaults in Portland is a bundle of papers relating to the Scarboro turnpike which I have not examined. Mr. Noah Pillsbury of Dunstan retains the last treasurer's book, opened Jan. 31, 1834, by Horatio Southgate, Esq., and closed April 1, 1860, when the turnpike corporation went out of existence.

Before me are several well preserved letters written by Dr. Robert Southgate, the first of the name at Dunstan. One of these is very lengthy, dated Sept. 13, 1817, addressed to Hon. Willim King and relates wholly to the turnpike and bridge, the substance of which I will here use:

"Mr. Maynard of this place informs me that Andrew Ritchie, Esq., has requested him to obtain my opinion relative to reducing the toll on the turnpike in order to regain the travel, as such a cause would be advantageous for us as well as the proprietors of Vaughn's bridge. I wrote Mr. Ritchie I thought it best to take off all the toll from the turnpike and then for the bridge to pay over to the turnpike corporation a respectable part of the tolls received at the bridge. The turnpike cost about half the sum it took to build the bridge, and usually there has been received at the turnpike gate about a third as much as at the bridge. Mr. Ritchie informed me that he had consulted with Mr. Gray (probably "Billy" Gray, a rich man of Salem) and "they" had concluded to offer the turnpike corporation $100 per year for ten years to 'lay open the turnpike gates.' Mr. Ritchie seems to be of the opinion that the turnpike is an incumbrance to the prosperity of the bridge, but such is not the case."

Dr. Southgate then enters into an argument to show that it was the opening of the new way via Stroudwater in 1815 that had hurt the bridge.

The doctor then states that he is informed that the collection at the bridge amount to $20 per week, and as an individual he would be willing to accept $300 in semi-annual payments from the bridge for a period of ten years, but would not act till William King had been heard from.

By a letter dated Aug. 1, 1818, it appears that Messrs. Ritchie and Gray were willing to pay the $300 yearly to the turnpike corporation to open their gates to the public.

January 31, 1834 the 77th six months' dividends of the turnpike was declared and the ownership of stock was as follows:

"Horatio Southgate, Esq., 14 shares, $70.
"Gov. William King, 5 shares, $26.
"Cyrus King's heirs, 7 shares, $35.
"Salmon Chase's heirs, 2 shares, $10.
"Benjamin Milliken, 2 shares, $10.
"Esther Lancaster, 1 share, $5.
"Moses Libby, 1 share, $5."
Total number of shares 33.

Some years the stock paid over $10 per share.

In 1856, or thereabouts, the county was petitioned to make the turnpike free for all time, and over the turnpike road the County Commissioners laid out a county way and awarded $2,000 damage to the turnpike stock holders.

January 1, 1857, the capital stock amounting to $2,000 was divided as follows:

"Horatio Southgate, Esq., 15 shares, $930.
"Cyrus King's heirs, 7 shares, $434.
"William King's heirs, 5 shares, $310.
"Seth Libby, 1 share, $62.
"John M. Milliken, 2 shares, $124.
"Moses Libby, 1 share, $62.
"William Pitt Preble Jr., 1 share, $62.
"L. D. M. Swett, 1 share, $62.
Total number of shares, 33, $2,046.

In addition to what the county paid the Town of Scarboro on April 1, 1860, handed the stockholders $500, when the final distribution of $614.59 was made as follows:

"Horatio Southgate, Esq., 24 shares.
"Cyrus King's heirs, 7 shares.
"John M. Milliken, 2 shares."
Total number of shares, 33.

I have stated that the building of the turnpike was a real King family affair, and so it was, as the records show, most of the stock remaining in the name of the final dissolution of the corporation.

The tracks of the Portland and Saco electric railway are now laid upon the old turnpike road bed, and otherways the general public pass over it. The ground is historical as it is all around. Upon it occurred the slaughter of the English settlers of more than two hundred years ago by the Indians. As the region is entered from Portland, Scottow's Hill forms the northerly boundary line of the horizon, towering above which appears the mansion house of Richard King, Jr., who was a brother to the

CONTINUED:

Governor, but a few rods from which Scottow and his associates held their courts in Scottow's garrison house and where Richard King, Jr., constructed his vessels, the story of one written at the time, I propose to tell later.

At the easterly termini of the turnpike, where the large clump of trees is seen, a fourth of a mile distant, in a southerly direction, the Vaughn mansion house stood which went to Andrew Ritchie, Esq., the father to the wife of Gen. Neal Dow, also to the second wife of Henry Smith, who was the father to the celebrated Rev. Henry Boynton Smith, then to Seth Storer, Esq., by purchase.

The Storer mill has now disappeared that stood close to the highway-mill dam, pond and nearly the whole of the stream are gone.

To be continued.

GRANDPA'S SCRAP BOOK

Week of June 11—13, 1903.

THE KING FAMILY OF SCARBORO.

WILLIAM KING.

The First Governor of Maine.

By Leonard B. Chapman.

NO. LXVIII.

[Note. In the next to the closing paragraph, in the article of last week, the name of Andrew Ritchie, Esq., should have been John Maynard.]

A SCOTTOW HILL VESSEL.

There is a tradition at Dunstan that Richard King, Jr., an elder brother to William King, built vessels on Scottow Hill. Look that way at the high land in passing in an electric car over the old turnpike and repeat the tradition and the entertainer would be viewed as a romancer, but the following, copied from a well preserved manuscript letter, in an excellent hand, must convince the doubter of the truthfulness of the tradition:

"Brunswick, Oct'r. 7th, 1816.
"Gen. William King, Esq.,
"Bath.

"Sir: In the year 1810, your Brother Richard applied to me to aid him who was then under embarrassments on account of sundry claims against him occasioned by the building a vessel and I contracted with him for a half of the vessel at a fair price, became responsible for his debts, rigged the vessel, & in connection with him went to Rhode Island & from there to New York, with a determination to sell the craft. We had a fair price tendered at Rhode Island & I urged your Brother by every influence in my power to accept the offer as it was rather more than the amount of the bills, but so sanguine was he that he could obtain more, he insisted upon proceeding to New York where he also refused another offer but not so favorable as the former, immediately upon which some very unfavorable intelligence arrived from France which sunk the value of the vessel twenty-five per cent. We deemed it most prudent to discharge the crew; but the vessel continued to depreciate for several months, and winter coming upon us, Mr. Codman procured a market for, her at about $2,300—nearly a thousand dollars less than we might have had for her at Rhode Island.

"I opened a store in the country about the same time I engaged with your Brother, some ten miles from Scarboro, & owed for half the stock, but being absent so long the young man left in charge embezzl'd the goods, died very suddenly, and thus involving myself and family in ruin. Previous to my leaving home I supplied your Brother & his son with clothing for the voyage & his family during his absence with provisions to the amount of notes as follows:

"One note,		$36.97
"Interest,	$10.96	
"One note,		24.64
"Interest,	6.69	
"One note,		3.50
"Interest,	.82	
	$18.47	$65.11

"He has uniformly held out the prospect that you would pay the above named claims, observing that his interest is under your control. I am now extremely embarrasssed & so much 'so that I broke up my family last fall, Mrs. Emerson in connection with myself suffering during the winter from solitary confinement, not communicating my distressed condition to my two sons—Rufus & William, the former having disbursed on my account more than a thousand dollars & William twelve hundred. My prospects for the coming winter are deplorable, but I am not willing to call upon my sons any further.

"If you will accept the following named proposal, altho' involving an unreasonable sacrifice on my part, it will result in my favor & will be received gratefully as an act of beneficence.

"I will discount the whole amount of interest and accept an order on Mr. Green & my son for the amount of the principal. If this is not acceptable I will take one half of the principal, and an order on your Brother for the other half in produce of his farm & chiefly in potatoes.

"I will thank you for an answer tomorrow, hoping you will accept the first named proposition.
"Your Ob't Serv't,
"Jos. Emerson."

Under the heading of "Trade Partners" I noticed Joseph Emerson and presented a letter of his written to William King in 1806 relative to his son William becoming a clerk to William King, which he did, then a partner in trade with Peter H. Green, at Bath, where they conducted a very large mercantile business.

Joseph Emerson seems to have been a man of culture. His penmanship was excellent, he spelled correctly, and his grammar was of the best—far in advance of some of the specimens of college graduates. And thus it was with William Emerson, the son of Joseph.

A letter dated at Dunstan, Sept. 2, 1805, and written by Octavia Southgate and addressed to Mrs. Dr. Benj. J. Porter, her aunt, at Topsham, furnishes a clue to the time when the Richard King, Jr., residence on Scottow's Hill, as now seen, was erected. The original, in the hand of Miss Octavia S., who became the wife of William Browne, is in the possession of a gentleman in New York city. It commenced thus:

"Scarboro."

"My dear Aunt Porter:

"Uncle Richard King is very sick of a fever. He has been confined to the house a week. He wishes if possible that Mamma King would come up. [William's Mother]. We are in hopes he is not dangerous and feel less alarmed about him because we have often seen him attacked thus violently. Mamma Southgate wishes me to mention that you may inform Uncle William that Uncle Richard is considerably embarrassed in his affairs. He has gone on very well with his building thus far, but he can't discharge his obligations to his workmen without disposing of some of his realestate and he thinks of selling his marsh. Papa thinks if this can be avoided it would be a seasonable relief to him. If uncle William could assist him in his affairs it might contribute to his restoration of health."

* * * * *

From a letter written by Hon. Cyrus King—a brother to William and Richard, Jr.—it appears that Richard, Jr., constructed his residence upon a piece of his father's estate, and William advanced his brother, Richard, Jr., $1,000, the heirs securing William by a mortgage deed upon the premises. So the King residence on Scottow's Hill, in the door yard of which Richard, Jr., built the vessel that caused Mr. Joseph Emerson so much pain—the historical residence so plainly seen by the patrons of the new electric railway—is but a year or so younger than the old turnpike road, the amended charter for which was obtained just a century ago.

Upon page 81, Vol. IV, Series II, Collections of the Maine Historical Society, under the caption of Rev. Joseph Emerson, may be seen a notice of the Emerson name of a very interesting nature, which closes as follows:

"Edward settled in York, Maine, had two wives; first, Miss Orven of Boston, Mass., second, Mrs. Bourne of Kennebunk. He had several sons: Edward, Bulkley, William, Samuel, Joseph, Joseph again, a Harvard College graduate, who settled in Scarboro, engaged in mercantile business on a large scale, and a worthy man. (Reverend Mr. Tilton.")

The contributor of this item was evidently Rev. Nathan Tilton, a graduate of Harvard, settled over the Dunstan Congregational church society Dec. 10, 1800, where he labored twenty-seven years. He died there Oct. 4, 1851, aged 79 years. Mary, his wife, died, August 6, 1851, aged 85 years. Both have memorial slabs.

They had a son who was very odd in his ways, particularly in the school room, when he was "master," who taught the ideas of the young of Scarboro "how to shoot."

To be continued.

Week of Feb. 18—20, 1904.

GRANDPA'S SCRAP BOOK

SLEMONS.

An Old and Respected Name Hereabouts.

By Leonard B. Chapman.

The exact date the first person bearing the name of Slemons made his appearance hereabouts is not known, nor is the name of the place from which he came known, but it is conjectured that he was among the immigrants that came over in 1718, or was an offspring of one, most of whom finally settled in Londonderry, N. H. The colony came from the north of Ireland, intending to settle on the Kennebec river, but the Indians being troublesome most of them left there, a few stopping in Cape Elizabeth. In a letter dated April 17, 1753, Robert Temple states that many of the colony removed to Pennsylvania, and a considerable part of them to Londonderry.

In 1735 the name of Robert Slemons first appears here upon public records as a taxpayer on personal property in Cape Elizabeth.

In 1742 Robert purchased fifty-one acres of land, located at Stroudwater, upon which was a small house.

Sept. 16, 1744, Robert's son, William Slemons, was united in marriage with Catherine Porterfield, and father and son made other land purchases and erected the dwelling now occupied by Mr. Fred A. Johnson.

To William Robert Slemons deeded his entire property though he had a married daughter residing in Biddeford by the name of Elizabeth, who was the second wife of one Thomas Kilpatrick.

Before me are scores of original letters and documents all in an excellent state of preservation; but I can use here but one which is of much genealogical value and reads as follows:

"Philadelphia, Pa., May 26, 1798.
"Dr. Sir—

"I met in this city a Congressman* who says he knows you, and so I make bold to write, hoping to have with you later on an intimate acquaintance.

"I am aware there are branches of our family and name in your country, for I have heard my father, Thomas Slemons, say (who is now dead about six years) that about fifteen or twenty years ago, a young Gentleman of our name, and a relative, came all the way to Lancaster County in Pennsylvania to see and know more of his dear relatives. Now, dear sir, as I believe you are the design of my writing I hope the acquaintance may be intimate, for the name of Slemons is very dear to me wherever I find it. You may doubtless have heard of me and know my origin. I am a grandson of old Thomas Slemons, the head father of our branch of the family, and am a son of his son Thomas who was named for him; was bred in Pequea, Lancaster County, on the place where my grandfather first settled. Upon this same place my mother, who is a widow, still resides and has with her two sons and an only daughter.

"Now, my dear friend, I have only to request most earnestly that you write me, informing of the state and number of my dear relatives in the country where you live, and I'll remain your, perhaps, unknown,
"John B. Slemons.
"To Mr. Thomas Slemons."

"N. B. To be candid, I am a Clergyman of about twenty-three years of age. I am this year a Missionary sent by the general Assembly to the back parts of the State of New York, and I wish you in the month of June to send me a letter to the town of Skenectady. Send a letter here to me at Lancaster Post Office.
"J. B. S."

*The Representative in Congress was Peleg Wadsworth, a merchant, who erected the Longfellow house.

An item in William Slemon's will dated Dec. 13, 1784 reads as follows:

"I give and bequeath to my well beloved son, Thomas Slemons, all my movable effects without and within doors, (the reserve for my Wife excepted), and all the Debts and Demands due me in Specie or otherwise; and also the Farm that I now live on [the Fred A. Johnson farm] with the Buildings and appurtenances, (ten acres excepted) also twelve acres of marsh in Scarboro, and also one fourth part of my Grist Mill at Stroudwater and another fourth at my wife's decease, and one third part of a point of Land called Ship Yard, all in Fee Simple, to him and his heirs and assigns forever."

This Thomas Slemons did not marry. Andrew Pepperell Frost who resided in the house later known as the "Brewer House," now remembered by many, married Thomas Slemon's sister, with whom Thomas spent his last days and departed this life. This is the Thomas to whom the letter as above presented was addressed and the Thomas who journeyed on horseback (family tradition) to Pennsylvania in search of relatives.

Upon a fly leaf of an old account book of Andrew P. Frost I find the following interesting data:

"Dec. 3, 1796. A settlement with Thomas Slemons who had been a boarder three years."

"Dec. 19, 1796. Ann Webb, (Ann Riggs), wife of Henry Webb, mariner, of Stroudwater was a widow."

"Oct. 6, 1795. Departed this life my beloved wife at about 7 o'clock p. m., aged 37 years." She was Eleanor Slemons.

"Feb. 7, 1796. Then my Honored Mother departed this life at 4 o'clock p. m. Aged 80 years." She was the widow of Chas. Frost, Esq.

"Oct. 18, 1797. Departed this life, Rev. Thomas Browne, at about 9 o'clock, aged 63 years."

"June 8, 1798. Departed this life Thomas Slemons at 3 o'clock in the morning, aged 43 years."

"At the funeral of Brother Slemons, 2 qts. New Rum; plate; painting and sheet, eleven shillings."

"May 24, 1805. Departed this life at 7 o'clock p. m. Andrew P. Frost, aged 52 years."

Capt. Thomas Seal, whose wife was A. P. F.'s daughter, adm. on the Frost estate.

Week of Feb. 25-27, 1904.

GRANDPA'S SCRAP BOOK

BRIMBLECOM.

A Name That Was Once Prominent in Westbrook.

By Leonard B. Chapman.

The following cannot fail to interest the friends of Westbrook Seminary as the Rev. Samuel Brimblecom, father of the writer of the letter here presented, was the first preceptor of the institution and the first to officiate in the Universalist Chapel erected in 1830, then in Westbrook but now within the territorial limits of the city of Portland, in consequence of the changes of town and city limits, and now exhibited to the public in a very unsightly condition caused unnecessarily by the removal, in a vandal-like manner, of the ledge-rock around the edifice, since the territorial enlargement of Portland—a proceeding that should have been prohibited at its beginning. For a period of two years blast after blast partaking of the infernal regions has not only rocked the building and broken to a large extent the glass but, made nearly everything pertaining to it lamentable without a reasonable cause, thus producing a legacy those who made the purchase of the Universalist Society that the citizens of Westbrook might have a suitable place for town meetings and the transaction of town business never dreamed of for a minute. Verily, the sentiment of the requiem indulged in by those having the official oversight of the work of devastation is indeed soul-harrowing rather than soul-soothing to the citizens of the locality and people generally who desire to hold in reverence the worthy customs of our ancestors by a display of ocular evidence when it can be done without the sacrifice of treasure or principle.

Santa Clara, California,
Jan. 25th, 1904.

My Dear Sir:

It is with pleasure I acknowledge the Portland Press duly received. I found much interest in the article on Westbrook Seminary and am pleased that it is in such a flourishing condition. It seems to me an ideal location for a school, pleasant and advantageous in every way for young people, and must be very attractive.

The familiar names in the paper made me homesick as they always do. The place where we now live has many pleasing features, and in climate and variety of productions is perhaps as perfect as any in the world. It is a cheerful, radiant climate, that should really tend to create happiness and contentment.

As soon as the last installment of crops—(pears and grapes)—are off the ground, the autumn rains begin to fall, and everywhere the grass becomes green, and spring has come! The birds begin to sing, and in Feb. the first trees bloom—the almond. So there is no time when all nature is resting, but each takes its turn in enlivening the scene. Yet—after all—I look upon New England as the cream of the world, and the wave-washed shores where I was born as very sacred.

I am going to take the liberty to send you a copy of the "In Memoriam" of my youngest brother, which is issued by our nieces, and has just reached me. They sent by express some extra copies with the request that they be forwarded to his friends and ours with whom they were unacquainted. Their home has always been in and about Chicago and they are but slightly acquainted in the East or far West.

This brother went through four years of the Civil War without "a scratch," but the great West was less kind. The heart difficulty from which he died was the result of freezing in one of the fierce blizzards of that inclement region, many years ago, and had caused him great suffering. But he was of a heroic nature, and never murmured, nor left his post of duty, and was greatly beloved everywhere for his joyous and indomitable spirit.

Ever with most friendly regard,
Lucy A. Brimblecom.

Week of March 3–5, 1904.

RANDPA'S SCRAP BOOK

GILMAN.

An Old-time Clergyman of North Yarmouth.

By Leonard B. Chapman.

Upon the northerly side of the electric rail-way, between Portland and Yarmouth, and a mile westerly of the Falls Village, may be seen a two-story dwelling house, very pleasantly located upon the northerly side of the way, fronting southerly. Two years ago, when I last observed it, in the month of October, the place was a picture of neatness. The occupants had migrated, but the window shutters were open, and I took the liberty to trespass upon the enclosure so far as to look through the unprotected window glass into several of the rooms where I saw much of an old-fashioned nature not only of an amusing but of an instructive character; but I cannot now attempt a description, so will only say that the internal arrangement was in strict accord with the external at the time of my visit, the date, 1771, appearing over the front door, evidently indicating the time the residence was erected, which was that of Rev. Tristram Gilman who departed this life nearly a century ago.

Upon the opposite side of the highway are two cemeteries, the one nearest the Gilman residence still being, to a small extent, in use; the other, the most ancient of the town of Yarmouth, now appearing in a woefully neglected state, is out of use. The first contains several grave memorial slabs and monuments possessed of interesting genealogical data, as does the last here noticed which is far less in quantity. In the more modern of the two may be seen a granite, uncut slab of about ten by twelve feet lying upon the ground by the side of which is erected a small slab inscribed as follows:

RUSSELL.
GILMAN.
1785.

Upon a slab of modern manufacture adjacent may be seen an inscription that reads as follows:

REV. TRISTRAM GILMAN,
born in Exeter, N. H.,
Nov. 24, 1735.
Graduate of Harvard College
1757.
For forty years
Minister of this Parish
from 1769, until his death,
April 1, 1809.

ELIZABETH SAYER,
his wife,
born in Wells, Me.,
Sept. 12, 1747.
Died Nov. 20, 1790.

The righteous shall be in everlasting remembrance.

Erected by their Grandchildren.
1887.

It appears that Parson Gilman was ordained as the fourth settled minister of North Yarmouth Dec. 8, 1769, the ancient town having been since divided and Yarmouth, in which the Gilman parsonage stands, created, and the most ancient of the two cemeteries was located upon the "church common" which lot was set apart in 1727, not only for church and burial purposes but as a training field, the stocks and the whipping-post, and at this late date may be seen the grave memorial of Benjamin Ingersoll within the enclosure whose ancestors once owned the Stroudwater fresh water mill privilege which was in 1680, Benjamin deeding to Col. Thomas Westbrook, March 19, 1734, a hundred acres of land upon an acre of which is located the Mary Brown Home.

Parson Gilman succeeded in the ministry at North Yarmouth Rev. Edward Brooks, a Harvard college graduate, settled there in 1764, July 4th, the ancestor of Bishop Brooks, recently deceased, but Brooks being too worldly to suit his parish remained but four years, when he quit the ministry, returned to Medford, Mass., where he died. His wife was a sister to Rev. Thomas Browne who was settled over the fourth, or Stroudwater parish, in 1764, where he officiated thirty years, the meeting house standing where the Mary Brown Home is now seen.

Parson Gilman preached for a period of twenty years without making any perceptible impression "w there was a most wonderful reviv The whole town was shaken up one hundred and forty-five were admitted to the church, prior to the month of Sept. 1793.

Some time since the Suburban Weeklies presented the Parson Gilman obituary that appeared in the Eastern Argus at the time of his death.

The following is an abstract from the Christian Mirror of Oct 17, 1840:

"Died in Wells, Oct. 6, Nicholas Gilman, aged 47 years, third son of Rev. Tristram Gilman of the First Church of North Yarmouth. He came to Wells in 1801. In 1821 he was appointed a Justice of the Peace which office he held till his death. He represented the town in the state legislature six years; was town clerk and treasurer eighteen years; and was one of the seventeen who organized into the second church on the 22d of Aug., 1831, at which time he was chosen a clerk, and in 1833, was chosen deacon."

Week of March 10-12, 1904.

RANDPA'S SCRAP BOOK

CUTTER.

The First Settled Minister of North Yarmouth.

By Leonard B. Chapman.

While Rev. Ammi [spelled also Ami] R. Cutter was the first settled minister of the town he was not the first clergyman there. Rev. Samuel Seabury preceded him in 1727 and continued to officiate till Nov. of 1729. He was invited to "settle" but declined.

In the month of April of 1729, a tax was assessed for the purpose of building a meeting-house, and on the 24th day of April, 1730, a meeting was held in the house that had been commenced then without a floor or windows. There was no road from the saw mill to the lot so the lumber was floated from the place known as the Falls or Lower Village to Larrabee's Landing. It was not till five years later the house was clapboarded, and in 1738 the town voted five pounds to pay for beating a bass drum on the hill back of the Parson Gilman residence, noticed last week, when meetings were to be held.

Rev. Mr. Cutter was a graduate of Harvard college in 1725, and began to preach in the unfinished meeting house Nov. 10, 1729, and was ordained Nov. 18, 1730, a sumptuous repast being provided as was the custom at that time.

The town gossip relating to his religious views and preaching is very meager upon public records. Parson Smith of Portland Neck records under date of January 11, 1733, that "Mr. Cutter gave great offence by his rank Arminianism." Again: "There was in the month of August, 1735, a Council at North Yarmouth respecting Mr. Cutter."

At a town meeting held Dec. 12, of that year, "Mr. Cutter was finally dismissed." He then entered in the town and vicinity upon the practice of medicine.

The agreement was that he should receive for preaching a salary of one hundred and twenty ounces of silver annually and the ministerial lot if he remained five years.

He lived in a house located "ninety feet easterly of the meeting house, built in 1734, of hewn timbers of hard wood, loop-holed, surrounded by a wall of hard wood timber, ten feet high, sixty feet wide and eighty feet long with two watch-boxes for rifles on its walls, and was called the "Cutter Fort."

One hundred and ninety feet to the west was the Loring Fort. Ammunition was stored in the loft of the meeting house, and a guard was kept posted when the Indians were troublesome on Gilman Rock.

But few people who now pass and repass upon the electric railroad tracks are aware of the historic events of the situation.

One writer states that Parson Cutter "cared more for the fleece than for the flock; more for silver than for souls; that he was a man of eccentric genius and a lover of learning rather than of preaching."

From North Yarmouth he went to the west side of the Saco river (now Hollis) at Salmon Falls, to a fort erected by the government in which Capt. Thomas Smith, father of Rev. Thomas Smith, of Portland Neck, was located as truck-master. Capt. Smith died Feb. 18, 1742, and Parson Cutter succeeded him. Smith was a merchant from Boston, and the position was one of honor and profit. At the place of trade, to which the Indians flocked, Parson Cutter compiled an Indian vocabulary of much merit.

The ministerial lot which Parson Cutter received comprised five hundred acres of land.

Dr. Ammi R. Cutter of Portsmouth, N. H., was a son and Levi Cutter, Esq., who was mayor of Portland from 1834 to 1840 was a grandson.

One "Levi Cutter, Esq.," was an overseer of Bowdoin college from 1818 till 1856. This may have been the mayor of Portland.

Wm. Cutter, born in Yarmouth, May 15, 1801, son of Levi Cutter, mayor of Portland, graduated at Bowdoin college A. M. class of 1821, was for a while a merchant in Portland then removed to Bedford, N. Y., where he engaged in literary work and died Feb. 8, 1867. A notice of him and a sample of his work may be seen in "Poets of Maine," page 66.

Edward Francis Cutter, born in Portland, Jan. 20, 1810, graduated A. M. from Bowdoin college 1828, became a D. D. officiating at Warren, Belfast and Rockland, and died March 27, 1880, at Charleston, S. C. Quite a number of his sermons are in print, including an eulogy on Abraham Lincoln delivered at Rockland, April 19, 1865.

The following is taken from a grave memorial in Yarmouth:

In Memory of
Rev.
Ammi Rubamah
CUTTER,
First Minister of
North Yarmouth,
born in West Cambridge,
died Louisburg, Cape Breton,
March 16 [1746]. Aged 44.

His wife
Dorothy Bradbury
Died June 18, 1776,
Aged 86.

Their daughter, Elizabeth
CUTTER,
Died 1792, aged 50.

Capt.
William Cutter,
son of
Rev. A. R. & D. Cutter,
was killed by the falling of a tree,
June 28, 1776,
aged 39 years.

His wife,
Mehitable Gray Cutter

died March 19, 1808,
aged 68 years.

Their son,
Samuel Cutter,
died March 23, 1776,
aged 4 years.

Levi Cutter,
son of Ammi & Hannah Cutter,
died Nov. 7, 1821,
aged 28 years.

Caroline,
dau. of A. & H. Cutter,
died Feb. 17, 1830, aged 29 years,
widow of Watson Gray Drinkwater, who died at Point Peter, Guadalupe, July 26, 1827. Their dau., Caroline W. Drinkwater, died Dec. 27, 1847, aged 20 years.

Ammi Cutter,
son of
William & Mehitable
Cutter,
died Sept. 18, 1825,
aged 55 years.

His wife,
Hannah G.,
only daughter of Ephraim
and Sarah Greely,
died June 8, 1819,
aged 44 years.

Their child Sarah died Sept. 17, 1794, aged 18 days.
Philip died in Havana, July 26, 1820, aged 22 years.

Week of March 17—19, 1904.

RANDPA'S SCRAP BOOK

JOHNSON—HATCH.

Curiosities in Grave-stone Characters and Inscriptions.

By Leonard B. Chapman.

The frequenter of cemeteries for genealogical memoranda often observe inscriptions as well as epitaphs that are odd and difficult to decipher. Something of the kind may be seen in the comparatively new cemetery in Westbrook located a mile southeasterly of Saccarappa, as follows:

CAPT. NATHANIEL HATCH.
1750-1832.

ELIZABETH [Hatch]
1758 1812.

ABIGAIL [Nason]
1772-1854.
[Two wives.]

Harriet. 1794-1811.
FATHER.
George Hatch—1797-1870.
MOTHER.
1810-1862.

John W. 1830-1853.
Mary E. 1831-1854.

Martha, wife of McDonald.
1845-1876.

The foregoing is not all copied from one stone but the several that occupy the half of a neatly kept lot.

Upon the other half may be seen stones inscribed as follows:

JOHNSON.

Father.	1777-1847.
Mother.	1780-1865.
Gardner.	1805-1883.
Mary.	1811-1845.
Abbie.	1812.1864.
Rufus.	1815-1891.
Harriet.	1826.1856.

To those in possession of the facts the foregoing is plain and means something—to the casual observer, or partially informed, the whole is of little value, without explanation, a little of which I will try and give.

James Johnson came from the North of Ireland to Scarboro where he ran a ferry-boat. He had sons, James and John, and daughters, two of whom, I believe, have erroneously been set down by some one who has endeavored to produce Johnson family history, as daughters of James Johnson, Jr., who was their brother, Florence, who married, Dec. 1, 1743, in Scarboro, Robert Patten, and settled in Bath, and Eleanor, who married John Mains of Biddeford, intention being made public Dec. 25, 1748.

Oct. 2, 1747, James Johnson, Jr., of Scarboro, a weaver, as well as a farmer, purchased land a mile westerly of Stroudwater, now located in the Deering district of Portland. His son, George, born 1728, married Mary, a daughter of Francis Jackson, of Cape Elizabeth, who resided a half mile southerly, upon what is now known as the Saco road, or street. The intention was made known June 25, 1752. The same year in which they were married, they jointly acknowledged the church covenant. She was a sister to Sarah (Jackson) Brewer whose daughter, Eleanor (Brewer) Rand, built the house which is now seen on Garrison street at Stroudwater in a very dilapidated condition.

In 1753, James Johnson, Jr., conveyed to his son George forty acres of his hundred acre purchase, adjoining William Porterfield's land, "whereon he now dwelleth."

June 19, 1771, George sold his lot "with buildings" to his brother, John Johnson, Jr.

One of George's sons was named Jeremiah Johnson. Sept. 27, 1797, his father sold him a forty acre lot where the homestead may now be seen in excellent repair for a dwelling of its age, located between the Saco road and the Stroudwater river where the Johnson mill stood for many years but now gone, a mile or two southwesterly of Saccarappa.

Jeremiah Johnson married July 26, 1804, Hannah, dau. of Capt. Nathaniel Hatch whose name appears in the foregoing. Their children—a record made from fragments:

1—Gardner, b. 1805, d. on the homestead farm, 1883. He did not marry.
2—Nathaniel H., intention of m. July 10, 1831, with Priscilla D. Sawyer of Buxton, was made public. She d. He m. Oct. 23, 1845, Mary Meserve of Scarboro.
3—Elizabeth H. m. William Johnson, a son of Richard and Eunice (Trickey) Johnson. Int. Jan. 1, 1834. She d. Jan. 4, 1838, aged 29 years. He m. second.
4—Mary b. 1811. She did not marry. Died 1845.
5—Abbie b. 1812. She did not marry. Died 1865.
6—Rufus. He was a great mechanical genius. He built, in 1862, the church organ now in use in the Mary Brown Home. Born 1815; d. 1891.
7—Harriet. She did not marry. Born 1826; d. 1856.

Joseph Hatch came to Gorham, this state, from Barnstable. His wife was Sarah Sawyer, dau. of John and Sarah. Their intention is not, nor is the marriage event, recorded in Gorham.

Nathaniel Hatch was their eldest child, b. in Gorham, Sept. 27, 1749, m. June 12, 1777, Elizabeth Hatch of Cape Elizabeth, to which place they removed a couple of years after the marriage event, then returned to Gorham, where they have the birth of child Betsey recorded, April 14, 1778. At Cape Elizabeth, Hannah, b. there April 22, 1780; Sally, Jan. 10, 1783; then at Gorham, Nathaniel, Sept. 30, 1789, m. and d. in Va.; Harriet, b. Sept. 5, 1794, d. Nov. 4, 1821, and George, b Nov. 3, 1797, who m. Mary Staples, 2nd, Emily Higgins. Hannah b. Cape Elizabeth, April 22, 1780, m., as I have shown, Jeremiah Johnson.

Capt. Hatch must have removed from Gorham to the Johnson neighborhood, or the region known by the name, in Westbrook, about 1790, where the large brick house he erected and in which he last resided may be seen, surrounded by most excellent land.

After retiring from the labors of the mariner he became a preacher of the Methodist denomination and was a "thunderer" as one of the aged citizens described him to me some years since

His wife died May 24, 1812, and he married Abigail Nason. He d. April 2, 1832, aged 82.

There was a burying place on the Westbrook farm but when the cemetery lot was purchased, to which I have alluded, the old memorial slabs of Hatches and Johnsons were destroyed.

Betsey (or Elizabeth) Hatch, b. in Gorham, April 14, 1778, m. William Roberts, the Roberts's going from Long Creek, C. E., in 1781, to Gorham. Their children;

1—Charles Roberts, b. Jan. 20, 1804, m. Elanor Chenery of Bradley's Corner, Deering.
2—William Roberts, b. May 8, 1807.
3—Harriet, b. April 1, 1813.

Mrs. Betsy (or Elizabeth) (Hatch) died and William Roberts married again and their daughter married Dr. Eben Strout who died in Deering, on Steven's Plains. She died and the doctor married Theresa Mason of Bethel. The widow and a daughter by the first marriage reside in New York where she is a successful music teacher.

NOTES

NOTES

NOTES

INDEX

INDEX NOTES

This index lists: people by last name, first name; places, such as, Scarborough, Westbrook, Saccrappa, Stroudwater, etc.; issue dates; and article titles. There are headings for Indians mention and interesting locations, such as, Back Cove (Skillin Farm). References to cemeteries has a seperate heading also.

When using the index to locate a person, read the complete article. Individuals are constantly mentioned over and again.

Abbott
   Amos, 94, 194
   Benjamin, 184
   Charles, 184
   David, 184
   Miranda, 184
   Naomy Royals (Burnham), 184
   Nathaniel, 164
   Sarah, 184
   William, 184
Adams
   Abigail (Pennell), 224, 226, 228
   Annah Eliz. Nichols (Bailey), 177
   Cornelius, 1
   Dr. I. Alja, 177
   Elizabeth (Maxfield), 37
   Frank, 37
   Harriet Briggs, 1
   Isaac, 1, 138
   Jacob, 18-19, 20.2, 290
   Jane, 20.2
   John Quincy, 313, 318
   Joseph, 18, 235, 266
   Margaret, 1
   Mrs. Abigail, 62
   Peggy, 18
   Rev. John G., 94
   Ruth, 137-138, 228
   Sally (Lewis), 235
   Thankful, 18
   William Davis, 1
Akers
   Thomas, 40
Alden
   Admiral James, 282
   Alpheus S., 195(2), 264
   Caleb, 195
   Capt. James, 280
   Capt. John, 280
   Charles, 38
   David, 195, 280
   Dea. David, 195
   Elizabeth (Tate), 279(2), 280
   Elizabeth E. (Stevens), 264
   George Forest, 195, 264
   Hannah (White), 195
   Henry Shaw, 195, 264
   Isabel (Frances), 193, 195
   Isabel Frances, 264(2)
   Isabell, 55
   Isabella B. (Frances), 195
   J., 42
   James, 279-280
   James Madison, 280
   James Madison, Jr., 280
   Jesse D., 193, 264
   Jesse Dunbar, 146, 193, 195
   John, 195(2)
   Joseph, 195
   Judith (Paddeford), 195
   Maj. Jesse D., 195
   Maria, 282
   Mary, 238
   Mary (Simmons), 195
   Mary Alden, 280
   Nancy (Quinby), 38

   Parmelia P. (Philips), 280
   Priscilla (Mullins), 195
   Rhoda (Leach), 195
   Robert T., 282
   Robert Tate, 280
   Sarah A., 282
   Sarah B., 282
   Sarah Rose, 195
   Susannah (Dunbar), 195
   Walter Franklin, 195, 264
Aldrich
   Jessie, 195
Alger
   Andrew, 243(2)
   Andrew, Jr., 243
   Arthur, 243
   Elizabeth, 243(2)
   Joanna, 243(2)
   John, 243-244
   Mathew, 243
Allen
   Dr. Solomon, 92, 96, 100, 263, 265, 269
   Edward S., 22
   Elijah, 263
   Elizabeth Lee, 251, 257
   Emery, 250
   Hattie F., 37
   Hunt, 55
   James M., 8
   Jeanette, 265
   Joseph, 250
   Lizzie Barbour, 265
   Lucy, 192
   Olive (Higgins), 263
   Robert, 55
   William, D.D., 257
Allison
   May A., 8
Ames
   Rev. Benjamin, 139
Anderson
   Caroline Louisa, 253
   Daniel, 55
   Elizabeth Virginia, 253
Anderson-Jordan
   Hannah, 155
Andras
   Governor, 203
Andrews
   Elizabeth, 185, 233
   Ezra C., 254
   Samuel, II, 208
Angier
   Frances, 237
Archer
   Agnes, 197(2)
Armstrong
   Catherine, 309
   John, 150
   Simeon (Simon), 150
Arthur
   Eliza, 282
   Timothy S., 282
Atkins
   Joshua Young, 1
   Lucy E., 308

Sarah, 115
Atkinson
  Joseph P., 94
  Rev. Joseph, 139
Austin
  Edward, 302
  Eliza (King), 312
  John, 243
  John L., 295
  William, 312
Avery
  Ruth S. (Brackett), 11
  Thomas, 11
Ayer
  F.S., 1
  Sarah B., 221
Ayers
  Mary Ann, 192
Babb
  Alexander, 71, 78
  Bailey, 121
  Capt. John, 7
  Charles, 159
  Daniel, 266
  Elizabeth (Conant), 220
  Ellen, 266
  George, 71
  Henry, 90, 94(2)
  James, 56, 105, 108
  John, 7, 39, 90, 94
  Joseph, 266
  Lucy (Bailey), 159
  Lucy (Libby), 266
  Mrs. Rebecca, 7
  Peter, 46-47, 56, 89, 288
  Rhoda (Quinby), 39
  Samuel L., 266
  William, 47, 89, 94, 220
  William, Jr., 266
Babcock
  Ada, 130
Bacon
  Gardner, 191
  Mary J. H., 191
  Stephen, 91, 94
Badger
  James W., 112
Bagley
  Ann, 61
Bailey
  Abbie A. (Winslow), 308
  Abbie W. (Sawyer), 26
  Abby Nichols (White), 177
  Abigail, 6, 25-26, 32
  Abigail W., 26
  Abigail W. (Bailey), 26
  Alexander, 26(3)
  Alice, 308
  Alpheus, 33, 94, 177, 179
  Annah Eliz. Nichols, 177
  Annie, 26, 308
  Benjamin, 22(2), 24(2), 131, 159, 177, 188, 236, 288, 290, 293, 307
  Benjamin F., 24
  Benjamin, Jr., 24
  Betsey (Webb), 33, 172
  Betty, 25
  Capt. Francis H., 60
  Caroline (Hilton), 27
  Catherine (Stevens), 45
  Catherine F., 26
  Charles A., 308
  Charles C., 308
  Charles E., 43, 172, 180
  Charles Edward, 177
  Charles L., 26
  Clarence W., 26(2)
  Col. Jeremiah, 64, 69, 169, 177
  Cora A., 26
  Daniel, 4, 25(4), 26, 167, 288
  David, 89, 159, 232, 288, 290
  Dea. Benjamin, 93
  Dea. James, 25(2), 26(2), 33, 101, 124, 189
  Dea. John, 18, 24(2), 35, 60, 77, 101, 159, 174, 177, 232, 236, 239, 305
  Deborah, 25
  Deborah (Skillings), 25(2), 167
  Doritha, 69
  Dorothy, 50, 263
  Dr. George H., 128, 234
  Elbridge G., 26
  Eliza, 307(2)
  Elizabeth, 2, 5(2), 24(3), 38, 189, 309
  Elizabeth Ann, 177
  Elizabeth B. (Stevens), 177
  Elizabeth Brisco (Stevens), 33
  Emeline, 308
  Emma (Hatford), 26
  Emma L., 308
  Eunice (Jones), 177
  F.A., 78
  Ferdinand M., 26
  Florence Cutler, 177
  Frances H., 174
  Frank M., 26
  Fred O., 9
  George , 33, 172, 177
  George A., 179
  George Albert, 177(3)
  George E., 26
  George W., 26(2)
  Harriet Rebecca (Woodford), 9
  Harriet White, 177
  Helen, 60
  Helen M., 77
  Henrietta C. (Knight), 45
  Henry, 20.2
  Herbert, 308
  Ida M., 26
  Isaac, 6, 19, 78, 91, 97, 158
  Isaac W., 91, 94
  James, 25(4), 167
  James I., 188
  James P., 26, 78
  James Paine, 27
  Jane, 19, 307
  Jane (Brady), 35
  Jane (Curtis), 177
  Jane M., 308
  Jane M. (Bailey), 308
  Jeremiah, 44, 78
  Jeremiah P., 26

Jesse, 159
John, 23-24, 60, 89-89, 90(2), 174, 177, 179-180, 199, 221
John G., 25(2)
John Gideon, 25
John, Dea., 2
John, Jr., 18, 24, 35, 89, 223, 309
Joseph, 24, 159, 307-308
Joseph Edwards, 308
Joseph W., 25
Joseph, Jr., 24, 302, 306(2), 307(2), 311
Josiah, 3, 266
Josiah Stevens, 45
Lafayette, 26(2)
Lena F., 26
Leon C., 308
Leon M., 26
Louisa (Clark), 308
Louisa (Stevens), 6
Lucy, 159
Lucy E. (Atkins), 308
Lydia, 41, 50, 69, 223
Marcena, 308
Mary, 24, 223, 309
Mary (Haggett), 308
Mary A., 308
Mary M., 26
Minnetta E., 26
Miriam Lincoln (Hobert), 177, 179
Miss Helen M., 177
Monroe, 26
Mrs. Catherine, 45
Nabby, 26
Nancy Cony Winslow, 177
Nancy Paine, 27
Octavia (Libby), 22, 24
Olive (Brackett), 24, 307
Orren, 26
Orren M., 26
Peter Brackett, 308
Phebe Ann, 26
Rebecca, 35(2), 109, 159, 174(2), 223, 307(2)
Richard G., 164
Robert, 65
Sally, 25, 124, 127(2), 190
Sally (WAterhouse), 159, 302, 306-307
Samuel, 78
Samuel K., 45(2)
Samuel Smith, 45
Sarah, 25
Sarah, 307(2)
Sarah (Paine), 25-26
Sarah (Stevens), 4
Sarah A. (Doughty), 26
Sgt. John, 46
Sophia, 26
Stillman G., 45
Susan, 95
Susan M., 308
Thomas, 172
Walter, 308
Walter Webb, 177, 179
William, 24, 308
Winslow, 308
Baird
Charles, 278

Baker
Alexander, 193
Capt. Barnabas, 100
Elijah, 165
Elisha, 202
Jacob, 205
Jacob C., 208
John, 11, 100
Josiah, 57, 89, 290
Mary Revere Rose, 264
Mrs. Mary (Rose), 193
Mrs. Ruth, 100
Ruth (Elder), 205
Sarah (Wilson), 202
Susannah (Brackett), 10
Balden
William, 46
Baldwin
Nabby P. (Kenny), 17
William, 17
Ballard
B.W., 94
George Henry, 188
R.W., 55
Sarah Buckley (Stevens), 188
Bancroft
George, 257
Bangs
Sarah, 266
Banks
Maj. Moses, 48
Barber
James, 77
James, Jr., 78
John, 57, 188
John, Jr., 57
Nancy, 165
Barbor
Hugh, 89
John, 89
John, Jr., 89
Barbour
Adam, 197, 266
Alexander, 3
Ann, 61
Betsey (Lowe), 197
Betty (Knight), 197
Charles, 197(2)
Clementine (Dennett), 197
David, 165
Dorcas, 197
Edward, 3
Edward Russell, 197
Esther, 197
Eunice, 197
Hugh, 197
James, 3, 61, 155, 197
Jane (Robinson), 197
Joanna (Cobb), 197
Joanna, 197(2)
John, 197(2), 288, 290
Josiah, 3
Lucy (Tenney), 197
Margaret, 155
Margaret (Nelson), 155
Martha (Stevens), 3

Mary, 3, 197
Mary (Bean), 197
Mary (Porter), 197
Miriam, 197
Susan, 197
Susanna (Wilson), 197
Sylvia, 271
William, 197
Barker
Alexander, 10
Charles, 277
Dr. Jeremiah, 32, 66, 157, 169, 207, 286
Ellen (Brackett), 109
Leander, 109
Mary, 174
Mary (Williams), 169
Mary G., 169
Mrs. Charles, 57
Sarah Brown, 100
Solomon, 164
Barlow
Hugh, 57
Barnes
Phinahas, 208
Barrett
Abbie Southgate, 254
Abigail Browne (Southgate), 248, 254
Charles C., 254
Dr. John, 248, 254
John, Esq., 254
John, Jr., 254
Martha (Dickinson), 254
Barstow
Ellen (Morrill), 75
George S., 75
Bartlett
Caleb, 38, 168
Charles, 78, 90-91, 93-94, 121, 168, 264
Dorcas (Barbour), 197
Eleanor E. (Sparrow), 264
Elizabeth (Sparrow), 168
Esther (Barbour), 197
Ichabod, 205
Lemuel, 328
Moses, 197
Mrs. Elizabeth, 168
Robert, 77
Stephen, 197
Susan, 306
William, 78, 176
Bartol
Eliza Waite, 100
Baston
Fannie (North), 130
Batchelder
John, 165
Bates
Mrs. Ella, 123
Mrs. Ella M., 202
Baxter
J.P., 208
Bayley
Achsa, 101
Bethsheba, 101
Daniel, 101
David, 46

Hannah, 101(2)
John, 77, 101
John, Jr., 57, 101
Joseph, 101
Judith, 101(2)
Lydia, 101
Martha, 101
Mary, 101(2)
Mary (Clark), 101
Mrs. Martha, 101
Mrs. Priscilla, 101
Naomi, 101
Priscilla, 101
Rebecca, 101
Robert, 101
Robert, Jr., 101
Schah, 101
William, 46
Beadle
Jane, 283
Beal
Ezera T., 96
Beals
Joseph, 188
Josiah, 27
Nancy (Berry), 27
Bean
Adam, 197
Agnes (Archer), 197
Ann, 197
Betsey, 197
Elizabeth, 197
Elizabeth (Goodrich), 197
Hannah, 197
Harriet (Merrill), 197
Henry, 197
John, 197
Joseph, 197(2)
Judith (Stevens), 197
Lucy (Potter), 197
Mary, 197(2)
Mrs. Joanna, 197
Robert, 197
Bedell
J., 55(2)
Jeremiah, 194
Bedinger
Caroline Bowne (Lawrence), 282
Hon. Henry, 282
Beebe
Charles Francis, 283
Emma (Bowne), 283
Gerald Edwin, 283
Kenneth, 283
Walter Bowne, 283
Beedle
Jeremiah, 94
Beels
Josiah, 173
Nancy (Berry), 173
Bell
William, 164
Bemis
Augustus, 186
Bennett
Enoch B., 9

Esther Ann Bean (Stevens), 9
Hannah, 109
William, 55
Benson
Miss. Matilda, 57
Bernell
Alice C. (Buckley), 190
Edward A., 190
Berry
Abigail, 175
Capt., 46
Capt. George, 281
Daniel, 252
Dorcas (Shattrock), 175, 281
Elizabeth, 27, 173
Elizabeth (Blackstone), 175
George, 173, 175(2)
George, Jr., 26(2), 189, 281
Harriet Rogers, 281
Jane (Bowie), 175
Jeremiah, 175
Joanna, 175
Joanna (Doane), 175
Josiah, 26-27, 173, 175, 290
Lucy (Torrey), 173
Maj. George, 26-27, 173, 175
Maj. William, 157
Mary (Stickney), 281
Mayor George, 26
Merrill, 23, 252
Miriam, 175
Miriam P., 27, 173
Mrs. J., 110
Nancy, 27, 173
Obediah, 26, 173, 157, 290
Phebe, 221
Pricilla, 60
Priscilla, 80(2), 244
Rebecca, 26, 175, 189
Remember, 175
Sally, 175
Samuel, 175, 281
Sarah (Stickney), 173
Thankful, 173
Thankful (Butler), 26-27, 173
William, 47, 175
Best
Martin W., 45
Bicknell
Anna (Sloan), 173
Com. George A., 173
George Edward, 192
Rev. George W., 140, 192
Bigalow
Mrs. Mary (Smith), 182
Bigelow
Rufus, 306
Bigford
John, 302
Biggsbee
George, 101
Bisby
William, 306
Bishop, 264
Adeline, 3
Catherine, 3, 264

Edward, 3
Edwin, 3
George, 3(2), 52, 90, 94, 125, 170, 188, 264
Julia Ann, 3
Mary, 3
Mollie, 3
Nancy (Stevens), 3, 264
Thomas, 278
William, 3
Black
Abel, 250
Blackstone
Elizabeth, 175
Blair
John, 48
Blaisdell
Josiah, 208
Blake
Alexander, 94
Almira, 15(2)
Daniel, 164
Francis, 188
Frank, 15
H., 42
Henry, 15(2), 55, 78, 94, 164-165
James, 15(2), 158
James, Jr., 164
Jasper, 15, 45
John, 15, 45, 188, 287
John H., 45
John S., 15
Mary, 15
Nancy (Barber), 165
Sally, 45
Thomas, 92
William, 188
Blanchard
Amanda, 130
Sylvanus C., 208
Blaney
Abigail, 207
Blethen
Jonah, 46
Bodge
Abbie M., 191
Abigail (Nason), 191
Andrew T., 191
Aurelia A., 191
Dayton, 191
Elbridge S., 191
Elizabeth Ellen, 191
Emily Jane, 191
Francis F.O.J., 191
Francis O.J., 191(2)
James A., 191
Joseph G., 191
Louisa M., 191
Martha E. (Howard), 191
Thomas, 191
Thomas, Jr., 191
William A., 191
Bogert
Henry A., Esq., 282
Mary Bowne (Lawrence), 282
Boles
Mary, 79

Rev., 75
Boiles
    Rev. E.C., 139
Bolton
    William, 37
Boody
    Addie Louisa (Pennell), 229
    Benjamin, 211
    Frank Hale, 229
    Henry, 211
    Henry B., 211-212
    Henry H., 211
    Jane (Winslow), 211
    Mrs., 55
Booker
    James, 278
    John, 278
    Mrs. Isabella, 278
Boothby
    L.T., 119
    William, 69
Bosworth
    Capt. Robert, 322
Bourne
    A., 325
Bowie
    Jane, 175
Bowker
    James, 191
    Judith (Chase), 191
    Tryphosa, 191
Bowne
    Adelaide (Huntington), 282-283
    Agnes (Burchard), 283
    Annie (Townsend), 282
    Caroline, 282-283
    Caroline, 283
    Clarence Southgate, 283
    Clifford, 283
    Edward Randolph, 283
    Eliza (Rapalye), 282
    Eliza (Southgate), 249, 282(2), 283, 314
    Eliza H. (Clements), 282
    Eliza Southgate, 282
    Elizabeth H., 283, 283
    Emily (Embury), 283
    Emma, 283
    Emma (Smith), 282-283
    Frances, 283
    Francis D., 283
    Frederic, 282-282, 283(2)
    Gertrude (Travers), 283
    Helen, 283(3)
    Horatio, 282
    Ida (Sutton), 283
    James Bruce, 283
    Jessie (Draper), 283
    John, 259
    Katherine (Guild), 283
    Lillie, 283
    Lizzie (McAdams), 283
    Marion Southgate, 283
    Mary, 249, 282-282
    Mary Ann, 283(2)
    Mayor Walter, 314
    Millie (Garfield), 283
    Robert, 282
    Robert Southgate, 283
    Simon Rapalge, 283
    Simon Rapalye, 282
    Spencer Frederic, 283
    Walter, 249, 259, 282(2), 283(2)
    Walter, III, 282-282, 283(2)
    Walter, Jr., 249, 282-283
    William, 283
Boyd, 247
    Alice Stillman, 258
    Augusta Murray, 248(2), 314
    Capt. Joseph Coffin, 315
    Capt. Robert, 197
    Catharine C. (Wilkins), 247
    Catherine Charlotte (Wilkins), 253
    Charles Mayo, 253
    Charles Orlando, 247
    Edward Augustus, 248
    Eliza (Railey), 253
    Elizabeth (Wilson), 253
    Ellen Almira, 248(2)
    Frances Greenleaf, 247
    Frances W. (Whitmore), 253
    Frederick William, 253
    Harriet (Dummer), 247, 316
    Harriet E. (Churchill), 253
    Horace Erald, 247
    Isabella (Southgate), 247, 253(2)
    Isabella Susanna, 247
    James, 247, 258
    James J., 314-315
    James Joseph, 247, 316
    James Railey, D.D., 253
    Joanna, 332
    Joel Hall, 253
    Joseph C., 247, 253(2), 314(2)
    Joseph Coffin, 247, 253, 314
    Lloyd Tilghman, 253
    Louie, 258
    Margaret, 258
    Margaret A. (Hall), 247
    Margaret Ann (Hall), 253
    Margaret Hall, 258
    Mary, 258
    Mary (Southgate), 253
    Mary Eliza (Railey), 248
    Mary Southgate, 247, 253
    Miranda Elizabeth, 247
    Octavia Caroline, 248
    Rev. Frederick William, 248, 253
    Robert Southgate, 247, 253(2), 258, 315
    Samuel Stillman, 247, 253(2)
    Samuel Stillman, Esq., 258
    Samuel Stillman, Jr., 258
    Sarah (Farrington), 248
    Walter Browne, 247
    Walter Stewart, 253
    William Edward, 253
Boylston
    Dr. Zabdiel, 286
Brackett, 10
    Abbie Ann, 113
    Abigail, 10-10, 11(2)
    Abigail, 11
    Abigail, 12

Abigail, 105(2), 107
Abigail, 107, 109-110, 113
Abigail (Brackett), 105
Abigail (Chapman), 10, 105
Abigail Helen, 113
Abraham, 10-10, 11(3)
Abraham Drake, 11
Abram, 11
Adriand (Sherman), 108
Alice Burnham, 113
Alma Maria, 108
Alpheus Ditman, 113
Alpheus Lowell, 113
Amanda (Wight), 109
Amos L., 11
Ann M., 109
Annie L. (Ditman), 113
Annie May, 113
Anthony, 10-11, 22, 47-48, 105, 107
Anthony Howard, 113
Anthony, Jr., 10, 12, 44, 56, 77, 88-89, 105-106, 107(2), 109, 113
Arminta (Caswell), 109
Arthur Hamilton, 113
Aurelia (Leighton), 108
Azubah Partridge (Quinby), 311
Benjamiin, 11
Benjamin F., 11
Betsey, 263
Betsey A., 11, 23
Betsey Walker, 110
Calista, 113
Calista (Wight), 109-110
Capt. Anthony, 20.3
Capt. John, 3, 10, 38, 47-47, 48(2), 49, 82-83, 109-110, 112, 153-154, 220, 227, 235, 288, 311
Capt. Nathaniel, 24
Capt. William, 161
Chapman, 109(2)
Charles E., 11
Charles H., 110
Clara (Spencer), 113
Cpl. Anthony, 46
Daniel, 105, 107(2), 108
Daniel H., 109
David, 10, 105
Dorothy (Bailey), 263
Elbridge O., 110
Eliza (Leach), 110
Eliza (Longley), 11
Eliza M. (Hodgkins), 11
Elizabeth, 11, 109(2), 109(2)
Elizabeth (Brackett), 109
Elizabeth (Morrell), 107-108
Ellen, 109
Elura, 11
Emeline, 109
Enoch, 109
Enoch, 109
Enos L., 11
Esther, 11
Esther (Cox), 11, 47
Esther Plummer, 108
Eunice, 11
Eunice (Humphrey), 24

Franklin Pierce, 113
George, 109
George W., 109
Gilbert Mariner, 112-113
Hannah, 11
Hannah (Bennett), 109
Hannah (Lunt), 11
Hannah Frances, 10, 11
Harriet (Russell), 108
Harriet W., 110
Henry Campbell, 113
J.C., 194
Jacob Morrell, 108
James, 11, 48
Jane, 10
Jennie (Hackett), 110
Jeremiah, 10, 48, 105, 107(3)
Jeremiah Chapman, 108
Joan, 11
Joanna, 11(3)
John, 10, 48, 89-90, 105, 107(3), 108(2), 288
John Snow, 140, 288
John, Jr., 109(2)
Jonathan H., 109
Joseph, 12, 14
Joseph Henry, 11-12
Josephine Mariah, 113
Josephine Mariah (Brackett), 113
Joshua, 10(2), 11, 14, 47, 89, 105(2), 182
Joshua, Jr., 57
Josiah, 12(2)
Judith, 12
Judith (Sawyer), 2, 10
Laura (Parker), 108
Lavinia Downing, 113
Lionel O., 107
Lionlen, 108
Lizzie, 11
Lois (Talbot), 110
Louis, 109
Louis P., 109
Louisa Allen, 11
Lt. Joshua, 12
Lucretia, 109
Lucy, 48
Lucy (Cobb), 108
Luisa M. (Lunt), 11
Marcy, 11
Margaret E., 107
Margaret Elizabeth, 108
Mariah H., 11
Martha Ann (Lowell), 109
Mary, 24
Mary, 47
Mary, 48, 107
Mary, 109
Mary (Hunt), 110
Mary (Shaw), 11
Mary (Snow), 10, 140
Mary (Walker), 108
Mary Addia, 11
Mary Ann, 108
Mary Geneva, 113
Miranda C., 11
Miranda C. (Brackett), 11
Miriam P. (Berry), 173

Molly (Walker), 10
Mrs. Betty, 24
Mrs. Molly, 108
Mrs. Sarah Wood, 182
Nancy (Robinson), 11
Nancy C., 110
Nathaniel, 11, 22-23, 107
Olive, 24, 307
Olive Stevens, 113
Oliver, 112
Pamelia, 109
Peel Bodwell, 113
Peter, 14, 22(2), 23, 174, 308
Polly, 11, 22
Polly W., 110
Rebecca, 12
Rebecca (Bailey), 109
Reuben, 107(2), 108
Rev. S.B., 10
Rev. Silas B., 109(2)
Rev. Silas Blake, 110-111, 113
Robert Peel, 111
Roxanna, 110
Ruth S., 11
Sally, 48
Sally (Sawyer), 23
Samuel, 11
Samuel Mountfort, 108
Sarah, 6, 10(2), 11-11, 12(2), 38, 45, 109, 128
Sarah (Hobbs), 109
Sarah A., 23(2), 24
Sarah Ann (Burnham), 111
Sarah F., 11
Sarah Jane, 108
Seth, 23
Silas Blake, 112
Silas Frederick, 113
Simon, 23
Sophia, 23
Sophronia (Lunt), 108
Sophronia S., 110
Stephen B., 11
Stephen Moulton, 108
Sumner Burnham, 113
Susan, 17
Susannah, 11(2), 12
Susannah (Drake), 10
Sybil, 109
Thomas, 10, 22-22, 23(2), 24, 57, 89, 140, 288, 290
Velzora Eastman, 113
Virgil Neal, 113
Walker, 109(2), 112
Walter, 110, 112
Walter, Jr., 110
William, 14, 22, 48, 109-110, 112, 288
William Plummer, 108
William, Esq., 24
William, Jr., 24, 263
Zachariah, 10(2), 12, 20.1, 22(2), 24, 45, 57, 78, 89, 105-106, 164, 173, 188, 196, 308

Bradbury
Dorothy, 338
Mary A., 149
Nancy, 128(2)

Bradford
Alden, 295
George R., 98

Bradley
Amos, 133
Dea. Amos, 133
Dorcas, 137
Dr. Peleg, 133
Elizabeth, 133, 218
Enoch, 133
Enos, 133
Frances W., 51
Hannah, 133
Harriet Angier (Pierce), 238
Harriet L., 238
Joseph, 133
Joshua, 133
Leonard, 268
Martha, 133
Mary (Alden), 238
Mr. Charles A., 21
Mrs. Abigail Loring (Codman), 275
Mrs. Susannah Webb (Partridge), 274
Nehemiah, 133
Parson, 74, 106, 131, 149
Rev. Caleb, 90, 92, 95, 97, 100, 107, 131, 133(2), 134, 145-145, 146(2), 149, 151, 157-157, 158(2), 159(2), 160-160, 161(2), 164, 170-174, 179, 187, 205, 207(2), 211, 217, 231, 236-238, 248, 263, 266, 268, 279-280, 284, 305-306
Rhoda, 133
Ruth, 133
Sally (Crocker), 146
Sarah, 133
Sarah (Crocker), 275
William C., 99, 238
William L., 238

Bradstreet
Harriet Louisa, 225
Lydia (Nichols), 225
Simon, 225

Brady
Jane, 35

Brawn
Charles, 307
Eliza, 307
Jane, 307
John, 307
Mary, 307
Rebecca (Bailey), 307

Bray
Charles H., 204
Dr. Madison J., 279
Elizabeth (Johnson), 279

Bremblecome
Samuel, 263

Brewer
Capt. Dexter, 43, 80, 83, 97, 121, 207, 215, 291
Col. Samuel, 154
David, 43
Dexter, 78
Dr. John M., 121
Eleanor, 339
Emeline, 207
Jane, 80(2)
Jane (Frost), 83

Nettie, 149
Sarah (Jackson), 339
Bridges
Mrs. Sarah M., 192
Briggs
David, 284
Brimblecom
A.L. (Harrington), 122
Albert Jonas, 122
Anna (Huntington), 122
Augusta (Reynolds), 122
Capt. Samuel A., 141
Charles, 122(2)
Col. Samuel, 122
Edward, 122
Emily (Gragg), 122
Francis Alden, 122
Frederic, 122
Harriet (Buttrick), 122, 141
Harriet C. (Houghton), 122
Henry, 122
James Stedman, 122
Lucy A., 122, 336
Lucy Adeline, 122
Mary (Mansfield), 122
Rev. Samuel, 94, 98, 123, 139, 141, 263, 265, 268, 285, 336
Samuel, 122
Samuel A., 122
Sarah (Holden), 122
William, 122(2)
Brisco
Sally (Stevens), 264
Sarah (Revere), 193
Sarah (Rose), 194
Thomas, 13, 193-194
Broad
Abigail, 168
Abigail (Carter), 168
Almira, 7, 168
Amos, 168
Amos [NH], 7
Ann, 168
Ann A., 162
Augustus, 168
Betsey, 7
Caleb, 168
Daniel, 168
Edward B., 168
Elizabeth, 168
Elizabeth (Greene), 168
Elizabeth (Jewett), 168
Ens. Daniel, 164
Ephraim, 164, 166, 168(2)
Ephraim [C.E.], 7
Eunice, 166, 168(2)
Ezra, 168
George B., 168
Henry, 168
Joseph, 92, 168
Lucy, 168
Lucy (Skillings), 167
Margaret, 168(2)
Mary, 168
Mary (Skillin), 168
Mary Ann, 168

Mrs. Eunice, 166
Sarah, 168
Silas, 78, 90-91, 94, 121, 166, 168
Sile, 129
Sopha (Waterhouse), 70, 304
Sophia (Waterhouse), 168
Sophia Augustus, 168
Thaddeus, 166-167, 168(2)
Thomas, 7, 70, 78, 165, 168(2), 304
William, 168
William F., 168
Brooks
Abigail (Browne), 59
Bertha M. (Pennell), 231
Bishop, 337
Clara, 253, 258
Gov. John, L.L.D., 318
Hannah, 159, 231
Harry D., 231
J., 295
John, 306
Martha, 304(2)
Mrs. Edward (Smith), 182
Peter, 68
Rev. Edward, 59, 337
Broughton
Abigail, 105
Brown
Abbie S. (North), 130
Abigail, 65
Alice M., 257
Catherine G., 307, 311
Dea. Nathaniel, 130
Ezra, 208
Hannah, 66
Harry, 281
John, 24
Maj. Jacob, 48
Rebecca (Fly), 24
Rev. Thomas, 20.2, 236
Sarah, 65
Susanna, 65
Browne
Abigail, 59, 239, 241(2)
Bettie, 243
Bishop, 242
Capt. Thomas, 146, 240-241, 251-252, 294
Cotton, 59
Cotton B., 59
Cynthia Eliza (Denny), 242-243
David McComas, 242
Eliza (Southgate), 246-247
Elizabeth, 59, 146, 239(2), 241, 248
Elizabeth S., 256
Elizabeth S. (Southgate), 242
Ellen Octavia, 242(2)
Esther W. (Lane), 240
Eunice, 246
Frederic, 242
Frederic S., 243
Frederick Edward, 243
George Southgate, 243
Hannie, 243
Harriet, 242
Harriet Augusta, 242
Ichabod, 59

Joanna (Cotton), 59
John, 59(2)
John Cotton, 240
Julia (Chapman), 242
Kizzie C., 243
Martha, 59
Mary Ann, 240
Meriel, 59
Merrill Cutting, 240
Mrs. Ann, 240
Mrs. Lydia, 59
Mrs. Lydia (Howard), 239
Mrs. Martha (Oldham), 59
Nathaniel, 59
Octavia (Southgate), 146, 239, 241-243, 247,
       249-250, 256, 315
Octavia S., 242
Parson, 146
Peter C., 59
Rebecca, 146, 158, 239, 240-241, 313
Rev. George W.G., 242, 294
Rev. John, 59, 239
Rev. Thomas, 58-59, 64, 77, 81, 146, 158, 216,
       237, 239-243, 245, 247, 250, 256,
       288, 290, 313, 335
Rev. Thomas, Jr., 239
Samuel, 59
Sarah (Gillespie), 242
T. Quincy, 240
Tennie, 242
Thomas, 59, 239
Thomas, Jr., 240
Wallace, 247
Ward, 59
William, 146, 239-243, 247, 249-250, 256, 294,
       315
William Gray, 242
William Henry, 242
William, Jr., 241

Bryant
Daniel, 67
Hannah, 154
James, 89
John, 307
Mary, 240
Moses, 57

Buchanan
Walter Starr, 264

Buck
Clarence O., 8
Ida G. (Stevens), 8
Mrs. Cyrus, 182
Mrs. Theodore, 23

Buckley
Adeline B. (Woodford), 42, 190
Alice C., 190
Barzillea, 187
Berilla, 78
C.S., 52, 94
Capt. Charles Sumner, 125, 190
Charles, 55
Charles M., 125, 190
Edward M., 159
Edward Melvin, 190
Edward William, 190
Edwin, 42
Ernest Lynn, 190
Frederick H., 190
Gertrude, 190
Helen F., 42
Henry, 125, 190
Herbert, 125, 190
Laura, 125, 190
Laura Jane (Stevens), 125, 190
Martha Ann (Hicks), 190
Mary A., 190
Mary Ann, 190(2), 233, 264
Mrs. Martha, 187
Nancy G., 188
Nancy Goodrich, 28
Oliver, 20.3, 28, 32, 52, 55, 90-91, 93-94, 98,
       125, 131, 140-141, 159, 187-187,
       188(2), 191, 271
Oren, 188, 190
Orin, 94
Ralph, 190
Ralph E., 190
Sally (Reed), 159, 187-188
Sarah, 125
Sarah J., 190
Solomon, 187
Sumner, 125

Buckman
John, 134
William, 82

Buckminister
Joseph S., 248

Budd
Bethiah Ann, 303
Eliza Smith, 303
George Bailey, 304
Joseph Chamberlain, 304
Martha Chamberlain, 304
Mary Ann (Chamberlain), 303
Mary Jane Alexander, 303
William, 303
William Edward, 304

Bulkley
Nancy, 196

Bunker
Capt. George, 295
Sarah W., 264

Burbank
Ebeneza P., 100
Frances Mariah, 100
Sarah Mariah (Graves), 100

Burchard
Agnes, 283

Burgess
Eliza W. (Montgomery), 264
Henry s., 264

Burnell
Ferdenand, 10
Marcena G. (Stevens), 10

Burnes
Mrs. Samuel, 138

Burnett
Nathan, 159
Rebecca (Bailey), 159

Burnham
Alexis, 186
Amos, 183

Angeline, 184
Benjamin, 9, 66, 75-76, 78, 145, 164, 183(2), 184(2), 303, 307
Brittania, 186
Caroline (Kennard), 184
Charles, 184
Charlotte, 9
Cymene, 186
Daniel, 183(2)
David, 76, 183(3)
Elbridge Gerry, 186
Eliza, 185
Eliza A., 185
Ella J., 184
Emeline (Bailey), 308
Emily Ann, 186
Emily Augusta (Foss), 185
Enoch, 94, 122, 186, 194
Enoch Lincoln, 186
Eunice, 183
Frank P., 185
Fred L., 185
George Collins, 185
George W., 183-184, 185(2)
Harriet D., 185(2), 185
Henretta (Kelley), 184
Jane, 183
Jennette, 186
Job, 183(2)
Job, Jr., 183
Joel, 183
Joseph, 83
Judith (Virgin), 186
Leonard, 308
Levi, 133
Lucy, 9
Mary, 183
Mary (Mustard), 112
Mary A., 184
Mary A. (Nickery), 184
Mary Ann (Foster), 184
Mary Ann (Hamilton), 185
Mary E. (Foss), 185
Mercy (Harmon), 183
Moses, 183(2)
Mrs. Emily A., 185
Mrs. olive, 183
Mrs. Rebecca, 183
Naomy (Royals), 183(2), 184
Naomy Royals, 184
Nathaniel, 112
Olevia (Libby), 185
Olive, 183
Olive (Sawyer), 112
Olive B. (Foss), 185
Patrick Henry, 186
Paul Dyer, 184
Rebecca, 183
Rebeckah, 183
Robert, 183
Rose, 37
Roxanna (Richards), 184
Royal R., 184-184, 185(2)
Samuel, 183
Sarah Ann, 111
Solomon, 183

Stephen A., 184
Thomas, 183
Vista, 186
William D., 184
William M., 271
Burton
Hannie (Browne), 243
J.S., 243
Bussell
Mrs. William F. (Smith), 182
Butler
C.B., 330
Gen. Benjamin F., 311
Jeremiah, 52
John, 44
Nancy (Haskell), 44
Thankful, 26, 27, 173
Thomas, 327
Buttrick
Col. Jonas, 122
Harriet, 122, 141
Maj. John, 122
Butts
Samuel, 64, 224, 227, 232, 236, 287, 310
Buxton
Susan, 284
Cadwell
C.A., 281
Calef
Samuel, 294
Call
Nathan, 302
Camel
Benjamin C., 128
Cammet
William, 238
Campbell
Benjamin G., 133
Dr. Henry, 111
John, 108
Mrs. Charity, 133
Mrs. Rebecca, 108
Carle
Samuel, Jr., 244
Carleton
Moses, 326
Samuel L., 205
Carlton
Rev. Isaac, 285
Carney
Harriet A. (Stevens), 8
Willard C. G., 8
Carpenter
Adele, 283
Arthur, 283
Beatrice, 283
Caroline Bowne (Smith), 283
Charles Whitney, 283
Charles Whitney, Jr., 283
Florence, 283
George Washington, 283
Jesse, 283
Lillian, 283
Carson
Abigail (Libby), 185
Isaac, 185

Carter
  Abigail, 168
  Asa H., 98
  Eunice P., 281
  Ezra, 168, 205, 246
  Frances (Lawrence), 282
  Hannah, 312
  Rev. Frederick Brewerton, 282
Carver
  Eunice, 327
Caskallon
  Edward, 47
Caswell
  Arminta, 109
Cemetery
  Allen's Corner, Portland, 263, 265
  Bailey Burying Ground, 33, 42-43, 45(2), 308
  Black Point Cemetery, 272
  Brackett, 107
  Broughton, Ill., 112
  Conant Cemetery, 307, 310
  Congress Street, 92
  Copp's Hill, Boston, 193
  Dea. Bailey Burying Ground, 155
  Dunstan Cemetery, Scarborough, 247-248, 252, 256
  Eastern, 5, 59, 113, 161, 179, 181, 197, 225, 240, 242, 280-281, 287, 313
  Evergreen, 14, 44, 91, 124, 141, 146, 149, 154, 177, 179, 185, 209-210, 225, 229, 240, 253, 258, 265, 271, 277, 281
  Flushing Cemetery, New York, 282
  Forest Ave., 189, 191(2), 194
  George Street, 20.5-20.6, 27, 173, 183, 227
  Hobbs Cemetery, West Falmouth, 263
  Larrabee, 231
  Lunt Cemetery, Westbrook, 233
  Magdalene, 204-205
  Mitchell's Hill, Portland, 146, 275
  North Hampton, Massachusetts, 257
  Old East Deering, 21
  Old Orchard Beach, 151
  Old Skillings Burying Place, 25
  Pine Grove, 9-10, 13, 42, 45, 51, 91, 116, 120, 125-126, 146, 154, 174, 187-188, 190(2), 191-192, 196, 275
  Saccarappa Village Cemetery, 34-35, 38, 40, 48, 220-221, 226, 228-229, 251, 275, 310, 339
  Skillings Long Creek, 166
  Stroudwater, 9, 29, 34-35, 39, 41, 48-51, 59, 61, 64, 67-70, 79-81, 82(2), 83, 124, 141, 146, 148, 150-151, 157, 167, 169(2), 174, 201, 216-217, 223-224, 239, 263, 271, 275-276, 279, 290, 303, 305
  Stroudwater Merrill cemetery, 172
  Village Cemetery, Westbrook, 212
  Webb Cemetery, 176, 274
  Western Cemetery, Portland, 252, 273, 281
  Windham Hill Cemetery, 279
  Windham Road (Forest Ave.), 13, 42, 45, 128, 130-131
Chadbourn
  Elizabeth (Wescott), 266
  William T., 266

Chadwell
  Mary B., 226
Chadwick
  Abigail, 245
  Eunice (Willard), 245
  Mary, 245
  Rev. Benjamin, 239, 245(2)
  Sopiah, 245
Chamberlain
  Aaron, 159, 279, 302-303
  Abigail, 303
  Bethiah (Pearson), 303
  Eliza, 303
  Elizabeth (Waterhouse), 159, 302-303
  Emeline D., 303
  Mary Ann, 303
Chandler
  Lydia, 127
Chapin
  Rev. Horace B., 137
  Rev. Perez, 137
Chaplin
  Rev. Perez, 135
Chapman
  A.P., 64, 91
  Abigail, 10, 105(2), 105, 107
  Abigail (Broughton), 105
  Albion P., 63, 309
  Anthony, 206
  Clara, 5(3), 5
  Edward, 36, 46(2), 56, 60, 80, 89-90, 105(2), 108, 167
  Edward K., 171
  Eleanor (Small), 105
  Elizabeth (Starbird), 51
  Gore B., 5, 8
  Gore Bugbee, 5
  Hannah (Quinby), 163
  Henry, 40, 202
  John E., 5
  Joseph, 206
  Julia, 242
  Julia Ann (Stevens), 5, 8
  L.B., 153
  Leonard Bond, 20.1
  Lydia, 21, 30, 51
  Lydia (Starbird), 30, 211
  Mary, 30
  Mary (Wilborn), 105
  Moses, 173
  Nancy, 30, 211
  Nathaniel, 47, 105, 108
  Polly (Jose), 108
  Rufus C., 5
  Ruth, 108, 220
  Samuel, 30, 163, 305
  Samuel A., 120
  Shadrach, 30, 211
  Shore, 182
  Simon, 108
  Wilford G., Esq., 5
Chase
  Adah E., 266
  Capt. Jonathan, 126
  Daniel, 111
  David, 164

    Ethel May, 130
    Hannah, 126, 196, 304
    Hannah E., 266
    John, 55
    John H., 130(2)
    Judith, 191
    Salmon, 333
    Sarah Louise, 130
    Sarah Louise (Chase), 130
    Sarah Louise (North), 130
    Thirah (Emery), 126
Chatben, 90
Checkley
    Rev. Mr., 59
Chenery
    Catherine M., 218(2)
    Daniel D., 41, 44, 49, 61, 77-78, 106-107, 289
    Daniel Dole, 157, 218
    Edward, 41, 51(2), 218
    Eleanor, 339
    Ida, 150
    John J., 51, 78, 100, 107
    John J., Mrs., 1
    Joseph, 41(2), 49, 90, 94, 96(2), 157(2), 218(2), 219
    Joseph, Jr., 218
    Margaret (Woodford), 51
    Mart T. (Dole), 218
    Mary (Dole), 157, 214
    Mary E. (Woodford), 51
    Mrs. Mary E., 78
    Phoebe, 149
    Rebecca (Johnson), 49, 218
Chesley
    Albert A., 21, 75, 168
    Charles, 168
    Mary Ann (Broad), 168
    Sarah, 304
Chick
    Nathan, 46, 89-90
Chickering
    Dwight, 99
Chipman
    John, Esq., 59
    Oren G., 63
Chism
    John, 302
Choat
    Daniel, 55
Choate
    David, 76
    Rufus, 206
Choatt
    Benjamin, 164
Churchill
    Harriet E., 253, 258
    James C., 98
Chute
    Thomas, 34
    Warren B., 22
Claise
    Thomas, 78-79
Clapp
    Asa, 241
Claridge
    Lucy A., 5

Clark
    Dr. Charles E., 163
    Edmund, 20.1
    Eleanor (Frost), 83, 275
    Elizabeth, 154
    Elizabeth (Fly), 307
    Jacob, 252, 307
    John, 188, 263
    Louisa, 308
    Luther, Esq., 100
    Mary, 101
    Morris, 307
    Peter T., 62, 78, 83, 275
    Sally (Hicks), 263
    Samuel, 252
    Seth, 157
    Sgt. Morris, 47-48
Clarke
    Mrs. C.A., 57
    Rev. Ephriam, 239
Clary
    Caroline, 3
    Clara, 3
    Dolla (Stevens), 3
    Eleanor, 3
    Sally, 3(2)
    Samuel, 3(2), 13
    Williams, 3
Clay
    Hanson M., 184
Cleeve
    George, 20, 20.2, 102, 198, 286
    Mary, 23
Clement
    Jeremiah, 77
Clements
    Eliza H., 282
Cloise
    George, 79
    Hannah, 79
    Mary, 79, 79
    Susannah, 79
    Thomas, 78-78, 79(2)
Cloudman
    Daniel C., 266
    Dorothy (Tate), 277
    Esther B. (Quinby), 266
    George C., 214-215
    Louise, 221
    Sewall, 277
Clough
    Josiah R., 164
Cloutman
    Catharine (Partridge), 309
    Dorothy L. (Tate), 304
    Eliza B., II (Waterhouse), 304
    Elizabeth, 304
    John T., 304
    John T., Jr., 304
    Mary Ann (Waterhouse), 304
    Mrs. Mary, 304
    Paul, 304
    Sewall, 304
    Timothy, 309
Cloyce
    Thomas, 199

Cobb
  Andrew, 46
  Betsey (Brackett), 263
  Brig. Gen. William, 163
  Capt. William, 262
  Chipman, 56, 62, 287
  Daniel, Jr., 76, 183
  Dianth, 179
  E., 331
  Edward, 211, 248
  Enoch, 165, 263
  Eunice (Quinby), 163
  George, 164, 263
  Isaac, 165
  Jediah, 226
  Joanna, 197
  Joseph, 140
  Lucretia (Brackett), 109
  Lucy, 9, 108
  Lucy (Webb), 76, 183
  Moses, 109
  Mrs. Abigail, 25
  Mrs. Lucy, 76
  Samuel, 62, 287
  Sgt. Chipman, 46
  Smith Woodward, 25
Cobby
  Jane, 231
  John, 231
Cochran
  Timothy, 164
Codman
  Ann (Jones), 225
  Charles E., 226
  Constance, 259
  Don, 226
  George C., 12, 215, 225-227, 232
  George Calvin, 225
  Harriet Louisa (Bradstreet), 225
  Horatio Southgate, 259
  John E., 226
  Lucretia (Smith), 225
  Mary, 225
  Mrs. Abigail Loring, 274, 275
  Randolph A.L., Esq., 228
  Richard, 225
  Sophia Munroe (Smith), 259
  William, 225
  William Coombs, 259
  William Coombs, III, 259
  William Henry, 225
Coffin
  Dr. N., 20.3
  Henry, 63
  James, 304
  Martha (Waterhouse), 304
  Rev. Paul, 247, 304
Colby
  William W., 190
Cole
  Benjamin, 226
  Susannah (Pennell), 226
Colesworthy
  D. C., 178
Collens
  John, 188

Colley
  Joseph, 137
Collins
  Lydia, 8
  Mary (Fickett), 66
  Mathew, 243
  Richard, 66
  Zenobia, 50
Colt
  Elizabeth H. (Bowne), 283
  Experience (Wheeler), 250
  H.D., 283
  John, Jr., 250
  Martha, 250
  Rev. Joseph, 250
Conant
  Ann, 220
  Ann, 220
  Ann, 309
  Ann (Haskell), 220
  Ann (Schofield), 220
  Bartholomew, 57, 220-221, 223
  Daniel, 77, 220-222
  Elizabeth, 220
  Hannah (Frink), 220
  Hannah (Worcester), 220
  Joseph, 57, 89, 199, 220-221, 223, 230
  Joseph, Jr., 57, 220
  Mary, 220, 309
  Mary (Peabody), 220, 309
  Ruth (Chapman), 108, 220
  Samuel, 46, 56, 89-90, 220, 235, 309
  William, 47, 220-221
Condid
  Rev., 157
Connell
  John G., 208
Connor
  Harriet White (Bailey), 177
  Seldon, 177
Cony
  Nancy, 176
Cook
  Francis, 222
  Gerry, 52, 55, 94, 133
  Jane, 222
  John, 47
  Mary (Maxfield), 41
  Mary Jane (Hallsbury), 133
  Nathan, 41
  Philip, 47
Cooke
  Robert, 243
Coolbroth
  Abigail, 185
  Lemuel, 319
Coombs
  Olive, 279
Copps
  Joseph, 63-64, 78, 310
  Mary, 63
  Mrs. Abigail, 64
  Mrs. Peggy, 64
  Nabby (Gould), 63
  Samuel, 63-65
  Samuel, Jr., 64

William, 78
Cordman
  John B., Esq., 3
Corey
  Martha E. (Goodrich), 196
Cottle
  Ann, 214
  Edward, 214
Cotton
  Africa, 15
  Africa P., 5
  Joanna, 59
  Rev. Roland, 59
  Sarah (Stevens), 5, 15
  William, 102
Coulbourn
  John, 22
Coverly
  Mary, 73, 274
  Mrs. Mary, 274, 275
Cowan
  Charles F., 149
Cox
  Capt. Joseph, 91
  Charles Edward, 19, 91
  Charlotte (Sawyer), 91
  Dorcas, 134, 171
  E., 55
  Emily, 152
  Enoch, 19, 91(2)
  Esther, 11(2), 47
  Isaac, 38, 175
  Jane Stevens, 19, 91
  John, 11, 153
  Joseph, 19, 52, 78, 91(3), 94, 151
  Josiah, 76, 180, 236, 290, 293, 305
  Lemuel, 2, 19, 91
  Lydia, 65, 66
  Martha (Quinby), 38, 175
  Martha (Stevens), 2
  Mary, 149, 151, 153
  Moses, 4
  Mrs. Charlotte, 91
  Sally, 4
  Sarah, 19
  Susanna Sawyer, 19
  Susannah S., 91
Cradiford
  Nathaniel, 89
Craig
  Alice (Wilson), 202
  John, 202
  Margaret Ann (Hawkes), 312
Crawford
  Thomas, 317
  William H., 318
Creasey
  Daniel, 241
Creddiford
  James, 66, 192
  Jimmy, 129
Cressey
  Rev. Noah, 134
Crispan
  Charles, 30
Crocker

Edward D., 161
Enoch, 161
Jonathan H., 317
Sally, 146
Sarah, 275
Crockett
  Abraham, 46
  Daniel, 48
  George, 48
  John, 6, 56
  John, Jr., 89
  Joshua, 46
  Nathaniel, 66, 240-241
  Richard, 46
  Samuel, Jr., 164
  Sgt. John, 46
  William, 23
Crosby
  J.C., 283
  Marion Southgate (Bowne), 283
Cross
  Jane, 285
Cummings
  Abram, 296
  Andrew Jackson, 41
  Charles Maxfield, 41
  Charles Winslow, 41
  Elizabeth Abbott, 253
Cummings
  Elmer E., 260
Cummings
  Frances Caroline, 41
  Francis J., 41
  George Andrew, 41
  Joanna (Barbour), 197
  Jonathan, 197
  Miaetta Frances, 41
  Martha Ella, 41
  Mary Eliza Shaw, 41
  Susan Maria, 41
  Thomas, 241
Curtis
  Addie J., 305
  Jane, 177
  John B., 44, 78, 96, 100, 107, 148, 183, 203
Cushing
  Christopher, 317
  Ezekil, 102, 104
  Isaac, 222
  Lucia, 2
Cushman
  Alvan, 182
  Charles, 182
  George H., 182
  John S., 182
  Levi, 182
  Martha (Downing), 182
  Nancy (Smith), 182
  Nancy S., 182
  Rebecca, 222
  Sarah, 182
  Susan E. (Hasty), 182
Cutter
  Abiel, 91, 94
  Ammi Ruhamah, 338
  Capt. William, 338

    Caroline, 338
    Dorothy (Bradbury), 338
    Elizabeth, 338
    F.F., 94
    F.T., 91
    Hannah C. (Greely), 338
    Levi, 75, 248
    Levi, Esq., 338
    Mehitable (Gray), 338
    Philip, 338
    Rev. Ami R., 338
    Samuel, 338
    Sarah, 338
    Simon, 78
    William, 338
    Zilpha I.W., 257

Cutts
    Thomas, 294

Dain
    Esther, 19
    Frederick, 19
    Hannah (Proctor), 19
    James, 19
    John, 19(2)

Dalinge
    Jacob, 46
    Jacob, Jr., 46

Dalton
    Asa, 170
    Rev. Asa, 162
    Samuel, 78, 162, 188

Dame
    Rev. Charles, 137-138

Damm
    Abigail, 34

Damon
    Michael S., 252

Dana
    Edward, 253
    Francis Swan (Southgate), 253
    George, 211
    Rev. Samuel, 326
    Samuel, 326

Dandridge
    Isabella (Lawrence), 282
    Lemuel Pendleton, 282

Danforth
    Ens. Joshua, 154
    Lt. Gov., 287
    President, 78
    Thomas, 198

Daniels
    Isaiah, 23

Danty
    Thomas, 89

Date
    18940000, 50
    18940600, 22
    18940800, 20, 51
    18940806, 18
    18940900, 2-3, 5
    18940915, 4
    18941006, 6
    18941013, 8
    18941020, 9
    18941027, 10
    18941103, 10
    18941110, 12
    18941117, 13
    18941201, 13
    18941208, 14
    18941215, 15
    18941222, 16
    18941229, 17
    18950105, 22
    18950112, 24
    18950119, 25
    18950126, 26
    18950202, 27
    18950209, 28
    18950216, 29
    18950223, 30
    18950309, 31
    18950316, 32
    18950323, 33
    18950330, 34
    18950406, 35
    18950413, 36
    18950420, 38
    18950427, 38
    18950504, 40
    18950511, 41
    18950518, 42
    18950525, 43
    18950601, 44
    18950608, 45
    18950615, 46
    18950629, 47
    18950706, 48
    18950713, 49
    18950720, 52
    18950727, 53
    18950803, 55
    18950810, 56
    18950817, 57
    18950824, 59
    18950831, 58
    18950907, 60
    18950914, 61
    18950921, 62
    18950928, 63
    18951005, 64
    18951012, 65
    18951019, 66
    18951026, 67
    18951102, 68
    18951109, 69
    18951116, 70
    18951123, 71
    18951130, 72
    18951207, 73
    18951214, 74
    18951221, 75
    18951228, 75
    18960104, 76
    18960111, 77
    18960118, 78
    18960125, 79
    18960201, 80
    18960208, 81
    18960215, 82
    18960222, 83

18960229, 84	18970918, 148-149
18960307, 85	18971002, 149
18960314, 85	18971009, 150
18960321, 87	18971016, 151
18960328, 88	18971023, 152
18960404, 89	18971030, 152
18960411, 90	18971106, 153
18960418, 90	18971113, 154
18960425, 91	18971120, 155
18960502, 92	18971127, 156
18960509, 93	18971204, 157
18960516, 94	18971211, 158
18960523, 95	18971225, 158
18960530, 96	18980101, 159
18960606, 97	18980108, 159
18960613, 99	18980115, 160
18960627, 98	18980122, 161
18960704, 100	18980129, 161
18960711, 101	18980205, 162
18960718, 102	18980219, 162
18960725, 103	18980226, 163
18960801, 104	18980312, 164
18960808, 105	18980319, 165
18960815, 106	18980326, 166-167
18960822, 107	18980409, 168
18960829, 107	18980423, 169
18960905, 109	18980430, 170
18960912, 110	18980507, 171
18960919, 111	18980514, 172
18960926, 111	18980521, 173
18961003, 112	18980527, 174
18961010, 113	18980618, 177
18961017, 114	18980702, 179
18961024, 114	18980709, 179
18961031, 115	18980716, 180
18961107, 116	18980723, 182
18961114, 117	18980730, 182
18961121, 118	18980806, 183-184
18961128, 119	18980820, 185
18961205, 120	18980827, 186
18961212, 120	18980917, 188
18961219, 121	18980924, 190
18970102, 121	18981001, 189
18970123, 122	18981008, 191
18970130, 123	18981010, 187
18970206, 124	18981015, 192
18970213, 125	18981022, 193
18970220, 126	18981029, 194
18970227, 127	18981105, 195
18970306, 128	18981112, 196
18970313, 129	18981119, 197
18970320, 130	18981126, 198
18970327, 131	18981203, 199
18970403, 133	18981210, 200
18970410, 134	18981217, 201
18970417, 136	18981224, 202
18970424, 137	18981231, 203
18970501, 138	19000103 204
18970508, 141	19000113, 205
18970515, 140	19000120, 206
18970522, 140	19000127, 207
18970717, 142	19000203, 207
18970731, 144	19000210, 208
18970807, 145	19000217, 209
18970814, 146	19000224, 210
18970828, 147	19000303, 211

19000310, 212
19000317, 213
19000324, 214
19000331, 215
19000407, 216
19000414, 217
19000421, 218
19000428, 219
19000505, 220
19000512, 221
19000519, 223
19000526, 225
19000602, 224
19000609, 226
19000616, 227
19000623, 228
19000630, 229
19000707, 230
19000714, 231
19000721, 232
19000728, 233
19000804, 234
19000811, 235
19000818, 236
19000901, 237
19000908, 239
19000915, 240
19000922, 241
19000929, 242
19001006, 243
19001013, 244
19001020, 246
19001027, 247
19001103, 248
19001110, 250
19001117, 251
19001124, 252
19001201, 253
19001208, 254
19001215, 256
19001222, 254
19001229, 257
19010105, 258
19010112, 259
19010119, 260
19010126, 261
19010202, 262
19010209, 263
19010213, 264
19010223, 265
19010302, 266
19010309, 268
19010316, 269
19010323, 270
19010330, 272
19010406, 274
19010413, 275
19010420, 276
19010427, 277
19010504, 278
19010511, 279
19010518, 280
19010525, 281
19010601, 282
19010608, 283
19011019, 285

19011026, 285
19011102, 286
19011109, 286
19011116, 288
19011123, 289
19011130, 290
19011207, 291
19011214, 292
19011221, 293
19030103, 313
19030110, 314
19030117, 314
19030124, 311, 315
19030131, 316
19030207, 317
19030214, 318
19030221, 319
19030228, 320
19030307, 321
19030321, 322
19030328, 323
19030404, 324
19030411, 325
19030418, 326
19030425, 327
19030502, 328
19030509, 329
19030516, 330
19030523, 331
19030530, 332
19030606, 333
19030613, 334
19030704, 295
19030711, 296
19030718, 297
19030725, 298
19030801, 299
19030808, 300
19030815, 301
19030822, 302
19030912, 304
19030919, 305
19030926, 306
19031003, 307
19031010, 308
19031017, 310
19031031, 312
19031107, 313
19040220, 335
19040227, 336
19040305, 337
19040312, 338
19040319, 339
1915, 20.1
Davidson
   James, 317
Davis
   Christopher S., 96-97
   Clara (Chapman), 5
   D., 55
   Elizabeth (Nickerson), 150
   Frederick, 164, 254
   George R., 240-241
   Irene Elmore (Stevens), 126
   Jacob, 150
   Judge Woodbury, 206, 219

Lawrence, 150
Rebecca, 1
Richard H., 126
Samuel, 317(2), 325
Silvanus, 203
Stella May, 126
Sylvanus, 45, 287
Day
Eunice (Quinby), 161
Ezekiel, 161
Hannah (Smith), 161
Henry Ezekiel, 161
James E., 191
John Q., 161
Joseph, 161, 324
Maria F. (Howard), 191
Deacons
Dea. E.D. Woodford, 6
Dea. William Stevens, 8
Deak
George, 158
Jerusha (Dyer), 158
Dean
Rev., 60, 170
Rev. Samuel, 81, 105, 182, 239, 273, 297
Deane
Nathaniel, 329
Dearborn
Henry, 323
Henry A.S., Esq., 156
Dearing
Joshua I., 164
Deering
Capt. James, 20.3
Henry, 10
Henry, Esq., 252
James, 10, 105, 147
John, 64, 241
William, 197
Delano
Ann, 155, 263
Eleanor (Libby), 185
Ella A., 33
Joseph, 123
William, 185
Dennett
Clementine, 197
Liberty B., Esq., 234
Dennison
Mary, 266
Denny
Cynthia Eliza, 242(2)
Daniel, 246
Maj. James Wilkinson, 243
Dent
Zilpha A., 100
Zilpha A. (Dent), 100
Derby
Elias Hasket, 239
Richard, 239
Dickinson
Martha, 254
Dilanoe
Amavriah, 250
Dill
Cypress, 182

Cypress L., 66, 303
Cyprus, 159
Samuel F., 33
Dinsmore
Hannah (Fickett), 66
James, 331
John, 66
Silas, 94
Ditman
Annie L., 113
Doane
Ebenezer, 46
Edward, 46
Eunice, 264
Joanna, 175
Doe
Daniel, 305
Dole
Andrew T., 119, 218
Andrew Titcomb, 219
Capt. Daniel, 35-36, 157, 174, 198, 216, 223-224, 236, 244, 291-292
Catherine, 140, 172, 218
Catherine (Partridge), 41
Catherine M. (Chenery), 218-219
Daniel, 40-41, 172, 214-215, 219, 225, 232, 235, 288(2), 289-289, 290(2), 293
Daniel, Jr., 217, 220, 290
John, 18, 152, 214(2)
John, Jr., 214
Katherine (Partridge), 220
London, 218
Mart T., 218
Mary, 35, 157, 174, 214, 215, 223
Mary (Foster), 218-219
Moses, 96-97, 215(2), 218-218, 219(2)
Moses H., 120, 219
Rebeckah (Pearsons), 214
Rhoda, 217
Richard, 157, 214, 217
Sarah (Pearson), 157, 215, 223, 235
Sarah (Pearsons), 214
Sophia Mitchell (Fosdick), 218, 219
William, 214
Dore
John, 94
Doughty
Hannah, 29, 189
Hannah (Hicks), 263
Hezehiah, 26
James, 47, 265
Jane, 189, 263
Joseph, 263
Martha (Wilson), 202
Nathan, 23
Sarah A., 26
Thomas, 202
Douty
Cpl. James, 48
George, 48, 90
James, 12, 57, 90
James, Jr., 90
Jonathan, 90
Thomas, 57
Dow
Augustus, 177

Col. Neal, 311
Dea. Hiram H., 78, 180, 216, 269, 288
Gen. Neal, 251, 334
Hiram, 55
Maria Caroline (Maynard), 251
Moses G., 100, 147
Moses G., Esq., 41, 120
Nancy Cony Winslow (Bailey), 177
Neal, 5
Downes
Harriet (Stevens), 6
Downing
Martha, 182
Drake
Abraham, 10
Susannah, 10
Draper
Jessie, 283
William B., 283
Dresser
Elizabeth A., 150
Wentworth, 245
Drew, 174
Annie C., 132
William A., 98
Drinkwater
Capt. Samuel, 285
Dudley
Benjamin, 153
Benjamin F., 150, 153
Clarabella, 150
Clarissa (Libby), 153
Edward, 150, 328-329
Elizabeth, 150
Ellen S., 150
Emily (Cox), 152
Emily C. (Mason), 153
Emily Cox (Mason), 150
George Edward, 150
Gilbert F., 150
Hannah W. (Luch), 153
Ida (Chenery), 150
James, 159
Mary F. (Fellows), 150
Nathaniel, 326-327, 332
William K., 330
William P., 150
Dummer
Harriet, 247, 316, 316
Jeremiah, 316
Mehitable (Moody), 316
Dunbar
Susannah, 195
Dunham
John, 55, 126
Olena, 126
Rufus, 28, 52, 55, 91, 94, 194
Dunn
Emeline (Brackett), 109
Eveline (Mitchell), 272
John W., 272
Josiah, 98
Samuel, 288
Dunning
Ebenezer P., 264
Sarah (Martin), 264

Duram
Humphrey, 20, 20.5
Duran
William, 6
Durant
Cornelius, 251
Durham
Humphrey, 20.2
Duston
Hannah, 133
Dwight
Eliza Waite (Bartol), 100
Rev. W.T., 100, 272
Dyer
A., 55
Alford, 20.2
Alfred, 27
Arthur, 164
Capt. Clement J., 132
Clement, 96
Elizabeth, 70
Ezekiel, 164
Isaac, 237
James, 55
Jerusha, 158
L.W., 22
Lydia, 27
Mary, 65
Moses, 123
Mrs. Rebecca (Smith), 182
Polly, 158
Robert, 158
Eastman
Eliza Ann (Quinby), 307
Joseph, 307
Rev. B. D., 111
Robert, 324
Eaton
Francis, Esq., 297
Nicholas, 164
Edes
Jeremiah, 122
Edwards
Charles, 154
Col. Clark S., 265
Eliza, 67
Thomas, 154
Elden
Gibeon, 221
Martha (Knight), 60
Mary C. (Partridge), 221
Ruth, 60
Elder
John, 266
Judith (Leighton), 263
Nancy (Mosher), 205
Nathaniel, 89
Ruth, 205
Samuel, 205
William, 165, 263
Eldridge
Pereze H., 93, 96
William, 55, 133
Elliot
Content, 22, 24
Ellsworth

Esther (Storer), 147
Jonathan, 147(2)
Mrs. Esther, 147
Elmer
Edward P., 196
Jerusha H. (Goodrich), 196
Elvins
Rev. Richard, 245
Richard, 245
Elwell
Edward H., 205
Embury
Emily, 283
Emerson
Andrew L., 204
Bulkley, 334
Edward, 334
Joseph, 295, 316, 334(2)
Rufus, 334
Samuel, 334
William, 316, 334(2)
Emery
Caroline, 277
Thirah, 126
William, 78
Epes
Abigail (Frost), 80, 86
Daniel, 80-80, 81(2), 90, 294
Estes
Silas, 263
Estis
Rev. Isaac, 270
Everett
Oliver, 121
Fagens
Joseph, 306
Mary (Whiting), 306
Farnum
Hannah, 221
Farrar
Bethiah, 37
Farrington
Sarah, 248(2)
William, 110
Fay
F. R., 22
Fayben
Joseph, 294
Fellows
Mary F., 150
Felton
Mrs. Miriam, 78
Fergerson
Charles, 66, 165, 238
James, 66
Mary (Slemons), 165
Thomas, Esq., 165
Ferguson
Charles, 77, 263
Mary (Slemons), 263
Fernald
Charles, 5
Fessenden
Abigail, 266
Daniel W., 205
William Pitt, 252, 284

Fickett
Abigail, 66(2)
Abigail (Brown), 65
Abigail (Fickett), 66(2)
Abner, 65(2), 71
Adeline, 70
Ann, 71
Asa, 67(2), 68-70
Benjamin, 65(5), 66(3), 183, 303
Betsey, 71
Charles, 24, 68(2), 69(2), 159, 302
Clarissa, 65
Clement, 71(2)
Cyrus, 70
Daniel, 65, 71
Deborah (Sawyer), 65
Dorcas (Plummer), 67-68
Ebenezer, 65-66, 71
Edward, 69
Eliza (Edwards), 67
Elizabeth, 67
Elizabeth, 70
Elizabeth, 70
Elizabeth, 75, 168
Elizabeth (Dyer), 70
Elizabeth (Larrabee), 51, 264
Elizabeth (Larraby), 69
Ellen, 68, 68
Enoch, 67, 70
Ephraim, 67
Ezera, 66
Fanie, 70
Frances, 68
Frances Augustus, 69
Francis, 68
Francis Augustus, 69
Frank, 68
G.S., 71
Gardner, 70
George, 68(3)
Hannah, 65-66
Hannah (Brown), 66
Harriet, 70
Isaac, 65-66
Isabella (Roberts), 66
J.B., 65
James, 68(2)
Jane, 70
Jason T., 65
Jennette, 68(2)
Jerome B., 65-66, 70
John, 65(5), 66-67
John, Jr., 65-66
Jonathan, 65-68, 70, 89, 290, 303-304
Jonathan, Jr., 65-66
Joseph, 65(2)
Joshua, 65(2)
Josiah, 66-67, 70, 72
Lucy (Stanford), 65-66
Lydia (Cox), 65-66
Margaret, 74(2)
Martha, 70
Mary, 65
Mary, 65
Mary, 67(2), 67, 70, 74
Mary (Dyer), 65

Mary (Hunnewell), 65
Mary (Moulton), 65
Mary (Swett), 70
Mehitable, 65, 65, 71, 74
Molly (Pennell), 65, 224, 226, 228
Moses, 66, 71
Mrs., 66
Mrs. Abigail, 65
Mrs. Betsey, 68, 70
Mrs. Elizabeth, 66
Mrs. Hannah, 65
Mrs. Molly, 62
Mrs. Nathan, 162
Nabby, 62
Nahum, 68(2), 69(2), 70
Nancy, 67
Natham, 264
Nathaniel, 65(2), 71
Nathan, 50
Nathaniel, 65(2), 66(2), 71, 228, 288
Nelly, 68(2)
Patience, 71, 228
Phebe, 67, 70, 76, 176
Polly, 71, 302(3)
Polly (Pennell), 65, 71
Robert, 70
Sally, 66
Sally (Fickett), 66
Sally (Warren), 66, 71
Samuel, 66-67, 70, 169
Sarah, 65
Sarah (Brown), 65
Sarah (Fickett), 65
Sarah (Sawyer), 66
Sarah (Stanford), 65
Scott, 70
Susan, 68
Susan, 68
Susanna (Brown), 65
Theophilus, 68(2)
Thomas, 65(3), 66(2), 67, 71
Vincent, 65(2), 66
Walter, 33, 35, 67-69, 70(2), 73, 78, 120
Walter, Esq., 121
Walton, 305
William, 65-65, 66(2)
Zebulon, 65-65, 66(2), 71
Field
Mary (Wilson), 202
Mary Ann, 42
Zachariah, 202
Fields
John, 164
Filker
Mrs. Ezra, 182
Fillebrown
Thomas, 327
Fillmore
President, 253
Fitch
Almira (Titcomb), 223
Luther, 223, 326
Luther, Esq., 263
Fletcher
A.W., 180
Flint
Jonathan, 20, 20.2
Thomas, 20
Fluent
Rufus, 78
Fluker
Thomas, 237
Fly
Capt. Isaac, 159
Dorcas, 307(2)
Eleanor, 307
Elizabeth, 24, 307-307
Hannah, 307
Isaac, 24, 78, 159, 302, 306-306, 307(2)
James, 307(2)
Jane, 24
Jerusha (Freeman), 307
Joanna (Libby), 307
John, 307(2)
Joseph, 24
Lucy, 307
Mary, 307(2)
Rebecca, 24
Sally, 24
Sally (Waterhouse), 302
Sarah, 307
Susannah, 307
Flye
Isaac, 164
Fobes
A.G., 52
Amasa, 91, 93-93, 94(2), 122
Amos, 90, 194
Charles S., 98
E.B., 55
Fogg
Esther, 302(2)
Hannah, 273
James, 109
Jeremiah, 305
Mary, 204
Mary (Brackett), 109
Seth, 65
Forbes
Albert, 55
Andrew J., 188, 190
Miriam Frances (Stevens), 188
Miss. Helen, 138
Mrs. Minnie F., 190
Ford
James, 252
Forder
James, 200
Richard, 171, 216, 262
Forest Ave.
Windham Road, 13, 42(2), 128(2), 131
Fosdick
Ann (Jones), 225
James, 225
Sophia Mitchell, 218, 219
Foss
Albert, 185
Charles A., 185
Clara (Woodford), 42
Emily Augusta, 185
Francis, 185
Harriet D. (Burnham), 185

Loretto Hartland, 42
Mary E., 185
Mrs. Mary, 185
Olive B., 185
William R., 129
Foster
Benjamin B., 38, 40, 78, 219
Freeman, 94
Hannah G., 172
Joseph H., 248
Mary, 218(2)
Mary Ann, 184
Moses H., 248
Rev. F., 94
Fowler
Daniel, 61, 155
Joseph, 315
Fox
Charles, 239
Daniel, 115
Eunice (McLellan), 239
Foxcroft
Joseph E., 297-298, 300-301
Rev. Samuel, 297
Foye
Sutton, 302
Frances
Caleb, 28, 193, 264
Harriet, 193
Harriet Revere, 264
Isabel, 193, 195
Isabella B., 195
James, 47
Maria, 193, 196
Mary, 170, 193, 265
Mary (Revere), 193
Mary (Rose), 264
Mary Rose, 265
Robert, 47
Sally, 193
Sarah B., 28
Francis
Nathaniel, 193
Frank
Melvin Porter, 284
Susan Augusta (Humphrey), 284
Fray
John J., 46
Frazier
Ann N., 317
John B., 320
Seth, 43, 76
Freeman
Daniel, 164
Enoch, 78, 90(2)
Eunice, 161, 163, 236
Frances (Smith), 283
Jerusha, 307
Joshua, 81, 236
Leonard Chester, 283
Lois (Pearson), 236
Louise, 283
Mabel, 283
Nathan, 91, 94
Samuel, 30, 235, 241, 283, 305
Samuel Harold, 283

Southgate Bowne, 283
Spencer Smith, 283
William, Esq., 20.3
French
Ann, 253
Frink
Dr. John N., 210
Hannah, 220
Mrs. Olivia E.S., 210
Frost
A.P., 64, 87(2)
Abigail, 37, 80(2), 81, 84-84, 86(3), 87
Abigail (Frost), 85
Abigail. Jr., 86
Andrew P., 60, 62, 78-80, 86, 224, 275, 290-291, 293
Andrew Pepperell, 335
Andrew Pepperrell, 80, 83(2), 84
Ann, 224
Catherine, 83
Frost
Catherine (Potefield), 83
Frost
Charles, 60, 79(2), 80, 85(3), 86-86, 87(4), 140, 147, 215
Charles, Esq., 80(2), 84, 230, 291, 294, 335
Charles, Jr., 82, 84-85
Charles, Jr., Esq., 85
Cpl. Charles, 48
Eleanor, 83(2), 275(2)
Eleanor (Frost), 83
Eleanor (Slemmons), 275
Eleanor (Slemons), 335
Eliza, 85(2), 87
George, 85-85, 86(2)
Harry, 85-87
Hon. John, 79, 84
James, 36, 46, 48, 56, 63, 105, 287
Jane, 80(2), 81-82, 84, 87
Joann, 165
Joanna, 56, 80, 82, 85, 87, 89, 288, 291
Joanna (Jackson), 79, 87
John, 79, 85(2), 87
Jonathan, 103
Joseph, 83, 86
Lydia, 29, 50
Maj. Charles, 29, 50, 79
Mary (Boles), 79
Mary (Pepperell), 79, 84, 87
Miss Joanna, 88
Miss Nabby, 81
Mrs. Hannah, 85
Mrs. Joanna, 79-80, 82
Nabby, 87
Nancy, 83
Nicholas, 79
Pepp, 158
Pepperell, 47
Peter, 5
Phebe C. (Hamilton), 87
Polly, 85
Sophia, 85
Timothy, Esq., 85
William, 80, 82(2), 83, 85-86, 87(2), 288(2), 289-289, 290(2), 291, 293
Wingate, 287

Fry
 James, 164
 Richard, 72
Frye
 Dean, 266
 John J., 26, 157, 173
 Richard, 261
Fultz
 Rev. W.H., 144
Furbish
 James, 98
Furgerson
 Charles, 202
Furlong
 Mrs. George W., 108
Gage
 Hanno W., 233
Galvin
 George Ilsley, 21
 Thomas P., 21
 Timothy, 30, 78
Gammon
 Lizzie, 37
 Miranda Southgate (King), 312
 Moses, 47-48
 Peter, 42
 Philip, 312
Gardner
 John, 132
 John D., 238
 Lois (North), 132
 William H., 121
Garfield
 Millie, 283
Garland
 Angeline (Burnham), 184
 Thomas B., 184
Garrett
 Richard, 169
 Temperance, 169
Gedney
 Mr., 78
Gerard
 Stephen, 276
Gerrish
 Charles, 48, 56
 Edward P., 254
 John J., Esq., 48
Gerry
 Elbridge, 239
Gey
 Mrs. Rebeckah, 65
Gibbs
 Andrew, 57, 288, 290
 Mary, 202(2)
 William, 57, 266, 288
Gibs
 Andrew, 89
 William, 89
Gidney
 Bartholomew, 200
Gilbert
 Caroline (Mason), 150
 John W., 150
Gillespie
 Sarah, 242

Gilman
 A.H., 252
 Edward, 56, 89(2)
 Edward, Jr., 46
 Elizabeth (Sayer), 337
 Joanna (Boyd), 332
 Nathaniel, 324, 332
 Nicholas, 337
 Rev. Tristram, 156, 239, 337
 Russell, 337
 Sgt. Edward, 46
Gilmore
 Simon, 78
Goddard
 Charles W., 205
Godfrey
 Benjamin, 46, 56
 Daniel, 18, 220
Gold
 Abel, 46
 Daniel, 47-48
Goldwait
 Mary, 316
Goodenow
 Rufus K., 119
Goodrich
 Caroline Maria, 196, 265
 Eli, 196
 Elizabeth, 197
 Jerusha H., 196(2)
 Joshua, 196
 Maria (Frances), 193, 196
 Maria Frances, 264
 Martha E., 196
 Nancy (Bulkley), 196
 Oliver B., 196
 Walter B., 45, 52(2), 55, 90(2), 91, 94, 125, 138-139, 146, 193, 196(2)
 Walter Buckley, 264
 Walter F., 52, 123
 Walter Franklin, 196, 264
Goodwin
 Dominicus, 294
 Ichabod, 294
 John, 19
Gookin
 Dorothy, 20.3
 Simon, 20.3
Goole
 Aaron, 56
Gordon
 Anna A., 245
 John, 221, 237
Gore
 Gov. Christopher, 318, 320
Gorham
 Abigail, 169
 Hon. William, 169
 Temperance (Garrett), 169
Gould
 Aaron, 89
 Abner, 166
 Betsey, 63
 Catharine (Starbird), 266
 Clarissa, 63
 Clement, 63, 228

Edward, 64
Edward L., 309
Eunice, 63
Eunice (Pennell), 63, 224, 226, 228
Gardner, 64, 76
Hon. William, 239
John, 63(2), 64, 228
Mary, 226
Mary (Copps), 63
Mary (Miles), 228
Mrs. Eunice, 62
Nabby, 63
Nathan, 82, 153, 201, 235, 279
Polly (Miles), 63
Samuel, 63, 78
Smith C., 266
Thomas, 91, 94
William, 63-64, 78

Gowell
Rev. W. H., 57

Gowen
Hannah, 263
James, 170
Levi, 170

Graffam
Caleb, 275
Clarence, 110
Eunice, 275
Mary (Wilson), 202
Peter, 202

Gragg
Emily, 122

Graham
Clara Octavia, 258
Dr. Neil Ferguson, 256
Elizabeth Brown, 258
Harriet A. (Southgate), 246
Harriet Augusta (Southgate), 256, 258
Harriet Ferguson, 258
Horatio Southgate, 258
Jennie, 126
Mary DuBois, 258
Neil Duncan, 258
Neil Ferguson, M.D., 258

Grant
Albion K. P., 33, 37
Edward Lyman, 33
Emma F., 37
George F., 37
Hattie F. (Allen), 37
Henry, 33
Isabella (Small), 37
James, 266
Mabel C., 37
Marsha Adelia, 33
Nathaniel Stevens, 33
Orman Franklin, 33
Sally (Stevens), 33
Samuel, 33
William, 33

Graves
Annie Thayer, 100
Charlotte Harwood, 100
Christopher, 186
Crispus, 263
Dwight Cushing, 100

Hattie Eliza, 100
Horace P., 100
Horace Porter, 100
Isabella (Hutchinson), 263
Maria Louise, 100
Mary Chandler, 100
Mrs. Mercy, 100
Nathaniel, 100
Samuel Bartol, 100
Sarah Ann (Gurling), 100
Sarah Brown (Barker), 100
Sarah Maria, 100
Sarah Mariah, 100
William, 96(2), 97, 100, 269
William Henry, 100
William Wallace, 100(2)

Gray
Hon. William, 326
John, 188
Lt. William, 294
Mehitable, 338
Samuel, 59
Silas, 158
William, 240
William, Jr., 239

Greaton
Col. John, 83

Greeley
Eliphalet, 204, 248

Greely
Hannah C., 338

Green
Abigail (Brackett), 105
Daniel, 109, 113, 182
Jesse, 78
John, 47
Mrs. Sarah Wood (Brackett), 182
Nathaniel W., 186
Peter H., 316, 334

Green
Sarah, 182

Greene
Elizabeth, 168
Roscoe G., 206

Greenleaf
Amos, 3, 55
Henry, 3
Jane, 3
John, 46
Joseph, 3

Greenwood
A., 317

Gregg
Rev., 115
Rev. William, 136, 270
William, 208

Grey
John, 90

Griffin
Philena, 57

Gripes
John, 47

Grouse
Makel, 47

Grover
Amos, 241

Eli, 241
Susan (Tyler), 241
Growin
Samuel, 302
Guild
Katherine, 283
Gunnison
Rev. John, 285
Gurling
Sarah Ann, 100
Hackett
Gertrude (Buckley), 190
Henry W., 190
Jennie, 110
Haggett
Mary, 308
Haines
Emma, 234
Hale
Benjamin, 319
Caroline (King), 319
Cyrus, 319
Nathaniel, 266
Haley
Rhoda, 25
Hall
Amos, 263
Ann, 155
Betsey, 4
Cornelius, 45
Farnum, 300
Frances Ellen, 42
George A., 109
George F., 42
Helen F. (Buckley), 42
Hellena (Woodford), 42
Henry Clay, 42
Hezekiah, 4
Joel, 253
Joseph, 57, 89, 317
Lemuel, 250
Margaret A., 247
Margaret Ann, 253
Martha (Colt), 250
Mary, 86, 263
Mary (Riggs), 155
Mary Ann (Field), 42
Mary Jane, 42
Miriam, 263
Moses, 20.3
Mrs. Ira L., 57
Nathaniel, 59
Pamelia (Brackett), 109
Philo, 42, 90, 94
Robert, 42
Silas L., 42, 152
Stephen, 111, 250
Susannah, 250
Thomas, 155
Hallsbury
Mary Jane, 133
Ham
John, 317
Hamblen
Martha, 285
Hamilton

Abiel, 306
Capt. Charles B., 197
George Montague, 278
Jonas, 41, 218
Mary (Barbour), 197
Mary Ann, 185
Mercy, 129
Phebe C., 87
Silas, 41, 78
Hammond
George, 48
George W., 232(3), 233
Thomas, 204, 232
Hancock
Hannah, 116
John, 116, 158
Louisa, 17
Hannah
Alexander, 9
Franzella K. (Stevens), 9
Hanningham
Esther, 63
Hanscom
Charlotte (Waterhouse), 305
Esther, 116
Humphrey, 182, 305
William, 305
Hanson
Abigail (Hayes), 304
Alfred L., 305
Alonzo, 305
Betsey (Waterhouse), 70, 304
Celia, 70
Celia Lowell, 305
Charlotte E. (Kelley), 305
Daniel Lowell, 305(2)
Dr. Moses, 305
George, 305
Hannah (Gowen), 263
Ichabod, 304
Jane, 43
John Lowell, 305
Lewis, 305
Mary (Sawyer), 305
Mary Ann, 305(2)
Mary E. (Sawyer), 305
Moses, 70, 304(2), 305(2)
Nicholas, 311
Olive J. (Stevens), 211
Rebecca (Swett), 305
Sally (Lowell), 304-305
Sarah (Chesley), 304
Thomas, 263
Timothy, 304
W., 55
Harding
Capt. Robert, 321
Miss. Low, 138
Hardy
Isaac, 57, 89
Harford
Solomon, 319
Harmon
Benjamin, 74
Capt. Nathaniel, 251
Edward, 250

George, 245
Joanna (Skillin), 263
John, 307
Maria Frances (Knight), 307
Mercy, 183
Mrs. Mary Elizabeth, 74
Thomas, 263
Warren, 62-64, 105, 224, 309
Z. K., 9
Z.K., 177
Harper
Eleanor (Winslow), 211
Samuel, 63(2), 90, 94(2)
Harrington
A.L., 122
Harris
Mark, 204
Nathan, 90, 94
Susan, 8
Hart
Rev. Heury, 172
Harvey
Col. John, 309
John, 310-311
Joseph, 311(2)
Mary, 310
Sally, 311
Sarah, 310
Hasack
Dr. David, 305
Haskell
Almirad, 44
Ann, 35, 220, 273
Ann (Partridge), 221
Benjamin, 46, 56, 60, 89, 155, 175, 239, 262, 288, 290
Daniel, 35
Dea. Solomon, 34
Dea. Thomas, 155
Doritha, 171
Edmund, 231(2)
Eleanor (Quinby), 34
Elizabeth, 35
Eunice (Starbird), 38, 40
George, 78, 221
Hannah, 44, 44
Hannah (Robins), 44
Jane (Larrabee), 231
Joanna, 171
Job, 4
John, 43(2), 44(4), 46, 97
Jonathan, 18, 44(4)
Joseph W., 78
Mark, 34(2), 35, 159
Mary, 44, 155, 155, 163(2), 236, 310
Mary (Riggs), 155
Mrs. Eleanor (Quinby), 310
Mrs. Mark, 37
Mrs. Sarah, 40-41
Nabby, 44
Nancy, 44
Nathaniel, 15, 22, 37, 40, 164
Nathaniel, Jr., 78
Polly, 4, 23
Polly (Partridge), 41
Rachel, 61, 155

Rev. W.H., 144
Rev. William H., 285
Sally (Berry), 175
Sarah (Stevens), 15
Sgt. John, 46
Sgt. Solomon, 46
Solomon, 34, 38, 41, 56, 60(2), 88-89, 239, 288-289, 290(2), 310
Solomon, Jr., 37, 41, 309
Susan, 44
Thomas, 2, 34, 56, 60, 78, 89-90, 105, 230, 239, 310(2)
Thomas B., 22
William, 240
Hastings
Daniel, 332
Hasty
Robert, 295
Susan E., 182
Hatch
Abigail (Nason), 339
Betsey, 339
Capt. Nathaniel, 339(2)
Elizabeth, 339(2)
Elizabeth, 339
Elizabeth (Bean), 197
Elizabeth (Hatch), 339
George, 339(2)
Hannah, 339, 339
Harriet, 339(2)
John W., 339
Joseph, 339
Mary E., 339
Nathaniel, 98, 266, 339
Sally, 339
Sarah (Sawyer), 339
Hatford
Emma, 26
Haughton
Naham, 324
Hawes
Andrew, 24, 74, 120, 140, 234
Andrew, Esq., 149, 162, 203, 236, 276
Hon. Andrew, 105
Martin, 43
Hawkes
Aaron, 312
Fidelia (King), 312
Margaret Ann, 312
Mary E., 312
Mrs. Ezra (Smith), 182
Sarah P., 221
Hawkins
Lorenzo P., 114
Mary, 72
Hayes
Abigail, 304
David, 99
Healy
James Augustine, 209
Hearn
Rose E., 37
Height
George, 295
Henderson
Delia, 282

Henry, 282
Hendrick
 Elmer T., 130
 Emma S. (North), 130
 Frank S., 130
 Martin T., 130
Herrick
 Capt. Benjamin, 130
 Daniel, 67(2)
 Martha (Small), 67
 Mary (Fickett), 67
 Oliver, 298
 Polly, 67, 75
 Susan B., 130
Hersey
 Henry W., 254
 Simeon, 52
Hibbs
 James, 131
Hichborn
 Deborah, 193
Hicks
 Ann, 33
 Edwin, 33
 Frances Ellen, 33
 Francis, 78, 90, 94
 Frank Melvin, 190
 Hannah, 263(2)
 James, 33(2)
 James Wallace, 33
 Julia, 33, 277
 Lemuel, 57, 288
 Maria, 33
 Martha Ann, 190
 Sally, 263
 Samuel, 48, 89, 188
 Sophia, 190
 Sophia (Stevens), 33
 Watson, 33
 William, 33, 78, 164, 190
Higgins
 Elisha, 52, 55
 Elisha, Jr., 18, 90-91, 94, 140
 Olive, 263
 Tamzia, 19
Hight
 Amos, 245
Hill
 Jacob, 205
 Jeremiah, 294
 John, 89, 202, 226
 Mark L., 321
Hillard
 Seth, 68
Hilton
 Caroline, 27
 Jane, 182
 Mary, 20.3
 Polly (Wilson), 202
 Simeon, 20.3
 Theophilus, 202
Hinde-Roper
 Gen. H.T., 259
 Gertrude, 257, 259(2)
Hinds
 Albert Henry, 120

Daniel A., 150
E.P., 98
Priscilla Grace (Libby), 120
Sophaetta (Mason), 150
Walter, 244
Hinginham
 Esther, 62, 231
Hix
 Samuel, 290
Hobart
 Frances (Stevens), 33
 John, 32-33
 Miles, 33
Hobbs
 Col. Josiah, 263
 Daniel, 89, 263
 Jeremiah, 56, 89, 263
 Joseph, 262
 Josiah, 262-263
 Lt. Josiah, 164
 Maj., 186
 Mary, 32, 201, 271
 Mary (Kilpatrick), 262
 Mrs. Joanna, 263
 Mrs. Mary, 263
 Sarah, 109
Hobert
 John, 70
 Miles, 177, 179
 Miriam Lincoln, 177, 179
 Rev. Caleb, 136-138
Hodgdon
 Elizabeth (Smith), 182
 Joseph, 244
 Samuel, 182
Hodge
 James, 302
Hodgkins
 Eliza M., 11
Hodgdon
 Eunice, 51
Holbrook
 Samuel, 104
Holden
 Daniel, 26
 Miss. Abbie, 138
 Nathan, 96
 Rebecca (Sawyer), 26
 Sarah, 122
Holmes
 Hon. John, M.C., 313
Homes
 John, 55
 William, 44, 100, 107
Hooper
 Rev. W.W., 139-140
Hopkins
 Mrs. S.B., 78
 Nathan, 89
 Rev. Mark R., 111
Horton
 Nancy, 51
Houdlet
 Chas. 302
Houghton
 Harriet C., 122

Rev. F.M., 140
Houstoun
　George, 57
Hovey
　Elizabeth A. (Stevens), 8
　Emerson W., 8
How
　Daniel, 306
　Mary E., 231
Howard
　Abijah, 26
　Abizer, 189, 191
　Abizer, Jr., 191(2), 192
　Albion, 188
　Ann (Reed), 191
　Arthur P., 189
　Caroline (Weeks), 191
　Charles, 191
　Ellen, 192
　Ellen (Moore), 192
　Franklin S., 191
　Hiram, 55
　James B., 191
　Louisa S., 192
　Maria F., 191
　Martha E., 191-191
　Mary A., 191
　Mary J. H. (Bacon), 191
　Mrs. Lydia, 239
　Oliver B., 26
　Oliver Buckley, 192
　Rosetta, 191
　Sally, 26, 191
　Sarah, 191(2)
　Simeon, 188, 191
　Thomas, 90, 94
　Tryphosa (Bowker), 191
　William H., 191
Howe
　Lydia, 185
　Marle, 264
Hubbard
　Rebeckah, 235, 237
Huchinson
　Isabella, 263
Huckins
　James, 180
　Pauline (Webb), 180
　Stephen, 180
Hudson
　Sally, 252
　Thomas, 165
Humphrey
　Augusta M. (Weston), 284
　Dea. John, 284-285
　Eunice, 23(2)
　Henry P., 284
　Rosetta (Howard), 191
　Susan Augusta, 284, 284
　William, 90
　William R., 191
Hunnewell
　Charles, 37
　Mary, 65
Hunscome
　A. Leroy, 176

Hunt
　Abby (Smith), 182
　Caroline, 157, 173, 207
　David, 226
　Dr. Caleb, 157, 169, 173
　Dr. Henry, 55, 121, 202, 207
　Dr. Jacob, 30, 64, 66, 92, 121, 157, 174, 207, 290
　Emeline (Brewer), 207
　F.W., 182
　George S., 75
　Henry, 197
　Henry J., 123
　Jacob, 164
　Jaeob, 174
　Mary, 110
　Sally (Rea), 157, 173, 207
Huntington
　Adelaide, 283(2)
　Anna, 122
Huntress
　Pearson, 48
Hurley
　John, 266
Huse
　James, 98
Hussey
　Daniel F., 33
　Frances Ellen (Hicks), 33
　Rev. L., 94
　Rev. Leander, 139
Husting
　John, 266
Huston
　Alfred R., 26, 173
　Ann, 202(2)
　George, 89
　John, 47, 165
　Olive, 202
　Paul, 57, 89
　Rufus, 77, 122
　Ruth, 202
Huston
　John, 48
Hutchinson
　Josepha, 214
Hutchinson
　Hiram, 256
　Isabella, 263
　Mrs. Mary Ann, 256
　Renie Caroline, 256
　Sarah Elizabeth, 248, 256
Ilsley
　Capt., 46
　Daniel, 290
　Ellen E., 132
　Enoch, 12, 66, 182, 290(2), 293
　George, 262
　Henry W., 132
　Hosea, 96
　Isaac, 20, 35
　Joanna, 21
　Joseph, 132
　Nathaniel, 96
　Robert, 77
　Stephen E., 132
Indians

Ammoncongin, 203, 215
Capisic, 203, 215, 286
Jane, 243
Naguasqua, 243
Scitterygusset, 203, 215, 286
Ugagoyuskitt, 243
Uphanum, 243 (Indian Jane)
Wickwarrawaske, 243
Ingalls
Benjamin, 78, 105-106
George, 78, 163
Isaiah, 45
John, 78, 163
Joseph, 78-79, 287
Lt. George, 198
Samuel, 78, 199
St. George, 78
Ingalson
Lydia, 155
Ingarsoll
George, 20
Ingersoll
Benjamin, 337
Daniel, 200
George, 20.2(2), 20.5, 200
Ingles
Archibald, 278
Ingraham
Ann, 278
Joseph Holt, 73, 123, 275, 278
Mary (Tate), 275
Irish
Gen. James, 300
James, 17
James, Jr., 301
Sarah (Kenny), 17
Jackson
Abigail (Damm), 34
Abigail (Stevens), 34
Amanda S., 34
Andrew, 295
Florence M., 34
Francis, 34
George, 87
George W., 34
Henry, 16, 78
Henry B., 34
Henry S., 41, 269
Henry Small, 34
Ida Lizzie, 34
Jeremiah, 16
Joanna, 79, 87
Lillian, 308
Lucy T., 34
Mary, 48, 339
Mary (McKenney), 34
Mrs. Joanna, 87
Nellie G., 34
Sally, 26
Sarah, 339
Sarah (Sawyer), 16
Thomas, 34, 46, 90(2), 120
Thomas W., 31, 69, 75
Jacksons
Frances, 201
Jacobs

Daniel, 11
E. Milton, 34, 120
Elias, 67-68
Elias M., 69, 305
Ellen (Fickett), 68
George B., 67, 69
Sarah F. (Brackett), 11
Jagger
Ann Louise (Lawrence), 282
Rt. Rev. Thomas A., 282
Jamerson
Mary, 50
Jameson
Rev., 75, 115
Rev. Thomas, 96, 270, 272
Sally, 39
Jefferson
President, 301
Jeffords
Rufus, 164
Jellison
Alexander, 185
Ann (Libby), 185
Capt. James, 185
Harriet D. (Burnham), 185
Jenkins
Rev. Charles, 5, 270
Jenks
Elizabeth (Sawyer), 2
John, 57
Jewett
Elder Nehemiah, 20.1
Elizabeth, 168
Henry C., 123
Rev. Caleb, 239
Rev. Henry C., 92, 133, 266, 268, 272
Jocelyn
Abram, 243
Henry, 312
Johanson
Fred A., 202
Johnson, 339
Abbie, 339
Abigail (Frost), 37
Alexander, 7, 49
Amelia (Webb), 180
Andrew J., 33
Andrew R., 7
Ann, 279, 281(2), 282
Ann (Tate), 279
Benjamin, 169
Capt. James, 235
Capt. Robert, 7
Caroline, 33
Charles, 279(2), 282
Charles Pope, 279
Daniel, 174
David, 7
Dorcas, 49
Elbridge, 146
Eleanor, 49, 150, 339
Eleanor (Lamb), 49
Elizabeth, 49, 279
Elizabeth (Porterfield), 49-50, 227
Elizabeth H., 339
Elizabeth H. (Johnson), 339

Eunice (Trickey), 218, 271, 339
F.A., 40
Fannie, 7
Flora, 48
Florence, 339
Fred A., 46, 50, 60, 77, 88, 335
Gardner, 339
George, 7, 46-47, 48(2), 61, 88-90, 182, 227, 339
George Tate, 279
George Woodbury, 32, 66, 201
George, Jr., 48
Hannah, 49
Hannah (Hatch), 339
Hannah (Johnson), 49
Harriet, 7, 339
Hepsbath (Norton), 180
Isaac, 33, 37, 61, 90, 94, 125, 194
James, 7, 32, 48-48, 49(2), 50, 55-56, 60-61, 78, 180, 201, 227, 239, 262, 290, 339
James, Esq., 271(2)
James, Jr., 46, 56, 89, 339
Jane, 49(2)
Jeremiah, 78, 266, 339
John, 7, 46, 49, 56, 60-61, 73, 89-90, 239, 262, 288, 339
John H., 168
John L., 7
John Lamb, 49
John, Jr., 46, 56, 88-89, 290, 339
Joseph, 7, 48, 302
Lt. James, 47-48
Lucinda (Trull), 279
Maj. John, 279
Margaret, 49
Margaret, 279
Martha Tate, 279
Mary, 339
Mary (Barker), 174
Mary (Jackson), 48, 339
Mary (Meserve), 339
Mary Frances (Maxfield), 37
Mary G. (Barker), 169
Mary R., 233
Matthew, 49
May, 7
Mr. Randall, 21
Mrs. Abigail, 37
Mrs. Eunice, 7
Mrs. M.A., 57
Mrs. Marion, 7
Mrs. Robert, 7
Nathan, 7
Nathaniel H., 339
Olive (Coombs), 279
Polly (Smith), 182
Priscilla D. (Sawyer), 339
Randall, 7(2), 37, 77-78, 90-91, 94
Rebecca, 49, 218
Richard, 7, 49, 73, 218, 271, 339
Robert, 7, 46, 56, 89-90, 288, 290
Sally, 49(2), 271
Sally (Johnson), 49
Samuel, 180
Samuel Tate, 279
Sgt. George, 46
Sgt. James, 46

Sgt. John, 46
Thomas, 7(2)
Thomas, Jr., 7
William, 49

Jones
A., 55
Ann, 225(2)
Capt. John, 61, 92, 140-141, 155, 169, 218
Capt. John, Jr., 168
Catherine, 225
Daniel S., 188
Eleanor (Libby), 185
Elizabeth, 94
Eunice, 177
George, 78
Harriet J. (Winslow), 168
J. Winslow, 308
Jabez, 236, 305
James, 324
Jane, 6

Jones
John, 18

Jones
John, 90-91, 94, 244
John, Esq., 94
Lucy (Riggs), 61
Lucy Caroline, 168
Lydia, 272
Margaret (Broad), 168
Mary, 168, 225
Mary (Hall), 86
Mary (Riggs), 61
Miranda, 93
Mr. Stephen, 20.3
Mrs. John, 168
Phineas, 12-13, 16, 20.2-20.3, 225
Richard, 225
Sally, 62, 229
Samuel, 185
Sarah, 225
Sarah, 273
Sarah (Smith), 225
Stephen, 13, 199
Susanna, 155
Thaddeus B., 168
Thomas, 46, 86, 90, 94
William, 225

Jordan
Abigail, 303
Alma Maria (Brackett), 108
Benjamin, 58
Calvin, 63
Dea. William, 51
Eleanor (Tate), 21, 276-277
Eliza, 5, 8
Eliza (Woodford), 51
Hannah, 263
Hon. Samuel, 98, 125, 234
Ichabod, 251
James, 108
John, 78, 90, 92, 94, 164, 306
Luther, 63
Nathaniel, 277
Noah, 78
Rev. Robert, 102
Rev. William T., 49

Richworth, 294
S., 55
Samuel, 52, 55, 145, 194, 212
Susan (Bartlett), 306
Tristram, 294
William, 49, 51-52, 55

Jordan
Jane Elizabeth, 125

Jose
Joanna, 116
Polly, 108

Josslin
Israel, 101

Judkins
Nellie, 37

Jumper
Rebecca, 26

Kelley
Charlotte E., 305
Florence Cutler (Bailey), 177
Henrietta, 184
Rev. T. J., 177

Kellogg
Rev. Elijah, 134, 272

Kemp, 60
J., 55

Kendrick
Charlotte, 304

Kennard
Caroline, 184
Sally, 263

Kenney
Freeman, 23
Lt. William, 165
Molly (Stevens), 165
Samuel, 22, 164, 263
Samuel, Jr., 22
Sopiah (Wormell), 263
Stetson, 23
William, 22, 164

Kenny
Clarissa, 17
Frances A., 17
Freeman, 17
Isaac Stevens, 17
Louisa, 17
Louisa (Hancock), 17
Molly (Stevens), 17
Nabby P., 17
Samuel, 17
Sarah, 17
Sophia W., 17
Stetson, 17(2)
Susan (Brackett), 17
William, 16-17
William, Jr., 17

Kent
Rev. Cephas H., 134

Kilpatrick
Elizabeth (Slemons), 335
Mary, 262
Thomas, 335

Kimball
Christopher S., 18
Cotton, 18, 20.2
Eunice, 20.1

George, 144
John, 107, 292
Lucy (Fly), 307
Rufus, 307
Sarah, 6
Sarah Saunders, 8
William G., 292

King
Ann Frazier, 319
Ann N. (Frazier), 317
Benjamin Samuel Black, 312
Betsey Lyden, 319
Caroline, 319
Charles R., 316
Cyrus, 295, 312-313, 333
Eliza, 312
Fidelia, 312
Gov. William, 314
Hannah (Carter), 312
Hannah Larrabee, 312
Hon. Cyrus, 334
Hon. Marquis F., 169
Hon. Rufus, 314
Hon. William, Esq., 295, 315
James G., 316
James Gore, 315
Jennie (Thompson), 125
John A., 314
Joseph Leland, 312
Mary, 246, 247, 252(5), 312, 314
Mary (Goldwait), 316
Mary E., 313
Miranda Southgate, 312
Mrs. Ann M., 316
Mrs. Ann N., 313
Mrs. William, 313
Richard, 47, 244(2), 334(2)
Richard, Jr., 312, 334
Ring, 246
Rufus, 312, 315-316
Silas, 312
William, 246, 294, 296, 298-301, 313, 316-318, 320-321, 323-327, 330, 332-334
William, Esq., 316

Kingman
Deliverance, 222
Eliza, 222
John, 222
Mary (Mitchell), 222
Samuel, 222

Kingsbury
Lucy, 154

Kingsley
Mary DuBois (Graham), 258
Silas Henry, 258

Kinson
John A., 63
Judith (Knight), 63

Knapp
Eunice (Carver), 327
James, 20.2
Joseph, 326-326, 327(2)
Ruth, 327
Simeon, 327

Knight
Abigail (Munson), 169

Alexander, 165
Amos, 290
Asa, 64, 78, 173
Benjamin, 79
Betsey (Thompson), 42
Betty, 197
Capt. Isaac, 240
Capt. John, 47
Capt. Samuel, 12
Charles, 42
Charlotte, 147, 225
Cpl. Enoch, 48
David, 164
Doratha (Haskell), 171
Dorcas (Cox), 171
Dorcas C., 9
Edward, 171
Edward Franklin, 307
Eliza, 42, 42, 190
Elizabeth, 47, 60, 171
Elizabeth (Pierce), 45, 171
Elizabeth (Slemmons), 60
Elizabeth (Slemons), 167
Emily Jane, 263
Enoch, 107, 266
Erastus, 171
Eunice, 62, 171(2), 226(3)
Fannie, 42
George, 46, 60(2), 73, 167
George Joseph, 307
George, III, 288
Hannah, 60
Henrietta C., 45
Henry, 57(2), 60, 62, 164, 188, 239, 288, 290
Henry, Jr., 57, 60, 159, 171
Isaac, 1, 18, 42
James, 47
Joanna (Storer), 147, 171
Job, 266
John, 47-48, 60, 167
John S., 158
John, Jr., 78
Johnson W., 208
Jonathan, 169
Joseph, 46, 79, 307
Joseph, Fifer, 48
Joshua, 47, 57, 290
Joshua S., 132
Josiah, 94, 266
Judith, 63(2)
Keziah, 47
Lavina, 42
Lt. Nathan, 46
Lt. Nathaniel, 46
Mehitable (Sawyer), 171
Margaret, 156
Maria, 42
Maria Frances, 307
Mariah (North), 132
Mark, 20.2, 57, 60, 62, 171(2), 263, 290
Marshall, 42
Martha, 60
Martha Adelaide, 307
Martha C. (Quinby), 307
Mary, 42, 47, 60
Mary (Westbrook), 60, 244

Mary W., 266
Mehitable, 15, 171
Merrill, 266
Miss. Kate, 138
Moses, 57, 172, 266
Moses, Jr., 266
Mrs. Jennie, 23
Mrs. Joanna, 147
Mrs. Ruth E., 167
Nathan, 47, 60, 167, 169, 244(2)
Nathaniel, 35, 42(2), 47(2), 56, 60(3), 80, 148, 167(2), 169, 203, 239, 246, 288
Nathaniel, Jr., 46, 290
Peter M., 165, 172, 266
Pricilla (Berry), 60
Priscilla, 60
Priscilla (Berry), 80, 244
Richard, 57, 165, 266
Robert, 173
Roland, 78
Rose, 221
Rowland, 164
Ruth (Elden), 60
Samuel, 46, 57, 82, 288, 290
Sarah, 42, 47(2), 60, 244
Sarah (Bangs), 266
Sarah Eliza, 307
Sgt. William, 46
Stephen, 77, 165
Storer S., 197
Theodore, 42
Theopolis, 164
Thomas, 19, 20.3, 47, 147(2), 169, 171
Thomas, Jr., 45, 159, 171
Westbrook, 169
William, 172
William, Jr., 46, 165
Zebulon, 48, 171
Knights
George, III, 89
Henry, 89, 171
Henry, Jr., 89
John, 231
Joshua, 89
Mark, 89
Moses, 89
Nathaniel, 89-90
Nathaniel, Jr., 89
Peter, 172
Richard, 89
Samuel, 89
Thomas, 219
William, 220
Knox
Amos P., 77
General, 249, 252
Henry, 154
Cunningham
Esther, 63
LaFayette, 150
General, 154
Lake
Thomas, 287
Lamb
Eleanor, 49
Hannah (Porterfield), 50

John, 50
Robert S., 110
Samuel, 78
Sarah, 231
Sophronia S. (Brackett), 110
William, 46, 56, 89
William, Jr., 288, 290
Lancaster
Dorothy, 272-273
Esther, 333
John, 273
Lydia (Jones), 272
Rev. Thomas, 158, 170, 239, 272-273
Sewall, 273
Thomas, Jr., 273
Lane
Capt. John, 319
Esther W., 240
Eunice (Barbour), 197
John W., 205
Rev., 96
Rev. Joseph, 97, 99, 136, 158
Lang
Susan, 266
Lapham
Dr. William B., 27, 175
Larabee
B., 55
Capt. Chase, 55
John, 55
Larkeman
Eben, 44
Mary (Haskell), 44
Larrabee
Benjamin, 20.3, 50, 94, 182, 231
David, 50
Elizabeth, 51, 50-51, 264
Jane, 231
Jane (Cobby), 231
Lettice (Trickey), 50
Lydia (Bailey), 50
Margaret, 50
Mary, 50
Mary Ann, 50
Sarah (Lamb), 231
William, 50(2), 51
Larraby
Benjamin, 69
Charlotte, 69
Daniel, 69
Edmond, 69
Elizabeth, 69, 69
Isaac, 20.3
Lettice (Porterfield), 69
Lydia (Bailey), 69
Mary Ann, 69
William, 69(2)
William P., 69
Larry
Abbie, 130
Lary
Samuel, 266
Latham
Dr. Daniel Stevens, 9
Dr. John Stevens, 9
Samuel D., 8

Laurie
Annie, 307
Lawrence
Ann Louise, 282
Capt. Abraham, 214
Caroline Bowne, 282
Effingham, 282
Eliza Southgate, 282
Elizabeth (Watson), 282
Emily, 282
Frances, 282
Hon. John Watson, 282
Isabella, 282
John, 282
John W., 249
John Watson, 282
Mary (Bowne), 249, 282
Mary Bowne, 282
Peter, 46
Rebecca, 282
Robert, 203
Leach
Almon, 55
Eliza, 110
James M., 208
Rhoda, 195
Leavitt
Abbie, 144
Capt. William, 172, 197
George B., 46, 49, 61
Leonora, 265
Maj. Isaac, 265
Mary, 265
Lee
Dr. Joseph, 301
Hon. Silas, 301, 315
Silas, Esq., 299, 302, 324
Leeman
George, 74
Leighton
Andrew, 164
Aurelia, 108
Capt., 186
Capt. Isaac, 165
Capt. Jediah, 158
Edward, 165, 263
Emeline A. (Roberts), 308
George, 164
Hannah (Hicks), 263
Hannah (Wilson), 202
Henry, 308
Joseph, 202
Judith, 263
Lt. Nathaniel, 164
Mrs. Mary, 158
Nelson, 192
Thaddeus, 165
Leland
Joseph, 312, 333
Lemont
Dea. James, 317
Thomas, 317
Leonard
Albert, 75
Margaret, 75
Nancy, 75

Nancy (Stevens), 75
Samuel, 75
Lewis
  Archelaus, 43, 47, 93, 140-141, 146, 212, 221, 232, 236-237, 241, 290-291, 293
  Archelaus, Jr., 238
  Capt. Benjamin H., 133
  Capt. John L., 146, 240-242, 313
  Elizabeth (Browne), 146, 237, 239, 241
  Eveline, 237
  Frances (Angier), 237
  Frances (McClink), 237
  Frances E., 238(2)
  George, 20.2
  George R., 240
  Hon. Archelaus, 151, 305
  John, 305, 313
  John L., 239
  Jotham, 20.2
  Maj. Archelaus, 35, 294
  Mary, 20.2
  Mary (Bryant), 240
  Philip, 20.2
  Polly (Watts), 313
  Rebecca (Browne), 146, 239-241
  Rebeckah (Hubbard), 235, 237
  Rebeckah (Mayo), 235
  Sally, 235
  Sarah (Lindsey), 313
  Sgt. Archeleus, 48
  Thaddeus M., 238
  William, 240
Libby
  Abigail, 185
  Abigail (Coolbroth), 185
  Abraham, 116
  Andrew, 65, 185
  Ann, 185
  Annie S. (Pennell), 231
  Asa, 185
  B.F., 110
  Betsey (McKenney), 117
  C. Thompson, 116
  Capt. David, 116-117
  Capt. Moses, 153
  Charles, 276(2)
  Charles Thornton, 333
  Charles Thorton, 20.1
  Clarissa, 153
  Daniel, 185
  David, 116, 201, 203
  Dea. Arthur, 150
  Dorcas (Means), 116
  Ebenezer, 185, 333
  Eleanor, 185(2), 201-201, 271
  Eleanor (Libby), 201
  Elijah, 185
  Elizabeth (McKenney), 116
  Elizabeth A. (Dresser), 150
  Esther, 273(2), 275-275, 277(2)
  Esther (Hanscom), 116
  Esther (Libby), 273
  Esther Libby, 277
  Eunice, 185(2)
  Fannie (Prescott), 117
  Fannie Margaret, 120

Frank Beverly, 231(2)
Franklin W., 45
Fred, 75
Fred H., 182
George, 2, 55-56, 94, 116-118, 120, 162, 173, 194
George, Esq., 90, 155
George, Jr., 120
Hannah, 231, 273, 276(2)
Hannah (Hancock), 116
Hannah (Libby), 231
Ichabod, 65(2), 71
Jethro, 273, 276
Joanna, 307
Joanna (Jose), 116
Joel, 185(2)
John, 116, 276
Jonathan, 295
Joseph, 78, 164
Joshiah, 294
Lothrop, 55
Louisa (Winslow), 185
Lt. Andrew, 82, 201, 271
Lucy, 266
Luther, 231
Lydia (Howe), 185
Mary, 45, 203
Mary (Fickett), 65
Mary (Tate), 279
Mary Ann (Mason), 150
Mary E. (Tounge), 231
Mary Kidder, 120
Matthias, 273, 275
Maud P., 8
Mayor Joseph, 333
Mehitable (Nash), 185(2)
Moses, 333
Mrs. Frank, 110
Mrs. Hannah Woodbury (Moody), 276
Nancy B. (Stevens), 45
Nancy J. (Pulsifer), 185
Nathaniel, 78
Octavia, 22, 24
Olevia, 185
Olevia J., 185
Oscar, 45
Oscar S., 45
Peter, 39
Phebe (Webb), 263
Priscilla, 120
Priscilla Grace, 120
Reuben, 333
Rosanna H. (McNelly), 120
Samuel, 245, 263
Seth, 294, 333
Storer, 45
Sumner, 192
Tamson (Quinby), 39
Thomas, 201
William, 72, 78, 203, 279
Limington
  Andrew, 91
Lincoln
  Abraham, 119
  D.W., Esq., 156
  Royal, 96

Lindsey
  Sarah, 313
Linscott
  John, 307
  Martha Adelaide (Knight), 307
Lithgrow
  Charles, 313
Little
  Abba Isabella, 253, 258
  Hon. Josiah S., 254, 258
Little
  James S., 208
Littlefield
  Nathaniel S., 206
Livermore
  Daniel, 246
  Mary (Southgate), 246
Lobdell
  Capt. Isaac, 171, 306
  Isaac, 221, 277
  Marcia, 205
  Mary G., 306
  Stetson, 21, 30, 221
Location
  Abbott's Corner, 12
  Allen's Corner, 12
  Back Cove, 5, 11-12, 18-20.2, 20.5, 56, 58, 78, 114, 155, 158, 174
  Bailey's Island, 74
  Barren Hill, South Portland, 71
  Barron Hill, So. Portland, 65-66
  Bennington Patent, 83
  Black Point, Scarborough, 65, 116, 159, 187, 201, 312
  Blue Point River, 243
  Bridge at Concord, MA, 122
  Broad Tavern, 129, 162, 164-166
  Capisic, 78
  Coyle's Gully, 20.2, 20.5, 56, 58
  Deer Isle, 37
  Deering Street, 56
  Dunstan, 47, 68, 167, 198, 201(2), 241, 243, 248, 294, 333
  Dunstan Abbey, 246, 248
  Dunstan, Scarborough, 60
  Ferry Village, South Portland, 183, 294
  Fickett Mansion, 121
  Garrison House, Stroudwater, 66
  George St., Back Cove, 173
  George Street, 20, 20.5
  Harrow House, 66, 121, 200-201
  House Island, 57
  Jocelyn's Hill, 243-244
  Libby River, 116
  Libby's Corner, Deering, 117
  Londonderry, N.H., 150
  Long Creek, 25, 46, 58, 166, 201, 227
  Lunt's Corner, 16, 20.5, 45
  Michael Mitton's House, 60
  Milbridge, Maine, 66
  Morrill's Corner, 16, 20.5
  Narragaugus, 71
  Narraguagus, Maine, 66
  New Gloucester, 5
  Nonesuch, Scarborough, 83, 116, 244
  Oak Hill, Scarborough, 251
  Oawascoage River, 243
  Ocean Ave., 20.5
  Ocean St., Back Cove, 173
  Pine Point, Scarborough, 184
  Pitch Pine Plains, 12
  Presumpscot River Canal, 204
  Pride's Corner, 24
  Prout's Neck, Scarborough, 231, 257, 273
  Province of Lygonia, 198
  Royals Homestead, 183
  Saccarappa, 38(2), 40
  Scottow's Hill, 116
  Sebago Lake Canal, 204
  Shaw's Corner [Morrill's], 18
  Skillings Farm, 56
  Skillings Lease, 201
  State Reform School Farm, 58, 76
  Stevens Plains, 5, 12(2), 22, 32, 42, 45
  Stevens' Ave. Tavern, 124
  Stroudwater, 21, 24, 29, 41, 43
  Vaughn Mansion, 251
  Wescott's Falls, 115
  Westbrook, 21
  Woodford's Corner, 20.5
Locke
  Nathaniel, 202
Logan
  C., 318
Lombard
  Daniel, 78, 94
  Rev. Solomon, 81
Londer
  Jonathan, 184
  Mary A. (Burnham), 184
Longfellow
  G.A., 91, 94
  Henry, 242
  Moses, 38
  Stephen, 57, 297
  Stephen, Esq., 238
Longley
  Eliza, 11
Loosen
  Clarabella (Dudley), 150
  Otto W., 150
Lord
  Charles, 90
  George W., 8
  Mrs. Miriam, 86
  Rev. Charles, 131
  William G., 165
Loring
  Eleanor (Trickey), 271
  Ignatius, 275
  Laban, 317
  Mary (Richmond), 286
  Rachel, 286
  Rev. Joseph, 285
  Richard, 271(2)
Lovell
  John L., 191
  Mary A. (Howard), 191
Low
  John, 89
Lowe
  Betsey, 197

Olive L. (Roberts), 308
Robert B., 308
Lowell
   Betsey (Waterhouse), 304
   Capt. Abner, 304
   Caroline, 266
   Edward, Sr., 109
   Elizabeth (Brackett), 109
   John, 108
   John P., 109
   Martha Ann, 109
   Mercy (Paine), 304
   Sally, 304(2)
Luch
   Hannah W., 153
Lunt
   Abigail (Brackett), 107
   Amos, 311
   Augusta S., 17
   Charity, 19
   Daniel, 19, 20.2, 47, 49, 288, 290
   George W., 233
   Hannah, 11
   Hattie E., 17
   Jane, 20-21, 157
   Job, 12, 20, 105, 107, 113
   John, 48
   Joshua, 55
   Louisa Kenny (Nason), 17
   Luisa M., 11
   Mary, 20
   Mary A., 233
   Mary Slemmons, 7
   Mrs. Charity, 20
   Peter, 21, 164
   Sally, 159
   Samuel, 18, 20, 20.2(2)
   Samuel H., 17, 94
   Sgt. Daniel, 48
   Sophronia, 108
   Zelia A., 233
Lyman
   Sylvanus R., 208
MOrrill
   Elizabeth, 75
Mabury
   Simeon, 94
   Simon, 91
Magoon
   David C., 324
Mahan
   Catherine (Frost), 83
   John, 83
Mains
   Eleanor (Johnson), 339
   James, 94
   John, 339
Manchester
   Stephen, 48
Mandall
   Rev. D.J., 94
Mandell
   Rev. David, 139
Maner
   Ascena (Milliken), 68
   John, 68

Mange
   Sarah J., 70, 304
Mann
   Dr. A.A., 111
   Edmund, 64
   Rebecca, 41
   Thomas, 89
Mansfield
   Mary, 122
Marble
   Frederick, 78
March
   Ann, 202(2)
   Capt., 186
   Edward, 266
   James, 333
   Lt. Col. Samuel, 48
   Mary (Brackett), 47
   Peletiah, 290
   Peltiah, 47
   Samuel, 108
Marean
   Dea. Joshua H., 269
   Joshua H., 78, 93, 96, 100
Marriner
   Eunice, 76
   Stephen, 48
Marrow
   Isabella (Hutchinson), 263
   Joseph, 263
Marston
   Benjamin, 284
   Mrs. Sarah, 240
   Zachariah, 240
   Zachariah, Jr., 241
Martin
   Ann M., 211
   David, 231
   Hannah (Pennell), 231
   Mrs. Alexander, 122
   Penelope, 213
   Sarah, 264
Mason
   Albert H., 150
   Alden P., 150
   Ann M. (Brackett), 109
   Artemus, 109
   Azor, 148
   Caroline, 150
   Carrie L., 150
   Charles, 150
   Danial, Esq., 154
   Daniel, 44, 148(2), 149(2), 154
   Daniel, Jr., 148(2), 149
   Edward, 205
   Eliza Ann (Pierce), 150
   Elizabeth (Clark), 154
   Elizabeth (Stone), 148
   Emily C., 153
   Emily Cox, 150
   Eunice N. (Winship), 150
   Frank W., 150
   George W., 150
   Georgian, 150
   Hannah, 154
   Hannah (Bryant), 154

Harriet (Tolman), 150
Henry A., 149
Herbert, 149
Herbert D., 149
Hugh, 154
Isaac, 90-91, 93-93, 94(2), 154-155
James, 149
James M., 149
James Means, 154
Joel, 148
Joseph, 154
Julia T., 149
Leroy B., 22
Lewis, 148
Lucy (Kingsbury), 154
Margaret, 154
Martha I., 149
Mary A. (Bradbury), 149
Mary Ann, 150
Moses, 91, 154
Mrs. Ellen F., 149
Mrs. Esther, 148-149
Myram P. (Morton), 150
Nancy, 148
Nehemiah, 148(2), 154
Nettie (Brewer), 149
Noble, 148
Pauline Adams, 150
Phoebe (Chenery), 149
Rebecca (Perley), 154
Sally (Riggs), 155
Samuel, 78, 148(2), 149(3), 150-151, 153, 173
Sarah (Brackett), 109
Sarah (Riggs), 91, 154
Seth, 154(2)
Sopha (Means), 151
Sophaetta, 150
Sophia (Means), 149(2), 151
Sumner R., 154
Thersa, 339
Thomas, 78
Varlow, 148
William F., 152
William Frederick, 150
Woodson, 109

Maston
Ebenezer, 263
Mrs. Adeline, 263

Matha
Rev. Cotton, 286

Mathews
John, 90

Maxfield
Adelaide B., 41
Almira, 41
Andrew, 35
Andrew J., 37
Angel (Poland), 37
Ann, 34
Apphia, 34
Caroline C., 37
Charles, 24, 34-35, 41, 73-74, 176, 272
Daniel, 34-34, 35(2), 41
Daniel V., 37
Daniel W., 41
Eliakim, 34, 41

Eliza Ann, 41
Eliza Haskell, 34
Elizabeth, 34-37
Ellen R., 37
George, 34, 41
George Webster, 37
Henrietta M., 37
Isabella (Webster), 34
James, 41
Josiah, 33-37, 41(2), 78
Josiah B., 37
Julia Ann (Mitchell), 41
Lancia, 41
Lizzie (Gammon), 37
Louisa S., 41
Lydia (Bailey, 35
Lydia (Bailey), 41, 223
Marcia (Stevens), 36
Maria (Hicks), 33
Maria (Stevens), 16
Mary, 34
Mary, 41
Mary (Waterhouse), 41
Mary (Wescott), 34, 37
Mary Frances, 37
Mary Jane, 35(2), 41
Nancy (Partridge), 41
Rebecca, 41
Rebecca (Mann), 41
Rose (Burnham), 37
Rose E. (Hearn), 37
Susan, 34(2)
Susannah (Webb), 34, 37
Wallace, 37, 37
Webster, 34
William, 34-34, 35(2), 37, 41(3)

Maxwell
Irene, 226

May
Col. John, 239

Mayberry
S.P., 22, 252
Sally (Quinby), 38
Thomas, 38
William, 34, 37

Maybury
John, 202
Rachel (Wilson), 202

Mayew
Capt. Ebenezer, 82

Maynard
Edward, 251
John, 251
Maria Caroline, 251, 251
Sally, 251, 251
Thomas, 251
William L., 251

Mayo
Elonzo, 90
Rebeckah, 235

Mayse
John, 302

McAdams
Lizzie, 283

McClink
Frances, 237

McCobb
    D., 98
    James, 254
McCollister
    Rev. S.H., 139
McDavitt
    Ina Lord, 312
    Mary E. (Hawkes), 312
McDonald
    Catherine (Bishop), 264
    David, 47
    Eli, 264
    John, 47-48
    Leonora, 192
    Sarah, 277
    Susie, 69
McDougal
    David, 76
    James, 76
    Mary (Patrick), 76
    Richard, 76
McGowan
    John A., 22
    Rev. William Knight, 57
McGowen
    Joseph A., 22
McGregor
    Rebecca (Merrill), 134, 172
    Rev., 133
    Rev. David, 134, 138, 172
McKenney
    Betsey, 117
    Elizabeth, 116
    Mary, 34(2), 115
McKown
    Capt. Robert, 320
McLellan
    Abigail, 247, 254
    Abigail (Browne), 241
    Alexander, 49
    Arthur, 241
    Capt. Arthur, 240
    Caroline, 239, 239
    Eunice, 239
    Hugh, 239, 241, 256
    Jane, 239
    John, 273
    Joseph, 239, 294
    Margaret (Johnson), 49
    Maria Maileville (Smith), 257
    Mary, 239
    Nabby, 239, 253(2), 256
    Rev. Charles H., D.D., 257(2)
    Sarah (Jones), 273
    Stephen, 239, 241
McLellen
    Abigail (Browne), 239
    Hugh, 239
McNelly
    Mrs. Fanny, 120
    Rosanna H., 120
    William, 120
Meader
    Mr., 115
Meador
    Moses, 132

Means
    Capt. James, 149-149, 150(2), 151-152, 160
    Charles, 151
    Col. James, 148, 176, 221, 228, 236, 263, 287
    Cpl. James, 48
    Dorcas, 116
    Eleanor (Johnson), 150
    George, 151
    James, 77, 90, 150-151, 152(2), 153-154, 180
    John, 150-151
    Jones, 30
    Mary, 151-152
    Mary (Cox), 149, 151
    Mrs. Mary, 152
    Robert, 150-150, 151(2)
    Samuel, 149
    Sopha, 151-151
    Sophia, 149(2), 151
    Thomas, 150
Mellen
    Grenville, 247, 252
    Mary King (Southgate), 247, 252
    Octavia Grenville, 252
    Prentess, 295
    Prentiss, 252
    Sally (Hudson), 252
Merrell
    Charles C., 109
    James, 88
Merrill
    Abba Isabella (Little), 253
    Abigail Brackett), 11
    Adams, 134, 172
    Albert J., 6
    Alden, 195, 264
    Alec Boyd, 258
    Annetta Jane, 9
    Benjamin, 253
    Capt., 186
    Charles B., 254
    Charles Putnam, 258
    Clara (Brooks), 253, 258
    Clara Alden, 195, 264
    Col. Charles Benjamin, 253
    Col. Charles Benjamin, A.M., 258
    Daniel Chamberlain, 258
    Dr. John, 247, 253, 254(2), 258, 315
    Dr. John Cummings, 253
    Dr. John, Jr., 315
    Edmund, 47, 288
    Eleanor (Patrick), 76
    Elizabeth Abbott (Cummings), 253
    Emily, 132
    Emily (North), 132
    Emma Louise, 195, 264
    Enos, 186
    Frank Thayer, 265
    Franklin Thayer, 195
    George Arthur, 195, 264
    George William, 264
    Giles, 134
    Harriet, 197
    I.G., 97
    Isaac D., 132
    Isaac D., Jr., 132
    Isabella Little, 258

Isabella Southgate, 253
J. Ambrose, 254
James, 11, 25, 57, 60, 62, 77, 88-89, 114, 134, 172, 239, 263
James, Jr., 186
Jesse Alden, 264
Jessie (Aldrich), 195
John, 90, 96, 250
John Cummings, M.D., 258
John Edward, 132
John Fuller Appleton, 258
John Q. Adams, 195
Joseph, 197, 284
Josiah Little, 258
Judith, 226
Judith (Brackett), 12
Leonard, 303
Louisa S. (Howard), 192
Lydia (Waterhouse), 303
Major James, 172
Marion (Stevens), 6
Mary (Boyd), 258
Mary Ann, 51
Mary Bliss, 195, 264
Mary Boyd, 253, 258
Mary Southgate, 258
Mary Southgate (Boyd), 247, 253
Miriam, 284
Miriam (Barbour), 197
Moses H., 192
Mrs. Abigail, 172
Nathan, 57, 89
Nathaniel, 12, 165
Paul, 195
Paul Aldrich, 264
Rebecca, 134, 172
Reuben, 134
Rev. Donatus, 131
Rev. Josiah G., 272
Richard King, 258
Royal, 195
Samuel, 134
Sarah Rose, 264
Sarah Rose (Alden), 195
Sophia N., 132
Thomas, 90, 94, 253
Thomas, Jr., 173
William, 195
William P., 197
Meserve
Mary, 339
Miles
Capt. William, 63, 228
Harry ["Gentleman of Color"], 41
Judith (Knight), 63
Mary, 228
Polly, 63
Rev. Edward C., 285
Milk
Capt., 46
Miller
John, 49
Milliken
Amanda (Stevens), 68
Arthur, 44, 78, 94, 266
Asa, 319
Ascena, 68
Benjamin, 333
Caroline (Lowell), 266
Charles, 68
Edward, 244(3), 333
Elizabeth, 68
Elizabeth (Alger), 243
Eunice, 157, 173
Frances, 68
Frances F., 68(2), 70
George, 68
James, 68
Jemina, 244
Jeremiah, 333
John, 243-244, 246
John M., 164, 333(2)
John M., Jr., 68
John Mulbury, 68
Jonathan, 244
Joseph, 244
Martha (Spaulding), 68
Mrs. Abigail, 244
Mrs. Martha, 244
Mrs. Sarah, 244
Nahum, 68
Nathaniel, 244(2)
Samuel, 244(2), 262, 333
Susan (Fickett), 68
William, 68
Millions
Sally, 93
Mills
Betsey Walker (Brackett), 110
Joanna (Alger), 243
John, 243
Moses, 329
O'Neal R., 110
Miltimore
Docas (Noyes), 134
Dorcas (Bradley), 137
Mrs. Mary O., 134
Rev. William, 134, 136, 186, 272
Mitchell
Andrew, 188
Dea. Jacob, 222
Deborah, 222
Deborah (Mitchell), 222
Deliverance (Kingman), 222
Edward, 222
Eliza (Kingman), 222
Elizabeth, 222
Eveline, 272
Experience, 222
Frederic L., 222
Isaac, 222
Jacob, 222(2)
Jane (Cook), 222
Jeremiah, 208
Julia Ann, 41
Lydia, 222
Mary, 222, 222(2)
Mrs. Ann, 41
Nathaniel, 204
Noah, 222
Peleg, 41(2), 107, 147, 176, 218, 272
Rachel (Loring), 286

Rebecca, 222
Rebecca (Cushman), 222
Sarah, 222
Seth, 222
Susannah, 222
Susannah (Pope), 222
Thomas, 222
Mitton
Michael, 20.2, 60
Nathaniel, 20.2
Monday
Polly, 149
Monroe
President, 104
President James, 237
Mons
Nile, 89
Montgomery
Eliza W., 264
Nathaniel, 311
Montgromery
John A., 266
Mary (Dennison), 266
Moody
Daniel, 276
Edward, 155
Enoch, 90
Joshua, 199, 225
Mary (Codman), 225
Mehitable, 316
Mrs. Hannah Woodbury, 276
Rachel (Riggs), 155
Samuel, 202
William, 155
Moore
Abigail (Brackett), 11
Collins, 11
Eleazer, 256
Ellen, 192
Esther (Brackett), 11
Eunice (Libby), 185
Joan F., 182
Levi, 11
Mary, 248, 256
William, 185
More
Robert, 90
Morey
Nicholas, 101
Morrell
Capt. Levi, 286
Elizabeth, 107(2), 108
Joshua, 134
Peter, Esq., 263
Robert, 287
Morrill
Anson P., 118-119
Capt. William, 265
Edmund N., 265
Eleanor (Stevens), 75
Ellen, 75
George A., 22
Hon. Edmund N., 37
Levi, 52, 55, 90, 94, 212
Lizzie Barbour (Allen), 265
Margaret Ann, 75

Mary, 264
Mary (Hall), 263
Mary (Leavitt), 265
Mary (Webb), 265
Mary S., 197, 265(2)
Nathaniel L., 263
Paul, 75(2)
Rufus, 52, 55, 90, 94, 125, 194, 264
Rufus, Jr., 265
Rufus, Sr., 265
Sally (Webb), 264-265
Samuel, 75
Mors
Anthony, 57
Morse
Andrew, 293
Anthony, 19, 60, 89, 239, 288-290
Ephriam, 19
Jane (Adams), 20.2
Jane (Bailey), 19
Jonathan, 10, 45
Nathaniel, 165
Sarah (Brackett)(Sawyer), 10
Thomas, 18-19, 20.2
Morton
Albert, 120
Ann Maria, 266
Ann Maria (Morton), 266
Ann Maria (Stevens), 31, 211
Capt. George, 70, 150, 264
Edith M., 150
George, 264
George M., 266
George W., 31
George, Jr., 72
Hannah, 33, 33
Mary Ann (Purington), 264
Myram P., 150
Nancy, 155
Nelson, 150
Solomon, 31
Susie (McDonald), 69
Wilma N., 150
Moses
Benjamin, 311
J.F., 55
Maria D., 189, 190
Nathaniel, 333
Mosher
Nancy, 205
Mosier
A.J., 51
Daniel, 10
Jane (Brackett), 10
Julia Harris (Woodford), 51
Motely
Mary Ann, 50
Moulton
Mary, 65
Mountfort
Edmund, 19
Edward, 19
Elizabeth, 19
Mrs. Hannah, 19
Samuel, 19, 146
Mowatt

Burning of Portland, 189
Capt., 214
Moxfield
   Charles, 220
   Josiah, 220
   Nancy (Partridge), 220
Mullins
   Priscilla, 195
Munjoy
   George, 58, 79, 199, 203, 286
   Mrs. Mary, 199
Munroe
   Cynthia, 127
   David, 127
   Edmund, 257
   Mrs. Adeline A., 210
   Ruth (Niles), 127
   Sophia Sewall (Wood), 257
   Susan D., 251
   Susan Dwight, 257
Munson
   Abigail, 169
Murray
   Catherine S., 45
   James T., 282-283
   Joel, 266
   Joel H., 45
   Mary (Stevens), 45
   Mary Ann (Bowne), 282-283
   Nancy (Stevens), 266
Mussett
   Joseph, 46
Mussey
   James, 101
Mustard
   Mary, 112
Muzzett
   Abigail (Chapman), 105
Nash
   Charlotte, 63
   Elizabeth (Andrews), 185
   Eunice, 226
   John, 185
   Mehitable, 185(2)
   Mrs. Mary, 130
Nason
   Abigail, 191, 339
   Bathsheba (Partridge), 309
   Chesley D., 91, 229
   Eunice (Wilson), 202
   Frances A. (Kenny), 17
   Isaac, 46, 56, 89, 165
   Jonathan, 46, 89
   Joseph, 191
   Louisa, 17
   Louisa (Kenny), 17
   Louisa Kenny, 17
   Mary S., 17
   Noah, 99
   Rev. Reuben, 261
   Richard, 56, 202
   Richard, Jr., 46, 89
   Thomas, 17
   Uriah, 48, 309
Nay
   Frank J., 37

Nellie (Judkins), 37
Wallace (Maxfield), 37
Neal
   Eliza, 247, 248
   Elizabeth, 256
   James, 248
   John, Esq., 253, 255
   Mrs. Abigail C., 248
Neilson
   John, 2
Nelson
   John, 78
   Joseph W., 221
   Lydia Ellen (Partridge), 221
   Margaret, 155
   Rev. F.T., 138, 140
   Rev. Frederick T., 146
Newbegin
   Jonathan, 71, 266
   Polly (Fickett), 71
Newcomb
   Erwin B., 229
   Nettie Sophia (Pennell), 229
Newman
   Ebenezer, 158
   Ed, 75
   Edward, 18, 55, 133, 148, 194
   John, 55, 129
   Miss. Mary A., 78
   Polly (Dyer), 158
Nicholls
   Francis, 78
Nichols
   Lydia, 225
   Parson, 213
   Rev. Ichabod, 255
Nickerson
   Elizabeth, 150
Nickery
   Mary A., 184
Niles
   Ruth, 127
Nixon
   Gen. John, 154
Noble
   Nathan, 89
Noise
   Hannah, 163
Norh
   Elijah, 18
North
   Abbie (Larry), 130
   Abbie S., 130(2)
   Ada (Babcock), 130
   Alice, 140
   Amanda (Blanchard), 130
   Annie, 130
   Annie C. (Drew), 132
   Bernice Washington, 130
   Capt. Samuel, 133
   Charles A., 130
   Charles D., 130
   Dora Ada, 130
   Edna May, 130
   Edward, 130
   Elijah, 13, 42, 49, 128, 131, 140, 159, 187-188

Elisha, 13, 49(2), 128-131, 133(2)
Eliza E. (Sampson), 132
Emily, 132
Emily Herrick, 130
Emma S., 130
Eunice (Snow), 132
F.O., 140
Fannie, 130
Frank A., 132
Frank W., 130
Fred O., 140
Frederick O., 132
Gertrude, 130
Grace Gordon (Young), 132
Harriet W., 130
Harry C., 130
John H., 132
Josiah S., 75, 133(2)
Josiah Stevens, 49, 130
Lois, 132
Mabel, 130
Maria A., 132
Mariah, 132
Martha (Woodford), 42, 131, 159, 187
Martha J., 132, 140
Mary A. (Winslow), 130
Mary Emma, 130
Mrs., 75, 133
Mrs. Lois, 128
Mrs. Mary (Nash), 130
Nabby (Stevens), 128, 130
Nancy (Bradbury), 128, 130
Orin B., 132
Orin, Jr., 132
Rhoda, 132
Rosilla, 130, 130
Sally (Read), 187
Samuel, 130, 133
Sarah Louise, 130
Silas, 132
Sophia, 132
Sophia (Warren), 131
Susan B. (Herrick), 130

Norton
Hepsbath, 180
James, 208
Mary Ann, 229

Norwell
Joseph, 157

Nowell
Betsey (Bean), 197
Zachariah, 197

Noyes
Albert T., 76
Alfred, 110
Amos, 48
Cpl. Amos, 47
Docas, 134
Elizabeth, 3
Hannah, 311
Harriet W. (Brackett), 110
Jacob, 64
Jane L., 9-9
Joseph, 10, 89, 147
Josiah, 90
Margaret (Stevens), 76

Nancy C. (Brackett), 110
Peter, 311
Peter, Esq., 290
Tristram, 110

Nutter
Anthony, 78
Nathan, 98

O'Brion
Edward C., 120
Thomas, 107

Oakman
Elias, 243
Joanna (Alger), 243

Oldham
Mrs. Martha, 59

Oliver
Capt. James, 323

Ordway
Reuben, 254

Osborne
Mary E. (Pennell), 231
Susan, 231

Osgood
E.S., 22
Joseph, 261

Packard
Mrs. Matilda M., 19

Packwood
Joan (Brackett), 11
Robert, 11

Paddeford
Judith, 195

Page
Albion, 130
Edward H., Esq., 317
Jonathan, 324
Rev. Caleb F., 97
Rosilla (North), 130
Samuel, 324

Pain
Elizabeth (Fickett), 75
Richard, 75

Paine
Elizabeth (Patrick), 76
Henry W., 206
Mercy, 304
Richard, 76
Ruth (Adams), 228
Sarah, 25(2)
Sarah M., 264
Uriah, 228

Palmer
Elizabeth (Alger), 243
Richard, 50

Parker
Abbie S. (North), 130
Abigail (Chamberlain), 303
Abigail (Fessenden), 266
Andrew J., 176
Deputy Sheriff, 175
Dr. Alexander M., 189
Edgar B., 130
Emma H., 130
Grace, 130
Hattie May, 130
James, 43, 69, 91, 159, 303

John, 263
Joseph, 73
Joseph C., 33(2), 40, 277
Julia (Tate), 33
Laura, 108
Louise, 130
Sally (Kennard), 263
Susie, 130
William, 57, 266
William H., 130
Willie Stevens, 130
Parkman
Samuel, 277
Parsons
Curtis H., 8
Judge, 174
Lucy M. (Stevens), 8
Rev. Eben G., 136
Walter Chenery, 9
Partridge
David, 220
Adeline (Quinby), 221
Albion K.P., 221
Andrew J., 221
Ann, 217(2)
Ann (Conant), 220, 309
Azabah, 38
Azubah, 309(2), 309
Bathsheba, 309
Benjamin Q., 221
Benjamin, Q., 38
Benoni, 308
Capt. Jesse, 24, 35, 38, 83, 151, 174(2), 220-221, 223, 279, 294, 309
Capt. Nathaniel, 274
Caroline P., 221
Catharine, 309
Catherine, 41
Catherine (Armstrong), 309
Charles L., 221
David, 47-48, 309
Frank, 221
Franklin, 268
George W., 38, 221
Hannah (Farnum), 221
Harriet N. (Snow), 221
Isabel (Proctor), 221
Jesse, 36, 49, 227, 288, 290, 293
John, 308
John W., 221
Joseph, 38(3), 220-221
Joseph P., 221
Jotham, 47, 223, 309
Katherine, 217(2)
Louise (Cloudman), 221
Lt. Jesse, 47-48
Lydia (Quinby), 220
Lydia Ellen, 221
Mary (Bailey), 223, 309
Mary (Conant), 220, 309
Mary (Rich), 221
Mary Ann (Buckley), 190
Mary C., 221
Mehitable (Wheelock), 308
Mrs. Susan Smith (Webb), 274
Mrs. Susannah Smith (Webb), 274

Mrs. Susannah Webb, 274
Nancy, 38, 41, 220
Nancy (Proctor), 221
Nathan, 48, 220-221, 308-309
Natnan, 220
Phebe (Berry), 221
Polly, 41
Preserved, 308-309
Rebecca (Bailey), 35, 223, 309
Resinah, 38
Rhoda, 34, 217, 309
Rose (Knight), 221
Rosina, 309(2)
Sarah B. (Ayer), 221
Sarah P. (Hawkes), 221
William, 190
Zipporah, 309
Patrick
Betsey, 72, 76
Charles, 65(2), 71-75, 89
David, 43, 46, 48, 56, 71-73, 74(2), 75, 203, 211, 276
David, Jr., 46
Eleanor, 72, 72-76, 273, 276
Elizabeth, 72-76
Elizabeth (Potter), 74
Elizabeth P., 74
Hariot, 74-74
Margaret, 43, 67, 72(2), 76(2), 75, 183, 203
Mary, 72-72, 76(2)
Mehitable (Fickett), 65, 74
Mrs., 158
Mrs. Mary, 276
Mrs. Mary, 72, 75, 203
William, 72-74
Patridge
Jesse, 89
Preserved, 89
Patten
Florence (Johnson), 339
Matthew, 151
Robert, 339
Patterson
Angelina A., 5-5
Gen. John, 154
Pattishall
Richard, 20.2
Payson
Ann Louise (Shipman), 213
Caroline Shipman, 213
Charles, 213
Edward, 212-213
Edward, D.D., 213
Elizabeth, 213
George, 213
Henry M., 213
Louisa Shipman, 213
Penelope (Martin), 213
Rev. Edward, 213, 250
Rev. Seth, 213
Peabody
Josiah, 48
Mary, 220, 309
Peaks
Mary (Thomes), 176
Mrs. Mary, 76

Nancy, 176
Sally, 9
Sophia, 43, 76
Pearson
Ann, 223
Bethiah, 303
Capt. Moses, 215, 220, 223
Elizabeth, 223
Eunice, 2
Lois, 236
Moses, 2, 18, 102, 157, 216, 236
Sarah, 157, 215, 223, 235
Pearsons
George, 109
Jeremiah, Jr., 214
Moses, 214
Rebeckah, 214
Sarah, 214, 214
Sybil (Brackett), 109
Peckham
Rev. Samuel H., 284
Peirce
Charles, 163
Joseph, 163
Rebecca, 162
Rebecca (Quinby), 163
Samuel, 163
Peirce (See Also Pierce), 162
Pennel
Clement, 63, 89
Pennell
Abigail, 228(3)
Abigail (Taylor), 231
Addie F. (Quinby), 229
Addie Louisa, 229
Alexander, 229
Almira, 62, 229
Ann (Tuckey), 231
Annie S., 231
Bertha M., 231
Charles, 62, 229, 231
Charlotte (Nash), 63
Clement, 46, 60, 62(2), 65, 224-225, 227-229, 231, 239
Clement, Jr., 62-63, 226
Corinda (Small), 229
Dixey, 230
Dixey Stone, 230
Dixie S., 226, 230
Elizabeth (Stone), 63, 226
Ephraim, 63
Ephriam, 229
Esther (Hinginham), 62, 231
Eunice, 63, 228(3)
Eunice (Knight), 62, 171, 226, 228-229
Eunice (Nash), 226
Eunice (Thomes), 229
Frank H., 231
George, 62, 229
Hannah, 231
Hannah (Brooks), 231
Hannah (Ward), 63, 226
Hannah W., 226
Hattie Jane, 229
Henry, 62, 229, 284
Henry B., 63

Irene (Maxwell), 226
James, 226, 230(2), 231
Jane F., 231
Jeremiah, 48, 226-227
John, 62, 231
John P., 229
John, Jr., 46, 227
Jones, 62, 229
Jones M., 229
Joseph, 48, 63
Joseph, 226
Joseph, 226-227, 230, 288
Joseph Henry, 229
Josiah, 231
Judith (Merrill), 226
Luther, 226, 229
Marcia, 231
Mary (Gould), 226
Mary Ann (Norton), 229
Mary E., 231(3)
Mary Susan (Weston), 284
Mathew, 231
Molly, 65, 228(3)
Mrs. Ruth, 225
Nancy, 62, 225(2)
Nettie Sophia, 229
Polly, 65, 71
Rachel (Riggs), 224
Robert B., 226
Ruth (Riggs), 62, 224, 226
Sally (Jones), 62, 229
Samuel, 226
Sarah (Sterns), 229
Sarah F., 229
Sophia, 62
Sophia J., 226(2)
Sophia J. (Pennell), 226, 229
Stephen, 284
Susan S. (Smith), 226
Susannah, 226
Thomas, 46, 56, 62(4), 63, 224(2), 226-228, 229(3), 231
William L., 63, 214, 225-225, 226(2), 229-230, 232
William M., 22
Pepperell
Mary, 79, 84, 87
Sir William, Baronet, 79(2)
Perkins
Charles P., 150
Mrs. Caroline, 152
Wid. Carrie L. (Thompson), 150
William, 150
Perley
Abraham, 154
Louis (Brackett), 109
Mrs. Rebecca, 154
Rebecca, 154
Samuel, Esq., 226
William, 109
Perry
John, 62
Perry
Gen. John J., 118
Porterfield
William, 90

Peters
   Elizabeth P. , 74
   Elizabeth P. (Patrick), 74
   William B., 74
Peterson
   George, 329
Pettingill
   Benjamin, 164
Phagrins
   Joseph, 175
   Mary (Whitney), 175
Philips
   John, 203
   Parmelia P., 280
Phinney
   Clement, 212, 214
   Col. Edmund, 48, 154, 235
   James, 285
   Jane (Cross), 285
   John, 164
   Martha (Hamblen), 285
Phipps
   Persis, 233
   Sir William, 243
Pickney
   Gen. C.C., 250
   General, 249
   Thomas, 250
Piece
   Joshua, 140
Pierce
   Abigail, 29
   Abigail Doughty (Shaw), 29
   Alden, 150
   Ann (Haskell), 273
   Archelaus L., 238
   Arthur Dorr, 238
   Benjamin, 29(2), 50
   Betsey (Storer), 147, 159
   Charles, 21, 28-28, 29(2), 30(2), 31, 44, 50, 64, 123, 162, 174
   Charles French, 238
   Cordelia (Stevens), 28-29
   Daniel, 29(2), 115
   Daniel Thompson, 238
   Daniel Thompson, Jr., 238
   Edward, 29(2), 30-31
   Eleazer, 29
   Eliza Ann, 150
   Eliza L., 238
   Elizabeth, 29, 45, 171
   Emeline I., 28
   Eveline (Lewis), 237
   Eveline L., 238
   Florence, 28
   Frances E. (Lewis), 238(2)
   Franklin, 242
   George Ann, 238
   George Washington, 238
   Hannah, 302
   Harriet, 238
   Harriet Angier, 238
   Humphrey, 29
   Joanna (Haskell), 171
   John, 29
   Joseph, 29-30
   Joshua, 140
   Josiah, 75, 238
   Josiah, Esq., 237
   Josiah, Jr., 238
   Levi, 29
   Levi Q., 28
   Lewis, 238
   Lewis, Esq., 288
   Lydia (Frost), 29
   Mary, 29-31, 51
   Mrs. Betsey, 147
   Mrs. Levi Q., 125
   Nancy, 238
   Peggy, 74
   Peggy (Porterfield), 28-29, 31, 69
   Peggy (Trickey), 50
   Rebecca, 30
   Rev. Thomas, 159, 171, 246, 273
   Richard Skinner, 238
   Samuel, 29
   Susan, 238
   Thomas, 29, 44-45, 147(2), 159, 171, 187
Pike
   Charles, 329
   Daniel, 126
   Emma, 251, 257
   Eveline, 155
   Helen L., 126
   Polly W. (Brackett), 110
   Samuel D., 266
   Seth, 110
   Timothy, 38, 266
Pillsbury
   Noah, 333
Pitt-Fessenden
   William, 118
Plaisted
   Mrs. Mary (Smith), 182
Plumer
   Josiah, 40
   Major, 78
Plummer
   C.F., 22
   Charles A., 167
   Dorcas, 67(2)
   James, 261
   Jeremiah, 295
   Josiah, 202
   Moses, 67
Poland
   Angel, 37
Polleys
   W., 55
Pomeroy
   Ann, 192
   Rev. Thaddeus, 137, 270
Poor
   Nathaniel, 325
Pope
   Caroline (McLellan), 239
   Elijah, 214
   Joseph, 239
   Susannah, 222
Porter
   Betsey Lyden (King), 319
   Capt. Richard K., 322

Dr. Aaron, 312
Dr. Benjamin F., 312
Dr. Benjamin J., 320, 333
Dr. Benjamin James, 324
Dr. Benjamin Jones, 316, 319
Freeman, 52, 55, 190, 233, 264
Joanna (Barbour), 197
Joshua, 78
Porter
Mary, 197
Porter
Mary Ann (Buckley), 190, 233, 264
Mrs. Dr. Benjamin J., 334
Nehemiah, 197
Rufus K. J., 326-328
Ruth (Knapp), 327
Samuel B., 190
Thersa Ellen, 190
Porterfield
Ann, 263
Capt. John, 50, 263
Catharine, 279
Catherine, 335
Catherine (Slemmons), 50
Dorothy (Bailey), 50
Elizabeth, 50(2), 51, 227
Elizabeth (Wilson), 50
Hannah, 50
James, 77
John, 48, 77, 90, 94(2), 290
Lettice, 69
Mary, 50
Mary, 50
Mary (Jamerson), 50
Mary (Larrabee), 50
Mary Ann (Larrabee), 50
Peggy, 28(2), 31, 69, 162
William, 46, 50(4), 94, 339
William, Jr., 50, 290
Pote, 18
Capt. William, 27, 239
Dorothy, 20
Elizabeth (Berry), 27, 173
Jeremiah, 27
Mrs., 134
William, 18, 20.2(2), 20.3, 56, 58
Potefield
Catherine, 83
Poterfield
Capt. John, 69
Catheren, 40
Catherine (Slemmons), 69
Doritha (Bailey), 69
James, 164
Mary Ann (Larraby), 69
Robert, 89(2)
William, 69
Potter
Elizabeth, 74, 246
Lucy, 197
Mrs. Rebecca, 246
Nathaniel, 246
Pratt
Ann (Porterfield), 263
Ann (Trickey), 50
B.F., 282

Charles, 50, 90-91, 263(2)
Charles, Jr., 94
Cushing, 90, 94
Cushing, Jr., 90
David, 7
Elizabeth (Woodbury), 263
Ellen, 282
Henry, 78, 90, 94
Nancy, 271
Nancy (Peaks), 176
Susan B., 266
Zenas, 30, 58, 76, 286
Preble
Agnes (Archer), 197
Capt. Enoch, 21, 30
Eben, 197
Enoch, 78
Gen. Jedediah, 287
William Pitt, Jr., 333
Prentiss
Artemus, 18, 188
Sargent S., 253
Prescott
Fannie, 117
Mrs. Elizabeth, 117
Stephen, 117
Prichard
John, 102
Pride
Abigail (Berry), 175
Benjamin, 175
Frederick, 17
James, 290
Jonah, 281
Joseph, 20.1-20.2, 57, 60, 89, 170(2), 175, 288
Margaret Baker, 263
Mrs. Mary, 281
Nathan, 170
Peter, 78, 263
Sally, 202
Samuel, 175
Sophia W. (Kenny), 17
William, 57, 89
William, 170
William, Jr., 78
Priest
John, 48
Prince
Albert, 98
Helen F. (Woodford), 42
Joel, 155
Lucius, 42
Sally (Riggs), 155
William, 208
Procter
John, 57, 89
William, 57, 89
Proctor
Capt. Nathaniel, 19
Charity, 20
Elizabeth (Quinby), 39
Hannah, 19
Isabel, 221
James, 39
Joanna (Berry), 175
John, 19

Mrs. Esther, 19
Mrs. Sarah, 19
Nancy, 221
Nathaniel, 19
Samuel A., 38, 175
William, 288
Prout
Timothy, 262
Puff
Peter, 47
Pullen
Washington, 329
Pulsifer
Nancy J., 185
Purington
John, 101
Mary Ann, 264
Putnam
Hon. William L., 252, 258
Quimby
Abel, 197
Joseph, 159
Quinby
Aaron, 221
Abel, 38, 40(2)
Abel, Jr., 40
Abigail, 39
Addie F., 229
Adeline, 221
Ann (Titcomb), 223
Annie (Laurie), 307
Annie Laurie, 307
Azubah (Partridge), 309-310
Azubah Partridge, 311
Benjamin, 38, 40(2), 90-91, 93-93, 94(2), 310
Benjamin, Jr., 38, 310
Betsey (Walker), 39-40
Capt. Isaac F., 24, 307, 311
Capt. Isaac Fly, 38
Capt. John, 30, 43, 155, 161(2), 163, 236(2), 237, 290, 294, 305
Catherine G. (Brown), 307, 311
Charles, 38(2), 39-40, 90, 94, 232
Charles E., 311
Charlotte, 24, 38, 40
Charlotte A., 307
Eleanor, 34
Eleanor (Starbird), 38, 40, 310
Eliza (Bailey), 307, 311
Eliza Ann, 307
Elizabeth, 39, 159
Elizabeth (Bailey), 24, 38, 309
Elizabeth (Fly), 24
Elizabeth Ann, 24
Emanuel Swedenburg, 307
Esther B., 266
Eunice, 38, 161, 161-163
Eunice (Freeman), 161, 163, 236
Franklin, 38
Frederick, 38, 266
George, 38, 40
George W., 40
George Washington, 38(2)
Hannah, 163-163
Hannah (Noise), 163
Hannah (Noyes), 311
Henry Brewer, 155
Henry C., 40, 155
Henry Cole, 155
Henry Quinby, 307
Hiram, 38-40
Isaac Franklin, 307
Jacob, 38, 40, 310
Jacob, Jr., 38
Jane (Brewer), 80
Jane E., 87
John, 64, 236, 293
John Laurie, 307
Joseph, 24(4), 30, 38(2), 48, 155, 161, 163(2), 165, 236, 307, 309-309, 310(2), 311
Joseph B., 24, 307(2)
Joseph Bailey, 307
Joseph Kilby, 307
Joseph), 39
Joseph, Jr., 163, 288, 307, 309, 311(2)
Joseph, Sr., 311
Levi, 38, 163, 174, 223
Lucretia, 38
Lydia, 38, 220
Martha, 38, 175
Martha C., 307
Mary, 38, 40, 163-163, 311
Mary (Haskell), 155, 163(2), 236, 310
Mary (Quinby), 311
Mary (Roberts), 39
Mary (Titcomb), 223
Moses, 38-39, 40(3), 64, 93-93, 94(2), 98, 121, 125, 139-140, 155, 223, 310
Moses, Esq., 40(2), 91-92, 204, 263
Moses, III, 40
Mrs., 40
Mrs. Abel, 40
Mrs. Abigail, 40
Mrs. Benjamin, 40
Mrs. Eleanor, 310
Mrs. Hannah, 38
Mrs. Jane, 80
Mrs. Moses, 40
Mrs. Sally, 38
Nancy, 38-38, 38(2)
Nathan, 38(3), 40, 309-310
Nathaniel, 24
Polly, 40
Rebecca, 163
Resinah (Partridge), 38
Rhoda, 39
Rosina (Partridge), 309-310
Sally, 38
Sally (Jameson), 39
Sally (Waterhouse), 309
Sarah, 40, 163
Sarah (Brackett), 38
Simeon, 38(2), 40(3), 310
Sophronia, 38, 266
Sylvia Laurie, 307
Sylphia Laura, 307
Tamson, 39
Thankful, 40
Thomas, 80, 120, 155, 163
Rackleff
Chandler, 55, 94
Racklyf

Benjamin, 189
Joshua, 189
Racklyft
Joshua, 16
Railey
Eliza, 253
Mary Eliza, 248(2)
Rand
Alvin B., 32
Elder Samuel, 130
Eleanor (Brewer), 339
James Brewster, 70
Rev. Samuel, 133
Samuel, 188
Randall
Robert S., 240-241
Rapalye
Eliza, 282
Helen, 282
Simon, 282
Ray
Fabins M., 234
Hon. F.M., 176, 207
Jonathan, 3, 164
Nobby (Stevens), 3
Samuel, 78
Raymond
Addie M., 233
Charles, 91, 94
Elizabeth (Andrews), 233
George H., 233
Hattie E., 233
Helen M., 233
John, 233
Jonas, 211-212, 214, 233(2), 234
King S., 233
Mary R. (Johnson), 233
Polly (Smith), 233
Samuel, 233
Samuel Tarbox, 233
Reynolds
Leonard O., 55
Rea
Dr. Caleb, Jr., 207
Sally, 157, 173, 207
Sarah (White), 207
Read
Eunice (Hodsdon), 51
Harriet B. (Woodford), 51
James N., 269
Jane (Woodford), 51
John, 51(2), 52, 55
Mr. James N., 269
Mrs. H.B., 78
Mrs. Jane B., 78
Nancy (Horton), 51
Nancy Paine (Bailey), 27
Noah, 51, 211
Rufus, 27, 78
Sally, 187, 187
William, 187-188
Record
Cynthia (Munroe), 127
Irene (Stevens), 126-127, 196
Lewis Miner, 127
Lydia (Chandler), 127

Mrs. Thomas G., 127
Rev. L.L., 98, 139
Rev. Lewis L., 126
Rev. Lewis Leonard, 127
Thomas, 127
Willie, 127
Redington
Asa, 324
Reed
Ann, 191
Harriet Rebecca (Stevens), 9
James N., 9
Sally, 131, 159, 187, 188
Thomas B., 22
Reese
Rev., 139
Rev. W. I., 92
Rev. W.I., 91
Remick
Benjamin, 30, 123-124
Restall
Charles, 57
George, 57
Miss. Laura, 57
Mrs. Mary, 57
Retchie
Andrew, Esq., 251
Revere
Deborah, 193
Deborah (Hichborn), 193
Elizabeth, 193
Francis, 193
John, 193(2)
Mary, 193(2), 193
Paul, Jr., 193(2)
Paul, Sr., 193
Sarah, 193
Thomas, 193
Reynolds
Alice Alberta, 33
Augusta, 122
Edward Everett, 33
Lena Eugene, 33
Leonard O., 33
Millie M., 33
Williams, 33
Rhemic
Benjamin, 174
Rice
Ephraim, 295
Mary (Stevens), 5
Mathias, 294
Simon T., 5
Rich
Henry, 168
Henry A., 168
Rich
Mary, 221
Richards
Albion Royal, 185
Annie Olevia, 185
Eliza (Burnham), 185
Enoch, 161-162
George William, 185
Harriet Elizabeth, 185
Richards

Roxanna, 184
Richards
  William, 185
Richardson
  Artemus L., 132
  David, 33
  Frank, 286
  John, 319
  Joshua, 148-149
  Marsha Adelia (Grant), 33
  N. Putnam, 254
Richmond
  Mary, 286
Ricker
  Helen (Bowne), 282-283
  Joseph R., 234
  Sylvanus Smith, 282-283
Rider
  John, 20.2
  Phineas, 20, 20.2(2), 20.5
Rigby
  Edward, Esq., 198
Riggs
  Abigail, 61
  Ann, 9, 76, 182, 335
  Ann (Bagley), 61
  Ann (Barbour), 61
  Ann (Delano), 155, 263
  Ann (Hall), 155
  Capt. Joseph, 289
  Charles J., 155
  Elbridge G., 62-63, 149(2), 155, 310
  Enoch, 41, 48
  Eveline (Pike), 155
  George, 155
  Hannah, 61
  Hannah (Anderson-Jordan), 155
  Hannah (Jordan), 263
  James, 62, 90-91, 94, 154-154, 155(2)
  James, Jr., 263
  Jeremiah, 46, 56, 60-61, 78-79, 89, 106, 155(3), 169, 239, 288, 290
  Jeremiah, Jr., 45, 61, 155
  Joseph, 41, 46, 56-57, 60(2), 61-62, 77, 239, 288, 290
  Lucy, 61
  Lydia (Ingalson), 155
  Margaret, 155
  Margaret (Barbour), 155
Riggs
  Mary, 61, 155(2)
  Mrs. Elbridge G., 64
  Nancy, 155
  Nancy (Morton), 155
  Polly (Monday), 149
  Rachel, 62
  Rachel, 155, 224
  Rachel (Haskell), 61, 155
  Rebecca, 155
  Ruth, 62, 62, 226(2)
  Sally, 155(2)
  Sarah, 91, 154
  Sgt. Jeremiah, 46
  Stephen, 45-46, 61, 63-64, 90, 94, 154-154, 155(3), 158-159, 188, 288, 290
  Stephen Jones, 155

Steven, 155
Sumner, 155
Susanna (Jones), 155
Thomas, 77, 155(2), 263
Thomas J., 55
Wheeler, 61
Riley
  Sally (Fly), 24
Rines
  J. Henry, 270
Ring
  David, 317
Ritchie
  Andrew, Esq., 333
Rivorie
  Apollas, 264
Robbins
  Emeline D. (Chamberlain), 303
  F.E.C., 1, 140
  Mrs. F.E.C., 138
  William H., 303
Roberts
  Elizabeth (Hatch), 339
  Almira (Waterhouse), 70, 304
  Benjamin, 78
  Charles, 339
  Clyde S., 308
  Dorcas (Johnson), 49
  Eleanor (Chenery), 339
  Ellen (Babb), 266
  Emeline A., 308
  George Capson, 25
  Gilbert F., 308
  Harriet, 339
  Ina M., 308
  Isabella, 66
  James W.C., 308
  Joshua D., 266
  Joshua S., 308
  Lillian (Jackson), 308
  Mary, 39
  Nellie F. (Sanborn), 308
  Olive L., 308
  Percy L., 308
  Philip C., 308
  Sarah (Buckley), 125
  Sarah J. (Buckley), 190
  Susan M. (Bailey), 308
  William, 49, 70, 125(2), 304, 339(2)
  William H., 190
Robie
  Rev. Thomas, 285
Robins
  Hannah, 44
Robinson
  Capt. Joshua, 197
  Eben, 8
  Eben S., 5
  Frankliin, 8
  George, 5
  Jane, 197
  John, 48
  Martha A., 8
  Martha Amelia (Stevens), 8
  Martha C. (Stevens), 5
  Nancy, 11

Samuel, 8
Thomas, 241, 294
Woodbury, 8
Roody
Henry H., 70
Rose
Edward, 193
Mary, 264
Mary (Revere), 193
Mrs. Mary, 193
Philip, 193
Sarah, 194(2)
Rounds
James, 50
Mary (Porterfield), 50
Sally, 39, 260
William, 50
Rowe
Richard, 155
Royals
Naomy, 183(2), 184
Rumford
Count, 238
Rundlet
Chas., 302
Russell
Edward, 295
Harriet, 108
John H., 183
Submit C., 183
Rust
Armistad Tomson Mason, 282
Dr. W.A., 119
Eliza Southgate (Lawrence), 282
Ryland
Sarah (Bailey), 307
Thomas A., 307
Sadler
Mrs. Harriet M., 210
Rev. Levi L., 210
Sampson
Edward, 125, 190
Eliza E., 132
Jeremiah B., 266
Laura (Buckley), 125, 190
Mary W. (Knight), 266
Oakes, 306
Sanborn
Dr. William, 186
John, 56, 90
Nellie F., 308
William, 164
Sangstad
Elizabeth Brown (Graham), 258
Olaf, 258
Sargent
Epes, 198
J., 55
Martha, 202(2)
Mrs. Mary, 198
William M., 20.1
Saunders
Lucy (Smith), 225
Samuel, 18, 20.2
Thomas, Esq., 225
Sawyer

Abbie W., 26, 26
Abraham, 2(2), 20.3
Abram, 18
Alexander, 26
Alfred, 132
Amos, 16
Ann, 26
Ann (Stevens), 26
Anthony, 159, 290
Augusta (Stevens), 15-16
Brackett, 78
Capt. Isaac, 12
Charles, 26, 55
Charles S., 132
Charlotte, 19, 91
Daniel, 26
David, 175
Deborah, 65
Dorcas, 16, 175
Eben, 55
Eben B., 132
Eben Barton, 132
Ebenezer Hilton, 26, 175, 189
Edward, 2
Elizabeth, 2, 26
Elizabeth (Bailey), 26
Frederick, 3, 55, 133
George, 26(4), 94
George H., 308
Hannah, 16
Harriet, 16, 33
Henry, 78
Hiram, 15-17, 22, 33, 132
Isaac, 2(2), 4, 6, 10, 18-20.2, 20.3(4), 51, 91, 132, 237, 288, 290, 293
Isaac, Jr., 10, 45, 188
Jane, 6, 16
Jeremiah, 26, 189
Joanna, 16
Joel, 26
John, 48, 226, 288, 339
John R., 234
Jonathan, 3, 20.3, 288
Jonathan, Jr., 3
Joseph, 158
Joseph M., 78
Joshua, 2
Josiah, 26
Judith, 2, 10, 12
Julia A. (Witham), 132
Lewis, 3
Louis H., 26
Lucy, 91
Lucy Ann C., 3
M.P., 232
Mahitable, 171
Mark, 132
Martha, 2, 26
Martha, Mrs., 2
Mary, 305, 316
Mary A. (Bailey), 308
Mary Abbie (Witham), 132
Mary E., 305
Merrill, 12
Miriam (Stevens), 3
Mrs. Charles (Smith), 182

Mrs. Harriet, 78
Mrs. Susannah, 20.3
N.K., 55, 94
Nathaniel, 16, 26, 78
Nathaniel K., 26, 189, 234
Olive, 112
Peggy, 51
Priscilla D., 339
Rebecca, 26, 166(2)
Rebecca (Berry), 26, 175, 189
Rebecca (Jumper), 26
Rev. Moses, 270
Rhoda (North), 132
Ruth, 132
Sally, 3, 23, 22, 26
Sally (Jackson), 26
Samuel, 158
Samuel Cox, 3
Sarah, 16, 66, 339
Sarah (Brackett), 10
Sarah (Thompson), 16, 175
Stephen, 46
Susannah, 2(2), 8, 227
Susannah (Brackett), 12
Thomas, 2, 12, 20.3, 45, 97, 305
Thomas, Jr., 170
William, 16(2), 26
William B., 26
Zachariah, 16(2), 17, 132, 175, 189, 290
Zachariah, Jr., 188
Zebulon, 159

Sayer
Elizabeth, 337

Scammon
Adah E. (Chase), 266
Hon. Seth, 246
Nathaniel, 294
Samuel, 294
William, 55
William M., 126, 266

Schofield
Ann, 220

Scott
Andrew, 197
Elizabeth, 246
Mary, 197, 202(2)
Mary (Bean), 197
Sarah, 246
Walter, 197
William H., 78, 246

Scottow
Joshua, 312

Seabury
Rev. Samuel, 338

Seal
Ann (Frost), 224
Capt. T., 55, 63, 91-92, 105, 121
Capt. Thomas, 44, 62, 64, 83, 309, 335
John, 64
Nancy (Frost), 83
Thomas, 90, 94, 173, 224
William, 83

Searl
Rev. Joseph, 78, 96, 136

Sennet
Nicholas, 180

Suckey (Webb), 180

Sewall
Dummer, Esq., 317, 324
Joseph, 306
Kiah B., Esq., 161
Rev. Jotham, 138

Shackley
Aaron, 221
Caroline P. (Partridge), 221

Shattrock
Dorcas, 175, 281

Shattuck
Dr. George C., 254

Shaw
Abigail Doughty, 29, 29
Alpheus, 122, 189, 272
Alpheus, Esq., 263
Bela, 29, 78, 189, 263
Belah, 1
Daniel Winslow, 34
David, 317
Eliza Haskell (Maxfield), 34
Frances Allen, 29
Hannah (Doughty), 29, 189
James, 272
Jane (Doughty), 189, 263
John L., 138
Joshua, 306
Martha Dunbar, 29
Mary, 11
Mary G. (Lobdell), 306
Miss. Esther, 146
Nathaniel, 34
Solomon, 263
Sumner, 29
William, 306

Sheldon
Ambrose, 308
Marcena (Bailey), 308
Rev. Anson W., 135-136

Shepard
Charles Hamilton, 282
Emily (Lawrence), 282
John, 202
John Hannibal, 296
Martha (Wilson), 202

Sherman
Adriand, 108

Shier
Velius, 47

Shinn
Rev. Q.H., 140

Shipman
Ann Louise, 213

Shirley
Joshua, 280

Short
Elizabeth (MOrrill), 75
William E., 75

Shoulders
Nicholas, 47

Silsby
Capt. Samuel A., 182

Simington
Andrew, 94

Simmons

Jas. S., 324
Mary, 195
Simon
Simeon, 150
Simonton
Thomas, 58
Simpson
Dr. Robert, 278
Edward, 278
James, 235
Skeminel
Valentine, 47
Skillin, 10, 271
Abbie Elizabeth (Stevens), 33
Andrew, 7
Benjamin, 7, 20.1-20.1, 20.2(3), 20.3(4)
Betsey [CE], 7
Capt., 46
Capt. John, 7
Capt. Samuel, 82, 166
Catherine, 7
Daniel [C.E.], 7, 49
Elizabeth, 7
Elizabeth (Johnson), 49
Enoch, 176
Frances E., 7
Glenn B., 20.3
Hannah [CE], 7
Hannah M., 7
Hezekiah [C.E.], 7
Isaac, 7, 20.2-20.3, 49, 56, 89, 294
James, 7
Jane, 7, 20.2
Jane (Johnson), 49
Jason [C.E.], 7
Joanna, 263
John, 7(2)
Joseph, 20.1
Joseph [C.E.], 7
Lydia, 20.2
Maj. Samuel, 7
Mary, 7(2), 20.2, 168
Mrs. Ann, 7
Mrs. Isaac, 7
Mrs. Jane, 7
Mrs. Lydia, 7
Mrs. Polly, 7
Nathan, 176
Nathaniel, 70
Nehemiah, 20.1
Reuben, 7
Rufus [C.E.], 7
Samuel, 33
Silas, 7, 49
Silas, Esq., 7
Simeon, 7
Statira, 271
Thomas, 20.2-20.2, 20.3(2), 20.5
Thomas, Jr., 20.1-20.3
Thomas, Sr., 20.1
Tiza, 7
William H. [C.E.], 7
Zebulon, 7
Skilling
Isaac, 57
Lt. Samuel, 166

Skillings, 18, 41
Capt. Samuel, 46, 77
Cyrus, 264
Deborah, 25(2), 167
Elizabeth, 25
Eunice (Doane), 264
G., 280
Josiah, 46
Lt. Samuel, 201
Lucy, 167
Rebecca, 201, 275
Rebecca (Sawyer), 167
Rhoda (Haley), 25
Samuel, 25(2), 166-167, 227
Samuel, Jr., 46
Silas, 22
Skillins, 272
Slemmons
Abbie, 39
Abigail (Quinby), 39
Catherine, 39, 50, 69
Eleanor, 275
Elizabeth, 60
George, 39
Harriet, 39
John, 39
Oliver, 39
Robert, 39-40
Sally (Rounds), 39
Sarah, 39
Sgt. Robert, 46
William, 46, 66, 73, 83, 98
William, Jr., 38
Slemons
Capt. Thomas, 164
Catherine (Porterfield), 40, 279, 335
Eleanor, 335
Elizabeth, 167, 335
George, 164
Hezekiah, 164
John, 259, 261
John B., 335
Lt. William, 164
Lydia Maria (Stevens), 211
Maj. Thomas, 164
Martha, 274, 279
Mary, 165, 263
Mary (Quinby), 163
Polly (Quinby), 40
Robert, 40, 164, 202, 260, 288, 335
Sally (Rounds), 260
Thomas, 335(2)
William, 77(2), 88-90, 123, 163-164, 279, 288, 290, 335
William, Jr., 78, 94
William Robert, 335
William, Jr., 40, 90, 290
Sloan
Adam, 73, 157, 173
Anna, 173
Caroline (Hunt), 157, 173, 207
Dr. John, 157, 173, 207
Eunice (Milliken), 157, 173
Small
Abner, 192
Abner Franklin, 192

Albert S., 192
Ann (Pomeroy), 192
Atkins, 191
Augustus, 192
Benjamin, 203
Benjamin F., 191
Charles, 192
Clorendo, 192
Col. George, 37
Corinda, 229
Daniel, 46, 89, 115, 203, 266
David, 46, 56
Dea. Samuel, 114
Dorcas, 115
Edward, 115, 203
Edward Buckley, 192
Eleanor, 36, 105
Elizabeth, 203
Emeline G., 192
Emma J., 191
Francis, 78, 106, 114-115, 203, 215, 286
George B., 191-192
Henry, 115(2)
Hiram H., 192
Isabella, 37
James, 36, 90
John, 114-115
John Lane, 192
Joseph, 35-36, 56, 89, 203(2), 266
Joseph, Jr., 35, 46, 204
Lauriston Ward, 114, 203
Leonard, 192
Leonora (McDonald), 192
Lt. Joseph, 46
Lucinda, 191
Lucy (Allen), 192
Major John, 114
Martha, 67
Mary (Fogg), 204
Mary (Libby), 203
Mary (McKenney), 115
Mary Ann (Ayers), 192
Mary Elizabeth, 192
Mary Ellen, 191
Mrs. Anna, 114
Mrs. Dolly, 37
Mrs. Howard, 238
Nathaniel, 191
Rachel, 115
Samuel, 203, 305
Sarah (Atkins), 115
Sarah (Howard), 191(2)
Sarah Ann, 192
Sarah E., 192
Thomas, 90, 192
Thomas H., 192
W., 55
William H., 191(3)
William Runnels, 192
Zachariah, 266
Zacheus, 115
Zebulon, 192
Smith
Charles, 66
Rev Thomas, 225
Smith

Abby, 182
Abraham, 328, 331
Adj't George, 48
Alice Durant, 257
Alice M. (Brown), 257
Alonzo, 182
Arixene (Southgate), 247, 250, 254
Arixene Southgate, 257(2)
C.B., 248
Capt. John K., 154
Capt. Jonathan, 64, 67
Capt. Thomas, 338
Caroline Bowne, 283
David, 77
Deborah, 25
Deborah (Bailey), 25
Dr. J. V., 132
Ebenezer, 182
Edmund Munroe, 257, 259
Elder Elias, 187-188
Eleanor Roberts Munroe, 259
Elias, 171
Eliza (Chamberlain), 303
Eliza Southgate (Bowne), 282
Elizabeth, 182
Elizabeth (Bradley), 218
Elizabeth Lee (Allen), 251, 257
Emma, 283(2)
Emma (Pike), 251, 257
Ephraim, 302
F.O.J., 1, 92
Frances, 283
Francis O.J., 98(2), 204, 206, 209-210
Smith
Francis O.J., 211
Smith
Francis Ormand Jonathan, 205
Frederick Southgate, 251, 257
Gen. John Kirby, 180, 182
Gen. John Kilby, 76, 151, 176
George, 25(3)
Gertrude (Hinde-Roper), 257, 259
Hannah, 161
Henry, 144, 182, 247, 250-251, 254, 283, 334
Henry Goodwin, 257
Henry Maynard, 257
Hon Jonathan, 234
Hon. F.O.J., 18
Hon. Jonathan, 31, 121
Horatio Southgate, 251, 259
Horatio Southgate, M.D., 257
Isaac, 250, 283
James, 164
Jane (Beadle), 283
Jane (Hilton), 182
Joan F. (Moore), 182
John, 182, 250
John Coit, 251
John K., 151
John K., Jr., 182
John Kirby, 180
John Kirby, Jr., 181
John T., 254
Jonathan, 18, 20.2, 55, 77, 90, 92, 94, 212
Lucretia, 225
Lucy, 225

Marcia (Lobdell), 205
Maria Maileville, 257
Martha J. (North), 132, 140
Mathew Hale, 171
Mrs. (Fickett), 66
Mrs. Charles, 182
Mrs. Edward, 182
Mrs. Elizabeth P., 157
Mrs. Ezra, 182
Mrs. Mary, 182(2)
Mrs. Rebecca, 182
Mrs. William F., 182
Nancy, 182
Nicholas, 46, 56
Niles, 89
Parson, 20.1-20.2
Polly, 182, 233
Prof. Henry Boynton, 257
Pyng, 77
Rebecca, 182
Rev. Henry Boynton, 251, 334
Rev. Henry Boynton, D.D., 254
Rev. John, 250
Rev. Thomas, 10, 46, 56, 60-61, 140, 297, 338
Robert Malcolm Munroe, 259
Sally, 182
Sally (Maynard), 251
Sally (Webb), 76, 176, 180
Samuel E., 98
Samuel Emerson, 326
Sarah, 225
Sarah (Green), 182
Sarah Ellen, 182
Sophia Munroe, 257, 259
Spencer Henry, 282-283
Susan D. (Munroe), 251
Susan Dwight (Munroe), 257
Susan Elizabeth, 257
Susan S., 226
Susannah, 274
Susannah (Hall), 250
Thomas, 78, 303
William, 181-182
William Allen, 257
William H., 154
William Henry, 182(2)
William W., 181-182
Zilpha I.W. (Cutter), 257

Snow
Elizabeth, 281
Eunice, 132
Harriet N., 221
John, 10, 20, 102, 114, 173
Mary, 10, 140
Rev. J.C., 140
Temple, 221

Soule
Rufus, 206

Southgate
Abba Isabella (Little), 258
Abigail (McLellan), 247, 254
Abigail Browne, 248(2), 254
Amos, 246
Anita Mary, 256
Ann (French), 253
Arixene, 247, 254(2)
Bishop, 146, 241, 254
Caroline Louisa (Anderson), 253
Charles Joseph, 256
Charles McLellan, 253
Clara Sophia, 256
Dr. Robert, 146, 241(2), 243, 246-247, 252-252, 253(2), 254(2), 256, 258, 282-283, 294, 333
Dr. Robert, Esq., 312
Edward, 256
Edward Payson, 249
Eleanor, 256
Eliza, 246, 247, 249, 283(3), 314, 314
Eliza (Neal), 247-248
Elizabeth, 246(2), 248
Elizabeth (Browne), 248
Elizabeth (Neal), 256
Elizabeth (Potter), 246
Elizabeth (Scott), 246
Elizabeth (Steward), 246
Elizabeth S., 242
Elizabeth S. (Browne), 256
Elizabeth Virginia (Anderson), 253
Ellen, 249
Emily, 248
Eunice (Browne), 246
Frances, 256
Frances (Swan), 248
Francis Swan, 253, 253
Frederic, 256
Frederic Charles, 256
Frederick, 247, 250
Frederick Charter, 253
Grace Helen, 256
Grace Talcott, 256
Hannah, 246
Harriet A., 246
Harriet Augusta, 256(2)
Harriet E. (Churchill), 258
Harriet Randolph (Talcot), 249, 256
Henry, 256
Henry Martin, 249
Henry Talcott, 256
Hiram Horatio, 256
Horatio, 239, 246-247, 248(3), 253(2), 254, 256-257
Horatio, Esq., 333
Horatio, Jr., 254, 256
Hugh McLellan, 253
Hutchinson, 256
Isabella, 247, 253(2), 314
James, 246
John, 246(2)
John Barrett, 249
Julia, 249
Julia Abby, 249
Margaret, 246
Margaret Hall (Boyd), 258
Merriam Agnes, 256
Mary, 246, 246, 253
Mary (King), 246-247, 249-250, 252-254
Mary (Moore), 248, 256
Mary (Webster), 247-248
Mary Frances (Swan), 253
Mary King, 247-252, 256
Mary Webster, 248

Miranda, 247
Moses, 246
Nabby (McLellan), 239, 248, 253, 256
Octavia, 146, 239, 241(3), 241, 247, 249(2), 256-256, 315, 334
Randolph, 256
Rebecca, 246
Renie Caroline (Hutchinson), 256
Rev. Bishop, 249
Rev. Frederic, 256
Rev. Frederick, 248
Rev. Horatio, Jr., 248
Rev. John Barrett, 256
Rev. Robert, 248, 253
Rev. William Scott, 246, 249, 256
Richard, 246(3), 248
Richard King, 256
Robert, 247-250, 258, 314
Robert Swan, 253
Robert, Esq., 333
Rt. Rev. Horatio, D.D., 254, 256
Ruth, 246
Samuel, 246
Sarah, 246
Sarah (Scott), 246
Sarah Elizabeth (Hutchinson), 248, 256
Steward, 246(3)
William, 246, 256
William S., 256
William Scott, 256
Southworth
Rev. Francis, 305
Sparrow
Eleanor (Trickey), 50
Eleanor E., 264
Elizabeth, 168
John, 162, 238, 287
Jonathan, 34, 43, 50, 107, 162, 172, 236, 238, 263, 287
William, 43, 68, 107, 238
Spaulding
Martha, 68
Spencer
Clara, 113
Spingent
Nathaniel, 286
Sprague
Oliver, 11
Polly (Brackett), 11
Springer
James, 244
Sprout
Col. Ebenezer, 154
St. Clair
Gen., 181
Stanford
Lucy, 65, 66
Sarah, 65
Stanton
William, 208
Stanwood
William, 324
Starbird
Annie (Bailey), 308
Catharine, 266
Edward D., 62(2), 64, 155, 224, 287

Eleanor, 38, 40, 310
Elias, 48
Elizabeth, 51
Ellery, 308
Eunice, 38, 40
Henry P., 94
Jethro, 89
John, 46-48, 56, 90, 288, 290
Levi, 62, 78, 90, 94, 225, 229
Levi Russell, 224
Lydia, 30, 211
Nancy (Pennell), 62, 225, 229
Nathan, 56
Nathaniel, 46(2)
Samuel, 36, 47-48
Thomas, 77, 224, 288
Starr
Almena Maria, 264
Almena Maria (Stevens), 28
Charles Granville, 264
Charles Richard, 264
Jennie, 264
Judge Charles R., 28
Stebbins
William, 283
Stephenson
Alexander B., 182
Fred C., 204
Sterne
William, 300
Sterns
Sarah, 229
Stevens
Abbie, 15
Abbie Elizabeth, 33
Abigail, 8, 32
Abigail, 34(2)
Abigail (Bailey), 6, 25, 32
Albert A., 5
Alberta Appleton, 126
Alfred, 27-28, 42, 52, 55, 90, 94, 188, 190
Alfred Augustus, 189
Almena Maria, 28, 264
Alvertene Buckley, 264
Amanda, 68-67
Angelina A. (Patterson), 5
Ann, 26
Ann Maria, 31, 211
Annetta Jane (Merrill), 9
Annie Irene, 126
Arthur W., 126
Augusta, 15, 16
Augustus E., 28, 190
Augustus Ervin, 264
Benjamin, 2(2), 3(2), 4, 8(2), 9-10, 12, 20.2, 51, 145, 183, 188
Benjamin F., 9(2)
Buckley, 126
Capt. Isaac S., 5-6, 8, 13, 17, 22, 25-25, 26(2), 27-28, 42, 45(2), 51, 124-125, 128, 130, 175, 177, 188, 196, 237, 290
Capt. Isaac Sawyer, 13
Capt. Joshua, 5
Capt. Joshua, 6
Capt. Joshua, 8, 227
Caroline, 5-6

Carrie William, 264
Catherine, 45
Charles, 6, 76, 78, 94
Charles B., 211-212, 214
Charles Bartlett, 211
Charles L., 9
Charlotte, 75, 133
Charlotte (Webb), 9, 51, 145, 183
Clara (Chapman), 5
Clara (Chapman)(Davis), 5
Cloracy, 15
Cora Bell, 126
Cordelia, 28(4)
Cornelia, 5-6
Cornelia B., 8
Daniel, 5-6, 8(2)
Daniel H., 8
Daniel Pike, 126
David, 8, 34, 43(2), 64, 74, 76(2), 78, 164, 211
Dea. William, 9
Doily, 8
Dolla, 3-3
Dr. John P., 5, 8
E.C., 190
Eben Collins, 8
Eben Stanwood, 5, 8
Ebenezer C., 5
Ebenezer Collins, 5, 8
Edward Clifton, 189
Edward P., 9(2)
Edward Payson, 8
Edward Wilford, 5
Eleanor, 75
Eliza (Jordan), 5, 8
Eliza A., 33
Elizabeth, 32, 67
Elizabeth (Bailey), 2, 4-5
Elizabeth A., 8
Elizabeth B., 177, 179
Elizabeth Brisco, 33
Elizabeth E., 264
Ella A. (Delano), 33
Ella E. (Woodford), 42
Ella Eliza (Woodford), 189
Ellen N., 32
Ellen North, 33
Emeline, 27-28
Emeline (Treadwell), 188
Emily Sargent, 264
Emma, 190
Ervin Greenwood, 264
Eunice, 5-5, 8(2)
Eunice (Marriner), 76
Eunice (Stevens), 5, 8
Eunice Caroline, 8
Eunice Maria, 8
Fannie Revere, 264
Frances, 5-6, 8, 32-33, 67
Frances Greenwood, 265
Frank G., 28, 52, 190
Franklin W., 33
Franklin Whitman, 33
Franzella K., 9
Fred Jarvus, 264
Frederick, 67
George Byron, 126

George L., 33, 35
George Leonard, 33
George M., 55, 94, 266
George Mead, 126, 164, 196
George Mellon, 5
George W., 8
George Washington, 8
George William, 126
Georgiana, 33
Graham Chase, 126
Granville M., 27-28, 32, 190, 264
Granville M., Jr., 264
Hannah (Chase), 126, 196
Hannah (Morton), 33
Hannah (Weir), 5, 15, 263
Hannah E. (Chase), 266
Harriet, 6-6, 15
Harriet (Sawyer), 16, 33
Harriet A., 8
Harriet Rebecca, 9
Harry, 164
Hattie Francis, 264
Helen Gertrude, 126
Helen L. (Pike), 126
Helen P., 126
Henry, 9, 211
Henry Francis, 264
Henry Hunt, 33
Henry Jewett, 6
Hudson, 15
Ida G., 8
Irene, 126(2), 196
Irene Elmore, 126
Isaac, 5, 8, 17, 20.3, 67, 125-126, 170-171, 188, 262-263
Isaac G., 12
Isaac S., 16, 189, 227, 288
Isaac S., Capt., 1
Isaac Sawyer, 4
Isaac, Jr., 13, 15
Isaac. S., 187
Jane (Jones), 6
Jane (Sawyer), 6
Jane L., 6
Jane L. (Noyes), 9
Jennie (Graham), 126
Jennie May, 126
Jennie Tyler, 264
Joel, 8
John, 2, 78
John Appleton, 126
John B., 45
John Fairfield, 33(2)
Jonathan, 4-6, 8(2), 9
Joseph, 6(2), 8, 18(2), 20.2-20.3, 147
Joshua, 2-2, 3(2), 4-4, 5(2), 8(2), 20.2-20.3, 290
Joshua, Capt., 3
Josiah, 13, 45(2), 125-126, 164-165, 188
Judith, 197
Julia Ann, 5, 8
Laura Jane, 125, 190
Lemuel, 9, 188
Lemuel, 4, 8, 10, 76
Leonard, 32-33, 35
Levi, 32
Levi Bradish, 16, 33

Lewis, 15
Lilla Cathleen, 28
Lillie B., 8
Lizzie Tyler, 264
Lorene, 15
Lottie (Turner), 189
Louisa, 6, 125
Lt. Orin B., 190
Lucretia, 76
Lucy, 6, 13, 42, 51
Lucy (Cobb), 9
Lucy (Webb), 183
Lucy A. (Claridge), 5
Lucy Ann, 76
Lucy M., 8
Lucy Maria, 33
Lydia, 8
Lydia (Collins), 8
Lydia Maria, 211
Marcena G., 10
Marcia, 36
Margaret, 76
Margaret, 75
Margaret (Fickett), 74-75
Margaret (Patrick), 43, 67, 74, 76, 183, 203
Maria, 16, 32
Maria D. (Moses), 189
Maria Elizabeth, 33
Mariah H. (Brackett), 11
Merriam, 8
Marion, 5(2)
Martha, 2(2), 5-6, 8(2)
Martha (Sawyer), 2
Martha Amelia, 8
Martha C., 5
Martha Ellen, 33
Martha Gordon, 265
Mary, 5-5, 8, 15, 45
Mary (Toby), 6
Mary E., 8
Mary Elizabeth, 126
Mary Fletcher, 264
Mary M., 33
Mary Maling, 264
Maud P. (Libby), 8
Mehitable (Knight), 15, 171
Michael, 9, 48, 67, 75-76, 120, 183(2)
Miriam, 3-3, 8
Miriam Frances, 188
Miriam P. (Berry), 27
Miss Almena, 94
Molly, 13, 17, 165
Mrs. Caroline, 35, 70
Mrs. Daniel Cobb (Webb), 183
Mrs. Emeline, 190
Mrs. Hannah, 13
Mrs. Mehitable, 13
Mrs. Sally, 125
Mrs. Sarah, 13
Mrs. Susannah, 6
Nabby, 8, 13, 128(2)
Nancy, 3-3, 8, 75, 264, 266
Nancy (Chapman), 30, 211
Nancy B., 45
Nancy G. (Buckley), 188
Nancy Goodrich (Buckley), 28
Nancy L., 9
Nancy W., 51
Nathaniel, 6, 13, 16, 25-26, 28, 32, 36, 78, 121, 164
Nellie C., 5
Nobby, 3-3
Olena (Dunham), 126
Olive J., 211
Oren Buckley, 188
Paul, 8
Paul T., 11
Philip Herman, 264
Pitt, 42
Polly (Herrick), 67, 75
Rev. Joseph B., 137, 285
Rufus B., 119
S. B., 52, 94
S.B., 91
Sally, 5, 8(2), 33, 32, 264
Sally (Bailey), 25, 124-125, 127, 190
Sally (Blake), 45
Sally (Frances), 193
Sally (Peaks), 9
Sally (Sawyer), 26
Samuel, 67(2), 75(2), 77
Samuel Augustus, 264
Samuel B., 27, 32, 90, 98, 146, 193(2)
Samuel Butler, 27-28
Samuel Henry, 264
Sarah, 4(2), 13-13, 15(2), 22
Sarah (Brackett), 6, 12, 45, 128
Sarah (Kimball), 6
Sarah B., 55
Sarah B. (Frances), 28
Sarah Buckley, 188
Sarah K., 8
Sarah Knight, 264
Sarah Saunders (Kimball), 8
Sgt. Joshua, 48, 227
Smith Cobb, 76
Sophia, 10, 33, 32(2)
Sophia (Hicks), 190
Sophia (Peaks), 43, 76
Susan (Harris), 8
Susannah, 3, 8
Susannah (Sawyer), 2-3, 227
Tabitha (Toby), 4, 9
Thompson, 126
Tristram, 73-73, 74(2), 75-76, 183, 203, 211
Tristram C., 30, 43, 67, 77, 211
Tristram Coffin, 75
Tristram, Jr., 43
William, 2, 4-5, 8(2), 9, 13, 25-27, 55, 78, 94, 124-124, 125(2), 127, 164, 190, 196
William H., 22
William K., 8
William Pitt, 189-190
William W., 126
William Wallace, 126
Zachariah B., 1, 13, 26, 28, 40, 42, 90, 94, 98, 125, 188(2), 189, 194
Zachariah Brackett, 27
Steves
T.C., 30
Steward
Elizabeth, 246

Mrs. Elizabeth, 246
William, 246
Stickney
Mary, 281
Sarah, 173
Stiles
John, 78
Moses, 78, 90, 94(2)
Stoddard
Hariot (Patrick), 74
Hariot Amelia, 74
Harriet, 74
William, 74(2)
Stone
Daniel, 324
Dr. Eben, 26, 234
Elizabeth, 63, 148, 226
Rev. Nathaniel, 136
Storer
Bellamy, 253
Betsey, 147, 159
Charlotte (Knight), 147, 225
Esther, 147
Joanna, 147, 171
Joseph, 147(3), 149, 159, 174, 188, 225(2)
Miriam, 147(2)
Mrs. Joanna, 147
Seth, Jr., Esq., 251, 334
Strong
Caleb, 295
Strout
Christa, 102
Christopher, 114
David, 58
Dr. Eben, 339
George, 164
John, 89
Patience (Fickett), 71, 228
Solomon, 71, 228
Thersa (Mason), 339
Stuart
Asa, 234
Charles A., 185, 234
Emma (Haines), 234
Mary Elizabeth, 234
Solomon, Esq., 185, 234
Sturdivant
Gardner, 108
Sulivan
Austin D., 33
Sullivan
Hon. James, 152
James, 295
Sutton
Allen M., 283
Helen (Bowne), 283
Ida, 283
Swan
Benjamin, 253
Frances, 248
Mary Frances, 253
Swanton
John B., 324
Swasyey
Horatio J., 208
Sweetser

A., 55
Swenson
Kizzie C. (Browne), 243
S.Y., 243
William Gray, 243
Swett
Capt. Joshua, 159
Dr. Stephen, 48
Hon. Leonard, 175
J., 55
Joshua, 57
I.D.M., 333
Mary, 70
Rebecca, 305
Samuel, 250
Stephen, 57, 89, 272
Susannah, 37
Swinton
John B., 316
Talbot
Ambrose, 101
Archie L., 101
Lois, 110
Talcot
Harriet Randolph, 249, 256
Talcott
Andrew, 256
Mrs. Harriet, 256
Tallman
Peleg, 298, 324
Tate
Ada E., 33
Ann, 275, 279
Augustus, 41, 120, 171, 216, 221, 262, 273, 277
Capt. George, 216, 274-281
Capt. Robert, 279-281
Capt. Samuel, 275
Caroline (Emery), 277
Catharine, 279
Charles, 277
Dorothy, 277
Dorothy L., 304
Eleanor, 21, 276(2), 279, 281
Eleanor (Patrick), 72, 273, 276
Elizabeth, 279(3)
Esther (Libby), 273, 276-277
Esther Libby (Libby), 277
Eunice (Graffam), 275
George, 46, 48, 56, 73-74, 94, 151, 162, 180, 203, 221, 273, 276-276, 277(2), 279
George, Jr., 274, 277-278
Hannah (Libby), 273, 276
Henry, 277
John, 33, 276-277
Julia, 33
Julia (Hicks), 33, 277
Martha (Slemons), 274, 279
Mary, 274
Mary, 275, 279
Mary (Coverly), 73
Mary (Fickett), 74
Mary (Trickey), 275
Mary Ann, 275
Mrs. Mary (Coverly), 274-275
Robert, 47, 274, 277-278
Samuel, 274, 276-277, 279

Sarah (McDonald), 277
Sarah Maria, 275, 277
Washington, 76, 273, 277
William, 46, 72, 162, 273-274, 276(2), 277(2)
William Major, 275
Taylor
Abigail, 231
Asa, 18-19
Emily Ann, 19
Freeman Todd, 19
Henrietta M. (Maxfield), 37
Russell, 37
William, 231
Temple
Robert, 335
Tenney
Lucy, 197
Tewksbury
Samuel H., 204
Thambs
William, 164
Thames
Benjamin, 90
John, 90(2)
Thatcher
Josiah, 294
Therell
James, 56
Thomas
Caesar [African-American], 17
Dr. Calvin, 277
Hon. W.W., 287
Hon. William Widgery, 299
John, 56
W.W., 76
William, 23
Thombs
John, Jr., 46
Nathaniel, 188
Thomes
Benjamin, 90
Caesar, 14
Capt. Isaac, 176
Capt. Samuel, 70, 76, 176
Capt. William, 176
Edward M., 117
Eleanor (Tyler), 176
Eunice, 229
Ezera, 108
Isaac, 76
Job, 78
John, 56, 62, 90, 117, 288, 290
John, Jr., 90
Joshua, 78
Mary, 76, 176
Mrs. Charity, 78
Phebe (Fickett), 70, 76, 176
Samuel, 70
Sarah Jane (Brackett), 108
Sgt. Thomas, 46
Thompson
Abba Valentine, 265
Abner B., 208
Annie, 110
Archibald, 125, 265
Bartholomew, 46, 90
Betsey, 42
Capt. John, 265
Capt. T.C., 110
Carrie, 125
Carrie L. (Mason), 150
David, 47, 55
Edwin D., 110
Frank B., 125
Frederick H., 265
George Homer, 125
George W., 265
Hannibal, 265
J.A., 55, 94
James, 23, 46, 90
James A., 125
James W., 125
Jane Elizabeth (Jordon), 125
Jeanette (Allen), 265
Jennie, 125
Jesse Murdock, 125
Joseph, 102, 139
Joseph P., 169
Julia S., 265
Leonora, 265
Leonora (Leavitt), 265
Louisa, 125
Louisa (Stevens), 125
Louise M., 265
Lyman S., 125
Mary Jane, 265
Miles, 90, 288, 290
Nellie, 125
Nicholas, 46, 90
Niles, 90
Rev. Zenas, 28, 52, 94, 137, 139, 194, 196, 222, 263, 265, 267-268
Samuel, 150
Sarah, 16, 175, 280
T.B., 94
Wid. Carrie L., 150
William, Esq., 333
Zenas, 123, 265
Zenas, Jr., 265
Thomes
John, 47
John, Jr., 48
Samuel, 47
Thorn
Edward G., 237
Elizabeth, 237
Greenlief, 237
Job, 90, 94
Jobe, 237
William, 55
William J., 237
Thurnburg
Charles, 31
Olaf N., 29, 31
Thurston
Thomas, 245
Tibbetts
Abbie, 44
Almirad (Haskell), 44
Frances, 44
Hannah, 44
Mark, 44

Miss. Abbie, 12
Mrs. Almira, 44
Nathan, 44(2), 88, 106, 203
Nathan W., 44
Rufus, 44(2)
Sarah (Bailey), 307
Tilghman
Augusta Murray (Boyd), 248, 314
Frederick B., 314
Gen. Lloyd, 314
Lloyd, 248, 314
Lloyd, Jr., 314
Mrs. Augusta M., 314
Sidell, 314
Tillerson
Mrs. Caroline, 182
Tilter
Valentine, 47
Tilton
Rev. Nathan, 245, 295, 334
Titcomb
Almira, 174, 223
Andrew, 35, 174(3), 217, 223-224, 309
Andrews Phillips, 223
Ann, 174, 223
Ann (Cottle), 214
Ann (Pearson), 223
Benjamin, 223
Dea., 223
Mary, 174
Mary, 223
Mary (Dole), 35, 174, 223
Mrs., 158
Mrs. Mary, 174
Mrs. Rebecca, 224
Rebecca (Bailey), 35, 174(2)
Rhoda (Dole), 217
Sally, 174
Sarah, 223
William, 174, 214, 223
Title
1st Parish of Deering (Cont.), 57
1st. Cong. Meeting House, 97
A Scottow's Hill Vessel, 334
Abizer Howard, 189, 191-192
All Souls Church, 138
Allen's Corner Sabbath School, 144
Alpheus S. Alden, 146
An Old Corporation, 121
An Old Record, 140
Annexation, 43
Anthony Brackett, 12
Anthony Brackett, Jr., 105-106, 107(2), 109-110, 111(3), 112
Armament of Ancient Stroudwater, 121
Author, History of Scarborough, 256
Back Cove, 10
Back Cove Stevens Family, 3
Bailey, 24-26
Barbour, 197
Benjamin Burnham, 183-185
Benjamin Pierce, 29
Benjamin Remick, 123
Benjamin Stevens, 2
Birthday-Book, 264
Black Point Ferry, Scarborough, 262

Bradley's Journal, 75
Brimblecom, 336
Broad Tavern, 166-168
Capisic, 286
Capt. George Tate, 274-281
Capt. Isaac S. Stevens, 15
Capt. Isaac Sawyer Stevens, 13
Capt. James Means, 150(2), 152(2), 153
Capt. John Brackett's Company, 48
Capt. John L. Lewis, 313
Capt. Joshua Stevens, 4
Capt. Samuel A. Brimblecom, 141
Capt. Samuel Skillin, 46
Capt. William Webster, 156
Charles Frost, 78-84, 85(2), 87
Charles Peirce, 163-164
Charles Pierce, 30, 162
Clement Pennell, 62
Col. James Webb, 176-176, 177(2), 179(2)
Capt. Henry Webb, 182
Cutter, 338
David Patrick, 72-76
Destructive Fire, 38
Dr. Jeremiah Barker, 169
Dr. John Sloan, 157
Dr. Robert Southgate, 246-248, 250-253, 254(2), 256-259, 282-283
Drew Execution, 175
Dunstan, 243-244
Ecclesiastical, 134, 136-137
Falmouth 3rd Parish Records, 77
Falmouth Artillery, 165
Falmouth in 1838, 158
Fort Preble, 156
Fort Scammel, 156
Francis O.J. Smith's Tomb, 210
Francis Small, 203
Gen. John Kirby Smith, 180, 182
George Calvin Codman, 225
George Libby, 116-120
Gilman, 337
Glimpses of the Past, 159(2), 160-160, 161(2), 162, 170-175
Grandfather's Clock, 186
Grandmarm Porterfield, 50
Gray, 130
Haskell, 44
Henry Knight, 60
Highways, 18
Historical Memoranda, 146, 158
Information Wanted, 140
Isaac Stevens, 14
Jacob Adams, 19
James Johnson, 61
James Merrill, 62
James Pennell, 230-231
Jeremiah Riggs, 61
John Fickett, 65-66, 67(2), 69-71
John Johnson, 61
Johnson - Hatch, 339
Jonathan Stevens, 5
Joseph Chenery, 157
Long Island, 57
Major Archelaus Lewis, 235-237
Major John Small, 114
Margaret Knight, 156

Market Square, 25
Marriage Events, 157
Mason, 148-149, 154
Massachusetts Bradley Family, 133
Matrimonial, 263, 265
Maxfield, 35
Mill Owners, 90
Minute Men, 47
Morrill's Corner, 22
Mr. Josiah S. North, 49
Nathaniel Knight, 60
Ninety-Four Years Ago, 260
North, 128-131, 133
Old Westbrook, 266, 268-269
Oliver Buckley, 187-188, 190
Papermaking at Stroudwater, 261
Parson Bradley's Journal, 115
Paul Revere, Senior, 193-196
Pierce, 31
Pine Grove, 52
Pine Grove Cem. Lot Owners, 55
Pine Grove Cemetery, By-Laws, 53
Presumpscot Falls, 186
Quimby, 38
Quinby, 40
Re. Joseph Lane, 99
Re. Thomas Browne, 239
Re. Tristram Gilman, 156
Religious Revival, 95
Rev. Caleb Bradley, 270, 272, 285
Rev. Caleb Bradley's Journal, 114
Rev. Lewis L. Record, 127
Rev. Samuel Brimblecom, 122
Rev. Thomas Browne, 58-64, 240-242
Robert Bayley, 101
Saccarappa Church Soc., 96
Sawyers, 16-17
Ships owned by W. King, 319
Skillin's Journal, 6
Skillings Claim, 25
Slemons, 335
Small, 36
Small Pox, 286
Stephen Riggs, 155
Stevens, 8-10, 28, 32-33
Stevens Family, 45
Stevens' Plain, 13
Storer Mansion, 147
Stroud. Par. Slave Owners, 89
Stroudwater, 198-203
Stroudwater Congregation, 85
Stroudwater Hall, 120
Stroudwater Infantry, 165
Stroudwater Parish, 88(2), 90
The Bodge Family, 191
The Doctors Hunt, 207
The First Parish of Deering, 56
The Grant Family, 37
The Great Bridge, 102-104
The Hamlet of Woodfords, 18
The King Family of Scarborough, 294-301, 312-313, 314(2), 315-334
The Maxfield Family, 41
The Mitchell Family, 222
The Paysons, 213
The Pennells, 228-229

The Scarborough Turnpike Road, 333
The Small Family, 191
The Stroudwater Parish, 288-293
The Webb Family, 37
The Weight of Authority, 20.1
The Woodford Brothers, 51
The Woodfords, 145
Things and Persons, 156
Thomas Cloise, 78
Thomas Haskell, 60
Timothy Galvin, 21
Town of Gray, 284
Town of Kingfield, 326
Trickey Family, 201
Universalist Society, 91-92, 93(2)
Vaughn's Bridge, 294
Waterhouse, 302, 304-308, 310-311
Westbrook, 204(2), 206-212, 214-221, 223-234
Westbrook Seminary, 98, 142, 285
Westbrook Seminary Contrib., 142-143
Westbrook Universalist Church, 90
William Graves, 100
William Kenney, 22
William L. Pennell, 224
William Maxfield, 34
William Stevens, 124-126
Woodfords, 20
Woodfords - part second, 19
Woodfords Family, 42
Zachariah B. Stevens, 27
Tobie
Betsey (Fickett), 71
C.C., 94
Elbridge, 10
Richard, 71
Toby
Eunice (Webb), 183
Mary, 6
Submit, 4
Tabitha, 4(2)
Tabitha, 8(2)
William, 4, 183
Todd
James, 208
Tole
Levi, 90
Mary (Quinby), 39
Tolman
Harriet, 150
Tompson
Hannah (Fogg), 273
Samuel, 273
Tomson
Nicholas, 57
Toothaker
Abner, 112
Topliff
Albion P., 250
Torrey
David, 189, 234
Lucy, 173
Tounge
Mary E., 231
Tower
Fred L., 138
Towle

Levi, 94
Townsend
   Annie, 282
Trask
   Ansel C., 63, 155
   Anson C., 154
   Clarissa (Gould), 63
   Daniel, 63
   Rev. J.H., 63
Travers
   Gertrude, 283
Treadwell
   Emeline, 188
Trickey
   Ann, 50
   Charles, 50
   Charles P., 58, 236, 271
   Daniel, 7, 49, 78, 271
   David, 7, 32, 78, 90, 201, 271(2), 290
   Edward, 50, 69
   Eleanor, 50, 271-271
   Eleanor (Libby), 271
   Elizabeth, 271
   Enoch, 201, 271
   Enock, 58
   Eunice, 218, 271, 339
   Francis, 201
   James, 50, 208
   Lettice, 50
   Mary, 50
   Mary, 271, 275
   Mary (Hobbs), 32, 201, 271
   Mary Ann (Motely), 50
   Mrs. Lucy S., 7
   Mrs. Mary, 275
   Nancy (Pratt), 271
   Otis, 271
   Peggy, 50
   Rebecca (Skillings), 201, 275
   Robert, 271
   Sally, 7
   Sally (Johnson), 49, 271
   Statira, 271
   Statira (Skillin), 271
   Sylvia (Barbour), 271
   Thomas, 50
   William, 50, 78, 271
   Zebulon, 7, 32, 46, 56, 66, 90(2), 176, 180, 200-201, 216, 271(2), 275
   Zebulon, Jr., 201, 271
   Zenobia (Collins), 50
Trowbridge
   Catharine T., 282
   Catherine (Walker), 281
   Henry, Jr., 248
   John H., 281-282
   Mary Webster (Southgate), 248
True
   Adams, 208
   Ebenezer, 6
   George W., 98
   John K., 98(2)
   John R., 52
Trufant
   David, 317
Trull
   Lucinda, 279
Tucker
   G.W., 98
   James B., 78
   Richard, 20, 198
Tuckey
   Ann, 231
Tukey
   Eliza (Waterhouse), 303
   George, 78
   George, Jr., 78, 303
Tuksbury
   Ervin R., 172
Turner
   Capt., 137
   Lottie, 189
Twitchell
   A.A., 37
   Mabel C. (Grant), 37
   Moses, 226
Tyler
   Eleanor, 176
   Rev. Bennett, 270, 272
   Susan, 241
Tyng
   Sarah, 58
Upham
   Edward E., 254
Usher
   Samuel, 330
Vaill
   Rev. Joseph, 136
Valentine
   Hon. Leander, 37, 40, 234
   Leander, 229
   Maj. William, 232
   Otis, 90, 94
   William, 37, 78, 90, 94
Van Buren
   Martin, 314
Varney
   Cyrus B., 138
Vaughan
   Elliot, 251
   Lt. Gov. George, 251
   William, 251
Vaughn
   William, 294, 333
Vincent
   Rev. Marion R., D.D., 257
Virgin
   Judith, 186
Wadsworth
   Henry, 248
   Peleg, 335
Waite
   Hannah (Southgate), 246
   James, 264
   John, 20.2, 158, 236, 241, 263
   Nathaniel, 246
   Sarah M. (Paine), 264
Wakefield
   Nathaniel, 78
Wakely, 20.5
Walden
   Nathaniel, 90, 94

Waldo
    Brig. Gen. Samuel, 45
    Col., 20.3
    Col. Samuel, Jr., 58, 121
    Francis, 71, 236-237, 305
    Gen. Samuel, 58-59, 62, 72, 198, 203, 237, 262, 287, 305
    Mrs. Sarah, 81
    Samuel, 63, 69, 81, 90, 200, 215, 236, 261
    Sarah, 41, 61, 182
    Sarah (Tyng), 58
Waldron
    F.A., 184
    Nathaniel, 77
Walker
    Ann (Fickett), 71
    Ann (Johnson), 279, 281
    Betsey, 39(2), 133
    Calvin S., 233
    Catherine, 281
    Charles, 164
    Charles B., 233
    Daniel, 182
    Dea., 10
    Edward S., 233(2), 281
    Eleanor (Tate), 279
    Elizabeth (Bailey), 26, 189
    Elizabeth (Snow), 281
    Ernest W., 233
    Eunice G. (Whitten), 266
    Gardner, 78, 279, 281(2), 282
    George, 57, 90, 108, 189, 288, 290
    Harriet Rogers (Berry), 281
    Henry B., 233(2), 234, 281
    Henry Percy, 233
    Isaac, 90-91, 94(2)
    Isaac G., 91, 94
    John, 108
    Joseph, 279, 281(2)
    Josiah, 71(2)
    Mary, 108
    Mary A. (Lunt), 233
    Molly, 10
    Moses B., 98
    Mrs. Elizabeth, 108
    Persis (Phipps), 233
    Peter H., 281-282
    Robert, 112
    Sally (Smith), 182
    Sewall V., 266
    William P., 194
    William Phipps, 281
    Zelia A. (Lunt), 233
Wallace
    Capt. Anice, 57
Walton
    Ann (Bean), 197
    Hannah (Bean), 197
    Mark, 197
Ward
    Elijah, 48
    George W., 26-27
    Hannah, 63, 226
    Lucy, 7
    Thomas J., 27
Wardsworth
    Peleg, 294
Warren
    Adriel, 47
    Adriel, Jr., 48
    David, 48
    Elizabeth, 48
    George, 100
    George, Jr., 30
    Gilbert, 46
    James, 48
    Jane, 48
    John, 46, 48, 50, 56, 66, 90, 221
    John, Jr., 48(2)
    Lewis P., 221
    Margaret, 48
    Nancy, 48
    Nathaniel, 48(2), 221
    Polly, 48
    Rev. William, 138
    Robert, 48, 91, 94
    Sally, 48, 66, 71
    Samuel D., 232
    Sphia, 131
Washington
    Augustine, 248
    Bushrod, 248
    Gen., 158
    George, 154
Wass
    John, 20.1
Waterhouse
    Aaron, 303
    Abigail (Jordan), 303
    Addie J. (Curtis), 305
    Adelaide Lorinda, 304
    Almira, 70, 304
    Alpheus, 70, 304-304, 305(2)
    Amos W., 69
    Benjamin, 78, 306
    Betsey, 70, 304(2)
    Capt. John, 159(2), 161, 303-304
    Catherine, 304
    Celia (Hanson), 70
    Celia F., 305
    Celia Lowell (Hanson), 305
    Charles, 304
    Charles William, 304
    Charles, II, 304
    Charlotte, 70, 305, 304
    Charlotte (Kendrick), 304
    Eliza, 303
    Eliza B., 304
    Eliza B., II, 304, 304
WAterhouse
    Elizabeth, 159, 302(2)
Waterhouse
    Elizabeth, 302
    Elizabeth (Fickett), 70, 168
    Esther (Fogg), 302, 305
    Ezekiel, 306
    Francis Augustus (Fickett), 69
    Fred, 302, 305
    Frederick, 66, 70, 123, 159, 182, 199, 304
    George, 47, 205
    George Hight, 304
    George Warren, 304

    Hannah (Brooks), 159
    Hannah (Chase), 304
    Hannah (Pierce), 302
    James W., 306
    John, 302(2), 304
    John P., 311
    John, II, 304
    Joseph, 303, 306
    Joseph Hatch, 302(2), 305
    Joseph Hote, 159
    Lucinda, 304
    Lydia, 303
    Martha, 304
    Martha, 304
    Martha (Brooks), 302, 304
    Mary, 41, 303
    Mary Ann, 304, 304
    Moses, 245
    Mrs. Elizabeth, 304
    Naylor, 304
    Polly (Fickett), 302, 304-305
    Richard, 245
    Robert, 70(2), 75, 159, 168, 302(2), 303-304, 305(2)
    Robert, Jr., 70
    Sally, 24
Waterhouse
    Sally, 159, 302, 306, 307, 309
    Samuel B., 304
    Sarah J. (Mange), 70, 304
    Sopha, 70, 304
    Sophia, 168
    Thomas, 304
    William, 24(2), 66, 70, 123, 159(2), 169, 174, 302-304
    William, III, 304
    William, Jr., 174, 302(2), 303, 311
    William, Sr., 307, 311
Waterman
    Eveline L. (Pierce), 238
    John A., 205
    John Anderson, 238
Waters
    Claredon, 266
    Daniel, 79
    Mary, 82
    Mary (Cloise), 79
    Sophronia (Quinby), 266
Watson
    David H., 308
    Eliphalet, 309
    Elizabeth, 282
    Emma L. (Bailey), 308
    Hannah Frances (Brackett), 10
    John, 333
    Joseph H., 264
    Marie (Howe), 264
    Thomas, 282
    William E., 10
    Zipporah (Partridge), 309
Watts
    Dr. Edward, 313
    Dr. Edward, 81
    Mrs. Mary, 81
    Polly, 313, 313
Wayte

    Benjamin, 90
Weatherby
    Daniel, 302
Webb
    Amelia, 180
    Ann (Riggs), 9, 76, 182, 335
    Bethiah (Farrar), 37
    Betsey, 33, 172
    Capt. Henry, 145, 182-182, 183(2)
    Capt. Seth, 37
    Charlotte, 9, 51, 145, 183
    Clarissa (Kenny), 17
    Col. James, 9, 33, 76, 151, 175-176, 179, 182, 294
    Col. Jason Webb, 172
    Daniel, 24
    David, 90, 307
    Edward C., 265
    Eli, 37, 146, 265
    Elizabeth Ann, 9
    Eunice, 183
    Henry, 9, 48, 66(2), 76, 176, 335
    James, 9, 17, 37, 48, 78, 180, 290, 293
    Jane (Bailey), 307
    Jane (Fly), 24
    John, 37, 48, 176
    John, Jr., 176
    Jonathan, 73(2), 180, 274, 307
    Joshua, 38, 40
    Judge Nathan, 37, 265
    Lucy, 76, 183, 183
    Mahlon T., 37
    Mary, 265
    Mary (Coverly), 274
    Mary (Thomes), 76
    Mrs., 175
    Mrs. Daniel Cobb, 183
    Mrs. Susan Smith, 274
    Mrs. Susannah Smith, 274
    Nancy (Cony), 176
    Nathan, 34
    Pauline, 180
    Phebe, 263
    Sally, 76, 76, 176, 176, 180, 264, 265
    Samuel, 37
    Seth, 37
    Sophia, 179
    Suckey, 180
    Susannah, 34-37, 37
    Susannah (Smith), 274
    Susannah (Swett), 37
    William, 46, 56, 164
Webber
    Capt. Aaron, 134
    Jeremiah, 107-108
    Margaret E. (Brackett), 107
    Margaret Elizabeth (Brackett), 108
    Mrs. Clarisa, 134
Webster
    Capt. William, 156
    Daniel, 248
    Dr. Noah, 248
    Isabella, 34
    Maj. Stephen, 161
    Mary, 247, 248
    Noah, 248

Weeb
  John, 57
Weeks
  Caroline, 191
  Eleanor (West), 175
  Samuel, 175
Weir
  Hannah, 5, 15
Welch
  James, 250
Weldon
  John, 78
Wentworth
  Capt. John, 12
Wescott
  Betsey, 7
  Betty (Bailey), 25
  Elizabeth, 266
  George E., 33
  Josiah, 7
  Lydia, 7
  Mary, 7, 34-37
  Mary (Trickey), 271
  Mary Ann, 7
  Mrs. [Post], 7
  Richard, 25, 46
  William, 271
  William [Post], 7
  William, Jr., 46
  Zebulon, 271
West
  Eleanor, 175
  Ella J. (Burnham), 184
  George, 184
Westbrook
  Col., 20.1
  Col. Thomas, 46-47, 60-62, 66, 79-80, 102, 105-106, 121, 151, 163, 167, 169, 182, 198-199, 200, 201, 216, 262, 287, 290, 306, 311, 337
  John, 163, 305
  Mary, 60, 60, 244
  Thomas, 78, 103, 261
  Thomas, Esq., 244
Westmore
  James, 48
Weston
  Augusta M., 284, 284
  Caroline K., 284
  Emma Carlton, 284
  Mary Susan, 284
  Rev. Daniel, 134, 270-271, 284
  Rev. I.P., 99
  Susan (Buxton), 284
Weymouth
  Eunice (Libby), 185
  James, 185
Wheeler
  Experience, 250
Wheelock
  Mehitable, 308
Wheelwright
  Rev. John B., 131
Wheldon
  John, 198
Whipple
  Carlile, 264
  Sarah W. (Bunker), 264
Whitcomb
  Col. Asa, 181
White
  Abby Nichols, 177
  Abigail (Blaney), 207
  Capt. John, 207
  Hannah, 195
White
  Peter, 47
  Philip, 20.2
White
  Sarah, 207
White
  Zachariah, 20.2(2)
Whitefield
  Abigail, 245
  Rev. George, 140, 245
Whitefoot
  John, 20.2(2)
Whiting
  Mary, 306
  Rev. Thurston, 299
  Thurston, 300
Whitman
  Abraham W., 21
  Ezekiel, 295
Whitmore
  Frances W., 253
Whitney
  Abel, 44
  Hannah (Haskell), 44
  Hannah (Tibbetts), 44
  Hannah W., 44
  John H., 44
  Lt. John, 154
  Mary, 175
Whitten
  Ellen Octavia (Browne), 242
  Eunice G., 266
  Samuel, 98
  William, 242
Whittier
  Edwin N., M.D., 238
  Nancy (Pierce), 238
Widgery
  William, 294, 299
Wier
  Hannah, 263
Wiggin
  Charles, 90
Wigglesworth
  Col. Edward, 181
Wight
  Amanda, 109
  Calista, 110(2)
Wilborn
  Mary, 105
Wilcox
  Susan (Lang), 266
  Thomas, 266
Wild
  Rev. John, 285
Wilder
  John, 104

Wiley
  Frank B., 266
  Susan B. (Pratt), 266
Wilkins
  Catharine C., 247
  Catherine Charlotte, 253
  Col. James C., 253
Willard
  Ebenezer, 44
  Eunice, 245, 245
  Frances E., 245
  Joseph, 245
  Mrs. Freeman, 110
  Prof. Joseph, 245
  Rev. Samuel, 245
  Rev. Samuel, Jr., 245
  Susan (Haskell), 44
Williams
  Capt. Hart, 154
  Mary, 169
  Rev. Ebenezer, 172, 239, 262
Willis
  Hon. William, 20.1
  Jonas, 197
  Susan (Barbour), 197
Wilson
  Albert M., 24
  Alice, 202
  Almira, 24
  Angeline, 24
  Ann (Huston), 202
  Ann (March), 202
  Benjamin, 24
  Capt. Aaron, 188
  Capt. Nathaniel, 293
  Charles, 202
  Cpl. John, 46
  Cyrus, 164
  Elizabeth, 50, 253
  Eunice, 202(2)
  George, 55
  Gowen, 40, 202(2)
  Gowen, Jr., 202
  Hannah, 202
  Henry, 24(2), 188
  Ichabod, 47, 202
  Jason, 55
  John, 56, 90, 134, 200, 226
  John M., 92
  John M., Esq., 202
  Joseph, 48, 202
  Levi, 164
  Maj. Nathaniel, 202
  Major, 24
  Mark, 48, 202, 288, 290
  Martha, 202(2)
  Martha (Sargent), 202
  Mary, 24, 202(3)
  Mary (Gibbs), 202
  Mary (Scott), 202
  Mary Ann, 24
  Nathaniel, 57, 90, 202, 288(2), 289-289, 290(2)
  Nathaniel, Jr., 202
  Olive (Huston), 202
  Polly, 202
  Rachel, 202
  Rev. E. P., 202
  Ruth (Huston), 202
  Sally (Pride), 202
  Sarah, 202(2)
  Scott, 202
  Susanna, 197
  Virgil C., 22, 24, 202
Wing
  Samuel S., 208
Wingate
  Joseph, Jr., 296
  Joshua, Jr., 323
Winship
  Eunice (Gould), 63
  Eunice N., 150(2)
  Isaac, 63
Winslow
  Aaron, 211
  Adam, 164
  Albert, 179-180
  Andrew, 172
  A., 94
  Aaron, 55, 90
  Abbie A., 308
  Amos, 77
  Capt. Aaron, 232-233
  Daniel, 208(2)
  Daniel, 98
  Dianth (Cobb), 179
  Edward, 64
  Eleanor, 211
  Fanny, 211
  Harriet J., 168
  Hezekiah, 211, 266
  Isaac, 45
  James, 214
  Jane, 211
  Jane C.B., 266
  Jane C.B. (Winslow), 266
  Job, Jr., 266
  John, 211
  John T., 42
  Jonathan, 211
  Joseph, 130
  Julia Abby (Southgate), 249
  Louisa, 185
  Mary A., 130
  Miles, 266
  Nancy C., 180
  Nancy Carrie, 179
  Nathan, 211
  Richard, 211
  Sophia (Webb), 179
  Thomas, 249
  William H., 179
Winter
  Isaac, 2
Wire
  Joseph, 12
  Rebecca (Brackett), 12
Wise
  A.R., 266
  Elizabeth (Pearson), 223
  Joseph, 223
Wiswell
  Rev. John, 172

Thomas, 162
Wite
    Mark, 115
Witham
    Julia A., 132
    Mary Abbie, 132
Witten
    Ellen Octavia (Browne), 242
    George, 242
    James, 242
    Mary, 242
    Sadie, 242
Wood
    Abiel, 326
    Abiel, Jr., 323
    Experience, 202
    Hon. John M., 241
    Joseph, 323
    Sophia Sewall, 257
Woodbury
    Capt. Warren B., 57
    Elizabeth, 263
    Hannah, 276
    Ira T., 219
    Israel, 276
    N.L., 55, 212
    Nathan L., 52
    Nathaniel L., 206
Woodford
    Addison P., 96-97
    Addison P., Rev., 1
    Adeline B., 42, 190
    Albert H., 9
    Anson, 97
    Charles D., 51
    Charles F., 42(2)
    Chauncey, 1, 42(2), 51, 131
    Chauncy, 16, 49
    Clara, 42
    Darius, 51(2)
    Dea. Addison, 42
    Dea. E.D., 100, 130
    Dea. Ebenezer D., 10, 19, 42(2), 51, 131, 193(2)
    Dorcas C. (Knight), 9
    Dr. Ebenezer D., 265
    E.D., 52, 96
    Ebenezer D., 1, 20.3, 49, 51, 97, 140, 146, 170, 194
    Edward, 42, 51
    Eliza, 42, 51
    Eliza (Knight), 42, 190
    Ella E., 42
    Ella Eliza, 189
    Frances W. (Bradley), 51
    Harriet B., 51
    Harriet Frances, 51
    Harriet Rebecca, 9
    Helen F., 42
    Hellena, 42, 42
    Isaac, 42-43
    Isaiah, 42(2), 49, 51
    Israel, 145
    Jane, 42, 51
    Jane, (Hanson), 43
    Joseph, 42(3), 43, 190
    Josiah, 1, 43, 51, 131

    Julia Harris, 51
    Lorenzo, 42
    Lucy (Stevens), 42, 51
    Margaret, 42(2), 51
    Marshall (Knight), 42
    Martha, 42, 42, 131, 159, 187
    Mary, 42, 51
    Mary (Frances), 170, 193, 265
    Mary Ann, 51
    Mary Ann (Merrill), 51
    Mary E., 51
    Mary Frances, 51
    Mrs. H.B., 78
    Mrs. Mary, 10
    Nancy L. (Stevens), 9
    Nancy W. (Stevens), 51
    Oren, 51
    Orin F., 42
    Peggy (Sawyer), 51
    Philip, 96
    Philip Rose, 51
    Silas, 42-43
    Thomas, 42, 97
    Thomas D., 51, 96, 269
    William, 3, 9(2), 51, 227
Woodfords
    Eben, 20.2
Woodfords
    Nancy W., 145
    William, 145
Woodfords
    Chauncey, 145
    Dea. Ebenezer D., 145
    Josiah, 145
    William, 145
Woodward
    Thomas, 113
    Velzora Eastman (Brackett), 113
Woolsley
    Arixene Southgate (Smith), 257, 258
    Charles W., 257
    Col. Charles William, 258
Worcester
    Hannah, 220
Wormell
    Sopiah, 263
Worster
    Stewart, 66
Wright
    Corcelia Ellen, 33
    Frances, 33
    John, 182
    Maria Elizabeth (Stevens), 33
    Shore (Chapman), 182
    Thomas, 33
Wyer
    Elijah, 44
    Nabby (Haskell), 44
Yeaton
    Aaron, 303
    Jacob, 303
    Mary (Waterhouse), 303
York
    David, 7
    Samuel, 7
    Submit, 4

Young
    Grace Gordon, 132
    Henry, 167
    Joe, 242
    John, 48
    Rev. Joab, 162
    Tennie (Browne), 242

Zane
    Abram V., 256
    Grace Helen (Southgate), 256

www.ingramcontent.com/pod-product-compliance
Lightning Source LLC
Chambersburg PA
CBHW081145290426
44108CB00018B/2446